As Per Latest CBSE Syllabus 2022-23
Issued on 21 April, 2022...

COMPLETE STUDY | COMPLETE PRACTICE | COMPLETE ASSESSMENT

Physics

CBSE Class 11

Authors
Kamal Upreti
Jayant Kumar Jha

ARIHANT PRAKASHAN (School Division Series)

ARIHANT PRAKASHAN
School Division Series
All Rights Reserved

ॐ **ADMINISTRATIVE & PRODUCTION OFFICES**

Regd. Office

'Ramchhaya' 4577/15, Agarwal Road, Darya Ganj, New Delhi -110002
Tele: 011- 47630600, 43518550; Fax: 011- 23280316

ॐ **Head Office**

Kalindi, TP Nagar, Meerut (UP) - 250002, Tel: 0121-7156203, 7156204

ॐ **SALES & SUPPORT OFFICES**

Agra, Ahmedabad, Bengaluru, Bareilly, Chennai, Delhi, Guwahati, Hyderabad, Jaipur, Jhansi, Kolkata, Lucknow, Nagpur & Pune.

PO No : TXT-XX-XXXXXXX-X-XX

Published By Arihant Publications (India) Ltd.

For further information about the books published by Arihant, log on to www.arihantbooks.com or e-mail at info@arihantbooks.com

Follow us on

PRODUCTION TEAM

Publishing Managers
Mahendra Singh Rawat &
Keshav Mohan

Project Coordinator
Yojna Sharma

Cover Designer
Bilal Hashmi

Inner Designer
Mazher Chaudhary

Page Layouting
Rajbhaskar Rana

Proof Readers
Princi Mittal, Ankit Poonia

9 789326 196246

THE FIRST WORD

All_in_**one** Physics Class 11th has been written keeping in mind the needs of students studying in Class 11th CBSE. This book has been made in such a way that students will be fully guided to prepare for the exam in the most effective manner, securing higher grades. The purpose of this book is to equip any CBSE Student with a sound knowledge of Physics at Class 11th Level. It covers the whole syllabus of Class 11th Physics divided into chapters as per the CBSE Curriculum. This book will give you support during the course as well as guide you on Revision and Preparation for the exam itself. The material is presented in a Clear & Concise form and there are questions for you to practice.

KEY FEATURES

- To make the students understand the chapter completely, each chapter has been divided into Individual Topics and each such topic has been treated as a separate chapter. Each topic has Detailed Theory, supported by Solved Examples, Notes, Remarks, Tables, Flow Charts, etc.

- Each topic has questions in the format in which they are asked in the examination like Objective Type, Very Short Answer Type Questions, Short Answer Type Questions, Long Answer Type Questions. These questions cover NCERT & NCERT Exemplar Questions and other Important Questions from examination point of view.

- For the students to check their understanding of the chapter, Chapter Practice of each chapter has been given.

- Chapterwise Study is not the only feature of this book, after the chapterwise study, it has 5 Sample Question Papers.

All-in-One Physics for CBSE Class 11th has all the material required for Learning, Understanding, Practice & Assessment and will surely guide the students to the Way of Success.

We are highly thankful to ARIHANT PRAKASHAN, MEERUT for giving us such an excellent opportunity to write this book. Huge efforts have been made from our side to keep this book error free, but inspite of that if any error or whatsoever is skipped in the book then that is purely incidental, apology for the same, please write to us about that so that it can be corrected in the further edition of the book. The role of Arihant DTP Unit and Proof Reading team is praise worthy in making of this book. Suggestions for further improvement of the book will also be welcomed.

At the end, we would like to say BEST OF LUCK to our readers!

Authors

02

The value of a physical quantity is generally expressed as the product of a number and its unit. The unit is simply a particular example of the quantity concerned which is used as a reference.

e.g. The speed v of a particle may be expressed as $v = 25$ m / s = 90 km/h, where metre per second and kilometre per hour are alternative units for expressing the same value of the quantity speed.

UNITS AND MEASUREMENT

|TOPIC 1|
System of Units

In order to define units for all fundamental quantities or base quantities, we use the term fundamental units or base units and then to define units for all other quantities as products of powers of the base units that we call derived units. Hence, a complete set of these units, i.e. both the base units and derived units, is known as the system of units.

PHYSICAL QUANTITIES

All those quantities which can be measured directly or indirectly and in terms of which the laws of physics can be expressed are called physical quantities.

Physical quantities can be further divided into two types:

(i) Fundamental Quantities

Those physical quantities which are independent of other physical quantities and are not defined in terms of other physical quantities, are called fundamental quantities or base quantities.

> **CHAPTER CHECKLIST**
> - Physical Quantities
> - Physical Unit
> - Need for Measurement
> - Measurement of Length
> - Measurement of Mass
> - Measurement of Time
> - Accuracy and Precision of Instruments
> - Errors in Measurement
> - Combination of Errors
> - Significant Figures
> - Dimensional Formulae and Dimensional Equations

| TOPIC PRACTICE 1 |

OBJECTIVE Type Questions
|1 Mark|

1. A is the fundamental quantity. Here, A refers to
   (a) mass
   (b) velocity
   (c) acceleration
   (d) linear momentum

Sol. (a) Mass is the fundamental quantity as it does not depend upon other physical quantities. However, other three quantities, i.e. velocity, acceleration and linear momentum are not fundamental quantities as these show their dependency on fundamental quantities. (1)

2. How many wavelength of Kr^{86} are there in 1 m?
   (a) 1553164.13   (b) 1650763.73
   (c) 2348123.73   (d) 652189.63

Sol. (b) The number of wavelengths of Kr^{86} in 1 m is 1650763.73.

3. The solid angle subtended by the periphery of an area 1 cm² at a point situated symmetrically at a distance of 5 cm from the area is
   (a) 2×10^{-2} steradian   (b) 4×10^{-2} steradian
   (c) 6×10^{-2} steradian   (d) 8×10^{-2} steradian

Sol. (b) Solid angle, $d\Omega = \dfrac{dA}{r^2} = \dfrac{1 \text{ cm}^2}{(5 \text{ cm})^2}$
   $= 0.04$ steradian
   $= 4 \times 10^{-2}$ steradian

4. Which of the following is not a physical quantity?
   (a) Time   (b) Impulse
   (c) Mass   (d) Kilogram

|TOPIC 2|
Measurement and Errors

NEED FOR MEASUREMENT

All engineering phenomena deal with definite and measured quantities, and so depend on the making of the measurement. We must be clear and precise in making these measurements. To make a measurement, magnitude of the physical quantity (unknown) is compared.

e.g. Weighing a material compares it with a standard weight of one kilogram. The result of the comparison is expressed in terms of multiples of the known quantity, i.e., so many kilograms.

Thus, the record of a measurement consists of three parts i.e. the dimension of the quantity, the unit which represents a standard quantity and a number which is the ratio of the measured quantity to the standard quantity.

ORDER OF MAGNITUDE

The order of magnitude of a quantity gives us a value nearest to the actual value of the quantity, in terms of suitable power of 10.

e.g. The radius of earth is 6400 km i.e. 64×10^6 m. Taking 6.4 as 10, size of earth is 10^7 m.

Hence, the order of magnitude of size of earth is 7. In order to measure the distance, it varies from radius of proton $(10^{-15}$ m) to size of universe $(10^{26}$ m).

> **Note**
> The order of magnitude of a quantity does not tell us the absolute value or exact value of the quantity. It gives an idea about how big or how small a given physical quantity is.

MEASUREMENT OF LENGTH

The length may be defined as the distance of separation between two points in space.

There are two methods for the measurement of length

Direct Method

In this method, measurement of length involves the use of
   (i) a metre scale for distances from 10^{-3} m to 10^2 m.
   (ii) a vernier calliper for distance upto 10^{-4} m.
   (iii) a screw gauge and a spherometer for distance upto 10^{-5} m.

Indirect Methods

These methods are used to measure large distances such as the distance of a planet or a star from the earth. There are various indirect methods to measure large distance such as Echo method, Parallax method, LASER method, RADAR method, etc.

ASSESS YOUR TOPICAL UNDERSTANDING

OBJECTIVE Type Questions
|1 Mark|

1. Which one of the following is not a unit of British system of units?
   (a) Foot   (b) Metre
   (c) Pound   (d) Second

2. Which of the following statement is incorrect regarding mass?
   (a) It is a basic property of matter
   (b) The SI unit of mass is candela
   (c) The mass of an atom is expressed in u
   (d) None of these

3. Pascal is the unit of
   (a) force   (b) stress   (c) work   (d) energy

4. The surface area of a solid cylinder of radius 2.0 cm and height A is equal to 1.5×10^4 (mm)². Here, A refers to
   (a) 0.9 cm   (b) 10 cm   (c) 30 cm   (d) 15 cm

5. If the value of force is 100 N and value of acceleration is 0.001 ms⁻², what is the value of mass in this system of units?
   (a) 10^5 kg   (b) 10^4 kg
   (c) 10^6 kg   (d) 10^6 kg

VERY SHORT ANSWER Type Questions
|1 Mark|

10. Explain the concept of mass, length and time which is related to basic or fundamental quantities in Mechanics.

11. How do we make the choice of a standard/unit of measurement?

12. Why MKS system had to be rationalised to obtain SI?

13. What is a coherent system of units?

SHORT ANSWER Type Questions
|2 Marks|

14. Briefly, explain the measuring process of any physical quantity.

15. Why 'metre' has been defined in terms of wavelength and 'second' in terms of periods of radiation or rotation?

16. Calculate the surface area of a solid cylinder of diameter 4 cm and height 20 cm in mm².
   [Ans. 27657.1 mm²]

Answer
1. (b)   2. (b)   3. (b)   4. (b)   5. (c)
6. (c)   7. (d)   8. (c)   9. (c)

TOPICAL ARRANGEMENT

To make the student understand the chapter completely, each chapter has been divided into **Individual Topics** and each such topic has been treated as a separate chapter. Each topic has detailed theory, supported by Illustrations, Solved Examples, tables, flow charts etc.

TOPIC PRACTICE

Each Topic Practice has questions group as Objective Type, Very Short Answer Type Questions, Short Answer Type Questions, Long Answer Type Questions. These questions cover NCERT Questions and other Important Question from examination point of view.

ASSESS YOUR TOPICAL UNDERSTANDING

At the end of each topic, their are some unsolved questions grouped as markswise. By practising them, a student can assess his knowledge about the concerned topic.

> for CBSE Class 11th Examination, it is hoped that this book will reinforce and extend your ideas about the subject and finally will place you in the row of toppers.

CHAPTER PRACTICE

Along with **Topic practice** to give students complete practice of the chapter as a whole **Chapter practice** of each chapter having questions arranged as per their marks have been given in each chapter.

CHAPTER PRACTICE

OBJECTIVE Type Questions
|1 Mark|

1. Which one of the following physical quantities is not a fundamental quantity?
   (a) Luminous intensity
   (b) Thermodynamic temperature
   (c) Electric current
   (d) Work

2. Among the given following system of unit which is not based on unit of mass, length and time?
   (a) CGS (b) FPS (c) MKS (d) SI

3. Find the value of $12.9 \, g - 7.05 \, g$.
   (a) 5.84 g (b) 5.8 g (c) 5.86 g (d) 5.9 g

4. Calculate the relative errors in measurement of mass $1.02 \, g \pm 0.01g$ and $9.89g \pm 0.01 g$.
   (a) ± 1% and ± 0.2%   (b) ±1% and ± 0.1%
   (c) ± 2% and ± 0.3%   (d) ±3% and ± 0.4%

5. The numbers 2.745 and 2.735 on rounding off to 3 significant figures will give   [NCERT Exemplar]
   (a) 2.75 and 2.74   (b) 2.74 and 2.73
   (c) 2.75 and 2.73   (d) 2.74 and 2.74

Answer
1. (d) 2. (d) 3. (b) 4. (b) 5. (d)
6. (a) 7. (a) 8. (a) 9. (a) 10. (c)

VERY SHORT ANSWER Type Questions
|1 Mark|

11. How many protons would make 1 kg? (Mass of proton $= 1.67 \times 10^{-27}$ kg)   [Ans. 5.99×10^{26}]

12. Wavelength of a laser light is 6463 Å. Express it in nm and micron.   [Ans. 646.3 nm, 0.6463 µ]

13. Find the value of 1 J of energy in CGS system of units.   [Ans. 10^{7} CGS units]

SHORT ANSWER Type Questions
|2 Marks|

14. The moon is observed from two diametrically opposite points A and B on the earth. The angle θ subtended at the moon by the two directions of observations is 1°54'. If the diameter of the earth is 1.276×10^{7} m. What is the distance of the moon from the earth?   [Ans. 3.84×10^{8} m]

15. A laser signal is beamed towards a planet from earth and its echo is received 680 s later. If distance of planet be 1.02×10^{11} m, what is the speed of laser light?   [Ans. 3×10^{8} m/s]

16. The relative density of a material is found by weighing the body first in air and then in water. If the weight in air is (10 ± 0.1) N and weight in water is (5.0 ± 0.1) N. What would be the maximum percentage error in relative density?   [Ans. 5%]

17. Find the value of the following upto the appropriate significant figures in the following.
   (a) 3.27 + 33.5472   (b) 53.312 − 53.3
   (c) 2.02 × 23   (d) 3.908 × 5.5
   [Ans. (a) 36.82 (b) zero (c) 46 (d) 21]

SAMPLE QUESTION PAPERS

To make the students practice in the real sense, we have provided **5 Sample Question Papers**, exactly based on the latest CBSE pattern & CBSE syllabus.

SUMMARY

- **Behaviour of gases** Gases at low pressure and high temperature much above that at which they liquify (or solidify), follow a relation.
  $$pV = Nk_B T \text{ or } \frac{pV}{NT} = k_B = \text{constant}$$
  For different gases, $\frac{p_1 V_1}{N_1 T_1} = \frac{p_2 V_2}{N_2 T_2} = \frac{p_3 V_3}{N_3 T_3} ... = k_B = \text{constant}$ where, k_B = Boltzmann's constant and its value in SI unit is 1.38×10^{-23} J/K.

- **Boyle's law** It states that for a given mass of a gas at constant temperature, the volume of that mass of a gas is inversely proportional to its pressure.
  i.e. $$V = \frac{1}{p}$$
  $$\Rightarrow \quad p_1 V_1 = p_2 V_2 = p_3 V_3 ... = \text{constant}$$

- **Charles' law** It states that for a given mass of an ideal gas at constant pressure, volume (V) of a gas is directly proportional to its absolute temperature T
  i.e. $$V \propto T$$
  $$\Rightarrow \quad \frac{V_1}{T_1} = \frac{V_2}{T_2} = \frac{V_3}{T_3} ... = \text{constant}$$

- **Dalton's law of partial pressure** It states that the total pressure of a mixture of non-interacting ideal gases is the sum of partial pressures exerted by individual gases in the mixture.
  i.e. $$p = p_1 + p_2 + p_3 + ...$$
  Dalton's law, $p = p_1 + p_2 + p_3 + ...$

- **Graham's law of diffusion** It state that the rate of diffusion of a gas is inversely proportional to the square root of its density.
  $$r = \frac{1}{\sqrt{\rho}}$$
  where, r = rate of diffusion and ρ = density of the gas.

SUMMARY

To give the students Revision of the chapter as a whole, a **Summary** of each chapter has been given. Through this Summary students can revise the formulae and important point through out whole chapter at a glance.

SAMPLE QUESTION PAPER 1

A HIGHLY SIMULATED SAMPLE QUESTION PAPER FOR CBSE CLASS XI EXAMINATIONS

PHYSICS (FULLY SOLVED)

GENERAL INSTRUCTIONS

1. All questions are compulsory. There are 33 questions in all.
2. This question paper has five sections: Section A, Section B, Section C, Section D and Section E.
3. **Section A** contains ten very short answer questions and four assertion reasoning MCQs of 1 mark each, **Section B** has two case based questions of 4 marks each, **Section C** contains nine short answer questions of 2 marks each, **Section D** contains five short answer questions of 3 marks each and **Section E** contains three long answer questions of 5 marks each.
4. There is no overall choice. However internal choice is provided. You have to attempt only one of the choices in such questions.

TIME : 3 HOURS MAX. MARKS : 70

SECTION-A

All questions are compulsory. In case of internal choices, attempt anyone of them.

1. To break a wire, a force of 10^{6} Nm^{-2} is required. If the density of the material is 3×10^{3} kgm^{-3}, then calculate the length of the wire which will break by its own weight.

2. A body is rotating with angular velocity, $\omega = (3\hat{i} - 4\hat{j} - \hat{k})$. What is the linear velocity of a point having position vector $r = (5\hat{i} - 6\hat{j} + 6\hat{k})$?

3. What is the torque of a force $7\hat{i} + 3\hat{j} - 5\hat{k}$ about the origin whose position vector is $\hat{i} - \hat{j} + \hat{k}$?

4. Find the dimensions of a/b in the equation $F = a\sqrt{x} + bt^{2}$, where F is force, x is distance and t is time.
   Or
   5.74 g of a substance occupies 1.2 cm^{3}. Express its density by keeping the significant figures in view.

5. Temperature remaining constant, the pressure of a gas is decreased by 20%. What is the percentage change in volume?
   Or
   An ideal gas at 27°C is heated at constant pressure so as to triple its volume. What is the increase in temperature of the gas?

6. Can transverse waves be produced in air?

7. An ideal gas has molar specific heat capacity at constant volume equal to $\frac{3}{2}R$. Find the molar specific heat capacity at constant pressure.

8. What is the function of the wooden box in the sonometer?
   Or
   A truck is moving with a speed of 90 kmh^{-1} towards a hill. Truck blows horn at a distance of 1800 m from the hill and a echo is heard after 8 s. Calculate the speed of sound (in ms^{-1}).

FULLY SOLVED

CONTENTS

Physics Class 11

LATEST SYLLABUS

Time: 3 Hrs   Total Marks : 70

Units	Title	No. of Periods	Marks
Unit I	Physical World and Measurement *Chapter 2 : Units and Measurements*	08	
Unit II	Kinematics *Chapter 3 : Motion in a Straight Line* *Chapter 4 : Motion in a Plane*	24	23
Unit III	Laws of Motion *Chapter 5 : Laws of Motion*	14	
Unit IV	Work, Energy and Power *Chapter 6 : Work, Energy and Power*	14	
Unit V	Motion of System of Particles and Rigid Body *Chapter 7 : System of Particles and Rotational Motion*	18	17
Unit VI	Gravitation *Chapter 8 : Gravitation*	12	
Unit VII	Properties of Bulk Matter *Chapter 9 : Mechanical Properties of Solids* *Chapter 10 : Mechanical Properties of Fluids* *Chapter 11 : Thermal Properties of Matter*	24	
Unit VIII	Thermodynamics *Chapter 12 : Thermodynamics*	12	20
Unit IX	Behaviour of Perfect Gases and Kinetic Theory of Gases *Chapter 13 : Kinetic Theory*	08	
Unit X	Oscillations and Waves *Chapter 14 : Oscillations* *Chapter 15 : Waves*	26	10
	TOTAL	**160**	**70**

UNIT I Physical World and Measurement   (08 Periods)

Chapter 2 : Units and Measurements

Need for measurement: Units of measurement; systems of units; SI units, fundamental and derived units. significant figures. Dimensions of physical quantities, dimensional analysis and its applications.

UNIT II Kinematics (24 Periods)

Chapter 3 : Motion in a Straight Line

Frame of reference, Motion in a straight line: speed and velocity. Elementary concepts of differentiation and integration for describing motion, uniform and non-uniform motion, average speed and instantaneous velocity, uniformly accelerated motion, velocity - time and position-time graphs. Relations for uniformly accelerated motion (graphical treatment).

Chapter 4 : Motion in a Plane

Scalar and vector quantities; position and displacement vectors, general vectors and their notations; equality of vectors, multiplication of vectors by a real number; addition and subtraction of vectors, Unit vector; resolution of a vector in a plane, rectangular components, Scalar and Vector product of vectors. Motion in a plane, cases of uniform velocity and uniform acceleration-projectile motion, uniform circular motion.

UNIT III Laws of Motion (14 Periods)

Chapter 5 : Laws of Motion

Intuitive concept of force, Inertia, Newton's first law of motion; momentum and Newton's second law of motion; impulse; Newton's third law of motion. Law of conservation of linear momentum and its applications. Equilibrium of concurrent forces, Static and kinetic friction, laws of friction, rolling friction, lubrication. Dynamics of uniform circular motion: Centripetal force, examples of circular motion (vehicle on a level circular road, vehicle on a banked road).

UNIT IV Work, Energy and Power (14 Periods)

Chapter 6 : Work, Energy and Power

Work done by a constant force and a variable force; kinetic energy, work-energy theorem, power. Notion of potential energy, potential energy of a spring, conservative forces: non-conservative forces: motion in a vertical circle; elastic and inelastic collisions in one and two dimensions.

UNIT V Motion of System of Particles and Rigid Body (18 Periods)

Chapter 7 : System of Particles and Rotational Motion

Centre of mass of a two-particle system, momentum conservation and centre of mass motion. Centre of mass of a rigid body; centre of mass of a uniform rod. Moment of a force, torque, angular momentum, law of conservation of angular momentum and its applications. Equilibrium of rigid bodies, rigid body rotation and equations of rotational motion, comparison of linear and rotational motions. Moment of inertia, radius of gyration, values of moments of inertia for simple geometrical objects (no derivation).

UNIT VI Gravitation (12 Periods)

Chapter 8 : Gravitation

Kepler's laws of planetary motion, universal law of gravitation. Acceleration due to gravity and its variation with altitude and depth. Gravitational potential energy and gravitational potential, escape velocity, orbital velocity of a satellite.

UNIT VII Properties of Bulk Matter   (24 Periods)

Chapter 9 : Mechanical Properties of Solids

Elastic behaviour, Stress-strain relationship, Hooke's law, Young's modulus, bulk modulus, shear modulus of rigidity, Poisson's ratio; elastic energy.

Chapter 10 : Mechanical Properties of Fluids

Pressure due to a fluid column; Pascal's law and its applications (hydraulic lift and hydraulic brakes), effect of gravity on fluid pressure. Viscosity, Stokes' law, terminal velocity, streamline and turbulent flow, critical velocity, Bernoulli's theorem and its applications. Surface energy and surface tension, angle of contact, excess of pressure across a curved surface, application of surface tension ideas to drops, bubbles and capillary rise.

Chapter 11 : Thermal Properties of Matter

Heat, temperature, thermal expansion; thermal expansion of solids, liquids and gases, anomalous expansion of water; specific heat capacity; Cp, Cv - calorimetry; change of state - latent heat capacity. Heat transfer-conduction, convection and radiation, thermal conductivity, qualitative ideas of Blackbody radiation, Wein's displacement Law, Stefan's law.

UNIT VIII Thermodynamics   (12 Periods)

Chapter 12 : Thermodynamics

Thermal equilibrium and definition of temperature (zeroth law of thermodynamics), heat, work and internal energy. First law of thermodynamics, isothermal and adiabatic processes. Second law of thermodynamics: reversible and irreversible processes.

UNIT IX Behaviour of Perfect Gases and
Kinetic Theory of Gases   (08 Periods)

Chapter 13 : Kinetic Theory

Equation of state of a perfect gas, work done in compressing a gas. Kinetic theory of gases - assumptions, concept of pressure. Kinetic interpretation of temperature; rms speed of gas molecules; degrees of freedom, law of equi-partition of energy (statement only) and application to specific heat capacities of gases; concept of mean free path, Avogadro's number.

UNIT X Oscillations and Waves   (26 Periods)

Chapter 14 : Oscillations

Periodic motion - time period, frequency, displacement as a function of time, periodic functions. Simple harmonic motion (S.H.M) and its equation; phase; oscillations of a loaded spring-restoring force and force constant; energy in S.H.M. Kinetic and potential energies; simple pendulum derivation of expression for its time period.

Chapter 15 : Waves

Transverse and longitudinal waves, speed of travelling wave, displacement relation for a progressive wave, principle of superposition of waves, reflection of waves, standing waves in strings and organ pipes, fundamental mode and harmonics, Beats.

01

The value of a physical quantity is generally expressed as the product of a number and its unit. The unit is simply a particular example of the quantity concerned which is used as a reference.

e.g. The speed v of a particle may be expressed as $v = 25$ m / s = 90 km/h, where metre per second and kilometre per hour are alternative units for expressing the same value of the

UNITS AND MEASUREMENTS

|TOPIC 1|
System of Units

In order to define units for all fundamental quantities or base quantities, we use the term fundamental units or base units and then to define units for all other quantities as products of powers of the base units that we call derived units. Hence, a complete set of these units, i.e. both the base units and derived units, is known as the system of units.

PHYSICAL QUANTITIES

All those quantities which can be measured directly or indirectly and in terms of which the laws of physics can be expressed are called physical quantities.

Physical quantities can be further divided into two types:

(i) Fundamental Quantities

Those physical quantities which are independent of other physical quantities and are not defined in terms of other physical quantities, are called fundamental quantities or base quantities.

e.g. Mass, length, time, temperature, luminous intensity, electric current and the amount of substance, etc.

(ii) Derived Quantities

Those quantities which can be derived from the fundamental quantities are called derived quantities. e.g. Velocity, acceleration and linear momentum, etc.

CHAPTER CHECKLIST

- Physical Quantities
- Physical Unit
- Significant Figures and Rounding off
- Dimensional Formulae and Dimensional Equations

MEASUREMENT OF PHYSICAL QUANTITIES

The measurement of physical quantity is the process of comparing this quantity with a standard amount of the physical quantity of the same kind, called its unit.

Hence, to express the measurement of a physical quantity, we need to know two things

(i) The unit in which the quantity is measured.

(ii) The numerical value or the magnitude of the quantity(n), i.e. the number of times that unit (u) is contained in the given physical quantity.

or $$\boxed{Q = nu}$$

Numerical Value Inversely Proportional to the Size of Unit

The numerical value (n) is inversely proportional to the size (u) of the unit.

$$n \propto \frac{1}{u} \ \Rightarrow \ nu = \text{constant}.$$

e.g. The magnitude of a quantity remains the same, whatever may be the unit of measurement.

Hence, $1 \, \text{kg} = 1000 \, \text{g}$

We may write as $Q = n_1 u_1 = n_2 u_2$

where n_1, n_2 are the numerical values and u_1, u_2 are the two units of measurement of the same quantity.

PHYSICAL UNIT

The standard amount of a physical quantity chosen to measure the physical quantity of the same kind is called a physical unit.

The essential requirements of physical unit are given as below:

(i) It should be of suitable size.

(ii) It should be easily accessible.

(iii) It should not vary with time.

(iv) It should be easily reproducible.

(v) It should not depend on physical conditions like pressure, volume, temperature, etc.

The physical unit can be classified into two ways that can be given as below :

Fundamental Units

The physical units which can neither be derived from one another, nor they can be further resolved into more simpler units are called fundamental units. The units of fundamental quantities, i.e. length, mass and time are called fundamental units or base units.

Derived Units

The units of measurement of all other physical quantities which can be obtained from fundamental units are called derived units.

e.g. $$\text{Speed} = \frac{\text{Distance}}{\text{Time}}$$

$\therefore$ $$\text{Unit of speed} = \frac{\text{Unit of distance}}{\text{Unit of time}}$$

$$= \frac{\text{m}}{\text{s}} = \text{ms}^{-1}$$

Unit of speed (i.e. ms^{-1}) is a derived unit.

THE INTERNATIONAL SYSTEM OF UNITS

A system of units is the complete set of units, both fundamental and derived for all kinds of physical quantities.

The common systems of units used in mechanics are given below

(i) **FPS System** It is the British engineering system of units, which uses foot as the unit of length, pound as the unit of mass and second as the unit of time.

(ii) **CGS System** It is based on Gaussian system of units, which uses centimetre, gram and second for length, mass and time, respectively.

(iii) **MKS System** It uses metre, kilogram and second as the fundamental units of length, mass and time, respectively.

(iv) **International System of Units** (SI Units) The system of units, which is accepted internationally for measurement is the System Internationaled' Units (French for International System of Units) abbreviated as SI.

The SI, with standard scheme of symbols, units and abbreviations, was developed and recommended by **General Conference on Weights and Measures** in 1971 for international usage in scientific, technical, industrial and commercial work.

This system of units makes revolutionary changes in the MKS system and is known as **rationalised MKS system.** It is helpful to obtain all the physical quantities in Physics.

In SI system, there are seven base units and two supplementary units as listed below:

SI base quantities and units

Base quantity	SI units		
	Name	Symbol	Definition
Length	Metre	m	One metre is the length of the path travelled by light in vacuum during a time interval of 1/299,792,458 of a second. (1983)
Mass	Kilogram	kg	One kilogram is equal to the mass of the international prototype of the kilogram (a platinum-iridium alloy cylinder) kept at international Bureau of Weights and Measures at Sevres, near Paris, France. (1889)
Time	Second	s	One second is the duration of 9,192,631,770 periods of the radiation corresponding to the transition between the two hyperfine levels of the ground state of the cesium-133 atom. (1967)
Electric current	Ampere	A	One ampere is that constant current which, if maintained in two straight parallel conductors of infinite length, of negligible circular cross-section, and placed 1 m apart in vacuum, would produce a force between these conductors equal to 2×10^{-7} N/m of length. (1948)
Thermodynamic temperature	Kelvin	K	One kelvin is the fraction 1/273.16 of the thermodynamic temperature of the triple point of water. (1967)
Amount of substance	Mole	mol	One mole is the amount of substance of a system which contains as many elementary entities as there are atoms in 0.012 kg of carbon-12. (1971)
Luminous intensity	Candela	cd	One candela is the luminous intensity in a given direction of a source that emits monochromatic radiation of frequency 540×10^{12} Hz and that has a radiant intensity in that direction of 1/683 watt per steradian. (1979)

Some supplementary quantities and their SI units

Supplementary quantity	SI units		
	Name	Symbol	Definition
Plane angle	Radian	rad	One radian is the angle subtended at the centre of a circle by an arc equal in length to the radius of the circle. i.e. $d\theta = \dfrac{ds}{r}$ 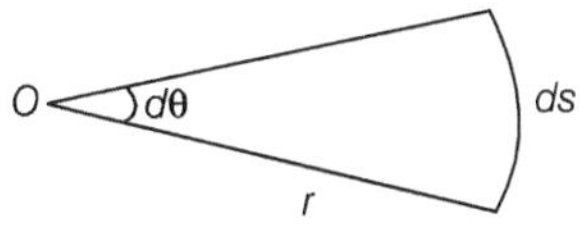
Solid angle	Steradian	sr	One steradian is the solid angle subtended at the centre of a sphere, by that surface of the sphere, which is equal in area, to the square of radius of the sphere. i.e. $d\Omega = \dfrac{dA}{r^2}$ 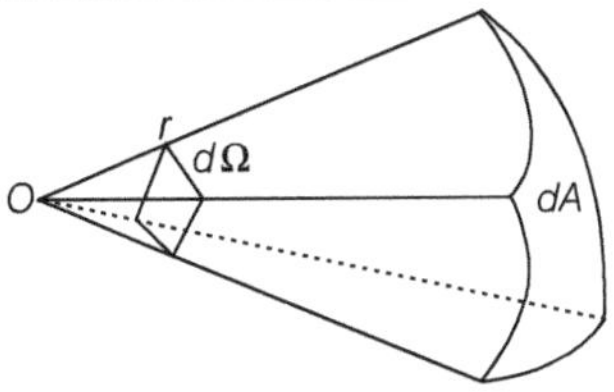

Note
- The FPS system is not a metric system. This system is not in much use these days.
- The drawback of CGS system is that many of the derived units on this system are inconveniently small.
- The advantages of MKS system is that some of the derived units are of convenient size.

SI derived units with special names

Physical Quantity	SI unit			
	Name	Symbol	Expression in terms of other units	Expression in terms of SI base units
Frequency	Hertz	Hz	–	s^{-1}
Force	Newton	N	–	$kg\ m\ s^{-2}$ or $kg\ m/s^2$
Pressure, stress	Pascal	Pa	N/m^2 or $N\ m^{-2}$	$kg\ m^{-1}s^{-2}$ or $kg/s^2\ m$
Energy, work, quantity of heat	Joule	J	Nm	$kg\ m^2s^{-2}$ or $kg\ m^2/s^2$
Power, radiant flux	Watt	W	J/s or $J\ s^{-1}$	$kg\ m^2\ s^{-3}$ or $kg\ m^2/s^3$
Quantity of electricity, electric charge	Coulomb	C	–	As
Electric potential, potential difference, electromotive force	Volt	V	W/A or WA^{-1}	$kg\ m^2\ s^{-3}\ A^{-1}$ or $kg\ m^2/s^3\ A$
Capacitance	Farad	F	C/V	$A^2\ s^4\ kg^{-1}m^{-2}$
Electric resistance	Ohm	Ω	V/A	$kg\ m^2\ s^{-3}A^{-2}$
Conductance	Siemens	S	A/V	$m^{-2}\ kg^{-1}s^3\ A^2$
Magnetic flux	Weber	Wb	Vs or J/A	$kg\ m^2s^{-2}\ A^{-1}$
Magnetic field, magnetic flux density, magnetic induction	Tesla	T	Wb/m^2	$kg\ s^{-2}\ A^{-1}$
Inductance	Henry	H	Wb/A	$kg\ m^2s^{-2}A^{-2}$
Luminous flux, luminous power	Lumen	lm	–	cd/sr
Illuminance	Lux	lx	lm/m^2	$m^{-2}\ cd\ sr^{-1}$
Activity (of a radio nuclide/ radioactive source)	Becquerel	Bq	–	s^{-1}
Absorbed dose, absorbed dose index	Gray	Gy	J/kg	m^2/s^2 or $m^2\ s^{-2}$

Some SI derived units expressed by means of SI units

Physical quantity	SI unit		
	Name	Symbol	Expression in terms of SI base units
Magnetic moment	Joule per tesla	JT^{-1}	$m^2\,A$
Dipole moment	Coulomb metre	$C\,m$	$s\,A\,m$
Dynamic viscosity	Poiseuille or pascal second or newton second per square metre	Pl or Pa s or $N\,s\,m^{-2}$	$m^{-1}\,kg\,s^{-1}$
Torque, couple, moment of force	Newton metre	$N\,m$	$m^2\,kg\,s^{-2}$
Surface tension	Newton per metre	N/m	$kg\,s^{-2}$
Power density, irradiance, heat flux density	Watt per square metre	W/m^2	$kg\,s^{-3}$
Heat capacity, entropy	Joule per kelvin	J/K	$m^2\,kg\,s^{-2}\,K^{-1}$
Specific heat capacity, specific entropy	Joule per kilogram kelvin	$J/kg\,K$	$m^2\,s^{-2}\,K^{-1}$
Specific energy, latent heat	Joule per kilogram	J/kg	$m^2\,s^{-2}$
Radiant intensity	Watt per steradian	$W\,Sr^{-1}$	$kg\,m^2\,s^{-3}\,Sr^{-1}$
Thermal conductivity	Watt per metre kelvin	$W\,m^{-1}\,K^{-1}$	$m\,kg\,s^{-3}\,K^{-1}$
Energy density	Joule per cubic metre	J/m^3	$kg\,m^{-1}\,s^{-2}$
Electric field strength	Volt per metre	V/m	$m\,kg\,s^{-3}\,A^{-1}$
Electric charge density	Coulomb per cubic metre	C/m^3	$m^{-3}\,A\,s$
Electricity flux density	Coulomb per square metre	C/m^2	$m^{-2}\,A\,s$
Permittivity	Farad per metre	F/m	$m^{-3}\,kg^{-1}\,s^4\,A^2$
Permeability	Henry per metre	H/m	$m\,kg\,s^{-2}\,A^{-2}$
Molar energy	Joule per mole	J/mol	$m^2\,kg\,s^{-2}\,mol^{-1}$
Angular momentum, Planck constant	Joule second	$J\,s$	$kg\,m^2\,s^{-1}$
Molar entropy, molar heat capacity	Joule per mole kelvin	$J/mol\,K$	$m^2\,kg\,s^{-2}\,K^{-1}\,mol^{-1}$
Exposure (X-rays and γ-rays)	Coulomb per kilogram	C/kg	$kg^{-1}\,s\,A$
Absorbed dose rate	Gray per second	Gy/s	$m^2\,s^{-3}$
Compressibility	Per pascal	Pa^{-1}	$m\,kg^{-1}\,s^2$
Elastic moduli	Newton per square metre	N/m^2 or $N\,m^{-2}$	$kg\,m^{-1}\,s^{-2}$
Pressure gradient	Pascal per metre	Pa/m or $N\,m^{-3}$	$kg\,m^{-2}\,s^{-2}$
Surface potential	Joule per kilogram	J/kg or $N\,m/kg$	$m^2\,s^{-2}$
Pressure energy	Pascal cubic metre	$Pa\,m^3$ or $N\,m$	$kg\,m^2\,s^{-2}$
Impulse	Newton second	$N\,s$	$kg\,m\,s\,s^{-1}$
Angular impulse	Newton metre second	$N\,m\,s$	$kg\,m^2\,s^{-1}$
Specific resistance	Ohm metre	$\Omega\,m$	$kg\,m^3\,s^{-3}\,A^{-2}$
Surface energy	Joule per square metre	J/m^2 or N/m	$kg\,s^{-2}$

PROBLEM SOLVING STRATEGY
(UNIT CONVERSION)

(i) **Identify the relevant concept** Unit conversion is important to recognise what it's needed. In most cases, you are best off using the fundamental SI units (length in metres, mass in kilograms and time in seconds) within a problem.

(ii) **Set up the problem** Units are multiplied and divided just like ordinary algebraic symbols. It gives us an easy way to convert a quantity from one set of units to another.

(iii) **Execute the problem** e.g., We say that 1 min = 60 s. So, the ratio of (1 min)/(60 s) equal to 1/60, as does its reciprocal (60 s)/(1 min). We may multiply a quantity by either of these factors without changing the quantity's by physical meaning. To find the number of seconds in 3 min, we write as

$$3 \text{ min} = (3 \text{ min})\left(\frac{60 \text{ s}}{1 \text{ min}}\right) = 180 \text{ s}$$

(iv) **Evaluate your answer** Check whether your answer is reasonable. Is the result 3 min = 180 s reasonable? Is your answer is consistent with an unit of conversion?

EXAMPLE |1| Conversion of Units

Calculate the angle of

(i) 1° (degree)

(ii) 1″ (second of arc or arc sec) in radian.   [NCERT]

Sol. (i) $1° = \frac{2\pi}{360} \text{ rad} = \frac{\pi}{180} = \frac{22}{7 \times 180}$

$$= 1.746 \times 10^{-2} \text{ rad}$$

(ii) $1 \text{ arc sec} = 1'' = \frac{1'}{60} = \frac{1°}{60 \times 60}$

$$= \frac{1}{60 \times 60} \times \frac{\pi}{180} \text{ rad}$$

$$= 4.85 \times 10^{-6} \text{ rad}$$

Rules for Writing SI Units

- Small letters are used for symbols of units.
- Symbols are not followed by a full stop.
- The initial letter of a symbol is capital only when the unit is named after a scientist.
- The full name of a unit always begins with a small letter even if it has been named after a scientist.
- Symbols do not take plural form.

ADVANTAGES OF SI OVER OTHER SYSTEMS OF UNITS

(i) **SI is a coherent system of units** All derived units can be obtained by simple multiplication or division of fundamental units without introducing any numerical factor.

(ii) **SI is a rational system of units** It uses only one unit for a given physical quantity. e.g, all forms of energy are measured in joule. On the other hand, in MKS system, the mechanical energy is measured in joule, heat energy in calorie and electrical energy in watt hour.

(iii) **SI is a metric system** The multiples and submultiples of SI units can be expressed as powers of 10.

$$\text{i.e. } a \times 10^{\pm b}.$$

(iv) **SI is an absolute system of units** It does not use gravitational units. The use of 'g' is not required.

Some General Units (Outside from SI)

Name	Symbol	Value in SI Unit
Minute	min	60 s
Hour	h	60 min = 3600 s
Day	d	24 h = 86400 s
Year	y	365.25 d = 3.156 × 10^7 s
Degree	°	1° = (π/180) rad
Litre	L	1 dm^3 = 10^{-3} m^3
Tonne	t	10^3 kg
Carat	c	200 mg
Bar	bar	0.1 MPa = 10^5 Pa
Curie	Ci	3.7 × 10^{10} s^{-1}
Roentgen	R	2.58 × 10^{-4} C/kg
Quintal	q	100 kg
Barn	b	100 fm^2 = 10^{-28} m^2
Area	a	1 dam^2 = 10^2 m^2
Hectare	ha	1 hm^2 = 10^4 m^2
Standard atmospheric pressure	atm	101325 Pa = 1.013 × 10^5 Pa

ABBREVIATIONS IN POWERS OF TEN

When the magnitudes of the physical quantities are very large or very small, it is convenient to express them in the multiples or submultiples of the SI units.

The various prefixes used for powers of 10 are listed below in table

Prefixes for Powers of Ten

Multiple	Prefix	Symbol	Sub-multiple	Prefix	Symbol
10^1	deca	da	10^{-1}	deci	d
10^2	hecto	h	10^{-2}	centi	c
10^3	kilo	k	10^{-3}	milli	m
10^6	mega	M	10^{-6}	micro	μ
10^9	giga	G	10^{-9}	nano	n
10^{12}	tera	T	10^{-12}	pico	p
10^{15}	peta	P	10^{-15}	femto	f
10^{18}	exa	E	10^{-18}	atto	a

e.g.
1 megaohm, $M\Omega = 10^6 \, \Omega$
1 milliampere or $1 \, mA = 10^{-3} \, A$
1 kilometre, $1 \, km = 10^3 \, m$
1 microvolt or $1\mu V = 10^{-6} \, V$
1 decagram, $1 \, da \, g = 10 \, g$
1 nanosecond or $1 \, ns = 10^{-9} \, s$
1 centimetre, $1 \, cm = 10^{-2} \, m$
1 picofarad or $1 \, pF = 10^{-12} \, F$

CGS, MKS and SI are Decimal Systems of Units

As we know that, CGS, MKS and SI are metric or decimal systems of units. This is because the multiplies and sub-multiplies of their basic units are related to the practical units by powers of 10.

SOME IMPORTANT PRACTICAL UNITS

For Length/Distance

(i) **Astronomical Unit** It is the mean distance of the earth from the sun. $1 \, AU = 1.496 \times 10^{11} \, m$.

(ii) **Light year** It is the distance travelled by light in vacuum in one year. $1 \, ly = 9.46 \times 10^{15} \, m$

(iii) **Parallactic second** It is the distance at which an arc of length 1 astronomical unit subtends an angle of 1 second of arc. $1 \, parsec = 3.084 \times 10^{16} \, m = 3.26 \, ly$

(iv) **Micron or micrometer**, $1 \, \mu m = 10^{-6} \, m$

(v) **Nanometer**, $1 \, nm = 10^{-9} \, m$

(vi) **Angstrom unit**, $1 \, Å = 10^{-10} \, m$

(vii) **Fermi** This unit is used for measuring nuclear sizes $1 \, Fm = 10^{-15} \, m$

EXAMPLE |2| **Length Conversion**
How many parsec are there in one metre?

Sol. Given, $1 \, parsec = 3.084 \times 10^{16} \, m$

or $3.084 \times 10^{16} \, m = 1 \, parsec$

$$\therefore \quad 1m = \frac{1}{3.084 \times 10^{16}} \, parsec$$

$$= 3.25 \times 10^{-17} \, parsec$$

EXAMPLE |3| **Relation between different unit of length**
Deduce relations between astronomical unit, light year and parsec. Arrange them in decreasing order of their magnitudes.

Sol. We know that $\quad 1 \, AU = 1.5 \times 10^{11} \, m$

$$1 \, ly = 9.46 \times 10^{15} \, m$$

$$1 \, par \, sec = 3.08 \times 10^{16} \, m$$

$$\therefore \quad \frac{1 \, ly}{1 \, AU} = \frac{9.46 \times 10^{15}}{1.5 \times 10^{11}} = 6.3 \times 10^4$$

$$1 \, ly = 6.3 \times 10^4 \, AU \qquad \text{...(i)}$$

Conversion of light year into parsec

$$\text{i.e.,} \quad \frac{1 \, parsec}{1 \, ly} = \frac{3.08 \times 10^{16}}{9.46 \times 10^{15}} = 3.26$$

$$\therefore \quad 1 \, parsec = 3.26 \, ly \qquad \text{...(ii)}$$

Comparing results from Eqs. (i) and (ii), we get
$1 \, parsec > 1 \, ly > 1 \, AU$

For Mass

(i) Pound, $1 \, lb = 0.4536 \, kg$

(ii) Slug, $1 \, Slug = 14.59 \, kg$

(iii) Quintal, $1 \, q = 100 \, kg$

(iv) Tonne or Metric ton, $1 \, t = 1000 \, kg$

(v) Atomic mass unit (it is defined as the 1/12th of the mass of one $^{12}_{6}C$ atom) $1 \, amu = 1.66 \times 10^{-27} \, kg$

For Time

(i) **Solar day** It is the time taken by the earth to complete one rotation about its own axis w.r.t. the sun.

(ii) **Sedrial year** It is the time taken by the earth to complete one rotation about its own axis w.r.t. a distant star.

(iii) **Solar year** It is the time taken by the earth to complete one revolution around the sun in its orbit.

1 solar year = 365.25 average solar days

= 366.25 sedrial days

(iv) **Tropical year** The year in which there is total solar eclipse is called **tropical year.**

(v) **Leap year** The year which is divisible by 4 and in which the month of February has 29 days is called a **leap year.**

(vi) **Lunar month** It is the time taken by the moon to complete one revolution around the earth in its orbit.

1 lunar month = 27.3 days

(*vii*) **Shake** It is the smallest practical unit of time.

1 shake = 10^{-8} s

EXAMPLE |4| A Clock

Which type of phenomena can be used as a measure of time? Give three examples.

Sol. A phenomena which repeats itself at regular intervals can be used as a measure of time.

Some examples are given below

(i) oscillation of a pendulum

(ii) rotation of earth around its axis

(iii) revolution of earth around the sun

For Areas

(i) Barn, 1 barn = 10^{-28} m^2

(ii) Acre, 1 acre = 4047 m^2

(iii) Hectare, 1 hectare = 10^4 m^2

For Other Quantities

(i) Litre (for volume), 1 L = 10^3 cc = 10^{-3} m^3

Where, cc represents cubic centimetre, i.e. cm^3.

(ii) Gallon (for volume),

In USA, 1 gallon = 3.7854 L

In UK, 1 gallon = 4.546 L

(iii) Pascal (for pressure), 1 Pa = 1 Nm^{-2}

Pressure exerted by earth's, atmosphere.

1 atm = 1.01×10^5 Pa

(iv) Bar (for pressure),

1 bar = 1 atm = 1.01×10^5 Pa = 760 mm of Hg

(v) Torr (for pressure),

1 torr = 1 mm of Hg column = 133.3 Pa

(vi) Electron volt,

1 eV = 1.6×10^{-19} J

(vii) Erg (for energy/work),

1 erg = 10^{-7} J

(viii) Kilowatt hour (for energy),

1 kWh = 3.6×10^6 J

(ix) Horse power (for power),

1 HP = 746 W

(x) Dioptre (for power of a lens),

1 D = 1 m^{-1}

(xi) Degree (for angle), $1° = \dfrac{\pi}{180}$ rad

| TOPIC PRACTICE 1 |

OBJECTIVE Type Questions

1. *A* is the fundamental quantity. Here, *A* refers to
   (a) mass
   (b) velocity
   (c) acceleration
   (d) linear momentum

Sol. (a) Mass is the fundamental quantity as it does not depend upon other physical quantities. However, other three quantities, i.e. velocity, acceleration and linear momentum are not fundamental quantities as these show their dependency on fundamental quantities.

2. How many wavelength of Kr^{86} are there in 1 m?
   (a) 1553164.13   (b) 1650763.73
   (c) 2348123.73   (d) 652189.63

Sol. (b) The number of wavelengths of Kr^{86} in 1 m is 1650763.73.

3. The solid angle subtended by the periphery of an area 1 cm^2 at a point situated symmetrically at a distance of 5 cm from the area is
   (a) 2×10^{-2} sr   (b) 4×10^{-2} sr
   (c) 6×10^{-2} sr   (d) 8×10^{-2} sr

Sol. (b) Solid angle, $d\Omega = \dfrac{dA}{r^2} = \dfrac{1 \text{ cm}^2}{(5 \text{ cm})^2}$

$= 0.04$ sr

$= 4 \times 10^{-2}$ sr

4. Which of the following is not a physical quantity?
   (a) Time   (b) Impulse
   (c) Mass   (d) Kilogram

Sol. (d) Kilogram represents the unit of a physical quantity. But other three, i.e. time, impulse and mass are the physical quantities.

5. The quantity having the same unit in all system of unit is
   (a) mass
   (b) time
   (c) length
   (d) temperature

Sol. (b) Time is the quantity which has the same unit in all systems of unit, i.e. second. Other three quantities, i.e. mass, length and temperature have different units in different systems.

6. SI unit of capacitance is
   (a) ohm-second
   (b) Wb
   (c) coulomb (volt)$^{-1}$
   (d) A-m^2

Sol. (c) SI unit of capacitance is coulomb (volt)$^{-1}$. However, ohm-second is the unit of inductance, Wb is the unit of magnetic flux and A-m^2 is the uinit of magnetic moment.

7. The damping force on an oscillator is directly proportional to the velocity. The unit of the constant of proportionality is
   (a) kg ms^{-1} (b) kg ms^{-2} (c) kg s^{-1} (d) kg s

Sol. (c) Given, damping force $\propto$ velocity
$$F \propto v \Rightarrow F = kv$$
$$\Rightarrow \quad k = \frac{F}{v}$$
$$\text{Unit of } k = \frac{\text{Unit of } F}{\text{Unit of } v} = \frac{\text{kg-ms}^{-2}}{\text{ms}^{-1}} = \text{kg s}^{-1}$$

8. Number of fermi in one metre is
   (a) 10^6 F (b) 10^{17} F (c) 10^{15} F (d) 10^{14} F

Sol. (c) 1 fermi (F) $= 10^{-15}$ m
   or $\quad 1\text{m} = \frac{1}{10^{-15}} = 10^{15}$ F

9. Number of degrees present in one radian is
   (a) 58° (b) 57.3° (c) 56.3° (d) 56°

Sol. (b) We know that,
$$\pi \text{ radian} = 180°$$
$$1 \text{ radian} = \frac{180}{\pi} = \frac{180}{22} \times 7 = 57.3°$$

VERY SHORT ANSWER Type Questions

10. Is it possible to have length and velocity both as fundamental quantities? Why?

Sol. No, since length is fundamental quantity and velocity is the derived quantity.

11. How many astronomical units make one metre?

Sol. 1 m $= 6.67 \times 10^{-12}$ AU

12. How many light years make 1 parsec?

Sol. 3.26 light years make 1 parsec.

13. Which of these is largest : astronomical unit, light year and parsec?

Sol. Parsec is larger than light year which in turn is larger than an astronomical unit.

14. Which unit is used to measure size of a nucleus?

Sol. The size of nucleus is measured in fermi.
   1 fermi $= 10^{-15}$ m

15. What is the difference between nm, mN and Nm?

Sol. nm stands for nanometre, 1 nm $= 10^{-9}$ m, mN stands for milli-newton, 1 mN $= 10^{-3}$ N, Nm stands for newton metre.

16. How many amu make 1 kg?

Sol. 1 amu $= 1.66 \times 10^{-27}$ kg
$$\therefore \quad 1 \text{ kg} = \frac{1}{1.66 \times 10^{-27}} = 0.6 \times 10^{27} \text{ amu}$$

17. Human heart is an inbuilt clock. Comment.

Sol. True, because human heart beats at a regular rate.

18. Define one Barn. How it is related with metre?

Sol. One barn is a small unit of area used to measure area of nuclear cross-section.
$$\therefore \quad 1 \text{ barn} = 10^{-28} \text{ m}^2$$

SHORT ANSWER Type Questions

19. Express an acceleration of 10 m/s^2 in km/h^2.

Sol. Acceleration $= \dfrac{10 \text{ m}}{(1\text{s})^2} = \dfrac{10 \times 10^{-3}}{\left[\dfrac{1}{60 \times 60} \text{h}\right]^2}$
$$= (3600)^2 \times 10^{-2} \text{ km/h}^2$$
$$= 1.29 \times 10^5 \text{ km/h}^2$$

20. Does AU and Å represent the same unit of length?

Sol. No, AU and Å represent two different units of length.
   1 AU = 1 astronomical unit $= 1.496 \times 10^{11}$ m
   1 Å = 1 angstrom $= 10^{-10}$ m

21. Find the value of one light year in giga metre.

Sol. We know that,
$$1 \text{ ly} = 9.46 \times 10^{15} \text{ m}$$
   Also, $\quad 1 \text{ Gm} = 10^9$ m
$$\therefore \quad 1 \text{ ly} = \frac{9.46 \times 10^{15}}{10^9} = 9.46 \times 10^6 \text{ Gm}$$

22. If the velocity of light is taken as the unit of velocity and year as the unit of time, what must be the unit of length? What is it called?

Sol. Unit of length = Unit of velocity × Unit of time

$$= 3 \times 10^8 \, ms^{-1} \times 1 \, year$$

$$= 3 \times 10^8 \, ms^{-1} \times 365 \times 24 \times 60 \times 60 \, s$$

$$= 9.45 \times 10^{15} \, ms^{-1} = 1 \, ly$$

23. How many metric tons are there in teragram?

Sol. In 1 teragram $= 10^{12}$ g

In 1 metric ton $= 10^3 kg = 10^3 \times 10^3 = 10^6$ g

∴ Number of metric tons are in teragram

$$= \frac{10^{12} \, g}{10^6 \, g} = 10^6$$

24. What is common between bar and torr?

Sol. Both bar and torr are the units of pressure.

1 bar = 1 atmospheric pressure

= 760 mm of Hg column

$= 10^5 N/m^2$

1 torr = 1 mm of Hg column

∴ 1 bar = 760 torr

25. The mass of a proton is 1.67×10^{-27} kg. How many protons would make 1 g?

Sol. Number of protons $= \dfrac{\text{Total mass}}{\text{Mass of each proton}}$

$$= \frac{10^{-3}}{1.67 \times 10^{-27}} = 5.99 \times 10^{23}$$

LONG ANSWER Type I Questions

26. Why length, mass and time are chosen as base quantities in mechanics?

Sol. In mechanics, length, mass and time are chosen as the base quantities because

(i) there is nothing simpler to length, mass and time.

(ii) all other quantities in mechanics can be expressed in terms of length, mass and time.

(iii) length, mass and time cannot be derived from one another.

27. Express the average distance of earth from the sun in (i) light year (ii) parsec.

Sol. Average distance of earth from the sun is (r)

i.e. $r = 1 \, AU = 1.496 \times 10^{11}$ m

$$= \frac{1.496 \times 10^{11}}{9.46 \times 10^{15}} \, ly = 1.58 \times 10^{-5} \, ly$$

Also, $r = \dfrac{1.496 \times 10^{11}}{3.08 \times 10^{16}}$ parsec

$$= 4.86 \times 10^{-6} \text{ parsec}$$

28. The radius of atom is of the order of 2 Å and radius of a nucleus is of the order of fermi. How many magnitudes higher is the volume of atom as compared to the volume of nucleus?

Sol. R_A, i.e. radius of atom is $2 \, \text{Å} = 2 \times 10^{-10}$ m

R_N, i.e. radius of nucleus is 1 fermi $= 10^{-15}$ m

$$\frac{V_A}{V_N} = \frac{\frac{4}{3}\pi R_A^3}{\frac{4}{3}\pi R_N^3} = \left[\frac{R_A}{R_N}\right]^3$$

$$= \left[\frac{2 \times 10^{-10}}{10^{-15}}\right]^3 = 8 \times 10^{15}$$

29. The unit of length convenient on the atomic scale is known as an angstrom and is denoted by Å.

$1 \, \text{Å} = 10^{-10}$ m. The size of the hydrogen atom is about 0.5 Å. What is the total atomic volume in m^3 of a mole of hydrogen atoms? **[NCERT]**

Sol. Radius of a hydrogen atom $(r) = 0.5 \, \text{Å} = 0.5 \times 10^{-10}$ m

Volume of each hydrogen atom $(V) = \dfrac{4}{3}\pi r^3$

$$= \frac{4}{3} \times 3.14 \times (0.5 \times 10^{-10})^3$$

$$= 5.234 \times 10^{-31} m^3$$

Number of atoms in 1 mole of hydrogen

= Avogadro's number (N)

$$= 6.023 \times 10^{23}$$

∴ Atomic volume of 1 mole of hydrogen atoms (V')

= Volume of a hydrogen atom × Number of atoms

$V' = V \times N$

$$= 5.236 \times 10^{-31} \times 6.023 \times 10^{23} m^3$$

$$= 3.152 \times 10^{-7} \text{ m}$$

30. Why has second been defined in terms of periods of radiations from cesium-133?

Sol. Second has been defined in terms of periods of radiation, because

(i) this period is accurately defined.

(ii) this period is not affected by change of physical conditions like temperature, pressure and volume etc.

(iii) the unit is easily reproducible in any good laboratory.

ASSESS YOUR TOPICAL UNDERSTANDING

OBJECTIVE Type Questions

1. Which one of the following is not a unit of British system of units?
   (a) Foot
   (b) Metre
   (c) Pound
   (d) Second

2. Which of the following statement is incorrect regarding mass?
   (a) It is a basic property of matter
   (b) The SI unit of mass is candela
   (c) The mass of an atom is expressed in u
   (d) None of the above

3. Pascal is the unit of
   (a) force
   (b) stress
   (c) work
   (d) energy

4. The surface area of a solid cylinder of radius 2.0 cm and height A cm is equal to 1.5×10^4 (mm)^2. Here, A refers to
   (a) 0.9 cm
   (b) 10 cm
   (c) 30 cm
   (d) 15 cm

5. If the value of force is 100 N and value of acceleration is 0.001 ms^{-2}, what is the value of mass in this system of units?
   (a) 10^3 kg
   (b) 10^4 kg
   (c) 10^5 kg
   (d) 10^6 kg

6. Young's modulus of steel is 1.9×10^{11} N /m^2. When expressed in CGS units of dyne/cm^2, it will be equal to (1N $= 10^5$ dyne, 1 m$^2 = 10^4$ cm^2)
   [NCERT Exemplar]
   (a) 1.9×10^{10}
   (b) 1.9×10^{11}
   (c) 1.9×10^{12}
   (d) 1.9×10^{13}

7. If the size of bacteria is 1μ, then the number of bacteria in 1 m length will be
   (a) one hundred
   (b) one crore
   (c) one thousand
   (d) one million

8. Among the given following units which one is not unit of length?
   (a) Angstrom
   (b) Fermi
   (c) Barn
   (d) Parsec

9. Age of the universe is about 10^{10} yr, whereas the mankind has existed for 10^6 yr. For how many seconds would the man have existed if age of universe were 1 day?
   (a) 9.2 s
   (b) 10.2 s
   (c) 8.6 s
   (d) 10.5 s

Answer

1. (b)	2. (b)	3. (b)	4. (b)	5. (c)
6. (c)	7. (d)	8. (c)	9. (c)	

VERY SHORT ANSWER Type Questions

10. Explain the concept of mass, length and time which is related to basic or fundamental quantities in mechanics.

11. How do we make the choice of a standard/unit of measurement?

12. Why MKS system had to be rationalised to obtain SI?

13. What is a coherent system of units?

SHORT ANSWER Type Questions

14. Briefly, explain the measuring process of any physical quantity.

15. Why 'metre' has been defined in terms of wavelength and 'second' in terms of periods of radiation or rotation?

16. Calculate the surface area of a solid cylinder of diameter 4 cm and height 20 cm in mm^2.
    [Ans. 27657.1 mm^2]

17. The density of air is 1.293 kg/m^3. Express it in CGS units. **[Ans. 0.001293 g/cc]**

18. What is the average distance of earth from the sun? **[Ans. 1.496×10^{11} m]**

19. An Astronomical Unit (AU) is the average distance between earth and the sun, approximately 1.50×10^8 km. The speed of light is about 3×10^8 m/s. Express the speed of light in astronomical unit per minute. **[Ans. 0.12 AU/min]**

LONG ANSWER Type I Questions

20. The radius of gold nucleus is 41.3 fermi. Express its volume in m^3. **[Ans. 2.95×10^{-40} m^3]**

21. Which unit can be used for measuring of very small masses?

22. "Five litres of benzene will weigh more in summer or winter". Comment.

23. Is the measure of an angle dependent upon the unit of length?

24. The height of mercury column in a barometer in Calcutta a laboratory was recorded to be 75 cm. Calculate this pressure in SI and CGS units using the following data.
Specific gravity of mercury = 13.6, Density of watch $= 10^3$ kg/m^3, $g = 9.8$ m/s^2 at Calcutta. Pressure $= h\rho g$ in usual symbols. **[Ans.** 10^{10^4} N/m^2, 10×10^5 dyne/cm^2**]**

25. The normal duration of ISc Physics practical period in Indian colleges is 100 minutes. Express this period in microcenturies. 1 microcentury$= 10^{-6} \times 100$ years. How many microcenturies did you leep yesterday? **[Ans.** 1.9 microcenturies**]**

|TOPIC 2|
Significant figures & Rounding off

SIGNIFICANT FIGURES

Normally, the reported result of measurement is a number that includes all digits in the number that are known reliably plus first digit that is uncertain. The digits that are known reliably plus the first uncertain digit are known as **significant digits** or **significant figures.**

e.g. When a measured distance is reported to be 374.5 m, it has four significant figures 3, 7, 4 and 5. The figures 3, 7, 4 are certain and reliable, while the digit 5 is uncertain.

Clearly, the digits beyond the significant digits reported in any result are superfluous.

The rules for determining the number of significant figures are

Rule 1 All non-zero digits are significant.
e.g. $x = 1234$ has four significant figures.

Rule 2 All the zeros between two non-zero digits are significant, no matter where, the decimal point is, if at all.
e.g. $x = 1007$ has four significant figures and $x = 10.07$ also contains four significant figures.

Rule 3 If the number is less than one, the zero(s) on the right of decimal point and to the left of first non-zero digit are not significant.
e.g. In 0.005704, the underlined zeros are not significant. The zero between 7 and 4 is significant. The number of significant figures is 4.

Rule 4 In a number without a decimal point, the terminal or trailing zeros are not significant.
e.g. $x = 3210$ has three significant figures, the trailing zeros are not significant.

Rule 5 The trailing zero(s) in a number with a decimal point are significant.
e.g. 3.500 has four significant figures.

Rule 6 The multiplying or dividing factors, which are neither rounded numbers nor numbers representing measured values are exact. They have infinite number of significant digits as per the condition.
e.g. In radius, $r = \dfrac{d}{2}$ and circumference, $s = 2\pi r$, the factors 2 is an exact number. It can be written as 2.0, 2.00 and 2.000, etc. as required.

Rule 7 The number of significant figures does not depend on the system of units. So, 16.4 cm, 0.164 m and 0.000164 km, all have three significant figures.

Ambiguity in Significant Figures

There can be some confusion regarding the trailing zeros. Suppose a measured length is reported as $x = 4.700$ m. Clearly, the zeros are meant to convey the precision of measurement and are therefore, significant. If we can rewrite the same length as $x = 0.004700$ km; $x = 470.0$ cm and $x = 4700$ mm.

As per rule 4, we would erroneously conclude that $x = 4700$ mm has two significant digits. While $x = 0.004700$ km has four significant digits and a mere change of units cannot change the number of significant figures (Rule 7).

To remove such ambiguities in determining the number of significant figures, the best way is to report every measurement in scientific notation (in the power of 10).

In this notation, every number can be expressed as
$$a \times 10^b$$
where, a is the number between 1 to 10 and b is any positive or negative exponent (or power) of 10.

Then, the number can be expressed approximately as 10^b in which exponent (or power) b of 10 is called order of magnitude of the quantity.
$$x = 4.700 \text{ m} = 4.700 \times 10^{-3} \text{ km}$$

In this case, the number of significant digit is 4, as the power of 10 is irrelevant to the determination of significant figures.

EXAMPLE |1| Uncertainty in Measurement

Write down the number of significant figure in the following.

(i) 0.072   (ii) 12.000   (iii) 0.060

(iv) 3.08×10^{11} (v) 1.2340   (vi) 0.04

Sol. (i) Two   (ii) Five   (iii) Two

(iv) Three   (v) Five   (vi) One

ROUNDING OFF

The result of computation with approximate numbers, which contain more than one uncertain digit, should be rounded off. While rounding off measurements, we use the following rules by convention:

Rule 1 If the digit to be dropped is less than 5, then the preceding digit is left unchanged.

e.g. $x = 7.82$ is rounded off to 7.8.

Rule 2 If the digit to be dropped is more than 5, then the preceding digit is raised by one.

e.g. $x = 6.87$ is rounded off to 6.9.

Rule 3 If the digit to be dropped is 5 followed by digits other than zero, then the preceding digit is raised by one. e.g. $x = 16.351$ is rounded off to 16.4.

Rule 4 If the digit to be dropped is 5 or 5 followed by zeros, then the preceding digit is left unchanged, if it is even.

e.g. $x = 3.250$ becomes 3.2 on rounding off.

Rule 5 If the digit to be dropped is 5 or 5 followed by zeros, then the preceding digits is raised by one, if it is odd.

e.g. $x = 3.750$ is rounded off to 3.8.

EXAMPLE |2| Precise Value

Round off the following number as indicated

(i) 18.35 upto 3 digits = 18.4

(ii) 143.45 upto 4 digits = 143.4

(iii) 189.67 upto 3 digits = 190

(iv) 321.1355 upto 5 digits = 321.14

(v) 31.325×10^{-5} upto 4 digits = 31.32×10^{-5}

(vi) 101.55×10^{6} upto 4 digits = 101.6×10^{6}

RULES FOR ARITHMETICAL OPERATIONS WITH SIGNIFICANT FIGURES

Any result is calculated by compounding (i.e. adding/ subtracting/multiplying/dividing) two or more variables, which might have been measured with different degrees of accuracy. Inaccuracy in the measurement of any one variable affects the accuracy of the final result.

Therefore, the result of arithmetical operations performed with measurements cannot be more accurate than the original measurement themselves. The following rules for arithmetic operations with significant figures that make final result more consistent with the precision of the measured values.

Addition and Subtraction

In both, addition and subtraction, the final result should retain as **many decimal places** as are there in the number with the **least decimal** places. e.g. The sum of three measurement of length 2.1 m, 1.78 m and 2.046 m is 5.926 m, which is rounded off to 5.9 m (upto smallest number of decimal places in the three measurements).

Similarly, if $x = 12.587$ m, and $y = 12.5$ m, then $(x - y)$ is $12.587 - 12.5 = 0.087$ m, which is rounded off to 0.1 m, upto smallest number of decimal places in y.

Multiplication and Division

In multiplication or division, the final result should retain as many significant figures, as are there in the original number with the least significant figures.

e.g. The speed of light is 3.00×10^{8} m/s and one year has 3.1557×10^{7} s, then light year is given by

$$= 3.00 \times 10^{8} \times 3.155 \times 10^{7}$$
$$= 9.4685 \times 10^{15} \text{ m}$$
$$= 9.5 \times 10^{15} \text{ m}$$

[Rounded off upto 2 significant figures]

EXAMPLE |3| A Rolling Cube

Each side of a cube is measured to be 7.203 m. What are the total surface area and the volume of the cube to appropriate significant figures? **[NCERT]**

Sol. Given, Side of the cube = 7.203 m

Total surface area $= 6 \times (\text{side})^2 = 6 \times (7.203)^2$

$$= 311.299254 \text{ m}^2 = 311.3 \text{ m}^2$$

[Rounded off to 4 significant figures]

Volume $= (\text{side})^3 = (7.203)^3$

$$= 373.714754 \text{ m}^3 = 373.7 \text{ m}^3.$$

[Rounded off to 4 significant figures]

EXAMPLE |4| Density of a Substance

5.74 g of a substance occupies 1.2 cm^3. Express its density keeping significant figures in view. **[NCERT]**

Sol. Density $= \dfrac{\text{Mass}}{\text{Volume}} = \dfrac{5.74 \text{ g}}{1.2 \text{ cm}^3}$

$= 4.783 \text{ g cm}^{-3}$

$= 4.8 \text{ g cm}^{-3}$

[Rounded off upto 2 significant figures]

RULES FOR DETERMINING UNCERTAINTY IN THE RESULTS OF ARITHMETIC CALCULATIONS

Rule 1 Suppose, we use a metre scale to measure length and breadth of a thin rectangular sheets as 15.4 cm and 10.2 cm, respectively.

Each measurement has three significant figures and a precision upto first place of decimal. Therefore, we can write length $(l) = (15.4 \pm 0.1)$ cm

$= 15.4 \pm \left(\dfrac{0.1}{15.4} \times 100 \right) = 15.4 \text{ cm} \pm 0.6\%$

Similarly, breadth $(b) = (10.2 \pm 0.1)$ cm

$= 10.2 \pm \left(\dfrac{0.1 \times 100}{10.2} \right)\% = 10.2 \text{ cm} \pm 1\%$

Thus, the error of the product i.e. area of thin sheet is $15.4 \times 10.2 \pm (0.6 + 1.0) \text{ cm}^2$

$= 157.08 \text{ cm}^2 \pm 1.6\%$

$= 157.08 \text{ cm}^2 \pm \left(\dfrac{1.6}{100} \times 157.08 \right) \text{cm}^2$

$= (157.08 \pm 2.51) \text{ cm}^2.$

As per rule, the final value of area can contain only three significant figures and error can contain only one significant figures, we can write the final result as $A = (157 \pm 3) \text{ cm}^2$

Rule 2 If a set of experimental data is specified to n significant figures, a result obtained by combining the data will also be valid to n significant figures.

e.g. $x = 13.7$ m and $y = 8.08$ m, both have three significant figures.

Now, $x - y = 13.7 - 8.08 = 5.62$ m

So, the final result should retain as many decimal places as, there is the number with least decimal places. Therefore, rounding off to one place of a decimal, we get $x - y = 5.6$ cm

Rule 3 The relative error of a value of number specified to n significant figures depends not only on n, but also on the number itself.

e.g. $\quad m_1 = (1.04 \pm 0.01)$ kg

and $\quad m_2 = (9.24 \pm 0.01)$ kg

Relative error in 1.04 kg is

$\pm \left(\dfrac{0.01}{1.04} \right) \times 100 = \pm 1\%$

Similarly, the relative error in 9.24 kg is

$\pm \left(\dfrac{0.01}{9.24} \right) \times 100 = \pm 0.1\%$

Thus, the relative error depends on the number itself.

Rule 4 In a multi-step computation, the intermediate results should be calculated to one more significant figure in every measurement, then the number of digits in the least precise measurement.

e.g. $x = 9.58$ has three significant digits. Now, reciprocal of x is $\dfrac{1}{x} = \dfrac{1}{9.58} = 0.104$, rounded off to three significant digits. When we take reciprocal of 0.104, we get 9.62, rounded off to three significant digits.

However, if we calculate $\dfrac{1}{x} = \dfrac{1}{9.58} = 0.1044$, rounded off to four significant figures, then

$\dfrac{1}{0.1044} = 9.58$, rounded off to three significant digits.

Thus, retaining one more extra digits in intermediate steps of complex calculations would avoid additional errors in the process of rounding off the numbers.

EXAMPLE |5| **Appropriate Numbers of Significant Number**

Solve the following and express the result to an appropriate number of significant figures.

(i) Add 6.2g, 4.33g and 17.456g

(ii) Subtract 63.54 kg from 187.2 kg

(iii) $75.5 \times 125.2 \times 0.51$

(iv) $\dfrac{2.13 \times 24.78}{458.2}$

Sol. (i) $6.2 \text{ g} + 4.33 \text{ g} + 17.456 \text{ g} = 27.986 = 28.0 \text{ g}$

[rounded off to first decimal place]

(ii) $187.2 \text{kg} - 63.54 \text{kg} = 123.66 \text{kg} = 123.7 \text{kg}$

[rounded off to first decimal place]

(iii) $75.5 \times 125.2 \times 0.51 = 4820.826 = 4800$

[rounded off upto two significant figures]

(iv) $\dfrac{2.13 \times 24.78}{458.2} = 0.115193 = 0.115$

[rounded off to three significant figures]

EXAMPLE |6|

The length, breadth and height of a rectangular block of wood were measured to be

$$l = 12.13 \pm 0.02 \text{ cm}, \quad b = 8.16 \pm 0.01 \text{ cm}$$

and $\quad h = 3.46 \pm 0.01 \text{ cm}$

Determine the percentage error in the volume of the block upto correct significant figures.

Sol. Volume of block, $V = lbh$

The percentage error in the volume is given by

$$\frac{\Delta V}{V} \times 100 = \left(\frac{\Delta l}{l} + \frac{\Delta b}{b} + \frac{\Delta h}{h} \right) \times 100$$

$$= \left(\frac{0.02}{12.13} + \frac{0.01}{8.16} + \frac{0.01}{3.46} \right) \times 100$$

$$= \frac{200}{1213} + \frac{100}{816} + \frac{100}{346}$$

$$= 0.1649 + 0.1225 + 0.2890$$

$$= 0.58\%$$

[rounded off to two significant figures]

| TOPIC PRACTICE 2 |

OBJECTIVE Type Questions

1. The ratio of the volume of the atom to the volume of the nucleus is of the order of
   (a) 10^{15} (b) 10^{25} (c) 10^{20} (d) 10^{10}

Sol. (a) Radius of atom $= 10^{-10}$ m

Radius of nucleus $= 10^{-15}$ m

$$\text{Ratio} = \frac{10^{-10}}{10^{-15}} = 10^5$$

$$\text{Ratio of volume} = (10^5)^3 = 10^{15}$$

2. The number of significant figures in the numbers 4.8000×10^4 and 48000.50 are respectively,
   (a) 5 and 6   (b) 5 and 7   (c) 2 and 7   (d) 2 and 6

Sol. (b) 4.8000×10^4 has 4, 8, 0, 0, 0 $\Rightarrow$ 5 significant digits.

48000.50 has 4, 8, 0, 0, 0, 5, 0 $\Rightarrow$ 7 significant digits.

3. If 3.8×10^{-6} is added to 4.2×10^{-5} giving due regard to significant figures, then the result will be
   (a) 4.58×10^{-5} (b) 4.6×10^{-5}
   (c) 45×10^{-5} (d) None of these

Sol. (b) By adding 3.8×10^{-6} and 42×10^{-6}, we get

$$= 45.8 \times 10^{-6} = 4.58 \times 10^{-5}$$

As least number of significant figures in given values are 2, so we round off the result to 4.6×10^{-5}.

4. The mass and volume of a body are 4.237 g and 2.5 cm^3, respectively. The density of the material of the body in correct significant figures is

[NCERT Exemplar]
   (a) 1.6048 g cm^{-3} (b) 1.69 g cm^{-3}
   (c) 1.7 g cm^{-3} (d) 1.695 g cm^{-3}

Sol. (c) In this question, density should be reported to two significant figures.

$$\text{Density} = \frac{4.237 \text{g}}{2.5 \text{ cm}^3}$$

$$= 1.6948$$

As rounding off the number, we get density $= 1.7$

VERY SHORT ANSWER Type Questions

5. If all measurements in an experiment are taken upto same number of significant figures, then which measurement is responsible for maximum error?

Sol. The maximum error will be due to
   (i) measurement which is least accurate.
   (ii) measurement of the quantity which has maximum power in the formula.

6. Round off to four significant figures
   (i) 36.879 (ii) 1.0084

Sol. (i) 36.88   (ii) 1.008

7. In a number without decimal, what is the significance of zeros on the right of non-zero digits?

Sol. All such zeros are not significant. e.g. $x = 678000$ has only three significant figures.

8. Solve with due regard to significant figures $\sqrt{6.5 - 6.32}$

Sol. $\sqrt{6.5 - 6.32} = \sqrt{0.18} = \sqrt{0.4242}$, upto one decimal place $= 0.43$ (having 2 significant figures).

SHORT ANSWER Type Questions

9. A jeweller put a diamond weighing 5.42 g in a box weighing 1.2 kg. Find the total weight of the box and the diamond to correct number of significant figures.

Sol. Weight of diamond $= 5.42$ g $= 0.00542$ kg

Total weight $= 1.2 + 0.00542$

$$= 1.20542 \text{ kg} = 1.2 \text{ kg}$$

10. The voltage across a lamp is $V = (6.0 \pm 0.1)$ volt and the current passing through it $I = (4 \pm 0.2)$ ampere. Find the power consumed by the electric lamp upto correct significant figures. Given that power, $P = VI$

Sol. As, $V = (6.0 \pm 0.1)$ V, $\quad I = (4.0 \pm 0.2)$A

Power, $P = VI = 6.0 \times 4.0 = 24$ W

and maximum error in power measurement

$$\frac{\Delta P}{P} = \frac{\Delta V}{V} + \frac{\Delta I}{I} = \frac{0.1}{6.0} + \frac{0.2}{4.0}$$

$$= 0.017 + 0.050 = 0.067$$

$$\Delta P = 0.067 \times P$$

$$= 0.067 \times 24 = 1.6 \text{ W}$$

Power consumed by the electric lamp within error limit is (24 ± 1.6) W.

LONG ANSWER Type I Questions

11. The mass of a box measured by a grocer's balance is 2.3 kg. Two gold pieces of masses 20.15 g and 20.17 g are added to the box. What is (i) the total mass of the box (ii) the difference in the mass of the pieces to correct significant figures?　　　　　　　　　　**[NCERT]**

Sol. Given, mass of the box $(m) = 2.3$ kg

Mass of first gold piece $(m_1) = 20.15$ g $= 0.02015$ kg

Mass of second gold piece $(m_2) = 20.17$ g $= 0.02017$ kg

(i) Total mass of the box $(M) = m + m_1 + m_2$

$$= 2.3 + 0.02015 + 0.02017$$

$$= 2.34032 \text{ kg}$$

As the mass of the box has least decimal place i.e. one decimal place, therefore, total mass of the box can have only one decimal place. Rounding off the total mass of the box up to one decimal place, we get

Total mass of the box $(M) = 2.3$ kg

(ii) Difference in masses of gold pieces

$$(\Delta m) = m_2 - m_1$$

$$= 20.17 - 20.15 = 0.02 \text{ g}$$

(The masses of two gold pieces has two decimal places, therefore, it is correct up to two places of decimal.)

12. A physical quantity P is related to four observables a, b, c and d are as follows $P = a^3 b^2 / \sqrt{cd}$

The percentage errors of measurement in a, b, c and d are 1%, 3%, 4% and 2%, respectively. What is the percentage error in the quantity P? If the value of P calculated using the above relation turns out to be 3.763, to what value should you round off the result?　　　　　　　　**[NCERT]**

Sol. Given, $\qquad P = a^3 b^2 / \sqrt{cd}$

Maximum relative error in physical quantity P is given by

$$\frac{\Delta P}{P} = \pm \left[3\left(\frac{\Delta a}{a}\right) + 2\left(\frac{\Delta b}{b}\right) + \frac{1}{2}\left(\frac{\Delta c}{c}\right) + \left(\frac{\Delta d}{d}\right) \right]$$

$\therefore$ Maximum percentage error in P is given by

$$\frac{\Delta P}{P} \times 100 = \pm \left[3\left(\frac{\Delta a}{a} \times 100\right) + 2\left(\frac{\Delta b}{b} \times 100\right) \right.$$
$$\left. + \frac{1}{2}\left(\frac{\Delta c}{c} \times 100\right) + \left(\frac{\Delta d}{d} \times 100\right) \right]$$

Given $\dfrac{\Delta a}{a} \times 100 = 1\%, \dfrac{\Delta b}{b} \times 100 = 3\%$

$\dfrac{\Delta c}{c} \times 100 = 4\%, \dfrac{\Delta d}{d} \times 100 = 2\%$

$\therefore \dfrac{\Delta P}{P} \times 100 = \pm \left[3 \times (1) + 2 \times (3) + \dfrac{1}{2} \times (4) + (2) \right]$

$$= \pm [3 + 6 + 2 + 2] \% = \pm 13\%$$

As the result (13%) has two significant figures, therefore, the value of $P = 3.763$ should have only two significant figures. Rounding off the value of P up to two significant figures, we get $P = 3.8$

13. State the number of significant figures in the following　　　　　　　　　　　　　　**[NCERT]**

(i) 0.007 m^2　　　　　　(ii) 2.64×10^{24} kg

(iii) 0.2370 g/cm^3　　(iv) 6.320 J

(v) 6.032 N/m^2　　　(vi) 0.0006032 m^2

Sol. The number of significant figures in the given quantities are given below.

(i) In 0.007, the number of significant figures is 1 because in a number less than 1, the zero's on the right of the decimal point but to the let of the first non-zero digit are not significant.

(ii) In 2.64×10^{24}, the number of significant figures is 3 because all non-zero digits are significant, power of 10 are not taken in significant figure.

(iii) In 0.2370, the number of significant figures is 4, as all non-zero digits left to decimal and trailing zero are significant.

(iv) In 6.320, the number of significant figures is 4 (reason is same as in part 'iii').

(v) In 6.032, the number of significant figures is 4 (reason is same as in part 'iii').

(vi) In 0.0006032, the number of significant figures is 4 (reason is same as in part 'i').

14. Write down the number of significant figures in the following

(i) 5238 N　　　　　　(ii) 4200 kg

(iii) 34.000 m　　　　(iv) 0.02340 N/m

Sol. (i) 5238 N has four significant digits.

(ii) $4200 \text{ kg} = 4.200 \times 10^3$ kg has four significant figures

(iii) 34.000 m has five significant digits.

(iv) 0.02340 N/m has four significant digits.

15. Compute the following with regards to significant figures.

(i) 4.6×0.128　　　　(ii) $\dfrac{0.9995 \times 1.53}{1.592}$

(iii) $876 + 0.4382$

Sol. (i) $4.6 \times 0.128 = 0.5888 = 0.59$

The result has been rounded off to have two significant digits (as in 4.6)

(ii) $\dfrac{0.9995 \times 1.53}{1.592} = 0.96057 = 0.961$

The result has been rounded off to three significant digits (as in 1.53).

(iii) $876 + 0.4382 = 876.4382 = 876$

As, there is no decimal point in 876, therefore, result of addition has been rounded off to no decimal point.

16. The length, breadth and thickness of a rectangular sheet of metal are 4.234 m, 1.005 m and 2.01 cm, respectively. Give the area and volume of the sheet to correct significant figures. **[NCERT]**

☼ If different values of a same quantity are given in different units, then first of all convert them in same units without changing the number of significant figures.

Sol. Given, length $(l) = 4.234$ m, Breadth $(b) = 1.005$ m

Thickness $(t) = 2.01$ cm $= 0.0201$ m

Area of sheet $(A) = 2(l \times b + b \times t + t \times l)$

$= 2[(4.234 \times 1.005) + (1.005 \times 0.0201)$
$\qquad\qquad + (0.0201 \times 4.234)]$

$= 2 \times 4.3604739 = 8.7209478$ m^2

As, thickness has least number of significant figures 3, therefore, rounding off area up to three significant figures, we get Area of sheet $(A) = 8.72$ m^2

Volume of sheet $(V) = l \times b \times t$

$= 4.234 \times 1.005 \times 0.0201$

$= 0.0855289$

Rounding off up to three significant figures, we get

Volume of the sheet $= 0.0855$ m^3

LONG ANSWER Type II Questions

17. The sun is a hot plasma (ionised matter) with its inner core at a temperature exceeding 10^7 K and its outer surface at a temperature of about 6000 K. At these high temperatures, no substance remains in a solid or liquid phase. In what range do you expect the mass density of the Sun to be, in the range of densities of solids and liquids or gases? Check if your guess is correct from the following data. **[NCERT]**

Mass of the Sun $= 2.0 \times 10^{30}$ kg
and radius of the Sun $= 7.0 \times 10^8$ m.

Sol. Given, mass of the sun $(M) = 2.0 \times 10^{30}$ kg

Radius of the Sun $(R) = 7.0 \times 10^8$ m

Density of the Sun $= \dfrac{\text{Mass of the Sun } (M)}{\text{Volume of the Sun } (V)}$

$$\left[\because \text{Density} = \dfrac{\text{Mass}}{\text{Volume}} \right]$$

$\rho = \dfrac{M}{\dfrac{4}{3}\pi R^3} = \dfrac{3}{4}\dfrac{M}{\pi R^3} = \dfrac{3 \times 2.0 \times 10^{30}}{4 \times 3.14 \times (7.0 \times 10^8)^3}$

$= \dfrac{3 \times 10^{30}}{6.28 \times 343 \times 10^{24}} = 1.392 \times 10^3$

$\rho \approx 1.4 \times 10^3$ kg/m^3

This density is of the order of density of solids and liquids and not of gases.

The temperature of inner core of the sun is 10^7 K while the temperature of the outer layers is nearly 6000 K. At so high temperature, no matter can exist in its solid or liquid state. Every matter is highly ionised and present as a mixture of nucleus, free electrons and ions which is called plasma. The density of plasma is so high due to inward gravitational attraction on outer layers due to inner layers of the sun.

18. Estimate the average mass density of sodium atom assuming its size to be about 2.5 Å (Use the known values of Avogadro's number and the atomic mass of sodium). Compare it with the density of sodium in its crystalline phase 970 kg/m^3. Are the two densities of the same order of magnitude? If so, why? **[NCERT]**

Sol. Given, radius of sodium atom,

$r = 2.5$ Å $= 2.5 \times 10^{-10}$ m $\qquad [\because 1 \text{ Å} = 10^{-10}$ m$]$

Volume of sodium atom $= \dfrac{4}{3}\pi r^3$

$= \dfrac{4}{3} \times 3.14 \times (2.5 \times 10^{-10})^3 = 65.42 \times 10^{-30}$ m^3

Number of atom in one mole of sodium

$= $ Avogadro's number (N)

$N = 6.023 \times 10^{23}$

∴ Atomic volume of sodium

$= $ Volume of one atom of sodium

$\times$ Number of atoms

$= 65.42 \times 10^{-30} \times 6.023 \times 10^{23} = 3.94 \times 10^{-5}$ m^3

Mass of a mole of sodium $= 23$ g $= 23 \times 10^{-3}$ kg

∴ Average mass density of sodium $= \dfrac{\text{Mass}}{\text{Volume}}$

$\rho = \dfrac{23 \times 10^{-3}}{3.94 \times 10^{-5}} \approx 5.84 \times 10^2$ kg/m^3 ≈ 584 kg/m^3

Density of sodium in crystalline phase

$= 970$ kg/m^3 $= 9.7 \times 10^2$ kg/m^3

The two densities are of the same order of magnitude because in solid state, atoms are tightly packed.

ASSESS YOUR TOPICAL UNDERSTANDING

OBJECTIVE Type Questions

1. Size of the universe is of the order of
   (a) 10^{40} m   (b) 10^{26} m   (c) 10^{18} m   (d) 10^{14} m

2. To determine the number of significant figures, scientific notation is
   (a) a^b (b) $a \times 10^b$ (c) $a \times 10^2$ (d) $a \times 10^4$

3. In 4700 m, significant digits are
   (a) 2   (b) 3   (c) 4   (d) 5

4. The number of significant figures in 0.06900 is
   [NCERT Exemplar]
   (a) 5   (b) 4   (c) 2   (d) 3

5. The sum of the numbers 436.32, 227.2 and 0.301 in appropriate significant figures is
   [NCERT Exemplar]
   (a) 663.821   (b) 664   (c) 663.8   (d) 663.82

6. Choose the correct option.
   (a) $3.00 - 2.5 = -5.0$ (b) $3.00 - 2.5 = 0.50$
   (c) $3.00 + 2.5 = 5.50$ (d) $3.00 + 2.5 = 5.500$

Answer

1.	(b)	2.	(b)	3.	(a)	4.	(b)	5.	(b)
6.	(b)								

VERY SHORT ANSWER Type Question

7. What do you mean by order of magnitude of a length?

LONG ANSWER Type II Questions

8. What is the difference between 5.0 and 5.00?

9. What is meant by significant figures? Give any four rules for counting significant figures.

|TOPIC 3|
Dimensions of a Physical Quantity

The dimensions of a physical quantity are the powers (or exponents) to which the units of base quantities are raised to represent a derived unit of that quantity. There are seven base quantities and are represented with square brackets [ ] such as length [L], mass [M], time [T], electric current [A], thermodynamic temperature [K], luminous intensity [cd] and amount of substances [mol].

e.g. The volume occupied by an object is expressed as the product of length. So, its dimension is given by

$$V = [L] \times [L] \times [L] = [L^3]$$

As there is no mass and time in volume, so the dimension of volume is expressed as

$$V = [M^0 L^3 T^0]$$

Similarly, for force, it is the product of mass and acceleration. It can be expressed as

$$F = \text{mass} \times \text{acceleration} = \text{mass} \times \frac{\text{length}}{(\text{time})^2}$$

∴ The dimension of force is given by

$$F = [M] \times \frac{[L]}{[T]^2} = [MLT^{-2}]$$

Note

Using the square bracket [ ] round a quantity means that we are dealing with the 'dimensions of' the quantity.

DIMENSIONAL FORMULAE AND DIMENSIONAL EQUATIONS

The expression which shows how and which of the fundamental quantities represent the dimension of the physical quantity is called the **dimensional formula** of the given physical quantity.

e.g. Some of the dimensional formulae are as given below

$$\text{Acceleration} = [M^0 L^1 T^{-2}]$$

$$\text{Mass density} = [ML^{-3} T^0]$$

$$\text{Volume} = [M^0 L^3 T^0]$$

The equation obtained by equating a physical quantity with its dimensional formula is called the **dimensional equation** of the given physical quantity.

e.g. Some of the dimensional equations are as given below

$$\text{Linear momentum} = \text{mass} \times \text{velocity} = [M^1 L^1 T^{-1}]$$

$$\text{Impulse} = \text{Force} \times \text{time} = [M^1 L^1 T^{-1}]$$

$$\text{Moment of Inertia} = \text{mass} \times \text{radius of gyration}$$
$$= [M^1 L^2 T^0]$$

Problem Solving Strategy
(Finding Dimensional Formulae)

1. First read the problem carefully and then find out whether we have given with the formulae or any law to describe in it.
2. Write the formulae of a physical quantity for which the dimensions to be known.
3. Convert the formulae of derived physical quantity into fundamental quantities, e.g. acceleration= Length/Time
4. Write the corresponding symbols for fundamental quantities, e.g. mass = [M], length = [L],
   time = [T], etc.
5. Make proper algebraic combination and get the result.
6. Try to arrange the dimensions in order i.e. [M], [L], [T] .....

EXAMPLE |1| Dimension of Gravitational Constant

Find out the dimensions of universal gravitational constant used in Newton's law of gravitation.

Sol. According to Newton's law of gravitation, the force F, between two masses m_1 and m_2 separated by distance r can be given as $F = G\dfrac{m_1 m_2}{r^2}$

Where, G = universal gravitational constant

$$G = \frac{Fr^2}{m_1 m_2} = \frac{\text{Newton} \times (\text{metre})^2}{(\text{kg})^2}$$

$$G = \frac{(\text{mass} \times \text{acceleration}) \times (\text{metre})^2}{(\text{mass})^2}$$

$$= \frac{1}{\text{mass}} \left(\frac{\text{Change in velocity}}{\text{Time}} \right) \times (\text{Length})^2$$

$$G = \frac{(\text{Length})^2}{\text{Mass} \times \text{Time}} \times \frac{\text{Distance}}{\text{Time}}$$

$$G = \frac{[L]^2}{[M] \times [T]} \times \frac{[L]}{[T]} = [M^{-1} \, L^3 \, T^{-2}]$$

Dimensional Formula of Some of the Important Mechanical Quantities

Physical quantity	Relation with other quantities	Dimensional formula	SI unit
Area	length × breadth	$L \times L = L^2 = [M^0 \, L^2 \, T^0]$	m^2
Volume	length × breadth × height	$L \times L \times L = L^3 = [M^0 \, L^3 \, T^0]$	m^3
Density	$\dfrac{\text{mass}}{\text{volume}}$	$\dfrac{M}{L^3} = [M^1 \, L^{-3} \, T^0]$	$kg \, m^{-3}$
Specific gravity	$\dfrac{\text{density of body}}{\text{density of water at 4°C}}$	$\dfrac{M/L^3}{M/L^3} = 1 = [M^0 \, L^0 \, T^0] \rightarrow$ no dimensions	No units
Speed or velocity	$\dfrac{\text{distance or displacement}}{\text{time}}$	$\dfrac{L}{T} = LT^{-1} = [M^0 \, L^1 \, T^{-1}]$	ms^{-1}
Linear momentum	mass × velocity	$M \times LT^{-1} = [M^1 \, L^1 \, T^{-1}]$	$kg \, ms^{-1}$
Acceleration	$\dfrac{\text{change in velocity}}{\text{time taken}}$	$\dfrac{L/T}{T} = LT^{-2} = [M^0 \, L^1 \, T^{-2}]$	ms^{-2}
Acceleration due to gravity (g)	$\dfrac{\text{change in velocity}}{\text{time taken}}$	$\dfrac{L/T}{T} = LT^{-2} = [M^0 \, L^1 \, T^{-2}]$	ms^{-2}
Force	mass × acceleration	$M \times LT^{-2} = [M^1 L^1 T^{-2}]$	N (newton)
Impulse	force × time	$M \, LT^{-2} \times T = [M^1 \, L^1 \, T^{-1}]$	Ns
Pressure	force/area	$\dfrac{MLT^{-2}}{L^2} = [M^1 \, L^{-1} \, T^{-2}]$	Nm^{-2}
Universal constant of gravitation (G)	From Newton's law of gravitation. $F = \dfrac{Gm_1 m_2}{r^2}$ or $G = \dfrac{Fr^2}{m_1 m_2}$, where F is force between masses m_1, m_2 at a distance r	$G = \dfrac{[MLT^{-2}] \, L^2}{MM} = [M^{-1} \, L^3 \, T^{-2}]$	$Nm^2 \, kg^{-2}$
Work	force × distance	$M \, LT^{-2} \times L = [M^1 \, L^2 \, T^{-2}]$	J (joule)
Energy (All types)	work	$[M^1 \, L^2 \, T^{-2}]$	J (joule)

Physical quantity	Relation with other quantities	Dimensional formula	SI unit
Moment of force	force $\times$ distance	$MLT^{-2} \times L = [M^1 L^2 T^{-2}]$	N-m
Power	$\dfrac{\text{work}}{\text{time}}$	$\dfrac{ML^2 T^{-2}}{T} = [M^1 L^2 T^{-3}]$	W (watt)
Surface tension	$\dfrac{\text{force}}{\text{length}}$	$\dfrac{MLT^{-2}}{T} = [M^1 L^0 T^{-2}]$	Nm^{-1}
Surface energy	Energy of free surface	$[M^1 L^2 T^{-2}]$	J
Force constant	$\dfrac{\text{force}}{\text{displacement}}$	$\dfrac{MLT^{-2}}{T} = [M^1 L^0 T^{-2}]$	Nm^{-1}
Thrust	force	$[M^1 L^1 T^{-2}]$	N (newton)
Tension	force	$[M^1 L^1 T^{-2}]$	N (newton)
Stress, Pressure	$\dfrac{\text{force}}{\text{area}}$	$\dfrac{MLT^{-2}}{L^2} = [M^1 L^{-1} T^{-2}]$	Nm^{-2}
Strain	$\dfrac{\text{change in dimension}}{\text{original dimension}}$	$\dfrac{L}{L} = [M^0 L^0 T^0]$	No units
Coefficient of elasticity	$\dfrac{\text{stress}}{\text{strain}}$	$\dfrac{M^1 L^{-1}T^{-2}}{1} = [M^1 L^{-1} T^{-2}]$	Nm^{-2}
Radius of gyration (K)	distance	$L = [M^0 L^1 T^0]$	m
Moment of inertia (I)	mass (radius of gyration)^2	$ML^2 = [M^1 L^2 T^0]$	$kg\,m^2$
Angle (θ) or Angular displacement (θ)	$\dfrac{\text{length} (l)}{\text{radius} (r)}$	$\dfrac{L}{L} = 1 = [M^0 L^0 T^0]$	radian
Angular velocity (ω)	$\dfrac{\text{angle} (\theta)}{\text{time} (t)}$	$\dfrac{1}{T} = T^{-1} = [M^0 L^0 T^{-1}]$	$rad\,s^{-1}$
Angular acceleration (α)	$\dfrac{\text{change in angular velocity}}{\text{time taken}}$	$\dfrac{1/T}{T} = T^{-2} = [M^0 L^0 T^{-2}]$	$rad\,s^{-2}$
Angular momentum	$I\omega$	$[ML^2][T^{-1}] = [M^1 L^2 T^{-1}]$	$kg\,m^2\,s^{-1}$
Torque	$I\alpha$	$[ML^2][T^{-2}] = [M^1 L^2 T^{-2}]$	N-m
Wavelength (λ)	length of one wave, i.e., distance	$L = [M^0 L^1 T^0]$	m
Frequency (v)	number of vibrations/sec	$\dfrac{1}{T} = T^{-1} = [M^0 L^0 T^{-1}]$	s^{-1} or Hz (hertz)
Angular frequency (ω)	$2\pi \times$ frequency	$T^{-1} = [M^0 L^0 T^{-1}]$	radian/sec
Velocity of light in vacuum (c)	$\dfrac{\text{distance travelled}}{\text{time taken}}$	$\dfrac{L}{T} = [M^0 L^1 T^{-1}]$	ms^{-1}
Velocity gradient	$\dfrac{\text{velocity}}{\text{distance}}$	$\dfrac{LT^{-1}}{T} = T^{-1} = [M^0 L^0 T^{-1}]$	s^{-1}
Rate of flow	$\dfrac{\text{volume}}{\text{time}}$	$\dfrac{L^3}{T} = L^3 T^{-1} = [M^0 L^3 T^{-1}]$	$m^3 s^{-1}$
Planck's constant (h)	$\dfrac{\text{energy} (E)}{\text{frequency} (v)}$	$\dfrac{ML^2 T^{-2}}{T^{-1}} = [M^1 L^2 T^{-1}]$	J-s
Linear mass density (m)	$\dfrac{\text{mass}}{\text{length}}$	$\dfrac{M}{L} = [M^1 L^{-1} T^0]$	$kg\,m^{-1}$

Physical quantity	Relation with other quantities	Dimensional formula	SI unit
Distance travelled in nth second	$\dfrac{\text{distance}}{\text{time}}$	$\dfrac{L}{T} = [M^0\ L^1\ T^{-1}]$	ms^{-1}
Avogadro's number (N)	Number of atoms/ molecules in one gram atom/mole	$[M^0\ L^0\ T^0]$	$mole^{-1}$
Magnetic dipole moment (M)	$M = IA$	$AL^2 = [M^0\ L^2\ T^0\ A^1]$	Am^2
Pole strength (m)	$m = \dfrac{M}{2l}$	$\dfrac{AL^2}{L} = AL = [M^0\ L^1\ T^0\ A^1]$	Am
Magnetic permeability of free space (μ_0)	From Coulomb's law in magnetism, $F = \dfrac{\mu_0}{4\pi}\dfrac{m_1 m_2}{r^2}$, where m_1, m_2 are strengths of two poles; $[\mu_0] = \dfrac{4\pi[F][r^2]}{m_1 m_2}$	$\dfrac{[MLT^{-2}][L^2]}{[AL]^2} = [M^1\ L^1\ T^{-2}\ A^{-2}]$	Hm^{-1}
Resistance (R)	$\dfrac{\text{potential difference}}{\text{current}}$	$\dfrac{ML^2T^{-3}A^{-1}}{A} = [M^1\ L^2\ T^{-3}\ A^{-2}]$	Ω (ohm)
Capacitance (C)	$\dfrac{\text{charge}}{\text{potential difference}}$	$\dfrac{AT}{M\ L^2\ T^{-3}\ A^{-1}} = [M^{-1}\ L^{-2}\ T^4\ A^2]$	F (farad)
Surface density of charge	$\sigma = \dfrac{\text{charge}}{\text{area}}$	$\dfrac{AT}{L^2} = [M^0\ L^{-2}\ T^1\ A^1]$	Cm^{-1}
Electric dipole moment (p)	$q\,(2a)$	$AT\,(L) = [M^0\ L^1\ T^1\ A^1]$	Cm
Specific Resistance or resistivity (ρ)	$\dfrac{Ra}{l}$	$\dfrac{[ML^2T^{-3}A^{-2}]\,[L^2]}{L} = [M^1\ L^3\ T^{-3}\ A^{-2}]$	ohm·m
Conductance (G)	$\dfrac{1}{R}$	$\dfrac{1}{[ML^2T^{-3}A^{-2}]} = [M^{-1}\ L^{-2}\ T^3\ A^2]$	ohm^{-1}
Conductivity (σ)	$\dfrac{1}{\rho}$	$\dfrac{1}{[M^1L^3T^{-3}A^{-2}]} = [M^{-1}\ L^{-3}\ T^3\ A^2]$	ohm^{-1}
Electric flux	Electric field $\times$ area	$[M^1L^1T^{-3}A^{-1}]\,[L^2] = [M^1\ L^3\ T^{-3}\ A^{-1}]$	$Nm^2\ C^{-1}$
Faraday constant	Avogadro number $\times$ elementary charge	$\dfrac{1}{mol} \times AT = [M^0\ L^0\ T^1\ A^1\ mol^{-1}]$	C
Mass defect (Δm)	Sum of masses of nucleons – mass of nucleus	$[M^1\ L^0\ T^0]$	kg
Binding energy of nucleus	(mass defect) $\times$ (speed of light)^2	$M\,[LT^{-1}]^2 = [ML^2T^{-2}]$	J

EXAMPLE |2| Pull Over Buddy

Derive the dimensions formula of physical quantities.

(i) Tension
(ii) Velocity gradient
(iii) Linear mass density
(iv) Impulse

Sol. (i) Tension = force = mass × acceleration
$$[M] \times [LT^{-2}] = [MLT^{-2}]$$

(ii) Velocity gradient $= \dfrac{\text{Velocity}}{\text{Distance}} = \dfrac{[LT^{-1}]}{[L]} = [T^{-1}]$

(iii) Linear mass density $= \dfrac{\text{Mass}}{\text{Length}} = \dfrac{[M]}{[L]} = [ML^{-1}]$

(iv) Impulse = force × time $= [MLT^{-2}] \times [T] = [MLT^{-1}]$

DIMENSIONAL ANALYSIS AND ITS APPLICATIONS

The dimensional analysis helps us in deducing the relations among different physical quantities and checking the accuracy, derivation and dimensional consistency or its homogeneity of various numerical expressions.

Its applications are as given below

1. Checking the dimensional consistency of equations
2. Conversion of one system of units into another
3. Deducing relation among the physical quantities

1. Checking the Dimensional Consistency of Equations

The magnitudes of physical quantities may be added together or subtracted from one another only if they have the same dimensions.

Thus, mass cannot be added to velocity or an electric current cannot be subtracted from time. We use the principle of homogeneity of dimensions to check the consistency and correctness of an equation.

The **principle of homogeneity of dimension** states that a physical quantity equation will be dimensionally correct, if the dimensions of all the terms occurring on both sides of the equation are same.

e.g. Let us check the dimensional consistency of the equation of motion as

$$s = ut + \frac{1}{2}at^2$$

Dimensions of different terms are

$$[s] = [L]$$

$$[ut] = [LT^{-1}][T] = [L]$$

$$\left[\frac{1}{2}at^2\right] = [LT^{-2}]/[T^2] = [L]$$

As all the terms on both sides of the equations have the same dimensions, so the given equation is dimensionally correct.

EXAMPLE |3| Test of Consistency

Check whether the given equation is dimensionally correct $\dfrac{1}{2}mv^2 = mgh$.

[NCERT]

Sol. The dimensions of LHS
$$= [M][LT^{-1}]^2 = [ML^2T^{-2}]$$

The dimensions of RHS $= [M][LT^{-2}][L] = [ML^2T^{-2}]$

The dimensions of LHS and RHS are same and hence the consistency is verified.

EXAMPLE |4| Analysis of an Equation

Check the dimensional consistency of the following equations.

(i) de-Broglie wavelength, $\lambda = \dfrac{h}{mv}$

(ii) Escape velocity, $v = \sqrt{\dfrac{2GM}{R}}$

Sol. (i) Given, $\lambda = \dfrac{h}{mv}$

LHS as wavelength is a distance $\lambda = [L]$

Also RHS, $\dfrac{h}{mv} = \dfrac{\text{Planck's constant}}{\text{Mass} \times \text{Velocity}}$

$$= \frac{[ML^2T^{-1}]}{[M] \times [LT^{-1}]} = [L]$$

$\therefore$ LHS = RHS

Hence, the given equation is dimensionally correct.

(ii) Here, $v = \sqrt{\dfrac{2GM}{R}}$

LHS $v = [LT^{-1}]$ RHS $= \left[\dfrac{2GM}{R}\right]^{1/2}$

$G = [M^{-1}L^3T^{-2}]$, $R = [L]$, $M = [M]$

$$= \left[\frac{M^{-1}L^3T^{-2}M}{L}\right]^{1/2} = [L^2T^{-2}]^{1/2} = [LT^{-1}]$$

$\therefore$ Dimensions of LHS = Dimensions of RHS

Hence, the equation is dimensionally correct.

2. Conversion of One System of Units into Another

As we know numerical value is inversely proportional to the size of the unit but the magnitude of the physical quantity remains the same, whatever be the system of its measurement.

i.e. $n_1 u_1 = n_2 u_2 \Rightarrow n_2 = \dfrac{n_1 u_1}{u_2}$ ...(i)

Where, u_1 and u_2 are two units of measurement of the quantity and n_1 and n_2 are their respective numerical values. If M_1, L_1 and T_1 are the fundamental units of mass, length and time in one system and while for other system, M_2, L_2 and T_2 are the fundamental units of mass, length and time then $u_1 = [M_1^a L_1^b T_1^c]$ and $u_2 = [M_2^a L_2^b T_2^c]$

From Eq. (i) $n_2 = \dfrac{n_1 [M_1^a L_1^b T_1^c]}{[M_2^a L_2^b T_2^c]} = n_1 \left[\dfrac{M_1}{M_2}\right]^a \left[\dfrac{L_1}{L_2}\right]^b \left[\dfrac{T_1}{T_2}\right]^c$

$$\boxed{n_2 = n_1 \left[\dfrac{M_1}{M_2}\right]^a \left[\dfrac{L_1}{L_2}\right]^b \left[\dfrac{T_1}{T_2}\right]^c}$$

EXAMPLE |5| Energy Estimation

A calorie is a unit of heat or energy and it equals about 4.2 J, where $1 \text{ J} = 1 \text{kg-m}^2/\text{s}^2$. Suppose we employ a system of units in which the unit of mass equals α kg, the unit of length is β m, the unit of time is γ s. Show that a calorie has a magnitude $4.2\, \alpha^{-1} \beta^{-2} \gamma^2$ in terms of new units.

[NCERT]

Sol. The dimensional formula of energy = $[ML^2 T^{-2}]$

Let M_1, L_1, T_1 and M_2, L_2, T_2 are the units of mass, length and time in given two systems.

∴ $M_1 = 1$ kg, $M_2 = \alpha$ kg
$L_1 = 1$ m, $L_2 = \beta$ m
$T_1 = 1$ s, $T_2 = \gamma$ s

For any physical quantity, the product of its magnitude and unit is always constant.

$n_1 u_1 = n_2 u_2$

or $n_2 = n_1 \dfrac{u_1}{u_2} = 4.2 \times \dfrac{[M_1 L_1^2 T_1^{-2}]}{[M_2 L_2^2 T_2^{-2}]}$

$= 4.2 \left[\dfrac{M_1}{M_2}\right] \times \left[\dfrac{L_1}{L_2}\right]^2 \times \left[\dfrac{T_1}{T_2}\right]^{-2}$

$= 4.2 \left[\dfrac{1}{\alpha}\text{kg}\right] \times \left[\dfrac{1}{\beta}\text{m}\right]^2 \times \left[\dfrac{1}{\gamma}\text{s}\right]^{-2}$

$n_2 = 4.2 \alpha^{-1} \beta^{-2} \gamma^2$ new unit

∴ 1 cal $= 4.2 \alpha^{-1} \beta^{-2} \gamma^2$ new unit

EXAMPLE |6| Power Estimation

Find the value of 60J per min on a system that has 100 g, 100 cm and 1 min as the base units.

Sol. Given, $P = \dfrac{60 \text{ joule}}{1 \text{min}} = \dfrac{60 \text{ joule}}{60 \text{ s}} = 1$ watt

which is the SI unit of power

Dimensional formula of power is $[ML^2 T^{-3}]$.

∴ $a = 1, b = 2$ and $c = -3$

SI	New System
$n_1 = 1$	$n_2 = ?$
$M_1 = 1$ kg $= 1000$ g	$M_2 = 100$ g
$L_1 = 1$ m $= 100$ cm	$L_2 = 100$ cm
$T_1 = 1$ s	$T_2 = 1$ min $= 60$ s

$n_2 = n_1 \left[\dfrac{M_1}{M_2}\right]^a \left[\dfrac{L_1}{L_2}\right]^b \left[\dfrac{T_1}{T_2}\right]^c$

$= 1 \left[\dfrac{1000}{100}\right]^{-1} \left[\dfrac{100}{100}\right]^{-2} \left[\dfrac{1}{60}\right]^{-3}$

$= 2.16 \times 10^6$

∴ $60 \text{ J min}^{-1} = 2.16 \times 10^6$ new units of power.

3. Deducing Relation among the Physical Quantities

The method of dimensions is used to deduce the relation among the physical quantities. We should know the dependence of the physical quantity on other quantities.

We will explain with the following illustration.

Consider a simple pendulum having a bob attached to a string that oscillates under the action of the force of gravity.

Suppose, the time period t of oscillation of the simple pendulum depends on its length (l), mass of the bob (m) and acceleration due to gravity (g).

Let $t = km^a l^b g^c$ ...(i)

Where a, b, c are the dimensions and k is dimensionless constant of proportionality.

Considering dimensions on both sides in terms of M, L, T, we get

$$[M^0 L^0 T^1] = M^a L^b [LT^{-2}]^c$$
$$= M^a L^{b+c} T^{-2c}$$

Applying the principle of homogeneity of dimensions, we get

$$a = 0, -2c = 1 \Rightarrow c = \dfrac{-1}{2},$$

$$b + c = 0 \Rightarrow b = -c \Rightarrow b = \dfrac{1}{2}$$

Substituting the values of a, b and c in Eq. (i), we get

$$t = km^0 l^{1/2} g^{-1/2} = k\sqrt{\dfrac{l}{g}}$$

$\Rightarrow$ $t = k\sqrt{\dfrac{l}{g}}$

So, dimensional analysis is very useful in deducing relations among the interdependent physical quantities. It can only test the dimensional validity but not the exact relationship between physical quantities in any given equation.

Problem Solving Strategy
(Derive an Expression)

1. Read the problem carefully and understand the concept of the problem before proceeding further.
2. Write all physical quantities which are known and unknown and list them.
3. Identify the physical parameter for all physical quantities.
4. Equation, the relationships between the physical quantities, should be written down next.
   Naturally, the selected equation should be consistent with the physical principles identified in the previous step.
5. Solve the set of equation for the unknown quantities in terms of the known. Do this algebraically, without substituting values until the next step ,except where terms are zero.
6. Substitute the known values, together with their units obtain *a* numerical value with units for each unknown.
7. Check your answer. Do the units match? Is the answer reasonable? Is your answer consistent with an order of magnitude estimate?

Limitations of Dimensional Analysis

(i) It does not give any information whether a physical quantity is a scalar or a vector.

(ii) It gives no information about the dimensionless constant in the formula e.g. 1, 2, 3 ... π etc.

(iii) We cannot drive the formula containing the trigonometrical function logarithmic function, exponential function which have no dimensions.

(iv) If a quantity depends on more than three factors, having dimensions, the formula cannot be derived.

This is because, equating the powers of M, L and T on either side of the dimensional equation, then we can obtain three equations from which we can compute three unknown dimensions.

EXAMPLE |7| An Oscillating Bob

Consider a simple pendulum, having a bob attached to a string, that oscillates under the action of the force of gravity. Suppose that the period of oscillation of the simple pendulum depends on

(i) mass m of the bob,

(ii) length l of the pendulum and

(iii) acceleration due to gravity g at the place.

Derive the expression for its time period using method of dimensions. **[NCERT]**

Sol. Let us assume that $T \propto m^a l^b g^c$

or $\qquad T = k m^a l^b g^c \qquad$ ...(i)

where, k is a dimensionless constant.

The dimensions of various quantities are

$$[T] = T, [m] = M,$$
$$[l] = L, [g] = LT^{-2}$$

Substituting these dimensions in Eq. (i), we get

$$T = [M]^a [L]^b [LT^{-2}]^c$$

or $\quad M^0 L^0 T^1 = M^a L^{b+c} T^{-2c}$

Equating the exponents of M, L and T on both sides, we get

$$a = 0, b + c = 0, -2c = 1$$

On solving, $a = 0, \quad b = \dfrac{1}{2}, \quad c = -\dfrac{1}{2}$

$\therefore \qquad T = k m^0 l^{1/2} g^{-1/2} = k \sqrt{\dfrac{l}{g}}$

From experiments, $k = 2\pi$

Therefore, $\qquad T = 2\pi \sqrt{\dfrac{l}{g}}.$

EXAMPLE |8| A Stretched Spring

A body of mass m hung at one end of the spring executes SHM. Prove that the relation $T = 2\pi m/k$ is incorrect, where k is the force constant of the spring. Also, derive the correct relation.

Sol. It is given that $T = \dfrac{2\pi m}{k}$

LHS, $\qquad T = [T]$

RHS, $\qquad \dfrac{2\pi m}{k} = \dfrac{[M]}{[MT^{-2}]} = [T^2]$

$$\left[\because k = \dfrac{\text{Force}}{\text{Length}} = \dfrac{[MLT^{-2}]}{[L]} = [MT^{-2}] \right]$$

$\therefore \qquad \text{LHS} \neq \text{RHS}$

Hence, the relation is incorrect.

To find the correct relation, suppose $T = k m^a k^b$, then

$$[T]^1 = [M]^a [MT^{-2}]^b = M^{a+b} T^{-2b}$$

$\therefore \qquad a + b = 0, -2b = 1$

On solving, we get $b = \dfrac{-1}{2}, a = \dfrac{1}{2}$

$\therefore \qquad T = k m^{1/2} k^{-1/2}$

Hence, $\qquad T = k \sqrt{\dfrac{m}{k}}$

EXAMPLE |9| **Vibration of Stretched String**

The frequency 'v' of vibration of stretched string depends upon

(i) its length l,
(ii) its mass per unit length 'm' and
(iii) the tension T in the string

Obtain dimensionally an expression for frequency v.

Sol. Let the frequency of vibration of the string be given by

$$v = K l^a m^b T^c \qquad \text{...(i)}$$

where $K = $ a dimensionless constant

Dimensions of the various quantities are

$$v = [T^{-1}], l = [L], T = [T],$$
$$\text{Force} = [MLT^{-2}]$$

and $$m = \frac{\text{mass}}{\text{length}} = [ML^{-1}]$$

Substituting these dimensions in Eq. (i), we get

$$[T^{-1}] = [L]^a [ML^{-1}]^b [MLT^{-2}]^c$$

or $$[M^0 L^0 T^{-1}] = [M^{b+c} L^{a-b+c} T^{-2c}]$$

Equating the dimensions of M, L and T, we get

$$b + c = 0, a - b + c = 0 \text{ and } -2c = -1$$

on solving, $$a = -1, b = -\frac{1}{2} \text{ and } c = \frac{1}{2}$$

$$\therefore \qquad (v) = K l^{-1} m^{-1/2} T^{1/2}$$

or $$(v) = \frac{K}{l} \sqrt{\frac{T}{m}}$$

EXAMPLE |10| **Time Period of Oscillation a Small Drop**

The time of oscillation T of a small drop of a liquid under surface tension (whose dimensions are those of force per unit length) depends upon the density d, the radius r and the surface tension σ. Derive dimensionally the relationship $T \propto \sqrt{dr^3/\sigma}$.

Sol. Let the time of oscillation of a small drop of a liquid is given by

$$T \propto d^a r^b d^c$$
$$T = k d^a r^2 d^2 \qquad \text{...(i)}$$

where, $K = $ a dimensionless constant

Dimension of the various quantities are

$$\sigma = [MT^{-2}], d = [ML^{-3}], r = [L]$$

Substituting these dimensions in Eq. (i), we get,

i.e. $$[M^0 L^0 T^1] = k[ML^{-3}]^a [L]^b [MT^{-2}]^c$$
$$= [M^{a+c} L^{-3a+b} T^{-2c}]$$

Equating the dimensions of M, L and T, we get,

$$a + c = 0, -2c = 1, -3a + b = 0$$

We get,

$$c = -1/2, a = 1/2 \text{ and } b = 3/2$$
$$T \propto d^{1/2} r^{3/2} \sigma^{-1/2}$$

i.e. $$T \propto \sqrt{\frac{dr^3}{\sigma}}$$

| TOPIC PRACTICE 3 |

OBJECTIVE Type Questions

1. Which of the following has unit but no dimension?
   (a) Angle   (b) Strain
   (c) Relative velocity   (d) Relative density

   Sol. (a) Angle has unit of radian but has no dimensions

   because, $$\theta = \frac{l}{r}$$

   i.e., it is the ratio of two quantities of same dimensions.

2. Which of the following has same dimension as that of Planck constant?
   (a) Work
   (b) Linear momentum
   (c) Angular momentum
   (d) Impulse

   Sol. (c) As, $E = hv$

   or $$h = \frac{E}{v} = \left[\frac{ML^2 T^{-2}}{T^{-1}}\right] = [ML^2 T^{-1}]$$

   Angular momentum $= mvr = [M][LT^{-1}][L] = [ML^2 T^{-1}]$

3. Which of the following sets have different dimensions?
   (a) Dipole moment, Electric field and Electric flux
   (b) Pressure, Young's modulus, Stress
   (c) Heat, Work, Energy
   (d) Emf, Potential difference and potential

   Sol. (a) Heat, work and energy are same things, so they have same dimensions.

   Emf, potential difference and potential have the same dimensions.

   $$\text{Pressure} = \frac{\text{force}}{\text{area}}, \text{stress} = \frac{\text{force}}{\text{area}}$$

   $$Y = \frac{\text{Stress}}{\text{Strain}} = \frac{\text{force / area}}{\text{dimensionless}} = \text{force / area}$$

   So, they have same dimensions.

   But dimension of Dipole moment $= [M^0 L^1 T^1 A^1]$

   dimenslion of electric field $= [M^1 L^1 T^{-3} A^{-1}]$

   and dimension of electric flux $= [M^1 L^3 T^{-3} A^{-1}]$

   hence they are different.

4. Obtain the dimensional equation for universal gas constant.
(a) $[M\,L^2T^{-2}\,mol^{-1}K^{-1}]$
(b) $[ML^3\,T^{-1}\,mol^{-2}\,K^{-2}]$
(c) $[M^2LT^{-1}\,mol^{-1}\,K^{-1}]$
(d) $[M^3LT^{-2}\,mol^{-1}\,K^{-2}]$

Sol. (a) According to ideal gas equation for universal gas constant.
i.e., $pV = nRT$, where n is the number of moles of gases.

$$R = \frac{(p)(V)}{(n)(T)} = \frac{[ML^{-1}\,T^{-2}]\,[L^3]}{[mol]\,[K]}$$

$$= [ML^2T^{-2}\,mol^{-1}K^{-1}]$$

5. Given, force $= \dfrac{\alpha}{\text{Density} + \beta^3}$.

What are the dimensions of α, β?
(a) $[ML^2\,T^{-2}]$, $[ML^{-1/3}]$
(b) $[M^2L^4T^{-2}]$, $[M^{1/3}L^{-1}]$
(c) $[M^2L^{-2}\,T^{-2}]$, $[M^{1/3}\,L^{-1}]$
(d) $[M^2\,L^{-2}T^{-2}]$, $[ML^{-2}]$

Sol. (c) Dimensions of β^3 = Dimensions of density = $[ML^{-3}]$

$$\beta = [M^{1/3}\,L^{-1}]$$

Also, α = Force $\times$ Density = $[MLT^{-2}]\,[ML^{-3}]$
$= [M^2L^{-2}T^{-2}]$

6. In the formula $x = 3yz^2$, x and z have dimensions of capacitance and magnetic induction, respectively. The dimensions of y in MKS system are
(a) $[M^{-2}\,L^{-2}\,T^4A^4]$ (b) $[M^{-3}\,L^{-3}\,T^4A^5]$
(c) $[M^{-3}\,L^{-2}\,T^8A^4]$ (d) $[M^{-1}L^{-4}T^2A^4]$

Sol. (c) Given, $[x]$ = capacitance = $[M^{-1}\,L^{-2}\,T^4\,A^2]$

$[z]$ = magnetic induction = $[MA^{-1}\,T^{-2}]$

So, $[y] = \dfrac{[M^{-1}L^{-2}T^4A^2]}{[MA^{-1}\,T^{-2}]^2} = [M^{-3}\,L^{-2}\,T^8A^4]$

7. When 1 m, 1 kg and 1 min are taken as the fundamental units, the magnitude of the force is 36 units. What will be the value of this force in CGS system?
(a) 10^5 dyne (b) 10^3 dyne (c) 10^8 dyne (d) 10^4 dyne

Sol. (b) As, dimensional formula of force = $[MLT^{-2}]$

$n_1 = 36$, $M_1 = 1$ kg, $L_1 = 1$m, $T_1 = 1$ min $= 60$ s
$n_2 = ?$, $M_2 = 1$ g, $L_2 = 1$ cm, $T_2 = 1$ s
So, conversion of 36 units into CGS system

i.e., $n_2 = n_1 \left[\dfrac{M_1}{M_2}\right]^a \left[\dfrac{L_1}{L_2}\right]^b \left[\dfrac{T_1}{T_2}\right]^c$

$$n_2 = n_1 \left[\frac{1\ kg}{1g}\right]^1 \left[\frac{1\ m}{1\ cm}\right]^1 \left[\frac{1\ min}{1\ s}\right]^{-2}$$

$$= 36 \left[\frac{1000\ g}{1\ g}\right]\left[\frac{100\ cm}{1\ cm}\right]^1\left[\frac{60\ s}{1\ s}\right]^{-2} = 10^3\ \text{dyne}$$

VERY SHORT ANSWER Type Questions

8. Write the dimensional formula of wavelength and frequency of a wave.

Sol. Wavelength $[\lambda] = [L]$, Frequency $[v] = [T^{-1}]$

9. Obtain the dimensional formula for coefficient of viscosity.

Sol. Coefficient of viscosity $(\eta) = \dfrac{Fdx}{A.dv} = \dfrac{[MLT^{-2}]\,[L]}{[L^2]\,[LT^{-1}]}$

$$= [ML^{-1}T^{-1}]$$

10. What is the dimensional formula for torque?

Sol. $[ML^{-2}T^{-2}]$

11. Write three pairs of physical quantities, which have same dimensional formula.

Sol. (i) Work and energy   (ii) Energy and torque
(iii) Pressure and stress

12. Express a joule in terms of fundamental unit.

Sol. Energy = $[ML^{-2}T^{-2}]$
Hence, $1\,J = 1$ kg $\times$ 1 m$^2 \times$ 1 s$^{-2} = 1$ kgm^{2}s^{-2}

13. Are all constants dimensionless?

Sol. No, it is not possible.

14. Name some physical quantities which are dimensionless.

Sol. Solid angle, relative density, strain, Reynold's number and Poisson's ratio.

15. Is Avogadro's number a dimensionless quantity?

Sol. No, it has dimensions. In fact, its dimensional formula is $[mol^{-1}]$.

16. If $x = a + bt + ct^2$, where x is in metres and t is second, what is the dimensional formula of c?

Sol. Here, $x = [L]$
$t = [T]$; $x = ct^2$
$[L] = c \times [T^2]$
$\Rightarrow$ $\dfrac{[L]}{[T^2]} = c \Rightarrow c = [LT^{-2}]$

17. What are the dimensions of a and b in the relation : $F = a + bx$, where F is force and (x) is distance?

Sol. $[a] = [F] = [MLT^{-2}]$, $[b] = \left[\dfrac{F}{x}\right] = \left[\dfrac{MLT^{-2}}{L}\right] = [MT^{-2}]$

SHORT ANSWER Type Questions

18. Find the dimensional formulae of (i) Kinetic energy and (ii) Pressure.

Sol. (i) $KE = \frac{1}{2}mv^2$ i.e., dimensional formula of KE is $[ML^2T^{-2}]$

(ii) Pressure $= \frac{Force}{Area} = \frac{[MLT^{-2}]}{[L^2]} = [ML^{-1}T^{-2}]$

19. State dimensional formulae for stress, strain and Young's modulus.

Sol. Strain is dimensionless quantity.

Dimensional formula for stress is $[ML^{-1}T^{-2}]$

Young's modulus has same dimensional formula as stress i.e. $[ML^{-1}T^{-2}]$

20. Using the relation $E = h\nu$, obtain the dimensions of Planck's constant.

Sol. We know that dimensional formula of energy E of photon is $[M^1L^2T^{-2}]$ and dimensional formula of frequency ν is $[T^{-1}]$

$$[h] = \frac{[E]}{[\nu]} = \frac{[M^1L^2T^{-2}]}{[T^{-1}]}$$
$$= [M^1L^2T^{-1}]$$

21. Magnitude of force F experienced by a certain object moving with speed v is given by $F = kv^2$, where k is constant. Find the dimensions of K.

Sol. Since, $F = kv^2$.

Hence, $[k] = \frac{[F]}{[v^2]} = \frac{[MLT^{-2}]}{[LT^{-1}]^2}$

$$= [M^1L^{-1}]$$

22. The rotational kinetic energy of a body is given by $E = \frac{1}{2}I\omega^2$, where ω is the angular velocity of the body. Use the equation to obtain dimensional formula for moment of inertia I. Also write its SI unit.

Sol. The given relation is $E = \frac{1}{2}I\omega^2$

$$I = \frac{[E]}{[\omega^2]} = \frac{[ML^2T^{-2}]}{[T^{-1}]^2}\left[\frac{ML^2T^{-2}}{T^{-2}}\right] = [ML^2]$$

Its SI unit is joule.

23. Distinguish between dimensional variables and dimensional constants. Give example too.

Sol. Dimensional variables are those quantities which have dimensions and whose numerical value may change. Speed, velocity, acceleration etc., are dimensional variables.

Dimensional constants are quantities having dimensions but having a constant value, e.g., gravitation constant (G), Planck's constant (H), Stefan's constant (σ) etc.

24. A book with many printing errors contains four different formulae for the displacement y of a particle undergoing a certain periodic motion **[NCERT]**

(i) $y = a\sin\frac{2\pi t}{T}$ (ii) $y = a\sin vt$

(iii) $y = \left(\frac{a}{T}\right)\sin\left(\frac{t}{a}\right)$

(iv) $y = \left(\frac{a}{\sqrt{2}}\right)\left(\sin\frac{2\pi t}{T} + \cos\frac{2\pi t}{T}\right)$

(where, a = maximum displacement of the particle, v = speed of the particle, T = time period of motion). Rule out the wrong formulae on dimensional grounds.

Sol. According to the principle of homogeneity of dimensions, if the dimensions of each term adding or subtracting in a given relation are same then it is correct, if not then it is wrong. The dimension of LHS of each relation is [L], therefore, the dimension of RHS should be [L] and the argument of the trigonometrical function i.e. angle should be dimensionless.

(i) As $\frac{2\pi t}{T}$ is dimensionless, therefore, dimension of RHS = [L]. This formula is correct.

(ii) Dimension of RHS = $[L]\sin[LT^{-1}][T] = [L]\sin[L]$

As angle is not dimensionless here. Therefore, this formula is wrong.

(iii) Dimension of RHS = $\frac{[L]}{[T]}\sin\frac{[T]}{[L]} = [LT^{-1}]\sin[TL^{-1}]$

As angle is not dimensionless here, therefore this formula is wrong.

(iv) Dimension of RHS = $[L]\left[\sin\frac{[T]}{[T]} + \cos\frac{[T]}{[T]}\right]$

$$= [L]$$

As angle is dimensionless and dimension of RHS is equal to the dimension of LHS, therefore, this formula is correct.

25. A famous relation in Physics relates 'moving mass' m to the 'rest mass' m_0 of a particle in terms of its speed v and speed of light c. (This relation first arose as a consequence of special relativity due to Albert Einstein). A boy recalls the relation almost correctly but forgets where to put the constant c. He writes $m = \frac{m_0}{(1-v^2)^{1/2}}$. Guess, where to put the missing c? **[NCERT]**

Sol. The relation is written by the boy $m = \frac{m_0}{(1-v^2)^{1/2}}$

According to the principle of homogeneity of dimensions, the dimensions on either side of a relation must be same i.e., the powers of M, L, T on either side of a relation must be same.

Dimension of m is equal to the dimension of m_0, therefore, the denominator $(1 - v^2)^{1/2}$ should be dimensionless. In denominator 1 is dimensionless but factor v^2 is not dimensionless.

To make it dimensionless, we have to divide it by the same physical quantity with same power, therefore, it should be v^2/c^2, to become dimensionless.

Hence, the correct relation should be $m = \dfrac{m_0}{\left(1 - \dfrac{v^2}{c^2}\right)^{1/2}}$

26. If $x = a + bt + ct^2$, where x is in metre and t in second, what are the units of a, b and c?

Sol. As $x = a + bt + ct^2$, where x is in metre and t in second. Hence, in accordance with the principle of homogeneity of dimensions, we have

Unit of $a = x = $ metre

Unit of $b = $ unit of $\dfrac{x}{t} = $ m/s and

Unit of $c = $ unit of $\dfrac{x}{t^2} = $ m/(s)^2

27. A man walking briskly in rain with speed v must slant his umbrella forward making an angle θ with the vertical. A student derives the following relation between θ and v : $\tan\theta = v$ and checks that the relation has a correct limit as $v \to 0$, $\theta \to 0$, as expected. (We are assuming there is no strong wind and that the rain falls vertically for a stationary man). Do you think this relation can be correct? If not, guess the correct relation. **[NCERT]**

Ans. Relation derived by the man, $\tan\theta = v$

The left hand side of the relation is dimensionless as it is a trigonometrical function.

The dimension of right hand of the relation = $[LT^{-1}]$

The dimension of LHS is not equal to the dimension of RHS. Therefore, this relation is not correct.

To be dimensionless, the RHS should be $\dfrac{v}{u}$.

Hence, the correct relation becomes $\tan\theta = \dfrac{v}{u}$

28. Check the correctness of the relation $v^2 - u^2 = 2as$ by method of dimensions. The symbol have their usual meaning.

Sol. The relation is given as $v^2 - u^2 = 2as$

On LHS Dimension of $v^2 = [L^2T^{-2}]$

and $u^2 = [LT^{-1}]^2 = [L^2T^{-2}]$

RHS $2as = [LT^{-2}][L] = [L^2T^{-2}]$

As dimensions of both terms on LHS are equal to the dimensions of RHS, the relation is dimensionally correct.

29. The speed of sound in a solid is given by the formula

$$v = \sqrt{\dfrac{E}{\rho}}$$

where, E is coefficient of elasticity and ρ is density of given solid. Check the relation by method of dimensional analysis.

Sol. In the given relation dimensions of LHS terms v are $[LT^{-1}]$.

Dimensional formula for E and ρ are $[ML^{-1}T^{-2}]$ and $[ML^{-3}]$.

Dimensions of RHS = $\sqrt{\dfrac{ML^{-1}T^{-2}}{ML^{-3}}} = \sqrt{L^2T^{-2}} = [LT^{-1}]$

As dimensions of LHS and RHS of the equation are same. Hence the equation is dimensionally correct.

30. If force F, length L and time T are taken as fundamental units then what be the dimensions of mass?

Sol. Suppose dimensions of mass M be $[F^aL^bT^c]$. Then, we have

$$[M] = [MLT^{-2}]^a[L]^b[T]^c$$
$$= M^aL^{a+b}T^{-2a+c}$$
$$a = 1, a + b = 0, -2a + c = 0$$
$$b = -a = -1, c = 2a = 2$$

Hence, dimensions of mass M are $[F^1L^{-1}T^2]$.

LONG ANSWER Type I Questions

31. In the relation $p = (a/b)e^{-(az/\theta)}$, p is the pressure, Z is the distance, and θ is the temperature. What is the dimensional formula of p?

Sol. Since, $e^{-(aZ/\theta)}$ is dimensionless, we have $aZ/\theta = 1$

or $a = \dfrac{\theta}{Z} = \dfrac{K}{L} = [L^{-1}K]$

We find that $a/b = $ dimensions of p and $b = [ML^{-1}T^{-2}]$.

Therefore, dimensional formula of p is obtained as

$$p = \dfrac{a}{[ML^{-1}T^{-2}]} = \dfrac{[L^{-1}K]}{[ML^{-1}T^{-2}]} = [M^{-1}L^0T^2K]$$

32. The SI unit of energy is J = kgm^{2}s^{-2}, that of speed v is ms^{-1} and acceleration a is ms^{-2}. Which of the formulae for kinetic energy (K) given below can you rule out on the basis of dimensional arguments (m stands for the mass of the body)?

(i) $K = m^2v^3$ (ii) $K = (1/2)mv^2$

(iii) $K = ma$ (iv) $K = (3/16)mv^2$

(v) $K = \left(\dfrac{1}{2}\right)mv^2 + ma$

[NCERT]

Sol. As SI unit of energy, $J = kg m^2 s^{-2}$,

So, $\quad$ [energy]$= [ML^2T^{-2}]$

(i) $[m^2v^2] = [M^2][LT^{-1}]^2 = [M^2L^2T^{-2}]$

(ii) $[1/2 m^2 v^2] = [M][LT^{-1}]^2 = [ML^2T^{-2}]$

(iii) $[ma] = [M][LT^{-2}] = [MLT^{-2}]$

(iv) $[3/16 mv^2] = [M][LT^{-1}]^2 = [ML^2T^{-2}]$

(v) The quantities $(1/2)mv^2$ and ma have different dimensions and hence, cannot be added.

Since, the kinetic energy K has the dimensions of $[ML^2T^{-2}]$, formulae (i), (iii) and (v) are clearly ruled out.

Dimensional analysis cannot tell which of the two, (ii) or (iv), is the correct formula. From the actual definition of kinetic energy, only (ii) is the correct formula for kinetic energy.

33. How will you convert a physical quantity from one unit system to another by method of dimensions?

Ans. If a given quantity is measured in two different unit system, then $Q = n_1 u_1 = n_2 u_2$

Let the dimensional formula of the quantity be $[M^a L^b T^c]$, then we have $n_1 [M_1^a L_1^b T_1^c] = n_2 [M_2^a L_2^b T_2^c]$

Here M_1, L_1, T_1 are the fundamental unit of mass, length and time in first unit system and M_2, L_2, T_2 in the second unit system.

Hence, $n_2 = n_1 \left[\dfrac{M_1}{M_2}\right]^a \left[\dfrac{L_1}{L_2}\right]^b \left[\dfrac{T_1}{T_2}\right]^c$

This relation helps us to convert a physical quantity from one unit system to another.

34. Find the value of 60 W on a system having 100 g, 20 cm and 1 min as the fundamental units.

Sol. $n_1 = 60$ W, power is $[M^1 L^2 T^{-3}]$

In first system, $M_1 = 1$ kg, $L_1 = 1$ m, and $T_1 = 1$s

In second system, $M_2 = 100$ g, $L_2 = 20$ m,

and $\quad\quad\quad\quad\quad\quad T_2 = 1$ min $= 60$ s

So, $n_2 = n_1 \left[\dfrac{M_1}{M_2}\right]^1 \left[\dfrac{L_1}{L_2}\right]^1 \left[\dfrac{T_1}{T_2}\right]^{-3}$

$= 60 \left[\dfrac{1000 \text{ g}}{100 \text{ g}}\right]\left[\dfrac{100 \text{ cm}}{20 \text{ cm}}\right]\left[\dfrac{1 \text{ s}}{60 \text{ s}}\right]^{-3}$

$= 60 \times \dfrac{1000}{100} \times \dfrac{100}{20} \times \dfrac{100}{20} \times 60 \times 60 \times 60$

$= 3.24 \times 10^9$ units

35. The wavelength λ associated with a moving particle depends upon its mass m, its velocity v and Planck's constant h. Show dimensional relation between them.

Sol. Suppose wavelength λ associated with a moving particle depends upon (i) its mass (m), (ii) its velocity (v) and (iii) Planck's constant (r)

$$\lambda = k m^a v^b h^c$$

where, k is a dimensionless constant.

Writing dimensions of various terms, we get

$[M^0 L^1 T^0] = [M]^a [LT^{-1}]^b [ML^2 T^{-1}]^c$

$\quad\quad\quad = M^{a+c} L^{b+2c} T^{-b-c}$

Comparing power of M, L and T on two sides of equation, we have

$a + c = 0, b + 2c = 1, -b - c = 0$

We get $a = -1, b = -1, c = +1$

Hence, the relation becomes $\lambda = \dfrac{kh}{mv}$

36. The orbital velocity v of a satellite may depend on its mass m, distance r from the centre of earth and acceleration due to gravity g. Obtain an expression for orbital velocity.

Sol. Suppose orbital velocity of satellite be given by the relation $\quad\quad v = k m^a r^b g^c$

where, k is a dimensionless constant and a, b, c are unknown powers.

Writing dimensions on two sides of equation, we have

$[M^0 L^1 T^{-1}] = [M]^a [L]^b [LT^{-2}]^c$

$\quad\quad\quad = [M^a L^{b+c} T^{-2c}]$

Applying principle of homogeneity of dimensional equation, we find that

$a = 0 \implies b + c = 1 \implies -2c = -1$

On solving these equations, we find that

$a = 0, b = +\dfrac{1}{2}$ and $c = +\dfrac{1}{2}$

$v = k r^{1/2} g^{1/2} \implies v = k\sqrt{rg}$

LONG ANSWER Type II Questions

37. A large fluid star oscillates in shape under the influence of its own gravitational field. Using dimensional analysis, find the expression for period of oscillation (T) in terms of radius of star (R). Mean density of fluid (ρ) and universal gravitational constant (G).

Sol. Suppose period of oscillation T depends on radius of star R, mean density of fluid ρ and universal gravitational constant (G) as

$T = kR^a \rho^b G^c$, where k is a dimensionless constant

$[M^0 L^0 T^1] = [L]^a [ML^{-3}]^b [M^{-1}L^3 T^{-2}]^c$

$\quad\quad\quad = [M^{b-c} L^{a-3b+3c} T^{-2c}]$

Comparing powers of M, L and T, we have
$$b - c = 0$$
$$a - 3b + 3c = 0 \text{ and } -2c = 1$$
On simplifying these equations, we get
$$c = -1/2, \ b = -1/2, \ a = 0$$
Thus, we have $T = k\rho^{-1/2}G^{-1/2} = \dfrac{k}{\sqrt{\rho G}}$

38. Find an expression for viscous force F acting on a tiny steel ball of radius r moving in a viscous liquid of viscosity η with a constant speed v by the method of dimensional analysis.

Sol. It is given that viscous force F depends on (i) radius r of steel ball, (ii) coefficient of viscosity η of viscous liquid (iii) Speed v of the ball

i.e., $F = kr^a\eta^b v^c$, where k is dimensionless constant

Dimensional formula of force
$$F = [MLT^{-2}], \ r = [L]$$
$$\eta = [M^1 L^{-1} T^{-1}] \text{ and } v = [LT^{-1}], \text{ we have}$$
$$[MLT^{-2}] = [L]^a [M^1 L^{-1} T^{-1}]^b [LT^{-1}]^c$$
$$= [M^a L^{a-b+c} T^{-b-c}]$$

Comparing powers of M, L and T on either side of equation, we get
$$a = 1$$
$$a - b + c = 1$$
$$-b - c = -2$$
On solving, these above equations, we get
$$a = 1, \ b = 1 \text{ and } c = 1$$
Hence, the relation becomes
$$F = kr\eta v$$

39. A great physicist of this century (PAM Dirac) loved playing with the numerical values of fundamental constants of nature. This led him to an interesting observation. Dirac found that from the basic constants of atomic physics m_e, m_p and the gravitational constant G, he could arrive at a number with the dimension of time.

Further, it was a very large number, its magnitude being close to the present estimate on the age of the universe (~ 15 billion yr).

From the table of fundamental constants in this book, try to see if you too can construct this number (or any other interesting number you can think of). If its coincidence with the age of the universe were significant, what would this imply for the constancy of fundamental constants?

Sol. Few basic constants of atomic physics are given below.

Charge of an electron $(e) = 1.6 \times 10^{-19}$ C

Speed of light in vacuum $(c) = 3 \times 10^8$ m/s

Gravitational constant $(G) = 6.67 \times 10^{-11}$ N-m^2/kg^2

Mass of electron $(m_e) = 9.1 \times 10^{-31}$ kg

Mass of proton $(m_p) = 1.67 \times 10^{-27}$ kg

Permittivity of free space $(\varepsilon_0) = 8.85 \times 10^{-12}$ N-m^2/C^2

On trying with these basic constants, we can get a quantity whose dimension is equal to the dimension of time. One such quantity is
$$x = \dfrac{e^4}{16\pi^2 \varepsilon_0^2 m_p m_e^2 c^3 G}$$

On writing dimensions of each quantity on RHS,
$[x]$
$$= \dfrac{[AT]^4}{[M^{-1}L^{-3}T^4A^2]^2 \times [M] \times [M]^2 \times [LT^{-1}]^3 \times [M^{-1}L^3T^{-2}]}$$
$$= [M^{2-1-2+1} L^{6-3-3} T^{4-8+2+3} A^{4-4}]$$
$$= [M^{3-3} L^{6-6} T^{9-8} A^{4-4}]$$
$$= [M^0 L^0 T A^0] = [T]$$

Now, substituting values of all constants in the given relation,
$$x = \dfrac{(1.6 \times 10^{-19})^4}{16 \times (3.14)^2 \times (8.854 \times 10^{-12})^2 \times (1.67 \times 10^{-27})}$$
$$\times (9.1 \times 10^{-31})^2 \times (3 \times 10^8)^3 \times (6.67 \times 10^{-11})]$$
$$= 2.18 \times 10^{16} \text{ s}$$
$$= 6.9 \times 10^8 \text{ yr} = 10^9 \text{ yr}$$
$$= 1 \text{ billion yr}$$

The estimates value of the quantity x is close to the age of the universe.

ASSESS YOUR TOPICAL UNDERSTANDING

OBJECTIVE Type Questions

1. The dimensional formula of Avagadro's number is
   (a) $[M^1L^1T^1]$
   (b) $[mole^{-1}]$
   (c) $[mole]$
   (d) $[M^0L^1T^0]$

2. Dimension formula of ΔQ, heat supplied to the system is
   (a) $[ML^2T^{-2}]$
   (b) $[MLT^{-2}]$
   (c) $[ML^2T^{-1}]$
   (d) $[MLT^1]$

3. Which of the following is not a dimensional constant?
   (a) Gravitational constant
   (b) π
   (c) Planck's constant
   (d) Gas constant (R)

4. Which of the following has neither units nor dimensions?
   (a) Angle
   (b) Energy
   (c) Relative density
   (d) Relative velocity

5. Which physical quantities have same dimension?
   (a) Force and power
   (b) Torque and energy
   (c) Torque and power
   (d) Force and torque

6. On checking the dimensional consistency of equation, it is based on the principle of
   (a) homogeneity of equations
   (b) homogeneity of dimensions
   (c) homogeneity of expressions
   (d) homogeneity of formula

7. Force (F) and density (d) are related as $F = \dfrac{\alpha}{\beta + \sqrt{d}}$.
   Then, the dimensions of α and β are
   (a) $[M^{3/2} L^{-1/2}T^{-2}]$, $[ML^{-3} T^0]$
   (b) $[M^{3/2} L^{-1/2}T^{-2}]$, $[M^{1/2} L^{-3/2} T^0]$
   (c) $[M^2L^2T^{-1}]$, $[ML^{-1}T^{-3/2}]$
   (d) $[M\ LT^{-2}]$, $[ML^{-2}T^{-2/3}]$

8. The density of a material in CGS system is $10\ \text{g cm}^{-3}$. If unit of length becomes 10 cm and unit of mass becomes 100 g, the new value of density will be
   (a) 10 units   (b) 100 units   (c) 1000 units   (d) 1 unit

Answer

1.	(b)	2.	(a)	3.	(b)	4.	(c)	5.	(b)
6.	(b)	7.	(b)	8.	(b)				

VERY SHORT ANSWER Type Questions

9. Write the dimensional formula corresponding to (i) Photon and (ii) Calories.

10. Name at least seven physical quantities whose dimensions are $[ML^{-2}T^{-2}]$.

11. Write the dimensional formula of torque.

12. Name the physical quantity of the dimensions given that
    (i) $[ML^{-1}T^{-1}]$,
    (ii) $[M^{-1}L^3T^{-2}]$,
    (iii) $[ML^2T^{-3}]$ and
    (iv) $[ML^0T^{-2}]$

SHORT ANSWER Type Questions

13. Write the dimensional formula of
    (i) Thrust
    (ii) Velocity gradient
    (iii) Angular velocity

14. Write the dimensions of (a) Radius of gyration (b) Moment of force, (c) Moment of inertia, (d) Work done, (e) Strain, (f) Stress.

15. What are the advantages of expressing physical quantities in terms of dimensional equations?

16. How can you check the correctness of a dimensional equation?

17. Are all dimensionally correct equations numerically correct? Give one example.

18. Let us consider the equation $\dfrac{1}{2}mv^2 = mgh$, where M is mass, v is the velocity of the body, g is the acceleration due to gravity and h is the height. Check whether the equation dimensionally correct.
    [**Ans.** Correct]

19. In CGS system, the value of Stefan's constant (σ) is 5.67×10^{-5} ergs^{-1}cm^{-2}K^{-4}. Write down its value in SI units. **[Ans.** 5.67×10^{-8} Js^{-1}m^{-2}K^{-4}**]**

LONG ANSWER Type I Questions

20. Find the dimensions of constant 'a' and 'b' occurring in van der Waals' equation.

$$\left[p + \frac{a}{V^2}\right][V - b] = RT$$

[Ans. $a = [M^1 L^5 T^{-2}], b = [L^3]$**]**

21. In Poiseuille's equation, $V = \pi\rho r^4 / 8\eta l$, determine the dimension of η.

22. Write the dimensions of a and b in the relation $E = b - x^2/at$, where E, x and t represent energy, distance and time, respectively.

23. The resistivity ρ of the material depends on the length l, diameter d and resistance R of the wire. Derive the relation for resistivity using the method of dimensions.

$$\left[\textbf{Ans. } \rho = k\left(\frac{Rd^2}{l}\right)\right]$$

LONG ANSWER Type II Questions

24. Assume that the mass (M) of the largest stone that car moved by the following river depends only upon the velocity v and the density ρ of the water, alongwith the acceleration due to gravity g. Show that m varies with sixth power of the velocity of the flow. **[Ans.** $M = kv^6$**]**

25. The escape velocity v of a body depends upon (i) the acceleration due to gravity of the planet and (ii) the radius of the planet R. Establish dimensionally the relationship v, g and R. **[Ans.** $v = k\sqrt{gR}$**]**

26. Explain the principle of homogeneity of dimensions. What are its uses? Illustrate by giving one example of each.

27. Using the principle of homogeneity of dimensions find which of the following is correct.

(i) $T^2 = 4\pi^2 r^2$, (ii) $T^2 = \dfrac{4\pi^2 r^3}{G}$ and

(iii) $T^2 = \dfrac{4\pi^2 r^3}{4M}$

SUMMARY

- All the quantities in terms of which laws of physics are described and whose measurement is necessary, are called physical quantities.
- **Types of physical quantities**
  - (i) **Fundamental quantities** The physical quantities which can be treated as independent of other physical quantities and are not usually defined in terms of other physical quantities are called fundamental quantities. e.g. mass, length, time etc.
  - (ii) **Derived quantities** Those physical quantities which are derived from fundamental quantities are called derived quantities. e.g. velocity, acceleration, force etc.
- **Unit** The standard amount of a physical quantity chosen to measure the physical quantity of the same kind is called a physical unit.
- **Types of physical units**
  - (i) **Fundamental units** The physical units which can neither be derived from one another, nor they can be further resolved into more simpler units are called fundamental units. e.g. kg, metre, second etc.
  - (ii) **Derived units** All other units which can be expressed in terms of fundamental units are called derived units e.g. m/s, m / s^2, etc.
- The comparision of any physical quantity with its standard unit is called **measurment**.
- **Rules for finding significant figures**
- The dimensions of a physical quantity are powers (or exponents) to which the base quantities are raised to represent the quantity.
- The expression which shows how and which of the base quantities represent the dimensions of a physical quantity is called the dimensional formula.
- The equation which expresses a physical quantity in terms of the fundamental units of mass, length and time is called dimensional equation.
- If the dimensions of left hand side of an equation are equal to the dimensions of right hand side of the equation, then the equation is dimensionally correct. This is known as homogeneity principle. Mathematically [LHS] = [RHS]

CHAPTER PRACTICE

OBJECTIVE Type Questions

1. Which one of the following physical quantities is not a fundamental quantity?
   (a) Luminous intensity
   (b) Thermodynamic temperature
   (c) Electric current
   (d) Work

2. Among the given following system of unit which is not based on unit of mass, length and time?
   (a) CGS   (b) FPS   (c) MKS   (d) SI

3. Find the value of 12.9 g $- 7.05$ g.
   (a) 5.84 g
   (b) 5.8 g
   (c) 5.86 g
   (d) 5.9 g

4. The numbers 2.745 and 2.735 on rounding off to 3 significant figures will give   [NCERT Exemplar]
   (a) 2.75 and 2.74
   (b) 2.74 and 2.73
   (c) 2.75 and 2.73
   (d) 2.74 and 2.74

5. The length and breadth of a rectangular sheet are 16.2 cm and 10.1 cm, respectively. The area of the sheet in appropriate significant figures and error is
   (a) 164 ± 3 cm^2
   (b) 163.62 ± 2.6 cm^2
   (c) 163.6 ± 2.6 cm^2
   (d) 163.62 ± 3 cm^2

6. If the unit of force is 100 N, unit of length is 10 m and unit of time is 100 s. What is the unit of mass in this system of units?
   (a) 10^5 kg
   (b) 10^7 kg
   (c) 10^2 kg
   (d) 10^9 kg

7. If P, Q, R are physical quantities, having different dimensions, which of following combinations can never be meaningful quantity?
   (a) $\left(\dfrac{P-Q}{R}\right)$
   (b) $PQ - R$
   (c) $\dfrac{PQ}{R}$
   (d) $\dfrac{PR - Q^2}{R}$

8. If R and L represent resistance and self-inductance respectively, which of the following combinations has the dimensions of frequency?
   (a) $\dfrac{R}{L}$
   (b) $\dfrac{L}{R}$
   (c) $\sqrt{\dfrac{R}{L}}$
   (d) $\sqrt{\dfrac{L}{R}}$

9. In the gas equation $\left(p + \dfrac{a}{V^2}\right)(V - b) = RT$, the dimensions of a are
   (a) $[ML^3T^{-2}]$
   (b) $[M^{-1}L^3T^{-1}]$
   (c) $[ML^5T^{-2}]$
   (d) $[M^{-1}L^{-5}T^2]$

ASSERTION AND REASON

Direction (Q. Nos. 10-14) *In the following questions, two statements are given- one labelled Assertion (A) and the other labelled Reason (R). Select the correct answer to these questions from the codes (a), (b), (c) and (d) as given below*
   (a) Both Assertion and Reason are true and Reason is the correct explanation of Assertion.
   (b) Both Assertion and Reason are true but Reason is not the correct explanation of Assertion.
   (c) Assertion is true but Reason is false.
   (d) Assertion is false but Reason is true.

10. **Assertion** The unit based for measuring nuclear cross-section is 'barn'.
    Reason 1 barn $= 10^{-14}$ m^2.

11. **Assertion** Pressure has the dimensions of energy density.
    Reason Energy density $= \dfrac{\text{Energy}}{\text{Volume}}$

12. **Assertion** The method of dimensions analysis cannot validate the exact relationship between physical quantities in any equation.
    Reason It does not distinguish between the physical quantities having same dimensions.

13. **Assertion** Let us consider an equation
    $$(1/2)\, mv^2 = mgh$$
    where, m is the mass of the body, v is velocity, g is the acceleration due to gravity and h is the height.
    Reason Equation is dimensionally correct.

14. **Assertion** A cesium atomic clock is used at NPL, New Delhi to maintain the Indian standard of time.

Reason The cesium atomic clocks are very accurate and precise.

CASE BASED QUESTIONS

Direction (Q. Nos. 15-16) *This question is case study based question. Attempt any 4 sub-parts from given question.*

15. **Measuring Experiment**

The true value of a certain length is near 3.678 cm. In one experiment, using a measuring instrument of resolution 0.1 cm, the measured value is found to be 3.5 cm, while in another experiment using a measuring device of greater resolution, say 0.01 cm, the length is determined to be 3.38 cm.

(i) Which measuring experiment is more accurate?
  (a) First   (b) Second
  (c) Either (a) or (b) (d) Neither (a) nor (b)

(ii) Which measuring experiment is more precise?
  (a) First   (b) Second
  (c) Either (a) or (b) (d) Neither (a) nor (b)

(iii) A device which is used for measurement of length to an accuracy of about 10^{-4} m is
  (a) screw gauge
  (b) spherometer
  (c) vernier calliper
  (d) Either (a) or (b)

(iv) Instrument contains some uncertainty. This uncertainty is
  (a) error
  (b) mistake
  (c) precision
  (d) accuracy

(v) The accuracy in measurement may depend on
  (a) limit, resolution
  (b) precision, limit
  (c) limit, accuracy
  (d) precision, accuracy

16. **Dimensions Analysis**

All quantities in mechanics are represented in terms of base units of length, mass and time. Additional base unit of temperature (kelvin) is used in heat and thermodynamics. In magnetism and electricity, the additional base unit of electric current is ampere.

(i) The dimensions of universal gravitational constant are
  (a) $[ML^{-3}T^2]$ (b) $[ML^2T^{-3}]$
  (c) $[M^{-1}L^3T^{-2}]$ (d) $[M^2L^2T^{-2}]$

(ii) The coefficient of thermal conductivity has the dimensions
  (a) $[ML^{-1}T^3K^3]$ (b) $[ML^{-1}T^{-3}K^{-1}]$
  (c) $[MLT^{-3}K^{-1}]$ (d) $[MLT^{-3}K]$

(iii) Dimensions of resistance are
  (a) $[MLT^{-3}A^{-1}]$ (b) $[ML^2T^{-3}A^{-1}]$
  (c) $[M^2LT^{-3}A^{-1}]$ (d) $[ML^2T^{-3}A]$

(iv) Given, force $= \dfrac{\alpha}{\text{Density} + \beta^3}$.

What are the dimensions of α, β?
  (a) $[ML^2T^{-2}]$, $[ML^{-1/3}]$
  (b) $[M^2L^4T^{-2}]$, $[M^{1/3}L^{-1}]$
  (c) $[M^2L^{-2}T^{-2}]$, $[M^{1/3}L^{-1}]$
  (d) $[M^2L^{-2}T^{-2}]$, $[ML^{-2}]$

(v) Which of the following has unit but no dimension?
  (a) Angle   (b) Strain
  (c) Relative velocity (d) Relative density

Answer

1. (d)	2. (d)	3. (b)	4. (d)	5. (a)
6. (a)	7. (a)	8. (a)	9. (c)	10. (c)
11. (a)	12. (a)	13. (a)	14. (a)	

15. (i) (a) (ii) (b) (iii) (d) (iv) (a) (v) (a)
16. (i) (c) (ii) (c) (iii) (b) (iv) (c) (v) (a)

VERY SHORT ANSWER Type Questions

17. Wavelength of a laser light is 6463 Å. Express it in nm and micron. **[Ans.** 646.3 nm, 0.6463 μ]

18. Find the value of 1 J of energy in CGS system of units. **[Ans.** 10^7 CGS units]

SHORT ANSWER Type Questions

19. Find the value of the following upto the appropriate significant figures in the following.
  (a) $3.27 + 33.5472$ (b) $53.312 - 53.3$
  (c) 2.02×23 (d) 3.908×5.5
  [Ans. (a) 36.82 (b) zero (c) 46 (d) 21]

20. If unit of force, velocity and energy are 100 dyne, 10 cm/s and 400 ergs, respectively. What will be the unit of mass, length and time?

[**Ans.** 4 g, 4 cm, 0.4]

21. If p represents radiation pressure, c represents the speed of light and q represents the radiation energy per unit area per unit time.

Calculate the non-zero integers such that $p^x q^y c^z$ is dimensionless.

LONG ANSWER Type I Questions

22. How many significant figures are there in the following results for quantities measured in the laboratory?

(a) 3.0120   (b) 123.0 km   (c) 0.006235 s

(d) 0.23×10^{-3} (e) 100.007 g   (f) 143000 km

23. If velocity of sound in air v depends on the modulus of elasticity E and density ρ.

Find expression of v.

$$\left[\textbf{Ans.}\ v = k\sqrt{\frac{E}{\rho}}\right]$$

24. Check the relation $S = ut + \frac{1}{2}at^2$ by method of dimension.

25. If the time period (T) of vibration of a liquid drop depends on surface tension (s) and radius (r) of the drop, and density (ρ) of the liquid. Derive an expression for T using dimensional analysis.

$$\left[\textbf{Ans.}\ T = \frac{pr^3}{s}\right]$$

26. The depth x to which a bullet penetrates a human body depends upon (i) coefficient of

elasticity η and (ii) kinetic energy E_k. By the method of dimensions, show that $x \propto \left[\dfrac{E_k}{\eta}\right]^{1/3}$

27. Rule out or accept the following formula for kinetic energy on the basis of dimensional arguments.

(i) $R = \dfrac{3}{16}mv^2$ (ii) $K = \dfrac{1}{2}mv^2 + ma$

[**Ans.** $x = 1, y = -1, z = 1$]

28. Miss Rita in her Physics class was explaining how to use a vernier calliper to measure small dimension. Her student Anubha was confused that why didn't we used a metre scale for the purpose. She asked Miss Rita who explained her that a proper instrument and unit should be used to get accurate measurement. Large dimensions such as distance of earth from Sun is measured in light year (ly) whereas size of nucleus is measured in fermi (fm).

(i) What values of Anubha and her teacher do you appreciate?

(ii) Give the physical quantities of following units.

(a) Parsec   (b) Joule

(iii) Give the physical quantities measured by following instrument

(a) Barometer   (b) Pyrometer

LONG ANSWER Type II Question

29. Specific resistance ρ of a thin circular wire of radius r in cm, resistance R in Ω and length L in cm is given by $\rho = (\pi r^2 R)/L$. If $r = (0.26 \pm 0.01)$ cm, $R = (30 \pm 2)\,\Omega$ and $L = (75.00 \pm 0.01)$ cm, find the percentage error in ρ upto correct significant figures.   [**Ans.** 14%]

02

Motion in a straight line is also called rectilinear motion. It involves no change in direction so its study is relatively simple. Under this head, we will study motion of object either along *X*-axis or along *Y*-axis.

MOTION IN A STRAIGHT LINE

|TOPIC 1|
General Introduction of Motion

Mechanics is a branch of physics in which we study the motion of objects.

There are three branches of mechanics that examine the motion of an object such as

Statics It is a branch of mechanics in which we study the objects at rest. In statics, time factor does not play any role.

Kinematics It describes the motion of objects without looking at the cause of the motion. Here, time factor plays an important role.

Dynamics It relates the motion of objects to the forces which cause them. The time factor also plays an important role.

REST

If the position of an object does not change w.r.t. its surrounding with the passage of time, it is said to be at **rest**. e.g. Book lying on the table, a person sitting on a chair, etc.

CHAPTER CHECKLIST

- Rest
- Motion
- Point Object
- Scalar and Vector Quantities
- Position, Path Length and Displacement
- Velocity
- Acceleration
- Position-Time Graphs for Positive, Negative and Zero Acceleration
- Velocity-Time Graphs for an Accelerated Motion
- Kinematic Equations for Uniformly Accelerated Motion

MOTION

If the position of an object is continuously changing w.r.t. its surrounding, then it is said to be in the **state of motion**. Thus, motion can be defined as a change in position of an object with time. It is common to everything in the universe. In our daily life, we see a train moving on rails, the walking man, the crawling insects, water flowing down a dam, etc., showing that the object is in motion.

Types of Motion

On the basis of the nature of path followed, motion is classified as

Rectilinear Motion The motion in which a particle moves along a straight line is called **rectilinear motion**.

e.g. Motion of a sliding body on an inclined plane.

Circular Motion The motion in which a particle moves in a circular path is called **circular motion**.

e.g. A string whirled in a circular loop.

Oscillatory Motion The motion in which a particle moves to and fro about a given point is known as **oscillatory motion**.

e.g. Simple pendulum

On the basis of the number of coordinates required to define the motion, motion is classified as

One-dimensional Motion The motion of an object is considered as 1-D if only one coordinate is needed to specify the position of the object.

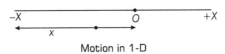

Motion in 1-D

In 1-D motion, the object moves along a straight line. In this type of motion, there are only two directions (backward and forward, upward and downward) in which an object moves and these directions are specified by + and − signs.

e.g. A boy running on a straight road, etc.

Two-dimensional Motion The motion of an object is considered as 2-D if two coordinates are needed to specify the position of the object. In 2-D motion, the object moves in a plane.

Motion in 2-D

e.g. A satellite revolving around the earth, etc.

Three-dimensional Motion The motion of an object is considered as 3-D if all the three coordinates are needed

to specify the position of the object. This type of motion takes place in three-dimensional space.

e.g. Butterfly flying in garden, the motion of water molecules, etc.

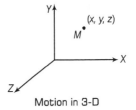

Motion in 3-D

POINT OBJECT

An object is considered as point object if the size of the object is much smaller than the distance it moves in a reasonable duration of time.

e.g.

(i) A train under a journey of several hundred kilometres can be regarded as a point object.

(ii) Earth can be regarded as a point object for studying its motion around the sun.

The following example helps us to decide about a point object.

EXAMPLE |1| **Body as a Point Object**

In which of the following examples of motion, can the body be considered approximately a point object?

[NCERT]

(i) A railway carriage moving without jerks between two stations.

(ii) A monkey sitting on the top of a man cycling smoothly on a circular track.

(iii) A spinning cricket ball that turns sharply on hitting the ground.

Sol. Any object can be considered as a point object if the distance travelled by it is very large in comparison to its dimensions.

(i) A railway carriage is moving without jerks between two stations, it means stations are at large distance, therefore railway carriage can be taken as a point object.

(ii) Man along with monkey is cycling smoothly which indicates that the distance travelled by the man is very large, therefore monkey can be taken as a point object.

(iii) The distance travelled by the ball is not so large therefore, spinning cricket ball cannot be taken as a point object.

SCALAR AND VECTOR QUANTITIES

Physical quantities are studied under two heads, i.e. scalars and vectors. Both types of quantities can be defined as follows

   (i) **Scalars** If only the magnitude is required to specify a physical quantity, that physical quantity is known as **scalar quantity** or **scalars.**

   e.g. Mass, length, time, speed, etc.

   (ii) **Vectors** If magnitude as well as direction both are required to specify a physical quantity, that physical quantity is known as **vector quantity** or **vectors.**

   e.g. Displacement, velocity, acceleration, etc.

POSITION, PATH LENGTH AND DISPLACEMENT

In order to specify position, we need to use a reference point, a set of axes and a frame of reference.

Position

It is defined as the point where an object is situated. Position can be determined by the coordinate axis that is, marked in units of length and that has positive and negative directions.

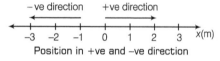

Position in +ve and −ve direction

e.g. If an object is situated at − 1 m, then minus sign indicates that the position has negative direction but if the object is at 0 m position then it will be said to be at rest.

The position of the object can be specified with reference to a conveniently chosen origin. For motion in a straight line, position to the right of the origin is taken as positive and to the left as negative.

Frame of Reference

We choose a rectangular coordinate system of three mutually perpendicular axes as x, y and z. The point of intersection of these three axes is called **origin** (O) and considered as the **reference point.**

The x, y, z-coordinates describe the position of the object w.r.t. the coordinate system. To measure time, we need a clock. This coordinate system alongwith a clock constitutes a **frame of reference.**

So, the frame of reference is a coordinate system with a clock w.r.t. which, an observer can describe the position, displacement, acceleration of an object.

Frame of reference are of two types

   (i) **Inertial frame of reference** These are the frame of reference in which, Newton's first law of motion is applicable.

   (ii) **Non-inertial frame of reference** These are the frame of reference in which, Newton's first law of motion is not applicable.

> ### Accelerated and Unaccelerated Frames
> * Generally, accelerated frames (with respect to earth) are non-inertial and unaccelerated frames (with respect to earth) are inertial.
> * The frames at rest or in uniform motion are inertial and frames in non-uniform motion are non-inertial.
> * To apply Newton's second law in the non-inertial frames, we use the concept of pseudo force.

Path Length/Distance

The length of the path covered by an object in a given time-interval, is known as its **path length** or **distance travelled.** Its SI unit is metre.

e.g. Suppose an object moves along x-axis to a distance of 100 m from the origin O in time (t). Then, the path length is 100 m.

Now, if the object returns to the origin in time (t'), then the path length is $100 + 100 = 200$ m.

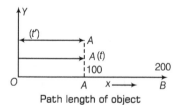

Path length of object

EXAMPLE |2| Total Path Length of a Scooter

A scooter is moving along a straight line AB covers a distance of 360 m in 24 s and returns back from B to C and covers 240 m in 18 s. Find the total path length travelled by the scooter.

Sol. From the above question, we draw the following figure.

$$A \xrightarrow[\overleftarrow{360 \text{ m}}]{\overset{\overrightarrow{240 \text{ m}}}{\underset{C}{}}} B$$

Total path length = $AB + BC = 360 + 240 = 600$ m

Displacement

The change in position of an object in a particular direction is termed as **displacement**, i.e. the difference between the final and initial positions of the object. It is denoted by Δx. Mathematically, it is represented by

$$\boxed{\text{Displacement, } \Delta x = x_2 - x_1}$$

where, x_1 and x_2 are the initial and final position of the object, respectively.

Cases

(i) If $x_2 > x_1$, then Δx is positive.
(ii) If $x_1 > x_2$, then Δx is negative.
(iii) If $x_1 = x_2$, then Δx is zero.

i.e. **the displacement of an object in motion can be positive, negative or zero.**

Displacement is a **vector quantity** as it possesses both, the magnitude and direction.

Note

- The magnitude of displacement may or may not be equal to the path length traversed by an object.
- The magnitude of the displacement for a course of motion may be zero but the corresponding path length will never be zero.

Differences between Distance and Displacement

S.No.	Distance	Displacement
1.	Length of the path is distance.	Magnitude of displacement is the length of the shortest possible path between initial and final positions.
2.	It is a scalar quantity.	It is a vector quantity.
3.	The distance covered by an object for some time interval cannot be zero.	The displacement of an object can be zero.
4.	The distance travelled by an object is always positive.	The displacement of an object can be positive, negative and zero

EXAMPLE |3| **Motion of a Boy**

A boy starts moving from -20 m towards $+ x$-axis as shown in figure. He turns at time instant t_2 and starts moving towards $- x$-axis. At time t_3, he reached at -50 m as shown in the figure. Find the displacement and distance for the time interval (i) t_1 to t_2 and (ii) t_1 to t_3.

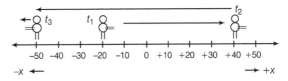

💡 For distance, we observe the actual path length and for displacement we observe the change in position.

Sol. (i) For t_1 to t_2,
Distance covered $= 20 + 40 = 60$ m
Displacement $= 40 - (-20)$
$\qquad = +60$ m (towards $+ x$-axis)

(ii) For t_1 to t_3,
Distance covered $= 60 + 90 = 150$ m
Displacement $= -50 - (-20)$
$\qquad = -30$ m (towards $- x$-axis)

UNIFORM MOTION IN A STRAIGHT LINE

A body is said to be in a uniform motion if it travels equal distance in equal intervals of time along a straight line.

e.g. A vehicle running with the constant speed of 10 m/s will cover equal distances of 10 m in every second, so its motion will be uniform.

Note

For a uniform motion along a straight line in a given direction, the magnitude of the displacement is equal to the actual distance covered by the object.

Non-uniform Motion

A body is in non-uniform motion if it travels equal displacement in unequal intervals of time.

During the non-uniform motion, the speed of the body or its direction of motion or both change with time.

e.g. The velocity of the vehicle is different at different instants, so it has non-uniform motion.

SPEED AND VELOCITY

Speed

The distance covered by an object divided by the time taken by the object to cover that distance is called the **speed** of that object.

$$\boxed{\text{Speed} = \frac{\text{Distance travelled}}{\text{Time taken}}}$$

Speed is a **scalar quantity**. The speed of the object for a given interval of time is always positive.

Unit of speed The unit of speed in MKS (SI) is m/s and in CGS as cm/s.

Dimensional formula $[M^0LT^{-1}]$.

Uniform Speed

If an object is moving with a uniform speed, it means that it covers equal distance in equal interval of time.

Variable or Non-Uniform Speed

If an object is moving with a non-uniform speed, it means that it covers equal distances in unequal intervals of time.

Velocity

The rate of change of position of an object with time is called the **velocity** of that object.

i.e. $\quad$ Velocity $= \dfrac{\text{Displacement}}{\text{Time}}$

Velocity is a **vector** quantity.

Unit of velocity The unit of velocity is cms^{-1} in CGS and ms^{-1} in MKS or SI.

Dimensional formula The dimensional formula of velocity is $[M^0LT^{-1}]$.

Uniform Velocity

An object could have uniform velocity if it covers equal displacement in equal interval of time. If an object have equal displacement in equal interval of time, it means that it is moving with uniform velocity.

Non-uniform Velocity

If an object is moving with a non-uniform velocity, then it will have unequal displacements in equal interval of time.

Note The velocity of an object can be positive, zero and negative according to its displacement is positive, zero and negative.

Average Speed and Average Velocity

Average Speed

Average speed of an object is defined as the total distance travelled by the object divided by the total time taken.

$$\text{Average speed, } v_{av} = \dfrac{\text{Total distance travelled}}{\text{Total time taken}}$$

Average Velocity

Average velocity of a body is defined as the change in position or displacement (Δx) divided by the time interval (Δt) in which that displacement occur.

$\therefore$ Average velocity of the body is given by

$$\mathbf{v}_{av} = \dfrac{\Delta x}{\Delta t}$$

Average Velocity *vs* Average Speed

- For average speed, find net distance covered and divide it by time taken.
- Average velocity is net displacement divided by time taken.
- So, just find out the net displacement and divide it by time taken for that displacement.
- Average velocity could be zero or positive or negative but average speed is always positive for a moving body.

Instantaneous Speed and Instantaneous Velocity

Instantaneous Speed

Speed at an instant is defined as the limit of the average speed as the time interval (Δt) becomes infinitesimally small or approaches to zero.

Mathematically, instantaneous speed at any instant of time (t) is expressed as

$$\text{Instantaneous speed, } s_i = \underset{\Delta t \to 0}{\text{Lim}} \dfrac{\Delta s}{\Delta t} \text{ or } s_i = \dfrac{ds}{dt}$$

$\qquad\qquad$ [ds is the distance covered in time dt]

where, $\dfrac{ds}{dt}$ is the differential coefficient of s w.r.t. t.

EXAMPLE |4| **Instantaneous Speed of the Particle**
If the average speed of the particle is $[2t^2\,\hat{\mathbf{i}} + 3t\,\hat{\mathbf{j}}]$, then find out the instantaneous speed of the particle.

Sol. Given, position of the particle, $s = [2t^2\hat{i} + 3t\hat{j}]$

$$s_i = \dfrac{ds}{dt} = \dfrac{d}{dt}[2t^2\hat{i} + 3t\hat{j}]$$

Instantaneous speed of the particle is $s_i = 4t\,\hat{i} + 3\hat{j}$

Instantaneous Velocity

Velocity at an instant is defined as the limit of average velocity as the time interval (Δt) becomes infinitesimally small or approaches to zero.

Mathematically, instantaneous velocity at instant of time (t) is given by

$$v_i = \lim_{\Delta t \to 0} \dfrac{\Delta x}{\Delta t} \text{ or } v_i = \dfrac{dx}{dt}$$

where, dx is displacement for time dt.

Note $\text{Lim}_{\Delta t \to 0} \frac{\Delta x}{\Delta t}$ is called **differential coefficient** of displacement x w.r.t. time t. i.e. $\frac{dx}{dt}$.

The value of instantaneous velocity can be calculated graphically also as given below.

Suppose an object is moving along a straight line with variable velocity. Let the position-time graph of this motion is represented by a curve as shown in the figure.

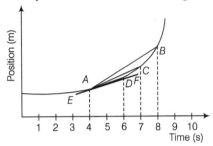

Graphical interpretation of instantaneous velocity

From the graph, the average velocity of the object over the time interval $\Delta t = 4$s, (i.e. from 4s to 8s) is the slope of straight line AB. If we decrease the interval of time Δt from 4s to 3s, then the line becomes AC. Similarly, at time interval Δt is 2s and the line becomes AD. As Δt approaches to zero, the point B approaches point A.

Thus, the line AB becomes the tangent of EF to the curve at D. Hence, the slope of the tangent with time axis gives the value of instantaneous velocity. Generally, we use numerical method to find the value of instantaneous velocity as the limiting process becomes clear.

Note The magnitude of instantaneous velocity is always equal to the instantaneous speed for a particular instant.

EXAMPLE | 5| Instantaneous velocity of a particle

The displacement (in m) of a particle moving along x-axis is given by $x = 18t + 15t^2$. Find the instantaneous velocity at $t = 0$ and $t = 2$s.

Sol. Given, Displacement,
$$x = 18t + 15t^2$$
Instantaneous velocity,
$$v_i = \frac{dx}{dt} = 18 + 30t$$
Instantaneous velocity at
$$t = 0, \; v = 18 + 30 \times 0 = 18 \text{ m/s}$$
$$t = 2s, \; v = 18 + 30 \times 2 = 78 \text{ m/s}$$

EXAMPLE |6| Instantaneous velocity by graphical method

Find the instantaneous velocity at $t = 3.5$ s from the graph given below.

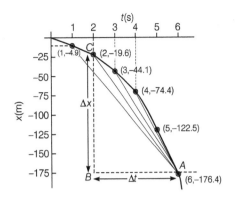

Sol. At $t = 3.5$,

We know that instantaneous velocity of a particle
$$v = \lim_{\Delta t \to 0} \frac{\Delta x}{\Delta t}$$

In the words to calculate instantaneous velocity, we have to reduce Δt to approximately zero (i.e. infinitesimal small) and find the corresponding value of $\Delta x/\Delta t$. Following table will illustrate the process.

$\Delta t'$	t_1'	t_2'	$x'(t_1)$	$x'(t_2)$	Δx	$\Delta x/\Delta t$
2	4.5	2.5	−103	−34	69	34.5
1	4	3	86	56	30	30.0
.5	3.75	3.25	119	60	59	29.55
.1	3.55	3.45	78	64	14	29.52
.01	3.505	3.495	81	69	12	29.51

So, the value of $\frac{\Delta x}{\Delta t}$ tends to come close to the value of 29.5 when we reduce Δt to very small around 3.5. Therefore, instantaneous value of velocity at 3.5 will be 29.5 m/s. The value of $x(t_1)$ and $x(t_2)$ have been obtained from the given graph.

TOPIC PRACTICE 1

OBJECTIVE Type Questions

1. **Which of the following statements is true for a car moving on the road?**
   (a) With respect to the frame of reference attached to the ground, the car is at rest
   (b) With respect to the frame of reference attached to the person sitting in the car, the car is at rest
   (c) With respect to the frame of reference attached to the person outside the car, the car is at rest
   (d) None of the above

Sol. (b) For a car in motion, if we describe this event w.r.t. a frame of reference attached to the person sitting inside the car, the car will appear to be at rest as the person inside the car (observer) is also moving with same velocity and in the same direction as car.

2. The coordinates of object with respect to a frame of reference at $t = 0$ are $(-1, 0, 3)$. If $t = 5$ s, its coordinates are $(-1, 0, 4)$, then the object is in
(a) motion along z-axis   (b) motion along x-axis
(c) motion along y-axis
(d) rest position between $t = 0$ s and $t = 5$ s

Sol. (a) Given, at $t = 0$ s, position of an object is $(-1, 0, 3)$ and at $t = 5$ s, its coordinate is $(-1, 0, 4)$. So, there is no change in x and y-coordinates, while z-coordinate changes from 3 to 4. So, the object is in motion along z-axis.

VERY SHORT ANSWER Type Questions

3. What is the condition for an object to be considered as a point object?

Sol. An object can be considered as a point object, if the distance travelled by it is very large than its size.

4. Can a tumbling beaker that has slipped off the edge of a table considered as a point object?
[NCERT]

Sol. No, because the size of the beaker is not negligible as compared to the height of the table.

5. Does the displacement of an object depend on the choice of the position of origin of the coordinate system?

Sol. No, the displacement of the object does not depend on the choice of the position of the origin.

6. For which condition, the distance and the magnitude of displacement of an object have the same values?

Sol. The distance and the magnitude of displacement of an object have the same values, when the body is moving along a straight line path in a fixed direction.

7. Which speed is measured by speedometer of your scooter?

Sol. Instantaneous speed of the scooter is measured by the speedometer.

8. The position coordinate of a moving particle is given by $x = 6 + 18t + 9t^2$, where x is in metres and t in seconds. What is the velocity at $t = 2$ s?

:bulb: We know that, velocity is rate of change of displacement i.e. $v = \dfrac{dx}{dt}$

Sol. Given, $x = 6 + 18t + 9t^2$

$$v_t = \dfrac{dx}{dt} = 18 + 18t$$

At $t = 2$,
$$v_2 = 18 + 18 \times 2$$
$$= 54 \text{ m/s}$$

9. For which condition, the average velocity will be equal to the instantaneous velocity?

Sol. When a body moves with a uniform velocity, then
$$v_{av} = v_{inst}$$

SHORT ANSWER Type Questions

10. From the given example, find if the motion is one or two or three-dimensional.
(i) A kite flying in the sky
(ii) A cricket ball hit by a player
(iii) Moon revolving around the earth and
(iv) The motion of a stone in a circle

Sol. (i) A flying kite in the sky comes under **three**-dimensional motion.
(ii) A cricket ball hit by a player comes under **two**-dimensional motion.
(iii) Moon revolving around the sun-earth comes under **two**-dimensional motion.
(iv) The motion of the stone in circular motion comes under **two**-dimensional motion.

11. For what condition, an object could be considered as a point object? Describe in brief.

Sol. An object could be considered as a point object if it covers a distance much larger than its own size.
e.g. If a bus of 5 m in size move 100 km, then the bus can be considered as a point object.

12. A drunkard walking in a narrow lane takes 5 steps forward and 3 steps backward, followed again 5 steps forward and 3 steps backward, and so on. Each step is 1 m long and requires 1 s. Determine how long the drunkard takes to fall in a pit 13 m away from the start. [NCERT]

Sol. The effective distance travelled by drunkard in 8 steps
$= 5 - 3 = 2$ m
Therefore, he takes 32 steps to move 8 m.
Now, he will have to cover 5 m more to reach the pit, for which he has to take only 5 forward steps.
Therefore, he will have to take $= 32 + 5 = 37$ steps to move 13 m. Thus, he will fall into the pit after taking 37 steps i.e. after 37 s from the start.

13. For the motion shown in the figure, find the displacement of car between the time intervals t_1 and t_3.

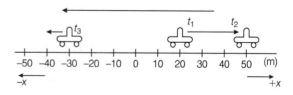

Sol. A car moving towards $+x$-axis. At time t_1 it is at $+20$ m. It turns at $+50$ m and starts moving towards $-x$-axis. At time t_3, it reached at -30 m.

The displacement of car in the interval $(t_3 - t_1) = \Delta t$ is $-30 - (+20) = -50$ m (negative sign shows the direction of displacement is towards $-x$-axis).

14. The position x of a body is given by $x = A \sin(\omega t)$. Find the time at which the displacement is maximum.

Sol. The value of position x will be maximum, when the value of $\sin(\omega t)$ is maximum, for this
$$\sin(\omega t) = 1 = \sin \pi/2$$
or
$$\omega t = \frac{\pi}{2} \implies t = \left(\frac{\pi}{2\omega}\right)$$

15. If the displacement of a body is zero, is distance necessarily zero? Answer with one example.

Sol. *No*, because the distance covered by an object is the path length of the path covered by the object. The displacement of an object is given by the change in position between the initial position and final position.

e.g. A boy starts from his home and moves towards market along a straight path. Then, he returns to home from the same path. Here, displacement is zero but distance is non-zero.

16. The position of an object is given by $x = 2t^2 + 3t$. Find out that its motion is uniform and non-uniform.

Sol. As given, $\qquad x = 2t^2 + 3t$

By differentiating x w.r.t. t, we get

Velocity, $\qquad v = \dfrac{dx}{dt} = \dfrac{d}{dt}(2t^2 + 3t)$
$$v = (4t + 3)$$

As velocity is time dependent, it means that motion is non-uniform.

17. The data regarding the motion of two different objects P and Q are given in the following table. Examine them carefully and state whether the motion of the objects is uniform or non-uniform.

Time	Distance travelled by object P (in m)	Distance travelled by object Q (in m)
9:30 am	10	12
9:45 am	20	19
10:00 am	30	23
10:15 am	40	35
10:30 am	50	37
10.45 am	60	41
11:00 am	70	44

Sol. We can see that the object P covers a distance of 10 m in every 15 min. In other words, it covers equal distance in equal intervals of time. So, the motion of object P is uniform. On the other hand, the object Q covers 7 m from 9:30 am to 9:45 am, 4 m from 9:45 am to 10:00 am and so on. In other words, it covers unequal distances in equal intervals of time. So, the motion of object Q is non-uniform.

18. Is earth inertial or non-inertial frame of reference?

Sol. Since, earth revolves around the sun and also spins about its own axis, so it is an accelerated frame of reference. Hence, earth is a non-inertial frame of reference.

However, if we do not take large scale motion such as wind and ocean currents into consideration, we can say that approximation the earth is an inertial frame.

19. A body is moving in a straight line along x-axis. Its distance from the origin is given by the equation $x = at^2 - bt^3$, where x is in metre and t is in second. Find its instantaneous speed at $t = 2$ s.

Sol. The given equation $x = at^2 - bt^3$

Instantaneous speed $v = \dfrac{dx}{dt} = \dfrac{d}{dt}(at^2 - bt^3) = 2at - 3bt^2$

At $t = 2$ s , $v = 4a - 12b$ m/s

20. The position of an object moving along x-axis is given by $x = a + bt^2$, where $a = 8.5$ m, $b = 2.5$ m and t is measured in seconds. What is its velocity at $t = 0$ s and $t = 2.0$ s? **[NCERT]**

Sol. We know that , $v = \dfrac{dx}{dt}$

On differentiating w.r.t. t, we get
$$v = \dfrac{d}{dt}(a + bt^2) = 2bt = 5t \text{ m/s} \quad [\because b = 2.5 \text{ m}]$$

At $t = 0, v = 0, \ t = 2$s and $v = 10$ m/s

LONG ANSWER Type I Question

21. No distinction is necessary when we consider instantaneous speed and magnitude of velocity. The instantaneous speed is always equal to the magnitude of instantaneous velocity. Why?

Sol. Instantaneous speed (v_{ins}) of the particle at an instant is the first derivative of the distance with respect to time at that instant of time i.e. $v_{ins} = \dfrac{dx}{dt}$.

Since, in instantaneous speed, we take only a small interval of time (dt) during which direction of motion of a body is not supposed to change, hence there is no difference between total path length and magnitude of displacement for small interval of time dt.

Hence, instantaneous speed is always equal to magnitude of instantaneous velocity.

ASSESS YOUR TOPICAL UNDERSTANDING

OBJECTIVE Type Question

1. The displacement of a car is given as -240 m. Here, negative sign indicates
   (a) direction of displacement
   (b) negative path length
   (c) position of car is at point whose coordinate is -120
   (d) no significance of negative sign

Answer

  1. (a)

SHORT ANSWER Type Question

2. A particle moves from one position to another position to the left of the origin in a straight line. Can the displacement of a particle be positive? Explain.

LONG ANSWER Type I Questions

3. What do you understand by non-uniform motion? Explain instantaneous velocity of an object in one-dimensional motion.

4. The displacement x of a particle moving in one dimension is related to time t by the relation $x = \sqrt{2t^2 - 3t}$, where x is in metre and t in second.

   Find the displacement of the particle when its velocity is zero.

   $$\left[\textbf{Ans. } \sqrt{-\frac{9}{8}} \text{ m}\right]$$

|TOPIC 2|
Uniformly Accelerated Motion

ACCELERATION

The existence of acceleration was given by Galileo in his different thoughts. **Acceleration of a body can be expressed as the rate of change of velocity with time.** By acceleration, we can understand that how fast or slow the velocity of an object is changing. Acceleration is a **vector quantity.**

$$\boxed{\text{Acceleration} = \frac{\text{Change in velocity}}{\text{Time taken}}}$$

Its SI unit is metre per second square (m/s^2) and CGS is cm/s^2. The dimensional formula is $[M^0L^1T^{-2}]$.

Note

• Acceleration therefore, may result from a change in speed (magnitude), a change in direction or changes in both.

• If the signs of velocity and acceleration is same (both positive or both negative), the body will accelerate and when the signs of velocity and acceleration are opposite, it means that the body is retarding.

EXAMPLE |1| **Retarding Bus**

Starting from a stationary position, a bus attains a velocity of 6 m/s in 30 s. Then, the driver of the bus applies a brake such that the velocity of the bus comes down to 4 m/s in the next 5 s. Calculate the acceleration of the bus in both the cases.

Sol. Case I Initial velocity of the bus, $u = 0$

Final velocity, $v = 6$ m/s; Time taken, $t = 30$ s

$$\therefore \text{ Acceleration} = \frac{\text{Change in velocity}}{\text{Time taken}}$$

$$= \frac{\text{Final velocity} - \text{Initial velocity}}{\text{Time taken}} = \frac{v - u}{t} = \frac{6 - 0}{30}$$

$$= 0.2 \text{ m/s}^2$$

Case II Initial velocity, $u = 6$ m/s

Final velocity, $v = 4$ m/s

$$\therefore \quad \text{Acceleration} = \frac{v - u}{t} = \frac{4 - 6}{5} = -0.4 \text{ m/s}^2$$

Thus, the acceleration in both the cases are 0.2 m/s^2 and -0.4 m/s^2

Average Acceleration

The average acceleration over a time interval is defined as **the change in velocity divided by the time interval.**

Suppose that at any time (t_1) a body has velocity $(\mathbf{v}_1)$. At a later time (t_2), it has velocity $(\mathbf{v}_2)$. Thus,

Change in velocity, $\Delta\mathbf{v} = \mathbf{v}_2 - \mathbf{v}_1$

Time during which velocity has changed, $\Delta t = t_2 - t_1$

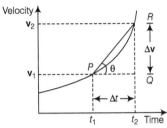

Velocity-time graph to calculate average acceleration

$$\mathbf{a}_{av} = \text{slope of straight line } PR = \frac{RQ}{PQ}$$

Average acceleration, $\mathbf{a}_{av} = \dfrac{\Delta\mathbf{v}}{\Delta t} = \dfrac{\mathbf{v}_2 - \mathbf{v}_1}{t_2 - t_1}$

The slope of velocity-time graph gives acceleration.

Instantaneous Acceleration

It is defined as the acceleration of a body at a certain instant or the limiting value of average acceleration when time interval becomes very small or tends to zero.

So, Instantaneous acceleration, $\mathbf{a}_{inst} = \lim\limits_{\Delta t \to 0} \dfrac{\Delta\mathbf{v}}{\Delta t} = \dfrac{d\mathbf{v}}{dt}$

where $\dfrac{d\mathbf{v}}{dt}$ is the differential coefficient of $\mathbf{v}$ w.r.t. t.

Elementary Concept of Integration for Describing Motion

We know that, $v = \dfrac{ds}{dt}$, $a = \dfrac{dv}{dt}$ or $v\dfrac{dv}{ds}$

If the displacement is given and we have to find the velocity and acceleration, then we use differentiation. If the acceleration is given and we have to find the velocity and displacement, then we use integration. To find the average value of square of velocity

$$\overline{v^2} = \frac{\displaystyle\int_{t_1}^{t_2} v^2 dt}{\displaystyle\int_{t_1}^{t_2} dt} \quad \Rightarrow \quad \overline{v^4} = \frac{\displaystyle\int_{t_1}^{t_2} v^4 dt}{\displaystyle\int_{t_1}^{t_2} dt}$$

If velocity is a function of displacement, $v = f(x)$, for average of v from $x = x_1$ to $x = x_2$

$$\Rightarrow \quad \overline{v} = \frac{\displaystyle\int_{x_1}^{x_2} v\, dt}{\displaystyle\int_{x_1}^{x_2} dt}$$

The above procedure can be applied to find the average value of any quantity like velocity, acceleration, force, etc.

EXAMPLE |2| Calculation of Average Acceleration

From the figure given, find the average acceleration between points A and B.

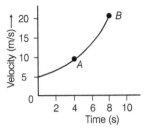

Sol. We draw the graph as

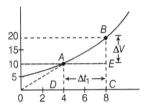

Average acceleration, $\mathbf{a}_{av} = \text{slope of line } AB = \dfrac{BE}{AE}$

$$BE = \Delta\mathbf{v} = \mathbf{v}_2 - \mathbf{v}_1 = 20 - 10 = 10 \text{ m/s}$$

$$AE = \Delta t = t_2 - t_1 = 8 - 4 = 4 \text{ s}$$

$$\therefore \qquad \mathbf{a}_{av} = \frac{10}{4} = 2.5 \text{ m/s}^2$$

EXAMPLE |3| Calculation of instantaneous acceleration

The velocity of a particle is given by $v = 2t^2 - 3t + 10$ m/s. Find the instantaneous acceleration at $t = 5$ s.

Sol. Given, $v = 2t^2 - 3t + 10$ m/s

$$\mathbf{a}_{in} = \frac{dv}{dt} = 4t - 3 \text{ m/s}^2$$

If $t = 5$, $\mathbf{a}_{in} = 5 \times 4 - 3 = 17 \text{ m/s}^2$

EXAMPLE |4| Average and Instantaneous Acceleration

A particle is moving in a straight line. Its displacement at any instant t is given by $x = 10\,t + 15t^3$, where x is in metres and t is in seconds. Find

(i) the average acceleration in the interval $t = 0$ to $t = 2$ s and

(ii) instantaneous acceleration at $t = 2$ s.

Sol. Given equation, $x = 10t + 15\,t^3$

and the variables are (i) $t = 0$ to $t = 2$s (ii) $t = 2$ s

Velocity of particle, $\mathbf{v} = \dfrac{dx}{dt}$

$$\mathbf{v} = \frac{d}{dt}(10t + 15t^3) = 10 + 45t^2$$

At $t = 0$, $\mathbf{v}_0 = 10 + 45(0) = 10 \text{ m/s}$,

At $t = 2$ s, $\mathbf{v}_2 = 10 + 45 \times (2)^2$

$$= 10 + 180 = 190 \text{ m/s}$$

$$\Delta \mathbf{v} = \mathbf{v}_2 - \mathbf{v}_0 = 190 - 10 = 180 \text{ m/s}$$

$$\Delta t = 2 - 0 = 2 \text{ s}$$

$\therefore \qquad \mathbf{a}_{av} = \dfrac{\Delta \mathbf{v}}{\Delta t} = \dfrac{180}{2} = 90 \text{ m/s}^2$

$$\mathbf{a} = \dfrac{d}{dt}(10 + 45\, t^2) = 90t$$

At $t = 2$ s, $\mathbf{a} = 90 \times 2 = 180 \text{ m/s}^2$

The instantaneous acceleration of a particle at 2s is 180 m/s^2.

Uniform Acceleration

If an object is moving with uniform acceleration, it means that the change in velocity is equal for equal intervals of time.

Non-uniform Acceleration

If an object has variable or non-uniform acceleration, it means that the change in velocity is unequal in equal intervals of time.

EXAMPLE |5| Uniform Acceleration

The displacement x of a particle varies with time t as $x = 4t^2 - 15t + 25$.

(i) Find the position, velocity and acceleration of the particle at $t = 0$.

(ii) Can we call the motion of the particle as one with uniform acceleration?

Sol. (i) Given position, $x = 4t^2 - 15t + 25$

Velocity, $v = \dfrac{dx}{dt} = \dfrac{d}{dt}(4t^2 - 15t + 25) = 8t - 15$

Acceleration, $a = \dfrac{dv}{dt} = \dfrac{d}{dt}(8t - 15) = 8$

At time $t = 0$, we have

$$x = 4t^2 - 15t + 25$$

$$= 4(0) - 15(0) + 25 = 25 \text{ m}$$

$$v = 8t - 15 = 8(0) - 15$$

$$= -15 \text{ m/s and } a = 8 \text{ m/s}^2$$

(ii) Yes, the particle has a uniform acceleration because it does not depend on time t.

POSITION-TIME GRAPHS FOR POSITIVE, NEGATIVE AND ZERO ACCELERATION

(i) **Positive Acceleration** When distance covered by a moving object goes on increasing with time, the object is said to have positive acceleration.

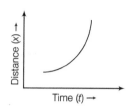

(ii) **Negative Acceleration** When distance covered by a moving object goes on decreasing with time, the object is said to have negative acceleration.

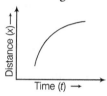

(iii) **Zero Acceleration** When the moving object covers equal distance in equal time, the object is said to have zero acceleration.

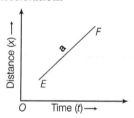

VELOCITY-TIME GRAPHS FOR AN ACCELERATED MOTION

(i) **Zero Acceleration** In case of zero acceleration, the velocity of the object does not change with time.

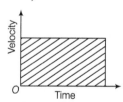

Note

The area under v-t graph gives displacement.

(ii) **Positive Acceleration**

(a) If the object is moving with positive acceleration having zero initial velocity, then **the velocity-time graph is a straight line starting from origin.**

In case of positive acceleration, the velocity of the object goes on increasing with time.

(b) If the object is moving with positive acceleration having some initial velocity, then **the velocity- time graph is a straight line starting from P.**

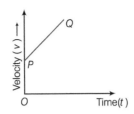

(iii) **Increasing Acceleration** In case of increasing acceleration, the velocity of the object goes on increasing exponentially (non-linearly). If the object is moving with increasing acceleration having zero initial velocity. The slope of v-t graph gives the **instantaneous acceleration.**

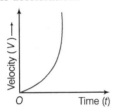

(iv) **Negative Acceleration**

(a) In case of negative acceleration, the velocity of the object decreases linearly with time.

If the object is moving with negative acceleration, have some positive initial velocity, then **the velocity-time graph is a straight line having negative slope.**

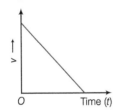

(b) If the object is moving with negative acceleration have some negative initial velocity, then **the velocity-time graph is a straight line starting from P as point of negative velocity.**

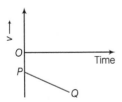

(c) If the object is moving with negative acceleration have some positive initial velocity, the direction of its motion can change at time (t). **The slope of velocity-time graph will remain constant for uniform acceleration.**

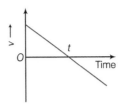

EXAMPLE |6| Analysis of Velocity-Time Graph

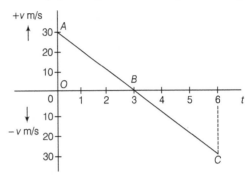

With the help of above velocity-time graph, find the

(i) displacement in first three seconds and

(ii) acceleration for the above graph.

💡 Area under the v-t graph gives the measurement of displacement. Thus, displacement = Area under v-t graph.

Sol. (i) Displacement in first three seconds = Area of $\triangle OAB$

$$= \frac{1}{2}(OB)\times(OA) = \frac{1}{2}(3)\times(+30) = +45\,\text{m}$$

(ii) Acceleration = Slope of v-t graph

As, v-t graph is a straight line. So, consider the slope of line AB.

$$\therefore \quad \text{Slope of line } AB = \frac{y_2 - y_1}{x_2 - x_1} = \frac{0-30}{3} = -10\,\text{m/s}^2$$

So, the acceleration is negative.

EXAMPLE |7| Uniform and Non-uniform Accelerated Motion of a Particle

The velocity-time graph of a particle in one-dimensional motion is shown in figure. Which of the following formulae are correct for describing the motion of the particle over the time interval t_1 to t_2?

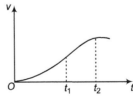

(i) $x(t_2) = x(t_1) + v(t_1)(t_2 - t_1) + \frac{1}{2}a(t_2 - t_1)^2$

(ii) $v(t_2) = v(t_1) + a(t_2 - t_1)$

(iii) $v_{av} = \left[\dfrac{x(t_2) - x(t_1)}{(t_2 - t_1)}\right]$ (iv) $a_{av} = \dfrac{[v(t_2) - v(t_1)]}{(t_2 - t_1)}$

(v) $x(t_2) = x(t_1) + v_{av}(t_2 - t_1) + \dfrac{1}{2} a_{av}(t_2 - t_1)^2$

(vi) $x(t_2) - x(t_1) =$ Area under v-t curve bounded by the t-axis and the dotted line shown. **[NCERT]**

Sol. The slope of the given graph over the time interval t_1 to t_2 is not constant and is not uniform. It means acceleration is not constant or uniform, therefore relations (*i*), (*ii*) and (*v*) are not correct which is uniform accelerated motion, but relations (*iii*), (*iv*) and (*vi*) are correct, because these relations are true for both uniform or non-uniform accelerated motion.

KINEMATIC EQUATIONS FOR UNIFORMLY ACCELERATED MOTION

If the change in velocity of an object in each unit of time is constant, then object is said to be moving with constant acceleration and such a motion is called **uniformly accelerated motion.**

If an object moves along a straight line with a constant acceleration a. Let u be the initial velocity at $t = 0$ and v be the final velocity of the object after time (t).

(i) Velocity-Time Relation

The slope of velocity-time graph gives the acceleration of the object.

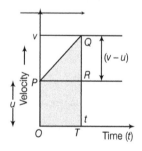

$\therefore \qquad a =$ Slope of PQ

$$a = \dfrac{QR}{PR} = \dfrac{v - u}{t}$$

$\Rightarrow \qquad a = \dfrac{v - u}{t}$

$\Rightarrow \qquad\qquad\qquad v - u = at$

$\boxed{\text{Velocity-Time relation, } v = u + at}$

(ii) Position-Time Relation

The area under the velocity-time graph gives the displacement.

Displacement of an object in time interval t is given by

$x =$ Area of $\Delta PQR +$ Area of rectangle $OPRT$

$$= \dfrac{1}{2} QR \times PR + OP \times PR$$

$$= \dfrac{1}{2} (v - u)t + ut$$

$$= \dfrac{1}{2} (at)t + ut \qquad [\because v - u = at]$$

$$= \dfrac{1}{2} at^2 + ut$$

$\Rightarrow \qquad x = \dfrac{1}{2} at^2 + ut$

$\boxed{\text{Position-time relation } x = ut + \dfrac{1}{2} at^2}$

(iii) Position-Velocity Relation

Again the displacement in time interval (t) is given by

$x =$ area of trapezium $OPQT$.

$$= \dfrac{1}{2} (OP + QT) \times OT$$

$$x = \dfrac{1}{2} (u + v) \times t \qquad \text{...(i)}$$

From $\qquad v - u = at$

$$t = \dfrac{v - u}{a} \qquad \text{...(ii)}$$

On substituting the value of t in Eq. (i), we get

$$x = \dfrac{1}{2} (u + v) \times \dfrac{(v - u)}{a}$$

$\Rightarrow \qquad v^2 - u^2 = 2ax$

$\Rightarrow \qquad \boxed{\text{Position-velocity relation, } v^2 = u^2 + 2ax}$

Displacement of the Particle in nth Second

Let an object is moving with initial velocity u under constant acceleration a.

To find the displacement in nth second, we subtract the position of particle at $(n - 1)$th second from the position of the particle at nth second.

Displacement in nth second $= s_n - s_{n-1}$

$$s\,(n\text{th}) = \left[un + \dfrac{1}{2} a\,(n^2)\right] - \left[u(n - 1) + \dfrac{1}{2} a\,(n - 1)^2\right]$$

$$= un + \dfrac{1}{2} an^2 - un + u - \dfrac{1}{2} a\,(n - 1)^2$$

$$= u + \dfrac{a}{2}[n^2 - (n - 1)^2]$$

$$= u + \frac{a}{2}(n^2 - n^2 - 1 + 2n)$$

Displacement in the nth second, $s(n\text{th}) = u + \frac{a}{2}(2n - 1)$

Above expression shows displacement in the nth second.

Steps to Solve Problems Based on Accelerated Motion

The following steps are recommended for solving problem involving accelerated motion.

Step I Make sure all the units in the problem are consistent. That is, if distances are measured in meters, be sure that velocities have units of meters per second and accelerations have units of meters per second square.

Step II Make a list of all the quantities given in the problem and a separate list of those to be determined.

Step III Think about what is going on physically in the problem and then select from the list of kinematic equations the one or ones that will enable you to determine the unknowns.

EXAMPLE |8| Mixture of Acceleration and Retardation

A motor car starts from rest and accelerates uniformly for 10s to a velocity of 20 m/s. After that car runs at a constant speed and is finally brought to rest in 40m with a constant aceleration. Total distance covered is 640 m. Find the value of acceleration, retardation and total time taken.

Sol. Let x_1, x_2 and x_3 be distances covered in three parts of the motion.

For first part of the motion, we have

$$u = 0, \, t = 10\text{s}, \, v = 20 \text{ m/s}$$

As $\quad v = u + at$

$\therefore \quad 20 = 0 + a \times 10$

Acceleration, $\quad a = 2 \text{ m/s}^2$

Distance, $\quad x_1 = ut + \frac{1}{2}at^2$

$$= 0 \times 10 + \frac{1}{2} \times 2 \times (10)^2 = 100 \text{ m}$$

For second part of the motion, we have

$$x_1 = 100\text{m}, \, x_3 = 40\text{m}$$

As $\quad x_1 + x_2 + x_3 = 640$

$\therefore \quad 100 + x_2 + 40 = 640$

or $\quad x_2 = 500\text{m}$

This distance is covered with a uniform speed of 20 m/s.

$\therefore$ Time taken $= \dfrac{500}{20} = 25$ s

For third part of the motion, we have

$$u = 20 \text{ m/s}, \, v = 0, \, x = x_3 = 40\text{m}$$

As $\quad v^2 - u^2 = 2ax$

$\therefore \quad (0)^2 - (20)^2 = 2 \times a \times 40$

or $\quad a = -\dfrac{400}{80} = -5\text{m/s}^2$

$\therefore$ Retardation $= 5\text{m/s}^2$

Time taken, $t = \dfrac{v - u}{a} = \dfrac{0 - 20}{-5} = 4\text{s}$

Total time taken $= 10 + 25 + 4 = 39$ s

EXAMPLE |9| Equations of Motion by Calculus Method

Obtain equation of motion for constant acceleration using method of calculus. **[NCERT]**

Sol. From the definition of average acceleration,

$$a = \frac{dv}{dt} \Rightarrow dv = a \, dt$$

Integrating both sides and taking the limit for velocity u to v and for time 0 to t.

$$\int_u^v dv = \int_0^t a \, dt = a \int_0^t dt = a[t]_0^t \qquad [\because a \text{ is constant}]$$

$$v - u = at$$

$$v = u + at$$

Now, from the definition of velocity, $v = \dfrac{dx}{dt} \Rightarrow dx = v \, dt$

Integrating both sides and taking the limit for displacement x_0 to x and for time 0 to t.

$$\int_{x_0}^x dx = \int_0^t v \, dt = \int_0^t (u + at) dt = v_0 [t]_0^t + a\left[\frac{t^2}{2}\right]_0^t$$

$$x - x_0 = ut + \frac{1}{2}at^2$$

$$x = x_0 + ut + \frac{1}{2}at^2$$

Now, we can write

$$a = \frac{dv}{dt} = \frac{dv}{dx}\frac{dx}{dt} = v\frac{dv}{dx}$$

or $\quad v \, dv = a \, dx$

Integrating both sides and taking the limit for velocity u to v and for displacement x_0 to x.

$$\int_u^v v \, dv = \int_{x_0}^x a \, dx$$

$$\frac{v^2 - u^2}{2} = a(x - x_0)$$

$$v^2 = u^2 + 2a(x - x_0)$$

This method is also be used for motion with non-uniform acceleration.

Non-uniformly Accelerated Motion

When acceleration of particle is not constant or acceleration is a function of time, then following relations hold for one-dimensional motion.

(i) $v = \dfrac{ds}{dt}$ (ii) $a = \dfrac{dv}{dt} = v\dfrac{dv}{dx}$

(iii) $ds = v\,dt$ and   (iv) $dv = a\,dt$ or $v\,dv = a\,dx$

EXAMPLE |10| Non-uniformaly Accelerated Motion

Two particles move along x-axis. The position of particle 1 is given by $x = 6.00t^2 + 3.00t + 2.00$ (in metre and in seconds); acceleration of particle 2 is given by $a = -8.00\,t$ (in m/s^2 and seconds) and at $t = 0$, its velocity is 20 m/s. When the velocities of the particles match, find their velocities.

Sol. List all informations about particle 1 and particle 2.

For particle 1,
$$x_1 = 6.00\,t^2 + 3.00\,t + 2.00$$

For particle 2,
$$a_2 = -8.00\,t,$$
$$v_2 = 20 \text{ m/s at } t = 0 \text{ s}$$

We know that, $v(t) = \dfrac{dx}{dt}$
$$v(t) = 12\,t + 3 + 0$$
$$v(t) = 12\,t + 3$$

For particle 2,
We know that, $\int a(t)\,dt = v(t)$

$\Rightarrow$ $\quad v(t) = \int -8.00\,dt = -8\int t\,dt = \dfrac{-8\,t^2}{2} + C$

$$v(t) = -4\,t^2 + C$$

If $v(t) = 20$ m/s and $t = 0$ s, then
$$20\,\text{m/s} = -4\,(0)^2 + C$$

$\Rightarrow$ $\quad 20 = 0 + C \Rightarrow C = 20$

So, $\quad v_2(t) = -4t^2 + 20$

Since, the particles' velocities have to match, you have to set the two equations equal to each other
$$v_1(t) = v_2(t)$$
$$12\,t + 3 = -4\,t^2 + 20$$
$$4\,t^2 + 12\,t - 17 = 0$$

Since, you could not factor out, you probably know to use the quadratic formula

$$= \dfrac{-b \pm \sqrt{b^2 - 4ac}}{2a} = \dfrac{-12 \pm \sqrt{(12)^2 - 4(4)(-17)}}{2(4)}$$

$$= \dfrac{-12 \pm \sqrt{144 + 272}}{8}$$

$$t = \dfrac{-12 \pm \sqrt{416}}{8} = \dfrac{-12 \pm 20.3}{8}$$

$$t = -4.04 \text{ s or } t = 1.04 \text{ s}$$

As, time cannot be negative, $t = 1.04$ s.

Find the velocities of different particles.
$$v(t_1) = 12\,(1.04) + 3 = 15.48 \text{ m/s}$$
$$v(t_2) = -4\,(1.04)^2 + 20 = 15.67 \text{ m/s}$$

EQUATIONS OF MOTION FOR THE MOTION OF AN OBJECT UNDER GRAVITY

When an object is thrown upwards or fall towards the earth, then its motion is called **motion under gravity** because in these conditions (upward or downward), the acceleration of the body is equal to the acceleration due to gravity.

In case of motion under gravity, the equations of motion are given below

$$v = u + (\pm g)\,t \qquad \qquad \text{...(i)}$$
$$h = ut + \dfrac{1}{2}(\pm g)\,t^2 \qquad \text{...(ii)}$$
$$v^2 = u^2 + 2(\pm g)\,h \qquad \text{...(iii)}$$

In case of upward motion, acceleration due to gravity (g) is taken as **positive** and for downward motion, g is taken as **negative**.

Feeling Weightlessness

There is a misconception that in free fall, no force acted on us since we are not able to feel our weight. Actually we feel our weight due to the reaction we get from earth. As in free fall, we are not pushing anything, so we are not getting any reaction (Newton's third law) and feeling weightlessness.

EXAMPLE |11| Free Fall

Discuss the motion of an object under free fall. Neglect air resistance. **[NCERT]**

Sol. An object released near the surface of the earth is accelerated downward under the influence of the force of gravity. The magnitude of acceleration due to gravity is represented by g. If air resistance is neglected, the object is said to be in **free fall**. If the height through which the object falls is small as compared to the earth's radius, g can be taken constant, equal to 9.8 ms^{-2}. Free fall is thus a case of motion with uniform acceleration.

We assume that the motion is in y-direction, more correctly in $(-y)$ direction because we choose upward direction as positive. Since, the acceleration due to gravity is always downward, it is in the negative direction and we have

$$a = -g = -9.8\,\text{m s}^{-2}$$

The object is released from rest at $y = 0$. Therefore, $u = 0$ and the equations of motion become

$$v = 0 - gt = -9.8t \text{ ms}^{-1}$$

$$h = 0 - 1/2gt^2 = -4.9t^2 \text{ m}$$

$$v^2 = 0 - 2gh = -19.6h \text{ m}^2\text{s}^{-2}$$

These equations give the velocity and the distance travelled as a function of time and also the variation of velocity with distance.

The variation of acceleration, velocity and distance with time have been plotted in Fig. (a), (b) and (c).

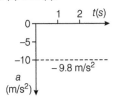

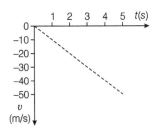

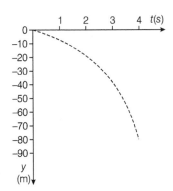

Note Here, magnitude of displacement and distance is equal.

EXAMPLE |12| Motion of a Ball under Gravity

A ball is thrown vertically upwards with a velocity of 20 m/s from the top of a multi storey building. The height of the point from where the ball is thrown 25 m from the ground.

(i) How high will the ball rise?

(ii) How long will it be before the ball hits the ground? Take, $g = 10 \text{ m/s}^2$ **[NCERT]**

Sol. (i) Consider vertical upward motion of ball upto highest point, we have

$$u = 20 \text{ m/s}, v = 0,$$

$$a = -10 \text{ m/s}^2, t = t_1,$$

$$x = ? \text{ (say)}$$

Using theorem, $v^2 = u^2 + 2ax$

$$x = \frac{v^2 - u^2}{2a} = \frac{0 - (20)^2}{2 \times (-10)} = 20 \text{ m}$$

(ii) As shown in figure, we have upward motion A to B in time (t_1) and downward motion (B to C) in time (t_2). Velocity at B is zero

$$\therefore \qquad v = u - gt$$

$$0 = 20 - 10t_1 \Rightarrow t_1 = 2s$$

From the top, the ball falls freely under acceleration due to gravity.

$$\therefore \qquad x = x_0 + ut + \frac{1}{2}gt_2^2$$

$$x = 0, x_0 = 45 \text{ m}, u = 0 \text{ and } g = 10 \text{ m/s}^2$$

$$0 = 45 + 0 + \frac{1}{2}(-10)t_2^2 = 45 - 5t_2^2$$

$$t_2^2 = 9 \Rightarrow t_2 = 3s$$

$\therefore$ Total time taken by the ball to hit the ground

$$t = t_1 + t_2 = 2 + 3 = 5 \text{ s}$$

Method II

In this method we shall consider net displacement = Final position − Initial position = 25m.

Using the formula $\qquad x = ut + \frac{1}{2}gt^2$

$$\Rightarrow \qquad -25 = +20t - \frac{1}{2}gt^2 = +20t - 5t^2$$

$$\Rightarrow \qquad t^2 - 4t - 5 = 0$$

$$(t - 5)(t + 1) = 0 \Rightarrow t = 5 \text{ s}$$

Galileo's Law of Odd Numbers

Galileo was the first to make quantitative studies of free fall. This law states that the distances traversed by a freely falling body during equal intervals of time stand to one another in the same ratio as the odd numbers beginning with unity, i.e. $1 : 3 : 5 : 7$.

EXAMPLE |13| Prove Galileo's Law of Odd Numbers

Sol. Let us divide the time interval of motion of an object under free fall into many equal intervals τ and find out the distances traversed during successive intervals of time. Since $u = 0$, then $y = -\frac{1}{2}gt^2$

To calculate the position of the object after different time intervals $0, \tau, 2\tau, 3\tau, \ldots$ which are given in the second column of the table shown below.

t	y	y in Terms of $y_0 = (-1/2)g\,\tau^2$	Distance Traversed in Successive Intervals	Ratio of Distances Traversed
0	0	0		
τ	$(-1/2)g\,\tau^2$	y_0	y_0	1
2τ	$-4(1/2)g\,\tau^2$	$4\,y_0$	$3\,y_0$	3
3τ	$-9(1/2)g\,\tau^2$	$9\,y_0$	$5\,y_0$	5
4τ	$-16(1/2)g\,\tau^2$	$16\,y_0$	$7\,y_0$	7
5τ	$-25(1/2)g\,\tau^2$	$25\,y_0$	$9\,y_0$	9
6τ	$-36(1/2)g\,\tau^2$	$36\,y_0$	$11\,y_0$	11

The third column gives the positions in the unit of y_0. The fourth column shows the distances traversed in successive τs. At last, the fifth column find the distances are in simple ratio $1 : 3 : 5 : 7$. **Hence proved**

Stopping Distance for a Vehicle

When brakes are applied to a moving vehicle, the distance it travels before coming to halt is called **stopping distance**.

It is also an important factor for road safety. Its value depends upon the speed at which the vehicle is running and the efficiency of the braking system.

Let the distance travelled by the vehicle before it stops be d_s.

Using the equation of motion,

$$v^2 = u^2 + 2\,ax$$

If $v = 0$ and $x = d_s$, then

$$\boxed{\text{Stopping distance, } d_s = \frac{-u^2}{2\,a}}$$

Thus, the stopping distance is proportional to the square of the initial velocity. If we double the initial velocity, its stopping distance increase by a factor of 4 for same deceleration.

EXAMPLE |14| Halt a Car

A car moving with a speed of 50 km/h can be stopped by brakes after covering 6 m. What will be the minimum stopping distance, if the same car is moving at a speed of 100 km/h?

Sol. In first case,

$$u = 50 \,\text{km/h} = 50 \times \frac{5}{18}$$

$$= \frac{125}{9} \,\text{m/s}, \ v = 0, \ x = 6 \,\text{m}$$

Using the relation, $v^2 - u^2 = 2ax$

$$0 - \left(\frac{125}{9}\right)^2 = 2a \times 6$$

$$\Rightarrow \quad a = \frac{-125 \times 125}{81 \times 2 \times 6} = -16.27 \,\text{m/s}^2 \approx 16 \,\text{m/s}$$

In second case,

$$u = 100 \,\text{km/h} = 100 \times \frac{5}{18} = \frac{250}{9} \,\text{m/s}$$

$$v = 0, \ a = -16 \,\text{m/s}^2 \text{and } x = ?$$

Using the relation, $v^2 - u^2 = 2ax$

$$0 - \left(\frac{250}{9}\right)^2 = 2 \times (-16)\,x$$

$$\Rightarrow \quad x = \frac{250 \times 250}{81 \times 2 \times 16} = 24.1 \,\text{m}$$

Reaction Time

When a situation demands our immediate action, it takes sometime before we really respond. **Reaction time is** defined as the time a person takes to observe, think and act.

e.g. If a person is driving a car and suddenly a boy appears on the road, then the time elapsed before he applies the brakes of the car is the reaction time.

Reaction time depends on
  (i) an individual presence of mind
  (ii) the complexity of the situation

Calculation of Reaction Time

We can find reaction time by the following experiment. Suppose your friend is holding a long rod vertically in the gap between the thumb and fore-finger of your right hand. He has to drop that rod and you have to catch and hold the falling rod. You will see that rod is caught after moving a distance x.

Let this distance x be 0.21 m. If t is the reaction time, then $u = 0$, $a = 9.8 \,\text{m/s}^2$, $x = 0.21 \,\text{m}$, $t = ?$

Using the relation, $x = ut + \dfrac{1}{2}at^2$

$$\Rightarrow \quad 0.21 = 0 + \frac{1}{2} \times 9.8 \times t^2$$

$$\Rightarrow \quad t = \sqrt{\frac{2 \times 0.21}{9.8}} = 0.2 \,\text{s}$$

TOPIC PRACTICE 2

OBJECTIVE Type Questions

1. The velocity of a particle moving along a straight line is described by equation
$$v = 12 - 3t^2$$
where, x is in metre and t in s. The retardation of the particle when its velocity becomes zero, is
(a) 24 ms^{-2} (b) zero (c) 6 ms^{-2} (d) 12 ms^{-2}

Sol. (d) We know acceleration $a = \dfrac{dv}{dt}$

So, $v = 12 - 3t^2$ and $a = -6t$
At $t = 2$ s, $v = 0$ and $a = -6 \times 2$
$a = 12 \text{ ms}^{-2}$

So, retardation of the particle $= 12 \text{ ms}^{-2}$.

2. A lift is coming from 8th floor and is just about to reach 4th floor. Taking ground floor as origin and positive direction upwards for all quantities, which one of the following is correct?

[NCERT Exemplar]

(a) $x < 0, v < 0, a > 0$ (b) $x > 0, v < 0, a < 0$
(c) $x > 0, v < 0, a > 0$ (d) $x > 0, v > 0, a < 0$

Sol. (a) As the lift is coming in downward directions displacement will be negative. We have to see whether the motion is accelerating or retarding.
When the lift reaches 4th floor is about to stop hence, motion is retarding in nature hence, $x < 0; a > 0$.
As displacement is in negative direction, velocity will also be negative i.e., $v < 0$.
This can be shown on the adjacent graph.

3. The object is released from rest under gravity at $y = 0$. The equation of motion which correctly expresses the above situation is
(a) $v = -9.8 \, t \text{ ms}^{-1}$
(b) $v = (9.8 - 9.8 \, t) \text{ m/s}$
(c) $v^2 = -19.6 \, y^2 \text{ m}^2\text{s}^{-2}$
(d) $v^2 = (v_0^2 + 29.6 \, y) \text{ m}^2 / \text{s}^2$

Sol. (a) For free fall, $v_0 = 0$, $a = -g = -9.8 \text{ ms}^{-2}$

The equations of motion are
$$v = -9.8 \, t \text{ ms}^{-1} \qquad \text{(using } v = v_0 + at\text{)}$$
$$v^2 = 2 \times (-9.8) \times y \qquad \text{(using } v^2 = v_0^2 + 2ay\text{)}$$
$$= -19.6y \text{ m}^2\text{s}^{-2}$$

4. The average velocities of the objects A and B are v_A and v_B, respectively. The velocities are related such that $v_A > v_B$.

The position-time graph for this situation can be represented as

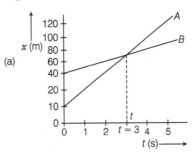

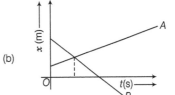

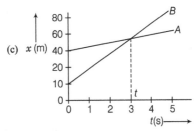

(d) None of the above

Sol. (a) Since, the velocities of the particles are positive, the slope of the straight line in $(x$-$t)$ graph must be positive. Since, $v_A > v_B$, the slope of straight line representing A must be greater than the slope of the straight line representing B i.e., graph representing A is more steeper. Even though, A starts with lower value of position coordinate than B, it overtakes, B at $t = 3$ s.

VERY SHORT ANSWER Type Questions

5. If position of a particle at instant t is given by $x = 2t^3$, find the acceleration of the particle.

Sol. Given, $x = 2t^3$, velocity, $v = \dfrac{dx}{dt} = \dfrac{d(2t^3)}{dt} = 6t^2$

∴ Acceleration, $a = \dfrac{dv}{dt} = \dfrac{d(6t^2)}{dt} = 12t$

6. When a body accelerates by βt, what is the velocity after time t, when it starts from rest?

Sol. Given, acceleration $a = \beta t$

It can be written as $\int dv = \int \beta t\, dt$

On integrating, we get $v = \dfrac{\beta t^2}{2} + C = \dfrac{\beta t^2}{2}$ $[\because C = 0]$

7. Give an example of uniformly accelerated linear motion.

Sol. Motion of a body under gravity.

8. Constant acceleration means that x-t graph will have constant slope? Yes/No

Sol. Acceleration means that velocity is non-uniform. So, x-t graph will be curved.

9. Draw v-t graph for non-uniform accelerated motion.

Sol.

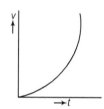

Here, acceleration is increasing.

10. Consider that the acceleration of a moving body varies with time. What does the area under acceleration-time graph for any time interval represent?

Sol. The area under acceleration-time graph for any time interval represents the change of velocity of the body during that time interval.

11. A car starts accelerating from rest for sometime, maintains the velocity for sometime and then comes to rest with uniform deceleration. Draw v-t graph.

Sol.

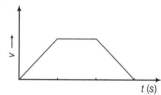

12. Write an expression for distance covered in nth second for a uniformly accelerated motion.

Sol. If a is the uniform acceleration, then

$$s(n\text{th}) = u + \frac{1}{2} a\,(2n - 1)$$

where, s (nth) is the distance covered in nth second, u is the initial velocity.

13. Find the acceleration and velocity of a ball at the instant it reaches its highest point if it was thrown up with velocity v.

Sol. Acceleration is 9.8 m/s^2 (downwards) and velocity is zero at the highest point.

SHORT ANSWER Type Questions

14. The displacement of a particle is given by at^2. What is dependency of acceleration on time?

Sol. Let x be the displacement. Then, $x = at^2$

$\therefore$ Velocity of the object, $v = \dfrac{dx}{dt} = 2at$

Acceleration of the object, $a = \dfrac{dv}{dt} = 2a$

It means that a is constant.

15. A bus starting from rest moves with a uniform acceleration of 0.1 m/s^2 for 2 min. Find (i) the speed acquired and (ii) the distance travelled.

Sol. $u = 0$, $a = 0.1$ m/s^2 and $t = 2$ min 120 s

(i) $v = u + at = 0 + 0.1 \times 120 = 12$ m/s

(ii) $s = ut + \dfrac{1}{2} at^2 = 0 + \dfrac{1}{2} \times 0.1 \times (120)^2$

$= \dfrac{1}{2} \times 0.1 \times 120 \times 120 = 720$ m

16. Points P, Q and R are in a vertical line such that $PQ = QR$. A ball at P is allowed to fall freely. What is the ratio of the times of descent through PQ and QR?

Sol. Let t_1 and t_2 be the times of descent through PQ and QR, respectively.

Let $\qquad PQ = QR = h$

Then, $\qquad h = \dfrac{1}{2} g\, t_1^2$ and $2h = \dfrac{1}{2} g\,(t_1 + t_2)^2$

By dividing, we get

$$\frac{1}{2} = \frac{t_1^2}{(t_1 + t_2)^2}$$

or $\qquad \dfrac{1}{\sqrt{2}} = \dfrac{t_1}{t_1 + t_2}$

Hence, $\quad t_1 : t_2 = 1 : (\sqrt{2} - 1)$

17. Which of the following is true for displacement?
(i) It cannot be zero.
(ii) Its magnitude is greater than the distance travelled by the object.

Sol. Both these statements are not true, because
(i) Its magnitude can be zero.
(ii) Its magnitude is either less than or equal to the distance travelled by the object.

18. What are uses of a velocity-time graph?

Sol. From a velocity-time graph, we can find out
  (i) The velocity of a body at any instant.
  (ii) The acceleration of the body and
  (iii) The net displacement of the body in a given time-interval.

19. The velocity of a particle is given by equation
$$v = 4 + 2(C_1 + C_2 t)$$
where, C_1 and C_2 are constant. Find the initial velocity and acceleration of the particle.

Sol. The given equation is $v = 4 + 2(C_1 + C_2 t)$
$$\Rightarrow \qquad v = (4 + 2C_1) + 2C_2 t$$
Comparing the above equations with equation of motion
$$v = u + at$$
Initial velocity, $u = 4 + 2C_1$
Acceleration of the particle $= 2C_2$

20. The speed-time graph for a car is shown in figure below.

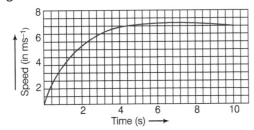

  (i) Find how far the car travels in the first 4 s? Shade the area on the graph that represents the distance travelled by the car during the period.
  (ii) Which part of the graph represent uniform motion of the car?

Sol. (i) The shaded portion of the car represents the distance travelled by the car in the first four seconds.

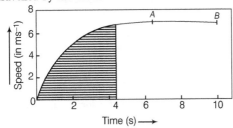

The car travels with a non-uniform speed which is accelerated in nature.
  (ii) The straight line portion of the graph represents the uniform motion of the car i.e. from point A to B.

21. At $t = 0$, a particle is at rest at origin. Its acceleration is 2 m/s^2 for the first 3s and -2 m/s^2 for next 3s.
Plot the acceleration *versus* time and velocity *versus* time graph.

Sol. The acceleration-time graph is

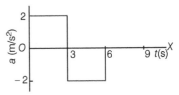

The area enclosed between *a-t* curve gives change in velocity for the corresponding interval.
At $t = 0$, $v = 0$, hence final velocity at $t = 3$ s will increase to 6 m/s. In next 3 s, the velocity will decrease to zero.
Thus, the velocity-time graph is

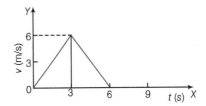

22. The distance travelled by a body is proportional to the square of time. What type of motion this body has?

Sol. Let x be the distance travelled in time t. Then,
$$x \propto t^2 \qquad \text{[given]}$$
$$x = kt^2 \quad \text{[here, } k = \text{constant of proportionality]}$$
We know that velocity is given
$$v = \frac{dx}{dt} = 2kt$$
and acceleration is given by
$$a = \frac{dv}{dt} = 2k \qquad \text{[constant]}$$
Thus, the body has uniform accelerated motion.

LONG ANSWER Type I Questions

23. Suggest a suitable physical situation for each of the following graph. **[NCERT]**

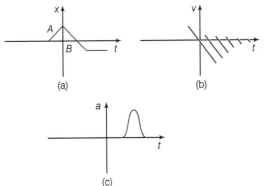

Sol. (i) In Fig. (a), the *x-t* graph shows that initially *x* is zero i.e. at rest, then it increases with time, attains a constant value and again reduces to zero with time, then it increases in opposite direction till it again attains a constant value i.e. comes to rest.

The similar physical situation arises when a ball resting on a smooth floor is kicked which rebounds from a wall with reduced speed. It then moves to the opposite wall which stops it.

(ii) In Fig. (b), the velocity changes sign again and again with passage of time and every time some speed is lost. The similar physical situation arises when a ball is thrown up with some velocity, returns back and falls freely. On striking the ground, it rebounds with reduced speed each time it strikes against the ground.

(iii) In Fig. (c), initially the body moves with uniform velocity. Its acceleration increases for a short duration and then falls to zero and thereafter the body moves with a constant velocity. The similar physical situation arises when a cricket ball moving with a uniform speed is hit with a bat for a very short interval of time.

24. Figure gives the *x-t* plot of a particle executing one-dimensional simple harmonic motion. Give the signs of position, velocity and acceleration variables of the particles at *t* = 0.3 s, 1.2 s, – 1.2 s.

[NCERT]

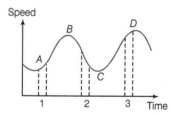

In SHM, the acceleration $a = -\omega^2 x$ i.e. acceleration is directly proportional to the displacement and opposite in direction.

Sol. In the SHM, acceleration $a = -\omega^2 x$, where ω (i.e. angular frequency) is constant.

(i) At time *t* = 0.3 s, *x* is negative, the slope of *x-t* plot is negative, hence **position and velocity are negative.** Since $a = -\omega^2 x$, hence acceleration is positive.

(ii) At time *t* = 1.2 s, *x* is positive, the slope of *x-t* plot is also positive, hence position and velocity are positive. Since $a = -\omega^2 x$, hence **acceleration is negative**

(iii) At *t* = – 1.2 s, *x* is negative, the slope of *x-t* plot is also negative. But since both *x* and *t* are negative here, hence **velocity is positive**. Finally, acceleration *a* is **also positive**.

25. Figure shows the *x-t* plot of a particle in one-dimensional motion. Three different equal intervals of time are shown. In which interval the average speed is greatest and in which it is the least? Give the sign of average speed for each interval.   **[NCERT]**

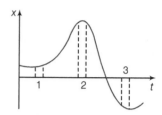

The slope of *x-t* graph represents the average speed in that interval of time i.e. higher the slope of *x-t* graph, higher is the average speed.

Sol. We know that average speed in a small interval of time is equal to the slope of *x-t* graph in that interval of time.

The average speed is the greatest in the interval 3 because slope is greatest and the average speed is least in interval 2 because slope is least there.

The average speed is positive in intervals 1 and 2 because slope of *x-t* is positive there and **average speed is negative in interval** 3 because the slope of *x-t* is negative.

26. Figure gives a speed-time graph of a particle in one-dimensional motion. Three different equal intervals of time are shown. In which interval is the average acceleration greatest in magnitude? In which interval is the average speed greatest? Choosing the positive direction as the constant direction of motion, give the signs of *u* and *a* in the three intervals. What are the accelerations at the points *A*, *B*, *C* and *D*?   **[NCERT]**

The slope of *v-t* graph represents the acceleration i.e. higher the slope of *v-t* graph, higher the acceleration.

Sol. We know that average acceleration in a small interval of time is equal to slope of velocity-time graph in that interval. As the slope of velocity-time graph is maximum in interval 2 as compared to other intervals 1 and 3, hence the magnitude of average acceleration is greatest in interval 2. The **average speed is greatest in interval 3** for obvious reasons.

In interval 1, the slope of velocity-time graph is positive, hence **acceleration *a* is positive**. The speed *u* is positive in this interval due to obvious reasons.

In interval 2, the slope of velocity-time graph is negative, hence **acceleration *a* is negative**. The speed *u* is positive in this interval due to obvious reasons.

In interval 3, the velocity-time graph is parallel to time axis, therefore **acceleration a is zero** in this interval but v **is positive** due to obvious reasons.

At points A, B, C and D, the velocity-time graph is parallel to time axis. Therefore, acceleration a **is zero at all the four points**.

27. Figure shows x-t plot of one-dimensional motion of a particle. Is it correct to say from the graph that the particle moves in a straight line for $t < 0$ and on a parabolic path for $t > 0$?

If not, suggest a suitable physical context for this graph. **[NCERT]**

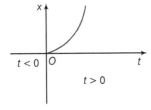

Sol. No, because the x-t graph does not represent the trajectory of the path followed by a particle. From the graph, it is noted that at $t = 0$, $x = 0$.

Context The above graph can represent the motion of a body falling freely from a tower under gravity.

28. Two trains A and B of length 400 m each are moving on two parallel tracks with a uniform speed of 72 km h^{-1} in the same direction with A ahead of B. The driver of B decides to overtake A and accelerates by 1 ms^{-2}. If after 50 s, the guard of B just brushes past the driver of A, what was the original distance between them? **[NCERT]**

Sol. For a train A, $u = 72$ kmh^{-1}

$$= \frac{72 \times 1000}{60 \times 60} = 20 \text{ ms}^{-1}$$

$$t = 50 \text{ s}, a = 0, x = x_A$$

As, $x = ut + \dfrac{1}{2} at^2$

$$\therefore \ x_A = 20 \times 50 + \frac{1}{2} \times 0 \times 50^2 = 1000 \text{ m}$$

For train B, $u = 72$ km$/$h $= 20$ ms^{-1},

$$a = 1 \text{ m/s}^2, t = 50 \text{s}, x = x_B$$

As, $x = ut + \dfrac{1}{2} at^2$

$$\therefore \qquad x_B = 20 \times 50 + \frac{1}{2} \times 1 \times 50^2 = 2250 \text{m}$$

Taking the guard of the train B in the last compartment of the train B, it follows that original distance between the two trains = length of train A + length of train B.

$= 800$

or original distance between the two trains is given by

$$= x_B - x_A = 2250 - 1000 = 1250$$

or original distance between the two trains

$$= 1250 - 800 = 450 \text{ m}$$

29. A jet plane beginning its take off moves down the runway at a constant acceleration of 4.00 m/s^2.

   (i) Find the position and velocity of the plane 5.00 s after it begins to move.

   (ii) If a speed of 70.0 m/s is required for the plane to leave the ground, how long a runway is required?

Sol. Because the acceleration is constant, we can apply the equations of motion derived above.

   (i) We take the origin of the x-axis to be the initial position of the plane, so that $x_0 = 0$.

   It is useful to begin by listing all the data given in the problem.

$$a = 4.00 \text{ m} / \text{s}^2$$

$$v = 0, x = 0$$

   The problem may be stated in terms of the symbols as follows

   Find x and v at $t = 5.00$ s

   When x and u are zero, these two equations reduce

   to $\qquad v = at \quad$ and $\quad x = \dfrac{1}{2} at^2$

   At $\ t = 5.00$ s

$$v = (4.00 \text{ m/s}^2)(5.00\text{s}) = 20.0 \text{ m/s}$$

$$x = \frac{1}{2}(4.00 \text{ m/s}^2)(5.00\text{s})^2$$

$$x = 50.0 \text{ m}$$

   (ii) The problem here may be stated as

   Find x when $v = 70.0$ m/s

   It contains the single unknown x, as well as a and v, which are known with $u = 0$, $v_x^2 = 2a_x x$

   Solving for x, we obtain

$$x = \frac{v^2}{2a} = \frac{(70.00 \text{ m/s})^2}{2(4.00 \text{ m/s}^2)} = 613 \text{ m}$$

30. A car starting from rest, accelerates at the rate f through a distance s, then continues at constant speed for sometime t and then decelerate at the rate $f/2$ to come to rest. If the total distance is $5s$, then prove that $s = \dfrac{1}{2} ft^2$.

Sol. **For accelerated motion,**

$$u = 0, a = f, s = s$$

As $\qquad v^2 - u^2 = 2as,$

$\therefore \qquad v_1^2 - 0^2 = 2fs \Rightarrow v_1 = \sqrt{2fs},$

Distance travelled, $s_2 = v_1 t = t\sqrt{2fs}$

For decelerated motion,

$$u = \sqrt{2fs}, \; a = -f/2, \; v = 0$$

As $\quad v^2 - u^2 = 2as,$

$\therefore \quad 0^2 - (\sqrt{2fs})^2 = 2 \times (-f/2) s_3$

Distance travelled, $s_3 = 2s$

Given, $\quad s + s_2 + s_3 = 5s$

$\Rightarrow \quad s + t\sqrt{2fs} + 2s = 5s \Rightarrow t\sqrt{2fs} = 2s$

$\Rightarrow \qquad\qquad s = \dfrac{1}{2} ft^2$

31. A player throws a ball upwards with an initial speed of 29.4 ms^{-1}.
    (i) What is the direction of acceleration during the upward motion of the ball?
    (ii) What are the velocity and acceleration of the ball at the highest point of its motion?
    (iii) Choose $x = 0$ and $t = 0$ be the location and time at its highest point, vertically downward direction to be the positive direction of x-axis and give the signs of position, velocity and acceleration of the ball during its upward and downward motion.
    (iv) To what height does the ball rise and after how long does the ball return to the player's hands? (Take $g = 9.8$ ms^{-2} and neglect air resistance) **[NCERT]**

Sol. (i) Since, the ball is moving under the effect of gravity, the direction of acceleration due to gravity is always vertically downwards.
    (ii) At the highest point, the velocity of the ball becomes zero and acceleration is equal to the acceleration due to gravity $= 9.8$ ms^{-2} in vertically downward direction.
    (iii) When the highest point is chosen as the location for $x = 0$ and $t = 0$ and vertically downward direction to be the positive direction of x-axis and upward direction as negative direction of x-axis.
    During upward motion, sign of position is negative, sign of velocity is negative and sign of acceleration is positive. During downward motion, sign of position is positive, sign of velocity is positive and sign of acceleration is also positive.
    (iv) Let t be the time taken by the ball to reach the highest point where height from ground be s.
    Taking vertical upward motion of the ball, we have $u = -29.4$ ms^{-1}, $a = 9.8$ ms^{-2}, $v = 0$, $s = S$, $t = ?$
    As, $\quad v^2 - u^2 = 2as$
    $\therefore \quad 0 - (-29.4)^2 = 2 \times 9.8 \times S$
    or $\qquad S = \dfrac{-(29.4)^2}{2 \times 9.8} = -44.1$ m

Here, negative sign shows that the distance is covered in upward direction.

As, $\qquad v = u + at$

$\therefore \qquad 0 = -29.4 + 9.8 \times t$

or $\qquad t = \dfrac{29.4}{9.8} = 3$s

It means time of ascent $= 3$ s

When an object moves under the effect of gravity alone, the time of ascent is always equal to the time of descent.

Therefore, total time after which the ball returns to the player's hand $= 3 + 3 = 6$ s.

32. Read each statement below carefully and state with reasons and examples if it is true or false.

    A particle in 1-D motion
    (i) with zero speed at an instant may have non-zero acceleration at that instant.
    (ii) with zero speed may have non-zero velocity.
    (iii) with constant speed must have zero acceleration.
    (iv) with positive value of acceleration must be speeding up. **[NCERT]**

Sol. (i) True, when a body is thrown vertically upwards in the space, then at the highest point, the body has zero speed but has downward acceleration equal to the acceleration due to gravity.
    (ii) False, because velocity is the speed of body in a given direction. When speed is zero, the magnitude of velocity of body is zero, hence velocity is zero.
    (iii) True, when a particle is moving along a straight line with a constant speed, its velocity remains constant with time. Therefore, acceleration (i.e. change in velocity/time) is zero.
    (iv) False, if the initial velocity of a body is negative, then even in the case of positive acceleration, the body speeds down. A body speeds up when the acceleration acts in the direction of motion.

33. A ball is dropped from a height of 90 m on a floor. At each collision with the floor, the ball loses one tenth of its speed. Plot the speed-time graph of its motion between $t = 0$ to 12 s. (Take, $g = 10$ ms^{-2}) **[NCERT]**

Sol. Taking vertical downward motion of ball from a height 90 m, we have $u = 0$, $a = 10$ m/s^2, $s = 90$ m, $t = ?$; $u = ?$

$$t = \sqrt{\dfrac{2s}{a}} = \sqrt{\dfrac{2 \times 90}{10}} = 3\sqrt{2} \; s = 4.24 \text{ s}$$

$$u = \sqrt{2as} = \sqrt{2 \times 10 \times 90} = 30\sqrt{2} \text{ m/s}$$

Rebound velocity of ball,

$$u' = \dfrac{9}{10} u = \dfrac{9}{10} \times 30\sqrt{2} = 27\sqrt{2} \text{ m/s}$$

Time to reach the highest point is

$$t' = \frac{u'}{a} = \frac{27\sqrt{2}}{10} = 2.7\sqrt{2} = 2.7\sqrt{2} = 3.81 \text{ s}$$

Total time $= t + t' = 4.24 + 3.81 = 8.05\text{s}$

The ball will take further 3.81 s to fall back to floor, where its velocity before striking the floor $= 27\sqrt{2}$ m/s

Velocity of ball after striking the floor

$$= \frac{9}{10} \times 27\sqrt{2} = 24.3\sqrt{2} \text{ m/s}$$

Total time elapsed before upward motion of ball

$$= 8.05 + 3.81 = 11.86\text{s}$$

Thus, the speed-time graph of this motion is shown in the figure.

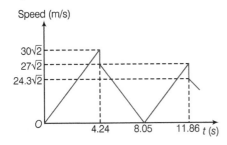

34. State which of the following situations are possible and give an example for each of these?

(i) An object with a constant acceleration but with zero velocity.

(ii) An object moving in a certain direction with acceleration in the perpendicular direction.

Sol. Both the situations are possible

(i) When an object is projected upwards, its velocity at the top-most point is zero even though the acceleration on it is 9.8 m /s ^{2}(g).

(ii) When a stone tied to a string is whirled in a circular path, the acceleration acting on it is always at right angles i.e. perpendicular to the direction of motion of stone (we will study about it in chapter 'motion in a plane').

35. A body is projected vertically upwards from A, the top of a tower it reaches the ground in it t_1 second. If it is projected vertically downwards from A with the same velocity it reaches the ground in t_2 second. If it falls freely, from A, prove that it would reach the ground in $\sqrt{t_1 t_2}$ second.

Sol. Using relations

Consider upwards as negative and downwards as positive.

$$h = -u t_1 + \frac{1}{2} g t_1^2 \qquad \text{...(i)}$$

and

$$h = u t_2 + \frac{1}{2} g t_2^2 \qquad \text{...(ii)}$$

On subtracting Eqs. (i) from (ii), we get

or $\qquad 0 = u(t_2 + t_1) + \frac{1}{2} g t_2^2 - \frac{1}{2} g t_1^2$

or $u(t_2 + t_1) + \frac{1}{2} g (t_2 + t_1)(t_2 - t_1) = 0$

or $\qquad u + \frac{1}{2} g (t_2 + t_1) = 0$

or $\qquad u = -\frac{g}{2}(t_2 - t_1) \qquad \text{...(iii)}$

From Eqs. (i) and (iii), we get

Now, $\quad h = \frac{g t_1}{2}(t_2 - t_1) + \frac{1}{2} g t_1^2 = \frac{1}{2} g t_1 t_2 \qquad \text{...(iv)}$

Again, when the body falls freely.

$$h = \frac{1}{2} g t^2; \quad \frac{1}{2} g t_1 t_2 = \frac{1}{2} g t^2 \qquad \text{[from Eq. (iv)]}$$

or $\qquad t = \sqrt{t_1 t_2} \qquad$ **Hence proved**

LONG ANSWER Type II Questions

36. A train takes 4 min to go between stations 2.25 km apart starting and finishing at rest. The acceleration is uniform for the first 40 s and the deceleration is uniform for the last 20 s.

Assuming the velocity to be constant for the remaining time, calculate the maximum speed, acceleration and retardation, use only the graphical method.

Sol. The velocity-time graph of the train's motion is shown in the following figure

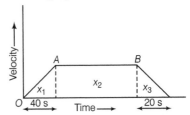

Let v represents the maximum speed of the train if x_1 be the distance covered during the first 40 s, then

$$\frac{v}{2} \times 40 = x_1 \text{ or } x_1 = 20 v$$

Since total time is 4 min, i.e. 240 s therefore, the time corresponding to velocity-time graph AB is $(240 - 40 - 20)$ s i.e. 180 s. If x_2 be the distance covered during this time, then $x_2 = 180 v$.]

If x_3 be the distance covered during the last 20 s, then

$$x_3 = \frac{v}{2} \times 20 = 10 v$$

Now, $\quad x_1 + x_2 + x_3 = 20 v + 180 v + 10 v$

or $\qquad 2250 = 210 v$

or $\qquad v = \frac{225}{21} \text{ ms}^{-1} = 10.7 \text{ ms}^{-1}$

$$\text{Acceleration} = \frac{v}{40} = \frac{10.7}{40} \text{ ms}^{-2} = 0.2675 \text{ ms}^{-2}$$

$$\text{Retardation} = \frac{v}{20} = \frac{10.7}{20} \text{ m s}^{-2} = 0.535 \text{ ms}^{-2}$$

37. A train passes a station A at 40 kmh^{-1} and maintains its speed for 7 km and is then uniformly retarded, stopping at B which is 8.5 km from A. A second train starts from A at the instant the first train passes and being accelerated some part of the journey and uniformly retarded for the rest, stops at B at the same times as the first train. Calculate the maximum speed of the second train, use only the graphical method.

Sol. Area $AEFG = AE \times AG \Rightarrow 7 = 40 \times AG$

or
$$AG = \frac{7}{40} \text{ h}$$

Area FGB gives the distance covered under retardation, it is $(8.5 - 7)$ km $= 1.5$ km

$$\text{Area of } \Delta FGB = \frac{1}{2} GB \times FG \Rightarrow GB = \frac{2 \times 1.5}{40} \text{ h} = \frac{3}{40} \text{ h}$$

$$\text{Total time} = \left(\frac{7}{40} + \frac{3}{40}\right) \text{h} = \frac{1}{4} \text{ h}$$

$$\text{Area of } \Delta ACB = \frac{1}{2} AB \times CD$$

$$8.5 = \frac{1}{2} \times \frac{1}{4} \times v$$

$$v = 8.5 \times 8 \text{ kmh}^{-1} = 68 \text{ kmh}^{-1}$$

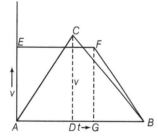

38. A three wheeler starts from rest, accelerates uniformly with 1 ms^{-2} on a straight road for 10 s, and then moves with uniform velocity. Plot a graph between the distance covered by the vehicle during the nth second $(n = 1, 2, 3, ...)$ versus n. What do you expect the plot to be during accelerated motion a straight line or a parabola? **[NCERT]**

Sol. Here, $u = 0$, $a = 1 \text{ ms}^{-2}$

Distance covered in nth second is

$$D_n = u + \frac{a}{2}(2n - 1)$$

$$D_n = 0 + \frac{1}{2}(2n - 1) = 0.5(2n - 1) \qquad ...(i)$$

Putting $n = 1, 2, 3, ...$, we can find the value of D_n. The various values of n and corresponding values of D_n are shown below

n	1	2	3	4	5	6	7	8	9	10
D_n	0.5	1.5	2.5	3.5	4.5	5.5	6.5	7.5	8.5	9.5

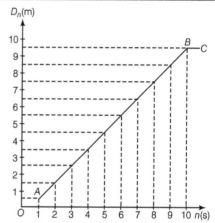

On plotting a graph between D_n and n, we get a straight line AB as shown in figure. From Eq. (i), $D_n \propto n$ so the graph is a straight line. After 10 s, the graph is a straight line BC parallel to time axis.

39. Two stones are thrown up simultaneously from the edge of a cliff 200 m high with initial speeds of 15 ms^{-1} and 30 ms^{-1}. Verify that the graph shown in figure, correctly represents the time variation of the relative position of the second stone with respect to the first.

Neglect the air resistance and assume that the stones do not rebound after hitting the ground. Take, $g = 10$ ms^{-2}. Give the equations for the linear and curved part of the plot. **[NCERT]**

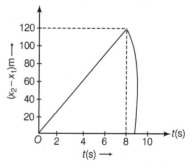

Sol. Taking vertical upward motion of the first stone for time t, we have

$$x_0 = 200 \text{ m}, \, u = 15 \text{ m/s},$$
$$a = -10 \text{ m} / \text{s}^2, \, t = t, \, x = x_1$$

As, $\quad x = x_0 + ut + \dfrac{1}{2} at^2$

$\therefore \quad x_1 = 200 + 15 t + \dfrac{1}{2}(-10) t^2$

or $\quad x_1 = 200 + 15 t - 5 t^2 \qquad$ ...(i)

Taking vertical upward motion of the second stone for time t, we have

$$x_0 = 200 \text{ m}, u = 30 \text{ ms}^{-1},$$
$$a = -10 \text{ ms}^{-2}, t = t, x = x_2$$

Then, $\quad x_2 = 200 + 30 t - \dfrac{1}{2} \times 10 t^2$

$$= 200 + 30 t - 5 t^2 \qquad \text{...(ii)}$$

When the first stone hits the ground, $x_1 = 0$, from Eq (i).

So, $\qquad t^2 - 3t - 40 = 0$

or $\qquad (t - 8)(t + 5) = 0$

$\therefore$ Either $t = 8$ s or -5 s

Since, $t = 0$ corresponds to the instant, when the stone was projected. Hence, negative time has no meaning in this case. So, $t = 8$ s.

When the second stone hits the ground, $x_2 = 0$, from Eq (ii).

So, $0 = 200 + 30 t - 5 t^2$ or $t^2 - 6 t - 40 = 0$

or $\qquad (t - 10)(t + 4) = 0$

Therefore, either $t = 10$ s, or $t = -4$ s

Since, $t = -4$ s is meaningless, so $t = 10$ s.

Relative position of second stone w.r.t. first is

$$= x_2 - x_1 = 15 t \qquad \text{...(iii)}$$

Since, $(x_2 - x_1)$ and t are linearly related, therefore, the graph is a straight line till $t = 8$ s.

For maximum separation, $t = 8$ s, so maximum separation $= 15 \times 8 = 120$ m

After 8 s only, second stone would be in motion for 2 s, so the graph is in accordance with the quadratic equation, $x_2 = 200 + 30 t - 5 t^2$ for the interval of time 8 s to 10 s.

40. The speed-time graph of a particle moving along a fixed direction is shown below in figure. Obtain the distance travelled by the particle between (i) $t = 0$ s to 10 s (ii) $t = 2$ s to 6 s. What is the average speed of the particle over the intervals in (i) and (ii)? **[NCERT]**

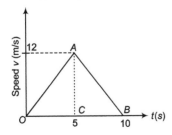

Sol. (i) Distance travelled by the particle between time interval $t = 0$ s to $t = 10$ s

$= $ Area of triangle OAB

$= \dfrac{1}{2} \times$ Base $\times$ Height $= \dfrac{1}{2} \times OB \times AC$

$= \dfrac{1}{2} \times 10 \times 12 = 60$ m

Average speed of the particle for this time interval

$= \dfrac{\text{Total distance travelled}}{\text{Total time taken}}$

$= \dfrac{60}{10} = 6$ m/s

(ii) From the part OA of the given graph (in accelerated motion)

When $t = 0, u = 0, \ t = 5$ s, $v = 12$ m/s

Using equation of motion,

$$v = u + at$$
$$12 = 0 + a \times 5$$

or $\qquad a = \dfrac{12}{5}$ m/s $= 2.4$ m/s^2

Speed of the particle at the end of $t = 2$ s

$$v' = u + at = 0 + 2.4 \times 2 = 4.8 \text{ m/s}$$

Now, distance travelled in accelerated motion from $t = 2$ s to $t = 5$ s i.e. in 3 s, for which initial speed is $u = v' = 4.8$ m/s

Using equation of motion,

$$s_1 = ut + \dfrac{1}{2} at^2$$

$$= 4.8 \times 3 + \dfrac{1}{2} \times 2.4 \times (3)^2 = 14.4 + 10.8$$

$$s_1 = 25.2 \text{ m}$$

From the part AB of the given graph (retarded motion)

Initial speed at $t = 5$ s, $u = 12$ m/s

Time taken, $t = (10 - 5) = 5$ s

Final speed at $t = 10$ s, $v = 0$

Using equation, $v = u + at$

$$0 = 12 + a \times 5$$

or $\qquad a = -\dfrac{12}{5} = -2.4$ m/s^2

Now, distance travelled by the particle in retarded motion from $t = 5$ s to $t = 6$ s i.e. in 1 s,

$$s_2 = ut + \dfrac{1}{2} at^2$$

$$= 12 \times 1 + \dfrac{1}{2}(-2.4) \times 1$$

$$= 12 - 1.2 = 10.8 \text{ m}$$

$\therefore$ Total distance travelled by the particle from $t = 2$ s to $t = 6$ s

$$s = s_1 + s_2$$

$$= 25.2 + 10.8 = 36.0 \text{ m}$$

Average speed of the particle for this time interval

$$= \frac{\text{Total distance travelled}}{\text{Total time taken}}$$

$$= \frac{36}{(6-2)} = \frac{36}{4} = 9 \text{ m/s}$$

41. A motor car moving at a speed of 72 km/h cannot come to a stop is less than 3.0 s while for a truck time interval is 5.0 s. On a highway, the car is behind the truck both moving at 72 km/h. The truck gives a signal that it is going to stop at emergency. At what distance the car should be from the truck so that it does not bumb onto (collide with) the truck? Human response time is 0.5 s. **[NCERT Exemplar]**

Sol. Given, speed of the car as well as truck = 72 km/h

$$= 72 \times \frac{5}{18} \text{ m/s} = 20 \text{ m/s}$$

Retarded motion for truck

$$v = u + a_t\, t$$
$$0 = 20 + a_t \times 5$$
or
$$a_t = -4 \text{ m/s}^2$$

Retarded motion for the car

$$v = u + a_c\, t$$
$$0 = 20 + a_c \times 3$$
or
$$a_c = -\frac{20}{3} \text{ m/s}^2$$

Let car be at a distance x from truck, when truck gives the signal and t be the time taken to cover this distance.

As human response time is 0.5 s, therefore time of retarded motion of car is $(t - 0.5)$ s.

Velocity of car after time t,

$$v_c = u - at = 20 - \left(\frac{20}{3}\right)(t - 0.5)$$

Velocity of truck after time t,

$$v_t = 20 - 4t$$

To avoid the car bumb onto the truck, $v_c = v_t$

$$20 - \frac{20}{3}(t - 0.5) = 20 - 4t$$

or
$$4t = \frac{20}{3}(t - 0.5)$$

or
$$t = \frac{5}{3}(t - 0.5)$$

or
$$3t = 5t - 2.5$$

or
$$t = \frac{2.5}{2} = \frac{5}{4} \text{ s}$$

Distance travelled by the truck in time t,

$$s_t = u_t\, t + \frac{1}{2} a_t\, t^2$$

$$= 20 \times \frac{5}{4} + \frac{1}{2} \times (-4) \times \left(\frac{5}{4}\right)^2$$

$$s_t = 25 - 3.125 = 21.875 \text{ m}$$

Distance travelled by the car in time t

= Distance travelled by the car in 0.5 s (without retardation) + Distance travelled by car in $(t - 0.5)$ s (with retardation)

$$s_c = (20 \times 0.5) + 20\left(\frac{5}{4} - 0.5\right) - \frac{1}{2}\left(\frac{20}{3}\right)\left(\frac{5}{4} - 0.5\right)^2$$

$$= 23.125 \text{ m}$$

$$\therefore \quad s_c - s_t = 23.125 - 21.875$$

$$= 1.250 \text{ m}$$

Therefore, to avoid the bumb onto the truck, the car must maintain a distance from the truck more than 1.250 m.

42. A ball is thrown upward with an initial velocity of 100 m/s. After how much time will it return? Draw velocity-time graph for the ball and find from the graph.
  (i) Maximum height attained by ball and
  (ii) Height of the ball after 15 s. Take, $g = 10 \text{ ms}^{-2}$

Sol. Here, $u = 100 \text{ ms}^{-1}$, $g = -10 \text{ ms}^{-1}$

At highest point, $v = 0$

As $v = u + gt \Rightarrow 0 = 100 - 10 \times t$

$\therefore$ Time taken to reach highest point

$$t = \frac{100}{10} = 10 \text{ s}$$

The ball will return to the ground at $t = 20$ s.

Velocities of the ball at different instants of time will be as follows.

At $t = 0$, $v = 100 - 10 \times 0 = 100 \text{ ms}^{-1}$

At $t = 5$ s, $v = 100 - 10 \times 5 = 50 \text{ ms}^{-1}$

At $t = 10$ s, $v = 100 - 10 \times 10 = 0$

At $t = 15$ s, $v = 100 - 10 \times 15 = -50 \text{ ms}^{-1}$

At $t = 20$ s, $v = 100 - 10 \times 20 = -100 \text{ ms}^{-1}$

The velocity time-graph will be as shown in figure.

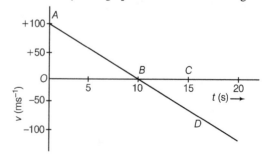

(i) Maximum height attained by ball

= Area of $\triangle AOB$

$= \frac{1}{2} \times 10s \times 100\ ms^{-1} = 500\ m$

(ii) Height attained after 15 s

= Area of $\triangle AOB$ + Area of $\triangle BCD$

$= 500 + \frac{1}{2}\ (15 - 10) \times (-50)$

$= 500 - 125 = 375\ m$

ASSESS YOUR TOPICAL UNDERSTANDING

OBJECTIVE Type Questions

1. The slope of the straight line connecting the points corresponding to (v_2, t_2) and (v_1, t_1) on a plot of velocity *versus* time gives
   (a) average velocity   (b) average acceleration
   (c) instantaneous velocity (d) None of these

2. The kinematic equations of rectilinear motion for constant acceleration for a general situation, where the position coordinate at $t = 0$ is non-zero, say x_0 is
   (a) $v = v_0 + at$
   (b) $x = x_0 + v_0 t + \frac{1}{2} at^2$
   (c) $v^2 = v_0^2 + 2a(x - x_0)$
   (d) All of the above

3. A car is moving with a velocity of $30\ ms^{-1}$. On applying the brakes, the velocity decreases to $15\ ms^{-1}$ in 2 s. The acceleration of the car is
   (a) $+7.5\ ms^{-2}$
   (b) $-7.7\ ms^{-2}$
   (c) $-7.5\ ms^{-2}$
   (d) $+15\ ms^{-2}$

4. An object starts from rest and moves with uniform acceleration a. The final velocity of the particle in terms of the distance x covered by it is given as
   (a) $\sqrt{2ax}$ (b) $2ax$ (c) $\sqrt{\frac{ax}{2}}$ (d) $\sqrt{ax}$

Answer

1. (b) | 2. (d) | 3. (c) | 4. (a)

VERY SHORT ANSWER Type Questions

5. Can a body have zero velocity and finite acceleration?

6. Is it possible for a body to be accelerated without speeding up or slowing down? If it is so, give example.

7. Plot a graph of velocity-time, for the condition if an object is moving with increasing acceleration and having zero initial velocity.

SHORT ANSWER Type Questions

8. A particle in one dimensional motion with positive value of acceleration must be speeding up. Is it true? Explain.

9. The acceleration-time graph for a body is shown in the adjoining. Plot the corresponding velocity-time graph.

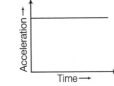

10. Establish a kinematic equation $s = ut + \frac{1}{2} at^2$ from velocity-time graph for a uniformly accelerated motion.

LONG ANSWER Type I Questions

11. State which of the following situations are possible and give an example for each of these?
    (i) An object with a constant acceleration but with zero velocity.
    (ii) An object moving in a certain direction with an acceleration in the perpendicular direction.

12. A passenger is standing d metres away from a bus. The bus begins to move with constant acceleration (a). To catch the bus, the passenger runs at a constant speed (v) towards the bus. What must be the minimum speed of the passenger so that he may catch the bus?
    [Ans. $\sqrt{2ad}$]

13. A particle starts moving from position of rest under a constant acceleration. If it travels a distance x in t second, what distance will it travel in next t second?
    [Ans. $3x$]

LONG ANSWER Type II Questions

14. The two ends of a moving train with a constant acceleration passes a certain point with velocities u and v. Show that the velocity with which the middle point of the train passes the same point is $\sqrt{\dfrac{u^2 + v^2}{2}}$.

15. A car starts from rest and accelerates uniformly for 10 s to a velocity of 8 m/s, then it runs at a constant velocity and is finally brought to rest in 64 m with a constant retardation. The total distance covered by the car is 584 m. Find the values of acceleration, retardation and total time taken.

   [**Ans.** $0.8 \text{ m}/\text{s}^2$, 0.5 m/s^2, 86 s]

16. (i) Draw position-time graphs for
    (a) Accelerated motion (b) Retarded motion
    (ii) A juggler throws balls into air. He throws one whenever the previous one is at its highest point. How high do the balls rise if he throws n balls in each second? Take acceleration due to gravity as g.

   [**Ans.** $\dfrac{g}{2n^2}$]

SUMMARY

- **Motion** is the change in position of an object with time.

- If the object size is much smaller than the distance it moves in a reasonable time, then it is called **point object**.

- **Displacement** is the measure of change in position of an object with time in a particular direction $\Delta x = x_2 - x_1$

- **Velocity** is the rate of change in position or displacement of an object with time. Its SI unit is m/s.

- **Speed** is the ratio of the path length or the distance covered by an object to the time taken.

- **Acceleration** is the rate of change of velocity with time.

- **Kinematics equations for uniformly accelerated motion** (Symbols have their usual meaning)

  1. $v = u + at$ 2. $x = x_0 + ut + \dfrac{1}{2}at^2$ 3. $v^2 = u^2 + 2ax$

- Displacement of a particle in the nth second is given by $S_n = u + \dfrac{a}{2}(2n - 1)$

- Equation of motion under gravity is given by (Symbols have their usual meaning)

  1. $v = u + (\pm g)t$ 2. $h = ut + \dfrac{1}{2}(\pm g)t^2$ 3. $v^2 = u^2 + 2(\pm g)h$

- **Stopping distance** for a vehicle is given as $d_s = \dfrac{-u}{2a}$

- If a body travels equal distance in equal interval of time along a straight line, then the body is said to be in uniform motion in a straight line.

- If a body travels equal distance in unequal intervals of time then it is said to be in non-uniform motion.

- For a non-uniformly accelerated motion, $v = \dfrac{ds}{dt}$, $a = \dfrac{dv}{dt}$

- Average velocity is given by, $v_{av} = \dfrac{\Delta x}{\Delta t} = \dfrac{x_2 - x_1}{t_2 - t_1}$

- **Average speed** is the total distance travelled divided by the total time taken.

- **Instantaneous speed** is the limit of the average speed as the time interval becomes infinitesimally small or approaches to zero. It is given by
  $s_{in} = \lim\limits_{Tt \to 0} \dfrac{\Delta s}{\Delta t} = \dfrac{ds}{dt}$

- **Average acceleration** is the ratio of change in velocity of the object to the time interval. It is given by, $a_{av} = \dfrac{\Delta v}{\Delta t} = \dfrac{v_2 - v_1}{t_2 - t_1}$

- **Instantanous acceleration** is the acceleration of a body at a certain instant or the limiting value of average acceleration when time interval tends to zero. It is given by, $a_{in} = \lim\limits_{\Delta t \to 0} \dfrac{\Delta v}{\Delta t} = \dfrac{dv}{dt}$

CHAPTER PRACTICE

OBJECTIVE Type Questions

1. If the velocity of a particle is $v = At + Bt^2$, where A and B are constants, then the distance travelled by it in 1s is

   (a) $3A + 7B$
   (b) $\dfrac{3}{2}A + \dfrac{7}{3}B$
   (c) $\dfrac{A}{2} + \dfrac{B}{3}$
   (d) $\dfrac{3}{2}A + 4B$

2. At a metro station, a girl walks up a stationary escalator in time t_1. If she remains stationary on the escalator, then the escalator take her up in time t_2. The time taken by her to walk up on the moving escalator will be [NCERT Exemplar]

   (a) $(t_1 + t_2)/2$
   (b) $t_1 t_2 /(t_2 - t_1)$
   (c) $t_1 t_2 /(t_2 + t_1)$
   (d) $t_1 - t_2$

3. In one dimensional motion, instantaneous speed v satisfies $0 \le v < v_0$. [NCERT Exemplar]

   (a) The displacement in time T must always take non-negative values
   (b) The displacement x in time T satisfies $-v_0 T < x < v_0 T$
   (c) The acceleration is always a non-negative number
   (d) The motion has no turning points

4. An object is moving with an initial velocity of 30 ms^{-1} with uniform acceleration. The velocity of object increases to 40 ms^{-1} in next 5 s. The v-t graph which least represents this situation is

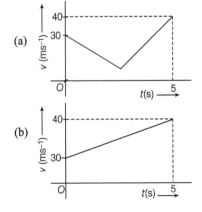

   (a)

   (b)

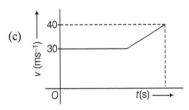

   (c)

   (d) None of the above

ASSERTION AND REASON

Direction (Q. Nos 5-9) *In the following questions, two statements are given- one labelled Assertion (A) and the other labelled Reason (R). Select the correct answer to these questions from the codes (a), (b), (c) and (d) as given below*

   (a) Both Assertion and Reason are true and Reason is the correct explanation of Assertion.
   (b) Both Assertion and Reason are true but Reason is not the correct explanation of Assertion.
   (c) Assertion is true but Reason is false.
   (d) Assertion is false but Reason is true.

5. **Assertion** In real life, in a good number of situations, the object is treated as a point object.
   Reason The object is treated as point object, so far as the size of the object is much smaller than the distance it moves in a reasonable duration of time.

6. **Assertion** For motion along a straight line and in the same direction, the magnitude of average velocity is equal to the average speed.
   Reason For motion along a straight line and in the same direction, the magnitude of displacement is equal to the path length.

7. **Assertion** For uniform motion, velocity is the same as the average velocity at all instants.
   Reason In uniform motion along a straight line, the object covers equal distances in equal intervals of time.

8. **Assertion** In realistic situation, the x-t, v-t and a-t graphs will be smooth. This means physically that acceleration and velocity cannot change values abruptly at an instant.
   Reason Changes are always continuous.

9. **Assertion** A body may be accelerated even when it is moving uniformly.

   Reason When direction of motion of the body is changing, then body may have acceleration.

CASE BASED QUESTIONS

Direction (Q. Nos. 10) *This question is case study based question. Attempt any 4 sub-parts from given question.*

10. *x-t* **Graph**

The *x-t* graph represents the motion of a car at different time instants. With reference to the below graph, choose the correct for the question given below.

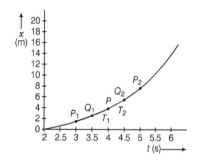

(i) The slope of the line $P_1 P_2$ for the interval $t = 3$ s to $t = 5$ s gives

(a) average velocity
(b) instantaneous velocity
(c) average speed
(d) Either (a) or (c)

(ii) The slope of the line $P_1 P_2$ for the int

I. For the time interval $t = 3.5$ s to $t = 4.5$ s, the value of average velocity is given by the slope of the line $Q_1 Q_2$.

II. The slope of the tangent $(T_1 T_2)$ at point P gives the velocity of the car at time instant $t = 4$ s.

III. The slope of the tangent at point P gives the instantaneous velocity of the car.

(a) Both I and II   (b) Only I
(c) Only III   (d) I, II and III

(iii) Which of the following statements is correct with reference to the above graph as the time interval Δt approaches zero, *i.e.*, $\Delta t \to 0$?

I. The line $P_1 P_2$ becomes tangent to the position-time curve at the point P.

II. The slope of the tangent $(T_1 T_2)$ at point P gives the velocity of the car at time instant $t = 4$ s.

III. The slope of the tangent at point P gives the instantaneous velocity of the car.

(a) Both I and II
(b) Only I
(c) Only III
(d) I, II and III

(iv) Figure shows the $(x-t)$ plot of a particle in one-dimensional motion. Two different equal intervals of time are speed in time intervals 1 and 2 respectively. Then,

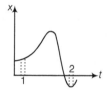

(a) $v_1 > v_2$
(b) $v_2 > v_1$
(c) $v_1 = v_2$
(d) Data insufficient

(v) Among the four graphs shown in the figure, there is only one graph for which average velocity over the time interval $(0, T)$ can vanish for a suitably chosen T. Which one is it?

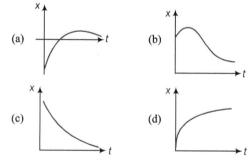

Answer

1. (c)	2. (c)	3. (b)	4. (b)	5. (a)
6. (a)	7. (b)	8. (a)	9. (d)	

10. (i) (a)   (ii) (d)   (iii) (d)   (iv) (b)   (v) (b)

VERY SHORT ANSWER Type Questions

11. Can earth be regarded as a point object when it describes its yearly journey around the sun?

12. Write the expression for distance covered in nth second by a uniformly accelerated body.

13. Why does a parachute descend slowly?

14. What does speedometer record: the average speed or the instantaneous speed?

15. Draw displacement-time graph for a uniformly accelerated motion. What is its shape?

SHORT ANSWER Type Questions

16. Two bodies of different masses m_1 and m_2 are dropped from two different heights a and b. What is the ratio of time taken by the two bodies to drop through these distances?
    [**Ans.** $\sqrt{a} : \sqrt{b}$]

17. If the velocity of a particle is given by $v = \sqrt{180 - 16x}$ m/s, what will be its acceleration?
    [**Ans.** $-8 \, \text{m/s}^2$]

18. The speed-time graph for a car is shown in figure below

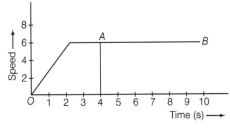

(i) Find how far does the car travel in the first 4s. Shade the area on the graph that represents the distance travelled by the car during the period. [**Ans.** 18 m]

(ii) Which part of the graph represents uniform motion of the car?

19. A body moving with a uniform acceleration describes 12 m in 3rd s of its motion and 20 m in the 5ths. Find the velocity after 10 s.
    [**Ans.** $v = 42$ m/s]

20. A car accelerates from rest at a constant rate α for some time, after which it decelerates at a constant rate β to come to rest. If t is total time elapsed, then calculate

(i) the maximum velocity attained by the car

(ii) the total distance travelled by the car

[**Ans.** (a) $\dfrac{\alpha\beta t}{\alpha + \beta}$, (b) $\dfrac{1}{2}\dfrac{\alpha\beta t^2}{(\alpha + \beta)}$]

LONG ANSWER Type I Questions

21. Discuss the motion of an object under free fall and draw (i) acceleration-time (ii) velocity-time and (iii) position-time graph for this motion.

22. A car moving with a speed of 50 km/h can be stopped by brakes after at least 6 m. What will be the minimum stopping distance, if the same car is moving at a speed of 100km/h? [**Ans.** 24 m]

23. Derive an expression for stopping distance of a vehicle in terms of initial velocity v_0 and deceleration a.

24. A train moves from one station to another in 2 h time. Its speed during the motion is shown in graph. Determine the maximum acceleration during the journey. Also, calculate the distance covered during the time interval from 0.75 h to 1 h.

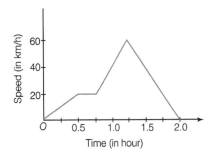

[**Ans.** $a = 160 \ \text{km}/\text{h}^2, s = 10$ km]

25. Establish the relation $x(t) = ut + \dfrac{1}{2}at^2$ by calculus method.

26. The distance covered by an object between timings t_1 and t_2 is given by area under the v-t graph between t_1 and t_2. Prove that the above statement also holds when an object is moving with negative acceleration has velocities positive at time t_1 and negative at t_2.

LONG ANSWER Type II Questions

27. Derive the three equations of motion by calculus method. Express the conditions under which they can be used.

28. A ball is dropped from a height of 100 m on a floor. At each collision with floor, the ball loses one-tenth of its speed. Plot the speed-time graph of its motion between $t = 0$ s and $t = 12$ s.

29. A parachutist bails out from an airplane and after dropping through a distance of 40 m, he opens the parachute and decelerates at 2 m/s². If he reaches the ground with a speed of 2 m/s, how long does he float in the air? At what height did he bail out from the plane?   [**Ans.** 15.86 s, 235m]

30. The velocity-time graph of a particle moving along a straight line as shown in figure by curve *OABCD*. Calculate the distance covered by the particle between (i) $t = 0$ to 18 s (ii) $t = 2$ s to $t = 12$ s and the maximum value of acceleration during this interval.

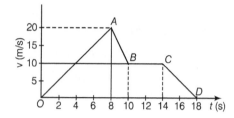

[**Ans.** (i) 170 m, (ii) 125 m, -5 m/s²]

03

Earlier, we have studied the motion of an object along a straight line. In this chapter, we will study the motion of an object in two dimensions (in plane) and in three dimensions (in space). As a simple case of motion in a plane, we shall discuss motion with constant acceleration and treat it in details as projectile and circular motion.

MOTION IN A PLANE

|TOPIC 1|
Scalars and Vectors

A study of motion will involve the introduction of a variety of quantities that are used to describe the physical world. e.g. Distance, speed, displacement, velocity, acceleration, force, mass, momentum, work, power, energy, etc.

In order to describe the motion of an object to be in two-dimensional and in three-dimensional, we need to understand the concept of vectors first.
Many quantities that have both magnitude and direction need a special mathematical language i.e. the language of vectors to describe such quantities. On the basis of magnitude and direction, all the physical quantities are classified into two groups as scalars and vectors.

SCALAR QUANTITIES

These are the physical quantities which have only magnitude but no direction. It is specified completely by a single number, alongwith the proper unit.

e.g. Temperature, mass, length, time, work, etc.

Note

+ The rules for combining scalars follow simple rules of algebra. Scalars can be added, subtracted, multiplied and divided just as the ordinary numbers.
+ The quantities with same units can be *added* or subtracted, but the quantities of different units can be multiplied or divided to make sense in scalars.

VECTOR QUANTITIES

These are the physical quantities which have both magnitudes and directions and obey the triangle/parallelogram laws of addition and subtraction.

It is specified by giving its magnitude by a number and its direction. e.g. Displacement, acceleration, velocity, momentum, force, etc. A vector is represented by a **bold face** type and also by **an arrow** placed over a letter

i.e. $\quad\quad$ **F, a, b** or $\vec{F}, \vec{a}, \vec{b}$

The length of the line gives the magnitude and the arrowhead gives the direction.

Note

The magnitude of a vector is often called its absolute value, indicated by $|\mathbf{v}| = v$.

e.g. Suppose a body has a velocity 40 m/s due East. If 1 cm is chosen to represent a velocity of 10 m/s, a line OP of 4 cm in length and drawn towards East with arrowhead at P will completely represent the velocity of the body.

The point P is called **head** or **terminal point** and point O is called **tail** or **initial point** of the vector **OP**.

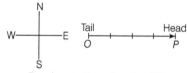

Representation of vector OP

Vectors are classified into two types such as

1. Polar Vectors

Vectors which have a starting point or a point of application are called **polar vectors**. e.g. Force, displacement, etc.

2. Axial Vectors

Vectors which represent the rotational effect and acts along the axis of rotation are called **axial vectors**.

e.g. Angular velocity, angular momentum, torque, etc.

The axial vector will have its direction along its axis of rotation depending on its anti-clockwise or clockwise rotational effect.

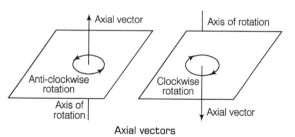

Axial vectors

Note

The physical quantities which have no specified direction and have different values in different directions are called tensors. e.g. Moment of inertia, stress, surface tension, pressure, etc.

Important Definitions Related to Vectors

(i) Modulus of a Vector

The magnitude of a vector is called **modulus** of that vector. For a vector **A**, it is represented by $|\mathbf{A}|$ or A.

(ii) Unit Vector

A vector having magnitude equal to unity but having a specific direction is called a **unit vector**. A unit vector of **A** is written as $\hat{\mathbf{A}}$ and read as A cap. It is expressed as

$$\hat{\mathbf{A}} = \frac{\mathbf{A}}{|\mathbf{A}|} = \frac{\mathbf{A}}{A} = \frac{\text{Vector}}{\text{Magnitude of the vector}}$$

$$\boxed{\mathbf{A} = |\mathbf{A}|\hat{\mathbf{A}}}$$

Hence, any vector can be expressed as the magnitude times the unit vector along its own direction.

In cartesian coordinates, $\hat{\mathbf{i}}, \hat{\mathbf{j}}$ and $\hat{\mathbf{k}}$ are the unit vectors along x-axis, y-axis and z-axis.

The magnitude of a unit vector is unity and has no unit or dimensions.

(iii) Null Vector

A vector with magnitude zero and having an arbitrary direction is called a **null vector.**

This vector is also known as **zero vector** and denoted by 0 (zero). e.g. The velocity vector of a stationary object, the acceleration vector of an object moving with uniform velocity.

(iv) Equal Vectors

Two vectors are said to be equal if they have equal magnitude and same direction.

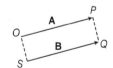

A and **B** are equal vectors

Consider two vectors **A** and **B** which are represented by two equal parallel lines drawn in the same magnitude and direction.

Thus, $\quad\quad$ **OP = SQ** $\quad$ or $\quad$ **A = B**

Vectors do not have fixed locations. When we displace a vector parallel to itself, then the vector does not change, such vectors are known as **free vectors**.

e.g. The velocity vector of a particle moving along a straight line is a free vector.

(v) Negative Vector

Two vectors are said to be the negative of each other if their magnitudes are equal but directions are opposite.

The negative vector of **A** is represented as −**A**.

Negative vector

(vi) Collinear Vectors

The two or more vectors are said to be collinear, when they act along the same lines or parallel lines. e.g. Tug of war.

Collinear vectors

If **A** and **B** are two collinear vectors, then they can be represented along a line in the same direction [Fig. a] or along the parallel lines in same direction [Fig. b] or along parallel lines in opposite direction [Fig. c]. Two collinear vectors having the same directions are called **parallel vectors**. In this case, the angle between those two vectors will be zero. Similarly, the two collinear vectors having the opposite directions are called **anti-parallel vectors**. In this case, the angle between those two vectors will be 180°.

(vii) Coplanar Vectors

The vectors lying in the same plane are called **coplanar vectors**. Three vectors **A**, **B** and **C** are lying in the same plane of paper as shown in figure, hence they are coplanar vectors.

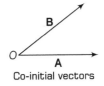

Coplanar vectors

(viii) Co-initial Vectors

The vectors which have the same initial point are called co-initial vectors.

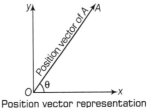

Co-initial vectors

Two vectors **A** and **B** have been drawn from the common initial point O. Therefore, **A** and **B** are called **co-initial vectors**.

(ix) Orthogonal Unit Vectors

If two or three unit vectors are perpendicular to each other, they are known as **orthogonal unit vectors**.

The unit vectors along x-axis, y-axis and z-axis are denoted by $\hat{\mathbf{i}}, \hat{\mathbf{j}}$ and $\hat{\mathbf{k}}$. These are orthogonal unit vectors.

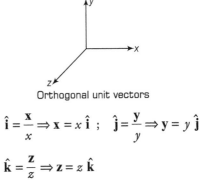

Orthogonal unit vectors

$$\hat{\mathbf{i}} = \frac{\mathbf{x}}{x} \Rightarrow \mathbf{x} = x\,\hat{\mathbf{i}} \;\; ; \;\; \hat{\mathbf{j}} = \frac{\mathbf{y}}{y} \Rightarrow \mathbf{y} = y\,\hat{\mathbf{j}}$$

$$\hat{\mathbf{k}} = \frac{\mathbf{z}}{z} \Rightarrow \mathbf{z} = z\,\hat{\mathbf{k}}$$

(x) Localised Vectors

Those vectors whose initial point is fixed are known as **localised vectors**. e.g. Position vector of a particle (initial point lies at the origin).

(xi) Non-localised Vectors

Those vectors whose initial point is not fixed are known as **non-localised vectors**. e.g. Velocity vector of a particle moving along a straight line.

POSITION AND DISPLACEMENT VECTORS

Position Vector

A vector which gives position of an object with reference to the origin of a coordinate system is called **position vector**. It is represented by a symbol **r**.

Consider the motion of an object in xy-plane with origin at O. Suppose an object is at point A at any instant t.

Then, **OA** is the position vector of the object at point A. i.e. **OA** = **r**

Position vector representation

The position vector provides two informations such as

(i) It tells us about the minimum distance of an object from the origin O.

(ii) It tells us about the direction of the object w.r.t. origin.

Displacement Vector

The vector which tells how much and in which direction an object has changed its position in a given interval of time is called **displacement vector.**

Displacement vector is the straight line joining the initial and final positions and does not depend on the actual path undertaken by the object between the two positions.

Consider an object moving in the xy-plane. Suppose it is at point A at any instant t and at point B at any later instant t'. Then, vector **AB** is the displacement vector of the object in time t to t'.

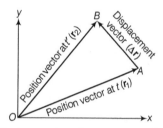

Displacement vector representation

If the coordinates of points A and B are (x_1, y_1) and (x_2, y_2), then the position vector of the object at point A, $\mathbf{r}_1 = x_1\hat{\mathbf{i}} + y_1\hat{\mathbf{j}}$ and the position vector of the object at point B, $\mathbf{r}_2 = x_2\hat{\mathbf{i}} + y_2\hat{\mathbf{j}}$

∴ The displacement vector for AB can be given as

$$\Delta\mathbf{r} = \mathbf{r}_2 - \mathbf{r}_1$$

$$\boxed{\text{Displacement vector, } \Delta\mathbf{r} = (x_2 - x_1)\hat{\mathbf{i}} + (y_2 - y_1)\hat{\mathbf{j}}}$$

(i) Magnitude of the displacement vector is given by

$$|\Delta\mathbf{r}| = \Delta r = \sqrt{(x_2 - x_1)^2 + (y_2 - y_1)^2}$$

The magnitude of displacement is either less or equal to the path length of an object between two points.

(ii) Magnitude of vectors for three-dimensional is given by

$$\Delta r = \sqrt{(x_2 - x_1)^2 + (y_2 - y_1)^2 + (z_2 - z_1)^2}$$

MULTIPLICATION OF A VECTOR BY A REAL NUMBER (OR SCALAR)

When we multiply a vector **A** by a real number λ, then we get a new vector along the direction of vector **A**. Its magnitude becomes λ times the magnitude of the given vector.

Similarly, if we multiply vector **A** with a negative real number $-\lambda$, then we get a vector whose magnitude is λ times the magnitude of vector **A** but direction is opposite to that of vector **A**.

Hence, $\boxed{\lambda(A) = \lambda A}$ and $\boxed{-\lambda(A) = -\lambda A}$

e.g. (i) Consider a vector **A** is multiplied by a real number $\lambda = 3$ or -4, we get 3A or -4 A

A   A

3 A -4 A

Multiplication of a vector by a real number

(ii) If we multiply a constant velocity vector by time, we will get a displacement vector in the direction of velocity vector.

RESULTANT VECTOR

The resultant vector of two or more vectors is defined as the single vector which produces the same effect as two or more vectors (given vectors) combinedly produces.

There are two cases

Case I   **When two vectors are acting in the same direction.**

Consider the vectors **A** and **B** are acting in the same direction as shown below

A

B

Then, the resultant of these two vectors is given by a vector having direction as same as that of **A** or **B** and the magnitude of the resultant vector will be equal to the sum of respective vectors i.e. $(A + B)$.

Thus, $\boxed{\text{Resultant vector, } \mathbf{R} = \mathbf{A} + \mathbf{B}}$

$R = A + B$

Case II **When two vectors are acting in mutually opposite directions.**
Consider the vectors **A** and **B** are acting in mutually opposite direction as shown below.

A →

← B

Then, the resultant of these two vectors is given by a vector having direction same as that of vector with larger magnitude. The magnitude of the resultant vector will be equal to $|A - B|$.

A →
B

Thus, $\boxed{\text{Resultant vector, } \mathbf{R} = \mathbf{A} - \mathbf{B}}$

   (i) If $\mathbf{B} > \mathbf{A}$, then direction of **R** is along **B**.
   (ii) If $\mathbf{A} > \mathbf{B}$, then direction of **R** is along **A**.

Conditions for Zero Resultant Vector

If three vectors acting on a point object at the same time are represented in magnitude and direction by the three sides of a triangle taken in the same order, their resultant is zero. The object is said to be in equilibrium.

Consider the three vectors **A**, **B** and **C** acting on an object at the same time represented by **OP**, **PQ** and **QO**, respectively.

Then, $\dfrac{\mathbf{A}}{\mathbf{OP}} = \dfrac{\mathbf{B}}{\mathbf{PQ}} = \dfrac{\mathbf{C}}{\mathbf{QO}}$

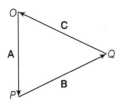

Vectors **A**, **B** and **C** acting along **OP**, **PQ** and **QO** respectively

Similarly, if number of vectors acting on an object at the same time are represented in magnitude and direction by the various sides of a closed polygon taken in the same order, their resultant vector is zero and the object will be in equilibrium.

Vectors represented by a closed polygon

Resultant vector, $\mathbf{R} = \mathbf{OA} + \mathbf{AB} + \mathbf{BC} + \mathbf{CD}$
$+ \mathbf{DE} + \mathbf{EF} + \mathbf{FG} + \mathbf{GO} = 0$

> **Conditions for Equilibrium of an Object**
> - There is no linear motion of the object i.e. the resultant force on the object is zero.
> - There is no rotational motion of the object i.e. the torque due to forces on the object is zero.
> - There is minimum potential energy of the object for stable equilibrium.

ADDITION OF VECTORS
(GRAPHICAL METHOD)

Two vectors can be added if both of them are of same nature e.g. A displacement vector cannot be added to a force but can be added to displacement vector only.

Graphical method of addition of vectors helps us in visualising the vectors and the resultant vectors.

This method contains following laws

1. Triangle Law of Vector Addition

This law states that **if two vectors can be represented both in magnitude and direction by the two sides of a triangle taken in the same order, then their resultant is represented completely, both in magnitude and direction, by the third side of the triangle taken in the opposite order.**

Consider two vectors **A** and **B** that lie in a plane as shown in Fig. (a). Draw a vector **OM** equal and parallel to vector **A** as shown in Fig. (b). From head of **OM**, draw a vector **MN** equal and parallel to vector **B**. Then, the resultant vector is given by **ON** which joins the tail of **A** and head of **B**.

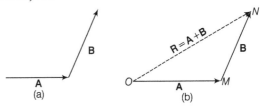

Triangle law of vector addition

The resultant of **A** and **B** is $\mathbf{ON} = \mathbf{OM} + \mathbf{MN}$

or $\boxed{\text{Resultant vector, } \mathbf{R} = \mathbf{A} + \mathbf{B}}$

EXAMPLE |1| Displacement of Vectors
A boy travels 10 m due to North and then 7 m due to East. Find the displacement and direction of the body.

Sol. Let the boy start moving from point O as shown in figure.
where,   **OA** = 10 m, due North
                    AB = 7 m, due East

According to triangle law of vector addition, **OB** is the resultant displacement.

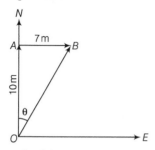

The magnitude of the resultant displacement,

$$|\mathbf{OB}| = OB = \sqrt{(OA)^2 + (AB)^2} = \sqrt{(10)^2 + (7)^2}$$

$$= \sqrt{100 + 49} = 12.21 \text{ m}$$

Since, the resultant displacement makes an angle θ with the North direction. Then,

$$\theta = \tan^{-1}\left(\frac{AB}{OA}\right) = \tan^{-1}\left(\frac{7}{10}\right) = 35°$$

2. Parallelogram Law of Vector Addition

This law states that **if two vectors acting on a particle at the same time are represented in magnitude and direction by two adjacent sides of a parallelogram drawn from a point** their resultant vector is represented in magnitude and direction by the diagonal of the parallelogram drawn from the same point.

Consider two vectors **A** and **B** that lie in a plane as shown in Fig. (a). From a common point O, draw a vector **OP** equal and parallel to **A** and vector **OR** equal and parallel to **B**. Complete the parallelogram **OPQR** as shown in Fig. (b). Then, the resultant vector is given by **OQ**.

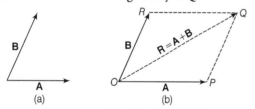

(a)   (b)

Parallelogram law of vector addition

According to parallelogram law of vector addition,

$$\mathbf{OQ} = \mathbf{OP} + \mathbf{OR}$$

or $\boxed{\text{Resultant vector, } \mathbf{R} = \mathbf{A} + \mathbf{B}}$

EXAMPLE |2| Velocities in Different Directions
A body is simultaneously given two velocities of 30 m/s due East and 40 m/s due North, respectively. Find the resultant velocity.

Sol. Let the body be starting from point O as shown.

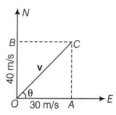

$\mathbf{v}_A = 30 \text{ m/s}$, due East; $\mathbf{v}_B = 40 \text{ m/s}$, due North
According to parallelogram law, **OC** is the resultant velocity. Its magnitude is given by

$$\mathbf{v} = \sqrt{v_A^2 + v_B^2}$$

$$= \sqrt{(30)^2 + (40)^2}$$

$$= \sqrt{900 + 1600}$$

$$= 50 \text{ m/s}$$

Since, the resultant velocity **v** makes an angle θ with the East direction. Then, $\theta = \tan^{-1}\dfrac{CA}{OA}$

$$= \tan^{-1}\left(\frac{40}{30}\right) = 53°8'$$

3. Polygon Law of Vector Addition

This law states that **when the number of vectors are represented in both magnitude and direction by the sides of an open polygon taken in an order**, then their resultant is represented in both magnitude and direction by the closing side of the polygon taken in opposite order.

Consider four vectors **A**, **B**, **C** and **D** be acting in different directions that lie in a plane as shown in Fig. (a). Draw a vector **OP** parallel and equal to vector **A**. Move vectors **B**, **C** and **D** parallel to themselves, so that the tail of **B** touches the head of **A**, the tail of **C** touches the head of **B** and the tail of **D** touches the head of **C** as shown in Fig. (b).

According to the polygon law of vector addition, the closing side OT of the polygon taken in the reverse order represent the resultant **R**.

Thus, $\mathbf{R} = \mathbf{A} + \mathbf{B} + \mathbf{C} + \mathbf{D}$

(a)   (b)

Polygon law of vector addition

Properties of Addition of Vectors

   (i) It follows commutative law, i.e. $A + B = B + A$

  (ii) It follows associative law,
$$(A + B) + C = A + (B + C)$$

  (iii) It obeys distributive law, $\lambda(A + B) = \lambda A + \lambda B$

  (iv) $A + 0 = A$

EXAMPLE |3| Displacement in Different Directions

A particle has a displacement of 12 m towards East and 5 m towards the North and then 6 m vertically upwards. Find the magnitude of the sum of these displacements.

Sol. Suppose initially the particle is at origin O. Then, its displacement vectors are

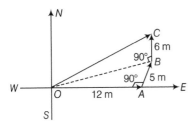

$$OA = 12\,m,\; AB = 5\,m,\; BC = 6\,m$$

According to polygon law of vector addition, **OC** is the resultant displacement.

∴ From $\Delta\, OAB$, have
$$\mathbf{OB} = \sqrt{OA^2 + AB^2} = \sqrt{(12)^2 + (5)^2} = 13\,m$$

Again from $\Delta\, OBC$, we have
$$\mathbf{OC} = \sqrt{OB^2 + BC^2} = \sqrt{(13)^2 + (6)^2} = \sqrt{205} = 14.32\,m$$

SUBTRACTION OF TWO VECTORS (GRAPHICAL METHOD)

If a vector **B** is to be subtracted from vector **A**, then we have to invert the vector **B** and then add it with vector **A** according to laws of addition of two vectors.

Hence, the subtraction of vector **B** from a vector **A** is defined as the addition of vector $(-B)$ (i.e. negative of vector **B**) to vector **A**.

It is expressed as $R = A + (-B) = A - B$

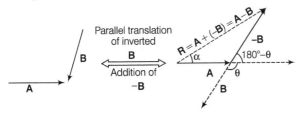

Graphical method of subtraction of two vectors

Properties of Subtraction of Vectors

   (i) Subtraction of vectors does not follow commutative law, i.e. $\qquad A - B \neq B - A$

  (ii) It does not follow associative law, i.e.
$$A - (B - C) \neq (A - B) - C$$

  (iii) It follows distributive law, $\lambda(A - B) = \lambda A - \lambda B$

EXAMPLE |4| Forces Act in Different Directions

Two forces of 5 N towards East and −7 N towards South acts on a particle. Find the resultant force.

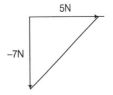

Sol. The two forces be $A = 5\,N$ and $B = -7\,N$

Then, the magnitude of the resultant force is given by
$$F = \sqrt{A^2 + (-B)^2} = \sqrt{5^2 + (-7)^2}$$
$$F = \sqrt{25 + 49} = \sqrt{74} = 8.6\,N$$

RESOLUTION OF VECTORS IN PLANE (IN TWO DIMENSIONS)

The process of splitting a single vector into two or more vectors in different directions which collectively produce the same effect as produced by the single vector alone is known as **resolution of a vector**.

The various vectors into which a single vector is splitted are known as **components of vectors**. Resolution of a vector into two component vectors along the directions of two given vectors is unique.

To understand the resolution of vector in the components vectors, let us discuss the vector as a combination of unit vectors.

Any vector **r** can be expressed as a linear combination of two unit vectors $\hat{i}$ and $\hat{j}$ at right angle i.e. $\mathbf{r} = x\hat{i} + y\hat{j}$

The vectors $x\hat{i}$ and $y\hat{j}$ are called the **perpendicular components** of **r**. The scalars x and y are called components or resolved parts of r in the directions of x-axis and y-axis.

∴

$$\boxed{\text{Resultant vector, } \mathbf{r} = \sqrt{x^2 + y^2}}$$

If θ is the inclination of **r** with x-axis, then

$$\boxed{\text{Angle, } \theta = \tan^{-1}\left(\frac{y}{x}\right)}$$

Resolving a Vector into Two Component Vectors Along Given Directions

Now, draw **OQ** to represent the resultant vector **R** in magnitude and direction. From point O, draw a line **OP** parallel to the vector **A** and from point P, draw a line **PQ** parallel to vector **B**.

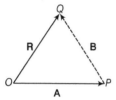

Then, these two lines intersect at point P as shown below.

From triangle law of vector addition, we have

$$\mathbf{OQ} = \mathbf{OP} + \mathbf{PQ}$$

But **OP** and **PQ** are two component vectors of **R** in the direction of **A** and **B** respectively. Let **OP** = λ**A** and **PQ** = μ**B**, where λ and μ are two real numbers. This is also illustrated in the figure as shown below.

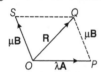

Now, the resultant vector becomes

$$\mathbf{R} = \lambda\mathbf{A} + \mu\mathbf{B}$$

Rectangular Components of a Vector in a Plane

When a vector in a plane is splitted into two component vectors at right angle to each other. Then, the component vectors are called **rectangular components** of that vector. The resultant vector is given by

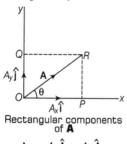

Rectangular components of **A**

$$\mathbf{A} = A_x\hat{\mathbf{i}} + A_y\hat{\mathbf{j}}$$

where, $\boxed{\text{Magnitude of vector, } A = \sqrt{A_x^2 + A_y^2}}$

We can also find the angle (θ) between them.

From

$$\tan\theta = \left(\frac{A_y}{A_x}\right)$$

$$\Rightarrow \boxed{\text{Angle, } \theta = \tan^{-1}\left(\frac{A_y}{A_x}\right)}$$

Where, A_y and A_x are the splitted vectors component of **A** in the direction of $\hat{\mathbf{j}}$ and $\hat{\mathbf{i}}$, respectively.

EXAMPLE |5| Resultant of Two Vectors

The greatest and the least resultant of two forces acting at a point are 29 N and 5 N, respectively. If each force is increased by 3 N. Find the resultant of two new forces acting at right angle to each other.

Sol. Let P and Q be the two forces.

Greatest resultant, $R_1 = P + Q = 29$ N

Least resultant, $R_2 = P - Q = 5$ N

$$P + Q = 29 \qquad \qquad \dots(i)$$
$$P - Q = 5 \qquad \qquad \dots(ii)$$

Solving Eqs. (i) and (ii), we get

$$P = 17 \text{ N}, Q = 12 \text{ N}$$

When each force is increased by 3N, then

$$P' = P + 3 = 17 + 3 = 20 \text{ N}$$
$$\Rightarrow \qquad Q' = 12 + 3 = 15 \text{ N}$$

The resultant of new forces is

$$R' = \sqrt{(20)^2 + (15)^2} = \sqrt{400 + 225} = 25 \text{ N}$$

Let the resultant **R**, makes an angle θ with **A**, then

$$\tan\theta = \frac{15}{20} = 0.75$$

$$\Rightarrow \qquad \theta = \tan^{-1}(0.75) = 36°52'$$

Thus, the resultant of two new forces P' and Q' are 25 N and angle between them is 36°52'.

EXAMPLE |6| Person Walks in Different Directions

A person walks in the following pattern 3.1 km North, then 2.4 km West and finally 5.2 km South.

(i) Sketch the vector diagram that represents this motion.

(ii) How far the person will be from its initial point?

(iii) In what direction would a bird fly in a straight line from the same starting point to the same final point?

💡 Label the displacement vectors **A**, **B** and **C** (and denote the result of their vector sum as **r**) now, choose East as the $\hat{\mathbf{i}}$ direction (+x direction) and North as the $\hat{\mathbf{j}}$ direction (+y direction). All distances are understood to be in kilometres.

The vectors **B** and **C** are taken as negative because according to our assumption, person walks in −x and −y directions.

Sol. (i) The vector diagram representing the motion is shown below.

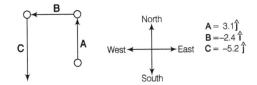

$$\mathbf{A} = 3.1\hat{\mathbf{j}}$$
$$\mathbf{B} = -2.4\,\hat{\mathbf{i}}$$
$$\mathbf{C} = -5.2\,\hat{\mathbf{j}}$$

(ii) The final point is represented by
$$\mathbf{r} = \mathbf{A} + \mathbf{B} + \mathbf{C} = 3.1\hat{\mathbf{j}} - 2.4\hat{\mathbf{i}} - 5.2\hat{\mathbf{j}}$$
$$= -2.4\hat{\mathbf{i}} - 2.1\hat{\mathbf{j}}$$

whose magnitude is $|\mathbf{r}| = \sqrt{(-2.4)^2 + (-2.1)^2} \approx 3.2$ km

Hence, the person will be 3.2 km away from the initial point.

(iii) There are two possibilities for the angle.
$$\theta = \tan^{-1}\left(\frac{A_y}{A_x}\right) = \tan^{-1}\left(\frac{-3.1}{-2.4}\right) = 41° \text{ or } 221°$$

$\because$ r is in the third quadrant, hence $\theta = 221°$

Resolution of a Space Vector
(In Three Dimensions)

Similarly, we can resolve a general vector $\mathbf{A}$ into three components along x, y and z-axes in three dimensions (i.e. space). Let α, β and γ are the angles between $\mathbf{A}$ and the x, y and z-axes, respectively as shown in figure.

Let $\hat{\mathbf{i}}, \hat{\mathbf{j}}, \hat{\mathbf{k}}$ be the unit vectors, along x, y and z-axes, respectively.

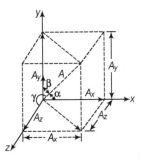

While resolving, we have,
$$A_x = A\cos\alpha,\ A_y = A\cos\beta,\ A_z = A\cos\gamma$$

$\therefore$ Resultant vector, $\mathbf{A} = A_x\hat{\mathbf{i}} + A_y\hat{\mathbf{j}} + A_z\hat{\mathbf{k}}$

Magnitude of vector $\mathbf{A}$ is $A = \sqrt{A_x^2 + A_y^2 + A_z^2}$ ...(i)

Position vector r is given by $\mathbf{r} = x\hat{\mathbf{i}} + y\hat{\mathbf{j}} + z\,\hat{\mathbf{k}}$

Remember that
$$\cos\alpha = \frac{A_x}{\sqrt{A_x^2 + A_y^2 + A_z^2}} = l$$

$$\cos\beta = \frac{A_y}{\sqrt{A_x^2 + A_y^2 + A_z^2}} = m$$

$$\cos\gamma = \frac{A_z}{\sqrt{A_x^2 + A_y^2 + A_z^2}} = n$$

Here, l, m and n are known as **direction cosines** of $\mathbf{A}$.
Putting the values of Ax, Ay and Az in Eq. (i), we get
$$A^2 = A^2\cos^2\alpha + A^2\cos^2\beta + A^2\cos^2\gamma$$
$$A^2 = A^2(\cos^2\alpha + \cos^2\beta + \cos^2\gamma)$$
or $\quad\cos^2\alpha + \cos^2\beta + \cos^2\gamma = 1$

It means, sum of the squares of the direction cosines of a vector is always unity.

Note

The angles α, β and γ are angles in space. They are between pairs of lines, which are not coplanar.

EXAMPLE |7| Three Components of a Vector

The figure shows three vectors $\mathbf{OA}, \mathbf{OB}$ and $\mathbf{OC}$ which are equal in magnitude (say, F). Determine the direction of $\mathbf{OA} + \mathbf{OB} - \mathbf{OC}$.

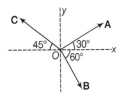

Sol. Given, $|\mathbf{OA}| = |\mathbf{OB}| = |\mathbf{OC}| = \mathbf{F}$

Angles are 30°, 45° and 60°.
Resolve all the vector components individually

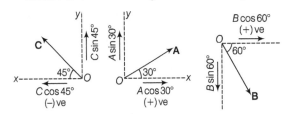

$$\mathbf{R}_x = \mathbf{R}_{x_1} + \mathbf{R}_{x_2} + \mathbf{R}_{x_3}$$

Sum of vectors in x-direction (i.e. R_x) and sum of vectors in y-direction (i.e. R_y)

$$\mathbf{R}_x = A\cos 30° + B\cos 60° - C\cos 45°$$
$$= \frac{F\sqrt{3}}{2} + \frac{F}{2} - \frac{F}{\sqrt{2}} \qquad [\because A = B = C = F]$$
$$= \frac{F}{2\sqrt{2}}(\sqrt{6} + \sqrt{2} - 2)$$

$$\mathbf{R}_y = A\sin 30° + C\cos 45° - B\sin 60°$$
$$= \frac{F}{2} + \frac{F}{\sqrt{2}} - \frac{F\sqrt{3}}{2} = \frac{F}{2\sqrt{2}}(\sqrt{2} + 2 - \sqrt{6})$$

Determination of magnitude,

$$R = \sqrt{R_x^2 + R_y^2}$$

$$= \sqrt{\left[\frac{F}{2\sqrt{2}}(\sqrt{6} + \sqrt{2} - 2)\right]^2 + \left[\frac{F}{2\sqrt{2}}(\sqrt{2} + 2 - \sqrt{6})\right]^2}$$

$$= \sqrt{F^2(0.435) + F^2(0.116)}$$

$$= \sqrt{F^2(0.550)} = F\sqrt{0.550}$$

$$\Rightarrow R = 0.74 \ F$$

Determination of direction

$$\tan\theta = \frac{R_y}{R_x} = \frac{\dfrac{F}{2\sqrt{2}}(\sqrt{2} + 2 - \sqrt{6})}{\dfrac{F}{2\sqrt{2}}(\sqrt{6} + \sqrt{2} - 2)}$$

$$= \frac{0.97}{1.85} \approx 0.524$$

$$\theta \approx 27.65$$

This is the angle which **R** makes with x-axis.

EXAMPLE |8| Resolution of Forces

Can the walk of a man be an example of resolution of forces?

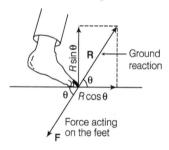

Sol. Walking of a man is an example of resolution of forces. A man while walking presses the ground with his feet backward by a force **F** at an angle θ with ground, in action.

The ground in reaction exerts an equal and opposite force **R** $(= \mathbf{F})$ on the feet.

Its horizontal component $H = R\cos\theta$ enables the person to move forward while the vertical component $V = R\sin\theta$ balances his weight because R is resolved into two rectangular components.

Application of resolution of vector

It is easier to pull a lawn mower than to push.

Addition of Vectors (Analytical Method)

Consider two vectors **A** and **B** inclined at an angle θ be acting on a particle at the same time. Let they be represented in magnitude and direction by two sides **OP** and **PQ** of ΔOPQ, taken in the same order (take from above). Then, according to triangle law of vector addition,

the resultant (**R**) is given by the closing side **OQ**, taken in opposite order.

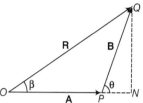

Draw QN perpendicular to OP produced.

From ΔQNP, $\dfrac{PN}{PQ} = \cos\theta$

$\Rightarrow \quad PN = PQ\cos\theta = B\cos\theta \quad [\because PQ = B] \ \dots(i)$

and $\qquad \dfrac{QN}{PQ} = \sin\theta$

$\Rightarrow \quad QN = PQ\sin\theta = B\sin\theta \qquad \dots(ii)$

In right angled ΔONQ, we have

$$OQ^2 = QN^2 + NO^2 = QN^2 + (OP + PN)^2$$

or $\quad R^2 = (B\sin\theta)^2 + (A + B\cos\theta)^2$

$$= B^2\sin^2\theta + A^2 + B^2\cos^2\theta + 2AB\cos\theta$$

$$= A^2 + B^2 + 2AB\cos\theta$$

$$\Rightarrow \quad \boxed{\text{Resultant, } R = \sqrt{A^2 + B^2 + 2AB\cos\theta}}$$

This represents the magnitude of resultant vector **R**.

If the resultant vector **R** makes an angle (β) with the direction of vector **A**, then from right angle ΔQNO,

$$\tan\beta = \frac{QN}{ON} = \frac{QN}{OP + PN} = \frac{B\sin\theta}{A + B\cos\theta}$$

or $\quad \boxed{\text{Direction of resultant } \mathbf{R}, \ \tan\beta = \dfrac{B\sin\theta}{A + B\cos\theta}}$

Regarding the Magnitude of R

(i) When $\theta = 0°$, then $R = A + B$ (maximum).

(ii) When $\theta = 90°$, then $R = \sqrt{A^2 + B^2}$.

(iii) When $\theta = 180°$, then $R = A - B$ (minimum).

This can be extended to any number of vectors if vectors **a**, **b** and **c** are given, then

$$\mathbf{a} = a_x\hat{\mathbf{i}} + a_y\hat{\mathbf{j}} + a_z\hat{\mathbf{k}}$$

$$\mathbf{b} = b_x\hat{\mathbf{i}} + b_y\hat{\mathbf{j}} + b_z\hat{\mathbf{k}}$$

$$\mathbf{c} = c_x\hat{\mathbf{i}} + c_y\hat{\mathbf{j}} + c_z\hat{\mathbf{k}}$$

where, $\mathbf{r}_x = a_x + b_x + c_x$, $\mathbf{r}_y = a_y + b_y + c_y$

$$\mathbf{r}_z = a_z + b_z + c_z$$

EXAMPLE |9| Law of Sine and Law of Cosine

Find the magnitude and direction of the resultant of two vectors **A** and **B** in terms of their magnitudes and angle θ between them. **[NCERT]**

Sol. Let the vectors **OP** and **OQ** represent two vectors **A** and **B** which are at angle θ with each other as shown in figure.

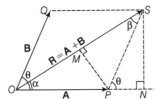

As we know the magnitude of the resultant vector **R** is

$$R = \sqrt{A^2 + B^2 + 2AB\cos\theta}$$

This is known as **law of cosine**.

If the resultant vector **R** makes an angle α with the direction of vector **A**. Then,

In ΔOSN, $SN = OS \sin\alpha = R\sin\alpha$ and

In ΔPSN, $SN = PS \sin\theta = B\sin\theta$

Thus, $\dfrac{R}{\sin\theta} = \dfrac{B}{\sin\alpha}$ ...(i)

Similarly, $PM = A\sin\alpha = B\sin\beta$

$$\dfrac{A}{\sin\beta} = \dfrac{B}{\sin\alpha}$$ ...(ii)

From Eqs. (i) and (ii), we get

$$\dfrac{R}{\sin\theta} = \dfrac{A}{\sin\beta} = \dfrac{B}{\sin\alpha}$$

This is known as **law of sines**.

EXAMPLE |10| Resultant of Two Vectors

Two vectors **C** and **D** having magnitude 5 units and angle θ = 30° with each other. Find the resultant vector.

Sol. We have to find the resultant of given two vectors **C** and **D**. For the magnitude of resultant vector

$$R = |\mathbf{R}| = |\mathbf{C} + \mathbf{D}| = \sqrt{C^2 + D^2 + 2CD\cos\theta}$$

$$= \sqrt{(5)^2 + (5)^2 + 2 \times 5 \times 5 \times \cos 30°}$$

$$= \sqrt{25 + 25 + 25\sqrt{3}}   \left(\because \cos 30° = \dfrac{\sqrt{3}}{2}\right)$$

$$= 5\sqrt{2 + \sqrt{3}} \text{ units}$$

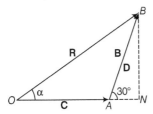

Now, for the direction of resultant vector

$$\tan\alpha = \dfrac{D\sin\theta}{C + D\cos\theta} = \dfrac{5 \times \sin 30°}{5 + 5 \times \cos 30°}$$

$$\tan\alpha = \dfrac{5 \times 1/2}{5 + 5 \times \dfrac{\sqrt{3}}{2}} = \left(\dfrac{1}{2 + \sqrt{3}}\right) = 2 - \sqrt{3} = 0.268$$

$$\Rightarrow \qquad \alpha = \tan^{-1}(0.268) \approx 15°$$

EXAMPLE |11| Resultant of Three Vectors

Three vectors are given by

$$\mathbf{A} = A_x\hat{i} + A_y\hat{j} + A_z\hat{k}$$
$$\mathbf{B} = B_x\hat{i} + B_y\hat{j} + B_z\hat{k}$$
$$\mathbf{C} = C_x\hat{i} + C_y\hat{j} + C_z\hat{k}$$

Determine the magnitude of resultant vector.

Sol. Given, $\mathbf{A} = A_x\hat{i} + A_y\hat{j} + A_z\hat{k}$

$$\mathbf{B} = B_x\hat{i} + B_y\hat{j} + B_z\hat{k}$$
$$\mathbf{C} = C_x\hat{i} + C_y\hat{j} + C_z\hat{k}$$

We can add these easily by analytical method.

The resultant of these three vectors are $\mathbf{R} = \mathbf{A} + \mathbf{B} + \mathbf{C}$

$$A_x\hat{i} + A_y\hat{j} + A_z\hat{k} + B_x\hat{i} + B_y\hat{j} + B_z\hat{k} + C_x\hat{i} + C_y\hat{j} + C_z\hat{k}$$

$$= (A_x + B_x + C_x)\hat{i} + (A_y + B_y + C_y)\hat{j} + (A_z + B_z + C_z)\hat{k}$$

The magnitude of **R** is given by,

$$R = \sqrt{(A_x + B_x + C_x)^2 + (A_y + B_y + C_y)^2 + (A_z + B_z + C_z)^2}$$

EXAMPLE |12| Resultant Velocity of a Boat

A motor boat is racing towards North at 25 km/h and the water current in that region is 10 km/h in the direction of 60° East to South. Find the resultant velocity of the boat.

[NCERT]

Sol. Given, velocity of motor boat, $v_b = 25$ km/h (towards North)

Velocity of water current, $v_c = 10$ km/h (towards East to South)

Direction, $\theta = 180° - 60° = 120°$

We know that,

$$v = \sqrt{v_b^2 + v_c^2 + 2v_b v_c \cos\theta}$$

$$v = \sqrt{(25)^2 + (10)^2 + 2 \times 25 \times 10 \times \cos 120°}$$

$$v = \sqrt{625 + 100 + 500\left(-\dfrac{1}{2}\right)}, \quad v = 21.8 \text{ km/h}$$

Suppose the resultant velocity v makes angle φ with the North direction. Then,

$$\tan\phi = \dfrac{v_c\sin 120°}{v_b + v_c\cos 120°} = \dfrac{10 \times (\sqrt{3}/2)}{25 + 10 \times (-1/2)} = 0.433$$

$$\therefore \qquad \phi = \tan^{-1}(0.433) = 23.4°$$

Subtraction of Vectors (Analytical Method)

There are two vectors **A** and **B** at an angle θ. If we have to subtract **B** from **A**, then first invert the vector **B** and then add with **A** as shown in figure.

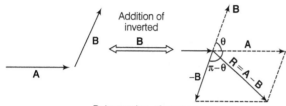

Subtraction of vectors

The resultant vector is $\mathbf{R} = \mathbf{A} + (-\mathbf{B}) = \mathbf{A} - \mathbf{B}$
The magnitude of resultant in this case is

$$R = |\mathbf{R}| = \sqrt{A^2 + B^2 + 2AB\cos(\pi - \theta)}$$

$$\boxed{\text{Resultant, } R = \sqrt{A^2 + B^2 - 2AB\cos\theta}}$$

Here, θ = angle between **A** and **B**

Regarding the magnitude of R

(i) When $\theta = 0°$, then $R = A - B$ (minimum).

(ii) When $\theta = 90°$, then $R = \sqrt{A^2 + B^2}$.

(iii) When $\theta = 180°$, then $R = A + B$ (maximum).

EXAMPLE |13| **Finding the Subtraction of Vectors**

Two vectors of magnitude 3 units and 4 units are at angle 60° between them. Find the magnitude of their difference.

Sol. Let the vectors are **A** and **B**.
Given, $|\mathbf{A}| = 3$ unit, $|\mathbf{B}| = 4$ unit and $\theta = 60°$
The magnitude of resultant of **A** and **B**

$$R = |\mathbf{R}| = \sqrt{A^2 + B^2 - 2AB\cos\theta}$$
$$= \sqrt{3^2 + 4^2 - 2 \times 3 \times 4\cos 60°}$$
$$R = \sqrt{25 - 12} = \sqrt{13} = 3.61 \text{ units}$$

EXAMPLE |14| **Sum and Difference Together**

Consider vectors A and B having equal magnitude of 5 units and are inclined each other by 60°. Find the magnitude of sum and difference of these vectors.

Sol. Given, $\mathbf{A} = 5$ units, $\mathbf{B} = 5$ units, $\theta = 60°$
$$\mathbf{A} + \mathbf{B} = ? \text{ and } \mathbf{A} - \mathbf{B} = ?$$

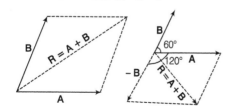

The magnitude of the resultant vectors of the sum,

$$R = \sqrt{A^2 + B^2 + 2AB\cos\theta}$$
$$= \sqrt{5^2 + 5^2 + 2 \times 5 \times 5 \times \cos 60°} = 5\sqrt{3} \text{ unit}$$

The magnitude of the resultant vector of the difference,

$$R = \sqrt{A^2 + (-B)^2 + 2AB\cos\theta}$$
$$R = \sqrt{5^2 + 5^2 + 2 \times 5 \times 5\cos 120°},$$
$$R = 5 \text{ unit}$$

DOT PRODUCT OR SCALAR PRODUCT

It is defined as the product of the magnitudes of vectors **A** and **B** and the cosine of the angle θ between them. It is represented by

$$\mathbf{A} \cdot \mathbf{B} = AB\cos\theta$$

(a) **B** cos θ is the projection of **B** onto **A**.
(b) **A** cos θ is the projection of **A** onto **B**.

Case I When the two vectors are parallel, then $\theta = 0°$.
We have, $\mathbf{A} \cdot \mathbf{B} = AB\cos 0° = AB$

Case II When the two vectors are mutually perpendicular, then $\theta = 90°$.
We have, $\mathbf{A} \cdot \mathbf{B} = AB\cos 90° = 0$

Case III When the two vectors are anti-parallel, then $\theta = 180°$.
We have, $\mathbf{A} \cdot \mathbf{B} = AB\cos 180° = -AB$

Dot Product of Two Vectors in Terms of Their Components

It is defined as the product of the magnitude of one vector and the magnitude of the component of other vector in the direction of first vector.

If $\mathbf{a} = a_1\hat{\mathbf{i}} + a_2\hat{\mathbf{j}} + a_3\hat{\mathbf{k}}$ and $\mathbf{b} = b_1\hat{\mathbf{i}} + b_2\hat{\mathbf{j}} + b_3\hat{\mathbf{k}}$

then $\mathbf{a} \cdot \mathbf{b} = (a_1\hat{\mathbf{i}} + a_2\hat{\mathbf{j}} + a_3\hat{\mathbf{k}}) \cdot (b_1\hat{\mathbf{i}} + b_2\hat{\mathbf{j}} + b_3\hat{\mathbf{k}})$

$$= (a_1 \cdot b_1)\hat{\mathbf{i}}^2 + (a_1 \cdot b_2)\hat{\mathbf{i}} \cdot \hat{\mathbf{j}} + (a_1 \cdot b_3)\hat{\mathbf{i}} \cdot \hat{\mathbf{k}}$$
$$+ (a_2 \cdot b_1)\hat{\mathbf{j}} \cdot \hat{\mathbf{i}} + (a_2 \cdot b_2)\hat{\mathbf{j}}^2 + (a_2 \cdot b_3)\hat{\mathbf{j}} \cdot \hat{\mathbf{k}}$$
$$+ (a_3 \cdot b_1)\hat{\mathbf{k}} \cdot \hat{\mathbf{i}} + (a_3 \cdot b_2)\hat{\mathbf{k}} \cdot \hat{\mathbf{j}} + (a_3 \cdot b_3)\hat{\mathbf{k}}^2.$$

$$= a_1 \cdot b_1 + a_2 \cdot b_2 + a_3 \cdot b_3$$

where, $\hat{i} \cdot \hat{i} = \hat{j} \cdot \hat{j} = \hat{k} \cdot \hat{k} = 1$

$$\hat{i} \cdot \hat{j} + \hat{i} \cdot \hat{k} + \hat{j} \cdot \hat{i} + \hat{k} \cdot \hat{i} = 0$$

Properties of Dot Product

(i) $\mathbf{a} \cdot \mathbf{a} = (a)^2$

(ii) $\mathbf{a} \cdot \mathbf{b} = \mathbf{b} \cdot \mathbf{a}$

(iii) $\mathbf{a} \cdot (\mathbf{b} + \mathbf{c}) = \mathbf{a} \cdot \mathbf{b} + \mathbf{a} \cdot \mathbf{c}$

(iv) $(\mathbf{c} \cdot \mathbf{a}) \cdot \mathbf{b} = \mathbf{c} \cdot (\mathbf{a} \cdot \mathbf{b})$

(v) $\mathbf{a} \cdot \mathbf{b} = |\mathbf{a}||\mathbf{b}|\cos\theta$

EXAMPLE |15| Dot Product of Two Vectors

Find the angle between the vectors

$$\mathbf{A} = \hat{i} - 2\hat{j} - \hat{k} \text{ and } \mathbf{B} = -\hat{i} + \hat{j} - 2\hat{k}$$

Sol. The angle between two vectors is included in the expression of dot product or scalar product.

$$\mathbf{A} \cdot \mathbf{B} = AB\cos Q \qquad ...(i)$$

The magnitude of **A** is given by

$$A = \sqrt{(1)^2 + (-2)^2 + (-1)^2} = \sqrt{6} \qquad ...(ii)$$

The magnitude of **B** is given by

$$B = \sqrt{(-1)^2 + (1)^2 + (-2)^2} = \sqrt{6} \qquad ...(iii)$$

We can separately evaluate the left side of Eq. (i) by writing the vectors in unit vector notation and using the distributive law.

$$\mathbf{A} \cdot \mathbf{B} = (\hat{i} + 2\hat{j} - \hat{k}) \cdot (-\hat{i} + \hat{j} - 2\hat{k})$$

$$= (1 \cdot -1)(\hat{i} \cdot \hat{i}) + (1 \cdot 1)(\hat{i} \cdot \hat{j}) + (1 \cdot -2)(\hat{i} \cdot \hat{k}) + (2 \cdot -1)$$

$$(\hat{j} \cdot \hat{i}) + (2 \cdot 1)(\hat{j} \cdot \hat{j}) + (2 \cdot -2)(\hat{j} \cdot \hat{k}) + (-1 \cdot -1)$$

$$(\hat{k} \cdot \hat{i}) + (-1 \cdot 1)(\hat{k} \cdot \hat{j}) + (-1 \cdot -2)(\hat{k} \cdot \hat{k})$$

$$\mathbf{A} \cdot \mathbf{B} = 3 \begin{bmatrix} \because \ \hat{i} \cdot \hat{i} = 1, \hat{i} \cdot \hat{j} = 0, \hat{i} \cdot \hat{k} = 0 \\ \hat{j} \cdot \hat{j} = 1, \hat{j} \cdot \hat{i} = 0, \hat{j} \cdot \hat{k} = 0 \\ \hat{k} \cdot \hat{k} = 1, \hat{k} \cdot \hat{i} = 0, \hat{k} \cdot \hat{j} = 0 \end{bmatrix}$$

Substituting the values of **A** from Eq. (ii) and **B** from Eq. (iii) and $\mathbf{A} \cdot \mathbf{B} = 6$ in Eq. (i), we get

$$3 = (\sqrt{6})(\sqrt{6})\cos\theta$$

$$\Rightarrow \quad \cos\theta = \frac{3}{6} = \frac{1}{2} \Rightarrow \theta = \cos^{-1}\left(\frac{1}{2}\right) = 60°$$

EXAMPLE |16| Application of Dot Product Method

A force of $(7\hat{i} + 6\hat{k})$ N makes a body move on a rough plane with a velocity of $(3\hat{i} + 4\hat{k})$ ms^{-1}. Calculate the power in W.

Sol. Using $\hat{k} \cdot \hat{k} = 1, \hat{i} \cdot \hat{j} = 0$

$$\therefore \text{ Power, } P = \mathbf{F} \cdot \mathbf{v} = (7\hat{i} + 6\hat{k}) \cdot (3\hat{i} + 4\hat{k})$$

$$= 21 + 24 = 45 \text{ W} \qquad [\because \ \hat{i} \cdot \hat{k} = 0]$$

VECTOR PRODUCT OR CROSS PRODUCT

It is defined as the product of the magnitudes of vectors **A** and **B** and the sine of the angle θ between them.

It is represented as

Cross product of vectors **A** and **B**, $\mathbf{A} \times \mathbf{B} = AB\sin\theta \ \hat{n}$

where $\hat{n}$ is a unit vector in the direction of $\hat{i}$.

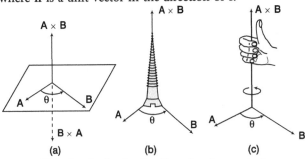

Right hand rules for direction of vector product

Cross Product of Two Vectors in Terms of Their Components

If $\mathbf{a} = a_1\hat{i} + a_2\hat{j} + a_3\hat{k}$ and $\mathbf{b} = b_1\hat{i} + b_2\hat{j} + b_3\hat{k}$, then

$$\mathbf{a} \times \mathbf{b} = \begin{vmatrix} \hat{i} & \hat{j} & \hat{k} \\ a_1 & a_2 & a_3 \\ b_1 & b_2 & b_3 \end{vmatrix}$$

$$= (a_2b_3 - a_3b_2)\hat{i} - (a_1b_3 - a_3b_1)\hat{j} + (a_1b_2 - a_2b_1)\hat{k}$$

where, $\hat{i} \times \hat{i} = \hat{j} \times \hat{j} = \hat{k} \times \hat{k} = 0$

and $\hat{i} \times \hat{j} = \hat{k}, \hat{j} \times \hat{k} = \hat{i}, \hat{k} \times \hat{i} = \hat{j},$

$$\hat{j} \times \hat{i} = -\hat{k}, \hat{k} \times \hat{j} = -\hat{i}, \hat{i} \times \hat{k} = -\hat{j}$$

Case I Cross product of two parallel or anti-parallel vectors is zero.

Case II Cross product of two mutually perpendicular vector is equal to product of the magnitude of two vectors.

If **A** and **B** are two sides of Δ, then area of $\Delta = \frac{1}{2}|\mathbf{A} \times \mathbf{B}|$

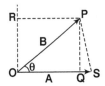

Representation of vectors **A** and **B**

As, area of $\Delta = \dfrac{1}{2} \times$ base $\times$ height $= \dfrac{1}{2} OS \times PQ$

$$\left(\begin{array}{l} \because \quad \sin\theta = \dfrac{PQ}{OP} \\ \Rightarrow \ PQ = OP\sin\theta = B\sin\theta \text{ and } OS = A \end{array} \right)$$

$$= \dfrac{1}{2} A \times B\sin\theta = \dfrac{1}{2} AB\sin\theta = \dfrac{1}{2}|A \times B|$$

Properties of Cross Product

(i) $a \times b = -b \times a$

(ii) $a \times (b + c) = a \times b + a \times c$

(iii) $(a \times b) + (c \times d) = (a \times c) + (a \times d) + (b \times c) + (b \times d)$

(iv) $ma \times b = a \times mb$

(v) $(b + c)a = b \times a + c \times a$

(vi) $a \times a = 0$

(vii) $a \times (b - c) = a \times b - a \times c$

(viii) $|a \times b|^2 = |a|^2 |b|^2 - |a \cdot b|^2$

(ix) $a \times (b \times c) = (c \cdot a)b - (b \cdot a)c$

EXAMPLE |17| Cross Product of Two Vectors

The vector **A** has a magnitude of 5 unit, **B** has a magnitude of 6 unit and the cross product **A** and **B** has the magnitude of 15 unit. Find the angle between **A** and **B**.

Sol. If the angle between **A** and **B** is θ, then cross product will have a magnitude,

$$|A \times B| = AB\sin\theta$$
$$\Rightarrow \qquad 15 = 5 \times 6 \sin\theta$$
$$\sin\theta = \dfrac{1}{2} \ \Rightarrow \ \theta = 30°$$

Representation of Unit Vectors in a Circle

Unit vectors along three axes of cartesian coordinate system (i.e. $\hat{i}, \hat{j}, \hat{k}$) can be represented on a circle in such a way that if we rotate our eyes in anti-clockwise product of two consecutive vector will produce the third unit vector.

e.g. $\qquad \hat{i} \times \hat{j} = \hat{k}$ and $\hat{j} \times \hat{i} = -\hat{k}$

and similarly for other possibilities.

Scalar Product of Vectors

The scalar product of vectors produce pseudo scalars, such as volume, power etc. The vector product of two vectors produces a pseudo vector. It is also called axial vector. The direction of this vector is perpendicular to the plane containing the multiple vectors.

| TOPIC PRACTICE 1 |

OBJECTIVE Type Questions

1. Which one of the following statements is true?
   [NCERT Exemplar]
   (a) A scalar quantity is the one that is conserved in a process
   (b) A scalar quantity is the one that can never take negative values
   (c) A scalar quantity is the one that does not vary from one point to another in space
   (d) A scalar quantity has the same value for observers with different orientation of the axes

   Sol. (d) A scalar quantity is independent of direction hence has the same value for observers with different orientations of the axes.

2. Consider the quantities, pressure, power, energy, impulse, gravitational potential, electrical charge, temperature, area. Out of these, the only vector quantity/ies is/are **[NCERT Exemplar]**
   (a) impulse, pressure and area
   (b) impulse
   (c) area and gravitational potential
   (d) impulse and pressure

   Sol. (b) We know that, impulse, $J = F.\Delta t = \Delta p$, where F is force, Δt is time duration and Δp is change in momentum. As Δp is a vector quantity, hence only impulse is also a vector quantity.

3. The relation between the vectors **A** and $-2\mathbf{A}$ is that,
   (a) both have same magnitude
   (b) both have same direction
   (c) they have opposite directions
   (d) None of the above

   Sol. (c) Multiplying a vector **A** by a negative number λ gives a vector λ**A**, whose directions opposite to the direction of **A** and it's magnitude is $-\lambda$ times $|A|$.

4. A and B are two inclined vectors. R is their sum. Choose the correct figure for the given description.

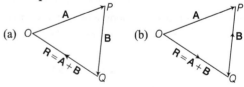

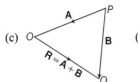
(c)

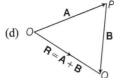
(d)

Sol. (d) Correct figure is

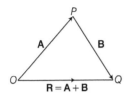

5. The component of a vector r along X-axis will have maximum value if **[NCERT Exemplar]**
   (a) **r** is along positive y-axis
   (b) **r** is along positive x-axis
   (c) **r** makes an angle of 45° with the x-axis
   (d) **r** is along negative y-axis

Sol. (b) Let r makes an angle θ with positive x-axis.
Component of r along X-axis

$$r_x = |\mathbf{r}| \cos \theta$$
$$(r_x)_{maximum} = |\mathbf{r}|(\cos \theta)_{maximum}$$
$$= |\mathbf{r}| \cos 0° = |\mathbf{r}|$$
$$(\because \cos \theta \text{ is maximum of } \theta = 0°)$$

As $\theta = 0°$,
r is along positive x-axis.

VERY SHORT ANSWER Type Questions

6. Three vectors not lying in a plane can never end up to give a null vector. Is it true? **[NCERT]**

Sol. Yes, because they cannot be represented by the three sides of a triangle taken in the same order.

7. When do we say two vectors are orthogonal?

Sol. If the dot product of two vectors is zero, then the vectors are orthogonal.

8. The total path length is always equal to the magnitude of the displacement vector of a particle. Why? **[NCERT]**

Sol. It is only true if the particle moves along a straight line in the same direction, otherwise the statement is false.

9. Under what condition, the three vectors give zero resultant?

Sol. If three vectors acting on a point object at the same time are represented in magnitude and direction by the three sides of a triangle taken in the same order, their resultant is zero.

The object is said to be in equilibrium.

10. What is the property of two vectors **A** and **B** such that **A + B = C** and **A + B = C**?

Sol. The two vectors are parallel and acting in the same direction i.e. $\theta = 0°$

11. What is the value of m in $\hat{\mathbf{i}} + m\hat{\mathbf{j}} + \hat{\mathbf{k}}$ to be unit vector?

Sol. For unit vector $|\hat{\mathbf{i}} + m\hat{\mathbf{j}} + \hat{\mathbf{k}}| = \sqrt{1 + m^2 + 1} = 1$
$$m^2 + 2 = 1$$
$$m^2 = -1 \Rightarrow m = \sqrt{-1}$$
$\therefore$ m is imaginary.

12. Two equal forces having their resultant equal to either. At what angle are they inclined?

Sol. $A = F, B = F, R = F, \theta = ?$
$$R = \sqrt{A^2 + B^2 + 2AB \cos \theta}$$
$$\Rightarrow \quad R^2 = A^2 + B^2 + 2AB \cos \theta$$
$$F^2 = F^2 + F^2 + 2F^2 \cos \theta$$
$$1 = 2(1 + \cos \theta)$$
$$\Rightarrow \quad \cos \theta = \frac{1}{2} - 1 = \frac{-1}{2}$$
$$\theta = \cos^{-1}\left(-\frac{1}{2}\right) = 120°$$

13. What is the angle made by vector, $\mathbf{A} = 2\hat{\mathbf{i}} + 2\hat{\mathbf{j}}$ with x-axis?

Sol. For the vector, $A_x = 2, A_y = 2$
We know that angle is given by
$$\theta = \tan^{-1}\left(\frac{A_y}{A_x}\right) = \tan^{-1}\left(\frac{2}{2}\right)$$
$$\theta = \tan^{-1}(1) = 45°$$

14. The magnitude of vectors **A**, **B** and **C** are 12, 5 and 13 units respectively and **A + B = C**, find the angle between **A** and **B**.

Sol. We know that, $C^2 = A^2 + B^2$ or $13^2 = 12^2 + 5^2$
Thus, the angle between **A** and **B** is 90°.

15. What are the minimum number of forces which are numerically equal whose vector sum can be zero?

Sol. Two only, provided that they are acting in opposite directions.

16. Under what condition the three vectors cannot give zero resultant?

Sol. When the three vectors are not lying in one plane, they cannot produce zero resultant.

17. If $|\mathbf{A} + \mathbf{B}| = |\mathbf{A} - \mathbf{B}|$, what is the angle between A and B?

Sol. $|\mathbf{A} + \mathbf{B}| = |\mathbf{A} - \mathbf{B}|$

$$\sqrt{A^2 + B^2 + 2AB\cos\theta} = \sqrt{A^2 + B^2 - 2AB\cos\theta}$$

$\Rightarrow \quad 4AB\cos\theta = 0 \Rightarrow \cos\theta = 0$

Hence, $\cos\theta = \cos 90°$ or $\theta = \pi/2$

18. Can the scalar product of two vectors be negative?

Sol. Yes, it will be negative if the angle between the two vectors lies between $90°$ to $270°$.

19. If $|\mathbf{A} \times \mathbf{B}| = \mathbf{A} \cdot \mathbf{B}$, what is the angle between A and B?

Sol. As we know, $\mathbf{A} \times \mathbf{B} = AB\sin\theta$

$$\mathbf{A} \cdot \mathbf{B} = AB\cos\theta$$

According to the question

$$AB\sin\theta = AB\cos\theta$$

$\Rightarrow \qquad \dfrac{\sin\theta}{\cos\theta} = 1 \Rightarrow \tan\theta = 1 \Rightarrow \theta = 45°$

20. What is the angle between A and B, if A and B denote the adjacent sides of a parallelogram drawn from a point and the area of the parallelogram is 1/2 AB?

Sol. Area of parallelogram $|\mathbf{A} \times \mathbf{B}| = AB\sin\theta = \dfrac{1}{2}AB$ [given]

$\therefore \qquad \sin\theta = \dfrac{1}{2} = \sin 30°$ or $\theta = 30°$

21. If $\mathbf{A} \cdot \mathbf{B} = |\mathbf{A} \times \mathbf{B}|$, find the value of angle between A and B.

Sol. As $\mathbf{A} \cdot \mathbf{B} = |\mathbf{A} \times \mathbf{B}|$

$\therefore AB\cos\theta = AB\sin\theta$ or $\tan\theta = 1$ or $\theta = \pi/4$

22. Can the walking on a road be an example of resolution of vectors?

Sol. Yes, when a man walks on the road, he presses the road along an oblique direction. The horizontal component of the reaction helps the man to walk on the road.

23. When the sum of the two vectors are maximum and minimum?

Sol. The sum of two vectors is maximum, when both the vectors are in the same direction and is minimum when they act in opposite direction.

As, $R = \sqrt{A^2 + B^2 + 2AB\cos\theta}$

(i) For R to be maximum, $\cos\theta = +1$

$$\theta = 0°$$

$$R_{max} = \sqrt{A^2 + B^2 + 2AB} = A + B$$

(ii) For R to be minimum,

$$\cos\theta = -1 \text{ or } \theta = 180°$$

$$R_{min} = \sqrt{A^2 + B^2 + 2AB(-1)} = A - B$$

SHORT ANSWER Type Questions

24. We can order events in time and there is no sense of time, distinguishing past, present and future. Is time a vector?

Sol. We know that time always flows on and on i.e. from past to present and then to future.

Therefore, a direction can be assigned to time. Since, the direction of time is unique and it is unspecified or unstated. That is why, time cannot be a vector though it has a direction.

25. Two forces whose magnitudes are in the ratio 3 : 5 give a resultant of 28 N. If the angle of their inclination is $60°$. Find the magnitude of each force.

Sol. Let A and B be the two forces.

Then, $A = 3x$, $B = 5x$, $R = 28$ N and $\theta = 60°$

Thus, $\dfrac{A}{B} = \dfrac{3}{5}$

Now, $R = \sqrt{A^2 + B^2 + 2AB\cos\theta}$

$\Rightarrow \quad 28 = \sqrt{9x^2 + 25x^2 + 30\,x^2\cos 60°} = 7x \Rightarrow x = 4$

$\therefore$ Forces are $A = 12$ N and $B = 20$ N.

26. Suppose you have two forces F and F. How would you combine them in order to have resultant force of magnitudes?

    (i) Zero   (ii) F

Sol. (i) If they act at opposite direction, resultant is zero.

(ii) For the resultant to be $\mathbf{F}$,

$$F^2 = F^2 + F^2 + 2F^2\cos\theta$$

$\Rightarrow \qquad \cos\theta = \dfrac{-1}{2}$

$\Rightarrow \qquad \theta = 120°$

27. Determine that vector which when added to the resultant of $\mathbf{A} = 3\hat{i} - 5\hat{j} + 7\hat{k}$ and $\mathbf{B} = 2\hat{i} + 4\hat{j} - 3\hat{k}$ gives unit vector along y-direction.

Sol. We are given, $\mathbf{A} = 3\hat{i} - 5\hat{j} + 7\hat{k}$ and $\mathbf{B} = 2\hat{i} + 4\hat{j} - 3\hat{k}$

Thus, the resultant vector is given by

$$\mathbf{R} = \mathbf{A} + \mathbf{B} = (3\hat{i} - 5\hat{j} + 7\hat{k}) + (2\hat{i} + 4\hat{j} - 3\hat{k})$$

$$= 5\hat{i} - \hat{j} + 4\hat{k}$$

But the unit vector along y-direction $= \hat{j}$

$\therefore$ Required vector $= \hat{j} - (5\hat{i} - \hat{j} + 4\hat{k})$

$$= -5\hat{i} + 2\hat{j} - 4\hat{k}$$

28. Explain the property of two vectors **A** and **B** if $|\mathbf{A} + \mathbf{B}| = |\mathbf{A} - \mathbf{B}|$.

Sol. As we know that, $|\mathbf{A} + \mathbf{B}| = \sqrt{A^2 + B^2 + 2AB \cos \theta}$

and $|\mathbf{A} - \mathbf{B}| = \sqrt{A^2 + B^2 - 2AB \cos \theta}$

But as per question, we have

$\sqrt{A^2 + B^2 + 2AB\cos\theta} = \sqrt{A^2 + B^2 - 2AB\cos\theta}$

Squaring both sides, we have $(4\, AB \cos \theta) = 0$

$\Rightarrow \qquad \cos \theta = 0 \quad$ or $\quad \theta = 90°$

Hence, the two vectors **A** and **B** are perpendicular to each other.

29. Two forces 5 kg-wt. and 10 kg-wt. are acting with an inclination of 120° between them. Find the angle when the resultant makes with 10 kg-wt.

Sol. Given, $A = 5$ kg-wt, $B = 10$ kg-wt, $\theta = 120°$ then $\beta = ?$

$$\tan \beta = \frac{B \sin \theta}{A + B \cos \theta} = \frac{10 \sin 120°}{5 + 10 \cos 120°} = \frac{5 \sin 60°}{10 - 5 \cos 60°}$$

$$= \frac{5 \times \sqrt{3}/2}{10 - 5/2} = \frac{1}{\sqrt{3}} = \tan 30°$$

$\therefore \qquad \beta = 30°$

30. The sum and difference of two vectors are perpendicular to each other. Prove that the vectors are equal in magnitude.

Sol. As the vectors $\mathbf{A} + \mathbf{B}$ and $\mathbf{A} - \mathbf{B}$ are perpendicular to each other, therefore

$$(\mathbf{A} + \mathbf{B}) \cdot (\mathbf{A} - \mathbf{B}) = 0$$
$$\mathbf{A} \cdot \mathbf{A} - \mathbf{A} \cdot \mathbf{B} + \mathbf{B} \cdot \mathbf{A} - \mathbf{B} \cdot \mathbf{B} = 0$$
or $\qquad\qquad A - B = 0 \qquad [\because \mathbf{A} \cdot \mathbf{B} = \mathbf{B} \cdot \mathbf{A}]$
$\Rightarrow \qquad\qquad A = B$

31. The dot product of two vectors vanishes when vectors are orthogonal and has maximum value when vectors are parallel to each other. Explain.

Sol. We know that, $\mathbf{A} \cdot \mathbf{B} = AB \cos \theta$, when vectors are orthogonal, $\theta = 90°$.

So, $\mathbf{A} \cdot \mathbf{B} = AB \cos 90° = 0$, when vectors are parallel, then, $\theta = 0°$.

So, $\qquad \mathbf{A} \cdot \mathbf{B} = AB \cos 0° = AB$ (maximum)

32. The angle between vectors **A** and **B** is 60°. What is the ratio of $\mathbf{A} \cdot \mathbf{B}$ and $|\mathbf{A} \times \mathbf{B}|$?

Sol. The dot product, $\mathbf{A} \cdot \mathbf{B} = AB \cos \theta$ and cross product $|\mathbf{A} \times \mathbf{B}| = AB \sin \theta$.

$\therefore$ Ratio is $\dfrac{\mathbf{A} \cdot \mathbf{B}}{|\mathbf{A} \times \mathbf{B}|} = \dfrac{AB \cos \theta}{AB \sin \theta} = \cot \theta$

$$= \cot 60° = \frac{1}{\sqrt{3}}$$

As, $\qquad \theta = 60°, \cot 60° = \dfrac{1}{\sqrt{3}}$

33. Can a flight of a bird, an example of composition of vectors. Why?

Sol. Yes, the flight of a bird is an example of composition of vectors. As the bird flies, it strikes the air with its wings W, W along WO. According to Newton's third law of motion, air strikes the wings in opposite directions with the same force in reaction. The reactions are **OA** and **OB**. From law of parallelogram vectors, **OC** is the resultant of **OA** and **OB**. This resultant upwards force **OC** is responsible for the flight of the bird.

LONG ANSWER Type I Questions

34. Can you associate vectors with?
  (i) The length of a wire bent into a loop
  (ii) A plane area
  (iii) A sphere **[NCERT]**

Sol. (i) We cannot associate a vector with the length of a wire bent into a loop.
  (ii) We can associate a vector with a plane area.
      Such a vector is called **area vector** and its direction is represented by outward drawn normal to the area.
  (iii) We cannot associate a vector with volume of sphere, however, a vector can be associated with the area of sphere.

35. On a certain day, rain was falling vertically with a speed of 35 m/s. A wind started blowing after sometime with a speed of 12 m/s in East to West direction. In which direction should a boy waiting at a bus stop hold his umbrella? **[NCERT]**

Sol. In figure

Velocity of rain, $\mathbf{V}_R = OA = 35$ m/s,

[vertically downward]

Velocity of wind, $\mathbf{V}_W = OB = 12$ m/s, [East to West]

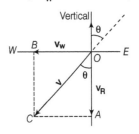

The magnitude of the resultant velocity is
$$v = \sqrt{(v_R)^2 + (v_W)^2}$$
$$= \sqrt{(35)^2 + (12)^2} = 37 \text{ m/s}$$

Let the resultant velocity, $\mathbf{v}(= \mathbf{OC})$ make an angle θ with the vertical. Then,
$$\tan\theta = \frac{AC}{OA} = \frac{v_W}{v_R} = \frac{12}{35} = 0.343$$
$$\therefore \qquad \theta = \tan^{-1}(0.343) \simeq 19°$$

36. There are two displacement vectors, one of magnitude 3 m and the other of 4 m. How would the two vectors be added so that the magnitude of the resultant vector be (i) 7 m (ii) 1 m and (iii) 5 m?

Sol. The magnitude of resultant $\mathbf{R}$ of two vectors $\mathbf{A}$ and $\mathbf{B}$ is given by, $R = \sqrt{A^2 + B^2 + 2AB \cos\theta}$
$$= \sqrt{3^2 + 4^2 + 2 \times 3 \times 4 \cos\theta}$$

(i) R is 7 m, if $\theta = 0°$
(ii) R is 1 m, if $\theta = 180°$
(iii) R is 5 m, if $\theta = 90°$

37. If unit vectors $\hat{\mathbf{a}}$ and $\hat{\mathbf{b}}$ are inclined at angle θ, then prove that $|\hat{\mathbf{a}} - \hat{\mathbf{b}}| = 2\sin\dfrac{\theta}{2}$. **[NCERT]**

Sol. For any vector a $\Rightarrow |\mathbf{a}|^2 = \mathbf{a} \cdot \mathbf{a}$
$$\therefore \quad |\hat{\mathbf{a}} - \hat{\mathbf{b}}|^2 = (\hat{\mathbf{a}} - \hat{\mathbf{b}}) \cdot (\hat{\mathbf{a}} - \hat{\mathbf{b}})$$
$$= \hat{\mathbf{a}} \cdot \hat{\mathbf{a}} - \hat{\mathbf{a}} \cdot \hat{\mathbf{b}} - \hat{\mathbf{b}} \cdot \hat{\mathbf{a}} + \hat{\mathbf{b}} \cdot \hat{\mathbf{b}}$$
$$= 1 - 2\hat{\mathbf{a}} \cdot \hat{\mathbf{b}} + 1 \quad [\because \hat{\mathbf{a}} \cdot \hat{\mathbf{a}} = 1 \times 1 \times \cos 0° = 1]$$
$$= 2 - 2 \times 1 \times 1 \times \cos\theta$$
$$= 2(1 - \cos\theta)$$
$$= 2 \cdot 2\sin^2\frac{\theta}{2} = 4\sin^2\frac{\theta}{2} \quad [\because 1 - \cos 2\theta = 2\sin^2\theta]$$

Hence, $|\hat{\mathbf{a}} - \hat{\mathbf{b}}| = 2\sin\dfrac{\theta}{2}$.

38. Show that vectors $\mathbf{A} = 2\hat{\mathbf{i}} - 3\hat{\mathbf{j}} - \hat{\mathbf{k}}$ and $\mathbf{B} = -6\hat{\mathbf{i}} + 9\hat{\mathbf{j}} + 3\hat{\mathbf{k}}$ are parallel.

Sol. The given vectors are
$$\mathbf{A} = 2\hat{\mathbf{i}} - 3\hat{\mathbf{j}} - \hat{\mathbf{k}}$$
and
$$\mathbf{B} = -6\hat{\mathbf{i}} + 9\hat{\mathbf{j}} + 3\hat{\mathbf{k}}$$

Then, the vectors are parallel, if $\mathbf{A} \times \mathbf{B} = 0$
$$\therefore \quad \mathbf{A} \times \mathbf{B} = \begin{vmatrix} \hat{\mathbf{i}} & \hat{\mathbf{j}} & \hat{\mathbf{k}} \\ 2 & -3 & -1 \\ -6 & 9 & 3 \end{vmatrix}$$
$$= \hat{\mathbf{i}}(-9 + 9) - \hat{\mathbf{j}}(6 - 6) + \hat{\mathbf{k}}(18 - 18) = 0$$

But $|\mathbf{A} \times \mathbf{B}| = 0$
or $AB \sin\theta = 0 \qquad [\because \mathbf{A} \neq 0 \text{ and } \mathbf{B} \neq 0]$
$\therefore \quad \sin\theta = 0 \text{ or } \theta = 0$
Hence, the vectors $\mathbf{A}$ and $\mathbf{B}$ are parallel.

LONG ANSWER Type II Questions

39. State with reasons, whether the following algebric operations with scalar and vector physical quantities are meaningful.
  (i) Adding any two scalars.
  (ii) Adding a scalar to a vector of the same dimensions.
  (iii) Multiplying any vector by any scalar.
  (iv) Multiplying any two scalars.
  (v) Adding any two vectors.
  (vi) Adding a component of a vector to the same vector. **[NCERT]**

Sol. (i) No, adding any two scalars is not meaningful because only the scalars of same dimensions i.e. having same unit can be added.

(ii) No, adding a scalar to a vector of the same dimensions is not meaningful because a scalar cannot be added to a vector.

(iii) Yes, multiplying any vector by any scalar is meaningful. When a vector is multiplied by a scalar, we get a vector, whose magnitude is equal to the product of magnitude of vector and the scalar and direction remains the same as the direction of the given vector.
e.g. A body of mass 4 kg is moving with a velocity 20 m/s towards East, then, product of velocity and mass gives the momentum of the body which is also a vector quantity.
$$\mathbf{p} = m\mathbf{v} = 4 \text{ kg} \times (20 \text{ m/s}) (\text{East}) = 80 \text{ kg-m/s, East}$$

(iv) Yes, multiplying any two scalars is meaningful. Density ρ and volume V both are scalar quantities. When density is multiplied by volume, then we get $\rho \times V = m$, mass of the body, which is a scalar quantity.

(v) No, adding any two vectors is not meaningful because only vectors of same dimensions i.e. having same unit can be added.

(vi) Yes, adding a component of a vector to the same vector is meaningful because both vectors are of same dimensions.

40. On an open ground, a motorist follows a track that turns to his left by an angle of 60° after every 500 m. Starting from a given turn, specify the displacement of the motorist at the third, sixth and eighth turn. Compare the magnitude of the displacement with the total path length covered by the motorist in each case.

> As motorist is taking turn to his left at an angle 60° after every 500 m, therefore, he is moving on a regular hexagon.

Sol. The distance after which motorist take a turn = 500 m
As motorist takes a turn at an angle of 60° each time, therefore motorist is moving on a regular hexagonal path. Let the motorist starts from point A and reaches at point D at the end of third turn and at initial point A at

the end of sixth turn and at point C at the end of eighth turn.

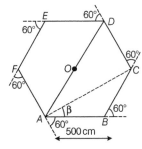

Displacement of the motorist at the third turn = AD

$$= AO + OD = 500 + 500 = 1000 \text{ m}$$

Total path length = $AB + BC + CD$

$$= 500 + 500 + 500 = 1500 \text{ m}$$

$$\therefore \quad \frac{\text{Magnitude of displacement}}{\text{Total path length}} = \frac{1000}{1500} = \frac{2}{3} = 0.67$$

At the sixth turn motorist is at the starting point A.

$\therefore$ Displacement of the motorist at the sixth turn = 0

Total path length = $AB + BC + CD + DE + EF + FA$

$$= 500 + 500 + 500 + 500 + 500 + 500 = 3000 \text{ m}$$

$$\therefore \quad \frac{\text{Magnitude of displacement}}{\text{Total path length}} = \frac{0}{3000} = 0$$

At the eighth turn, the motorist is at point C.

$\therefore$ Displacement of the motorist = AC

Using triangle law of vector addition,

$$AC = \sqrt{AB^2 + BC^2 + 2AB \cdot BC \cos 60°}$$

$$= \sqrt{(500)^2 + (500)^2 + 2 \times 500 \times 500 \times \frac{1}{2}}$$

$$= \sqrt{3 \times (500)^2} = 500\sqrt{3} \text{ m}$$

$$AC = 500 \times 1.732 \text{ m} = 866 \text{ m}$$

If it is inclined at an angle β from the direction of **AB**,

then $\tan\beta = \dfrac{500\sin 60°}{500 + 500\cos 60°} = \dfrac{500 \times \dfrac{\sqrt{3}}{2}}{500 + 500 \times \dfrac{1}{2}}$

$$= \dfrac{500 \times \dfrac{\sqrt{3}}{2}}{500\left(1 + \dfrac{1}{2}\right)} = \dfrac{\dfrac{\sqrt{3}}{2}}{\dfrac{3}{2}} = \dfrac{1}{\sqrt{3}} = \tan 30°$$

or $\beta = 30°$

$\therefore$ Displacement of the motorist at the end of eighth turn is 866 m making an angle 30° with the initial direction of motion.

Total path length = $8 \times 500 = 4000 \text{ m}$

$$\therefore \quad \frac{\text{Magnitude of displacement}}{\text{Total path length}} = \frac{500\sqrt{3}}{4000} = \frac{\sqrt{3}}{8} = 0.22$$

41. Establish the following inequalities geometrically or otherwise.

(i) $|\mathbf{A} + \mathbf{B}| \le |\mathbf{A}| + |\mathbf{B}|$ (ii) $|\mathbf{A} + \mathbf{B}| \ge ||\mathbf{A}| - |\mathbf{B}||$

(iii) $|\mathbf{A} - \mathbf{B}| \le |\mathbf{A}| + |\mathbf{B}|$ (iv) $|\mathbf{A} - \mathbf{B}| \ge ||\mathbf{A}| - |\mathbf{B}||$

When does the equality sign above apply?

[NCERT]

Sol. Consider two vectors **A** and **B** be represented by the sides **OP** and **OQ** of a parallelogram *OPSQ*. According to parallelogram law of vector addition, $(\mathbf{A} + \mathbf{B})$ will be represented by **OS** as shown in figure.

Thus, $OP = |\mathbf{A}|, \ OQ = PS = |\mathbf{B}|$

and $OS = |\mathbf{A} + \mathbf{B}|$

(i) To prove $|\mathbf{A} + \mathbf{B}| \le |\mathbf{A}| + |\mathbf{B}|$

We know that the length of one side of a triangle is always less than the sum of the lengths of the other two sides. Hence from Δ *OPS*, we have

$$OS < OP + PS$$

$\Rightarrow \quad OS < OP + OQ$

or $\quad |\mathbf{A} + \mathbf{B}| < |\mathbf{A}| + |\mathbf{B}|$ ...(i)

If the two vectors **A** and **B** are acting along the same straight line and in the same direction.

or $\quad |\mathbf{A} + \mathbf{B}| = |\mathbf{A}| + |\mathbf{B}|$ ...(ii)

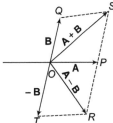

Combining the conditions mentioned in Eqs. (i) and (ii), we have $|\mathbf{A} + \mathbf{B}| \le |\mathbf{A}| + |\mathbf{B}|$

(ii) To prove $\quad |\mathbf{A} + \mathbf{B}| \ge ||\mathbf{A}| + |\mathbf{B}||$

From Δ *OPS*, we have

$$OS + PS > OP \text{ or } OS > |OP - PS|$$

or $\quad OS > |OP - OQ|$ ... (iii)

$$[\because PS = OQ]$$

The modulus of $(OP - PS)$ has been taken because the LHS is always positive but the RHS may be negative if $OP < PS$. Thus, from Eq. (iii) we have

$$|\mathbf{A} + \mathbf{B}| > ||\mathbf{A}| - |\mathbf{B}|| \quad \text{...(iv)}$$

If the two vectors **A** and **B** are acting along a straight line in opposite directions, then

$$|\mathbf{A} + \mathbf{B}| = ||\mathbf{A}| - |\mathbf{B}|| \quad \text{...(v)}$$

Combining the conditions mentioned in Eqs. (iv) and (v) we get $\quad |\mathbf{A} + \mathbf{B}| \ge ||\mathbf{A}| - |\mathbf{B}||$

(iii) To prove $|\mathbf{A} - \mathbf{B}| \le |\mathbf{A}| + |\mathbf{B}|$

In figure, $\mathbf{A} = (\mathbf{OP}), \ -\mathbf{B} = \mathbf{OT} = \mathbf{PR}$ and $(\mathbf{A} - \mathbf{B}) = \mathbf{OR}$

From $\triangle ORP$, we note that $OR < OP + PR$.

or $\qquad |\mathbf{A} - \mathbf{B}| < |\mathbf{A}| + |-\mathbf{B}|$

or $\qquad |\mathbf{A} - \mathbf{B}| < |\mathbf{A}| + |\mathbf{B}|$ ...(vi)

If the two vectors are acting along a straight line. But in the opposite direction, then

$$|\mathbf{A} - \mathbf{B}| = |\mathbf{A}| + |\mathbf{B}| \qquad \text{...(vii)}$$

Combining the conditions mentioned in Eqs. (vi) and (vii), we get $\quad |\mathbf{A} - \mathbf{B}| \le |\mathbf{A}| + |\mathbf{B}|$

(iv) To prove $\quad |\mathbf{A} - \mathbf{B}| \ge \big||\mathbf{A}| + |\mathbf{B}|\big|$

In figure from $\triangle\, OPR$, we note that $\qquad [\because OT = PR]$

$OR + PR > OP \quad$ or $\quad OR > |OP - PR|$

or $\qquad OR > |OP - OT|$ ...(viii)

The modulus of $(OP - OT)$ has been taken because LHS is positive and RHS may be negative if $OP < OT$. From Eq. (viii) , we have

$$|\mathbf{A} - \mathbf{B}| > \big||\mathbf{A}| - |\mathbf{B}|\big| \qquad \text{...(ix)}$$

If the two vectors $\mathbf{A}$ and $\mathbf{B}$ are acting along the same straight line in the same direction, then

$$|\mathbf{A} - \mathbf{B}| = |\mathbf{A}| - |\mathbf{B}| \qquad \text{...(x)}$$

Combining the conditions mentioned in Eqs. (ix) and (x), we get $\quad |\mathbf{A} - \mathbf{B}| \ge |\mathbf{A}| - |\mathbf{B}|$

42. $\hat{\mathbf{i}}$ and $\hat{\mathbf{j}}$ are unit vectors along X and Y-axes, respectively. What is the magnitude and direction of vectors $\hat{\mathbf{i}} + \hat{\mathbf{j}}$ and $\hat{\mathbf{i}} - \hat{\mathbf{j}}$? What are the components of a vector $A = 2\hat{\mathbf{i}} + 3\hat{\mathbf{j}}$ along the direction $\hat{\mathbf{i}} + \hat{\mathbf{j}}$ and $\hat{\mathbf{i}} - \hat{\mathbf{j}}$? (You may use graphical method).

The modulus of a vector $\mathbf{A} = A_x\hat{\mathbf{i}} + A_y\hat{\mathbf{j}}$ is given by $A = |\mathbf{A}| = \sqrt{A_x^2 + A_y^2}$. If vector is inclined at an angle θ, from x-axis, then $\tan\theta = \dfrac{A_y}{A_x}$

Sol. (i) Magnitude of $(\hat{\mathbf{i}} + \hat{\mathbf{j}}) = \sqrt{(1)^2 + (1)^2} = \sqrt{2}$

If vector $(\hat{\mathbf{i}} + \hat{\mathbf{j}})$ makes an angle θ, with the x-axis, then

$\tan\theta = \dfrac{A_y}{A_x} = \dfrac{1}{1} = 1 = \tan 45°$ or $\theta = 45°$

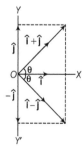

(ii) Magnitude of

$$(\hat{\mathbf{i}} - \hat{\mathbf{j}}) = \sqrt{(1)^2 + (-1)^2} = \sqrt{2}$$

If vector $(\hat{\mathbf{i}} - \hat{\mathbf{j}})$ makes an angle θ, with x-axis, then

$$\tan\theta = \dfrac{A_y}{A_x} = \dfrac{(-1)}{1} = -1$$

$$= -\tan 45° \Rightarrow \theta = -45° \text{ with } \hat{\mathbf{i}}$$

Hence, vector $(\hat{\mathbf{i}} - \hat{\mathbf{j}})$ makes an angle of $45°$ from x-axis in negative direction.

(iii) To determine the component of $\mathbf{A} = 2\hat{\mathbf{i}} + 3\hat{\mathbf{j}}$ in the direction of $(\hat{\mathbf{i}} + \hat{\mathbf{j}})$.

Let $\qquad \mathbf{B} = (\hat{\mathbf{i}} + \hat{\mathbf{j}})$

$$\mathbf{A} \cdot \mathbf{B} = AB\cos\theta = (A\cos\theta)\cdot B$$

or $\qquad A\cos\theta = \dfrac{\mathbf{A}\cdot\mathbf{B}}{B}$

$\therefore$ Magnitude of the component of $\mathbf{A}$ in the direction of

$$\mathbf{B} = A\cos\theta = \dfrac{\mathbf{A}\cdot\mathbf{B}}{B} = \dfrac{(2\hat{\mathbf{i}} + 3\hat{\mathbf{j}})\cdot(\hat{\mathbf{i}} + \hat{\mathbf{j}})}{\sqrt{(1)^2 + (1)^2}}$$

$$= \dfrac{2\hat{\mathbf{i}}\cdot\hat{\mathbf{i}} + 3\hat{\mathbf{j}}\cdot\hat{\mathbf{j}}}{\sqrt{2}}$$

$$= \dfrac{2 + 3}{\sqrt{2}} = \dfrac{5}{\sqrt{2}}$$

(iv) Unit vector along $(\hat{\mathbf{i}} + \hat{\mathbf{j}})$, $\hat{\mathbf{n}} = \dfrac{(\hat{\mathbf{i}} + \hat{\mathbf{j}})}{|\hat{\mathbf{i}} + \hat{\mathbf{j}}|} = \dfrac{(\hat{\mathbf{i}} + \hat{\mathbf{j}})}{\sqrt{2}}$

Component of $\mathbf{A}$ along $(\hat{\mathbf{i}} + \hat{\mathbf{j}})$

$= $ Magnitude of the component of $\mathbf{A}$ along $(\hat{\mathbf{i}} + \hat{\mathbf{j}})\cdot\hat{\mathbf{n}}$

$$= \dfrac{5}{\sqrt{2}}\cdot\dfrac{(\hat{\mathbf{i}} + \hat{\mathbf{j}})}{\sqrt{2}} = \dfrac{5}{2}(\hat{\mathbf{i}} + \hat{\mathbf{j}})$$

Magnitude of the component of $\mathbf{A}$ in the direction of

$$(\hat{\mathbf{i}} - \hat{\mathbf{j}}) = \dfrac{(2\hat{\mathbf{i}} + 3\hat{\mathbf{j}})\cdot(\hat{\mathbf{i}} - \hat{\mathbf{j}})}{|\hat{\mathbf{i}} - \hat{\mathbf{j}}|} = \dfrac{2\hat{\mathbf{i}}\cdot\hat{\mathbf{i}} - 3\hat{\mathbf{j}}\cdot\hat{\mathbf{j}}}{\sqrt{(1)^2 + (-1)^2}}$$

$$= \dfrac{2 - 3}{\sqrt{2}} = -\dfrac{1}{\sqrt{2}}$$

Unit vector along $(\hat{\mathbf{i}} - \hat{\mathbf{j}})$

$$\hat{\mathbf{n}} = \dfrac{(\hat{\mathbf{i}} - \hat{\mathbf{j}})}{|\hat{\mathbf{i}} - \hat{\mathbf{j}}|} = \dfrac{(\hat{\mathbf{i}} - \hat{\mathbf{j}})}{\sqrt{2}}$$

$\therefore$ Component of $\mathbf{A}$ along $(\hat{\mathbf{i}} - \hat{\mathbf{j}})$

$= $ Magnitude of the component of $\mathbf{A}$ along $(\hat{\mathbf{i}} - \hat{\mathbf{j}})\cdot\hat{\mathbf{n}}$

$$= -\dfrac{1}{\sqrt{2}}\cdot\dfrac{(\hat{\mathbf{i}} - \hat{\mathbf{j}})}{\sqrt{2}} = -\dfrac{1}{2}(\hat{\mathbf{i}} - \hat{\mathbf{j}})$$

ASSESS YOUR TOPICAL UNDERSTANDING

OBJECTIVE Type Questions

1. Choose the correct option(s).
   (a) To represent two-dimensional motion we need vectors
   (b) To represent one-dimensional motion we use positive and negative signs
   (c) To represent 3-dimensional motion we need vectors
   (d) All (a), (b) and (c)

2. $|\lambda \mathbf{A}| = \lambda |\mathbf{A}|$, if
   (a) $\lambda > 0$
   (b) $\lambda < 0$
   (c) $\lambda = 0$
   (d) $\lambda \neq 0$

3. If $\mathbf{A}$ is a vector with magnitude $|\mathbf{A}|$, then the unit vector $\hat{a}$ in the direction of vector $\mathbf{A}$ is
   (a) $A\,\mathbf{A}$
   (b) $\mathbf{A} \cdot \mathbf{A}$
   (c) $\mathbf{A} \times \mathbf{A}$
   (d) $\dfrac{\mathbf{A}}{|\mathbf{A}|}$

4. Given, $|\mathbf{A} + \mathbf{B}| = P$, $|\mathbf{A} - \mathbf{B}| = Q$. The value of $P^2 + Q^2$ is
   (a) $2(A^2 + B^2)$
   (b) $A^2 - B^2$
   (c) $A^2 + B^2$
   (d) $2(A^2 - B^2)$

5. Choose the correct option regarding the given figure.

   (a) $\mathbf{B} = \mathbf{A}$
   (b) $\mathbf{B} = -\mathbf{A}$
   (c) $|\mathbf{B}| = |\mathbf{A}|$
   (d) $|\mathbf{B}| \neq |\mathbf{A}|$

Answer
1. (d) | 2. (a) | 3. (d) | 4. (a) | 5. (d)

VERY SHORT ANSWER Type Questions

6. How is a vector represented?

7. What is a zero vector? Explain the need of a zero vector.

8. State parallelogram law of vector addition. Show that the resultant of two vectors A and B inclined at an angle θ is
$$R = \sqrt{A^2 + B^2 + 2AB \cos \theta}.$$

9. Is the working of a sling based on the parallelogram law of vector addition, why?

SHORT ANSWER Type Questions

10. A vector $\mathbf{A}$ of magnitude A is turned through an angle α. Calculate the change in the magnitude of vector.

    [**Ans.** $2A \sin \alpha/2$]

11. A hiker begins a trip by walking 25.0 km South-East from her base camp. On the second day she walks 40.0 km in direction 60.0° North to East, at which point she discovers a forest ranger's tower?
    (i) Determine the component of the hiker's displacements in the first and second days.
    (ii) Determine the component of the hiker's total displacement for the trip.
    (iii) Find the magnitude and direction of the displacement from base camp.

    [**Ans.** (i) $A_x = 17.7$ km, $A_y = -17.7$ km, $B_x = 20.0$ km, $B_y = 34.6$ km
    (ii) $R_x = 37.7$ km, $R_y = 16.9$ km,
    (iii) $R = 41.3$ km and $\theta = 24.1°$]

12. Is $\mathbf{A} + \mathbf{B}$ and $\mathbf{A} - \mathbf{B}$ lie in the same plane?

LONG ANSWER Type I Questions

13. Is finite rotation of a vector?

14. Find the angle made by vector, $\mathbf{A} = 2\hat{\mathbf{i}} + 2\hat{\mathbf{j}}$ with X-axis.

    [**Ans.** $\theta = 45°$]

15. It is easier to pull than to push a lawn roller. Why? [2]

16. Determine a unit vector which is perpendicular to both $\mathbf{A} = 2\hat{\mathbf{i}} + \hat{\mathbf{j}} + \hat{\mathbf{k}}$ and $\mathbf{B} = \hat{\mathbf{i}} - \hat{\mathbf{j}} + \hat{\mathbf{k}}$

    $\left[\textbf{Ans.} \dfrac{3\hat{\mathbf{i}} - 3\hat{\mathbf{j}} - 3\hat{\mathbf{k}}}{\sqrt{27}}\right]$

LONG ANSWER Type II Questions

17. A car is moving along a straight road with a uniform speed v. At a certain time, it is at a point Q-marked on the road. Suppose point O is taken as a fixed point, then show that $\mathbf{OQ} \times \mathbf{v}$ is independent of the position Q.

18. If $\mathbf{A}$ and $\mathbf{B}$ are two vectors such that $|\mathbf{A} \times \mathbf{B}| = \sqrt{3}\ \mathbf{A} \cdot \mathbf{B}$. Then,
    (i) Find the angle θ between $\mathbf{A}$ and $\mathbf{B}$
    (ii) Also, find the value of $|\mathbf{A} \times \mathbf{B}|$.

    [**Ans.** (i) 60°, (ii) $\sqrt{A^2 + B^2 + AB}$]

|TOPIC 2|
Motion in a Plane

Here, we will discuss how to describe motion of an object in two dimensions using vectors.

POSITION, DISPLACEMENT AND VELOCITY VECTORS

Position Vector

A vector that extends from a reference point to the point at which particle is located is called **position vector**.

Let r be the position vector of a particle P located in a plane with reference to the origin O in xy-plane as shown in figure.

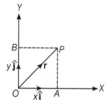

Representation of position vector

$$OP = OA + OB$$

$$\boxed{\text{Position vector, } \mathbf{r} = x\hat{\mathbf{i}} + y\hat{\mathbf{j}}}$$

In three dimensions, the position vector is represented as

$$r = x\hat{\mathbf{i}} + y\hat{\mathbf{j}} + z\hat{\mathbf{k}}$$

Displacement

Consider a particle moving in xy-plane with a uniform velocity $\mathbf{v}$, Suppose O is the origin for measuring time and position of the particle. Let, the particle be at position A at time t_1 and at position B at time t_2, respectively. The position vectors are $\mathbf{OA} = \mathbf{r}_1$ and $\mathbf{OB} = \mathbf{r}_2$.

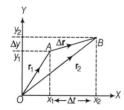

Representation of displacement vector

Then, the displacement of the particle in time interval $(t_2 - t_1)$ is $\mathbf{AB}$. From triangle law of vector addition, we have

$$\mathbf{OA} + \mathbf{AB} = \mathbf{OB} \Rightarrow \mathbf{AB} = \mathbf{OB} - \mathbf{OA}$$

$$\mathbf{AB} = \mathbf{r}_2 - \mathbf{r}_1 \qquad \dots \text{(i)}$$

If the position coordinates of the particle at points A and B are (x_1, y_1) and (x_2, y_2), then

$$\therefore \qquad \mathbf{r}_1 = x_1\hat{\mathbf{i}} + y_1\hat{\mathbf{j}}$$

and $$\mathbf{r}_2 = x_2\hat{\mathbf{i}} + y_2\hat{\mathbf{j}}$$

Substituting the values of $\mathbf{r}_1$ and $\mathbf{r}_2$ in Eq. (i), we have

$$\mathbf{AB} = (x_2\hat{\mathbf{i}} + y_2\hat{\mathbf{j}}) - (x_1\hat{\mathbf{i}} + y_1\hat{\mathbf{j}})$$

$$\boxed{\text{Displacement, } \mathbf{AB} = (x_2 - x_1)\,\hat{\mathbf{i}} + (y_2 - y_1)\,\hat{\mathbf{j}}}$$

Similarly, in three dimensions the displacement can be represented as

$$\Delta\mathbf{r} = (x_2 - x_1)\,\hat{\mathbf{i}} + (y_2 - y_1)\hat{\mathbf{j}} + (z_2 - z_1)\,\hat{\mathbf{k}}$$

Velocity

The rate of change of displacement of an object in a particular direction is called its velocity.

It is of two types

Average Velocity

It is defined as the ratio of the displacement and the corresponding time interval.

Thus, average velocity $= \dfrac{\text{displacement}}{\text{time taken}}$

$$\boxed{\text{Average velocity, } \mathbf{v}_{av} = \frac{\Delta\mathbf{r}}{\Delta t} = \frac{\mathbf{r}_2 - \mathbf{r}_1}{t_2 - t_1}}$$

Velocity can be expressed in the component form as

$$\mathbf{v}_{av} = \frac{\Delta x}{\Delta t}\hat{\mathbf{i}} + \frac{\Delta y}{\Delta t}\hat{\mathbf{j}}$$

$$= v_x\hat{\mathbf{i}} + v_y\hat{\mathbf{j}}$$

where, v_x and v_y are the components of velocity along x-direction and y-direction, respectively.

The magnitude of $\mathbf{v}_{av}$ is given by $\mathbf{v}_{av} = \sqrt{v_x^2 + v_y^2}$

and the direction of $\mathbf{v}_{av}$ is given by angle θ

$$\tan\theta = \frac{v_y}{v_x}$$

$$\Rightarrow \boxed{\text{Direction of average velocity, } \theta = \tan^{-1}\left(\frac{v_y}{v_x}\right)}$$

EXAMPLE |1| Average Velocity of Train

A train is moving with a velocity of 30 km/h due East and a car is moving with a velocity of 40 km/h due North. What is the velocity of car as appear to a passenger in the train?

Sol. Given, $\mathbf{v}_T = 30$ km/h due East

$\quad\quad \mathbf{v}_C = 40$ km/h due North

$\quad\quad \mathbf{v}_{CT} = ?, \theta = ?$

According to question,

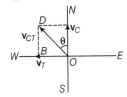

In the figure,

$$\mathbf{v}_{CT} = OD = \sqrt{OB^2 + BD^2} = \sqrt{v_T^2 + v_C^2}$$

Then, $v_{CT} = \sqrt{(30)^2 + (40)^2} = \sqrt{900 + 1600} = 50$ km/h

$$\tan \theta = \frac{BD}{OD} = \frac{v_C}{v_T} \Rightarrow \tan\theta = \frac{30}{40}$$

$$\theta = \tan^{-1}\left(\frac{30}{40}\right) = 36°52' \text{ West of North}$$

Instantaneous Velocity

The velocity at an instant of time (t) is known as **instantaneous velocity**.

The average velocity will become instantaneous, if Δt approaches to zero. The instantaneous velocity is expressed as

$$\boxed{\text{Instantaneous velocity, } \mathbf{v}_i = \lim_{\Delta t \to 0} \frac{\Delta \mathbf{r}}{\Delta t} = \frac{d\mathbf{r}}{dt}}$$

The limiting process can be easily understood with the help of figure.

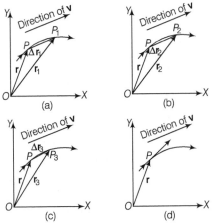

Limiting processes of instantaneous velocity

In the above figure, the curve represents the path of an object. The object is at point P on the path at time t. P_1, P_2 and P_3 are the positions of the object after time intervals $\Delta t_1, \Delta t_2$ and Δt_3, where $\Delta t_1 > \Delta t_2 > \Delta t_3$.

As the time interval Δt approaches zero, the average velocity approaches the velocity $\mathbf{v}$. The direction of $\mathbf{v}$ is parallel to the line tangent to the path.

Note

The direction of instantaneous velocity at any point on the path of an object is tangential to the path at that point and is in the direction of motion.

EXAMPLE |2| Instantaneous Velocity of a Particle

A particle starts from origin at $t = 0$ with a velocity $5\hat{\mathbf{i}}$ m/s and moves in xy-plane under action of a force which produces a constant acceleration of $(3\hat{\mathbf{i}} + 2\hat{\mathbf{j}})$ m/s^2.

(i) What is the y-coordinate of the particle at the instant its x-coordinate is 84 m?

(ii) What is the speed of the particle at this time?

[NCERT]

Sol. (i) Given, $v_0 = 5\hat{\mathbf{i}}$ m/s, $a = 3\hat{\mathbf{i}} + 2\hat{\mathbf{j}}$ m/s^2

(i) $y(t) = ?$, $x(t) = 84$ m   (ii) Speed $v = ?$

Then, $y(t) = v_0 t + \frac{1}{2} at^2$ and $v = \sqrt{v_x^2 + v_y^2}$

$$y(t) = 5\hat{\mathbf{i}} t + \frac{1}{2}(3\hat{\mathbf{i}} + 2\hat{\mathbf{j}}) t^2$$

$$= \left(5t + \frac{3}{2}t^2\right)\hat{\mathbf{i}} + t^2\hat{\mathbf{j}}$$

On comparing, $x(t) = 5t + \frac{3}{2}t^2$

$\Rightarrow \quad\quad\quad y(t) = 1t^2$

(ii) The speed of the particle can be find by differentiating the position vector w.r.t. time.

If $x(t) = 84$ m, then $t = 6$ s

$\therefore \quad y(6) = 36$ m

$$v = \frac{dy}{dt} = \frac{d(5t + \frac{3}{2}t^2)\hat{\mathbf{i}} + t^2\hat{\mathbf{j}}}{dt} = (5 + 3t)\hat{\mathbf{i}} + 2t\hat{\mathbf{j}}$$

At $\quad t = 6$s, $v = 23\hat{\mathbf{i}} + 12\hat{\mathbf{j}}$

$\therefore \quad\quad v = \sqrt{(23)^2 + (12)^2} = 26$ m/s

Acceleration

It is defined as the ratio of change in velocity and the corresponding time interval. It can be expressed as

$$\text{Acceleration, } \mathbf{a} = \frac{\text{Change in velocity}}{\text{Time taken}} = \frac{\Delta \mathbf{v}}{\Delta t}$$

$$\boxed{\text{Acceleration, } \mathbf{a} = \frac{\mathbf{v}_2 - \mathbf{v}_1}{t_2 - t_1}}$$

Average Acceleration

It is defined as the change in velocity $(\Delta \mathbf{v})$ divided by the corresponding time interval (Δt). It can be expressed as

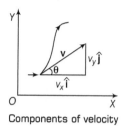

Components of velocity

Average acceleration, $\mathbf{a}_{av} = \dfrac{\Delta \mathbf{v}}{\Delta t} = \dfrac{\Delta v_x \hat{\mathbf{i}} + \Delta v_y \hat{\mathbf{j}}}{\Delta t}$

$= \dfrac{\Delta v_x}{\Delta t} \hat{\mathbf{i}} + \dfrac{\Delta v_y}{\Delta t} \hat{\mathbf{j}}$

$$\boxed{\text{Average acceleration, } \mathbf{a}_{av} = a_x \hat{\mathbf{i}} + a_y \hat{\mathbf{j}}}$$

Which is expressed in component form.

In terms of x and y, a_x and a_y can be expressed as

$$a_x = \dfrac{d}{dt}\left(\dfrac{dx}{dt}\right) = \dfrac{d^2 x}{dt^2} \quad \text{and} \quad a_y = \dfrac{d}{dt}\left(\dfrac{dy}{dt}\right) = \dfrac{d^2 y}{dt^2}$$

EXAMPLE |3| Average Acceleration of Particle

A particle is moving Eastwards with a velocity of 5 m/s in 10 second, the velocity changes to 5 m/s Northwards. Find the average accelaration of the particle in this time interval.

Sol.

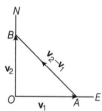

According to triangle law of vector addition,

$$\mathbf{OA} + \mathbf{AB} = \mathbf{OB}$$
$$\mathbf{AB} = \mathbf{OB} - \mathbf{OA} = \mathbf{v}_2 - \mathbf{v}_1$$
$$= \text{Change in velocity}$$

$\therefore \qquad |\mathbf{v}_2 - \mathbf{v}_1| = AB = \sqrt{(\mathbf{OA})^2 + (\mathbf{OB})^2}$

$$= \sqrt{(5)^2 + (5)^2} = 5\sqrt{2} \text{ m/s}$$

Hence, average acceleration $= \dfrac{|\mathbf{v}_2 - \mathbf{v}_1|}{t}$

$$= \dfrac{5\sqrt{2}}{10} = \dfrac{1}{\sqrt{2}} \text{ m/s}^2$$

Along North-West direction.

Instantaneous Acceleration

It is defined as the limiting value of the average acceleration as the time interval approaches to zero.

It can be expressed as

$$\mathbf{a}_i = \lim_{\Delta t \to 0} \dfrac{\Delta \mathbf{v}}{\Delta t} = \dfrac{d\mathbf{v}}{dt}$$

$$\boxed{\text{Instantaneous acceleration, } \mathbf{a}_i = a_x \hat{\mathbf{i}} + a_y \hat{\mathbf{j}}}$$

where, $a_x = \dfrac{dv_x}{dt}, a_y = \dfrac{dv_y}{dt}$

The magnitude of instantaneous acceleration is given by

$$a_i = \sqrt{a_x^2 + a_y^2}$$

The limiting process can be easily understood with the help of figure.

The object is at point P at time t. P_1, P_2 and P_3 represent the positions of the object after time intervals $\Delta t_1, \Delta t_2$ and Δt_3, respectively. The time interval at the different positions in such way that $\Delta t_1 > \Delta t_2 > \Delta t_3$.

The velocity vectors at points P, P_1, P_2 and P_3 are also shown in figures.

In each case of Δt, the change in velocity $\Delta \mathbf{v}$ is obtained by using triangle law of vector addition. The direction of the average acceleration is also shown as parallel to $\Delta \mathbf{v}$.

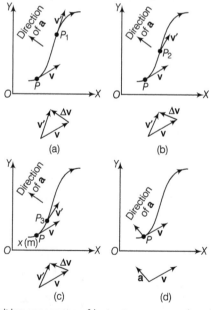

Limiting processes of instantaneous acceleration

The average acceleration for three intervals (a) Δt_1, (b) Δt_2 and (c) Δt_3, $(\Delta t_1 > \Delta t_2 > \Delta t_3)$. (d) In the limit $\Delta t \to 0$, the average acceleration becomes the instantaneous acceleration called simply **acceleration**.

From the given figures, it can be evaluated as the time interval Δt decreases from (a) to (d), the direction of $\Delta \mathbf{v}$ and hence that of **a** changes. In Fig. (d), the time interval $\Delta t \rightarrow 0$, hence, the average acceleration becomes the instantaneous acceleration having direction as shown in figure.

Note

In two or three-dimensions, velocity and acceleration vectors can have any angle between 0° to 180° whereas in one dimension, the velocity and acceleration of an object are always along the same straight line (may be in same direction or in opposite direction).

EXAMPLE |4| Position Vector

The position of a particle is given by
$$\mathbf{r} = 3.0\,t\,\hat{\mathbf{i}} + 2.0\,t^2\hat{\mathbf{j}} + 5.0\,\hat{\mathbf{k}}$$
where, t is in seconds and the coefficients have the proper units for $\mathbf{r}$ to be in metres.

(i) Find $v(t)$ and $a(t)$ of the particles.

(ii) Find the magnitude and direction of $v(t)$ at $t = 2.0$ s.

[NCERT]

Sol. Position of particle, $\mathbf{r} = 3.0\,t\,\hat{\mathbf{i}} + 2.0\,t^2\hat{\mathbf{j}} + 5.0\,\hat{\mathbf{k}}$

(i) $v(t) = ?$ and $a(t) = ?$

(ii) $v(t) = ?$, if $t = 1.0$ s, $\theta = ?$

(i) $\mathbf{v}(t) = \dfrac{d\mathbf{r}}{dt} = \dfrac{d}{dt}(3.0\,t\,\hat{\mathbf{i}} + 2.0t^2\,\hat{\mathbf{j}} + 5.0\,\hat{\mathbf{k}})$

$= 3.0\,\hat{\mathbf{i}} + 4.0t\,\hat{\mathbf{j}}$

$\mathbf{a}(t) = \dfrac{d\mathbf{v}}{dt} = -4.0\,\hat{\mathbf{j}}\ \text{ms}^{-2}$

(ii) At $t = 2.0$ s

$\mathbf{v}(t) = 3.0\,\hat{\mathbf{i}} - 8.0\,\hat{\mathbf{j}}$

$v = \sqrt{v_x^2 + v_y^2} = \sqrt{(3.0)^2 + (-8)^2} = \sqrt{73} = 8.54\ \text{ms}^{-2}$

$\theta = \tan^{-1}\left(\dfrac{v_y}{v_x}\right)\tan^{-1}\left(\dfrac{8}{3}\right) = -2.667 = -\tan 69.5°$

$\theta = 69.5°$ below X-axis

Motion in a Plane with Uniform Velocity

A body is said to be moving with uniform velocity, if it suffers equal displacements in equal intervals of time, however small. Consider an object moving with uniform velocity $\mathbf{v}$ in xy-plane. Let $\mathbf{r}(0)$ and $\mathbf{r}(t)$ be its position vectors at $t = 0$ and $t = t$, respectively.

Then, $\quad \mathbf{v} = \dfrac{\mathbf{r}(t) - \mathbf{r}(0)}{t - 0} \Rightarrow \mathbf{r}(t) = \mathbf{r}(0) + \mathbf{v}t \quad$ ...(i)

In terms of rectangular coordinates, we get

$$\mathbf{v} = v_x\hat{\mathbf{i}} + v_y\hat{\mathbf{j}}, \quad v = \sqrt{v_x^2 + v_y^2}$$

$$\mathbf{r}(0) = x(0)\hat{\mathbf{i}} + y(0)\hat{\mathbf{j}} \quad \text{and} \quad \mathbf{r}(t) = x(t)\hat{\mathbf{i}} + y(t)\hat{\mathbf{j}}$$

On substituting these values in Eq. (i), we have

$$x(t)\hat{\mathbf{i}} + y(t)\hat{\mathbf{j}} = x(0)\hat{\mathbf{i}} + y(0)\hat{\mathbf{j}} + (v_x\hat{\mathbf{i}} + v_y\hat{\mathbf{j}})t$$

$$x(t)\hat{\mathbf{i}} + y(t)\hat{\mathbf{j}} = [x(0) + v_x t]\hat{\mathbf{i}} + [y(0) + v_y t]\hat{\mathbf{j}}\ \text{...(ii)}$$

By equating the coefficients of $\hat{\mathbf{i}}$ and $\hat{\mathbf{j}}$, we have

$$x(t) = x(0) + v_x t \quad \text{and} \quad y(t) = y(0) + v_y t$$

These two equations represent uniform motion along X-axis and Y-axis, respectively.

Eq. (ii) shows that the uniform motion in two dimensions can be expressed as the sum of two uniform motions along two mutually perpendicular directions.

Motion in a Plane with Constant Acceleration

A body is said to be moving with uniform acceleration, if its velocity vector suffers the same change in the same interval of time, however small.

Let an object is moving in xy-plane and its acceleration **a** is constant. At time $t = 0$, the velocity of an object be $\mathbf{v}_0$ (say) and $\mathbf{v}$ be the velocity at time t.

According to definition of average acceleration, we have

$$\mathbf{a} = \dfrac{\mathbf{v} - \mathbf{v}_0}{t - 0} = \dfrac{\mathbf{v} - \mathbf{v}_0}{t}$$

$\Rightarrow \qquad \boxed{\mathbf{v} = \mathbf{v}_0 + \mathbf{a}t}$

In terms of rectangular components, we can express it as

$$v_x = v_{ox} + a_x t \text{ and } v_y = v_{oy} + a_y t$$

It can be concluded that each rectangular component of velocity of an object moving with uniform acceleration in a plane depends upon time as, if it were the velocity vector of one-dimensional uniformly accelerated motion.

Now, we can also find the position vector ($\mathbf{r}$). Let $\mathbf{r}_0$ and $\mathbf{r}$ be the position vectors of the particle at time $t = 0$ and $t = t$ and their velocities at these instants be $\mathbf{v}_0$ and $\mathbf{v}$. Then, the average velocity is given by

$$\mathbf{v}_{av} = \dfrac{\mathbf{v}_0 + \mathbf{v}}{2}$$

Displacement is the product of average velocity and time interval. It is expressed as

$$\mathbf{r} - \mathbf{r}_0 = \left(\dfrac{\mathbf{v} + \mathbf{v}_0}{2}\right)t = \left[\dfrac{(\mathbf{v}_0 + \mathbf{a}t) + \mathbf{v}_0}{2}\right]t$$

$\Rightarrow \qquad \mathbf{r} - \mathbf{r}_0 = \mathbf{v}_0 t + \dfrac{1}{2}\mathbf{a}t^2$

$\Rightarrow \qquad \boxed{\mathbf{r} = \mathbf{r}_0 + \mathbf{v}_0 t + \dfrac{1}{2}\mathbf{a}t^2}$

In terms of rectangular components, we have

$$x\hat{\mathbf{i}} + y\hat{\mathbf{j}} = x_0\hat{\mathbf{i}} + y_0\hat{\mathbf{j}} + (v_{0x}\hat{\mathbf{i}} + v_{0y}\hat{\mathbf{j}})t + \frac{1}{2}(a_x\hat{\mathbf{i}} + a_y\hat{\mathbf{j}})t^2$$

Now, equating the coefficients of $\hat{\mathbf{i}}$ and $\hat{\mathbf{j}}$,

$$x = x_0 + v_{0x}t + \frac{1}{2}a_x t^2$$

$$y = y_0 + v_{0y}t + \frac{1}{2}a_y t^2$$

Note

Motion in a plane (two-dimensional motion) can be treated as two separate simultaneous one-dimensional motions with constant acceleration along two perpendicular directions.

EXAMPLE |5| Particle Starts from Origin

A particle starts from origin at $t = 0$ with a velocity $15\,\hat{\mathbf{i}}$ m/s and moves in xy-plane under the action of a force which produces a constant acceleration of $15\hat{\mathbf{i}} + 10\hat{\mathbf{j}}$ m/s^2. Find the y-coordinate of the particle at the instant. Its x-coordinate is 125 m.

Sol. The position of the particle is given by

$$r(t) = v_0 t + \frac{1}{2}at^2 = 15\hat{\mathbf{i}}t + \frac{1}{2}(15\hat{\mathbf{i}} + 10\hat{\mathbf{j}})t^2$$

$$= (15t + 7.5t^2)\hat{\mathbf{i}} + 5\hat{\mathbf{j}}t^2$$

$$\therefore \quad x(t) = 15t + 7.5t^2 \implies y(t) = 5t^2$$

If $\quad x(t) = 125$ m, $t = ?$

$$125 = 15t + 7.5t^2 \implies 1.5t^2 + 3t - 25 = 0$$

$$t = 3.2\,\text{s}$$

$$\therefore \quad y(t) = 5 \times (3.2)^2 = 51.2\,\text{m}$$

PROJECTILE MOTION

Projectile motion is a form of motion in which an object or particle is thrown with some initial velocity near the earth's surface and it moves along a curved path under the action of gravity alone. The path followed by a projectile is called its **trajectory**.

An object that is in flight after being thrown is called projectile.

    (i) A tennis ball or a baseball in a flight.

    (ii) A bullet fired from a rifle.

    (iii) A body dropped from the window of a moving train.

    (iv) A jet of water flowing from a hole near the bottom of water tank.

    (v) A javelin thrown by an athlete.

Assumptions before the Study of Projectile Motion

    (i) There is no frictional resistance of air.

    (ii) The effect due to rotation of earth and the curvature of the earth is negligible.

    (iii) The acceleration due to gravity is constant both in magnitude and direction, at all points during the motion of projectile.

Mathematical Analysis of Projectile Motion

Let OX be a horizontal line on the ground, OY be a vertical line perpendicular to ground and O be the origin for XY-axes on a plane. Suppose an object is projected from point O with velocity (u), making an angle (θ) with the horizontal direction OX, such that $x_0 = 0$ and $y_0 = 0$ when $t = 0$.

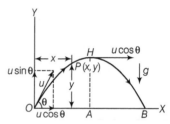

A projectile motion

While resolving velocity (u) into two components, we get (a) $u\cos\theta$ along OX and (b) $u\sin\theta$ along OY

As the horizontal component of velocity $(u\cos\theta)$ is constant throughout the motion, so there is a constant acceleration and hence force is in the horizontal direction, if air resistance is assumed to be zero. As the vertical components of velocity $(u\sin\theta)$ decreases continuously with height, from O to H, due to downward force of gravity and becomes zero.

At point H, the object has only horizontal component velocity $(u\cos\theta)$. It attains a maximum height at AH. OB is the maximum horizontal range.

Note

The horizontal and vertical components of projectile motion was stated by Galileo.

Equation of Path of a Projectile

Suppose at any time t_1, the object reaches at point $P(x, y)$.

So, x = horizontal distance travelled by object in time t.

y = vertical distance travelled by object in time t.

Motion Along Horizontal Direction (OX)

The velocity of an object in horizontal direction i.e. OX is constant, so the acceleration a_x in horizontal direction is zero.

$\therefore$ Position of the object at time t along horizontal direction is given by $x = x_0 + u_x t + \frac{1}{2} a_x t^2$

But $x_0 = 0, u_x = u \cos\theta, a_x = 0$ and $t = t$

$\therefore \qquad\qquad x = u \cos\theta \, t$

$\Rightarrow \qquad \boxed{\text{Time, } t = \dfrac{x}{u \cos\theta}} \qquad \dots \text{(i)}$

Motion Along Vertical Direction (OY)

The vertical velocity of the object is decreasing from O to H due to gravity, so acceleration a_y is g.

$\therefore$ Position of the object at any time t along the vertical direction i.e. OY is given by

$$y = y_0 + u_y t + \frac{1}{2} a_y t^2$$

But $\quad y_0 = 0, u_y = u \sin\theta, a_y = -g$

and $\qquad t = t$

So, $\qquad y = u \sin\theta \, t + \frac{1}{2}(-g) t^2$

$$= u \sin\theta \, t - \frac{1}{2} g t^2 \qquad \dots \text{(ii)}$$

Substituting the value of t from Eq. (i) in Eq. (ii), we get

$$y = u \sin\theta \left(\frac{x}{u \cos\theta}\right) - \frac{1}{2} g \left(\frac{x}{u \cos\theta}\right)^2$$

$$= x \tan\theta - \frac{1}{2} g \left(\frac{x}{u \cos\theta}\right)^2$$

$$\boxed{\text{Total vertical distance, } y = x \tan\theta - \left(\frac{1}{2} \frac{g}{u^2 \cos^2\theta}\right) x^2}$$

This equation represents a parabola and is known as equation of trajectory of a projectile..

Note
The path of a projectile projected at some angle with the horizontal (i.e. ground) is a parabolic path.

Time of Flight

It is defined as the total time for which projectile is in flight i.e. time during the motion of projectile from O to B. It is denoted by T.

Total time of flight consists of two parts such as

(a) Time taken by an object to go from point O to H. It is also known as **time of ascent** (t).

(b) Time taken by an object to go from point H to B. It is also known as **time of descent** (t).

Total time can be expressed as

$$T = t + t = 2t \implies t = \frac{T}{2}$$

The vertical component of velocity of object becomes zero at the highest point H.

Let us consider vertical upward motion of an object from O to H, we have

$$u_y = u \sin\theta, \, a_y = -g, t = \frac{T}{2} \text{ and } v_y = 0$$

Since, $\quad v_y = u_y + a_y t \implies 0 = u \sin\theta - g \frac{T}{2}$

$$\boxed{\text{Total time of flight, } T = \frac{2 u \sin\theta}{g}}$$

Note
For a projectile, time of ascent equals time of descent.

Maximum Height of a Projectile

It is defined as the maximum vertical height attained by an object above the point of projection during its flight. It is denoted by H.

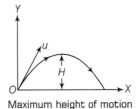

Maximum height of motion

Let us consider the vertical upward motion of the object from O to H.

We have,

$$u_y = u \sin\theta, \, a_y = -g, y_0 = 0, y = H, t = \frac{T}{2} = \frac{u \sin\theta}{g},$$

Using this relation, $\quad y = y_0 + u_y t + \frac{1}{2} a_y t^2$

We have, $H = 0 + u \sin\theta \, \dfrac{u \sin\theta}{g} + \dfrac{1}{2}(-g)\left(\dfrac{u \sin\theta}{g}\right)^2$

$$= \frac{u^2}{g} \sin^2\theta - \frac{1}{2} \frac{u^2 \sin^2\theta}{g}$$

$$\boxed{\text{Maximum height, } H = \frac{u^2 \sin^2\theta}{2g}}$$

Horizontal Range of a Projectile

The horizontal range of the projectile is defined as the horizontal distance covered by the projectile during its time of flight. It is denoted by R.

If the object having uniform velocity $u\cos\theta$ (i.e. horizontal component) and the total time of flight T, then the horizontal range covered by the objective.

$$\therefore \quad R = u\cos\theta \times T = u\cos\theta \times 2u\frac{\sin\theta}{g}$$

$$= \frac{u^2}{g} 2\sin\theta\cos\theta$$

$$\boxed{\text{Horizontal range, } R = \frac{u^2\sin 2\theta}{g}}$$

$$[\because \sin 2\theta = 2\sin\theta\cos\theta]$$

The horizontal range will be maximum, if

$$\sin 2\theta = \text{maximum} = 1$$
$$\sin 2\theta = \sin 90° \text{ or } \theta = 45°$$

$$\therefore \quad \boxed{\text{Maximum horizontal range, } R_m = \frac{u^2}{g}}$$

EXAMPLE |6| Motions of a Soccer Ball

A soccer player kicks a ball at an angle of 30° with an initial speed of 20 m/s. Assuming that the ball travels in a vertical plane. Calculate (i) the time at which the ball reaches the highest point, (ii) the maximum height reached, (iii) the horizontal range of the ball and (iv) the time for which the ball is in the air. $g = 10 \text{ m/s}^2$.

Sol. Given, $\theta = 30°, u = 20$ m/s, $g = 10$ m/s^2

(i) $t = ?$ (ii) $H = ?$
(iii) $R = ?$ (iv) $T = ?$

(i) $t = \dfrac{T}{2} = \dfrac{u\sin\theta}{g} = \dfrac{20 \times \sin 30°}{10} = 2 \times \dfrac{1}{2} = 1$ s

(ii) $H = \dfrac{u^2\sin^2\theta}{2g} = \dfrac{(20)^2 \times \sin^2 30°}{2 \times 10} = 5$ m

(iii) $R = \dfrac{u^2\sin 2\theta}{g} = \dfrac{(20)^2 \times \sin 2 \times 30°}{10} = 34.64$ m

(iv) $T = \dfrac{2u\sin\theta}{g} = \dfrac{2 \times 20 \times \sin 30°}{10} = 2$ s

EXAMPLE |7| A Pace Bowler

A cricket ball is thrown at a speed of 28 ms^{-1} in a direction 30° above the horizontal. Calculate

(i) the maximum height
(ii) the time taken by the ball to return to the same level and
(iii) the distance from the thrower to the point where the ball returns to the same level. **[NCERT]**

Sol. (i) The maximum height attained by the ball is

$$H_m = \frac{(v_0\sin\theta_0)^2}{2g}$$

$$= \frac{(28\sin 30°)^2}{2(9.8)} = \frac{14 \times 14}{2 \times 9.8} = 10.0 \text{ m}$$

(ii) The time taken by the ball to return the same level is

$$T = (2v_0\sin\theta_0)/g = (2 \times 28 \times \sin 30°)/9.8$$

$$= 28/9.8 = 2.9 \text{ s}$$

(iii) The distance from the thrower to the point where the ball returns to the same level is

$$R = \frac{(v_0^2\sin 2\theta_0)}{g} = \frac{28 \times 28 \times \sin 60°}{9.8} = 69 \text{ m}$$

Projectile Fired at an Angle with the Vertical

Let a particle be projected vertically with an angle θ with vertical and its muzzle speed (i.e. speed of projection) is u. The projectile has two components of its velocity at all the points during its motion.

The components are along X-axis (horizontal) and along Y-axis (vertical). Clearly, the angle made by the velocity of projectile at point of projection is $(90° - \theta)$ with the horizontal. In this case

(i) Time of flight $= \dfrac{2u\sin(90° - \theta)}{g} = \dfrac{2u}{g}\cos\theta$

(ii) Maximum height $= \dfrac{u^2\sin^2(90° - \theta)}{2g}$

$$= \frac{u^2\cos^2\theta}{2g}$$

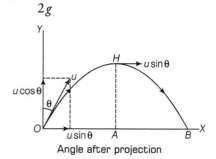

Angle after projection

(iii) Horizontal range

$$= \frac{u^2}{g}\sin 2(90° - \theta)$$

$$= \frac{u^2}{g}\sin(180° - 2\theta) = \frac{u^2}{g}\sin 2\theta$$

(iv) Path of projectile

$$y = x \tan (90° - \theta) - \frac{1}{2} \frac{gx^2}{u^2 \cos^2 (90° - \theta)}$$

$$= x \cot \theta - \frac{gx^2}{2u^2 \sin^2 \theta}$$

(v) Velocity at any time, t

$$= \sqrt{[u\cos(90 - \theta)]^2 + [u\sin(90 - \theta) - gt]^2}$$

$$= \sqrt{u^2 + g^2 t^2 - 2ugt \sin (90° - \theta)}$$

$$= \sqrt{u^2 + g^2 t^2 - 2u \, gt \cos \theta}$$

This velocity makes an angle β with the horizontal direction, then

$$\tan \beta = \frac{u \sin (90° - \theta) - gt}{u \cos (90° - \theta)}$$

$$= \frac{u \cos \theta - gt}{u \sin \theta}$$

EXAMPLE |8| **Projection of a Particle**

A particle is projected horizontally with a speed v from the top of a plane inclined at angle θ with the horizontal. How far from the point of projection will the particle hit the plane?

Sol. To solve this problem, we take X and Y axes as shown in figure.

Consider the motion of particle from A to B.
Motion of particle along X-axis is given by
$$x = ut \qquad \text{...(i)}$$
where, t = time to reach the particle from A to B.
Motion of particle along Y-axis is given by
$$y = \frac{1}{2}gt^2 \qquad \text{...(ii)}$$
Eliminating t from Eqs. (i) and (ii), we get
$$y = \frac{1}{2}g\frac{x^2}{u^2}$$
and $$y = x \tan\theta$$
Thus, $\frac{gx^2}{2u^2} = x\tan\theta$, giving, $x = 0$ or $\frac{2u^2 \tan\theta}{g}$, $x = 0$ at
point A and point B correspond to $x = \frac{2u^2 \tan\theta}{g}$, then
$$y = x \tan\theta = \frac{2u^2 \tan^2\theta}{g}$$

Now, $AB = \sqrt{x^2 + y^2}$

$$= \frac{2u^2}{g}\tan\theta \sqrt{1 + \tan^2\theta} = \frac{2u^2}{g}\tan\theta \sec\theta$$

Effect of Air Resistance on Projectile Motion

- As we have seen that in projectile motion, we assume that air resistance has no effect on its motion. Friction, force due to viscosity, air resistance are all dissipative forces.
- A projectile that traverses a parabolic path would slow duration its idealised trajectory in the presence of air resistance. It will not hit the ground with the same speed with which it was projected.
- In the absence of air resistance, it is only the y-component that undergoes a continuous change. However, in the presence of air resistance, both of X and Y-component would get affected.

UNIFORM CIRCULAR MOTION

When an object follows a circular path at a constant speed, the motion of the object is called **uniform circular motion**. The word uniform refers to the speed which is uniform (constant) throughout the motion. Although the speed does not vary, the particle is accelerating because the velocity changes its direction at every point on the circular track.

The figure shows a particle P which moves along a circular track of radius r with a uniform speed u.

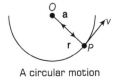

A circular motion

Examples

(i) Motion of the tip of the second hand of a clock.
(ii) Motion of a point on the rim of a wheel rotating uniformly.

Terms Related to Circular Motion

Angular Displacement

It is defined as the the angle traced out by the radius vector at the centre of the circular path in the given time. It is denoted by $\Delta\theta$ and expressed in radian. It is a dimensionless quantity. Its a vector quantity, direction is given by Right-hand rule.

Angular Velocity

It is defined as the time rate of change of its angular position, denoted by ω and is measured in radian per second. Its dimensional formula is $[M^0 L^0 T^{-1}]$. It is a vector quantity.

If a point object moving along a circular path, with centre (i.e. axis of rotation) at O. Let the object move from P to Q in a small time interval Δt, where $\angle POQ = \Delta \theta$.

Now, angular velocity $\omega = \dfrac{\text{Angle traced}}{\text{Time taken}}$

$$= \lim_{\Delta t \to 0} \frac{\Delta \theta}{\Delta t} = \frac{d\theta}{dt}$$

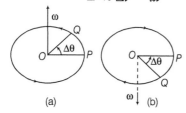

(a) (b)

Time Period

It is defined as the time taken by a particle to complete one revolution along its circular path. It is denoted by T and is measured in second.

Frequency

It is defined as the number of revolutions completed per unit time. It is denoted by f and is measured in Hz.

Angular Acceleration

It is defined as the time rate of change of angular velocity of a particle. It is measured in radian per second square and has dimensions $[M^0 L^0 T^{-2}]$.

It is denoted by α, where

$$\alpha = \lim_{\Delta t \to 0} \frac{\Delta \omega}{\Delta t} = \frac{d\omega}{dt}$$

Relation between Time Period and Frequency

Let f be the frequency of an object in circular motion, then the object will complete one revolution in $\dfrac{1}{f}$ second

which is known as time period (T).

$$\boxed{\text{Time period, } T = \frac{1}{f}}$$

Relation among Angular Velocity, Frequency and Time Period

Suppose a point object illustrating a uniform circular motion with frequency (f) and time period (T). Then, the object completes one revolution, the angle traced at its axis of circular motion is 2π in radian.

If time $t = T, \theta = 2\pi$ radian.

Thus, the angular velocity ω is given by

$$\boxed{\text{Angular velocity, } \omega = \frac{\theta}{t} = \frac{2\pi}{T} = 2\pi f}$$

Relation between Linear Velocity (v) and Angular Velocity (ω)

Suppose the particle moving on circular track of radius r is showing angular displacement $\Delta \theta$ in Δt time and in this time period, it covers a distance Δs along the circular track, then

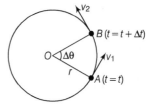

Representation of linear velocity and angular velocity

$$\omega = \frac{\Delta \theta}{\Delta t} \qquad \ldots(i)$$

and $$v = \frac{\Delta s}{\Delta t} \qquad \ldots(ii)$$

But $$\Delta s = r\,\Delta \theta \qquad \ldots(iii)$$

(Since, angle = arc/radius)

From above three equations, we get

$$\boxed{\text{Linear velocity, } v = r\frac{\Delta \theta}{\Delta t} = r\,\omega}$$

Centripetal Acceleration

The acceleration associated with uniform circular motion is called a **centripetal acceleration**. Consider a particle of mass (m) moving with a constant speed (v) and uniform angular velocity (ω) on a circular path of radius (r) with centre at O. Suppose at any time t, the particle be at P, where $\mathbf{OP} = r_1$ and at time $t + \Delta t$ the particle be at Q, where $\mathbf{OQ} = r_2$ and $\angle POQ = \Delta \theta$ as shown in the figure. But $|\mathbf{r_1}| = |\mathbf{r_2}| = r$

Angular speed of the particle, $\omega = \dfrac{\Delta \theta}{\Delta t} \qquad \ldots(i)$

Let $\mathbf{v}_1$ and $\mathbf{v}_2$ be the velocity vectors of the particle at locations P and Q respectively. The magnitude and direction of $\mathbf{v}_1$ and $\mathbf{v}_2$ is represented by the tangent $\mathbf{PA}$ and $\mathbf{QB}$.

Since the particle is moving with a uniform speed (v), the length of tangents at P and Q are equal

i.e. $$|\mathbf{PA}| = |\mathbf{QB}| = |\mathbf{v}|$$

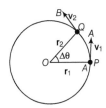

Centripetal acceleration

These two vectors have been separately shown in the following figures

A triangle made of vectors

From triangle law of vectors, we have

$$\mathbf{P'A'} + \mathbf{A'B'} = \mathbf{P'B'}$$

$$\Rightarrow \qquad \mathbf{A'B'} = \mathbf{P'B'} - \mathbf{P'A'}$$

$$= \mathbf{v}_2 - \mathbf{v}_1 = \Delta\mathbf{v}$$

If $\Delta t \to 0$, then A' lies close to B'. Then, $A'B'$ can be taken as an arc $A'B'$ of circle of radius $P'A' = |\mathbf{v}|$

$$\therefore \qquad \Delta\theta = \frac{A'B'}{P'A'} = \frac{|\Delta\mathbf{v}|}{|\mathbf{v}|}$$

From Eq. (i), we have

$$\omega \Delta t = \frac{|\Delta\mathbf{v}|}{|\mathbf{v}|}$$

$$\Rightarrow \qquad \omega|\mathbf{v}| = \frac{|\Delta\mathbf{v}|}{\Delta t}$$

$$\Rightarrow \qquad \frac{|\Delta\mathbf{v}|}{\Delta t} = (\omega r)\,\omega = \omega^2 r \qquad [\because v = \omega r]$$

As $\Delta t \to 0$, then $\dfrac{|\Delta\mathbf{v}|}{\Delta t}$ represents the magnitude of

centripetal acceleration at P which is given by

$$|\mathbf{a}| = \frac{|\Delta\mathbf{v}|}{\Delta t} = \omega^2 r = \left[\frac{v}{r}\right]^2 r = \frac{v^2}{r}$$

Centripetal acceleration, $a = \dfrac{v^2}{r}$

It is towards the centre of circle.

Radius of Curvature

- Any curved path can be assume to be a part of circular arc. Radius of curvature at a point is defined as the radius of that circular arc which fits at the particular point on the curve as shown in figure.

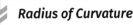

- In the expression, $a_c = v^2/R$, the term R is known as radius of curvature.

EXAMPLE |9| Trapped Insect

An insect trapped in a circular groove of radius 12 cm moves along the groove steadily and completes 7 revolutions in 100 s.

(i) What is the angular speed and the linear speed of the motion?

(ii) Is the acceleration vector, a constant vector? What is its magnitude? **[NCERT]**

Sol. The given question is based on uniform circular motion. Here, radius $R = 12$ cm.

The angular speed ω is given as

$$\omega = 2\pi / T = 2\pi \times 7 / 100 = 0.44 \text{ rad/s}$$

and linear speed v is $v = \omega R = 0.44 \times 12 = 5.3 \text{ cm s}^{-1}$

The direction of velocity v is along the tangent to the circle at every point. The acceleration is directed towards the centre of the circle. Since, this direction changes continuously acceleration, here is not a constant vector.

However, the magnitude of acceleration is constant.

$$a = \omega^2 R = (0.44)^2 \times 12 = 2.3 \text{ cm s}^{-2}$$

EXAMPLE |10| Centripetal Acceleration of a body

A body of mass 10 kg revolves in a circle of diameter 0.4 m making 1000 revolutions per minute. Calculate its linear velocity and centripetal acceleration.

Sol. $m = 10$ kg, $d = 0.4$ m, $r = 0.2$ m,

Revolutions per min, $\nu = 1000/\text{min} = \dfrac{1000}{60}$ s,

Linear velocity, $v = ?$, centripetal acceleration, $a = ?$

$$\omega = 2\pi\nu = 2\pi \times \frac{1000}{60} = \frac{100\,\pi}{3} \text{ rad/s}$$

$$v = r\omega = 0.2 \times \frac{100\,\pi}{3} = \frac{20\,\pi}{3} \text{ m/s}$$

$$a = r\omega^2 = 0.2 \times \left(\frac{100\,\pi}{3}\right)^2 = \frac{2000\,\pi^2}{9} \text{ m/s}^2$$

TOPIC PRACTICE 2

OBJECTIVE Type Questions

1. In a two dimensional motion, instantaneous speed v_0 is a positive constant. Then, which of the following are necessarily true? [NCERT Exemplar]
   (a) The acceleration of the particle is zero
   (b) The acceleration of the particle is bounded
   (c) The acceleration of the particle is necessarily in the plane of motion
   (d) The particle must be undergoing a uniform circular motion

Sol. (c) As given motion is two dimensional motion and given that instantaneous speed v_0 is positive constant. Acceleration is rate of change of velocity (instantaneous speed) hence it will also be in the plane of motion.

2. Figure shows the orientation of two vectors **u** and **v** in the xy-plane. [NCERT Exemplar]

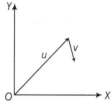

If $\mathbf{u} = a\hat{\mathbf{i}} + b\hat{\mathbf{j}}$ and $\mathbf{v} = p\hat{\mathbf{i}} + q\hat{\mathbf{j}}$
Which of the following is correct?
(a) a and p are positive while b and q are negative
(b) a, p and b are positive while q is negative
(c) a, q and b are positive while p is negative
(d) a, b, p and q are all positive

Sol. (b) Clearly from the diagram, $\mathbf{u} = a\hat{\mathbf{i}} + b\hat{\mathbf{j}}$

As **u** is in the first quadrant, hence both components a and b will be positive.

For $\mathbf{v} = p\hat{\mathbf{i}} + q\hat{\mathbf{j}}$, as it is in positive x-direction and located downward, hence x-component, p will be positive and y-component, q will be negative.

3. Three particles A, B and C projected from the same point with the same initial speeds making angle 30°, 45° and 60°, respectively with the horizontally. Which of the following statements is correct?
   (a) A, B and C have unequal ranges
   (b) Ranges of A and C are less than that of B
   (c) Ranges of A and C are equal and greater than that of B
   (d) A, B and C have equal ranges

Sol. (b) When a body is projected at an angle θ with the horizontal with initial velocity u, then the horizontal range R of projectile is $R = \dfrac{u^2 \sin 2\theta}{g}$.

Clearly, for maximum horizontal range $\sin 2\theta = 1$ or $2\theta = 90°$ or $\theta = 45°$. Hence, in order to achieve maximum range, the body should be projected at 45°.

In this case $R_{max} = \dfrac{u^2}{g}$

Hence, ranges of A and C are less than that of B.

4. The ceiling of a hall is 30 m high. A ball is thrown with 60 ms^{-1} at an angle θ, so that maximum horizontal distance may be covered. The angle of projection θ is given by
   (a) $\sin \theta = \dfrac{1}{\sqrt{8}}$ (b) $\sin \theta = \dfrac{1}{\sqrt{6}}$
   (c) $\sin \theta = \dfrac{1}{\sqrt{3}}$ (d) None of these

Sol. (b) Given, $u = 60$ ms^{-1}

$\therefore$ Maximum height, $H = \dfrac{u^2 \sin^2 \theta}{2g}$

$\Rightarrow \qquad 30 = \dfrac{(60)^2 \sin^2 \theta}{2g}$

$\Rightarrow \qquad \sin^2 \theta = \dfrac{30 \times 2g}{60 \times 60} = \dfrac{10}{60}$

$\Rightarrow \qquad \sin \theta = \dfrac{1}{\sqrt{6}}$

5. Two cars of masses m_1 and m_2 are moving in circles of radii r_1 and r_2, respectively. Their speeds are such that they make complete circles in the same time t. The ratio of their centripetal accelerations is
   (a) $m_1 r_1 : m_2 r_2$ (b) $m_1 : m_2$
   (c) $r_1 : r_2$ (d) 1:1

Sol. (c) As, centripetal acceleration is given as, $a_c = \dfrac{v^2}{r}$

For the first body of mass m_1, $a_{c_1} = \dfrac{v_1^2}{r_1}$

For the second body of mass m_2, $a_{c_2} = \dfrac{v_2^2}{r_2}$

Also time to complete one revolution by both body is same.

Hence, $\dfrac{2\pi r_1}{v_1} = \dfrac{2\pi r_2}{v_2}$

$\Rightarrow \qquad \dfrac{v_1}{v_2} = \dfrac{r_1}{r_2}$ ...(i) i.e., $a_{c_1} : a_{c_2} = \dfrac{v_1^2}{r_1} \times \dfrac{r_2}{v_2^2}$ [from Eq. (i)]

$$= \dfrac{r_1^2}{r_2^2} \times \dfrac{r_2}{r_1} = \dfrac{r_1}{r_2} = r_1 : r_2$$

VERY SHORT ANSWER Type Questions

6. Can a body move on a curved path without having acceleration? Why?

Sol. No, a body cannot move on a curved path without acceleration because while moving on a curved path, the velocity of the body changes with time as the direction changes at each point.

7. A particle cannot accelerate if its velocity is constant, why?

Sol. When the particle is moving with a constant velocity, there is no change in velocity with time and hence, its acceleration is zero.

8. The magnitude and direction of the acceleration of a body both are constant. Will the path of the body be necessarily be a straight line?

Sol. No, the acceleration of a body remains constant, the magnitude and direction of the velocity of the body may change.

9. Give a few examples of motion in two dimensions.

Sol. A ball dropped from an aircraft flying horizontally, a gun short fired at some angle with the horizontal etc.

10. A football is kicked into the air vertically upwards. What is its (i) acceleration and (ii) velocity at the highest point?
[NCERT Exemplar]

Sol. (i) Acceleration at the highest point
= $-g$
(ii) Velocity at the highest point = 0.

11. Can there be motion in two dimensions with an acceleration only in one dimension?

Sol. Yes, in a projectile motion, the acceleration acts vertically downwards, while the projectile follows a parabolic path.

12. A stone is thrown vertically upwards and then it returns to the thrower. Is it a projectile?

Sol. No, it is not a projectile, because a projectile should have two component velocities in two mutually perpendicular directions but in this case, the body has velocity only in one direction while going up or coming down.

**13. At what point in its trajectory does a projectile have its
(i) minimum speed and   (ii) maximum speed?**

Sol. (i) Projectile has minimum speed at the highest point of its trajectory.
(ii) Projectile has maximum speed at the point of projection.

14. The direction of the oblique projectile becomes horizontal at the maximum height. What is the cause of it?

Sol. At the maximum height of projectile, the vertical component velocity becomes zero and only horizontal component velocity of projectile is there.

15. Two bodies are projected at an angle θ and $(\pi/2 - \theta)$ to the horizontal with the same speed. Find the ratio of their time of flight.

Sol. The times of flights are

$$T_1 = \dfrac{2u \sin\theta}{g}$$

and $T_2 = \dfrac{2u \sin\left(\dfrac{\pi}{2} - \theta\right)}{g} = \dfrac{2u \cos\theta}{g}$

∴ $\dfrac{T_1}{T_2} = \dfrac{\sin\theta}{\cos\theta} = \tan\theta$

16. Is the rocket in flight is an illustration of projectile?

Sol. No, because it is propelled by combustion of fuel and does not move under the effect of gravity alone.

17. Why does a tennis ball bounce higher on hills than in plains?

Sol. Maximum height attained by a projectile $\propto 1/g$. As the value of g is less on hills than on plains, so a tennis ball bounces higher on hills than on plains.

18. Galileo, in his book 'Two new sciences', stated that for elevations which exceed or fall short of $45°$ by equal amounts, the ranges are equal. Prove this statement.   [NCERT]

Sol. For a projectile launched with velocity v_0 at an angle θ_0,

the range is given by $R = \dfrac{v_0^2 \sin 2\theta_0}{g}$. Now, for angles,

$(45° + \alpha)$ and $(45° - \alpha)$, $2\theta_0$ is $(90° + 2\alpha)$ and $(90° - 2\alpha)$, respectively. The values of $\sin(90° + 2\alpha)$ and $\sin(90° - 2\alpha)$ are the same, equal to that of $\cos 2\alpha$. Therefore, ranges are equal for elevations which exceed or fall short of $45°$ by equal amount α.

19. A stone tied at the end of string is whirled in a circle. If the string breaks, the stone flies away tangentially. Why?

Sol. When a stone is going around a circular path, the instantaneous velocity of stone is acting as tangent to the circle. When the string breaks, the centripetal force stops to act. Due to inertia, the stone continues to move along the tangent to circular path. So, the stone flies off tangentially to the circular path.

20. A body is moving on a circular path with a constant speed. What is the nature of its acceleration?

Sol. The nature of its acceleration is centripetal, which is perpendicular to motion at every point and acts along the radius and directed towards the centre of the curved circular path.

21. What will be the net effect on maximum height of a projectile when its angle of projection is changed from 30° to 60°, keeping the same initial velocity of projection?

Sol. As, $\qquad H \propto \sin^2\theta$

$\Rightarrow \qquad \dfrac{H_1}{H_2} = \dfrac{(\sin 30°)^2}{(\sin 60°)^2} = \dfrac{1}{4} \times \dfrac{4}{3} = \dfrac{1}{3}$

or $\qquad H_2 = 3H_1$

The maximum effect of a projectile is three times the initial vertical height.

SHORT ANSWER Type Questions

22. An aircraft is flying at a height of 3400 m above the ground. If the angle subtended at a ground observation point by the aircraft positions 10 s apart is 30°, what is the speed of the aircraft? **[NCERT]**

Sol. In figure, O is the observation point at the ground, A and B are the positions of aircraft for which $\angle AOB = 30°$. Draw a perpendicular OC on AB. Here $OC = 3400$ m and $\angle AOC = \angle COB = 15°$. Time taken by aircraft from A to B is 10 s. **[1/2]**

In $\triangle AOC$, $AC = OC \tan 15°$

$\qquad = 3400 \times 0.2679$

$\qquad = 910.86$ m

$AB = AC + CB = AC + AC = 2AC$

$\qquad = 2 \times 910.86$ m

Speed of the aircraft

$\qquad v = \dfrac{\text{distance } AB}{\text{time}} = \dfrac{2 \times 910.86}{10}$

$\qquad = 182.17 \text{ ms}^{-1} = 182.2 \text{ ms}^{-1}$

23. A passenger arriving in a new town wishes to go from the station to a hotel located 10 km away on a straight road from the station. A dishonest cabman takes him along a circutious path 23 km long and reaches the hotel in 28 min. What is (i) the average speed of the taxi and (ii) the magnitude of average velocity? Are the two equal? **[NCERT]**

Sol. Given, shortest distance between the station and the hotel = 10 km

$\therefore$ Displacement of the taxi = 10 km

Distance travelled by the taxi = 23 km

Time taken by the taxi = 28 min = $\dfrac{28}{60} = \dfrac{7}{15}$ h

(i) Average speed of the taxi

$\qquad = \dfrac{\text{Total distance travelled}}{\text{Total time taken}}$

$\qquad = \dfrac{23}{(7/15)} = \dfrac{345}{7}$ km/h $= 49.3$ km/h

(ii) Magnitude of average velocity

$\qquad = \dfrac{\text{Magnitude of the total displacement}}{\text{Total time taken}}$

$\qquad = \dfrac{10}{(7/15)} = \dfrac{150}{7}$ km/h $= 21.43$ km/h

No, the average speed of the taxi is not equal to the magnitude of the average velocity of the taxi.

24. A bullet fired at an angle of 30° with the horizontal hits the ground 3 km away. By adjusting its angle of projection, can one hope to hit a target 5 km away? Assume the muzzle speed to be fixed, and neglect air resistance. **[NCERT]**

Sol. Horizontal range,

$$R = \dfrac{u^2 \sin 2\theta}{g}$$

or $\qquad 3 = \dfrac{u^2 \sin 60°}{g} = \dfrac{u^2}{g} \sqrt{3}/2$

or $\qquad \dfrac{u^2}{g} = 2\sqrt{3}$

Since, the muzzle velocity is fixed

Therefore, maximum horizontal range,

$$R_{\max} = \dfrac{u^2}{g} = 2\sqrt{3} = 3.464 \text{ km}$$

So, the bullet cannot hit the target.

25. Find the angle of projection at which horizontal range and maximum height are equal.

Sol. Horizontal range = Maximum height (given)

$\therefore \qquad \dfrac{u^2}{g} \sin 2\theta = \dfrac{u^2 \sin^2\theta}{2g}$

$\Rightarrow \quad 2\sin\theta \cos\theta = \dfrac{\sin^2\theta}{2} \qquad [\because \sin 2\theta = 2\cos\theta \sin\theta]$

$\qquad \tan\theta = 4$

$\Rightarrow \qquad \theta = 75°58'$

26. A football is kicked 20 m/s at a projection angle of 45°. A receiver on the goal line 25 m away in the direction of the kick runs the same instant to meet the ball. What must be his speed, if he has to catch the ball before it hits the ground?

Sol. Given, $u = 20$ m/s, $\theta = 45°$, $d = 25$ m

Horizontal range is given by

$$R = \frac{u^2}{g}\sin 2\theta = \frac{(20)^2}{9.8}\sin 2(45°)$$

$$= \frac{400}{9.8} \times 1 = 40.82 \text{ m}$$

Time of flight, $T = \frac{2u\sin\theta}{g} = \frac{2 \times 20}{9.8}\sin 45°$

$$= 2.886 \text{ s}$$

The goal man is 25 m away in the direction of the ball, so to catch the ball, he is to cover a distance

$$= 40.82 - 25 = 15.82 \text{ m in time } 2.886 \text{ s}.$$

∴ Velocity of the goal man to catch the ball,

$$v = \frac{15.82}{2.886} = 5.48 \text{ m/s}$$

27. How does the knowledge of projectile help, a player in the baseball game?

Sol. In the baseball game, a player has to throw a ball so that it goes a certain distance in the minimum time. The time would depend on velocity of ball and angle of throw with the horizontal. Thus, while playing a baseball game, the speed and angle of projection have to be adjusted suitably so that the ball covers the desired distance in minimum time. So, a player has to see the distance and air resistance while playing with a baseball game.

28. A biker stands on the edge of a cliff 490 m above the ground and throws a stone horizontally with an initial speed of 15 m/s. Neglecting air resistance, find the time taken by the stone to reach the ground and the speed with which it hits the ground. Consider $g = 9.8 \text{ m/s}^2$. **[NCERT]**

Sol. Given, $h = 490$ m, $u_x = 15$ m/s,

$$a_y = 9.8 \text{ m/s}, a_x = 0, u_y = 0$$

Time taken by the stone is

$$t = \sqrt{\frac{2h}{g}} = \sqrt{\frac{2 \times 490}{9.8}} = 10 \text{ s}$$

$$v_x = u_x + a_x t = 15 + 0 \times 10 = 15 \text{ m/s}$$
$$v_y = u_y + a_y t = 0 + 9.8 \times 10 = 98 \text{ m/s}$$
$$v = \sqrt{v_x^2 + v_y^2} = \sqrt{15^2 + 98^2} = 99.14 \text{ m/s}$$

29. A cricketer can throw a ball to a maximum horizontal distance of 100 m. With the same speed, how high above the ground can the cricketer throw the same ball? **[NCERT]**

💡 Horizontal range is maximum when angle of projection is 45°.

Sol. Let u be the velocity of projection of the ball. The ball will cover maximum horizontal distance when angle of projection with horizontal, $\theta = 45°$. Then, $R_{max} = u^2/g$.

Here, $u^2/g = 100$ m

In order to study the motion of the ball along vertical direction, consider a point on the surface of Earth as the origin and vertical upward direction as the positive direction of Y-axis. Taking motion of the ball along vertical upward direction, we have

$$u_y = u, a_y = -g, v_y = 0, t = ?, y_0 = 0, y = ?$$

As, $v_y = u_y + a_y t$

∴ $0 = u + (-g)t \Rightarrow t = u/g$

Also, $y = y_0 + u_y t + \frac{1}{2}a_y t^2$

∴ $y = 0 + u(u/g) + \frac{1}{2}(-g)u^2/g^2$

$$= \frac{u^2}{g} - \frac{1}{2}\frac{u^2}{g} = \frac{1}{2}\frac{u^2}{g} = \frac{100}{2} = 50 \text{ m}$$

$$\left[\because \frac{u^2}{g} = 100\right]$$

30. A stone tied to the end of a string 80 cm long is whirled in a horizontal circle with a constant speed. If the stone makes 14 revolutions in 25 s, what is the magnitude and direction of acceleration of the stone? **[NCERT]**

💡 In uniform circular motion, a centripetal acceleration, $a_c = \frac{v^2}{r} = r\omega^2$ acts on the body whose direction is always towards the centre of the path.

Sol. Here, $r = 80$ cm $= 0.8$ m, $f = 14/25 \text{ s}^{-1}$

∴ $\omega = 2\pi f = 2 \times \frac{22}{7} \times \frac{14}{25} = \frac{88}{25}$ rad/s

The centripetal acceleration

$$a = \omega^2 r = \left(\frac{88}{25}\right)^2 \times 0.80$$

$$= 9.90 \text{ ms}^{-2}$$

The direction of centripetal acceleration is along the string directed towards the centre of circular path.

31. An aircraft executes a horizontal loop of radius 1 km with a steady speed of 900 kmh⁻¹. Compare its centripetal acceleration with the acceleration due to gravity. **[NCERT]**

Sol. Here, $r = 1$ km $= 1000$ m,

$v = 900$ kmh$^{-1} = 900 \times (1000$ m$)/(60 \times 60$ s$) = 250$ ms^{-1}

Centripetal acceleration, $a = \dfrac{v^2}{r} = \dfrac{(250)^2}{1000}$

Now, $\dfrac{a}{g} = \dfrac{(250)^2}{1000} \times \dfrac{1}{9.8} = 6.38$

32. A skilled gun man always keeps his gun slightly tilted above the line of sight while shooting. Why?

Sol. When a bullet is fired from a gun with its barrel directed towards the target, it starts falling downwards on account of acceleration due to gravity.

Due to which the bullet hits below the target. Just to avoid it, the barrel of the gun is lined up little above the target, so that the bullet after travelling in parabolic path hits the distant target.

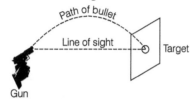

33. Prove that the horizontal range is same when angle of projection is
   (i) greater than 45° by certain value and
   (ii) less than 45° by the same value.

Sol. The horizontal range of the projectile is given by

$$R = \dfrac{u^2 \sin 2\theta}{g}$$

(i) If angle of projection $\theta = 45° + \alpha$ and $R = R_1$

then, $R_1 = \dfrac{u^2 \sin 2(45° + \alpha)}{g} = \dfrac{u^2}{g} \cos 2\alpha$ ...(i)

(ii) If angle of projection
   $\theta = 45° - \alpha$ and $R = R_2$

$\therefore$ $R_2 = \dfrac{u^2 \sin 2(45° - \alpha)}{g} = \dfrac{u^2}{g} \cos 2\alpha$ ...(ii)

Comparing Eqs. (i) and (ii), we have
$$R_1 = R_2$$
                        Hence proved.

LONG ANSWER Type I Questions

34. The position of a particle is given by
$\mathbf{r} = 3.0t\,\hat{\mathbf{i}} - 2.0\,t^2\hat{\mathbf{j}} + 4.0\,\hat{\mathbf{k}}$ where, t is in seconds and the coefficients have the proper units for $\mathbf{r}$ to be in metres.
   (i) Find the $\mathbf{v}$ and $\mathbf{a}$ of the particle.
   (ii) What is the magnitude and direction of velocity of the particle at $t = 2$ s?   **[NCERT]**

Sol. (i) Velocity, $\mathbf{v} = \dfrac{d\mathbf{r}}{dt} = \dfrac{d}{dt}(3.0\,t\,\hat{\mathbf{i}} - 2.0\,t^2\hat{\mathbf{j}} + 4.0\,\hat{\mathbf{k}})$

$= [3.0\,\hat{\mathbf{i}} - 4.0\,t\,\hat{\mathbf{j}}]$ ms^{-1}

Acceleration, $\mathbf{a} = \dfrac{d\mathbf{v}}{dt} = \dfrac{d}{dt}(3.0\,\hat{\mathbf{i}} - 4.0\,t\,\hat{\mathbf{j}})$

$= 0 - 4.0\,\hat{\mathbf{j}}$

$= -4.0\,\hat{\mathbf{j}}$ ms^{-2}

(ii) At time, $t = 2$ s, $\mathbf{v} = 3.0\,\hat{\mathbf{i}} - 4.0 \times 2\,\hat{\mathbf{j}} = 3.0\,\hat{\mathbf{i}} - 8.0\,\hat{\mathbf{j}}$

$\therefore$ $v = \sqrt{(3.0)^2 + (-8)^2} = \sqrt{73} = 8.54$ ms^{-1}

If θ is the angle which $\mathbf{v}$ makes with X-axis, then

$$\tan\theta = \dfrac{v_y}{v_x} = \dfrac{-8}{3} = -2.667 = -\tan 69.5°$$

$\therefore$ $\theta = 69.5°$ below the X-axis.

35. The position vector of a particle is
$$(\mathbf{r} = 2.0\hat{\mathbf{i}} + t^2\hat{\mathbf{j}} + 3.0\hat{\mathbf{k}})$$
where, t is in seconds and the coefficients have the proper units for r to be in metres. What will be the value of $\mathbf{v}(t)$ and $\mathbf{a}(t)$ for the particle and the magnitude and direction of $v(t)$ at $t = 2.0$ s?
                       [NCERT]

Sol. The position vector, $\mathbf{r} = 2.0\hat{\mathbf{i}}t + t^2\,\hat{\mathbf{j}} + 3.0\,\hat{\mathbf{k}}$

$\therefore$ $\mathbf{v}(t) = \dfrac{d\mathbf{r}}{dt} = \dfrac{d}{dt}(2.0\hat{\mathbf{i}}t + t^2\,\hat{\mathbf{j}} + 3.0\hat{\mathbf{k}})$

$\mathbf{v}(t) = 2.0\hat{\mathbf{i}} + 2t\,\hat{\mathbf{j}}$

$\mathbf{a}(t) = \dfrac{d\mathbf{v}(t)}{dt} = \dfrac{d}{dt}(2.0\hat{\mathbf{i}} + 2t\hat{\mathbf{j}}) = 2\hat{\mathbf{j}}$

At $t = 2.0$ s, the magnitude of the $\mathbf{v}(t)$ can be given as

$\mathbf{v}(t) = 2.0\,\hat{\mathbf{i}} + 2 \times 2\hat{\mathbf{j}} = 2.0\,\hat{\mathbf{i}} + 4\hat{\mathbf{j}}$

$v = \sqrt{4 + 16} = \sqrt{20}$ and direction is

$$\theta = \tan^{-1}\left(\dfrac{v_y}{v_x}\right) = \tan^{-1}\left(\dfrac{4}{2}\right) \approx 63°$$

36. A vector has magnitude and direction
   (i) Does it have a location in the space?
   (ii) Can it vary with time?
   (iii) Will two equal vectors $\mathbf{a}$ and $\mathbf{b}$ at different locations in space necessarily have identical physical effects? Give examples in support of your answer.   **[NCERT]**

Sol. (i) A vector in general has no definite location in space because a vector remains unaffected whenever it is displaced anywhere in space provided its magnitude and direction do not change. However, a position vector has a definite location in space.

(ii) A vector can vary with time e.g. the velocity vector of an accelerated particle varies with time.

(iii) Two equal vectors at different locations in space do not necessarily have same physical effects. e.g. two equal forces acting at two different points on a body which can cause the rotation of a body about an axis will not produce equal turning effect.

37. Read each statement below carefully and state with reasons, if it is true or false.

  (i) The magnitude of a vector is always a scalar.

  (ii) Each component of a vector is always a scalar.

  (iii) The average speed of a particle (defined as total path length divided by the time taken to cover the path) is either greater or equal to the magnitude of average velocity of the particle over the same interval of time. **[NCERT]**

Sol. (i) **True,** because magnitude is a pure number.

  (ii) **False,** each component of a vector is also a vector.

  (iii) **True,** because the total path length is either greater than or equal to the magnitude of the displacement vector.

38. Figure shows a pirateship 560 m from a fort defending a harbour entrance. A defence cannon, located at sea level, fires balls at initial speed, $u_0 = 82$ m/s.

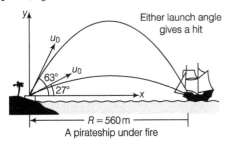

A pirateship under fire

  (i) At what angle, θ_0 from the horizontal must a ball be fired to hit the ship?

  (ii) What is the maximum range of the cannon balls?

  ☼ A fired cannon ball is a projectile. We relate angle and the horizontal displacement i.e. range as it moves from cannon to ship.

Sol. (i) A fired cannon ball is a projectile and we want an equation that relates the launch angle θ_0 to the ball horizontal displacement i.e. range as it moves from the cannon to the ship.

$$\therefore \quad \theta_0 = \frac{1}{2}\sin^{-1}\left(\frac{gR}{u_0^2}\right) = \frac{1}{2}\sin^{-1}\left(\frac{9.8 \times 560}{(82)^2}\right)$$

$$= \frac{1}{2}\sin^{-1}(0.816) = 27°$$

If one angle is 27°, then other angle $(90° - \theta_0)$ is

$$= 90° - 27° = 63°$$

(ii) Maximum range at $\theta_0 = 45°$

$$\therefore \qquad R = \frac{u^2}{g}\sin 2\theta_0 = \frac{(82)^2}{9.8} \times \sin 90°$$

$$= 686 \text{ m}$$

39. A boy stands at 78.4 m from a building and throws a ball which just enters a window 39.2 m above the ground. Calculate the velocity of projection of the ball.

Sol. Consider a boy standing at P throw a ball with a velocity u at an angle θ with the horizontal which just enters window W.

As the boy is at 78.4 m from the building and the ball just enters the window 39.2 m above the ground.

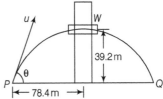

$$\therefore \text{ Maximum height, } H = \frac{u^2 \sin^2 \theta}{2g}$$

$$\Rightarrow \qquad 39.2 = \frac{u^2 \sin^2 \theta}{2g} \qquad \qquad \dots(i)$$

and horizontal range, $R = \dfrac{u^2 \sin 2\theta}{g}$

$$\Rightarrow \qquad 2 \times 78.4 = \frac{u^2 \sin 2\theta}{g} \qquad \dots(ii)$$

Dividing Eq. (i) by Eq. (ii), we get

$$\frac{u^2 \sin^2 \theta}{2g} \times \frac{g}{u^2 \, 2\sin\theta \cos\theta} = \frac{39.2}{2 \times 78.4}$$

$$\Rightarrow \qquad \frac{1}{4}\tan\theta = \frac{1}{4}$$

$$\Rightarrow \qquad \theta = 45°$$

Substituting $\theta = 45°$ in Eq. (ii), we get

$$\frac{u^2 \sin 90°}{9.8} = 2 \times 78.4$$

$$\Rightarrow \qquad u = \sqrt{2 \times 78.4 \times 9.8} = 39.2 \text{ m/s}$$

40. An aeroplane is flying in a horizontal direction with a velocity of 600 km/h and at a height of 1960 m. When it is vertically above the point A on the ground, a body is dropped from it. The body strikes the ground at point B. Calculate the distance AB.

  ☼ Find the time taken by the body to fall at the given height

$$y = h = u_{0y}t + \frac{1}{2}gt^2$$

  But initial vertical velocity is zero. Then, find the horizontal distance travelled by the body x.

Sol. Velocity of the aeroplane in the horizontal direction is

$$u_{0y} = 600 \text{ km/h} = 600 \times \frac{5}{18} = \frac{500}{3} \text{ m/s}$$

Velocity remains constant throughout the flight of the body.

$$u_{0y} = 0 \text{ and } y = h = 1960 \text{ m}$$

Let $t = $ time taken by the body to reach the ground

Now, $$y = u_{0y}t + \frac{1}{2}gt^2$$

Here, $$y = h = 1960 \text{ m}, u_{0y} = 0$$

$\therefore$ $$1960 = \frac{1}{2} \times 9.8 \times t^2$$

$\Rightarrow$ $$t = \sqrt{\frac{1960}{4.9}} = \sqrt{400} = 20 \text{ s}$$

Distance travelled by the body in the horizontal direction,

$$AB = x = v_{ax}\, t = \frac{500}{3} \times 20$$

$$= \frac{10000}{3} = 3333 \text{ m} = 3.33 \text{ km}$$

41. A clever strategy in a snowball fight is to throw two snowballs at your opponent in quick succession. The first one with a high trajectory and the second one with a lower trajectory and shorter time of flight, so that they both reach the target at the same instant. Suppose your opponent is 20.0 m away.

You throw both snowballs with the same initial speed v_0 but θ_0 is 60.0° for the first snowball and 30.0° for the second. If they are both to reach their target at the same instant, how much time must elapse between the release of the two snowballs?

Sol. We need to find the time of flight for each snowball. The time t_R is determined by v_{y0}, the vertical component of initial velocity, then

$$t_R = \frac{2v_{y0}}{g} = \frac{2v_0 \sin\theta_0}{g}$$

To find t_R we need to know, in addition to the initial angle θ_0 (as given), the initial speed v_0, which is not given. We can find v_0 by applying the range equation

$$R = \frac{v_0^2 \sin 2\theta_0}{g}$$

Solving for v_0, we obtain $v_0 = \sqrt{\dfrac{Rg}{\sin 2\theta_0}}$

We obtain the same value for v_0 whether we use,

$$\theta_0 = 30.0° \text{ or } \theta_0 = 60.0°$$

Since, $\sin 2(30.0°) = \sin 2(60.0°)$

$$v_0 = \sqrt{\frac{(20.0 \text{ m}) (9.80 \text{ m}/\text{s}^2)}{\sin 60.0°}} = 15.0 \text{ m/s}$$

Now, we can find t_R for each snowball

$$t_g = \frac{2v_{y0}}{g} \Rightarrow t_g = \frac{2v_0 \sin\theta_0}{g}$$

For the first snowball,

$$t_R = \frac{2 (15.0 \text{ m}/\text{s}\, (\sin 60.0°)}{9.80 \text{ m}/\text{s}^2} = 2.65 \text{ s}$$

For the second snow ball,

$$t_R' = \frac{2(15.0 \text{ m}/\text{s}) (\sin 30.0°)}{9.80 \text{ m}/\text{s}^2} = 1.53 \text{ s}$$

Thus, you should wait a time Δt before making your second throw, where Δt is the difference in the times of flight, $\Delta t = t_R - t_R' = 2.65 \text{ s} - 1.53 \text{ s} = 1.12 \text{ s}$

42. The ceiling of a long hall is 25 m high. What is the maximum horizontal distance that a ball thrown with a speed of 40 m/s can go without hitting the ceiling of the hall? **[NCERT]**

💡 Maximum height attained by a projectile is given

by $H = \dfrac{u^2 \sin^2 \theta}{2g}$

and horizontal range is given by $R = \dfrac{u^2 \sin 2\theta}{g}$

Sol. Given, initial velocity $(u) = 40 \text{ m/s}$

Height of the hall $(H) = 25 \text{ m}$

Let the angle of projection of the ball be θ, when maximum height attained by it be 25 m.

Maximum height attained by the ball

$$H = \frac{u^2 \sin^2 \theta}{2g} \Rightarrow 25 = \frac{(40)^2 \sin^2 \theta}{2 \times 9.8}$$

or $$\sin^2 \theta = \frac{25 \times 2 \times 9.8}{1600} = 0.3063$$

or $$\sin\theta = 0.5534 = \sin 33.6°$$

or $$\theta = 33.6°$$

$\therefore$ Horizontal range $(R) = \dfrac{u^2 \sin 2\theta}{g}$

$$= \frac{(40)^2 \sin 2 \times 33.6°}{9.8} = \frac{1600 \times \sin 67.2°}{9.8}$$

$$= \frac{1600 \times 0.9219}{9.8} = 150.5 \text{ m}$$

43. Read each statement below carefully and state, with reasons, if it is true or false.
  (i) The net acceleration of a particle in circular motion is always along the radius of the circle towards the centre.
  (ii) The velocity vector of a particle at a point is always along the tangent to the path of the particle at that point.
  (iii) The acceleration vector of a particle in uniform circular motion averaged over one cycle is a null vector. **[NCERT]**

Sol. (i) False, because the net acceleration of a particle is towards the centre only in case of a uniform circular motion.

(ii) True, because while leaving the circular path, the particle moves tangentially to the circular path.

(iii) True, because the direction of acceleration vector in a uniform circular motion is directed towards the centre of circular path. It is constantly changing with time. The resultant of all these vectors will be a zero vector.

44. A cyclist is riding with a speed of $27 \, \text{kmh}^{-1}$. As he approaches, a circular turn on the road of radius 80 m, he applies brakes and reduces his speed at the constant rate of $0.5 \, \text{ms}^{-2}$. What is the magnitude and direction of the net acceleration of the cyclist on the circular turn?

[NCERT]

Sol. Here, $v = 27 \, \text{kmh}^{-1} = 27 \times (1000 \, \text{m}) \times (60 \times 60 \, \text{s})^{-1}$

$= 7.5 \, \text{ms}^{-1}, \, r = 80 \, \text{m}$

Centripetal acceleration, $a_c = \dfrac{v^2}{r} = \dfrac{(7.5)^2}{80} = 0.7 \, \text{ms}^{-2}$

Let the cyclist applies the brakes at the point P of the circular turn, then tangential acceleration a_T will act opposite to velocity.

Acceleration along the tangent, $a_T = 0.5 \, \text{ms}^{-2}$

Angle between both the accelerations is 90°

Therefore, the magnitude of resultant acceleration

$a = \sqrt{a_c^2 + a_T^2} = \sqrt{(0.7)^2 + (0.5)^2} = 0.86 \, \text{ms}^{-2}$

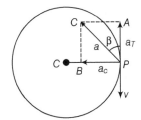

Let the resultant acceleration make an angle β with the tangent i.e. the direction of net acceleration of the cyclist then, $\tan \beta = \dfrac{a_c}{a_T} = \dfrac{0.7}{0.5} = 1.4 \quad \text{or} \quad \beta = 54° \, 28'$

45. A particle starts from the origin at $t = 0$ with a velocity of $10.0 \, \hat{j} \, \text{m/s}$ and moves in the xy-plane with a constant acceleration of $(8.0 \, \hat{i} + 2.0 \, \hat{j}) \, \text{ms}^{-2}$.

(i) At what time is the x-coordinate of the particle 16 m? What is the y-coordinate of the particle at that time ?

(ii) What is the speed of the particle at that time?

[NCERT]

Sol. Here, $\mathbf{u} = 10.0 \, \hat{j} \, \text{ms}^{-1}$ at $t = 0$.

$$\mathbf{a} = \dfrac{d\mathbf{v}}{dt} = (8.0 \, \hat{i} + 2.0 \, \hat{j}) \, \text{ms}^{-2}$$

So, $\qquad d\mathbf{v} = (8.0 \, \hat{i} + 2.0 \, \hat{j}) \, dt$

Integrating it within the limits of motion i.e. as time changes from 0 to t, velocity changes from u to v, we have

$$\mathbf{v} - \mathbf{u} = (8.0 \, \hat{i} + 2.0 \, \hat{j}) \, t$$

$\Rightarrow \qquad \mathbf{v} = \mathbf{u} + 8.0t \, \hat{i} + 2.0t \, \hat{j}$

As, $\qquad \mathbf{v} = \dfrac{d\mathbf{r}}{dt} \Rightarrow d\mathbf{r} = \mathbf{v} \, dt$

So, $\qquad d\mathbf{r} = (\mathbf{u} + 8.0 \, t \, \hat{i} + 2.0t \, \hat{j}) \, dt$

Integrating it within the conditions of motion i.e. as time changes from 0 to t, displacement is from 0 to r, we have

$$\mathbf{r} = \mathbf{u} \, t + \dfrac{1}{2} \times 8.0 \, t^2 \, \hat{i} + \dfrac{1}{2} \times 2.0 \, t^2 \, \hat{j}$$

or $\quad x \, \hat{i} + y \, \hat{j} = 10 \, \hat{j} \, t + 4.0 \, t^2 \, \hat{i} + t^2 \, \hat{j}$

$$= 4.0 \, t^2 \, \hat{i} + (10 \, t + t^2) \, \hat{j}$$

Here, we have, $x = 4.0 \, t^2$ and $y = 10 \, t + t^2$

$\therefore \qquad t = (x/4)^{\frac{1}{2}}$

(i) At $x = 16 \, \text{m}, \quad t = (16/4)^{\frac{1}{2}} = 2 \text{s}$

$$y = 10 \times 2 + 2^2 = 24 \, \text{m}$$

(ii) Velocity of the particle at time t is

$$\mathbf{v} = 10 \, \hat{j} + 8.0 \, t \, \hat{i} + 2.0t \, \hat{j}$$

When $t = 2$ s, then,

$$\mathbf{v} = 10 \, \hat{j} + 8.0 \times 2 \, \hat{i} + 2.0 \times 2 \, \hat{j} = 16 \, \hat{i} + 14 \, \hat{j}$$

$\therefore \text{Speed} = |\mathbf{v}| = \sqrt{16^2 + 14^2} = 21.26 \, \text{ms}^{-1}$

46. The maximum height attained by a projectile is increased by 10% by increasing its speed of projection, without changing the angle of projection. What will the percentage increase in the horizontal range?

Sol. As, maximum height, $H = \dfrac{u^2}{2g} \sin^2 \theta$

Consider ΔH be the increase in H when u changes by Δu, it can be obtained by differentiating the above equation, we get

$$\Delta H = \dfrac{2u \, \Delta u \sin^2 \theta}{2g} = \dfrac{2 \, \Delta u}{u} \, H$$

$\Rightarrow \qquad \dfrac{\Delta H}{H} = \dfrac{2 \, \Delta u}{u}$

Given, % increase in H is 10%, so

$$\dfrac{\Delta H}{H} = \dfrac{10}{100} = 0.1 \Rightarrow \dfrac{2\Delta u}{u} = 0.1$$

As, $\qquad R = \dfrac{u^2 \sin 2\theta}{g}$

∵ $\quad \Delta R = \dfrac{2u\,\Delta u}{g}\sin 2\theta \;\Rightarrow\; \dfrac{\Delta R}{R} = \dfrac{2\,\Delta u}{u} = 0.1$

∴ % increase in horizontal range $= \dfrac{\Delta R}{R} \times 100$

$\qquad = 0.1 \times 100 = 10\%$

47. The range of a rifle bullet is 1000 m, when θ is the angle of projection. If the bullet is fired with the same angle from a car travelling at 36 km/h towards the target, show that the range will be increased by $142.9\sqrt{\tan\theta}$ m.

💡 When the bullet is fired from the moving car, the horizontal component velocity of the bullet increases with the velocity of car. But the vertical component of the velocity remains uneffected.

Sol. Given, $R = 1000$ m

∴ Horizontal range of the bullet fired at an angle θ is

$R = \dfrac{u^2 \sin 2\theta}{g} \;\Rightarrow\; 1000 = \dfrac{u^2\, 2\sin\theta\,\cos\theta}{g}$ ...(i)

Bullet is fired from the car moving with 36 km/h i.e.10 m/s, then horizontal component of the velocity of bullet $= u\sin\theta + 10$

Vertical component of the velocity of the bullet $= u\sin\theta$
Then, new range of the bullet is

$R_1 = \dfrac{2}{g}(u\sin\theta)(u\cos\theta + 10)$

$\quad = \dfrac{2}{g}u^2 \sin\theta\,\cos\theta + \dfrac{20}{g}u\sin\theta$

$\Rightarrow \qquad R_1 = R + \dfrac{20}{g}u\sin\theta$

$\Rightarrow \qquad R_1 - R = \dfrac{20}{g}u\sin\theta$ ...(ii)

From Eq. (i), we have $u = \sqrt{\dfrac{1000 \times g}{2\sin\theta\,\cos\theta}}$ ...(iii)

Now, substituting the value of u in Eq. (ii), we get

$R_1 - R = \dfrac{20}{g}\sqrt{\dfrac{1000 \times g}{2\sin\theta\,\cos\theta}}\,\sin\theta = 20\sqrt{\dfrac{500 \times \sin\theta}{g\cos\theta}}$

$\qquad = 20\sqrt{\dfrac{500}{9.8}\tan\theta} = 142.9\sqrt{\tan\theta}$

LONG ANSWER Type II Questions

48. A fighter plane flying horizontally at an altitude of 1.5 km with speed 720 km h⁻¹ passes directly over an anticraft gun. At what angle from the vertical should the gun be fired from the shell with muzzle speed 600 ms⁻¹ to hit the plane? At what minimum altitude should the pilot fly the plane to avoid being hit? (Take, $g = 10$ ms⁻²)?

[NCERT]

Sol. From the figure, let O be the position of gun and A be the position of plane.

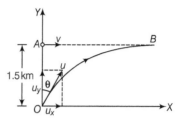

The speed of the plane,

$v = \dfrac{720 \times 1000}{60 \times 60} = 200$ ms⁻¹

The speed of the shell, $u = 600$ ms⁻¹

Let the shell hit the plane at B after time t if fired at an angle θ with the vertical from O. Then, the horizontal distance travelled by shell in time t is the same as the distance covered by the plane during the same period.

i.e. $u_x \times t = vt$ or $u\sin\theta\,t = vt$

or $\quad \sin\theta = \dfrac{v}{u} = \dfrac{200}{600} = 0.33333 = \sin 19.5°$

or $\qquad \theta = 19.5°$ with the vertical

The plane will not be hit by the bullet from the gun if it is flying at a minimum height which is the maximum height (H) attained by bullet after firing from gun.

Here, $H = \dfrac{u^2 \sin^2(90° - \theta)}{2g} = \dfrac{u^2 \cos^2\theta}{2g}$

$\qquad = \dfrac{(600)^2 \times (\cos 19.5°)^2}{2 \times 10}$

$\qquad\qquad [\because \sin\theta = 1/3,\ \cos\theta = \sqrt{8}/3]$

$\qquad = \dfrac{(600)^2 \times (\sqrt{8}/3)^2}{20} = 16000$ m $= 16$ km

49. A projectile is fired horizontally with a velocity of 98 ms⁻¹ from the hill 490 m high. Find (i) time taken to reach the ground (ii) the distance of the target from the hill and (iii) the velocity with which the body strikes the ground.

Sol. Let OX and OY be two perpendicular axes and $YO = 490$ m. A body projected horizontally from O with velocity $u\,(= 98$ ms⁻¹) meets the ground at A following a parabolic path shown in figure.

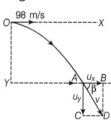

(i) Let T be the time of flight of the projectile i.e. time taken by projectile to go from O to A.

Taking vertical downward motion (i.e. motion along OY axis) of projectile from O to A, we have

$y_0 = 0,\ y = 490$ m, $u_y = 0,\ a_y = 9.8$ m/s², $t = T$

As, $\quad y = y_0 + u_y t + \dfrac{1}{2}a_y t^2$

$\therefore \quad 490 = 0 + 0 \times T + \dfrac{1}{2} \times 9.8 \times T^2 = 4.9\, T^2$

or $\quad T = \sqrt{\dfrac{490}{4.9}} = 10$ s

(ii) Taking horizontal motion (i.e. motion along OX axis) of projectile from O to A, we have

$x_0 = 0,\, x = R$ (say), $u_x = 98$ m/s, $t = T = 10$ s , $a_x = 0$

As, $x = x_0 + u_x t + \dfrac{1}{2} a_x t^2$

$\therefore \quad R = 0 + 98 \times 10 + \dfrac{1}{2} \times 0 \times 10^2 = 980$ m

(iii) Let $v_x,\, v_y$ be the horizontal and vertical component velocity of the projectile at A.

Using the relation,

$v_x = u_x + a_x t = 98 + 0 \times 10 = 98$ m/s

Represented by AB

Using the relation,

$v_y = u_y + a_y t = 0 + 9.8 \times 10 = 98$ m/s

Represented by AC.

$\therefore$ Resultant velocity

$v = \sqrt{v_x^2 + v_y^2} = \sqrt{98^2 + 98^2} = 98\sqrt{2}$ m/s

If β is the angle which $\mathbf{v}$ makes with the horizontal direction, then $\tan\beta = \dfrac{v_y}{v_x} = \dfrac{98}{98} = 1$ or $\beta = 45°$ with the horizontal.

50. A hunter aims his gun and fires a bullet directly at a monkey in a tree. At the instant, the bullet leaves the barrel of the gun, the monkey drops. Will the bullet hit the monkey? Substantiate your answer with proper reasoning.

Sol. Let the monkey stationed at A, be fired with a gun from O with a velocity u at an angle θ with the horizontal direction OX.

Draw AC, perpendicular to OX. Let the bullet cross the vertical line AC at B after time t and coordinates of B (x, y) be w.r.t. origin O as shown in figure.

$\therefore \qquad t = \dfrac{OC}{u\cos\theta} = \dfrac{x}{u\cos\theta} \qquad$ ...(i)

[where, $OC = x$]

In $\triangle OAC$, $AC = OC \tan\theta = x\tan\theta$ ...(ii)

Clearly, $CB = y =$ the vertical distance travelled by the bullet in time t.

Taking motion of the bullet from O to B along Y-axis, we have $y_0 = 0,\, y = y,\, u_y = u\sin\theta,\, a_y = -g,\, t = t$

As, $y = y_0 + u_y t + \dfrac{1}{2} a_y t^2$

$\therefore \qquad y = 0 + u\sin\theta\, t + \dfrac{1}{2}(-g)\, t^2$

$\qquad = u\sin\theta\, t - \dfrac{1}{2} gt^2 \qquad$ ...(iii)

$\therefore AB = AC - BC = x\tan\theta - y$

$\qquad = x\tan\theta - \left(u\sin\theta t - \dfrac{1}{2} gt^2\right)$

$\qquad = x\tan\theta - \left(u\sin\theta \times \dfrac{x}{u\cos\theta} - \dfrac{1}{2} gt^2\right)$

[from Eq. (i)]

$AB = x\tan\theta - x\tan\theta + \dfrac{1}{2} gt^2 = \dfrac{1}{2} gt^2$

It means the bullet will pass through the point B on vertical line AC at a vertical distance $\dfrac{1}{2} gt^2$ below point A.

The distance through which the monkey falls vertically in time $t = \dfrac{1}{2} gt^2 = AB$. It means the bullet and monkey will pass through the point B simultaneously. Therefore, the bullet will hit the monkey.

51. A marble rolls along a table at a constant speed of 1.00 m/s and then falls off the edge of the table to the floor 1.00 m below. (i) How long does the marble take to reach the floor? (ii) At what horizontal distance from the edge of the table does the marble land? (iii) What is its velocity as it strikes the floor?

Sol. Projectile motion of the marble begins as it leaves the table as shown. Since, the marble is initially moving horizontally, $v_{y_0} = 0$ and $v_{x_0} = 1.00$ m/s. We must consider the origin to be at the edge of the table, so that $x_0 = y_0 = 0$

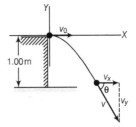

(i) $\quad t = ?$, if $y = -1.00$ m; $y = \dfrac{-1}{2} gt^2 \qquad [\because v_{x_0} = 0]$

$\Rightarrow \quad t = \sqrt{\dfrac{-2y}{g}} = \sqrt{\dfrac{(-2)(-1.00)}{9.8}} = 0.452$ s

(ii) $x = ?$, when $t = 0.452$ s

$\therefore \quad x = v_{x_0} t = 1.00 \times 0.452$ s $= 0.452$ m

(iii) $v = ?$, $\theta = ?$ at $t = 0.452$ s

The x-component of velocity is constant throughout the motion, $v_x = v_{x_0} = 1.00$ m/s

The y-component of velocity

$v_y = v_{y_0} - gt = 0 - 9.8 \times .452 = -4.43$ m/s

$\therefore\ v = \sqrt{v_x^2 + v_y^2} = \sqrt{(1.00)^2 + (-4.43)^2} = 4.54$ m/s

$\theta = \tan^{-1}\left|\dfrac{v_y}{v_x}\right| = \dfrac{4.43}{1.00} = 77.3°$

As the velocity hits the floor, its velocity is 4.54 m/s directed 77.3° below the horizontal.

52. A quarterback, standing on his opponents 35-yard line, throws a football directly down field, releasing the ball at a height of 2.00 m above the ground with an initial velocity of 20.0 m/s, directed 30.0° above the horizontal. (i) How long does it take for the ball to cross the goal line, 32.0 m from the point of release? (ii) The ball is thrown too hard and so passes over the head of the intended receiver at the goal line. What is the ball's height above the ground as it crosses the goal line?

Sol. To better visualise the solution described here, we first sketch the trajectory as shown in figure.

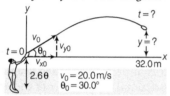

(i) The problem here is to find t when $x = 32.0$ m. We can use $(x = v_{x_0} t)$, if we first find v_{x0}. From figure, we see that $v_{x_0} = v_0 \cos \theta_0 = (20.0$ m/s$)(\cos 30.0°)$
= 17.3 m/s

Using the relation and solve for t.

$x = v_{x_0} t$

$t = \dfrac{x}{v_{x0}} = \dfrac{32.0\text{ m}}{17.3\text{ m/s}} = 1.85$ s

(ii) We want to find y when $x = 32.0$ m, or since we have already found the time in part (a), we can state this, find y when $t = 1.85$ s. Using the relation,

$y = v_{y_0} t - \dfrac{1}{2} gt^2$

where $v_{y_0} = v_0 \sin \theta_0 = (20.0$ m/s$)(\sin 30.0°)$
= 10.0 m/s

Thus, $y = (10.0$ m/s$)(1.85$ s$) - \dfrac{1}{2}(9.80$ m/s$^2)(1.85$ s$)^2$

= 1.73 m

Since, $y = 0$ is 2.00 m above the ground, this means the ball is 3.73 m above the ground as it crosses the goal line too much high to be caught at that point.

53. (i) Show that for a projectile, the angle between the velocity and the X-axis as function of time is given by

$$\theta_{(t)} = \tan^{-1}\left(\dfrac{v_{oy} - gt}{v_{ox}}\right)$$

where, the various symbols have their usual meanings.

(ii) Show that projection angle θ_0 for a projectile launched from the origin is given by

$$\theta_0 = \tan^{-1}\left(\dfrac{4h_m}{R}\right)$$

where the symbols have their usual meanings.

[NCERT]

Sol. (i) Let v_{ox} and v_{oy} be the initial component velocities of the projectile at O along OX direction and OY direction respectively, where OX is horizontal and OY is vertical. Let the projectile go from O to P in time t and v_x, v_y be the component velocity of projectile at P along horizontal and vertical directions as shown in figure.

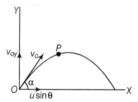

Then, $v_y = v_{oy} - gt$ and $v_x = v_{ox}$

If θ is the angle which the resultant velocity $\mathbf{v}$ makes with horizontal direction, then

$\tan \theta = \dfrac{v_y}{v_x} = \dfrac{v_{oy} - gt}{v_{ax}}$

$\Rightarrow\qquad \theta = \tan^{-1}\left(\dfrac{v_{oy} - gt}{v_{ox}}\right)$

(ii) In angular projection,

Maximum vertical height, $h_m = \dfrac{u^2 \sin^2 \theta_0}{2g}$

Horizontal range,

$R = \dfrac{u^2 \sin^2 \theta_0}{g} = \dfrac{u^2}{g} 2\sin\theta_0 \cos\theta_0$

So, $\dfrac{h_m}{R} = \dfrac{\tan \theta_0}{4}$ or $\tan \theta_0 = \dfrac{4 h_m}{R}$

or $\theta_0 = \tan^{-1}\left(\dfrac{4 h_m}{R}\right)$

ASSESS YOUR TOPICAL UNDERSTANDING

OBJECTIVE Type Questions

1. In a two dimensional motion, instantaneous speed v_0 is a positive constant. Then, which of the following are necessarily true? **[NCERT Exemplar]**
   (a) The average velocity is not zero at any time
   (b) Average acceleration must always vanish
   (c) Displacements in equal time intervals are equal
   (d) Equal path lengths are traversed in equal intervals

2. A particle starts from origin at $t = 0$ with a velocity $5.0\hat{i}$ ms^{-1} and moves in XY-plane under action of force which produces a constant acceleration of $(3.0\hat{i} + 2.0\hat{j})$ ms^{-2}. What is the y-coordinate of the particle at the instant when its x-coordinate is 84 m?
   (a) 36 m   (b) 24 m
   (c) 39 m   (d) 18 m

3. Two projectiles A and B thrown with speeds in the ratio $1 : \sqrt{2}$ acquired the same height. If A is thrown at an angle of $45°$ with the horizontal, then angle of projection of B will be
   (a) $0°$ (b) $60°$
   (c) $30°$ (d) $45°$

4. If a person can throw a stone to maximum height of h metre vertically, then the maximum distance through which it can be thrown horizontally by the same person is
   (a) $\dfrac{h}{2}$ (b) h
   (c) $2h$ (d) $3h$

5. The displacement of a particle moving on a circular path of radius r when it makes $60°$ at the centre is
   (a) $2r$ (b) r
   (c) $\sqrt{2}r$ (d) None of these

6. What is the position vector of a point mass moving on a circular path of radius of 10 m with angular frequency of 2 rads^{-1} after $\pi/8$ s? Initially the point was on Y-axis.
   (a) $5 \cdot (\hat{i} + \hat{j})$ (b) $5\sqrt{2}(\hat{i} + \hat{j})$
   (c) $\hat{i} + \hat{j}$ (d) $\dfrac{1}{\sqrt{2}}(\hat{i} + \hat{j})$

VERY SHORT ANSWER Type Questions

7. Show graphically the displacement vector for a motion in two dimensions. Also, write an expression for displacement vector in terms of its rectangular components.

8. A body is projected with speed u at an angle θ to the horizontal to have maximum range. What is the velocity at the highest point? $\left[\text{Ans. } \dfrac{u}{\sqrt{2}}\right]$

9. Is the maximum height attained by projectile is largest when its horizontal range is maximum?

SHORT ANSWER Type Questions

10. A boy can jump on the moon six times as high as on the earth. Why?

11. What will be the effect on maximum height of a projectile when its angle of projection is changed from $30°$ to $60°$, keeping the same initial velocity of projection?

12. A glass marble slides from rest from the top most point of a vertical circle of radius r along a smooth chord. Does the time of descent depend upon the chord chosen?

13. A railway carriage moves over a straight track with acceleration a. A passenger in the carriage drops a stone. What is the acceleration of the stone w.r.t. the carriage and the earth? $[\text{Ans. } \sqrt{a^2 + g^2}]$

14. When a rifle is fired at a distant target, the barrel is not lined up exactly on the target. Why?

LONG ANSWER Type I Questions

15. The speed of a projectile u reduces by 50% on reaching maximum height. What is the range on the horizontal plane? $\left[\text{Ans. } \dfrac{u^2}{g} \times \dfrac{\sqrt{3}}{2}\right]$

16. When a knife is sharpened with the help of a rotating grinding stone, the spark always travel tangentially to it. Why?

17. An aircraft flying horizontally at a height of 2 km with a speed 200 m/s passes directly over head an anti-aircraft gun. At what angle from the vertical

Answer

1. (d)	2. (a)	3. (c)	4. (c)	5. (b)
6. (b)				

should the gun be fired so that a shell with muzzle speed 600 m/s may hit the plane ? Calculate the safe height of the plane so that the shell may not hit it. (Take, $g = 10$ m /s^2)   [**Ans.** $\theta = 19.5°$, $H = 16$ km]

18. A projectile is fired at an angle θ with the vertical with velocity u as shown in the figure.

Write the expression for

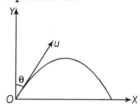

(i) maximum height   (ii) total time of flight
(iii) horizontal range

Also, write equation of the path of the projectile.

19. At what angle should a body be projected with a velocity 24 m/s just to pass over the obstacle 16 m high at a horizontal distance of 32 m?
(Take, $g = 10$ m / s^2)
[**Ans.** $67°54'$ or $48°40'$]

20. The velocity of a particle, when it is at the greatest height is $\sqrt{2/5}$ times its velocity when it is at half of its greatest height. Determine its angle of projection.
[**Ans.** $\theta = 60°$]

LONG ANSWER Type II Questions

21. Derive an expression for horizontal range of a projectile. Also, show that there are two angles of projection for the same horizontal range.

22. A particle is projected in air at an angle β to a surface which itself is inclined at an angle α to the horizontal as shown in figure.

Find (i) time of flight (ii) expression for the range on the plane surface i.e. L and (iii) the value of β at which range will be maximum.

[**Ans.** (i) $T = \dfrac{2u_0 \sin\beta}{g\cos\alpha}$ (ii) $R = \dfrac{2u_0^2 \sin\beta \cos(\alpha+\beta)}{g\cos^2\alpha}$
and (iii) $\beta = \dfrac{\pi}{4} - \dfrac{\alpha}{2}$]

23. What is the angular velocity of the hour hand of a clock ?

24. Derive an expression for centripetal acceleration of an object in uniform circular motion in a plane. What will be the direction of the velocity and acceleration at any instant?

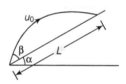

SUMMARY

- **Scalar quantities** are quantities with magnitudes only. Examples are distance, speed, mass and temperature.

- **Vector quantities** are quantities with magnitude and direction both. Examples are displacement, velocity and acceleration. They obey special rules of vector algebra.

- A **null** or **zero vector** is a vector with zero magnitude. Since the magnitude is zero, we don't have to specific its direction.

- **Negative vector** Two vectors are said to be negative of each other if their magnitudes are equal but directions are opposite.

- **Collinear vectors** The vectors which either act along the same line or along parallel lines are called collinear vectors.

- **Coplanar vectors** The vectors which act in the same plane are called coplanar vectors.

- **Position vector** A vector which gives position of an object with reference to the origin of a coordinate system is called position vector. It is given by $\mathbf{r} = x\hat{\mathbf{i}} + y\hat{\mathbf{j}}$

- **Displacement vector** It is that vector which tells how much and in which direction an object has changed its position in a given time interval.

- **Multiplication of vector by a real number** When a vector **A** is multiplied by a real number λ, we get $\lambda(A) = \lambda A$ and $-\lambda(A) = -\lambda A$.

- **Addition of vectors** Vectors can by added by using Triangle law / Parallelogram law / Polygon law

- **Properties of vector addition**
  - (i) Vectors representing physical quantities of same nature can only be added.
  - (ii) Vector addition is **commutative** $\mathbf{A} + \mathbf{B} = \mathbf{B} + \mathbf{A}$
  - (iii) Vector addition is **associative** $(\mathbf{A} + \mathbf{B}) + \mathbf{C} = \mathbf{A} + (\mathbf{B} + \mathbf{C})$
- **Subtraction of vectors** The subtraction of a vector $\mathbf{B}$ from vector $\mathbf{A}$ is defined as the addition of vector $-\mathbf{B}$ to $\mathbf{A}$.
  Thus, $\mathbf{A} - \mathbf{B} = \mathbf{A} + (-\mathbf{B})$
- **Resolution of a vector** The process of splitting a vector into two or more vectors is known as resolution of the vector.
- A vector $\mathbf{A}$ can be expressed as $\mathbf{A} = A_x \hat{\mathbf{i}} + A_y \hat{\mathbf{j}}$

  where A_x, A_y are its components along x-axis and y-axis. If vector $\mathbf{A}$ makes an angle θ with the x-axis, then $A_x = A\cos\theta$, $A_y = A\sin\theta$ and $A = |\mathbf{A}| = \sqrt{A_x^2 + A_y^2}$, $\tan\theta = \dfrac{A_y}{A_x}$.

- Any vector in three dimensions can be expressed in terms of its rectangular components as
  $$\mathbf{A} = A_x \hat{\mathbf{i}} + A_y \hat{\mathbf{j}} + A_z \hat{\mathbf{k}}$$
  Its magnitude, $A = \sqrt{A_x^2 + A_y^2 + A_z^2}$

- **Scalar or dot product** The scalar or dot product of two vectors $\mathbf{A}$ and $\mathbf{B}$ is defined as the product of the magnitudes of $\mathbf{A}$ and $\mathbf{B}$ and cosine of the angle θ between them. Thus $\mathbf{A} \cdot \mathbf{B} = |\mathbf{A}||\mathbf{B}|\cos\theta = AB\cos\theta$
  It can be positive, negative or zero depending upon the value of θ.

- **Vector or cross product** For two vectors $\mathbf{A}$ and $\mathbf{B}$ inclined at an angle θ, the vector or cross product is defined as
  $$\mathbf{A} \times \mathbf{B} = AB\sin\theta\,\hat{\mathbf{n}}$$
  where $\hat{\mathbf{n}}$ is a unit vector perpendicular to the plane of $\mathbf{A}$ and $\mathbf{B}$ and its direction is that in which a right handed screw advances when rotated from $\mathbf{A}$ to $\mathbf{B}$.

- Equations of motion in vector form. For motion with constant acceleration,
  - (i) $\mathbf{v} = \mathbf{v}_0 + \mathbf{a}t$
  - (ii) $\mathbf{r} = \mathbf{r}_0 + \mathbf{v}_0 t + \dfrac{1}{2}\mathbf{a}\,t^2$
  - (iii) $v^2 - v_0^2 = 2\mathbf{a} \cdot (\mathbf{r} - \mathbf{r}_0)$

- The motion in a plane with uniform acceleration can be treated as the superposition of two separate simultaneous one-dimensional motions along two perpendicular directions.

- An object that is in flight after being projected is called a projectile.
  The path of a projectile is parabolic and is given by $y = (\tan\theta_0) - \dfrac{gx^2}{2(v_o\cos\theta_o)^2}$

- **Projectile fired at an angle with the horizontal** Suppose a projectile is fired with velocity u at an angle θ with the horizontal. Let it reach the point (x, y) after time t. Then
  - (i) Components of initial velocity $u_x = u\cos\theta$, $u_y = u\sin\theta$
  - (ii) Components of acceleration at any instant $a_x = 0$, $a_y = -g$
  - (iii) Position after time t, $x = (u\cos\theta)\,t$, $y = (u\sin\theta)\,t - \dfrac{1}{2}gt^2$
  - (iv) Equation of trajectory: $y = x\tan\theta - \dfrac{g}{2u^2\cos^2\theta}\cdot x^2$
  - (v) Maximum height, $H = \dfrac{u^2\sin^2\theta}{2g}$
  - (vi) Time of flight, $T = \dfrac{2u\sin\theta}{g}$
  - (vii) Horizontal range, $R = \dfrac{u^2\sin 2\theta}{g}$
  - (viii) Maximum horizontal range is attained at $\theta = 45°$ and its value is $R_{max} = \dfrac{u^2}{g}$

(ix) Velocity after time t, $v_x = u \cos \theta$, $v_y = u \sin \theta - gt$

$$\therefore \qquad v = \sqrt{v_x^2 + v_y^2} \text{ and } \tan \beta = \frac{v_y}{v_x}$$

(x) The velocity with which the projectile reaches the horizontal plane through the point of projection same as the velocity of projection.

- **Uniform circular motion** When a body moves along a circular path with uniform speed, its motion is said to uniform circular motion.
- **Angular displacement** It is the angle swept out by a radius vector in a given time interval.

$$\theta \, (\text{Rad}) = \frac{\text{Arc}}{\text{Radius}} = \frac{s}{r}$$

- **Angular velocity** The angle swept out by the radius vector per second is called angular velocity.

$$\omega = \frac{\theta}{t} \text{ or } \omega = \frac{\theta_2 - \theta_1}{t_2 - t_1}$$

- **Time period and frequency** Time taken for one complete revolution is called time period (T).
  The number of revolutions completed per second is called frequency.

$$\omega = \frac{2\pi}{T} = 2\pi\nu$$

Relationship between v and ω. It is given by $v = r\omega$

- Angular acceleration and its relation with linear acceleration. The rate of change of angular velocity is called angular acceleration. It is given by Linear acceleration $= \text{Radius} \times \text{Angular acceleration}$

$$\alpha = \frac{\omega_2 - \omega_1}{t_2 - t_1}; \quad a = r\alpha$$

- **Centripetal acceleration** A body moving along a circular path is acted upon by an acceleration directed towards the centre along the radius. This acceleration is called centripetal acceleration. It is given by

$$\alpha = \frac{v_2 - v_1}{r} = r\varpi^2$$

CHAPTER PRACTICE

OBJECTIVE Type Questions

1. The angle between $\mathbf{A} = \hat{\mathbf{i}} + \hat{\mathbf{j}}$ and $\mathbf{B} = \hat{\mathbf{i}} - \hat{\mathbf{j}}$ is

   [NCERT Exemplar]

   (a) 45°   (b) 90°   (c) − 45°   (d) 180°

2. The quantities A_x and A_y are called x and y-components of the vector $\mathbf{A}$. Note that A_x is itself not a vector, but $A_x\,\hat{\mathbf{i}}$ is a vector, and so is $A_y\hat{\mathbf{j}}$. Using simple trigonometry, we can express A_x and A_y in terms of the magnitude of $\mathbf{A}$ and the angle it makes with the x-axis

   $$A_x = A\cos\theta, \quad A_y = A\sin\theta$$

   Choose the correct figure on the basis of given description.

   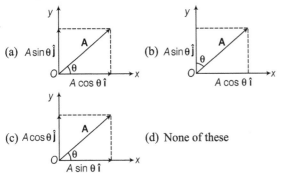

   (a) $A\sin\theta\hat{\mathbf{j}}$ (b) $A\sin\theta\hat{\mathbf{j}}$ (c) $A\cos\theta\hat{\mathbf{j}}$ (d) None of these

3. The direction of instantaneous velocity is shown by

   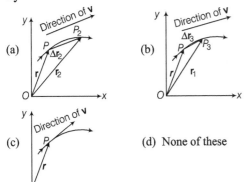

   (a)   (b)   (c)   (d) None of these

4. The speed of a projectile at the maximum height is 1/2 its initial speed. Find the ratio of range of projectile to the maximum height attained.

   (a) $4\sqrt{3}$ (b) $\dfrac{4}{\sqrt{3}}$ (c) $\dfrac{\sqrt{3}}{4}$ (d) 6

5. The horizontal range of a projectile fired at an angle of 15° is 50 m. If it is fired with the same speed at an angle of 45°, its range will be

   (a) 60 m   (b) 71 m   (c) 100 m   (d) 141 m

6. Two cars A and B move along a concentric circular path of radius r_A and r_B with velocities v_A and v_B maintaining constant distance, then $\dfrac{v_A}{v_B}$ is equal to

   (a) $\dfrac{r_B}{r_A}$ (b) $\dfrac{r_A}{r_B}$ (c) $\dfrac{r_A^2}{r_B^2}$ (d) $\dfrac{r_B^2}{r_A^2}$

ASSERTION AND REASON

Direction (Q.Nos. 7-13) In the following questions, two statements are given- one labelled Assertion (A) and the other labelled Reason (R). Select the correct answer to these questions from the codes (a), (b), (c) and (d) as given below

(a) Both Assertion and Reason are true and Reason is the correct explanation of Assertion.

(b) Both Assertion and Reason are true but Reason is not the correct explanation of Assertion.

(c) Assertion is true but Reason is false.

(d) Assertion is false but Reason is true.

7. **Assertion** Force and area are vectors.
   Reason Pressure is a vector.

8. **Assertion** Displacement vector is defined with respect to origin.
   Reason Position vector is defined with respect to origin.

9. **Assertion** The value of a_x depends on $\dfrac{dv}{dt}$.
   Reason Acceleration means rate of change of velocity.

10. **Assertion** When a body is dropped or thrown horizontally from the same height, it would reach the ground at the same time.
    Reason Horizontal velocity has no effect on the vertical direction.

11. **Assertion** The maximum horizontal range of projectile is proportional to square of velocity.

    Reason The maximum horizontal range of projectile is equal to maximum height attained by projectile.

12. **Assertion** The range of a projectile is maximum at 45°.
    Reason At $\theta = 45°$, the value of $\sin \theta$ is maximum.

13. **Assertion** Speed is constant in uniform circular motion.

    Reason Acceleration is constant in uniform circular motion.

CASE BASED QUESTIONS

Directions (Q. Nos. 14-15) *This questions is case study based question. Attempt any 4 sub-parts from given question.*

14. **Projectile Motion**

    Projectile motion is a form of motion in which an object or particle is thrown with some initial velocity near the earth's surface and it moves along a curved path under the action of gravity alone. The path followed by a projectile is called its trajectory, which is shown below.

    While resolving velocity (u) into two components, we get (a) $u \cos\theta$ along OX and (b) $u \sin \theta$ along OY.

    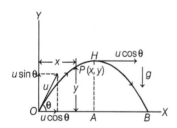

    (i) The example of such type of motion is
    (a) motion of car on a banked road
    (b) motion of boat in sea
    (c) a javelin thrown by an athlete
    (d) motion of ball thrown vertically upward

    (ii) The acceleration of the object in horizontal direction is
    (a) constant   (b) decreasing
    (c) increasing   (d) zero

    (iii) The vertical component of velocity at point H is
    (a) maximum
    (b) zero

    (c) double to that at O
    (d) equal to horizontal component

    (iv) A cricket ball is thrown at a speed of 28 m/s in a direction 30° with the horizontal.

    The time taken by the ball to return to the same level will be
    (a) 2.0 s   (b) 3.0 s
    (c) 4.0 s   (d) 2.9 s

    (v) In above case, the distance from the thrower to the point where the ball returns to the same level will be
    (a) 39 m   (b) 69 m   (c) 68 m   (d) 72 m

15. **Uniform Circular Motion**

    When an object follows a circular path at a constant speed, the motion of the object is called uniform  circular motion. The word uniform refers to the speed which is uniform (constant) throughout the motion. Although, the speed does not vary, the particle is accelerating because the velocity changes its direction at every point on the circular track.

    The figure shows a particle P which moves along a circular track of radius r with a uniform speed v.

    (i) A circular motion
    (a) is one-dimensional motion
    (b) is two-dimensional motion
    (c) it is represented by combination of two variable vectors
    (d) Both (b) and (c)

    (ii) The displacement of a particle moving on a circular path when it makes 60° at the centre is
    (a) $2r$ (b) r
    (c) $\sqrt{2}r$ (d) None of these

    (iii) Two cars A and B move along a concentric circular path of radius r_A and r_B with velocities v_A and v_B maintaining constant distance, then $\dfrac{v_A}{v_B}$ is equal to

    (a) $\dfrac{r_B}{r_A}$ (b) $\dfrac{r_A}{r_B}$ (c) $\dfrac{r_A^2}{r_B^2}$ (d) $\dfrac{r_B^2}{r_A^2}$

    (iv) A particle is moving with a constant speed v in a circle. What is the magnitude of average velocity after half rotation?
    (a) $2v$ (b) $\dfrac{2v}{\pi}$ (c) $\dfrac{v}{2}$ (d) $\dfrac{v}{2\pi}$

(v) What is the centripetal acceleration of a point mass which is moving on a circular path of radius 5 m with speed 23 ms^{-1}?
(a) 106 ms^{-2}
(b) 90 ms^{-2}
(c) 60 ms^{-2}
(d) None of the above

Answer

1.	(b)	2.	(a)	3.	(c)		4.	(b)	5.	(c)
6.	(b)	7.	(c)	8.	(d)		9.	(d)	10.	(a)
11.	(c)	12.	(c)	13.	(c)					

14.	(i)	(c)	(ii)	(a)	(iii)	(b)	(iv)	(d)	(v)	(b)
15.	(i)	(d)	(ii)	(b)	(iii)	(b)	(iv)	(b)	(v)	(a)

VERY SHORT ANSWER Type Questions

16. When the component of a vector **A** along the direction of **B** is zero, what can you conclude about the two vectors?

17. Displacement vector is fundamentally a position vector. Comment on this statement.

18. Is it necessary to mention the direction of vector having zero magnitude?

19. Does the nature of a vector change when it is multiplied by a scalar? Explain with example.

20. Draw the conclusion about B if A − B = A + **B**.

21. For what angle between P and Q, the value of $P + Q$ is maximum?

22. Can the walk of a man be an example of resolution of vectors? If yes, how?

23. Can there be two vectors, where the resultant is equal to either of them?

SHORT ANSWER Type Questions

24. Suppose you are driving in a convertible car with the top removed. The car is moving to the right at a constant velocity. As the figure illustrates, you point a toy rifle straight upward and trigger it. In the absence of air resistance, where would the bullet land (i) behind you, (ii) ahead of you or (iii) in the barrel of the rifle?

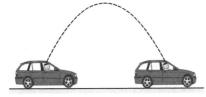

25. A rabbit runs across a parking lot on which a set of coordinates axes has been drawn. The coordinates (in metres) of the rabbit's position as functions of time t (in seconds) are given by

$x = -0.31 t^2 + 7.2 t + 28$ and $y = 0.22 t^2 - 9.1 t + 30$

At $t = 15$ s, what is the rabbit's position vector **r** in unit vector notation and in magnitude angle notation?

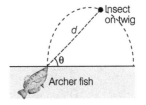

(i) Draw a graph for rabbit's path for $t = 0$ to 25 s.
(ii) Find the rabbit's velocity v at time $t = 15$ s.
(iii) Find the rabbit's acceleration a at time $t = 15$ s.
[**Ans.** (ii) **v** $= 3.3$ m / s, $\theta = -130°$
(iii) $a = 0.76$ m /s^2, $\theta = -145°$]

26. When a large star becomes a supernova, its core may be compressed so tightly that it becomes a neutron star, with a radius of about 20 km. If a neutron star rotates once every second, (i) what is the speed of a particle on the star's equator and (ii) what is the magnitude of the particle's centripetal acceleration? (iii) If the neutron star rotates faster, do the answer to (i) and (ii) increase, decrease or remain the same?
[**Ans.** (i) $a = 1.3 \times 10^5$ m / s, (ii) 7.9×10^5 m /s^2 and (iii) increase]

27. A woman rides a carnival ferris wheel at radius 15 m, completing five turns about its horizontal axis every minute. What are (i) the period of the motion, (ii) the magnitude and (iii) direction of her centripetal acceleration at the highest point (iv) magnitude and (v) direction of her centripetal acceleration at the lowest point?
[Ans. (i) 12s, (ii) 4.1 m /s^2, (iii) down and (iv) up]

28. A boy whirls a stone in a horizontal circle of radius 1.5 m and at height 2.0 m above level ground. The string breaks, and the stone flies off horizontally and strikes the ground after travelling a horizontal distance of 10 m.

What is the magnitude of the centripetal acceleration of the stone during the circular motion? [**Ans.** 160 m/s^2]

29. Around 1939-1940, Emanuel Zacchini took human-cannon ball act to an extreme. After being shot from a cannon, it soared over three Ferris wheels and into a net as shown in figure. Assume that it is launched with a speed of 26.5 m/s and at an angle of 53.0°. (i) Treating it as a particle, calculate its clearance over the first wheel. (ii) If he reached maximum height over the middle wheel, by how much did he clear it? (iii) How far from the cannon should the net's centre have been positioned (neglect air drag)?

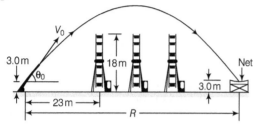

[**Ans.** (*a*) 5.3 m, (*b*) 7.9 m and (*c*) 69 m]

30. Upon spotting an insect on a twig overhanging water, an archer fish squirts water drops at the insect to knock it into the water as shown in figure. Although the fish sees the insect along a straight-line path at angle ϕ and distance d a drop must be launched at a different angle θ_0. if its parabolic path is to intersect the insect.

    If $\phi = 36.0°$ and $d = 0.900$ m, what launch angle θ_0 is required for the drop to be at the top of the parabolic path when it reaches the insect?

    [**Ans.** $\theta = 55.5°$]

31. A dart is thrown horizontally with an initial speed of 10 m/s toward point P, the bull's eyes on a dart board. It hits at point Q on the rim, vertically below P, 0.19 s later. (i) What is the distance PQ? (ii) How far away from the dart board is the dart released?

    [**Ans.** (i) 18 cm and (ii) 1.9 m]

LONG ANSWER Type I Questions

32. A rifle that shoots bullets at 460 m/s is to aim at a target 45.7 m away. If the centre of the target is level with the rifle, how high above the target must the rifle barrel be pointed so that the bullet hits dead centre? [**Ans.** 4.84 cm]

33. Water from a sprinkler comes out with a constant velocity u in all the directions. What is the maximum area of the grassland that can be watered at any time? [**Ans.** $\pi u^4 / g^2$]

34. What is the speed of an aircraft if the pilot remains in contact with the seat, even while looping in vertical plane?

35. Prove that the path of one projectile as seen from another projectile is a straight line.

36. A bullet P is fired from a gun when the angle of elevation of the gun is 30°. Another bullet Q is fired from the gun when the angle of elevation is 60°. The vertical height attained in the second case is x times the vertical height attained in the first case. What is the value of x? [**Ans.** 3]

37. Two billiard balls are rolling on a flat table. One has the velocity components $v_x = 1$ ms^{-1}, $v_y = \sqrt{3}$ ms^{-1} and the other has components $v'_x = 2$ ms^{-1} and $v'_y = 2$ ms^{-1}. If both the balls start moving from the same point, what is the angle between their paths? [**Ans.** 15°]

38. If R is the horizontal range for θ inclination and h is the maximum height reached by the projectile, show that the maximum range is given by $\dfrac{R^2}{8h} + 2h$.

LONG ANSWER Type II Questions

39. A hunter aims his gun and fires a bullet directly at a monkey on a tree. At the instant, the bullet leaves the barrel of the gun, the monkey drops. Will the bullet hit the monkey? Substantiate your answer with proper reasoning.

40. While firing, one has to aim a little above the target and not exactly on the target. Explain.

41. A ball rolls of the top of a stairway with horizontal velocity of 1.8 m/s. The steps are 0.24 m high and 0.2 m wide. Which step will the ball hit first? Take, $g = 9.8$ m/s^2 [**Ans.** Fourth step]

42. Justify that a uniform circular motion is an accelerated motion.

43. A particle is thrown over a triangle from one end of a horizontal base that grazing the vertex falls on the other end of the base. If α and β be the base angles and θ be the angle of projection, then show that $\tan \theta = \tan \alpha + \tan \beta$

44. A machine gun is mounted on the top of a tower 100 m high. At what angle should the gun be inclined to cover a maximum range of firing on the ground below? The muzzle speed of the bullet is 150 m/s. Take, $g = 10$ m/s^2

    [**Hint** $R = u_x \times t = 150 \cos \theta \ (15 \sin \theta + \sqrt{225 \sin^2 \theta + 20})$]

    [**Ans.** $\theta = 44°$]

04

Motion is an integral part of most of the natural phenomena. Galaxies, Stars, Planets, Satellites all are in continuous motion. Motion of these bodies is governed and regulated by certain laws. Laws hidden behind these motions in nature were discovered first by Issac Newton. Therefore, these laws are known as Newton's laws of motion.

LAWS OF MOTION

|TOPIC 1|
Newton's Laws of Motion

Motion is the common and most important phenomenon in nature. In case of macroscopic bodies (natural system), it is easily observable. But if we go down to atomic or even nuclear level, motion is not observable but motion is very much there. Motion may be as simple as throwing a ball high up into air. Whatever is the type of motion, we have to study the forces which generate motion.

FORCE

Force may be defined as an external agency (a push or a pull) which changes or tends to change the state of rest or of uniform motion or the direction of motion of a body.

The dimensions of force are $[MLT^{-2}]$ and its SI unit is **Newton.**

A force applied on an object can produce four types of effects such as

  (i) Force can start or stop a motion.

 (ii) Force can change speed of an object, making it to move slower or faster.

(iii) Force can change the direction of motion of an object.

(iv) Force can change the shape of an object.

> **Some Important Points about Force**
> - A bar magnet can attract an iron nail from a distance. This shows that external agencies of force (gravitational and magnetic forces) can exert force on a body even from a distance.
> - Force is a polar vector as it has a point of application.
> - The vector sum of the forces acting on an object is called the net force.

What happens if a body is moving in uniform motion along a straight line, (e.g. if a box is moving with a constant velocity on an ice slab)? Is an external force required to keep a body in uniform motion? For this, we will understand Aristotle's Fallacy and Galileo's law of inertia.

ARISTOTLE'S FALLACY AND GALILEO GALILEI

The Greek philosopher, Aristotle (384 BC-322 BC) gave the view that if a body is moving, some external force is required to keep it moving.

e.g. When an arrow shot from a bow keeps flying since the air behind the arrow keeps pushing it. Thus, according to Aristotelian's law, **an external force is necessary to keep a body in uniform motion.**

Aristotle's statement is based on the fact that ever presenting resistive forces will always stop the motion. So, to keep a body in motion, an external force is needed (i.e. the force to counter the resistive force). An example of rolling ball that stops due to friction could be considered.

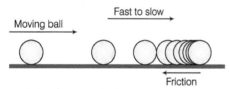

Motion of a ball on a horizontal plane

The opposing force such as friction (in case of solids) and viscous forces (in case of fluids) are always present in the natural world. However, Aristotle's views were proved wrong by Galileo about two thousand years later on. It was observed that the external forces were necessary to counter the opposing forces of friction to keep bodies in uniform motion.

If there were no friction, no external force would be needed to maintain the state of uniform motion of a body. Hence, Galileo proposed his **law of inertia.**

LAW OF INERTIA

Galileo first asserted that objects move with constant speed when no external forces act on them. He arrived at this revolutionary conclusion on the basis of following simple experiments

(a) Galileo's Experiments with Single Inclined Plane

Galileo first studied the motion of objects on an inclined plane.

He observed that

(i) When an object moves down on inclined plane, its speed increases.

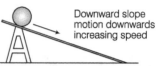

Downward motion of the object

(ii) When the object is moved up on the inclined plane, its speed decreases, i.e. retards.

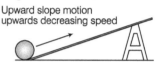

Upward motion of the object

(iii) When an object is moving on a horizontal plane, there should be no acceleration nor retardation, i.e. constant speed.

Horizontal motion of the object

(b) Galileo's Experiments on Two Inclined Planes Combined Together

Galileo also observed that in the case of an oscillating pendulum, the bob always reaches the same height on either side of the mean position. Galileo conducted another experiment by using a double inclined plane. In this experiment, two inclined planes are arranged as facing each other.

(i) When an object rolls down one of the inclined planes, it climbs up the other. It almost reaches the same height but not completely because of friction. In ideal case, when there is no friction, the final height of the object is same as the initial height as shown in figure.

Both planes are inclined at same angle

(ii) When the slope of the second inclined plane is decreased, the object still reaches the same final height but the object has to travel a longer distance to attain the same height.

Inclination of second plane is reduced

(iii) When the slope of the second inclined plane is made zero (i.e. the second plane is made horizontal) the object travels an infinite distance in the ideal situation. This is possible only if the object moves forever with uniform velocity on the horizontal surface.

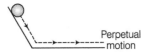

Inclination of second plane reduced to zero

From his experiments, Galileo concluded the law of inertia and states that the state of rest and the state of motion with constant velocity are equivalent in the absence of external forces.

INERTIA

The term inertia means resistance of any physical object. It is defined as the inherent property of a material body by virtue of which it remains in its state of rest or of uniform motion in a straight line. This term was first used by Galileo.

Various Types of Inertia

The various types of inertia are as below

(i) Inertia of Rest

It is defined as the tendency of a body to remain in its position of rest.

e.g. A person standing in a train falls backward when the train suddenly starts moving forward. It depicts, when train moves, the lower part of his body begins to move alongwith the train while the upper part of his body continues to remain at rest due to inertia.

(ii) Inertia of Motion

It is defined as the tendency of a body to remain in its state of uniform motion in a straight line.

e.g. When a moving bus suddenly stops or apply the brake, a person standing in it falls forward. As the bus stops, the lower part of his body comes to rest alongwith the bus while upper part of his body continues to remain in motion due to inertia and falls forward.

(iii) Inertia of Direction

It is defined as inability of a body to change by itself its direction of motion.

e.g. An umbrella protects us from rain.

The rain drops falling vertically downwards cannot change their direction of motion and wet us, with the umbrella on.

NEWTON'S LAWS OF MOTION

Sir Isaac Newton (1642-1727) made a systematic study of motion and extended the views of Galileo. He arrived at three laws of motion which are called **Newton's law of motion.** These laws are as follows

Newton's First Law of Motion

This law states that **every body continues in its state of rest or of uniform motion in a straight line unless it is compelled by some external force to change that state.**

The state of rest or uniform linear motion both imply zero acceleration. The first law of motion can therefore be simply expressed as:

If the net external force on a body is zero, its acceleration is zero. Acceleration can be non-zero, only if there is a net external force on the body. Newton's first law defines force qualitatively.

The Newton's first law is categorised in three parts

(i) **First part** If a body at rest continues in its state of rest. An external force has to be applied on it to make it move.

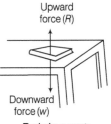

e.g. A book on the table will continue to remain there unless we displace it means a book at rest on a horizontal surface of table, it is subjected to two external forces, the force due to gravity (due to its weight w) acting downward and the upward force on the book by the table, i.e. the normal force R. Since, the book is observed to be at rest, the net external force on it must be zero, i.e. $w = R$ as shown in figure.

(ii) **Second part** If a body is in motion it continues moving in a straight path with a uniform speed unless an external force is applied.

This part seems to be contrary to our every day experience. A rolling ball comes to rest on a rough ground. This is because of

Rolling ball on the floor

force of friction. The ball moves through a larger distance on a smooth floor.

If the friction was zero, the ball would continue its motion forever.

This part also depicts that to increase or decrease the speed of a body moving in a straight line, a force has to be applied on it in the direction of motion or opposite to the direction of motion.

(iii) **Third part** says that a body moving with a uniform speed in a straight line cannot change tself its direction of motion.

Moon changes its direction continuously

To change its direction of motion, a force has to be applied normal to this direction of motion.
Consider the motion of the moon continuously changes. The force needed to change the direction is provided by the gravitational attraction of the earth on the moon.

Newton's First Law Defines the Inertia

According to Newton's first law of motion, everybody continues in its state of rest or uniform motion unless an external force acts upon it. This depicts that a body by itself cannot change its state of rest or of uniform motion along a straight line.

Thus, first law defines inertia and so it is rightly inspired by the **law of inertia**.

EXAMPLE |1| A Spaceship
An astronaut accidentally gets separated out of his small spaceship accelerating in interstellar space at a constant rate of 100 m/s² . What is the acceleration of the astronaut the instant after he is outside the spaceship? (Assume that there are no nearby stars to exert gravitational force on him). **[NCERT]**

Sol. Since, there are no nearby stars to exert gravitational force on him and the small spaceship exerts negligible gravitational attraction on him. The net force acting on the astronaut, once he is out of the spaceship, is zero. By the first law of motion, the acceleration of the astronaut is zero.

MOMENTUM

Momentum of a body is the quantity of motion possessed by the body. It is defined to be the product of its mass m and velocity $\mathbf{v}$ and is denoted by $\mathbf{p}$.

$$\text{Momentum, } \mathbf{p} = m\mathbf{v}$$

Unit and Dimensional Formula
SI unit of momentum $= \text{kg m/s or kg ms}^{-1}$
CGS unit of momentum $= \text{g cm/s or g cm s}^{-1}$
The dimensional formula of momentum is $[\text{MLT}^{-1}]$. It is a vector quantity.

Variation of Momentum

Case I Let two objects each of mass m are moving with different velocities v_1 and v_2 with $v_1 > v_2$, then

$$p_1 = mv_1$$
and
$$p_2 = mv_2$$
$$\therefore \quad \frac{p_1}{p_2} = \frac{mv_1}{mv_2} = \frac{v_1}{v_2}$$
$$\Rightarrow \quad \frac{p_1}{p_2} = \frac{v_1}{v_2}$$

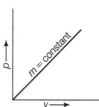

As $v_1 > v_2$, so $p_1 > p_2$

Result It is graphically represented in figure. Thus, **the momenta of bodies having equal masses are proportional to their velocities**.

Case II Let a heavier object of mass m_1 and lighter object of mass m_2.
Suppose both the objects are moving with the same velocity v.

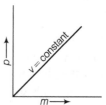

Then, $p_1 = m_1v$ and $p_2 = m_2v$

$$\therefore \quad \frac{p_1}{p_2} = \frac{m_1 v}{m_2 v} = \frac{m_1}{m_2}$$

$$\Rightarrow \quad \frac{p_1}{p_2} = \frac{m_1}{m_2}$$

As a result $m_1 > m_2$

So, $p_1 > p_2$

It is graphically represented in figure. Thus, **the momentum of bodies having equal velocities are proportional to their masses.**

Case III Let two objects having equal linear momenta. Thus,

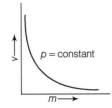

$$p_1 = p_2 = p \Rightarrow m_1 v_1 = m_2 v_2$$

$$\Rightarrow \quad \frac{v_2}{v_1} = \frac{m_1}{m_2}$$

As a result $m_1 > m_2$

So, $v_1 < v_2$

It is graphically represented by figure. Thus, **the velocities of bodies having equal linear momenta are inversely proportional to their masses.**

Some Everyday Phenomena Based on Momentum

The following common examples are

(i) Consider a light-weight vehicle, i.e. car and a heavy weight vehicle i.e. truck parked on a horizontal road. We require a greater force to push the truck than the car to bring at the same speed in same time. Also, a greater opposing force is required to stop the truck than the car at the same time if they are moving with the same speed.

(ii) Speed is another important parameter to consider. A bullet fired by a gun can easily pierce human tissue before it stops, resulting in casuality. The same bullet fired with moderate speed will not cause much damage.

Thus, for a given mass, the greater the speed, the greater is the opposing force needed to stop the body in a certain time. Taken together, the product of mass and velocity, that is momentum eventually is

relevant variable of motion. The greater the change in the momentum in a given time, the greater is the force that needs to be applied.

(iii) If two stones, one light and other heavy are dropped from the top of a building, a person on the ground will find it easier to catch the light stone than the heavy stone. This is due to the mass of a body is thus an important parameter that determines the effect of force on its motion.

(iv) Suppose a stone is rotated with uniform speed in a horizontal plane by means of a string, the magnitude of momentum is fixed. But its direction changes. This is due to a force needed to cause this change in momentum vector.

A fastened stone with the string is rotating

This force is provided by our hand through the string. Experience suggests that our hand needs to exert a greater force if the stone is rotated at greater speed or in a circle of smaller radius or both. This corresponds to greater acceleration or greater rate of change in momentum vector. That means the greater rate of change in momentum vector, the greater is the force applied.

Newton's Second Law of Motion

This law states that **the rate of change of momentum of a body is directly proportional to the external force applied on the body and the change takes place in the direction of the applied force.** Let **F** be external force applied on the body in the direction of motion of the body for time interval Δt, then the velocity of a body of mass m changes from **v** to $\mathbf{v} + \Delta \mathbf{v}$, i.e. change in momentum $\Delta \mathbf{p} = m\Delta \mathbf{v}$.

According to Newton's second law,

$$\mathbf{F} \propto \frac{\Delta \mathbf{p}}{\Delta t} \quad \text{or} \quad \mathbf{F} = k \frac{\Delta \mathbf{p}}{\Delta t}$$

where, k is a constant of proportionality.

If limit $\Delta t \to 0$, then the term $\frac{\Delta \mathbf{p}}{\Delta t}$ becomes the derivative $\frac{d\mathbf{p}}{dt}$.

Thus, $$\mathbf{F} = k \frac{d\mathbf{p}}{dt}$$

For a body of fixed mass m, we have

$$\mathbf{F} = k \frac{d(m\mathbf{v})}{dt} = km \frac{d\mathbf{v}}{dt}$$

$$\mathbf{F} = km\mathbf{a} \qquad \left(\because \frac{dv}{dt} = a \right)$$

Let, $k = 1$

So, Force, $\mathbf{F} = m\mathbf{a}$

In scalar form, this equation can be written as

$$F = ma$$

∴ 1 unit force = 1 unit mass × 1 unit acceleration

A unit force may be defined as the force which produces unit acceleration in a body of unit mass.

The force is a vector quantity and its SI unit is Newton.

One newton is defined as that much force which produces an acceleration of 1 m/s^2 in a body of mass 1 kg.

$$1\,\text{N} = 1\,\text{kg} \times 1\,\text{m/s}^2$$
$$1\,\text{N} = 1\,\text{kg m/s}^2$$

In CGS system, absolute unit of force is dyne. One dyne is that much force which produces an acceleration of 1 cm/s^2 in a body of mass 1 g.

$$1\,\text{dyne} = 1\,\text{g} \times 1\,\text{cm/s}^2$$
$$1\,\text{dyne} = 1\,\text{gcm/s}^2$$

In SI unit, gravitational unit of force is kilogram weight (kg-wt). It is defined as that much force which produces an acceleration of 9.80 m/s^2 in a body of mass 1 kg.

$$1\,\text{kg-wt} = 1\,\text{kgf} = 9.8\,\text{N}$$

In CGS system, gravitational unit of force is gram weight (g-wt) or gram force (gf). It is defined as that force which produces an acceleration of 980 cm/s^2 in a body of mass 1 g.

$$1\,\text{g-wt} = 1\,\text{gf} = 980\,\text{gcm/s}^2$$

Relation between Newton and Dyne

$$1\,\text{N} = 1\,\text{kg} \times 1\,\text{m/s}^2 = 1000\,\text{g} \times 100\,\text{cm/s}^2$$
$$= 10^5\,\text{g cm/s}^2 \qquad [1\,\text{dyne} = 1\,\text{g cm/s}^2]$$
$$1\,\text{N} = 10^5\,\text{dyne}$$

Note

• A gravitational unit is g times the corresponding absolute unit.

• A gravitational unit of force is used to express the weight of a body. e.g. The weight of a body of mass 10 kg is 10 kg-wt or 10 kgf. For this reason, the gravitational units are also called practical units.

EXAMPLE |2| **Playing with the X-ray**

If an electron is subjected to a force of 10^{-25} N in an X-ray machine, then find out the time taken by the electron to cover a distance of 0.2 m. Take mass of the electron = 10^{-30} kg.

Sol. The acceleration of the electron

$$a = \frac{F}{m} = \frac{10^{-25}}{10^{-30}} = 10^5\,\text{m/s}^2$$

The time taken by the electron (t) to cover the distance (s) of 0.2 m can be given by

$$s = ut + \frac{1}{2}at^2$$

$$0.2 = 0 + \frac{1}{2} \times 10^5 \times t^2$$
$$t^2 = 0.4 \times 10^{-5} = 4 \times 10^{-6}\,\text{s}^2$$
$$t = 2 \times 10^{-3}\,\text{s}$$

Newton's Second Law in Component Form and its Significance

In terms of their rectangular components, the force, momentum and acceleration vectors can be expressed as

$$\mathbf{F} = F_x\hat{\mathbf{i}} + F_y\hat{\mathbf{j}} + F_z\hat{\mathbf{k}}$$
$$\mathbf{p} = p_x\hat{\mathbf{i}} + p_y\hat{\mathbf{j}} + p_z\hat{\mathbf{k}}$$

and

$$\mathbf{a} = a_x\hat{\mathbf{i}} + a_y\hat{\mathbf{j}} + a_z\hat{\mathbf{k}}$$

From the formula of force in vector form, for constant m,

$$\mathbf{F} = \frac{d\mathbf{p}}{dt} = m\mathbf{a}$$

∴ $$F_x\hat{\mathbf{i}} + F_y\hat{\mathbf{j}} + F_z\hat{\mathbf{k}} = \frac{d}{dt}(p_x\hat{\mathbf{i}} + p_y\hat{\mathbf{j}} + p_z\hat{\mathbf{k}})$$
$$= m(a_x\hat{\mathbf{i}} + a_y\hat{\mathbf{j}} + a_z\hat{\mathbf{k}})$$

Equating the components along the three coordinate axes, we get

$$F_x = \frac{dp_x}{dt} = ma_x, \quad F_y = \frac{dp_y}{dt} = ma_y$$

and

$$F_z = \frac{dp_z}{dt} = ma_z$$

The above three equations represent the component form of Newton's second law.

EXAMPLE |3| **Acceleration of the Puck**

A hockey puck with a mass of 0.3 kg slides on the horizontal frictionless surface of an ice rink. Two forces act on the puck as shown in figure. The force F_1 has a magnitude of 5 N and F_2 has a magnitude of 8 N. Determine the acceleration of the puck.

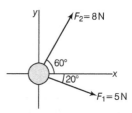

 Using trigonometry, find the x-component and y-component of both the forces exerted on the puck. Add x-components together to get the x-component of the resultant force and then do the same with the y-components. Divide by the mass of the puck to get the accelerations in the x and y-directions.

Sol. Given, $F_1 = 5$N, $F_2 = 8$N, $m = 0.3$ kg and acceleration $a = ?$ The resultant force in the x-direction exerted on the puck,

$$\Sigma F_x = F_{1x} + F_{2x} = F_1 \cos 20° + F_2 \cos 60°$$
$$= (5\ N)(0.940) + (8\ N)(0.500)$$
$$= 8.70\ N$$

The resultant force in the y-direction exerted on the puck,

$$\Sigma F_y = F_{1y} + F_{2y} = - F_1 \sin 20° + F_2 \sin 60°$$
$$= -(5\ N)(0.342) + (8\ N)(0.8666) = 5.22\ N$$

Now, we can use Newton's second law in component form to find the x and y-components of acceleration

$$a_x = \frac{\Sigma F_x}{m} = \frac{8.70\ N}{0.3\ kg} = 29.0\ m/s^2$$

and

$$a_y = \frac{\Sigma F_y}{m} = \frac{5.22\ N}{0.3\ kg} = 17.4\ m/s^2$$

Magnitude, $a = \sqrt{(29.0)^2 + (17.4)^2}\ m/s^2$

$$= 33.8\ m/s^2$$

and its direction is

$$\theta = \tan^{-1}(a_y/a_x) = \tan^{-1}(17.4/29.0) = 31.0°$$

relative to the positive x-axis.

EXAMPLE |4| Magnitude of the Force

A force applied on an object of mass 1 kg produces an acceleration of 8 m/s². When a force of the same magnitude is applied to a carton of ice cream of mass m_2, it produces an acceleration of 12 m/s² .What is the mass of the carton of ice cream and the magnitude of the force?

Apply ΣF = ma to each object and solve for the mass of the ice cream carton and the magnitude of the force.

Sol. Given, $a_2 = 12$m/s² and Force $F = ?$

Apply Σ **F** = m **a** to each object.

$$F_1 = m_1 a_1$$
and
$$F_2 = m_2 a_2$$
$$F_1 = F_2 = F$$
or
$$m_1 a_1 = m_2 a_2$$
$$\Rightarrow \qquad \frac{m_2}{m_1} = \frac{a_1}{a_2} = \frac{8}{12}$$
$$m_2 = \frac{8}{12} = 0.67\ kg$$
$$F = m_1 a_1 = 1 \times 8 = 8N$$

EXAMPLE |5| Dangerous Bullet

A bullet of mass 0.04 kg moving with a speed of 90 m/s enters a heavy wooden block and is stopped after a distance of 60 cm. What is the average resistive force exerted by the block on the bullet?   [NCERT]

Sol. Given, $\quad s = 60$ cm $= 0.6$ m, $u = 90$ m/s

The retardation a of the bullet is given by

$$a = -\frac{u^2}{2s} = \frac{-90 \times 90}{2 \times 0.6}$$
$$\Rightarrow \qquad a = -6750\ m/s^2$$

The retarding force by the second law of motion is

$$F = ma$$
where,
$$F = 0.04 \times 6750$$
$$F = 270\ N$$

Actual resistive force and retardation of the bullet may not be uniform. It indicates only average force.

EXAMPLE |6| Force Acting on a Particle

The motion of a particle of mass m is described by $y = ut + \frac{1}{2} gt^2$. Find the force acting on the particle.   [NCERT]

Sol. We know, $y = ut + \frac{1}{2} gt^2$

Now, by differentiating the above equation w.r.t. t, we get

$$v = \frac{dy}{dt} = u + gt$$

and acceleration, $a = \frac{dv}{dt} = g$

Then, the force is given by

$$F = ma = mg$$

Thus, the given equation describes the motion of a particle under acceleration due to gravity and y is the position coordinate in the direction of g.

IMPULSE

The measure of the action of a large force acting for a duration of time to produce a finite change in momentum is called an **impulse**. Impulse is defined as the product of the average force and the time interval for which the force acts on the body. It is denoted by **I**.

Thus, \qquad Impulse = Average force × time

Impulse is a vector quantity. The direction of impulse is same as that of the force.

Its SI unit is newton-second (N-s).

Its dimensional formula is $[MLT^{-1}]$.

Expression for an Impulse

Consider a constant force **F** which acts on a body for time dt. The impulse is given by

$$d\mathbf{I} = \mathbf{F}\, dt$$

If the force acts on the body for a time interval from t_1 to t_2, the impulse is given by

$$\mathbf{I} = \int d\mathbf{I} = \int_{t_1}^{t_2} \mathbf{F}\, dt$$

If F_{av} is the average force, then

$$I = F_{av} \int_{t_1}^{t_2} dt = F_{av} \, [t]_{t_1}^{t_2}$$

$$I = F_{av} \, [t_2 - t_1]$$

$$\text{Impulse, } I = F_{av} \, \Delta t$$

According to Newton's second law of motion,

$$F = \frac{d\mathbf{p}}{dt}$$

$$\Rightarrow \qquad F \, dt = d\mathbf{p}$$

Integrating both sides with limits, we get

$$\int_0^t F \, dt = \int_{P_1}^{P_2} d\mathbf{p}$$

$$\Rightarrow \qquad F \times t = \mathbf{p}_2 - \mathbf{p}_1$$

$$\Rightarrow \qquad \text{Impulse, } I = \mathbf{p}_2 - \mathbf{p}_1$$

Thus, **the impulse of a force is equal to the total change in momentum produced by the force.**

(Following are some of the practical aspects of impulse.

(i) When a ball hits a wall and bounces back, the force on the ball by the wall acts for a very short time. When the two are in contact, the force is large enough to reverse the momentum of the ball. Often, in these situations, the force and the time duration are difficult to ascertain separately.

However, the product of force (F) and time (t) which is the change in momentum of the body remains measurable quantity.

(ii) An athelete is advised to stop slowly after finishing a fast race, so that time of stop increases and hence force experienced by him decreases.

(iii) Boggies of a train are provided with buffers to avoid severe jerks during shunting of the train. Due to presence of buffers, time of impact increases. Thus, force during jerks decreases.

In all the examples described above, the formula for impulse that is $m(v - u) = F \times t$ is utilised. I_0 achieve the same change in momentum, when t is increased, F required decreases. It results into less injury to body.

(iv) A cricket player lowers his hands while catching a ball. This is due to the player has to apply a retarding force to stop the moving ball (i.e. to change the momentum of the moving ball).

If the player does not lower his hands while catching the ball, the time to reduce the momentum of ball to zero, is small.

So, a large retarding force has to be applied to change the momentum of the moving ball $\left(\because F = \dfrac{d\mathbf{p}}{dt} \right)$.

Hence, his hands are injured. On the other hand, when the player lowers his hands while catching the ball, the time to stop the ball is increased.

Hence, less retarding force has to be applied to cause the same change in the momentum of the moving ball. Therefore, the hands of the player are not injured as shown in given figure.

Change in momentum of the ball

EXAMPLE |7| A Straight Drive

A batsman hits back a ball straight in the direction of the bowler without changing its initial speed of 12 m/s. If the mass of the ball is 0.15 kg, determine the impulse imparted to the ball. (Consider a ball in linear motion). **[NCERT]**

Sol. Given, $m = 0.15$ kg, $v = 12$ m/s, $u = -12$ m/s

Change in momentum $= \mathbf{p}_2 - \mathbf{p}_1 = m[v - u]$

$$= 0.15 \, [12 - (-12)] = 0.15 \times 24$$

$$\mathbf{p}_2 - \mathbf{p}_1 = 3.60 \text{ kg-m/s}$$

Impulse, $\qquad I = \mathbf{p}_2 - \mathbf{p}_1 \Rightarrow I = 3.6 \text{ N-s}$

EXAMPLE |8| Fall of a Ball

Consider a ball falling from a height of 2 m and rebounding to a height of 0.5 m. If the mass of the ball is 60 g, find the impulse and the average force between the ball and the ground. The time for which the ball and the ground remained in contact was 0.2 s.

Sol. The initial velocity of the ball at P is zero. Let the final velocity of the ball at Q is v.

Given $s = 2$ m, then

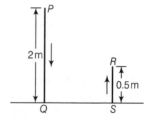

$$v^2 = u^2 + 2as$$
$$v^2 = 0 + 2 \times 9.8 \times 2 = 4 \times 9.8$$
$$v = \sqrt{39.2} \text{ m/s} = 6.26 \text{ m/s}$$

Let u' be the velocity of rebound of the ball.
Given, $s' = 0.5$ m, the final velocity at R is zero
$$v'^2 = u'^2 + 2as$$
$$0 = u'^2 + 2 \times (-9.8) \times 0.5$$
$$u' = -\sqrt{9.8} \text{ m/s} = -3.13 \text{ m/s}$$

Now, Impulse = Change in momentum
$$= mv - (-mu') = m(v + u')$$
$$= \frac{60}{1000}(6.26 + 3.13)$$
$$= 0.06 \times 9.39 = 0.563 \text{ N-s}$$

$\therefore$ Average force $= \dfrac{\text{Impulse}}{\text{Time}} = \dfrac{0.563}{0.2} = 2.817$ N

Newton's Third Law of Motion

When we press a coiled spring, the spring is compressed by the force of our hand. In turn, the compressed spring exerts a force on our hand, and we can feel it. Also, the earth pulls a stone downwards due to gravity. But according to Newton, the stone exerts an equal and opposite force on the earth. We do not notice it since the earth is very massive and the effect of a small force on its motion is negligible.

Thus, forces always occur in pairs as a result of mutual interaction between two bodies. Thus, **Newton's third law states that for every action, there is always an equal and opposite reaction.**

In simple terms, the third law can be stated as follows

Force in nature always occurs in pairs. Force on body A by body B is equal and opposite to the force on the body B by A.

As shown in figure if $\mathbf{F}_{BA}$ is the force exerted by body A on B and $\mathbf{F}_{AB}$ is the force exerted by B on A, then according to Newton's third law,

$$\mathbf{F}_{AB} = -\mathbf{F}_{BA}$$

Force on A by $B = -$ Force on B by A
The condition is shown in figure.

F_{AB} F_{BA}
Forces acting on bodies A and B
(A colliding with B)

Some important implications about the third law of motion

(i) **Newton's third law of motion is applicable irrespective of the nature of the forces** The forces of action and reaction may be mechanical, gravitational, electric or of any other nature.

(ii) **Action and reaction always act on two different bodies** If they acted on the same body, the resultant force would be zero and there could never be accelerated motion.

(iii) **The force of action and reaction cannot cancel each other** This is because action and reaction, though equal and opposite forces always act on different bodies and so cannot cancel each other.

(iv) **No action can occur in the absence of a reaction** In a tug of war, one team can pull the rope only if the other team is pulling the other end of the rope, no force can be exerted if the other end is free.

One team can exert the force of action because the other team provides the force of reaction.

Some Important Concepts about Newton's Third Law of Motion

(i) While walking we press the ground (action) with our feet slightly slanted in the backward direction. The ground exerts an equal and opposite force on us. The vertical component of the force of reaction balances our weight and the horizontal component enables us to move forward as shown in figure.

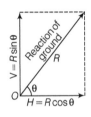

Applied force by the feet and its reaction
force along with its components

(ii) **Rotatory lawn sprinkler** The action of rotatory lawn sprinkler is based on third law of motion. As water forces way its of the nozzle, it exerts an equal and opposite force in the backward direction, causing the sprinkler to rotate in the opposite direction. Thus, water is scattered in all directions as shown in figure.

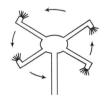

Water rotatory lawn sprinkler

EXAMPLE |9| Play with Billiard Ball

Two identical billiard balls strike a rigid wall with the same speed but at different angles and get reflected without any change in a speed as shown in figure.

(i) What is the direction of the force on the wall due to each ball?

(ii) What is the ratio of the magnitudes of impulses imparted to the balls by the wall? **[NCERT]**

Sol. Let m be the mass of the ball and u be the speed of each ball before and after collision with the ball. Choosing xy- axes as shown in figure.

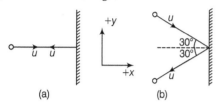

(a)   (b)

(i) **Case (a)** In Fig. (a),

$$p_{x_{initial}} = mu \Big\} \text{ on } x\text{-axis}$$
$$p_{x_{final}} = -mu$$

On y-axis $p_{y_{initial}} = 0$, $p_{y_{final}} = 0$

and we know that impulse

I = change in momentum $(\mathbf{p}_2 - \mathbf{p}_1)$

∴ x-component of impulse

$$= p_{x_{final}} - p_{x_{initial}} = -mu - mu = -2mu$$

y-component of impulse

$$= p_{y_{final}} - p_{y_{initial}} = 0 - 0 = 0$$

Since, impulse and force are in the same direction, therefore, force on the ball due to the wall is along negative x-axis.

By Newton's third law of motion, the force on the wall due to the ball is normal to wall along the positive x-direction.

Case (b) In Fig. (b),

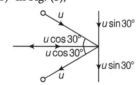

On x-axis, $p_{x_{initial}} = mu \cos 30°$

$p_{x_{final}} = -mu \cos 30°$

On y-axis $p_{y_{initial}} = -mu \sin 30°$

$p_{y_{final}} = -mu \sin 30°$

x-component of impulse $= p_{x_{final}} - p_{x_{initial}}$

$$= -mu \cos 30° - mu \cos 30°$$
$$= -2mu \cos 30°$$

y-component of impulse $= p_{y_{final}} - p_{y_{initial}}$

$$= -mu \sin 30° + mu \sin 30° = 0$$

The direction of force on the wall is same as in case (a) i.e. normal to wall along positive x-direction.

(ii) The ratio of the magnitude of the impulse imparted to the balls in cases a and b is

$$= \frac{-2mu}{-2mu \cos 30°}$$
$$= \frac{1}{\cos 30°} = \frac{1}{\sqrt{3}/2} = \frac{2}{\sqrt{3}} = 1.2$$

EXAMPLE |10| Change in Momentum

A truck is moving with a speed of 20 m/s along a straight line. Suddenly, some sand starts falling from the back side of the truck at the rate of 20 g/s. Find the value of external force required to make the truck move with the constant velocity of 20 m/s.

Sol. Since, truck is losing weight or mass without any change in velocity, its momentum changes. When there is a change in momentum, there is creation of force (according to Newton's second law applied in reverse). Since, truck is becoming lighter, it will be accelerated in forward direction. That means force in it will be created in forward direction.

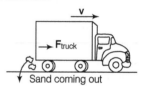

The value of this force could be found out with the formula of Newton's second law, when **v** is constant (at an instant) but mass is varying.

$$|\mathbf{F}|_{truck} = |\mathbf{v}| \frac{dm}{dt}$$

That much amount of force have to be applied on the truck in the backward direction to keep the truck moving with constant velocity

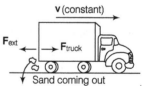

$$\mathbf{F}_{ext} = \mathbf{F}_{truck} = v \frac{dm}{dt}$$
$$\mathbf{F}_{ext} = 20 \text{ m/s } [20 \times 10^{-3} \text{ kg /s}] = 0.4 \text{ N (backward)}$$

Apparent Weight of a Man in a Lift

Let us consider a man of mass m is standing on a weighing machine placed in an elevator/lift. The actual weight mg of the man acts on the weighing machine and offers a reaction R given by the reading of the weighing machine.

This reaction R exerted by the surface of contact on the man is the apparent weight of the man. Now, we consider how R is related to mg in the different conditions.

(i) When the lift moves upwards with acceleration a as shown in figure, the net upward force on the man is

$$R - mg = ma \implies R = ma + mg$$

$$\boxed{\text{Apparent weight, } R = m(g + a)}$$

So, when a lift accelerates upwards, the apparent weight of the man inside it increases.

(ii) When the lift moves downwards with acceleration a as shown in figure, net downward force on the man is

$$mg - R = ma$$

$$\boxed{\text{Apparent weight, } R = m(g - a)}$$

So, when a lift accelerates downwards, the apparent weight of the man inside it decreases.

(iii) When the lift is at rest or moving with uniform velocity v downward or upward as shown in figure.

Then, acceleration $a = 0$. So, net force on the man is

$$R - mg = m \times 0 \implies R = mg$$

or $\boxed{\text{Apparent weight} = \text{actual weight}}$

So, **when the lift at rest and the apparent weight of the man is the actual weight of him.**

(iv) When the lift falls freely under gravity if the supporting cable of the lift breaks. Then, $a = g$.

The net downward force on the man is

$$R = m(g - g) \implies \boxed{R = 0}$$

Thus, **the apparent weight of the man becomes zero.**

This is because both the lifts are moving downwards with the same acceleration g and so there are no forces of action and reaction exists between the man and lift. Hence, a person develops a feeling of weightlessness when the lift falls freely under gravity.

EXAMPLE |11| Feeling Weightlessness

A man of mass 70 kg stands on a weighing scale in a lift which is moving

(i) upwards with uniform speed of 10 m/s?

(ii) downwards with a uniform acceleration of 5 m/s^2?

(iii) upwards with uniform acceleration of 5 m/s^2. What would be the readings on the scale in each case?

(iv) What would be the reading if the lift mechanism failed and it hurtled down freely under gravity?   [NCERT]

When a man is standing on a weighing scale, it will read the normal reaction R as apparent weight.

Sol. Given, mass of man $(m) = 70$ kg

In each case the weighing scale will read the reaction R, i.e. the apparent weight.

(i) As lift is moving upward with a uniform speed, therefore, its acceleration $a = 0$

∴ Normal reaction $w = R = mg = 70 \times 10$ N $= 700$ N

w acts vertically downwards and R acts vertically upwards.

∴ Reading on weighing scale $= \dfrac{700}{10} = 70$ kg

(ii) Acceleration of the lift, $a = 5$ m/s$^2 (\downarrow)$

∴ Normal reaction, $R = m(g - a) = 70(10 - 5)$ N
$$= 70 \times 5 \text{ N} = 350 \text{ N}$$

∴ Reading on weighing scale $= \dfrac{350 \text{ N}}{10 \text{ m/s}^2} = 35$ kg

(iii) Acceleration of the lift, $a = 5$ m/s$^2 (\uparrow)$

∴ Normal reaction, $R = m(g + a)$
$$= 70(10 + 5) = 1050 \text{ N}$$

∴ Reading on weighing scale $= \dfrac{1050 \text{ N}}{10 \text{ m/s}^2} = 105$ kg

(iv) Acceleration of the lift when it is falling freely under gravity

$$a = g (\downarrow)$$

∴ Normal reaction, $R = m(g - a) = m(g - g) = 0$

∴ Reading on weighing scale $= 0$

Note

There will be feeling of weightlessness. We feel our weight because of reaction force. When reaction is zero, we feel weightlessness, though our weight is still there.

CONSERVATION OF MOMENTUM

This principle is a consequence of Newton's second and third law of motion.

According to this principle

"In the absence of an external force the total momentum of a system remains constant or conserved and does not change with time"

If $\qquad\qquad \mathbf{F}_{ext} = 0$

Or in an isolated system (i.e. a system having no external force) mutual forces (called internal forces) between pairs of particles in the system causes momentum change in individual particle. But as the mutual forces for each pair are equal and opposite, the linear momentum of individual particle cancel in pairs and the total momentum remains unchanged. This fact is known as the **law of conservation of momentum.**

The total momentum of an isolated system of interacting particle is conserved. Now, we will show that the total momentum of a system remains constant in the absence of external force. Internal forces acting among constituent particles of a system do not affect momentum of system as a whole.

Explanation of Conservation of Momentum

Let us consider the momenta of two particles system of masses m_1 and m_2 are $\mathbf{p}_1$ and $\mathbf{p}_2$ respectively, then the net momentum of the whole system

$$\mathbf{p} = \mathbf{p}_1 + \mathbf{p}_2 \qquad \ldots(i)$$

Suppose $\mathbf{F}_1$ and $\mathbf{F}_2$ are two forces acting on particles of masses m_1 and m_2. Let in a small time interval Δt the change produced by the forces $\mathbf{F}_1$ and $\mathbf{F}_2$ are $\Delta \mathbf{p}_1$ and $\Delta \mathbf{p}_2$. Thus, net change in momentum

$$\Delta \mathbf{p} = \Delta \mathbf{p}_1 + \Delta \mathbf{p}_2$$

or $\qquad \dfrac{\Delta \mathbf{p}}{\Delta t} = \dfrac{\Delta \mathbf{p}_1}{\Delta t} + \dfrac{\Delta \mathbf{p}_2}{\Delta t}$

or $\qquad \dfrac{d\mathbf{p}}{dt} = \dfrac{d\mathbf{p}_1}{dt} + \dfrac{d\mathbf{p}_2}{dt} \qquad$ [as $\Delta t \to 0$]

or $\qquad \dfrac{d\mathbf{p}}{dt} = \mathbf{F}_1 + \mathbf{F}_2 \qquad \ldots(ii)$

where, $\qquad \mathbf{F}_1 = \mathbf{F}_{1\,ext} + \mathbf{F}_{1\,int}$
and $\qquad \mathbf{F}_2 = \mathbf{F}_{2\,ext} + \mathbf{F}_{2\,int}$

$\qquad \dfrac{d\mathbf{p}}{dt} = (\mathbf{F}_{1\,ext} + \mathbf{F}_{1\,int}) + (\mathbf{F}_{2\,ext} + \mathbf{F}_{2\,int})$

or $\qquad \dfrac{d\mathbf{p}}{dt} = (\mathbf{F}_{1\,ext} + \mathbf{F}_{2\,ext}) + (\mathbf{F}_{1\,int} + \mathbf{F}_{2\,int}) \quad \ldots(iii)$

From Newton's third law, the internal forces always occur in pair so

$$(\mathbf{F}_{1\,int} + \mathbf{F}_{2\,int}) = 0$$

or $\qquad\qquad (\mathbf{F}_{1\,int} = -\mathbf{F}_{2\,int})$

From Eq. (iii), we get

Thus, $\qquad \dfrac{d\mathbf{p}}{dt} = (-\mathbf{F}_{2\,int} + \mathbf{F}_{2\,int}) + (-\mathbf{F}_{1\,ext} + \mathbf{F}_{2\,ext})$

or $\qquad \dfrac{d\mathbf{p}}{dt} = 0 + \mathbf{F}_{1\,ext} + \mathbf{F}_{2\,ext} \quad$ or $\quad \dfrac{d\mathbf{p}}{dt} = \mathbf{F}_{ext}$

where, $\qquad \mathbf{F} = \mathbf{F}_{1\,ext} + \mathbf{F}_{2\,ext}, \mathbf{F}_{ext} = 0$

Then, $\qquad\qquad \dfrac{d\mathbf{p}}{dt} = 0$

or $\qquad\qquad$ Momentum, $\mathbf{p} = $ constant

This equation shows that the law of conservation of linear momentum holds true, i.e. linear momentum of the system remains conserved.

Conservation of momentum theorem is applicable for $\mathbf{F}_{ext} = 0$, it does not depend on internal forces.

e.g.

(i) Let us consider a bullet fired from a gun. Then, force on the bullet by the gun is $\mathbf{F}$ and according to third law of motion, the force on the gun by bullet will be $-\mathbf{F}$. The two forces act for a common interval of time Δt.

According to second law, $\mathbf{F} \Delta t$ is the change in momentum of the bullet and $-\mathbf{F} \Delta t$ is the change in momentum of the gun. Because bullet and gun are initially at rest and then change in momentum of the system is zero, so the sum of their final momenta must be zero.

Thus, if $\mathbf{p}_b$ is the momentum of the bullet after firing and $\mathbf{p}_g$ is the recoil momentum of the gun, then $\mathbf{p}_g = -\mathbf{p}_b$ or $\mathbf{p}_b + \mathbf{p}_g = 0$

(ii) Let a bomb be at rest, then its momentum will be zero. If the bomb explodes into two equal parts, then the parts fly off in exactly opposite directions with the same speed so that the total momentum is still zero. Here no external force is applied on the system of particles (bomb). Forces created are internal only.

EXAMPLE |12| Newton's Third Law from Newton's Second Law

Show that Newton's third law of motion is contained in the second law.

Sol. Let $\mathbf{F}_{BA}$ be the force (action) exerted by A on B and $\dfrac{d\mathbf{p}_B}{dt}$ be the resulting change of the momentum of B.

Let F_{AB} be the force (reaction) exerted by B on A and $\dfrac{d\mathbf{p}_A}{dt}$ be the resulting change of momentum of A.

According to Newton's second law, $F = \dfrac{d\mathbf{p}}{dt}$

Then, $\mathbf{F}_{BA} = \dfrac{d\mathbf{p}_B}{dt}$ and $\mathbf{F}_{AB} = \dfrac{d\mathbf{p}_A}{dt}$

$\therefore \quad \mathbf{F}_{BA} + \mathbf{F}_{AB} = \dfrac{d\mathbf{p}_B}{dt} + \dfrac{d\mathbf{p}_A}{dt} = \dfrac{d}{dt}(\mathbf{p}_B + \mathbf{p}_A)$ ...(i)

Without any external force, the rate of change of momentum of the whole system must be zero.

i.e. $\dfrac{d}{dt}(\mathbf{p}_B + \mathbf{p}_A) = 0$

So, $\mathbf{F}_{BA} + \mathbf{F}_{AB} = 0$ or $\mathbf{F}_{BA} = -\mathbf{F}_{AB}$

or   Action = − reaction

and it is a Newton's third law of motion. Hence, Newton's third law of motion is contained in the second law of motion.

So, Newton's second law of motion is the real law of motion.

EXAMPLE |13| Conservation of Momentum

A moving neutron with speed 10^6 m/s collides with a deuteron at rest and sticks to it. Find the speed of the combination if masses of the neutron and deuteron are 1.67×10^{-27} kg and 3.34×10^{-27} kg, respectively.

Sol. Given, for neutron,

Mass, $m_1 = 1.67 \times 10^{-27}$ kg

Speed, $u_1 = 10^6$ m/s

For deuteron,

Mass, $m_2 = 3.34 \times 10^{-27}$ kg

Speed, $u_2 = 0$ [∵ the deuteron is at rest]

From principle of conservation of momentum,

$m_1 u_1 + m_2 u_2 = (m_1 + m_2) v$

$1.67 \times 10^{-27} \times 10^6 + 3.34 \times 10^{-27} \times 0$

$\qquad = (3.34 + 1.67) \times 10^{-27} \times v$

$v = \dfrac{1.67 \times 10^{-27} \times 10^{+6}}{5.01 \times 10^{-27}} = 33.33 \times 10^4$ m/s

Equilibrium of a Particle

Forces which are acting at the same point or on a particle are called **concurrent forces**. These forces are said to be in equilibrium when their resultant is zero.

F₂ ●————————● F₁

Representation of concurrent forces

(i) If two forces $\mathbf{F}_1$ and $\mathbf{F}_2$ act on a particle, then they will be in equilibrium if $\mathbf{F}_1 = -\mathbf{F}_2$ i.e. two forces on the particle must be equal and opposite.

(ii) Three concurrent forces $\mathbf{F}_1, \mathbf{F}_2$ and $\mathbf{F}_3$ will be in equilibrium when the resultant of two forces $\mathbf{F}_1$ and $\mathbf{F}_2$ is equal and opposite to the third force $\mathbf{F}_3$.

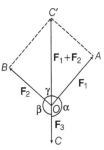

Equilibrium under concurrent forces

Given, figure shows that three concurrent forces $\mathbf{F}_1, \mathbf{F}_2$ and $\mathbf{F}_3$ are acting at a point O and represented by OA, OB and OC, respectively. Let us complete the parallelogram $OAC'B$.

The diagonal OC' of the parallelogram represents $\mathbf{F}_1 + \mathbf{F}_2$, the resultant of $\mathbf{F}_1$ and $\mathbf{F}_2$ from law of parallelogram of forces.

If OC' is equal and opposite to OC, then

$\mathbf{F}_1 + \mathbf{F}_2 = -\mathbf{F}_3$ or $\mathbf{F}_1 + \mathbf{F}_2 + \mathbf{F}_3 = 0$

i.e. three concurrent forces are in equilibrium when the resultant of any two of them is equal and opposite to the third.

A particle under the action of forces $\mathbf{F}_1, \mathbf{F}_2, \mathbf{F}_3, \ldots, \mathbf{F}_n$ will be in equilibrium if these forces can be represented by the sides of a closed n sided polygon in the same sense, i.e.

$\mathbf{F}_1 + \mathbf{F}_2 + \mathbf{F}_3 + \ldots + \mathbf{F}_n = 0$

This equation implies that

$\mathbf{F}_{1x} + \mathbf{F}_{2x} + \mathbf{F}_{3x} + \ldots + \mathbf{F}_{nx} = 0$
$\mathbf{F}_{1y} + \mathbf{F}_{2y} + \mathbf{F}_{3y} + \ldots + \mathbf{F}_{ny} = 0$
$\mathbf{F}_{1z} + \mathbf{F}_{2z} + \mathbf{F}_{3z} + \ldots + \mathbf{F}_{nz} = 0$

where, $\mathbf{F}_{1x}, \mathbf{F}_{1y}$ and $\mathbf{F}_{1z}$ are the rectangular components of $\mathbf{F}_1$ along x, y and z-directions.

LAMI'S THEOREM

According to this theorem, when three concurrent forces $\mathbf{F}_1, \mathbf{F}_2$ and $\mathbf{F}_3$ acting on a body are in equilibrium, then

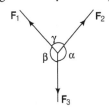

Three concurrent forces acting at some angles

$$\dfrac{F_1}{\sin \alpha} = \dfrac{F_2}{\sin \beta} = \dfrac{F_3}{\sin \gamma}$$

where, α = angle between $\mathbf{F}_2$ and $\mathbf{F}_3$

β = angle between $\mathbf{F}_3$ and $\mathbf{F}_1$

γ = angle between $\mathbf{F}_1$ and $\mathbf{F}_2$

Proof

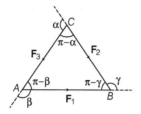

As shown in above figure, the forces F_1, F_2 and F_3 can be represented by sides of $\triangle ABC$, taken in the same order. Applying law of sines to $\triangle ABC$, we get

$$\frac{F_1}{\sin(\pi - \alpha)} = \frac{F_2}{\sin(\pi - \beta)} = \frac{F_3}{\sin(\pi - \gamma)}$$

or

$$\frac{F_1}{\sin \alpha} = \frac{F_2}{\sin \beta} = \frac{F_3}{\sin \gamma} \quad [\because \sin(\pi - \theta) = \sin \theta]$$

EXAMPLE |14| Lami's Theorem
The below figure is the part of a horizontal stretched net. Section AB is stretched with a force of 10 N, then determine the forces in the sections BC and BF.

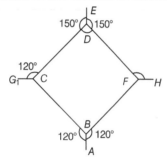

Sol. By drawing the free body diagram of point B.
Let the force in the section BC and BF are F_1 and F_2 respectively.

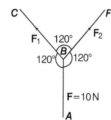

Three concurrent
forces acting at
some angles

$$\frac{F_1}{\sin 120°} = \frac{F_2}{\sin 120°} = \frac{F}{\sin 120°}$$

From Lami's theorem $F_1 = F_2 = F = 10\,\text{N}$

TOPIC PRACTICE 1

OBJECTIVE Type Questions

1. Suppose the earth suddenly stops attracting objects placed near surface. A person standing on the surface of the earth will
   (a) remain standing
   (b) fly up
   (c) sink into earth
   (d) Either (b) or (c)

Sol. (a) If downward force on the earth stops, so upward self adjusting force also stop. In vertical direction, there is no force. Due to inertia person resists any change to its state of rest. Person will remain standing.

2. An astronaut accidentally gets separated out of his small spaceship accelerating in interstellar space at a constant rate of 100 ms^{-2}. What is the acceleration of the astronaut at the instant after he is outside the spaceship? (Assume that there are no nearby starts to exert gravitational force on him)
   (a) 0
   (b) 1
   (c) ∞
   (d) Data insufficient

Sol. (a) Since, there are no near by stars to exert gravitational force on him and the small spaceship exert negligible gravitational attraction on him, the net force acting on the astronaut, once he is out of the spaceship is zero.

3. A ball is travelling with uniform translatory motion. This means that **[NCERT Exemplar]**
   (a) it is at rest
   (b) the path can be a straight line or circular and the ball travels with uniform speed
   (c) all parts of the ball have the same velocity (magnitude and direction) and the velocity is constant
   (d) the centre of the ball moves with constant velocity and the ball spins about its centre uniformly

Sol. (c) In a uniform translatory motion, all parts of the ball have the same velocity in magnitude and direction and this velocity is constant.

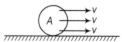

The situation is shown in adjacent diagram, where a body A is in uniform translatory motion.

4. A metre scale is moving with uniform velocity. This implies **[NCERT Exemplar]**

(a) the force acting on the scale is zero, but a torque about the centre of mass can act on the scale

(b) the force acting on the scale is zero and the torque acting about centre of mass of the scale is also zero

(c) the total force acting on it need not be zero but the torque on it is zero

(d) neither the force nor the torque need to be zero

Sol. (b) To solve this question we have to apply Newton's second law of motion, in terms of force and change in momentum.

We known that, $F = \dfrac{dp}{dt}$

given that meter scale is moving with uniform velocity, hence, $dp = 0$

Force, $F = 0$.

As all part of the scale is moving with uniform velocity and total force is zero, hence, torque will also be zero.

5. Conservation of momentum in a collision between particles can be understood from **[NCERT Exemplar]**

(a) conservation of energy

(b) Newton's first law only

(c) Newton's second law only

(d) Both Newton's second and third law

Sol. (d) In case of collision between particles equal and opposite forces will act on individual. (by Newton's third law)

From second law of motion, if external force is zero, then momentum is consered.

6. A body of mass 2kg travels according to the law $x(t) = pt + qt^2 + rt^3$ where, $q = 4\text{ms}^{-2}$, $p = 3\text{ms}^{-1}$ and $r = 5\text{ms}^{-3}$. The force acting on the body at $t = 2\text{s}$ is **[NCERT Exemplar]**

(a) 136 N   (b) 134 N

(c) 158 N   (d) 68 N

Sol. (a) Given, mass = 2 kg

$$x(t) = pt + qt^2 + rt^3$$

$$v = \dfrac{dx}{dt} = p + 2qt + 3rt^2$$

$$a = \dfrac{dv}{dt} = 0 + 2q + 6rt$$

at $t = 2\text{s}$; $a = 2q + 6 \times 2 \times r$

$$= 2q + 12r$$

$$= 2 \times 4 + 12 \times 5$$

$$= 8 + 60 = 68 \text{ m/s}$$

Force $= F = ma$

$$= 2 \times 68 = 136 \text{ N}$$

7. In equilibrium of particle when net external force of the particle is zero. Then, the particle is

(a) at rest

(b) moving with uniform velocity

(c) moving with uniform acceleration

(d) Both (a) and (b)

Sol. (d) In equilibrium, net force is zero, there force, acceleration is zero, hence particle is either at rest or in motion with uniform velocity.

VERY SHORT ANSWER Type Questions

8. Bodies of larger mass need greater initial effort to put them in motion. Why?

Sol. According to the Newton's second law of motion, $F = ma$, for given acceleration a, if m is large, F should be more i.e. greater force will be required to put a larger mass in motion.

9. A force of 1 N acts on a body of mass 1 g. Calculate the acceleration produced in the body.

Sol. Given, $F = 1\text{N}$, $m = 1\text{ g} = 10^{-3}\text{ kg}$

Now, $F = ma$

$$\Rightarrow \quad a = \dfrac{F}{m} = \dfrac{1}{10^{-3}} = 10^3 \text{ m/s}^2$$

10. Calculate the force acting on a body which changes the momentum of the body at the rate of $1\,\text{kg-m/s}^2$.

Sol. We know that, F = rate of change of momentum

$$F = 1 \text{ kg-m/s}^2 = 1\text{N}$$

11. The distance travelled by a moving body is directly proportional to time. Is any external force acting on it?

Sol. When $S \propto t$, so acceleration = 0, Therefore, no external force is acting on the body.

12. A force of 36 dyne is inclined to the horizontal at an angle of 60°. Find the acceleration in a mass of 18 g that moves in a horizontal direction.

Sol. Given, $F = 36$ dyne at an angle of 60°.

∴ Component of force along x-direction

$$F_x = F \cos 60° = 36 \times \dfrac{1}{2} = 18 \text{ dyne}$$

But $\quad F_x = ma_x$,

$$a_x = \dfrac{F_x}{m} = \dfrac{18}{18} = 1 \text{ cm/s}^2$$

13. A body is acted upon by a number of external forces. Can it remain at rest?

Sol. Yes, if the external forces acting on the body can be represented in magnitude and direction by the sides of a closed polygon taken in the same order.

14. If force is acting on a moving body perpendicular to the direction of motion, then what will be its effect on the speed and direction of the body?

Sol. No change in speed, but change in direction is possible. Forces acting on a body in circular motion is an example.

15. An impulse is applied to a moving object with a force at an angle of 20° w.r.t. velocity vector, what is the angle between the impulse vector and change in momentum vector?

Sol. Impulse and change in momentum are along the same direction. Therefore, angle between these two vectors is zero degree.

SHORT ANSWER Type Questions

16. Why are porcelain objects wrapped in paper or straw before packing for transportation? [NCERT]

Sol. Porcelain objects are wrapped in paper or straw before packing to reduce the chances of damage during transportation. During transportation sudden jerks or even fall can take place. Forces are created at the point of collision and the force takes longer time to reach the porcelain objects through paper or straw for same change in momentum as $F = \Delta p / \Delta t$ and therefore a lesser force acts on object.

17. A woman throws an object of mass 500 g with a speed of 25 m/s.
  (i) What is the impulse imparted to the object?
  (ii) If the object hits a wall and rebounds with half the original speed, what is the change in momentum of the object? [NCERT]

Sol. Given, Mass of the object $(m) = 500\,g = 0.5$ kg
Speed of the object $(v) = 25$ m/s
(i) Impulse imparted to the object
    = change in the momentum
    $= mv - mu = m(v - u)$
    $= 0.5(25 - 0) = 12.5$ N-s
(ii) Velocity of the object after rebounding $= -\dfrac{25}{2}$ m/s
    $v' = -12.5$ m/s
∴ Change in momentum $= m(v' - v)$
    $= 0.5(-12.5 - 25) = -18.75$ N-s

18. A passenger of mass 72.2 kg is riding in an elevator while standing on a platform scale. What does the scale read when the elevator cab is (i) descending with constant velocity (ii) ascending with constant acceleration, 3.5 m/s²?

Sol. Given, mass, $m = 72.2$ kg
Gravity acceleration, $g = 9.8$ m/s²
Scale reading = apparent weight = $R = ?$
(i) While descending with constant velocity, $a = 0$
    ∴ $R = mg$
              $R = 72.2 \times 9.8$
    ⇒ $R = 707.56$ N
(ii) While ascending with $a = 3.2$ m/s²
    $R = m(g + a)$
    $R = 72.2(9.8 + 3.2) = 938.6$ N

19. A person of mass 50 kg stands on a weighing scale on a lift. If the lift is descending with a downwards acceleration of 9 m/s², what would be the reading of the weighing scale? $(g = 10$ m/s²$)$

☀ When a lift descends with a downward acceleration a, the apparent weight of a body of mass m is given by
  $w' = R = m(g - a)$ [NCERT Exemplar]

Sol. Given, Mass of the person, $m = 50$ kg
Descending acceleration, $a = 9$ m/s²
Acceleration due to gravity, $g = 10$ m/s²
Apparent weight of the person,
    $R = m(g - a) = 50(10 - 9) = 50$ N
∴ Reading of the weighing scale $= \dfrac{R}{g} = \dfrac{50}{10} = 5$ kg

20. A person driving a car suddenly applies the brakes on seeing a child on the road ahead. If he is not wearing seat belt, he falls forward and hits his head against the steering wheel. Why?
                                                    [NCERT]

Sol. When a person driving a car suddenly applies the brakes, the lower part of the body slower down with the car while upper part of the body continues to move forward due to inertia of motion. If driver is not wearing seat belt, then he falls forward and his head hit against the steering wheel.

21. Why does a child feel more pain when she falls down on a hard cement floor, than when she falls on the soft muddy ground in the garden?
                                                    [NCERT]

Sol. When a child falls on a cement floor, her body comes to rest instantly.
But $F \times \Delta t$ = change in momentum = constant.
As time of stopping Δt decreases, therefore. F increases and hence child feel more pain. When she falls on a soft muddy ground in the garden, the time of stopping increases and hence F decreases and she feels lesser pain.

LONG ANSWER Type I Questions

22. A pebble of mass 0.05 kg is thrown vertically upwards. Give the direction and magnitude of the net force on the pebble

    (i) during its upward motion.

    (ii) during its downward motion.

    (iii) at the highest point where it is momentarily at rest.

Do your answer change if the pebble was thrown at an angle of 45° with the horizontal direction? Ignore air resistance.   **[NCERT]**

Sol. When an object is thrown vertically upward or it falls vertically downward under gravity, then an acceleration $g = 10 \, m/s^2$ acts downward due to the earth's gravitational pull.

Mass of pebble $(m) = 0.05$ kg

(i) During upward motion

Net force acting on pebble $(F) = ma = 0.05 \times 10$ N

$= 0.50$ N   (vertically downward)

(ii) During downward motion

Net force acting on pebble $(F) = ma = 0.05 \times 10$ N

$= 0.50$ N   (vertically downward)

(iii) At the highest point

Net force acting on pebble

$(F) = ma = 0.05 \times 10$ N

$= 0.50$ N   (vertically downward)

If pebble was thrown at an angle of 45° with the horizontal direction, then acceleration acting on it and therefore force acting on it will remain unchanged, i.e. 0.50 N (vertically downward). In case (c), at the highest point the vertical component of velocity will be zero but horizontal component of velocity will not be zero.

23. A stream of water flowing horizontally with a speed of 15 m/s gushes out of a tube of cross-sectional area 10^{-2} m^2 and hits a vertical wall nearby. What is the force exerted on the wall by the impact of water, assuming it does not rebound?   **[NCERT]**

Sol. Given, speed of the stream of water, $v = 15$ m/s

Area of cross-section of the tube, $A = 10^{-2}$ m^2

Volume of water coming out per second from the tube

$V = Av = 10^{-2} \times 15 = 15 \times 10^{-2}$ m^3

Density of water $= 10^3$ kg/m^3

∴ Mass of the water coming out of the tube per second

$m = V\rho$ $\left[\because \text{Density} = \dfrac{\text{mass}}{\text{volume}} \right]$

$= 15 \times 10^{-2} \times 10^3$ kg

$= 150$ kg/s

Force exerted on the wall by the impact of water

= change in momentum per second

$= mv = 150 \times 15$ N

$= 2250$ N

24. Ten one-rupee coins are put on top of each other on a table. Each coin has mass m. Give the magnitude and direction of

    (i) the force on the 7th coin (counted from the bottom) due to all the coins on its top,

    (ii) the force on the 7th coin by the 8 coin, (counted from the bottom)

    (iii) the reaction of the 6th coin on the 7th coin. (counted from the bottom)   **[NCERT]**

Sol. ∵ Mass of each coin $= m$

Number of total coins $= 10$

(i) Force acting on 7th coin (counted from the bottom)

= Weight of the coins above it

= Weight of 3 coins

$= 3 \, mg$ N (downward)

(ii) Force acting on 7th coin by the 8th coin = weight of the 8 coins + weight of two coins supported by 8 coins

$= mg + 2mg$

$= 3 \, mg$ N (downward)

(iii) Reaction of the 6th coin on the 7th coin

$= -$ (force exerted on 6th coin)

$= -$ (weight of 4 coins)

$= -4 \, mg$ N (vertically upward)

25. A helicopter of mass 1000 kg rises with a vertical acceleration of 15 m/s^2. The crew and the passengers weigh 300 kg. Give the magnitude and direction of the

    (i) force on floor by the crew and passengers.

    (ii) action of the rotor of the helicopter on the surrounding air

    (iii) force on the helicopter due to the surrounding air, take $g = 10$ m/s^2.   **[NCERT]**

Sol. ∵ Mass of the helicopter, $m_1 = 1000$ kg

Mass of the crew and the passengers, $m_2 = 300$ kg

Acceleration of the helicopter, $a = 15$ m/s^2

Acceleration due to gravity, $g = 10$ m/s^2

(i) Let R_1 be the reaction applied by the floor on the crew and the passengers.

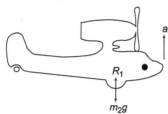

$$\therefore \quad R_1 - m_2 g = m_2 a$$

or $\quad R_1 = m_2 g + m_2 a = m_2(g+a) = 300\,(10+15)$
$$= 7500 \text{ N (upward direction)}$$

(ii) Action of the rotor of the helicopter on the surrounding air
$$= (m_1 + m_2)\,g + (m_1 + m_2)a$$
$$= (m_1 + m_2)(g + a)$$
$$= (1000 + 300) \times (10 + 15)$$
$$= 1300 \times 25 = 32500 \text{ N}$$

Force (action) of the rotor of the helicopter on the surrounding air = 32500 N (downward)

(iii) According to Newton's third law of motion, for every action there is an equal and opposite reaction.

$\therefore$ Force on the helicopter due to the surrounding air
$$= 32500 \text{ N} \quad \text{(upward direction)}$$

26. A girl riding a bicycle along a straight road with a speed of 5 m/s throws a stone of mass 0.5 kg which has a speed of 15 m/s with respect to the ground along her direction of motion. The mass of the girl and bicycle is 50 kg. Does the speed of the bicycle change after the stone is thrown? What is the change in speed, if so?

[NCERT Exemplar]

Sol. Total mass of girl, bicycle and stone,
$$m_1 = (50 + 0.5) \text{ kg} = 50.5 \text{ kg}$$
Velocity of bicycle, $u_1 = 5$ m/s
Mass of stone, $m_2 = 0.5$ kg
Velocity of stone, $u_2 = 15$ m/s
Mass of girl and bicycle, $m = 50$ kg
Yes, the speed of the bicycle changes after the stone is thrown.
Let, after throwing the stone the speed of bicycle be v m/s.
According to the law of conservation of linear momentum,
$$m_1 u_1 = m_2 u_2 + mv$$
$$50.5 \times 5 = 0.5 \times 15 + 50 \times v$$
$$252.5 - 7.5 = 50v \quad \text{or} \quad v = \frac{245.0}{50}$$
$$v = 4.9 \text{ m/s}$$
Change in speed $= 5 - 4.9 = 0.1$ m/s

LONG ANSWER Type II Questions

27. Give the magnitude and direction of the net force acting on

    (i) a drop of rain falling down with a constant speed.

    (ii) a cork of mass 10 g floating on water.

    (iii) a kite skillfully held stationary in the sky.

    (iv) a car moving with a constant velocity of 30 km/h on a rough road.

    (v) a high speed electron in space far from all gravitational (material) objects and free of electric and magnetic fields. **[NCERT]**

💡 Force $F = ma$, therefore force acting on a particle in unaccelerated ($a = 0$) motion is zero.

Sol. (i) As drop of rain is falling downward with a constant speed, therefore its acceleration is zero.
According to Newton's second law of motion, net force acting on drop $F = ma = 0$.

    (ii) In floating condition, the weight of the body is balanced by the upthrust. Therefore, net force acting on a cork floating on water = 0.

    (iii) As kite is held stationary in the sky, therefore acceleration of the kite is zero. Therefore, net force acting on the kite $F = ma = 0$.

    (iv) As car is moving with a constant velocity, therefore, its acceleration is zero i.e. $a = 0$ therefore, net force acting on the car $F = ma = 0$.

    (v) As electron is in a space where there is no electric field, magnetic field and gravitational (material) objects, therefore, no electric, magnetic and gravitational force is acting on it. Hence, net force acting on electron is zero.

28. Give the magnitude and direction of the net force acting on a stone of mass 0.1 kg.

    (i) Just after it is dropped from the window of a stationary train.

    (ii) Just after it is dropped from the window of a train running at a constant velocity of 36 km/h.

    (iii) Just after it is dropped from the window of a train accelerating with 1 m/s².

    (iv) Lying on the floor of a train which is accelerating with 1 m/s², the stone being at rest relative to the train. Neglect air resistance throughout. **[NCERT]**

💡 When any object is thrown from a train, the influence of train on the object becomes zero at the same moment, i.e. there is no effect of acceleration of train on the object.

Sol. $\because$ Mass of stone $(m) = 0.1$ kg

(i) When stone is dropped from the window of a stationary train, it falls freely under gravity.

$\therefore$ Net force acting on stone (F)

$$= mg = 0.1 \times 10$$
$$= 1.0 \text{ N (vertical downward)}$$

(ii) Just after the stone is dropped from the window of a train running at a constant velocity, i.e. acceleration of the train is zero. So, no force acts on the stone due to motion it falls freely under gravity.

The force acts on it is due to its weight only, i.e. acceleration of the train is zero, so no force acts, on the stone due to this motion.

(iii) The train accelerates horizontally by 1 m/s², but as the stone is left it moves under gravity only so the net force on it will be due to gravity only.

(iv) As the stone is accelerating with the train, so there must be a net horizontal force on it. Its weight also acts but is balanced by reaction force of the floor.

$$F = m \times a_{\text{(train)}} = 0.1 \times 1 = 0.1 \text{ N}$$

29. Figure shows (x, t), (y, t) diagram of a particle moving in 2-dimensions.

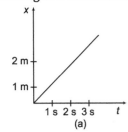 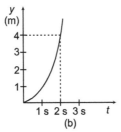

(a)　　　　　(b)

If the particle has a mass of 500 g, find the force (direction and magnitude) acting on the particle.

[NCERT Exemplar]

Sol. Given, mass of the particle $(m) = 500 \text{ g} = 0.5 \text{ kg}$

x-t graph of the particle is a straight line.

Hence, particle is moving with a uniform velocity along x-axis, i.e. its acceleration along x-axis is zero and hence, force acting along x-axis is zero.

y-t graph of particle is a parabola. Therefore, particle is in accelerated motion along y-axis.

At $t = 0$, $u_y = 0$

Along y-axis, at $t = 2$ s, $y = 4$ m

Using equation of motion, $y = u_y t + \dfrac{1}{2} a_y t^2$

$$4 = 0 \times 2 + \frac{1}{2} \times a_y \times (2)^2$$

or $\qquad a_y = 2 \text{ m/s}^2$

$\therefore$ Force acting along y-axis $(f_y) = ma_y$

$$= 0.5 \times 2 = 1.0 \text{ N} \quad \text{(along } y\text{-axis)}$$

30. Figure below shows the position-time graph of a particle of mass 4 kg. What is the (i) force on the particle for $t < 0$, $t > 4$s, $0 < t < 4$s? (ii) impulse at $t = 0$ and $t = 4$s? (Consider one-dimensional motion only).

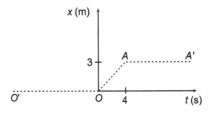

[NCERT]

💡 Velocity = slope of position-time graph
and impulse = change in momentum = $mv - mu$.

Sol. (i) (a) For $t < 0$, the position-time graph is OO', for which displacement of the particle is zero, therefore, particle is at rest at the origin. Hence, acceleration and force acting on particle will also be zero.

(b) For $t > 4$s, the position-time graph AA' is parallel to time axis. Therefore, for $t > 4$s particle remains at a fixed distance of 3 m from the origin. It means particle is at rest. Therefore, acceleration and force acting on particle will be zero.

(c) For $0 < t < 4$s, the position-time graph OA is a straight line inclined at an angle from time axis, which is representing uniform motion of the particle, i.e. the particle is moving with a constant velocity. Therefore, acceleration and force acting on the particle will be zero.

(ii) Impulse at $t = 0$

(a) Impulse = change in momentum

$$= mv - mu = m(v - u)$$

Before $t = 0$, particle is at rest, hence $u = 0$

After $t = 0$, particle is moving with a constant velocity.

Velocity of the particle = slope of position-time graph

$$= \frac{3 \text{ m}}{4 \text{ s}} = 0.75 \text{ m/s}$$

$\therefore$ Impulse = change in momentum

$$= 4(0.75 - 0) = 3 \text{ kg-m/s}$$

(b) Impulse at $t = 4$s

Before $t = 4$s, particle is moving with a constant speed, $u = 0.75$ m/s

After $t = 4$s, particle is again at rest

$\because \qquad v = 0$

$\therefore \qquad$ Impulse = Change in momentum = $m(v - u)$

$$= 4(0 - 0.75)$$
$$= -3 \text{ kg-m/s}$$

31. A block of mass 25 kg is raised by a 50 kg man in two different ways as shown in figure. What is the action on the floor by the man in the two cases? If the floor yields a normal force of 700 N, which mode should the man adopt to lift the block without the floor yielding? **[NCERT]**

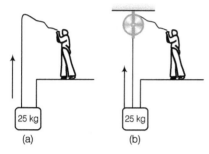

(a)   (b)

Sol. ∵ Mass of block, $m = 25$ kg

Mass of the man, $M = 50$ kg

Force required to lift the block (F) = weight of the block

$$F = mg = 25 \times 10 = 250 \text{ N}$$

Weight of the man, $w = Mg = 50 \times 10 = 500$ N

Case (a)

If the block is raised by the man as shown in Fig. (a), then, force is applied by the man in the upward direction due to which apparent weight of the man increases. When man applies force on block in upward direction, block applies force on man in downward direction, according to 3rd law of motion. Therefore, action on the floor by the man = $F + w$

$$= 250 + 500 = 750 \text{ N}$$

Case (b)

If the block is raised by the man as shown in Fig. (b), then, force is applied by the man in the downward direction due to which apparent weight of the man decreases. Therefore, action on the floor by the man

$$= mg - F$$

$$= 500 - 250 = 250 \text{ N}$$

The floor yields a normal force of 700 N. Action on the floor in case (a) exceeds 700 N, and less than 700 N in case (b). Therefore, mode (b) has to be adopted by the man to lift the block.

32. Explain why?

(i) A horse cannot pull a cart and run in empty space.

(ii) Passengers are thrown forward from their seats when a speeding bus stops suddenly.

(iii) It is easier to pull a lawn mower than to push it.

(iv) A cricketer moves his hands backwards while holding a catch. **[NCERT]**

Sol. (i) When a horse is trying to pull a cart, he pushes the ground backward at an angle from the horizontal. According to Newton's third law of motion, the

ground also apply equal reaction force on the feet of the horse in opposite direction. The vertical component of reaction balances the weight of the horse and horizontal component is responsible for motion of the cart. In empty space, there is no reaction force, therefore, a horse cannot pull a cart.

(ii) When bus is moving, the passengers sitting in it are also in motion and moving with the speed of the bus. When bus stops suddenly then lower part of the body of passengers which is in contact with the bus slow down with the bus but upper part of the bodies of the passengers continue to remain in motion in initial direction due to its inertia of motion and hence are thrown forward.

(iii) In pulling a lawn mower, a force F is applied in upward direction, making an angle θ with the horizontal [Fig. (a)]. Its vertical component in upward direction decreasing the effective weight of the mower.

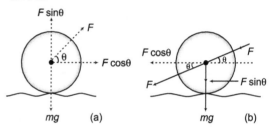

(a)   (b)

In pushing a lawn mower, a force F is applied in downward direction, making an angle θ with the horizontal [Fig. (b)]. Its vertical component is in downward direction increasing the effective weight of the mower. Therefore, it is easier to pull a lawn mower than to push it.

(iv) In holding a catch, the impulse imparted to the hands $= F \times \Delta t$ = change in momentum of the ball when a cricketer lowers his hands to take a catch, he increases the time taken to stop the ball. As time t increases the force F applied on the hands of the cricketer by the ball decreases and his hands feel less hurt.

33. Figure below shows the position-time graph of a body of mass 0.04 kg. Suggest a suitable physical context for this motion. What is the time between two consecutive impulses received by the body?

What is the magnitude of each impulse? **[NCERT]**

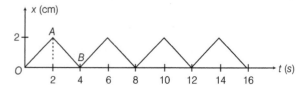

Sol. Mass of the body, $m = 0.04$ kg

The position-time graph OA from $t = 0$ to $t = 2$s is a straight line, therefore body is moving with a constant velocity.

Velocity of the body, $v = $ Slope of x-t graph

$$= \frac{2-0}{2-0} = 1 \text{ cm/s}$$

$$= 10^{-2} \text{m/s} \quad [\because 1 \text{ cm} = 10^{-2} \text{m}]$$

Part AB of position-time graph is also a straight line, therefore, velocity of the body

$$v' = \frac{0-2}{0-2} = -1 \text{ cm/s} = -10^{-2} \text{cm/s}$$

Negative sign shows that the direction of velocity is reversed after 2s and it is being repeated.

A suitable physical context for this motion is a ball moving with a constant velocity of 10^{-2} m/s between two walls located at $x = 0$ and at $x = 2$m and rebounded repeatedly on striking each wall.

Magnitude of the impulse imparted to the ball after every two seconds

= change in momentum of the ball

$$= mv - mv' = m(v - v')$$

$$= 0.04 \, [10^{-2} - (-10^{-2})]$$

$$= 8 \times 10^{-4} \text{kg-m/s}$$

ASSESS YOUR TOPICAL UNDERSTANDING

OBJECTIVE Type Questions

1. If the running bus stop suddenly our feet stop due to friction which does not allow relative motion between the feet and floor of the bus. But the rest of the body continues to move forward due to
   (a) momentum
   (b) force
   (c) inertia
   (d) impulse

2. A cricket ball of mass 150 g has an initial velocity $\mathbf{u} = (3\hat{\mathbf{i}} + 4\hat{\mathbf{j}}) \text{ ms}^{-1}$ and a final velocity $\mathbf{v} = -(3\hat{\mathbf{i}} + 4\hat{\mathbf{j}}) \text{ ms}^{-1}$, after being hit. The change in momentum (final momentum–initial momentum) is (in kg-ms^{-1}) **[NCERT Exemplar]**
   (a) zero
   (b) $-(0.45\hat{\mathbf{i}} + 0.6\hat{\mathbf{j}})$
   (c) $-(0.9\hat{\mathbf{j}} + 1.2\hat{\mathbf{j}})$
   (d) $-5(\hat{\mathbf{i}} + \hat{\mathbf{j}})\hat{\mathbf{i}}$

3. In the previous problem (2), the magnitude of the momentum transferred during the hit is
   [NCERT Exemplar]
   (a) zero
   (b) 0.75 kg-m s^{-1}
   (c) 1.5 kg-m s^{-1}
   (d) 14 kg-m s^{-1}

4. A body with mass 5 kg is acted upon by a force $\mathbf{F} = (-3\hat{\mathbf{i}} + 4\hat{\mathbf{j}})$ N. If its initial velocity at $t = 0$ is $v = (6\hat{\mathbf{i}} - 12\hat{\mathbf{j}}) \text{ms}^{-1}$, the time at which it will just have a velocity along the y-axis is
   (a) never   (b) 10 s   (c) 2 s   (d) 15 s

5. Which of the following statements is not true regarding the Newton's third law of motion?
   (a) To every action there is always an equal and opposite reaction
   (b) Action and reaction act on the same body

(c) There is no cause-effect relation between action and reaction
(d) Action and reaction forces are simultaneous

6. A book is lying on the table. What is the angle between the action of the book on the table and reaction of the table on the book?
   (a) 0°
   (b) 30°
   (c) 45°
   (d) 180°

7. Two forces $F_1 = 3\hat{\mathbf{i}} - 4\hat{\mathbf{j}}$ and $F_2 = 2\hat{\mathbf{i}} - 3\hat{\mathbf{j}}$ are acting upon a body of mass 2 kg. Find the force F_3 which when acting on the body will make it stable.
   (a) $5\hat{\mathbf{i}} + 7\hat{\mathbf{j}}$
   (b) $-5\hat{\mathbf{i}} - 7\hat{\mathbf{j}}$
   (c) $-5\hat{\mathbf{i}} + 7\hat{\mathbf{j}}$
   (d) $5\hat{\mathbf{i}} - 7\hat{\mathbf{j}}$

Answer

1.	(c)	2.	(c)	3.	(c)	4.	(b)	5.	(b)
6.	(d)	7.	(c)						

VERY SHORT ANSWER Type Questions

8. According to Newton's third law, every force is accompanied by an equal and opposite force. How can a movement ever take place?

9. A man suspends a fish from the spring balance held in his hand and the balance reads 9.8 N. While shifting the balance to his other hand, the balance slips and falls down. What will be the reading of the balance during the fall? **[Ans. zero]**

10. Action and reaction are equal and opposite. Why cannot they cancel each other?

11. Calculate the impulse necessary to step 1500 kg car travelling at 90 km/h. **[Ans. 37500 kg-m/s]**

SHORT ANSWER Type Questions

12. A force of 128 If acts on a mass of 490 g for 10 s. What velocity will it give to the mass?

    [**Ans.** 25.6 m/s]

13. A force of 16 N acts on a ball of mass 80 g for 1 μs. Calculate the acceleration and the impulse.

    [**Ans.** 200 m/s^2, 1.6×10^{-5} kg-m/s]

14. Two billiard balls each of mass 0.5 kg moving in opposite directions with speed 6 m/s collide and rebound with the same speed. What is the impulse imparted to each ball due to the other?

    [**Ans.** 3 kg-m/s]

15. A body of mass 25 kg is moving with a constant velocity of 5 m/s on a horizontal frictionless surface in vacuum. What is the force acting on the body?

    [**Ans.** zero]

LONG ANSWER Type I Questions

16. A body of mass 5 kg is acted upon by two perpendicular forces 8 N and 6 N. Find the magnitude and direction of the acceleration.

    [**Ans.** 2 m/s^2, Making an angle $\tan^{-1}(4/3)$ from 6 N force]

17. A batsman deflects a ball by an angle of 45° without changing its initial speed, which is equal to 54 km/h. What is the impulse imparted to the ball? Mass of the ball is 0.15 kg.

    [**Ans.** 4.16 kg-m/s]

18. Earth is rotating frame of reference, even then it is considered as inertial frame of reference for all practical purposes. Explain why?

19. Given the action force, describe the reaction force for each situation.

(i) You push forward on a book with 5.2 N.

    [**Ans.** 5.2 N backward]

(ii) A boat exerts a force of 450 N on the water.

    [**Ans.** 450 N on the boat]

(iii) A hockey player hits the boards with a force of 180 N toward the boards.

    [**Ans.** 180 N on the hockey stick]

LONG ANSWER Type II Questions

20. A hammer weighing 1 kg moving with the speed of 20 m/s strikes the head of a nail driving it 20 cm into a wall. Neglecting the mass of the nail, calculate

(i) the acceleration during the impact

    [**Ans.** −2000 m/s^2]

(ii) the time interval during the impact and

    [**Ans.** 0.01s]

(iii) the impulse

    [**Ans.** −20 N]

21. A male astronaut 82 kg and a female astronaut 64 kg are floating side by side in space.

(i) Determine the acceleration of each astronaut if the woman pushes on the man with a force of 16 N (left).

    [**Ans.** a_M = 0.2 m/s^2, a_W = .25 m]

(ii) How will your answers change if the man pushes with 16 N (Right) on the woman instead?

    [**Ans.** No change]

(iii) How will your answers change if they both reach out and push on each other's shoulders with a force of 16 N?

    [**Ans.** a_M = 2.62 m/s^2, a_W = 2 m/s^2]

| TOPIC 2 |
Common Forces in Mechanics and Circular Motion

COMMON FORCES IN MECHANICS

In mechanics, we encounter several kinds of forces.

(i) The gravitational force is all pervasive. Every object on the earth experiences the force of gravity due to earth. It is a **non-contact force**.

(ii) All the other forces common in mechanics are **contact forces**. A contact force on an object arises due to contact with some other object solid or fluid.

When bodies are in contact (e.g. a book resting on a table, a system of rigid bodies connected by rods), there are mutual contact forces (for each pair of bodies) satisfying the third law of motion.

The component of contact force normal to the surfaces in contact is called **normal reaction**. The component parallel to the surfaces in contact is called **friction**.

(iii) Contact forces arise also when solids are in contact with fluids.

e.g. For a solid immersed in a fluid, there is an upward force exerted by the fluid on the solid which is known as **buoyant force** and it is equal to the weight of the fluid displaced.

The viscous force, (i.e. force opposing the motion of the fluid), air resistance are examples of contact force.

Buoyant force

(iv) Two other common contact forces are tension in the string and force due to spring.

i.e. When a spring is compressed or extended by an external force, a restoring force is generated. This restoring force (F) is usually proportional to the compression and elongation (for small displacements).

It is expressed as $F = kx$, where k is a spring constant and x is the displacement.

Tension force When a body of mass m is fastened with the string, then the weight of the body acts downwards while a force acts just opposite to the downwards force for balancing the downwards force, this force is called **tension**.

$$T = mg$$

Spring force

where,

g = acceleration due to gravity,
T = tension in the string.

Tension force

Note
- Gravitational force is the only non-contact force that we use in mechanics.
- If the rope is not light, we will consider its weight as well.

FRICTION

Whenever a body moves or tends to move over the surface of another body, a force comes into play which acts parallel to the surface of contact and opposes the relative motion. This opposing force is called **friction**.

Consider a wooden block placed on a horizontal surface and give it a gentle push. The block slides through a small distance and comes to rest, then according to Newton's second law, a retarding force must be acting on the block. This retarding force or opposing force is called **friction** or **friction force**. As shown in figure, the force of friction always acts tangential to the surface in contact and in a direction opposite to the direction of (relative) motion of the body.

Friction in different directions

TYPES OF FRICTION

There are mainly two types of friction such as

1. Internal Friction

It arises on account of relative motion between two layers of a liquid. Internal friction is also referred as **viscosity** of liquid.

2. External Friction

It arises when two bodies in contact with each other try to move or there is an actual relative motion between the two bodies. This external friction is also called **contact friction**.

Further, external friction is of three types as given below

(i) Static Friction

Let us consider a wooden block placed over a horizontal table. Apply a small force F on it as shown in figure. The block does not move. The force of friction f_s comes into action which balances the applied force F.

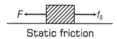
Static friction

Thus, force of friction which comes into play between two bodies before one body actually starts moving over the other is called **static friction** and it is denoted by f_s.

Therefore, static friction opposes the **impending motion** i.e. the motion that would take place under the applied force, if friction were absent. The static friction does not exist by itself. When there is no applied force, there is no static friction. It is a self adjusting force.

(ii) Limiting Friction

As we increase the applied force on the block, static friction f_s also increases to balance the applied force and the block does not move.

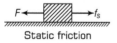
Static friction

Once the applied force is increased beyond a certain limit, the block just begins to move. At this stage, static friction is maximum.

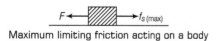
Maximum limiting friction acting on a body

Hence, maximum force of static friction which comes into play when a body just starts moving over the surface of another body is called **limiting friction**. Thus, $f_s \leq f_{s\,(max)}$.

There are four laws of limiting friction such as

(a) The value of the limiting friction depends upon the nature of the two surfaces in contact and their state of roughness.

(b) The force of limiting friction is tangential (parallel) to the two surfaces in contact and acts opposite to the direction in which the body would start moving on applying the force.

(c) The value of limiting friction is independent of the area of the surface in contact so long as the normal reaction remains the same.

(d) The value of limiting friction $(f_{s\,(max)})$ between two given surfaces is directly proportional to the normal reaction (R) between the two surfaces

i.e. $f_{s\,(max)} \propto R$ or $f_{s\,(max)} = \mu_s R$

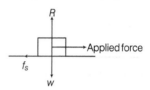

where, $R = w = mg,$ m = mass of the block

or $\mu_s = \dfrac{f_{s\,(max)}}{R} = \dfrac{\text{Limiting friction}}{\text{Normal reaction}}$

The proportionality constant μ_s is called **coefficient of static friction**. It is defined as the ratio of limiting friction to the normal reaction.

EXAMPLE |1| A Force Applied on a Sledge

A horizontal force of 980 N is required to slide a sledge weighing 1200 kgf over a flat surface. Calculate the coefficient of friction.

Sol. Given, $f_s = 980$ N, $R = Mg = 1200\,\text{kgf} = 1200 \times 9.8$ N

Now, coefficient of static friction

i.e. $\mu_s = \dfrac{f_s}{R} = \dfrac{980}{1200 \times 9.8} = 0.83$

EXAMPLE |2| A Force of Friction

A block of mass 2 kg is placed on the floor, the coefficient of static friction is 0.4. A force of 2.5 N is applied on the block as shown in figure. Calculate the force of friction between the block and the floor.

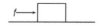

Sol. Here $m = 2\,kg, \mu_s = 0.4, g = 9.8\,m/s^2$

The value of limiting friction

$$F_{s(max)} = \mu_s R = \mu_s\, mg = 0.4 \times 2 \times 9.8 = 7.84\,N$$

As the applied force of 2.5 N is less than the limiting friction (7.84 N), so the block does not move.

In this situation, Force of friction = Applied force = 2.5 N

Angle of Friction

The angle of friction may be defined as the angle which the resultant of the limiting friction and the normal reaction makes with the normal reaction.

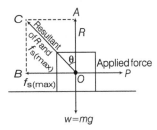

$w = mg$

In the above figure, OA represents the normal reaction R which balances the weight of the body. OB represents the limiting friction. P is the applied force and OC is the resultant of limiting friction and normal reaction. The angle θ between the normal reaction R and the resultant OC is the angle of friction.

The value of angle of friction depends on the nature of materials of the surfaces in contact and the nature of the surfaces (smooth or rough).

Relation between angle of friction (θ) and coefficient of friction (μ_s).

In ΔAOC, $\tan\theta = \dfrac{AC}{OA} = \dfrac{OB}{OA} = \dfrac{f_{s(max)}}{R}$

But $\dfrac{f_{s(max)}}{R} = \mu_s$ = coefficient of static friction

$\therefore$ $\tan\theta = \mu_s$ or $\theta = \tan^{-1}(\mu_s)$

Hence, **coefficient of static friction is equal to tangent of the angle of friction.**

EXAMPLE |3| Angle of Friction

A force of 49 N is just sufficient to pull a block of wood weighing 10 kg on a rough horizontal surface, so calculate the coefficient of friction and angle of friction.

Sol. Here, F = applied force= 49 N

$m = 10$ kg, $g = 9.8\,m/s^2$

Coefficient of friction, $\mu = \dfrac{F}{R} = \dfrac{F}{mg} = \dfrac{49}{10 \times 9.8} = 0.5$

As $\tan\theta = \mu = 0.5$

$\therefore$ $\theta = \tan^{-1}(0.5) = 26°34'$

Angle of Repose

Angle of repose is defined as the minimum angle of inclination of a plane with the horizontal, such that a body placed on the plane just begins to slide down the incline. It is represented by α and its value depends on material and nature of the surfaces in contact.

Consider a body of mass m placed on an inclined plane. The angle of inclination α of the inclined plane is so adjusted that a body placed on it just begins to slide down. Thus, α is the angle of repose the various forces acting on the body are

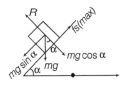

(i) The weight mg of the body acting vertically downwards.

(ii) The limiting friction $f_{s(max)}$ acting along the inclined plane in the upward direction. It balances the component $mg\sin\alpha$ of the weight mg perpendicular to the inclined plane. Thus,

$$f_{s(max)} = mg\sin\alpha \qquad \dots(i)$$

(iii) The normal reaction R acting at right angle to the inclined plane in the upward direction. It balances the weight $mg\cos\alpha$ of the weight mg perpendicular to the inclined plane. Thus

$$R = mg\cos\alpha \qquad \dots(ii)$$

Dividing the Eq. (i) by Eq. (ii), we get

$$\dfrac{f_{s(max)}}{R} = \dfrac{mg\sin\alpha}{mg\cos\alpha}$$

or $\mu_s = \tan\alpha$

Thus, the coefficient of static friction is equal to the tangent of the angle of repose.

As $\mu_s = \tan\theta = \tan\alpha$

$\therefore$ $\theta = \alpha$

Thus, the angle of friction is equal to the angle of repose.

(iii) Kinetic Friction

When we increase the applied force slightly beyond limiting friction, the actual motion starts and force of friction decreases. This means that the applied force is now greater than the force of limiting friction. The force of friction at this stage is called **kinetic friction** or **dynamic friction** which is actually a little bit less than the value of limiting friction.

Hence, kinetic friction or dynamic friction is the opposing force that comes into play when one body is actually moving over the surface of another body. Thus, kinetic friction opposes the **relative motion**.

There are four laws of kinetic friction such as

(a) The kinetic friction opposes the relative motion and has a constant value which depends on the nature of two surfaces in contact.

(b) The value of kinetic friction f_k is independent of the area of contact so long as the normal reaction remains the same.

(c) The kinetic friction does not depend on velocity.

(d) The value of kinetic friction f_k is directly proportional to the normal reaction R between the two surfaces.

i.e. $$f_k \propto R$$

or $$f_k = \mu_k R$$

$$\mu_k = \frac{f_k}{R} = \frac{\text{Kinetic friction}}{\text{Normal reaction}}$$

The proportionality constant μ_k is called **coefficient of kinetic friction** and it is defined as the ratio of kinetic friction to the normal reaction.

Note
- This can be shown as $f_k < f_{s(\max)}$ or $\mu_k R < \mu_s R$
  $$\therefore \qquad \mu_k < \mu_s$$
- Thus, the coefficient of kinetic friction is less than the coefficient of static friction.

EXAMPLE |4| Coefficient of Kinetic Friction

A hockey puck is given an initial speed of 20 m/s on a frozen pond as shown in figure. The puck remains on the ice and slides 120 m before coming to rest. Determine the coefficient of kinetic friction between the puck and the ice.

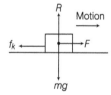

💡 After the puck is given an initial velocity, the external forces acting on it are the weight mg, the normal force R and the force of kinetic friction f_k. The acceleration of the puck can be found from $v^2 = u^2 + 2ax$, with the final speed v equal to zero because after 120 m the puck comes to rest.

Sol. Given,

The initial speed, $u = 20$ m/s

Distance travelled, $x = 120$ m

$$v^2 = u^2 + 2ax \qquad \text{[third equation of motion]}$$
$$0 = (20 \text{ m/s})^2 + 2a \,(120 \text{ m})$$
$$a = -1.67 \text{ m/s}^2$$

The negative sign shows that the acceleration is towards left, i.e. opposite the direction of the velocity.

$$\Sigma F_y = R - w = 0 \implies R = w = mg$$

Thus, $$f_k = \mu_k R = \mu_k mg$$
$$\Sigma F_x = -f_k = ma$$
$$\implies \mu_k mg = m \,(-1.67 \text{ m/s}^2)$$

$$\mu_k = \frac{1.67 \text{ m/s}^2}{9.80 \text{ m/s}^2} = 0.170$$

EXAMPLE |5| Force on the Block

A block P of mass 4 kg is placed on another block Q of mass 5 kg, and the block Q rests on a smooth horizontal table. For sliding block P on Q, horizontal force of 12 N is required to be applied on P. How much maximum force can applied on Q so that both P and Q move together? Also, find out acceleration produced by this force.

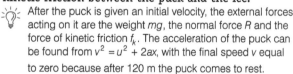

Sol. Here, $m_1 = 4$ kg, $m_2 = 5$ kg

Force applied on block $P = 12$ N

This force must be equal to the kinetic friction applied on P by Q.

$$\therefore \qquad 12 = F_k = \mu_k R = \mu_k m_1 g$$
or $$12 = \mu_k \times 4g \quad \text{or} \quad \mu_k = \frac{12}{4g} = \frac{3}{g}$$

acceleration of $P = \dfrac{12}{4} = 3$ m/s

When force F is applied on Q to create common motion in P & Q, the forces created (friction) is shown in the diagram above. F_1 force will be created on P and F_2 force will be created on Q.

Considering forces on Q, we have
$$F - F_2 \text{ (net force)} = m_2 \times a = m_2 \times 3$$
Since, $F_1 = F_2 = \mu_1 m_1 g$
$$F - \mu_k m_1 g = m_2 \times 3$$
$$F = \mu_k m_1 g + m_2 \times 3 = \frac{3}{g} \times 4 \times g + 5 \times 3 = 12 + 15 = 27 \text{ N}$$

As this force moves both the blocks together on a smooth table, so the acceleration produced is
$$a = \frac{F}{m_1 + m_2} = \frac{27}{4 + 5} = 3 \text{ m/s}$$

EXAMPLE |6| Kinetic Friction Between Deck and the Disc

Consider a shuffleboard cue which is being used by a cruiseship passenger. To push the shuffleboard disc of mass 0.50 kg horizontally along the deck so that the disc leaves the cue with a speed of 6 m/s, what will be the coefficient of kinetic friction between the deck and the disc if the disc slides a distance of 10 m before coming to rest?

When the disc is separated from the cue, the force of kinetic friction is the only horizontal force acting on the disc. Since, the frictional force is constant, the acceleration is also constant.

Sol. ∵ Mass of the disc, $m = 0.50$ kg

Initial velocity, $u = 6$ m/s

Displacement, $x = 10$ m

Coefficient of kinetic friction, $\mu_k = ?$

Draw a FBD for the disc after it leaves the cue.

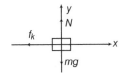

Apply $\Sigma F_y = ma_y$ to the disc and solve for normal reaction N.

$$\Sigma F_y = ma_y$$
$$N - mg = 0$$
$$N = mg = 0.5 \times 9.8 = 4.9 \text{ N}$$

The kinetic friction f_k can be found out by using the equation given below $f_k = \mu_k\, mg$

Now, apply $\Sigma F_x = ma_x$ to the disc and solve for a_x.

$$-f_k = ma_x \quad \text{or} \quad -\mu_k mg = ma_x$$
$$a_x = -\mu_k g$$

Now, use the third equation of motion.

$$v^2 = u^2 + 2ax \quad 0 = 6^2 + 2(-\mu_k g)10$$

$$\mu_k = \frac{36}{2 \times 9.8 \times 10} = \frac{36}{196} = 0.184$$

Types of Kinetic Friction

(i) Sliding Friction

The force of friction that comes into play when a body slides over the surface of another body is called **sliding friction**.

e.g. When a flat block is moved over the flat surface of a table, then the opposing force acting on it is known as sliding friction.

Laws of sliding friction are

(a) The sliding friction opposes the applied force and has a constant value, depending upon the nature of the two surfaces in relative motion.

(b) The force of sliding friction is directly proportional to the normal reaction R.

(c) The sliding frictional force is independent of the area of the contact between the two surfaces so long as the normal reactions remain the same.

(d) The sliding friction does not depend upon the velocity.

EXAMPLE |7| Enjoy the Ride of a Trolley

What is the acceleration of the block and trolley system shown in a figure. If the coefficient of kinetic friction between the trolley and the surface is 0.04, what is the tension in the string? (take $g = 10$ ms^{-2}). Neglect the mass of the string. **[NCERT]**

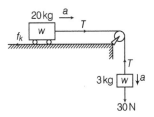

 As the string is inextensible and the pulley is smooth, the 3 kg block and the 20 kg trolley both have same magnitude of acceleration.

Sol. Applying the second law of motion to the block.

$$30 - T = 3a \qquad \text{...(i)}$$

Apply the second law of motion to the trolley.

$$T - f_k = 20a$$

Now, $\qquad f_k = \mu_k R = \mu_k\, mg$

Here, $\qquad \mu_k = 0.04$

$$f_k = 0.04 \times 20 \times 10 = 8 \text{ N}$$

Thus, the equation for the motion of the trolley is

$$T - 8 = 20a \qquad \text{...(ii)}$$

On adding Eqs.(i) and (ii), we get

$$22 = 23a$$

or $\qquad a = \dfrac{22}{23} = 0.96 \text{ m/s}^2$

From Eq. (i),

$$30 - T = 3 \times 0.96$$
$$T = 30 - 2.88 = 27.12 \text{ N}$$

(ii) Rolling Friction

The force of friction that comes into play when a body rolls over the surface of another body is called **rolling friction**. e.g. When a wheel, circular disc or a ring or a sphere or a cylinder roll over a surface, the force that opposes it is the rolling friction.

When a wheel rolls without slipping over a horizontal plane, the surfaces at contact do not rub each other. The relative velocity of the point of contact of the wheel with respect to the plane is zero, if there is no slipping. There is no sliding or static friction in such an ideal situation.

We need to overcome rolling friction only which is much smaller than sliding friction. For this reason, wheel has been considered as one of the greatest inventions. It conversly sliding into rolling friction thus lowers friction.

Cause of Rolling Friction Let us consider a wheel rolling along a road. As the wheel rolls, it exerts a large pressure due to its small area.

This causes a depression in the surface below and a mount or bump in front of it is shown in figure. In addition to this, the rolling wheel has a continuously detach itself from the surface on which it rolls. This is opposed by the adhesive force between the two surfaces in contact.

On account of these factors, a force originates which retards the rolling motion. This retarding force is known as **rolling friction**.

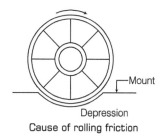

Cause of rolling friction

Ways for Reducing Friction

The various ways of reducing friction are

(i) **Lubrication** They are used to reduce kinetic friction in a machine. Lubricants like oil, grease, etc. fill the irregularities of the surface to make them smoothers. Thus, friction decreases.

(ii) **Polishing** They are used to make the surface smoother.

(iii) **Ball Bearing** The ball bearing arrangement consists of two co-axial cylinders P and R between which suitable number of hard steel balls are arranged. When the wheel rotates the ball B rotates in the direction as shown.

   The wheel thus rolls on the balls instead of sliding on the axle. Thus, power dissipation is reduced.

Ball bearing arrangement

(iv) A thin cushion of air maintained between solid surfaces in relative motion.

(v) **Streamlining** Friction due to air is considerably reduced by streamlining the shape of the body moving through air.

DYNAMICS OF CIRCULAR MOTION

Earlier, we have studied that acceleration of a body moving in a circle of radius r with uniform speed v is $\dfrac{v^2}{r}$ directed towards the centre. From second law of motion, the force F_c is given by

$$\text{Centripetal force, } F_c = \frac{mv^2}{r}$$

where, m is the mass of the body. This force directed forward the centre is called **centripetal force**.

But $\dfrac{v^2}{r}$ is centripetal acceleration or radial acceleration.

$$\therefore \quad \boxed{\text{Centripetal force, } F_c = mr\omega^2} \qquad [\because v = \omega r]$$

For a stone rotated in a circle by a string, the centripetal force is provided by the tension in the string.

The centripetal force for motion of a planet around the sun is the gravitation force on the planet due to the sun.

For a car taking a circular turn on a horizontal road, the centripetal is the force of friction.

EXAMPLE |8| **Check out the Revolving Satellite**
An artificial satellite of mass 2500 kg is orbiting around the earth with a speed of 4 kms^{-1} at a distance of 10^4 km from the earth. Calculate the centripetal force acting on it.

Sol. Given, $r = 10^4 \text{ km} = 10^4 \times 1000 \text{ m} = 10^7 \text{ m}$,
$$m = 2500 \text{ kg},$$
$$v = 4 \text{ kms}^{-1} = 4 \times 10^3 \text{ ms}^{-1}$$

Now, centripetal force is $F = \dfrac{mv^2}{r}$

$$F = \frac{2500 \times (4 \times 10^3)^2}{10^7} = \frac{2500 \times 16 \times 10^6}{10^7}$$

$$F = \frac{250 \times 16 \times 10^7}{10^7} = 4000 \text{ N}$$

Interesting Applications of Laws of Motion

The circular motion of a car on a flat and banked road are explained below

(i) Circular Motion of a Car on Level Road

When a vehicle goes round a curved road, it requires some centripetal force. While rounding the curve, the wheels of the vehicle have a tendency to leave the curved path and regain the straight line path. The force of friction between the road and the tyres provided the centripetal force required to keep the car in motion around the curve.

There are three forces acting on the car such as

(i) The weight of the car mg, acting vertically downwards.

(ii) Normal reaction R of the road on the car, acting vertically upwards.

(iii) Frictional force F, along the surface of the road, i.e. towards the centre of the turn.

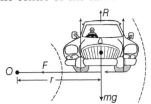

Motion of a car on a circular level road

Let us consider a car of weight mg going around a circular level road of radius r with velocity v as shown in figure. While taking the turn, the tyres of the car tend to leave the road and go away from the centre of the curve.

The force of friction F is acting on the tyre and R is the normal reaction of the ground.

As there is no acceleration in the vertical direction, then

$$R - mg = 0 \implies R = mg$$

For circular motion, the centripetal force is along the surface of the road towards the centre of the turn. The static friction opposes the impending motion of the car moving away from the circle. Thus, $\dfrac{mv^2}{r} \leq F$

where v is the velocity of car while turning and r is the radius of the circular track.

As, $$F = \mu_s R = \mu_s mg$$

F is limiting friction here to get maximum velocity possible of car

where, μ_s is the coefficient of static friction between tyres and the road.

$$\therefore \qquad \frac{mv^2}{r} \leq \mu_s mg \implies v \leq \sqrt{\mu_s rg}$$

or $\boxed{\text{Maximum velocity of the vehicle, } v_{max} = \sqrt{\mu_s rg}}$

Hence, the maximum velocity with which a vehicle can go round a level curve without skidding is

$$v = \sqrt{\mu_s rg}.$$

EXAMPLE |9| Rounding off a Flat Curve

A bend in a level road has a radius of 100 m. Find the maximum speed which a car turning this bend may have without skidding, if the coefficient of friction between the tyres and road is 0.8.

Sol. The maximum speed which the car can have without skidding is given by

$$\mu = \frac{v^2}{rg} \implies v = \sqrt{\mu rg}$$

Here, $r = 100$ m, $\mu = 0.8$, $g = 9.8$ ms^{-2}

$$v = \sqrt{0.8 \times 100 \times 9.8} = \sqrt{4 \times 2 \times 2 \times 49}$$

$$v = 2 \times 2 \times 7 = 28 \text{ m/s}$$

EXAMPLE |10| Cyclist Slip on Turn

A cyclist speeding at 18 km/h on a level road takes a sharp circular turn of radius 3m without reducing the speed. The coefficient of static friction between the tyres and the road is 0.1. Will the cyclist slip while taking the turn? [NCERT]

Sol. Here, $v = 18$ km/h $= \dfrac{18 \times 1000}{60 \times 60} = 5$ m/s

$$r = 3 \text{ m}, \mu_s = 0.1$$

On a level road, frictional force alone can provide the centripetal force.

Therefore, condition for the cyclist not to slip is that

$$\frac{mv^2}{r} \leq F_s \; (= \mu_s R = \mu_s \, mg); \; v^2 \leq \mu_s rg$$

As $\qquad v^2 = (5)^2 = 25 \text{ m}^2\text{s}^{-2}$

and $\quad \mu_s \, rg = 0.1 \times 3 \times 10 = 3 \text{ m}^2\text{s}^{-2}$

$\therefore$ The condition is not satisfied. Hence, the cyclist will slip.

(ii) Motion of a Car on a Banked Road

The large amount of friction between the tyres and the road produces considerable wear and tear of the tyres. To avoid this, the curved road is given an inclined sloping upwards towards the outer circumference. This reduces wearing out of the tyres because the horizontal component of normal reaction provides the necessary centripetal force.

The system of raising the outer edge of a curved road above its inner edge is called **banking of the curved road**. So, the angle through which the outer edge of the curved road is raised above the inner edge is called **angle of banking**.

Let us consider a car of weight mg going along a curved path of radius r with speed v on a road banked at an angle θ, as shown in figure.

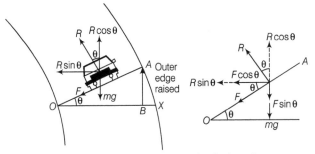

Circular motion of a car on a banked road

The forces acting on the car are
  (i) Weight mg acting vertically downwards.
  (ii) Normal reaction R acting upwards in a direction perpendicular to inclined plane making angle θ with the horizontal plane.
  (iii) Force of friction F acting downwards along the inclined plane because car tends to slip outwards.

Reaction R can be resolved into two rectangular components
  (i) $R\cos\theta$, along vertically upward direction.
  (ii) $R\sin\theta$, along the horizontal towards the centre of the curved road .

Force of friction F, can also be resolved into two rectangular components.
  (i) $F\cos\theta$, along the horizontal, towards the centre of curved road.
  (ii) $F\sin\theta$, along vertically downward direction.

Since, there is no motion along vertical, so
$$R\cos\theta = mg + F\sin\theta \qquad \text{...(i)}$$

Let v is velocity of the car. The centripetal force is now provided by the components $R\sin\theta$ and $F\cos\theta$, i.e.
$$R\sin\theta + F\cos\theta = \frac{mv^2}{r} \qquad \text{...(ii)}$$

We know $F = \mu_s R$, then we can write Eqs. (i) and (ii) as
$$R\cos\theta = mg + \mu_s R\sin\theta \qquad \text{...(iii)}$$
and $\quad R\sin\theta + \mu_s R\cos\theta = \frac{mv^2}{r} \qquad \text{...(iv)}$

From Eq. (iii), we get
or $\qquad R\cos\theta - \mu_s R \cdot \sin\theta = mg$
or $\qquad R(\cos\theta - \mu_s \sin\theta) = mg$
or $\qquad R = \dfrac{mg}{\cos\theta - \mu_s \sin\theta} \qquad \text{...(v)}$

From Eq. (iv), we get
$$R(\sin\theta + \mu_s \cos\theta) = \frac{mv^2}{r} \qquad \text{...(vi)}$$

From Eq. (v) and (vi), we get
$$\frac{mg(\sin\theta + \mu_s \cos\theta)}{\cos\theta - \mu_s \sin\theta} = \frac{mv^2}{r}$$
$$\therefore \qquad v^2 = \frac{rg(\sin\theta + \mu_s \cos\theta)}{(\cos\theta - \mu_s \sin\theta)}$$
$$v^2 = \frac{rg\cos\theta\left(\dfrac{\sin\theta}{\cos\theta} + \dfrac{\mu_s \cos\theta}{\cos\theta}\right)}{\cos\theta\left(\dfrac{\cos\theta}{\cos\theta} - \mu_s \dfrac{\sin\theta}{\cos\theta}\right)}$$

$$v^2 = \frac{rg\cos\theta(\tan\theta + \mu_s)}{\cos\theta(1 - \mu_s \tan\theta)}$$
$$v^2 = \frac{rg(\tan\theta + \mu_s)}{(1 - \mu_s \tan\theta)}$$

Maximum velocity of vehicle on banked road, $v = \sqrt{\dfrac{rg(\mu_s + \tan\theta)}{(1 - \mu_s \tan\theta)}} \qquad \text{...(vii)}$

Special case When there is no friction between the road and the tyres, then the safe limit for maximum velocity is $\mu_s = 0$,

Substituting the value of μ_s in Eq. (vii), we get
$$v = \sqrt{\frac{rg(0 + \tan\theta)}{1 - (0 \times \tan\theta)}}$$
$$v = \sqrt{rg\tan\theta} \qquad \text{...(viii)}$$

This is the speed at which car does not slide down even if, track is smooth. If track is smooth and speed is less than $\sqrt{rg\tan\theta}$, vehicle will move down so that r gets decreased and if speed is more than this vehicle will move up.

The angle of banking θ for minimum wear and tear of tyres is given by Eq. (viii), we get

$$\tan\theta = \frac{v^2}{rg} \quad \text{or} \quad \boxed{\text{Angle of banking, } \theta = \tan^{-1}\left(\frac{v^2}{rg}\right)}$$

EXAMPLE |11| Formula One Racing Track

A circular race track of radius 300 m is banked at angle of 15°. If the coefficient of friction between the wheels of a race car and the road is 0.2, what is the (i) optimum speed of the race car to avoid wear and tear on its tyres and (ii) maximum permissible speed to avoid slipping?
[tan 15° = 0.2679]   [NCERT]

💡 On a banked road, the horizontal component of the normal force and the frictional force contribute to provide centripetal force to keep the car moving on a circular turn without slipping. At the optimum speed, the normal reaction's component is enough to provide the needed centripetal force and the frictional force is not needed. Friction force increases the slope of increasing the velocity on banked surface.

Sol. The optimum speed v_0 is given by equation
$$v_0 = (R\,g\tan\theta)^{1/2}$$

Here, $\quad R = 300$ m, $\theta = 15°$, $g = 9.8$ ms^{-2}, $\mu_s = 0.2$,
We have
$$v_0 = 28.1 \text{ ms}^{-1}$$

The maximum permissible speed v_{max} is given by equation.

$$v_{max} = \left(Rg \frac{\mu_s + \tan\theta}{1 - \mu_s \tan\theta} \right)^{1/2}$$

$$v_{max} = \left(\frac{300 \times 9.8 \times (0.2 + \tan 15°)}{1 - (0.2 \times \tan 15°)} \right)^{1/2}$$

$$v_{max} = \left(\frac{2940 \times (0.4679)}{0.9464} \right)^{1/2}$$

$$= (1453.535)^{1/2} = 38.1 \text{ ms}^{-1}$$

EXAMPLE |12| Train goes over Circular Path

The radius of curvature of a railway track at a place, where the train is moving at a speed of 72 kmh^{-1} is 625 m. The distance between the rails is 1.5 m. Find the angle and the elevation of the out rail so that there may be no side pressure on the rails. Take, $g = 9.8$ m/s^2

[$\tan^{-1}(0.00653) = 3.74°$, $\sin 3.74° = 0.06522$]

Sol. Here, $r = 625$ m, $v = 72$ kmh^{-1}

$$v = 72 \times \frac{5}{18} \text{ m/s}$$

$$v = 20 \text{ m/s}, \ g = 9.8 \text{ m/s}^2, \ l = 1.5 \text{ m}$$

Now, angle of elevation of outer rail

i.e $\qquad \tan\theta = \dfrac{v^2}{rg}$

$$\tan\theta = \frac{20 \times 20}{625 \times 9.8} = .00653$$

$$\theta \ \tan^{-1} = (0.00653)$$

$$\theta = 3.74°$$

Also, elevation of outer rail $h = l\sin\theta$

$$h = 1.5 \sin 3.74°$$

$$h = 0.0978 \text{ m} = 9.78 \text{ cm}$$

EXAMPLE |13| Banked Curve

If a car having speed 50 km/h can round the curve banked at an angle θ. Find out the value of θ, if radius of the curve is 40 m and consider the friction is negligible. [$\tan^{-1}(0.5) = 26.5$]

💡 In the given case, only two forces act on the car i.e. gravity and the normal force. Since, the car is travelling in a circle at constant speed, the acceleration is in the centripetal direction. The vector sum of the two forces is in the direction of the acceleration.

Sol. Write the given quantity and the quantity to be known.

$$v = 50 \text{ km/h} = 50 \times \frac{5}{18} \text{ m/s} = 13.88 \text{ m/s}$$

$$r = 40 \text{ m}, \ \theta = ?$$

Draw the FBD of the car.

Now, apply $\Sigma F_g = ma_y$ to the car

$$R\cos\theta - mg = 0 \ \Rightarrow \ R = \frac{mg}{\cos\theta}$$

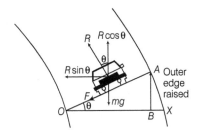

Similarly, apply $\Sigma F_x = ma_x$ to the car

$$R\sin\theta = \frac{mv^2}{r}$$

Put the value of R and then solve for θ.

$$\frac{mg}{\cos\theta} \cdot \sin\theta = \frac{mv^2}{r}$$

$$\Rightarrow \qquad \tan\theta = \frac{v^2}{rg}; \theta = \tan^{-1}\left(\frac{v^2}{rg} \right)$$

Put the all given values to get θ.

$$\theta = \tan^{-1}\left[\frac{(13.88)^2}{40 \times 9.8} \right] = \tan^{-1}(0.4917)$$

$$\theta = 26.18°$$

Solving Problems in Mechanics

A typical problem in mechanics usually does not merely involve a single body under the action of given forces. More often, we will need to consider an assembly of different bodies exerting forces on each other. Besides, each body in the assembly experiences the force of gravity. To solve a typical problem in mechanics, we use the following steps

• Draw a diagram showing schematically the various parts of the assembly of bodies, the links, supports, etc.

• Choose a convenient part of the assembly as one system.

• Draw a separate diagram which shows this system and all the forces on the system by the remaining part of the assembly. Also include the forces on the system by other agencies. A diagram of this type is known as **free body diagram**.

• In free body diagram, mark the magnitude and direction of the forces that are either given or you are sure of and the rest should be treated as unknowns to be determined using laws of motion.

• If necessary, we can follow the same procedure for any other part of the system. The equations of laws of motion obtain for different parts of the system can be solved to obtain the desired results.

EXAMPLE |14| Action-reaction Pairs

A wooden block of mass 2 kg rests on a soft horizontal floor. When an iron cylinder of mass 25 kg is placed on top of the block, the floor yields steadily and the block and the cylinder together go down with an acceleration of $0.1 \, \text{m/s}^2$. What is the action of the block on the floor (i) before and (ii) after the floor yields? Take $g = 10 \, \text{m/s}^2$. Identify the action-reaction pairs in the problem. **[NCERT]**

Sol. ∵ Mass of the block = 2 kg

Mass of the cylinder = 25 kg

Acceleration of the system = $0.1 \, \text{m/s}^2$

$$g = 10 \, \text{m/s}^2$$

The force of gravitational attraction of the earth, i.e. weight of the block is equal to mg.

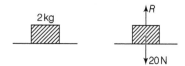

$$w = mg \implies w = 2 \times 10 \implies w = 20 \, \text{N}$$

According to Newton's first law, net force on the block is zero, i.e. $R = 20 \, \text{N}$

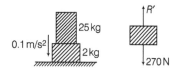

Force of gravity due to the earth, i.e.

$$w = mg = (25 + 2) \times 10 = 270 \, \text{N}$$

$$270 - R' = 27 \times 0.1$$

$$\implies \qquad R' = 270 - 2.7 = 267.3 \, \text{N}$$

EXAMPLE |15| Pulley-block System

Consider two masses m_1 and m_2 connected by a light and inextensible string passing over a smooth light pulley which is fixed by a rigid cord, from a rigid support as shown in figure. This device is also known as Atwood's machine. Find the tension in the rope and acceleration of each block.

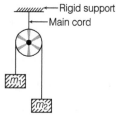

Sol. To study the motion of the blocks, let us draw the free body diagram (FBD) of various parts of the system, by assuming $m_2 > m_1$. FBD and dynamics of block m_1

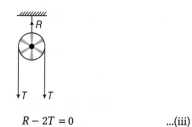

$$T - m_1 g = m_1 a \qquad \qquad ...(i)$$

FBD and dynamics of block m_2,

$$m_2 g - T = m_2 a \qquad \qquad ...(ii)$$

FBD of pulley

$$R - 2T = 0 \qquad \qquad ...(iii)$$

where, R is reaction on the axle of pulley. Since, pulley is fixed, therefore, $a = 0$ for it.

From the solution of simultaneous Eqs. (i), (ii) and (iii) we get, the value of acceleration a, tension T and pressure R on the axle of pulley.

Thus, from adding Eqs. (i) and (ii), we get acceleration a

$$T - m_1 g = m_1 a$$

and $\qquad m_2 g - T = m_2 a$

or $T - m_1 g + m_2 g - T = m_1 a + m_2 a$

$$m_2 g - m_1 g = a (m_1 + m_2)$$

or $\qquad a = \dfrac{(m_2 - m_1) g}{(m_1 + m_2)} \qquad \qquad ...(iv)$

On substituting a in Eqs. (i) or (ii), we get

$$T = \left(\dfrac{2 \, m_1 m_2 \, g}{m_1 + m_2} \right) \qquad \qquad ...(v)$$

and pressure on pulley from Eq. (iii), we get

$$R = 2T$$

$$R = 2 \times \dfrac{2 \, m_1 m_2 \, g}{m_1 + m_2} = \dfrac{4 \, m_1 m_2 g}{m_1 + m_2} \qquad \qquad ...(vi)$$

EXAMPLE |16| Motion of Two Bodies

A body of mass m_1 equal to 20 kg is placed on a smooth horizontal table. This body is connected to a string which passes over a frictionless pulley. The string also carries another body of mass m_2 equal to 10 kg at the other end. Find out the acceleration which will be produced when the nail fixed on the table is removed, also find out the tension in the string during the motion of the bodies. What is the result, when the bodies stop? Take $g = 10$ N/kg.

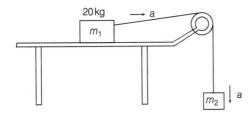

Sol. When the nail fixed on the table is removed, system of two bodies moves with an acceleration a in the forward direction. The acceleration can be found by using Newton's second law.

Draw the FBD for each body as shown in the figure

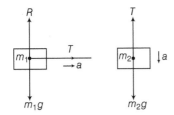

For mass m_1,

$$T = m_1 a \qquad \text{...(i)}$$

For mass m_2,

$$m_2 g - T = m_2 a \qquad \text{...(ii)}$$

Adding Eqs. (i) and (ii), we get

$$m_1 a + m_2 a = m_2 g$$

$$a = \frac{m_2 g}{m_1 + m_2}$$

$$= \frac{10 \times 10}{20 + 10} = \frac{100}{30}$$

$$= 3.33 \text{ m/s}^2$$

Tension, $T = m_1 a = 10 \times 3.33 = 33.3$ N

When the bodies stop, acceleration, a will be zero. Suppose, the tension becomes T. As the net force on each body is zero, so for body m_2

$$T = m_2 g$$
$$= 10 \times 10$$
$$= 100 \text{ N}$$

EXAMPLE |17| Connected Bodies

Two bodies of masses 10 kg and 20 kg respectively kept on a smooth, horizontal surface are tied to the ends of a light string. A horizontal force $F = 600$ N is applied to (i) A, (ii) B along the direction of string. What is the tension in the string in each case? **[NCERT]**

Sol. (i) **When force is applied on A, then**

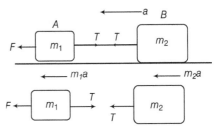

$\because$ Mass of body A $(m_1) = 10$ kg
Mass of body B $(m_2) = 20$ kg
Force applied $(F) = 600$ N
For body A, $F - T = m_1 a$ ...(i)
For body B, $T = m_2 a$ ...(ii)
Adding Eqs. (i) and (ii), we get

$$F = (m_1 + m_2) a$$

or $\qquad a = \dfrac{F}{m_1 + m_2} = \dfrac{600}{(10 + 20)} = 20 \text{ m/s}^2$

Substituting value of a in Eq. (ii), we get

$$T = m_2 a = 20 \times 20 \text{ N} = 400 \text{ N}$$

(ii) **When force is applied on B, then**

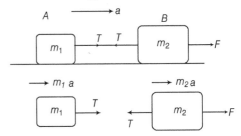

For body A, $\qquad T = m_1 a$ ...(iii)
For body B, $\qquad F - T = m_2 a$ ...(iv)
Adding Eqs. (iii) and (iv), we get

$$F = (m_1 + m_2) a$$

or $\qquad a = \dfrac{F}{m_1 + m_2}$

$$= \dfrac{600}{10 + 20} = 20 \text{ m/s}^2$$

Substituting the value of a in Eq. (iii), we get

$$T = m_1 a = 10 \times 20 = 200 \text{ N}$$

EXAMPLE |18| Tension in the Strings

Consider the body of mass m is suspended by two strings making angles α and β with the horizontal as shown in figure. If the body is in equilibrium, then find out the tension in the strings.

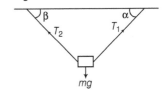

Sol. Draw the free body diagram firstly as shown in figure. Mention all the horizontal and vertical components of tensions T_1 and T_2.

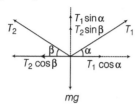

As the body is in equilibrium, the various forces must add to zero. Taking horizontal components of forces.

$$T_1 \cos \alpha = T_2 \cos \beta$$
$$\Rightarrow \quad T_2 = T_1 \frac{\cos \alpha}{\cos \beta}$$

Now, taking the vertical components of forces.

$$T_1 \sin \alpha + T_2 \sin \beta = mg$$
$$T_1 \sin \alpha + T_1 \frac{\cos \alpha}{\cos \beta} \sin \beta = mg$$

Now, solve the equations for T_1 to find out the value of T_1.

$$T_1 = \frac{mg}{\sin \alpha + \dfrac{\cos \alpha}{\cos \beta} \sin \beta}$$

$$= \frac{mg \cos \beta}{\sin \alpha \cos \beta + \cos \alpha \sin \beta}$$

$$\therefore \quad T_1 = \frac{mg \cos \beta}{\sin (\alpha + \beta)}$$

$$[\because \ \sin(A + B) = \sin A \cos B + \cos A \sin B]$$

Now, find out the value of T_2 by using above equation.

$$T_2 = T_1 \frac{\cos \alpha}{\cos \beta} = \frac{mg \cos \beta}{\sin (\alpha + \beta)} \times \frac{\cos \alpha}{\cos \beta}$$

$$= \frac{mg \cos \alpha}{\sin (\alpha + \beta)}$$

EXAMPLE |19| Tension in the Strings

Determine the tensions T_1 and T_2 in the strings as shown in the figure.

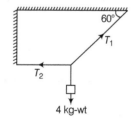

Sol. We redraw the above figure

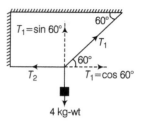

While resolving the tension T_1 along horizontal and vertical directions. As, in equilibrium,

$$T_1 \sin 60° = 4 \text{kg-wt} = 4 \times 9.8 \text{ N} \quad \text{...(i)}$$
$$T_1 \cos 60° = T_2 \quad \text{...(ii)}$$

Solving Eq. (i), we get

$$T_1 = \frac{4 \times 9.8}{\sin 60°} = 45.26 \text{ N}$$

Solving Eq. (ii), we get

$$T_2 = T_1 \cos 60°$$
$$= 45.26 \times 0.5$$
$$= 22.63 \text{ N}$$

EXAMPLE |20| Horizontal Force Applied on Rope Hanging Vertically

See in figure a mass of 6 kg is suspended by a rope of length 2 m from the ceiling. A force of 50 N in the horizontal direction is applied at the mid-point P of the rope as shown. What is the angle, the rope makes with the vertical in equilibrium? (Take $g = 10 \text{ ms}^{-2}$). Neglect the mass of the rope. **[NCERT]**

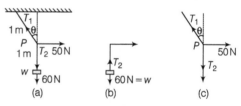

Sol. Fig. (b) is the free body diagram of w and Fig. (c) is the free body diagram of point P.

Consider the equilibrium of the weight w. Clearly,

$$T_2 = 6 \times 10 = 60 \text{ N}$$

Consider the equilibrium of the point P under the action of three forces, the tensions T_1 and T_2 and the horizontal force 50 N. The horizontal and vertical components of the resultant force must vanish separately.

$$T_1 \cos \theta = T_2 = 60 \text{ N}$$
and $$T_1 \sin \theta = 50 \text{ N}$$

Which gives that $\tan \theta = \dfrac{5}{6}$

or $$\theta = \tan^{-1}\left(\frac{5}{6}\right) = 40°$$

TOPIC PRACTICE 2

OBJECTIVE Type Questions

1. Which force is dissipative force?
   (a) Electrostatic force   (b) Magnetic force
   (c) Gravitational force   (d) Frictional force

   Sol. (d) Frictional force is a non-conservative force because work done by it is dissipated (wasted) as heat energy. This is not the case with other forces.

2. A trolley is carrying a box on its surface having coefficient of static friction equal to 0.3. Now the trolley starts moving with increasing acceleration. Find the maximum acceleration of the trolley so that the box does not slide back on the trolley.
   (a) 2 ms^{-2} (b) 3 ms^{-2}
   (c) 4 ms^{-2} (d) 5 ms^{-2}

   Sol. (b) As trolley accelerates forward, a pseudo force acts on the box in reverse. It prevents its slippage in backward direction, as friction starts acting on it. But as friction can be increased to a maximum value of μmg. So maximum acceleration that is possible for block before it starts slipping $= \mu g = 0.3 \times 10 = 3 \text{ ms}^{-2}$

3. If a car is moving in uniform circular motion, then what should be the value of velocity of a car, so that car will not moving away from the circle,
   (a) $v < \sqrt{\mu_s \, Rg}$ (b) $v \leq \sqrt{\mu_s \, Rg}$
   (c) $v < \sqrt{\mu_k Rg}$ (d) None of these

   Sol. (b) For car moving in circle of radius R, with velocity v, mass $= m$,
   centripetal force required $=$ Frictional force $\leq \mu_s N$
   $$\frac{mv^2}{R} \leq \mu_s mg \qquad (\because N = mg)$$
   $$v \leq \sqrt{\mu_s Rg}$$

4. A particle of man 2 kg is moving on a circular path of radius 10 m with a speed of 5 ms^{-1} and its speed is increasing at rate of 3 ms^{-1}. Find the force acting on the particle.
   (a) 5 N   (b) 10 N
   (c) 12 N   (d) 14 N

   Sol. (a) Radial acceleration (centripetal acceleration)
   $$= \frac{v^2}{r} = \frac{5 \times 5}{10} = 2.5 \text{ ms}^{-2}$$
   Force acting $=$ mass $\times$ acceleration
   $$= 2 \times 2.5 = 5 \text{ N}$$

5. Two masses $m_1 = 1$ kg and $m_2 = 2$ kg are connected by a light inextensible string and suspended by means of a weightless pulley as shown in figure.

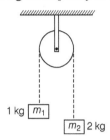

1 kg $\boxed{m_1}$

$\boxed{m_2}$ 2 kg

   Assuming that both the masses start from rest, the distance travelled by 2 kg mass in 2 s is
   (a) $\dfrac{20}{9}$ m   (b) $\dfrac{40}{9}$ m
   (c) $\dfrac{20}{3}$ m   (d) $\dfrac{1}{3}$ m

   Sol. (c) Given, $m_1 = 1$ kg, $m_2 = 2$kg and $g = 10 \text{ ms}^{-2}$
   Acceleration, $\quad a = \left(\dfrac{m_2 - m_1}{m_1 + m_2}\right)g$
   $$= \left(\dfrac{2-1}{1+2}\right)10 = \dfrac{10}{3}$$
   $$\left[\because s = ut + \frac{1}{2}at^2 \text{ and } u = 0 \text{ ms}^{-1}\right]$$
   Distance, $\quad s = \dfrac{1}{2} \times a \times t^2$
   $$= \dfrac{1}{2} \times \dfrac{10}{3} \times 4 = \dfrac{20}{3} \text{ m}$$

6. If a box is lying in the compartment of an accelerating train and box is stationary relative to the train. What force cause the acceleration of the box?
   (a) Frictional force in the direction of train
   (b) Frictional force in the opposite direction of train
   (c) Force applied by air
   (d) None of the above

   Sol. (a) Frictional force in the direction of train causes the acceleration of the box lying in the compartment of an accelerating train.

VERY SHORT ANSWER Type Questions

7. Why is static friction called a self-adjusting force?

   Sol. As the applied force increases, the static friction also increases and becomes equal to the applied force to make the object stationary. That is why static friction is called a self-adjusting force.

8. A body is moving in a circular path such that its speed always remains constant. Should there be a force acting on the body?

Sol. When a body is moving along a circular path, speed always remains constant and a centripetal force is acting on the body.

9. What is the acceleration of a train travelling at 50 ms^{-1} as it goes round a curve of 250 m radius?

Sol. Given, velocity, $v = 50$ ms^{-1}
Radius, $r = 250$ m

Centripetal acceleration, $a = \dfrac{v^2}{r}$

$$a = \dfrac{50 \times 50}{250} = 10 \text{ ms}^{-2}$$

10. A heavy point mass tied to the end of string is whirled in a horizontal circle of radius 20 cm with a constant angular speed. What is angular speed if the centripetal acceleration is 980 cms^{-2}?

Sol. Here, radius $r = 20$ cm

Centripetal acceleration, $= 980$ cms^{-2}

We know that centripetal acceleration, $a = r\omega^2$

$$\omega = \sqrt{\dfrac{a}{r}} = \sqrt{\dfrac{980}{20}}$$

$$\omega = \sqrt{49} = 7 \text{ rad/s}$$

11. Carts with rubber tyres are easier to ply than those with iron tyres. Explain.

Sol. The carts with rubber tyres are easier to ply than those with iron types because the coefficient of friction between rubber and concrete is less than that between iron and the road.

12. The mountain road is generally made winding upwards rather than going straight up. Why?

Sol. When we go up a mountain, the opposing force of friction $F = \mu R = \mu mg \cos \theta$.
where θ is angle of slope with horizontal. To avoid skidding, F should be large.
∴ $\cos \theta$ should be large and hence, θ must be small. Therefore, mountain roads are generally made winding upwards. The road straight up would have large slope.

13. The outer rail of a curved railway track is generally raised over the inner. Why?

Sol. When the outer rail of a curved railway track is raised over the inner, the horizontal component of the normal reaction of the rails, provides the necessary centripetal force for the train to enable it moving along the curved path.

SHORT ANSWER Type Questions

14. A body placed on a rough inclined plane just begins to slide, when the slope of the plane equal to 1 in 4. Calculate the coefficient of friction.

Sol. The slope of the plane equal to 1 in 4 implies that if $BC = 4$ and $AB = 1$. Suppose that the plane is inclined at angle θ with the horizontal AC. From the relation between the coefficient of friction and angle of repose, we have

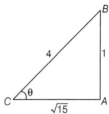

$\mu = \tan \theta$ \qquad [here, θ is angle of repose]

$$\mu = \dfrac{AB}{AC} = \dfrac{AB}{\sqrt{BC^2 - AB^2}}$$

$$= \dfrac{1}{\sqrt{4^2 - 1^2}} = \dfrac{1}{\sqrt{16 - 1}}$$

$$\mu = \dfrac{1}{\sqrt{15}}$$

$$\mu = 0.258$$

15. A block of mass m is held against a rough vertical wall by pressing it with a finger. If the coefficient of friction between the block and the wall is μ and the acceleration due to gravity is g, calculate the minimum force required to be applied by finger to hold the block against the wall? \hfill **[NCERT Exemplar]**

Sol. Given, mass of the block $= m$

Coefficient of friction between the block and the wall $= \mu$

Let a force F be applied on the block to hold the block against the wall. The normal reaction of mass be N and force of friction acting upward be f.

In equilibrium, vertical and horizontal forces should be balanced separately.

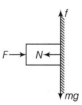

∴ \qquad $f = mg$ \hfill ...(i)

and \qquad $F = N$ \hfill ...(ii)

But force of friction $(f) = \mu N$
$$= \mu F \quad \text{[using Eq. (ii)]} \quad \text{...(iii)}$$
From Eqs. (i) and (iii), we get
$$\mu F = mg \quad \text{or} \quad F = \frac{mg}{\mu}$$

16. A body of mass 2 kg is being dragged with a uniform velocity of $2\ ms^{-1}$ on a rough horizontal plane. The coefficient of friction between the body and the surface is 0.2. Calculate the amount of heat generated per second. Take $g = 9.8\ ms^{-2}$ and $J = 4.2\ Jcal^{-1}$.

Sol. Given, $m = 2\ kg, u = 2\ ms^{-1}, \mu = 0.2$

Force of friction, $\quad F = \mu R$
$$F = \mu mg \qquad [\because R = mg]$$
$$F = 0.2 \times 2 \times 9.8$$
$$F = 3.92\ N$$
Distance moved per second $s = ut$
$$s = 2 \times 1 = 2$$
Work done by friction per second, $W = Fs$
$$W = 3.92 \times 2 = 7.84\ J$$
Heat produced, $\quad H = \frac{W}{J} \Rightarrow H = \frac{7.84}{4.2}$
$$H = 1.87\ cal$$

17. If the speed of stone is increased beyond the maximum permissible value and the string breaks suddenly, which of the following correctly describes the trajectory of the stone after the string breaks

    (i) the stone moves radially outwards,

    (ii) the stone flies off tangentially from the instant the string breaks,

    (iii) the stone flies off at an angle with the tangent whose magnitude depends on the speed of the particle?   **[NCERT]**

Sol. The second part correctly describes the trajectory of the stone after the spring breaks because when a stone tied to one end of a string is whirled round in a circle then velocity of the stone at any point is along the tangent at that point. If the string breaks suddenly, then stone flies off tangentially, along the direction of its velocity.

LONG ANSWER Type I Questions

18. Figure below shows a man standing stationary with respect to a horizontal conveyor belt that is accelerating with $1\ m/s^2$.

What is the net force on the man? If the coefficient of static friction between the man's shoes and the belt is 0.2, up to what acceleration of the belt can the man continue to be stationary relative to the belt? (Mass of the man = 65 kg).

                                                                                                          [NCERT]

Sol. Acceleration of the conveyor belt, $a = 1\ m/s^2$

As man is standing stationary with respect to the horizontal conveyor belt therefore, acceleration of the man = acceleration of the belt

$\therefore \qquad\qquad\qquad a = 1\ m/s^2$

Mass of the man, $m = 65\ kg$

$\therefore$ Net force acting on the man $F = ma = 65 \times 1 = 65\ N$

This force is actually the force of friction (static) between man and the belt. Force of friction is actually supporting motion of man.

The direction of this force is in the direction of motion of the belt. Coefficient of friction between the man's shoes and the belt $\mu = 0.2$

Let a' be the acceleration of the belt upto which the man can continue to be stationary relative to the belt.

In this condition

$\therefore \qquad ma' = $ maximum static friction

$$ma' = \mu R = \mu mg \qquad \left[\because \mu = \frac{\text{Limiting friction}}{\text{Normal reaction}}\right]$$

or $\qquad a' = \mu g = 0.2 \times 9.8 = 1.96\ m/s^2$

19. A stone of mass 0.25 kg tied to the end of a string is whirled round in a circle of radius 1.5 m with speed 40 rev/min in a horizontal plane. What is the tension in the string? What is the maximum speed with which the stone can be whirled around if the string can withstand a maximum tension of 200 N?   **[NCERT]**

💡 When a stone tied to one end of a string is whirled in a circle, then required centripetal force is provided by the tension in the string.

Sol. Mass of stone, $m = 0.25\ kg$, Radius of the string, $r = 1.5\ m$

Frequency, $\nu = 40\ rev/min = \frac{40}{60}\ rev/s = \frac{2}{3}\ rev/s$

Centripetal force required for circular motion is obtained from the tension in the string.

$\therefore$ Tension in the string = centripetal force
$$T = mr\omega^2$$
$$= mr(2\pi\nu)^2 \qquad [\because \omega = 2\pi\nu]$$
$$= mr4\pi^2\nu^2$$
$$T = 0.25 \times 1.5 \times 4 \times \left(\frac{22}{7}\right)^2 \times \left(\frac{2}{3}\right)^2 = 6.6\ N$$

Maximum tension which can be withstand by the string

$$T_{max} = 200 \text{ N} = \frac{mv^2_{max}}{r}$$

$$v_{max} = \sqrt{\frac{T_{max} \times r}{m}} = \sqrt{\frac{200 \times 1.5}{0.25}}$$

$$= 34.6 \text{ m/s}$$

20. A stone of mass m tied to the end of a string revolves in a vertical circle of radius R. The net forces at the lowest and highest points of the circle directed vertically downwards are (choose the correct alternative).

Lowest point	Highest point
(i) $mg - T_1$	$mg + T_2$
(ii) $mg + T_1$	$mg - T_2$
(iii) $mg + T_1 - (mv_1^2)/R$	$mg - T_2 + (mv_2^2)/R$
(iv) $mg - T_1 - (mv_1^2)/R$	$mg + T_2 + (mv_2^2)/R$

Here, T_1, T_2 and (v_1, v_2) denote the tension in the string (and the speed of the stone) at the lowest and the highest point respectively. **[NCERT]**

Sol. Let tension in the string be T_1 and T_2 at lowest and highest points of the vertical circle.

At lowest point T_1 acts towards the centre of the circle ($\because$ at the lowest point string will be stretched downward due to weight of the stone) and mg acts vertically downward (weight of an object always acts downward)

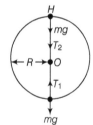

$\therefore$ Net force acting on the stone in downward direction $(F_L) = mg - T_1$

At highest point Both T_2 and mg act vertically downward ($\because$ at the highest point string is stretched away from the centre) towards the centre of the vertical circle. Net force acting on the stone in downward direction $(F_H) = mg + T_2$

$\therefore$ Correct option is (i).

21. An aircraft executes a horizontal loop at a speed of 720 km/h with its wings banked at 15°. What is the radius of the loop? **[NCERT]**

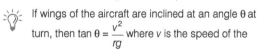
If wings of the aircraft are inclined at an angle θ at turn, then $\tan \theta = \frac{v^2}{rg}$ where v is the speed of the aircraft and r is the radius of the circular turn.

Sol. Speed of the aircraft, $v = 720$ km/h

$$= 720 \times \frac{5}{18} \text{ m/s} \quad \left[\because 1 \text{ km/h} = \frac{5}{18} \text{ m/s} \right]$$

$$= 200 \text{ m/s}$$

Angle of banking, $\theta = 15°$

Acceleration due to gravity, $g = 9.8$ m/s^2

At turn, $\tan \theta = \frac{v^2}{rg}$

or $r = \frac{v^2}{g \tan \theta} = \frac{(200)^2}{9.8 \times \tan 15°} = \frac{40000}{9.8 \times 0.2679}$

$r = 15240$ m $= 15.24 \times 10^3$ m $= 15.24$ km

22. A train rounds an unbanked circular bend of radius 30 m at a speed of 54 km/h. The mass of the train is 10^6 kg. What provides the centripetal force required for this purpose, the engine or the rails? What is the angle of banking required to prevent wearing out of the rail? **[NCERT]**

The centripetal force required by the train to cross the circular bend is provided by the lateral thrust exerted by the outer rails on the wheels. According to Newton's third law of motion, the train also exerts an equal and opposite force on the rails causing its wear and tear.

Sol. Radius of circular bend, $r = 30$ m

Speed of the train, $v = 54$ km/h

$$= 54 \times \frac{5}{18} \text{ m/s} \quad \left[\because 1 \text{ km/h} = \frac{5}{18} \text{ m/s} \right]$$

$$= 15 \text{ m/s}$$

Mass of the train, $m = 10^6$ kg

Let θ be the angle of banking required to prevent wearing out the rails, then

$$\tan \theta = \frac{v^2}{rg} = \frac{(15)^2}{30 \times 9.8}$$

$$= \frac{225}{30 \times 9.8} = 0.7653$$

$$\theta = \tan^{-1}(0.7653) = 37.4°$$

23. A rocket with a lift-off mass 20000 kg is blasted upwards with an initial acceleration of 5.0 m/s^2. Calculate the initial thrust (force) of the blast. **[NCERT]**

Sol. Initial mass of the rocket,

$m = 20000$ kg

Initial acceleration $a = 5.0$ m/s^2 in upwards direction

Let initial thrust of the blast be T.

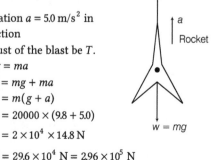

$\therefore \qquad T - mg = ma$

or $\qquad T = mg + ma$

$$= m(g + a)$$

$$= 20000 \times (9.8 + 5.0)$$

$$= 2 \times 10^4 \times 14.8 \text{ N}$$

$$= 29.6 \times 10^4 \text{ N} = 2.96 \times 10^5 \text{ N}$$

24. You may have seen in a circus a motorcyclist driving in vertical loops inside a death well (a hollow spherical chamber with holes, so the spectators can watch from outside). Explain clearly, why the motorcyclist does not drop down when he is at the uppermost point, with no support from below. What is the minimum speed required at the uppermost position to perform a vertical loop if the radius of the chamber is 25 m?   **[NCERT]**

Sol. When the motorcyclist is at the uppermost point of the death well, then weight of the cyclist as well as the normal reaction R of the ceiling of the chamber is in downward direction. These forces are balanced by the outward centrifugal force acting on the motorcyclist.

$$\therefore \qquad R + mg = \frac{mv^2}{r}$$

where, v = speed of the motorcyclist

m = mass of (motorcycle + driver)

r = radius of the death well.

As the forces acting on the motorcyclist are balanced, therefore, motorcyclist does not fall down.

The minimum speed required to perform a vertical loop is given by

$$mg = \frac{mv^2_{min}}{r}$$

[$\because$ In the case weight of the object = centripetal force]

or $\qquad v_{min} = \sqrt{rg} = \sqrt{25 \times 9.8}$

$$= 15.65 \text{ m/s}$$

LONG ANSWER Type II Questions

25. A block of mass 15 kg is placed on a long trolley. The coefficient of static friction between the block and the trolley is 0.18. The trolley accelerates from rest with 0.5 m/s² for 20s and then moves with uniform velocity. Discuss the motion of the block as viewed by (i) stationary observer on the ground (ii) an observer moving with the trolley.   **[NCERT]**

Sol. Mass of the block, $m = 15$ kg

Coefficient of friction between the block and the trolley

$$\mu = 0.18$$

Acceleration of the trolley, $a = 0.5 \text{ m/s}^2$

Time, $t = 20$ s

(i) As block is placed on the trolley, therefore, friction force is applied on the block by the trolley

$$F = ma = 15 \times 0.5 = 7.5 \text{ N}$$

Force on the block is the friction applied by trolley on the block, its direction is in the direction of motion of the trolley.

For the stationary observer on the ground, the block will appear to move with acceleration initially and then with uniform velocity as given in the question.

(ii) For an observer on the trolley, the block is always at rest either initially or finally. Trolley always becomes inertial frame with respect to block because both have the same acceleration initially and same velocity finally.

26. The rear side of a truck is open and a box of 40kg mass is placed 5 m away from the open end as shown. The coefficient of friction between the box and the surface below it, is 0.15. On a straight road, the truck starts from rest and accelerates with 2 m/s².

At what distance from the starting point does the box fall off the truck? (ignore the size of the box).   **[NCERT]**

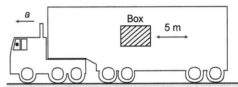

Sol. $\because$ Mass of the box, $m = 40$ kg

Coefficient of friction between the box and the surface,

$$\mu = 0.15$$

Acceleration of the truck, $a = 2 \text{ m/s}^2$

Truck is a non-inertial frame for the box, so motion of box can be studied by assuming a pseudo force acting on it in a direction opposite to the direction of acceleration of truck i.e. in backward direction.

pseudo force applied by the truck on the box due to its accelerated motion, $F = ma = 40 \times 2 = 80$ N

Due to this pseudo force on the box, the box tries to move in backward direction but limiting friction force opposes its motion.

Limiting friction force between the box and the surface

$$= \mu R = \mu mg$$

$$f = 0.15 \times 40 \times 9.8 \text{ N}$$

$$= 58.8 \text{ N} \qquad \text{[in forward direction]}$$

Net force acting on box in backward direction

$$F' = F - f = 80 - 58.8 \text{ N}$$

$$= 21.2 \text{ N}$$

Acceleration produced in the box in backward direction

$$a' = \frac{F'}{m} = \frac{21.2}{40} \text{ ms}^{-2}$$

$$a' = 0.53 \text{ ms}^{-2}$$

Using equation of motion for travelling $s = 5$ m to fall off the truck, $\qquad s = ut + \frac{1}{2}at^2$

$$5 = 0 \times t + \frac{1}{2} \times 0.53 \times t^2$$

or $$t = \sqrt{\frac{5 \times 2}{0.53}} = \sqrt{\frac{1000}{53}} = 4.34 \text{ s}$$

Distance travelled by the truck in time,

$$t = 4.34 \text{ s}$$

$$s' = ut + \frac{1}{2}at^2 = 0 \times t + \frac{1}{2} \times 2 \times (4.34)^2$$

$$= (4.34)^2 = 18.84 \text{ m}$$

27. Two bodies A and B of masses 5 kg and 10 kg in contact with each other rest on a table is against a rigid wall as shown in figure. The coefficient of friction between the bodies and the table 0.15. A force of 200 N is applied horizontally at A.

What are (i) the reaction of the partition or wall (ii) the action- reaction forces between A and B? What happens when the partition is removed? Does the answer to (ii) change, when the bodies are in motion? Ignore difference between μ_s and μ_k. **[NCERT]**

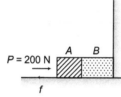

Sol. Mass of body $A(m_1) = 5$ kg

Mass of body $B(m_2) = 10$ kg

Coefficient of friction between the bodies and the table $(\mu) = 0.15$

Force applied horizontally at A, $F = 200$ N

(i) **Reaction of partition**

Limiting friction acting to the left

$$f = \mu R = \mu (m_1 + m_2)g$$
$$= 0.15 (5 + 10) \times 9.8 = 22.05 \text{ N}$$

∴ Net force acting on the partition towards the right

$$F' = F - f$$
$$= 200 - 22.05 = 177.95 \text{ N}$$

According to the Newton's third law of motion, Reaction of partition = Net force acting on the partition

$$= 177.95 \text{ N} \quad \text{[towards the left]}$$

(ii) **Action-reaction forces between A and B**

Let f_1 be the force of limiting friction acting on body A and F_1 be the net force applied by body A on body B.

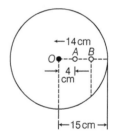

$$f_1 = \mu R_1$$
$$= \mu m_1 g \qquad [\because R_1 = m_1 g]$$
$$= 0.15 \times 5 \times 9.8$$
$$= 7.35 \text{ N (towards the left)}$$

∴ Net force applied by body A on body B,

$$F_1 = F - f_1 = 200 - 7.35$$
$$= 192.65 \text{ N} \qquad \text{[towards the right]}$$

According to Newton's third law of motion, reaction force applied by body B on body, i.e.

$$A = F_1 = 192.65 \text{ N} \quad \text{(towards left)}$$

28. A disc revolves with a speed of $33\frac{1}{3}$ rev/min and has a radius of 15 cm. Two coins are placed at 4 cm and 14 cm away from the centre of the record. If the coefficient of friction between the coins and the record is 0.15, which of the coins will revolve with the record? **[NCERT]**

Sol. Given, $(v) = 33\frac{1}{3} = \frac{100}{3}$ rev/min $= \frac{100}{3 \times 60}$ rev/s $= \frac{5}{9}$ rev/s

∴ Angular velocity $(\omega) = 2\pi v = 2 \times \frac{22}{7} \times \frac{5}{9} = \frac{220}{63}$ rad/s

Radius of the disc $(r) = 15$ cm.

Distance of first coin A from the centre $(x_1) = 4$ cm

Distance of the second coin B from the centre $(x_2) = 14$ cm

Coefficient of friction between the coins and the record $= 0.15$.

If force of friction between the coin and the record is sufficient to provide the centripetal force, then coil will revolve with the record.

∴ To prevent slipping (or to revolve the coin alongwith record) the force of friction $f \geq$ centripetal force (f_c)

or $$\mu mg \geq mr\omega^2$$

or $$\mu g \geq r\omega^2$$

For first coin A

$$r\omega^2 = \frac{4}{100} \times \left(\frac{220}{63}\right)^2 = \frac{4 \times 220 \times 220}{100 \times 63 \times 63}$$

$$= 0.488 \text{ m/s}^2$$

and $$\mu g = 0.15 \times 9.8 = 1.47 \text{ m/s}^2$$

Here, $\mu g > r\omega^2$, therefore, this coin will revolve with the record.

For second coin B

$$r\omega^2 = \frac{14}{100} \times \left(\frac{220}{63}\right)^2 = \frac{14 \times 220 \times 220}{100 \times 63 \times 63} = 1.707 \text{ m/s}$$

and $$\mu g = 1.47 \text{ m/s}$$

Here, $\mu g < r\omega^2$, therefore, centripetal force will not be obtained from the force of friction, hence this coin will not revolve with the record.

29. A 70 kg man stands in contact against the inner wall of a hollow cylindrical drum of radius 3 m rotating about its vertical axis with 200 rev/min. The coefficient of friction between the wall and his clothing is 0.15. What is the minimum rotational speed of the cylinder to enable the man to remain stuck to the wall (without falling) when the floor is suddenly removed? **[NCERT]**

Sol. Given, Radius of the cylindrical drum $(r) = 3$ m

Coefficient of friction between the wall and his clothing $(\mu) = 0.15$. Frequency $(\nu) = 200$ rev/min

$$= \frac{200}{60} \text{ rev/s} = \frac{10}{3} \text{ rev/s}$$

The normal reaction of the wall on the man acting horizontally provides the required centripetal force.

$$R = mr\omega^2 \qquad \text{...(i)}$$

The frictional force F, acting upwards balances his weight

i.e. $\qquad F = mg \qquad \text{...(ii)}$

The man will remain stuck to the wall without slipping, if

$$\mu R \geq F \quad \text{or} \quad F \leq \mu R$$

$$mg \leq \mu \times mr\omega^2 \quad \text{or} \quad \omega^2 \geq \frac{g}{\mu r}$$

$$\omega \geq \sqrt{\frac{g}{\mu R}}$$

For minimum angular speed of rotation,

$$\omega_{min} = \sqrt{\frac{g}{\mu R}} = \sqrt{\frac{9.8}{0.15 \times 3}} = 4.67 \text{ rad/s}$$

30. When a body slides down from rest along a smooth inclined plane making an angle of 45° with the horizontal, it takes time T. When the same body slides down from rest along a rough inclined plane making the same angle and through the same distance, it is seen to take time pT, where p is some number greater than 1. Calculate the coefficient of friction between the body and the rough plane. **[NCERT Exemplar]**

Sol. On smooth inclined plane Acceleration of a body sliding down a smooth inclined plane, $a = g\sin\theta$

Here, $\qquad \theta = 45°$

$\therefore \qquad a = g\sin 45° = \frac{g}{\sqrt{2}}$

Let the travelled distance be s.

Using the equation of motion, $s = ut + \frac{1}{2}at^2$, we get

$$s = 0 \cdot t + \frac{1}{2}\frac{g}{\sqrt{2}}T^2 \quad \text{or} \quad s = \frac{gT^2}{2\sqrt{2}} \qquad \text{...(i)}$$

On rough inclined plane

Acceleration of the body,

$$a = g(\sin\theta - \mu\cos\theta)$$
$$= g(\sin 45° - \mu\cos 45°)$$
$$= \frac{g(1-\mu)}{\sqrt{2}} \qquad \left[\text{as } \sin 45° = \frac{1}{\sqrt{2}}\right]$$

Again using equation of motion, $s = ut + \frac{1}{2}at^2$, we get

$$s = 0(pT) + \frac{1}{2}\frac{g(1-\mu)}{\sqrt{2}}(pT)^2$$

or $\qquad s = \frac{g(1-\mu)p^2T^2}{2\sqrt{2}} \qquad \text{...(ii)}$

From Eqs. (i) and (ii), we get

$$\frac{gT^2}{2\sqrt{2}} = \frac{g(1-\mu)p^2T^2}{2\sqrt{2}}$$

or $\quad (1-\mu)p^2 = 1 \quad \text{or} \quad 1-\mu = \frac{1}{p^2}$

or $\qquad \mu = \left(1 - \frac{1}{p^2}\right)$

31. A monkey of mass 40 kg climbs on a rope which can stand a maximum tension of 600 N. In which of the following cases will the rope break? The monkey

(i) climbs up with an acceleration of 6 m/s².

(ii) climbs down with an acceleration of 4 m/s².

(iii) climbs up with a uniform speed of 5 m/s.

(iv) falls down the rope nearly freely under gravity. (Ignore the mass of the rope) and take $g = 10$ m/s². **[NCERT]**

Tension in the rope will be equal to the apparent weight of the monkey (R).

Sol. Given, Mass of the monkey, $m = 40$ kg

Maximum tension which can be withstood by the rope $(T)_{max} = 600$ N

(i) When monkey climbs up with an acceleration $a = 6$ m/s², then

$$T - mg = ma; \quad T = mg + ma$$

$$T = m(g + a) = 40(10 + 6) = 640 \text{ N}$$

In this condition, $T > T_{max}$ therefore, the rope will break.

(ii) When monkey climbs down with an acceleration $a = 4 \text{ m/s}^2$, then

$$mg - T = ma$$

or $\quad T = mg - ma = m(g - a)$

$$= 40(10 - 4) \text{ N} = 240 \text{ N}$$

In this condition, $T < T_{max}$,
Therefore, the rope will not break.

(iii) When monkey climbs up with a uniform speed of 5 m/s, then its acceleration a is zero.

$$\therefore \quad T = mg = 40 \times 10 = 400 \text{ N}$$

In this condition $T < T_{max}$, therefore, the rope will not break.

(iv) When monkey falls down freely under gravity, then its acceleration in downward direction is g.

$$\therefore \quad T = m(g - a) = m(g - g) \quad [\because a = g]$$
$$= 0$$

In this condition, monkey will be in a state of weightlessness and tension in the rope is zero.

Therefore, the rope will not break.

In this problem, T actually represents friction force which is generated, when the monkey pushes the rope in downward direction with a view to climb up.

32. In a rotor, a hollow vertical cylinder rotates about its axis and a person rests against the inner wall. At a particular speed of the rotor, the floor below the person is removed and the person hangs resting against the wall without any floor.

If the radius of the rotor is 2 m and the coefficient of static friction between the wall and the person is 0.2.

(i) Find the minimum speed at which the floor may be removed.

(ii) What type of speciality is associated with this question? [take, $g = 10 \text{ m/s}^2$]

Sol. The situation is shown in figure below

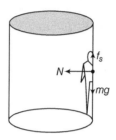

(i) When the floor is removed, the forces on the person are

(a) weight mg downward.

(b) normal force N due to the wall towards the centre.

(c) frictional force f_s parallel to the wall, upwards.

The person is moving in a circle with a uniform speed, so its acceleration is v^2/r towards the centre.

Newton's law for the horizontal direction (second law) and for the vertical direction (first law) give

$$N = mv^2/r \qquad \qquad ...(i)$$

and $\qquad f_s = mg \qquad \qquad ...(ii)$

For the minimum speed, when the floor may be removed, the friction is limiting one and, so equals $\mu_s N$.

This gives $\quad \mu_s N = mg$

or $\qquad \dfrac{\mu_s mv^2}{r} = mg \qquad$ [using Eq. (i)]

or $\qquad v = \sqrt{\dfrac{rg}{\mu_s}} = \sqrt{\dfrac{2m \times 10 \text{ m/s}^2}{0.2}}$

$$= 10 \text{ m/s}$$

(ii) Speciality is that without the floor an object a body may be 0 align with a vertical wall provided, it is set to be in circular motion (horizontal) with properly required speed.

ASSESS YOUR TOPICAL UNDERSTANDING

OBJECTIVE Type Questions

1. When a box is in stationary position with respect to train moving with no acceleration, then relative motion is opposed by .... Which provides the same velocity to the box as that of the train, keeping it stationary relative to the train.
   (a) static friction
   (b) kinetic friction
   (c) No friction because there will be no relative velocity
   (d) None of the above

2. A boy prevents fall of his book on the ground by pressing it against a vertical wall. If weight of his book is 10 kg and μ_s of the wall is 0.2. Find the minimum force needed by him in his attempt.
   (a) 300 N   (b) 400 N
   (c) 500 N   (d) 600 N

3. When a car is taking a circular turn on a horizontal road, the centripetal force is the force of
   (a) friction   (b) weight of the car
   (c) weight of the tyres (d) None of these

4. When a car is moving along a circle on a level road, then centripetal force is provided by f, where f denotes as
   (a) $f < \mu_s\, N = \dfrac{mv^2}{r}$ (b) $\dfrac{mv^2}{r} = f \le \mu_s N$
   (c) $f = \mu_s\, N = \dfrac{mv^2}{r}$ (d) $f = \mu_k\, N = \dfrac{mv^2}{r}$

5. Three blocks of masses m_1, m_2 and m_3 kg are placed in contact with each other on a frictionless table. A force F is applied on the heaviest mass m_1, so the acceleration of m_3 will be

   (a) $\dfrac{F}{m_1}$ (b) $\dfrac{F}{m_1 + m_2}$
   (c) $\dfrac{F}{m_2 + m_3}$ (d) $\dfrac{F}{m_1 + m_2 + m_3}$

Answer

  1. (c) | 2. (c) | 3. (a) | 4. (b) | 5. (d)

VERY SHORT ANSWER Type Questions

6. What type of friction is involved when an axle rotates in a sleeve?

7. A stone is tied to one end of a string and rotated in a vertical circle. What is the difference in tension of the string at lowest and highest points of the vertical circle?

8. A ball of 1 g released down an inclined plane describe a circle of radius 10 cm in the vertical plane on reaching the bottom. What is the minimum height of the inclined plane?   [**Ans.** 25 cm]

9. For uniform circular motion, does the direction of the centripetal force depend on the sense of rotation, i.e. clockwise or anti-clockwise rotation?

SHORT ANSWER Type Questions

10. Distinguish between sliding friction and rolling friction.

11. A block slides down a rough incline of angle 30° with an acceleration $g/4$. Find the coefficient of kinetic friction.   [**Ans.** $1/2\sqrt{3}$]

12. State two advantages of friction in daily life.

13. How sliding friction is converted into rolling friction?

14. State the laws of kinetic friction. Define coefficient of kinetic friction.

LONG ANSWER Type I Questions

15. A body of mass 10 kg is placed on an inclined plane of angle 30°. If the coefficient of static friction is $\dfrac{1}{\sqrt{3}}$. Find the force required to just push the body up the inclined surface.   [**Ans.** 100 N]

16. A block of mass 2 kg is placed on the floor. The coefficient of limiting friction is 0.4. If a force of 3.6 N is applied on the block parallel to the floor. Find the acceleration of the block. What is the force of friction between the block and floor?
          [**Ans.** zero, 3.6 N]

17. A small body tied to one end of the string is whirled in a vertical circle.
    (i) Represent the forces on a diagram when the string makes an angle θ with initial position.
    (ii) Find the tension and velocity at the highest and lowest point, respectively.

LONG ANSWER Type II Questions

18. A trolley of mass 20 kg rests on a horizontal surface. A massless string tied to the trolley passes over a frictionless pulley and a load of 5 kg is suspended from other end of string. If coefficient of kinetic friction between trolley and surface be 0.1, find the acceleration of trolley and tension in the string. (take $g = 10$ ms^{-2}). [**Ans.** 44 N]

19. A circular motion addict of mass 80 kg sides a ferris wheel around in a vertical circle of radius 10 m at a constant speed of 6.1 m/s. (i) What is the period of motion? What is the magnitude of the normal force on the addict from the seat when both go through (ii) the highest point of the circular path and (iii) lowest point? [**Ans.** (i) 10 s, (ii) 4.9×10^2 N and (iii) 1.1×10^3 N]

20. A curve of radius 120 m is banked at an angle of 18°. At what speed can it be negotiated under icy conditions where friction is negligible? [**Ans.** 2×10^1 m/s]

21. A stone of mass 0.20 kg is tied to one end of a string of length 80 cm, holding the other end, the stone is whirled into a vertical circle. What is the minimum speed of the stone at the lowest point so that it just completes the circle. What is the tension in string at lowest point of the circular path? ($g = 10$ m/s^2) [**Ans.** 6.32 m/s, 12 N]

22. Derive an expression for acceleration of a body down a rough inclined plane.

SUMMARY

- Force is an external agency (a pull or a push) which changes or tends to change the state of rest or of uniform motion or the direction of motion of a body. Its SI units is Newton and dimensional formula is [MLT^{-2}].
- Sir Issac Newton made a systematic study of motion and proposed three laws of motion.
- **Newton's first law of motion** states that every body continues in its state of rest or of uniform motion in a straight line unless it is compelled by some external force to change that state.
- **Newton's second law of motion** states that the rate of change of momentum of a body is directly proportional to the external force applied on the body and the change takes place in the direction of the applied force.
$$F = k\frac{d\rho}{dt} = ma$$
- **Newton's third law of motion** states that for every action there is always an equal and opposite reaction $F_{AB} = -F_{BA}$.
- **Momentum** is quantity of motion possessed by the body. It is the product of its mass and velocity.
$$p = mv$$
SI units is kg-m/s and dimensional formula is [MLT^{-1}].
- **Impulse** is the product of the average force and the time interval for which the force acts on the body
$$I = \mathbf{F} \times \Delta t = \mathbf{p}_2 - \mathbf{p}_1.$$
Its SI unit N-s and dimensional formula is [MLT^{-1}].
- In a lift going upwards or downwards, our feeling of weight (called apparent weight) changes as follows due to different values of reaction force of ground

$R = ma + mg$	[in lift going upwards]
$R = mg - ma$	[in lift going downwards]
$R = 0$	[lift falls freely under gravity]

- **Conservation of momentum**, if there are no external forces acting on a system, the total momentum of the system remains constant .

$$F_{ex} = 0, \text{ then } \Delta \mathbf{p} = \text{constant}$$
$$\mathbf{p} = \mathbf{p}_1 + \mathbf{p}_2$$

- **Equilibrium of a particle** the forces which are acting at the same point or on a particle are called concurrent forces. These forces are said to be in equilibrium when their resultant is zero.

- **Lami's theorem** According to this theorem when three concurrent forces F_1, F_2 and F_3 acting on a body are in equilibrium, then

$$\frac{F_1}{\sin \alpha} = \frac{F_2}{\sin \beta} = \frac{F_3}{\sin \gamma}$$

- **Some common forces in mechanics** are
  Gravitational force $F_g = mg$
  Weight $w = mg$,   Tension force, $T = mg$, Spring force $F = k\,x$ and Buoyant force friction.

- **Friction** is the opposing force which comes into play when a body moves or tries to move over the surface of another body.

- **Internal friction** are arises due to relative motion between two layers of liquid.

- **External friction** are arises when two bodies in contact with each other try to move or there is an actual relative motion between the two bodies.

- **Static Friction** The opposing force which comes into play between two bodies before one body actually starts moving over the other. It is denoted by f_s.

- **Limiting friction** The maximum opposing force which comes into play when a body just starts moving over the surface of another body. There are four laws of limiting friction.

$$\mu_s = \frac{f_s}{R} = \frac{\text{Limiting friction}}{\text{Normal reaction}}$$

- **Kinetic friction** The opposing force that comes into existence when one object is actually moving over the surface of the other object. it is also known as dynamic friction.

$$\mu_s = \frac{f_R}{R} = \frac{\text{Kinetic friction}}{\text{Normal reaction}}$$

- **Angle of friction** (θ) may be defined as the angle which the resultant of the limiting friction and the normal reaction makes with the normal reaction.

- **Angle of repose** is defined as the minimum angle of inclination of a plane with the horizontal such that a body placed on the plane just begins to slide down the ineline. It is represented by α

- **Types of kinetic friction sliding friction** The force that comes into play when a body slides over the surface of another body.

- **Rolling Friction** The force of friction that comes into play when a body rolls over the surface of another body.

- For circular motion of car on level road
  Centripetal force $F_c = mr\omega^2 = \dfrac{mv^2}{r}$ and $v_{max} = \sqrt{\mu r_g}$

- For motion of a car on banked road $v_{max} = \sqrt{\dfrac{r_g (u_s \tan \theta)}{T - (u_s \tan \theta)}}$

  Angle of banking, $\theta = \tan^{-1}\left(\dfrac{v^2}{r\,g}\right)$

CHAPTER PRACTICE

OBJECTIVE Type Questions

1. Who gave the idea that when a particle is moving with uniform velocity, there is no need of any force, if frictional force is zero?
   - (a) Aristotle
   - (b) Newton
   - (c) Galileo
   - (d) Einstein

2. A hockey player is moving northward and suddenly turns westward with the same speed to avoid an opponent. The force that acts on the player is   [NCERT Exemplar]
   - (a) frictional force along westward
   - (b) muscle force along southward
   - (c) frictional force along south-West
   - (d) muscle force along south-West

3. A car of mass m starts from rest and acquires a velocity along east, $\mathbf{v} = v\hat{i}\ (v > 0)$ in two seconds. Assuming the car moves with uniform acceleration, the force exerted on the car is   [NCERT Exemplar]
   - (a) $\dfrac{mv}{2}$ eastward and is exerted by the car engine
   - (b) $\dfrac{mv}{2}$ eastward and is due to the friction on the tyres exerted by the road
   - (c) more than $\dfrac{mv}{2}$ eastward exerted due to the engine and overcomes the friction of the road
   - (d) $\dfrac{mv}{2}$ exerted by the engine

4. If F is the force applied (as $F > f_k$), then acceleration of the body of mass M when body is on horizontal surface   [NCERT Exemplar]
   - (a) $\dfrac{f_k}{M}$
   - (b) $\dfrac{F - F_k}{M}$
   - (c) $\dfrac{F}{M}$
   - (d) None of these

5. If 3 forces $\mathbf{F}_1$, $\mathbf{F}_2$ and $\mathbf{F}_3$ act on a particle, then in equilibrium ...
   - (a) $\mathbf{F}_{21} + \mathbf{F}_2 + \mathbf{F}_3 = 0$
   - (b) $\mathbf{F}_1 + \mathbf{F}_2 + \mathbf{F}_3 = 0$
   - (c) $\mathbf{F}_{21} + \mathbf{F}_2 + \mathbf{F}_3$
   - (d) None of these

6. The coefficient of friction between tyres and the road is 0.1. Find the maximum speed allowed by traffic police for cars to cross a circular turn of radius 10 m to prevent accident.
   - (a) $\sqrt{10}$ ms^{-1}
   - (b) $\sqrt{20}$ ms^{-1}
   - (c) 5 ms^{-1}
   - (d) 9 ms^{-1}

7. A particle is moving on a circular path of 10 m radius. At any instant of time, its speed is 5ms^{-1} and the speed is increasing at a rate of 2 ms^{-2}. The magnitude of net acceleration at this instant is
   - (a) 5 ms^{-2}
   - (b) 2 ms^{-2}
   - (c) 3.2 ms^{-2}
   - (d) 4.3 ms^{-2}

ASSERTION AND REASON

Direction (Q. Nos. 8-17) *In the following questions, two statements are given- one labelled Assertion (A) and the other labelled Reason (R). Select the correct answer to these questions from the codes (a), (b), (c) and (d) as given below*
   - (a) Both Assertion and Reason are true and Reason is the correct explanation of Assertion.
   - (b) Both Assertion and Reason are true but Reason is not the correct explanation of Assertion.
   - (c) Assertion is true but Reason is false.
   - (d) Assertion is false but Reason is true.

8. **Assertion** A body is momentarily at rest still some force is acting on it at that time.
   Reason When a force acts on a body, it may not have some acceleration.

9. **Assertion** During the action of an impulsive force, change in the momentum is very high even though force acts for a very short period.
   Reason The amount of force is very high.

10. **Assertion** Action and Reaction forces do not cancel out each other.
    Reason It is because both do not act on the same body.

11. **Assertion** Angle of repose is equal to angle of limiting friction.
    Reason When a body is just at the point of motion, the force of friction in this stage is called as limiting friction.

12. Assertion It is always necessary that external agency of force is in contact with the object while applying force on object.

Reason A stone released from top of a building accelerates downward due to gravitational pull of the earth.

13. Assertion At the microscopic level, all bodies are made of charged constituents (nuclei and electrons) and various contact forces arise.

Reason These forces are due to elasticity of bodies, molecular collisions and impacts, etc.

14. Assertion Objects in motion generally experience friction, viscous drag, etc.

Reason On the earth, if an object is at rest or in uniform linear motion, it is not because there are no forces acting on it but because the various external forces cancel out, *i.e.* add upto zero net external force.

15. Assertion A seasoned cricketer allows a longer time for his hands to stop the ball, while catching the ball. His hand is not hurt.

Reason The novice (new player) keeps his hand fixed and tries to catch the ball almost instantly. He needs to provide a much greater force to stop the ball instantly and this hurts.

16. Assertion Product of mass and velocity (*i.e.* momentum) is basic to the effect of force on motion.

Reason Same force for same time causes the same change in momentum for different bodies.

17. Assertion Newton's third law of motion is applicable only when bodies are in motion.

Reason Newton's third law applies to all types of forces, e.g., gravitational, electric or magnetic forces, etc.

CASE BASED QUESTIONS

Direction (Q. Nos. 18-19) *These questions are case study based questions. Attempt any 4 sub-parts from each question.*

18. Force of Friction on Connected Bodies

When bodies are in contact, there are mutual contact forces satisfying the third law of motion. The component of contact force normal to the surfaces in contact is called normal reaction. The component parallel to the surfaces in contact is called friction.

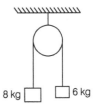

In the figure, 8 kg and 6 kg are hanging stationary from a rough pulley and are about to move. They are stationary due to roughness of the pulley.

(i) Which force is acting between pulley and rope?
(a) Gravitational force   (b) Tension force
(c) Frictional force   (d) Buoyant force

(ii) The normal reaction acting on the system is
(a) 8 g   (b) 6 g   (c) 2 g   (d) 14 g

(iii) The tension is more on side having mass of
(a) 8 kg   (b) 6 kg
(c) Same on both   (d) Nothing can be said

(iv) The force of friction acting on the rope is
(a) 20 N   (b) 30 N   (c) 40 N   (d) 50 N

(v) Coefficient of friction of the pulley is
(a) $\dfrac{1}{6}$ (b) $\dfrac{1}{7}$ (c) $\dfrac{1}{5}$ (d) $\dfrac{1}{4}$

19. Friction

Starting from rest, a body slides down a $\theta = 45°$ inclined plane of length s in twice the time it takes to slide down the same distance in the absence of friction. The coefficient of friction between the body and the inclined plane is μ.

(i) What is the expression for the acceleration of body?
(a) $a = g(\sin\theta - \mu\cos\theta)$
(b) $a = g(\cos\theta - \mu\sin\theta)$
(c) $a = g\sin\theta$
(d) $a = \mu g\cos\theta$

(ii) Expression for time taken by body to slide down the plane is

(a) $\sqrt{\dfrac{2s}{g(\sin\theta - \mu\cos\theta)}}$

(b) $\sqrt{\dfrac{2s}{g(\sin\theta + \mu\cos\theta)}}$

(c) $\sqrt{\dfrac{2s}{g(\tan\theta - \mu)}}$

(d) None of the above

(iii) When friction is absent, time taken to slide down the plane

(a) $\sqrt{\dfrac{2s}{g\sin\theta}}$ (b) $\sqrt{\dfrac{2s}{g\cos\theta}}$

(c) $\sqrt{\dfrac{2s}{g\tan\theta}}$ (d) $\sqrt{\dfrac{2s}{g\cot\theta}}$

(iv) Which of the following relation is correct?

(a) $3\cos\theta = 4\mu\sin\theta$ (b) $3\sin\theta = 4\mu\cos\theta$
(c) $4\cos\theta = 3\mu\sin\theta$ (d) $4\sin\theta = 3\mu\cos\theta$

(v) Coefficient of friction μ is

(a) 0.5   (b) 0.75   (c) 0.25   (d) 0.35

Answer

1.	(c)	2.	(c)	3.	(b)	4.	(b)	5.	(b)
6.	(a)	7.	(c)	8.	(c)	9.	(a)	10.	(a)
11.	(a)	12.	(a)	13.	(b)	14.	(b)	15.	(a)
16.	(c)	17.	(d)								

18. (i) (c)   (ii) (d)   (iii) (a)   (iv) (a)   (v) (b)
19. (i) (a)   (ii) (a)   (iii) (a)   (iv) (b)   (v) (b)

VERY SHORT ANSWER Type Questions

20. $F = ma$, this expression represents Newton's second law. What is the condition behind this expression?

21. Write the formula of the speed of the car on a banked circular road, when friction force acting on the tyres is zero.

22. A boy is standing on the road, having a box on his head. Find the number of action-reaction pairs.

23. A box is lying on a rough floor. What is the maximum value of F_{ext} so that box do not slip relative to the floor?

$\mu_s = 0.2$ | 20 kg | $\rightarrow F_{max} = ?$ [**Ans.** 40 N]

24. A box is lying on the floor of a lift, which is in free fall, what is the value of normal reaction?

SHORT ANSWER Type Questions

25. Forces of 16 N and 12 N are acting on a mass of 200 kg in mutually perpendicular direction. Find the magnitude of acceleration produced. [**Ans.** 0.1 m/s^2]

26. The wheel of a truck has a radius of $r = 0.29$ m and is being rotated at 830 revolutions per minute (rpm) on a tyre balancing machine. Determine the speed (in m/s) at which the outer edge of the wheel is moving. [**Ans.** 0.1 m/s]

27. What is the smallest radius of an unbanked (flat) track around which a bicyclist can move if her speed is 29 km/h and the μ_s between tyres and track is 0.32? [**Ans.** 2.1 m]

28. A boy is trying to push a truck but not able to push it. His friend explains the situation with the help of Newton's third law. His friend says that according to Newton's third law action-reaction forces are equal and opposite, so they will cancel each other and the net force on the truck will become zero. That's why the truck will not move. Analyse the explanation of his friend and comment that his explanation is right or wrong.

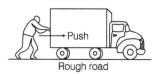

29. A shell of mass 0.020 kg is fired by a gun of mass 100 kg. If the muzzle speed of the shell is 80 m/s, what is the recoil speed of the gun? [**Ans.** 0.016 m/s]

LONG ANSWER Type I Questions

30. A bullet of mass 0.04 kg moving with a speed of 30 m/s enters a heavy wooden block and is stopped after a distance of 60 cm. What is the average resistive force exerted by the block on the bullet? [**Ans.** 270 N]

31. Briefly explain static friction, limiting friction and kinetic friction. How do they vary with the applied force?

32. For the given pulley block system, find the acceleration of 2 kg block.

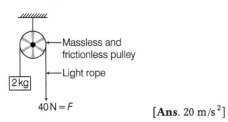

40 N = F   [**Ans.** 20 m/s^2]

33. Two blocks are placed over a horizontal smooth plane as shown in the figure. Find the minimum value of μ_2, so that block could move together.

$\mu_2 = ?$ $\boxed{2\,kg}$

$\boxed{4\,kg}$ $\rightarrow$ F = 18 N

$\mu_1 = 0$ [**Ans.** 0.6]

34. Find the maximum speed at which a car can turn around a curve of 30 m radius on a level road, given the coefficient of friction between the tyres and the road is 0.4. [$g = 10$ m/s^2]   [**Ans.** 11 m/s]

35. For traffic moving at 60 km/h, if the radius of a curve is 0.1 km, then what is the correct angle of banking of the road? [take $g = 10$ m/s^2]

[**Ans.** $\theta = \tan^{-1}\left(\dfrac{5}{18}\right) = 15°\,32'$]

36. Discuss the equilibrium of concurrent forces acting on a rigid body.

LONG ANSWER Type II Questions

37. A disc revolves in a horizontal plane at a steady rate of 3 revolutions per second. A coin of mass 6 g just remains on the disc if kept at a mean distance of 2 cm from the axis of rotation. What is the coefficient of friction between the coin and the disc? ($g = 10$ m/s^2)   [**Ans.** 0.725]

38. For the system below, find the values of T_1, T_2 and T_3. Also, find the acceleration of every block.

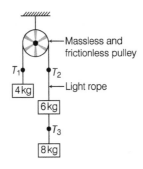

[**Ans.** $T_1 = \dfrac{56}{9}g$, $T_2 = \dfrac{56}{9}g$, $T_3 = \dfrac{16}{9}g$, $a = \dfrac{5}{9}g$]

In daily life, we generally use the terms work, energy and power. Work is any activity involving mental or physical effort.

Whereas, energy is our capacity to do work. The word power is also used in everyday life with different shades of meaning. In this chapter, we will study these terms from the vision of science.

WORK, ENERGY AND POWER

|TOPIC 1|
Work

The term work as understood in everyday life i.e. any physical or mental labour, has a different meaning in science. If a coolie is carrying a load on his head and waiting for the arrival of the train, he is not performing any work in the scientific sense.

DEFINITION OF WORK

Work is said to be done by a force, when the body is displaced actually through some distance in the direction of the applied force. Thus, work is done on a body only if the following two conditions are satisfied:

  (i) A force acts on the body.

  (ii) The point of application of the force moves in the direction of the force.

e.g. Work is done when an engine pulls a train, a man goes up a hill, a horse pulls a cart, etc.

Work Done by a Constant Force

Work done by the force (constant force) is the product of component of force in the direction of the displacement and the magnitude of the displacement.

If a constant force **F** is applied on a body and the body has a displacement **s** in the direction of the force as shown in figure.

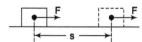

Work done, when force and displacement
are in the same direction

Then, the work done on the body by the force is given by

$$\boxed{\text{Work done, } W = \mathbf{F} \cdot \mathbf{s}}$$

Thus, work done by a force is the **dot product** of force and displacement.

Work Done When Force and Displacement are Inclined to Each Other

Sometimes the displacement **s** is not in the direction of **F** as shown in figure.

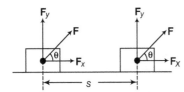

Work done when force and displacement
are inclined to each other

In such a case, we find the work done by resolving **F** into two rectangular components.

(i) $\mathbf{F}_x$ along the direction of displacement **s**, such that
$$|\mathbf{F}_x| = F\cos\theta$$

(ii) $\mathbf{F}_y$ along perpendicular to displacement **s**, such that
$$|\mathbf{F}_y| = F\sin\theta$$

The component $\mathbf{F}_y$ does not work as the body does not move up or down. All the work is done by the component $\mathbf{F}_x$.

$$\text{Work done } (W) = |\mathbf{F}| \cdot |\mathbf{s}| = (F\cos\theta)\cdot s$$

$$\boxed{\text{Work done, } W = Fs\cos\theta}$$

Thus, work done is the dot product of force and displacement vector. Hence, work is a scalar quantity.

Two cases can be considered for the maximum and minimum work.

Case I When **F** and **s** are in the same direction, i.e. $\theta = 0°$, then work done is

$$W = Fs\cos 0° = Fs(1) = Fs$$
i.e. maximum work done by the force.

Case II When **F** and **s** are perpendicular to each other, then

$$W = \mathbf{F} \cdot \mathbf{s} = Fs\cos 90° = Fs(0) = 0$$

i.e. no work done by the force, when a body moves in a direction perpendicular to the force.

Note
For a particular displacement, work done by a force is independent of type of motion i.e. whether it moves with constant velocity, constant acceleration or retardation.

Dimensions and Units of Work

As, work = force × distance $= [\text{MLT}^{-2}] \times [\text{L}]$
$$W = [\text{ML}^2\text{T}^{-2}]$$

This is the dimensional formula of work.
The units of work are of two types:
1. Absolute units   2. Gravitational units

1. Absolute Units

Work done is said to be one absolute unit, if an absolute unit of force displaces a body through a unit distance in the direction of the force.

(i) **Joule** It is the absolute unit of work in SI, named after British physicist James Prescott Joule (1811 – 1869).

One joule of work is said to be done when a force of one newton displaces a body through a distance of one metre in its own direction.

From work done $(W) = Fs\cos\theta$,
$$1\,\text{J} = 1\,\text{N} \times 1\,\text{m} \times \cos 0° = 1\,\text{N-m}$$

(ii) **Erg** It is the absolute unit of work in CGS system. One erg of work is said to be done if a force of one dyne displaces a body through a distance of one centimetre in its own direction.

From work done $(W) = Fs\cos\theta$
$$1\,\text{erg} = 1\,\text{dyne} \times 1\,\text{cm} \times \cos 0° = 1\,\text{dyne-cm}$$

Relation between Joule and Erg
$$1\,\text{J} = 1\,\text{N} \times 1\,\text{m}$$
$$= 10^5\,\text{dyne} \times 10^2\,\text{cm} = 10^7\,\text{dyne-cm}$$

or $\boxed{1\,\text{J} = 10^7\,\text{erg}}$

2. Gravitational Units

Work is said to be one gravitational unit if a gravitational unit of force displaces a body through a unit distance in the direction of the force.

(i) **Kilogram-metre** (kg-m) It is the gravitational unit of work in SI system. One kilogram-metre of work is said to be done when a force of one kilogram weight displaces a body through a distance of one metre in its own direction.

We know work done $(W) = Fs\cos\theta$
$$1\,\text{kg-m} = 1\,\text{kg wt} \times \cos 0°$$
$$= 9.8\,\text{N} \times 1\text{m} \times 1 = 9.8\,\text{J}$$
i.e. $1\,\text{kg-m} = 9.8\,\text{J}$

(ii) **Gram-centimetre** (g-cm) It is the gravitational unit of work in CGS system. One gram-centimetre of work is said to be done when a force of one gram-centimetre weight displaces a body through a distance of one centimetre in its own direction.

$\therefore$ $\quad$ 1 g-cm = 1 g-wt × 1 cm = 980 dyne × 1 cm

or $\quad$ 1 g-cm = 980 erg

EXAMPLE |1| A Lawn Roller

A lawn roller has been pushed by a gardener through a distance of 30 m. What will be the work done by him if he applies a force of 30 kg-wt in the direction inclined at 60° to the ground? Take, $g = 10$ m/s^2

Sol. Given, Displacement $s = 30$ m

Force, $F = 30$ kg-wt $= 30 \times 10 = 300$N

Angle between force and ground, $\theta = 60°$

The work done by the gardener,

$W = F \cdot s = Fs \cos \theta = 300 \times 30 \times \cos 60°$

$W = 4500$ J

EXAMPLE |2| A Coolie

A coolie is holding a bag by applying a force of 15 N. He moves forward and covers the horizontal distance of 8 m and then he climbs up and covers the vertical distance of 10 m. What will be the work done by him?

💡 The net work done by coolie is the sum of work done to cover the horizontal direction and the work done to climb up in the vertical direction.

Sol. Given, $F = 15$ N, $s_1 = 8$ m and $s_2 = 10$ m

As coolie is walking horizontally, therefore, the angle between the bag and distance covered is 90°.

$\therefore$ Work done to cover the distance of 8 m.

$W_1 = Fs_1 \cos \theta$

$= 15 \times 8 \cos 90° = 0$ J

When the coolie climb.

Thus, $\quad \theta = 0°$

The work done, $W_2 = Fs_2 \cos \theta$

$= 15 \times 10 \times \cos 0° = 150$ J

The net work done by him

$W = W_1 + W_2 = 0 + 150 = 150$ J

Nature of Work Done in Different Situations

Although work done is a scalar quantity, its value may be positive, negative or even zero, as discussed below:

1. Positive Work

If a force acting on a body has a component in the direction of the displacement, then the work done by the force is positive.

As shown in figure, when θ is acute, then $\cos \theta$ is positive i.e. $0 \leq \theta < 90°$.

$\therefore$ $\quad$ Work done $(W) = Fs \cos \theta = $ positive value

$[0 \leq \theta < 90°]$

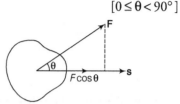

Positive work done $\theta <$ °

e.g.

(i) When a horse pulls a cart, the applied force and the displacement are in the same direction. So, work done by horse is positive.

(ii) When a load is lifted, then the lifting force and displacement act in the same direction. So, work done by the lifting force is positive.

(iii) When a spring is stretched, work done by the stretching force is positive.

2. Negative Work

If a force acting on the body has a component in the opposite direction of displacement, then work done is negative. As shown in figure, when θ is obtuse, then $\cos \theta$ is negative.

Work done $(W) = Fs \cos \theta = $ negative value

$[90° < \theta < 180°]$

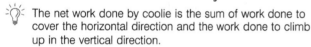

Negative work done $(\theta >$ °

e.g.

(i) When brakes are applied to a moving vehicle, the work done by the braking force is negative, this is because the braking force and the displacement act in opposite directions.

(ii) When a body is dragged along a rough surface, then work done by the frictional force is negative. This is because the frictional force acts in a direction opposite to that of the displacement.

(iii) When a body is lifted, then work done by gravitational force is negative. This is because the gravitational force acts vertically downwards while the displacement is in the vertically upward direction.

3. Zero Work

Work done by force is zero, if the body gets displaced in the direction perpendicular to the direction of the applied force.

Work done $(W) = Fs \cos 90° = Fs \cdot 0 = $ zero

e.g.

(i) Consider a body sliding over a horizontal surface. The work done by the force of gravity and the normal reaction of the surface will be zero.

This is because both the forces of gravity and reaction act normally to the displacement as shown in figure.

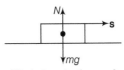

Work done by force of
gravity and normal force

(ii) Consider a body moving in a circle with constant speed. At every point of the circular path, the centripetal force and the displacement are mutually perpendicular as shown in figure.

So, the work done by the centripetal force is zero. The same argument can be applied to a satellite moving in a circular orbit.

Work done by
centripetal force

In this case, the gravitational force is always perpendicular to displacement. So, work done by gravitational force is zero.

(iii) As shown in figure, the tension in the string of simple pendulum is always perpendicular to displacement. So, work done by the tension is zero.

Work done by tension

EXAMPLE |3| Leaving Skid Marks

A cyclist comes to a skidding stop in 10 m. During this process, the force on the cycle due to the road is 200 N and is directly opposite to the motion. (i) How much work does the road do on the cycle? (ii) How much work does the cycle do on the road? **[NCERT]**

💡 Work done on the cycle by the road is the work done by the stopping force of friction on the cycle due to the road.

Sol. (i) The stopping force and the displacement make an angle of $180°$ with each other. Thus, work done by the road or the work done by the stopping force is

$$W_r = Fs \cos \theta$$
$$= 200 \times 10 \times \cos 180° = -2000 \text{ J}$$

Negative sign shows that work done by road-on cycle.

(ii) According to Newton's third law, an equal and opposite force acts on the road due to the cycle. Its magnitude is 200 N. However, the road undergoes no displacement. So, work done by the cycle on the road is zero.

Work Done by a Variable Force

Let a variable force F acts on a body along the fixed direction, say x-axis. The magnitude of the force F depends on x, as shown by force-displacement graph in figure.

Let us calculate the work done when the body moves from the initial position x_i to the final position x_f under a force $F(x)$.

The displacement can be divided into a large number of small equal displacements, i.e. Δx. During small displacement Δx, the force F can be assumed to be constant. Then, the work done is

$$\Delta W = F(x)\Delta x = \text{Area of rectangle } abcd.$$

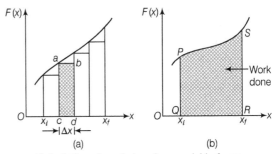

Calculation of work done by a variable force

Adding areas of all the rectangles in figure (a), we get the total work done as

$$W \cong \sum_{x_i}^{x_f} F(x) \Delta x$$

If the displacements are much small (i.e. are allowed to approach zero), then the number of terms in the sum increases without limit, but the sum approaches to definite value equal to the area under the curve. Thus, the total work done is

$$W = \lim_{\Delta x \to 0} \sum_{x_i}^{x_f} F(x) \Delta x = \int_{x_i}^{x_f} F(x)\, dx$$

$$W_{x_i \to x_f} = \int_{x_i}^{x_f} \mathbf{F} \cdot d\mathbf{x} = \int_{x_i}^{x_f} (F \cos \theta) \cdot dx$$

$$= \text{Area of } PQRS$$

$$\boxed{W_{x_i \to x_f} = \text{Area under the force-displacement curve}}$$

Hence, **for a varying force the work done is equal to the definite integral of the force over the given displacement as shown in figure.**

When the magnitude and direction of a force vary in three dimensions. So, it can be expressed in terms of rectangular components, we get

Force, $\mathbf{F} = F_x\hat{\mathbf{i}} + F_y\hat{\mathbf{j}} + F_z\hat{\mathbf{k}}$ and

Displacement, $\mathbf{dx} = dx\,\hat{\mathbf{i}} + dy\,\hat{\mathbf{j}} + dz\,\hat{\mathbf{k}}$

So, work done from x_i to x_f

$$\boxed{\text{Work done, } W = \int_{x_i}^{x_f} F_x\,dx + \int_{x_i}^{x_f} F_y\,dy + \int_{x_i}^{x_f} F_z\,dz}$$

where, F_x, F_y and F_z are the rectangular components of force in x, y and z-directions, respectively.

Note

When the body is in equilibrium (either static or dynamic), then resultant force is zero. Therefore, work done $W = 0$.

EXAMPLE |4| Work Done in Moving the Particles

Force $\mathbf{F} = [3x^2\,\hat{\mathbf{i}} + 4\,\hat{\mathbf{j}}]$ N with x in metres, acts on a particle. How much work is done on the particles as it moves from coordinates (2m, 3m) to (3m, 0m)?

Sol. Given, force $F = 3x^2\,\hat{\mathbf{i}} + 4\,\hat{\mathbf{j}}$

Coordinates $= \underset{x_i\ \ y_i}{(2m,\ 3m)}$ to $\underset{x_f\ \ y_f}{(3m,\ 0m)}$

Here, the force is variable force. Thus, work done is

$$W = \int_{x_i}^{x_f} F_x \cdot dx + \int_{y_i}^{y_f} F_y\,dy$$

$$= \int_2^3 3x^2\,dx + \int_3^0 4\,dy = 3\left[\frac{x^3}{3}\right]_2^3 + 4\,[y]_3^0$$

$$= \frac{3}{3} \times [27 - 8] + 4[0 - 3] = 19 - 12$$

$$W = 7.0\,\text{J}$$

EXAMPLE |5| Not Easy to Push a Trunk

A woman pushes a trunk on railway platform which has a rough surface. She applies a force of 100 N over a distance of 10 m. Thereafter, she gets progressively tired and her applied force reduces linearly with distance to 50 N. The total distance by which the trunk has been moved is 20 m. Plot the force applied by the woman and the frictional force, which is 50 N. Calculate the work done by the two forces over 20 m. **[NCERT]**

Sol. Plots of force F applied by the woman and the opposing frictional force F are shown in figure.

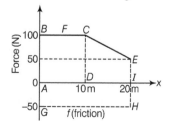

Clearly, at $x = 20$ m, $F = 50$ N

As we know the force of friction f opposes the applied force F, so it has been shown on the negative side of the force-axis.

Work done by the force F applied by the woman

$W_F = $ Area of rectangle $ABCD + $ Area of trapezium $CEID$

$$= 100 \times 10 + \frac{1}{2}(100 + 50) \times 10 = 1000 + 750$$

$$= 1750\,\text{J}$$

Work done by the frictional force,

$$W_f = \text{Area of rectangle } AGHI = (-50) \times 20 = -1000\,\text{J}$$

EXAMPLE |6| Work Done by Man using Variable Force

The force applied by a man in pushing a block varies with displacement as shown in figure. If the force is expressed in Newton and displacement in metres, find the work done by him.

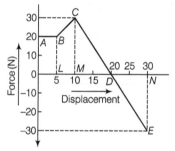

Sol. Given, displacement and forces are

At point B, $d_1 = 5$ m, $f_1 = 20$ N

At point C, $d_2 = 10$ m, $f_2 = 30$ N,

At point D, $d_3 = 20$ m, $f_3 = 0$ N,

At point E, $d_4 = 30$ m, $f_4 = -30$ N

Work done by the man $= ?$

Area under the rectangle $OABL$ is equal to work done W_{OABL}.

$$W_{OABL} = 20 \times 5 = 100\,\text{J}$$

$$[\because \text{Area} = \text{length} \times \text{breadth}]$$

Area under the trapezium $BCML$ is equal to work done W_{BCML}.

$$W_{BCML} = \frac{1}{2} \times [20 + 30] \times 5$$

$$\left[\because \text{area} = \frac{1}{2} \times (\text{sum of parallel side}) \times \text{height}\right]$$

$$W_{BCML} = \frac{1}{2} \times 50 \times 5 = 125\,\text{J}$$

Area under the $\Delta\,CDM$ is equal to work done W_{CDM}.

$$W_{CDM} = \frac{1}{2} \times 10 \times 30 = 150\,\text{J}$$

$$\left[\because \text{area} = \frac{1}{2} \times \text{base} \times \text{height}\right]$$

Area under the Δ DEN is equal to work done W_{DEN}.

$$W_{DEN} = \frac{1}{2} \times (10) \times -30 = -150 \text{ J}$$

$$\left[\because \text{area} = \frac{1}{2} \times \text{base} \times \text{height} \right]$$

Total amount of work done

$$= 100 \text{ J} + 125 \text{ J} + 150 \text{ J} - 150 \text{ J} = 225 \text{ J}$$

CONSERVATIVE FORCE

If the work done by the force in displacing an object depends only on the initial and final positions of the object and not on the nature of the path followed between the initial and final positions, such a force is known as **conservative force**.

e.g. **Gravitational force** is a conservative force.

Work Done by Conservative Forces

(i) Work done by or against a conservative force, in moving a body from one position to another, depends only on the initial and final positions of the body.

(ii) It does not depend upon the nature of the path followed by the body in going from initial position to the final position.

(iii) Work done by or against a force is said to be conservative, if the work done by the force in moving a particle along a closed path (round trip), net work done is zero.

Net Work Done by a Body in Moving Over the Round Trip

In case of gravitational force, if work done in moving the body from position P to Q, against the gravity (g → −Ve), then work done in moving the body from position Q to P, by gravity, as taken be positive. i.e.

$$W_{PQ} = -W_{QP}, W_{PQ} + W_{QP} = 0$$

Thus, net work done by a body in moving over the round trip $(P \to Q \to P)$ is zero.

EXAMPLE |7| Sliding Object

Figure shows two industrial spies sliding an initially stationary 250 kg floor safe, a displacement **d** of magnitude 10 m, straight towards their truck. The push $\mathbf{F}_1$ of spy A is 15 N directed at an angle of 30° downward from the horizontal, the pull $\mathbf{F}_2$ of spy B is 12 N directed at 40° above the horizontal plane.

The magnitudes and direction of these forces do not change as the safe moves, and the floor and safe make frictionless contact. [tan 40° = 0.8390, sin 40° = 0.6427]

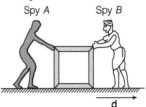

Spy A Spy B

(i) What is the net work done on the safe by forces $\mathbf{F}_1$ and $\mathbf{F}_2$ during the displacement **d** ?

(ii) During the displacement, what is the work W_g done on the safe by the gravitational force $\mathbf{F}_g$ and what is the work W_N done on the safe by normal $\mathbf{F}_N$ from the floor?

The net work done on the safe by forces $\mathbf{F}_1$ and $\mathbf{F}_2$ is the sum of works they do individually. Because we can treat the safe as a particle and the forces are constant in both magnitude and direction, we can use either ($W = Fd \cos \phi$) or ($W = \mathbf{F} \cdot \mathbf{d}$) to calculate those works. Since, we know the magnitudes and directions of the forces, we choose $W = Fd \cos \phi$. First draw the FBD of the safe.

Sol. (i)

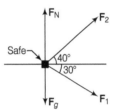

For first spy, $F_1 = 15$ N, $d = 10$ m and $\phi_1 = 30°$

Thus, work done

$$W_1 = F_1 d \cos \phi_1,$$
$$W_1 = 15 \times 10 \cos 30° = 130 \text{ J}$$

For Second spy, $F_2 = 12$ N, $d = 10$ m and $\phi_2 = 40°$

Thus, work done

$$W_2 = F_2 d \cos \phi_2$$

$$W_2 = 12 \times 10 \times \cos 40° \left[\because \cos 40° = \frac{\sin 40°}{\tan 40°} \right]$$

$$= 12 \times 10 \times 0.77 \cong 92 \text{ J}$$

Hence, net work done $W = W_1 + W_2 = 130 + 92 = 222$ J

(ii) These two forces (i.e. F_1 and F_2) are constant in both magnitude and direction, we can find out the work done on the safe by the gravitational force.

$$W_g = F_g d \cos 90°$$

Take $\phi = 90°$ because the direction of the gravitational force is perpendicular to the displacement of safe.

$$W_g = mgd \cos 90° = 0$$

and $\qquad W_N = F_N d \cos 90°$
$$= F_N d \cdot 0 = 0$$

$\therefore$ These forces are perpendicular to the displacement of safe, they do zero work.

NON-CONSERVATIVE FORCE

If work done by a force in displacing an object from one position to another, depends upon the path between the two positions. Such a force is known as **non-conservative force**.

Let W_1, W_2 and W_3 denote the net work done in moving a body from A to B along three different path $1, 2$ and 3 respectively as shown in figure. If the force is non-conservative, then $W_1 \neq W_2 \neq W_3$

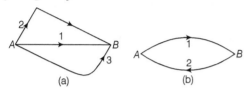

(a)   (b)

If Fig. (b), a particle is moving in a closed path $A \to 1 \to B \to 2 \to A$. If W_1 is work done in moving the particle from $A \to 1 \to B$, and W_2 is work done in moving the particle from $B \to 2 \to A$, then for a non-conservative force $|W_1| \neq |W_2|$

Hence, net work done along the closed path, $A \to B \to A$ is not zero.

The common examples of non-conservative forces are

  (i) Force of friction   (ii) Viscous force

  (iii) Tension

Work Done by Non-conservative Forces (Friction Forces)

As we know that friction force is always opposite to the relative motion so that the work done by friction may be positive, zero and negative.

Work Done due to Friction Forces

Case I	Case II	Case III
Fig. (a) shows a situation where a block is pulled by a force F which is insufficient to overcome the friction f_{max} i.e. $F < f_{max}$	Fig. (b) shows a situation where a block is pulled by a force F which is large to overcome friction f_{max} i.e. $F > f_{max}$. Here, the work done by friction force is negative.	Fig. (c) shows that block A is placed on block B and when block A is pulled with a force F, friction force does positive work on block B and negative work on block A.

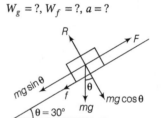

Case I	Case II	Case III
$F < f_{max}$	$F > f_{max}$	Work done $W_{Friction}$
$F < \mu_s N$	$f_{max} = Mg$	$= -$ ve for A.
$F < \mu_s Mg$		Work done $W_{Friction}$
$\therefore$ Work done,	$W = -\mu_k Mg\, s$	$= +$ ve for B.
$W = 0$		

EXAMPLE |8| **Sliding of Wooden Block on Inclined Plane**

A wooden block of mass 1 kg is pushed up a surface inclined to horizontal at angle of 30° by a force of 10 N parallel to the inclined surface [figure]. The coefficient of friction between block and the incline is 0.1. If the block is pushed up by 10 m along the incline. Calculate.

  (i) Work done against gravity.

  (ii) Work done against force of friction.

  (iii) Acceleration of block when it moves upward.

Sol. Given, $m = 1$ kg, $\theta = 30°$, $F = 10$ N, $\mu = 0.1$, $s = 10$ m,

$$W_g = ?, W_f = ?, a = ?$$

Work done against gravity,

$$W_g = mg \sin \theta \times s$$
$$W_g = mg \sin \theta \times s$$
$$= 1 \times 10 \sin 30° \times 10$$
$$= \frac{100}{2} = 50\,\text{J}$$

Work done against friction,

i.e. $W_f = F \times s$

$$W_f = F \times s = \mu R \times s$$
$$= \mu mg \cos \theta \times s$$
$$= 0.1 \times 1 \times 10 \cos 30° \times 10$$
$$= 10 \times 0.866 = 8.66\,\text{J}$$

Acceleration of block up the inclined plane, i.e.

$$F = ma + (mg \sin \theta + \mu\, mg \cos \theta)$$

$$\Rightarrow \quad a = \frac{F - (mg \sin \theta + \mu\, mg \cos \theta)}{m}$$

$$a = \frac{10 - \left(1 \times 10 \times \dfrac{1}{2} + 0.1 \times 10 \times 0.866\right)}{1}$$

$$= 4.13\,\text{m/s}^2$$

TOPIC PRACTICE 1

OBJECTIVE Type Questions

1. In which case, work done will be zero
   (a) a weight-lifter while holding a weight of 100 kg on his shoulders for 1 min
   (b) a locomotive against gravity when it is running on a level plane with a speed of 60 kmh^{-1}
   (c) a person holding a suitcase on his head and standing at a bus terminal
   (d) All of the above

Sol. (d) Work done by weight-lifter is zero because there is no displacement. In a locomotive, work done is zero because force and displacement are mutually perpendicular to each other.

While a person holding a suitcase, work done is zero because there is no displacement.

2. If the force and displacement of particle in the direction of force are doubled, then work done would be
   (a) double   (b) 4 times
   (c) half   (d) $\frac{1}{4}$ times

Sol. (b) ∵ Work = Force × Displacement   ...(i)
So, if the force and displacement of particle in the direction of force are doubled, then as per Eq. (i), their product will make the work done 4 times more than its initial value.

3. An electron and a proton are moving under the influence of mutual forces. In calculating the change in the kinetic energy of the system during motion, one ignores the magnetic force of one on another. This is, because   **[NCERT Exemplar]**
   (a) the two magnetic forces are equal and opposite, so they produce no net effect
   (b) the magnetic forces do not work on each particle
   (c) the magnetic forces do equal and opposite (but non-zero) work on each particle
   (d) the magnetic forces are necessarily negligible

Sol. (b) When electron and proton are moving under influence of their mutual forces, the magnetic forces will be perpendicular to their motion, hence no work is done by these forces.

4. A particle is pushed by forces $2\hat{i} + 3\hat{j} - 2\hat{k}$ and $5\hat{i} - \hat{j} - 3\hat{k}$ simultaneously and it is displaced from point $\hat{i} + \hat{j} + \hat{k}$ to point $2\hat{i} - \hat{j} + 3\hat{k}$. The work done is

   (a) 7 units   (b) -7 units
   (c) 10 units   (d) -10 units

Sol. (b) Net force, $\mathbf{F} = 2\hat{i} + 3\hat{j} - 2\hat{k} + 5\hat{i} - \hat{j} - 3\hat{k}$
$$= 7\hat{i} + 2\hat{j} - 5\hat{k}$$
Displacement, $\mathbf{d} = 2\hat{i} - \hat{j} + 3\hat{k} - \hat{i} - \hat{j} - \hat{k} = \hat{i} - 2\hat{j} + 2\hat{k}$
Work done = $\mathbf{F} \cdot \mathbf{d} = (7\hat{i} + 2\hat{j} - 5\hat{k}) \cdot (\hat{i} - 2\hat{j} + 2\hat{k})$
$$= 7 - 4 - 10 = -7 \text{ units}$$

5. A body is moving along a circular path. How much work is done by the centripetal force?
   (a) -1 J   (b) -2 J   (c) 3 J   (d) Zero

Sol. (d) For a body moving along a circular path, the centripetal force acts along the radius while the displacement is tangential, i.e. $\theta = 90°$, therefore, $W = Fs \cos 90° = 0$.

VERY SHORT ANSWER Type Questions

6. Is work done a scalar or a vector?

Sol. Work done by a force for a certain displacement is a scalar quantity.

7. Under what condition is the work done by a force is zero inspite of displacement being taking place?

Sol. Work done by a force is zero inspite of displacement being taking place, if displacement is in a direction perpendicular to that of force applied.

8. Can acceleration be produced without doing any work? Give example.

Sol. Yes, for uniform circular motion, no work done but a centripetal acceleration is present.

9. In a game of tug of war, one team is slowly giving way to the other. Which team is doing positive work and which team negative?

Sol. The winning team (i.e. the team which is pulling the other team towards itself) is doing positive work and the losing team (i.e. the team slowly giving way to the other) is doing negative work.

10. Does the amount of work done depend upon the fact that how fast is a load raised or moved in the direction of force?

Sol. The amount of work does not depend upon the fact that how fast is a load raised or moved in the direction of force.

11. A body is moving along a circular path. How much work is done by the centripetal force?

Sol. For a body moving along a circular path, the centripetal force acts along the radius while the displacement is tangential, i.e. $\theta = 90°$, therefore, $W = Fs \cos 90° = 0$.

SHORT ANSWER Type Questions

12. A body constrained to move along the Z-axis of a coordinate system is subject to a constant force $\mathbf{F}$ given by $\mathbf{F} = (-\,\hat{\mathbf{i}} + 2\hat{\mathbf{j}} + 3\hat{\mathbf{k}})$ N, where $\hat{\mathbf{i}}, \hat{\mathbf{j}}, \hat{\mathbf{k}}$ are unit vectors along the x, y and z-axes of the system, respectively. What is the work done by this force in moving the body a distance of 4 m along the z-axis? **[NCERT]**

Sol. Here, $\mathbf{F} = (-\,\hat{\mathbf{i}} + 2\hat{\mathbf{j}} + 3\hat{\mathbf{k}})$ N and $\mathbf{s} = (4\,\hat{\mathbf{k}})$ m

$$W = \mathbf{F} \cdot \mathbf{s} = \mathbf{F}_z \cdot \mathbf{s}_z = 3 \times 4 = 12 \text{ N-m} = 12 \text{ J}$$

13. A trolley of mass 300 kg carrying a sand bag of 25 kg is moving uniformly with a speed of 27 km/h on a frictionless track. After a while, sand starts leaking out of a hole on the floor of the trolley at the rate of 0.05 kgs^{-1}. What is the speed of the trolley after the entire sand bag is empty? **[NCERT]**

Sol. In present problem, there are no net external forces. The sand is slowly leaking downwards from the hole. Consequently, normal reaction acting vertically upwards also slowly decreases.

But it does not do any work because it is at right angle to trolley's motion. Thus, there is no change in speed of the trolley and it will continue among moving with a uniform speed of 27 kmh^{-1}.

14. Find the work done in pulling and pushing a roller through 100 m horizontally when a force of 1500 N is acting along a chain making an angle of 60° with ground. Assume the floor to be smooth.

Sol. Here, force $F = 1500$ N

and displacement, $s = 100$ m, $\theta = 60°$

$\therefore$ Work done, $W = Fs \cos \theta = 1500 \times 100 \times \cos 60°$

$$= 1500 \times 100 \times \frac{1}{2} = 75000 \text{ J} = 75 \text{ kJ}$$

15. Calculate the work done by a car against gravity in moving along a straight horizontal road. The mass of the car is 400 kg and the distance moved is 2 m. **[NCERT Exemplar]**

Sol. The work done by a car against gravity is zero because force of gravity is vertical and motion of car is along a straight horizontal road.

As angle θ between directions of force and displacement is 90°, hence work done is zero.

LONG ANSWER Type I Questions

16. A body of mass of 2 kg initially at rest moves under the action of an applied horizontally force of 7 N on a table with coefficient of kinetic friction = 0.1. Compute the **[NCERT]**

(i) work done by the applied force in 10 s,
(ii) work done by friction in 10 s,
(iii) work done by the net force on the body in 10 s,

Sol. Here, applied force $F = 7$ N

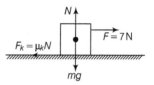

and opposing friction force, $f = \mu_k \cdot N = \mu_k \cdot mg$

$$= 0.1 \times 2 \times 9.8 = 1.96 \text{ N}$$

$\because$ Net accelerating force $= F - f = 7 - 1.96 = 5.04$ N

$\therefore$ Acceleration, $a = \dfrac{\text{force}}{\text{mass}} = \dfrac{5.04 \text{ N}}{2 \text{ kg}} = 2.52 \text{ ms}^{-2}$

(i) Distance covered in 10 s (assuming $u = 0$)

$$s = 0 + \frac{1}{2}at^2 = \frac{1}{2} \times 2.52 \times (10)^2 = 126 \text{ m}$$

$\therefore$ Work done by the applied force

$$W = Fs = 7 \times 126 = +882 \text{ J}$$

(ii) Work done by friction in 10 s

$$W' = fs \cos 180° = -1.96 \times 126 = -247 \text{ J}$$

(iii) Work done by net force in

$$10 \text{ s} = W - W' = 882 - 247 = +635 \text{ J}$$

17. A body of mass 3 kg is under a constant force, which causes a displacement S in metre in it, given by the relation $S = \dfrac{1}{3}t^2$, where t is in second. Find the work done by the force in 2 s.

Sol. Work done by the force = force $\times$ displacement

or $\qquad\qquad W = F \times S$ ...(i)

But from Newton's 2nd law, we have

Force = mass $\times$ acceleration

i.e. $\quad F = ma$ ...(ii)

Hence, from Eqs. (i) and (ii), we get

$$W = m\left(\frac{d^2s}{dt^2}\right)S \qquad \left[\because a = \frac{d^2s}{dt^2}\right] \text{ ...(iii)}$$

Now, we have $S = \dfrac{1}{3}t^2$

$\therefore \quad \dfrac{d^2s}{dt^2} = \dfrac{d}{dt}\left[\dfrac{d}{dt}\left(\dfrac{1}{3}t^2\right)\right] = \dfrac{d}{dt} \times \left(\dfrac{2}{3}t\right) = \dfrac{2}{3}\dfrac{dt}{dt} = \dfrac{2}{3}$

Hence Eq. (iii) becomes

$$W = \frac{2}{3}ms = \frac{2}{3} \times m \times \frac{1}{3}t^2 = \frac{2}{9}mt^2$$

We have, $m = 3$ kg, $t = 2$s

$\therefore \qquad W = \dfrac{2}{9} \times 3 \times (2)^2 = \dfrac{8}{3}$ J

18. A boy has a bag of sand of mass 20 kg. First of all, he keeps the bag on his head and moves 10 m. Second time, he drags the bag through 10 m on a frictionless surface with coefficient of friction $\mu = 0.1$. In which case, he does more work?

Sol. We know, work done is given by $W = Fs \cos \theta$

In first case, angle (θ) between F and s is 90° because weight of the bag, i.e. force acts perpendicular to the displacement.

$\therefore \qquad W = Fs \cos 90° = 0$

In second case, F and s are in the same direction, so $\theta = 0°$.

Here, $\qquad F = \mu \, mg = 0.1 \times 20 \times 9.8 = 19.6$ N

$\therefore \qquad W = 19.6 \times 10 \times \cos 0 = 196$ J

So, work done in second case is more.

19. A man weighing 50 kg supports a body of 25 kg on his head. What is the work done when he moves a distance of 20 m up an incline of 1 in 10? Take, $g = 9.8 \text{ m/s}^2$.

Sol. Here, mass of body $= 50 + 25 = 75$ kg

$$\sin \theta = \frac{1}{10}$$

Distance, $s = 20$ m, $g = 9.8 \text{ m/s}^2$

Force needed to be applied against gravity

i.e. $\qquad F = mg \sin \theta$

Work done, $\qquad W = Fs = mg \sin \theta \times s$

$$= 75 \times 9.8 \times \frac{1}{10} \times 20$$

$$= 1470 \text{ J}$$

20. A particle moves along the x-axis from $x = 0$ to $x = 5$m under the influence of a force given by $f(x) = 7 - 2x + 3x^2$. Calculate the work done.

Sol. As work done, $dW = Fdx$

$$W = \int_0^5 F \cdot dx = \int_0^5 (7 - 2x + 3x^2) dx$$

$$= \left[7x - \frac{2x^2}{2} + \frac{3x^3}{3} \right]_0^5$$

$$= 7(5 - 0) - (5^2 - 0) + (5^3 - 0) = 135 \text{ J}$$

LONG ANSWER Type II Questions

21. The sign of work done by a force on a body is important to understand. State carefully if the following quantities are positive or negative.

(i) Work done by a man in lifting a bucket out of a well by means of a rope tied to the bucket.

(ii) Work done by gravitational force in the above case.

(iii) Work done by friction on a body sliding down on inclined plane.

(iv) Work done by an applied force on a body moving on a rough horizontal plane with uniform velocity.

(v) Work done by the resistive force of air on a vibrating pendulum in bringing it to rest. **[NCERT]**

Sol. (i) Work done by the man against the force of gravity while lifting a bucket out of a well by means of a rope tied to the bucket is +ve, because force and displacement are in same direction.

(ii) Work done by gravitational force in the above case is −ve because direction of gravitational force is opposite to the displacement.

(iii) Work done is −ve because direction of friction force is opposite to sliding motion.

(iv) Work done by an applied force on a body moving on a rough horizontal plane is positive because force is being applied in the direction of motion so as to overcome friction.

(v) Work done is negative because the resistive force of air acts in a direction opposite to the direction of motion of the vibrating pendulum.

22. Calculate work done in raising a stone of mass 5 kg of specific gravity 3 immersed in water from a depth of 6 m to 1 m below surface of water. (Take, $g = 10 \text{ ms}^{-2}$)

Sol. As the stone weight acts downwards and upthrust acts upwards.

Thus, net weight of stone can be calculated.

$$\text{Specific gravity} = \text{Relative density} = \frac{\text{Density of stone}}{\text{Density of water}}$$

Thus, density of stone $= 3 \times 10^3 \text{ kg/m}^3$

$$\text{Volume of stone} = \frac{\text{Mass of stone}}{\text{Density of stone}}$$

$$= \frac{5}{3 \times 10^3} = \frac{5}{3} \times 10^{-3} \text{ m}^3$$

Upthrust on stone = Weight of liquid displaced

$$= \frac{5}{3} \times 10^{-3} \times \rho_{water} \times g$$

$$= \frac{5}{3} \times 10^{-3} \times 10^3 \times 10 = \frac{50}{3} \text{ N}$$

Thus, net weight of stone, $mg' = mg - \text{upthrust}$

$$mg' = \left(5 \times 10 - \frac{50}{3} \right) = \frac{100}{3} \text{ N}$$

Now, force required to raise the stone, $F = \frac{100}{3}$ N

Work required to raise the stone,

$$W = Fd = \frac{100}{3} \times 5 = \frac{500}{3} \text{ J} = 166.6 \text{ J}$$

23. A body of mass 0.3 kg is taken up an inclined plane length 10 m and height 5 m and then allowed to slide down the bottom again. The coefficient of friction between the body and the plane is 0.15. What is the

  (i) work done by gravitational force over the round trip?
  (ii) work done by the applied force over the upward journey?
  (iii) work done by the frictional force over the round trip?
  (iv) kinetic energy of the body at the end of trip?
  ($g = 10$ ms^{-2})

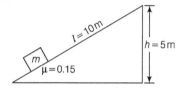

Sol. **Upward journey**

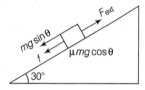

Let us calculate work done by different forces over upward journey.

Work by gravitational force

$$W_1 = (mg \sin\theta)s \cos 180°$$

$$W_1 = 0.3 \times 10 \sin 30° \times 10(-1)$$
$$W_1 = -15 \text{ J}$$

Work by force of friction

$$W_2 = (\mu\, mg \cos\theta)s \cos 180°$$
$$W_2 = 0.15 \times 0.3 \times 10 \cos 30° \times 10[-1]$$
$$W_2 = -3.879 \text{ J}$$

Work done by external force

$$W_3 = F_{ext} \times s \times \cos 0°$$
$$W_3 = [mg \sin\theta + \mu\, mg \cos\theta] \times 10 \times 1$$
$$W_3 = 18.897 \text{ J}$$

Downward journey

$$mg \sin 30° > \mu\, mg \cos 30°$$

Work done by the gravitational force

$$W_4 = mg \sin 30° \times s \cos 0°$$

$$W_4 = 0.3 \times 10 \times \frac{1}{2} \times 10 = +15 \text{ J}$$

Work done by the frictional force

$$W_5 = \mu mg \cos 30° \times s \cos 180°$$

$$= 0.15 \times 0.3 \times \frac{10\sqrt{3}}{2} \times 10 \times (-1)$$

$$= -3.897 \text{ J}$$

(i) Work done by gravitational force over the round trip
$$= W_1 + W_4 = 0 \text{ J}$$

(ii) Work done by applied force over upward journey
$$= W_3 = 18.897 \text{ J}$$

(iii) Work done by frictional force over the round trip
$$W_2 + W_5 = -3.897 + (-3.897) = -7.794 \text{ J}$$

(iv) Kinetic energy of the body at the end of the trip
$$W_4 + W_5 = 11.103 \text{ J}$$

ASSESS YOUR TOPICAL UNDERSTANDING

OBJECTIVE Type Questions

1. A body of mass 0.5 kg travels in a straight line by applying a force, $F = \dfrac{3}{2} ma^2 x^2$, where $a = 5$ m$^{-1/2}$s^{-1}.

   The work done by the net force during its displacement from $x = 0$ to $x = 2$ m is
   [NCERT Exemplar]

   (a) 1.5 J   (b) 50 J   (c) 10 J   (d) 100 J

2. Work done by gravitational force in one revolution of the earth around the sun on its elliptical path is zero because

   (a) force is always perpendicular to displacement
   (b) displacement is zero
   (c) displacement is positive
   (d) displacement is negative

3. Work done by a body against friction always results in

   (a) loss in kinetic energy
   (b) loss in potential energy
   (c) gain in kinetic energy
   (d) gain in potential energy

4. A bicyclist comes to a skidding stop in 10 m. During this process, the force on the bicycle due to the road is 200N and is directly opposed to the motion. The work done by the cycle on the road is **[NCERT Exemplar]**

   (a) + 2000J
   (b) − 200J
   (c) zero
   (d) − 20, 000J

5. A force $\mathbf{F} = 5\,\hat{\mathbf{i}} + 6\,\hat{\mathbf{j}} - 4\,\hat{\mathbf{k}}$ acting on a body produces a displacement $\mathbf{s} = 6\,\hat{\mathbf{i}} + 5\,\hat{\mathbf{k}}$. The work done by the force is
   - (a) 18 units
   - (b) 15 units
   - (c) 12 units
   - (d) 10 units

Answer

| 1. (b) | 2. (b) | 3. (a) | 4. (c) | 5. (d) |

VERY SHORT ANSWER Type Questions

6. Give the conditions under which a force is called conservative force.

7. A man raises a mass m to a height h and then shifts it horizontally by a length x. What is the work done against the force of gravity?

8. A mass is moving in a circular path with constant speed. What is the work done in $\frac{3}{4}$ th of a rotation? [**Ans.** zero]

SHORT ANSWER Type Questions

9. What is meant by zero work? Give any one example.

10. Mountain roads wind up gradually instead of going straight up the slope. Why?

11. A man moves on a straight horizontal road with a block of a mass 2 kg in his hand. If he moves a distance of 40 m with acceleration of $0.5\,\text{m/s}^2$. Calculate work done by the man on the block during motion. [**Ans.** 40J]

LONG ANSWER Type I Questions

12. What is a conservative and non-conservative forces? Explain various properties.

13. Define the term work. Show that work done is equal to the dot product of force and displacement vectors.

14. What is meant by positive work, negative work and zero work? Give one example of each.

15. What is the amount of work done by
   - (i) a weight-lifter in holding a weight of 120 kg on his shoulder for 30 s and
   - (ii) a locomotive against gravity, if it is travelling on a level plane? [**Ans.** zero, zero]

LONG ANSWER Type II Questions

16. What is a conservative force? Prove that gravitational force is conservative, while frictional force is non-conservative.

17. Obtain mathematically and graphically the work done by a variable force.

18. A simple pendulum of length 1m has a wooden bob of mass 1 kg. It is struck by a bullet of mass 10^{-2} kg moving with a speed of 2×10^2 m/s. The bullet gets embedded into the bob. Obtain the height to which the bob rises before swinging back. [Take, $g = 10\,\text{m/s}^2$] [**Ans.** 0.2 m]

|TOPIC 2|

Energy

The energy of a body is defined as its capacity or ability for doing work.
   - (i) Like work, energy is a scalar quantity having magnitude only and no direction.
   - (ii) The dimensions of energy are the same as the dimensions of work i.e. $[\text{M}^1\text{L}^2\,\text{T}^{-2}]$.
   - (iii) It is measured in the same unit as work i.e. joule in SI and erg in CGS system.

Energy can exist in various forms such as mechanical energy (potential energy and kinetic energy), sound energy, heat energy, light energy, etc. Some practical units of energy and their equivalence to joule is given in the table below

Some Other Units of Work or Energy

S. No.	Unit	Symbol	Value in SI
1.	Erg	erg	10^{-7} J
2.	Electron volt	eV	1.6×10^{-19} J
3.	Calorie	cal	4.186 J
4.	Kilowatt hour	kWh	3.6×10^6 J

KINETIC ENERGY

The energy possessed by a body by virtue of its motion is called **kinetic energy**. In other words, the amount of work done, i.e. a moving object can do before coming to rest is equal to its kinetic energy.

$$\therefore \quad \text{Kinetic energy}, KE = \frac{1}{2}mv^2$$

where, m is a mass and v is the velocity of a body, e.g.

  (i) A bullet fired from a gun can pierce a target due to its kinetic energy.
  (ii) The kinetic energy of a fast stream of water is used to run water mills.
  (iii) The kinetic energy of air is used to run wind mills.
  (iv) The kinetic energy of a hammer is used in driving a nail into a piece of wood.

The units and dimensions of KE are Joule (in SI) and $[ML^2T^{-2}]$ respectively.

Kinetic energy of a body is always positive. It can never be negative.

Kinetic energy of a body depends upon the frame of reference, e.g. KE of a person of mass m sitting in a train moving with velocity v is $\left[\frac{1}{2}mv^2\right]$ in the frame of earth and KE of the same person $= 0$, in the frame of the train.

EXAMPLE |1| A Ballistics Demonstration

In a ballistics demonstration, a police officer fires a bullet of mass 50.0 g with speed 200 ms^{-1} on soft plywood of thickness 2.00 cm. The bullet emerges with only 10% of its initial kinetic energy. What is the emergent speed of the bullet? **[NCERT]**

Sol. Here, $m = 50.0\,g = 0.05$ kg, $u = 200$ ms^{-1}

Initial KE $= \frac{1}{2}mu^2 = \frac{1}{2} \times 0.05 \times (200)^2 = 1000$ J

Final KE $= 10\%$ of 1000 J $= \frac{10 \times 1000}{100} = 100$ J

or $\frac{1}{2}mv^2 = 100$ J

$\therefore \quad v = \sqrt{\frac{2 \times 100}{m}} = \sqrt{\frac{2 \times 100}{0.05}} = 63.2$ ms^{-1}

Clearly, the speed reduces nearly by 68% and not by 90% by which the KE reduces.

Measurement of Kinetic Energy

Suppose a body is initially at rest and the force **F** is applied on the body to displace it through $d\mathbf{s}$ along the direction of the force. Then, the small work done as shown in figure.

A body displaced from A to B
by applying force

$$dW = \mathbf{F} \cdot d\mathbf{s} = Fds\cos 0° = Fds$$

According to Newton's second law of motion, we get

$$F = ma$$

where, a is acceleration produced on applying the force and m is the mass of the body.

$\therefore \qquad dW = mads = m\frac{dv}{dt}ds \qquad \left[\because a = \frac{dv}{dt}\right]$

or $\qquad dW = m\frac{ds}{dt}dv = mvdv \qquad \left[\because \frac{ds}{dt} = v\right]$

Therefore, total work done on the body in order to increase its velocity from zero to v.

$$W = \int_0^v mvdv = m\int_0^v vdv = m\left[\frac{v^2}{2}\right]_0^v = \frac{1}{2}mv^2$$

This work done appears as kinetic energy of the body.

i.e. $\boxed{\text{Kinetic energy}, KE = \frac{1}{2}mv^2}$

Hence, the kinetic energy of a body is equal to one-half the product of the mass of the body and the square of its velocity.

Note

We observed that KE $\propto m$ and also KE $\propto v^2$. Thus, a heavier body and a body moving faster possess greater energy. The reverse is also true.

EXAMPLE |2| Rocket Propulsion

A toy rocket of mass 0.1 kg has a small fuel of mass 0.02 kg which it burns out in 3 s. Starting from rest on horizontal smooth track it gets a speed of 20 ms^{-1} after the fuel is burnt out. What is the approximate thrust of the rocket? What is the energy content per unit mass of the fuel? (Ignore the small mass variation of the rocket during fuel burning). **[NCERT]**

Sol. Here, $m = 0.1$ kg, $u = 0$, $v = 20$ ms^{-1}, $t = 3$s

Thrust of the rocket $= ma = m\frac{v-u}{t}$

$= 0.1 \times \frac{20-0}{3} = \frac{2}{3}$ N $\left[\because v = u + at \text{ or } a = \frac{v-u}{t}\right]$

Kinetic energy gained by the rocket

$$K = \frac{1}{2}mv^2$$

$$= \frac{1}{2} \times 0.1 \times (20)^2 = 20 \text{ J}$$

Energy content per unit mass of the fuel

$$= \frac{\text{Total energy}}{\text{Mass of the fuel}} = \frac{20 \text{ J}}{0.02 \text{ kg}} = 1000 \text{ Jkg}^{-1}$$

Relation between Kinetic Energy and Linear Momentum

According to linear momentum,
we know $\qquad p = mv \qquad$ ...(i)
where, m is mass and v is the velocity of a body

and kinetic energy of the body $= \dfrac{1}{2} mv^2 = \dfrac{1}{2m}(m^2 v^2)$

$$KE = \frac{p^2}{2m} \qquad \text{[from Eq. (i)]}$$

or $\qquad p^2 = 2m\,KE$

$\Rightarrow \quad \boxed{\text{Linear momentum, } p = \sqrt{2m\,KE}}$

Let us consider three cases as given below.

(i) Further, if $p =$ constant, $KE \propto \dfrac{1}{m}$. This is shown in Fig. (a).

(ii) If $KE =$ constant, $p^2 \propto m$ or $p \propto \sqrt{m}$. This is shown in Fig. (b).

(iii) If $m =$ constant, $p^2 \propto KE$ or $p \propto \sqrt{KE}$. This is shown in Fig. (c).

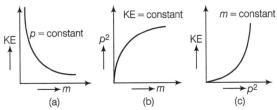

Graphical representation of kinetic energy and linear momentum

EXAMPLE |3| Radioactive Decay

A nucleus of radium ($^{226}_{88}$Ra) decays to $^{222}_{86}$Rn by the emission of α-particle ($^4_2$He) of energy 4.8 MeV. If mass of $^{222}_{86}$Rn $= 222.0$ amu and mass of $^4_2$He $= 4.003$ amu, then calculate the recoil energy of the daughter nucleus $^{222}_{86}$Rn.

[NCERT]

Sol. The nuclear decay may be represented as follows

Ra^{226} —Decay→ Rn^{222} + α-particle

At rest   KE = ?   KE = 4.8 MeV

The kinetic energy of a particle is given by

$$K = \frac{p^2}{2m}$$

$\therefore \qquad p = \sqrt{2mK}$

As momentum is conserved in the absence of an external force, so $\qquad mK =$ constant

or $\qquad m_{Rn} K_{Rn} = m_\alpha K_\alpha$

or $\qquad K_{Rn} = \dfrac{m_\alpha\,K_\alpha}{m_{Rn}} = \dfrac{4.003 \times 4.8}{222} = 0.0866$ MeV

WORK ENERGY THEOREM OR WORK ENERGY PRINCIPLE

It states that work done by the net force acting on a body is equal to the change produced in the kinetic energy of the body.

Work Energy Theorem for a Constant Force

When a force F acting on a body of mass m produces acceleration a in it. After covering distance s, suppose the velocity of the body changes from u to v. We use the equation of motion $v^2 - u^2 = 2as$

Multiply both sides by $\dfrac{1}{2} m$, we get

$$\frac{1}{2} mv^2 - \frac{1}{2} mu^2 = mas$$

By Newton's second law, $\qquad F = ma$

$\therefore \qquad \dfrac{1}{2} mv^2 - \dfrac{1}{2} mu^2 = Fs$

or $\qquad \boxed{K_f - K_i = W} \qquad [\because W = Fs]$

where, K_f and K_i are the final and initial kinetic energies of the body.

EXAMPLE |4| Pulling a Block

A 8 kg block initially at rest is pulled to the right along a frictionless horizontal surface by a constant, horizontal force of 12 N, as shown in figure. Find the velocity of the block after it has moved a distance of 3 m. Also, find out the acceleration of the block.

8 kg →$F = 12$N

3 m

The weight of the block is balanced by the normal force and neither of these forces does work, since the displacement is horizontal. Because there is no friction, the resultant external force is 12 N.

Sol. First of all draw the free body diagram of the block.

F_N

Friction force $f = 0$ ← 8 kg →$F = 12$N   8 kg

←—3m—→

8g

Find out the work done by the force 12 N.

$$W = F s = Fs \cos 0° = 12 \times 3 = 36 \text{ J}$$

The work done by the normal and the weight of body will be zero.

If K_f and K_i are the final and initial kinetic energies of the block respectively, then according to work energy theorem.

$$W = K_f - K_i = \frac{1}{2}mv^2 - \frac{1}{2}mu^2 = \frac{1}{2}mv^2$$

$$[\because \text{ initial velocity of the block } u = 0]$$

Velocity of the block,

$$v = \sqrt{\frac{2W}{m}} = \sqrt{\frac{2 \times 36}{8}} \qquad [\because \text{ given, } m = 8 \text{ kg}]$$

$$v = 3 \text{ m/s}$$

The acceleration of the block can be calculated using the kinematic equation.

$$v^2 = u^2 + 2as$$

$$\therefore \qquad a = \frac{v^2 - u^2}{2s} = \frac{9}{2 \times 3} = 1.5 \text{ m/s}^2$$

A Block over Another Block

When a block A is placed on block B which is accelerating towards right with respect to ground as shown in figure. Then, work done by weight (w) and normal reaction (N) are zero because they act perpendicular to the displacement of block A.

In inertial frame, we have, $W_{\text{friction}} + W_{\text{pseudo}} = \Delta \text{KE}$,

if block A is at rest with respect to block B, then $\Delta \text{KE} = 0$ and therefore, $W_{\text{pseudo}} = -W_{\text{friction}}$.

In non-inertial frame,

$$W_{\text{external}} + W_{\text{internal}} + W_{\text{pseudo}} + W_{\text{other}} = \Delta \text{KE}$$

Work energy theorem is true for any system of particles in the presence of all types of force (conservative or non-conservative).

When KE increases, then work done is positive and when KE decreases, then work done is negative.

Work Energy Theorem for a Variable Force

Suppose a variable force $\mathbf{F}$ acts on a body of mass m and produces displacement $d\mathbf{s}$ in its own direction ($\theta = 0°$). Then,.the small work done is

$$dW = \mathbf{F} \cdot d\mathbf{s} = Fds \cos 0° = Fds$$

The time rate of change of kinetic energy is

$$\frac{dK}{dt} = \frac{d}{dt}\left[\frac{1}{2}mv^2\right]$$

$$= \frac{1}{2} \times 2v \times m\frac{dv}{dt}$$

$$= m\frac{dv}{dt}(v) = (ma)v$$

$$\left[\because \text{ force, } F = ma \text{ and } v = \frac{ds}{dt}\right]$$

$$\therefore \qquad \frac{dK}{dt} = F \cdot \frac{ds}{dt}$$

Thus, $\qquad dK = F\,ds$

Integrating from the initial position (x_i) to final position (x_f), we have

$$\int_{K_i}^{K_f} dK = \int_{x_i}^{x_f} F\,ds$$

where, K_i and K_f are the initial and final kinetic energies corresponding to x_i and x_f, respectively.

or $\qquad \boxed{\text{Change in kinetic energy, } K_f - K_i = \int_{x_i}^{x_f} F\,ds}$

$$\therefore \qquad K_f - K_i = \text{work done on the body } (W)$$

$$= \text{increase in KE of body.}$$

This proves the work energy theorem for a variable force.

Note
- The work energy theorem is not independent of Newton's second law.
- Newton's second law in two or three dimensions is in vector form, but the work energy theorem is in scalar form.

EXAMPLE |5| **When a Pebble Hits the Ground**

Consider a drop of small pebble of mass 1.00 g falling from a cliff of height 1.00 km. It hits the ground with a speed of 50.0 ms^{-1}. What is the work done by the unknown resistive force? **[NCERT]**

Sol. We assume that the pebble is initially at rest on the cliff.

$$\therefore \qquad u = 0, m = 1.00 \text{ g} = 10^{-3} \text{ kg}$$

$$v = 50 \text{ ms}^{-1}, h = 1.00 \text{ km} = 10^3 \text{ m}$$

The change in KE of the pebble is

$$\Delta K = \frac{1}{2}mv^2 - \frac{1}{2}mu^2$$

$$= \frac{1}{2} \times 10^{-3} \times (50)^2 - 0 = 1.25 \text{ J}$$

Assuming that $g = 10 \text{ ms}^{-2}$ is constant, the work done by the gravitational force is

$$W_g = F \cdot h = mgh = 10^{-3} \times 10 \times 10^3 = 10.0 \text{ J}$$

If W_r is the work done by the resistive force on the pebble, then from the work energy theorem,

$$\Delta K = W_g + W_r$$

or $\qquad W_r = \Delta K - W_g$

$$= 1.25 - 10.0 = -8.75 \text{ J}$$

EXAMPLE |6| A Stretched Block on a Horizontal Plane

A block of mass $m = 1\,\text{kg}$, moving on a horizontal surface with speed $v_i = 2\ \text{ms}^{-1}$ enters a rough patch ranging from $x = 0.10\,\text{m}$ to $x = 2.01\,\text{m}$. The retarding force F_r on the block in this range is inversely proportional to x over this range.

$$F_r = \frac{-k}{x}\quad 0.1 < x < 2.01\ \text{m}$$
$$= 0\ \text{for}\ x < 0.1\ \text{m and}\ x > 2.01\ \text{m}$$

where, $k = 0.5\,\text{J}$. What is the final kinetic energy and speed v_f of the block as it crosses this patch? **[NCERT]**

Sol. By work energy theorem,

$$\Delta K = W_r\quad \text{or}\quad K_f - K_i = \int_{x_i}^{x_f} F_r\, dx$$

$$\therefore \qquad K_f = K_i + \int_{0.1}^{2.01} \frac{(-k)}{x}\, dx \qquad [\because F_r = -kx]$$

where, k = spring constant

$$K_f = \frac{1}{2} m v_i^2 - k \int_{0.1}^{2.01} \frac{1}{x}\, dx$$

$$= \frac{1}{2} \times 1 \times 2^2 - k\, [\ln x]_{0.1}^{2.01}$$

$$= 2 - 0.5\left[\ln \frac{2.01}{0.1}\right] = 2 - 0.5 \ln 20.1$$

$$= 2 - 0.5 \times 2.303 \log 20.1$$

$$= 2 - 0.5 \times 2.303 \times 1.3032$$

$$K_f = 2 - 1.5 = 0.5\,\text{J}$$

Final speed, $v_f = \sqrt{\dfrac{2K_f}{m}} = \sqrt{\dfrac{2 \times 0.5}{1}} = 1\ \text{ms}^{-1}$

POTENTIAL ENERGY

The potential energy of a body is defined as the energy possessed by the body by virtue of its position or configuration in some field.

Thus, the potential energy of a system that can be associated with the configuration of a system of objects that exert forces on one another. So, configuration of the system changes, then its potential energy changes.

e.g.
  (i) A body lying on the roof of a building has some potential energy. When allowed to fall down it can do work.
  (ii) When a spring is compressed or stretched, work done in compressing or stretching spring is stored in the spring in the form of potential energy.

Units and Dimensions of Potential Energy

The units and dimensions of potential energy are same as that of kinetic energy given as,

Dimensions $= [\text{ML}^2\text{T}^{-2}]$

Unit = Joule (J) in SI

> ### Potential Energy Converted into Kinetic Energy
> The notion of potential energy applies to only those forces where the work done against the force gets stored up as energy by virtue of position or configuration of the body when external constraints are removed.
>
> This energy appears as kinetic energy, when the position or configuration of the body gets change under the action of external constraints.

Gravitational Potential Energy

Gravitational potential energy of a body is the energy possessed by the body by virtue of its position above the surface of the earth.

Consider a body of mass m lying on the surface of the earth as shown in figure. Let g be the acceleration due to gravity at this place. For height much smaller than the radius of the earth ($h << R_E$) the value of g can be taken constant.

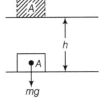

Gravitational potential energy of a body

Force needed to lift the body up with zero acceleration,

$$F = \text{weight of the body} = mg$$

Work done on the body in raising it through height h,

$$W = Fh = mgh$$

This work done against gravity is stored as the gravitational potential energy (U) of the body.

$$\therefore \qquad \boxed{\text{Gravitational potential energy, } U = mgh}$$

If h is taken as a variable, then the gravitational force F equal to the negative of derivative of U with respect to h.

Thus, $$F = -\frac{d(U)}{dh} = -mg$$

Here, the negative sign indicates that the gravitational force is downward.

Moreover, if a body of mass m is released from rest, from the top of a smooth (frictionless) inclined plane of height h, just before it hits the ground, its speed is given by the kinematic relation.

$$v^2 - (0)^2 = 2gh \quad \text{or} \quad v = \sqrt{2gh}$$

So, KE acquired by the body on reaching the ground,

$$\frac{1}{2} mv^2 = \frac{1}{2} m \times 2gh = mgh$$

$$= \text{work done by the gravitational force}$$

This equation shows that the gravitational potential energy of the object at height h, when it is released reveals itself as kinetic energy of the object on reaching the ground

$$v = \sqrt{2gh}$$

- For gravitational potential energy, the zero of potential energy is chosen to be the ground.
- The work done by the gravitational force does not depend on the angle of inclination of the inclined plane or the path of the falling body. It just depends on the initial and final position. Thus, gravitational force is a conservative force.

$$\therefore \qquad F(x) = \frac{-dU}{dx}$$

If x_i and x_f are the initial and final position of the object and U_i and U_f are the corresponding potential energies, then

$$\int_{x_i}^{x_f} F(x)\, dx = -\int_{U_i}^{U_f} dU = U_i - U_f$$

EXAMPLE |7| A Ball Hits the Ground
A ball falls from a height of 20 m. Find out of the velocity with which the ball hits the ground?

Sol. Given, $h = 20$ m, $v = ?$

When the ball hits the ground its kinetic energy is converted into potential energy.

$\therefore$ When it hits the ground KE = PE

$$\frac{1}{2}mv^2 = mgh$$

$$v = \sqrt{2gh} = \sqrt{2 \times 9.8 \times 20} = \sqrt{392} = 19.798 \text{ m/s}$$

Potential Energy of a Spring

There are many types of spring. Important among these are helical and spiral springs as shown in figure.

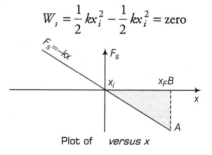

(a) Helical spring and (b) Spiral spring

Usually, we assume that the springs are massless. Therefore, work done is stored in the spring in the form of elastic potential energy of the spring. Thus, potential energy of a spring is the energy associated with the state of compression or expansion of an elastic spring.

Consider an elastic spring of negligibly small mass with its one end attached to a rigid support and its other end is attached to a block of mass m can slide over a smooth horizontal surface. At $x = 0$, the position is in the state of equilibrium as shown in Fig. (a), when the spring is stretched in Fig. (b) and compressed by pushing the block as shown in Fig. (c). So, spring force F_s begins to act in equilibrium position.

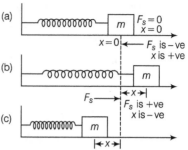

Equilibrium, stretched and compressed states of an elastic spring

For a small stretch or compression, spring obeys Hooke's law, i.e. restoring force $\propto$ stretch or compression

$$-F_s \propto x \quad \Rightarrow \quad F_s = -kx$$

where, k is called **spring constant**. Its SI unit is N/m. The negative sign shows F_s acts in the opposite direction of displacement x. The work done by the spring force for the small extension is $dW_s = F_s\, dx = -kx\, dx$

If the block is moved from an initial displacement x_i to final displacement x_f, then work done by spring force is

$$W_s = \int dW_s = -\int_{x_i}^{x_f} kx\, dx = -k\left[\frac{x^2}{2}\right]_{x_i}^{x_f}$$

or $\boxed{\text{Net work done by the spring, } W_s = \frac{1}{2}kx_i^2 - \frac{1}{2}kx_f^2}$

(i) If $x_i = 0$ (i.e. for mean position) then, work done by the spring force is

$$W_s = -\frac{1}{2}kx_f^2$$

(ii) If the block is pulled from x_i and allowed to return to x_i, then

$$W_s = \frac{1}{2}kx_i^2 - \frac{1}{2}kx_i^2 = \text{zero}$$

Plot of F_s versus x

Conclusion

(i) Spring force F_s is position dependent as it is clear in Hooke's law.
   i.e. $F_s = -kx$

(ii) The work done by the spring force depends on initial and final position.

(iii) The work done by the spring force in a cyclic process is zero.

(iv) It can be expressed as the difference between the initial and final values of a potential energy function. Hence, spring force is a **conservative force**.

Note
The potential energy of a body which is subjected to a conservative force is uncertain upto a certain limit. This is because the point of zero potential energy is a matter of choice. For the spring potential energy $\frac{1}{2}kx^2$, the zero of the potential energy is the equilibrium position of the oscillating mass.

EXAMPLE |8| Compresses a Spring

As shown in figure, a canister of mass $m = 0.40$ kg slides across a horizontal frictionless counter with speed $v = 0.50$ m/s. It then runs into and compresses a spring of spring constant $k = 750$ N/m. When the canister is momentarily stopped by the spring, by what distance d is the spring compressed ?

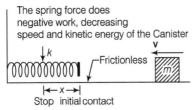

The spring force does negative work, decreasing speed and kinetic energy of the Canister

Stop   initial contact

The work W_s done on the canister by the spring force is related to the distance x by the relation $W_s = -\frac{1}{2}kx^2$.

The work W_s is also related to the kinetic energy of the canister by $(K_f - K_i = W)$
The canister's kinetic energy has an initial value of $K = \frac{1}{2}mv^2$ and a value of zero when the canister is momentarily at rest.

Sol. Write the work energy theorem for the canister as

$$K_f - K_i = \frac{1}{2}kx^2$$

Substituting according to the third key idea gives us the expression

$$0 - \frac{1}{2}mv^2 = -\frac{1}{2}kx^2$$

$$x = v\sqrt{\frac{m}{k}} = (0.50 \text{ m / s})\sqrt{\frac{0.40 \text{ kg}}{750 \text{ N / m}}}$$

$$= 0.50 \times 0.02 = 0.0115 \text{ m} = 1.15 \text{ cm}$$

MOTION IN A VERTICAL CIRCLE

Suppose a particle of mass m is attached to an inextensible light string of length L. The particle is moving in a vertical circle of radius L about a fixed point O.

It is imparted a velocity u in horizontal direction at lowest point A. Let v be its velocity at point B, the circle as shown in figure. Here we have $h = R(1 - \cos\theta)$

Now from conservation of mechanical energy, we have

$$\frac{1}{2}m(u^2 - v^2) = mgh \qquad \ldots(i)$$

The necessary centripetal force is provided by the resultant of tension T and $mg\cos\theta$.

$$\therefore \qquad T - mg\cos\theta = \frac{mv^2}{R} \qquad \ldots(ii)$$

As speed of the particle decreases with height, tension in the string is maximum at the bottom. The particle will complete the circle if the string does not slack even at the highest point.

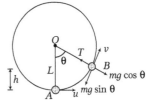

Motion of a particle in vertical circle

Now following conclusions can be made using above Eqs. (i) and (ii).

(i) **Minimum velocity at highest point** so that particle complete the circle $v_{\min} = \sqrt{gL}$, at this velocity, tension in the string is zero.

(ii) **Minimum velocity at lowest point** so that particle complete the circle, $v_{\min} = \sqrt{5gL}$, at this velocity, tension in the string is $6\,mg$.

(iii) **When string is horizontal**, then minimum velocity is $\sqrt{3Rg}$ and tension in this condition is $3\,mg$.

(iv) If velocity at lowest point is less than $\sqrt{5\,gR}$, then tension in the string becomes zero before reaching the highest point, now the particle will leave the circle and will move on parabolic path.

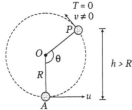

In this condition, if $\sqrt{2gR} < v < \sqrt{5\,gR}$ then tension in the string becomes zero but velocity is not zero, the particle will leave circle at $90° < \theta < 180°$ or $h > R$

(v) If velocity at lowest point is $0 < v \leq \sqrt{2\,gR}$, the particle will oscillate, in this condition velocity becomes zero but tension is not zero. The particle will oscillate in lower half of circle, *i.e.*, $0° < \theta < 90°$

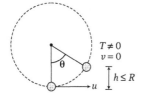

EXAMPLE |9| A Ballistic Bob

A bob of mass m is suspended by a light string of length L. It is imparted a horizontal velocity v_0 at the lowest point A such that it completes a semi-circular trajectory in the vertical plane with the string becoming slack only on reaching the topmost point, C. This is shown in figure obtain an expression for (i) v_0 (ii) the speeds at points B and C, (iii) the ratio of the kinetic energies (K_B/K_C) at B and C. Comment on the nature of the trajectory of the bob after it reaches the point C.

[NCERT]

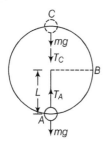

Sol. (i) Two external forces act on the bob, i.e. gravity and tension (T) in the string.

At the lowest point A, the potential energy of the system can be taken zero. So, at point A,

Total mechanical energy = Kinetic energy

$$E = \frac{1}{2}\,mv_0^2 \qquad \ldots(i)$$

If T_A is the tension in the string at point A, then from Newton's second law,

$$T_A - mg = \frac{mv_0^2}{L} \qquad \ldots(ii)$$

At the highest point C, the string slackens, so the tension T_C becomes zero. If v_C is the speed at point C, then by conservation of energy,

$$E = K + U \quad \text{or} \quad E = \frac{1}{2}\,mv_C^2 + 2\,mgL \qquad \ldots(iii)$$

From Newton's second law,

$$mg = \frac{mv_C^2}{L} \qquad \ldots(iv)$$

or $$mv_C^2 = mgL \qquad \ldots(v)$$

Using Eq. (v) in Eq. (iii), we get

$$E = \frac{1}{2}\,mgL + 2\,mgL = \frac{5}{2}\,mgL \qquad \ldots(vi)$$

From Eqs. (i) and (vi), we get

$$\frac{5}{2}\,mgL = \frac{m}{2}\,v_0^2 \text{ or } v_0 = \sqrt{5\,gL} \qquad \ldots(vii)$$

(ii)   From Eq. (iv), we have $v_C = \sqrt{gL}$

The total energy at B is $E = \frac{1}{2}\,mv_B^2 + mgL \qquad \ldots(viii)$

From Eqs. (i) and (viii), we get

$$\frac{1}{2}\,mv_B^2 + mgL = \frac{1}{2}\,mv_0^2$$

$$\frac{1}{2}\,mv_B^2 + mgL = \frac{1}{2}\,m \times 5gL \quad \text{[using Eq. (vii)]}$$

$$\therefore \qquad\qquad v_B = \sqrt{3gL}$$

(iii) The ratio of the kinetic energies at B and C is

$$\frac{K_B}{K_C} = \frac{(1/2)\,mv_B^2}{(1/2)\,mv_C^2} = \frac{3}{1} = 3:1$$

VARIOUS FORMS OF ENERGY

Energy can manifest itself in many forms. Some of these forms are as follows

(i) **Mechanical Energy** The sum of kinetic and potential energies is called as **mechanical energy.** KE is due to motion while the potential energy is due to position or configuration.

(ii) **Internal Energy** When the molecules of a body vibrate with respect to one another, the molecules possess potential energy due to their location against the intermolecular forces and possess kinetic energy because of motion. The sum of these kinetic and potential energies of all the molecules constituting the body is called its **internal energy.**

(iii) **Heat Energy** A body possess heat energy due to the disorderly motion of its molecules. Heat energy is also related to the internal energy of the body. In winter, we generate heat by rubbing our hands against each other.

(iv) **Chemical Energy**   A stable chemical compound has lesser energy than its constituent atoms, the difference being in the arrangement and motion of electron in the compound. This difference is called **chemical energy.**

If the total energy of the reactant is more than the product of the reaction, then heat is released and the reaction is said to be an **exothermic reaction.** If the reverse is true, then heat is absorbed and the reaction is **endothermic.**

(v) **Electrical Energy** Work is said to be done when electric charge moves from one point to another in an electric field or motion of a current carrying conductor inside a magnetic field. The energy is associated with an electric current. The flow of current causes bulbs to glows motor to run and electric heater to produce heat.

(vi) **Nuclear Energy** When U^{235} nucleus breaks up into lighter nuclei on being bombarded by a slow neutron, a tremendous amount of energy is released. Thus, the energy so released is called nuclear energy and this phenomenon is known as **nuclear fission**. **Nuclear reactors** and **nuclear bombs** are the sources of nuclear energy.

Equivalence of Mass and Energy

In 1905, Einstein discovered that mass can be converted into energy and *vice-versa*. He showed that mass(m) and energy(E) are equivalent and related by the relation given,

$$\boxed{E = mc^2}$$

where, m is mass that disappears. E is energy that appears and c is velocity of light in vacuum.

Conversely, when energy E disappears, a mass $m\ (= E/c^2)$ appears. Thus, according to modern physics, mass and energy are not conserved separately, but are conserved as a single entity called **mass energy**. So, the law of conservation of mass and law of conservation of energy have been unified by this relation into a single law of conservation of mass energy.

As speed of light in vacuum is approximately 3×10^8 m/s. Thus, a staggering amount of energy is associated with a mere one kilogram of matter.

i.e. $\quad\quad E = 1 \times (3 \times 10^8)^2 = 9 \times 10^6\, \text{J}$

Thus, it is equivalent to the annual electrical output of a large (3000 MW) power generating station.

EXAMPLE |10| **Nuclear Fusion Reaction**
Estimate the amount of energy released in the nuclear fusion reaction

$$_1H^2 + _1H^2 \longrightarrow _2He^3 + _0n^1$$

Given that $M\ (_1H^2) = 2.0141\, \text{u}$,

$$M\ (_2He^3) = 3.0160\, \text{u}$$

Mn = 1.0087 u, where 1 u $= 1.661 \times 10^{-27}$ kg

Express your answer in units of MeV.

Sol. Given, $_1H^2 = 2.014$ u, $_2He^3 = 3.0160$ u, Mn $= 1.0087$ u

$$1\, \text{u} = 1.66 \times 10^{-27}\, \text{kg}$$

Energy released = ?
mass of reactant, mass $_r = 2 \times 2.0141 = 4.0282\, \text{u}$
mass of products, mass $_p = 3.0160 + 1.0087 = 4.0247\, \text{u}$
Loss of mass = mass $_p$ − mass $_r$

$$\Delta M = (4.0282 - 4.0247)\, \text{u}$$
$$= 0.0035\, \text{u}$$
$$= 0.0035 \times 1.66 \times 10^{-27}\, \text{kg}$$

Energy released $E = (\Delta m)c^2$

$$E = 0.0035 \times 1.66 \times 10^{-27} \times (3 \times 10^8)^2$$
$$= 52.2 \times 10^{-14}\, \text{J}$$

As we know 1 MeV $= 1.602 \times 10^{-13}$ J

$$\text{Energy released} = \frac{52.2 \times 10^{-14}}{1.602 \times 10^{-13}} = 3.26\, \text{MeV}$$

Table below gives an approximate energy associated with some of the important phenomena.

Energy Associated with Some Important Phenomena

Description	Energy (J)
Big Bang	10^{68}
Radio energy emitted by the galaxy during its lifetime	10^{55}
Rotational energy of the Milky Way	10^{52}
Energy released in a supernova explosion	10^{44}
Ocean's hydrogen in fusion	10^{34}
Rotational energy of the earth	10^{29}
Annual solar energy incident on the earth	5×10^{24}
Annual wind energy dissipated near earth's surface	10^{22}
Annual global energy usage by human	3×10^{20}
Annual energy dissipated by the tides	10^{20}
Energy release of 15-megaton fusion bomb	10^{17}
Annual electrical output of large generating plant	10^{16}
Thunderstorm	10^{15}
Energy released in burning 1000 kg of coal	3×10^{10}
Kinetic energy of a large jet aircraft	10^9
Energy released in burning 1 L of gasoline	3×10^7
Daily food in take of a human adult	10^7
Work done by a human heart per beat	0.5
Turning this page	10^{-3}
Flea hop	10^{-7}
Discharge of a single neutron	10^{-10}
Typical energy of a proton in a nucleus	10^{-13}
Typical energy of an electron in an atom	10^{-18}
Energy to break one bond in DNA	10^{-20}

Principle of Conservation of Energy

It states that, the energy can neither be created nor be destroyed but can only be converted from one form to another.

It is one of the fundamental laws and is applied in all the processes taking place in the universe.

Whenever energy in one form disappears, then equivalent amount of energy appears in some other form. Thus, the total energy remains constant. Therefore, principle of conservation of energy may be stated as below

Total energy of an isolated system always remains constant. Since, the universe as a whole may be viewed as an isolated system, total energy of the universe is constant. If one part of the universe loses energy, then other part must gain an equal amount of energy.

The principle of conservation of energy cannot be proved as such. However, no violation of this principle has been observed.

EXAMPLE |11| Life Span of a Nuclei

The nucleus Fe^{57} emits a γ-ray of energy 14.4 keV. If the mass of the nucleus is 56.935 amu, calculate the recoil energy of the nucleus. [Take, 1 amu = 1.66×10^{-27} kg]

[NCERT]

Sol. The nuclear decay may be represented as follows

$$\underset{\text{Excited state}}{Fe^{57}} \longrightarrow \underset{\text{Ground state}}{Fe^{57}} + h\nu \text{ (γ-ray photon)}$$

According to de-Broglie hypothesis, momentum of a photon of energy E is

$$p = \frac{E}{c} = \frac{14.4 \text{ keV}}{c}$$

$$= \frac{14.4 \times 1.6 \times 10^{-16} \text{ J}}{3 \times 10^8 \text{ ms}^{-1}}$$

$$p = 7.68 \times 10^{-24} \text{ kg ms}^{-1}$$

By conservation of momentum, the momentum of daughter nucleus, p = momentum of γ-ray photon

$$= 7.68 \times 10^{-24} \text{ kg ms}^{-1}$$

The recoil energy of the nucleus will be

$$K = \frac{p^2}{2m} = \frac{(7.68 \times 10^{-24})^2}{2 \times 56.935 \times 1.66 \times 10^{-27}}$$

$$= 0.32 \times 10^{-21} \text{ J} = \frac{0.312 \times 10^{-21}}{1.6 \times 10^{-16}} \text{ keV}$$

$$K = 1.95 \times 10^{-6} \text{ keV}$$

| TOPIC PRACTICE 2 |

OBJECTIVE Type Questions

1. An object of mass 10 kg is moving with velocity of 10 ms^{-1}. A force of 50 N acted upon it for 2 s. Percentage increase in its KE is
   (a) 25% (b) 50%
   (c) 75% (d) 300%

Sol. (d) Initial velocity = 10 ms^{-1}

Final velocity = $\frac{50}{10} \times 2 + 10 = 20 \text{ ms}^{-1}$

$$\left(\text{Acceleration} = \frac{50}{10} = 5 \text{ m/s}^2 \right)$$

Initial KE = $\frac{1}{2} \times 10 \times 10 \times 10 = 5 \times 10^2$ J

Final KE = $\frac{1}{2} \times 10 \times 20 \times 20 = 20 \times 10^2$ J

% increase = $\frac{(20-5) \times 10^2}{5 \times 10^2} \times 100 = 300\%$

2. Two masses of 1 g and 4 g are moving with equal kinetic energy. The ratio of the magnitudes of their momentum is
   (a) 4 : 1 (b) $\sqrt{2}$:1
   (c) 1 : 2 (d) 1 : 16

Sol. (c) As we know that linear momentum = $\sqrt{2mK}$

$$\left(\because K = \frac{p^2}{2m} \right)$$

For same kinetic energy, $p \propto \sqrt{m}$

$$\frac{p_1}{p_2} = \sqrt{\frac{m_1}{m_2}} = \sqrt{\frac{1}{4}} = \frac{1}{2} = 1:2$$

3. Which of the diagrams shown in figure most closely shows the variation in kinetic energy of the earth as it moves once around the sun in its elliptical orbit? **[NCERT Exemplar]**

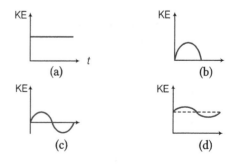

Sol. (d) When the earth is closest to the sun, speed of the earth is maximum, hence, KE is maximum. When the earth is farthest from the sun speed is minimum hence, KE is minimum but never zero and negative.

This variation is correctly represented by option (d).

4. Which of the diagrams in figure correctly shows the change in kinetic energy of an iron sphere falling freely in a lake having sufficient depth to impart it a terminal velocity?   **[NCERT Exemplar]**

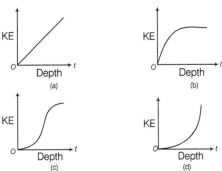

Sol. (b) First velocity of the iron sphere increases and after sometime becomes constant, called terminal velocity. Hence, accordingly first KE increases and then becomes constant which is best represented by (b).

VERY SHORT ANSWER Type Questions

5. Is it possible to exert a force which does work on a body without changing its kinetic energy. If, so give example.

Sol. Yes, when spring is compressed or when a body is pulled with a constant velocity on a rough horizontal surface.

6. What is the source of kinetic energy of the bullet coming out of the bullet of a rifle?

Sol. The source of kinetic energy of bullet is the potential energy of the compressed spring in the loaded rifle.

7. When an air bubble rises in water, what happens to its potential energy?

Sol. Potential energy of air bubble decreases because work is done by upthrust on the bubble.

8. A spring is cut into two equal halves. How is the spring constant of each half affected?

Sol. Spring constant of each half becomes twice the spring constant of the original spring.

9. What type of energy stored in (i) the wound spring of a watch (ii) a stretched bow while ready to project an arrow?

Sol. In both cases, energy is stored in the form of elastic potential energy due to change in configuration.

10. Does potential energy of a spring decrease/ increase when it is compressed or stretched?

Sol. When a spring is compressed or stretched, potential energy of the spring increases in both the cases. This is because work is done by us in compression as well as stretching.

SHORT ANSWER Type Questions

11. A bolt of mass 0.3 kg falls from the ceiling of an elevator moving down with an uniform speed of 7 ms^{-1}. It hits the floor of the elevator (length of the elevator = 3 m) and does not rebound. What is the heat produced by the impact? Would your answer be different if the elevator were stationary?   **[NCERT]**

Sol. Given, mass of bolt, $m = 0.3$ kg, height through which bolt falls $h = 3$ m.

When the bolt falls on floor of elevator and does not rebound, it suffers a loss of potential energy
$$\Delta U = mgh = 0.3 \times 9.8 \times 3 = 8.82 \text{ J}$$
∴ Amount of heat produced = Loss of potential energy = 8.82 J, because there is no gain in KE at all.

The answer is true when either the elevator is at rest or in state of uniform motion because potential energy of bolt has no connection with velocity of elevator.

12. A 0.5 kg block slides from the point A on a horizontal track with an initial speed $4\sqrt{5} \text{ ms}^{-1}$ towards a weightless horizontal spring of length 10 m and spring constant 2 N/m.

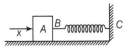

The initial track is frictionless and part BC under the unstretched length of spring has coefficient of kinetic friction $\mu_k = 0.2$, Calculate total distance by which the block move before coming finally to rest. ($g = 10 \text{ ms}^{-2}$).

Sol. Let the block compresses the spring by x before finally coming to rest on the rough part.

Total energy of the block on friction surface
= Work done against friction + Potential energy stored in spring.

$$\frac{1}{2} \times 0.5 \times 16 \times 5 = \mu_k \, mg \, s + \frac{1}{2} kx^2$$

$$20 = 0.2 \times 0.5 \times 10 \times x + \frac{1}{2} \times 2 \times x^2$$
$$20 = x + x^2$$
$$x^2 + x - 20 = 0$$
$$x^2 + 5x - 4x - 200 = 0$$
$$x(x+5) - 4(x+5) = 0$$
$$x = 4, \; x = -5$$

Hence, the compression of spring is 4 m.

13. **Can a body have energy without momentum? If yes, then explain how they are related with each other?**

Sol. Yes, when $p = 0$,

Then, $\qquad K = \dfrac{p^2}{2m} = 0$

But $E = K + U = U$ (potential energy), which may or may not be zero.

14. **A spring balance reads forces in Newtons. The scale is 20 cm long and read from 0 to 60 N. Find potential energy of spring when the scale reads 20 N.**

Sol. We can calculate the spring constant of spring, as it is extended by 20 cm under 60 N force.

$$F = kx \implies 60 = k \times 20 \times 10^{-2}$$
$$k = 300 \text{ N/m}$$

At a force of 20 N, the extension in spring is

$$F = kx \implies 20 = 300x$$
$$x = \frac{2}{30} = \frac{1}{15} \text{ m}$$

15. **A vertical spring with constant 200 N/m has a light platform on its top. When a 500 g mass is kept on the platform spring compresses 2.5 cm. Mass is now pushed down 7.50 cm further and released. How far above later position will the mass fly? ($g = 10 \text{ ms}^{-2}$).**

Sol. When the external force is removed after the push, the mass gets detached when spring obtain its natural length and say, mass m rises h height from the pushed position.

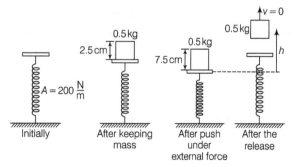

Loss in potential energy of spring = Gain in gravitational potential energy

$$\frac{1}{2} k [x^2] = mgh$$
$$\frac{1}{2} \times 200 [0.1]^2 = 0.5 \times 10 \times h$$
$$1 = 5h \implies h = 0.2 \text{ m}$$

16. **A body of mass 1.0 kg initially at rest is moved by a horizontal force of 0.5 N on a smooth frictionless table. Calculate the work done by the force in 10 s and show that this is equal to the change in kinetic energy of the body.**

Sol. Acceleration of a body,

$$a = F/m = \frac{0.5}{1.0} = 0.5 \text{ ms}^{-2}$$

Distance travelled, $s = ut + \dfrac{1}{2} at^2$

$$s = 0 + \frac{1}{2} \times 0.5 (10)^2 = 25 \text{ m}$$

Work done $= F \times s = 0.5 \times 25 = 12.5 \text{ J}$
$$v = u + at = 0 + 0.5 \times 10 = 5 \text{ ms}^{-1}$$

Change in KE $= (1/2)\, m\, (v^2 - u^2)$
$$= (1/2) \times 1.0 (5^2 - 0) = 12.51$$

17. **A body of mass 0.5 kg travels in a straight line with velocity $v = ax^{3/2}$, where $a = 5 \text{ m}^{-\frac{1}{2}} \text{s}^{-1}$. What is the work done by the net force during its displacement from $x = 0$ to $x = 2$ m ?** [NCERT]

Sol. Given, $m = 0.5 \text{ kg}, \; v = ax^{\frac{3}{2}}, \;$ where $a = 5 \text{ m}^{-\frac{1}{2}} \text{ s}^{-1}$.

We know that work done by net force acting on a body is equal to its change in KE. If velocity of body corresponding to $x = 0$ and $x = 2$ m be u and v respectively, then

$$W = \frac{1}{2} mv^2 - \frac{1}{2} mu^2 = \frac{1}{2} m(v^2 - u^2)$$

Now, $u = a \cdot (0)^{3/2} = 0$ and $v = a \cdot (2)^{3/2}$

$$\therefore \qquad W = \frac{1}{2} \times 0.5 \, [\{a(2)^{3/2}\}^2 - 0]$$
$$= \frac{1}{2} \times 0.5 \times a^2 \times (2)^3$$
$$= \frac{1}{2} \times 0.5 \times (5)^2 \times 8 = 50 \text{ J}$$

LONG ANSWER Type I Questions

18. **The bob of a pendulum is released from a horizontal position. If the length of the pendulum is 1.5 m, what is the speed with which the bob arrives at the lowermost point, given that it dissipated 5% of its initial energy against air resistance?** [NCERT]

Sol. On releasing the bob of pendulum from horizontal position, it falls vertically downward by a distance equal to length of pendulum i.e. $h = l = 1.5$ m.

As 5% of loss in PE is dissipated against air resistance, the balance 95% energy is transformed into KE. Hence,

$$\frac{1}{2} mv^2 = \frac{95}{100} \times mgh$$

$$\Rightarrow \qquad v = \sqrt{2 \times \frac{95}{100} \times gh}$$

$$= \sqrt{\frac{2 \times 95 \times 9.8 \times 1.5}{100}}$$

$$= 5.3 \text{ ms}^{-1}$$

19. Underline the correct alternative.

   (i) When a conservative force does positive work on a body, the potential energy of the body increases decreases/remains unaltered.

   (ii) Work done by a body against friction always results in a loss of its kinetic/potential energy.

   (iii) The rate of change of total momentum of a many particle system is proportional to the external force/ sum of the internal forces on the system. **[NCERT]**

Sol. (i) The potential energy decreases, because $\Delta U = - \int \mathbf{F} \cdot dx$. If work done by conservative force is positive, then obviously ΔU is $-$ ve.

   (ii) Friction always opposes motion. Hence, work done by a body against friction causes loss in its kinetic energy.

   (iii) The total (net) momentum can change only when some net external force acts on the system. Hence, its rate of change is proportional to the external force.

20. When a 300 g mass is hung from a vertical spring, it stretches from equilibrium by 10 cm. What work is required to stretch it by next 5 cm?

Sol. We can calculate spring constant of spring by first information.

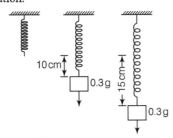

Work done by a vertical spring is

$$0.3 \text{ g} = k[10 \times 10^{-2}]$$

$$2 = k \times 0.1 \Rightarrow k = \frac{3}{0.1} = 30 \ \frac{\text{N}}{\text{m}}$$

Extra work required to stretch it by next 5 cm.

$$W = \frac{1}{2} k x_2^2 - \frac{1}{2} k x_1^2$$

$$W = \frac{1}{2} \times 30 \left[(15 \times 10^{-2})^2 - (10 \times 10^{-2})^2 \right]$$

$$W = 15 [225 - 100] \times 10^{-4} = 15 \times 125 \times 10^{-4} \text{ J}$$

$$W = 0.1875 \text{ J}$$

21. If momentum of a body increased by 300%, then what will be percentage increase in momentum of a body?

Sol. Consider a particle of mass m moving with a velocity v so, that its KE $= \frac{1}{2} mv^2$ and momentum, $p = mv$.

Thus, $\qquad$ KE $= \frac{p^2}{2m}$ or $p = \sqrt{2m\text{KE}}$

when KE is increased by 300%, then new KE

KE$' =$ KE $+ 300\%$ of $E =$ KE $+ 3$KE $= 4$KE

New momentum, $p' = \sqrt{2m\text{KE}'} = \sqrt{2m \times 4\text{KE}}$

$$= 2\sqrt{2m \text{ KE}} = 2p$$

$\therefore$ Percentage increase in momentum

$$= \frac{p'-p}{p} \times 100 = \frac{2p - p}{p} \times 100 = 100\%$$

22. A long spring of spring constant 500 N/m is attached to a wall horizontally and surface below the spring is rough with coefficient of friction 0.75. A 100 kg mass block moving with a speed $10\sqrt{2}$ ms^{-1} strikes the spring. Find the maximum compression of the spring. $(g = 10 \text{ ms}^{-2})$

Sol. When the block strikes the spring it carry some kinetic energy and all of that is spent against friction and stores in the compressed spring as potential energy.

$$v = 10\sqrt{2}\,\text{m/s}$$
$$k = 500\,\text{N/m} \quad \boxed{100\,\text{kg}}$$

Let the spring compresses by x.

Loss in kinetic energy of block = Gain in potential energy of the spring + Work done against friction.

$$\frac{1}{2} mv^2 = \frac{1}{2} k x^2 + \mu mg \, x$$

$$\frac{1}{2} \times 100 \times 200 = \frac{1}{2} \, 500 \, x^2 + 0.75 \times 100 \times 10 \times x$$

$$50 \times 200 = 250x^2 + 750x \ \Rightarrow \ 200 = 5x^2 + 15x$$

$$5x^2 + 15x - 200 = 0$$

$$x^2 + 3x - 40 = 0$$

$$x^2 + 8x - 5x - 40 = 0 \ \Rightarrow x (x + 8) - 5 (x + 8) = 0$$

$$x = 5 \text{ m}, \ x = - 8 \text{ m}$$

So, $\qquad\qquad x = 5 \text{ m}$

23. An electron and a proton are detected in a cosmic ray experiment, the first with kinetic energy 10 keV and the second with 100 keV. Which is faster, the electron or the proton? Obtain the ratio of their speeds. (Electron mass $= 9.11 \times 10^{-31}$ kg, proton mass $= 1.67 \times 10^{-27}$ kg, $1\text{eV} = 1.60 \times 10^{-19}$ J). **[NCERT]**

Sol. Here, $K_e = 10$ keV and $K_p = 100$ keV
$$m_e = 9.11 \times 10^{-31} \text{ kg}$$
and $m_p = 1.67 \times 10^{-27}$ kg

As $K = \dfrac{1}{2} mv^2$ or $v = \sqrt{\dfrac{2K}{m}}$,

Hence, $\dfrac{v_e}{v_p} = \sqrt{\dfrac{K_e}{K_p} \times \dfrac{m_p}{m_e}}$

$$= \sqrt{\dfrac{10 \text{ keV}}{100 \text{ keV}} \times \dfrac{1.67 \times 10^{-27} \text{ kg}}{9.11 \times 10^{-31} \text{ kg}}}$$

$\Rightarrow \qquad v_e = 13.54 v_p$

Thus, electron is travelling faster.

LONG ANSWER Type II Questions

24. A helicopter lifts a 72 kg astronaut 15 m vertically from the ocean by means of a cable. The acceleration of the astronaut is $\dfrac{g}{10}$. How much work is done on the astronaut by

    (i) the force from the helicopter and
    (ii) the gravitational force on him?
    (iii) what are the kinetic energy and
    (iv) the speed of the astronaut just before he reaches the helicopter? (Take, $g = 10 \text{ ms}^{-2}$)

Sol. Here, mass of astronaut $m = 72$ kg, vertical distance $h = 15$ m and acceleration of astronaut $a = \dfrac{g}{10}$.

(i) Force from the helicopter
$$F = mg + ma = mg + \dfrac{mg}{10} = \dfrac{11 \, mg}{10}$$
∴ Work done by force from the helicopter
$$W = F \times h = \dfrac{11 mg}{10} \times h$$
$$W = \dfrac{11 \times 72 \times 10 \times 15}{10} = 11880 \text{ J}$$

(ii) Work done by gravitational force
$$W' = (mg)(h)(\cos 180°)$$
$$W' = -mgh = -72 \times 10 \times 15$$
$$= -10800 \text{ J}$$

(iii) KE of astronaut K = network done on him
$$= W + W'$$
$$= (11880 - 10800) \text{ J} = +1080 \text{ J}$$

(iv) As $\text{KE} = \dfrac{1}{2} mv^2$, hence
$$v = \sqrt{\dfrac{2K}{m}} = \sqrt{\dfrac{2 \times 1080}{72}} = 5.48 \text{ ms}^{-1}$$

25. One end of a light spring of natural length d and spring constant k is fixed on a rigid wall and other end is fixed in a smooth ring of mass m as shown in figure. Initially, the spring is stretched such that it makes an angle of 37° with the horizontal.

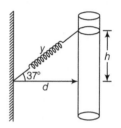

Now, the ring is stretched from rest, find the speed of the ring when it will become horizontal, assume that ring slides on the vertical wall without friction.

When the spring is released, it slides down under gravity. The potential energy stored in the stretched spring and the potential energy of the ring released which appear as gain in kinetic energy of the ring.

Sol. We can first calculate the stretch l the spring over natural length in the initial situation.

$$\cos 37° = \dfrac{d}{y}$$
$$y = \dfrac{d}{\cos 37°}$$
$$= \dfrac{d}{4/5} = \dfrac{5d}{4} = 1.25 \, d$$

Similarly, $\tan 37° = \dfrac{h}{d} \Rightarrow \dfrac{3}{4} = \dfrac{h}{d}$
$$h = \dfrac{3}{4} d$$

Now, we can apply conservation of energy.
Total energy initially = Total energy when spring is horizontal.
$$\dfrac{1}{2} kl^2 + mgh = \dfrac{1}{2} mv^2$$

$$\dfrac{1}{2} k (0.25d)^2 + mg \dfrac{3}{4} d = \dfrac{1}{2} mv^2$$

$$\frac{3}{4}mg\,d + \frac{1}{2}k\frac{d^2}{16} = \frac{1}{2}mv^2$$

$$v = d\sqrt{\frac{3g}{2d} + \frac{k}{16m}}$$

26. Answer the following

(i) The casing of a rocket in flight burns up due to friction. At whose expense is the heat energy required for burning obtained ? The rocket or the atmosphere.

(ii) Comets move around the Sun in highly elliptical orbits. The gravitational force on the comet due to the Sun is not normal to the comet's velocity in general. Yet the work done by the gravitational force over every complete orbit of the comet is zero. Why?

(iii) An artificial satellite orbiting the Earth in very thin atmosphere loses its energy gradually due to dissipation against atmospheric resistance, however small. Why then does its speed increase progressively as it comes closer and closer to the earth?

(iv) In Fig. (a) the man walks 2 m carrying a mass of 15 kg on his hands. In Fig. (b) he walks the same distance pulling the rope behind him.

The rope goes over a pulley and a mass of 15 kg hangs at its other end. In which case is the work done greater?

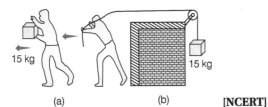

(a)   (b)   **[NCERT]**

Sol. (i) Heat energy required for burning of casing of rocket comes from the rocket itself. As a result of work done against friction the kinetic energy of rocket continuously decreases and this work against friction reappears as heat energy.

(ii) The gravitational force is a conservative force, hence, work done by the gravitational force over one complete (closed) orbit of comet is zero.

(iii) As an artificial satellite gradually loses its energy due to dissipation against atmospheric resistance, its potential energy decreases rapidly. As a result, kinetic energy of satellite slightly increases i.e. its speed increases progressively.

(iv) In figure, the man carries the mass of 15 kg on his hands and walks 2 m. In this case, he is actually doing work against the friction force.

Friction force contribution by mass,

$$f = \mu N = \mu mg \times 15 \times 9.8 \text{ N}$$

and work done against friction,

$$W_1 = fs = \mu \times 15 \times 9.8 \times 2 = 294\,\mu J$$

In figure (ii), the tension in string, $T = mg = 15 \times 9.8$ N
Hence, force applied by man for pulling the rope

$$F = T = 15 \times 9.8 \text{ N}$$

$\therefore$ Work done by man, $W_2 = Fs = 15 \times 9.8 \times 2 = 294$ J
and additional work has to be done against friction also.

Thus, it is clear that $W_2 > W_1$.

27. A 1 kg block situated on a rough incline is connected to a spring of spring constant 100 N m^{-1} as shown in figure. The block is released from rest with the spring in the unstretched position.

The block moves 10 cm down the incline before coming to rest. Find the coefficient of friction between the block and the incline. Assume that the spring has a negligible mass and the pulley is frictionless.

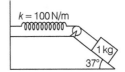

[Given, sin 37° = 0.6 and cos 37° = 0.8]   **[NCERT]**

Sol. Here, force constant $k = 100$ Nm^{-1}, mass of block
$m = 1$ kg, $\theta = 37°$ and distance moved by block
$x = 10$ cm $= 0.1$ m

As shown in figure, the net accelerating force acting on block is $\quad F = mg\sin\theta - f = mg\sin\theta - \mu N$

$$= mg\sin\theta - \mu\, mg\cos\theta$$

$\therefore$ Work done by the force F for motion of block

$$W = Fx = mg(\sin\theta - \mu\cos\theta)x$$

When the block stops, the work done is stored in the spring in the form of its potential energy

$$U = \frac{1}{2}kx^2$$

$\therefore \quad mg(\sin\theta - \mu\cos\theta)x = \frac{1}{2}kx^2$

$\Rightarrow \qquad \mu = \frac{1}{\cos\theta}\left[\sin\theta - \frac{kx}{2\,mg}\right]$

Substituting the values, we get

$$\mu = \frac{1}{\cos 37°}\left[\sin 37° - \frac{100 \times 0.1}{2 \times 1 \times 10}\right]$$

$$= \frac{1}{0.8}[0.6 - 0.5] = 0.125$$

ASSESS YOUR TOPICAL UNDERSTANDING

OBJECTIVE Type Questions

1. In daily life, intake of a human adult is 10^7 J, then average human consumption in a day is
   (a) 2400 kcal   (b) 1000 kcal
   (c) 1200 kcal   (d) 700 kcal

2. The potential energy of a spring when stretched through a distance x is 10 J. What is the amount of work done on the same spring to stretch it through an additional distance x?
   (a) 10 J   (b) 20 J
   (c) 30 J   (d) 40 J

3. The ratio of spring constants of two springs is 2 : 3. What is the ratio of their potential energy if they are stretched by the same force?
   (a) 2 : 3   (b) 3 : 2
   (c) 4 : 9   (d) 9 : 4

4. Which of the diagrams shown in figure represents variation of total mechanical energy of a pendulum oscillating in air as function of time?
   [NCERT Exemplar]

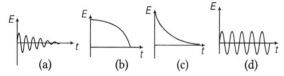

   (a)   (b)   (c)   (d)

5. A mass of 0.5 kg moving with a speed of 1.5 ms^{-1} on a horizontal smooth surface, collides with a nearly weightless spring of spring constant $k = 50$ Nm^{-1}. The maximum compression of the spring would be

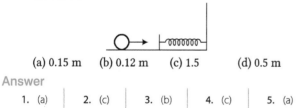

   (a) 0.15 m   (b) 0.12 m   (c) 1.5   (d) 0.5 m

Answer

| 1. (a) | 2. (c) | 3. (b) | 4. (c) | 5. (a) |

VERY SHORT ANSWER Type Questions

6. A spark is produced when two stones are struck against each other. Why?

7. Can energy be created or destroyed? Comment.

8. Name the largest and smallest practical unit of energy.

SHORT ANSWER Type Questions

9. Calculate the velocity of the bob of a simple pendulum at its mean position if it is able to rise to a vertical height of 10 cm. [$g = 9.8$ m/s^2]
   [**Ans.** 1.4 m/s]

10. What is the minimum amount of energy released in the annihilation of an electron-position pair? (Take, rest mass of electron-position $= 9.11 \times 10^{-3}$ kg and $c = 3 \times 10^8$ m/s) [**Ans.** 1.023 MeV]

11. What is meant by mass-energy equivalence? Discuss its significance in physics.

LONG ANSWER Type I Questions

12. Calculate the energy equivalent of 1 amu in MeV, taking 1 amu $= 1.66 \times 10^{-27}$ kg. [**Ans.** 933.75 MeV]

13. If 1000kg of water is heated from 0°C to 100°C. Calculate the increase in mass of water.
    [**Ans.** 4.66×10^{-9} kg]

14. Two bodies of unequal masses have same KE which one has greater linear momentum?

15. Define kinetic energy. Prove that KE associated with a mass m moving with velocity v is $\frac{1}{2}mv^2$.

LONG ANSWER Type II Questions

16. Explain, what is meant by potential energy of a spring? Obtain an expression for it and discuss the nature of its variation?

17. A stone of mass 0.4 kg is thrown vertically upward with a speed of 9.4 m/s. Find the potential and kinetic energies after half second.
    [**Ans.** 14.386 J and 4.802J]

18. If the linear momentum of a body increases by 20%, what will be the % increase in the kinetic energy of the body? [**Ans.** 44%]

19. A running man has half the kinetic energy that a boy of half his mass has. The man speeds up by 1.0 m/s and then same energy as the boy. What were the orignal speeds of the man and the boy?
    [**Ans.** 2.41 m/s, 4.828 m/s]

20. What is the work-energy theorem? Should it be named as work KE theorem? What exactly is work? Can it not be defined in terms of the expenses of energy? Explain your answer.

|TOPIC 3|
Power and Collision

POWER

Power of a person or machine is defined as the time rate at which work is done or energy is transferred by it.

If a person does work W in time t, then its average power is given by

$$\text{Average power } (P_{av}) = \text{Rate of doing work}$$
$$= \frac{\text{Work done}}{\text{Time taken}} = \frac{W}{t}$$

$$\boxed{\text{Average power, } P_{av} = \frac{W}{t}}$$

Thus, the average power of a force is defined as the ratio of the work, W to the total time t.

The **instantaneous power** of an agent is defined as the limiting value of the average power of an agent in a small time interval, when the time interval approaches to zero.

When work done by a force $\mathbf{F}$ for a small displacement $d\mathbf{r}$ is $dW = \mathbf{F} \cdot d\mathbf{r}$. Then, instantaneous power can be given as

i.e. $$P = \lim_{\Delta t \to 0} \frac{\Delta W}{\Delta t} = \frac{dW}{dt}$$

Now, $$dW = \mathbf{F} \cdot d\mathbf{r}$$

$$\therefore \qquad P = \mathbf{F} \cdot \frac{d\mathbf{r}}{dt}$$

Again $\dfrac{d\mathbf{r}}{dt} = \mathbf{v}$, instantaneous velocity of an agent.

Therefore, $$P = \mathbf{F} \cdot \mathbf{v}$$

Thus, the power of an agent at any instant is equal to the dot product of its force and velocity vectors at that instant.

Dimensional Formula of Power

Power is a scalar quantity, because it is the ratio of two scalar quantities work (W) and time (t). The dimensional formula of power is $[ML^2T^{-3}]$.

Units of Power

The SI unit of power is watt (W). The power of an agent is one watt if it does work at the rate of 1 joule per second.

$$1 \text{ watt} = \frac{1 \text{ joule}}{1 \text{ second}} = 1 \text{ Js}^{-1}$$

Another popular units of power are kilowatt and horsepower.

1 kilowatt = 1000 watt or $1 \text{ kW} = 10^3$ W

1 horsepower = 746 watt or $1 \text{ hp} = 746$ W

This unit is used to describe the output of automobiles, motorbikes, engines, etc.

Note

- Kilowatt hour (kWh) or Board of Trade (BOT) is the commercial unit of electrical energy.
- Relation between kWh and joule.
$$1 \text{ kWh} = 1 \text{ kW} \times 1 \text{ h} = 1000 \text{ W} \times 1 \text{ h}$$
$$= 1000 \text{ Js}^{-1} \times 3600 \text{ s}$$
or $$1 \text{ kWh} = 3.6 \times 10^6 \text{ J}$$

EXAMPLE |1| Weighing a Man in a Lift

An elevator which can carry a maximum load of 1800 kg (elevator + passenger) is moving up with a constant speed of 2 ms^{-1}. The frictional force opposing the motion is 4000 N. Determine the minimum power delivered by the motor to the elevator in watts as well as in horsepower. **[NCERT]**

Sol. The downward force on the elevator is
$$F = mg + F_f$$
where, F_f is the frictional force
$$= 1800 \times 10 + 4000$$
$$= 22000 \text{ N}$$
The motor must supply enough power to balance this force. Hence, $P = Fv = 22000 \times 2 = 44000$ W
$$= \frac{44000}{746} \text{ hp} \approx 59 \text{ hp}$$

EXAMPLE |2| Encounter with Two Cranes

A car of mass 2000 kg is lifted up a distance of 30 m by a crane in 1 min. A second crane does the same job in 2 min. Do the cranes consume the same or different amounts of fuel? What is the power supplied by each crane? Neglect power dissipation against friction. **[NCERT]**

Sol. Here, $m = 2000$ kg, $s = 30$ m
$$t_1 = 1 \text{ min} = 60 \text{ s}, \ t_2 = 2 \text{ min} = 120 \text{ s}$$
Work done by each crane,
$$W = Fs = mgs = 2000 \times 9.8 \times 30$$
$$= 5.88 \times 10^5 \text{ J}$$

As both the cranes do same amount of work, so both consume same amount of fuel.

Power supplied by first crane,
$$P_1 = \frac{W}{t_1} = \frac{5.88 \times 10^5}{60} = 9800 \text{ W}$$

Power supplied by second crane,
$$P_2 = \frac{W}{t_2} = \frac{5.88 \times 10^5}{120} = 4900 \text{ W}$$

EXAMPLE |3| Walking on Stairs

A boy of mass 40 kg walks up a flight of stairs to a vertical distance of 12 m, in a time interval of 40 s.

   (i) At what rate is the boy doing work against the force of gravity?

  (ii) If energy is transformed by the leg muscles of the students at the rate of 30 kJ every minute, what is the students power output?

Sol. (i) Given, $m = 40$ kg, $t = 40$ s

Energy $= 30$ kJ, power $= ?$

Student's power output $= ?$

Work done by the student against the force of gravity is equal to the gain in gravitational potential energy, so

Work done $(W) = mg\Delta h$

$$\text{Power} = \frac{\text{Work done}}{\text{Time taken } (\Delta t)}$$

$$P = \frac{W}{\Delta t} = \frac{40 \times 10 \times 12}{40} = 120 \text{ W}$$

(ii) Student's power output can be calculated as

$$\text{Power } (P) = \frac{\text{Energy transferred}}{\text{Time taken}}$$

$$P = 30 \text{ kJ/min} = \frac{30000 \text{ J}}{60 \text{ s}} = 500 \text{ W}$$

Mean Power of Projectile Motion on Horizontal Plane

As we know, mean power $= \dfrac{\text{Net gain in kinetic energy}}{\text{Total time of motion}}$

In projectile motion on horizontal plane, when a particle strikes the ground with the same speed with which it was projected, then kinetic energy of particle does not change. Hence, from initial point to final point, there is no gain in kinetic energy.

i.e.   Mean power $= 0$

COLLISION

A collision is an isolated event in which two or more colliding bodies exert strong forces on each other for a relatively short time. For a collision to take place, the actual physical contact is not necessary.

e.g. In Rutherford's scattering experiment, an alpha particle moves towards nucleus of an atom get deflected by the electrostatic force of repulsion without actual physical contact with the nucleus. So, the alpha particle undergone collision with the nucleus.

Collision between particles have been divided into two types

	Elastic Collision	Inelastic Collision
(i)	A collision in which there is absolutely no loss of kinetic energy.	A collision in which there occurs some loss of kinetic energy.
(ii)	Forces involved during elastic collision must be conserved in nature.	Some or all forces involved during collision may be non-conservative in nature.
(iii)	The mechanical energy is not converted into heat, light, sound etc.	A part of the mechanical energy is converted into heat, light, sound, etc.
(iv)	e.g. Collision between subatomic particles, collision between glass balls, etc.	e.g. Collision between two vehicles, collision between a ball and floor.

Conservation of Linear Momentum in Collision

Consider two bodies 1 and 2 collide against each other. They exert mutual impulsive forces on each other during the collision time Δt. The changes produced in momenta of the two bodies will be

$$\Delta \mathbf{p}_1 = \mathbf{F}_{12} \, \Delta t \text{ and } \Delta \mathbf{p}_2 = \mathbf{F}_{21} \, \Delta t$$

where, $\mathbf{F}_{12}$ is the force exerted on body 1 by body 2 and $\mathbf{F}_{21}$ is the force exerted on body 2 by body 1.

According to Newton's third law of motion, we have

$$\mathbf{F}_{12} = -\mathbf{F}_{21}$$

$\therefore$ $\mathbf{F}_{12} \, \Delta t = -\mathbf{F}_{21} \, \Delta t$

or $\mathbf{F}_{12} \, \Delta t + \mathbf{F}_{21} \, \Delta t = 0$

$$\Delta \mathbf{p}_1 + \Delta \mathbf{p}_2 = 0$$

$$\Delta (\mathbf{p}_1 + \mathbf{p}_2) = 0$$

$$\boxed{\mathbf{p}_1 + \mathbf{p}_2 = \text{constant}}$$

Hence, **total linear momentum is conserved at each instant during collision.**

Elastic Collision in One Dimension

It involves two bodies moving initially along the same straight line, striking against each other without loss of kinetic energy and continuing to move along the same straight line after collision.

Suppose two bodies A and B of masses m_1 and m_2 moving along the same straight line with velocities u_1 and u_2, respectively. Let $u_1 > u_2$.

After collision, bodies A and B moving with velocities v_1 and v_2 in the same direction such that $v_2 > v_1$ as shown in figure.

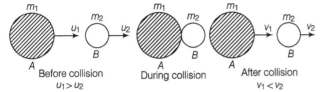

Before collision
$u_1 > u_2$

During collision

After collision
$v_1 < v_2$

Elastic collision in one dimension

As linear momentum is conserved in any collision, we get

$$m_1 u_1 + m_2 u_2 = m_1 v_1 + m_2 v_2 \qquad \text{...(i)}$$

or $\qquad m_1 u_1 - m_1 v_1 = m_2 v_2 - m_2 u_2$

or $\qquad m_1 (u_1 - v_1) = m_2 (v_2 - u_2) \qquad \text{...(ii)}$

Since, **KE is also conserved in an elastic collision**, we get

$$\frac{1}{2} m_1 u_1^2 + \frac{1}{2} m_2 u_2^2 = \frac{1}{2} m_1 v_1^2 + \frac{1}{2} m_2 v_2^2$$

or $\qquad m_1 u_1^2 - m_1 v_1^2 = m_2 v_2^2 - m_2 u_2^2$

or $\quad m_1 (u_1 + v_1)(u_1 - v_1) = m_2 (v_2 - u_2)(v_2 + u_2) \text{...(iii)}$

Dividing Eq. (iii) by Eq. (ii), we get

$$u_1 + v_1 = v_2 + u_2$$

or $\qquad u_1 - u_2 = v_2 - v_1 \qquad \text{...(iv)}$

Hence, in one-dimensional elastic collision, relative velocity of separation after collision is equal to relative velocity of approach before collision.

Velocities of the Bodies after the Collision

From Eq. (iv), we get

$$v_2 = u_1 - u_2 + v_1 \qquad \text{...(v)}$$

Putting this value of v_2 in Eq. (i), we get

$$m_1 u_1 + m_2 u_2 = m_1 v_1 + m_2 (u_1 - u_2 + v_1)$$
$$= m_1 v_1 + m_2 u_1 - m_2 u_2 + m_2 v_1$$

or $\qquad (m_1 - m_2) u_1 + 2 m_2 u_2 = (m_1 + m_2) v_1$

Velocity of body A after collision,

$$v_1 = \left(\frac{m_1 - m_2}{m_1 + m_2} \right) u_1 + \left(\frac{2m_2}{m_1 + m_2} \right) u_2 \qquad \text{...(vi)}$$

Putting the value of v_1 in Eq. (v), we get

Velocity of body B after collision,

$$v_2 = \left(\frac{m_2 - m_1}{m_1 + m_2} \right) u_2 + \left(\frac{2m_1}{m_1 + m_2} \right) u_1 \qquad \text{...(vii)}$$

Eqs. (vi) and (vii) give the final velocities of the colliding bodies in terms of their initial velocities.

The two cases under the action of same and different masses can be considered as given below.

Case I When two bodies of equal masses collide.

i.e. $\qquad m_1 = m_2 = m$ say

From Eq. (vi), $v_1 = \dfrac{2mu_2}{2m} = u_2$

= velocity of body of mass m_2 before collision

From Eq. (vii), $v_2 = \dfrac{2mu_1}{2m} = u_1$

= velocity of body of mass m_1 before collision.

Hence, when two bodies of equal masses undergo perfectly elastic collision in one dimension, their velocities are just interchanged.

Case II When a light body collides against a massive stationary body.

Here, $m_1 \ll m_2$ and $u_2 = 0$

Neglecting m_1 in Eq. (vi), we get

$$v_1 = -\frac{m_2 u_1}{m_2} = -u_1$$

From Eq. (vii), $v_2 \simeq 0$.

Hence, when a light body collides against a massive body at rest, the light body rebounds after the collision with an equal and opposite velocity while the massive body practically remains at rest.

In an elastic collision, the kinetic energy conservation holds only after the collision is over. It does not hold during the short duration of actual collision.

At the time of collision, the two colliding objects are deformed and may be momentarily at rest with respect to each other.

If the initial velocities and final velocities of both the bodies are along the same straight line, then it is called a one-dimensional collision or head-on collision.

EXAMPLE |4| **Head-on Collision**
Two ball bearings of mass m each moving in opposite directions with equal speed collide head on with each other. Predict the outcome of the collision, assuming it to be perfectly elastic. **[NCERT]**

Sol. Here, $\qquad m_1 = m_2 = m \text{ (say)}$

$$u_1 = v, u_2 = -v$$

We have taken $u_1 = v$ and $u_2 = -v$ because both the ball bearings moving with same velocity but in opposite directions.

As the collision is perfectly elastic, velocities after the collision will be

$$v_1 = \frac{m_1 - m_2}{m_1 + m_2} \cdot u_1 + \frac{2m_2}{m_1 + m_2} \cdot u_2$$

$$= \frac{m - m}{m + m} \cdot v + \frac{2m}{m + m} (-v) = 0 - v = -v$$

$$v_2 = \frac{2m_1}{m_1 + m_2} \cdot u_1 + \frac{m_2 - m_1}{m_1 + m_2} \cdot u_2$$

$$= \frac{2m}{m + m} \cdot v + \frac{m - m}{m + m} \cdot (-v) = v + 0 = v$$

Thus, the two balls bounce back with equal speed after the collision.

EXAMPLE |5| Slowing Down of Neutrons
In a nuclear reactor, a neutron of high speed (typically 10^7 ms^{-1}) must be slowed to 10^3 ms^{-1} so that it can have a high probability of interacting with isotope $^{325}_{92}$U and causing it to fission.
Show that a neutron can lose most of its kinetic energy in an elastic collision with a light nucleus like deuterium or carbon which has a mass of only a few times the neutron mass. The material making up the light nuclei, usually heavy water (D$_2$O) or graphite is called a moderator.

[NCERT]

Or

A body of mass M at rest is struck by a moving body of mass m. Prove that fraction of the initial KE of the mass m transferred to the struck body is $4mM/(m + M)^2$ in an elastic collision.

Sol. Here, m_1 = mass of neutron = m

m_2 = mass of target nucleus = M

$u_1 = u$ and $u_2 = 0$

Now, $v_2 = \frac{2m_1}{m_1 + m_2} \cdot u_1 + \frac{m_2 - m_2}{m_1 + m_2} \cdot u_2$

$$= \frac{2m}{m + M} \cdot u + 0 = \frac{2mu}{m + M}$$

Initial KE of mass m, $K_1 = \frac{1}{2} m_1 u_1^2 = \frac{1}{2} mu^2$

Final KE of mass M,

$$K_2 = \frac{1}{2} m_2 v_2^2 = \frac{1}{2} M \left(\frac{2mu}{m + M} \right)^2 = \frac{2 M m^2 u^2}{(m + M)^2}$$

Fraction of the initial KE transferred,

$$f = \frac{K_2}{K_1} = \frac{2 M m^2 u^2}{(m + M)^2} \times \frac{2}{mu^2} = \frac{4 mM}{(m + M)^2}$$

(i) For deuterium, $M = 2m$, therefore

$$f = \frac{4m \times 2m}{(m + 2m)^2} = \frac{8}{9} \simeq 0.9$$

About 90% of the neutron's energy is transferred to deuterium.

(ii) For carbon, $M = 12m$, therefore

$$f = \frac{4m \times 12 m}{(m + 12m)^2} = 0.284$$

About 28.4% of the neutron's energy is transferred to carbon.

Perfectly Inelastic Collision in One Dimension

When the two colliding bodies stick together and move as a single body with a common velocity after the collision, then the collision is **perfectly inelastic**.

As shown in figure, perfectly inelastic collision between two bodies of masses m_1 and m_2. The body of mass m_2 happens to be initially at rest ($u_2 = 0$). After the collision, the two bodies move together with common velocity v.

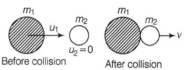

Before collision   After collision

Perfectly inelastic collision

As the total linear momentum of the system remains constant, therefore $p_i = p_f$

i.e. $\qquad m_1 u_1 + m_2 u_2 = (m_1 + m_2) v$

$\therefore \qquad v = \frac{m_1 u_1}{m_1 + m_2} \qquad [\because u_2 = 0]$

Total KE before collision,

$$E_1 = \frac{1}{2} m_1 u_1^2 \qquad \qquad ...(i)$$

Total KE after collision,

$$E_2 = \frac{1}{2} (m_1 + m_2) v^2 \qquad \qquad ...(ii)$$

On putting the value of v in Eq. (ii), we get

$$E_2 = \frac{1}{2} (m_1 + m_2) \left[\frac{m_1 u_1}{m_1 + m_2} \right]^2 = \frac{1}{2} \frac{m_1^2 u_1^2}{(m_1 + m_2)}$$

Loss of KE $= E_1 - E_2 = \frac{1}{2} m_1 u_1^2 - \frac{m_1^2 u_1^2}{2 (m_1 + m_2)}$

$$\Delta KE = \frac{m_1^2 u_1^2 + m_1 m_2 u_1^2 - m_1^2 u_1^2}{2 (m_1 + m_2)} = \frac{m_1 m_2 u_1^2}{2 (m_1 + m_2)}$$

$\therefore$ **ΔKE is a positive quantity.**

Therefore, kinetic energy is lost mainly in the form of light, sound and heat.

EXAMPLE |6| A Railway Carriage got an Accident

A railway carriage of mass 9000kg moving with a speed of 36km/h collides with a stationary carriage of the same mass. After the collision, the carriage get coupled and move together. What is their common speed after collision? What type of collision is this?

Sol. Given, $m_1 = 9000$ kg, $u_1 = 36$ km/h $= 36 \times \dfrac{5}{18} = 10$ m/s

$$m_2 = 9000 \text{ kg}, u_2 = 0, v_1 = v_2 = v$$

By conservation of momentum

$$m_1 u_1 + m_2 u_2 = (m_1 + m_2)v$$
$$9000 \times 10 + 9000 \times 0 = (9000 + 9000)v$$

or $$v = \dfrac{90000}{18000} = 5 \text{ m/s}$$

Total KE before collision $= \dfrac{1}{2}m_1 u_1^2 + \dfrac{1}{2}m_2 u_2^2$

$$= \dfrac{1}{2} \times 9000 \times 10 \times 10 + 0$$

$$= 450000 \text{ J}$$

Total KE after collision $= \dfrac{1}{2}(m_1 + m_2)v^2$

$$= \dfrac{1}{2} \times 2 \times 9000 \times (5)^2$$

$$= 225000 \text{ J}$$

Thus, total KE after collision < Total KE before collision
Hence, the collision is inelastic.

Elastic Collision in Two Dimensions or Oblique Collision

Consider two objects A and B of masses m_1 and m_2 kept on the x-axis as shown in figure. Initially, the object B is at rest and A moves towards B with a speed u_1. If the collision is not head-on (the force during the collision is not along the initial velocity), the objects move along different lines.

Suppose the object A moves with a velocity $\mathbf{v}_1$ making an angle θ with the x-axis and the object B moves with a velocity $\mathbf{v}_2$ making an angle ϕ with the same axis as shown in figure.

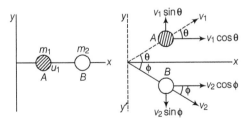

Elastic collision in two dimensions

Also, suppose $\mathbf{v}_1$ and $\mathbf{v}_2$ lie in xy-plane. Using conservation of momentum in x and y-directions, we get

$$m_1 u_1 = m_1 v_1 \cos\theta + m_2 v_2 \cos\phi$$
$$[\because u_2 = 0] \ ...(i)$$

$\because$ The initial momentum of m_1 and m_2 along y-axis is zero, then

$$0 = m_1 v_1 \sin\theta - m_2 v_2 \sin\phi \qquad ...(ii)$$

If the collision is elastic, the final kinetic energy is equal to the initial kinetic energy. Thus,

$$\dfrac{1}{2}m_1 u_1^2 = \dfrac{1}{2}m_1 v_1^2 + \dfrac{1}{2}m_2 v_2^2$$

or $$m_1 u_1^2 = m_1 v_1^2 + m_2 v_2^2 \qquad ...(iii)$$

The four unknown quantities v_1, v_2, θ and ϕ cannot be calculated by using the three equations (i), (ii) and (iii).

But by measuring one of the four unknowns, say θ experimentally. The value of other three unknowns can be solved.

The three cases can be considered as given below.

Case I Glancing collision In a glancing collision, the incident particle does not lose any kinetic energy and is scattered almost undeflected. Thus, for such collision, when $\theta \approx 0°$ and $\phi \approx 90°$

From Eqs. (i) and (ii), we get

$$u_1 = v_1 \text{ and } v_2 = 0$$

KE of the target particle $= \dfrac{1}{2}m_2 v_2^2 = 0$

Case II Head-on collision In this type of collision, the target particle moves in the direction of the incident particle, i.e. $\phi = 0°$. Then, Eqs. (i) and (ii), become

$$m_1 u_1 = m_1 v_1 \cos\theta + m_2 v_2 \text{ and } 0 = m_1 v_1 \sin\theta$$

Eq. (iii) for the kinetic energy remains unchanged.

Case III Elastic collision of two identical particles When two particles of same mass undergo perfectly elastic collision in two dimensions, i.e. $m_1 = m_2$.

Let us take $u_1 = u$

From Eq. (iii), $v_1^2 + v_2^2 = u^2 \qquad ...(iv)$

From Eq.(i) $v_1 \cos\theta + v_2 \cos\phi = u \qquad ...(v)$

From Eq. (ii), $v_1 \sin\theta - v_2 \sin\phi = 0 \qquad ...(vi)$

Using Eq. (v), we obtain from Eq. (iv)

$$v_1^2 + v_2^2 = (v_1 \cos\theta + v_2 \cos\phi)^2 = v_1^2 \cos^2\theta$$
$$+ v_2^2 \cos^2\phi + 2v_1 v_2 \cos\theta \cos\phi$$

$$\Rightarrow \quad v_1^2(1 - \cos^2\theta) + v_2^2(1 - \cos^2\phi)$$
$$= 2v_1 v_2 \cos\theta \cos\phi$$

$$v_1^2 \sin^2 \theta + v_2^2 \sin^2 \phi = 2v_1 v_2 \cos \theta \cos \phi \quad ...(vii)$$

From Eq. (vi), $v_2 \sin \phi = v_1 \sin \theta$

Put in Eq. (vii), $2v_1^2 \sin^2 \theta = 2v_1 v_2 \cos \theta \cos \phi$

or $\cos \theta = \dfrac{2v_1^2 \sin^2 \theta}{2v_1 v_2 \cos \phi} = \left[\dfrac{v_1}{v_2}\right] \times \dfrac{\sin^2 \theta}{\cos \phi} \quad ...(viii)$

We know $\cos (\theta + \phi) = \cos \theta \cos \phi - \sin \theta \sin \phi$

Using Eq. (viii) and Eq. (vi), we get

$$\cos (\theta + \phi) = \dfrac{v_1 \sin^2 \theta}{v_2 \cos \phi} \cos \phi - \dfrac{v_1}{v_2} \sin^2 \theta = 0$$

$\therefore \quad \theta + \phi = 90°$

Hence, we conclude that in a perfectly elastic collision, when a moving particle of mass m collides elastically in two dimensions with another particle of mass m, after collision the two particles will move at right angle to each other.

EXAMPLE |7| Collision at an Intersection

Consider the collision depicted in figure to be between two billiard balls with equal masses $m_1 = m_2$. The first ball is called the cue while the second ball is called the target. The billiard player wants to sink the target ball in a corner pocket, which is at an angle $\theta_2 = 37°$. Assume that the collision is elastic and that friction and rotational motion are not important. Obtain θ_1. **[NCERT]**

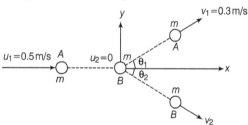

Sol. By conservation of momentum, we have

$$m\mathbf{u}_1 + 0 = m\mathbf{v}_1 + m\mathbf{v}_2$$

or $\mathbf{u}_1 = \mathbf{v}_1 + \mathbf{v}_2$ ...(i)

By conservation of energy, we have

$$\dfrac{1}{2} mu_1^2 = \dfrac{1}{2} mv_1^2 + \dfrac{1}{2} mv_2^2$$

or $u_1^2 = v_1^2 + v_2^2$ ...(ii)

From Eq. (i), we have

$$\mathbf{u}_1 \cdot \mathbf{u}_1 = (\mathbf{v}_1 + \mathbf{v}_2) \cdot (\mathbf{v}_1 + \mathbf{v}_2)$$
$$= \mathbf{v}_1 \cdot \mathbf{v}_1 + \mathbf{v}_1 \cdot \mathbf{v}_2 + \mathbf{v}_2 \cdot \mathbf{v}_1 + \mathbf{v}_2 \cdot \mathbf{v}_2$$

or $u_1^2 = v_1^2 + v_2^2 + 2\mathbf{v}_1 \cdot \mathbf{v}_2$

or $u_1^2 = u_1^2 + 2\mathbf{v}_1 \cdot \mathbf{v}_2$ [using Eq. (ii)]

or $\mathbf{v}_1 \cdot \mathbf{v}_2 = 0$

Thus, the angle between $\mathbf{v}_1$ and $\mathbf{v}_2$ is 90°.

or $\theta_1 + \theta_2 = 90°$

$\therefore \quad \theta_1 = 90° - \theta_2$
$$= 90 - 37° = 53°$$

Inelastic Collision in Two Dimensions

When two bodies travelling initially along the same straight line collide involving some loss of kinetic energy and move after collision along different directions in a plane.

Steps to be used for Solving Problems based on Two Dimensional Collision

Step I Firstly find out both x and y-coordinates. Its convenient to have either the x-axis or y-axis coincide with the direction of one of the initial velocities.

Step II Draw a diagram, labelling velocity vectors and masses.

Step III Write a separate conservation of momentum equation for each of the x and y-axes. In each case, total initial momentum in a given direction equal to the final momentum in that direction.

Step IV If the collision is in elastic, then write a general expression for the total energy before and after the collision.

Equate both the equations to get unknown value.

Step V There are two equations for inelastic collisions and three for elastic collision.

EXAMPLE |8| Inelastic Collision between Two Balls

A ball moving with a speed of 9 m/s strikes an identical ball at rest, such that after collision, the direction of each ball makes an angle of 30° with the original line of motion. Find the speed of the two balls after collision.

Sol. Given, $m_1 = m_2 = m,\ u_1 = 9$ m/s, $u_2 = 0$

$$\theta_1 = \theta_2 = 30°,\ v_1 = ?,\ v_2 = ?$$

According to principle of conservation of linear momentum.

$$m_1 u_1 + m_2 u_2 = m_1 v_1 \cos \theta_1 + m_2 v_2 \cos \theta_2$$

Along the direction of motion in x-axis

$$m \times 9 + 0 = mv_1 \cos 30° + mv_2 \cos 30°$$

$$9 = v_1 \dfrac{\sqrt{3}}{2} + v_2 \dfrac{\sqrt{3}}{2} = \dfrac{(v_1 + v_2)\sqrt{3}}{2}$$

$$v_1 + v_2 = \dfrac{18}{\sqrt{3}} \quad ...(i)$$

Along a direction of motion in y-axis

$$0 + 0 = m_1 v_1 \sin \theta_1 - m_2 v_2 \sin \theta_2$$

$$m_1 v_1 \sin \theta_1 = m_2 v_2 \sin \theta_2$$

$$\Rightarrow \qquad mv_1 \sin 30° = mv_2 \sin 30°$$
$$\Rightarrow \qquad v_1 = v_2 \qquad \text{...(ii)}$$

Substituting value from Eq. (ii) in Eq. (i), then find out values of v_1 and v_2

$$2v_1 = \frac{18}{\sqrt{3}}$$

$$\Rightarrow \qquad v_1 = \frac{9}{\sqrt{3}} \times \frac{\sqrt{3}}{\sqrt{3}}$$

$$= \frac{9\sqrt{3}}{3} = 3\sqrt{3} \text{ m/s}$$

Hence, two balls move with same velocity $= 3\sqrt{3}$ m/s after collision.

Coefficient of Restitution or Coefficient of Resilience

It is defined as the ratio of relative velocity of separation after collision to the relative velocity of approach before collision. It is denoted by e.

$$e = \frac{\text{Relative velocity of separation (after collision)}}{\text{Relative velocity of approach (before collision)}}$$

$$e = \frac{|v_2 - v_1|}{|u_1 - u_2|} = \frac{v_2 - v_1}{u_1 - u_2}$$

$$\boxed{\text{Coefficient of resilience, } e = \frac{v_2 - v_1}{u_1 - u_2}}$$

where u_1, u_2 are velocities of two bodies before collision and v_1, v_2 are their respective velocities after collision.

- The coefficient of restitution gives a measure of the degree of restitution of a collision. The value of e depends on the materials of the colliding bodies. e.g. for two glass balls, $e = 0.95$ and for the lead balls, $e = 0.20$.
- For a perfectly elastic collision, relative velocity of separation after collision is equal to relative velocity of approach before collision
  $$\therefore \qquad e = 1$$
  For a perfectly inelastic collision, relative velocity of separation after collision = 0 i.e. = 0
- For all other collisions, e lies between 0 and 1, i.e. $0 < e < 1$

Rebouncing of a Ball

If a ball is dropped from certain height h, then it rebounds from a floor as shown in figure.

So, height attained after n impacts is $h_n = e^{2n} h$. Then, total distance travelled before the body comes to rest is

$$s = h\left(\frac{1 + e^2}{1 - e^2}\right), \text{ where } e \text{ is coefficient of restitution.}$$

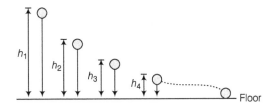

If we add impact heights at every instance, then it forms geometric progression.

Different Types of Collisions

Collision	Kinetic energy	Coefficient of restitution	Main domain
Elastic	Conserved	$e = 1$	Between atomic particles
Inelastic	Not conserved	$0 < e < 1$	Between ordinary objects
Perfectly inelastic	Maximum loss of KE	$e = 0$	During shooting
Super elastic	KE increases	$e > 1$	In explosions

EXAMPLE |9| Momentum of a Bob

A sphere of mass m moving with a velocity u hits another stationary sphere of same mass. What will be the ratio of the velocities of two spheres after the collision. Take e as the coefficient of restitution.

Sol. Here, $\qquad u_1 = u, u_2 = 0$

$$\therefore \qquad e = \frac{v_2 - v_1}{u_1 - u_2} = \frac{v_2 - v_1}{u - 0}$$

or $\qquad v_2 - v_1 = e\,u \qquad \text{...(i)}$

According to the law of conservation of momentum, we have

$$mu + m \times 0 = mv_1 + mv_2$$

or $\qquad v_1 + v_2 = u \qquad \text{...(ii)}$

On adding Eqs. (i) and (ii), we get

$$2v_2 = u + eu = u(1 + e)$$

or $\qquad v_2 = \frac{u(1 + e)}{2} \qquad \text{...(iii)}$

Substituting the value of v_2 in Eq. (ii), we have

$$v_1 = u - v_2$$

$$= u - \frac{u(1 + e)}{2}$$

$$= \frac{u(1 - e)}{2} \qquad \text{...(iv)}$$

Dividing Eq. (iii) by Eq. (iv), we get

$$\frac{v_2}{v_1} = \frac{1 + e}{1 - e}$$

TOPIC PRACTICE 3

OBJECTIVE Type Questions

1. A particle is acted by a constant power. Then, which of the following physical quantity remains constant?
   (a) Speed
   (b) Rate of change of acceleration
   (c) Kinetic energy
   (d) Rate of change of kinetic energy

   Sol. (d) By definition, $P = \dfrac{dW}{dt}$

   $\because$ Work done = Kinetic energy

   $\Rightarrow P = \dfrac{dW}{dt} = \dfrac{d(KE)}{dt} = $ constant

2. The power (P) of an engine lifting a mass of 100 kg upto a height of 10 m in 1 min is
   (a) 162.3 W   (b) 163.3 W
   (c) 164.3 W   (d) 165 W

   Sol. (b) Power $= \dfrac{\text{Work}}{\text{Time}} = \dfrac{mgh}{t}$

   Here, $m = 100$ kg, $h = 10$ m and $t = 1$ min $= 60$ s.

   $\therefore P = \dfrac{100 \times 9.8 \times 10}{60} = 163.3$ W

3. A man does a given amount of work in 10 s. Another man does the same amount of work in 20 s. The ratio of the output power of the first man to that of second man is
   (a) 1   (b) 1 : 2   (c) 2 : 1   (d) 3 : 1

   Sol. (c) Since, $P = \dfrac{W}{t}$

   So, if W is constant, then $P \propto \dfrac{1}{t}$

   i.e. $\dfrac{P_1}{P_2} = \dfrac{t_2}{t_1} = \dfrac{20}{10} \Rightarrow \dfrac{P_1}{P_2} = \dfrac{2}{1}$ or $P_1 : P_2 = 2 : 1$

4. A particle of mass m_1 moves with velocity v_1 collides with another particle at rest of equal mass. The velocity of second particle after the elastic collision is
   (a) $2v_1$ (b) v_1 (c) $-v_1$ (d) 0

   Sol. (b) Given, mass $m_1 = m_2 = m$ and velocity, $v = v_1$

   For elastic collision, $v_2 = \left(\dfrac{m_2 - m_1}{m_1 + m_2}\right) v_2 + \dfrac{2m_1 v_1}{m_1 + m_2}$

   After putting given values, we will get

   $v_2 = \dfrac{2m_1 v_1}{2m_1} \Rightarrow v_2 = v_1$

5. A body of mass 5 kg is thrown vertically up with a kinetic energy of 490 J. The height at which the kinetic energy of the body becomes half of the original value is
   (a) 12.5 m   (b) 10 m   (c) 2.5 m   (d) 5 m

   Sol. (d) According to the law of conservation of energy,

   $$\dfrac{1}{2}mv^2 = \dfrac{1}{2}\left(\dfrac{1}{2}mv^2\right) + mgh$$

   $\Rightarrow \quad 490 = 245 + 5 \times 9.8 \times h, \quad h = \dfrac{245}{49} = 5$ m

VERY SHORT ANSWER Type Questions

6. Calculate the power of an electric engine which can lift 20 tonne of coal per hour from a mine 180 m deep.

   Sol. Power $= \dfrac{\text{Work done}}{\text{Time taken}} = \dfrac{mgh}{t} = \dfrac{20 \times 1000 \times 9.8 \times 180}{60 \times 60}$

   $= 9800$ W $= 9.8$ kW

7. Is collision between two particles possible even without any physical contact between them?

   Sol. Yes, in atomic and subatomic particles collision without any physical contact between the colliding particles is taking place e.g. Rutherford's alpha particles scattering.

8. In what type of collision, maximum kinetic energy is transferred?

   Sol. Maximum kinetic energy is transferred when two bodies of equal mass collide.

9. If the momentum and total energy is conserved, then define the collision is occurred?

   Sol. Collision in which momentum and total energy remained conserved and total kinetic energy of the colliding particles remain constant both before and after the collision, is called **elastic collision**.

10. In which of the two types of collision i.e. elastic or inelastic, the momentum is conserved? What about KE?

    Sol. Momentum is conserved in both the types of collisions, but KE is conserved only in elastic collision.

11. Which physical terms remain conserved in an inelastic collision?

    Sol. In an inelastic collision, total momentum as well as total energy remain conserved.

12. Is the total linear momentum conserved during the short time of an elastic collision of two balls ?

    Sol. During the short interval of an elastic collision, total linear momentum is conserved.

13. What is the loss in kinetic energy after collision, if the target body is initially at rest?

Sol. Loss in kinetic energy on collision is $\dfrac{1}{2}\left(\dfrac{m_1 m_2}{m_1 + m_2}\right)u^2$, where u is the initial velocity.

SHORT ANSWER Type Questions

14. A molecule in a gas container hits a horizontal wall with speed $200\ ms^{-1}$ and angle $30°$ with the normal, and rebounds with the same speed. Is momentum conserved in the collision? Is the collision elastic or inelastic? **[NCERT]**

Sol. Yes, momentum remains conserved in the collision. To check whether the collision is elastic or inelastic, we consider the kinetic energy of the molecule.

We find that the initial kinetic energy $\left(\dfrac{1}{2}mu^2\right)$ is the

same as final KE. $\left(\dfrac{1}{2}mv^2\right)$ of the molecule as

$u = v = 200\ m/s$ i.e. thus the collision is elastic collision.

15. Two ball bearings of mass m each moving in opposite directions with equal speed v collide head-on with each other. Predict the outcome of the collision, assuming it to be perfectly elastic.

Sol. Here, $M_1 = M_2 = m,\ u_1 = v$ and $u_2 = -v$

Now, $v_1 = \dfrac{(M_1 - M_2)u_1 + 2M_2 u_2}{M_1 + M_2}$

$= \dfrac{(m - m)v + 2m(-v)}{m + m} = -v$

and $v_2 = \dfrac{(M_2 - M_1)u_2 + 2M_1 u_1}{M_1 + M_2}$

$= \dfrac{(m - m)(-v) + 2m v}{m + m} = v$

After collision, the two ball bearings will move with same speed but their directions of motion will be reversed.

16. The bob A of a pendulum released from $30°$ to the vertical hits another bob B of the same mass at rest on a table as shown in figure.

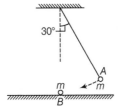

How high does the bob A rise after the collision? Neglect the size of the bobs and assume the collision to be elastic. **[NCERT]**

Sol. When the pendulum bob A reaches the position B, its velocity is horizontal and it strikes the mass m placed at

B. Since, the collision is one-dimensional and elastic, the bob exchange their velocities being of the same mass. The bob A does not rise at all and the bob B begins to move with the velocity of A.

17. A particle of mass 1 kg moving with a velocity $\mathbf{v}_1 = (3\hat{i} - 2\hat{j})$ m/s experience a perfectly inelastic collision with another particle of mass 2 kg having velocity $\mathbf{v}_2 = (4\hat{j} - 6\hat{k})$ m/s. Find the velocity and speed of the particle formed.

Sol. Given, $m_1 = 1$ kg, $\mathbf{v}_1 = (3\hat{i} - 2\hat{j})$ m/s, $m_2 = 2$ kg and

$$\mathbf{v}_2 = (4\hat{j} - 6\hat{k})\ \text{m/s}$$

When two particles experience a perfectly inelastic collision. They stick together and move with a common velocity $\mathbf{v}$ given by

$$\mathbf{v} = \dfrac{m_1\mathbf{v}_1 + m_2\mathbf{v}_2}{m_1 + m_2} = \dfrac{1(3\hat{i} - 2\hat{j}) + 2(4\hat{j} - 6\hat{k})}{1 + 2}$$

$$= (\hat{i} + 2\hat{j} - 4\hat{k})\ \text{m/s}$$

Speed of combined particle $v = \sqrt{1^2 + (2)^2 + (-4)^2} = \sqrt{21}$ m/s

18. Calculate the power of a motor which is capable of raising of water in 5 min from a well 120 m deep.

Sol. Here, the volume of water raised $V = 2000$ L

Density of water, $\rho = 1$ kg/L

$\therefore$ Mass of water raised, $m = V\rho = 2000 \times 1 = 2000$ kg

Power, $P = \dfrac{W}{t} = \dfrac{mgh}{t} = \dfrac{2000 \times 9.8 \times 120}{5 \times 60} = 7840$ W

$= 7.840$ kW   [1kW = 1000 W]

LONG ANSWER Type I Questions

19. A pump on the ground floor of a building can pump up water to fill a tank of volume 30 m^3 in 15 min. If the tank is 40 m above the ground, and the efficiency of the pump is 30%, how much electric power is consumed by the pump? **[NCERT]**

Sol. Here, volume of water lifted $V =$ volume of tank $= 30$ m^3, time $t = 15$ min $= 900$ s,

Height of tank, $h = 40$ m and efficiency of motor, $\eta = 30\%$

$\therefore$ Output of motor = work done to raise water

$$= mgh = V\rho gh$$

$\therefore$ Output power $= \dfrac{V\rho gh}{t} = \dfrac{30 \times 10^3 \times 9.8 \times 40}{900}$

$$= 1.307 \times 10^4\ \text{W}$$

$\therefore$ Input power $= \dfrac{\text{Output power}}{\eta} = +\dfrac{1.307 \times 10^4}{\dfrac{30}{100}}$

$$= \dfrac{1.307 \times 10^4 \times 100}{30} = 4.357 \times 10^4\ \text{W}$$

$$= 43.57\ \text{kW} \qquad\qquad [1kW = 1000W]$$

20. The blades of a windmill sweep out a circlef area A. (i) If the wind flows at a velocity v perpendicular to the circle, what is the mass of the air passing through it in time t? (ii) What is the kinetic energy of the air? (iii) Assume that the windmill converts 25% of the wind's energy into electrical energy, and that $A = 30\ m^2$, $v = 36\ km/h$ and the density of the air is 1.2 kg m^{-3}. What is the electrical power produced?

Sol. (i) Area swept by blades of windmill $= A$ and wind velocity $= v$

∴ Volume of air passing per unit time $= Av$

∴ Mass of air passing per unit time $= Av\rho$

and mass of air passing in time t, $M = Av\rho t$

(ii) KE of said quantity of air, $K = \dfrac{1}{2} Mv^2 = \dfrac{1}{2} A\rho t v^3$

(iii) If efficiency of windmill be 25%, then

Output electrical power = 25% of input power

$$= \frac{25}{100} \times \frac{1}{2} A\rho v^3$$

As $A = 30\ m^2$, $v = 36\ km/h = 36 \times \dfrac{5}{18}\ m/s$

$= 10\ m/s$ and $\rho = 1.2\ kgm^{-3}$

∴ Output electrical power $= \dfrac{25}{100} \times \dfrac{1}{2} \times 30 \times 1.2 \times (10)^3$

$= 4500\ W = 4.5\ kW$

$[1\ kW = 1000\ W]$

21. Which of the following potential energy curves in figure cannot possibly describe the elastic collision of two billiard balls? Here, r is the distance between centres of the balls. **[NCERT]**

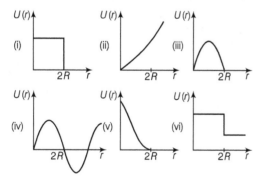

Sol. When two billiard balls collide then distance between their centres is $2R$. Due to impact of collision there is small temporary deformation of balls. In this process, KE of ball is gradually reduced to zero and converted into elastic potential energy of balls.

When KE is zero, the balls regain their original configuration due to elasticity. The phenomenon can be successfully explained only by potential energy curve

number (v), because here as $r < 2R$, the potential energy function $U(r)$ is increasing gradually on decreasing value of r.

22. Two identical ball bearings in contact with each other and resting on a frictionless table are hit head-on by another ball bearing of the same mass moving initially with a speed v. If the collision is elastic, which of the following (figure) is a possible result after collision? **[NCERT]**

Sol. We know that, when two bodies of same mass collide, they interchange their velocities. When first ball collides with the combinations of balls 2 and 3, the first ball comes to rest while ball number 2 moves with velocity v again it collides with ball number 3 and hence ball number 2 comes to rest while ball number 3 moves with velocity v.

Hence, the situation shown in Fig. (ii) is the correct result of collision.

23. A bullet of mass 0.012 kg and horizontal speed 70 ms^{-1} strikes a block of wood of mass 0.4 kg and instantly comes to rest with respect to the block. The block is suspended from the ceiling by means of thin wires. Calculate the height to which the block rises. Also, estimate the amount of heat produced to the block. **[NCERT]**

Sol. Here, mass of bullet $m = 0.012$ kg, initial speed of bullet $u = 70$ ms^{-1}, mass of wood block $M = 0.4$ kg.

As on collision, the bullet comes to rest w.r.t. block, it means that after collision bullet and block are moving with a common speed v.

From conservation law of momentum $mu = (M + m) v$

$$\Rightarrow \qquad v = \frac{mu}{(M+m)} = \frac{0.012 \times 70}{(0.4 + 0.012)}$$

$$= 2.04\ m\ s^{-1}$$

If the block now rises to a maximum height of h, then using conservation law of mechanical energy, we have

$$\frac{1}{2}(M+m)v^2 - 0 = (M+m)gh$$

$$\Rightarrow \qquad h = \frac{v^2}{2g} = \frac{(2.04)^2}{2 \times 9.8} = 0.212\ m = 21.2\ cm$$

24. A trolley of mass 200 kg moves with a uniform speed of 36 km/h on a frictionless track. A child of mass 20 kg runs on the trolley from one end to the other (10 m away) with a speed of 4 ms^{-1} relative to the trolley in a direction opposite to its motion, and jumps out of the trolley. What is the final speed of the trolley? How much has the trolley moved from the time the child begins to run? **[NCERT]**

Sol. Let there be an observer travelling parallel to the trolley with the same speed. He will observe the initial momentum of the trolley of mass M and child of mass m as zero. When the child jumps in opposite direction, he will observe the increase in the velocity of the trolley by Δv. Let u be the velocity of the child. He will observe child landing at velocity $(u - \Delta v)$.

Therefore, final momentum $= M\Delta v - m(u - \Delta v)$

From the law of conservation of momentum, we have

$$M\Delta v - m(u - \Delta v) = 0 \implies \Delta v = \frac{mu}{M + m}$$

Putting various values, we have

$$\Delta v = \frac{4 \times 20}{20 + 220} = 0.33 \text{ ms}^{-1}$$

∴ Final speed of trolley is 10.36 ms^{-1}

The child take 2.5 s to run on the trolley.

Therefore, the trolley moves a distance

$$= 2.5 \times 10.36 \text{ m} = 25.9 \text{ m}$$

25. A family uses 8 kW of power. (i) Direct solar energy is incident on the horizontal surface at an average rate of 200 W per square metre. If 20% of this energy can be converted to useful electrical energy, how large an area is needed to supply 8 kW? (ii) Compare this area to that of the roof of a typical house. **[NCERT]**

Sol. (i) Power used by family, $P = 8$ kW $= 8000$ W

As only 20% of solar energy can be converted to useful electrical energy, hence power to be supplied by solar energy $\frac{8000 \text{ W}}{20\%} = 40000$ W

As solar energy is incident at a rate of 200 Wm^{-2}, hence the area needed

$$A = \frac{40000 \text{ W}}{200 \text{ Wm}^{-2}} = 200 \text{ m}^2$$

(ii) The area needed is comparable to roof area of a large sized house.

26. A synchronous motor is used to lift an elevator and its load of 1500 kg to a height of 20 m. The time taken for job is 20 s. What is work done? What is the rate at which work is done? If the efficiency of the motor is 75%, at which rate is the energy supplied to the motor?

Sol. Given, mass, $m = 1500$ kg, $h = 20$ m, $\eta = 75\%$, $t = 20$ s

Work done, $W = mgh = 1500 \times 9.8 \times 20$
$$= 2.94 \times 10^5 \text{ J}$$

Rate of doing work $= \frac{W}{t} = \frac{2.94 \times 10^5}{20} = 1.47 \times 10^4$ W

As, efficiency, $\eta = \dfrac{\text{Output power}}{\text{Input power}}$

$$\frac{75}{100} = \frac{1.47 \times 10^4}{\text{Input power}}$$

Input power or the rate at which energy is supplied

$$= \frac{1.47 \times 10^4 \times 100}{75} = 1.96 \times 10^4 \text{ W}$$

LONG ANSWER Type II Questions

27. State if each of the following statements is true or false. Give reasons for your answer.

(i) In an elastic collision of two bodies, the momentum and energy of each body is conserved.

(ii) Total energy of a system is always conserved, no matter what internal and external forces on the body are present?

(iii) Work done in the motion of a body over a closed loop is zero for every force in nature.

(iv) In an inelastic collision, the final kinetic energy is always less than the initial kinetic energy of the system. **[NCERT]**

Sol. (i) False, in elastic collision the linear momentum and kinetic energy of the system as a whole is conserved, but momentum and kinetic energy of each of individual body change.

(ii) False, internal as well as external forces can change the kinetic energy. Again forces if conservative may change the potential energy of a system.

(iii) False, for non-conservative force the work done over a closed loop is not zero.

(iv) It is usually true but not always true. As an example in the explosion of a cracker final kinetic energy is greater than the initial kinetic energy.

Again final kinetic energy of gun-bullet system after firing is more than initial kinetic energy before collision.

28. Answer carefully with reasons

(i) In an elastic collision of two billiard balls, is the total kinetic energy conserved during the short time of collision of the balls i.e. when they are in contact? **[NCERT]**

(ii) Is the total linear momentum conserved during the short time of an elastic collision of two balls?

(iii) What are the answer to (i) and (ii) for an inelastic collision?

(iv) If the potential energy of two billiard balls depends only on the separation distance between their centres, is the collision elastic or inelastic? (Note : We are talking here of potential energy corresponding to the force during collision, not gravitational potential energy.)

Sol. (i) No, the total kinetic energy, does not remain conserved during the short time when two billiard balls are in contact. At that time, balls are at rest and their KE is zero. In fact, all this KE has been transformed into elastic potential energy of balls.

(ii) Yes, total linear momentum remains conserved during the short time of an elastic collision of two balls. The balls exert forces on one another due to which individual momenta of two balls change but total linear momentum remains conserved.

(iii) For an inelastic, collision kinetic energy is not conserved but total linear momentum is conserved even now.

(iv) As the potential energy depends only on the separation distance between the centres of balls, it means that conservative forces are in action (because PE changes due to conservative forces only). Hence, collision is surely inelastic collision.

29. Prove that when a particle suffers an oblique elastic collision with another particle of equal mass and initially at rest, the two particles would move in mutually perpendicular directions after collisions.

Sol. Let a particle A of mass m and having velocity u collides with particle B of equal mass but at rest. Let the collision be oblique elastic collision and after collision the balls A and B move with velocities v_1 and v_2 respectively inclined at an angle θ from each other.

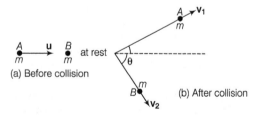

(a) Before collision

(b) After collision

Applying principle of conservation of linear momentum, we get

$$m\mathbf{u} = m\mathbf{v}_1 + m\mathbf{v}_2 \text{ or } \mathbf{u} = \mathbf{v}_1 + \mathbf{v}_2$$

or $$u^2 = (\mathbf{v}_1 + \mathbf{v}_2) \cdot (\mathbf{v}_1 + \mathbf{v}_2)$$
$$= v_1^2 + v_2^2 + 2v_1v_2 \cos\theta \qquad \text{...(i)}$$

Again as total KE before collision = total KE after collision

$$\therefore \qquad \frac{1}{2}mu^2 = \frac{1}{2}mv_1^2 + \frac{1}{2}mv_2^2$$
$$\Rightarrow \qquad u^2 = v_1^2 + v_2^2 \qquad \text{...(ii)}$$

Comparing Eqs. (i) and (ii), we get $2v_1v_2 \cos\theta = 0$

As in an oblique collision both v_1 and v_2 are finite, hence $\cos\theta = 0$

$$\Rightarrow \qquad \theta = \cos^{-1}(0) = \frac{\pi}{2}$$

Thus, particles A and B are moving in mutually perpendicular directions after the collision.

30. A particle of mass m moving with an initial velocity u collides inelastically with a particle of mass M initially at rest. If the collision is completely inelastic, then find expressions for (i) final velocity of combined entity and (ii) loss in kinetic energy during collision.

Sol. (i) Let a particle of mass m moving with an initial velocity u collides inelastically with another particle of mass M initially at rest. Let after collision, the combined entity moves with a velocity v. Then, from the conservation of linear momentum, we have

$$mu + 0 = (m + M)v$$
$$\Rightarrow \qquad v = \frac{mu}{m + M}$$

(ii) Initial kinetic energy of system before collision

$$K = \frac{1}{2}mu^2$$

and final kinetic energy of system after collision

$$K' = \frac{1}{2}(m + M)v^2 = \frac{1}{2}(m + M) \cdot \left(\frac{mu}{m + M}\right)^2$$

$\therefore$ Loss in kinetic energy during collision

$$= \frac{1}{2}\frac{m^2u^2}{(m + M)} = \frac{1}{2}\frac{m^2u^2}{(m + M)} \qquad \Delta K = K - K'$$

$$= \frac{1}{2}mu^2 - \frac{1}{2}\frac{m^2u^2}{(m + M)}$$

$$= \frac{1}{2}mu^2\left[1 - \frac{m}{M + m}\right] = \frac{1}{2}mu^2 \cdot \left(\frac{M}{M + m}\right)$$

and fractional loss in kinetic energy during collision

$$\frac{\Delta K}{K} = \frac{M}{M + m}$$

ASSESS YOUR TOPICAL UNDERSTANDING

OBJECTIVE Type Questions

1. A one kilowatt motor is used to pump water from a well 10 m deep. The quantity of water pumped out per second is nearly
   (a) 1kg   (b) 10 kg
   (c) 100 kg   (d) 1000 kg

2. A molecule in a gas container hits a horizontal wall with speed 200 ms^{-1} and angle 30° with the normal and rebounds with the same speed. Which statement is true?
   (a) Momentum is conserved
   (b) Elastic collision
   (c) Inelastic collision
   (d) Both (a) and (b)

3. A particle of mass 1g moving with a velocity $v_1 = 3\hat{i} - 2\hat{j}$ ms^{-1} experiences a perfectly elastic collision with another particle of mass 2 g and velocity $v_2 = 4\hat{j} - 6\hat{k}$ ms^{-1}. The velocity of the particle is
   (a) 2.3 ms^{-1} (b) 4.6 ms^{-1}
   (c) 9.2 ms^{-1} (d) 6 ms^{-1}

4. In an inelastic collision,
   (a) conservation of momentum is not followed
   (b) conservation of mechanical energy is not followed
   (c) conservation of mechanical energy is followed
   (d) None of the above

5. The power of a windmill having blade area equal to A and wind velocity equal to v is (ρ is density of air)
   (a) $\dfrac{A\rho v^3}{2}$ (b) $\dfrac{A\rho v^2}{2}$ (c) $\dfrac{A\rho v}{2}$ (d) $A\rho v^3$

Answer

| 1. (b) | 2. (d) | 3. (b) | 4. (c) | 5. (a) |

VERY SHORT ANSWER Type Questions

6. What is an oblique collision?

7. What happen when two identical objects moving in mutually opposite directions suffer elastic collision?

SHORT ANSWER Type Questions

8. Show that coefficient of restitution for one-dimensional elastic collision is equal to one.

9. An engine of 4.9 kw power is used to pump water from a well 50m deep. Calculate the quantity of water in kilolitres which it can pump out in one hour.

10. Is it possible for an individual to have
    (i) more power and less energy
    (ii) less power and more energy?

11. Prove that instantaneous power is given by the scalar product of force and velocity.

12. What are oblique collisions? Find the final velocities when two bodies of equal mass collide with each other.

LONG ANSWER Type I Questions

13. What do you meant by conservation of linear momentum?

14. Explain perfectly inelastic collision in one dimension.

15. Calculate the horsepower of a man who can chew ice at the rate of 30 g per minute.
    Given 1hp = 746 W, 1 J = 4.2 J/cal and latent heat of ice = 80 cal/gm   [**Ans.** 0. 225 HP]

16. What are power, instantaneous power and average power? Is there any relationship between power and impulse? Elucidate your answer?

17. A body of mass m moving with speed v collides elastically head-on with another body of mass m initially at rest. Show that moving body will come to a stop as a result of this collision.

LONG ANSWER Type II Questions

18. A mass m is moving with a speed u collides with a similar mass m at rest, elastically and obliquely prove that they will move in directions making an angle $\pi/2$ with each other.

19. A billiard ball of radius 1.5 cm moving with 1 m/s hits an identical ball at rest. If the impact parameter of the collision is 1.5 cm, find the speed and direction of each ball after the collision, assuming it to be elastic.
    [**Ans.** $v_1 = (1/2)$ m/s, $v_2 = (\sqrt{3}/2)$ m/s, $\theta = 60°$]

20. A body of mass M at rest is struck by a moving body of mass m. Show that the fraction of the initial kinetic energy of moving mass m transferred to the strucked body is $4\, Mn/(m + M)^2$.

21. Define the terms elastic and inelastic collision. What is the difference between a partially, inelastic collision and a completely inelastic collision?

SUMMARY

- Work is said to be done whenever a force acts on a body and the body moves through some distance in the direction of the force. It is the dot product of force and displacement i.e. $W = \mathbf{F} \cdot \mathbf{s} = Fs \cos \theta$, where θ is the angle between $\mathbf{F}$ and $\mathbf{s}$.

  (i) If $\theta = 90°$; then $W = 0$,

  (ii) $\theta < 90°$, then $W = +$ ve,

  (iii) $\theta > 90°$; then $W = -$ ve

- Work done is a scalar quantity measured in newton-metre. Its dimension is $[ML^2 T^{-2}]$.

- The SI unit of work is joule and the CGS unit of work is erg. $1 \text{ joule} = 10^7 \text{ erg}$

- Work done by variable force F is given by $W = \int F \cdot ds$

  $=$ Area under the force-displacement curve.

  (a) Forces are **conservative** if,

   (i) Work done in a closed path is zero.

   (ii) Work done is independent of path.

  (b) Forces are **non-conservative** if,

   (i) Work done in a closed path is not zero.

   (ii) Work done depends upon the path.

- The energy of a body is defined as its ability of doing work. It is a scalar quantity. Like work, SI unit of energy is joule and the CGS unit is erg.

- The energy possessed by a body by virtue of its motion is called kinetic energy. The KE of a body of mass m moving with velocity v is given by KE $= \frac{1}{2}mv^2$ or $\frac{p^2}{2m}$

- **According to work-energy theorem**, the work done by the net force acting on a body is equal to the change in kinetic energy of the body. $W =$ Change in KE $= \frac{1}{2}mv^2 - \frac{1}{2}mu^2$

- The energy possessed by a body by virtue of its position or configuration is called its **potential energy**.

  The gravitational potential energy of an object of mass m at height h from the earth's surface is given by $u = mgh$, where g is acceleration due to gravity.

- The energy associated with the state of compression or extension of an elastic (spring like) object is called elastic potential energy. If a spring is stretched through a distance x, then the elastic potential energy of the spring is given by

  $u = \frac{1}{2}kx^2$, where k is the force constant of the spring.

- **Power** is the rate of doing work. $P = \dfrac{\text{Energy}}{\text{Time}}$ or $\dfrac{\text{Work done}}{\text{Time}}$. It is a scalar quantity and it is measured in Js^{-1} or watt.

- A collision in which both the momentum and kinetic energy of the body remains conserved is called **elastic collision**.

- A collision in which only the momentum of the system is conserved but kinetic energy is not conserved is called **inelastic collision**.

- If the colliding bodies move along the same straight line path before and after the collision, then the collision is said to be one dimensional collision.

- If the two bodies do not move along the same straight line path before and after the collision, then the collision is said to be two dimensional or oblique collision.

- If two bodies of masses m_1 and m_2 moving with velocities u_1 and u_2 $(u_2 > u_1)$ in the same direction suffer head-on elastic collision such that v_1 and v_2 be their respective velocities after collision, then

  $v_1 = \left(\dfrac{m_1 - m_2}{m_1 + m_2}\right)u_1 + \left(\dfrac{2m_2}{m_1 + m_2}\right)u_2$

  and $v_2 = \left(\dfrac{2m_1}{m_1 + m_2}\right)u_1 + \left(\dfrac{m_2 - m_1}{m_1 + m_2}\right)u_2$

- If a body of mass m_1 moving with velocity u_1 collides with another body of mass m_2 and sticks to it (i.e. collision is perfectly inelastic collision), then the final common velocity is given by $v = \dfrac{m_1 u_1}{m_1 + m_2}$

- In such a case loss in kinetic energy of the system is $\Delta KE = \dfrac{m_1 m_2 u_1^2}{2(m_1 + m_2)}$

- If a particle of mass m_1 moving with velocity u_1 collides with another particle of mass m_2 at rest, then after the collision the two particles move with velocities v_1 and v_2, making angles θ_1 and θ_2 with x-axis
  $m_1 v_1 \sin \theta_1 = m_2 v_2 \sin \theta_2$ (along y-axis)
   $m_1 u_1 = m_1 v_1 \cos \theta + m_1 v_2 \cos \theta_2$ (along x-axis)

- The coefficient of restitution gives a measure of the degree of restitution of a collision and it is defined as the ratio of relative velocity of separation after collision to the relative velocity of approach before collision. It is denoted by e. i.e. $e = \dfrac{v_2 - v_1}{u_1 - u_2}$

- For a perfectly elastic collision, $e = 1$ and for a perfectly inelastic collision, $e = 0$

CHAPTER PRACTICE

OBJECTIVE Type Questions

1. The earth, moving around the sun in a circular orbit, is acted upon by a force and hence work done on the earth by the force is
   (a) zero   (b) + ve
   (c) − ve   (d) None of these

2. A force $F = - k/x^2$ $(x \neq 0)$ acts on a particle in X-direction. Find the work done by the force in displacing the particle from $x = - a$ to $x = 2a$.
   (a) $3k/2a$ (b) $4k/a^2$ (c) $- 3k/2a^2$ (d) $\dfrac{- 9k}{a^2}$

3. A force of 10 N is applied on an object of mass 2 kg placed on a rough surface having coefficient of friction equal to 0.2. Work done by applied force in 4 s is
   (a) 120 J   (b) 240 J
   (c) 250 J   (d) 100 J

4. A man squatting on the ground gets straight up and stand. The force of reaction of ground on the man during the process is   **[NCERT Exemplar]**
   (a) constant and equal to mg in magnitude
   (b) constant and greater than mg in magnitude
   (c) variable but always greater than mg
   (d) at first greater than mg and later becomes equal to mg

5. The potential energy, i.e., $U(x)$ can be assumed zero when
   (a) $x = 0$
   (b) gravitational force is constant
   (c) infinite distance from the gravitational source
   (d) All of the above

6. What is the ratio of kinetic energy of a particle at the bottom to the kinetic energy at the top when it just loops a vertical loop of radius r?
   (a) 5:1   (b) 2:3   (c) 5:2   (d) 7:2

7. Two bodies of masses m_1 and m_2 have same momentum. The ratio of their KE is
   (a) $\sqrt{\dfrac{m_2}{m_1}}$ (b) $\sqrt{\dfrac{m_1}{m_2}}$ (c) $\dfrac{m_1}{m_2}$ (d) $\dfrac{m_2}{m_1}$

8. If the linear momentum is increased by 50%, then kinetic energy will be increased by
   (a) 50%   (b) 100%   (c) 125%   (d) 25%

9. How much amount of energy is liberated to convert 1 kg of coal into energy?
   (a) 9×10^{16} J   (b) 9×10^{15} J
   (c) 3×10^{14} J   (d) 4×10^{6} J

10. In a hydroelectric power station, the water is flowing at 2 ms^{-1} in the river which is 100 m wide and 5 m deep. The maximum power output from the river is
    (a) 1.5 MW   (b) 2 MW   (c) 2.5 MW   (d) 3 MW

11. In a head on elastic collision of a very heavy body moving with velocity v with a light body at rest. Then, the velocity of heavy body after collision is
    (a) v (b) $2v$ (c) zero   (d) $\dfrac{v}{2}$

12. The height attained by a ball after 3 rebounds on falling from a height of h on floor having coefficient of restitution e is
    (a) $e^3 h$ (b) $e^4 h$ (c) $e^5 h$ (d) $e^6 h$

ASSERTION-REASON

Direction (Q.Nos. 13-17) *In the following questions, two statements are given- one labelled Assertion (A) and the other labelled Reason (R). Select the correct answer to these questions from the codes (a), (b), (c) and (d) as given below*
   (a) Both Assertion and Reason are true and Reason is the correct explanation of Assertion.
   (b) Both Assertion and Reason are true but Reason is not the correct explanation of Assertion.
   (c) Assertion is true but Reason is false.
   (d) Assertion is false but Reason is true.

13. **Assertion** Two springs of force constants k_1 and k_2 are stretched by the same force. If $k_1 > k_2$, then work done in stretching the first (W_1) is less than work done in stretching the second (W_2).

    Reason $F = k_1 x_1 = k_2 x_2$

14. **Assertion** If momentum of a body increases by 50%, its kinetic energy will increase by 125%.

    Reason Kinetic energy is proportional to square of velocity.

15. **Assertion** Stopping distance $= \dfrac{\text{Kinetic energy}}{\text{Stopping force}}$

    Reason Work done in stopping a body is equal to change in kinetic energy of the body.

16. **Assertion** Mass and energy are not conserved separately but are conserved as a single entity called 'mass-energy'.

    Reason This is because one can be obtained at the cost of the other as per Einstein's equation $E = mc^2$

17. **Assertion** Force applied on a block moving in one dimension is producing a constant power, then the motion should be uniformly accelerated.

    Reason This constant power multiplied with time is equal to the change in kinetic energy.

Answer

CASE BASED QUESTIONS

Direction (Q. Nos. 18) *This question is case study based questions. Attempt any 4 sub-parts from each question.*

18. **PE of Spring**

    There are many types of spring. Important among these are helical and spiral springs as shown in figure.

    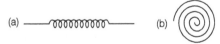

    Usually, we assume that the springs are massless. Therefore, work done is stored in the spring in the form of elastic potential energy of the spring. Thus, potential energy of a spring is the energy associated with the state of compression or expansion of an elastic spring.

    (i) The potential energy of a body is increases in which of the following cases?
    (a) If work is done by conservative force
    (b) If work is done against conservative force
    (c) If work is done by non-conservative force
    (d) If work is done against non- conservative force

(ii) The potential energy, i.e. $U(x)$ can be assumed zero when
(a) $x = 0$
(b) gravitational force is constant
(c) infinite distance from the gravitational source
(d) All of the above

(iii) The ratio of spring constants of two springs is $2 : 3$. What is the ratio of their potential energy, if they are stretched by the same force?
(a) $2 : 3$ (b) $3 : 2$ (c) $4 : 9$ (d) $9 : 4$

(iv) The potential energy of a spring increases by 15 J when stretched by 3 cm. If it is stretched by 4 cm, the increase in potential energy is
(a) 27 J   (b) 30 J
(c) 33 J   (d) 36 J

(v) The potential energy of a spring when stretched through a distance x is 10 J. What is the amount of work done on the same spring to stretch it through an additional distance x?
(a) 10 J   (b) 20 J   (c) 30 J   (d) 40 J

Answer

1. (a)	2. (a)	3. (b)	4. (d)	5. (d)
6. (a)	7. (d)	8. (c)	9. (a)	10. (b)
11. (a)	12. (d)	13. (a)	14. (a)	15. (a)
16. (a)	17. (d)			
18. (i) (b)	(ii) (d)	(iii) (b)	(iv) (a)	(v) (c)

VERY SHORT ANSWER Type Questions

19. How much work is done by mass M moving once around a horizontal circle of radius r?

20. Does the work done in moving a body depend upon how fast the body is moved?

21. Define spring constant of a spring. Give its SI unit.

22. Friction is a non-conservative force. Why?

23. What is coefficient of restitution?

24. A person walking on a horizontal road with a load on his head does no work. Why?

25. Find the work done in moving a particle along a vector $s = (2\hat{i} - 3\hat{j} + \hat{k})$ metre, if applied force is $\mathbf{F} = (\hat{i} - 2\hat{j} + 3\hat{k})$N.   [**Ans.** -6J]

SHORT ANSWER Type Questions

26. Calculate the kinetic energy of a body of mass 0.1 kg, if its linear momentum is 20 kg-m/s.
    [**Ans.** 2000 J]

27. Momentum of a body is doubled. What is the percentage increase in kinetic energy ? [**Ans.** 100%]

28. Find the average frictional force needed to stop a car weighing 800 kg running with an initial speed of 54 km/h with a distance of 25 m.
    [**Ans.** 3600 N]

29. A steel spring of spring constant 150 N/m is compressed from its natural position through a mud wall 1m thick, the speed of bullet drops to 100 m/s. Calculate the average resistance of the wall. Neglect friction of air.   [**Ans.** 0.12 J]

30. Two balls of mass m, each moving in opposite direction with a speed v collide head-on with each other. How will they move after collision, assuming it to be perfectly elastic?

LONG ANSWER Type I Questions

31. About 4×10^{10} kg of matter per second is converted into energy in the central core of the Sun. What is the power output of the Sun?
    [**Ans.** 3.6×10^{27} W]

32. A fast moving neutron make a head-on elastic collision with a stationary deuteron. What fraction of its initial kinetic energy is lost by the neutron during collision?
    $\left[\textbf{Ans. } \dfrac{8}{9}\right]$

33. Briefly describe the mechanism of the functioning of heavy water as moderator in nuclear reactors.

34. 1 mg of uranium is completely destroyed in an atomic bomb. How much energy is liberated?
    [**Ans.** 9×10^{10}]

35. A block of mass 1.2 kg moving at a speed of 20 cm/s collides head-on with a similar block kept at rest. The coefficient of restitution is 3/5, find the loss of kinetic energy during collision.
    [**Ans.** 7.7×10^{-3} J]

36. (i) What is the power of a centripetal force in circular motion?
    (ii) A pump can take out 7200 kg of water per hour from a well 100m deep. Calculate the power of the pump, assuming that its efficiency is 50%. ($g = 10$ ms^{-2})   [**Ans.** 4 kW]
    (iii) An elevator which can carry a maximum load of 1800 kg is moving up with a constant speed of 2m/s. The frictional force opposing the motion is 4000 N. Determine the maximum power delivered by the motor to the elevator in horse power.   [**Ans.** 59 hp]

37. (i) Define the term instantaneous power and write its relation with velocity.
    (ii) A machine gun fire 240 bullets per minute. If the mass of each bullet is 10 g and the velocity of the bullets is 600 ms^{-1}, then find power (in kW) of th gun. [**Ans.** 7.2 kW]
    (iii) A motor pumps up 1000 kg of water through length of 10 m in 5s. If the efficiency of the motor is 60%, then calculate the power of the motor in kilowatt.

LONG ANSWER Type II Questions

38. Two balls A and B of masses 0.3 kg and 0.2 kg respectively are moving along positive x-axis and negative x-axis with velocity 20 m/s. They collide and thereafter move in the direction opposite to their original direction. Find the velocity of A and B after collision. Also, calculate total KE of the balls before and after collision.   [**Ans.** 1.0 J]

39. A projectile proton with a speed of 500 m/s collide elastically with a target proton initially at rest. The two protons then move along perpendicular paths, with the projectile path at 60° from the original direction. After collision, what are the speed of (i) the target proton? (ii) The projectile proton?   [**Ans.** 433 m/s, 250 m/s]

40. A body of mass 2 kg makes an elastic collision with another body at rest and continuous to move in the original direction but one-fourth of its original speed. (i) what is the mass of the other body ? (ii) what is the speed of the two body centre of mass if initial speed of 2 kg body was 4.0 m/s?   [**Ans.** 1.2 kg, 2.5 m/s]

06

In earlier cases, we considered every object as point mass. Even the finite size objects are considered as point mass to understand their motion.

An extended body (any finite size body) is a system of particles. Hence, now we will consider the motion of system. To understand the motion of a system (extended body), we will understand the concept of centre of mass of a system of particles.

SYSTEM OF PARTICLES AND ROTATIONAL MOTION

|TOPIC 1|
Centre of Mass and Rotational Motion

RIGID BODY

Ideally, a body is said to be a rigid body when it has a perfectly definite shape and size. The distance between all pairs of particles of such a body do not change while applying any force on it.

e.g. A wheel can be considered as rigid body by ignoring a little change in its shape.

Kinds of Motion of a Rigid Body

A rigid body can possess pure translational motion, pure rotational motion or a combination of both these motions. Let us explore these kinds of motions one by one.

Pure Translational Motion

This type of motion in which every particle of the body moves through the same linear distance in a straight line and in a given time interval is known as **pure translational motion**.

CHAPTER CHECKLIST
• Rigid Body
• Centre of Mass
• Linear Momentum of a System of Particles
• Torque and Angular Momentum
• Equilibrium of a Rigid Body
• Centre of Gravity
• Moment of Inertia
• Rolling Motion

In pure translational motion, at any instant of time all particles of the body have the same velocity.

In pure translational motion, all the particles of body are moving along parallel paths.

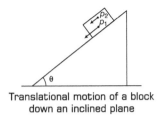

Translational motion of a block
down an inclined plane

Rotational Motion (Fixed Axis of Rotation)

In pure rotational motion, every particle of the rigid body moves in circles of different radii about a fixed line, which is known as **axis of rotation**. e.g.

(i) Consider an oscillating fan as shown in figure. When the fan rotates, the particle A revolves in a circle of radius r_1 and particle B revolves in a circle of radius r_2. Hence, the axis moves side wise, and these points are fixed.

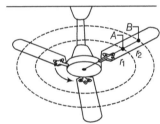

A rotating ceiling fan with the particles
and   moving in circular paths

(ii) The following figure shows the rotational motion of a rigid body about a fixed axis, i.e. z-axis.

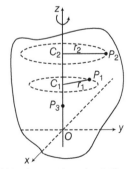

A rigid body rotating about the z-axis

The body is in xy-plane. Let P_1 be a particle of the rigid body arbitrarily chosen at a distance r_1 from the fixed axis, i.e. z-axis.

The particle P_1 describes a circle of radius r_1 with its centre C_1 on the fixed axis and the circle lies in a plane, perpendicular to the axis.

The another particle P_2 of the body describes a circle of radius r_2 with centre at C_2 lying on the same z-axis and lies in a plane perpendicular to the axis of rotation.

The circles described by P_1 and P_2 may lie in different planes, both these planes are perpendicular to the fixed axis. For any particle on the axis of rotation like $P_3, r = 0$. Therefore, such a particle remains stationary, while the body rotates.

Some of the examples of pure rotation about an axis are given as,

A potter's wheel, a giant wheel in a circus, a merry-go-round etc.

Note

- In pure rotational motion, the plane of the circle in which any particle moves, is always perpendicular to the fixed axis of rotation and has its centre on the axis.
- The particle on the axis of rotation remains stationary.

Precession

In **precession**, one end of axis of rotation is fixed and other end rotates about a circular path.

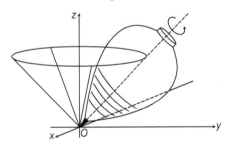

A spinning top is in precession

(i) The point of contact of the top with ground is fixed. The axis of rotation of the top at any instant passes through the point of contact.

(ii) We mostly deal with the case of fixed axis, so if not stated rotation will be about the fixed axis.

(iii) Oscillating table fan is also an example of precession.

Combination of Translational and Rotational Motions

A rigid body may have a rolling motion, which is a combination of rotation and translation.

e.g. Consider a cylinder rolls down an inclined plane, its motion is the combination of rotation about a fixed axis and translation.

When the cylinder shifts from top to bottom, the points P_1, P_2, P_3, P_4 on this cylinder have different velocities at a particular instant of time. But if the cylinder were to roll without slipping, the velocity of point of contact P_3 would be zero at any instant of time.

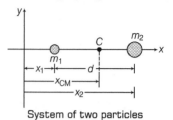

A cylinder rolling down

In rolling motion, body is rotating along a fixed line, an axis of rotation and that axis of rotation is in translatory motion. Hence, the motion of a rigid body in some way is either a pure translation or a combination of translation and rotation.

In general, motion of a rigid body is a combination of translation and rotation. As in case of our base ball bat.

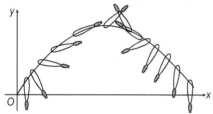

Base ball bat neither in pure translation nor in pure rotation but in the combination

Note

The motion of a rigid body which is not pivoted or fixed in some way is either pure translational or a combination of translational and rotational. The motion of a rigid body which is pivoted or fixed in some way is pure rotation.

CENTRE OF MASS

The centre of mass of a body or a system of bodies is the point which moves as though all of the mass were concentrated there and all external forces were applied to it.

Hence, a point at which the entire mass of the body or system of bodies is supposed to be concentrated is known as the **centre of mass**.

For a System of Two Particles

Let the distances of the two particles be x_1 and x_2 respectively from origin O. Let m_1 and m_2 be their masses. The centre of mass of the system is that point C which is at a distance x_{CM} from O, where x_{CM} is given by

$$x_{CM} = \frac{m_1 x_1 + m_2 x_2}{m_1 + m_2}$$

$$\boxed{\text{Centre of mass, } x_{CM} = \frac{m_1 x_1 + m_2 x_2}{M}}$$

where, $M = m_1 + m_2 = $ total mass of system.

Hence, the centre of mass of a two particles system is such that the product of total mass of the system and the position vector of centre of mass is equal to sum of the products of masses of the two particles and their respective position vectors.

System of two particles

x_{CM} can be regarded as the mass-weighted mean of x_1 and x_2. If the two particles have the same mass $m_1 = m_2 = m$, then

$$x_{CM} = \frac{m x_1 + m x_2}{2m} = \frac{x_1 + x_2}{2}$$

Thus, for two particles of equal mass, the centre of mass lies exactly midway between them.

EXAMPLE |1| A Two Body System

Two bodies of masses 1 kg and 2 kg are located at (1, 2) and $(-1, 3)$, respectively. Calculate the coordinates of the centre of mass.

Sol. Given, $m_1 = 1\,\text{kg}, \quad m_2 = 2\,\text{kg}$

$$x_1 = 1\,\text{m}, \quad x_2 = -1\,\text{m}$$
$$y_1 = 2\,\text{m}, \quad y_2 = 3\,\text{m}$$
$$\therefore \quad x_{CM} = \frac{m_1 x_1 + m_2 x_2}{m_1 + m_2} = \frac{1 \times 1 + 2 \times -1}{1 + 2}$$
$$= \frac{1-2}{3} = \frac{-1}{3} = -0.33$$
$$\text{and} \quad y_{CM} = \frac{m_1 y_1 + m_2 y_2}{m_1 + m_2} = \frac{1 \times 2 + 2 \times 3}{1 + 2}$$
$$= \frac{2+6}{3} = \frac{8}{3} = 2.66$$

Thus, the coordinates of centre of mass are $(-0.33, 2.66)$.

Note

The centre of mass of a system of two particles lies on the straight line joining the two particles.

For a System of n Particles

Suppose a system of n particles having masses $m_1, m_2, m_3, ..., m_n$ occupying x-coordinates $x_1, x_2, x_3, ..., x_n$.

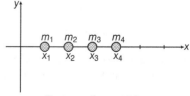

System of n particles

i.e. x_{CM} = x-coordinates of centre of mass of system

$$= \frac{m_1 x_1 + m_2 x_2 + m_3 x_3 + \cdots + m_n x_n}{m_1 + m_2 + m_3 + \cdots + m_n}$$

$$\boxed{\text{Centre of mass, } x_{CM} = \frac{\sum\limits_{i=1}^{n} m_i x_i}{\sum m_i}}$$

Consider three particles of masses m_1, m_2 and m_3 are lying at points $(x_1, y_1), (x_2, y_2)$ and (x_3, y_3), respectively. Then, the centre of mass of the system of these three particles lies at a point whose coordinates (X, Y) are given by

$$X = \frac{m_1 x_1 + m_2 x_2 + m_3 x_3}{m_1 + m_2 + m_3}$$

and

$$Y = \frac{m_1 y_1 + m_2 y_2 + m_3 y_3}{m_1 + m_2 + m_3}$$

For the particles of equal mass $m = m_1 = m_2 = m_3$, then

$$X = \frac{mx_1 + mx_2 + mx_3}{m + m + m} = \frac{x_1 + x_2 + x_3}{3}$$

and

$$Y = \frac{my_1 + my_2 + my_3}{m + m + m} = \frac{y_1 + y_2 + y_3}{3}$$

If particles are distributed in three-dimensional space, then the centre of mass has 3-coordinates, which are

$$x_{CM} = \frac{1}{M} \sum_{i=1}^{n} m_i x_i, \quad y_{CM} = \frac{1}{M} \sum_{i=1}^{n} m_i y_i$$

and

$$z_{CM} = \frac{1}{M} \sum_{i=1}^{n} m_i z_i$$

where, $M = m_1 + m_2 + \cdots = \sum_{i=1}^{n} m_i$ is the total mass of the system. The index i runs from 1 to n, m_i is the mass of the ith particle and the position of the ith particle is given by (x_i, y_i, z_i).

EXAMPLE |2| **An Equilateral Triangle**
Three masses 3 kg, 4 kg and 5 kg are located at the corners of an equilateral triangle of side 1m , then what are the coordinates of centre of mass of this system.

Sol. Suppose the equilateral triangle lies in the xy-plane with mass 3 kg at the origin.

Let (x, y) be the coordinates of centre of mass.

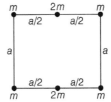

Clearly, $AB = \sqrt{(OB)^2 - (OA)^2} = \sqrt{(1)^2 - \left(\frac{1}{2}\right)^2} = \frac{\sqrt{3}}{2}$m

Now, $x_1 = 0, x_2 = 1m, x_3 = OA = 0.5m$

$m_1 = 3\,kg, m_2 = 4\,kg, m_3 = 5\,kg$

$\therefore \quad x = \frac{m_1 x_1 + m_2 x_2 + m_3 x_3}{m_1 + m_2 + m_3}$

$= \frac{3 \times 0 + 4 \times 1 + 5 \times 0.5}{3 + 4 + 5}$

$= \frac{6.5}{12} = 0.54\,m$

Again, $y_1 = 0, y_2 = 0, y_3 = AB = \frac{\sqrt{3}}{2}$,

$\therefore \quad y = \frac{m_1 y_1 + m_2 y_2 + m_3 y_3}{m_1 + m_2 + m_3}$

$= \frac{3 \times 0 + 4 \times 0 + 5 \times \left(\dfrac{\sqrt{3}}{2}\right)}{3 + 4 + 5}$

$= \frac{5 \times \sqrt{3}}{2 \times 12} = 0.36\,m$

Thus, the coordinate of centre of mass are (0.54 m, 0.36 m).

EXAMPLE |3| **Centre of Mass of Six Particles**
Six particles are placed at different points of a square as shown in the figure. Find the centre of mass for the system of six particles.

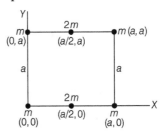

Sol. First of all consider a coordinate system for the given system of particles.

Now, apply the formula for the X-component of centre of mass.

$$X_{CM} = \frac{2m \times a/2 + 2m \times a/2 + m \times a + m \times a}{m + 2m + m + m + 2m + m}$$

$$= \frac{4ma}{8m} = \frac{a}{2}$$

Now, apply the formula for the Y-component of centre of mass.

$$Y_{CM} = \frac{m \times a + 2m \times a + m \times a}{8m} = \frac{4ma}{8m} = \frac{a}{2}$$

So, the coordinates of centre of mass should be written as

$$(X_{CM}, Y_{CM}) = \left(\frac{a}{2}, \frac{a}{2}\right)$$

Relation between Position Vectors of Particles and Centre of Mass

We can also define centre of mass in terms of vector. Let $\mathbf{r}_i$ be the position vector of the ith particle and $\mathbf{R}$ be the position vector of the centre of mass, then

$$\mathbf{r}_i = x_i \hat{\mathbf{i}} + y_i \hat{\mathbf{j}} + z_i \hat{\mathbf{k}}$$

and

$$\mathbf{R} = x\hat{\mathbf{i}} + y\hat{\mathbf{j}} + z\hat{\mathbf{k}}$$

> Position vector of the centre of mass, $\mathbf{R} = \dfrac{\sum\limits_{i=1}^{n} m_i \mathbf{r}_i}{m}$

If the origin of the frame of reference is considered at the centre of mass, then

$$\mathbf{R}_{CM} = 0$$

So,

$$\sum_{i=1}^{n} m_i \mathbf{r}_i = 0$$

Centre of Mass of Rigid Continuous Bodies

For a real body which is a continuous distribution of matter, point masses are then differential mass elements dm and centre of mass is defined as

$$x_{CM} = \frac{1}{M}\int x\, dm, \quad y_{CM} = \frac{1}{M}\int y\, dm$$

$$z_{CM} = \frac{1}{M}\int z\, dm$$

where, M is total mass of that real body.

If we choose the origin of coordinates axes at centre of mass then,

$$\int x\, dm = \int y\, dm = \int z\, dm = 0$$

Position of the Centre of Mass in the Absence of External Force

In the absence of an external force, the position of the centre of mass of a stationary system does not change. However, if under the influence of external forces, the position of different particles of masses $m_1, m_2, m_3, \ldots$ changes by $\Delta\mathbf{r}_1, \Delta\mathbf{r}_2, \ldots$ then shift in the position vector of the centre of mass is given by

$$\Delta\mathbf{r}_{CM} = \frac{m_1\Delta\mathbf{r}_1 + m_2\Delta\mathbf{r}_2 + \ldots + m_n\Delta\mathbf{r}_n}{m_1 + m_2 + \ldots + m_n} = \frac{\sum\limits_{i=1}^{n} m_i \Delta\mathbf{r}_i}{\sum\limits_{i=1}^{n} m_i}$$

EXAMPLE |4| **Particles at the Corner of a Square**

If four particles of mass 1kg, 2kg, 3kg and 4kg are placed at the four vertices A, B, C and D of square of side 1m. Find the position of the centre of mass of the particle.

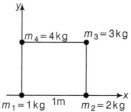

Sol. Observing the figure,

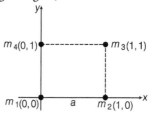

Coordinates of m_1, $x_1 = 0$, $y_1 = 0$

Coordinates of m_2, $x_2 = 1$, $y_2 = 0$

Coordinates of m_3, $x_3 = 1$, $y_3 = 1$

Coordinates of m_4, $x_4 = 0$, $y_4 = 1$

$$\therefore \quad x_{CM} = \frac{m_1 x_1 + m_2 x_2 + m_3 x_3 + m_4 x_4}{m_1 + m_2 + m_3 + m_4}$$

$$= \frac{(1)(0) + (2)(1) + (3)(1) + (4)(0)}{1 + 2 + 3 + 4}$$

$$= \frac{5}{10} = 0.5 \text{ m}$$

Now, $y_{CM} = \dfrac{m_1 y_1 + m_2 y_2 + m_3 y_3 + m_4 y_4}{m_1 + m_2 + m_3 + m_4}$

$$= \frac{(1)(0) + (2)(0) + (3)(1) + (4)(1)}{1 + 2 + 3 + 4}$$

$$= \frac{7}{10} = 0.7 \text{ m}$$

Thus, centre of mass is located at (0.5m, 0.7m).

Centre of Mass of a Uniform Thin Rod

Let us consider a uniform thin rod AB of mass M and length L. The rod is held along x-axis with its end A at the origin, where $x = y = 0$, as shown in figure. Suppose the element is placed side by side of length dx at distance i.e. x from the origin.

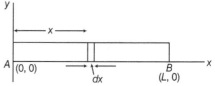

Calculation of centre of mass of a uniform thin rod

Then, mass of element $dm = \dfrac{M}{L} dx$

Let (x_{CM}, y_{CM}) be the coordinates of centre of mass of thin rod from origin. Then,

$$x_{CM} = \frac{1}{M} \int_0^L x \, dm = \frac{1}{M} \int_0^L x \left(\frac{M}{L}\right) dx = \frac{1}{L} \frac{x^2}{2}\Big|_0^L = \frac{L}{2}$$

Centre of mass, $x_{CM} = \dfrac{L}{2}$

and $\qquad y_{CM} = \dfrac{1}{M} \int y \, dm = 0 \quad [\because y = 0 \text{ for thin rod}]$

$$y_{CM} = 0$$

Thus, it means that the centre of mass of thin rod AB lies at point $\left(\dfrac{L}{2}, 0\right)$ i.e. centre between its ends A and B. Thus, the centre of mass coincides with geometric centre.

MOTION OF CENTRE OF MASS

As already defined for a system of n particles, we can relate position vector of centre of mass and that of individual masses as

$$M \cdot \mathbf{r}_{CM} = m_1 \mathbf{r}_1 + m_2 \mathbf{r}_2 + m_3 \mathbf{r}_3 + \cdots + m_n \mathbf{r}_n$$

Differentiating with respect to time, we get

$$M \cdot \frac{d}{dt} \mathbf{r}_{CM} = m_1 \frac{d}{dt} \mathbf{r}_1 + m_2 \frac{d}{dt} \mathbf{r}_2 + \cdots + m_n \frac{d}{dt} \mathbf{r}_n$$

As masses are constants and only position vectors are variables

$$\Rightarrow M \cdot \mathbf{v}_{CM} = m_1 \mathbf{v}_1 + m_2 \mathbf{v}_2 + m_3 \mathbf{v}_3 + \cdots + m_n \mathbf{v}_n$$

So, $\boxed{\text{Velocity about centre of mass, } \mathbf{v}_{CM} = \dfrac{\sum\limits_{i=1}^{n} m_i \mathbf{v}_i}{M}}$

where, $\mathbf{v} = \dfrac{d\mathbf{r}}{dt}$, rate of change of position vector is velocity.

Again differentiating the result, we get

$$M \frac{d}{dt} \mathbf{v}_{CM} = m_1 \frac{d}{dt} \mathbf{v}_1 + m_2 \frac{d}{dt} \mathbf{v}_2 + m_3 \frac{d}{dt} \mathbf{v}_3 + \cdots + m_n \frac{d}{dt} \mathbf{v}_n$$

As rate of change of velocity is acceleration, we write

$$a = \frac{dv}{dt}$$

$$M \mathbf{a}_{CM} = m_1 \mathbf{a}_1 + m_2 \mathbf{a}_2 + \cdots + m_n \mathbf{a}_n$$

So, $\boxed{\text{Acceleration about centre of mass, } \mathbf{a}_{CM} = \dfrac{\sum\limits_{i=1}^{n} m_i \mathbf{a}_i}{M}}$

But, $m_i \mathbf{a}_i$ is the resultant force on the ith particle, so

$$M \mathbf{a}_{CM} = \mathbf{F}_1 + \mathbf{F}_2 + \mathbf{F}_3 + \cdots + \mathbf{F}_n$$

or $\qquad M \mathbf{a}_{CM} = \mathbf{F}_{net, ext} \qquad \qquad \text{...(i)}$

where, $\mathbf{F}_{net, ext} = \mathbf{F}_1 + \mathbf{F}_2 + \mathbf{F}_3 + \cdots + \mathbf{F}_n$ is net force of all external forces that act on the system.

From the expression (i), it is clear that the centre of mass of a system of particles moves as if whole mass of the system was concentrated at the centre of mass and all the external forces were applied at that point.

Internal forces are action-reaction pairs and hence, cancels out and only vector sum of external forces remains.
e.g. If a rocket explodes in its path and fragment flies in all directions.

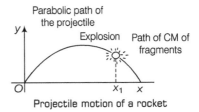

Projectile motion of a rocket

As explosion forces are internal to the system, they did not contribute to motion of centre of mass and centre of mass of rocket follows same parabolic trajectory that rocket would have followed if it **would not be exploded.**

So, motion of centre of mass of a system or object is not affected by any of internal forces or they occur always on action-reaction pairs and so their net contribution to acceleration of centre of mass is zero.

Note
The translational motion of extended bodies could be understand with the help of the motion of centre of mass of the system, by considering that the total mass of the system is concentrated on the centre of mass and as all the external forces are acting at the centre of mass.

LINEAR MOMENTUM OF A SYSTEM OF PARTICLES

For a system of n particles, total linear momentum is vector sum of linear momenta of individual particles. Where linear momentum of an individual particle is product of its mass and velocity ($\mathbf{p} = m\mathbf{v}$).

So, linear momentum of system is

$$\mathbf{p} = \mathbf{p}_1 + \mathbf{p}_2 + \mathbf{p}_3 + \cdots + \mathbf{p}_n$$

or $\qquad \mathbf{p} = m_1 \mathbf{v}_1 + m_2 \mathbf{v}_2 + m_3 \mathbf{v}_3 + \cdots + m_n \mathbf{v}_n \qquad \text{...(i)}$

From the concept of centre of mass, we know that

$$m_1 \mathbf{v}_1 + m_2 \mathbf{v}_2 + m_3 \mathbf{v}_3 + \cdots + m_n \mathbf{v}_n = M \cdot \mathbf{V}_{CM} \quad \text{...(ii)}$$

From Eqs. (i) and (ii), we get

$$\boxed{\text{Total linear momentum, } \mathbf{p} = M\mathbf{V}_{CM}} \qquad \ldots\text{(iii)}$$

Thus, the total momentum of a system of particles is equal to the product of the total mass and velocity of its centre of mass.

Newton's Second Law for System of Particles

Now, differentiating Eq. (iii) with respect to time, we get

$$\frac{d}{dt}\mathbf{p} = \frac{d}{dt}M\mathbf{V}_{CM}$$

or $\qquad \frac{d\mathbf{p}}{dt} = M\frac{d}{dt}\mathbf{V}_{CM} \quad$ [if M is constant]

or $\qquad \frac{d\mathbf{p}}{dt} = M\mathbf{A}_{CM} \qquad \ldots\text{(iv)}$

From centre of mass concept, we know

$$M\mathbf{A}_{CM} = \text{net external force} \qquad \ldots\text{(v)}$$

From Eqs. (iv) and (v), we get

$$\therefore \quad \boxed{\text{Net external force, } \mathbf{F}_{ext} = \frac{d\mathbf{p}}{dt}} \qquad \ldots\text{(vi)}$$

Above expression represents Newton's second law for system of particles. Here, $\mathbf{p}$ is net momentum of the system and $\mathbf{F}_{ext}$ is the net external force applied on the system.

Conservation of Linear Momentum for System of particles

If external force is not acting on the system of particles,

$$\mathbf{F}_{ext} = 0, \text{ then } \frac{d\mathbf{p}}{dt} = 0$$

or **rate of change of momentum is zero, i.e. momentum of system remains constant.**

So, $\qquad \mathbf{p}_{initial} = \mathbf{p}_{final}, \text{ if } \mathbf{F}_{ext} = 0 \qquad \ldots\text{(vii)}$

Above expression represents the law of conservation of linear momentum for system of particles.

If mass of the system is constant, then

$$M\mathbf{V}_{CM} = \text{constant} \qquad [\because \mathbf{F}_{ext} = 0]$$
$$\mathbf{V}_{CM} = \text{constant} \qquad \ldots\text{(viii)}$$

Eq. (viii) shows that if the mass of system of particles is constant and if **net external force on the system is zero, then the velocity of centre of mass of the system will remain constant.**

The vector equation $\frac{d\mathbf{p}}{dt} = 0$ or $p = $ constant is equivalent to three equations, $\mathbf{p}_x = C_1$, $\mathbf{p}_y = C_2$ and $\mathbf{p}_z = C_3$,

where $\mathbf{p}_x$, $\mathbf{p}_y$ and $\mathbf{p}_z$ are the components of the total linear momentum vector $\mathbf{p}$ along x, y and z-axes respectively C_1, C_2 and C_3 are constants.

EXAMPLE |5| Enjoying the Ride of a Trolley

A child sits stationary at one end of a long trolley moving uniformly with a speed v on smooth horizontal floor. If child gets up and runs about on the trolley in any manner, what is the speed of CM of the (trolley + child) system?

[NCERT]

Sol. When the child gets up and runs about on the trolley, he is exerting an internal force on the trolley-child system.

Thus, no external force acts on the system. So, centre of mass is not accelerated. Hence, centre of mass of trolley-child system remains same as before, i.e.v.

EXAMPLE |6| Acceleration of the Position Vectors

If two particles of masses $m_1 = 2$ kg and $m_2 = 3$ kg have position vectors $\mathbf{r}_1 = t\hat{i} + 2t^2\hat{j} + 2t\hat{k}$ and $\mathbf{r}_2 = \hat{i} + 2t^3\hat{j} + 5\hat{k}$ respectively, then the position vector of r_1 and r_2 is in metres and time is in seconds. Calculate the velocity and acceleration of centre of mass of two particles system.

Sol. Here, $m_1 = 2$ kg, $m_2 = 3$ kg and position vectors

$$\mathbf{r}_1 = t\hat{i} + 2t^2\hat{j} + 2t\hat{k}$$

and $\qquad \mathbf{r}_2 = \hat{i} + 2t^3\hat{j} + 5\hat{k}$

Now, velocity of first particle, $\mathbf{v}_1 = \dfrac{d}{dt}(\mathbf{r}_1)$

$$= \frac{d}{dt}(t\hat{i} + 2t^2\hat{j} + 2t\hat{k})$$
$$= \hat{i} + 4t\hat{j} + 2\hat{k}$$

Velocity of second particle,

$$\mathbf{v}_2 = \frac{d}{dt}(\mathbf{r}_2)$$
$$= \frac{d}{dt}(\hat{i} + 2t^3\hat{j} + 5\hat{k}) = 6t^2\hat{j}$$

$\therefore$ Velocity of centre of mass of two particles system is

$$\mathbf{v}_{CM} = \frac{m_1\mathbf{v}_1 + m_2\mathbf{v}_2}{m_1 + m_2}$$
$$= \frac{2\times(\hat{i} + 4t\hat{j} + 2\hat{k}) + 3\times(6t^2\hat{j})}{2 + 3}$$
$$= \frac{2\hat{i} + (8t + 18t^2)\hat{j} + 4\hat{k}}{5}$$
$$= \left[\frac{2}{5}\hat{i} + \frac{(8t + 18t^2)}{5}\hat{j} + \frac{4}{5}\hat{k}\right] m/s$$

Now, acceleration of first particle,

$$\mathbf{a}_1 = \frac{d}{dt}(\mathbf{v}_1) = \frac{d}{dt}(\hat{i} + 4t\hat{j} + 2\hat{k}) = 4\hat{j}$$

Acceleration of second particle

$$\mathbf{a}_2 = \frac{d}{dt}(\mathbf{v}_2) = \frac{d}{dt}(6\,t^2\hat{\mathbf{j}}) = 12t\,\hat{\mathbf{j}}$$

∴ Acceleration of centre of mass of two particles system is calculated as

$$\mathbf{a}_{CM} = \frac{m_1\mathbf{a}_1 + m_2\mathbf{a}_2}{m_1 + m_2}$$

$$= \frac{2(4\,\hat{\mathbf{j}}) + 3(12\,t\,\hat{\mathbf{j}})}{2+3}$$

$$\mathbf{a}_{CM} = \left[\frac{(8+36\,t)}{5}\,\hat{\mathbf{j}}\right] m/s^2$$

TORQUE AND ANGULAR MOMENTUM

The two physical quantities torque and angular momentum are to be discussed as vector products of two vectors.

Moment of Force (Torque)

Torque is also known as **moment of force** or **couple**. When a force acts on a particle, the particle does not merely move in the direction of the force but it also turns about some point.

So, we can define the torque for a particle about a point as the vector product of position vector of the point where the force acts and with the force itself. Let us consider a particle P and force $\mathbf{F}$ acting on it.

Let the position vector of point of application of force about O is $\mathbf{r}$.

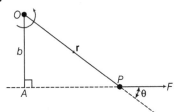

Particle showing torque, position vector and force

From figure, the torque τ acting on the particle relative to the fixed point O is a vector quantity and is defined as

$$\boxed{\text{Torque}, \tau = \mathbf{r} \times \mathbf{F}}$$

The magnitude of torque $|\tau|$ is

$$\tau = rF\sin\theta$$

$$= Fr\sin\theta$$

$$\tau = Fr_\perp = Fb \text{ (from figure)}$$

Here, $r_\perp$ is the perpendicular distance of the line of action of $\mathbf{F}$ from the point O.

Magnitude of torque can also be described as

$$\tau = rF\sin\theta$$

$$\tau = rF_\perp$$

Here, $F_\perp$ is the component of $\mathbf{F}$ in the direction perpendicular to $\mathbf{r}$.

Note

Torque could be zero ($\tau = 0$), if

$$r = 0 \quad \text{or} \quad F = 0 \quad \text{or} \quad \theta = 0, 180°$$

In SI system, torque is expressed in Newton-metre (N-m), it has same dimensions as that of workdone. Dimensions of torque are $[ML^2T^{-2}]$.

According to vector product, torque is perpendicular to the plane of $\mathbf{r}$ and $\mathbf{F}$ as shown below.

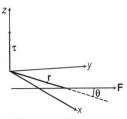

Plane showing torque perpendicular to force

If the body is rotating counterclockwise, then the torque is taken positive otherwise negative.

EXAMPLE |7| Finding the Torque

Find the torque of a force $7\hat{\mathbf{i}} + 3\hat{\mathbf{j}} - 5\hat{\mathbf{k}}$ about the origin. The force acts on a particle whose position vector is $\hat{\mathbf{i}} - \hat{\mathbf{j}} + \hat{\mathbf{k}}$. **[NCERT]**

Sol. Given, position vector

$$\mathbf{r} = \hat{\mathbf{i}} - \hat{\mathbf{j}} + \hat{\mathbf{k}}$$

Force, $\mathbf{F} = 7\hat{\mathbf{i}} + 3\hat{\mathbf{j}} - 5\hat{\mathbf{k}}$

Torque, $\tau = ?$

$$\tau = \mathbf{r} \times \mathbf{F} = \begin{vmatrix} \hat{\mathbf{i}} & \hat{\mathbf{j}} & \hat{\mathbf{k}} \\ 1 & -1 & 1 \\ 7 & 3 & -5 \end{vmatrix}$$

$$= (5-3)\hat{\mathbf{i}} - (-5-7)\hat{\mathbf{j}} + (3+7)\hat{\mathbf{k}} = 2\hat{\mathbf{i}} + 12\hat{\mathbf{j}} + 10\hat{\mathbf{k}}$$

Angular Momentum of a Particle

Angular momentum (L) can be defined as **moment of linear momentum** about a point.

The angular momentum of a particle of mass m moving with velocity $\mathbf{v}$ (having a linear momentum $\mathbf{p} = m\mathbf{v}$) about a point O is defined by the following vector product.

$$\mathbf{L} = \mathbf{r} \times \mathbf{p}$$

or $\boxed{\text{Angular momentum, } \mathbf{L} = m(\mathbf{r} \times \mathbf{v})}$

L is angular momentum of particle about point O.
r is position vector of the particle about point O.

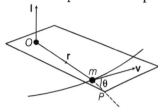

A particle moving about a point

Magnitude of angular momentum depends on the position of point O and is given by $L = mvr \sin \theta$
where, θ = angle between r and v
L can be represented as $L = rp \sin \theta = rp_\perp$

where, $p_\perp$ ($p \sin \theta$) is the component of p in a direction perpendicular to r.
and $L = pr \sin \theta = pr_\perp$
where, $r_\perp$ is the perpendicular distance of the linear momentum vector (p) from origin.

EXAMPLE |8| Revolving Electron in an Atom

In a hydrogen atom, electron revolves in a circular orbit of radius 0.53 Å with a velocity of 2.2×10^6 m/s with an angle 30°. If the mass of electron is 9×10^{-31} kg. Find its angular momentum.

Sol. Given, $r = 0.53 \text{Å} = 0.53 \times 10^{-10}$ m

$$m = 9 \times 10^{-31} \text{ kg}, v = 2.2 \times 10^6 \text{ m/s},$$
$$\theta = 30°, L = ?$$
$$L = mvr \sin \theta$$
$$= 9 \times 10^{-31} \times 2.2 \times 10^6 \times 0.53 \times 10^{-10} \times \sin 30°$$
$$= 5.247 \times 10^{-3} \text{ kg-m}^2/\text{s}$$

Relation between Torque and Angular Momentum

As angular momentum,
$$L = r \times p \text{ or } L = m (r \times v)$$
Differentiating with respect to time,
$$\frac{dL}{dt} = \frac{d}{dt} m(r \times v)$$
or
$$\frac{dL}{dt} = m\left(\frac{dr}{dt} \times v + r \times \frac{dv}{dt}\right)$$
[from product rule of differentiation]
But
$$\frac{dr}{dt} = v \text{ and } v \times v = 0$$
So,
$$\frac{dL}{dt} = m\left(r \times \frac{dv}{dt}\right)$$

But
$$\frac{dv}{dt} = a = \text{acceleration}$$
$$= m(r \times a) = (r \times ma) = r \times F$$
As
$$\tau = r \times F$$
∴
Rate of change of angular momentum, $\dfrac{dL}{dt} = \tau$

Above equation gives Newton's second law of motion in angular form, **rate of change of angular momentum is equal to the torque applied.**

Torque and Angular Momentum for a System of Particles

For a system of particles or a rigid body with n-particles, the total angular momentum of the system is the vector sum of the angular momenta of the individual particles.

$$L = L_1 + L_2 + L_3 + \cdots + L_n = \sum_{i=1}^{n} L_i$$

Differentiating the above expression with time,

$$\frac{dL}{dt} = \sum_{i=1}^{n} \frac{dL_i}{dt}$$

But $\sum_{i=1}^{n} \dfrac{dL_i}{dt}$ is the net torque on the system so, $\dfrac{dL}{dt} = \tau_{\text{net}}$

Above expression shows Newton's second law for system of particles which state that the net external torque τ_{net} acting on a system of particles is equal to the time rate of change of the system's total angular momentum L.

For ith particle, the torque is given by
$$\tau = r_i \times F_i$$
The force F_i on the ith particle is the vector sum of external forces F_i^{ext} acting on the particle and the internal forces F_i^{int} exerted on it by other particles of the system. Then, total torque is given by

$$\tau = \sum_i \tau_i = \sum_i r_i \times F_i = \tau_{\text{ext}} + \tau_{\text{int}}$$

where, $\tau_{\text{ext}} = \sum_i r_i \times F_i^{\text{ext}}$ and $\tau_{\text{int}} = \sum_i r_i \times F_i^{\text{int}}$

According to Newton's third law of motion, $\tau_{\text{int}} = 0$, then $\tau_{\text{ext}} = \tau$.
∴
$$\tau = \sum \tau_i$$

Rate of change of angular momentum, $\dfrac{dL}{dt} = \tau_{\text{ext}}$

Thus, **the time rate of the total angular momentum of a system of particles about a point is equal to the sum of the external torques acting on the system taken about the same point.**

> ### Relation between Angular Momentum and Moment of Inertia
> For a rigid body (about an fixed axis),
> $$L = \text{sum of angular momenta of all particles}$$
> $$= m_1 v_1 r_1 + m_2 v_2 r_2 + \ldots\ldots$$
> $$= m_1 r_1^2 \omega + m_2 r_2^2 \omega + \ldots\ldots \qquad [\because v = \omega r]$$
> $$= (m_1 r_1^2 + m_2 r_2^2 + m_3 r_3^2 + \ldots\ldots)\omega$$
> i.e. $\qquad L = I\omega$

Conservation of Angular Momentum

As, $\dfrac{d\mathbf{L}}{dt} = \tau_{net}$ for the rigid body which can be treated as a system of n-particles. If $\tau_{ext} = 0$, then $\dfrac{d\mathbf{L}}{dt} = 0$, that means L = constant with time.

Hence, **without any external torque, angular momentum of a system of particles remain constant.** This is known as the conservation of angular momentum.

If $\qquad \tau_{ext} = 0 \Rightarrow \boxed{\mathbf{L}_{initial} = \mathbf{L}_{final}}$

If $\mathbf{L}$ is constant, then its all three components will also be constant.

$$L_x = \text{constant},\ L_y = \text{constant},\ L_z = \text{constant}$$

Applications of Law of Conservation of Angular Momentum

- A circus acrobat performs beats involving spin by bringing her arms and legs closer to her body or *vice-versa*. On bringing the arms and legs closer to the body, her moment of inertia I decreases, hence angular velocity ω increases. The same principle is applied by ice skater or a ballet dancer.

- All helicopters are provided with two propellers. If there were only one propeller, the helicopter would rotate itself in opposite direction.

- A diver performs somersaults by jumping from a high diving board keeping his legs and arms out stretched first and then curling his body. On doing so, the moment of inertia I of his body decreases. As angular momentum remains constant, therefore, angular velocity ω of his body increases. He, then, performs somersaults. As the diver is about to touch the surface of water, he stretches out his limbs.

EXAMPLE |9| Angular Momentum of an Object

At a certain time, a 0.25 kg object has a position vector $\mathbf{r} = 2\hat{\mathbf{i}} - 2\hat{\mathbf{k}}$ m. At that instant, its velocity is $\mathbf{v} = -5\hat{\mathbf{i}} + 5\hat{\mathbf{k}}$ m/s and the force acting on it is $\mathbf{F} = 4\hat{\mathbf{j}}$ N.

(i) What is the angular momentum of the object about the origin?

(ii) What is torque on it?

Sol. Angular momentum, $\mathbf{L} = \mathbf{r} \times \mathbf{p} = \mathbf{r} \times m\mathbf{v} = m(\mathbf{r} \times \mathbf{v})$

Now, $\mathbf{r} \times \mathbf{v} = \begin{vmatrix} \hat{\mathbf{i}} & \hat{\mathbf{j}} & \hat{\mathbf{k}} \\ 2 & 0 & -2 \\ -5 & 0 & 5 \end{vmatrix}$

$= \hat{\mathbf{i}}[(0 \times 5) - (0 \times -2)] - \hat{\mathbf{j}}[(2 \times 5) - (-2 \times -5)]$
$\qquad\qquad + \hat{\mathbf{k}}[2 \times 0 - (0 \times -5)]$
$= 0$

So, angular momentum of particle is zero.

and $\tau = \text{torque} = \mathbf{r} \times \mathbf{F} = \begin{vmatrix} \hat{\mathbf{i}} & \hat{\mathbf{j}} & \hat{\mathbf{k}} \\ 2 & 0 & -2 \\ 0 & 4 & 0 \end{vmatrix} = 8\hat{\mathbf{i}} + 8\hat{\mathbf{k}}$ N-m

EXAMPLE |10| A Freely Rotating Body

A door is hinged at one end and is free to rotate about a vertical axis. Does its weight cause any torque about its axis? Give reason for your answer. **[NCERT Exemplar]**

Sol. As torque = $\mathbf{r} \times \mathbf{F}$

That means torque produced by force is in a plane perpendicular to plane containing $\mathbf{r}$ and $\mathbf{F}$.

So, if door is in xy-plane, torque produced by weight is in $\pm z$-direction.

It is never about an axis passing through y-direction.

EQUILIBRIUM OF A RIGID BODY

A rigid body is said to be in equilibrium, if both of its linear momentum and angular momentum are not changing with time.

Thus, equilibrium body does not possess linear acceleration or angular acceleration.

This means,

(i) The total force, i.e. the vector sum of all forces acting on the rigid body is zero.

$$\mathbf{F}_1 + \mathbf{F}_2 + \cdots + \mathbf{F}_n = \sum_{i=1}^{n} \mathbf{F}_i = 0$$

If the total force acting on the body is zero, then the linear momentum of body remains constant, so body must be in translatory equilibrium.

The above equations can be written in scalar form as

$$\sum_{i=1}^{n} F_{ix} = 0,\ \sum_{i=0}^{n} F_{iy} = 0 \text{ and } \sum_{i=0}^{n} F_{iz} = 0$$

where, F_{ix}, F_{iy} and F_{iz} are x, y and z-components of force $\mathbf{F}_i$.

(ii) The total torque, i.e. the vector sum of all torques acting on the body must be zero.

$$\tau_1 + \tau_2 + \tau_3 + \cdots + \tau_n = \sum_{i=1}^{n} \tau_i = 0$$

The above equation can be written in scalar form as

$$\sum_{i=0}^{n} \tau_{ix} = 0, \ \sum_{i=0}^{n} \tau_{iy} = 0$$

and

$$\sum_{i=0}^{n} \tau_{iz} = 0.$$

where, τ_{ix}, τ_{iy} and τ_{iz} are x, y and z-components of torque τ_i.

Note
Rotational equilibrium condition remains valid for any origin.

A body may remain in **partial equilibrium** as well. It means that body may remain only in **translational equilibrium** or only in **rotational equilibrium**.

(iii) The sum of the components of the torques along any axis perpendicular to the plane of the forces must be zero.

Rotational Equilibrium Only

If the net torque acting on the rigid body is zero but net force is non-zero, then rigid body is in **rotational equilibrium only**.

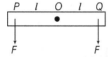

A rod under rotational equilibrium

Two equal forces are acting at the ends of a rod. In this case, the net torque produced by two forces will be zero, but net force is non-zero. It means that rigid body will have zero angular acceleration but non-zero linear acceleration.

Translational Equilibrium Only

If the net force acting on the rigid body is zero but net torque is non-zero, then rigid body is in **translational equilibrium only**.

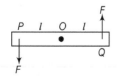

A rod under translational equilibrium

Two equal and opposite forces are acting at the ends of a rod. In this case the net force is zero, but both the forces will produce a non-zero torque. It means that rigid body will have zero linear acceleration but non-zero angular acceleration.

COUPLE

A pair of equal and opposite forces with parallel lines of action are known as a **couple**. A couple produces rotation without translation.

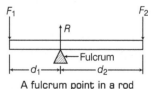

Equal and opposite forces

Let a couple with forces $-\mathbf{F}$ and $\mathbf{F}$ acting at A and B points with position vectors $\mathbf{r}_1$ and $\mathbf{r}_2$ with respect to some origin O.

The moment of couple = total torque

$$= \mathbf{r}_1 \times (-\mathbf{F}) + \mathbf{r}_2 \times \mathbf{F}$$

$$= \mathbf{r}_2 \times \mathbf{F} - \mathbf{r}_1 \times \mathbf{F} = (\mathbf{r}_2 - \mathbf{r}_1) \times \mathbf{F}$$

$\therefore$ $\boxed{\text{Moment of couple} = \mathbf{AB} \times \mathbf{F}}$

By triangle law, $\mathbf{r}_1 + \mathbf{AB} = \mathbf{r}_2$

So, $\mathbf{AB} = \mathbf{r}_2 - \mathbf{r}_1$

So, moment of couple is independent of origin.

Principle of Moment

When an object is in rotational equilibrium, then algebraic sum of all torques acting on it is zero. Clockwise torques are taken negative and anti-clockwise torques are taken positive.

e.g. Consider a rod of negligible mass is provided at some point like a see-saw or a lever. Pivot of lever is called **fulcrum**.

A fulcrum point in a rod

For translational equilibrium,

$$\Sigma F = 0 \text{ or } R - F_1 - F_2 = 0$$

For rotational equilibrium, $\Sigma \tau = 0$ or $F_1 d_1 - F_2 d_2 = 0$

In case of levers, F_1 is called load, d_1 is **load arm**, F_2 is called **effort**, d_2 is **effort arm**.

As, $F_1 d_1 - F_2 d_2 = 0$ or $F_1 d_1 = F_2 d_2$

or load × load arm = effort × effort arm.

This is called **principle of moment** for a lever.

Also, $\boxed{\text{Mechanical advantage}, \ \dfrac{F_1}{F_2} = \dfrac{d_2}{d_1}}$

The ratio $\dfrac{F_1}{F_2}$ is called **mechanical advantage** (MA).

Mechanical advantage greater than one is usually required as this means a small effort is required to lift a large load.

CENTRE OF GRAVITY

If a body is supported on a point such that total gravitational torque about this point is zero, then this point is called **centre of gravity** of the body.

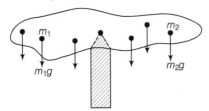

Calculation of centre of gravity supported at a point

As, total gravitational torque about centre of gravity (CG) is zero.

Then, $\tau_g = \sum\limits_{i=1}^{n} \tau_i = \Sigma\, \mathbf{r}_i \times mg = \mathbf{g}\cdot \Sigma m_i\,\mathbf{r}_i = 0$

$$\text{[if } g = \text{constant]}$$

So, $\Sigma m_i \mathbf{r}_i = 0$ $\quad$ [A$\mathbf{g} \neq 0$] ...(i)

Above equation shows that with centre of gravity as origin,

$$\Sigma m_i\,\mathbf{r}_i = 0$$

If r is position vector of centre of mass $= \dfrac{1}{M}\cdot \Sigma m_i \cdot \mathbf{r}_i$

If centre of mass lies at origin

$$0 = m_1\mathbf{r}_1 + m_2\mathbf{r}_2 + \cdots + m_n\mathbf{r}_n,\ \Sigma m_i\mathbf{r}_i = 0 \quad \text{...(ii)}$$

So, centre of gravity coincides with centre of mass if g is constant. But, above statement is not true for very large objects as g will vary and CG does not coincide with CM.

Note
- CM and CG are two different concepts. For small bodies, g will
- be constant at all points on the body.

Centre of Gravity of a Body having Irregular Shape

If we suspended the body from a point say P, the vertical line through P passes through centre of gravity. Then, suspend the body through other point Q.

The intersection of vertical lines gives centre of gravity.

EXAMPLE |11| A Non-uniform Rod

A non-uniform bar of weight w is suspended at rest by two strings of negligible weight as shown,

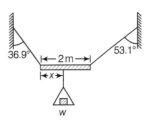

Angles made by strings with vertical are 36.9° and 53.1°, respectively. The bar is 2 m long. Calculate the distance x of the centre of gravity of bar from its left end.

[NCERT]

Sol. Bar is in equilibrium, so the total of forces and torque acting on it must be zero.

$\Rightarrow$ $\qquad\qquad\qquad \Sigma F = 0$

and $\qquad\qquad\qquad \Sigma \tau = 0$

Let, T_1 and T_2 are tensions in strings as shown

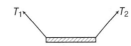

Then, force components are

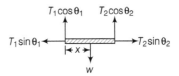

As, sum of vertical components is zero

$\therefore \qquad T_1 \cos\theta_1 + T_2\cos\theta_2 - w = 0$ $\qquad$ ...(i)

Sum of horizontal components is zero,

$\Rightarrow \qquad T_1\sin\theta_1 = T_2\sin\theta_2$ $\qquad$ ...(ii)

Sum of torques must be zero, (taking torque about left hand corner.)

$$w\cdot x = T_2\cos\theta_2 \times 4 \qquad \text{...(iii)}$$

From Eq. (ii), $T_1 = \dfrac{T_2 \sin\theta_2}{\sin\theta_1}$

Substituting in Eq. (i), we get

$$T_2 = w\sin\theta_1/\sin\theta_2\cos\theta_1 + \cos\theta_2\sin\theta_1$$

So, substituting for T_2 in Eq. (iii), we get

$$x = \dfrac{L\cdot\sin\theta_1\,\cos\theta_2}{\sin\theta_2\cos\theta_1 + \cos\theta_2\sin\theta_1}$$

$$= L\cdot\dfrac{\sin\theta_1\,\cos\theta_2}{\sin(\theta_1 + \theta_2)}$$

Here, $L = 2$m, $\theta_1 = 36.9°$, $\theta_2 = 53.1°$

So, $\theta_1 + \theta_2 = 90°$

So, $\qquad x = 2 \times \sin 36.9° \times \cos 53.1°$

$$= 2.20\text{ m}$$

EXAMPLE |12| **Analyse the Height of Large Objects**
Centre of gravity of a body on the earth coincides with its centre of mass for a small object and for a large object, it may not.

What is qualitative meaning of small and large in this regard? For which of the following two of them coincides, a building, a pond, a lake, a mountain. **[NCERT Exemplar]**

Sol. Centre of mass and centre of gravity are two different concepts. But if g does not vary from one part of body to other than CG and CM coincides.

So, when vertical height of the object is very small compared to radius of earth, we call object small, otherwise we call it extended. In above context, building and pond are small objects and a deep lake and a mountain are large extended objects.

EXAMPLE |13| **Non-concurrent Forces**
The vector sum of a system of non-collinear forces acting on a rigid body is given to be non-zero. If vector sum of all the torques due to this system of forces about a certain point is found to be zero, does this means that it is necessarily zero about any arbitrary point.

[NCERT Exemplar]

Sol. Given that $\sum\limits_{i=1}^{n} F_i = 0$

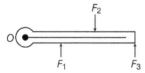

Sum of torques about a point O,

$\sum \mathbf{r}_i \times \mathbf{F}_i = 0$

Then, sum of torques about any other point A is

$\sum \tau = \sum (\mathbf{r}_i - \mathbf{a}) \times F_i = \sum \mathbf{r}_i F_i - \sum \mathbf{a} \times F_i$

Clearly, second term is non-zero. Hence, sum of torques about any other point may not be zero.

| TOPIC PRACTICE 1 |

OBJECTIVE Type Questions

1. For n particles in a space, the suitable expression for the x-coordinate of the centre of mass of the system is

   (a) $\dfrac{\Sigma m_i x_i}{m_i}$ (b) $\dfrac{\Sigma m_i x_i}{M}$ (c) $\dfrac{\Sigma m_i y_i}{M}$ (d) $\dfrac{\Sigma m_i z_i}{M}$

   Here, M is the total mass of the system.

Sol. (b) For system of n- particles in space, the centre of mass of such a system is at (X, Y, Z), where

$$X = \frac{\Sigma m_i x_i}{M}, \quad Y = \frac{\Sigma m_i y_i}{M} \text{ and } Z = \frac{\Sigma m_i z_i}{M}$$

Here, $M = \Sigma m_i$ is the total mass of the system. The index i runs from 1 to n.

$m_i \rightarrow$ Mass of the ith particle and position of ith particle is (x_i, y_i, z_i).

2. Which of the following points is the likely position of the centre of mass of the system shown in figure? **[NCERT Exemplar]**

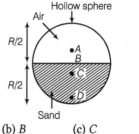

(a) A (b) B (c) C (d) D

Sol. (c) Centre of mass of a system lies towards the part of the system, having bigger mass. In the above diagram, lower part is heavier, hence CM of the system lies below the horizontal diameter.

3. A body is rotating with angular velocity $\omega = (3\hat{i} - 4\hat{j} - \hat{k})$. The linear velocity of a point having position vector $\mathbf{r} = (5\hat{i} - 6\hat{j} + 6\hat{k})$ is

   (a) $6\hat{i} + 2\hat{j} - 3\hat{k}$ (b) $-18\hat{i} - 23\hat{j} + 2\hat{k}$
   (c) $-30\hat{i} - 23\hat{j} + 2\hat{k}$ (d) $6\hat{i} - 2\hat{j} + 8\hat{k}$

Sol. (c) Here, $\omega = 3\hat{i} - 4\hat{j} - \hat{k}$, $\mathbf{r} = 5\hat{i} - 6\hat{j} + 6\hat{k}$

As, $\mathbf{v} = \omega \times \mathbf{r} = \begin{vmatrix} \hat{i} & \hat{j} & \hat{k} \\ 3 & -4 & -1 \\ 5 & -6 & 6 \end{vmatrix}$

$= \hat{i}(-24 - 6) + \hat{j}(-5 - 18) + \hat{k}(-18 + 20)$
$= -30\hat{i} - 23\hat{j} + 2\hat{k}$

4. Newton's second law for rotational motion of a system of particles can be represented as (L is the angular momentum for a system of particles)

   (a) $\dfrac{d\mathbf{p}}{dt} = \tau_{\text{ext}}$ (b) $\dfrac{d\mathbf{L}}{dt} = \tau_{\text{ext}}$
   (c) $\dfrac{d\mathbf{L}}{dt} = \tau_{\text{ext}}$ (d) $\dfrac{d\mathbf{L}}{dt} = \tau_{\text{int}} + \tau_{\text{ext}}$

Sol. (c) Newton's second law for rotational motion is

$$\tau = \tau_{\text{ext}} = \frac{d\mathbf{L}}{dt}$$

5. In the game of see-saw, what should be the displacement of boy B from right edge to keep the see-saw in equilibrium? ($M_1 = 40$ kg, $M_2 = 60$ kg)

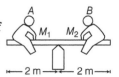

   (a) $\dfrac{4}{3}$ m   (b) 1 m   (c) $\dfrac{2}{3}$ m   (d) Zero

Sol. (c) For the equilibrium, $M_1 g \times r_A = M_2 g \times x$

$$(40 \times 10) \times 2 = (60 \times 10) x$$

$$x = \frac{8}{6} = \frac{4}{3} \text{ m}$$

So, 60 kg boy has to be displaced $= 2 - \frac{4}{3} = \frac{2}{3} \text{ m}$

VERY SHORT ANSWER Type Questions

6. Should there necessarily be any mass at centre of mass of system?

Sol. No, the centre of mass of a ring lies at its centre.

7. Is centre of mass a reality?

Sol. No, the centre of mass of a system is a hypothetical point which acts as a single mass particle of the system for an external force.

8. In which case centre of mass of a body lie outside it? Give one example.

Sol. If geometrical centre of a body lies outside it, then centre of mass of body lies outside the body.

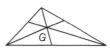

Centre of mass of a L-shaped lamina lies outside it on the line of symmetry.

9. A cricket bat is cut through its centre of mass into two parts as shown

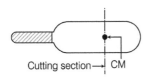

Then, state whether both parts are of same mass or not. Also, give reason.

Sol. Centre of mass of a body lies towards region of heavier mass. So, if bat is cut through its centre of mass, both parts are not of equal masses.

10. $(n-1)$ equal point masses each of mass m are placed at the vertices of a regular n-polygon. The vacant vertex has a position vector **a** with respect to the centre of the polygon. Find the position vector of centre of mass. **[NCERT Exemplar]**

Sol. Suppose, **b** be the position vector of centre of mass of regular n-polygon.

As $(n-1)$ equal point masses each of mass m are placed at $(n-1)$ vertices of regular polygon, therefore

$$\frac{(n-1) m b + m a}{(n-1+1)m} = 0 \Rightarrow (n-1) mb + ma = 0$$

$$\Rightarrow \qquad b = \frac{-a}{(n-1)}$$

11. Find centre of mass of a triangular lamina.
[NCERT]

Sol. For any planar solid, centre of mass always lies at its geometrical centre.

Geometrical centre of a triangle is intersection point of its media.

So, for any given triangular lamina

Centre of mass is at its centroid, point of intersection is media.

12. If no external torque act on a body, will its angular velocity remain conserved?

Sol. No, angular velocity is not conserved but angular momentum is conserved.

13. Which component of linear momentum does not contribute to angular momentum?

Sol. The radial component of linear momentum does not contribute to angular momentum.

14. If net torque on a rigid body is zero, does its linear momentum necessary remain conserved?

Sol. The linear momentum remain conserved if the net force on the system is zero.

15. What happens to the moment of force about a point, if the line of action of the force moves towards the point?

Sol. Moment of force
= force × the perpendicular distance of the line of action of force from the axis of rotation.
Hence, the moment of force about a point decreases if the line of action of the force moves towards that point.

16. The vector sum of a system of non-collinear forces acting on a rigid body is given to be non-zero. If the vector sum of all the torques due to the system of forces about a certain point is found to be zero, does this mean that it is necessarily zero about any arbitrary point?
[NCERT]

Sol. No, given $\sum_i \mathbf{F}_i \neq 0$

The sum of torques about a certain point O
$$\sum_i \mathbf{r}_i \times \mathbf{F}_i = 0$$
The sum of torques about any other point O'.
$$\sum_i (\mathbf{r}_i - \mathbf{a}) \times \mathbf{F}_i = \sum_i \mathbf{r}_i \times \mathbf{F}_i - \mathbf{a} \times \sum_i \mathbf{F}_i$$
Here, the second term need not vanish.

17. When is a body lying in a gravitation field in stable equilibrium?

Sol. A body in a gravitation field will be in stable equilibrium, if the vertical line through its centre of gravity passes through the base of the body.

18. Is centre of mass and centre of gravity body always coincide?

Sol. No, if the body is large such that g varies from one point to another, then centre of gravity is offset from centre of mass.

But for small bodies, centre of mass and centre of gravity lies at their geometrical centres.

19. Does the centre of mass of a solid necessarily lie within the body? If not, give an example.

Sol. No, the centre of mass of L-shaped rod lies in the region outside of rod.

20. A faulty balance with unequal arms has its beam horizontal. Are the weights of the two pans equal?

Sol. They are of unequal mass. Their masses are in the inverse ratio of the arms of the balance.

21. When a labourer cuts down a tree, he makes a cut on the side facing the direction in which he wants it to fall. Why?

Sol. The weight of tree exerts a torque about the point where the cut is made. This causes rotation of the tree about the cut.

22. Why a wrench of longer arm is preferred in comparison to a wrench of shorter arm?

Sol. The torque applied on the nut by the wrench is equal to the force multiplied by the perpendicular distance from the axis of rotation. Hence, to increase torque a wrench of longer arm is preferred.

23. Why in hand driven grinding machine, handle is put near the circumference of the stone or wheel?

Sol. For a given force, torque can be increased if the perpendicular distance of the point of application of the force from the axis of rotation is increased.

Hence, the handle put near the circumference produces maximum torque.

24. The bottom of a ship is made heavy. Why?

Sol. The bottom of a ship is made heavy so that its centre of gravity remains low. This ensures the stability of its equilibrium.

SHORT ANSWER Type Questions

25. A metre stick is balanced on a knife edge at its centre. When two coins, each of mass 5 g are put one on top of the other at the 12 cm mark, the stick is found to be balanced at 45.0 cm.

What is the mass of the metre stick ? **[NCERT]**

Sol. Let total mass of the metre stick be M kg.

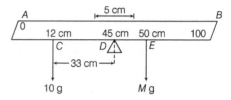

Distance between mid-point E and new centre of gravity (DE),

$$= 50 - 45 = 5 \text{ cm}$$

Distance between 12 cm mark and new centre of gravity (CD),

$$= 45 - 12 = 33 \text{ cm}$$

From principle of moments in equilibrium,

$$M \times DE = (2 \times 5) \times CD$$
$$M \times 5 = 10 \times 33 \quad \text{or} \quad M = 66 \text{ g}$$

∴ Mass of the metre stick is 66 g.

26. In HCl molecule, separation of nuclei of the two atoms is about 1.27Å (1Å $= 10^{-10}$m). Find the centre of mass of molecule given that a chlorine atom is about 35.5 times massive than a hydrogen atom.

[NCERT]

Sol. Mass of an atom is concentrated at its nucleus, they can be treated as point masses.

We take nucleus of hydrogen atom at origin and nucleus of chlorine atom on x-axis.

where,
m_1 = mass of hydrogen = 1
m_2 = mass of chlorine = 35.5
$x_1 = 0$, $x_2 = 1.27$ Å

As the system is symmetrical about x-axis, its centre of mass lies on x-axis.

Using
$$x_{CM} = \frac{m_1 x_1 + m_2 x_2}{m_1 + m_2} = \frac{1 \times 0 + 35.5 \times 1.27}{1 + 35.5}$$
$$= 1.235 \text{ Å}$$
$$= 1.235 \times 10^{-10} \text{m (from origin)}$$

So, centre of mass of HCl molecule is nearly 1.235 Å from the H-nucleus on the line joining H and Cl nuclei.

27. Does angular momentum of a body in translatory motion is zero?

Sol. Angular momentum of a body is measured with respect to certain origin.

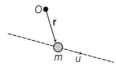

So, a body in translatory motion can have angular momentum.

It will be zero, if origin lies on the line of motion of particle.

LONG ANSWER Type I Questions

28. Give the location of the centre of mass of a
 (i) sphere
 (ii) cylinder
 (iii) ring and
 (iv) cube each of uniform mass density.

Does the centre of mass of a body necessarily lie inside the body? **[NCERT]**

Sol. (i) Centre of mass of a sphere lies at its geometrical centre.

 (ii) Centre of mass of a cylinder lies at its geometrical centre, i.e. at the mid-point of its axis of symmetry.

 (iii) Centre of mass of a ring lies at its geometrical centre.

 (iv) Centre of mass of a cube lies at its geometrical centre, i.e. at the point of intersection of its diagonals.

No, it is not necessary that centre of mass of a body lie inside it, because in some cases such as a ring, a hollow cylinder, a hollow sphere and a hollow cube centre of mass lies outside.

29. Figure shows momentum *versus* time graph for a particle moving along x-axis. In which region, force on the particle is large. Why?

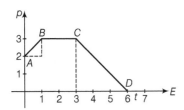

Sol. Net force is given by $F_{net} = \dfrac{dp}{dt}$

Also, rate of change of momentum = slope of graph.

As from graph, slope AB = slope CD

And slope (BC) = slope (DE) = 0

So, force acting on the particle is equal in regions AB and CD and in regions BC and DE (which is zero).

30. Find components along x, y and z-axes of the angular momentum **L** of a particle whose position vector is **r** and momentum is **p** with components p_x, p_y and p_z. Show if the particle moves only in xy-plane, the angular momentum has only a z-component. **[NCERT]**

Sol. Angular momentum of a particle is $\mathbf{l} = \mathbf{r} \times \mathbf{p}$

Let, $\mathbf{r} = x\hat{i} + y\hat{j} + z\hat{k}$, where (x, y, z) is the location of particle at some instant and $\mathbf{p} = p_x\hat{i} + p_y\hat{j} + p_z\hat{k}$, is the linear momentum of particle at that instant.

Then, angular momentum of particle is given by

$$\mathbf{L} = \mathbf{r} \times \mathbf{p} = \begin{vmatrix} \hat{i} & \hat{j} & \hat{k} \\ x & y & z \\ p_x & p_y & p_z \end{vmatrix}$$

$$= \hat{i}\,(p_z \cdot y - p_y \cdot z) - \hat{j}\,(p_z \cdot x - p_x \cdot z) + \hat{k}\,(p_y \cdot x - p_x \cdot y) \ldots(i)$$

So, components of angular momentum along x, y and z-axes are

$$L_x = p_z y - p_y z$$
$$L_y = p_z x - p_x z$$
and $$L_z = p_y x - p_x y, \text{ respectively}$$

Now, if particle is confined to xy-plane, then

$$\mathbf{r} = x\hat{i} + y\hat{i} \Rightarrow z = 0$$
and $$\mathbf{p} = p_x\hat{i} + p_y\hat{j} \Rightarrow p_z = 0$$

Substituting in Eq. (i), we get

$$\mathbf{L} = \hat{k}\,(p_y x - p_x y)$$

So, angular momentum only has a z-component. As angular momentum is cross-product of **r** and **p**.

∴ It is always perpendicular to plane containing **r** and **p**.

31. Two cylindrical hollow drums of radii R and $2R$, and of a common height h, are rotating with angular velocities ω (anti-clockwise) and ω (clockwise), respectively.

Their axes, fixed are parallel and in a horizontal plane separated by $(3R + \delta)$. They are now brought in contact $(\delta \to 0)$.

 (i) Show the frictional forces just after contact.

 (ii) Identify forces and torques external to the system just after contact.

 (iii) What would be the ratio of final angular velocities when friction ceases?

[NCERT Exemplar]

Sol. (i)

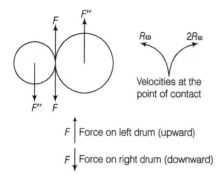

Velocities at the point of contact

F | Force on left drum (upward)

F | Force on right drum (downward)

(ii) $F' = F = F''$ where F and F'' are external forces through support.
$$F_{net} = 0$$
External torque $= F \times 3R$, anti-clockwise.

(iii) Let ω_1 and ω_2 be final angular velocities (anti-clockwise and clockwise respectively). Finally, there will be no friction.

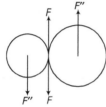

Hence, $R\omega_1 = 2R\omega_2 \Rightarrow \dfrac{\omega_1}{\omega_2} = 2$

32. A particle on a rotating disc have initial and final angular positions are

(i) -2 rad, $+6$ rad   (ii) -4 rad, -8 rad

(iii) 6 rad, -2 rad,

In which case, particle undergoes a negative displacement.

Sol. (i) Angular displacement is
$$\Delta\theta = \theta_f - \theta_i = 6 - (-2) = 8 \text{ rad}$$
(ii) $\Delta\theta = \theta_f - \theta_i = -8 \text{ rad} - (-4 \text{ rad}) = -4 \text{ rad}$
(iii) $\Delta\theta = -2 \text{ rad} - (+6 \text{ rad}) = -8 \text{ rad}$

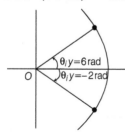

In cases (ii) and (iii), angular displacement is negative.

33. A particle of mass m is projected from origin O with speed u at an angle θ with positive x-axis. Find the angular momentum of particle at any time t about O before the particle strikes the ground again.

Sol. Let particle is at P at any instant t and its position vector is $\mathbf{r}$.
Then, $\qquad \mathbf{r} = x\,\hat{\mathbf{i}} + y\,\hat{\mathbf{j}}$
where, $\qquad x = u\cos\theta \cdot t$
and $\qquad y = u\sin\theta \cdot t - \dfrac{1}{2}gt^2$

and if $\mathbf{v}$ = velocity vector of particle at that instant.

Then, $\qquad \mathbf{r} = x\hat{\mathbf{i}} + y\hat{\mathbf{j}}$
where, $\qquad x = u\cos\theta.t$
and $\qquad y = u\sin\theta.t - \dfrac{1}{2}gt^2$

and if $\qquad \mathbf{v}$ = velocity vector of particle at that instant.

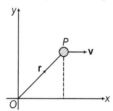

Then, $\qquad \mathbf{v} = \mathbf{v}_x\hat{\mathbf{i}} + \mathbf{v}_y\hat{\mathbf{j}}$
where, $\qquad v_x = u\cos\theta$
and $\qquad v_y = u\sin\theta - gt$

So, $\qquad \mathbf{r} = (u\cos\theta)t\,\hat{\mathbf{i}} + \left((u\sin\theta)\cdot t - \dfrac{1}{2}gt^2\right)\hat{\mathbf{j}}$

and $\qquad \mathbf{v} = u\cos\theta\,\hat{\mathbf{i}} + (u\sin\theta - gt)\,\hat{\mathbf{j}}$

So, $\qquad L$ = angular momentum of particle
$$= m\,(\mathbf{r} \times \mathbf{v})$$
$$= m\begin{vmatrix} \hat{\mathbf{i}} & \hat{\mathbf{j}} & \hat{\mathbf{k}} \\ u\cos\theta t & \left(u\sin\theta - \dfrac{1}{2}gt\right)t & 0 \\ u\cos\theta & (u\sin\theta - gt) & 0 \end{vmatrix}$$
$$= -\dfrac{1}{2}m\,(u\cos\theta)\,gt^2.\hat{\mathbf{k}}$$

So, angular momentum is along z-axis.

34. A car of weight 1800 kg. The distance between its front and back axles is 1.8 m. Its centre of gravity is 1.05 m behind the front axle. Determine the force exerted by the level ground on each front wheel and each back wheel.

[NCERT Exemplar]

💡 Moment of forces about centre of gravity is always zero.

Sol. Total mass of the car = 1800 kg

Let m and $(900 - m)$ kg be the masses of each front wheel and each back wheel, respectively.

Distance of centre of gravity from the front axle = 1.05 m
∴ Distance of centre of gravity from the back axle
= 1.80 − 1.05 = 0.75 m

Taking torque about centre of gravity,

$$m \times 1.05 = (900 - m) \times 0.75$$

or $\qquad 1.05\,m + 0.75\,m = 900 \times 0.75$

or $\qquad 1.80\,m = 900 \times 0.75$

or $\qquad m = \dfrac{900 \times 0.75}{1.80} = 375\,\text{kg}$

$\therefore \qquad (900 - m) = 900 - 375 = 525\,\text{kg}$

$\therefore$ Weight of each front wheel $(w_1) = m_1 g$

$$w_1 = 375 \times 9.8 = 3675\,\text{N}$$

Force exerted by the level ground on each front wheel.

= force exerted by each front wheel on the level ground

$$(w_1) = 3675\,\text{N}$$

Weight of each back wheel $(w_2) = m_2 g$

$$w_2 = 525 \times 9.8 = 5145\,\text{N}$$

$\therefore$ Force exerted by the level ground on each back wheel.

= force exerted by each back wheel on level ground

$$(w_2) = 5145\,\text{N}.$$

LONG ANSWER Type II Questions

35. Find position of centre of mass of a semicircular disc of radius r. **[NCERT Exemplar]**

Sol. As semicircular disc is symmetrical about its one of diameter, we take axes as shown. So, now we only have to calculate Y_{CM}. (As, X_{CM} is zero by symmetry and choice of origin).

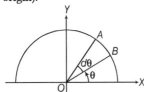

Axis of symmetry CM lies on this

Now, $\qquad Y_{CM} = \dfrac{\int y\,dm}{\int dm}$

From our text, $M \cdot Y_{CM} = \int y\,dm$

$$Y_{CM} = \frac{1}{M}\int y\,dm = \frac{\int y\,dm}{\int dm}$$

Now, for a small element OAB, as element is small and it can be treated as a triangle so,

Area of sector $OAB = \dfrac{1}{2} \times r \times r d\theta$

Height of triangle $= r$

Base of triangle $= AB = r d\theta$

So, its mass $dm = \dfrac{1}{2} r^2 d\theta \cdot \rho \qquad \left[\because \rho = \dfrac{\text{mass}}{\text{area}}\right]$

As centre of mass of a triangle is at a distance of $\dfrac{2}{3}$ from its vertex (at centroid, intersection of medians). So,

$y = \dfrac{2}{3} r\sin\theta$ (location of CM of small sector AOB).

So, $Y_{CM} = \dfrac{\displaystyle\int_0^\pi y\,dm}{\displaystyle\int_0^\pi \frac{1}{2}r^2\rho\,d\theta}$

$$= \dfrac{\displaystyle\int_0^\pi \frac{2}{3}r\sin\theta \times \frac{1}{2}r^2 d\theta \cdot \rho}{\displaystyle\int_0^\pi \frac{1}{2}r^2\rho\,d\theta}$$

$$= \dfrac{\frac{1}{2} \times \frac{2}{3}r^3 \cdot \rho \int_0^\pi \sin\theta\,d\theta}{\frac{1}{2}r^2\rho \cdot \int_0^\pi d\theta} = \dfrac{\frac{2r}{3}\int_0^\pi \sin\theta\,d\theta}{\int_0^\pi d\theta}$$

$$= \dfrac{\frac{2r}{3}[-\cos\theta]_0^\pi}{[\theta]_0^\pi} = \dfrac{\frac{-2r}{3}(\cos\pi - \cos 0^\circ)}{(\pi - \theta)}$$

$$= 4r/3\pi$$

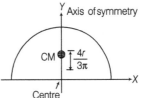

So, CM of disc is at a distance of $\dfrac{4r}{3\pi}$ from its centre on its axis of symmetry.

36. A disc of radius R is removed from a disc of radius $2R$ as shown.

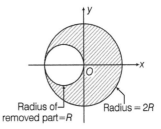

Find centre of mass of above disc with hole. **[NCERT]**

Sol. First consider the composite plate,

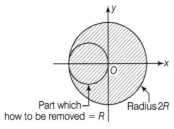

x-coordinate of centre of mass of composite plate is given by $x_{CM} = \dfrac{m_1 x_1 + m_2 x_2}{m_1 + m_2}$

where,

m_1 = mass of disc of radius $2R$

x_1 = position of centre of mass of disc with hole

m_2 = mass of part removed of radius R

x_2 = position of centre of mass of part removed.

Now, as centre of mass of composite plate is at origin, so

$$x_{CM} = 0 = \frac{m_1 x_1 + m_2 x_2}{m_1 + m_2}$$

or $m_1 x_1 + m_2 x_2 = 0$

Now, we are finding x_1.

So, $\quad x_1 = -\dfrac{m_2 x_2}{m_1}$

Now, $\quad \dfrac{m_2}{m_1} = \dfrac{\text{density} \times \text{volume of portion 2}}{\text{density} \times \text{volume of portion 1}}$

$$= \frac{\text{thickness} \times \text{area of portion 2}}{\text{thickness} \times \text{area of portion 1}}$$

$\Rightarrow \quad \dfrac{m_2}{m_1} = \dfrac{A_2}{A_1} = \dfrac{\pi R^2}{\pi (2R)^2 - \pi R^2} = \dfrac{1}{3}$

Also, $x_2 = -R$, (negative sign is w.r.t. coordinate axes)

Hence, $\quad x_1 = -\dfrac{m_2}{m_1} \cdot x_2$

$$= -\frac{1}{3}(-R) = \frac{1}{3}R$$

So, centre of mass located at $\left(x = \dfrac{1}{3}R, y = 0 \right)$ point.

37. Two particles each of mass m and speed v travel in opposite direction along parallel lines, separated by a distance d. Show that vector angular momentum of the two particles system is same whatever be the point about which angular momentum is taken. **[NCERT]**

Sol. A sketch of system of particles at any instant is shown. Let, O be the origin chosen.

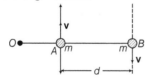

Then, angular momentum of particle at A is

$l_1 = \mathbf{OA} \times \mathbf{p} = \mathbf{OA} \times m\mathbf{v}$

$\quad = m(\mathbf{OA} \times \mathbf{v})$

and angular momentum of particle at B is

$l_2 = \mathbf{OB} \times \mathbf{p} = \mathbf{OB} \times (-m\mathbf{v})$

$\quad = -m(\mathbf{OB} \times \mathbf{v})$

So, total angular momentum of the system of particles is

$\mathbf{L} = l_1 + l_2$

$\quad = m(\mathbf{OA} \times \mathbf{v}) - m(\mathbf{OB} \times \mathbf{v})$

$\quad = m(\mathbf{OA} \times \mathbf{v} - \mathbf{OB} \times \mathbf{v})$

$\quad = m(\mathbf{OA} - \mathbf{OB}) \times \mathbf{v}$

$\quad = m(\mathbf{BA}) \times \mathbf{v}$

{As, $\mathbf{BA}$ = position vector of A − position vector of B}

Above expression is independent of choice of origin.

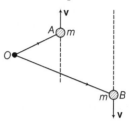

This is true even when particles are not in a straight line.

$\mathbf{L}_i = l_1 + l_2 = m(\mathbf{OA} \times \mathbf{v} - \mathbf{OB} \times \mathbf{v})$

$\quad = m(\mathbf{BA}) \times \mathbf{v}$

Which is same as previous result. So, angular momentum of system is independent of choice of origin.

38. A beam of uniform cross-section and uniform mass-density of mass 20 kg is supported at ends. A mass of 5 kg is placed at a distance of $L/5$ m from one of its end. If beam is L m long, what are reactions of supports?

💡 In dealing with problems of equilibrium of a rigid body (like beam in this question), first of all draw a free body diagram of the system, indicating all of the forces acting on the system.

Sol. In given case, our system looks like

Forces involved are (i) weight of beam $= F_1 = m_1 g$. (ii) weight of mass placed over beam $= F_2 = m_2 g$. (ii) Reactions of supports F_3 and F_4 which we have to found.

Free body diagram of our system is

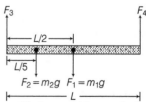

In static equilibrium problem, calculation involves the following equations

Sum of all vertical (or vertical component of) forces is zero, $\Sigma F_V = 0$

Sum of all horizontal forces or horizontal components of forces is zero, $\Delta F_H = 0$

Sum of all torques is zero.

$$\Sigma \tau = 0$$

You may take signs as

All forces along $+y$-direction are positive.

All forces along $+x$-direction are positive.

All forces along $-y$-direction are negative.

All forces along $-x$-direction are negative.

All anti-clockwise torques are positive.

All clockwise torques are negative.

In given problem, as the beam is in equilibrium,

$$\Sigma F_V = 0$$

or $\qquad F_3 + F_4 - F_2 - F_1 = 0$

or $\qquad F_3 + F_4 - m_2 g - m_1 g = 0 \qquad$ ...(i)

$$\Sigma F_H = 0$$

As there is no horizontal force involved here so, this does not give any equation.

and $\qquad\qquad \Sigma \tau = 0$

Let us choose rotation axis through right hand corner of beam.

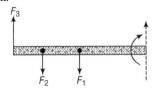

Sum of all torques is

$$F_2 \times \frac{4}{5} L + F_1 \times \frac{L}{2} - F_3 \times L = 0$$

(no torque due to force F_4)

From above equation,

$$\frac{4}{5} F_2 + F_1 - F_3 = 0$$

or $\qquad \frac{4}{5} m_2 g + m_1 g - F_3 = 0 \qquad$ ...(ii)

When all the equations are formed, solve them like linear simultaneous equations to get desired results.

In given problem, from Eq. (ii) we get

$$F_3 = \frac{4}{5} m_2 g + m_1 g$$

$$= \frac{4}{5} \times 5 \times 10 + 20 \times 10$$

$$= 20 \times 12 = 240 \, \text{N}$$

$$m_1 = 20 \, \text{kg}$$

and $\qquad m_2 = 5 \, \text{kg}$

$$g = 10 \, \text{m/s}^2$$

Substituting value of F_3, m_1 and m_2 in Eq. (i), we get

$$240 + F_4 - 5 \times 10 - 20 \times 10 = 0$$

or $\qquad\qquad\qquad F_4 = 50 + 200 - 240$

$$F_4 = 10 \, \text{N}$$

So, support reactions are 240 N on left support and 10 N on right support.

39. As shown in the figure, the two sides of a step ladder BA and CA are 1.6 m long and hinged at A. A rope DE, 0.05 m is tied half way up. A weight 40 kg is suspended from a point F, 1.2 m from B along the ladder BA. Assuming the floor to be frictionless and neglecting the weight of the ladder, find the tension in the rope and forces exerted by the floor on the ladder. (Take, $g = 9.8 \, \text{m/s}^2$) **[NCERT]**

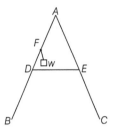

Sol. Different forces acting on the system are

(i) Normal reaction of the floor at point B, N_B acting in vertically upward direction.

(ii) Normal reaction of the floor at point C, N_C acting in vertically upward direction.

(iii) Weight at point F, acting vertically downward.

(iv) Tensions in the string, as the ladder will have a tendency to slide at point B and point C (as the floor is frictionless) so, at both points D and E the string will be stretched in outward direction, therefore the tensions at both points will be along inward.

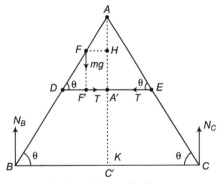

Given, length of each side of ladder

$$AB = AC = 1.6 \, \text{m}$$

Let the sides of the ladder subtend an angle θ with the horizontal and forces exerted by the floor on the ladder at points B and C be N_B and N_C, respectively.

Length of the rope $(DE) = 0.5 \, \text{m}$

Weight suspended $(w) = 40 \, \text{kg-f}$

$$= 40 \times 9.8 = 392 \, \text{N}$$

Distance $(BF) = 1.2 \, \text{m}$

$\therefore$ Distance $(AF) = AB - BF = 1.6 - 1.2 = 0.4 \, \text{m}$

$\angle ABC = \angle ADE = \angle ACB = \angle AED = \theta$

Let A' be the mid-point of the rope

$\therefore$ $\qquad DA' = \dfrac{0.5}{2} = 0.25$ m

$\therefore$ $\qquad DF' = F'A' = \dfrac{1}{2}DA' = \dfrac{1}{2} \times 0.25 = 0.125$ m

For translational equilibrium of the step ladder,

$$N_B + N_C = W$$
$$N_B + N_C = 392 \text{ N} \qquad \text{...(i)}$$

Taking moment of forces about point A for side AB,

$$N_B \times BC' = W \times F'A' + T \times AA'$$

But $\qquad BC' = AB\cos\theta$

and $\qquad AA' = AD\sin\theta$

$$N_B \times AB\cos\theta = W \times 0.125 + T \times AD\sin\theta \quad \text{...(ii)}$$

But from $\Delta DFF'$,

$$\cos\theta = \dfrac{DF'}{DF} = \dfrac{0.125}{0.4} = 0.3125$$
$$\theta = 72.8°$$

$\therefore$ $\qquad \cos\theta = \cos 72.8° = 0.3125$

$$\sin\theta = \sin 72.8° = 0.9553$$
$$\tan\theta = \tan 72.8° = 3.2350$$

Substituting values in Eq. (ii), we get

$$N_B \times 1.6 \times 0.3125 = (392 \times 0.125) + (T \times 0.8 \times 0.9553)$$

or $\qquad 0.5\,N_B = 0.764T + 49 \qquad \text{...(iii)}$

Now, taking moment of forces about point A, for side AC.

$$N_C \times CC' = T \times AA'$$

But $CC' = AC\cos\theta$ and $AA' = AE\sin\theta$

$\therefore$ $\qquad N_C \times AC\cos\theta = T \times AE\sin\theta$

$$N_C \times 1.6 \times 0.3125 = T \times 0.8 \times 0.9553$$
$$0.5\,N_C = 0.764\,T \qquad \text{...(iv)}$$

Substituting value from Eq. (iv) in Eq. (iii), we get

$$0.5\,N_B = 0.5\,N_C + 49$$
$$0.5\,(N_B - N_C) = 49$$
$$\dfrac{1}{2}(N_B - N_C) = 49$$
$$N_B - N_C = 98 \qquad \text{...(v)}$$

Adding Eqs. (i) and (v), we get

$$2N_B = 392 + 98 = 490$$

or $\qquad N_B = 245$ N

From Eq. (i),

$$N_C = 392 - 245 \text{ N} = 147 \text{ N}$$

From Eq (iv), $\qquad T = \dfrac{0.5 \times 147}{0.764} = 96.2$ N

40. From a uniform disc of radius R, a circular section of radius $\dfrac{R}{2}$ is cut out. The centre of the hole is at $\dfrac{R}{2}$ from the centre of the original disc. Locate the centre of gravity of the resulting flat body. **[NCERT]**

Sol. Let mass per unit area of the disc be m.

$\therefore$ Mass of the disc (M) = total area of disc $\times$ mass per unit area = $\pi R^2 m$.

Mass of the portion removed from the disc (M')

$$= \pi\left(\dfrac{R}{2}\right)^2 m$$

$\Rightarrow$ $\qquad \dfrac{\pi R^2}{4}m = \dfrac{M}{4}$

The centre of mass of the original disc is O and the centre of mass of the removed part is O_1 and let centre of mass of the remaining part be O_2.

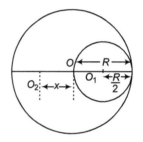

According to the question, figure can be drawn as

Here, $\qquad OO_1 = \dfrac{R}{2}$

The remaining portion of the disc can be considered as a system of two masses M at O and $-M' = -\dfrac{M}{4}$ at O_1.

If the distance of the centre of mass of the remaining part from the centre O is at a distance x, then

$$x = \dfrac{M \times 0 - M' \times \dfrac{R}{2}}{M - M'} = \dfrac{-\dfrac{M}{4} \times \dfrac{R}{2}}{M - \dfrac{M}{4}}$$

$$= -\dfrac{MR}{8} \times \dfrac{4}{3M} = -\dfrac{R}{6}$$

Therefore, centre of mass of the remaining part is at $\dfrac{R}{6}$ to the left of centre O.

ASSESS YOUR TOPICAL UNDERSTANDING

OBJECTIVE Type Questions

1. A system of particles is called a rigid body when
   (a) any two of particles of system may have displacements in opposite directions under action of a force.
   (b) Any two of particles of system may have velocities in opposite directions under action of a force.
   (c) Any two particles of system may have a non-zero relative velocity.
   (d) Any two particles of system may have displacements in same direction under action of a force.

2. For n-particles in a space, the suitable expression for the position vector of centre of mass is
   (a) $\dfrac{\Sigma m_i \mathbf{r}_i}{m_i}$
   (b) $m_i \mathbf{r}_i$
   (c) $\dfrac{\Sigma m_i \mathbf{r}_i}{M}$
   (d) $\dfrac{m_i \mathbf{r}_i}{m_i}$

3. For which of the following does the centre of mass lie outside the body? **[NCERT Exemplar]**
   (a) A pencil
   (b) A shotput
   (c) A dice
   (d) A bangle

4. Angular velocity vector is directed along
   (a) the tangent to the circular path
   (b) the inward radius
   (c) the outward radius
   (d) the axis of rotation

5. In translational equilibrium,
   (a) $\sum\limits_{i=1}^{n} \mathbf{F}_{net} = 0$
   (b) $\sum\limits_{i=1}^{n} \tau_{net} = 0$
   (c) Both (a) and (b) are the necessary conditions for the translational equilibrium
   (d) Particle may be in equilibrium when (a) and (b) are not fulfilled.

Answer
   1. (c)　|　2. (c)　|　3. (d)　|　4. (d)　|　5. (a)

VERY SHORT ANSWER Type Questions

6. What is the basic difference between pure translation motion and pure rotational motion?

7. A ball is moving with a velocity of 10 m/s. Suddenly, it breaks into two equal parts. What will be the speed of centre of mass of the system after explosion? **[Ans. 10 m/s]**

8. A particle is moving on the x-axis with a linear velocity of 2 m/s. What will be its angular momentum about the origin? **[Ans. zero]**

SHORT ANSWER Type Questions

9. It is difficult to open the door by pushing it or pulling it at the hinge. Why?

10. Which physical quantities are expressed by the following:
    (i) the rate of change of angular momentum?
    (ii) moment of linear momentum?

11. If no external torque acts on a body, will its angular velocity remains conserved?

12. Why is it easier to open a tap with two finger than with one finger?

13. Can the couple acting on a rigid body produce translatory motion?

14. Can be a body in translational motion have angular momentum? Why?

15. If a body is rotating, is it necessarily being acted upon by an external torque?

LONG ANSWER Type I Questions

|3 Marks|

16. Locate the centre of mass of uniform triangular lamina and a uniform cone.

17. Three identical spheres each of radius r and mass m are placed touching each other on a horizontal floor. Locate the position of centre of mass of the system.
    $\left[\text{Ans. } \left(r, \dfrac{r}{3}\right)\right]$

18. Explain the concept of torque. Obtain an expression for torque in polar coordinates.

LONG ANSWER Type II Questions

19. In given pulley mass system, mass $m_1 = 500$ g, $m_2 = 460$ g and the pulley has a radius of 5 cm. When released from rest, heavier mass falls through 7.50 cm in 5 s. There is no slippage between pulley and string.
    (i) What is magnitude of acceleration of masses?
    (ii) What is magnitude of pulley's angular acceleration?
    [**Ans.** $a = 6 \times 10^{-2}$ m/s^2, $\alpha = 1.20$ rad/s^2]

20. Find the centre of mass for a solid cone of base radius r and height h.
    [**Ans.** At height $\dfrac{h}{4}$ from the point O. O is at the centre of the base of the cone]

21. A metal 13 bar 70 cm long and 4 kg in mass supported on two knife edges placed 10 cm from each end. A 6 kg weight is suspended at 30 cm from one end. Find the reactions at the knife edges. Assume the bar to be of uniform cross-section and homogeneous.
    [**Ans.** 55 N and 43 N]

|TOPIC 2|
Moment of Inertia and Rolling Motion

MOMENT OF INERTIA

The property of a body by virtue of which it opposes the torque tending to change its state of rest or of uniform rotation about an axis is called **rotational inertia** or **moment of inertia.**

To understand moment of inertia, let us consider a rigid body rotating about a fixed axis. For a rotating rigid body, kinetic energy is the sum of kinetic energies of individual particles.

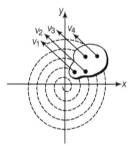

Rotation of a rigid body

So, kinetic energy of a rotating body,

$$K = \frac{1}{2} m_1 v_1^2 + \frac{1}{2} m_2 v_2^2 + \cdots + \frac{1}{2} m_n v_n^2$$

or

$$K = \sum_{i=1}^{n} \frac{1}{2} m_i v_i^2$$

Substituting $v = r\omega$, $K = \sum \frac{1}{2} m_i r_i^2 \omega^2$

where m_i is the mass of particle, v_i is the linear velocity.

As, the angular velocity ω is same for all the particles of rigid body.

So,

$$K = \frac{1}{2} \omega^2 \left(\sum_{i=1}^{n} m_i r_i^2 \right) \qquad \ldots(i)$$

The quantity $\sum (m_i r_i^2)$ depends on distribution of mass around axis of rotation. This quantity is called **moment of inertia** (I).

$$\boxed{\text{Kinetic energy, } K = \frac{1}{2} I \omega^2} \qquad \ldots(ii)$$

For translational motion, the kinetic energy of a particle of mass m and speed v is

$$\text{KE} = \frac{1}{2} m v^2 \qquad \ldots(iii)$$

By comparing Eqs. (ii) and (iii), we can get that moment of inertia in the rotational analogue of mass.

So, for a rotating body, its moment of inertia

$$I = \sum_{i=1}^{n} m_i r_i^2$$

Hence, moment of inertia of a rigid body about a fixed axis is defined as the sum of the products of the masses of the particles constituting the body and the squares of their respective distances from the axis of rotation.

Some Important Points about Moment of Inertia

- Moment of inertia is a measure of rotational inertia and it plays same role as played by mass in translational motion.

- So, for a particle of mass m revolving in a path of radius r, moment of inertia is $I = mr^2$.

Particle revolving in a path

- For a system of n particles, $I = \sum\limits_{i=1}^{n} m_i r_i^2$

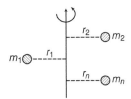

Number of particles revolving in a path

- For continuous mass distributions, treating a differentially small mass as a particle moment of inertia of complete body

$$I = \int r^2 dm$$

where, integral is taken for complete body.

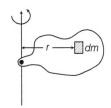

A small particle in a rigid body to find moment of inertia of the whole body

- A heavy wheel called flywheel is attached to the shaft of steam engine, automobile engine etc., because of its large moment of inertia, the flywheel opposes the sudden increase or decrease of the speed of the vehicle. It allows a gradual change in the speed and prevents jerky motion and hence ensure smooth ride of passengers.

- In a bicycle, bullock-cart etc., the moment of inertia is increased by concentrating most of the mass at the rim of the wheel and connecting the rim to the axle through the spokes.
  Even after we stop paddling, the wheels of a bicycle continue to rotate for sometime due to their large moment of inertia.

Relation between Rotational Kinetic Energy and Moment of Inertia

We have rotational kinetic energy

$$KE = \frac{1}{2}(\Sigma mr^2)\,\omega^2$$

$\because$
$$KE = \frac{1}{2}mv^2 = \frac{1}{2}mr^2\omega^2$$

For system of n particles, $KE = \frac{1}{2}(\Sigma\,mr^2)\,\omega^2$

But $$\Sigma\,mr^2 = I$$

Therefore, rotational $KE = \frac{1}{2}I\omega^2$

When $\omega = 1$, rotational $KE = \frac{1}{2}I$

or $\boxed{\text{Moment of inertia, } I = 2 \times \text{rotational KE}}$

Hence, **the moment of inertia of a rigid body about an axis of rotation is numerically equal to twice the rotational kinetic energy of the body when it is rotating with unit angular velocity about that axis.**

EXAMPLE |1| Increasing the Revolution

An energy of 484 J is spent in increasing the speed of a flywheel from 60 rpm to 360 rpm. Calculate moment of inertia of flywheel.

Sol. Energy spent, $W = 484\,J$

Initial speed, $\omega_1 = 60\,rpm = \dfrac{60}{60} \times 2\pi = 2\pi\,rad/s$

Final speed, $\omega_2 = 360\,rpm = \dfrac{360}{60} \times 2\pi = 12\pi\,rad/s$

Moment of inertia, $I = ?$

Energy spent, $W = E_2 - E_1 = \dfrac{1}{2}I\omega_2^2 - \dfrac{1}{2}I\omega_1^2$

$$= \frac{1}{2}I[(12\pi)^2 - (2\pi)^2] = 70I\,\pi^2$$

$\Rightarrow$
$$I = \frac{484}{70 \times \pi^2} = 0.7\,\text{kg-m}^2.$$

Radius of Gyration (K)

The radius of gyration of a body about an axis may be defined as the distance from the axis of a mass point whose mass is equal to the mass of whole body and whose moment of inertia is equal to the moment of inertia of the body about the axis. When square of radius of gyration is multiplied with the mass of the body, gives the moment of inertia of the body about the given axis.

$$I = MK^2$$

$$\boxed{\text{Radius of gyration, } K = \sqrt{\dfrac{I}{M}}}$$

where, K is radius of gyration of the body.

If we consider a rotating body, then its moment of inertia is

$$I = m_1 r_1^2 + m_2 r_2^2 + m_3 r_3^2 + \cdots + m_n r_n^2$$

Let $\quad m_1 = m_2 = m_3 = \cdots = m_n = m,$

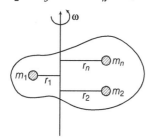

A rotating body with various masses

Then, $\quad I = m r_1^2 + m r_2^2 + m r_3^2 + \cdots + m r_n^2$

$$= m (r_1^2 + r_2^2 + r_3^3 + \cdots + r_n^2) \qquad \text{...(i)}$$

and by definition of radius of gyration,

$$I = m K^2 \qquad \text{...(ii)}$$

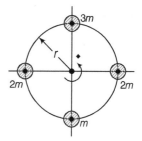

Total mass

A rotating body

So, from Eqs. (i) and (ii), we get

$$M K^2 = m (r_1^2 + r_2^2 + \cdots + r_n^2)$$

or $\quad K^2 = \dfrac{m}{M} (r_1^2 + r_2^2 + \cdots + r_n^2)$

$$K^2 = \dfrac{m}{mn} (r_1^2 + r_2^2 + \cdots r_n^2) \quad [\text{as } M = mn]$$

or $\quad \boxed{K = \sqrt{\dfrac{r_1^2 + r_2^2 + \cdots + r_n^2}{n}}}$

Hence, **radius of gyration of a body about a given axis is equal to root mean square distance of constituent particles from the given axis.**

Note

* Factors on which radius of gyration of a body depend
* Position and direction of the axis of rotation.
* Distribution of mass about the axis of rotation.

EXAMPLE |2| **Radius of Gyration when a number of Masses having Rotation**

Four masses are rotated about an axis as shown. Find radius of gyration of the system. **[NCERT]**

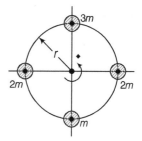

Sol. Moment of inertia of a mass about axis

$$= \text{mass} \times (\text{distance})^2$$

$\therefore$ Moments of inertia of masses are

$$I_1 = 2 m r^2$$

$\Rightarrow \qquad I_2 = 3 m \cdot r^2$

$$I_3 = 2 m \cdot r^2$$

$\Rightarrow \qquad I_4 = m \cdot r^2$

So, total moment of inertia of system of masses

$$= I_1 + I_2 + I_3 + I_4 = 8 m r^2$$

Total mass of system $= 8m$

If radius of gyration is K, then $I = M K^2$

or $\qquad K^2 = \dfrac{I}{M} = \dfrac{8 m r^2}{8 m}$

or $\qquad K = r$

Moment of Inertia in Some Standard Cases

Body	Figure	Moment of inertia	K	K^2/R^2
Thin circular ring, radius R		MR^2	R	1
Thin rod length, L		$\dfrac{1}{12}ML^2$	$\dfrac{L}{\sqrt{12}}$	
Circular disc, radius R		$\dfrac{1}{2}MR^2$	$\dfrac{R}{2}$	$\dfrac{1}{2}$
Hollow cylinder, radius R		MR^2	R	1
Solid cylindrical, radius R		$\dfrac{MR^2}{2}$	$\dfrac{R}{2}$	$\dfrac{1}{2}$
Solid sphere, radius R		$\dfrac{2}{5}MR^2$	$\sqrt{\dfrac{2}{5}}R$	$\dfrac{2}{5}$

KINETIC EQUATIONS OF ROTATIONAL MOTION ABOUT A FIXED AXIS

The three equations of linear motion are

(i) $v = u + at$

(ii) $s = ut + \frac{1}{2} at^2$

(iii) $v^2 - u^2 = 2as$

where, the symbols have their usual meaning.

In the similar way, we can write equations of motion for rotational motion such as

(i) $\omega = \omega_0 + \alpha t$ (ii) $\theta = \omega_0 t + \frac{1}{2} \alpha t^2$

(iii) $\omega^2 - \omega_0^2 = 2\alpha (\theta - \theta_0)$

where, θ_0 and ω_0 are the initial angular displacement and initial angular velocity of the body, respectively.

EXAMPLE |3| Angular Speed of Wheels

The angular speed of a motor wheel is increased from 1200 rpm to 3120 rpm in 16s.

(i) What is its angular acceleration, assuming the acceleration to be uniform?

(ii) How many revolutions does the engine make during this time? **[NCERT]**

Sol. (i) Given,

Initial revolution of the wheel, $N_0 = 1200$ rpm

Final revolution of the wheel, $N = 3120$ rpm

Time, $t = 16$ s

Angular acceleration, $\alpha = ?$

Number of revolutions of the engine $= ?$

Initial angular speed, $\omega_0 = \dfrac{2\pi N_0}{60} = \dfrac{2\pi \times 1200}{60}$

$= 40\pi$ rad/s

Final angular speed, $\omega = \dfrac{2\pi N}{60} = \dfrac{2\pi \times 3120}{60} = 104\pi$ rad/s

Angular acceleration, $\alpha = \dfrac{\omega - \omega_0}{t}$,

$\alpha = \dfrac{104\pi - 40\pi}{16} = 4\pi$ rad/s^2

(ii) Now, evaluate the angular displacement of the motor wheel because the number of revolutions of the wheel of the engine is

$$N_E = \frac{\theta}{2\pi}$$

The angular displacement in time t is

$$\theta = \omega_0 t + \frac{1}{2} \alpha t^2$$

$$\theta = 40\pi \times 16 + \frac{1}{2} \times 4\pi \times (16)^2 = 1152\pi \, \text{rad}$$

Determine the number of revolutions done by the wheel of the engine in time, $t = 16$ s.

$$N_E = \frac{\theta}{2\pi} = \frac{1152\pi}{2\pi}$$

$$N_E = 576$$

The revolutions per second can also be find out as

$$\frac{576}{16} = 36 \text{ rps}$$

EXAMPLE |4| A Constant Angular Acceleration of a Wheel

A wheel has a constant angular acceleration of 4.2 rad/s^2. During a certain 8.05 s interval, it turns through angle of 140 rad. Assuming that wheel started from rest, how long it had been in motion before the start of the 8.0 s?

Sol. Let $\omega_0 = $ initial angular speed at $t = 0$

Then, angle turned at end of 8.0 s is 140°.

Using $\theta = \omega_0 t + \frac{1}{2} \alpha t^2$

We have $\omega_0 = \dfrac{\theta - \frac{1}{2} \alpha t^2}{t}$

$\omega_0 = \dfrac{140 - \frac{1}{2}(4.2)(8.0)^2}{8.0}$

$\omega_0 = 0.7$ rad/s

Now, using $\omega = \omega_0 + \alpha t$ and taking $\omega = 0$.

We have, $t = \dfrac{\omega - \omega_0}{\alpha} = \dfrac{0 - \omega_0}{4.2}$

$= -\dfrac{0.7}{4.2} = -0.16$ s

So, wheel starts from rest 0.16 s before.

DYNAMICS OF ROTATIONAL MOTION ABOUT A FIXED AXIS

From the given table, we compare linear motion and rotational motion about a fixed axis, i.e. z-axis.

Comparison of Translational and Rotational Motion

Pure translation	Pure rotational
Position, x	Angular position, θ
Velocity, $v = \dfrac{dx}{dt}$	Angular velocity, $\omega = \dfrac{d\theta}{dt}$
Acceleration, $a = \dfrac{dv}{dt}$	Angular acceleration, $\alpha = \dfrac{d\omega}{dt}$
Mass, m	Rotational inertia, I

Pure translation	Pure rotational
Newton's second law, $F = ma$	Newton's second law, $\tau = I\alpha$
Work done, $W = \int F\, dx$	Work done, $W = \int \tau\, d\theta$
Kinetic energy, $K = \dfrac{1}{2}mv^2$	Kinetic energy, $K = \dfrac{1}{2}I\omega^2$
Power, $P = Fv$	Power, $P = \tau\omega$
Linear momentum, $p = mv$	Angular momentum, $L = I\omega$

In case of rotational motion about a fixed axis, we have

(i) We need to consider only those forces that lie in planes perpendicular to the axis. The forces which are parallel to the axis of rotation will give torques perpendicular to axis. As the axis is fixed, we will ignore torques perpendicular to the axis.

(ii) We consider only those components of the position vectors which are perpendicular to the axis of rotation. Components of position vectors along the axis will result in torques perpendicular to axis and thus be ignored.

Work Done by a Torque

Consider a rigid body rotating about a fixed axis. Let F_1 be the force acting on a particle of the body at point P_1 with its line of action in a plane perpendicular to the axis.

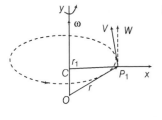

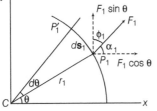

(a) The angular velocity vector ω is directed along the fixed axis

(b) Work done by a force acting on a particle of a body

The particle at P_1 describes a circular path of radius r_1 with centre C on the axis, $CP_1 = r_1$. At time Δt_1 the point moves to the position P_1' and displacement of the particle ds_1.

Work done by the force on the particle is given by

$$dW_1 = \mathbf{F}_1 \cdot ds_1 = F_1 ds_1 \cos\phi_1 = F_1 (r_1\, d\theta)\sin\alpha_1$$

where, ϕ_1 is the angle between $\mathbf{F}_1$ and the tangent at P_1 and α_1 is the angle between $\mathbf{F}_1$ and radius vector $\mathbf{OP}_1$; $\phi_1 + \alpha_1 = 90°$.

Torque due to $\mathbf{F}_1$ about the origin is given by

$$\tau_1 = \mathbf{OP}_1 \times \mathbf{F}_1$$

From Fig. (a) $OP_1 = OC + CP_1$ but OC is along the axis, therefore the torque resulting from it is excluded from our consideration.

Now, the effective torque due to F_1 is given by

$$\tau_1 = \mathbf{CP} \times \mathbf{F}_1$$

$\therefore$

$$dW_1 = \tau_1\, d\theta$$

If there are more than one forces acting on the body, then work done is given by

$$dW = (\tau_1 + \tau_2 + \tau_3 + \ldots)d\theta$$
$$= \tau\, d\theta \qquad [\because \tau_1 + \tau_2 + \tau_3 + \ldots = \tau]$$

Dividing both sides by dt, we get

$$\frac{dW}{dt} = \tau \frac{d\theta}{dt}$$

$\Rightarrow$ $\boxed{\text{Instantaneous power, } P = \tau W}$

The above expression indicates **instantaneous power**.

Relation between Torque and Moment of Inertia

The rotational kinetic energy of a rigid body is represented by

$$\text{KE} = \frac{1}{2}I\omega^2$$

If the body has an angular acceleration α, its rotational kinetic energy will be change.

We know $P = \dfrac{d}{dt}(\text{KE})$

[rate of change of KE is momentum]

$$= \frac{d}{dt}\left(\frac{1}{2}I\omega^2\right)$$

$$= \frac{1}{2}I\frac{d}{dt}(\omega^2) \qquad \text{[if I is constant]}$$

$$= \frac{1}{2}I(2\omega)\frac{d\omega}{dt}$$

$$P = I\omega\alpha \qquad \left[\because \alpha = \frac{d\omega}{dt}\right]$$

$$\tau\omega = I\omega\alpha \qquad [\because P = \tau\omega]$$

$\boxed{\text{Torque, } \tau = I\alpha} \qquad \text{[I is constant]}$

It is similar to the expression of Newton's second law for translational motion with constant mass.

EXAMPLE |5| Cord Wounded Round a Flywheel

A cord of negligible mass is wound round the rim of a flywheel of mass 20 kg and radius 20 cm. A steady pull of 25 N is applied on the cord as shown in the figure. The flywheel is mounted on a horizontal axle with frictionless bearings.

(i) Compute angular acceleration of the flywheel.

(ii) Find the work done by the pull, when 2 m of the cord is unwound.

(iii) Find also the KE of the flywheel at this point. Assume that the flywheel starts from rest.

(iv) Compare the answers of parts (ii) and (iii).

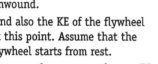

$m = 20$ kg
$R = 20$ cm

$F = 25$ N

Sol. (i) Torque, $\tau = FR = 25 \times 0.20 = 5$ N-m

$$[\because R = 20 \text{ cm} = 0.2 \text{ m}]$$

Moment of inertia, $I = \dfrac{MR^2}{2} = \dfrac{20 \times (0.2)^2}{2} = 0.4$ kg-m^2

Angular acceleration, $\alpha = \dfrac{\tau}{I} = \dfrac{5}{0.4} = 12.5$ rad /s^2

(ii) Work done by the pull, $W = F \times s = 25 \times 2 = 50$ J

(iii) KE $= \dfrac{1}{2} I\omega^2$

$$\omega^2 = \omega_0^2 + 2\alpha\,\theta = 0 + 2 \times 12.5 \times 10$$

$$\left[\because \omega_0 = 0, \theta = \dfrac{2}{0.2} = 10 \text{ rad}\right]$$

$\therefore \qquad$ KE $= \dfrac{1}{2} \times 0.4 \times 250 = 50$ J

(iv) From parts (ii) and (iii), KE $= W$

$\therefore$ No loss of energy due to friction.

EXAMPLE |6| Work Done by a Rotor

To maintain a rotor at a uniform angular speed of 200 rads^{-1}, an engine needs to transmit a torque of 180 N-m. What is the power required by engine? Assume 100% efficiency of engine.

Sol. Work done by torque in turning rotor by angle $d\theta$ is

$$= \tau\, d\theta$$

So, power delivered by engine

$$P = \dfrac{\text{Work done}}{\text{Time taken}} = \tau\, \dfrac{d\theta}{dt}$$

$$[dt = \text{time for turning by angle } d\theta.]$$

or $\qquad P = \tau\omega$

So, power required $= 180 \times 200 = 36000$ W

$$= 36 \text{ kW} \qquad [1 \text{ kW} = 1000 \text{ W}]$$

ANGULAR MOMENTUM IN CASE OF ROTATION ABOUT A FIXED AXIS

The general expression for total angular momentum of a system of particles is given by

$$\mathbf{L} = \sum_{i=1}^{n} \mathbf{r}_i \times \mathbf{p}_i = \sum_{i=1}^{n} \mathbf{r}_i \times m_i \times \mathbf{v}_i$$

$$= \sum_{i=1}^{n} \mathbf{r}_i \times m_i \times (\omega \times \mathbf{r}_i)$$

Using vector triple product, we get

$$\mathbf{L} = \sum_{i=1}^{n} m_i [(\mathbf{r}_i \cdot \mathbf{r}_i)\omega - (\mathbf{r}_i \cdot \omega) \cdot \mathbf{r}_i]$$

$$= \sum_{i=1}^{n} m_i [r_1^2 \omega - 0] = \sum_{i=1}^{n} m_i r_i^2 \omega$$

For any individual particle, the vectors of angular momentum and angular velocity are not necessarily parallel. In case of linear motion, linear momentum and linear velocity vectors are always parallel to each other.

In z-axis, the moment of inertia $I = \sum_{i=1}^{n} m_i \cdot r_1^2$ and

substituting in the above equation, we get

$$\mathbf{L} = L_z = I\omega \,\hat{\mathbf{k}}$$

Differentiating w.r.t. time, we get

$$\dfrac{d}{dt}\mathbf{L}_z = \dfrac{d}{dt}(I\omega)\hat{\mathbf{k}} \qquad \ldots(i)$$

For rotation about fixed axis, we have $\dfrac{d L_z}{dt} = \tau\,\hat{\mathbf{k}} \quad \ldots(ii)$

From Eqs. (i) and (ii), we have

$$\dfrac{d}{dt}(I\omega) = \tau \qquad \ldots(iii)$$

If moment of inertia does not change with time, the Eq. (ii) can be written as

$$\dfrac{I d\omega}{dt} = \tau \text{ or } I\alpha = \tau$$

$$\boxed{\text{Torque, } \tau = I\alpha}$$

EXAMPLE |7| A Rotating Table

A child stands at centre of a turntable with his arms out stretched. The turntable is set rotating with an angular speed of 40 rev/min.

(i) How much is the speed of child if he folds his hands and thereby reduces his MI to $2/5$ times of initial value? Assume turntable is frictionless.

(ii) Show that child's new kinetic energy of rotation is more than the initial kinetic energy. How do you account for this increase in kinetic energy? **[NCERT Exemplar]**

Sol. (i) As no external torque is involved with child + turntable system, so angular momentum of system remains constant.

or $\qquad\qquad I_i \omega_i = I_f \omega_f$

$I_i \omega_i =$ initial angular momentum, $I_f \omega_f =$ final angular momentum

Here, $\qquad \omega_i = 40$ rpm $\Rightarrow I_f = \dfrac{2}{5} I_i$

Substituting, we get

$$I_i \times 40 = \frac{2}{5} I_i \times \omega_f \text{ or } \omega_f = \frac{5 \times 40}{2} = 100 \text{ rpm}$$

(ii) Initial KE $= \frac{1}{2} I_i \omega_i^2 = \frac{1}{2} \times I_i \times (40)^2$

$$= \frac{1}{2} \times I_i \times 1600 = 800 \, I_i$$

Final KE $= \frac{1}{2} I_f \omega_f^2 = \frac{1}{2} \times \frac{2}{5} I_i \times (100)^2$

$$= \frac{1}{2} \times \frac{2}{5} \times I_i \times 100 \times 100 = 2000 \, I_i$$

Clearly, final KE > initial KE. This energy is obtained from conversion of muscular work in KE. Muscular work has to be done in folding of arms.

EXAMPLE |8| Conservation of Angular Momentum

A comet revolves around the Sun in a highly elliptical orbit having a minimum distance of 7×10^{10} m and a maximum distance of 1.4×10^{13} m. If its speed while nearest to the sun is 60 kms^{-1}, find its linear speed when situated farthest from the sun.

Sol. Let mass of comet be M and its angular speed be ω when situated at a distance r from the Sun, then its angular momentum $L = I \omega = Mr^2 \omega$

If v be the linear speed, then $L = Mr^2 \omega = Mrv$

In accordance with conservation law of angular momentum, we can write that $mr_1 v_1 = mr_2 v_2$

$$\therefore \quad v_2 = \frac{r_1 v_1}{r_2} = \frac{7 \times 10^{10} \times 60}{1.4 \times 10^{13}} = 0.3 \text{ km /s or } 300 \text{ m/s}$$

ROLLING MOTION

The rolling motion can be regarded as the combination of pure rotation and pure translation. It is also one of the most common motions observed in daily life.

e.g. The wheels of all vehicles running on a road having rolling motion. The translational motion of a system of particles is the motion of its centre of mass.

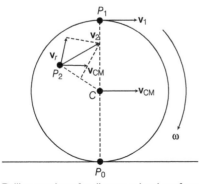

Rolling motion of a disc on a level surface

Suppose the rolling motion (without slipping) of a circular disc on a level surface. At any instant, the point of contact P_0 of the disc with the surface is at rest (as there is no slipping). If $\mathbf{v}_{CM}$ is the velocity of centre of mass which is the geometric centre C of the disc, then the translational velocity of disc in $\mathbf{v}_{CM}$ is parallel to the level surface.

If the rotation of disc is about its symmetric axis, it passes through C. Then, velocity $\mathbf{v}_2$ at point P_2 of disc is vector sum of $\mathbf{v}_{CM}$ and $\mathbf{v}_r$ which is linear velocity on account of rotation.

The magnitude of linear velocity is

$$\mathbf{v}_r = r \omega$$

The velocity $\mathbf{v}_r$ is directed perpendicular to r. The velocity $\mathbf{v}_2$ of point P_2 as the resultant $\mathbf{v}_{CM}$ and $\mathbf{v}_r$. At P_0, the linear velocity $\mathbf{v}_r$ due to rotation is directed opposite to the translational velocity $\mathbf{v}_{CM}$. The magnitude of $\mathbf{v}_r$ is P_0 is $R\omega$, where R is the radius of the disc. As P_0 is instantaneously at rest. So,

$$\boxed{\text{Velocity of centre of mass, } \mathbf{v}_{CM} = R\omega}$$

Thus, for the disc to roll without slipping, the essential condition is $\mathbf{v}_{CM} = R\omega$.

At top of the disc, $v_1 = \mathbf{v}_{CM} + R\omega = 2\mathbf{v}_{CM}$ and is directed parallel to the surface of level.

Kinetic Energy of a Rolling Body

The kinetic energy of a body rolling without slipping is the sum of kinetic energies of translational and rotational motion.

$\therefore$ Total KE of a rolling body

$$= \text{Rotational KE} + \text{Translational KE}$$

$$= \frac{1}{2} I \omega^2 + \frac{1}{2} m v_{CM}^2$$

where v_{CM} is the velocity of centre of mass and I is the moment of inertia about the symmetry axis of the rolling body. If R is the radius and K is the radius of gyration of the rolling body, then,

$$v_{CM} = R\omega$$

and $$I = mK^2$$

$$\therefore \quad K = \frac{1}{2} m v_{CM}^2 + \frac{1}{2} mK^2 \left[\frac{v_{CM}}{R} \right]^2$$

$$\boxed{\text{Kinetic energy, } K = \frac{1}{2} m v_{CM}^2 \left[1 + \frac{K^2}{R^2} \right]}$$

EXAMPLE |9| A Solid Sphere on an Inclined Plane

A solid sphere rolls down two different inclined planes of same height but different angles of inclination

(i) Will it reach the bottom with the same speed in each case?

(ii) Will it take longer to roll down one plane than the other?

(iii) If so, then which one? **[NCERT Exemplar]**

Sol. (i) Yes, (ii) Yes, (iii) On smaller inclination

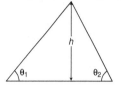

(i) Let mass of sphere = m

Radius of sphere = r

Height of inclined plane = h

At top, total energy is potential energy = mgh

At bottom, the sphere has both rotational and translational kinetic energies.

Hence, total energy at bottom of incline

$$= \frac{1}{2}mv^2 + \frac{1}{2}I\omega^2$$

Here, $I = \frac{2}{5}mr^2$ and $v = r\omega$

So, total energy at bottom

$$= \frac{1}{2}m(r\omega)^2 + \frac{1}{2} \times \frac{2}{5}mr^2 \times \omega^2$$

$$= \frac{7}{10}mr^2\omega^2 = \frac{7}{10}mv^2$$

As sphere is not slipping, no energy is lost in rolling down the plane

So, equating energy at bottom and at top

$$\frac{7}{10}mv^2 = mgh \quad \text{or} \quad v = \sqrt{\frac{10}{7}gh}$$

Hence, velocity of sphere depends only on height h and acceleration due to gravity g. So, velocity at bottom is same in both cases.

(ii) When sphere rolls down the plane, forces acting on sphere are as shown

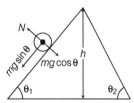

As only force down the plane is $mg \sin\theta$, acceleration down the plane is $g \sin\theta$.

If $\theta_2 > \theta_1$

Then, $g \sin\theta_2 > g \sin\theta_1$ or $a_2 > a_1$

Now, using $v = u + at$

and taking $u = 0$, $v = at$ or $t = \dfrac{v}{a}$

(iii) As v is same in both cases, $t \propto \dfrac{1}{a}$. As $a_2 > a_1$,

so $t_2 > t_1$.

Hence, sphere will take a longer time to reach the bottom of inclined plane having smaller inclination.

| TOPIC PRACTICE 2 |

OBJECTIVE Type Questions

1. The angular velocity of a wheel increases from 100 rps to 300 rps in 10 s. The number of revolutions made during that time is

   (a) 600   (b) 1500

   (c) 1000   (d) 2000

   Sol. (d) Angular displacement θ during time t, assuming constant acceleration be

   $$\theta = \frac{\omega_0 + \omega_t}{2}$$

   $$= \frac{100 + 300}{2} \times 10$$

   $$= 2000 \text{ revolutions}$$

2. If a girl rotating on a chair bends her hand as shown in figure the (neglecting frictional force).

   (a) I_{girl} will reduce

   (b) I_{girl} will increase

   (c) ω_{girl} will reduce

   (d) None of the above

   Sol. (a) As there is no external torque, if the girl bends her hands, her MI about the rotational axis will decrease. By conservation of angular momentum,

   if $L = I\omega$ = constant, then ω will increase.

3. When a disc rotates with uniform angular velocity, which of the following is not true?

   [NCERT Exemplar]

   (a) The sense of rotation remains same

   (b) The orientation of the axis of rotation remains same

   (c) The speed of rotation is non-zero and remains same

   (d) The angular acceleration is zero

   Sol. (d) We know that angular acceleration

   $$\alpha = \frac{d\omega}{dt}, \text{ given } \omega = \text{constant}$$

   where ω is angular velocity of the disc

   $$\Rightarrow \quad \alpha = \frac{d\omega}{dt} = \frac{0}{dt} = 0$$

   Hence, angular acceleration is zero.

VERY SHORT ANSWER Type Questions

4. Why is moment of inertia also called rotational inertia?

   Sol. The moment of inertia gives a measure of inertia in rotational motion.

   So, it is also called rotational inertia.

5. Does the moment of inertia of a rigid body change with the speed of rotation?

Sol. No, because the moment of inertia depends upon the axis of rotation and distribution of mass.

6. Two solid spheres of the same mass are made of metals of different densities. Which of them has a larger moment of inertia about the diameter? Why?

Sol. The sphere with smaller density will have larger radius and hence larger moment of inertia.

7. In a flywheel, most of the mass is concentrated at the rim. Explain why?

Sol. Concentration of mass at the rim increases the moment of inertia and thereby brings uniform motion.

8. What is the moment of inertia of a sphere of mass 20 kg and radius $\frac{1}{4}$ m about its diameter?

Sol. Moment of inertia of a sphere about its diameter,

$$I = \frac{2}{5}mR^2 = \frac{2}{5} \times 20 \times \left(\frac{1}{4}\right)^2 = 0.5 \text{ kg-m}^2$$

9. Does the radius of gyration depend upon the speed of rotation of the body?

Sol. No, it depends only on the distribution of mass of the body.

10. About which axis would a uniform cube have a minimum rotational inertia?

Sol. In a uniform cube, the mass is more concentrated about a diagonal.

11. A constant torque of 120 N-m rotates its point of action by an angle of 30°. What is the work done by the torque?

Sol. Work done by the torque, $W = t\theta$

$$= 120 \times \left(\frac{30 \times \pi}{180}\right) = 20\pi \text{ J}$$

12. A ballet dancer stretches her hand out for slowing down. Name the conservation obeyed.

Sol. This is based on the conservation of angular momentum.

13. A wheel of moment of inertia 50 kg-m² about its own axis is revolving at a rate of 5 revolutions per second. What is its angular momentum?

Sol. Here, $I = 50$ kg-m², $\omega = 5$ rps $= 5 \times 2\pi$ rad/s

∴ Angular momentum $L = I\omega = 50 \times 10\pi = 500\pi$ J-s

14. Can the mass of body be taken to be concentrated at its centre of mass for the purpose of calculating its rotational inertia?

Sol. No, the moment of inertia greatly depends on the distribution of mass about the axis of rotation.

15. If a cube is melted and is casted into a sphere, does moment of inertia about an axis through centre of mass increases or decreases.

Sol. Moment of inertia of a sphere is less than that of a cube of same mass.

SHORT ANSWER Type Questions

16. A person is standing on a rotating table with metal spheres in his hands. If he withdraw his hands to his chest, what will be the effect on his angular velocity?

Sol. When the person withdraws his hands to his chest, his moment of inertia decreases. No external torque is acting on the system. So, to conserve angular momentum, the angular velocity increases.

17. Why does a solid sphere have smaller moment of inertia than a hollow cylinder of same mass and radius about an axis passing through their axis of symmetry? [NCERT Exemplar]

Sol. All mass of a hollow cylinder lies at a distance R from axis of rotation. Whereas in case of a sphere, most of mass lies at a distance less than R from axis of rotation. As moment of inertia is $\Sigma M_i R_i^2$, so sphere as a lower value of moment of inertia.

18. Two boys of the same weight sit at the opposite ends of a diameter of a rotating circular table. What happens to the speed of rotation if they move nearer to the axis of rotation?

Sol. The moment of inertia of the system (circular table + two boys) decreases. To conserve angular momentum $(L = I\omega = \text{constant})$, the speed of rotation of the circular table increases.

19. If ice on poles melts, then what is the change in duration of day?

Sol. Molten ice from poles goes into ocean and so mass is going away from axis of rotation. So, moment of inertia of earth increases and to conserve angular momentum, angular velocity (ω) decreases. So, time period of rotation increases $(T = 2\pi/\omega)$. So, net effect of global warming is increasing in the duration of day.

20. The speed of a whirl wind in a tornado is alarmingly high. Why?

Sol. In a whirl wind, the air from nearby region gets concentrated in a small space thereby decreasing the value of moment of inertia considerably. Since, $I\omega = \text{constant}$, due to decrease in moment of inertia, the angular speed becomes quite high.

21. A solid cylinder of mass 20 kg rotates about its axis with angular speed of 100 rad/s. The radius of cylinder is 0.25 m. What is KE of rotation of cylinder? **[NCERT Exemplar]**

Sol. $M = 20$ kg, $\omega = 100$ rad/s, $R = 0.25$ m

Moment of inertia of cylinder about its own axis

$$= \frac{1}{2}MR^2 = \frac{1}{2} \times 20 \times (0.25)^2 = 0.625 \text{ kg-m}^2$$

Rotational KE $= \frac{1}{2}I\omega^2$

$$= \frac{1}{2} \times 0.625 \times (100)^2 = 3125 \text{ J}$$

22. If earth contracts to half its radius. What would be the length of the day?

Sol. The moment of inertia $\left(I = \frac{2}{5}MR^2\right)$ of the earth about

its own axis will become one-fourth and so its angular velocity will become four times ($L = I\omega =$ constant). Hence, the time period will reduce to one-fourth ($T = 2\pi/\omega$), i.e. 6 hours.

23. Explain how a cat is able to land on its feet after a fall taking the advantage of principle of conservation of angular momentum?

Sol. When a cat falls to ground from a height, it stretches its body alongwith the tail so that its moment of inertia becomes high. Since, $I\omega$ is to remain constant, the value of angular speed ω decreases and therefore the cat is able to land on the ground gently.

LONG ANSWER Type I Questions

24. A rope of negligible mass is wound round a hollow cylinder of mass 3 kg and radius 40 cm. What is angular acceleration of the cylinder, if the rope is pulled with a force of 30 N? What is linear acceleration of the rope? Assume no slipping. **[NCERT]**

Sol. Torque on cylinder, $\tau =$ force $\times$ radius

$$= 30 \times 0.4 = 12 \text{ N-m}$$

Moment of inertia of hollow cylinder about its axis

$$I = MR^2 = 3 \times (0.4)^2 = 0.48 \text{ kg-m}^2$$

Also, $\tau = I\alpha \Rightarrow \alpha = \dfrac{\tau}{I}$

$\therefore \qquad \alpha = \dfrac{12}{0.48} = 25 \text{ s}^{-2}$

Linear acceleration of rope

$$a = \frac{F}{m} = \frac{30}{3} = 10 \text{ m/s}^2$$

25. Torques of equal magnitude are applied to a hollow cylinder and a solid sphere, both having the same mass and radius. The cylinder is free to rotate about its standard axis of symmetry and the sphere is free to rotate about an axis passing through its centre. Which of the two will acquire a greater angular speed after a given time? **[NCERT]**

💡 Moment of inertia of the hollow cylinder about its axis of symmetry.
$$I_1 = MR^2$$
Moment of inertia of the solid sphere about its diameter, $\quad I_2 = \frac{2}{5}MR^2$

Sol. Let M and R be the mass and radius of the solid sphere and hollow cylinder.

Let torque τ of equal magnitude be applied on hollow cylinder and solid sphere. The angular accelerations produced in it are α_1 and α_2, respectively.

$\therefore \qquad \tau = I_1\alpha_1$ and $\tau = I_2\alpha_2$

Therefore, $\quad I_1\alpha_1 = I_2\alpha_2$

or $\qquad \dfrac{\alpha_1}{\alpha_2} = \dfrac{I_2}{I_1} = \dfrac{\frac{2}{5}MR^2}{MR^2} = \dfrac{2}{5}$

or $\qquad \alpha_2 = \dfrac{5}{2}\alpha_1 = 2.5\alpha_1 \qquad \ldots(i)$

Let after time t, ω_1 and ω_2 be the angular speeds of the hollow cylinder and solid sphere, respectively.

$\therefore \qquad \omega_1 = \omega_0 + \alpha_1 t \qquad \qquad \ldots(ii)$

and $\qquad \omega_2 = \omega_0 + \alpha_2 t = \omega_0 + 2.5\,\alpha_1 t \quad \ldots(iii)$

From Eqs. (ii) and (iii), we get $\omega_2 > \omega_1$

Therefore, solid sphere will acquire a greater angular speed after a given time.

26. A wheel in uniform motion about an axis passing through its centre and perpendicular to its plane is considered to be in mechanical (translational and rotational) equilibrium because no net external torque is required to sustain its motion.

However, the particles that constitute the wheel to experience a centripetal acceleration towards the centre. How do you reconcile this fact with the wheel begin in equilibrium?

How would you set a half wheel into uniform motion about an axis passing through the centre of mass of the wheel and perpendicular to its plane? Will you require external forces to sustain the motion? **[NCERT Exemplar]**

Sol. The centripetal acceleration in a wheel arise due to the internal elastic forces which in pairs cancel each other. So the system remains in equilibrium during rolling.

In a half wheel, the system is not symmetrical so, direction of angular momentum does not coincide with the direction of angular velocity and hence an external torque is required to maintain the rotation.

27. A solid cylinder of mass 20 kg rotates about its axis with angular speed (100 rad/s). The radius of cylinder is 0.25 m. What is the kinetic energy associated with the rotation of the cylinder? What is the magnitude of angular momentum of the cylinder about its axis?　　**[NCERT]**

Sol. Moment of inertia of cylinder about its axis = $\dfrac{1}{2}MR^2$

M = mass, R = radius

$$= \dfrac{1}{2} \times 20 \times (0.25)^2 \, \text{kg-m}^2$$

$$= 0.625 \ \text{kg-m}^2$$

Kinetic energy of rotating cylinder

$$= \dfrac{1}{2}\, I\omega^2 = \dfrac{1}{2}\, (0.625)\,(100)^2 \ \text{J}$$

$$= 3125 \, \text{J}$$

Angular momentum of cylinder about its own axis

$$= I\omega = 0.625 \times 100$$

$$= 62.5 \ \text{kg-m}^2/\text{s}$$

28. A hoop of radius 2 m weighs 100 kg. It rolls along a horizontal floor so that its centre of mass has a speed of 20 cm/s. How much work has to be done to stop it?　　**[NCERT Exemplar]**

Sol. Moment of inertia of hoop about its centre

$$I = MR^2$$

and energy of loop = translational kinetic energy of CM and rotational kinetic energy about axis through CM.

$$= \dfrac{1}{2}\, mv_{\text{CM}}^2 + \dfrac{1}{2}\, I\omega^2 \qquad \left[I = mR^2 \text{and } \omega = \dfrac{v}{R} \right]$$

$$= \dfrac{1}{2} mv_{\text{CM}}^2 + \dfrac{1}{2}\, mR^2 \times \dfrac{v_{\text{CM}}^2}{R^2} = mv_{\text{CM}}^2$$

Work done is stopping the hoop

$$= \text{total KE of loop}$$

$$= mv_{\text{CM}}^2 = 100 \times (0.2)^2 = 4 \ \text{J}$$

29. A bullet of mass 10 g and speed 500 m/s is fired into a door and gets embedded exactly at the centre of the door. The door is 1.0 m wide and weight 12 kg. It is hinged at one end and rotates about a vertical axis practically without friction. Find the angular speed of the door just after the bullet embeds into it.　　**[NCERT]**

Sol. Given, mass of bullet $(m) = 10\,\text{g} = 0.01$ kg

Speed of bullet $(v) = 500$ m/s

Width of the door $(l) = 1.0$ m

Mass of the door $(M) = 12$ kg

As bullet gets embedded exactly at the centre of the door, therefore its distance from the hinged end of the door,

$$r = \dfrac{l}{2} = \dfrac{1}{2}\,\text{m}$$

Angular momentum transferred by the bullet to the door,

$$L = mv \times r = 0.01 \times 500 \times \dfrac{1}{2} = 2.5 \ \text{Js}$$

Moment of inertia of the door about the vertical axis at one of its end,　$I = \dfrac{Ml^2}{3} = \dfrac{12 \times (1)^2}{3} = 4 \ \text{kg-m}^2$

But angular momentum, $L = I\omega$

$$2.5 = 4 \times \omega = \dfrac{2.5}{4} = 0.625 \ \text{rad/s}$$

30. A uniform circular disc of radius R is rolling on a horizontal surface. Determine the tangential velocity at

(i) upper most point　(ii) at centre of mass

(iii) at point of contact

Sol. Rolling is a combination of pure rotation and translation

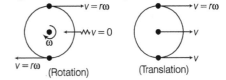

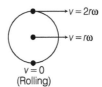

So, tangential velocity

(i) of uppermost point is $2\,r\omega$.

(ii) of centre of mass is $r\omega$.

(iii) of point of contact is zero.

31. A uniform disc of radius R is resting on a table on its rim. The coefficient of friction between disc and table is μ (figure). Now, the disc is pulled with a force F as shown in the figure. What is the maximum value of F for which the disc rolls without slipping?

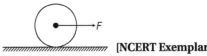

[NCERT Exemplar]

Sol. Let the acceleration of the centre of mass of disc be a, then

$$Ma = F - f$$

The angular acceleration of the disc is $\alpha = a/R$ (if there is no sliding).

Then, $\left(\dfrac{1}{2}MR^2 \right)\alpha = Rf \ \Rightarrow \ Ma = 2f$

Thus, $f = F/3$. Since, there is no sliding.

$\Rightarrow \qquad\qquad f \le \mu mg \ \Rightarrow \ F \le 3\mu Mg$

32. A cylinder of mass 10 kg and radius 15 cm is rolling perfectly on a plane of inclination 30°.

The coefficient of static friction, $\mu_s = 0.25$.

(i) How much is the force of friction acting on the cylinder?

(ii) What is the work done against friction during rolling?

(iii) If the inclination θ of the plane is increased, at what value of θ does the cylinder begin to skid and not roll perfectly? [NCERT]

Sol. Given, mass of the cylinder, $m = 10$ kg

Radius, $r = 15$ cm $= 0.15$ m

Inclination of plane, $\theta = 30°$

Coefficient of static friction, $\mu_s = 0.25$

(i) Force of friction acting on the cylinder on the inclined

plane, $\quad F = \dfrac{1}{3} mg \sin\theta = \dfrac{1}{3} \times 10 \times 9.8 \times \sin 30°$

$\quad\quad = \dfrac{1}{3} \times 10 \times 9.8 \times \dfrac{1}{2} = 16.3$ N

(ii) Force of friction acts perpendicular to the direction of displacement.

∴ Work done against friction during rolling

$\quad\quad W = Fs \cos 90° = 0$

(iii) For rolling without slipping,

$\quad\quad \mu = \dfrac{1}{3} \tan\theta$

or $\quad \tan\theta = 3\mu = 3 \times 0.25 = 0.75 = \tan 36°54'$

or $\quad\quad \theta = 36°54' = 37°$

33. Explain why friction is necessary to make the disc in figure rolling in the direction indicated.

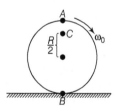

(i) Give the direction of frictional force at B and the sense of frictional torque before perfect rolling begins.

(ii) What is the force of friction after perfect rolling begins? [NCERT]

Sol. To roll a disc, one require a linear velocity which can be provided only by a tangential force. As frictional force is the only tangential force in this case, so it is necessary for the rolling of the disc. Initially, friction will be kinetic.

(i) As frictional force at B opposes the angular velocity of B. So, frictional force is in the forward direction, the sense of frictional torque is such as to oppose the angular motion and produce some linear motion, so

that the condition of pure rolling ($v_{CM} = R\omega$) should be fulfilled.

(ii) After pure rolling starts there will be no need of friction, so friction force will become zero.

LONG ANSWER Type II Questions

34. A solid disc and a ring, both of radius 10 cm are placed on a horizontal table simultaneously, with initial angular speed equal to 10π rads^{-1}.

Which of the two will start to roll earlier? The coefficient of kinetic friction is $\mu_k = 0.2$? [NCERT]

💡 In case of pure rotation without translation, the velocity of centre of mass is zero. The friction reduces the speed at the point of contact and as such accelerates the centre of mass till the velocity of centre of mass becomes equal to $v = R\omega$ and the instantaneous velocity at the contact point becomes zero.

Sol. Thus, the force of friction $\mu_k \, mg$ produces an acceleration a in the centre of mass. So, the equation of motion for centre of mass is

$$\mu_k mg = ma \quad\quad ...(i)$$

The torque due to force of friction is $\mu_k \, mg \times R$. It produces angular retardation given by

$$\mu_k \, mgR = -I\alpha \quad\quad ...(ii)$$

Rolling begins when $v = R\omega$

But $\quad\quad v = 0 + at = \mu_k gt \quad\quad ...(iii)$

$\quad\quad$ [from Eq. (i), $a = \mu_k g$]

and $\quad \omega = \omega_0 + \alpha t = \omega_0 - \dfrac{\mu_k mgR}{I} t \quad$ [using Eq. (ii)]

or $\quad \dfrac{v}{R} = \omega_0 - \dfrac{\mu_k mgR}{I} t \Rightarrow \dfrac{\mu_k gt}{R} = \omega_0 - \dfrac{\mu_0 mgRt}{I}$

or $\quad \dfrac{\mu_k gt}{R}\left[1 + \dfrac{mR^2}{I} \right] = \omega_0 \quad$ or $\quad t = \dfrac{R\omega_0}{\mu_k g\left(1 + \dfrac{mR^2}{I} \right)}$

For a disc, $I = mR^2/2$

∴ $\quad\quad t = \dfrac{R\omega_0}{3\mu_k g} = \dfrac{0.10 \times 10\pi}{3 \times 0.2 \times 9.8} = 0.53$ s

For a ring, $I = mR^2$

∴ $\quad\quad t = \dfrac{R\omega_0}{2\mu_k g} = \dfrac{0.10 \times 10\pi}{2 \times 0.2 \times 9.8} = 0.80$ s

Thus, the disc begins to roll earlier than the ring.

35. Two discs of moment of inertia I_1 and I_2 (about their axes normal to plane of disc and passing through centre) are rotating with angular speeds ω_1 and ω_2 are brought into contact face to face with their axes coinciding.

(i) What is angular speed of two discs system?

(ii) Show that the kinetic energy of combined system is less than the sum of initial kinetic energies of the two discs.

(iii) How do you account for loss of energy? [NCERT]

Sol. Let ω be the final angular velocity of two discs system.

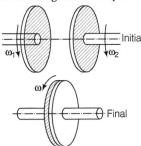

(i) According to conservation of angular momentum, we get

Total initial angular momentum = Final angular momentum

$$\Rightarrow \quad I_1\omega_1 + I_2\omega_2 = (I_1 + I_2)\,\omega$$

$$\Rightarrow \quad \omega = \left(\frac{I_1\omega_1 + I_2\omega_2}{I_1 + I_2}\right)$$

(ii) Initial KE of disc $= K_1 + K_2 = \dfrac{1}{2} I_1\omega_1^2 + \dfrac{1}{2} I_2\omega_2^2$

Final KE of disc system $= \dfrac{1}{2}(I_1 + I_2)\,\omega^2$

$$= \frac{1}{2}(I_1 + I_2)\cdot\left(\frac{I_1\omega_1 + I_2\omega_2}{I_1 + I_2}\right)^2$$

Loss of KE = Initial KE − Final KE

$$= \left(\frac{1}{2} I_1\omega_1^2 + \frac{1}{2} I_2\omega_2^2\right)$$

$$- \frac{1}{2}(I_1 + I_2)\cdot\left(\frac{I_1\omega_1 + I_2\omega_2}{I_1 + I_2}\right)^2$$

$$= \frac{1}{2(I_1 + I_2)}(I_1^2\omega_1^2 + I_1 I_2\omega_2^2 + I_1 I_2\omega_1^2$$

$$+ I_2^2\omega_2^2 - I_1^2\omega_1^2 - I_2^2\omega_2^2 - 2I_1 I_2\omega_1\omega_2)$$

$$= \frac{1}{2(I_1 + I_2)}(I_1 I_2\omega_2^2 + I_1 I_2\omega_1^2 - 2I_1 I_2\omega_1\omega_2)$$

$$= \frac{1}{2(I_1 + I_2)}\cdot I_1 I_2 \cdot(\omega_2^2 + \omega_1^2 - 2\omega_1\omega_2)$$

$$= \frac{I_1 I_2}{2(I_1 + I_2)}\cdot(\omega_1 - \omega_2)^2$$

As above quantity is positive, so a loss of energy occurs.

(iii) When 2 discs come in contact, they rub against each other till both reach same energy.

36. A man stands on a rotating platform with his arms stretched horizontally holding a 5 kg weight in each hand. The angular speed of the platform is 30 rpm. The man then brings his arms close to his body with the distance of each weight from the axis changing from 90 cm to 20 cm. The moment of inertia of the man together with the platform may be taken to be constant and equal to 7.6 kg-m^2.

    (i) What is his new angular speed? (Neglect friction)

    (ii) Is kinetic energy conserved in the process? If not, from where does the change come about? **[NCERT]**

Sol. (i) Moment of inertia of man and platform system

$$I_i = 7.6 \text{ kg-m}^2$$

Change in moment of inertia of man and platform system when he stretches his hands to a distance of 90 cm $= 2 \times mr^2 = 2 \times 5 \times (0.9)^2$

$$= 8.1 \text{ kg-m}^2$$

$$I_i = I + 8.1 = 7.6 + 8.1 = 15.7 \text{ kg-m}^2$$

Initial angular velocity, $\omega_i = 30$ rpm

Initial angular momentum of system,

$$L_i = I_i\omega_i = 15.7 \text{ kg-m}^2 \times 30 \text{ rpm}$$

When man folds his hands to a distance of 20 cm,

Moment of inertia of man $= 2 \times mr^2 = 2 \times 5 \times (0.2)^2$

$$= 0.4 \text{ kg-m}^2$$

So, final moment of inertia of man and platform system

$$= 7.6 + 0.4 = 8 \text{ kg-m}^2$$

Final angular momentum of system

$$L_f = I_f\omega_f = 8 \times \omega_f$$

Equating initial and final values

$$L_i = L_f$$

$$\Rightarrow \quad \omega_f = \frac{15.7 \times 30}{8}$$

$$= 58.88 \text{ rpm}$$

(ii) KE is not conserved in process.

$$K_{\text{final}} > K_{\text{initial}}$$

Muscular work done by the man in folding his arms is converted into KE.

37. A solid cylinder rolls up an inclined plane of angle of inclination 30°. At the bottom of inclined plane, the CM of cylinder has a speed of 5 m/s.

    (i) How far will the cylinder go up the plane? **[NCERT]**

    (ii) How long it will take to return to the bottom?

Sol. (i) Energy at point $A = \dfrac{1}{2} mv^2 + \dfrac{1}{2} I\omega^2$

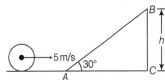

where, $I = \frac{1}{2}mr^2$ and $\omega = \frac{v}{r}$

So, energy at point $A = \frac{1}{2}mv^2 + \frac{1}{2} \times \frac{1}{2}mr^2 \times \frac{v^2}{r^2}$

$$= \frac{1}{2}mv^2 + \frac{1}{4}mv^2 = \frac{3}{4}mv^2$$

and energy at point $B = mgh$

Equating we get, $\frac{3}{4}mv^2 = mgh$

or $\qquad h = \frac{3}{4}\frac{v^2}{g} = \frac{3}{4} \times \frac{5^2}{9.8} = 1.91$ m

(ii) In ΔABC, $\qquad AB = \dfrac{h}{\sin 30°}$

or $\qquad AB = \dfrac{1.91}{0.5} = 3.82$ m

So, cylinder rolls a direction of 3.82 m up the incline.

38. A disc of radius R is rotating with an angular speed ω, about a horizontal axis. It is placed on a horizontal table. The coefficient of kinetic friction is μ_k.

    (i) What was the velocity of its centre of mass before being brought in contact with the table?

    (ii) What happens to the linear velocity of a point on its rim when placed in contact with the table?

    (iii) What happens to the linear speed of the centre of mass when disc is placed in contact with the table?

    (iv) Which force is responsible for the effects in (ii) and (iii)?

    (v) What condition should be satisfied for rolling to begin?

    (vi) Calculate the time taken for the rolling to begin. **[NCERT Exemplar]**

Sol. (i) Before the disc is brought in contact with table, it is only rotating about its horizontal axis. So, its centre of mass is at rest, i.e. $v_{CM} = 0$.

    (ii) When rim is placed in contact with the table, then its linear velocity at any point on the rim of disc will reduce due to kinetic friction.

    (iii) If rotating disc is placed in contact with the table, its centre of mass acquires some velocity (which was zero before contact) due to kinetic friction. So, linear velocity of CM will increase.

    (iv) Kinetic friction.

    (v) Rolling will begin when $v_{CM} = R\omega$.

    (vi) Acceleration produced in centre of mass due to friction $\quad a_{CM} = \dfrac{F}{m} = \dfrac{\mu_k mg}{m} = \mu_k g$

Angular acceleration produced by the torque due to friction. $\qquad \alpha = \dfrac{\tau}{I} = \dfrac{\mu_k mgR}{I}$

$\therefore \qquad\qquad v_{CM} = u_{CM} + a_{CM}t$

$\Rightarrow \qquad\qquad v_{CM} = \mu_k gt$

and $\qquad \omega = \omega_0 + \alpha t \Rightarrow \omega = \omega_0 - \dfrac{\mu_k mgR}{I}t$

For rolling without slipping,

$$\frac{v_{CM}}{R} = \omega_0 - \frac{\mu_k mgR}{I}t$$

$\Rightarrow \qquad \dfrac{\mu_k gt}{R} = \omega_0 - \dfrac{\mu_k mgR_t}{I}$

$$t = \frac{R\omega_0}{\mu_k g\left(1 + \dfrac{mR^2}{I}\right)}$$

39. Prove the result that the velocity v of translation of a rolling body (like a ring, disc, cylinder or sphere) at the bottom of an inclined plane of a height h is given by $v^2 = \dfrac{2gh}{(1 + K^2/R^2)}$ using dynamical consideration (i.e. by consideration of forces and torques). Note K is the radius of gyration of the body about its symmetry axis and R is the radius of the body. The body starts from rest at the top of the plane. **[NCERT]**

Sol. Let a body of mass M and radius R is rolling down a plane inclined at an angle θ with the horizontal and forces acting on the body are also shown in figure.

Let a be the downward acceleration of the body. The equations of motion for the body can be written as

$$N - Mg\cos\theta = 0$$
$$F = Ma = Mg\sin\theta - f$$

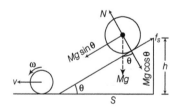

As the force of friction f provides the necessary torque for rolling, so

$$\tau = f \times R = I\alpha = MK^2\left(\frac{a}{R}\right)$$

or $\qquad f = M\dfrac{K^2}{R^2} \cdot a$

where, K is the radius of gyration of the body about its axis of rotation. Clearly,

$$Ma = Mg \sin \theta - M \frac{K^2}{R^2} \cdot a$$

or

$$a = \frac{g \sin \theta}{(1 + K^2/R^2)}$$

Let h be height of the inclined plane and s the distance travelled by the body down the plane. The velocity v attained by the body at the bottom of the inclined plane can be obtained as follows

$$v^2 - u^2 = 2as$$

or

$$v^2 - 0^2 = 2 \cdot \frac{g \sin \theta}{(1 + K^2/R^2)} \cdot s$$

or

$$v^2 = \frac{2gh}{1 + K^2/R^2} \qquad \left[\because \frac{h}{s} = \sin \theta\right]$$

or

$$v = \sqrt{\frac{2gh}{(1 + K^2/R^2)}}$$

40. Obtain an expression for linear acceleration of a cylinder rolling down an inclined plane and hence find the condition for the cylinder to roll down the inclined plane without slipping.

Sol. When a cylinder rolls down on an inclined plane, then forces involved are
(i) Weight mg (ii) Normal reaction N (iii) Friction f

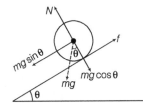

From free body diagram,

$$N - mg \cos \theta = 0$$

or

$$N = mg \cos \theta$$

Also, if a = acceleration of centre of mass down the plane, then

$$F_{net} = ma = mg \sin \theta - f \qquad \text{...(i)}$$

As friction produces torque necessary for rotation,

$$\tau = I\alpha = fR$$

$$\Rightarrow \qquad f = \frac{I\alpha}{R} = \frac{Ia}{R^2} \qquad \left[\therefore \alpha = \frac{a}{R}\right]$$

Substituting for f in Eq. (i), we get

$$ma = mg \sin \theta - \frac{Ia}{R^2}$$

$$\Rightarrow \qquad a = g \sin \theta - \frac{Ia}{mR^2}$$

For cylinder, $I = \frac{1}{2} mR^2$

$$\therefore \qquad a = g \sin \theta - \frac{a}{2}$$

$$\Rightarrow \qquad \frac{3a}{2} = g \sin \theta$$

$$\Rightarrow \qquad a = \frac{2g \sin \theta}{3}$$

and from Eq. (i), the value of friction is

$$f = mg \sin \theta - ma$$

$$= mg \sin \theta - \frac{2}{3} mg \sin \theta$$

$$= \frac{1}{3} mg \sin \theta$$

If μ_s = coefficient of static friction, then

$$\mu_s = \frac{f}{N} \quad \text{or} \quad \mu_s = \frac{1}{3} \tan \theta$$

$\therefore$ For perfect rolling, $\mu_s \geq \frac{1}{3} \tan \theta$

ASSESS YOUR TOPICAL UNDERSTANDING

OBJECTIVE Type Questions

1. One solid sphere A and another hollow sphere B are of same mass and same outer radius. Their moments of inertia about their diameters are respectively, I_A and I_B such that
   (a) $I_A = I_B$ (b) $I_A > I_B$
   (c) $I_A < I_B$ (d) None of these

2. In pure rotation,
   (a) all particles of the body move in a straight line
   (b) all particles of body move in concentric circles
   (c) all particles of body move in non-concentric circles
   (d) all particles of body have same speed

3. Sphere is in pure accelerated rolling motion in the figure shown,

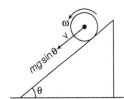

Choose the correct option.
(a) The direction of f_s is upwards
(b) The direction of f_s is downwards
(c) The direction of gravitational force is upwards
(d) The direction of normal reaction is downwards

4. A merry-go-round, made of a ring-like platform of radius R and mass M, is revolving with angular speed ω. A person of mass M is standing on it. At one instant, the person jumps off the round, radially away from the centre of the round (as seen from the round). The speed of the round of afterwards is

[NCERT Exemplar]

(a) 2ω
(b) ω
(c) $\dfrac{\omega}{2}$
(d) 0

Answer

1. (c)	2. (c)	3. (a)	4. (a)

VERY SHORT ANSWER Type Question

5. On which factors, moment of inertia of a rigid body depends?

SHORT ANSWER Type Question

6. A horizontal disc rotating about a vertical axis perpendicular to its plane and passing through centre makes 180 rpm. A small lump of wet mud of mass 10 g falls on disc lightly and sticks to it at a distance of 8 cm from its axis. If now the disc with mud makes 150 rpm only, calculate the moment of inertia of the disc.

[**Ans.** $I = 3.2 \times 10^{-8}$ kg-m^2]

7. Describe moment of inertia. Give two examples about how to find moment of inertia. Hence, describe radius of gyration.

8. Give three illustrations to show that moment of inertia is the rotational analogue of mass.

LONG ANSWER Type I Questions

9. Write three equations of motion for the rotational motion about a fixed axis.

10. Prove the relation $\tau = I\alpha$, for a rigid body rotating about a fixed axis.

11. A disc is rolling on a horizontal floor with an angular speed ω and translation speed v. What fraction of total kinetic energy is rotational kinetic energy?

12. A diver bends his body while jumping in the swimming pool, due to this his angular speed increases. On which law, this incidence is based upon?

13. A body is in pure rolling on a horizontal road. What will be the net velocity of the uppermost point of that rolling body? The radius of rolling body is R and its angular velocity about axis passing through centre of mass is ω.   [**Ans.** $2R\omega$]

LONG ANSWER Type II Questions

14. A sphere is rolling on a moving plank as shown in the above figure. What will be the velocity of centre of mass of the sphere?   [**Ans.** $(v + R\omega)$]

15. A uniform disc of radius R and mass m is resting on table on its rim. The coefficient of friction between rim and table is μ. Now, disc is pulled with force F. What is the maximum value of F for which the disc rolls without slipping?   [**Ans.** $F_{max} = 3\mu\, mg$]

16. A cylinder is released from rest from the top of an incline of inclination θ and length l. If the cylinder rolls without slipping. What will be its speed when it reaches the bottom?

$$\left[\textbf{Ans.}\ v = \sqrt{\frac{4}{3}gl\sin\theta}\,\right]$$

SUMMARY

- A body is said to be a rigid body when it has a perfectly definite shape and size. The distance between all pairs of particles of such a body do not change while applying any force on it.

- The centre of mass of a body or a system of bodies is the point which moves as through all of the mass were concentrated there and all external forces were applied to it.

- For a system of n-particles, the centre of mass is given by $x_{CM} = \dfrac{m_1 x_1 + m_2 x_2 + \ldots + m_n x_n}{m_1 + m_2 + \ldots + mn} = \dfrac{\displaystyle\sum_{i=1}^{n} m_i x_i}{\sum m_i}$

- If in a two particles system, particles of masses m_1 and m_2 are moving with velocities v_1 and v_2, respectively, then velocity of the centre of mass is given by $V_{CM} = \dfrac{m_1 v_1 + m_2 v_2}{m_1 + m_2}$

- If acceleration of the particles are a_1 and a_2 respectively, then acceleration of the centre of mass is given by $a_{CM} = \dfrac{m_1 a_1 + m_2 a_2}{m_1 + m_2}$

- The centre of mass of an object need not to lie within the object.

- The turning effect of a force about the axis of rotation is called moment of force or torque due to the force.
  Torque = Force × its perpendicular distance from the axis of rotation.

- The moment of linear momentum is called **angular momentum**. It is denoted by τ.
  Angular momentum (τ) = linear momentum (p) × its perpendicular distance from the axis of rotation (r).

- The rate of change of angular momentum of a system of particles about a fixed point is equal to the total external torque acting on the system about that point. $\tau_{total} = \dfrac{d}{dt}$

- **For translational equilibrium of a rigid body**, the vector sum of all the forces acting on a rigid body must be zero.
  i.e. $F_1 + F_2 + \ldots + F_n = \displaystyle\sum_{i=1}^{n} F_i = 0$

- **For rotational equilibrium**, the vector sum of torques of all the forces acting on the rigid body about the reference point must be zero.
  i.e. $\tau_1 + \tau_2 + \ldots + \tau_n = \displaystyle\sum_{i=1}^{n} \tau_i = 0$

- The moment of couple is equal to the product of either of the forces and the perpendicular distance, called the arm of the couple, between their lines of action.
  Moment of couple = Force × Arm of the couple
  or $\tau = Fd$

- In rotational equilibrium, Clockwise moment = Anti-clockwise moment
  or $F_1 \times d_1 = F_2 \times d_2$
  Or load × load arm = effort × effort arm

- The moment of inertia of a body about a given axis is equal to the sum of the products of the masses of its constituent particles and the square of their respective distances from the axis of rotation.
  Moment of inertia of a body is given by
  $I = m_1 r_1^2 + m_2 r_2^2 + m_3 r_3^2 + \ldots = \displaystyle\sum_{i=1}^{n} m_i r_i^2$
  Its unit is kg-m^2 and its dimensional formula is [ML^2].
  Moment of inertia, $I = 2 \times$ Rotational KE

- If $I = MK^2$
  Radius of gyration, $K = \sqrt{\dfrac{I}{M}}$

  For a body composed of particles of equal masses,
  $K = \sqrt{\dfrac{r_1^2 + r_2^2 + \ldots + r_4^2}{n}}$
  i.e. radius of gyration is equal to the root mean square distance of the particles from the axis of rotation.

- Angular momentum = Moment of inertia × Angular velocity i.e. $L = I_\omega$
  or Torque = Moment of inertia × Angular acceleration, i.e. $L = I_\infty$

- Rolling motion is very common in daily life. Motion of wheels of all modes of transportation is rolling motion. In fact, rolling motion is a combination of translation and rotation.

CHAPTER PRACTICE

OBJECTIVE Type Questions

1. The centre of mass of a system of two particles divides the distance between them.
   (a) In inverse ratio of square of masses of particles
   (b) In direct ratio of square of masses of particles
   (c) In inverse ratio of masses of particles
   (d) In direct ratio of masses of particles

2. A projectile is fired at an angle and it was following a parabolic path. Suddenly, it explodes into fragments. Choose the correct option regarding this situation.

   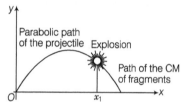

   (a) Due to explosion CM shifts upwards
   (b) Due to explosion CM shifts downwards
   (c) Due to explosion CM traces its path back to origin
   (d) CM continues to move along same parabolic path

3. For rotational equilibrium,
   (a) $\sum\limits_{i=1}^{n} \mathbf{F}_{net} = 0$ (b) $\sum\limits_{i=1}^{n} \tau_{net} = 0$
   (c) Both (a) and (b) are the necessary conditions for the rotational equilibrium
   (d) Both (a) and (b) are not necessary for rotational equilibrium

4. When acrobat bends his body (assume no external torque)
   (a) $I_{acrobat}$ decreases
   (b) $I_{acrobat}$ increases
   (c) $\omega_{acrobat}$ increases
   (d) Both (a) and (c)

   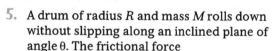

5. A drum of radius R and mass M rolls down without slipping along an inclined plane of angle θ. The frictional force
   (a) converts translational energy into rotational energy
   (b) dissipates energy as heat
   (c) decreases the rotational motion
   (d) decreases the rotational and translational motion

ASSERTION AND REASON

Direction (Q. Nos. 6-13) *In the following questions, two statements are given- one labelled Assertion (A) and the other labelled Reason (R). Select the correct answer to these questions from the codes (a), (b), (c) and (d) as given below*
   (a) Both Assertion and Reason are true and Reason is the correct explanation of Assertion.
   (b) Both Assertion and Reason are true but Reason is not the correct explanation of Assertion.
   (c) Assertion is true but Reason is false.
   (d) Assertion is false but Reason is true.

6. **Assertion** The CM of a body must lie on the body.
   Reason The CM of a body lie at the geometric centre of body.

7. **Assertion** The motion of the CM describes the translational part of the motion.
   Reason Translational motion always means straight line motion.

8. **Assertion** At the centre of earth, a body has centre of mass, but no centre of gravity.
   Reason Acceleration due to gravity is zero at the centre of earth.

9. **Assertion** Inertia and moment of inertia are same quantities.
   Reason Inertia represents the capacity of a body to oppose its state of motion of rest.

10. **Assertion** Moment of inertia of a particle is same, whatever be the axis of rotation.
    Reason Moment of inertia depends on mass and distance of the particle from the axis of rotation.

11. **Assertion** A particle moving on a straight line with a uniform velocity, its angular momentum is constant.
    Reason The angular momentum is zero when particle moves with a uniform velocity.

12. **Assertion** For a system of particles under central force field, the total angular momentum is conserved.
    Reason The torque acting on such a system is zero.

13. **Assertion** If bodies slide down an inclined plane without rolling, then all bodies reach the bottom simultaneously.

Reason Acceleration of all bodies are equal and independent of the shape.

CASE BASED QUESTIONS

Directions (Q. Nos. 14-15) *These questions are case study based questions. Attempt any 4 sub-parts from each question.*

14. **The Centre of Gravity**

The centre of gravity of a rigid body is a point through which the total weight of the body act. Centre of gravity can lie within the body or not. For small objects, centre of mass always coincides with centre of gravity. But in case of large bodies whose dimensions are comparable to the size of earth, centre of mass and centre of gravity will be at different locations.

In the given figure, balancing of a cardboard on the tip of a pencil is done. The point of support, G is the centre of gravity.

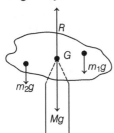

(i) If the $\mathbf{F}_{net, ext}$ is zero on the cardboard, it means
   (a) $R = Mg$ (b) $m_1 g = Mg$
   (c) $m_2 g = Mg$ (d) $R = m_1 / g$

(ii) Choose the correct option.
   (a) τ_{Mg} about CG $= 0$
   (b) τ_R about CG $= 0$
   (c) Net τ due to $m_1 g, m_2 g \cdots m_n g$ about CG $= 0$
   (d) All of the above

(iii) The centre of gravity and the centre of mass of a body coincide when
   (a) g is negligible   (b) g is variable
   (c) g is constant   (d) g is zero

(iv) If value of g varies, the centre of gravity and the centre of mass will
   (a) coincide
   (b) not coincide
   (c) become same physical quantities
   (d) None of the above

(v) Where will be the centre of gravity of the following rigid body?

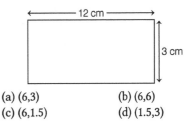

   (a) (6,3)   (b) (6,6)
   (c) (6,1.5)   (d) (1.5,3)

15. **Torque and Centre of Gravity**

Torque is also known as moment of force or couple. When a force acts on a particle, the particle does not merely move in the direction of the force but it also turns about some point. So, we can define the torque for a particle about a point as the vector product of position vector of the point where the force acts and with the force itself. In the given figure, balancing of a cardboard on the tip of a pencil is done. The point of support, G is the centre of gravity.

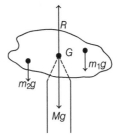

(i) If the $\mathbf{F}_{net, ext}$ is zero on the cardboard, it means
   (a) $R = Mg$ (b) $m_1 g = Mg$
   (c) $m_2 g = Mg$ (d) $R = m_1 / g$

(ii) Choose the correct option.
   (a) τ_{mg} about CG $= 0$
   (b) τ_R about CG $= 0$
   (c) Net τ due to $m_1 g, m_2 g \cdots m_n g$ about CG $= 0$
   (d) All of the above

(iii) The centre of gravity and the centre of mass of a body coincide when
   (a) g is negligible   (b) g is variable
   (c) g is constant   (d) g is zero

(iv) If value of g varies, the centre of gravity and the centre of mass will
   (a) coincide
   (b) not coincide
   (c) become same physical quantities
   (d) None of the above

(v) A body lying in a gravitational field is in stable equilibrium, if
   (a) vertical line through CG passes from top
   (b) horizontal line through CG passes from top
   (c) vertical line through CG passes from base
   (d) horizontal line through CG passes from base

Answer

1. (c)	2. (c)	3. (b)	4. (d)	5. (a)
6. (d)	7. (c)	8. (a)	9. (d)	10. (d)
11. (c)	12. (a)	13. (c)		
14. (i) (a)	(ii) (d)	(iii) (c)	(iv) (b)	(v) (c)
15. (i) (a)	(ii) (d)	(iii) (c)	(iv) (b)	(v) (c)

VERY SHORT ANSWER Type Questions

16. What is the significance of centre of mass?

17. Three point masses of 1 kg, 2 kg and 3 kg lie at $(1, 2), (0, -1)$ and $(2, -3)$, respectively. Calculate the coordinates of the centre of mass of the system. **[Ans. 7/6, -3/2]**

18. What is the condition for precession?

19. Find the value of torque if $\mathbf{F} = (4\hat{i} - 10\hat{j})$ N and $\mathbf{r} = (-5\hat{i} - 3\hat{j})$ m **[Ans. $62\,\hat{k}$ N-m]**

20. What is couple?

21. An automobile engine develops 100 kW when rotating at a speed of 1800 rpm. Find the torque produced. **[Ans. 531 N-m]**

22. State conservation of angular momentum theorem for a rigid body.

23. How to define rolling motion?

24. If the value of acceleration due to gravity (g) varies, will the centre of mass and centre of gravity coincide?

25. Write one example of conservation of angular momentum theorem.

SHORT ANSWER Type Questions

26. If two point masses are placed at $(+2\,m)$, and $(-2\,m)$, is it necessary that the centre of mass of system must lie at origin? **[Ans. No]**

27. Write two differences between centre of mass and centre of gravity.

28. State Newton's second law for rotational motion of a rigid body about a fixed axis.

29. A fan of moment of inertia is 0.6 kg-m^2 is to be run upto a working speed of 0.5 rps. What is the angular momentum of the fan? **[Ans 1.9 kg-m/s]**

LONG ANSWER Type I Questions

30. Moment of inertia of a thin rod of length l about an axis passing through its one end and perpendicular to its length is $MR^2/3$. Find the value of radius of gyration for the given scenario. **[Ans. $K = F/\sqrt{3}$]**

31. How to find kinetic energy of a rolling body?

32. A lay falls from the first floor of a building. He saw a pile of wool on the ground. He has a bag in his hand. Can he save himself with the help of that bag?

33. Derive the relation between angular momentum and moment of inertia for a rigid body rotating about a fixed axis.

34. Write three practical applications of conservation of angular momentum for a rigid body.

LONG ANSWER Type II Questions

35. Derive expressions for (i) Linear momentum, (ii) Newton's second law and (iii) Conservation of linear momentum for the system of particles.

36. Give location of centre of mass of (i) a sphere, (ii) cylinder, (iii) ring and (iv) a cube, each of uniform mass density. Does the centre of mass of a body necessarily lie inside the body?

37. Torques of equal magnitude are applied to a hollow cylinder and a solid sphere, both having same masses and radii. The cylinder is free to rotate about its standard axis of symmetry and sphere is free to rotate about an axis passing through its centre. Which of the two will acquire a greater angular speed after a given time?

07

Every object in the universe attracts every other object with a force which is called force of gravitation.

Galileo was the first to recognise the fact that all bodies, irrespective of their masses fall towards the earth with a constant acceleration. Kepler believed all heavenly bodies obey a mathematical order unlike anything on the earth.

GRAVITATION

|TOPIC 1|
Theory of Planetary Motion

In early days, people were observing the heavenly bodies like sun, moon, stars, planets etc., and their movement. It was the Italian physicist **Galileo**, (1564-1642), who recognised all the heavenly bodies like the sun, planets, the moon etc., are moving around the earth which is stationary and was taken as the centre of the universe.

The earliest recorded model for planetary motions proposed by **Ptolemy** about 2000 years ago was a **geocentric model**. It states that the description of the cosmos where the earth is at the orbital centre of all celestial bodies.

However, a more elegant model in which the sun was the centre around which the planet revolved the **heliocentric model**. This theory was later on supported by Galileo from his experimental study on the moon and other planets.

Tycho Brahe (1546-1601) spent his entire lifetime recording observations of the planets with the naked eyes. His assistants Johannes Kepler compiled his data and analysed. He extracted three elegant laws that are now known as Kepler's law.

CHAPTER CHECKLIST

- Theory of Planetary Motion
- Kepler's Laws of Planetary Motion
- Universal Law of Gravitation
- Principle of Superposition
- Gravitational Constant (Cavendish's Experiment)
- Acceleration due to Gravity of Earth
- Gravitational Potential
- Gravitational Potential Energy
- Escape Speed
- Earth Satellites
- Energy of an Orbiting Satellite

KEPLER'S LAWS OF PLANETARY MOTION

Kepler's laws of planetary motion are three scientific laws describing motion of planets around the sun.

Kepler's First Law of Orbits

According to this law, all planets move in elliptical orbits with the sun situated at one of the foci of the ellipse.

This law identifies that the distance between the sun and the earth is constantly changing as the earth goes around its orbit as shown in figure.

It shows an ellipse traced out by a planet around the sun, S. The closest point is P and the farthest point is A. P is called the **perihelion** and A is the **aphelion**. The length of the major axis is equal to the sum of the planet-sun distance at perihelion plus the planet-sun distance at aphelion. The length of the major axis is $2a$. Half the distance AP is length a of the semi-major axis.

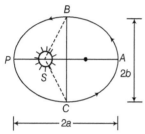

An ellipse traced out by a planet around the sun

Kepler's Second Law of Areas

According to this law, the speed of planet varies in such a way that the radius vector drawn from the sun to a planet sweeps out equal areas in equal interval of time.

i.e. The areal velocity of the planet around the sun is constant.

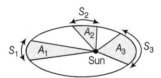

Laws of areas

The elliptical orbit of a planet around the sun is shown in figure. The areas A_1, A_2 and A_3 are swept out by the radius vector in equal intervals of time. According to Kepler's second law i.e. $A_1 = A_2 = A_3$

Note

Areal velocity may be defined as the area swept by the radius vector in unit time.

This law is identical with the law of conservation of angular momentum. Consider a small area ΔA described in a small time interval Δt and let the position of the planet be denoted by r.

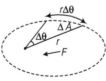

Now, $\qquad \Delta A = \dfrac{1}{2} r (r \Delta \theta)$

$\therefore \qquad \dfrac{\Delta A}{\Delta t} = \dfrac{1}{2} r^2 \dfrac{\Delta \theta}{\Delta t}$

Proceeding to limit as $\Delta t \to 0$, we get

$$\lim_{\Delta t \to 0} \dfrac{\Delta A}{\Delta t} = \dfrac{1}{2} r^2 \lim_{\Delta t \to 0} \dfrac{\Delta \theta}{\Delta t}$$

or $\qquad \dfrac{dA}{dt} = \dfrac{1}{2} r^2 \omega \qquad \left[\therefore \omega = \dfrac{\Delta \theta}{\Delta t} \right] \dots \text{(i)}$

Instantaneous angular momentum,

$$L = mr^2 \omega \qquad \dots \text{(ii)}$$

From Eqs. (i) and (ii), we get

$$\dfrac{dA}{dt} = \dfrac{L}{2m}$$

or $\qquad L = 2m \times \dfrac{dA}{dt} \qquad \dots \text{(iii)}$

The line of action of the gravitational force passes through the axis. Therefore, angle between $\mathbf{r}$ and $\mathbf{F}$ is $180°$.

Now, $\qquad \tau_{ext} = \mathbf{r} \times \mathbf{F} = rF \sin 180° \, \hat{\mathbf{n}} = 0$

$\therefore \qquad \tau_{ext} = 0$

$\qquad L = \text{constant} \qquad \left[\therefore \dfrac{dL}{dt} = \tau_{ext} \right] \dots \text{(iv)}$

From Eqs. (iii) and (iv), we get

$\therefore \qquad$ Areal velocity, $\dfrac{dA}{dt} = \text{constant}$

i.e. **The areal velocity of the planet around the sun is constant.** This proved the Kepler's second law of planetary motion.

Kepler's Third Law of Period

According to this law, the square of the time period of revolution of a planet around the sun is proportional to the cube of the semi-major axis of its elliptical orbit.

$T =$ time period of revolution of a planet

i.e. $\qquad \boxed{T^2 \propto a^3} \qquad \dots \text{(i)}$

As shown in figure, we have

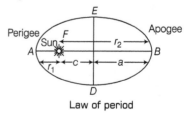

Law of period

$$AB = AF + FB$$
$$2a = r_1 + r_2$$
$$a = \dfrac{r_1 + r_2}{2}$$

So, putting the value of a in Eq. (i), we get

$$T^2 \propto \left(\frac{r_1 + r_2}{2}\right)^3$$

where, a = length of semi-major axis,

r_1 = shortest distance of planet from sun (perigee)

r_2 = longest distance of planet from sun (apogee).

Note

Kepler's laws are applicable not only to the solar system but also to the artificial satellites as well as to the moon going round the planets.

EXAMPLE |1| Angular Momentum of a Planet

Let the speed of the planet at the perihelion P in figure be v_P and the sun-planet distance SP be r_P. Relate $\{r_P, v_P\}$ to the corresponding quantities at the aphelion $\{r_A, v_A\}$. Will the planet take equal time to traverse BAC and CPB?

[NCERT]

Sol. At any point, radius vector and velocity vector of the planet are mutually perpendicular. Angular momentum of the planet at the perihelion P is

$$L_P = m_P r_P v_P$$

An ellipse traced out by a planet around the sun

Similarly, at the aphelion

$$L_A = m_P r_A v_A$$

By conservation of angular momentum,

$$L_P = L_A$$

or $\qquad m_P r_P v_P = m_P r_A v_A$

or $\qquad \dfrac{v_P}{v_A} = \dfrac{r_A}{r_P} = \dfrac{a+c}{a-c} = \dfrac{1+e}{1-e}$

As, $\qquad r_A > r_P$

So, $\qquad v_P > v_A.$

Here, $\qquad r_P = a - c$

$\qquad\qquad r_A = a + c$

and $\qquad$ eccentricity, $e = \dfrac{c}{a}$

To traverse BAC, area swept by radius vector

$$= \text{area } SBAC$$

To traverse CPB, area swept by radius vector = area $SBPC$

But, area $SBAC >$ area $SBPC$ as shown in figure.

From Kepler's second law, equal areas are swept in equal time. Hence, the planet will take a longer time to traverse BAC than CPB.

Kepler's Law of Period for the Solar System

Planets	Semi-major Axis r (10^{10} m)	Time Period T Years (y)	T^2/r^3 (10^{-34} y^2/m^3)
Mercury	5.79	0.241	2.99
Venus	10.8	0.615	3.00
Earth	15.0	1.00	2.96
Mars	22.8	1.88	2.98
Jupiter	77.8	11.9	3.01
Saturn	143	29.5	2.98
Uranus	287	84.0	2.98
Neptune	450	165.0	2.99
Pluto	590	248.0	2.99

EXAMPLE |2| Period of Neptune

Calculate the period of revolution of the neptune around the sun, given that diameter of its orbit is 30 times the diameter of the earth's orbit around the sun. Assume both the orbits to be circular.

Sol. According to Kepler's third law,

$$\frac{T_n^2}{T_e^2} = \frac{R_n^3}{R_e^3}$$

where subscripts n and e refer to the neptune and the earth respectively.

$\therefore \qquad T_n^2 = T_e^2 \times \left(\dfrac{R_n}{R_e}\right)^3 = 1 \times (30)^3$

[$\because$ time period of the earth's revolution = 1 year and ratio of radii (hence, diameters) of the neptune and the earth is 30]

$\therefore \qquad T_n = 1 \times \sqrt{(30)^3}$

$$T_n = 30\sqrt{30} = 164.3 \text{ yr}$$

EXAMPLE |3| Orbital Size of a Planet

Suppose there existed a planet that went around the sun twice as fast as the earth. What would be its orbital size as compared to that of the earth? **[NCERT]**

Sol. Let T_P and T_E denote the time periods of the planet and the earth, respectively. If R_P and R_E denote the corresponding orbital size as, then

$$\frac{T_P^2}{T_E^2} = \frac{R_P^3}{R_E^3}$$

or $\qquad \left(\dfrac{R_P}{R_E}\right)^3 = \left(\dfrac{T_P}{T_E}\right)^2 \Rightarrow \dfrac{R_P}{R_E} = \left(\dfrac{T_P}{T_E}\right)^{2/3}$

Since, $\qquad T_P = \dfrac{1}{2} T_E, \dfrac{T_P}{T_E} = \dfrac{1}{2}$

Thus, $\qquad \dfrac{R_P}{R_E} = \left(\dfrac{1}{2}\right)^{2/3} = 0.63$

Universal Law of Gravitation

It states that

Every body in this universe attracts each other body with a force whose magnitude is directly proportional to the product of their masses and inversely proportional to the square of the distance between their centres. This force acts along the line joining the centres of two bodies.

Consider two bodies of masses m_1 and m_2 with their centres mutually separated by a distance r as shown in figure. Let F be the force (in magnitude) of gravitational attraction between two bodies.

According to Newton's law of gravitation, we get

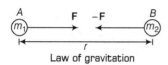

Law of gravitation

So, $$F \propto m_1 m_2 \qquad \qquad \ldots\text{(i)}$$

and $$F \propto \frac{1}{r^2} \qquad \qquad \ldots\text{(ii)}$$

From Eqs. (i) and (ii), we get

or $$F \propto \frac{m_1 m_2}{r^2}$$

or $$\boxed{\text{Gravitational force, } F = G \frac{m_1 m_2}{r^2}} \qquad \ldots\text{(iii)}$$

where, G is a constant of proportionality known as **gravitational constant**. It is also known as **universal gravitational constant**.

In CGS system, the value of G is 6.67×10^{-8} dyne cm^2 g^{-2} and its SI value is 6.67×10^{-11} Nm^{2}kg^{-2}.

Dimensional formula for G

$$G = \frac{F r^2}{m_1 m_2} = \frac{[\text{MLT}^{-2}][\text{L}^2]}{[\text{M}^2]}$$

$$= [\text{MLT}^{-2}][\text{L}^2][\text{M}^{-2}]$$

$$= [\text{M}^{-1}\text{L}^3\text{T}^{-2}]$$

Suppose $m_1 = m_2 = 1$ unit and $r = 1$ unit, then from Eq. (iii), we get

$$F = \frac{G \times 1 \times 1}{(1)^2} \implies F = G$$

Thus, universal gravitational constant (G) is numerically equal to the force of attraction acting between two bodies, each of unit mass separated by unit distance apart.

Important Points about Gravitational Force

- It is always attractive in nature while electric and magnetic force can be attractive or repulsive.
- It is independent of the intervening medium between the particles while electric and magnetic force depend on the nature of the medium between the particles.
- The gravitational force is a conservative force.
- The value of G does not depend on the nature and size of the masses.
- The force of attraction between a hollow spherical shell of uniform density and a point mass situated outside is just as if the entire mass of the shell is concentrated at the centre of the shell. Gravitational force possesses spherical symmetry.
- The force of attraction due to a hollow spherical shell of uniform density on a point mass situated inside it, is zero.

EXAMPLE |4| Attraction of Sphere

A sphere of mass 40 kg is attracted by a second sphere of mass 60 kg with a force equal to 4 mgf. If G is 6×10^{-11} Nm^2/kg^2, then calculate the distance between them. Consider acceleration due to gravity is $10\,\text{m/s}^2$.

Sol. Given, $M = 40\,\text{kg}, m = 60\,\text{kg}$,

$$F = 4\,\text{mgf} = 4 \times 10^{-6} \times 10 = 4 \times 10^{-5}\,\text{N},$$

$$G = 6 \times 10^{-11}\,\text{Nm}^2/\text{kg}^2, g = 10\,\text{m/s}^2.$$

According to universal law, $F = \dfrac{GMm}{r^2}$

$$\implies \quad r = \sqrt{\frac{GMm}{F}} = \sqrt{\frac{6 \times 10^{-11} \times 40 \times 60}{4 \times 10^{-5}}} = 0.06\,\text{m} = 6\,\text{cm}$$

Vector Form of Newton's Law of Gravitation

Consider two particles A and B of masses m_1 and m_2, respectively.

Let $\mathbf{r}_{12}$ = displacement vector from A to B,

$A \longleftarrow\!\!\!\!\underset{\mathbf{r}_{12}}{\longrightarrow} B$

$\mathbf{r}_{21}$ = displacement vector from B to A,

$A \longleftarrow\!\!\!\!\underset{\mathbf{r}_{21} = -\mathbf{r}_{12}}{\longrightarrow} B$

$\mathbf{F}_{21}$ = gravitational force exerted on B by A

$\mathbf{F}_{12}$ = gravitational force exerted on A by B

$A \underset{\mathbf{F}_{12}}{\longrightarrow} - - - - \underset{\mathbf{F}_{21}}{\longleftarrow} B$

On vector notation, Newton's law of gravitation is written as follows

$$\mathbf{F}_{12} = -G \frac{m_1 m_2}{r_{21}^2} \hat{\mathbf{r}}_{21} \qquad \ldots\text{(i)}$$

where, $\hat{\mathbf{r}}_{21}$ is a unit vector pointing towards A. The negative sign indicates that the direction of $\mathbf{F}_{12}$ is opposite to that of $\hat{\mathbf{r}}_{21}$. The negative sign also shows that the gravitational force is attractive in nature.

Similarly, $\qquad \mathbf{F}_{21} = -G \dfrac{m_1 m_2}{r_{12}^2} \hat{\mathbf{r}}_{12}$

where, $\hat{\mathbf{r}}_{12}$ is a unit vector pointing towards B.

But, $\qquad\qquad \hat{\mathbf{r}}_{21} = -\hat{\mathbf{r}}_{12}$

Also, $\qquad\qquad r_{21}^2 = r_{12}^2$

$\therefore \qquad\qquad \mathbf{F}_{21} = G \dfrac{m_1 m_2}{r_{21}^2} \hat{\mathbf{r}}_{21} \qquad \ldots(ii)$

Equating Eqs. (i) and (ii), we have

$$\mathbf{F}_{12} = -\mathbf{F}_{21}$$

As $\mathbf{F}_{12}$ and $\mathbf{F}_{21}$ are directed towards the centres of the two particles, so **gravitational force is a central force.**

PRINCIPLE OF SUPERPOSITION

Suppose $\mathbf{F}_1, \mathbf{F}_2, \ldots, \mathbf{F}_n$ be the individual forces due to the masses $m_1, m_2, m_3, \ldots, m_n$ which are given by the universal law of gravitation, then from the principle of superposition, each of these forces acts independently and uninfluenced by the other bodies as shown in figure.

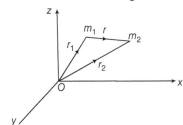

Gravitational force on   due to   is along
r, where the vector r is (r − r)

So, the resultant force $\mathbf{F}$ can be expressed in vector addition of various forces

$$\mathbf{F} = \mathbf{F}_{12} + \mathbf{F}_{13} + \mathbf{F}_{14} + \ldots + \mathbf{F}_{1n}$$

Superposition principle of gravitational forces

Clearly, $\mathbf{F} = -G \dfrac{m_1 m_2}{r_{12}^2} \hat{\mathbf{r}}_{21} - G \dfrac{m_1 m_3}{r_{13}^2} \hat{\mathbf{r}}_{31} - \ldots - G \dfrac{m_1 m_n}{r_{1n}^2} \mathbf{r}_{n1}$

$$\boxed{\text{Resultant force, } \mathbf{F} = -Gm_1 \left[\frac{m_2}{r_{12}^2} \hat{\mathbf{r}}_{21} + \frac{m_3}{r_{13}^2} \hat{\mathbf{r}}_{31} + \ldots + \frac{m_n}{r_{1n}^2} \hat{\mathbf{r}}_{n1} \right]}$$

EXAMPLE |5| Force on system of masses

Three equal masses of m kg each are fixed at the vertices of an equilateral triangle ABC (in figure)

(i) What is the force acting on a mass 2 m placed at the centroid G of the triangle?
(ii) What is the force, if the mass at the vertex A is doubled? (Take, $AG = BG = CG = 1\,\text{m}$) **[NCERT]**

Sol. In the given figure, ΔABC

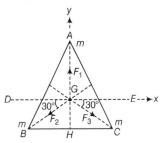

Mass of each body A, B and $C = m$

$$F_1 = \frac{G \times m \times 2\,m}{(1)^2} = 2Gm^2 \quad \text{along } GA$$

$$F_2 = \frac{G \times m \times 2m}{(1)^2} = 2Gm^2 \quad \text{along } GB$$

$$F_3 = \frac{G \times m \times 2m}{(1)^2} = 2Gm^2 \quad \text{along } GC$$

Then, $\angle EGC = \angle DGB = 30°$

Resolving F_2 and F_3 into x and y-axes components.

$F_2 \cos 30°$ along GD and $F_2 \sin 30°$ along GH

and $F_3 \cos 30°$ along GE and $F_3 \sin 30°$ along GH

Resultant force on the mass $2m$ at G.

Force at G is $F_1 - (F_2 \sin 30° + F_3 \sin 30°)$

$$F = 2Gm^2 - \left(2Gm^2 \times \frac{1}{2} + 2Gm^2 \times \frac{1}{2} \right) = 0$$

Gravitational force on mass 2 m at G due to mass $2m$ at A.

Net force, F_1' is $G \dfrac{2m \times 2m}{1^2} = 4Gm^2 \quad$ along GA

Net force acting at G due to masses A, B and C

$= F_1' - (F_2 \sin 30° + F_3 \sin 30°)$

$= 4\,Gm^2 - \left(2Gm^2 \times \dfrac{1}{2} + 2Gm^2 \times \dfrac{1}{2} \right)$

$= 2\,Gm^2 \quad$ along GA

EXAMPLE |6| Three Balls Positioned at the Corners of a Right Triangle

Consider the three billiard balls of masses 400 g are placed on a table at the corners of a right angle as shown in figure. Calculate the gravitational force vector on the ball of the mass m_1 resulting from other two balls. Also, find the magnitude and direction of this force.

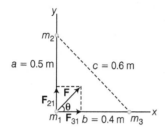

 The cue ball is attracted to other balls by the gravitational force. We can see graphically, the net force should point upward and towards right. Hence, we locate our coordinate axes by placing our origin at the position of the one ball as shown in figure.

Sol. Force exerted by m_2 on the cue ball of mass m_1.

$$m_1 = m_2 = m_3 = 400\,g = 0.4\,kg$$
$$a = 0.5\,m, b = 0.4\,m \text{ and } c = 0.6\ m$$

Gravitational constant,

$$G = 6.67 \times 10^{-11}\,Nm^2/kg^2$$

The force

$$\mathbf{F}_{21} = G\frac{m_2 m_1}{a^2}\hat{\mathbf{j}} = \frac{6.67 \times 10^{-11} \times 0.4 \times 0.4}{(0.5)^2} \cdot \hat{\mathbf{j}}$$

$$\mathbf{F}_{21} = 4.268 \times 10^{-11}\,\hat{\mathbf{j}}\,N$$

Similarly, $\mathbf{F}_{31} = \dfrac{Gm_3 m_1}{b^2}\hat{\mathbf{i}} = \dfrac{6.67 \times 10^{-11} \times 0.4 \times 0.4}{(0.4)^2}\hat{\mathbf{i}}$

$$\mathbf{F}_{31} = 6.67 \times 10^{-11}\,\hat{\mathbf{i}}\,N$$

The net gravitational force on the one ball,

$$\mathbf{F} = \mathbf{F}_{31} + \mathbf{F}_{21} = (6.67\,\hat{\mathbf{i}} + 4.26\,\hat{\mathbf{j}}) \times 10^{-11}\,N$$

The net gravitational force,

$$F = \sqrt{\mathbf{F}_{31}^2 + \mathbf{F}_{21}^2} = \sqrt{(6.67)^2 + (4.268)^2} \times 10^{-11}\,N$$

$$F = 7.918 \times 10^{-11}\,N$$

Also, $\tan\theta = \dfrac{F_y}{F_x} = \dfrac{\mathbf{F}_{21}}{\mathbf{F}_{31}} = \dfrac{4.268 \times 10^{-11}}{6.67 \times 10^{-11}} = 0.639$

$$\Rightarrow \qquad \theta = 32.6°$$

 Newton's Principia

Kepler had formulated his third law by 1619. The announcement of the underlying universal law of gravitation came about seventy years later with the publication in 1687 of Newton's masterpiece Philosophiae Naturalis Principia Mathematica, often simply called the Principia.

GRAVITATIONAL CONSTANT
(CAVENDISH'S EXPERIMENT)

The value of the gravitational constant G was first determined experimentally by English Scientist Henry Cavendish in 1798.

Two small lead spheres of mass m each are connected to the end of a rod of length L which is suspended from its mid-point by a fine quartz fibre, forming a torsion balance.

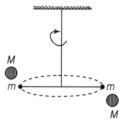

Two large lead spheres of mass M each are brought close to small ones but on opposite sides.

As, the small spheres move towards the larger ones under the gravitational attraction. Thus, the gravitational force on each small sphere due to big sphere is $F = \dfrac{GMm}{R^2}$,

where R is the distance between the centre of the large and its neighbouring small sphere.

Due to this force, the resultant gravitational force on the bar is zero but a gravitational torque acts on it. The value of gravitational torque on the bar

$$= \text{gravitational force} \times \text{length of the bar} = \frac{GMm}{R^2} \times L$$

Due to this gravitational torque, the bar is rotated through an angle θ, say about the wire as an axis and the wire gets twisted through an angle θ. If τ is the restoring torque per unit twist of the thin wire used, then restoring torque $= \tau\,\theta$. In equilibrium position,

Restoring torque = gravitational torque, $\tau\,\theta = \dfrac{GMm}{R^2} \times L$

$$\boxed{\text{Gravitational constant, } G = \frac{R^2 \tau \theta}{MmL}}$$

Knowing all the quantities on the right hand side from the experiment, the value of G can be determined. Since, Cavendish's experiment, the measurement of G has been improved upon. The currently accepted value of G is

$$G = 6.67 \times 10^{-11}\,N\text{-}m^2/kg^2$$

Note

G is an universal constant and its value does not vary with change in intervening medium or temperature or pressure, etc.

TOPIC PRACTICE 1

OBJECTIVE Type Questions

1. For a satellite in elliptical orbit which of the following quantities does not remain constant?
   (a) Angular momentum
   (b) Linear momentum
   (c) Areal velocity
   (d) All of the above

Sol. (b) In elliptical orbit, velocity keeps on changing both in magnitude and direction. Therefore, momentum does not remain constant $(P = mv)$.

2. Both the earth and the moon are subject to the gravitational force of the sun. As observed from the sun, the orbit of the moon   [NCERT Exemplar]
   (a) will be elliptical
   (b) will not be strictly elliptical because the total gravitational force on it is not central
   (c) is not elliptical but will necessarily be a closed curve
   (d) deviates considerably from being elliptical due to influence of planets other than the earth

Sol. (b) As observed from the sun, two types of forces are acting on the moon one is due to gravitational attraction between the sun and the moon and the other is due to gravitational attraction between the earth and the moon. Hence, total force on the moon is not central.

3. The velocity of the planet when it is closest to sun is
   (a) maximum
   (b) minimum
   (c) can have any value
   (d) None of the above

Sol. (a) From conservation of angular momentum,

$$\text{Velocity of planet}\,(v) \propto \frac{1}{\text{Distance of the planet from sun}\,(r)}$$

So, r_P is minimum for perihelion (P).
⇒ v_P is maximum.

4. Two sphere of masses m and M are situated in air and the gravitational force between them is F. The space around the masses is now filled with a liquid of specific gravity 3. The gravitational force will now be

   (a) F (b) $\dfrac{F}{3}$

   (c) $\dfrac{F}{9}$ (d) $3\,F$

Sol. (a) Gravitational force does not depend on the medium between the masses. So, it will remain same i.e., F.

5. If the gravitation force on body 1 due to 2 is given by $\mathbf{F}_{12}$ and on body 2 due to 1 is given as $\mathbf{F}_{21}$, then
   (a) $\mathbf{F}_{12} = \mathbf{F}_{21}$
   (b) $\mathbf{F}_{12} = -\mathbf{F}_{21}$
   (c) $\mathbf{F}_{12} = \dfrac{\mathbf{F}_{21}}{4}$
   (d) None of the above

Sol. (b) Since, gravitational forces are attractive $\mathbf{F}_{12}$ is directed opposite to $\mathbf{F}_{21}$ and they are also equal in magnitude.

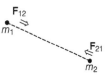

Hence, $\mathbf{F}_{21} = -\mathbf{F}_{12}$
or $\mathbf{F}_{12} = -\mathbf{F}_{21}$

VERY SHORT ANSWER Type Questions

6. How earth retains most of the atmosphere?

Sol. Earth retains most of the atmosphere due to force of gravity.

7. If earth be at one half its present distance from the sun, then how many days will there be in a year?

Sol. According to Kepler's third law
$$T^2 \propto R^3$$

Hence, $\dfrac{T_1^2}{T_2^2} = \dfrac{R_1^3}{R_2^3}$

⇒ $T_2^2 = \left[\dfrac{R_2}{R_1}\right]^3 T_1^2$

⇒ $T_2 = T_1 \left[\dfrac{R_2}{R_1}\right]^{3/2} = 365 \left(\dfrac{R/2}{R}\right)^{3/2}$

$$= 365 \times \dfrac{1}{2\sqrt{2}} = 129 \text{ days}$$

8. By which law is the Kepler's law of areas identical?

Sol. The law of conservation of angular momentum.

9. Do the force of friction and other contact forces arise due to gravitational attraction? If not, then what is the origin of these forces?

Sol. Contact forces have electrical region.

10. Is the Kepler's law kinematic?

Sol. Yes, because kepler's third law is the relation between distance and time.

11. Why does tides arise in the oceans?

Sol. Tides arise in the oceans due to the force of attraction between the moon and sea water.

12. Assume that the law of gravitation changes from inverse square to inverse cube. Does the angular momentum of a planet about the sun will remain constant?

Sol. The torque on a planet is zero so long as the force is a central force. The angular momentum of planet remains constant so long as torque remains zero.

13. You can shield a change from electrical forces by putting it inside a hollow conductor. Can you shield a body from the gravitational influence of nearby matter by putting it inside a hollow sphere or by some other means? **[NCERT]**

Sol. No, while electrical forces depend upon the medium, the gravitational forces do not depend upon medium. To sum up, the 'gravity screens' are not possible.

14. If you compare the gravitational force on the earth due to the sun to that due to the moon, you would find that sun's pull is greater than the moon's pull. However, the tidal effect of the moon's pull is greater than the tidal effect of the sun. Why? **[NCERT]**

Sol. The tidal effect depends inversely on the cube of the distance unlike force which depends inversely on the square of the distance. As the moon is closer to earth than the sun, so its tidal effect is greater than that of the sun. The ratio of these two effects is

$$\frac{T_m}{T_s} = \left(\frac{d_s}{d_m}\right)^3 = \left(\frac{1.5 \times 10^{11}}{3.8 \times 10^8}\right)^3 = 61.5 \times 10^6$$

15. Draw areal velocity versus time graph for mars. **[NCERT Exemplar]**

Sol. Areal velocity of planet revolving around the sun is constant with time (kepler's second law).

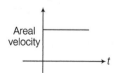

16. What is the direction of areal velocity of the earth around the sun? **[NCERT Exemplar]**

Sol. It is normal to the plane containing the earth and the sun as areal velocity.

$$\frac{\Delta A}{\Delta t} = \frac{1}{2} r \times v \Delta t$$

and directed according to right hand rule.

17. Out of aphelion and perihelion, where is the speed of the earth more and why? **[NCERT Exemplar]**

Sol. At perihelion, because the earth has to cover greater linear distance to keep the areal velocity constant.

18. From Kepler's second law and observations of the sun's motion as seen from the earth, we can conclude that the earth is closer to the sun during winter in the Northern hemisphere than during summer. Explain.

Sol. The earth is closer to the sun during winter. But heating effect is less because the sun's rays fall obliquely.

19. At what factor between the two particles gravitational force does not depend?

Sol. Gravitational force does not depend upon the medium between the two particles.

20. Are the Kepler's laws applicable only to the solar system?

Sol. No, they are applicable to the artificial satellites too.

21. Two particles of masses m_1 and m_2 attract each other gravitationally and are set in motion under the influence of the gravitational force? Will the centre of mass move?

Sol. Since, gravitational force is an internal force, therefore the centre of mass would not move.

22. When will the Kepler's law be applicable on the planets?

Sol. Kepler's law will be applicable whenever inverse square law is involved.

23. Work done in moving a particle round a closed path under the action of gravitation force is zero. Why?

Sol. Gravitational force is a conservative force which means that work done by it, is independent of path followed.

SHORT ANSWER Type Questions

24. Imagine what would happen if the value of G becomes
  (i) 100 times of its present value.
  (ii) $\frac{1}{100}$ times of its present value.

Sol. (i) Earth's attraction would be so large that you would be crushed to the earth.
  (ii) Earth's attraction would be so less that we can easily jump from the top of a multi-storey building.

25. In Kepler's law of periods, $T^2 = kr^3$, the constant, $k = 10^{-13}$ s^{2}m^{-3}. Express the constant k in days and kilometres. The moon is at a distance of 3.84×10^5 km from the earth. Obtain its time period of revolution in days.   **[NCERT]**

Sol. Given, $k = 10^{-13}$ s^2/m^3

As, 1 s $= \dfrac{1}{24 \times 60 \times 60}$ day and 1m $= \dfrac{1}{1000}$ km

$\therefore \quad k = 10^{-13} \times \dfrac{1}{(24 \times 60 \times 60)^2}(\text{day})^2 \dfrac{1}{(1/1000)^3} \text{km}^{-3}$

$= 1.33 \times 10^{-14} \,(\text{day})^2 \text{km}^{-3}$

For the moon, $r = 3.84 \times 10^5$ km

$\therefore \quad T^2 = kr^3 = 1.33 \times 10^{-14} \times (3.84 \times 10^5)^3 = 753.087$

$T = 27.3$ days

26. The time period of a satellite of earth is 5 h. If the separation between the earth and the satellite is increased to four times the previous value, then what will be the new time period?

Sol. $T_2 = T_1\left[\dfrac{R_2}{R_1}\right]^{3/2} = T_1[4]^{3/2} = 8T_1 = 40\text{h}$

27. A planet moving along an elliptical orbit is closest to the Sun at a distance r_1 and farthest away at a distance of r_2. If v_1 and v_2 are the linear velocities at these points respectively, then find the ratio $\dfrac{v_1}{v_2}$.

Sol. From the law of conservation of angular momentum

$mr_1v_1 = mr_2v_2$

$\Rightarrow \qquad r_1v_1 = r_2v_2 \text{ or } \dfrac{v_1}{v_2} = \dfrac{r_2}{r_1}$

28. The gravitational force between two spheres is x when the distance between their centres is y. What will be the new force, if the separation is made $3y$?

Sol. $F \propto \dfrac{1}{r^2}$. So, if r is increased by a factor of 3, F will be reduced by a factor of 9. Thus, the new force will be $\dfrac{x}{9}$.

29. A mass M is broken into two parts, m and $(M - m)$. How is m related to M so that the gravitational force between two parts is maximum?

Sol. Let $m_1 = m, m_2 = M - m$

$F = G\dfrac{m(M-m)}{r^2} = \dfrac{G}{r}(Mm - m^2)$

Differentiating w.r.t m, $\dfrac{dF}{dm} = \dfrac{G}{r^2}(M - 2m)$

for F to be maximum, $\dfrac{dF}{dm} = 0$

$\dfrac{G}{r^2}(M - 2m) = 0$

$M = 2m, \text{ or } m = \dfrac{M}{2}$

$\therefore \qquad m_1 = m_2 = M/2$

30. A mass of 1 g is separated from another mass of 1 g by a distance of 1 cm. How many g-wt of force exists between them?

Sol. $F = G\dfrac{m_1 m_2}{r^2}$

$= (6.67 \times 10^{-8})\left(\dfrac{1 \times 1}{1^2}\right)$ dyne

$= 6.67 \times 10^{-8}$ dyne $= \dfrac{6.67 \times 10^{-8}}{980}$

$= 7 \times 10^{-11}$ g-wt

LONG ANSWER Type I Questions

31. Two identical heavy spheres are separated by a distance 10 times their radius. Will an object placed at the mid-point of the line joining their centres be in stable equilibrium or unstable equilibrium? Give reasons for your answer.
          [NCERT Exemplar]

Sol. If F_L and F_R are the forces exerted on mass m lying at O (after displacing it from O to O'), by masses M lying on left and right, respectively. Then, from figure,

$F_L = G\dfrac{Mm}{(x + \Delta x)^2}$ and $F_R = G\dfrac{Mm}{(x - \Delta x)^2}$

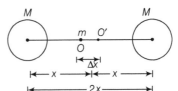

Since $F_R > F_L$, the net force on m is towards right. Hence, the equilibrium is unstable.

32. A geostationary satellite is orbiting the earth at a height of $5R$ above the surface of the earth, R being the radius of the earth. Find the time period of another satellite (in hours) at a height of $2R$ from the surface of the earth.

Sol. From Kepler's third law, $T^2 \propto r^3$

Hence, $T_1^2 \propto r_1^3$ and $T_2^2 \propto r_2^3$

So, $\dfrac{T_2^2}{T_1^2} = \dfrac{r_2^3}{r_1^3} = \dfrac{(3R)^3}{(6R)^3}$

$\Rightarrow \dfrac{T_2}{T_1} = \dfrac{1}{2\sqrt{2}} \qquad [\because T_1 = 12]$

$\therefore \qquad T_2 = \dfrac{12}{2\sqrt{2}} = \dfrac{6}{\sqrt{2}}$

33. Two stationary particles of masses M_1 and M_2 are a distance d apart. A third particle lying on the line joining the particles, experiences no resultant gravitational force. What is the distance of this particle from M_1?

Sol. The force on m towards M_1 is $F = G\dfrac{M_1 m}{r^2}$

The force on m towards M_2 is $F = G\dfrac{M_2 m}{(d-r)^2}$

M_1 •——————r——————• m ————— • M_2

$\overset{\longleftarrow\ r\ \longrightarrow}{}$

$\overset{\longleftarrow\qquad\ d\qquad\ \longrightarrow}{}$

Equating two forces, we have

$$G\frac{M_1 m}{r^2} = G\frac{M_2 m}{(d-r)^2}$$

$$\left(\frac{d-r}{r}\right)^2 = \frac{M_2}{M_1} \quad\text{or}\quad \frac{d}{r} - 1 = \frac{\sqrt{M_2}}{\sqrt{M_1}}$$

$$\Rightarrow \qquad \frac{d}{r} = \frac{\sqrt{M_2} + \sqrt{M_1}}{\sqrt{M_1}}$$

So, distance of an particle from m is

$$r = d\left(\frac{\sqrt{M_1}}{\sqrt{M_1} + \sqrt{M_2}}\right)$$

34. A saturn year is 29.5 times the earth year. How far is the saturn from the sun of the earth is 1.50×10^8 km away from the sun? **[NCERT]**

Sol. According to Kepler's third law of planetary motion, $T^2 \propto r^3$

Thus, $\qquad \dfrac{T_S^2}{T_E^2} = \dfrac{r_S^3}{r_E^3} \quad\text{or}\quad \left(\dfrac{T_S}{T_E}\right)^2 = \left(\dfrac{r_S}{r_E}\right)^3$

or $\qquad \left(\dfrac{r_S}{r_E}\right) = \left(\dfrac{T_S}{T_E}\right)^{2/3}$

or $\qquad r_S = \left(\dfrac{T_S}{T_E}\right)^{2/3} \times r_E$

As, $\dfrac{T_S}{T_E} = 29.5$ and $r_E = 1.5 \times 10^8$ km,

$$r_S = (29.5)^{2/3}(1.5 \times 10^8 \text{ km})$$

$$= 14.3 \times 10^8 \text{ km}$$

LONG ANSWER Type II Questions

35. A mass m is placed at P, a distance h along the normal through the centre O of a thin circular ring of mass M and radius r. If the mass is removed further away

such that OP becomes $2h$, by what factor the force of gravitation will decrease, if $h = r$? **[NCERT Exemplar]**

Sol. Consider a small element of the ring of mass dM, gravitational force between dM and m, distance x apart in figure i.e.

$$dF = \frac{G(dM)m}{x^2}$$

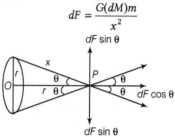

$d\mathbf{F}$ can be resolved into two rectangular components.
(i) $dF \cos\theta$ along PO and
(ii) $dF \sin\theta$ perpendicular to PO (given figure)
The total force (F) between the ring and mass (m) can be obtained by integrating the effects of all the elements forming the ring, whereas all the components perpendicular to PO cancel out, i.e. $\int dF \sin\theta = 0$, the component along PO add together to give F i.e.

$$F = \int dF \sin\theta = \int \frac{G(dM)m}{x^2}\left(\frac{h}{x}\right) = \frac{Gmh}{x^3}\int dM$$

i.e. $\qquad F = \dfrac{GMmh}{(r^2 + h^2)^{3/2}}$

$$[\because \int dM = M \text{ and } x = (r^2 + h^2)^{1/2}]$$

Since, $h = r$, $F = GMm\left(\dfrac{r}{2\sqrt{2}r^3}\right) = \dfrac{GMm}{2\sqrt{2}r^2}$

When h becomes $2r$, $F' = \dfrac{GMm(2r)}{(r^2 + 4r^2)^{3/2}} = \dfrac{2GMm}{5\sqrt{5}r^2}$

Thus, $\dfrac{F'}{F} = \left(\dfrac{2GMm}{5\sqrt{5}r^2}\right)\left(\dfrac{2\sqrt{2}r^2}{GMm}\right) = \dfrac{4\sqrt{2}}{5\sqrt{5}}$

36. Earth's orbit in an ellipse with eccentricity 0.016. Thus, earth's distance from the sun and speed as it moves around the sun varies from day to day. This means that the length of solar day is not constant through the year. Assume that the earth's spin axis is normal to its orbital plane and find out the length of the shortest and the longest day. A day should be taken from noon to noon. Does this explain variation of length of the day during the year? **[NCERT Exemplar]**

Sol. From the geometry of the ellipse of eccentricity e and semi-major axis a, the aphelion and perihelion distances are

$$r_a = a(1+e)$$
$$r_p = a(1-e)$$

or $\qquad \dfrac{r_a}{r_p} = \dfrac{1+e}{1-e}$

Since, angular momentum ($mr^2\omega$) is conserved.

$$r^2\omega = \text{constant i.e. } r_p^2\omega_p = r_a^2\omega_a$$

or $\qquad \dfrac{\omega_p}{\omega_a} = \dfrac{r_a^2}{r_p^2} = \left(\dfrac{1+e}{1-e}\right)^2$

$$= \left(\dfrac{1+0.0167}{1-0.0167}\right)^2 = 1.0691$$

or $\quad \left(\dfrac{\omega_p}{\omega}\right)\left(\dfrac{\omega}{\omega_a}\right) = 1.0691 \qquad\qquad ...(i)$

where, ω is the angular speed corresponding to mean solar day and can be considered to be the geometric mean of ω_p and ω_a.

i.e. $\qquad \omega_p \cdot \omega_a = \omega^2 \text{ or } \dfrac{\omega_p}{\omega} = \dfrac{\omega}{\omega_a} \qquad ...(ii)$

From Eqs. (i) and (ii), we get

$$\dfrac{\omega_p}{\omega} = \dfrac{\omega}{\omega_a} = \sqrt{1.0691} = 1.034$$

If $\omega = 1°/$ day (mean angular speed)

$\omega_p = 1.034°/\text{day and } \omega_a = \dfrac{1°}{1.034}/\text{day} = 0.967°/\text{day}$

Since 361° correspond to 24 h, $(360 + 1.034)°$ corresponds to 24.0023 h, i.e. 24 h 8.14″ and $(360 + 0.967)°$ corresponds to 23 h 59′ m 52″.

This does not explain the actual variation in the length of the day during the year.

37. A rocket is fired from the earth towards the sun. At what distance from the earth's centre is the gravitational force on the rocket zero? Mass of the sun = 2×10^{30} kg, mass of the earth

= 6×10^{24} kg. Neglect the effect of other planets etc. (Orbital radius = 1.5×10^{11} m). **[NCERT]**

Sol. We are given that

Mass of the sun, $M_s = 2 \times 10^{30}$ kg

Mass of the earth, $M_e = 6 \times 10^{24}$ kg

Distance between the centres of the sun and the earth,

$$r = 1.5 \times 10^{11} \text{ m}$$

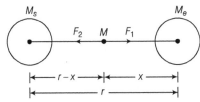

Let x be the distance of the required point from the centre of the earth. Clearly, at this point the gravitational force (F_1) on the rocket of mass m due to the earth = gravitational force (F_2) on the rocket due to the sun, i.e. $F_1 = F_2$.

or $\qquad \dfrac{GmM_e}{x^2} = \dfrac{GmM_s}{(r-x)^2}$

or $\qquad \dfrac{(r-x)^2}{x^2} = \dfrac{M_s}{M_e} = \dfrac{2 \times 10^{30} \text{ kg}}{6 \times 10^{24} \text{ kg}} = \dfrac{10^6}{3}$

or $\qquad \dfrac{r-x}{x} = \dfrac{10^3}{\sqrt{3}} \text{ or } \dfrac{r}{x} - 1 = \dfrac{10^3}{\sqrt{3}}$

or $\qquad \dfrac{r}{x} = \dfrac{10^3}{\sqrt{3}} + 1 \approx \dfrac{10^3}{\sqrt{3}}$

or $\qquad x = \dfrac{\sqrt{3}r}{10^3} = \dfrac{1.732(1.5 \times 10^{11}) \text{ m}}{10^3}$

$$= 2.6 \times 10^8 \text{ m}$$

ASSESS YOUR TOPICAL UNDERSTANDING

OBJECTIVE Type Questions

1. According to Kepler's law of planetary motion, if T represents time-period and r is orbital radius, then for two planets these are related as

(a) $\left(\dfrac{T_1}{T_2}\right)^3 = \left(\dfrac{r_1}{r_2}\right)^2$ (b) $\left(\dfrac{T_1}{T_2}\right)^{3/2} = \dfrac{r_1}{r_2}$

(c) $\left(\dfrac{T_1}{T_2}\right)^2 = \left(\dfrac{r_1}{r_2}\right)^3$ (d) $\left(\dfrac{T_1}{T_2}\right) = \left(\dfrac{r_1}{r_2}\right)^{2/3}$

2. As observed from the earth, the sun appears to move in an approximate circular orbit. For the motion of another planet like mercury as observed from the earth, this would

[NCERT Exemplar]

(a) be similarly true

(b) not be true because the force between the earth and mercury is not inverse square law

(c) not be true because the major gravitational force on mercury is due to the sun

(d) not be true because mercury is influenced by forces other than gravitational forces

3. Law of areas is valid only when gravitational force is

(a) conservative force   (b) central force

(c) attractive force   (d) weak force

4. A point mass m is placed outside a hollow spherical shell of mass M and uniform density at a distance d from centre of the big sphere. Gravitational force on point mass m at P is

(a) $\dfrac{GmM}{d^2}$

(b) Zero

(c) $\dfrac{2\,GmM}{d^2}$

(d) Data insufficient

5. The force of attraction due to a hollow spherical shell of mass M, radius R and uniform density, on a point mass m situated inside it is

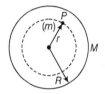

(a) $\dfrac{GmM}{r^2}$

(b) $\dfrac{Gm\,M}{R^2}$

(c) Zero

(d) Data insufficient

Answer

| 1. (c) | 2. (c) | 3. (b) | 4. (a) | 5. (c) |

VERY SHORT ANSWER Type Questions

6. What would happen to an orbiting planet if all of a sudden it comes to stand still?

7. We cannot move fingers without disturbing all stars, why?

8. In case of earth, at what points is its gravitational field zero?

9. How could we determine the mass of a planet such as venus which has no moon?

SHORT ANSWER Type Questions

10. If the earth be at one half of its present distance from the sun, then how many days will be there in a year? **[Ans.** 129 days]

11. Calculate the force of attraction between two bodies, each of mass 100 kg and 1 m apart on the surface of the earth. **[Ans.** 6.67×10^{-7} N]

LONG ANSWER Type I Questions

12. The distances of two planets from the sun are 10^{13} m and 10^{12} m, respectively. Calculate the ratio of time period and the speeds of the two planets.

$$\left[\textbf{Ans. } 10\sqrt{10}, \ \frac{1}{\sqrt{10}} \right]$$

13. If the earth is $\dfrac{1}{4}$ of its present distance from the sun, then what is the duration of the year?

[Ans. 0.125 yr]

14. A sphere of mass 40 kg is attracted by another sphere of mass 15 kg, with a force of $\dfrac{1}{40}$ mg-wt. Find the value of the gravitational constant if their centres are 0.40 m apart.

[Ans. 6.54×10^{-11} Nm^2 kg^{-2}]

15. The masses and coordinates of the three spheres are as follows; 20 kg, $x = 0.50$ m, $y = 1.0$ m, 40 kg, $x = -1.0$ m, $y = -1.0$ m, 60 kg, $x = 0$ m, $y = -0.50$ m. What is the magnitude of the gravitational force on a 20 kg sphere located at the origin due to the other spheres? **[Ans.** 3.2×10^{-7} N]

LONG ANSWER Type II Question

16. Consider two solid uniform spherical objects of the same density ρ. One has a radius R and the other a radius $2R$. They are in outer space where the gravitational fields from other objects are negligible. If they are at rest with their surfaces touching, then what is the contact force between the objects due to their gravitational attraction?

$$\left[\textbf{Ans. } \frac{128}{81} G\pi^2 R^4 \rho^2 \right]$$

|TOPIC 2|
Acceleration Due to Gravity and Gravitational Potential Energy

ACCELERATION DUE TO GRAVITY OF EARTH

The force of gravity acting on a body having unit mass placed on or near the surface of the earth is known as **acceleration due to gravity**. In other words, acceleration set up in the body when it falls freely under the effect of gravity is also known as acceleration due to gravity. It is represented by symbol g and its value is $9.8\ \text{m/s}^2$ on the surface of the earth.

At a given place, the value of acceleration due to gravity is the same for all bodies irrespective of their masses. However, it differs from place to place on the surface of the earth. It also varies with altitude and depth.

Hence, at a point outside the earth, the gravitational force is just as if the entire mass of the earth is concentrated at its centre.

e.g. Consider the earth to be made up of concentric shells and a point mass m situated at a distance r from the centre. The point P lies outside the sphere of radius r and the point P lies inside if the

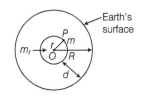

Determination of acceleration due to gravity of earth

shell's radius is greater than r. The smaller sphere exerts a force on a mass m at P as if its mass m_r is concentrated at the centre. The force on the mass m at P has a magnitude

$$F = \frac{Gm(m_r)}{r^2} \qquad \ldots(i)$$

Mass on the earth is $M = \dfrac{4\pi}{3}R^3\rho$

where, M = mass of the earth, R = radius of the earth and ρ = density of the earth.

Mass on sphere is $m_r = \dfrac{4\pi}{3}\rho r^3$

Substituting the value of m_r in Eq. (i), we have

$$F = \frac{Gm}{r^2}\frac{4\pi}{3}\rho r^3 = Gm\frac{M}{R^3}r$$

$$\Rightarrow \qquad F = G\frac{Mm}{R^2} \qquad [\because r = R]$$

From Newton's second law, we know, $F = mg$

$$\therefore \qquad g = \frac{F}{m} = \frac{GM}{R^2}$$

$$\boxed{\text{Acceleration due to gravity, } g = \frac{GM}{R^2}}$$

Substituting the values of $M = 6.4 \times 10^{24}$ kg and $R = 6.4 \times 10^6$ m, we get $g = 9.8$ m/s^2.

Note

- The value of g on the surface of the moon is equal to 1/6 times the value of g on the surface of the earth.
- The value of g is independent of mass, shape, size etc., of the body and depends upon the mass and radius of the earth.

EXAMPLE |1| Mass of the Moon
The acceleration due to gravity at the moon's surface is $1.67\ \text{ms}^{-2}$. If the radius of the moon is 1.74×10^6 m, then calculate the mass of the moon.

Sol. $g = \dfrac{GM}{R^2}$ or $M = \dfrac{gR^2}{G}$

This relation is true not only to the earth but for any heavenly body which is assumed to be spherical.

Now, $g = 1.67\ \text{ms}^{-2}, R = 1.74 \times 10^6$ m

$$G = 6.67 \times 10^{-11}\ \text{Nm}^{-2}\ \text{kg}^{-2}$$

$\therefore$ Mass of the moon, $M = \dfrac{1.67 \times (1.74 \times 10^6)^2}{6.67 \times 10^{-11}}$ kg

$$= 7.58 \times 10^{22}\ \text{kg}$$

EXAMPLE |2| Star Heavier than Sun
A star 2.5 times the mass of the sun and collapsed to a size of 12 km and rotates with a speed of 1.2 revolutions per second. (Extremely compact stars of this kind are known as neutron stars. Certain stellar objects, called pulsars, belong to this category.) Will an object placed on its equator remain stuck to its surface due to gravity? (mass of the sun = 2×10^{30} kg) [NCERT]

Sol. We are given mass of neutron star,

i.e. $M = 2.5 \times 2 \times 10^{30}$ kg

$$= 5 \times 10^{30}\ \text{kg}$$

Radius of star, $R = 12$ km $= 1.2 \times 10^4$ m

Frequency of rotation, $\nu = 1.5$

If g is the acceleration due to gravity on the surface of the star,

$$g = \frac{GM}{R^2} = \frac{6.67 \times 10^{-11} \times 5 \times 10^{20}}{(1.2 \times 10^4)^2} \text{ m/s}^2$$

$$= 2.3 \times 10^{12} \text{ m/s}^2$$

Centrifugal acceleration (a_c) produced in the object at the equator,

i.e. $\qquad a_c = R\omega^2$

$$= R \times (2\pi v)^2 = 4\pi^2 v^2 R$$

or $\qquad a_c = 4 \times 9.87 \times (1.5)^2 \times 1.2 \times 10^4 \text{ m/s}^2$

$$a_c = 1.1 \times 10^6 \text{ m/s}^2$$

Since $g > a_c$, the object will remain stuck to its surface due to gravity.

EXAMPLE |3| Mass of the Earth

A spherical mass of 20 kg lying on the earth's surface is attracted by another spherical mass of 150 kg with a force equal to the weight of 0.25 mg. The centre of the two masses are 0.30 m apart. Calculate the mass of the earth.

Sol.

$m_1 = 20$ kg $\qquad m_2 = 150$ kg

$r = 0.30$ m

Given, $\qquad m_1 = 20$ kg, $m_2 = 150$ kg

$$F = 0.25 \text{ mg- wt}$$

$$g = 9.80 \text{ ms}^{-2}$$

$$R = 6 \times 10^6 \text{ m}$$

Now, kg-wt multiply by 9.8 to get in Newton.

$F = 0.25$ mg-wt

$$= 0.25 \times 10^{-3} \text{ g-wt}$$

$$= 0.25 \times 10^{-3} \times 10^{-3} \text{ kg-wt}$$

$$= 0.25 \times 10^{-6} \text{ kg-wt}$$

$$= 0.25 \times 10^{-6} \times 9.8 \text{ N} \qquad [\because 1 \text{ kg-wt} = 9.8 \text{ N}]$$

From universal law, $F = G\dfrac{m_1 m_2}{r^2}$

or $\qquad G = \dfrac{Fr^2}{m_1 m_2}$

$$G = \frac{0.25 \times 10^{-6} \times 9.8 \times (0.3)^2}{20 \times 150}$$

$$G = 75 \times 9.80 \times 10^{-13} \text{ Nm}^2 \text{ kg}^{-2}$$

$\therefore \qquad g = \dfrac{GM}{R^2}$

$\therefore \qquad M = \dfrac{g \times R^2}{G} = \dfrac{9.80 \times (6 \times 10^6)^2}{75 \times 9.80 \times 10^{-13}}$

$$= 4.8 \times 10^{24} \text{ kg}$$

Acceleration due to Gravity above the Surface of Earth

Consider a body of mass m lying on the surface of the earth of mass M and radius R. Acceleration due to gravity at the surface of the earth.

i.e. $\qquad\qquad g = \dfrac{GM}{R^2} \qquad\qquad ...(i)$

Suppose the body is taken to a height h above the surface of the earth where the value of acceleration due to gravity is g_h as shown in figure.

Then, $g_h = \dfrac{GM}{(R+h)^2} \qquad ...(ii)$

Variation of g with altitude

where, $(R + h)$ is the distance between the centres of body and the earth.

Dividing Eq. (ii) by Eq. (i), we get

$$\frac{g_h}{g} = \frac{GM}{(R+h)^2} \times \frac{R^2}{GM}$$

or $\qquad \dfrac{g_h}{g} = \dfrac{R^2}{(R+h)^2} \qquad\qquad ...(iii)$

As $h << R$, we can derive an expression for g_h

$$\frac{g_h}{g} = \frac{R^2}{\left[R\left(1+\dfrac{h}{R}\right)\right]^2} = \frac{R^2}{R^2\left(1+\dfrac{h}{R}\right)^2}$$

or $\qquad \dfrac{g_h}{g} = \dfrac{1}{\left(1+\dfrac{h}{R}\right)^2} = \left(1+\dfrac{h}{R}\right)^{-2}$

> Acceleration due to gravity at height h, $g_h = \dfrac{g}{\left(1+\dfrac{h}{R}\right)^2}$

If $h << R$, therefore h/R is very small, then expanding the right hand side of the above equation by Binomial theorem and neglecting squares and higher power of h/R, we get

$$\frac{g_h}{g} = 1 - \frac{2h}{R}$$

> Acceleration due to gravity at height h, $g_h = g\left(1 - \dfrac{2h}{R}\right)$

$$...(iv)$$

or $\qquad\qquad gh = g - \dfrac{2h}{R}g$

or $\qquad\qquad g - g_h = \dfrac{2h}{R}g \qquad\qquad ...(v)$

From Eq. (v), we know that the value of acceleration due to gravity decreases with height.

Since, the value of g at a given place on the earth is constant and R is also constant,

∴ $$g - g_h \propto h$$

From the above equation, we note that if h increases, g_h must decrease because g is constant. **Thus, the value of acceleration due to gravity decreases with increase in height above the surface of the earth.**

With height h, the decrease in the value of g is

⇒ $$g - g_h = \frac{2hg}{R}$$

∴ Fractional decrease in the value of g is

⇒ $$\frac{g - g_h}{g} = \frac{2h}{R}$$

∴ % decrease in the value of g

$$= \left(\frac{g - g_h}{g}\right) \times 100 = \frac{2h}{R} \times 100\%$$

EXAMPLE |4| Gravitational Pull on a Body

A body weighs 63 N on the surface of the earth. What is the gravitational force on it due to the earth at a height equal to half the radius of the earth?   **[NCERT]**

Sol. Let g_h be the acceleration due to gravity at a height equal to half the radius of the earth $\left(h = \dfrac{R}{2}\right)$ and g is its value on the earth's surface. Let the body have mass m. We know that

$$\frac{g_h}{g} = \left(\frac{R}{R+h}\right)^2 \text{ or } \frac{g_h}{g} = \left(\frac{R}{R+\dfrac{R}{2}}\right)^2 = \left(\frac{2}{3}\right)^2 = \frac{4}{9}$$

Let w be the weight of body on the surface of the earth and w_h be the weight of the body at height h.

Then, $$\frac{w_h}{w} = \frac{mg_h}{mg} = \frac{g_h}{g} = \frac{4}{9}$$

or $$w_h = \frac{4}{9}w = \frac{4}{9} \times 63\,\text{N} = 28\,\text{N}$$

EXAMLE |5| Free Fall Acceleration From Space

If an object at the altitude of the space shuttle's orbit, about 400 km about the earth's surface, then find out the free fall acceleration of that object.

Sol. The acceleration, $$g = \frac{F}{m} = \frac{GMm/R^2}{m} = \frac{GM}{R^2}$$

If the object is at height h above the earth's surface, then

$$g_h = \frac{GM}{(R+h)^2}$$

⇒ $$g_h = \frac{6.67 \times 10^{-11} \times 5.98 \times 10^{24}}{(6.4 \times 10^6 + 0.4 \times 10^6)^2} = 8.70\,\text{m/s}^2$$

Acceleration due to Gravity below the Earth's Surface

Assume the earth to be a homogeneous sphere (i.e. a sphere of uniform density). Let ρ be the mean density of the earth and a body be lying on the surface of the earth where the value of acceleration due to gravity is g.

Then, $$g = \frac{GM}{R^2} \text{ or } g = \frac{G \times \dfrac{4}{3}\pi R^3 \rho}{R^2}$$

$$\left[\because \text{ mass of the earth, } M = \frac{4}{3}\pi R^3 \rho\right]$$

$$g = \frac{4}{3}\pi GR\rho \qquad \qquad \dots(i)$$

Now, the body be taken to a depth d below the free surface of the earth, where the acceleration due to gravity is g_d. Here, the force of gravity acting on the body is only due to the inner solid sphere of radius $(R - d)$.

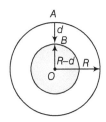

∴ $$g_d = \frac{GM'}{(R-d)^2}$$

Variation of g with depth

where M' is the mass of inner solid sphere of radius $(R-d)$.

or $$g_d = \frac{G}{(R-d)^2} \times \frac{4}{3}\pi (R-d)^3 \times \rho$$

or $$g_d = \frac{4}{3}\pi G (R-d)\rho \qquad \qquad \dots(ii)$$

Dividing Eq. (ii) by Eq. (i), we get

$$\frac{g_d}{g} = \frac{\dfrac{4}{3}\pi G(R-d)\rho}{\dfrac{4}{3}\pi GR\rho} = \frac{R-d}{R}$$

or $$\frac{g_d}{g} = 1 - \frac{d}{R}$$

$$\boxed{\text{Acceleration due to gravity at depth } d, \; g_d = g\left(1 - \frac{d}{R}\right)}$$

or $$g_d - g = -\frac{d}{R_t}g$$

or $$g - g_d = \frac{d}{R}g$$

Here, $(g - g_d)$ gives the decrease in the value of g.

Since, g is constant at a given place of the earth and R is also a constant.

$\therefore \qquad (g - g_d) \propto d$

From the above equation, it is clear that if d increases, g_d must decrease because g is constant. **Hence, the acceleration due to gravity decreases as we move down into the surface of the earth.** i.e. g decreases with the increase in depth d.

At the centre O of the earth, $d = R$

Thus, we get $\qquad g_d = g\left(1 - \dfrac{R}{R}\right) = $ zero

Hence, acceleration due to gravity at the centre of the earth is zero.

Hence, the weight of a body at the centre of the earth is zero though its mass is constant.

Decrease in the value of g with depth d is

$$g - g_d = \frac{g_d}{R}$$

$\therefore$ Fractional decrease in the value of g with depth

$$= \frac{g - g_d}{g} = \frac{d}{R}$$

$\therefore$ % decrease in the value of g

$$= \frac{g - g_d}{g} \times 100 = \frac{d}{R} \times 100\%$$

EXAMPLE |6| Variation in g at the Sea Level

What will be the value of g at the bottom of sea 7 km deep? Diameter of the earth is 12800 km and g on the surface of the earth is 9.8 ms^{-2}.

Sol. Depth of sea, $d = 7$ km, $g = 9.8$ ms^{-2}

Radius of the earth, $R = \dfrac{D}{2} = \dfrac{12800}{2}$ km $= 6400$ km

Value of g at bottom of sea

$$g_d = g\left(1 - \frac{d}{R}\right)$$

$$= 9.8\left(1 - \frac{7}{6400}\right) \text{ ms}^{-2}$$

$$g_d = \frac{9.8 \times 6393}{6400} \text{ ms}^{-2}$$

$$= 9.789 \text{ ms}^{-2}$$

Note

Acceleration due to gravity also vary due to the rotation of earth, if a body of mass m lying at a point whose latitude is λ, then rotation of earth (angular speed ω), the apparent acceleration due to gravity on body is given by $g' = g - \omega^2 R \cos^2 \lambda$

INTENSITY OF GRAVITATIONAL FIELD AT A POINT

It is the force experienced by a unit mass placed at that point.

Let, M be the mass of a body around which a gravitational field exists. In order to get the gravitational field intensity at a point P in the gravitational field, a test mass m is placed at the point P.

The test mass is supposed to be so small that it does not alter the gravitational field in any manner. If a test mass m at a point P in a gravitational field experience a force **F**, then

Gravitational field intensity

Intensity of gravitational field, $I = \dfrac{F}{m} = \dfrac{GMm/r^2}{m}$

$$\boxed{\text{Intensity of gravitational field, } I = \frac{GM}{r^2}}$$

where, r is the distance of P from the centre of the body producing the gravitation field.

If $r = \infty$, $I = 0$. It means the intensity of gravitational field is zero only at infinite distance from the body.

If a unit mass (m) is placed on the surface of earth, then the gravitational force acting on the test mass m will be equal to the weight w of the test mass.

Now, $\qquad I = \dfrac{w}{m} = \dfrac{mg}{m} = g \quad$ or $\quad I = g$

EXAMPLE |7| A Hemispherical Shell

The gravitational intensity at the centre of a hemispherical shell of uniform mass density, (in figure) has the direction indicated by arrow (i) a, (ii) b, (iii) c, (iv) zero. Choose the correct answer. **[NCERT]**

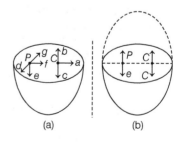

(a)   (b)

Hemispherical shell

Sol. Complete the hemisphere, Fig. (b). The gravitational intensity (gravitational force per unit mass) is zero at all points in a spherical shell. This implies that at any point inside the spherical shell, the gravitational forces are symmetrically placed. As gravitational potential v is constant, hence intensity, $E = -\dfrac{dv}{dr} = 0$ at C.

Thus, if the upper hemisphere is removed, the net gravitational force acting on the particle at C will be downward as shown by arrow c.

Hence, option (iii) is correct. It is to be remembered that the net gravitational force acting on particle C due to upper hemisphere (shown by dotted arrow), is equal and opposite to that acting due to lower hemisphere in order that the total gravitational force due to entire spherical shell is zero.

EXAMPLE |8| Gravitational Field Intensity

Two masses 800 kg and 600 kg, are at a distance 0.25 m apart. Calculate the magnitude of the gravitational field intensity at a point distance 0.20 m from the 800 kg mass and 0.15 m from the 600 kg mass.
Given, $G = 6.6 \times 10^{-11}$ Nm^2 kg^{-2}.

Sol. Let I_A be the gravitational field intensity at P due to 800 kg mass at A.

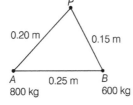

Then, $I_A = G \dfrac{800}{(0.2)^2}$

$= 2 \times 10^4$ along PA

Let I_B be the gravitational field intensity at P due to 600 kg mass at B

Then, $I_B = G \dfrac{600}{(0.15)^2}$ along PB

$= \dfrac{80000\,G}{3}$ along PB

The angle between I_A and I_B is 90°.

If I be the magnitude of the resultant intensity, then

$I = \sqrt{I_A^2 + I_B^2}$

$= \sqrt{(2 \times 10^4\, G)^2 + \left(\dfrac{80000\,G}{3}\right)^2}$

$= G\sqrt{4 \times 10^8 + \dfrac{64}{9} \times 10^8}$

$= 6.67 \times 10^{-11} \times 2 \times 10^4 \sqrt{1 + \dfrac{16}{9}}$

$= 6.67 \times 2 \times \dfrac{5}{3} \times 10^{-7}$ Nkg^{-1}

$I = 2.22 \times 10^{-6}$ Nkg^{-1}

GRAVITATIONAL POTENTIAL

Gravitational potential at a point in the gravitational field is defined as the amount of work done in bringing a body of unit mass from infinity to that point without acceleration

i.e. $V = -\dfrac{W}{m} = -\int \dfrac{\mathbf{F} \cdot \mathbf{dr}}{m} = -\int \mathbf{I} \cdot \mathbf{dr}$ $\quad \left[\text{as}, \dfrac{F}{m} = I\right]$

where, W is the amount of work done in bringing a body of mass m from infinity to that point and I is the intensity of field.

$\therefore$ $\qquad\qquad I = -\dfrac{dV}{dr}$

i.e. negative gradient of potential gives intensity of field or potential which is a scalar function of position whose space derivative gives intensity.

Negative sign indicates that the direction of intensity is in the direction where the potential decreases. Gravitational potential is a scalar quantity and SI is joule/kg and in CGS system is erg/g.

Dimensional formula for gravitational potential.

i.e. $\qquad V = \dfrac{W}{m} = \dfrac{[ML^2T^{-2}]}{[M]} = [M^0L^2T^{-2}]$

Expression for Gravitational Potential

Suppose the earth be perfect sphere of radius R and mass M, can be supposed to be concentrated at its centre O. Then, the gravitational potential at point Q can be calculated, where $OQ = r$ and $r > R$.

Take two points A and B, so $OA = x$ and $AB = dx$ as shown in figure.

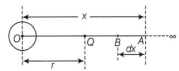

Calculation for gravitational potential

At point A, gravitational force of attraction on a body of unit mass will be $\qquad F = \dfrac{GM \times 1}{x^2} = \dfrac{GM}{x^2}$

Small amount of work done in bringing the unit mass body without acceleration through a small distance $(AB = dx)$ is

$$dW = Fdx = \dfrac{GM}{x^2}\,dx$$

Total amount of work done in bringing a body from infinity to point Q, we get

$$\text{Work done } (W) = \int_{\infty}^{r} \frac{GM}{x^2}\, dx = -\left[\frac{GM}{x}\right]_{\infty}^{r}$$

$$= -GM\left[\frac{1}{r} - \frac{1}{\infty}\right] = \frac{-GM}{r}$$

$$\therefore \qquad V = W$$

$$\boxed{\text{Gravitational potential, } V = \frac{-GM}{r}} \qquad \ldots(i)$$

where, V is total gravitational potential at point Q.

Special Cases

(i) When $r = \infty$ from Eq. (i), then $V_Q = 0$, hence gravitational potential is maximum (zero) at infinity.

(ii) At surface of the earth, $r = R$, then $V_Q = \dfrac{-GM}{R}$.

Note

Potential due to a large number of particles is given by scalar addition of all the potentials as shown in figure.

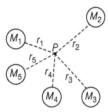

Superposition of different potentials

$$V = V_1 + V_2 + V_3 + \ldots$$
$$= \frac{-GM_1}{r_1} - \frac{GM_2}{r_2} - \frac{GM_3}{r_3} \ldots = -G\sum_{i=1}^{i=n}\frac{M_i}{r_i}$$

EXAMPLE |9| Potential on Geostationary Satellite
As you will learn in the text, a geostationary satellite orbits the earth at a height of nearly 36000 km from the surface of the earth. What is the potential due to the earth's gravity at the site of this satellite? (take the potential energy at infinity to be zero). Mass of the earth $= 6.0 \times 10^{24}$ kg, radius $= 6400$ km. **[NCERT]**

Sol. We are given that

Mass of the earth, $M = 6.0 \times 10^{24}$ kg

Radius of the earth, $R = 6400$ km

Height of the satellite from the earth's surface,
$\quad h = 36000$ km

Distance of the satellite from the centre of the earth,
$\quad r = R + h = 6400\ \text{km} + 36000\ \text{km}$
$\quad r = 42400\ \text{km} = 4.24 \times 10^7$ m

If V is the potential at the site of the satellite,

$$V = -\frac{GM}{r} = -\frac{(6.67 \times 10^{-11}) \times (6.0 \times 10^{24})}{(4.24 \times 10^7)}$$

$$V = -9.4 \times 10^6 \text{ J/kg}$$

EXAMPLE |10| Dependence of Gravity on Altitude
At a point above the surface of the earth, the gravitational potential is -5.12×10^7 J/kg and the acceleration due to gravity is 6.4 m/s^2. Assuming the mean radius of the earth to be 6400 km, calculate the height of the point above the earth's surface.

Sol. If r is the distance of the given point from the centre of the earth, then gravitational potential at the point,

$$V = -\frac{GM}{r} = -5.12 \times 10^7 \text{ J/kg}$$

Acceleration due to gravity at this point,

$$g = \frac{GM}{r^2} = 6.4 \text{ m / s}^2$$

Clearly, $\quad \dfrac{|V|}{g} = \dfrac{GM/r}{GM/r^2} = r$

Thus, $\quad r = \dfrac{5.12 \times 10^7 \text{ J/kg}}{6.4 \text{ m/s}^2} = 8 \times 10^6 \text{ m} = 8000 \text{ km}$

Obviously, height of the point from the earth's surface

$$= (r - R) = 8000 \text{ km} - 6400 \text{ km} = 1600 \text{ km}$$

GRAVITATIONAL POTENTIAL ENERGY

Gravitational potential energy of a body at a point is defined as the amount of work done in bringing the given body from infinity to that point against the gravitational force.

Let a body of mass m is placed at P in the gravitational field of a body of mass M.

Let r be the distance of P from the centre O of the body of mass M as shown in figure. Then, the total work done (W) by the gravitational field when a body of mass m is moved from infinity to a distance r from O is given by

$$W = -\frac{GmM}{r}$$

Gravitational potential energy

This work done is equal to the gravitational potential energy U of mass m.

$\therefore$ Gravitational potential energy, $U = -\dfrac{GMm}{r}$

Now, $\qquad U = -\dfrac{GMm}{r}$

$\Rightarrow$ Gravitational potential energy, $U = \left(-\dfrac{GM}{r}\right) \times m$

$\therefore$ **Gravitational potential energy = Gravitational potential $\times$ mass of the body.**

Some Cases

(i) According to the superposition principle, if there are three particles of masses m_1, m_2 and m_3 in an isolated system, then total gravitational potential energy of the system is

$$U = -\left(\frac{Gm_1 m_2}{r_{12}} + \frac{Gm_2 m_3}{r_{23}} + \frac{Gm_1 m_3}{r_{13}}\right)$$

(ii) If the body of mass m is moved from the surface of the earth to a point distance h above the surface of the earth.

Then, change in potential energy or work done against gravity will be

$$W = \Delta U = GMm\left(\frac{1}{r_1} - \frac{1}{r_2}\right)$$

Change in gravitational potential energy at height h

$$\Delta U = GMm\left(\frac{1}{R} - \frac{1}{R+h}\right)$$

$\qquad\qquad$ [as, $r_1 = R$ and $r_2 = R + h$]

$\Rightarrow \quad \Delta U = \dfrac{GMmh}{R^2\left(1 + \dfrac{h}{R}\right)} = \dfrac{mgh}{1 + \dfrac{h}{R}} \quad \left(\text{as, } \dfrac{GM}{R^2} = g\right)$

$$\Delta U = mgh\left(1 + \frac{h}{R}\right)^{-1} = mgh\left(1 - \frac{h}{R}\right)$$

$\because \qquad h \ll R$

$\therefore \quad \Delta U = mgh$

(iii) When $h = R$, then work done $= \dfrac{mgR}{1 + R/R} = \dfrac{1}{2}mgR$

EXAMPLE |11| Work Done by Uniform Axial Ring

A particle of mass 1 kg is placed at a distance of 4 m from the centre and on the axis of a uniform ring of mass 5 kg and radius 3 m. Calculate the work required to be done to increase the distance of the particle from 4 m to $3\sqrt{3}$ m.

Sol. $U_1 = -\dfrac{G \times 5 \times 1}{5}\,\text{J} \quad \text{or} \quad U_1 = -G\text{J}$

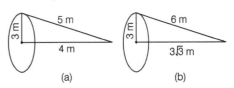

(a) $\qquad\qquad\qquad$ (b)

$$U_2 = \frac{-G \times 5 \times 1}{6}\,\text{J} = -\frac{5G}{6}\,\text{J}$$

Work done $= \left(-\dfrac{5G}{6}\right) - (-G) = G - \dfrac{5G}{6} = \dfrac{G}{6}.$

EXAMPLE |12| Potential Energy of a System of four Particles.

Find the potential energy of a system of four particles placed at the vertices of a square of side l. Also, obtain the potential at the centre of the square. **[NCERT]**

Sol.

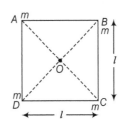

Here, $\qquad AB = BC = CD = DA = l$

$\qquad\qquad AC = BD = \sqrt{l^2 + l^2} = \sqrt{2l^2} = l\sqrt{2}$

$\therefore \qquad OA = OB = OC = OD = \dfrac{l\sqrt{2}}{2} = \dfrac{l}{\sqrt{2}}$

Applying principle of superposition

Total potential energy of the system of particles is

$U = U_{BA} + (U_{CB} + U_{CA}) + (U_{DA} + U_{DB} + U_{DC})$

$\quad = 4U_{BA} + 2U_{DB}$

$\qquad\qquad$ [$\because U_{BA} = U_{DA} = U_{DC} = U_{CB}, U_{CA} = U_{DB}$]

$\quad = 4\left(\dfrac{-Gmm}{l}\right) + 2\left(\dfrac{-Gmm}{l\sqrt{2}}\right)$

$\quad = \dfrac{-2\,Gm^2}{l}\left(2 + \dfrac{1}{\sqrt{2}}\right) = \dfrac{-2Gm^2}{l}(2 + 0.707)$

$U = \dfrac{-5.41}{l}Gm^2$

Total gravitational potential at the centre O,

$V = V_A + V_B + V_C + V_D$

$\quad = 4V_A = 4\left(\dfrac{-Gm}{l_{OA}}\right) = 4 \times \left(\dfrac{-Gm}{l/\sqrt{2}}\right)$

$V = \dfrac{-4\sqrt{2}\,Gm}{l}$

TOPIC PRACTICE 2

OBJECTIVE Type Questions

1. The earth is an approximate sphere. If the interior contained matter which is not of the same density everywhere, then on the surface of the earth, the acceleration due to gravity
   [NCERT Exemplar]
   (a) will be directed towards the centre but not the same everywhere
   (b) will have the same value everywhere but not directed towards the centre
   (c) will be same everywhere in magnitude directed towards the centre
   (d) cannot be zero at any point

Sol. (d) If we assume the earth as a sphere of uniform density, then it can be treated as point mass placed at its centre. In this case acceleration due to gravity $g = 0$, at the centre.

It is not so, if the earth is considered as a sphere of non-uniform density, in that case value of g will be different at different points and cannot be zero at any point.

2. If g is the acceleration due to gravity at the surface of the earth. The force acting on the particle of mass m placed at the surface is
   (a) mg (b) $\dfrac{GmM_e}{R_e^2}$
   (c) Data insufficient   (d) Both (a) and (b)

Sol. (d) Force on particle at surface is
$$F = mg$$
where, g = acceleration due to gravity at the earth's surface

Also, $$g = \dfrac{GM_e}{R_e^2}$$

$\Rightarrow$ $$F = mg = \dfrac{GmM_e}{R_e^2}$$

3. Earth is flattened at the poles and bulges at the equator. This is due to the fact that
   (a) the earth revolves around the sun in an elliptical orbit
   (b) the angular velocity of spinning about its axis is more at the equator
   (c) the centrifugal force is more at the equator than at poles
   (d) None of the above

Sol. (c) Higher centrifugal force causes bulging of earth at equator.

4. The gravitational potential at a distance r from the centre of the earth ($r > R$) is given by (consider, mass of the earth = M_e, radius of the earth = R)
   (a) $\dfrac{-GM_e}{R}$ (b) $\dfrac{GM_e}{R}$ (c) $\dfrac{-GM_e}{r}$ (d) $\dfrac{+GM_e}{r}$

Sol. (c) The gravitational potential at a distance r from the centre of the earth.
$$V(r) = -\dfrac{GM_e}{r}$$

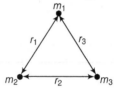

5. Gravitational potential energy of a system of particles as shown in the figure is

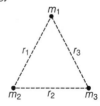

(a) $\dfrac{Gm_1 m_2}{r_1} + \dfrac{Gm_2 m_3}{r_3} + \dfrac{Gm_1 m_3}{r_3}$

(b) $\left(\dfrac{-Gm_1 m_2}{r_1}\right) + \left(\dfrac{-Gm_2 m_3}{r_2}\right) + \left(\dfrac{-Gm_1 m_3}{r_3}\right)$

(c) $\dfrac{-Gm_1 m_2}{r_1} - \dfrac{Gm_2 m_3}{r_2} + \dfrac{Gm_1 m_3}{r_3}$

(d) $\dfrac{Gm_1 m_2}{r_1} + \dfrac{Gm_2 m_3}{r_2} - \dfrac{Gm_1 m_3}{r_3}$

Sol. (b) For a system of particles, all possible pairs are taken and total gravitational potential energy is the algebraic sum of the potential energies due to each pair, applying the principle of superposition. Total gravitational potential energy

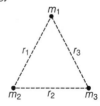

$$= \dfrac{-Gm_1 m_2}{r_1} - \dfrac{Gm_2 m_3}{r_2} - \dfrac{Gm_1 m_3}{r_3}$$

$$= \left(\dfrac{-Gm_1 m_2}{r_1}\right) + \left(\dfrac{-Gm_2 m_3}{r_2}\right) + \left(\dfrac{-Gm_1 m_3}{r_3}\right)$$

VERY SHORT ANSWER Type Questions

6. Where does a body weigh more; at the surface of the earth or in a mine?

Sol. The value of g in mine is less than that on the surface of the earth.

7. If the earth is regarded as a hollow sphere, then what is the weight of an object below surface of the earth?

Sol. The weight of an object below surface of the earth is zero.

8. What is the amount of work done in bringing a mass from the surface of the earth on one side to a point diametrically opposite on the other side?

Sol. Since, gravitational potential difference is zero, therefore the work done is zero.

9. If the force of gravity acts on all bodies in proportion to their masses, then why doesn't a heavy body fall faster than a light body?

Sol. Acceleration due to gravity is independent of the mass of the body.

10. What would happen if the force of gravity were to disappear suddenly?

Sol. The universe would collapse. We would be thrown away because of the centrifugal force. Eating, drinking and infact all activities would become impossible.

11. When a pendulum clock is taken to a mountain, it becomes slow. But a wrist watch controlled by a spring remains unaffected. Explain.

Sol. At the mountain, g decreases and time period of the pendulum clock increases at $T = 2\pi \sqrt{l/g}$. On the other hand, a spring in the wrist watch remains unaffected by the variation of g.

12. What is the apparent weight of a man of 60 kg who is standing in a lift which is moving up with a uniform speed?

Sol. Apparent weight = $mg = 60 \times 10$ N $= 600$ N

13. Would we have more sugar to the kilogram at the pole or at the equator?

Sol. $mg_p = m' g_e$ since, $g_p > g_e$,

∴ $m' > m$. So, we shall have greater mass of sugar at the equator.

14. Why a body weighs more at poles and less at equator?

Sol. The value of g is more at poles than at the equator. Therefore, a body weighs more at poles than at equator.

15. Give a method for the determination of the mass of the moon.

Sol. By making use of the relation,
$$g_m = \frac{GM_m}{R_m^2}$$

16. Define the effect of shape of the earth on the value of g.

Sol. At the surface of the earth, g is maximum at the poles and minimum at the equator i.e. the value of g decreases from poles to equator.

SHORT ANSWER Type Questions

17. Why a tennis ball bounces higher on hills than on plains?

Sol. As the acceleration due to gravity on hills is less than that on the surface of the earth (effect of height), therefore, a tennis ball bounces higher on hills than on plains.

18. The acceleration due to gravity on a planet is 1.96 ms^{-2}. If it is safe to jump from a height of 2 m on the earth, then what will be the corresponding safe height on the planet?

Sol. The safety of a person depends upon the momentum with which the person hits the planet. Since, the mass of the person is constant, therefore the maximum velocity v is the limiting factor.

19. Does the concentration of the earth's mass near its centre change the variation of g with height compared with a homogeneous sphere, how?

Sol. Any change in the distribution of the earth's mass will not affect the variation of acceleration due to gravity with height. This is because for a point outside the earth, the whole mass of the earth is effective and the earth behaves as a homogeneous sphere.

20. Determine the speed with which the earth would have to rotate on its axis so that a person on the equator would weigh $\frac{3}{5}$th as much as at present. Take the equatorial radius as 6400 km.

Sol. Acceleration due to gravity at the equator is
$$g_e = g - R\omega^2$$
$$mg_e = mg - mR\omega^2$$
or $\quad \frac{3}{5} mg = mg - mR\omega^2 \qquad \left[\because mg_e = \frac{3}{5} mg \right]$

∴ $\quad \omega = \sqrt{\frac{2g}{5R}} = \sqrt{\frac{2 \times 9.8}{5 \times 6400 \times 10^3}} = 7.8 \times 10^{-4}$ rad/s

21. What is the gravitational potential energy of a body at height h from the earth surface?

Sol. Gravitational potential energy, i.e.

$$U_h = -\frac{GMm}{R+h} = -\frac{gR^2m}{R+h} \qquad \left[\text{where, } g = \frac{GM}{R^2}\right]$$

$$= -\frac{gR^2m}{R\left(1+\dfrac{h}{R}\right)} = -\frac{mgR}{1+\dfrac{h}{R}}$$

22. A spherical planet has mass M_P and diameter D_P. A particle of mass m falling freely near the surface of this planet will **experience** an acceleration due to gravity, equal to whom?

Sol. Force is given by

$$F = \frac{GM_e m}{R^2} = \frac{GM_p m}{(D_p/2)^2} = \frac{4GM_p m}{D_p^2}$$

$$\frac{F}{m} = \frac{4GM_p}{D_p^2}$$

LONG ANSWER Type I Questions

23. Assuming the earth to be a sphere of uniform mass density, how much would body weigh half way down to the centre of the earth if it weighted 250 N on the surface? **[NCERT]**

> To calculate the weight of the body down the centre of the earth, we have to calculate the acceleration due to gravity at depth d from earth's surface which is given by
> $$g' = g\left(1 - \frac{d}{R}\right)$$

Sol. Weight of the body at the earth's surface

$$w = mg = 250\,\text{N} \qquad \text{...(i)}$$

Acceleration due to gravity at depth d from the earth's surface

$$g' = g\left(1 - \frac{d}{R}\right)$$

Here, $d = \dfrac{R}{2}$

$$\therefore \qquad g' = g\left(1 - \frac{R/2}{R}\right) = g\left(1 - \frac{1}{2}\right)$$

$$\Rightarrow \qquad g' = \frac{g}{2}$$

$\therefore$ Weight of the body at depth d

$$\Rightarrow \qquad w' = mg = \frac{mg}{2}$$

Using Eq. (i), we get

$$w' = \frac{250}{2} = 125\,\text{N}$$

$\therefore$ Weight of the body will be 125 N.

24. An object of mass m is raised from the surface of the earth to a height equal to the radius of the earth, that is, taken from a distance R to $2R$ from the centre of the earth. What is the gain in its potential energy? **[NCERT Exemplar]**

Sol. Gain in PE, $\Delta U = U_f - U_i$

$$= -\frac{GMm}{2R} - \left(-\frac{GMm}{R}\right)$$

$$= \frac{GMm}{R}\left(-\frac{1}{2} + 1\right) = \frac{GMm}{2R}$$

$$= \frac{(gR^2)m}{2R} = \frac{1}{2}mgR \qquad \left[\text{as } g = \frac{GM}{R^2}\right]$$

25. Derive an expression for work done against gravity.

Sol. Potential energy of the body on the surface of the earth

$$= \frac{-GMm}{R}$$

Potential energy of the body at a height h from the surface of the earth $= -\dfrac{GMm}{(R+h)}$

$$\text{Work done} = \left(-\frac{GMm}{R+h}\right) - \left(-\frac{GMm}{R}\right)$$

$$= \frac{GMm}{R} - \frac{GMm}{R+h}$$

$$= GMm\left(\frac{1}{R} - \frac{1}{R+h}\right)$$

$$= \frac{GMmh}{R(R+h)} = \frac{MgR^2h}{R(R+h)} \qquad \left[\because g = \frac{GM}{R^2}\right]$$

$$= \frac{(Mgh)R}{(R+h)} = \frac{Mgh}{1+\dfrac{h}{R}}$$

26. Two bodies of m and $4m$ are placed at a distance r. The gravitational field is zero at a point on the line joining the two masses. What will be the gravitational potential at this point? **[AIEEE 2011]**

Sol.

$$\frac{Gm}{x^2} = \frac{G(4m)}{(r-x)^2}$$

$$\frac{1}{x} = \frac{2}{r-x}$$

$$\Rightarrow \qquad r - x = 2x$$

$$\Rightarrow \qquad 3x = r \Rightarrow x = \frac{r}{3}$$

∴ The gravitational potential $= \dfrac{-Gm}{r/3} \dfrac{-G(4m)}{2r/3}$

$$= \frac{-3Gm}{r} \frac{-6Gm}{r} = \frac{-9Gm}{r}$$

27. The mass of a spaceship is 1000 kg. It is to be launched from the earth's surface out into free space. The value of g and R (radius of earth) are $10 \, \text{m/s}^2$ and 6400 km, respectively.

What is the required energy for this work done?

Sol. $W = 0 - \left[\dfrac{-GMm}{R} \right] = \dfrac{GMm}{R}$

$$= gR^2 \times \frac{m}{R} = mgR$$

$$= 1000 \times 10 \times 6400 \times 10^3$$

$$= 64 \times 10^9 \, \text{J} = 6.4 \times 10^{10} \, \text{J}$$

28. What will be the potential energy of a body of mass 67 kg at a distance of 6.6×10^{10} m from the centre of the earth? Find gravitational potential at this distance.

Sol. Mass of the earth, $M = 6.0 \times 10^{24}$ kg, $m = 67$ kg

$$G = 6.67 \times 10^{-11} \, \text{Nm}^2 \, \text{kg}^{-2}$$

Gravitational potential, $V = -\dfrac{GM}{R}$

$$= -\frac{6.67 \times 10^{-11} \times 6 \times 10^{24}}{6.6 \times 10^{10}}$$

$$V = -6.1 \times 10^3 \, \text{Jkg}^{-1}$$

29. Two heavy spheres, each of mass 100 kg and radius 0.10 m are placed 1.0 m apart on a horizontal table. What is the gravitational force and potential at the mid-point of the line joining the centres of the spheres? Is an object placed at that point in equilibrium? If so, is the equilibrium stable or unstable? **[NCERT]**

Sol. Let A and B be the two given spheres and O be the mid-point on the line joining their centres.

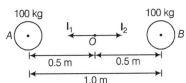

If $\mathbf{I}_1$ and $\mathbf{I}_2$ are the gravitational fields at O due to A and B respectively,

$$I_1 = \frac{G \times 100}{(0.5)^2}, \quad I_2 = \frac{G \times 100}{(0.5)^2}$$

Since, I_1 and I_2 are equal and opposite, then resultant gravitational field at O is zero.

If V is the gravitational potential at O due to A and B

$$V = -\frac{G \times 100}{0.5} - \frac{G \times 100}{0.5}$$

$$= -\frac{2G \times 100}{0.5}$$

or $\qquad V = \dfrac{-2 \times 6.67 \times 10^{-11} \times 100}{0.5}$

$$= -2.7 \times 10^{-8} \, \text{J/kg}$$

The object placed at O is in equilibrium as there is no net force acting on the object. But it will be in an unstable equilibrium as once displaced from O, it will not come back to O.

LONG ANSWER Type II Questions

30. Choose the correct alternatives.

(i) Acceleration due to gravity increases/ decreases with increasing altitude.

(ii) Acceleration due to gravity increases/ decreases with increasing depth (assume the earth to be a sphere of uniform density).

(iii) Acceleration due to gravity is independent of the mass of the earth/mass of the body.

(iv) The formula, $-GMm \left(\dfrac{1}{r_2} - \dfrac{1}{r_1} \right)$ is more/less accurate than the formula $mg(r_2 - r_1)$ for the difference of potential energy between two points r_2 and r_1 distance away from the centre of the earth. **[NCERT]**

Sol. (i) Acceleration due to gravity at altitude h from the earth's surface is given by

$$g' = \frac{g}{\left(1 + \dfrac{h}{R_e} \right)^2}$$

where, R_e is the radius of the earth.

Therefore, acceleration due to gravity decreases with increasing altitude.

(ii) Acceleration due to gravity at depth d from the earth's surface is given by

$$g' = g \left(1 - \frac{d}{R_e} \right)$$

Therefore, acceleration due to gravity decreases with increasing depth.

(iii) Acceleration due to gravity is independent of the mass of the body.

(iv) The formula, $-GMm \left(\dfrac{1}{r_2} - \dfrac{1}{r_1} \right)$

is more accurate than the formula $mg(r_2 - r_1)$ for the difference of potential energy between two points r_2 and r_1, distance away from the centre of the earth.

31. Two stars each of 1 solar mass ($= 2 \times 10^{30}$ kg) are approaching each other for a head on collision. When they are at a distance of 10^9 km, their speeds are negligible. What is the speed with which they will collide? The radius of each star is 10^4 km. Assume the stars to remain undistored until they collide (use the known value of G). **[NCERT]**

Sol. Here, mass of each star, $M = 2 \times 10^{30}$ kg

Radius of each star, $r = 10^7$ m

Initial potential energy of the stars when they are 10^{12} m apart $= -\dfrac{GM \times M}{10^{12}} = -\dfrac{GM^2}{10^{12}}$

[distance between two stars $= 10^{12}$ m]

When the stars are just going to collide, the distance between their centres = twice the radius of each star $= 2r = 2 \times 10^7$ m

Final potential energy of the stars when they are about to collide $= - G \dfrac{M \times M}{2 \times 10^7} = -\dfrac{GM^2}{2 \times 10^7}$

Change in potential energy of stars

$$= -\dfrac{GM^2}{10^{12}} - \left(-\dfrac{GM^2}{2 \times 10^7} \right) = \dfrac{GM^2}{2 \times 10^7} - \dfrac{GM^2}{10^{12}}$$

$$\approx \dfrac{GM^2}{2 \times 10^7} \left[\text{as } \dfrac{GM^2}{10^{12}} \ll \dfrac{GM^2}{2 \times 10^7} \right] \quad \text{...(i)}$$

Let v be the speed of each star just before colliding.

Final KE of the stars $= 2 \times \dfrac{1}{2} Mv^2 = Mv^2$

Initial KE of the stars $= 0$
(because when the stars are initially 10^{12} m apart, their speeds are negligible).

Change in KE of the stars $= Mv^2$ \quad ...(ii)

Using the law of conservation of energy, from Eqs. (i) and (ii), we get $\dfrac{GM^2}{2 \times 10^7} = Mv^2$

or $\quad v = \sqrt{\dfrac{GM}{2 \times 10^7}}$ or $v = \sqrt{\dfrac{6.67 \times 10^{-11} \times (2 \times 10^{30})}{2 \times 10^7}}$

or $\quad v = 2.6 \times 10^6$ m/s

ASSESS YOUR TOPICAL UNDERSTANDING

OBJECTIVE Type Questions

1. What is the value of acceleration caused by force of gravity on a stone placed on ground?
(a) 10 ms^{-2} (b) 9.8 ms^{-2}
(c) 0   (d) ~ 9.81 ms^{-2}

2. The radii of two planets are respectively R_1 and R_2 and their densities are respectively ρ_1 and ρ_2. The ratio of the accelerations due to gravity at their surfaces is
(a) $g_1 : g_2 = \dfrac{\rho_1}{R_1^2} : \dfrac{\rho_2}{R_2^2}$
(b) $g_1 : g_2 = R_1 R_2 : \rho_1 \rho_2$
(c) $g_1 : g_2 = R_1 \rho_2 : R_2 \rho_1$
(d) $g_1 : g_2 = R_1 \rho_1 : R_2 \rho_2$

3. The value of acceleration due to gravity at a height h above the surface of the earth of radius R is g', then
(a) $g' < g$ (b) $g' > g$
(c) $g' = g$ (d) $g' = g\left(1 - \dfrac{2h}{R}\right)$

4. The gravitational potential energy of a system consisting of two particles separated by a distance r is
(a) directly proportional to product of the masses of particles
(b) inversely proportional to the separation between them
(c) independent of distance r
(d) Both (a) and (b)

5. Two point masses m_1 and m_2 are separated by a distance r. The gravitational potential energy of the system is G_1. When the separation between the particles is doubled, the gravitational potential energy is G_2. Then, the ratio of $\dfrac{G_1}{G_2}$ is
(a) 1   (b) 2   (c) 3   (d) 4

Answer

1. (c) | 2. (d) | 3. (a) | 4. (d) | 5. (b)

VERY SHORT ANSWER Type Questions

6. If the radius of the earth is 6000 km, then what will be the weight of 120 kg body if taken to a height of 2000 km above sea level? **[Ans.** -67.5 kg-wt **]**

7. What is the value of gravitational potential at the surface of the earth, referred to zero potential at infinite distance? **[Ans.** -6.25×10^7 J / kg **]**

8. If the radius of the earth were increased by a factor of 3, then by what factor would its density have to be changed to keep g the same? **[Ans.** $\rho/3$ **]**

9. The particles of masses 0.2 kg and 0.8 kg are separated by 12 cm. At which point from the 0.2 kg particle, the gravitational field intensity due to the two particles is zero? **[Ans.** $d = 4$ cm **]**

SHORT ANSWER Type Questions

10. The mount everest is 8848 m above sea level. Estimate the acceleration due to gravity at this height, given that mean g on the surface of the earth is $9.8 \, \text{m/s}^2$. **[Ans.** $9.77 \, \text{m/s}^2$ **]**

11. What will be the value of g at the bottom of sea 7 km deep? Diameter of the earth is 12800 km and g on the surface of the earth is $9.8 \, \text{m/s}^2$. **[Ans.** $9.789 \, \text{m/s}^2$ **]**

12. If the earth was a perfect sphere of radius 6.37×10^6 m, rotating about its axis with a period of 1 day, then how much would the acceleration due to gravity (g) differ from the poles to the equator? **[Ans.** $3.37 \times 10^{-2} \, \text{m/s}^2$ **]**

LONG ANSWER Type I Questions
|3 Marks|

13. Calculate the earth's surface potential from the following data.
   (i) Radius of the earth, $R = 6.63 \times 10^6$ m
   (ii) Mean density of the earth,
      $\rho = 5.57 \times 10^3 \, \text{kgm}^{-3}$
   (iii) $G = 6.67 \times 10^{-11} \, \text{Nm}^2 \, \text{kg}^{-2}$
   [Ans. $-6.84 \times 10^7 \, \text{J kg}^{-1}$ **]**

14. At a point above the earth, the gravitational potential is $-5.12 \times 10^7 \, \text{J kg}^{-1}$ and acceleration due to gravity is $6.4 \, \text{ms}^{-2}$. Assuming the mean radius of the earth to be 6400 km, calculate the height of this point above the surface of the earth. **[Ans.** 7600 km **]**

LONG ANSWER Type II Questions

15. Two equal masses of 6.40 kg are separated by a distance of 0.16 m. A small body is released from a point P equidistant from the two masses and at a distance of 0.06 m from the line joining them.
   (i) Calculate the velocity of this body when it passes through Q.
   (ii) Calculate the acceleration of this body at P and Q if its mass is 0.1 kg.

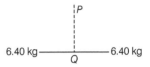

   [Ans. (i) $6.53 \times 10^{-5} \, \text{ms}^{-1}$ (ii) $5.12 \times 10^{-8} \, \text{ms}^{-2}$ **]**

16. What do you understand by gravitational field, intensity of gravitational field? Prove that gravitational intensity at a point is equal to the acceleration due to gravity at that point.

17. A body weighs 90 kg on the surface of the earth. How much will it weigh on the surface of the mars whose mass is $\frac{1}{9}$ th and radius $\frac{1}{2}$ of that of the earth? **[Ans.** 40 kg **]**

18. The Earth-moon distance is 3.8×10^5 km. The mass of the earth is 81 times that of moon. Determine the distance from the earth to the point where the gravitational fields due to the earth and the moon cancel out. **[Ans.** 3.42×10^5 km **]**

19. What should be the angular speed of earth, so that bodies lying on equator may appear weight less? **[Ans.** $1.25 \times 10^{-3} \, \text{rad s}^{-1}$ **]**

20. Find the intensity of gravitational field at a point lying at a distance x from the centre on the axis of a ring of radius 'a' and mass 'M'.

|TOPIC 3|
Escape Speed, Geostationary and Solar Satellites

ESCAPE SPEED

Escape speed on the earth (or any other planet) is defined as the minimum speed with which a body should be projected vertically upwards from the surface of the earth so that it just escapes out from gravitational field of the earth and never return on its own.

e.g. If you fire a projectile upward, usually it will slow down, stop momentarily and return to the earth. A certain minimum initial speed will cause it to move upward forever and coming to rest only at infinity.

Consider a body of mass m lying at a distance x from the centre of the earth. Let M be the mass and R be radius of the earth as shown in figure. According to Newton's law of gravitation, **the gravitational force F of attraction between the body and the earth** is given by

$$F = G\frac{Mm}{x^2}$$

If dW be the work done to displace the body through a small distance dx, then

$$dW = Fdx = \frac{GMm}{x^2}dx$$

Calculation for escape speed

Total work done in taking the body from the surface of the earth i.e. $x = R$ to $x = \infty$ is given by

$$W = \int dW = \int_R^\infty \frac{GMm}{x^2}dx$$

or $$W = GMm\int_R^\infty \frac{1}{x^2}dx$$

$$[\because GMm \text{ is the constant quantity}]$$

$\therefore$ $$W = GMm\int_R^\infty x^{-2}dx = GMm\left(\frac{x^{-2+1}}{-2+1}\right)_R^\infty$$

or $$W = GMm\left[\frac{x^{-1}}{-1}\right]_R^\infty = -GMm\left[\frac{1}{x}\right]_R^\infty$$

$$= -GMm\left[\frac{1}{\infty} - \frac{1}{R}\right]$$

$$W = \frac{GMm}{R} \qquad \left[\because \frac{1}{\infty} = 0\right]$$

If v_e is the required escape speed of the body, then kinetic energy imparted to the body $= \frac{1}{2}mv_e^2$

$\therefore$ $$\frac{1}{2}mv_e^2 = \frac{GMm}{R}$$

or $$v_e^2 = \frac{2GM}{R}$$

$$v_e = \sqrt{\frac{2GM}{R}} \qquad \ldots(i)$$

Thus, the escape speed of a body depends upon the mass and radius of the planet from which the body is projected.

$$g = \frac{GM}{R^2}$$

$\Rightarrow$ $$GM = gR^2$$

$\therefore$ $$v_e = \sqrt{\frac{2gR^2}{R}}$$

or $$v_e = \sqrt{2gR} \qquad \ldots(ii)$$

or $$\boxed{\text{Escape velocity, } v_e = \sqrt{2gR}}$$

where, R is the radius of the earth.
From Eq. (i),

$$v_e = \sqrt{\frac{2G}{R} \times \frac{4}{3}\pi R^3 \times \rho}$$

where, ρ is the mean density of the earth.

$$\boxed{\text{Escape velocity, } v_e = R\sqrt{\frac{8}{3}\pi G\rho}} \qquad \ldots(iii)$$

Escape Speed from Principle of Conservation of Energy

Let the object reach at infinity and its speed be v_f. The energy of an object is the sum of potential energy and kinetic energy. Then, the total energy of the projectile at infinity is given by

$$E(\infty) = W_1 + \frac{mv_f^2}{2} \qquad \ldots(i)$$

where, W_1 is gravitational potential energy of the object at infinity.

If the object was thrown initially with a speed v_i from a point at a distance $(h + R)$ from the centre of the earth, then its initial energy is given by

$$E(h + R) = \frac{1}{2} m v_i^2 - \frac{GmM}{h + R} + W_1 \quad \ldots(\text{ii})$$

According to principle of energy conservation Eqs.(i) and (ii) are equal. So, $\dfrac{mv_i^2}{2} - \dfrac{GmM}{(h + R)} = \dfrac{mv_f^2}{2}$

If $\dfrac{mv_f^2}{2}$ is zero, then $\dfrac{mv_i^2}{2} - \dfrac{GmM}{h + R} = 0$

Thus, the minimum speed required for an object to reach infinity i.e. escape from the earth corresponds to

$$\frac{1}{2} m (v_i^2)_{\min} = \frac{GmM}{h + R}$$

If the object is thrown from the surface of the earth, h is zero, so we get

$$(v_i)_{\min} = \sqrt{\frac{2GM}{R}}$$

Using the relation, $g = GM / R^2$, we get

$$\boxed{\text{Minimum speed, } (v_i)_{\min} = \sqrt{2gR}}$$

If $g = 9.8$ m/s^2 and $R = 6.4 \times 10^6$ m, then

$$(v_i)_{\min} = 11.2 \text{ km/s}$$

EXAMPLE |1| Escape Velocity on Solar System

Calculate the escape speed of a body from the solar system from following data

(i) Mass of the sun = 2×10^{30} kg.

(ii) Separation of the earth from the sun = 1.5×10^{11} m.

Sol. If M be the mass of the sun and R be the distance of the earth from the sun, then escape velocity,

$$v_e = \sqrt{\frac{2GM}{R}} = \sqrt{\frac{2 \times 6.67 \times 10^{-11} \times 2 \times 10^{30}}{1.5 \times 10^{11}}} \text{ m s}^{-1}$$

$$= \sqrt{\frac{4 \times 6.67}{1.5}} \times 10^4 \text{ ms}^{-1}$$

$$= 4.217 \times 10^4 \text{ ms}^{-1}$$

$$v_e = 42.17 \text{ kms}^{-1} \qquad [1 \text{ km} = 1000 \text{ m}]$$

$\therefore$ The escape speed for solar system is 42.17 kms^{-1}.

Note

Orbital velocity (v_0) of a satellite is the velocity required to put the satellite into its orbit around the earth, $v_0 = \sqrt{gR}$, i.e. $v_e = \sqrt{2} v_0$

EXAMPLE |2| A Rockey Sphere

Estimate the size of a rockey sphere with a density of 3.0 g/cm^3 from the surface of which you could barely throw a golf ball and have it never back. (assume your best throw is 40 m/s).

Sol. Let us consider that the rockey sphere has mass M and radius R. The escape speed for such a sphere is given by

$$v_e = \sqrt{\frac{2GM}{R}} = \sqrt{\frac{2G\left(\frac{4\pi}{3}\right)R^3 \rho}{R}} = \sqrt{\frac{8\pi G\rho}{3}} R$$

or $\qquad R = v_e \sqrt{\dfrac{3}{8\pi G\rho}}$

Here, $\rho = 3.0$ g/cm^3 = 3.0×10^3 kg/m^3, $v_e = 40$ m/s

Thus, $\quad R = 40 \sqrt{\dfrac{3}{8 \times 3.14 \times 6.67 \times 10^{-11} \times 3 \times 10^3}}$ m

or $\qquad R = 40 \times 772.6$ m = 30904 m = 30.904 km

EXAMPLE |3| Escape velocity for an atmospheric particle

Calculate the escape velocity for an atmospheric particle 1000 km above the earth's surface, given that the radius of the earth = 6.4×10^6 m and acceleration due to gravity on the surface of the earth = 9.8 m s^{-2}.

Sol.

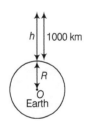

Here, Height, $h = 1000$ km, $R = 6.4 \times 10^6$ m, $g = 9.8$ ms^{-2}

$$h = 1000 \times 1000 = 10^6 \text{ m}$$

Escape velocity at a height h above the earth's surface

$$v_e = \sqrt{2g_h(R + h)}$$

Substitute the value of g_h in the above formula, we get

$$g_h = \frac{gR^2}{(R + h)^2}$$

$$\Rightarrow \quad v_e = \sqrt{\frac{2 \times gR^2}{(R + h)^2}(R + h)} = \sqrt{\frac{2gR^2}{R + h}}$$

$$v_e = \sqrt{\frac{2 \times 9.8 \times (6.4 \times 10^6)^2}{(6.4 + 1) 10^6}} \text{ ms}^{-1}$$

$$= 10.42 \text{ kms}^{-1}$$

EARTH SATELLITES

A satellite is a body which is constantly revolving in an orbit around a comparatively much larger body.

e.g. The moon is a natural satellite while INSAT-1B is an artificial satellite of the earth. Condition for establishment of satellite is that the centre of orbit of satellite must coincide with centre of the earth or satellite must move around great circle of the earth.

As we have already discussed that the centripetal force required for circular orbit is given by

$$F_e = \frac{mv^2}{R+h} \qquad \text{...(i)}$$

and is directeds toward the centre. This centripetal force is provided by the gravitational force which is expressed as,

$$F_g = \frac{GmM}{(R+h)^2} \qquad \text{...(ii)}$$

Equating both these Eqs. (i) and (ii), we get

$$v^2 = \frac{GM}{R+h}$$

Thus, v decreases as h increases. When, $h = 0$

$$\therefore \qquad v^2 = \frac{GM}{R} = gR \qquad \left[\because g = \frac{GM}{R^2}\right]$$

In every orbit, the satellite traverses a distance $2\pi(R+h)$ with speed v.

Then, its time period is given by

$$T = \frac{2\pi(R+h)}{v}$$

$$= \frac{2\pi(R+h)^{3/2}}{\sqrt{GM}} \qquad \text{...(iii)} \left[\because v^2 = \frac{GM}{R+h}\right]$$

On squaring both sides in Eq. (iii), we get

$$\boxed{T^2 = k(R+h)^3} \qquad \left[\because k = \frac{4\pi^2}{GM}\right]$$

Thus, it is Kepler's law of periods. For a satellite, very close to surface of earth, h can be neglected in comparison to R. If $h = 0$ and T is T_0, then

$$T_0 = 2\pi\sqrt{R/g}$$

For earth, $R = 6400$ km and $g = 9.8$ m/s^2

$$T_0 = 2\pi\sqrt{\frac{6.4\times10^6}{9.8}} \cong 85\text{ min}$$

EXAMPLE |4| Phobos and Delmos

The planet mars has two moons, phobos and delmos.

(i) Phobos has a period 7h, 39 min and an orbital radius of 9.4×10^3 km. Calculate the mass of mars.

(ii) Assume that earth and mars move in circular orbits around the sun with the martian orbit being 1.52 times the orbital radius of the earth. What is the length of the martian year in days?

Sol. (i) Given, $T = 7$ h 39 min $= 459\times60$ s

$$R = 9.4\times10^3 \text{ km} = 9.4\times10^6 \text{ m}, \ M_m = ?$$

$$\therefore \text{ Mass of mars, } M_m = \frac{4\pi^2}{G}\cdot\frac{R^3}{T^2}$$

$$= \frac{4\times(3.14)^2\times(9.4\times10^6)^3}{6.67\times10^{-11}\times(459\times60)^2}$$

$$= 6.48\times10^{23} \text{ kg}$$

(ii) From Kepler's third law, $\dfrac{T_m^2}{T^2} = \dfrac{R_{MS}^3}{R_{ES}^3}$

where, R_{MS} is the mass-sun distance and R_{ES} is the earth-sun distance

$$\therefore \qquad T_m = (1.52)^{3/2}\times365 = 684\text{ days}$$

EXAMPLE |5| Revolution of a Moon

Express the constant k in equation $T^2 = k(R+h)^3$ in days and kilometres. Given, $k = 10^{-13}$ s^2/m^3. The moon is at a distance of 3.84×10^5 km from the orbit. Obtain its time period of revolution in days. **[NCERT]**

Sol. $k = 10^{-13}\text{s}^2/\text{m}^3$

$$= 10^{-13}\left[\frac{1}{(24\times60\times60)^2}\text{d}^2\right]\left[\frac{1}{(1/1000)^3\text{ km}^3}\right]$$

$$= 1.33\times10^{-14}\text{d}^2/\text{km}^3$$

$$T^2 = k(R+h)^3 = 1.33\times10^{-14}\times(3.84\times10^5)^3 = 27.3\text{ days}$$

ENERGY OF AN ORBITING SATELLITE

When a satellite revolves around a planet in its orbit, it possesses both potential energy (due to its position against gravitational pull of the earth) and kinetic energy (due to orbital motion).

If m is the mass of the satellite and v is its orbital velocity. Then, KE of the satellite

$$K = \frac{1}{2}mv^2 = \frac{1}{2}m\frac{GM}{r}$$

$$\boxed{\text{Kinetic energy of satellite, } K = \frac{GMm}{2(R+h)}} \qquad \text{...(i)}$$

$$[\because r = R+h]$$

PE of the satellite, $U = mV$

$$\boxed{\text{Potential energy of satellite, } U = -\frac{GMm}{R+h}}$$ ...(ii)

Total mechanical energy of satellite, $E = K + U$

or $\quad E = \dfrac{GMm}{2(R+h)} - \dfrac{GMm}{(R+h)}$

$\quad\quad E = -\dfrac{GMm}{2(R+h)}$ ...(iii)

$\therefore \quad \boxed{\text{Total energy of satellite, } E = -\frac{GMm}{2(R+h)}}$

Satellites are always at finite distance from the earth and hence, their energy cannot be positive or zero.

Now, plot the graph between the kinetic, potential and total energies by considering the following conditions.

(i) Kinetic energy $(K) = -$ (total energy)

(ii) Potential energy $(U) = 2$ (total energy)

(iii) Potential energy $(U) = -2$ (kinetic energy) as shown in Fig (a).

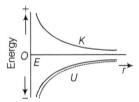

(a) Energy graph for a satellite

If the orbit of a satellite is elliptic as shown in Fig. (b), then, total energy $(E) = \dfrac{-GMm}{2a}$

$\quad\quad\quad\quad = $ constant,

where a is semi-major axis.

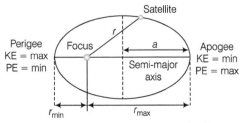

(b) Energy distribution in elliptical orbit

EXAMPLE |6| Transferring the Satellite

A 400 kg satellite is in a circular orbit of radius $2R$ about the earth. How much energy is required to transfer it to a circular orbit of radius $4R$? What are the changes in the kinetic and potential energies? **[NCERT]**

Sol. Given

Mass of satellite, $m = 400$ kg

The initial energy is given by, $E_i = \dfrac{-GMm}{4R}$

Final energy is given by, $E_f = \dfrac{-GMm}{8R}$

$\therefore$ Change in the total energy is given by

$$\Delta E = E_f - E_i = \frac{-GMm}{8R} - \left(\frac{-GMm}{4R}\right)$$

$$\Delta E = \frac{GMm}{8R} = \left(\frac{GM}{R^2}\right)\frac{mR}{8}$$

$$= \frac{gmR}{8} = \frac{9.81 \times 400 \times 6.37 \times 10^6}{8}$$

$$\Delta E = 3.13 \times 10^9 \text{ J}$$

The kinetic energy is reduced,

$\therefore \quad\quad \Delta K = K_f - K_i = -3.13 \times 10^3 \text{ J}$

Change in potential energy,

$\quad\quad \Delta U = -2 \times \Delta E = -2 \times 3.13 \times 10^9 = -6.25 \times 10^9 \text{ J}$

WEIGHTLESSNESS

The weight of a body is the force with which it is attracted towards the centre of the earth. When a body is stationary with respect to the earth, its weight equals to the gravity. This weight of the body is known as its **static** or **true weight**.

At one particular position, the two gravitational pulls may be equal and opposite and the net pull on the body becomes zero. This is zero gravity region or the null point and the body is said to be **weightless**.

The state of weightlessness can be observed in the following situations

(i) When objects fall freely under gravity.

e.g. A lift falling freely

(ii) When a satellite revolves in its orbit around the earth.

(iii) When bodies are at null points in outer space.

Weightlessness in a Satellite

A satellite which does not produce its own gravity moves around the earth in a circular orbit under the action of gravity. The acceleration of satellite is GM/r^2 towards the centre of the earth as shown in figure.

If a body of mass m is placed on a surface inside a satellite moving around the earth. Then, forces on the body are

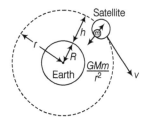

Weightlessness in a satellite

The gravitational pull of the earth $= \dfrac{GMm}{r^2}$

The reaction by the surface $= N$

By Newton's law, $\dfrac{GMm}{r^2} - N = ma$

$$\dfrac{GMm}{r^2} - N = m\left(\dfrac{GM}{r^2}\right)$$

$$N = 0$$

Thus, the surface does not exert any force on the body and hence, its apparent weight is zero.

Note

Condition of weightlessness can be experienced only when the mass of satellite is negligible so that it does not produce its own gravity.

e.g. Moon is a satellite of the earth but due to its own weight, it applies gravitational force of attraction on the body placed on its surface and hence, weight of the body will not be equal to zero at the surface of the moon.

The experiment of simple pendulum cannot be performed in the weightlessness state because

$$T = 2\pi\sqrt{\dfrac{L}{g}} = \infty \text{ as } g = 0$$

TOPIC PRACTICE 3

OBJECTIVE Type Questions

1. An object is thrown from the surface of the moon. The escape speed for the object is

   (a) $\sqrt{2g'R_m}$, where $g' =$ acceleration due to gravity on the moon and $R_m =$ radius of the moon

   (b) $\sqrt{2g'R_e}$, where $g' =$ acceleration due to gravity on the moon and $R_e =$ radius of the earth

   (c) $\sqrt{2gR_m}$, where $g =$ acceleration due to gravity on the earth and $R_m =$ radius of the moon

   (d) None of the above

   Sol. (a) Escape speed from the moon $= \sqrt{2g'R_m}$

   where,

   $g' =$ acceleration due to gravity on the surface of moon.

   $R_m =$ radius of the moon

2. The escape velocity of a body from the earth is v_e. If the radius of earth contracts to $1/4$ th of its value, keeping the mass of the earth constant, escape velocity will be

   (a) doubled   (b) halved
   (c) tripled   (d) unaltered

   Sol. (a) Given, escape speed $v_e = \sqrt{\dfrac{2GM_e}{R_e}}$

   where, $M_e =$ mass of the earth, $R_e =$ radius of the earth

   Now, radius of earth $= R' = R_e/4$

   $$\Rightarrow v'_e = \sqrt{\dfrac{2GM}{R'}} = \sqrt{4\left(\dfrac{2GM}{R_e}\right)} = 2\sqrt{\dfrac{2GM}{R_e}}$$

   or $v'_e = 2 v_e$

3. The kinetic energy of the satellite in a circular orbit with speed v is given as

   (a) $KE = \dfrac{-GmM_e}{2(R_e + h)}$ (b) $KE = \dfrac{GmM_e}{(R_e + h)}$

   (c) $KE = \dfrac{GmM_e}{2(R_e + h)}$ (d) $KE = -\dfrac{1}{2}mv^2$

   Sol. (c) KE of satellite $= \dfrac{1}{2}mv^2$

   $$= \dfrac{1}{2} m \left(\sqrt{\dfrac{GM_e}{(R_e + h)}}\right)^2$$

   $$= \dfrac{1}{2} \dfrac{GmM_e}{(R_e + h)}$$

4. Satellites orbiting the earth have finite life and sometimes debris of satellites fall to the earth. This is because   **[NCERT Exemplar]**

   (a) the solar cells and batteries in satellites run out

   (b) the laws of gravitation predict a trajectory spiralling inwards

   (c) of viscous forces causing the speed of satellite and hence height to gradually decrease

   (d) of collisions with other satellites

   Sol. (c) As the total energy of the earth satellite bounded system is negative $\left(\dfrac{-GM}{2a}\right)$.

where, a is radius of the satellite and M is mass of the earth.

Due to the viscous force acting on satellite, energy decreases continuously and radius of the orbit or height decreases gradually.

5. The orbital velocity of a satellite orbiting near the surface of the earth is given by

   (a) $v = \sqrt{gR_e}$, where $g = \dfrac{GM_e}{R_e^2}$

   (b) $v = \sqrt{gR_e}$, where $g = \dfrac{GM_e}{R_e}$

   (c) $v = \sqrt{\dfrac{gh}{R_e}}$, where $g = \dfrac{GM_e}{R_e^2}$

   (d) $v = \sqrt{gh}$, where $g = \dfrac{GM_e}{R_e}$

Sol. (a) Orbital velocity of satellite, $v = \sqrt{\dfrac{GM_e}{(R_e + h)}}$

If the satellite is close to the surface of the earth, $h = 0$

$\Rightarrow \quad v = \sqrt{\dfrac{GM_e}{R_e}} \Rightarrow v = \sqrt{\left(\dfrac{GM_e}{R_e^2}\right) R_e}$

$\qquad = \sqrt{gR_e}, \qquad\qquad \left[\because\ g = \dfrac{GM_e}{R_e^2}\right]$

VERY SHORT ANSWER Type Questions

6. Can we determine the mass of a satellite by measuring its time period?

Sol. No, we cannot determine the mass of a satellite by measuring its time period.

7. Why is the atmosphere much rarer on the moon than on the earth?

Sol. The value of escape velocity on the moon is small as compared to the value of the earth only $2.5\ \text{kms}^{-1}$. So, the molecules of air escape easily from the surface of moon, hence there is no atmosphere.

8. What velocity will you give to a donkey and what velocity to a monkey so that both escape the gravitational field of the earth?

Sol. The escape velocity does not depend upon the mass of the body.

$$v_e = \sqrt{2gR}$$

9. Two satellites are at different heights. Which would have greater velocity?

Sol. $v_o \propto \dfrac{1}{\sqrt{r}}$; so the satellite at smaller height would possess greater velocity.

10. A thief with a box in his hand jumps from the top of a building. What will be the load experienced by him during the state of free fall?

Sol. During the state of free fall, his acceleration is equal to the acceleration due to gravity. So, the thief will be in state of weightlessness. Hence, the load experienced by him will be zero.

11. Is it possible to put an artificial satellite in an orbit such a way that it always remains visible directly over New Delhi?

Sol. It is not possible. This is because New Delhi is not in the equatorial plane.

12. Does the speed of a satellite remain constant in a particular orbit (circular)?

Sol. Yes, as $v = \sqrt{\dfrac{GM}{r}}$, v depends only upon r. For a particular orbit, r is constant and so is v.

13. How much energy is required by a satellite to keep it orbiting? Neglect air resistance.

Sol. No energy is required. This is because the work done by centripetal force is zero.

14. An artificial satellite revolving around the earth does not need any fuel. On the other hand, the aeroplane requires fuel to fly at a certain height. Why?

Sol. The satellite move in air-free region, while the aeroplane has to overcome air resistance.

15. Assume that an artificial satellite release a bomb. Would the bomb ever strike the earth if the effect of air resistance is neglected?

Sol. The bomb would merely act as another satellite. It would never hit the earth due to state of weight lessness.

SHORT ANSWER Type Questions

16. Show that the orbital velocity of a satellite revolving the earth is $7.92\ \text{km s}^{-1}$.

Sol. Orbital velocity, $v_o = \sqrt{gR}$

$\qquad = \sqrt{9.8 \times 6.4 \times 10^6}$

$\qquad = 7.92\ \text{kms}^{-1}$

17. The orbiting velocity of an earth-satellite is $8\ \text{kms}^{-1}$. What will be the escape velocity?

Sol. Escape velocity, $v_e = \sqrt{2}\ v_o$

$\qquad v_e = \sqrt{2} \times 8$

$\qquad\quad = 11.31\ \text{kms}^{-1}$

18. A satellite does not need any fuel to circle around the earth. Why?

Sol. The gravitational force between satellite and the earth provides the centripetal force required by the satellite to move in a circular orbit. The satellite orbits around earth at such a higher height where air friction is neglible.

19. If the kinetic energy of a satellite revolving around the earth in any orbit is doubled, then what will happen to it?

Sol. The total energy of a satellite in any orbit, $E = -K$, where K is its KE in that orbit.

If its kinetic energy is doubled, i.e. an additional kinetic energy (K) is given to it, $E = -K + K = 0$ and the satellite will leave its orbit and go to infinity.

20. On what factor does the escape speed from a surface depend?

Sol. Value of escape speed at the surface of a planet is given by the relation

$$v_{es} = \sqrt{\frac{2GM}{R}} = \sqrt{2\,gR}$$

Thus, the value of escape speed from the surface of a planet depends upon (*i*) value of acceleration due to gravity g at the surface and (*ii*) the size (i.e. radius) R of the planet only. It is independent of all other factors.
e.g. The mass and size of the body to be projected, angle of projection, etc.

21. An astronaut, by mistake, drops his food packet from an artificial satellite orbiting around the earth. Will it reach the surface of the earth? Why?

Sol. The food packet will not fall on the earth. As the satellite as well as astronaut were in a state of weightlessness, hence, the food packet, when dropped by mistake, will also start moving with the same velocity as that of satellite and will continue to move along with the satellite in the same orbit.

22. If suddenly the gravitational force of attraction between the earth and a satellite revolving around it becomes zero, then what will happen to the satellite?

Sol. If suddenly the gravitational force of attraction between the earth and a satellite revolving around it becomes zero, satellite will not be able to revolve around the earth. Instead, the satellite will start moving along a straight line tangentially at that point on its orbit, where it is at the time of gravitational force becoming zero.

23. Which of the following symptoms is likely to affect an astronaut in space (a) swollen feet (b) swollen face, (c) headache, (d) orientational problem. **[NCERT]**

Sol. (a) We know that the legs carry the weight of the body in the normal position due to gravity pull. The astronaut in space is in weightlessness state. Hence, swollen feet may not affect his working.

(b) In the conditions of weightlessness, the face of the astronaut is expected to get more supply. Due to it, the astronaut may develop swollen face. As eyes, ears, nose, mouth etc., are all embedded in the face, hence swollen face may affect to great extent the seeing/hearing/smelling/eating capabilities of the astronaut in space.

(c) Headache is due to mental strain. It will persist whether a person is an astronaut in space or he is on earth. It means headache will have the same effect on the astronaut in space as on a person on earth.

(d) Space also has orientation. We also have the frames of reference in space. Hence, orientational problem will affect the astronaut in space.

24. The escape speed on the earth is 11.2 km/s. What is its value for a planet having double the radius and eight times the mass of the earth?

Sol. v_P (escape speed on a planet) $= \sqrt{\dfrac{GM_P}{R_P}}$

v_e (escape speed on the earth) $= \sqrt{\dfrac{GM_e}{R_e}}$

Clearly, $\dfrac{v_P}{v_e} = \sqrt{\dfrac{M_P}{M_e} \times \dfrac{R_e}{R_P}} = \sqrt{8 \times \dfrac{1}{2}} = 2$

or $\qquad v_P = 2v_e = 22.4$ km/s

25. The earth is acted upon by the gravitational attraction of the sun. Why don't the earth fall into the sun?

Sol. The earth is orbiting round the sun in a stable orbit (nearly circular) such that the gravitational attraction of the sun just provides the required centripetal force to the earth for its orbital motion. So, net force on the earth is zero and consequently, the earth does not fall into the sun.

26. The asteroid pallas has an orbital period of 4.62 yr. Find the semi-major axis of its orbit. Given, $G = 6.67 \times 10^{-11}$ Nm^{2}kg^{-2}, mass of the sun = 1.99×10^{30}kg and 1 yr $= 3.156 \times 10^7$ s.

Sol. $\qquad T^2 = \dfrac{4\pi^2 a^3}{GM_s}$

or $\qquad a = \left[\dfrac{GM_s T^2}{4\pi^2}\right]^{1/3}$

Substituting values, we get
$\qquad a = 4.15 \times 10^{11}$ m

27. **Does the change in gravitational potential energy of a body between two given points depend upon the nature of path followed, why?**

Sol. The change in gravitational potential energy of a body between two given points depends only upon the position of the given points and is independent of the path followed. is due to the fact that the gravitational force is a conservative force and work done by a conservative force depends only on the position of initial and final points and is independent of path followed.

LONG ANSWER Type I Questions

28. **Define period of revolution. Derive an expression of period of revolution or time period of satellite.**

Sol. Period of revolution of a satellite is the time taken by the satellite to complete one revolution round the earth. It is denoted by T.

$$\therefore \qquad T = \frac{\text{Circumference of circular orbit}}{\text{Orbital velocity}}$$

$$\text{or} \qquad T = \frac{2\pi r}{v_o}$$

$$\text{or} \qquad T = \frac{2\pi(R + h)}{v_o} \qquad [\because r = R + h]$$

$$\text{or} \qquad T = 2\pi(R + h)\sqrt{\frac{R + h}{GM}} \qquad \left[\because v_o = \sqrt{\frac{GM}{R + h}}\right]$$

$$\text{or} \qquad T = 2\pi\sqrt{\frac{(R + h)^3}{GM}}$$

$$\text{Also,} \qquad T = 2\pi\sqrt{\frac{(R + h)^2(R + h)}{GM}}$$

$$\text{or} \qquad T = 2\pi\sqrt{\frac{(R + h)^3}{gR^2}}$$

$$\because \qquad gR^2 = GM$$

$$\therefore \qquad T = 2\pi\sqrt{\frac{(R + h)^3}{gR^2}}$$

29. **A satellite orbits the earth at a height of 400 km above the surface. How much energy must be expanded to rocket, the satellite out of the earth's gravitational influence?**
Mass of the satellite = 200 kg, mass of the earth, $M = 6.0 \times 10^{24}$ kg, radius of the earth $= 6.4 \times 10^6$ m, $G = 6.67 \times 10^{-11}$ Nm^2/kg^2. [NCERT]

Sol. Mass of the earth, $M = 6.0 \times 10^{24}$ kg

Mass of the satellite, $m = 200$ kg

Radius of the earth, $R = 6.4 \times 10^6$ m

Height of the satellite above the earth's surface,

$$h = 400 \text{ km} = 0.4 \times 10^6 \text{ m}$$

Radius of the orbit of the satellite, $r = R + h$
$$= 6.4 \times 10^6 + 0.4 \times 10^6 = 6.8 \times 10^6 \text{ m}$$

Total energy of the satellite,

$$E = -\frac{GMm}{2r} = -\frac{6.67 \times 10^{-11} \times 6.0 \times 10^{24} \times 200}{2 \times 6.8 \times 10^6}$$

$$= -5.9 \times 10^9 \text{ J}$$

Negative total energy denoted that the satellite is round to the earth. Therefore, to pull the satellite out of the earth's gravitational influence, energy required $= 5.9 \times 10^6$ J. [1/2]

30. **Viscous force increase the velocity of a satellite. Discuss.**

Sol. Imagine a satellite of mass m moving with a velocity v in an orbit of radius r around a planet of mass M.

PE of the satellite, $U = -\dfrac{GMm}{r}$

KE of the satellite, $K = \dfrac{1}{2}mv^2 = \dfrac{GMm}{2r}$ [as $v = \sqrt{GM/r}$]

Total energy of the satellite, i.e.

$$E = K + U = \frac{GMm}{2r} - \frac{GMm}{r} = -\frac{GMm}{2r}$$

For the sake of clarity, take $\dfrac{GMm}{2r} = x$

Clearly, $\qquad U = -2x, K = x, E = -x$

The orbiting satellite loses energy due to viscous force acting on it due to atmosphere and as such it loses height.

Let the new orbital radius be $\dfrac{r}{2}$ (say)

Clearly, $\qquad U' = -4x, K' = 2x$
$$E' = -2x$$

Clearly, $E' < E, U' < U$ and $K' > K$. Since, kinetic energy has increased, the velocity of the satellite increases.

31. **Does the escape speed of a body from the earth depend on**
  (i) mass of the body
  (ii) the location from where it is projected
  (iii) the direction of projection
  (iv) the height of the location from where the body is launched? **[NCERT]**

Sol. (i) No, escape velocity is independent of the mass of the body.

 (ii) Yes, escape velocity depends (through slightly) on the location from where the body is projected because with location g changes and so should v_e $(=\sqrt{2gR})$ change.

 (iii) No, escape velocity is independent of the direction of projection.

 (iv) Yes, escape velocity depends (through slightly) on the height of location from where the body is projected as g depends on height.

32. The escape speed of a projectile on the earth's surface is 11.2 km/s. A body is projected out with thrice this speed. What is the speed of the body far away from the earth? Ignore the presence of the sun and other planets. **[NCERT]**

Sol. Let v_e be the escape velocity and v be the velocity of the body outside the gravitational field of the earth.

According to law of conservation of energy,

Initial KE of the body = energy spent by the body in crossing the earth's gravitational field + kinetic energy left with the body once outside the earth's gravitational field, i.e.

$$\frac{1}{2}m(3v_e)^2 = \frac{1}{2}mv_e^2 + \frac{1}{2}mv^2$$

or $\quad \frac{9}{2}mv_e^2 = \frac{1}{2}mv_e^2 + \frac{1}{2}mv^2 \quad$ or $\quad v^2 = 8v_e^2$

or $\quad v = \sqrt{8v_e^2} = 2\sqrt{2}\,v_e$

As $\quad v_e = 11.2$ km/s $\Rightarrow v = 2\sqrt{2} \times 11.2$ km/s

or $\quad v = 31.7$ km/s

33. How will you weigh the sun i.e. estimate its mass? The mean orbital radius of the earth around the sun is 1.5×10^8 km. **[NCERT]**

Sol. We can weight the sun i.e. find its mass (M) using Kepler's third law of planetary motion according to which

$$T^2 = \left(\frac{4\pi^2}{GM}\right)r^3 \text{ or } M = \frac{4\pi^2 r^3}{GT^2}$$

Here, r (radius of the earth's orbit around the sun)
$$= 1.5 \times 10^8 \text{ km} = 1.5 \times 10^{11} \text{m}$$

T (time period of earth's revolution around the sun)
$$= 1y = 3.156 \times 10^7 s$$

Thus, $M = \dfrac{39.5\,(1.5 \times 10^{11} \text{ m})^3}{(6.67 \times 10^{-11} \text{ Nm}^2 / \text{kg}^2)\,(3.156 \times 10^7 \text{ s})^2}$

[as $5\pi^2 = 39.5$]

$M = 2.0 \times 10^{30}$ kg

34. Let us assume that our galaxy consists of 2.5×10^{11} stars each of one solar mass. How long will a star at a distance of 50000 ly from the galactic centre take to complete one revolution? **[NCERT]**

Sol. Mass of the galaxy, $m = (2.5 \times 10^{11})$ solar mass
$$= (2.5 \times 10^{11})\,(2 \times 10^{30} \text{ kg})$$
$$= 5 \times 10^{41} \text{ kg}$$

Radius of the path of the star, $r = 50000$ ly
$$= 50000(9.46 \times 10^{15} \text{ m})$$
$$= 4.73 \times 10^{20} \text{ m}$$

If T is the time taken by the star to complete one revolution, then $T = \left(\dfrac{4\pi^2 r^3}{Gm}\right)^{1/2}$

$$T = \left[\frac{39.5\,(4.73 \times 10^{20} \text{ m})^3}{(6.67 \times 10^{-11} \text{ Nm}^2 / \text{kg}^2)\,(5 \times 10^{41} \text{ kg})}\right]^{1/2}$$

$T = 11.194 \times 10^{15}$ s

or $\quad T = \dfrac{11.194 \times 10^{15}}{3.156 \times 10^7}\,y = 3.55 \times 10^8\,y$

[as $1y = (365.24 \times 24 \times 60 \times 60)$ s $= 3.156 \times 10^7$ s]

35. Choose the correct alternatives.

(i) If the zero of potential energy is at infinity, the total energy of an orbiting satellite is negative of the kinetic/potential energy.

(ii) The energy required to rocket an orbiting satellite out of the earth's gravitational influence is more/less than the energy required in project a stationary object at the same height (as the satellite) of the earth's influence. **[NCERT]**

Sol. (i) Potential energy of satellite, $U = -\dfrac{GMm}{r}$

Kinetic energy of satellite, $K = \dfrac{GMm}{2r}$

Total energy, $E = U + K$

$$= \frac{-GMm}{r} + \frac{GMm}{2r}$$

$$= \frac{-GMm}{2r} = -K$$

i.e. negative of kinetic energy.

(ii) The energy required to rocket an orbiting satellite out of gravitational influence is less than the energy required to project a stationary object, because in case of orbiting satellite, the gravitational pull of the earth acting on it is balanced by centripetal force, so work is required only in rocketing it (no work is required against the gravitational pull).

36. A comet orbits the sun in highly elliptical orbit. Does the comet has a constant

(i) linear speed,
(ii) angular speed,
(iii) angular momentum,
(iv) kinetic energy,
(v) potential energy and
(vi) total energy throughout its orbit? Neglect any mass loss of the comet when it comes very close to the sun. **[NCERT]**

Sol. (i) According to law of conservation of angular momentum, $L = mvr =$ constant, therefore the comet moves faster when it is close to the sun and moves slower when it is farther away from the sun. Therefore, the speed of the comet does not remain constant.

(ii) As the linear speed varies, the angular speed also varies. Therefore, angular speed of the comet does not remain constant.

(iii) As no external torque is acting on the comet, therefore, according to law of conservation of angular momentum, the angular momentum of the comet remain constant.

(iv) Kinetic energy of the comet $= \dfrac{1}{2}mv^2$

As the linear speed of the comet changes, its kinetic energy also changes. Therefore, its KE does not remain constant.

(v) Potential energy of the comet changes as its kinetic energy changes.

(vi) Only angular momentum and total energy of a comet remain constant throughout its orbit.

37. Calculate the change in the energy of a 500 kg satellite when it falls from an altitude of 200 km to 199 km. If this change takes place during one orbit. Calculate the retarding force on the satellite.

Given, mass of the earth $= 6 \times 10^{24}$ kg and radius of the earth = 6400 km

Sol. Given, $\quad M_e = 6 \times 10^{24}$ kg, $r_e = 6400$ km

$r_1 = 6400 + 200 = 6600$ km $= 6.6 \times 10^6$ m

$r_2 = 6400 + 199 = 6599$ km $= 6.599 \times 10^6$ m

Change in energy $= GMm \left(\dfrac{1}{r_1} - \dfrac{1}{r_2} \right)$

$= 6.67 \times 10^{-11} \times 6 \times 10^{24} \times 500$

$\left(\dfrac{1}{6.6 \times 10^6} - \dfrac{1}{6.599 \times 10^6} \right)$

$= 2 \times 10^{17} \, (1.5152 \times 10^{-7} - 1.5154 \times 10^7) \, \text{J}$

$= -4 \times 10^6$ J

If this occurs during one orbit, then the energy lost
= force × distance.

If we take the distance as being the circumference of one orbit. Then,

Retarding force $= \dfrac{4 \times 10^6}{2\pi \times 6.6 \times 10^6}$

$= \dfrac{4 \times 10^6}{2 \times 6.6 \times 3.14 \times 10^6} = 0.1$ N

LONG ANSWER Type II Questions

38. A rocket is fired vertically with a speed of 5 km/s from the earth surface. How far from the earth does the rocket go before returning to the earth? Mass of the earth $= 6.0 \times 10^{24}$ kg. Mean radius of the earth $= 6.4 \times 10^6$ m; $G = 6.67 \times 10^{-11}$ Nm^2/kg^2.   **[NCERT]**

Sol. Here, speed of the rocket, $v = 5$ km/s $= 5 \times 10^3$ m/s

Mass of the earth, $M = 6.0 \times 10^{24}$ kg

Radius of the earth, $x = 6.4 \times 10^6$ m

Gravitational constant, $G = 6.67 \times 10^{-11}$ Nm^2/kg^2

Let m be the mass of the rocket and h be the maximum height gained by the rocket.

Change in potential energy of the rocket
= PE at a height h − PE at the surface of the earth

$= -\dfrac{GMm}{(R+h)} - \left(-\dfrac{GMm}{R} \right) = GMm \left(\dfrac{1}{R} - \dfrac{1}{R+h} \right)$

$= GMm \left[\dfrac{h}{R(R+h)} \right]$ ...(i)

Initial KE of rocket $= \dfrac{1}{2}mv^2$

Final KE of the rocket when at the height, $h = 0$

Thus, change in KE of the rocket $= \dfrac{1}{2}mv^2$ ...(ii)

According to law of conservation of energy, from Eqs. (i) and (ii), we get

$$GMm \left[\dfrac{h}{R(R+h)} \right] = \dfrac{1}{2}mv^2$$

or $\qquad \dfrac{v^2}{2GM} = \dfrac{h}{R^2 + Rh}$

or $\qquad v^2R^2 + v^2Rh = 2GMh$

or $\qquad h(2GM - v^2R) = v^2R^2$

or $\qquad h = \dfrac{v^2R^2}{2GM - v^2R}$

or $\quad h = \dfrac{(5 \times 10^3 \text{ m/s})^2 (6.4 \times 10^6 \text{ m})^2}{[\{2 \times (6.67 \times 10^{-11} \text{ Nm}^2 / \text{kg}^2)(6.0 \times 10^{24} \text{ kg})\}}$
$\qquad\qquad\qquad - \{(5 \times 10^3 \text{ m/s})^2(6.4 \times 10^6 \text{ m})\}]$

$= 1.6 \times 10^6$ m

Distance of the rocket from the centre of the earth
$= 6.4 \times 10^6$ m $+ 1.6 \times 10^6$ m $= 8 \times 10^6$ m

39. A rocket is fired vertically from the surface of the mars with the speed of 2 km/s. If 20% of its initial energy is lost due to Martian atmospheric resistance, how far will the rocket go from the surface of the mars before returning to it. Mass of the mars = 6.4×10^{23} kg; radius of the mars = 3395 km; $G = 6.67 \times 10^{-11}$ Nm^2/kg^2 **[NCERT]**

Sol. We are given that

Mass of the mars, $M = 6.4 \times 10^{23}$ kg

Radius of the mars, $R = 3395$ km $= 3.395 \times 10^6$ m

Velocity of the rocket, $v = 2$ km/s $= 2 \times 10^3$ m/s

Let h be the maximum height attained by the rocket. Change in potential energy of rocket.

PE = final potential energy – initial potential energy

$$= -G\frac{Mm}{(R+h)} - \left(-G\frac{Mm}{R}\right) = -G\frac{Mm}{(R+h)} + G\frac{Mm}{R}$$

$$= GMm\left(\frac{1}{R} - \frac{1}{R+h}\right) = GMm\frac{h}{R(R+h)}$$

Here, 20% of the kinetic energy of the rocket is lost due to Martian atmosphere.

KE of the rocket which is converted into its potential energy $= \dfrac{80}{100} \times \dfrac{1}{2}mv^2 = 0.4\,mv^2$

Applying law of conservation of energy,

$$\Rightarrow \qquad GMm\frac{h}{R(R+h)} = 0.4\,mv^2$$

$$\Rightarrow \qquad GM\frac{h}{R^2 + Rh} = 0.4\,v^2 \text{ or } h = \frac{R^2}{\left(\dfrac{GM}{0.4\,v^2}\right) - R}$$

$$\Rightarrow \qquad h = \frac{11.526 \times 10^{12}}{26.68 \times 10^6 - 3.395 \times 10^6} \text{ m}$$

$$\Rightarrow \qquad h = 495 \times 10^3 \text{ m} = 495 \text{ km}$$

40. A spaceship is stationed on the mars. How much energy must be expanded on the spaceship to launch it out of the solar system. The mass of the spaceship = 1000 kg; mass of the sun = 2×10^{30} kg; mass of the mars = 6.4×10^{23} kg; radius of the mars = 3395 km; radius of the orbit of mars = 2.28×10^8 km, $G = 6.67 \times 10^{-11}$ Nm^2/kg^2. **[NCERT]**

Sol. Given, mass of the sun, $M = 2 \times 10^{30}$ kg

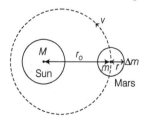

Mass of the mars, $m = 6.4 \times 10^{23}$ kg

Mass of spaceship, $\Delta m = 1000$ kg

Radius of orbit of the mars, $r_0 = 2.28 \times 10^{11}$ m

Radius of the mars, $r = 3.395 \times 10^6$ m

If v is the orbital velocity of mars.

$$\frac{mv^2}{r_0} = G\frac{Mm}{r_0^2} \quad \text{or} \quad v^2 = \frac{GM}{r_0}$$

Since, the velocity of the spaceship is the same as that of the mars.

Kinetic energy of the spaceship,

$$K = \frac{1}{2}(\Delta m)v^2 = \frac{1}{2}(\Delta m)\frac{GM}{r_0} = \frac{GM(\Delta m)}{2r_0}$$

$$\text{or } K = \frac{(6.67 \times 10^{-11})\,(2 \times 10^{30}) \times 1000}{2 \times (2.28 \times 10^{11})}\text{J} = 2.925 \times 10^{11} \text{ J}$$

Total potential energy of the spaceship.

U = potential energy of the spaceship due to its being in the gravitational field of the mars + potential energy of the spaceship due to its being in the gravitational field of the sun.

$$= -G\frac{m \times \Delta m}{r} - G\frac{M \times \Delta m}{r_0} = -G\Delta m\left(\frac{m}{r} + \frac{M}{r_0}\right)$$

$$\text{or } U = -6.67 \times 10^{-11} \times 10^3 \times \left(\frac{6.4 \times 10^{23}}{3.395 \times 10^6} + \frac{2 \times 10^{30}}{2.28 \times 10^{11}}\right)\text{J}$$

$$= -6.67 \times 10^{-8}\,(1.885 \times 10^{17} + 87.719 \times 10^{17})\text{ J}$$

$$= -6.67\,(89.604 \times 10^9)\text{ J} = -5.977 \times 10^{11} \text{ J}$$

Total energy of the spaceship,

$$E = K + U = 2.925 \times 10^{11}\text{ J} - 5.997 \times 10^{11} \text{ J}$$

$$= -3.072 \times 10^{11}\text{ J} = -3.1 \times 10^{11} \text{ J}$$

Negative energy denotes that the spaceship is bound to the solar system.

Thus, the energy needed by the spaceship to escape from the solar system $= 3.1 \times 10^{11}$ J.

41. If one satellite of Jupiter has an orbital period of 1.769 days and the radius of the orbit is 4.22×10^8 m. Show that the mass of jupiter is about one-thousandth that of the sun. **[NCERT]**

Sol. Here, orbital period of the satellite of jupiter, $T_s = 1.769$ days $= 1.769 \times 24 \times 60 \times 60$ s

Orbital period of the earth, $T_e = 1y = 365.25$ d

Radius of the orbit of the satellite, $r_s = 4.22 \times 10^8$ m

Radius of the orbit of the earth, $r_e = 1$ AU $= 1.496 \times 10^{11}$ m

According to Kepler's third law, $T^2 = \left(\dfrac{4\pi^2}{Gm}\right)r^3$

Let M_s and M_j represent the masses of the sun and the jupiter. For the Sun-Earth system,

$$T_e^2 = \left(\frac{4\pi^2}{GM_s}\right)r_e^3$$

For Jupiter-Satellite system,

$$T_s^2 = \left(\frac{4\pi^2}{GM_j}\right) r_s^3$$

Thus, $\quad \dfrac{T_e^2}{T_s^2} = \left(\dfrac{M_j}{M_s}\right)\left(\dfrac{r_e}{r_s}\right)^3 \quad$ or $\quad \dfrac{M_j}{M_s} = \left(\dfrac{T_e}{T_s}\right)^2 \left(\dfrac{r_s}{r_e}\right)^3$

or $\quad \dfrac{M_j}{M_s} = \left(\dfrac{365.25\text{d}}{1.769\text{ d}}\right)^2 \left(\dfrac{4.22 \times 10^8\,\text{m}}{1.496 \times 10^{11}\,\text{m}}\right)^3$

$\qquad = (4.26 \times 10^4)(22.4 \times 10^{-9}) \times 10^{-3}$

or $\quad M_j \approx 10^{-3}\, M_s$

Thus, M_j (mass of the jupiter) $= \dfrac{1}{1000} M_s$ (mass of the sun)

42. A satellite is in an elliptic orbit around the earth with aphelion of $6R$ and perihelion of $2R$, where $R = 6400$ km is the radius of the earth. Find eccentricity of the orbit. Find the velocity of the satellite at apogee and perigee. What should be done if this satellite has to be transferred to a circular orbit of radius $6R$? **[NCERT Exemplar]**

Sol. If r_a and r_p denote the distances of aphelion and perihelion of the elliptical orbit (of eccentricity) of the satellite, then from the geometry of the ellipse.

$$r_a = a(1 + e) \text{ and } r_p = a(1 - e)$$

[where, a is the semi-major axis of the ellipse]

As $r_a = 6R$ and $r_p = 2R$,

$$\frac{a(1 + e)}{a(1 - e)} = \frac{6R}{2R} = 3, \text{ where } e = \frac{1}{2}$$

If v_a and v_p are the velocities of the satellite (of mass m) at aphelion and perihelion respectively, then from the law of conservation of angular momentum,

$$mv_a r_a = mv_p r_p \text{ or } \frac{v_a}{v_p} = \frac{r_p}{r_a} = \frac{2R}{6R} = \frac{1}{3}$$

From the law of conservation of energy,

(KE + PE) at aphelion = (KE + PE) at perihelion

or $\quad \dfrac{1}{2}mv_a^2 - \dfrac{GMm}{r_a} = \dfrac{1}{2}mv_p^2 - \dfrac{GMm}{r_p}$

or $\quad v_p^2 - v_a^2 = -2GM\left(\dfrac{1}{r_a} - \dfrac{1}{r_p}\right)$

$\qquad = 2GM\left(\dfrac{1}{r_p} - \dfrac{1}{r_a}\right)$

or $\quad v_p^2\left(1 - \dfrac{v_a^2}{v_p^2}\right) = 2GM\left(\dfrac{r_a - r_p}{r_p r_a}\right)$

$\qquad = 2GM\left(\dfrac{6R - 2R}{6R \times 2R}\right) = \dfrac{2}{3}\dfrac{GM}{R}$

or $\quad v_p^2\left(1 - \dfrac{1}{9}\right) = \dfrac{2}{3}\dfrac{GM}{R} \quad$ or $\quad v_p = \sqrt{\dfrac{3}{4}\dfrac{GM}{R}}$

$\qquad = \dfrac{\sqrt{3}}{2}\sqrt{\dfrac{GM}{R}} = 0.8666\,(7.9\text{ km/s}) = 6.84\text{ km/s}$

Also, $\quad v_a = \dfrac{v_p}{3} = \dfrac{6.84\text{ km/s}}{3} = 2.28\text{ km/s}$

Velocity of the satellite in a circular orbit.

$$v_c = \sqrt{\frac{GM}{r}} = \sqrt{\frac{GM}{6R}} \qquad \text{[as } r = 6R\text{]}$$

or $\quad v_c = \dfrac{1}{\sqrt{6}}\sqrt{\dfrac{GM}{R}} = 0.408\,(7.9\text{ km/s})$

$\qquad = 3.22\text{ km/s}$

The amount by which velocity is to be increased in transferring the satellite into a circular orbit at apogee.

$$= v_c - v_a = 3.22\text{ km/s} - 2.28\text{ km/s} = 0.94\text{ km/s}$$

This is accomplished by suitably firing rockets from the satellites.

43. Two uniform solid spheres of equal radii R, but mass M and $4M$ have a centre of separation $6R$, as shown in figure. The two spheres are held fixed. A projectile of mass m is projected from the surface of the sphere of mass M directly towards the centre of the second sphere. Obtain an expression for the minimum speed v of the projectile so that it reaches the surface of the second sphere. **[NCERT]**

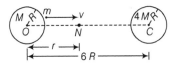

Sol. The two spheres exert gravitational forces on the projectile in mutually opposite directions. At the neutral point N, these two forces cancel each other. If $ON = r$, then

$$\frac{GMm}{r^2} = \frac{G(4M)m}{(6R - r)^2}$$

or $\quad (6R - r)^2 = 4r^2 \implies 6R - r = \pm 2r$

or $\quad r = 2R \text{ or } -6R$

The neutral point, $r = -6R$ is inadmissible.

$\therefore \qquad\qquad ON = r = 2R$

It will be sufficient to project the particle m with a minimum speed v which enables it to reach the point N. Therefore, the particle m gets attracted by the gravitational pull of $4M$.

The total mechanical energy of m at surface of left sphere is

$$E_i = \text{KE of } m + \text{PE due to left sphere}$$
$$+ \text{PE due to right sphere}$$

$$= \frac{1}{2} mv^2 - \frac{GMm}{R} - \frac{4\,GMm}{5R}$$

At the neutral point, speed of the particle becomes zero. The energy is purely potential.

$\therefore E_N$ = PE due to left sphere + PE due to right sphere

$$= -\frac{GMm}{2R} - \frac{4GMm}{4R}$$

By conservation of mechanical energy, $E_i = E_N$

or $\quad \frac{1}{2} mv^2 - \frac{GMm}{R} - \frac{4\,GMm}{5R} = -\frac{GMm}{2R} - \frac{4GMm}{4R}$

or $\quad v^2 = \frac{2GM}{R}\left(\frac{4}{5} - \frac{1}{2}\right) = \frac{3GM}{5R}$

$\therefore \quad v = \sqrt{\dfrac{3GM}{5R}}$

ASSESS YOUR TOPICAL UNDERSTANDING

OBJECTIVE Type Questions

1. A particle is kept at rest at a distance R_e (earth's radius) above the earth's surface. The minimum speed with which it should be projected so that it does not return is (mass of earth = M_e)
(a) $\sqrt{\dfrac{6M_e}{4R_e}}$ (b) $\sqrt{\dfrac{GM_e}{2R_e}}$ (c) $\sqrt{\dfrac{GM_e}{R_e}}$ (d) $\sqrt{\dfrac{2\,GM_e}{R_e}}$

2. The ratio of the magnitude of potential energy and kinetic energy of a satellite is
(a) 1:2 (b) 2:1
(c) 3:1 (d) 1:3

3. Which one of the following statements is correct?
(a) The energy required to rocket an orbiting satellite out of earth's gravitational influence is more than the energy required to project a stationary object at the same height (as the satellite) out of earth's influence
(b) If the zero of potential energy is at infinity, the total energy of an orbiting satellite is negative of potential energy
(c) The first artificial satellite sputnik I was launched in the year 2001
(d) The time period of rotation of the SYNCOMS (Synchronous communications satellite) is 24 hours.

4. The radius of the orbit of a satellite is r and its kinetic energy is K. If the radius of the orbit is doubled, then the new kinetic energy K' is
(a) $2K$ (b) $\dfrac{K}{2}$
(c) $4K$ (d) Data insufficient

Answer

1. (c) | 2. (b) | 3. (d) | 4. (b)

VERY SHORT ANSWER Type Questions

5. Determine the speed of a body from the moon. Take the moon to be a uniform sphere of radius 1.74×10^6 m and mass 7.36×10^{22} kg. [**Ans.** 2.38 km/s]

6. Calculate the mass of the sun, given that distance between the sun and the earth is 1.49×10^{11} m and $G = 6.67 \times 10^{-11}$ Nm^2/kg^2. [**Ans.** 1.972×10^{30} kg]

7. Calculate the velocity with which a body projected from the surface of the moon may escapes from its gravitational pull. [**Ans.** 2.5 km/s]

8. Why do different planets have different escape speeds?

9. Can a pendulum vibrate in an artificial satellite?

SHORT ANSWER Type Questions

10. Calculate the ratio of the kinetic energy required to be given to a satellite so that it escape the gravitational field of earth to the kinetic energy required to put the satellite in a circular orbit just above the free surface of the earth. [**Ans.** 2]

11. Two particles of equal mass m go round a circle of radius R under the action of their mutual gravitational attraction. What is the speed of each particle? $\left[\textbf{Ans.}\ \dfrac{1}{2}\sqrt{\dfrac{Gm}{R}}\right]$

12. An artificial satellite moving in a circular orbit around the earth has a total energy E_0. What is its potential energy? [**Ans.** $U = 2E_0$]

13. Two satellites have their masses in the ratio of 3 : 1. The radii of their circular orbits are in the ratio of 1 : 4. What is the ratio of total mechanical energy of A and B? [**Ans.** 12:1]

LONG ANSWER Type I Questions

14. A 400 kg satellite is in circular orbit of radius $2R_E$ about the earth. How much energy is required to transfer it to a circular orbit of radius $4R_E$? What are the changes in the kinetic and potential energies?

[**Ans.** -3.13×10^6 J, -6.26×10^9 J]

15. The world's first artificial satellite (Sputnik-I) launched by USSR was circling the earth at a distance of 896 km. Calculate its orbital speed and period of revolution.

[**Ans.** 7.417 km/s, 1 h 43 min 3 s]

16. If the earth has a mass nine times and radius twice that of the planet mars, calculate the maximum velocity required by a rocket to pull out of the gravitational force of the mars.

[**Ans.** 5.28 km/s]

17. An artificial satellite is going round the earth, close to the surface. What is the time taken by it to complete one round?

[**Ans.** 1.41 h]

LONG ANSWER Type II Questions

18. A spaceship is launched into a circular orbit close to the surface of the earth. What additional velocity has now to be imparted to the spaceship in the orbit to overcome the gravitational pull.

[**Ans.** 3.3 km/s]

19. If a satellite is revolving around a planet of mass M in elliptical orbit of major axis a, then show that the orbital speed of the satellite when it is at a distance r from the focus will be given by $v^2 = GM\left(\dfrac{2}{r} - \dfrac{1}{a}\right)$

20. The earth satellite makes a complete circular orbit in 1.5 h. Determine the altitude of satellite above the surface of the earth.

[**Ans.** 277.2 km]

SUMMARY

- **Kepler's laws of planetary motion.**

  (i) **Kepler's first law (law of orbit)** Every planet revolves around the sun in an elliptical orbit. The sun is situated at one focus of the ellipse.

  (ii) **Kepler's second law (law of area)** The radius vector drawn from the sun to a planet sweeps out equal areas in equal intervals of time, i.e. the areal velocity of the planet around the sun is constant.

  (iii) **Kepler's third law (law of period)** The square of the time period of revolution of a planet around the sun is directly proportional to the cube of semi-major axis of the elliptical orbit, i.e. $T^2 \propto r^3$, where r is the semi-major axis of the elliptical orbit of the planet around the sun.

  The period T and radius R of the circular orbit of a planet about the sun are related by

  $$T^2 = \left(\frac{4\pi^2}{G M_s}\right) R^3$$

  where, M_s is the mass of the sun. Most planets have nearly circular orbits about the sun. For elliptical orbits, the above equation is valid if R is replaced by the semi-major axis, a.

- **Universal law of gravitation** Every body in the universe attracts every other body with a force which is directly proportional to the product of their masses and inversely proportional to the square of the distance between them.

- **Universal law of gravitation**

  Gravitational force, $F = G\dfrac{m_1 m_2}{r^2}$

  Where, G = Constant of proportionality, = Universal Gravitational Constant
  $= 6.67 \times 10^{-11}$ Nm^{2}kg^{-2} (in SI unit)

  Dimensional formula of $G = [M^{-1}L^3T^{-2}]$

- **Principle of superposition** Resultant force, $F = -Gm_1\left[\dfrac{m_2}{r_{12}^2}\hat{r}_{21} + \dfrac{m_3}{r_{13}^2}\hat{r}_{31} + \ldots + \dfrac{m_n}{r_{1n}^2}\hat{r}_{n1}\right]$

- The acceleration due to gravity (g) is related with gravitational constant (G) by the relation, $g = \dfrac{GM}{R^2}$ where, M and R are the mass and radius of the earth, respectively.

- **Variation of acceleration due to gravity**

    (i) **Effect of altitude,** $g' = \dfrac{g R^2}{(R+h)^2}$ and $g' = g\left(1 - \dfrac{2h}{R}\right)$

    (ii) **Effect of depth,** $g' = g\left(1 - \dfrac{d}{R}\right)$

- Intensity of Gravitational field at a point is, $I = \dfrac{F}{m} = \dfrac{GM}{r^2}$

- **Gravitational potential,** $\qquad v = -\dfrac{w}{m} = -\int I \cdot dr \ \left[\text{as } \dfrac{F}{m} = I\right]$

- **Gravitational potential energy,** U = gravitational potential × mass of body $= -\dfrac{GM}{r} \times m$.

$$v_e = \sqrt{\dfrac{2GM}{R}} = \sqrt{2 g R}.$$ For Earth, the value of escape speed is $11.2\,\text{kms}^{-1}$.

For a point close to the Earth's surface, the escape speed and orbital speed are related as $v_e = \sqrt{2}\, v_o$, where v_o = the velocity required to put the satellite into its orbit.

   (i) **Orbital speed of a satellite** is the speed required to put the satellite into given orbit around Earth. Orbital speed of satellite, when it is revolving around earth at height h is given by $v_o = R\sqrt{\dfrac{g}{R+h}}$

   (ii) **Time period of satellite (T)** It is the time taken by satellite to complete one revolution around the earth.

$$T = \dfrac{2\pi (R+h)}{v_o} = \dfrac{2\pi}{R}\sqrt{\dfrac{(R+h)^3}{g}}$$

   (iv) **Total energy of satellite,**

$$E = -\dfrac{GM\,m}{(R+h)} + \dfrac{1}{2}m v_o^2 = -\dfrac{GM\,m}{(R+h)} + \dfrac{1}{2}m\left(\dfrac{GM}{R+h}\right) = -\dfrac{GM\,m}{2(R+h)}$$

   (v) **Binding energy of satellite** $= -E = \dfrac{GM\,m}{(R+h)}$.

- **Weightlessness** It is a situation in which the effective weight of the body becomes zero.

CHAPTER PRACTICE

OBJECTIVE Type Questions

1. The law of areas can be interpreted as
   (a) $\dfrac{\Delta A}{\Delta t} = \text{constant}$
   (b) $\dfrac{\Delta A}{\Delta t} = \dfrac{L}{m}$
   (c) $\dfrac{\Delta A}{\Delta t} = \dfrac{1}{2}(r \times P)$
   (d) $\dfrac{\Delta A}{\Delta t} = \dfrac{2L}{m}$

2. Three uniform spheres of mass M and radius R each are kept in such a way that each touches the other two. The magnitude of the gravitational force on any of the spheres due to the other two is
   (a) $\dfrac{\sqrt{3}}{4}\dfrac{GM^2}{R^2}$ (b) $\dfrac{3}{2}\dfrac{GM^2}{R^2}$ (c) $\dfrac{\sqrt{3}\,GM^2}{R^2}$ (d) $\dfrac{\sqrt{3}}{2}\dfrac{GM^2}{R^2}$

3. A point mass m is placed at the centre of the square $ABCD$ of side a units as shown below.

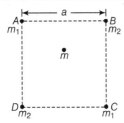

   The resultant gravitational force on mass m due to masses m_1 and m_2 plant on the vertices of square is
   (a) $\dfrac{Gm_1 m_2}{(a\sqrt{2})^2}$
   (b) $\dfrac{2Gm(m_1 + m_2)}{a^2}$
   (c) zero
   (d) $\dfrac{Gm(m_1 + m_2)}{(a\sqrt{2})^2}$

4. If the mass of the earth is doubled and its radius halved, then new acceleration due to the gravity g' is
   (a) $g' = 4\,g$ (b) $g' = 8\,g$ (c) $g' = g$ (d) $g' = 16\,g$

5. A planet has twice the density of earth but the acceleration due to gravity on its surface is exactly the same as on the surface of earth. Its radius in terms of radius of earth R will be
   (a) $R/4$
   (b) $R/2$
   (c) $R/3$
   (d) $R/8$

6. A particle of mass m is at the surface of the earth of radius R. It is lifted to a height h above the surface of the earth. The gain in gravitational potential energy of the particle is
   (a) $\dfrac{mgh}{\left(1 - \dfrac{h}{R}\right)}$
   (b) $\dfrac{mgh}{\left(1 + \dfrac{h}{R}\right)}$
   (c) $\dfrac{mgh\,R}{(R + h)}$
   (d) Both (b) and (c)

7. Three particles each of mass m are kept at vertices of an equilateral triangle of side L. The gravitational potential energy possessed by this system is
   (a) $\dfrac{-Gm^2}{L}$ (b) $\dfrac{-3\,Gm^2}{L}$ (c) $-\dfrac{2\,Gm^2}{L}$ (d) $\dfrac{+3\,Gm^2}{L}$

8. If the gravitational potential energy at infinity is assumed to be zero, the potential energy at distance $(R_e + h)$ from the centre of the earth is
   (a) $\text{PE} = \dfrac{GmM_e}{(R_e + h)}$
   (b) $\text{PE} = \dfrac{-GmM_e}{(R_e + h)}$
   (c) $\text{PE} = mgh$
   (d) $\text{PE} = \dfrac{-GmM_e}{2(R_e + h)}$

9. In our solar system, the inter-planetary region has chunks of matter (much smaller in size compared to planets) called asteroids. They **[NCERT Exemplar]**
   (a) will not move around the sun, since they have very small masses compared to the sun
   (b) will move in an irregular way because of their small masses and will drift away into outer space
   (c) will move around the sun in closed orbits but not obey Kepler's laws
   (d) will move in orbits like planets and obey Kepler's laws

10. Choose the wrong option. **[NCERT Exemplar]**
   (a) Inertial mass is a measure of difficulty of accelerating a body by an external force whereas the gravitational mass is relevant in determining the gravitational force on it by an external mass

(b) That the gravitational mass and inertial mass are equal is an experimental result

(c) That the acceleration due to gravity on the earth is the same for all bodies is due to the equality of gravitational mass and inertial mass

(d) Gravitational mass of a particle like proton can depend on the presence of neighbouring heavy objects but the inertial mass cannot

ASSERTION AND REASON

Direction (Q. Nos. 11-19) *In the following questions, two statements are given- one labelled Assertion (A) and the other labelled Reason (R). Select the correct answer to these questions from the codes (a), (b), (c) and (d) as given below*

(a) Both Assertion and Reason are true and Reason is the correct explanation of Assertion.

(b) Both Assertion and Reason are true but Reason is not the correct explanation of Assertion.

(c) Assertion is true but Reason is false.

(d) Assertion is false but Reason is true.

11. **Assertion** The force of attraction due to a hollow spherical shell of uniform density, on a point mass situated inside it is zero.

    Reason Various region of the spherical shell attract the point mass inside it in various directions. These forces cancel each other completely.

12. **Assertion** There is a popular statement regarding Cavendish: 'Cavendish weighed the earth'.

    Reason The measurement of G by Cavendish's experiment, combined with the knowledge of g and R_E enables one to estimates M_E from equation.

    $$g = \frac{GM_E}{R_E^2}$$

13. **Assertion** The velocity of the satellite decreases as its height above earth's surface increases and is maximum near the surface of the earth.

    Reason The velocity of the satellite is inversely proportional to its height above earth's surface.

14. **Assertion** The total energy of the satellite is always negative irrespective of the nature of its orbit *i.e.,* elliptical or circular and it cannot be positive or zero.

    Reason If the total energy is positive or zero, the satellite would leave its orbit.

15. **Assertion** As we go up the surface of the earth, we feel light weighed than on the surface of the earth.

Reason The acceleration due to gravity decreases on going up above the surface of the earth.

16. **Assertion** The escape speed for the moon is $2.3 \, \text{kms}^{-1}$ which is five times smaller than that for the earth.

    Reason The escape speed depends on acceleration due to gravity on the moon and radius of the moon and both of them are smaller than that of earth.

17. **Assertion** Moon has no atmosphere.

    Reason The escape speed for the moon is much smaller. Gas molecules, if formed on the surface of the moon having velocities larger than escape speed will escape the gravitational pull of the moon.

18. **Assertion** In the satellite everything inside is in a free fall.

    Reason Free falling objects have no net upwards force acting on them.

19. **Assertion** An object is weightless when it is in free fall and this phenomenon is called phenomenon of weightlessness.

    Reason In free fall, there is no upward force acting on the object.

CASE BASED QUESTIONS

Direction (Q. Nos. 20-21) *These questions are case study based questions. Attempt any 4 sub-parts from each question.*

20. **Cavendish's Experiment**

    The figure shows the schematic drawing of Cavendish's experiment to determine the value of the gravitational constant. The bar AB has two small lead spheres attached at its ends. The bar is suspended from a rigid support by a fine wire.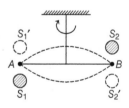

    Two large lead spheres are brought close to the small ones but on opposite sides as shown. The name of G from this experiment came to be $6.67 \times 10^{-11} \text{N-m}^2/\text{kg}^2$.

    (i) The big spheres attract the nearby small ones by a force which is

    (a) equal and opposite

    (b) equal but in same direction

    (c) unequal and opposite

    (d) None of the above

(ii) The net force on the bar is
  (a) non-zero
  (b) zero
  (c) Data insufficient
  (d) None of the above

(iii) The net torque on the bar is
  (a) zero
  (b) non-zero
  (c) F times the length of the bar, where F is the force of attraction between a big sphere and its neighbouring
  (d) Both (b) and (c)

(iv) The torque produces twist in the suspended wire. The twisting stops when
  (a) restoring torque of the wire equals the gravitational torque
  (b) restoring torque of the wire exceeds the gravitational torque
  (c) the gravitational torque exceeds the restoring torque of the wire
  (d) None of the above

(v) After Cavendish's experiment, there have been suggestions that the value of the gravitational constant G becomes smaller when considered over very large time period (in billions of years) in the future. If that happens, for our earth,
  (a) nothing will change
  (b) we will become hotter after billions of years
  (c) we will be going around but not strictly in closed orbits
  (d) None of the above

21. Angular Momentum

Let the speed of the planet at the perihelion P in above figure be v_P and the Sun planet distance SP be r_P. The corresponding quantity at the aphelion A is (r_A, v_A). The mass of the planet in m_P.

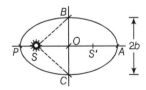

(i) The magnitude of the angular momentum at P is
  (a) $L_P = \dfrac{m_P\, r_P}{v_P}$ (b) $L_P = \dfrac{m_P v_P}{r_P}$
  (c) $L_P = m_P r_P v_P$ (d) $L_P = m_P v_P$

(ii) The magnitude of the angular momentum at A is
  (a) $L_A = m_P r_A v_A$ (b) $L_A = \dfrac{m_P r_A}{v_A}$
  (c) $L_A = m_P v_A$ (d) $L_A = \dfrac{m_P v_A}{r_A}$

(iii) The vectors $\mathbf{r}_P$ and $\mathbf{v}_P$ are
  (a) parallel   (b) mutually perpendicular
  (c) anti-parallel   (d) coincident

(iv) The relation for conservation of angular momentum at P and A is
  (a) $m_P r_P v_P = m_P r_A v_A$
  (b) $\dfrac{m_P r_P}{v_P} = \dfrac{m_P r_A}{v_A}$
  (c) $m_P v_P = m_P v_A$
  (d) $\dfrac{m_P v_P}{r_P} = \dfrac{m_P v_A}{r_A}$

(v) The magnitude of the angular momentum as the planet goes round the sun is
  (a) constant
  (b) variable
  (c) depends on magnitude of velocity
  (d) increases as planet goes near to sun

Answer

1. (a)	2. (a)	3. (c)	4. (b)	5. (b)
6. (d)	7. (b)	8. (b)	9. (d)	10. (d)
11. (a)	12. (a)	13. (a)	14. (a)	15. (a)
16. (a)	17. (a)	18. (b)	19. (a)	

20.	(i) (a)	(ii) (d)	(iii) (b)	(iv) (a)	(v) (c)
21.	(i) (c)	(ii) (a)	(iii) (b)	(iv) (a)	(v) (a)

VERY SHORT ANSWER Type Questions

22 Calculate the force of attraction between two balls, each of mass 1 kg, when their centres are 10 cm apart.   [**Ans.** 6.67×10^{-9} N]

23. If a planet exist whose mass and radius were both half those of the earth, what would be the value of acceleration due to gravity on its surface as compared to what it is on the surface of the earth?   [**Ans.** 2]

24. What would happen to an artificial satellite, if its orbital velocity is slightly decreased due to some defects in it?

25. If the diameter of the earth becomes two times its present value and its mass remains unchanged, then how would the weight of an object on the surface of the earth be affected?
[**Ans.** Weight would become one-fourth]

SHORT ANSWER Type Questions

26. How far away from the surface of the earth does the acceleration due to gravity become 4% of its value on the surface of the earth?
[**Ans.** 25600 km]

27. Find the percentage decrease in the weight of a body when taken 10 km below the surface of the earth.
[**Ans.** 0.25]

28. How much below the surface of the earth does acceleration due to gravity become 1% of the value at the earth's surface? [**Ans.** 6.32×10^3 km]

29. Determine the speed with which the earth would have to rotate on its axis so that a person on the equator would weigh 3/5 as much as present.
[**Ans.** 5 kms^{-1}]

30. State and explain Kepler's laws of planetary motion. Also, name the physical quantities which remain constant during the planetary motion.

31. Prove that the moon would depart forever if, its speed were increased by nearly 42%.

LONG ANSWER Type I Questions

32. A body is projected vertically upwards from the bottom of a crater of the moon of depth $\frac{R}{100}$, where R is the radius of the moon, with a velocity equal to the escape velocity on the surface of the moon. Calculate the maximum height attained by the body from the surface of the moon.
[**Ans.** 100 R]

33. A body is projected vertically upwards from the surface of the earth so as to reach a height equal to the radius of the earth. Neglecting resistance due to air, calculate the initial speed which should be imparted to the body.
[**Ans.** 7.89 kms^{-1}]

34. A satellite revolves around a planet in an orbit just above the planet's surface. Find the period of the satellite.
[**Ans.** 4.2×10^3 s]

35. Determine the velocity with which a body must be thrown vertically upward from the surface of earth so that it may reach a height of $10R$, where R is the radius of the earth.
$\left[\textbf{Ans.} \left(\dfrac{20\,GM}{11\,R} \right)^{1/2} \right]$

36. Prove that the gravitational field and gravitational potential at any point on the surface of the earth are g and gR, respectively. The earth may be assumed to be a sphere of uniform density.

37. A meteor is falling. How much gravitational acceleration would it experience when its height from the surface of the earth is equal to three times the radius of the earth?
$\left[\textbf{Ans.} \dfrac{g}{16} \right]$

LONG ANSWER Type II Questions

38. The planet Neptune travels around the Sun with a period of 165 yr. Show that the radius of its orbit is approximately thirty times that of the earth's orbit, both being considered as circular.
[**Ans.** $R_2 \approx 30R_1$]

39. A 70 kg boy stands 1 m away from a 60 kg boy. Calculate the force of gravitational attraction between them.
[**Ans.** 2.7972×10^{-7} N]

40. At what height above the surface of the earth, value of acceleration due to gravity is 36% of its value on the surface of the earth? Given radius of the earth = 6400 km.
[**Ans.** 4267 km]

41. A particle is fired vertically upward with a speed of 15 km/s. Find the speed of particle when it goes out of the earth's gravitational pull.
[**Ans.** 10 km/s]

42. Calculate the period of revolution of the neptune around the sun. Given that radius of its orbit is 30 times the earth's orbital radius around the sun.
[**Ans.** 164.3 yr]

43. Two steel balls whose masses are 5.2 kg and 0.25 kg are placed with their centres half a metre apart with what force do they attract each other?
[**Ans.** 3.468×10^{-10} N]

The materials having a definite shape and volume are known as solids or rigid bodies. They are of great importance for us as they are used in constructing buildings, bridges, railway tracks, automobiles, artificial limbs, electric poles, wires, ropes, etc. But in reality, these bodies can be deformed on applying force on them. Our aim is to study these materials under loads or forces and their mechanical properties. e.g. elasticity, plasticity, stress and strain etc., in this chapter.

MECHANICAL PROPERTIES OF SOLIDS

|TOPIC 1|
Elastic and Plastic Behaviour of Solids

ELASTIC BODY AND ELASTICITY

A body that returns to its original shape and size on the removal of the deforming force (when deformed within elastic limit) is called an **elastic body**. Quartz fibre, ivory ball and phosphor bronze are the elastic bodies.

The property of matter by virtue of which it regains its original shape and size, when the deforming forces have been removed is called **elasticity**. e.g. If we stretch a spring, and release, then it will regain its original size.

PLASTIC BODY AND PLASTICITY

A body that does not regain its original shape and size even after the removal of deforming force, is called a **plastic body**. Putty, paraffin wax, mud and quartz are nearly perfectly plastic bodies.

The property of a body by virtue of which it does not regain its original shape and size even after the removal of deforming force, is said to be a **plasticity**. e.g. If we stretch a piece of chewing gum and release, it will not regain its original shape and size.

Note

• All rigid bodies are elastic to some extent, which means we can change their dimensions slightly by pulling or pushing, them.
• No body is perfectly elastic or perfectly plastic. All the bodies found in nature lie between these two limits. When the elastic behaviour of a body decreases, its plastic behaviour increases.

CHAPTER CHECKLIST

• Elastic Body and Elasticity
• Plastic Body and Plasticity
• Stress
• Strain
• Hooke's Law
• Stress-strain Curve
• Elastic Modulus
• Energy Stored in a Deformed Body

Deforming Force

A force acting on a body, instead of producing a change in its state of rest or of uniform motion, produces a change in the shape of the body, such a force is called deforming force.

A rigid body can be noticeably stretched, compressed, bent or twisted by applying a suitable force. So, that a body can be deformed by a force. This can be easily shown by stretching a rubber band or by loading a spring.

Elastic Behaviour of Solids

The atoms in a solid are held together by interatomic or intermolecular forces. These forces keep solid in a stable equilibrium position. When a solid is deformed, the atoms or molecules are displaced from their equilibrium positions. Thus, deformation causes change in interatomic or intermolecular distances.

On removing deforming forces, the interatomic forces tend to drive the displaced atoms or molecules to their original equilibrium positions.

Spring Ball Model of Solids

Atoms in a solid may be regarded as mass points or small balls connected in three-dimensional space through springs. Then, springs represent the interatomic forces of attraction between balls. This is called spring ball model of a solid as shown in figure.

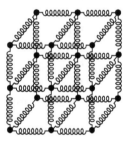

Normally, the balls occupy the positions of minimum potential energy or zero interatomic force. When any ball is displaced from its equilibrium or mean position, the various springs connected to it exert a restoring force on this ball. This force tends to bring the ball to its equilibrium position.

It shows the elastic behaviour of solid in terms of microscopic nature of the solid. Robert Hook, an English Physicist performed an experiment on springs and found that the elongation produced in a body is proportional to the applied force or load.

STRESS

When a deforming force is applied on a body, it changes the configuration of the body by changing the normal positions of the molecules or atoms of the body. As a result, an internal restoring force comes into play which tends to bring the body back to its initial configuration.

The internal restoring force acting per unit area of a deformed body is called **stress**.

i.e.
$$\text{Stress} = \frac{\text{Restoring force } (F)}{\text{Area of cross -section } (A)}$$

If there is no permanent change in the configuration of the body i.e. in the absence of plastic behaviour of the body, the restoring force is equal and opposite to the external deforming force applied. Thus, quantitatively, stress can be given as

$$\text{Stress, } S = \frac{\text{External deforming force}}{\text{Area of cross-section}}$$

Units and Dimensional Formula of Stress

Its SI unit is N/m^2 or pascal (Pa) and in CGS system unit is $dyne/cm^2$. The dimensional formula of stress is $[ML^{-1}T^{-2}]$

Note
- Stress is not a vector quantity. Since, unlike a force, the stress cannot be assigned a specific direction.
- Breaking stress is constant for a material.

On the basis of applied forces on the body, the stress can be classified as

1. Normal Stress or Longitudinal Stress

It is defined as the restoring force per unit area, acts perpendicular to the surface of the body. It is of two types

(i) Tensile Stress

When two equal and opposite forces are applied at the ends of a circular rod as shown in Fig. (a) to increase its length, then a restoring force equal to the applied force F normal to the cross-sectional area A of the rod comes into existence. This restoring force per unit area of cross-section is known as **tensile stress**.

$$\text{Tensile stress} = \frac{F}{A}$$

In case of tensile stress, there is increase in length of a body. Consider a rod of length L, the two equal forces F are applied in the direction as shown in figure, then the final length of the rod becomes $L + \Delta L$.

Thus, increase in length of the rod is ΔL.

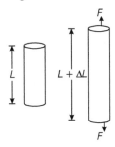

(ii) Compressive Stress

When two equal and opposite forces are applied at the ends of a rod as shown in Fig. (b) to decrease its length or compress it, then again restoring force equal to the applied force comes into existence. This restoring force per unit area of cross-section of the rod is known as **compressive stress**.

$$\text{Compressive stress} = \frac{F}{A}$$

In case of compressive stress, there is decrease in length of a body. If a rod of length L, the two equal forces F are applied in the direction as shown in figure , then the final length of the rod becomes $L - \Delta L$. Thus, decrease in length of the rod is ΔL.

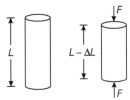

Under tensile stress or compressive stress, the net force acting on an object is zero but the object is deformed.

Note
Tensile stress or compressive stress is also termed as **longitudinal stress**.

2. Tangential or Shearing Stress

When a deforming force acts tangentially to the surface of a body, it produces a change in the shape of the body without any change in volume. This tangential force applied per unit area of cross-section is known as **tangential stress**.

$$\text{Tangential stress} = \frac{F}{A}$$

In case of tangential stress, the deforming force F is applied on top surface of the cubical body in tangential direction

due to which the upper face is deformed by an angle θ from its original position as shown in figure.

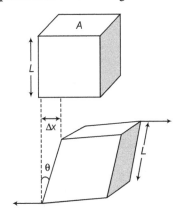

Deforming force on the surface of a body

3. Hydraulic or Bulk Stress

If a body is subjected to a uniform force from all sides, then the corresponding stress is called **hydraulic stress** or bulk stress. There is a change in volume of the body but not change in geometrical shape.

$$\text{Bulk stress} = \frac{F}{A}$$

In case of hydraulic stress, the force F is applied perpendicular to every point on the surface of body due to which the change in volume ΔV of a body occured.

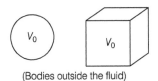

(Bodies outside the fluid)

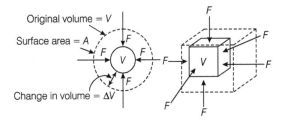

Original volume = V
Surface area = A
Change in volume = ΔV

(Bodies immersed in a fluid)

Hydraulic stress on different surfaces

Note
- The hydraulic stress is also known as volumetric stress.
- The effect of stress is to produce distortion or change in size, volume and shape (i.e. configuration of the body).

EXAMPLE |1| **Stress in a Wire**

Calculate the value of stress in a wire of steel having radius of 2 mm of 10 kN of force is applied on it.

Sol. Force, $F = 10\,\text{kN} = 1 \times 10^4\,\text{N}$

Radius, $r = 2\,\text{mm} = 2 \times 10^{-3}\,\text{m}$

Area, $A = \pi r^2 = \pi \times (2 \times 10^{-3})^2$

$$= 12.56 \times 10^{-6}\,\text{m}^2$$

$$\text{Stress} = \frac{\text{Force}}{\text{Area}} = \frac{1 \times 10^4\,\text{N}}{12.56 \times 10^{-6}\,\text{m}^2}$$

$$= 0.0796 \times 10^{10}$$

$$= 7.96 \times 10^8\,\text{N/m}^2$$

EXAMPLE |2| **Flying tackle**

A man carrying mass $M = 125$ kg makes a flying tackle at $v_1 = 4$ m/s on a stationary quarterback of mass $m = 85$ kg and his helmet makes solid contact with quarterback's femur.

(i) What is the final speed of two athletes immediately after contact and also determine the average force exerted on the quarterback's femur, when last collision occur at 0.100 s?

(ii) If area of cross-section of quarterback's femur is $5 \times 10^{-4}\,\text{m}^2$, then estimate the shear stress exerted on femur in the collision.

Sol.

(i) Here, $M = 125$ kg, $v_1 = 4$ m/s, $m = 85$ kg

Applying, conservation of linear momentum, we get

$$p_{\text{initial}} = p_{\text{final}} \text{ i.e. } Mv_i = (M + m)v_f$$

The value of final speed

$$v_f = \frac{Mv_i}{M + m} = \frac{125 \times 4}{(125 + 85)} = 2.38\,\text{m/s}$$

(ii) Average force exerted to the quarterback's femur

So, $\quad F_{\text{av}} \times \Delta t = M(v_f - v_i)$

i.e. $\quad F_{\text{av}} = \dfrac{M(v_f - v_i)}{\Delta t} = \dfrac{125\,(4 - 2.38)}{0.1}$

$$= \frac{125 \times 1.62}{0.1} = 2.03 \times 10^3\,\text{N}$$

Shearing stress $= \dfrac{F}{A} = \dfrac{2.03 \times 10^3}{5 \times 10^{-4}} = 4.06 \times 10^6\,\text{Pa}$

STRAIN

When a deforming force acts on a body, the body undergoes a change in its shape and size. The ratio of the change in configuration of the body to the original configuration is called **strain**.

$$\text{Strain} = \frac{\text{Change in configuration}}{\text{Original configuration}}$$

If there is a change in any of the configuration of the body due to the applied deforming force on it, then the body is said to be strained or deformed.

Strain is the ratio of two like quantities, so it has no unit and dimension.

According to a change in configuration i.e. change in length, volume or shape of the body, the strain can be classified as

1. Longitudinal Strain

It is defined as the change in length per unit original length, when the body is deformed by external forces.

$$\text{Longitudinal strain} = \frac{\text{Change in length}}{\text{Original length}} = \frac{\Delta L}{L}$$

EXAMPLE |3| **Percentage Strain in Rod**

Consider a steel rod having radius of 8 mm and the length of 2m. If a force of 150 kN stretches it along its length, then calculate the stress, percentage strain in the rod if the elongation in length is 7.46 mm.

Sol. If the rod stretches along its length, then the stress produced is the tensile stress whereas the strain produced is longitudinal strain.

Radius, $r = 8\,\text{mm} = 8 \times 10^{-3}\,\text{m}$, Length, $L = 2\,\text{m}$

Force, $F = 150\,\text{kN} = 15 \times 10^4\,\text{N}$

Area, $A = \pi r^2 = \pi \times (8 \times 10^{-3})^2 = 201 \times 10^{-6}\,\text{m}^2$

$\Delta L = 7.46\,\text{mm} = 7.46 \times 10^{-3}\,\text{m}$, Percentage strain = ?

$$\text{Stress} = \frac{F}{A} = \frac{15 \times 10^4}{201 \times 10^{-6}} = 0.0746 \times 10^{10}\,\text{N/m}^2$$

$$= 7.46 \times 10^8\,\text{N/m}^2$$

Longitudinal strain $= \dfrac{\Delta L}{L} = \dfrac{7.46 \times 10^{-3}}{2} = 3.73 \times 10^{-3}$

Percentage strain $= 3.73 \times 10^{-3} \times 100 = 0.37\,\%$

2. Volumetric Strain

It is defined as the change in volume per unit original volume, when the body is deformed by external forces.

$$\text{Volumetric strain} = \frac{\text{Change in volume}}{\text{Original volume}} = \frac{\Delta V}{V}$$

EXAMPLE |4| **Volumetric Strain in a Cube**

Consider a solid cube which is subjected to a pressure of $6 \times 10^5\,\text{N/m}^2$. Due to this pressure, each side of the cube is shortened by 2%. Find out the volumetric strain of the cube.

Sol. Let L be the initial length of the each side of the cube.

Volume, $V = L \times L \times L = L^3$

$= $ Initial volume (V_i say)

If the each side of the cube is shortened by 2%, then final length of the cube $= L - 2\%$ of L

$$= \left(L - \frac{2L}{100}\right) = L\left(1 - \frac{2}{100}\right)$$

$\therefore$ Final volume, $V_f = L^3\left(1 - \frac{2}{100}\right)^3 = V\left(1 - \frac{2}{100}\right)^3$

Change in volume, $\Delta V = V_f - V_i = V\left(1 - \frac{2}{100}\right)^3 - V$

$$= V\left[\left(1 - \frac{2}{100}\right)^3 - 1\right]$$

$$\frac{\Delta V}{V} = \left(1 - \frac{2}{100}\right)^3 - 1 \simeq \left[1 - \frac{2 \times 3}{100}\right] - 1$$

$$[\because (1-x)^n \simeq 1 - nx \text{ for } x << 1]$$

$\therefore$ Volumetric strain $= \dfrac{\Delta V}{V} = 1 - 0.06 - 1 = 0.06$

(take positive sign)

3. Shear Strain

If the deforming forces produce a change in the shape of the body, then the strain is called **shear strain**. Within elastic limit, it is measured by the ratio of the relative displacement of one plane to its distance from the fixed plane. It can also be measured by the angle through which a line originally perpendicular to the fixed plane as shown in figure.

Consider a cubical body which gets deformed under the effect of tangential force F. The vertical planes $ADEG$ and $BCFH$ are laterally shifted to positions $AD'E'G$ and $BC'F'H$ respectively through an angle θ. If $AD = L$ and $EE' = \Delta L$ (change in perpendicular distance of the displaced surface from the fixed surface $ADEG$)

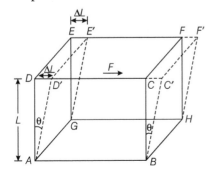

The angle θ is called **angle of shear**.

$$\boxed{\text{Shear strain } (\theta) = \tan\theta = \frac{\Delta L}{L}}$$

If $L = 1$m, then shear strain $= \Delta L$

So, shear strain is the relative displacement between two parallel planes, a unit distance apart.

The strain is the ratio of two like quantities, i.e. the change in dimension to the original or initial dimension, it has no unit or dimensional formula.

Note

- The strain produced in a spring is longitudinal as well as shear if the spring is stretched by suspending a load at its free end.
- The strain persists even when the stress is removed and thus lags behind the stress.

EXAMPLE |5| A Cubical Body Gets Deformed

If the angle of shear is 30° for a cubical body and the change in length is 250 cm, then what must be the volume of this cubical body?

Sol. Given, angle of shear $= 30°$

and change in length $\Delta L = 250$ cm $= 2.5$ m

$\therefore$ Shear strain, $\tan\theta = \dfrac{\Delta L}{L} \Rightarrow \tan 30° = \dfrac{2.5}{L}$

$$L = \frac{2.5}{\tan 30°} = \frac{2.5}{0.577} = 4.332 \text{ m}$$

Volume, $V = L^3 = 81.309 \text{ m}^3$

HOOKE'S LAW

From the experimental investigations, Robert Hooke, an English physicist (1635-1703 AD) in 1679 formulated a law known after him as Hooke's law which states that, the extension produced in the wire is directly proportional to the load applied within defined limit of elasticity.

So, $\boxed{\text{extension} \propto \text{load applied}}$

Later on, it was found that this law is applicable to all types of deformations such as compression, bending, twisting etc., and thus a modified form of Hooke's law was given as

Within elastic limit, the stress developed is directly proportional to the strain produced in a body.

i.e. Stress $\propto$ Strain $\Rightarrow$ Stress $= E \times$ Strain

or $\boxed{E = \dfrac{\text{Stress}}{\text{Strain}}}$

where E is a constant and is known as **modulus of elasticity** of the material of the body.

EXAMPLE |6| Hooke's law

After a fall, a 95 kg rock climber finds himself dangling from the end of a rope that had been 15 m long and 9.6 mm in diameter but has stretched by 2.8 cm. For the rope, calculate.

(i) the strain,   (ii) the stress and

(iii) the modulus of elasticity.

Sol. Here, $L = 1500$ cm is the unstretched length of the rope, $\Delta L = 2.8$ cm is the amount of length stretches.

$$\text{The strain} = \frac{\Delta L}{L} = \frac{2.8 \text{ cm}}{1500 \text{ cm}} = 1.9 \times 10^{-3}$$

$$\text{Stress} = \text{Force}/\text{Area}$$

Force, $F = $ force of gravity on the rock climber
$$= mg = 95 \times 9.8 \text{ N}$$

$$\text{Area, } A = \pi r^2 = \pi \times \left(\frac{D}{2}\right)^2 = \pi \times \left(\frac{9.6}{2} \times 10^{-3} \text{ m}\right)^2$$

$$\text{Stress} = \frac{95 \times 9.8}{\pi \times (4.8)^2 \times 10^{-6}} \simeq 1.29 \times 10^7 \text{ N/m}^2$$

$$\text{Hence, } E = \frac{\text{Stress}}{\text{Strain}} = \frac{1.3 \times 10^7}{1.9 \times 10^{-3}} = 6.84 \times 10^9 \text{ N/m}^2$$

STRESS-STRAIN CURVE

When a wire is stretched by a load as in Fig. (*a*), it is seen that for small value of load, the extension produced in the wire is proportional to the load.

Hence, $\quad\quad\quad$ stress $\propto$ strain

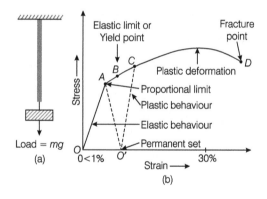

(i) In drawing, a stress *vs* strain graph, the stress is found to be proportional to strain (% elongation) up to point *A*. Thus, Hooke's law is fully obeyed in this region, the point *A* is known as point of **proportional limit**.

(ii) When stress is increased beyond *A*, then for small stress, there is a large strain in the wire upto point *B*.

(iii) When the load is gradually removed between points *O* to *B*, the wire return to its original length.

The wire regains its original dimension only when load applied is less than or equal to certain limit. This limit is called **elastic limit**. The point *B* on stress-strain curve is known as **elastic limit** or **yield point**.

The material of the wire in the region *OB* shows the elastic behaviour, hence known as **elastic region**.

 Elastic Limit

Elastic limit is the upper limit of deforming force up to which, if deforming force is removed, the body regains its original form completely and beyond which if deforming force is increased, the body loses its property of elasticity and gets permanently deformed. Elastic limit is the property of a body whereas elasticity is the property of material of a body.

(iv) If the stress or load increases beyond point *B*, the strain further increases. This increase in strain represented by *BC* part of the curve. Now, if the load is removed, the wire does not regain its original length. But the increase in the length of the wire is permanent.

In other words, there is permanent strain equal to *OO′* in the wire even when the stress is zero.

This permanent strain in the wire is known as permanent set.

(v) Now, as the stress beyond *C* is increased, there is large strain in the wire. This large increase in the strain for small stress is represented by *CD* part of the curve. The wire breaks at point *D* which is also known as **fracture point**.

The material of the wire from point *C* to point *D* shows the **plastic behaviour** or **plastic deformation**. The stress needed to cause the actual fracture of the material is known as **breaking stress** or **ultimate tensile strength**.

Note
- Hooke's law is valid only in the linear portion of the stress-strain curve. The law is not valid for large values of strain.
- Elastic limit and limit of proportionality are very close to each other, so that Hooke's law is nearly applicable upto elastic limit.
- In the yield region, strain is 15 to 20 times those that takes place upto the proportional limit occur during yielding.

Breaking Stress of Some Materials

Material	Breaking stress (in Nm^{-2})
Aluminium	2.2×10^8
Iron	3.0×10^8
Brass	4.7×10^8
Phosphor bronze	5.6×10^8
Steel	5 to 20×10^8
Glass	10×10^8

On the basis of elastic and plastic properties, materials can be classified in two ways.

(i) Ductile Materials

The materials which have large plastic range of extension are called **ductile materials**. As shown in the stress-strain curve, the fracture point is widely separated from the elastic limit.

Such materials undergo an irreversible increase in length before snapping. So, they can be drawn into thin wires e.g. copper, silver, iron, aluminium, etc.

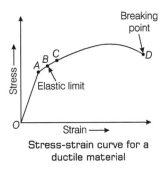

Stress-strain curve for a
ductile material

(ii) Brittle Materials

The materials which have very small range of plastic extension are called **brittle materials**. Such materials break as soon as the stress is increased beyond the elastic limit.

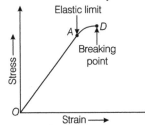

Stress-strain curve for a brittle material

Their breaking point lies just close to their elastic limit, as shown in figure e.g. cast iron, glass, ceramics, etc.

Malleability

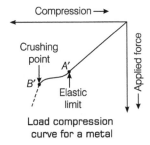

Load compression
curve for a metal

When a solid is compressed, a stage is reached beyond which it cannot regain its original shape after the deforming force is removed. This is the elastic limit point (A') for compression. The solid then behaves like a plastic body.

The yield point (B') obtained under compression is called **crushing point**. After this stage, metals are said to be **malleable** i.e. they can be hammered or rolled into thin sheets. e.g. gold, silver, lead, etc.

Elastomers

The materials which can be elastically stretched to large values of strain are called **elastomers**. e.g. rubber can be stretched to several times its original length but still it can regain its original length when the applied force is removed.

There is no well defined plastic region, rubber just breaks when pulled beyond a certain limit. Elastic region in such cases is very large, but the material does not obey Hooke's law. In our body, the elastic tissue of aorta (the large blood vessel carrying blood from the heart) is an elastomer, for which the stress-strain curve is shown in figure.

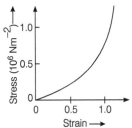

TOPIC PRACTICE 1

OBJECTIVE Type Questions

1. The property of a body by virtue of which it tends to regain its original size and shape of a body when applied force is removed, is known as
   (a) fluidity   (b) elasticity
   (c) plasticity   (d) rigidity

   Sol. (b) The property of a body, by virtue of which it tends to regain its original size and shape when the applied force is removed, is known as elasticity and the deformation caused is known as elastic deformation.

2. Elasticity is shown by materials because inter-atomic or inter-molecular forces
   (a) increases when a body is deformed
   (b) decreases when a body is deformed
   (c) remains same when a body is deformed
   (d) becomes non-zero when a body is deformed

Sol. (d) When a body is deformed, atoms/molecules are displaced from their equilibrium positions $(F = 0)$. As a result, there is a force $(F \neq 0)$ acts between them to restore their position.

3. The maximum load a wire can withstand without breaking, when its length is reduced to half of its original length, will   [NCERT Exemplar]
   (a) be double   (b) be half
   (c) be four times   (d) remain same

Sol. (d) We know that,
$$\text{Maximum stress} = \frac{\text{Maximum force}}{\text{Area of cross-section}}$$
When length of the wire changes, area of cross-section remains same.

Hence, maximum force will be same when length changes.

4. A wire is stretched to double its length. The strain is
   (a) 2   (b) 1   (c) zero   (d) 0.5

Sol. (b) Strain $= \dfrac{\text{Change in length}}{\text{Original length}} = \dfrac{2L - L}{L} = 1$

5. Stress-strain curves for the material A and B are shown below
   Then,
   (a) A is brittle material
   (b) B is ductile material
   (c) B is brittle material
   (d) Both (a) and (b)

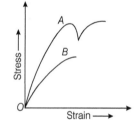

Sol. (c) B is brittle as there is no plastic region. However, A is ductile as it has large plastic range of extension.

VERY SHORT ANSWER Type Questions

6. Two identical solid balls, one of ivory and the other of wet-clay, are dropped from the same height on the floor. Which will rise to a greater height after striking the floor and why?

Sol. The ball of ivory will rise to a greater height because, ivory is more elastic than wet-clay.

7. Is stress a vector quantity?   [NCERT Exemplar]

Sol. No, because stress is a scalar quantity, not a vector quantity.
$$\text{Stress} = \frac{\text{Magnitude of internal reaction force}}{\text{Area of cross - section}}$$

8. A thick wire is suspended from a rigid support, but no load is attached to its free end. Is this wire under stress?

Sol. Yes, the wire is under stress due to its own weight.

9. Stress and pressure are both forces per unit area. Then, in what respect does stress differ from pressure?

Sol. Pressure is an external force per unit area, while stress is the internal restoring force which comes into play in a deformed body acting transversely per unit area of a body.

10. Which type of strain is there, when a spiral spring is stretched by a force?

Sol. Longitudinal strain and shear strain.

11. What does the slope of stress *versus* strain graph indicate?

Sol. The slope of stress (on y-axis) and strain (on x-axis) gives modulus of elasticity.
The slope of stress (on x-axis) and strain (on y-axis) gives the reciprocal of modulus of elasticity.

12. Is it possible to double the length of a metallic wire by applying a force over it?

Sol. No, it is not possible because within elastic limit, strain is only order of 10^{-3}, wires actually break much before it is stretched to double the length.

SHORT ANSWER Type Questions

13. A steel cable with a radius of 1.5 cm supports a chair lift at a ski area. If the maximum stress is not to exceed 10^8 N/m^2, then what is the maximum load the cable can support?   [NCERT]

Sol. Given, radius of steel cable $(r) = 1.5$ cm $= 1.5 \times 10^{-2}$ m
$$\text{Maximum stress} = 10^8 \text{ N/m}^2$$
Area of cross-section of steel cable $(A) = \pi r^2$
$$= 3.14 \times (1.5 \times 10^{-2})^2 \text{ m}^2$$
$$= 3.14 \times 2.25 \times 10^{-4} \text{ m}^2$$
$$\text{Maximum stress} = \frac{\text{Maximum force}}{\text{Area of cross-section}}$$
or Maximum force $=$ Maximum stress $\times$ Area of cross-section
$$= 10^8 \times (3.14 \times 2.25 \times 10^{-4}) \text{ N}$$
$$= 7.065 \times 10^4 = 7.1 \times 10^4 \text{ N}$$

14. A wire of length 2.5 m has a percentage strain of 0.012% under a tensile force. Determine the extension in the wire.

Sol. Here, original length, $L = 2.5$ m
$$\text{Strain} = \frac{\Delta L}{L} = 0.012\% = \frac{0.012}{100}$$
$$\Delta L = \text{Strain} \times L$$
or $\quad \Delta L = \text{extension} = \dfrac{0.012}{100} \times L$
$$= \frac{0.012 \times 2.5}{100}$$
$$= 3 \times 10^{-4} \text{ m}$$
$$= 0.3 \text{ mm}$$

LONG ANSWER Type I Questions

15. Two strips of metal are riveted together at their ends by four rivets, each of diameter 6 mm. What is the maximum tension that can be exerted by the riveted strip if the shearing stress on the rivet is not to exceed 6.9×10^7 Pa? Assume that each rivet is to carry one-quarter of the load. **[NCERT]**

Sol. Diameter of each rivet, $D = 6$ mm

$\therefore$ Radius, $r = \dfrac{D}{2} = 3$ mm $= 3 \times 10^{-3}$ m

Maximum shearing stress on each rivet $= 6.9 \times 10^7$ Pa

Let w be the maximum load that can be subjected to the riveted strip. As each rivet carry one-quarter of the load.

Therefore, load on each rivet $= \dfrac{w}{4}$

Maximum shearing stress $= \dfrac{\text{Maximum shearing force}}{\text{Area}}$

$\therefore \quad 6.9 \times 10^7 = \dfrac{w/4}{\pi r^2}$

or $\quad w = 6.9 \times 10^7 \times 4\pi r^2$

or $\quad w = 6.9 \times 10^7 \times 4 \times 3.14 \times (3 \times 10^{-3})^2$

$= 6.9 \times 4 \times 3.14 \times 9 \times 10$

$= 7.8 \times 10^3$ N

16. Anvils made of single crystals of diamond, with the shape as shown in figure are used to investigate the behaviour of materials under very high pressure. Flat faces at the narrow end of the anvil have a diameter of 0.5 mm and the wide ends are subjected to a compressional force of 50000 N. What is the pressure at the tip of the anvil? **[NCERT]**

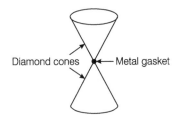

Diamond cones ← Metal gasket

Sol. Given, compressional force, $F = 50000$ N

Diameter, $D = 0.5$ mm $= 5 \times 10^{-4}$ m

$\therefore \quad$ Radius, $r = \dfrac{D}{2} = 2.5 \times 10^{-4}$ m

Pressure at the tip of the anvil $(p) = \dfrac{\text{Force}}{\text{Area}}$

$\therefore \quad p = \dfrac{F}{\pi r^2} = \dfrac{50000}{3.14 \times (2.5 \times 10^{-4})^2}$

$= 2.5 \times 10^{11}$ Pa

17. A bar of cross-section A is subjected to equal and opposite tensile forces at its ends. Consider a plane section of the bar whose normal makes an angle θ with the axis of the bar.
(i) What is the tensile stress on this plane?
(ii) What is the shearing stress on this plane?
(iii) For what value of θ is the tensile stress maximum?
(iv) For what value of θ is the shearing stress maximum?

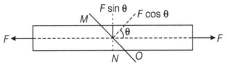

Sol. (i) The resolved part of F along the normal is the tensile force on this plane and the resolved part parallel to the plane is the shearing force on the plane.

$\because$ Area of MO plane section $= A \sec\theta$

$\text{Tensile stress} = \dfrac{\text{Force}}{\text{Area}} = \dfrac{F\cos\theta}{A\sec\theta}$

$= \dfrac{F}{A}\cos^2\theta \quad \left[\because \sec\theta = \dfrac{1}{\cos\theta}\right]$

(ii) Shearing stress applied on the top face

So, $\quad F = F\sin\theta$

$\text{Shearing stress} = \dfrac{\text{Force}}{\text{Area}} = \dfrac{F\sin\theta}{A\sec\theta} = \dfrac{F}{A}\sin\theta\cos\theta$

$= \dfrac{F}{2A}\sin 2\theta \quad [\because \sin 2\theta = 2\sin\theta\cos\theta]$

(iii) Tensile stress will be maximum when $\cos^2\theta$ is maximum i.e. $\cos\theta = 1$ or $\theta = 0°$.

(iv) Shearing stress will be maximum when $\sin 2\theta$ is maximum i.e. $\sin 2\theta = 1$ or $2\theta = 90°$ or $\theta = 45°$.

LONG ANSWER Type II Questions

18. Two long metallic strips are joined together by two rivets each of radius 0.1 cm (see Fig.). Each rivet can withstand a maximum shearing stress of 3.0×10^8 Nm^{-2}. Calculate the maximum tangential force a strip can exert.

Sol. Let F be the tensile force applied. Since, each rivet shares the stretching force equally, so the shearing force on each rivet $= F/2$.

If A is the area of each rivet, then shearing stress on each rivet $= \dfrac{F}{2A}$. Now, maximum shearing stress on each strip $= 3.0 \times 10^8$ Nm^{-2}

i.e. $\quad \dfrac{F_{\max}}{2A} = 3.0 \times 10^8$ Nm^{-2}

where, F_{max} is maximum tangential force.

or $\quad F_{max} = 3.0 \times 10^8 \times 2A = 6.0 \times 10^8 \times \pi r^2$

$\therefore \qquad r = 0.1$ cm $\Rightarrow 0.1 \times 10^{-2}$

$\qquad r = 1 \times 10^{-3}$ m

$\Rightarrow \quad F_{max} = 6.0 \times 10^8 \times \dfrac{22}{7} \times (1 \times 10^{-3})^2 = 1885$ N

19. A steel wire of length $2l$ and cross-sectional area A is stretched within elastic limit as shown in figure. Calculate the strain and stress in the wire.

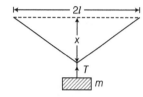

Sol. Total length $L = 2l$. Increase in length of the wire, when it is stretched from its mid-point.

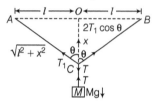

From Pythagoras theorem, $BC^2 = l^2 + x^2$

$$BC = \sqrt{l^2 + x^2}$$

Similarly, $\quad AC = \sqrt{l^2 + x^2}$

Change in length of the wire

$\Delta L = (AC + CB) - AB = (\sqrt{l^2 + x^2} + \sqrt{l^2 + x^2}) - 2l$

$\qquad = 2(l^2 + x^2)^{1/2} - 2l = 2l\left(1 + \dfrac{x^2}{l^2}\right)^{1/2} - 2l \qquad$ ...(i)

Since $x \ll l$, so using Binomial expansion, we have

$$\left(1 + \dfrac{x^2}{l^2}\right)^{1/2} = \left(1 + \dfrac{x^2}{2l^2}\right)$$

[neglecting terms containing higher powers of x]

$\therefore \qquad \Delta L = 2l\left(1 + \dfrac{x^2}{2l^2}\right) - 2l = \dfrac{x^2}{l}$

Hence, strain $= \dfrac{\Delta L}{L} = \dfrac{x^2}{l \times 2l} = \dfrac{x^2}{2l^2}$

$\because \qquad T = 2T_1 \cos\theta \quad \therefore \quad T_1 = \dfrac{Mg}{2\cos\theta} \qquad [\because T = Mg]$

Putting $\cos\theta = \dfrac{x}{\sqrt{l^2 + x^2}}$

$T_1 = \dfrac{Mg}{2x}(\sqrt{l^2 + x^2}) = \dfrac{Mgl}{2x}\left(1 + \dfrac{x^2}{l^2}\right)^{1/2}$

$\qquad = \dfrac{Mgl}{2x}\left(1 + \dfrac{x^2}{2l^2}\right) \qquad$ [using $(1+x)^x = 1 + xx$]

$\because \qquad x \ll l \quad \therefore \quad \dfrac{x^2}{2l^2} \to 0 \quad$ Thus, $1 + \dfrac{x^2}{2l^2} = 1$

$\therefore \qquad T_1 = \dfrac{Mgl}{2x}$

Stress in the wire $= \dfrac{T_1}{A} = \dfrac{Mgl}{2xA}$

ASSESS YOUR TOPICAL UNDERSTANDING

OBJECTIVE Type Questions

1. Elasticity is due to
(a) decrease of PE with separation between atoms/molecules
(b) increase of PE with separation between atoms/molecules
(c) asymmetric nature of PE curve
(d) None of the above

2. A uniform bar of square cross-section is lying along a frictionless horizontal surface. A horizontal force is applied to pull it from one of its ends, then
(a) the bar is under same stress throughout its length
(b) the bar is not under any stress because force has been applied only at one end
(c) the bar simply moves without any stress in it
(d) the stress developed gradually reduces to zero at the end of the bar where no force is applied

3. A spring is stretched by applying a load to its free end. The strain produced in the spring is
(a) volumetric $\qquad$ **[NCERT Exemplar]**
(b) shear
(c) longitudinal and shear
(d) longitudinal

4. A wire of diameter 1 mm breaks under a tension of 1000 N. Another wire of same material as that of the first one, but of diameter 2 mm breaks under a tension of
(a) 500 N $\quad$ (b) 1000 N $\quad$ (c) 10000 N $\quad$ (d) 4000 N

5. The length of a wire increases by 1% by a load of 2 kg-wt. The linear strain produced in the wire will be
(a) 0.02 $\qquad$ (b) 0.001 $\qquad$ (c) 0.01 $\qquad$ (d) 0.002

6. A uniform cube is subjected to volume compression. If each side is decreased by 1%, then bulk strain is
   (a) 0.01   (b) 0.06   (c) 0.02   (d) 0.03

Answers
   1. (c) | 2. (d) | 3. (b) | 4. (d) | 5. (c)
   6. (d)

VERY SHORT ANSWER Type Questions

7. Following are the graphs of elastic materials. Which one correspond to that of brittle material?

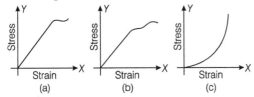

   (a)   (b)   (c)

8. Metal wires after being heavily loaded do not regain their lengths completely. Explain, why?

9. The breaking force for a wire is F. What will be the breaking forces for two parallel wires of this size?

SHORT ANSWER Type Questions

10. A wire fixed at the upper end stretches by length l by applying a force F. What is the work done in stretching the wire?

11. The ratio stress/strain remains constant for a small deformation. What happens to this ratio, if deformation is made very large?

12. A wire is replaced by another wire of same length and material but of twice diameter.
    (i) What will be the effect on the increase in its length under a given load?
    (ii) What will be the effect on the maximum load which it can bear?

LONG ANSWER Type I Question

13. Show graphically the change of potential energy and kinetic energy of a block attached to a spring which obeys Hooke's law.

LONG ANSWER Type II Question

14. The stress-strain graph for a metal wire is shown in figure. Up to the point E, the wire returns to its original state O along the curve EPO when it is gradually unloaded. Point B corresponds to the fracture of the wire.

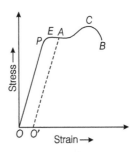

    (i) Up to which point on the curve is Hooke's law obeyed? This point is sometimes called proportionality limit.
    (ii) Which point on the curve corresponds to elastic limit and yield point of the wire?
    (iii) Indicate the elastic and plastic regions of the stress-strain graph.
    (iv) Describe what happens when the wire is loaded up to a stress corresponding to the point A on the graph and then unloaded gradually. In particular, explain the dotted curve.
    (v) What is peculiar about the portion of the stress-strain graph from C to B ? Up to what stress can the wire be subjected without causing fracture?

|TOPIC 2|
Modulus of Elasticity or Elastic Modulus

ELASTIC MODULUS

The modulus of elasticity or coefficient of elasticity of a body is defined as the ratio of stress to the corresponding strain within the elastic limit.

$$\boxed{\text{Modulus of elasticity} = \frac{\text{Stress}}{\text{Strain}}}$$

Its SI unit is Nm^{-2} or Pascal (Pa) and its dimensional formula is $[ML^{-1}T^{-2}]$.

- Modulus of elasticity depends on the nature of the material of the body.
- Modulus of elasticity of a body is independent of its dimensions (i.e. length, area, volume etc.)
- Dimensional formula of modulus of elasticity is same as that of the stress or pressure.

There are three types of modulus of elasticity

1. Young's Modulus of Elasticity

Within the elastic limit, the ratio of longitudinal stress to the longitudinal strain is called Young's modulus of the material of the wire.

i.e. Young's modulus $(Y) = \dfrac{\text{Longitudinal stress}}{\text{Longitudinal strain}}$

$$\boxed{\text{Young's modulus, } Y = \frac{\text{Tensile (or compressive) stress } (\sigma)}{\text{Longitudinal strain } (\varepsilon)}}$$

Consider a wire of radius r and length L. Let a force F be applied on the wire along its length i.e. normal to the surface of the wire as shown in figure.

If ΔL be the change in length of the wire,

Longitudinal stress = F/A, where A is the area of cross-section of the wire.

Longitudinal strain = $\Delta L / L$

∴ Young's modulus,

$$Y = \frac{F/A}{\Delta L/L} = \frac{FL}{A\Delta L} \qquad ...(i)$$

If the extension is produced by the load of mass m, then $F = mg$

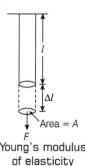
Young's modulus of elasticity

Here, wire has a circular elasticity. So, area of cross-section of the wire,

$$A = \pi r^2$$

From Eq. (i), it can be written as

$$Y = \frac{mgL}{\pi r^2 \Delta L}$$

or $\boxed{\text{Young's modulus, } Y = \dfrac{FL}{\pi r^2 \Delta L}}$

If $L = 1m$, $A = 1m^2$ and $\Delta L = 1m$, then $Y = F$

Thus, **Young's modulus of elasticity is equal to the force required to extend a wire of unit length and unit area of cross-section by unit amount**

Extension is proportional to the deforming force and length of rod. Greater the force, larger the deformation and longer the rod larger, the extension.

EXAMPLE |1| An Elongated Wire

If a wire of length 4 m and cross-sectional area of $2m^2$ is stretched by a force of 3 kN, then determine the change in length due to this force. Given Young's modulus of material of wire is 110×10^9 N / m^2.

Sol. Given, area of cross-section, $A = 2\,m^2$

Force, $F = 3\,kN = 3 \times 10^3$ N

Length, $L = 4$ m

Young's modulus, $Y = 110 \times 10^9$ N / m^2

Change in length, $\Delta L = ?$

Apply, $Y = \dfrac{FL}{A\Delta L}$

$\Rightarrow \quad \Delta L = \dfrac{FL}{AY} = \dfrac{3 \times 10^3 \times 4}{2 \times 110 \times 10^9} = 0.0545 \times 10^{-6}$ m

$\Delta L = 54.5 \times 10^{-3}$ mm

EXAMPLE |2| Foucault Pendulum

In a physics department, a Foucault pendulum consists of a 130 kg steel ball which swings at the end of a 8.0 m long steel cable having the diameter of 3.0 mm. If the ball was first hung from the cable, then determine how much did the cable stretch?

☀ The amount by which the cable stretches depends on the elasticity of the steel cable. Young's Modulus for steel is given as $Y = 20 \times 10^8$ N/m^2

Sol. Given, Diameter, $D = 3.0$ mm $= 3.0 \times 10^{-3}$ m

Length, $L = 8.0$ m; Mass, $m = 130$ kg

Radius, $r = \dfrac{D}{2} = \dfrac{3.0 \times 10^{-3}}{2} = 1.5 \times 10^{-3}$ m

The area of cross-section of the cable

$$A = \pi r^2 = \pi \times (1.5 \times 10^{-3})^2 = 7.065 \times 10^{-6} \, m^2$$

Thus, $F = w = mg = 130 \times 9.8$

$F = 1274$ N

The change in length

$$Y = \frac{\text{Stress}}{\text{Strain}} = \frac{F/A}{\Delta L/L} \Rightarrow \Delta L = \frac{LF}{AY}$$

$$\Delta L = \frac{8.0 \times 1274}{7.065 \times 10^{-6} \times 20 \times 10^{8}} = 0.72 \, m = 720 \, mm$$

EXAMPLE |3| Finding Young's Modulus

The ball of 200 g is attached to the end of a string of an elastic material (say rubber) and having length and cross-sectional area of 51 cm and 22 mm², respectively. Find the Young's modulus of this material if string is whirled round, horizontally at a uniform speed of 50 rpm in a circle of diameter 104 cm.

Sol. Mass of the ball, $M = 200$ g $= 0.2$ kg

Area of cross-section, $A = 22 \, mm^2 = 22 \times 10^{-6} \, m^2$

Radius of the circle, $r = \dfrac{D}{2} = \dfrac{104}{2} = 52$ cm $= 0.52$ m

Length of the string, $l = 51$ cm $= 0.51$ m

Revolution per second, $= 50 \times 60$ rps $= 3000$ rps

Certain petal force, $F = mr\omega^2 = 0.2 \times 0.52 \times (2\pi \times N)^2$

$$F = 36.95 \times 10^6 \, N$$

The change in length Δl

$\Delta l = $ radius of the circle $-$ length of the string

$= 0.52 - 0.51$

$\Delta l = 0.01$ m

Young's modulus of the material

$$Y = \frac{F}{A}\frac{l}{\Delta l} = \frac{36.95 \times 10^6}{22 \times 10^{-6}} \times \frac{0.51}{0.01} = 85.67 \times 10^{12} \, Nm^{-2}$$

Determination of Young's Modulus of the Material of a Wire

A simple experimental arrangement used for the determination of Young's modulus of the material of a wire is shown in Fig. (a).

Constructional Details

The experiment consists of two long straight wires of same length and equal radius suspended side by side from a fixed rigid support. The wire A, called the **reference wire**, carries a main milliammeter scale M and below it a heavy fixed load. This load keeps the wire tight and free from kinks.

The wire B, called the **experimental wire**, carries a Vernier scale at its bottom.

The Vernier scale can slide against the main scale attached to the reference wire. A hanger is attached at the lower end of the Vernier scale. Slotted half kg weights can be slipped into this hanger.

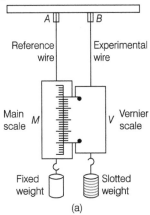

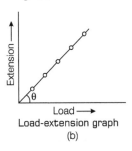

(a)

Experimental arrangement for the determination of Young's modulus

Observations

With the help of a **screw gauge**, the radius of the experimental wire is measured at several places. Let r be the initial average radius and L be the initial length of the experimental wire.

A small initial load, say 1 kg, is put on the hanger. This keeps the experimental wire straight and kink free. The Vernier scale reading is noted. A half kg weight is added to the hanger. The wire is allowed to elongate for a minute. The Vernier scale reading is again noted.

The difference between the two vernier readings gives the extension produced due to the extra weight added. The weight is gradually increased in few steps and every time we note the extension produced.

Area of cross-section of the wire $B = \pi r^2$

and stretching force $= mg$

A graph is plotted between the load applied and extension produced. It will be a straight line passing through the origin, as shown in Fig. (b).

Load-extension graph

(b)

Mathematical Interpretation

Let M be the mass that produced an elongation ΔL in the wire. Thus, the applied force is equal to Mg, where g is the acceleration due to gravity. The slope of the load-extension line $= \tan\theta = \dfrac{\Delta L}{Mg}$

Longitudinal stress $= \dfrac{Mg}{\pi r^2}$ and longitudinal strain $= \dfrac{\Delta L}{L}$

The Young's modulus of the material of the experimental wire will be

$$Y = \frac{\text{Longitudinal stress}}{\text{Longitudinal strain}} = \frac{Mg}{\pi r^2} \cdot \frac{L}{\Delta L} = \frac{L}{\pi r^2 \tan\theta}$$

Thus, Y can be determined.

$$\boxed{\text{Young's modulus, } Y = \frac{L}{\pi r^2} \times \frac{1}{\text{Slope of the graph}}}$$

EXAMPLE |4| Elongation of Copper Wire

A copper wire is stretched by 10 N force. If radius of wire decreases by 2%. How will Young's modulus of wire be affected?

Sol. Since, Young's modulus depends only on the nature of material and not on its dimensions. So, the value of Young's modulus of the copper wire is not changed when its radius decreases. Thus, Young's modulus of the wire remains the same.

2. Bulk Modulus of Elasticity

Within the elastic limit, the ratio of normal stress to the volumetric strain is called bulk modulus of elasticity. In other words, the ratio of hydraulic stress to the hydraulic strain is called bulk modulus.

Consider a body of volume V and surface area A. Suppose a force F acts uniformly over the whole surface of the body and it decreases the volume by ΔV as shown in figure.

The Bulk modulus of elasticity is given by

$$B = \frac{\text{Normal stress}}{\text{Volumetric strain}} = \frac{F/A}{\Delta V/V}$$

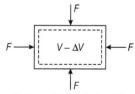

Bulk modulus of elasticity

$$\therefore \text{Bulk modulus, } B = \frac{-F}{A}\frac{V}{\Delta V}$$

$$\Rightarrow \boxed{\text{Bulk modulus, } B = -\frac{pV}{\Delta V}}$$

where, $p = \dfrac{F}{A}$ is the normal pressure.

Note
- Negative sign shows that the volume decreases with the increase in stress. But for a system in equilibrium, the value of bulk modulus is always positive.
- Bulk modulus for a perfect rigid body and ideal liquid is infinite.

Compressibility

The reciprocal of the Bulk modulus of a material is called its compressibility.

Compressibility, $k = \dfrac{1}{B} = \dfrac{-\Delta V}{pV}$

SI unit of compressibility $= N^{-1}m^2$

CGS unit of compressibility $= dyne^{-1}cm^2$

The dimensional formula of compressibility is $[M^{-1}LT^2]$.

EXAMPLE |5| Volumetric Analysis

What will be the decrease in volume of 100 cm^3 of water under pressure of 100 atm if the compressibility of water is 4×10^{-5} per unit atmospheric pressure?

Sol. Bulk modulus $(B) = \dfrac{1}{\text{Compressibility}} = \dfrac{1}{k}$

$$= \frac{1}{4 \times 10^{-5}} = 0.25 \times 10^5 \text{ atm}$$
$$= 0.25 \times 10^5 \times 1.013 \times 10^5 \text{ N/m}^2$$
$$= 2.533 \times 10^9 \text{ N/m}^2$$

Volume, $V = 100\,\text{cm}^3 = 10^{-4}\,\text{m}^3$

Pressure, $p = 100\,\text{atm} = 100 \times 1.013 \times 10^5 \text{ N/m}^2$
$$= 1.013 \times 10^7\,\text{N/m}^{-2}$$

Now, apply $\dfrac{1}{B} = k = \dfrac{\Delta V}{pV}$

$$\therefore \quad \Delta V = \frac{pV}{B} = \frac{1.013 \times 10^7 \times 10^{-4}}{2.533 \times 10^9}$$
$$\Delta V = 0.4 \times 10^{-6}\,\text{m}^3 = 0.4\,\text{cm}^3$$

3. Modulus of Rigidity or Shear Modulus

Within the elastic limit, the ratio of tangential stress (shear stress) to shear strain is called modulus of rigidity. It is denoted as G or η. Let us consider a cube whose lower face is fixed and a tangent force F acts on the upper face whose area is A, as shown in figure.

$\therefore$

$$\boxed{\text{Tangential stress (shear stress)} = \frac{F}{A}}$$

Let the vertical sides of the cube shifts through an angle θ, called shear strain.

$\therefore$ Modulus of rigidity is given by

$$\eta \text{ or } G = \frac{\text{Tangential stress (shear stress)}}{\text{Shear strain}}$$

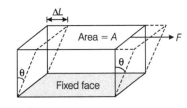

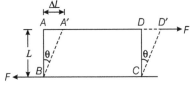

According to diagram, by displacing its upper face through distance $AA' = \Delta L$

Let $AB = DC = L$ and $\angle ABA' = \theta$,

$$\eta = \frac{F/A}{\theta} = \frac{F}{A\theta}$$

Shear strain, $\theta \approx \tan\theta = \dfrac{AA'}{AB} = \dfrac{\Delta L}{L}$

$$\boxed{\text{Shear modulus, } \eta = \frac{F}{A} \cdot \frac{L}{\Delta L}}$$

EXAMPLE |6| Shear Deformation Under Action of Tangential Force

Consider an Indian rubber cube having modulus of rigidity of 2×10^7 dyne/cm^2 and of side 8 cm. If one side of the rubber is fixed, while a tangential force equal to the weight of 300 kg is applied to the opposite face, then find out the shearing strain produced and distance through which the strain side moves.

Sol. Given, modulus of rigidity, $\eta = 2 \times 10^7$ dyne/cm^2

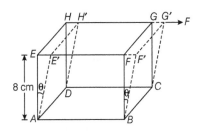

Side of the cube, $l = 8$ cm

Area, $A = l^2 = 64$ cm^2

Force or load, $F = 300$ kgf $= 300 \times 1000 \times 981$ dyne

As, $\eta = \dfrac{F}{A\theta}$

$\Rightarrow$ $\theta = \dfrac{F}{A\eta}$

$$\theta = \frac{300 \times 1000 \times 981}{64 \times 2 \times 10^7} \approx 0.23 \text{ rad}$$

As, $\eta = \dfrac{F}{A} \dfrac{l}{\Delta l}$

$\Rightarrow$ $\dfrac{\Delta l}{l} = \theta$

$\Rightarrow$ $\Delta l = l\theta = 8 \times 0.23$

$\Delta l = 1.84$ cm

EXAMPLE |7| Shear Modulus is Less than Young's Modulus

The shear modulus of a material is always considerably smaller than the Young's modulus for it. What does it signify?

Sol. η of a material is smaller than its Y. As, we know that it is easier to slide layers of atoms of solids over one another than to pull them apart or to squeeze them to close together.

Note

• Shear modulus for ideal liquid is zero.
• A solid has all types of moduli of elasticity i.e. Y, B and η. But fluids (i.e. liquids and gases) has only Bulk modulus of elasticity.

Stress, Strain and Various Elastic Moduli

S.No.	Types of stress	Stress	Strain	Change in Shape	Change in Volume	Elastic modulus	Name of modulus	State of Matter
1.	Tensile or compressive	Two equal and opposite forces perpendicular to opposite faces ($\sigma = F/A$)	Elongation or compression parallel to force direction ($\Delta L/L$) (longitudinal strain)	Yes	No	$Y = (F \times L)/(A \times \Delta L)$	Young's modulus	Solid
2.	Shearing	Two equal and opposite forces parallel to opposite surfaces (forces in each case) such that total forces and total torque on the body vanishes ($\sigma_s = F/A$)	Pure shear, θ	Yes	No	$G = (F \times \theta)/A$	Shear modulus	Solid
3.	Hydraulic	Forces perpendicular everywhere to the surface, force per unit area (pressure) same everywhere	Volume change (compression or elongation) ($\Delta V/V$)	No	Yes	$B = -p(\Delta V/V)$	Bulk modulus	Solid, liquid and gas

POISSON'S RATIO

When a wire is loaded, its length increases but its diameter decreases. The strain produced in the direction of applied force is called **longitudinal strain** and strain produced in the perpendicular direction is called **lateral strain**.

Within the elastic limit, the ratio of lateral strain to the longitudinal strain is called **Poisson's ratio**.

Let the length of the loaded wire increases from L to $L + \Delta L$ and its diameter decreases from D to $D - \Delta D$.

$$\text{Longitudinal strain} = \frac{\Delta L}{L}$$

$$\text{Lateral strain} = \frac{-\Delta D}{D}$$

$$\text{Poisson's ratio } \sigma = \frac{\text{Lateral strain}}{\text{Longitudinal strain}}$$

$$= \frac{-\Delta D/D}{\Delta L/L}$$

$$\boxed{\text{Poisson's ratio, } \sigma = \frac{-L}{D} \cdot \frac{\Delta D}{\Delta L}}$$

The negative sign indicates that longitudinal and lateral strain are in opposite sense, it has no unit and dimensions.

$$\begin{cases} -1 < \sigma < 0.5 & \text{for theoretical purpose} \\ 0 < \sigma < 0.5 & \text{for practical purpose} \end{cases}$$

Poisson's ratio is a constant provided a material remains elastic, homogeneous and isotropic in nature.

EXAMPLE |8| Poisson's Ratio

A material having Poisson's ratio 0.2. A load is applied on it, due to which it suffers the longitudinal strain 3.0×10^{-3}, then find out the percentage change in its volume.

Sol. Given, Poisson's ratio, $\sigma = 0.2$

$$\text{Longitudinal strain} = \frac{\Delta L}{L} = 3.0 \times 10^{-3}$$

As, $$\sigma = -\frac{\Delta D/D}{\Delta L/L} \text{ or } \sigma = \frac{-\Delta R/R}{\Delta L/L}$$

$$\Rightarrow \quad \frac{\Delta R}{R} = -\sigma \times \frac{\Delta L}{L} = -0.6 \times 10^{-3}$$

Volume, $V = \pi R^2 L$

Then, percentage change in volume,

$$\left(\frac{\Delta V}{V} \times 100\right) = \left(\frac{2\Delta R}{R} + \frac{\Delta L}{L}\right) \times 100$$

$$= [2 \times (-0.6 \times 10^{-3}) + 3.0 \times 10^{-3}] \times 100$$

$$= 0.18 \%$$

Relation between Y, B, η **and** σ

The different elastic constants exhibit the following relationship.

(i) $Y = 3B(1 - 2\sigma)$ (ii) $Y = 2\eta(1 + \sigma)$

(iii) $\sigma = \dfrac{3B - 2\eta}{2\eta + 6B}$ (iv) $\dfrac{9}{Y} = \dfrac{1}{B} + \dfrac{3}{\eta}$

FACTORS AFFECTING ELASTICITY OF MATERIAL

The following factors affect the elasticity of a material

   (i) **Hammering and rolling** In both of these processes, the crystal grains are broken into small units and the elasticity of the material increases.

  (ii) **Annealing** This process result in the formation of larger crystal grains and elasticity of the material decreases.

 (iii) **Presence of impurities** Depending on the nature of impurity, the elasticity of material can be increased or decreased.

 (iv) **Temperature** Elasticity of most of the materials decreases with increase in the temperature but elasticity of invor steel (alloy) does not change with change of temperature.

Elastic After Effect

When the deforming force is removed from the elastic bodies, the bodies tend to return to their respective original state. It has been found that some bodies return to its original state immediately, others take appreciably long time to do so. The delay in regaining the original position is known as elastic after effect.

Note

A quartz fibre returns immediately to its normal state, when the twisting torque acting on it ceases to act. On the other hand, a glass fibre will take hours to return to its original state.

Elastic Fatigue

The elastic fatigue is defined as the loss in the strength of a material caused due to repeated alternating strains to which the material is subjected.

e.g. A hard wire can be broken by bending it repeatedly in opposite directions, as it loses strength due to elastic fatigue. For the same reason, the railway bridges are declared unsafe after a reasonably long period to avoid the risk of a mishappening.

ENERGY STORED IN A DEFORMED BODY

When a wire is stretched, interatomic forces come into play which oppose the change in configuration of the wire. Hence, work has to be done against these restoring forces. The work done in stretching the wire is stored in it as its elastic potential energy.

Let a force F applied on a wire of length L increases its length by ΔL. Initially, the internal restoring force in the wire is zero. When the length is increased by ΔL, the internal force increases from 0 to F. (applied force)

∴ Average internal force for an increase in length

$$\Delta L \text{ of wire} = \frac{0 + F}{2} = \frac{F}{2}$$

Work done on the wire,

$$W = \text{Average force} \times \text{Increase in length}$$
$$= \frac{F}{2} \times \Delta L$$

This work done is stored as elastic potential energy U in the wire,

$$U = \frac{1}{2} F \times \Delta L = \frac{1}{2} \text{Stretching force} \times \text{Increase in length}$$

Let A be the area of cross-section of the wire.

Then,

$$U = \frac{1}{2} \frac{F}{A} \times \frac{\Delta L}{L} \times AL$$

Elastic potential energy,

$$\boxed{U = \frac{1}{2} \text{Stress} \times \text{Strain} \times \text{Volume of wire}}$$

Elastic potential energy per unit volume of the wire or elastic energy density is

$$\mu = \frac{U}{\text{Volume}} = \frac{1}{2} \text{Stress} \times \text{Strain}$$

But   stress = Young's modulus × Strain

Elastic energy density,

$$\boxed{\mu = \frac{1}{2} \text{Young's modulus} \times (\text{Strain})^2}$$

EXAMPLE |9| Elastic Potential Energy of a Wire
When the load of a wire is increased from 3 kg wt to 5 kg wt, the length of that wire changes from 0.61 mm to 1.02 mm. Calculate the change in the elastic potential energy of the wire.

Sol. Here, $F_1 = 3 \text{ kg-f} = 3 \times 9.8 \text{ N} = 29.4 \text{ N}$

$$\Delta l_1 = 0.61 \text{ mm} = 6.1 \times 10^{-4} \text{ m}$$
$$F_2 = 5 \text{ kg-f} = 5 \times 9.8 = 49 \text{ N}$$
$$\Delta l_2 = 1.02 \text{ mm} = 1.02 \times 10^{-3} \text{ m}$$
$$\therefore \quad U_1 = \frac{1}{2} F_1 \cdot \Delta l_1 = \frac{29.4 \times 6.1 \times 10^{-4}}{2} = 8.96 \times 10^{-3} \text{ J}$$
$$\text{and} \quad U_2 = \frac{1}{2} F_2 \cdot \Delta l_2 = \frac{49 \times 1.02 \times 10^{-3}}{2}$$
$$= 24.99 \times 10^{-3} \text{ J}$$

∴ Change in elastic potential energy of the wire,

$$\Delta U = U_2 - U_1$$
$$= 24.99 \times 10^{-3} - 8.96 \times 10^{-3} = 16.03 \times 10^{-3} \text{ J}$$

APPLICATIONS OF ELASTIC BEHAVIOUR OF SOLIDS

(i) Any metallic part of a machinery is never subjected to a stress beyond the elastic limit of the material.

In case, the metallic part of the machinery is subjected to a stress beyond the elastic limit, it will get permanently deformed and hamper its working.

(ii) The thickness of metallic ropes used in cranes to lift and move heavy weights is decided on the basis of the elastic limit of the rope and the factor of safety.

Note

Factor of safety also known as Safety Factor (SF), is a term describing the structural capacity of a system beyond the expected loads or actual loads.

(iii) In designing a bridge or beam that has to be designed such that it can withstand the load of the following traffic, the force of winds and its own weight. In both cases, the over coming of the problem of bending of a bridge or beam under a load is of prime importance. The bridge or beam should not bend too much or break.

Consider a beam of length l and of rectangular cross-section having breadth b and depth d. When the beam is loaded in the middle with a load w, then it gets depressed by an amount δ given by

Depression its beam, $\delta = \dfrac{wl^3}{4\, Ybd^3}$

where, $Y =$ Young's modulus of elasticity.

Since, the value of depression δ varies inversely as its breadth (b) and as the cube of its depth (d), the depression can be reduced more effectively by increasing the depth of the beam rather than increasing its breadth.

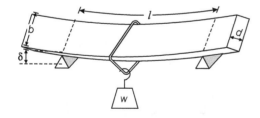

Bending Resistance and Elastic Modulus

A beam can support load by producing resistance against bending. Larger the bending resistance, greater the load bearing capacity. So, the bending resistance is directly proportional to elastic modulus of the material, shape of the cross-section of beam and ultimate stress of the material.

(iv) Maximum height of a mountain on earth (~10 km) can be estimated from the elastic behaviour of earth. A mountain base is not under uniform compression and this provides some shearing stress to the rocks under which they can flow. To illustrate this, consider a mountain of height h, the force per unit area due to the weight of the mountain at its base is $h\rho g$, where ρ is density of material of mountain and g is the acceleration due to gravity. The material at the bottom experiences this force in the vertical direction. The elastic limit for a typical rock is 30×10^7 Nm^{-2}. Equating this to $h\rho g$.

$$h\rho g = 30 \times 10^7$$
$$h \times 3 \times 10^3 \times 10 = 30 \times 10^7$$
$$h = 10 \text{ km}$$

TOPIC PRACTICE 2

OBJECTIVE Type Questions

1. Which of the following statements is incorrect?
   (a) Young's modulus and shear modulus are relevant only for solids.
   (b) Bulk modulus is relevant for liquids and gases.
   (c) Metals have larger values of Young's modulus than elastomers.
   (d) Alloys have larger values of Young's modulus than metals.

Sol. (d) Metals have larger values of Young's modulus than alloy and elastomers.

2. When a pressure of 100 atmosphere is applied on a spherical ball of rubber, then its volume reduces to 0.01%. The bulk modulus of the material of the rubber in dyne cm^{-2} is
   (a) 10×10^{12} (b) 100×10^{12} (c) 1×10^{12} (d) 20×10^{12}

Sol. (c) 1 atm $= 10^5$ Nm^{-2}

$\therefore$ 100 atm $= 10^7$ Nm^{-2} and $\Delta V = 0.01\% \, V$

$\therefore \quad \dfrac{\Delta V}{V} = 0.0001$

$B = \dfrac{p}{\Delta V / V} = \dfrac{10^7}{0.0001} = 1 \times 10^{11} \text{ } Nm^{-2} = 1 \times 10^{12} \, \dfrac{\text{dyne}}{cm^2}$

3. Modulus of rigidity of ideal liquids is
   [NCERT Exemplar]
   (a) infinity
   (b) zero
   (c) unity
   (d) some finite small non-zero constant value

Sol. (b) No frictional (viscous) force exists in case of ideal fluid, hence, tangential forces are zero, so there is no stress developed.

4. A material has Poisson's ratio 0.5. If a uniform rod of it suffers a longitudinal strain of 2×10^{-3}, then the percentage change in volume is
   (a) 0.6
   (b) 0.4
   (d) 0.2
   (d) zero

Sol. (d) As, the Poisson's ratio of material is 0.5, so there is no change in volume.

5. The graph shows the behaviour of a length of wire in the region for which the substance obeys Hooke's law. P and Q represent

   (a) $P = $ applied force, $Q = $ extension
   (b) $P = $ extension, $Q = $ applied force
   (c) $P = $ extension, $Q = $ stored elastic energy
   (d) $P = $ stored elastic energy, $Q = $ extension

Sol. (c) The graph between applied force and extension will be straight line because in elastic range,

   Applied force $\propto$ extension

   But the graph between extension and stored elastic energy will be parabolic in nature.

   As, $\qquad U = \dfrac{1}{2} kx^2 \quad \text{or} \quad U \propto x^2$

VERY SHORT ANSWER Type Questions

6. What is the Young's modulus for a perfect rigid body?

Sol. Young's modulus $(Y) = \dfrac{F}{A} \times \dfrac{l}{\Delta l}$

   For a perfectly rigid body, change in length $\Delta l = 0$

   $\therefore \qquad Y = \dfrac{F}{A} \times \dfrac{l}{0} = \infty$

   Therefore, Young's modulus for a perfectly rigid body is ∞.

7. A metal bar of length L, area of cross-section A, Young's modulus Y and coefficient of linear expansion α, is clamped between two stout pillars. What is the force exerted by the bar when it is heated through $t°C$?

Sol. $Y = \dfrac{FL}{Al}$, where $l = L\alpha \Delta t$ and $l = $ change in length.

   $Y = \dfrac{FL}{AL\alpha \Delta t} = \dfrac{F}{A\alpha \Delta t} = \dfrac{F}{A\alpha \Delta t}$

   $\therefore \qquad F = YA\alpha \cdot \Delta t$

8. A wire increases by 10^{-3} of its length when a stress of 10^8 Nm^{-2} is applied to it. What is the Young's modulus of the material of the wire?

Sol. Given, $\Delta L = 10^{-3} L$, with L as the original length

   $\text{Strain} = \dfrac{\Delta L}{L} = 10^{-3}$ and $\text{Stress} = \dfrac{F}{A} = 10^8 \text{ N/m}^2$

   $\because \qquad Y = \dfrac{\text{Stress}}{\text{Strain}} = \dfrac{F/A}{\Delta L / L}$

   $\qquad Y = \dfrac{1 \times 10^8}{10^{-3}} = 10^{11} \text{ N/m}^2$

9. What is Bulk modulus for a perfectly rigid body?

Sol. Bulk modulus $(B) = \dfrac{p}{\Delta V / V} = \dfrac{pV}{\Delta V}$

   For perfectly rigid body, change in volume $\Delta V = 0$

   $\therefore \qquad B = \dfrac{pV}{0} = \infty$

   Therefore, Bulk modulus for a perfectly rigid body is ∞.

SHORT ANSWER Type Questions

10. A wire of length L and radius r is clamped rigidly at one end. When the other end of the wire is pulled by a force f, its length increases by l. Another wire of the same material of length $2L$ and radius $2r$, is pulled by a force $2f$. Find the increase in length of this wire.

   💡 In this problem, we have to apply Hooke's law and then elongation in each wire will be compared.

Sol. The situation is shown in the diagram.

   Now, Young's modulus $(Y) = \dfrac{f}{A} \times \dfrac{L}{l}$

   For first wire, $\quad Y = \dfrac{f}{\pi r^2} \times \dfrac{L}{l} \qquad$ ...(i)

   For second wire, $Y = \dfrac{2f}{\pi (2r)^2} \times \dfrac{2L}{l'}$

   $\qquad = \dfrac{f}{\pi r^2} \times \dfrac{L}{l'} \qquad$ ...(ii)

   For Eqs. (i) and (ii), $\dfrac{f}{\pi r^2} \times \dfrac{L}{l} = \dfrac{f}{\pi r^2} \times \dfrac{L}{l'}$

   $\therefore \qquad l = l'$

   [$\because$ both wires are of same material, hence, Young's modulus will be same].

11. Two wires made of same material are subjected to forces in the ratio 1 : 4. Their lengths are in the ratio 2 : 1 and diameters in the ratio 1 : 3. What is the ratio of their extensions?

Sol. According to Hooke's law,

   Modulus of elasticity, $E = \dfrac{F}{\pi r^2} \times \dfrac{l}{\Delta l}$ or $\Delta l = \dfrac{Fl}{\pi r^2 E}$

   or $\qquad \Delta l \propto \dfrac{Fl}{r^2} \qquad$ [$\because E$ is same for two wires]

$$\therefore \qquad \frac{\Delta l_1}{\Delta l_2} = \frac{F_1}{F_2} \times \frac{l_1}{l_2} \times \frac{r_2^2}{r_1^2} = \frac{1}{4} \times \frac{2}{1} \times \left(\frac{3}{1}\right)^2 = \frac{9}{2}$$

So, $\qquad \Delta l_1 : \Delta l_2 = 9 : 2$.

12. The stress-strain graphs for materials A and B are shown in Fig. (a) and Fig. (b).

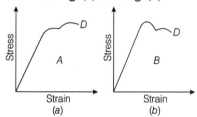

$$\begin{array}{cc} \text{(a)} & \text{(b)} \end{array}$$

The graphs are drawn to the same scale.
  (i) Which of the materials has greater Young's modulus?
  (ii) Which of the two is the stronger material?

[NCERT]

Sol. (i) In the two graphs, the slope of graph in Fig. (a) is greater than the slope of graph in Fig. (b), so material A has greater Young's modulus.

  (ii) Material A is stronger than material B because it can withstand more load without breaking. For material A, the break even point (D) is higher.

13. A wire elongates by l mm when a load W is hanged from it. If the wire goes over a pulley and two weights W each are hung at the two ends, then what will be the elongation of the wire in mm?

Sol. According to Hooke's law,

Modulus of elasticity, $E = \dfrac{W}{A} \times \dfrac{L}{l}$

where, L = original length of the wire
$\qquad A$ = cross-sectional area of the wire

$\therefore$ Elongation, $\Delta l = \dfrac{WL}{E}$ ...(i)

On either side of the wire, tension is W and length is $l/2$.

$$\Delta l = \frac{W \, L/2}{AE} = \frac{WL}{2AE} = \frac{l}{2} \qquad \text{[from Eq. (i)]}$$

$\therefore$ Total elongation in the wire $= \dfrac{l}{2} + \dfrac{l}{2} = l$

14. Two wires A and B are of the same material. Their lengths are in the ratio 1:2 and the diameters in the ratio 2:1. If they are pulled by the same force, then what will be the ratio of their increase in lengths?

Sol. We know, $\Delta L = \dfrac{FL}{AY}$, $\dfrac{L_A}{L_B} = \dfrac{1}{2}$ and $\dfrac{r_A}{r_B} = \dfrac{2}{1}$ (given)

[$\because$ the wires A and B are pulled by the same force and they are made up of same material, hence, $F_A = F_B = F$, $Y_A = Y_B = Y$]

$$\frac{\Delta L_A}{\Delta L_B} = \frac{L_A}{\pi r_A^2} \times \frac{\pi r_B^2}{L_B}$$

$$\frac{\Delta L_A}{\Delta L_B} = \frac{L_A}{L_B} \times \left(\frac{r_B}{r_A}\right)^2 \Rightarrow \frac{\Delta L_A}{\Delta L_B} = \frac{1}{2} \times \left(\frac{1}{2}\right)^2 = \frac{1}{8}$$

$$\frac{\Delta L_A}{\Delta L_B} = \frac{1}{8}$$

15. The Young's modulus for steel is much more than that for rubber. For the same longitudinal strain, which one will have greater tensile stress? [NCERT Exemplar]

Sol. Young's modulus $(Y) = \dfrac{\text{Stress}}{\text{Longitudinal strain}}$

For same longitudinal strain, $Y \propto$ stress

$\therefore \qquad \dfrac{Y_{\text{steel}}}{Y_{\text{rubber}}} = \dfrac{(\text{stress})_{\text{steel}}}{(\text{stress})_{\text{rubber}}}$ ...(i)

But $\qquad Y_{\text{steel}} > Y_{\text{rubber}}$

$\therefore \qquad \dfrac{Y_{\text{steel}}}{Y_{\text{rubber}}} > 1$

Therefore, from Eq. (i), we get

$$\frac{(\text{stress})_{\text{steel}}}{(\text{stress})_{\text{rubber}}} > 1$$

or $\qquad (\text{stress})_{\text{steel}} > (\text{stress})_{\text{rubber}}$

16. Figure shows the strain-stress curve for a given material. What are (i) Young's modulus and (ii) approximate yield strength for this material? [NCERT]

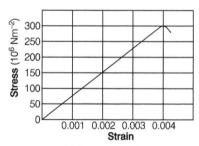

💡 The slope of straight line portion of strain-stress curve for a given material represents its Young's modulus.
The maximum stress that a material can sustain is called its yield strength.

Sol. (i) Young's modulus of the given material (Y)
$= $ Slope of strain-stress curve
$$Y = \frac{150 \times 10^6}{0.002} = 75 \times 10^9 \text{ N/m}^2$$
$$= 7.5 \times 10^{10} \text{ N/m}^2$$

(ii) Yield strength of the given material
$= $ Maximum stress, the material can sustain
$= 300 \times 10^6 \text{ N/m}^2$
$= 3 \times 10^8 \text{ N/m}^2$

17. Calculate the percentage increase in length of a wire of diameter 2.5 mm stretched by a force of 100 kg weight. Young's modulus of elasticity of wire is 12.5×10^{11} dyne/sq. cm.

Sol. Here, $2r = 2.5\,\text{mm} = 0.25\,\text{cm}$ or $r = 0.125$ cm

$\therefore \qquad a = \pi r^2 = \dfrac{22}{7} \times (0.125)^2$ sq. cm

$\qquad F = 100\,\text{kg} = 100 \times 1000\,\text{g}$

$\qquad F = 10 \times 1000 \times 980$ dyne

$\qquad Y = 12.5 \times 10^{11}$ dyne/sq. cm

As $\qquad Y = \dfrac{F \times l}{a \times \Delta l}$

$\therefore \qquad \dfrac{\Delta l}{l} = \dfrac{F}{aY}$

Hence, % increase in length

$$= \dfrac{\Delta l}{l} \times 100 = \dfrac{F}{aY} \times 100$$

$$= \dfrac{(100 \times 1000 \times 980) \times 7 \times 100}{22 \times (0.125)^2 \times 12.5 \times 10^{11}}$$

$$= 0.1812\%$$

18. A solid sphere of radius R made of a material of bulk modulus B is surrounded by a liquid in a cylindrical container. A massless piston of area A floats on the surface of the liquid.

When a mass M is placed on the piston to compress the liquid, find fractional change in the radius of the sphere?

Sol. When mass M is placed on the piston, the excess pressure, $p = Mg/A$. As this pressure is equally applicable from all the direction on the sphere, hence there will be decrease in volume due to decrease in radius of sphere. Volume of the sphere, $V = \dfrac{4}{3}\pi R^3$.

Differentiating it, we get,

$$\Delta V = \dfrac{4}{3}\pi (3R^2)\Delta R = 4\pi R^2 \Delta R$$

$\therefore \qquad \dfrac{\Delta V}{V} = \dfrac{4\pi R^2 \Delta R}{\dfrac{4}{3}\pi R^3} = \dfrac{3\Delta R}{R}$

We know that, $B = \dfrac{P}{dV/V} = \dfrac{Mg}{A} \Big/ \dfrac{3\Delta R}{R}$

or $\qquad \dfrac{\Delta R}{R} = \dfrac{Mg}{3BA}$

19. The Marina trench is located in the Pacific ocean and at one place, it is nearly 11 km beneath the surface of water. The water pressure at the bottom of the trench is about 1.1×10^8 Pa. A steel ball of initial volume 0.32 m^3 is dropped into the ocean and falls to the bottom of trench. What is the change in the volume of the ball when it reaches to the bottom if the Bulk modulus of steel is 1.6×10^{11} N/m^2? **[NCERT]**

Sol. Depth $(h) = 11\,\text{km} = 11 \times 10^3$ m

Pressure at the bottom of the trench $(p) = 1.1 \times 10^8$ Pa

Initial volume of the ball $(V) = 0.32$ m^3

Bulk modulus of steel $(B) = 1.6 \times 10^{11}$ N/m^2

Bulk modulus of steel $(B) = \dfrac{p}{(\Delta V / V)} = \dfrac{pV}{\Delta V}$

$$\Delta V = \dfrac{pV}{B} = \dfrac{1.1 \times 10^8 \times 0.32}{1.6 \times 10^{11}}$$

$$\Delta V = 2.2 \times 10^{-4}\,\text{m}^3$$

20. To what depth must a rubber ball be taken in deep sea so that its volume is decreased by 0.1%? (The Bulk modulus of rubber is 9.8×10^8 N/m^2; and the density of seawater is 10^3 kg/m^3.)

Sol. Bulk modulus of rubber $(B) = 9.8 \times 10^8$ N/m^2

Density of seawater $(\rho) = 10^3$ kg/m^3

Percentage decrease in volume,

$$\left(\dfrac{\Delta V}{V} \times 100\right) = 0.1 \text{ or } \dfrac{\Delta V}{V} = \dfrac{0.1}{100}$$

or $\qquad \dfrac{\Delta V}{V} = \dfrac{1}{1000}$

Let the rubber ball be taken up to depth h.

$\because$ Change in pressure $(p) = h\rho g$

$\therefore$ Bulk modulus $(B) = \dfrac{p}{(\Delta V/V)} = \dfrac{h\rho g}{(\Delta V/V)}$

or $\quad h = \dfrac{B \times (\Delta V/V)}{\rho g} = \dfrac{9.8 \times 10^8 \times \dfrac{1}{1000}}{10^3 \times 9.8} = 100\,\text{m}$

21. The maximum stress that can be applied to the material of a wire used to suspend on elevator is 1.3×10^8 Nm^{-2}. If the mass of the elevator is 900 kg and it moves up with an accleration of 2.2 ms^{-2}, then what is the minimum diameter of the wire?

Sol. As the elevator moves up, the tension in the wire,

$$F = mg + ma = m(g + a) = 900 \times (9.8 + 2.2) = 10800\,\text{N}$$

Stress in the wire $= \dfrac{F}{A} = \dfrac{F}{\pi r^2}$

Clearly, when the stress is maximum, r is minimum.

$\therefore$ Maximum stress $= \dfrac{F}{\pi r_{min}^2}$

or $\qquad r_{min}^2 = \dfrac{F}{\pi \times \text{Maximum stress}}$

$$= \frac{10800}{3.14 \times 1.3 \times 10^8} = 0.2645 \times 10^{-4}\,m$$

or $r_{min} = 0.5142 \times 10^{-2}\,m$

Minimum diameter

$$= 2r_{min} = 2 \times 0.5142 \times 10^{-2}$$

$$= 1.0284 \times 10^{-2}\,m$$

LONG ANSWER Type I Questions

22. A steel wire of length 4.7 m and cross-sectional area $3.0 \times 10^{-5}\,m^2$ stretches by the same amount as a copper wire of length 3.5 m and cross-sectional area $4.0 \times 10^{-5}\,m^2$ under a given load. What is the ratio of the Young's modulus of steel to that of copper? **[NCERT]**

Sol. Given, **for steel wire**, length $(l_1) = 4.7\,m$

Area of cross-section $(A_1) = 3.0 \times 10^{-5}\,m^2$

For copper wire

Length $(l_2) = 3.5\,m$

Area of cross-section $(A_2) = 4.0 \times 10^{-5}\,m^2$

Let F be the given load under which steel and copper wires be stretched by the same amount Δl.

Young's modulus $(Y) = \dfrac{F/A}{\Delta l/l} = \dfrac{F \times l}{A \times \Delta l}$

For steel, $\quad Y_s = \dfrac{F \times l_1}{A_1 \times \Delta l}$ ...(i)

For copper, $\quad Y_c = \dfrac{F \times l_2}{A_2 \times \Delta l}$ ...(ii)

Dividing Eq. (i) by Eq. (ii), we get

$$\frac{Y_s}{Y_c} = \frac{F \times l_1}{A_1 \times \Delta l} \times \frac{A_2 \times \Delta l}{F \times l_2}$$

$$= \frac{l_1}{l_2} \times \frac{A_2}{A_1} = \frac{4.7}{3.5} \times \frac{4.0 \times 10^{-5}}{3.0 \times 10^{-5}}$$

$$\frac{Y_s}{Y_c} = \frac{18.8}{10.5} = 1.79 = 1.8$$

23. Identical springs of steel and copper are equally stretched. On which, more work will have to be done? **[NCERT Exemplar]**

Sol. Work done in stretching a wire is given by

$$W = \frac{1}{2}F \times \Delta l$$

As springs of steel and copper are equally stretched. Therefore, for same force (F),

$$W \propto \Delta l \qquad \text{...(i)}$$

Young's modulus $(Y) = \dfrac{F}{A} \times \dfrac{l}{\Delta l}$

or $\quad \Delta l = \dfrac{F}{A} \times \dfrac{l}{Y}$

As both springs are identical,

$\therefore \qquad \Delta l \propto \dfrac{1}{Y} \qquad$ ...(ii)

From Eqs. (i) and (ii), we get $W \propto \dfrac{1}{Y}$

$\therefore \qquad \dfrac{W_{steel}}{W_{copper}} = \dfrac{Y_{copper}}{Y_{steel}} < 1 \qquad [\text{as } Y_{steel} > Y_{copper}]$

or $\qquad W_{steel} < W_{copper}$

Therefore, more work will be done for stretching copper spring.

24. A uniform heavy rod of weight W, cross-sectional area A and length l is hanging from a fixed support. Young's modulus of the material of the rod is Y. Neglecting the lateral contraction, find the elongation produced in the rod.

Sol. As shown in figure, consider a small element of thickness dx at distance x from the fixed support. Force acting on the element dx is

$$F = \text{Weight of length } (l - x) \text{ of the rod}$$

$$= \frac{W}{l}(l - x)$$

Elongation of the element

$$= \text{Original length} \times \frac{\text{Stress}}{Y}$$

$$= dx \times \frac{F/A}{Y} = \frac{W}{l\,Ay}(l - x)dx$$

Total elongation produced in the rod

$$= \frac{W}{l\,AY}\int_0^l (l - x)dx = \frac{W}{l\,Ay}\left[lx - \frac{x^2}{2}\right]_0^l$$

$$= \frac{W}{l\,Ay}\left[l^2 - \frac{l^2}{2}\right] = \frac{Wl}{2Ay}$$

25. One end of a nylon rope, of length 4.5 cm and diameter 6 mm, is fixed to a free limb. A monkey, weighing 100 N, jumps to catch the free end and stays there. Find the elongation of the rope and the corresponding change in the diameter. Given Young's modulus of nylon $= 4.8 \times 10^{11}\,N/m^2$ and Poisson's ratio of nylon $= 0.2$.

Sol. Here, $l = 4.5\,m;\ D = 6\,mm = 6 \times 10^{-3}\,m$

$F = Mg = 100\,N,$

$Y = 4.8 \times 10^{11}\,N/m^2;\ \Delta l = ?;\ \Delta D = ?$

$Y = \dfrac{F}{(\pi D^2/4)} \times \dfrac{l}{\Delta l}$

or $\Delta l = \dfrac{4Fl}{\pi D^2 Y} = \dfrac{4 \times 100 \times 4.5}{3.14 \times (6 \times 10^{-3})^2 \times (4.8 \times 10^{11})}$

$= 3.315 \times 10^{-5}$ m

$\sigma = \dfrac{\Delta D / D}{\Delta l / l}$ (in magnitude)

or $\Delta D = \sigma \dfrac{\Delta l}{l} \times D$

$= 0.2 \times \dfrac{(3.315 \times 10^{-5})}{4.5} \times (6 \times 10^{-3})$

$= 8.84 \times 10^{-9}$ m

26. A mild steel wire of length 1 m and cross-sectional area 0.5×10^{-2} cm^2 is stretched, well within its elastic limit, horizontally between two pillars. A mass of 100 g is suspended from the mid-point of the wire. Calculate the depression at the mid-point. Given Young's modulus for steel $(Y_s) = 2 \times 10^{11}$ Pa.

[NCERT]

When a load w is suspended from a stretched wire of length l, then depression at the mid-point is given by

$$\delta = \dfrac{w\,l^3}{12\pi r^4 Y}$$

where, r = radius of the wire,
Y = Young's modulus of the material of the wire.

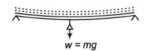

$$w = mg$$

Sol. Given, length $(l) = 1$ m

Area of cross-section $(A) = 0.5 \times 10^{-2}$ cm^2

$= 0.5 \times 10^{-6}$ m^2

Mass $(m) = 100$ g $= 0.1$ kg

$\therefore$ Load $(w) = mg = 0.1 \times 9.8$ N $= 0.98$ N

Young's modulus for steel $(Y) = 2 \times 10^{11}$ Pa

Area $(A) = \pi r^2$

or $r^2 = \dfrac{A}{\pi}$

$= \dfrac{0.5 \times 10^{-6}}{\pi}$

Depression in a wire when a load is suspended at its centre

$\delta = \dfrac{w\,l^3}{12\pi r^4 Y} = \dfrac{0.98 \times (1)^3}{12\pi \times \left(\dfrac{0.5 \times 10^{-6}}{\pi}\right)^2 \times 2 \times 10^{11}}$

$\delta = \dfrac{0.98 \times \pi}{12 \times 0.25 \times 2 \times 10^{-1}} = 5.12$ m

27. Determine the volume contraction of a solid copper cube, 10 cm on an edge, when subjected to a hydraulic pressure of 7×10^6 Pa. Bulk modulus for copper $= 140 \times 10^9$ Pa. **[NCERT]**

Sol. Given, each side of cube $(l) = 10$ cm $= 0.1$ m

Hydraulic pressure $(p) = 7 \times 10^6$ Pa

Bulk modulus for copper $(B) = 140 \times 10^9$ Pa

Volume contraction $(\Delta V) = ?$

Volume of the cube $(V) = l^3 = (0.1)^3 = 1 \times 10^{-3}$ m^3

Bulk modulus for copper $(B) = \dfrac{p}{\Delta V / V}$

$= \dfrac{pV}{\Delta V}$

or $\Delta V = \dfrac{pV}{B}$

$\Delta V = \dfrac{7 \times 10^6 \times 1 \times 10^{-3}}{140 \times 10^9} = \dfrac{1}{20} \times 10^{-6}$ m^3

$= 0.05 \times 10^{-6}$ m$^3 = 5 \times 10^{-8}$ m^3

LONG ANSWER Type II Questions

28. What is the density of water at a depth where pressure is 80.0 atm, given that its density at the surface is 1.03×10^3 kg/m^3, compressibility of water is 45.8×10^{-11} Pa^{-1}. **[NCERT]**

Sol. Density of water at the surface $(\rho_0) = 1.03 \times 10^3$ kg/m^3

Pressure $(p) = 80.0$ atm $= 80.0 \times 1.013 \times 10^5$ Pa

[$\because$ 1 atm $= 1.013 \times 10^5$ Pa]

Compressibility of water $\left(\dfrac{1}{B}\right) = 45.8 \times 10^{-11}$ Pa^{-1}

Let V and V' be the volumes of certain mass of water at the surface and at a given depth. The density of water at the given depth be ρ'.

Volume of water at the surface, $V = \dfrac{m}{\rho}$

At the given depth, $V' = \dfrac{m}{\rho'}$

$\therefore$ Change in volume, $\Delta V = V - V' = m\left(\dfrac{1}{\rho} - \dfrac{1}{\rho'}\right)$

Volumetric strain $= \dfrac{\Delta V}{V}$

$= m\left(\dfrac{1}{\rho} - \dfrac{1}{\rho'}\right) \times \dfrac{\rho}{m}$

$= \left(1 - \dfrac{\rho}{\rho'}\right)$

$$\text{Compressibility} = \frac{1}{\text{Bulk modulus } (B)}$$

$$= \frac{1}{\dfrac{\Delta p}{(\Delta V / V)}} = \frac{\Delta V}{\Delta p V}$$

$$45.8 \times 10^{-11} = \left(1 - \frac{\rho}{\rho'}\right) \times \frac{1}{80 \times 1.013 \times 10^5}$$

$$45.8 \times 10^{-11} \times 80 \times 1.013 \times 10^5 = 1 - \frac{1.03 \times 10^3}{\rho'}$$

$$3.712 \times 10^{-3} = 1 - \frac{1.03 \times 10^3}{\rho'}$$

$$\frac{1.03 \times 10^3}{\rho'} = 1 - 3.712 \times 10^{-3}$$

or $\quad \rho' = \dfrac{1.03 \times 10^3}{1 - 0.003712} = 1.034 \times 10^3 \text{kg/m}^3$

29. A rigid bar of mass 15 kg is supported symmetrically by three wires each 2 m long. These at each end are of copper and middle one is of iron. Determine the ratio of their diameters if each is to have the same tension. Young's modulus of elasticity for copper and steel are $110 \times 10^9 \text{N/m}^2$ and $190 \times 10^9 \text{N/m}^2$, respectively.   **[NCERT]**

Sol. Young's modulus of copper $(Y_1) = 110 \times 10^9 \text{N/m}^2$

Young's modulus of steel $(Y_2) = 190 \times 10^9 \text{N/m}^2$

Let d_1 and d_2 be the diameters of copper and steel wires. Since, tension in each wire is same, therefore each wire has same extension. As each wire is of same length, hence each wire has same strain.

$$\text{Young's modulus } (Y) = \frac{\text{Stress}}{\text{Strain}} = \frac{F/A}{\text{Strain}}$$

or $\quad Y = \dfrac{F}{\left(\dfrac{\pi d^2}{4}\right) \times \text{Strain}} = \dfrac{4F}{\pi d^2 \times \text{Strain}}$

$\because \quad Y \propto \dfrac{1}{d^2} \Rightarrow d^2 \propto \dfrac{1}{Y}$

$\therefore \quad \dfrac{d_1^2}{d_2^2} = \dfrac{Y_2}{Y_1}$

or $\quad \dfrac{d_1}{d_2} = \sqrt{\dfrac{Y_2}{Y_1}} = \sqrt{\dfrac{190 \times 10^9}{110 \times 10^9}}$

$$= \sqrt{\dfrac{19}{11}} = \sqrt{1.73} = 1.31$$

$\therefore \qquad d_1 : d_2 = 1.31 : 1$

30. A 14.5 kg mass, fastened to one end of a steel wire of unstretched length 1 m is whirled in a vertical circle with an angular frequency of 2 rev/s at the bottom of the circle. The cross-sectional area of the wire is 0.065 cm².

Calculate the elongation of the wire when the mass is at the lowest point of its path.   **[NCERT]**

Sol. Given, mass $(m) = 14.5$ kg

Length of wire $(l) = 1$ m

Angular frequency $(\nu) = 2$ rev/s

Angular velocity $(\omega) = 2\pi\nu$

$$= 2\pi \times 2 \text{ rad/s} = 4\pi \text{ rad/s}$$

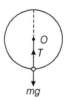

Area of cross-section of wire $(A) = 0.065 \text{ cm}^2$

$$= 6.5 \times 10^{-6} \text{ m}^2$$

Young's modulus for steel $(Y) = 2 \times 10^{11} \text{ N/m}^2$.

At lowest point of the vertical circle,

$$T - mg = ml\omega^2$$

or $\quad T = mg + ml\omega^2$

$$= (14.5 \times 9.8) + 14.5 \times 1 \times (4\pi)^2$$

$$= 14.5(9.8 + 16\pi^2)$$

$$= 14.5(9.8 + 16 \times 9.87) \qquad [\because \pi^2 = 9.87]$$

$$= 14.5 \times 167.72 \text{ N} = 2431.94 \text{ N}$$

$$\text{Young's modulus } (Y) = \frac{\text{Stress}}{\text{Strain}} = \frac{(T/A)}{\Delta l / l} = \frac{Tl}{A \cdot \Delta l}$$

$\therefore \qquad \Delta l = \dfrac{T \cdot l}{A \cdot Y} = \dfrac{2431.94 \times 1}{6.5 \times 10^{-6} \times 2 \times 10^{11}}$

$$= 1.87 \times 10^{-3} \text{ m} = 1.87 \text{ mm}$$

31. Four identical hollow cylindrical columns of mild steel support a big structure of mass 50000 kg. The inner and outer radii of each column are 30 cm and 60 cm, respectively. Assuming the load distribution to be uniform, calculate the compressional strain of each column. Young's modulus, $Y = 2.0 \times 10^{11}$ Pa.   **[NCERT]**

Sol. Given, total mass supported by cylindrical columns (m)

$$= 50000 \text{ kg}$$

$\because$ Total weight supported by cylindrical columns

$$= mg = 50000 \times 9.8 = 490000 \text{ N}$$

$\therefore$ Load acting on each cylindrical support

$$F = \frac{mg}{4} = \frac{490000}{4} \text{ N} = 122500 \text{ N}$$

Inner radius of each column $(r_1) = 30 \text{ cm} = 0.3 \text{ m}$

Outer radius of each column $(r_2) = 60 \text{ cm} = 0.6 \text{ m}$

$\therefore$ Area of cross-section of each cylindrical column

$$A = \pi r_2^2 - \pi r_1^2 = \pi (r_2^2 - r_1^2)$$

$$= 3.14 [(0.6)^2 - (0.3)^2] = 3.14 \times 0.27 \text{ m}^2$$

Young's modulus $(Y) = 2 \times 10^{11}$ Pa

Compressional strain of each column = ?

$$\text{Young's modulus } (Y) = \frac{\text{Compressional stress}}{\text{Compressional strain}}$$

or Compressional strain $= \dfrac{\text{Compressional stress}}{\text{Young's modulus}}$

$$= \frac{F/A}{Y} = \frac{F}{AY}$$

$$= \frac{122500}{(3.14 \times 0.27) \times 2 \times 10^{11}}$$

$$= 0.722 \times 10^{-6} = 7.22 \times 10^{-7}$$

32. Two wires of diameter 0.25 cm, one made of steel and other made of brass are loaded as shown in Fig. The unloaded length of steel wire is 1.5 m and that of brass wire is 1.0 m. Young's modulus of steel is 2.0×10^{11} Pa. Compute the elongations of steel and brass wires.
$(1 \text{ Pa} = 1 \text{ N/m}^2)$. **[NCERT]**

Sol. Given, diameter of wires $(2r) = 0.25$ cm

$\therefore \qquad r = 0.125 \text{ cm} = 1.25 \times 10^{-3}$ m

For steel wire,

Load $(F_1) = (4 + 6)$ kgf

$\qquad = 10 \times 9.8 \text{ N} = 98$ N

Length of steel wire $(l_1) = 1.5$ m

Young's modulus $(Y_1) = 2.0 \times 10^{11}$ Pa

Young's modulus $(Y) = \dfrac{F_1 \times l_1}{A_1 \times \Delta l_1}$

$\therefore$ Change in length $(\Delta l_1) = \dfrac{F_1 \times l_1}{A_1 \times Y_1} = \dfrac{F_1 \times l_1}{\pi r_1^2 \times Y_1}$

$$= \frac{98 \times 1.5}{3.14 \times (1.25 \times 10^{-3})^2 \times 2.0 \times 10^{11}}$$

$$= 1.5 \times 10^{-4} \text{ m}$$

For brass wire,

Load $(F_2) = 6$ kgf $= 6 \times 9.8 \text{ N} = 58.8$ N

Length of brass wire $(l_2) = 1.0$ m

Young's modulus $(Y_2) = 0.91 \times 10^{11}$ Pa

Change in length $(\Delta l_2) = \dfrac{F_2 \times l_2}{\pi r_2^2 \times Y_2}$

$$= \frac{58.8 \times 1.0}{3.14 \times (1.25 \times 10^{-3})^2 \times 0.91 \times 10^{11}}$$

$$= 1.3 \times 10^{-4} \text{ m}$$

33. A rod of length 1.05 m having negligible mass is supported at its ends by two wires of steel (wire A) and aluminium (wire B) of equal lengths as shown in Fig. The cross-sectional areas of wires A and B are 1 mm^2 and 2 mm^2, respectively. Young's modulus of elasticity for steel and aluminium are 2×10^{11} and 7×10^{11} N/m^2, respectively.

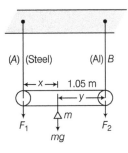

At what point along the rod should a mass m be suspended in order to produce (i) equal stresses and (ii) equal strains in both steel and aluminium wires. **[NCERT]**

Sol. Let the length of wires A and B is equal to L and their area of cross-section be A_1 and A_2, respectively.

Given, $\qquad A_1 = 1 \text{ mm}^2 = 1 \times 10^{-6} \text{ m}^2$

$$A_2 = 2 \text{ mm}^2 = 2 \times 10^{-6} \text{ m}^2$$

$$Y_{\text{steel}} = 2 \times 10^{11} \text{ N/m}^2$$

$$Y_{\text{Al}} = 7.0 \times 10^{10} \text{ N/m}^2$$

Let F_1 and F_2 be the tensions in the two wires, respectively.

(i) When equal stresses are produced, then

$$\frac{F_1}{A_1} = \frac{F_2}{A_2}$$

or $\qquad \dfrac{F_1}{F_2} = \dfrac{A_1}{A_2} = \dfrac{1 \times 10^{-6}}{2 \times 10^{-6}}$ or $\dfrac{F_1}{F_2} = \dfrac{1}{2}$ ...(i)

Let mass m be suspended at distance x from steel wire A.

Taking moment of forces about the point of suspension of mass from the rod, we get

$$F_1 \times x = F_2 \times (1.05 - x)$$

or $\qquad \dfrac{F_1}{F_2} = \dfrac{(1.05 - x)}{x}$ ...(ii)

From Eqs. (i) and (ii), we get

$$\frac{1}{2} = \frac{(1.05 - x)}{x}$$

$$x = 2.10 - 2x$$

or $\qquad 3x = 2.10$

or $\qquad x = 0.70$m

$\therefore$ The mass m must be suspended at a distance 0.70 m from steel wire A.

(ii) Young's modulus $(Y) = \dfrac{\text{Stress}}{\text{Strain}}$

$\therefore \qquad \text{Strain} = \dfrac{\text{Stress}}{Y} = \dfrac{F/A}{Y}$

For steel wire A, $(\text{Strain})_{\text{steel}} = \dfrac{F_1}{A_1 Y_1}$

For aluminium wire B,

$$(\text{Strain})_{Al} = \frac{F_2}{A_2 Y_2}$$

When equal strains are produced in both wires, then

$$\frac{F_1}{A_1 Y_1} = \frac{F_2}{A_2 Y_2}$$

or

$$\frac{F_1}{F_2} = \frac{A_1 Y_1}{A_2 Y_2} \qquad \qquad \text{...(iii)}$$

$\therefore$ From Eqs. (ii) and (iii), we get

$$\frac{(1.05 - x)}{x} = \frac{A_1 Y_2}{A_2 Y_2}$$

$$= \frac{1 \times 10^{-6}}{2 \times 10^{-6}} \times \frac{2 \times 10^{11}}{7 \times 10^{10}}$$

$$\frac{(1.05 - x)}{x} = \frac{10}{7}$$

$$10x = 7.35 - 7x$$

$$\Rightarrow \qquad 17x = 7.35 \text{ or } x = \frac{7.35}{17}$$

$$x = 0.43 \text{ m}$$

$\therefore$ The mass m must be suspended at a distance 0.43 m from the steel with A.

34. A rubber string 10 m long is suspended from a rigid support at its one end. Calculate the extension in the string due to its own weight. The density of rubber is 1.5×10^3 kg/m³ and Young's modulus for the rubber is 5×10^6 N/m². The breaking stress for a metal is 7.8×10^9 N/m².

Calculate the maximum length of the wire made of this metal which may be suspended without breaking. The density of metal $= 7.8 \times 10^3$ kg/m³.

Sol. $l = 10$ m, $\rho = 1.5 \times 10^3$ kg/m³

$Y = 5 \times 10^6$ N/m²

We know, $Y = \dfrac{Fl}{A\Delta l}$

Efficient force $= Mg$

Consider a small length dy at a distance y from free end.

The length above this, $(l - y)$ will experience a force of

$$F_{dy} = \frac{M}{l}(dy).gdy$$

$\therefore$ Extension $dl = \dfrac{Fl}{AY}$

$$\Rightarrow \qquad dl = \frac{(l - y)}{AY} \cdot \frac{M}{l} gdy = \frac{Mg}{lAY}(l - y)dy$$

$$\left.\begin{array}{l}\text{Net extension due} \\ \text{to its own weight}\end{array}\right\} = \int dl$$

$$= \frac{Mg}{AYl}\int_0^l (l - y)dy = \frac{Mg}{lAY}\left[ly - \frac{y^2}{2}\right]_0^l = \frac{Mgl}{2AY}$$

Net extension $= \dfrac{Mgl}{2AY} = \dfrac{Mgl^2}{2YV} = \dfrac{\rho g l^2}{2Y}$

Extension of rubber string

$$= \frac{1.5 \times 10^3 \times 10 \times 10^2}{2 \times 5 \times 10^6} = 0.15 \text{ m}$$

Breaking stress for a metal $= 7.8 \times 10^9$ N/m²

Density $= 7.8 \times 10^3$ kg/m³.

$$\text{Stress} = \frac{\text{Force}}{\text{Area}} = \frac{Mg}{A} = \frac{Mgl}{Al} = \frac{Mgl}{\text{Volume}} = \rho g l$$

If $\rho g l >$ Breaking stress, the wire will break.

$$\therefore \qquad l \leq \frac{7.8 \times 10^9}{\rho g}, l \leq \frac{7.8 \times 10^9}{7.8 \times 10^3 \times 10}$$

i.e. $\qquad l \leq 10^5$ m

Maximum length of wire $= 10^5$ m

35. Compute the Bulk modulus of water from the following data; initial volume = 100.0 L, pressure increase = 100.0 atm (1 atm = 1.013 $\times 10^5$ Pa), final volume = 100.5 L. Compare the Bulk modulus of water with that of air (at constant temperature). Explain in simple terms, why the ratio is so large? **[NCERT]**

Sol. Given, initial volume $(V_1) = 100.0$ L

Final volume $(V_2) = 100.5$ L

$\therefore$ Increase in volume $(\Delta V) = V_2 - V_1$

$$= 100.5 - 100.0 = 0.5 \text{ L}$$

$$= 0.5 \times 10^{-3} \text{ m}^3 \qquad [\because 1 \text{ L} = 10^{-3}\text{m}^3]$$

Increase in pressure,

$$(\Delta p) = 100.0 \text{ atm}$$

$$= 100.0 \times 1.013 \times 10^5 \text{ Pa}$$

$$[\because 1 \text{ atm} = 1.013 \times 10^5 \text{Pa}]$$

$$= 1.013 \times 10^7 \text{ Pa}$$

Bulk modulus of water

$$(B_w) = \frac{\Delta p}{(\Delta V / V)}$$

$$= \frac{\Delta p V}{\Delta V} = \frac{1.013 \times 10^7 \times 100 \times 10^{-3}}{0.5 \times 10^{-3}}$$

$$= \frac{10.13}{5} \times 10^9 \text{ Pa}$$

$$= 2.026 \times 10^9 \text{ Pa}$$

Bulk modulus of air $(B_a) = 1.0 \times 10^5$ Pa

$$\therefore \qquad \frac{\text{Bulk modulus of water }(B_w)}{\text{Bulk modulus of air }(B_a)} = \frac{2.026 \times 10^9}{1.0 \times 10^5}$$

$$= 2.026 \times 10^4$$

This ratio is too large as gases are more compressible than those of liquids. In liquids, interatomic forces are more strong than that for gases.

36. The edge of an aluminium cube is 10 cm long. One face of the cube is firmly fixed to a vertical wall. A mass of 100 kg is then attached to the opposite face of the cube.

The shear modulus of aluminium is 25 GPa. What is the vertical deflection of this face?

[NCERT]

Sol.

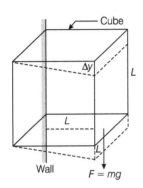

Given, side of a cube (l) = 10 cm = 0.1 m

Area of its each face (A) = l^2 = $(0.1)^2$ = 0.01 m^2

Load (m) = 100 kg

Tangential force acting on one face of the cube,

$$F = mg = 100 \times 9.8 = 980 \, \text{N}$$

Shear stress acting on this face = $\dfrac{F}{A} = \dfrac{980}{0.01} \, \text{N/m}^2$

$$= 9.8 \times 10^4 \, \text{N/m}^2$$

Shear modulus of aluminium (η) = 25 GPa

$$= 25 \times 10^9 \, \text{N/m}^2$$

Shear modulus (η) = $\dfrac{\text{Shearing stress}}{\text{Shearing strain}}$

or shearing strain $\left(\dfrac{\Delta L}{L}\right) = \dfrac{\text{Shearing stress}}{\text{Shear modulus}}$

or $\quad \Delta L = \dfrac{\text{Shearing stress}}{\text{Shear modulus}} \times L = \dfrac{9.8 \times 10^4}{25 \times 10^9} \times 0.1$

$$= 0.0392 \times 10^{-5} \, \text{m}$$

$$= 3.92 \times 10^{-7} \, \text{m}$$

ASSESS YOUR TOPICAL UNDERSTANDING

OBJECTIVE Type Questions

1. On applying a stress of 20×10^8 Nm^{-2}, the length of a perfectly elastic wire is doubled. Its Young's modulus will be
   (a) 40×10^8 Nm^{-2}
   (b) 20×10^8 Nm^{-2}
   (c) 10×10^8 Nm^{-2}
   (d) 5×10^8 Nm^{-2}

2. A wire of length 2 m is made from 10 cm^3 of copper. A force F is applied so that its length increases by 2 mm. Another wire of length 8 m is made from the same volume of copper. If the force F is applied to it, its length will increase by
   (a) 0.8 cm
   (b) 1.6 cm
   (c) 2.4 cm
   (d) 3.2 cm

3. In steel, the Young's modulus and the strain at the breaking point are 2×10^{11} Nm^{-2} and 0.15, respectively. The stress at the breaking point for steel is therefore
   (a) 1.33×10^{11} Nm^{-2}
   (b) 1.33×10^{12} Nm^{-2}
   (c) 7.5×10^{-13} Nm^{-2}
   (d) 3×10^{10} Nm^{-2}

4. Elasticity of a material can be altered by
   (a) annealing
   (b) hammering
   (c) adding impurities
   (d) All of these

5. Two wires of the same material and length but diameter in the ratio 1 : 2 are stretched by the same load. The ratio of elastic potential energy per unit volume for the two wires is
   (a) 1 : 1
   (b) 2 : 1
   (c) 4 : 1
   (d) 16 : 1

Answers

| 1. (b) | 2. (d) | 3. (d) | 4. (d) | 5. (d) |

VERY SHORT ANSWER Type Questions

6. What are the factors on which the modulus of elasticity depends?

7. What is the value of bulk modulus for an incompressible liquid?

SHORT ANSWER Type Questions

8. A wire elongates by 8 mm when a load of 9 kg is suspended from it. What is the elongation when its radius is doubled, if all other quantities are the same as before? **[Ans. 2 mm]**

9. Find the change in volume which 1cc of water at the surface will undergo, when it is taken to the bottom of the lake 100m deep, given that volume elasticity is 22000 atmospheres **[Ans. 0.00044 cc]**

10. A square lead slab of side 50 cm and thickness 10 cm is subjected to a shearing force (on its narrow edge) of 9.0×10^4 N. The lower edge is reveted to the floor. How much will the upper edge be displaced? Modulus of rigidity of lead = 5.6×10^9 N/m²

[**Ans.** 0.16 mm]

LONG ANSWER Type I Questions

11. A cube of aluminium of each side 4 cm is subjected to a tangential (shearing) force. The top face of the cube is sheared through 0.012 cm with respect to the bottom face.
Find (i) shearing strain (ii) shearing stress and (iii) the shearing force. Given, $\eta = 2.08 \times 10^{11}$ dyne cm⁻².

12. Two cylinders A and B of radii r and $2r$ are soldered co-axially. The free end of A is clamped and the free end of B is twisted by an angle ϕ. Find twist at the junction taking the material of two cylinders to be same and of equal length.

13. A metal bar of length L and area of cross-section A, is rigidly clamped between two walls. The Young's modulus of its material is Y and the coefficient of linear expansion is α. The bar is heated so that its temperature is increased from 0 to $\theta°$C. Find the force exerted at the ends of the bar.

14. A wire of length l and area of cross-section A is stretched by the application of a force. If the Young's modulus is Y, then what is the work done per unit volume?

LONG ANSWER Type II Questions

15. A slightly tapering wire of length l and end radii a and b on both sides is subjected to the stretching forces F on both sides as shown in figure. If Y is the Young's modulus of the wire, then calculate the extension produced in the wire.

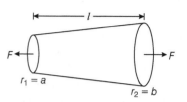

16. Four identical cylindrical columns of steel support a big structure of mass 50000 kg. The inner and outer radii of each column are 30 cm and 40 cm, respectively. Assume the load distribution to be uniform, calculate the compressional strain of each column. The Young's modulus of steel is 2.0×10^{11} Pa.

17. A composite wire of diameter 1 cm consisting of copper and steel wire of lengths 2.2 m and 2.0 m, respectively.
Total extension of the wire, when stretched by a force is 1.2 mm. Calculate the force, given that Young's modulus for copper is 1.1×10^{11} Pa and for steel is 2.0×10^{11} Pa.

18. A light rod of length 2m is suspended from the ceiling horizontally by means of two vertical wires of equal length tied to its ends.
One of the wires is made of steel and is of cross-sectional area 0.1 sq cm and the other is of brass of cross-sectional area 0.2 sq cm. Find out the position along the rod at which a weight may be hung to produce
(i) equal stress in both wires,
(ii) equal strain in both wires.
Given, Y for steel = 20×10^{11} dyne cm⁻² and Y for brass = 10×10^{11} dyne cm⁻².

SUMMARY

- Materials having a definite shape and volume are known as **solids** or rigid bodies.
- A body that returns to its original shape and size on the removal of deforming force is called elastic body and this property is called **elasticity**.
- If a body does not show any tendency to regain its original shape and size even after the removal of deforming force are called plastic body and this property is called **plasticity**.
- The internal restoring force acting per unit area of a deformed force is called **stress**.

  i.e
  $$\text{Stress} = \frac{F}{A}$$

  SI unit of stress is N/m^2 or pascal
- The restoring forces per unit area act perpendicular to the surface of the body are called **normal forces**.
- When there is an increase in the length or the extension of the body in the direction of the force applied then it is called **tensile stress**.
- When there is a decrease in the length or the compression of the body due to the deforming force applied normally on the body then it is called **compressive stress.**
- If a body is subjected to a uniform force from all sides, then the corresponding stress is called **bulk stress** or **hydraulic stress** or volumetric stress.
- **Strain** is defined as the ratio of change in configuration to the original configuration.
- The materials which can be elastically stretched to large values of strain are called **elastomers**.
- **Longitudinal strain** (ε) is the change in length per unit original length, when the body is deformed by external forces,

  i.e.
  $$\varepsilon = \frac{\Delta L}{L}$$

- **Volumetric strain** is the change in volume per unit original volume, when the body is deformed by external forces. i.e. $\varepsilon = \frac{\Delta V}{V}$.

- **Shearing strain** is the deforming forces produce a change in the shape of the body, i.e. $\theta = \tan\theta = \frac{\Delta L}{L}$.

- The material which have large plastic range of extension are called **ductile material.**
- The materials which have very small range of plastic extension are called **brittle material.**
- Within elastic limit, the stress developed is directly proportional to the strain produced in a body. This is **Hooke's law.**
- From **Hooke's law**, stress $\propto$ strain.
  $$\Rightarrow \qquad \text{Stress} = E \times \text{Strain, here } E \text{ is modulus of elasticity.}$$
- The ratio of longitudinal stress (σ) to the longitudinal strain (ε) within the elastic limit is called **Young's modulus** (Y).

  i.e.
  $$Y = \frac{\sigma}{\varepsilon}$$

- Ratio of normal stress to the volumetric strain within the elastic limit is called **Bulk Modulus** (B)

  i.e. $B = \frac{F}{A} / \frac{\Delta v}{v} = \frac{1}{k}$, where $k = $ compressibility
- The ratio of tangential stress to the shear strain within elastic limit is called shear modulus or **modulus of rigidity** (η).

  i.e.
  $$\eta = \frac{F}{A} \cdot \frac{L}{\Delta L}$$

- The ratio of lateral strain to the longitudinal strains within the elastic limit it is called **Poisson's ratio.**
- Potential energy stored in a deformed body.

CHAPTER PRACTICE

OBJECTIVE Type Questions

1. In solids, inter-atomic forces are
   (a) totally repulsive
   (b) totally attractive
   (c) combination of (a) and (b)
   (d) None of the above

2. The nature of molecular forces resembles with the nature of the
   (a) gravitational force   (b) nuclear force
   (c) electromagnetic force   (d) weak force

3. A and B are two wires. The radius of A is twice that of B. They are stretched by the same load. Then, the stress on B is
   (a) equal to that on A (b) four times that on A
   (c) two times that on A (d) half that on A

4. On suspending a weight Mg, the length l of elastic wire having area of cross-section A, becomes double the initial length. The instantaneous stress action on the wire is
   (a) Mg/A (b) $Mg/2A$
   (c) $2Mg/A$ (d) $4Mg/A$

5. A cube of aluminium of side 0.1 m is subjected to a shearing force of 100 N. The top face of the cube is displaced through 0.02 cm with respect to the bottom face. The shearing strain would be
   (a) 0.02   (b) 0.1   (c) 0.005   (d) 0.002

6. A steel rod of length 1 m and radius 10 mm is stretched by a force 100 kN along its length. The stress produced in the rod is $Y_{\text{Steel}} = 2 \times 10^{11}\,\text{Nm}^{-2}$.
   (a) $3.18 \times 10^6\,\text{Nm}^{-2}$ (b) $3.18 \times 10^7\,\text{Nm}^{-2}$
   (c) $3.18 \times 10^8\,\text{Nm}^{-2}$ (d) $3.18 \times 10^9\,\text{Nm}^{-2}$

7. The upper end of a wire of radius 4 mm and length 100 cm is clamped and its other end is twisted through an angle of 30°. Then, angle of shear is
   (a) 12°   (b) 0.12°   (c) 1.2°   (d) 0.012°

8. A copper and a steel wire of the same diameter are connected end to end. A deforming force F is applied to this composite wire which causes a total elongation of 1 cm. The two wires will have
   (a) the same stress and strain
   (b) the same stress but different strain
   (c) the same strain but different stress
   (d) different strains and stress

9. A wire of length L and radius r is rigidly fixed at one end. On stretching the other end of the wire with a force F, the increase in its length is l. If another wire of same material but of length $2L$ and radius $2r$ is stretched with a force of $2F$, the increase in its length will be
   (a) l (b) $2l$
   (c) $l/2$ (d) $l/4$

10. In the given figure, if the dimension of the wire are the same and materials are different, Young's modulus is more for

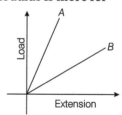

   (a) A (b) B (c) Both   (d) None of these

ASSERTION AND REASON

Direction (Q.Nos. 11-16) *In the following questions, two statements are given- one labelled Assertion (A) and the other labelled Reason (R). Select the correct answer to these questions from the codes (a), (b), (c) and (d) as given below*
   (a) Both Assertion and Reason are true and Reason is the correct explanation of Assertion.
   (b) Both Assertion and Reason are true but Reason is not the correct explanation of Assertion.
   (c) Assertion is true but Reason is false.
   (d) Assertion is false but Reason is true.

11. **Assertion** Stress is the internal force per unit area of a body.
    Reason Rubber is less elastic than steel.

12. **Assertion** When a solid is deformed, the atoms or molecules are displaced from their equilibrium position.
    Reason Due to change in inter-atomic spacing, intermolecular/interatomic forces arise.

13. **Assertion** The restoring force F, on a stretched string for extension x is related to potential energy U as
    $$F = \frac{-dU}{dx}$$
    Reason $F = -kx$ and $U = (1/2)kx^2$, where k is a spring constant for the given stretched string.

14. **Assertion** The strain produced by a hydraulic pressure is volumetric in nature.
    Reason It is a ratio of change in volume (ΔV) of the original volume (V).

15. **Assertion** Young's modulus for a perfectly plastic body is zero.
    Reason For a perfectly plastic body, restoring force is zero.

16. **Assertion** Ropes are always made of a number of thin wires braided together.
    Reason It helps to ease in manufacture, flexibility and strength.

CASE BASED QUESTIONS

Direction (Q. Nos. 17-18) *These questions are case study based questions. Attempt any 4 sub-parts from each question. Each question carries 1 mark.*

17. **Restoring Force due to Stress**

    When a bar of cross-section A is subjected to equal and opposite tensile forces at its ends, then a restoring force equal to the applied force normal to its cross-section comes into existence. This restoring force per unit area of cross-section is known as tensile stress. While when the deforming force acts tangentially to the surface, then this tangential force applied per unit area of cross-section is known as tangential stress. Consider a plane section of the bar whose normal makes an angle θ with the axis of the bar.

    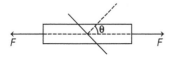

(i) Which of the following property of the bar does not change due to this force?
   (a) Area   (b) Volume
   (c) Shape   (d) Size

(ii) What is the tensile stress on this plane?
   (a) $(F/A)\cos^2\theta$ (b) F/A
   (c) $(F/A)\tan\theta$ (d) $(F/A)\sec^2\theta$

(iii) What is the shearing stress on this plane?
   (a) $\dfrac{F}{2A}\sin 2\theta$ (b) $\dfrac{F}{A}\cos 2\theta$
   (c) $\dfrac{F}{2A}\cos^2\theta$ (d) $\dfrac{F}{4A^2}$

(iv) For what value of θ is the tensile stress maximum?
   (a) $0°$ (b) $90°$
   (c) $45°$ (d) $30°$

(v) For what value of θ is the shearing stress maximum?
   (a) $45°$ (b) $30°$
   (c) $90°$ (d) $60°$

18. **Young's Modulus Experiment**

    A typical experimental arrangement to determine the Young's modulus of a material of wire under tension is shown in figure. It consists of two long straight wires of same length and equal radii suspended side-by-side from a fixed rigid support. The wire A (called the reference wire) carries a millimeter main scale M and a pan to place a weight.

    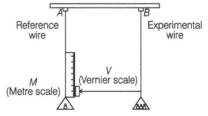

    The wire B (called the experimental wire) of uniform area of cross-section also carries a pan in which known weights can be placed, vernier scale is attached to a pointer at the bottom of experimental wire B and main scale is fixed to the reference wire A.

(i) When a weight is placed in the pan, which type of stress is produced in it,
   (a) Tensile
   (b) Tangential
   (c) Bulk
   (d) Compressive

(ii) The reference wire is used to compensate for any change in length due to change in
(a) length of experimental wire
(b) volume of experimental wire
(c) room temperature
(d) weight of pan

(iii) The difference between which two readings gives the elongation produced in the wire.
(a) Main
(b) Vernier
(c) Reference
(d) Original wire

(iv) Suppose M be the mass of wire that produced an elongation ΔL in the wire, then the applied force is equal to
(a) Mg
(b) Ma
(c) Mv
(d) Mv^2

(v) The Young's modulus of an experimental wire is
(a) $Mg \times L/(\pi r^2 \times \Delta L)$
(b) $Mg \times (\pi r^2 \times \Delta L)/L$
(c) $(\Delta L \times \pi r^2)/Mg \times L$
(d) $Mg \times \pi r^2 \times L/(\Delta L)^2$

Answers

1. (c)	2. (c)	3. (b)	4. (c)	5. (d)
6. (c)	7. (b)	8. (b)	9. (a)	10. (a)
11. (b)	12. (a)	13. (a)	14. (b)	15. (a)
16. (a)				

17.	(i) (b)	(ii) (a)	(iii) (a)	(iv) (a)	(v) (a)
18.	(i) (a)	(ii) (c)	(iii) (b)	(iv) (a)	(v) (a)

VERY SHORT ANSWER Type Questions

19. A wire 50 cm long and 1 sq mm in cross-section has the Young's modulus, $Y = 2 \times 10^{10}$ Nm^{-2}. How much work is done in stretching the wire through 1 mm?
[**Ans.** 2×10^{-2} J]

20. The star Sirius has a mass of 7×10^{30} kg, its distance from the earth is 8×10^{16} m and the mass of the earth is 6×10^{24} kg. Calculate the cross-section of a steel cable that can withstand the gravitational pull between the Sirius and the earth. Given, $G = 6.67 \times 10^{-11}$ Nm^{2}kg^{-2} and breaking stress $= 10^{10}$ Nm^{-2}.
[**Ans.** 44m^2]

21. A solid sphere of radius R made of a material of Bulk modulus B is surrounded by a liquid in a cylindrical container. A massless piston of area

A floats on the surface of the liquid. When a mass M is placed on the piston to compress the liquid, find fractional change in the radius of the sphere.
$$\left[\textbf{Ans.}\ \left(\frac{\Delta R}{R} = \frac{Mg}{3AB}\right)\right]$$

22. A uniform pressure p is exerted on all sides of a solid cube at temperature $t°$ C. By what amount should the temperature of the cube be raised in order to bring its volume back to the volume it had before the pressure was applied, if the Bulk modulus and coefficient of volume expansion of the material are B and γ, respectively?
$$\left[\textbf{Ans.}\ \left(\frac{p}{\gamma B}\right)\right]$$

SHORT ANSWER Type Questions

23. Determine the fractional change in volume as the pressure of the atmosphere 1.0×10^5 Pa around a metal block is reduced to zero by placing the block in vacuum. The Bulk modulus for the block is 1.25×10^{11} Nm^{-2}.
[**Ans.** 8×10^{-7}]

24. (a) Which is more elastic, rubber or glass? Why?
(b) Identical springs of steel and copper are equally stretched. On which spring, more work will have to be done?

25. A lift is tied with thick iron wires and its mass is 1000 kg. If the maximum acceleration of lift is 1.2 ms^{-2} and the maximum safe stress is 1.4×10^8 Nm^{-2}, then find the minimum diameter of the wire. Take, $g = 9.8$ ms^{-2}.
[**Ans.** 0.01 m]

LONG ANSWER Type I Questions

26. Two parallel steel wires A and B are fixed to rigid support at the upper ends and subjected to the same load at the lower ends. The lengths of the wires are in the ratio 4:5 and their radii are in the ratio 4:3. The increase in the length of the wire A is 1 mm. Calculate the increase in the length of the wire B.
[**Ans.** 2.22 mm]

27. Assume that if the shear stress in steel exceeds about 4×10^8 N/m^2, the steel reptures.
Determine the shearing force necessary to (a) shear a steel bolt 1.00 cm in diameter and (b) punch a 1 cm diameter hole in a steel plate 0.500 cm thick.
[**Ans.** 3.14×10^4 N, 6.28×10^4 N]

28. A uniform heavy rod of weight w, cross-sectional area A and length l is hanging from a fixed support. Young's modulus of the material of the rod is Y. Neglecting the lateral contraction, find the elongation produced in the rod.

$$\left[\textbf{Ans. } \frac{wl}{2A\,Y}\right]$$

LONG ANSWER Type II Questions

29. What is the length of a wire that breaks under its own weight when suspended vertically?

Breaking stress $= 5\times10^{7}$ Nm^{-2} and density of the material of the wire $= 3\times10^{3}$ kg/m^{3}.

[**Ans.** 1.67 km]

30. A silica glass rod has a diameter of 1 cm and is 10 cm long. The ultimate strength of glass is 50×10^{6} Nm^{-2}. Estimate the largest mass that can be hung from it without breaking it. Take, $g = 10$ Nkg^{-1}.   [**Ans.** 392.5 kg]

31. Two different types of rubber are found to have the stress-strain curves shown below in figure.

(i) In which significant ways do these curves differ from the stress-strain curve of a metal wire.

(ii) A heavy machine is to be installed in a factory. To absorb vibrations of the machine, a block of rubber is placed between the machinery and the floor. Which of the two rubbers A and B would you prefer to use for this purpose? Why?

(iii) Which of the two rubber materials would you choose for a car tyre?

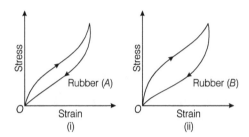

32. Two wires of equal cross-section but one made of steel and the other copper are joined end to end. When the combination is kept under tension, the elongation in the two wires is found to be equal. Given Young's moduli of steel and copper are 2.0×10^{11} Nm^{-2} and 1.1×10^{11} Nm^{-2}. Find the ratio between the lengths of steel and copper wires.   [**Ans.** 20 : 11]

09

Liquids and gases are collectively known as fluids. Fluid flows under the action of an applied force and does not have a shape of its own. It takes the shape of the vessel in which it is placed.

In this chapter, we shall study hydrostatics and hydrodynamics. The study of fluids at rest is known as hydrostatics or **fluid statics**. The study of fluids in motion is named as **hydrodynamics** or **fluid dynamics**.

MECHANICAL PROPERTIES OF FLUIDS

|TOPIC 1|
Hydrostatics

The key property of fluids is that they offer very little resistance to shear stress; their shape changes by application of very small shear stress.

THRUST

The molecules of a fluid kept in a container are in random motion due to their thermal velocities. So, they constantly collide with the walls of the container and rebounding from them, suffering a change in momentum normal to the colliding walls due to which some normal change in momentum is transferred to the walls.

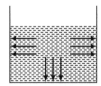

Liquid in a container is exerting thrust

The normal change in momentum transferred to the walls of the container per unit time by the molecules of the fluid is called thrust of the fluid on the container.

Liquid in Equilibrium

When a liquid is in equilibrium, then the net force acting on the liquid always acts perpendicular to its surface.
It can be easily proved as below

Consider a liquid kept in a vessel. Let us suppose that the liquid is in the equilibrium of rest and the net force F makes an angle θ with the direction parallel to the surface of liquid as shown in the figure.

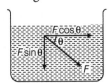

Parallel and perpendicular
components of the force F

The force F can be resolved into two components such as
  (i) $F \cos \theta$ as tangential component acts parallel to the surface of liquid.
  (ii) $F \sin \theta$ as normal component acts perpendicular to the surface of liquid.

Since, the liquid is at rest (i.e. there is no flow of liquid), the tangential component acts parallel to the surface of the liquid must be zero.

i.e. $F \cos \theta = 0$

As F cannot be zero, we have $\cos \theta = 0 \Rightarrow \theta = 90°$

Hence, if a liquid is in equilibrium state of rest, then the net force acting on it is always perpendicular to its surface.

PRESSURE

The pressure of liquid at a point is the thrust (or normal force) exerted by the liquid at rest per unit area around that point. If the total force F acts normally over a flat area A, then, the pressure is

$$p = \frac{\text{thrust}}{\text{area}} \quad \text{or} \quad \boxed{\text{Pressure, } p = \frac{F}{A}}$$

The unit of pressure is **dyne/cm^2** in CGS system and **N/m^2** in SI system and dimensional formula of pressure is $[ML^{-1}T^{-2}]$.

Pressure of 1 N/m^2 is called **1 pascal** in the honour of the French scientist **Blaise Pascal** (1623-1662) who carried out the pioneering studies on fluid pressure.

$$1 \text{Pa (or } 1 \text{N/m}^2) = 10 \text{ dyne/cm}^2$$

The another common unit of pressure is atmosphere (atm). 1 atm is defined as the pressure exerted by the atmosphere at sea level.

$$1 \text{ atm} = 1.013 \times 10^5 \text{ Pa}.$$

If the force is not distributed uniformly over the given surface, then pressure will be different at different points. If a force ΔF acts normally on a small area ΔA surrounding a given point, then pressure at that point will be

$$p = \lim_{\Delta A \to 0} \frac{\Delta F}{\Delta A} = \frac{dF}{dA}$$

Pressure is a scalar quantity, because liquid pressure at a particular point in liquid has same magnitude in all directions. This shows that a definite direction is not associated with liquid pressure.

EXAMPLE |1| **Pressure Exerted by Human Body**
The two thigh bones (femurs), each of cross-sectional area 10 cm^2 support the upper part of a human body of mass 40 kg. Estimate the average pressure sustained by the femurs.   **[NCERT]**

Sol. Given, $A = 20 \times 10^{-4}$ m^2

Weight of body acting vertically downwards

Force on bones, $F = 40$ kg-wt $= 400$ N   [$\because$ $g = 10$ m/s^2]

$$p_{av} = \frac{F}{A} = \frac{400}{20 \times 10^{-4}}$$

$$= 2 \times 10^5 \text{ N/m}^2$$

EXAMPLE |2| **Fluid Pressure Measurement**
Consider a spring having spring constant of 81.75 N/m of pressure measuring device. A force acting on the piston compresses the spring downward and the area of the piston is 3 m^2. Find out the compression in the spring, if the upthrust force exerted by the fluid on the piston is 12 N.

Sol. As the force acting on the piston compresses the spring. This force will be balanced by the force acting upward by the fluid known as **upthrust force**.

$$\therefore \qquad p = \frac{F}{A} = \frac{kx}{A}$$

Given, $F = 12$ N, $A = 3$ m^2 and $k = 81.75$ N/m

From $F = kx$

$$\Rightarrow \qquad x = \frac{F}{k} = \frac{12}{81.75}$$

$$x = 0.146 \text{ m}$$

Hence, compression in the spring is $x = 14.6$ cm

Practical Applications of Pressure

(i) A sharp knife cuts better than a blunt one.

(ii) A camel walks easily on sand while it is difficult to walk on a sand for man.

(iii) Railway tracks are laid on large sized wooden or iron sleepers.

(iv) A sharp needle peers the skin easily but not a dull needle although the force applied in both the cases is the same.

DENSITY AND RELATIVE DENSITY

Density of a substance is defined as mass per unit volume of the substance. It is denoted by ρ.

If M be the mass of a substance of volume V, then density of that substance is given by

$$\boxed{\text{Density, } \rho = \frac{M}{V}}$$

The SI unit of density is kg/m^3 and dimensional formula is $[ML^{-3}]$.

Relative density (or specific gravity) of substance is defined as the ratio of the density of that substance to the density of water at 4°C, i.e.

$$\boxed{\text{Relative density} = \frac{\text{Density of substance}}{\text{Density of water at 4°C}}}$$

It has no unit and no dimensions. It is a positive **scalar quantity**.

The density of water at 4°C is maximum and equal to 1000 kg/m^3.

PASCAL'S LAW

The French scientist **Blaise Pascal** observed that *pressure in a fluid at rest is the same at all points if they are at same height.*

This is known as **Pascal's law**.

Proof of Pascal's Law

It can be proved by using two principles as given below:

(i) The force on any layer of a fluid at rest is normal to the layer.

(ii) Newton's first law of motion

In given figure, consider an element in the interior of a fluid at rest. This element *ABC-DEF* is in the form of a right angled prism. This prismatic element is very small so that every part of it can be considered at the same depth from the liquid surface and therefore, the effect of the gravity is the same at all these points.

Let we extend this element for our clarification. The forces on this element are those exerted by the rest of the fluid and they must be normal to the surfaces of the element as discussed earlier. Suppose, the fluid exert pressures p_a, p_b and p_c on the faces *BEFC*, *ADFC* and *ADEB*, respectively, of this element and the corresponding normal forces on these faces are F_a, F_b and F_c.

Let A_a, A_b and A_c be the respective areas of the three faces.

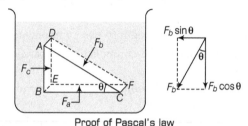

Proof of Pascal's law

In right triangle ABC, $\angle ACB = \theta$

Along horizontal direction, $F_b \sin \theta = F_c$

Along vertical direction, $F_b \cos \theta = F_a$ ...(i)

From the geometry, we have

$A_b \sin \theta = A_c$ and $A_b \cos \theta = A_a$ ...(ii)

From the above equations, we have

$$\frac{F_b \sin \theta}{A_b \sin \theta} = \frac{F_c}{A_c} \text{ and } \frac{F_b \cos \theta}{A_b \cos \theta} = \frac{F_a}{A_a}$$

$$\therefore \quad \frac{F_a}{A_a} = \frac{F_b}{A_b} = \frac{F_c}{A_c}$$

$$\Rightarrow \quad \boxed{p_a = p_b = p_c}$$

Hence, the pressure exerted by the fluid at rest on a body in the fluid is same in all directions. Thus, pressure is not a vector quantity because no direction can be assigned to it.

e.g. Consider a horizontal bar of uniform cross-section is placed in the fluid at rest. The bar is in equilibrium because the horizontal forces exerted at its two ends are balanced or the pressures at the two ends are equal. This proves that for a liquid in equilibrium, the pressure is same at all points in a horizontal plane.

Variation of Pressure with Depth

Consider a fluid at rest having density ρ contained in a cylindrical vessel as shown in figure. Let the two points A and B separated by a vertical distance h.

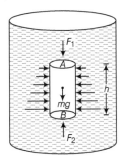

Fluid under gravity

Now, we consider an imaginary cylinder of fluid of cross-sectional area a, such that points A and B lie on its upper and lower circular faces, respectively. Then, weight of fluid cylinder acting downwards,

$$w = m \times g = \text{volume} \times \text{density} \times g = Ah\rho g$$

where, $V = A \times h$

As the fluid is at rest, the resultant horizontal forces should be zero and the resultant vertical forces should balance the weight of the element.

$\therefore$ Net downward force = net upward force

$$F_1 + w = F_2$$

where, F_1 is the force acting downwards at the top and F_2 is the force acting upward at the bottom.

$$F_2 - F_1 = w$$
$$p_2 A - p_1 A = Ah\rho g$$
$$A(p_2 - p_1) = A(h\rho g)$$

$$\boxed{\text{Pressure difference, } p_2 - p_1 = h\rho g}$$

Hence, the pressure difference depends on the vertical height (i.e. distance between point A and point B), density of the fluid and the acceleration due to gravity.

If point A is shifted to the fluid surface, which is open to the atmosphere, then replace p_1 by atmospheric pressure p_a and p_2 by p, we get

$$\boxed{\text{Pressure, } p = p_a + h\rho g}$$

Thus, the pressure p at depth below the surface of a liquid open to the atmosphere is greater than atmospheric pressure by an amount $\rho g h$.

This excess of pressure at depth h in liquid $p - p_a = h\rho g$, i.e. called **gauge pressure** at point B, while point A is at the liquid surface.

Thus, gauge pressure at a point in a fluid is the difference of total pressure at that point and atmospheric pressure.

EXAMPLE |3| **A Swimmer Experiences the Pressure**
What is the pressure on a swimmer 10 m below the surface of a lake? **[NCERT]**

Sol. Here, $h = 10$ m and $\rho = 1000$ kg/m^3
$$g = 10 \text{ m/s}^2$$
$$p = p_a + \rho g h$$
$$= 1.01 \times 10^5 \text{ Pa} + 1000 \text{ kg/m}^3 \times 10 \text{ m/s}^2 \times 10 \text{ m}$$
$$= 2.01 \times 10^5 \text{ Pa} \simeq 2 \text{ atm}$$

EXAMPLE |4| **Pressure at a depth in ocean**
At a depth 1000 m in an ocean
(i) What is the absolute pressure?
(ii) What is the gauge pressure?
(iii) Find the force acting on the window of area 20 cm $\times$ 20 cm of a submarine at this depth, the interior of which is maintained at sea-level atmospheric pressure. (The density of sea water is 1.03×10^3 kgm^{-3}, $g = 10$ ms^{-2}) **[NCERT]**

Sol. Given, $h = 1000$ m and $\rho = 1.03 \times 10^3$ kg/m^3
We know, $p = p_a + \rho g h$
$$p = 1.01 \times 10^5 + 1.03 \times 10^3 \times 10 \times 1000$$
$$p = 104.01 \times 10^5 \text{ Pa} \approx 104 \text{ atm}$$
Now, $p_g = p - p_a$
$$p_g = 104 \text{ atm} - 1 \text{ atm}$$
$$p_a = 1 \text{ atm}$$
$\because \qquad p_g = 103 \text{ atm}$
The pressure outside the submarine while pressure inside, it is p_a.
Given, $A = 400$ cm$^2 = 0.04$ m^2.
The net pressure acting on the window is gauge pressure, then $p_g = \dfrac{F}{A}$
$\Rightarrow \qquad F = p_g A$
or $\qquad F = 103 \times 10^5 \times 0.04 = 4.12 \times 10^5$ N

Hydrostatic Paradox

Let us take three vessels A, B and C of different shapes which are open both at the top and the bottom ends. These vessels are connected with a common pipe at the bottom as shown in figure below.

Now, fill the three vessels with the same liquid. The reading, we note that pressure will be same even though the quantity of liquid in different vessels is different.

It means the liquid pressure at a point is independent of the quantity of liquid but depends upon the depth of point below the liquid surface.

This is known as **hydrostatic paradox.**

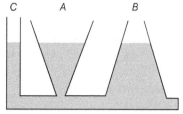

Three vessels *A*, *B* and *C* containing different amounts of liquids

Hence, the pressure exerted by a liquid depends only on the height of fluid column and is independent of the shape of the containing vessel.

Atmospheric Pressure and Gauge Pressure

The gaseous envelope surrounding the earth is called **earth's atmosphere.** The pressure exerted by the atmosphere is called **atmospheric pressure.** The force exerted by air column of air on a unit area on the earth's surface is equal to the atmospheric pressure, it is denoted by p_a.

The value of atmospheric pressure on the surface of the earth at sea level called 1 atmosphere (1 atm), it is nearly about $1.013 \times 10^5 \, \text{N}/\text{m}^2$.

The earth's atmosphere exerts a huge pressure, which can be demonstrated by the following methods.

Mercury Barometer

An Italian scientist **Evangelista Torricelli** (1608-1647), first devised an instrument to measure atmospheric pressure. It is known as **barometer.** A long glass tube closed at one end and filled with mercury is inverted into a trough of mercury.

We find that mercury column in the tube has height of about **76 cm** above the mercury level in the trough.

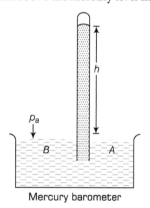

Mercury barometer

If the given tube is inclined or raised up or lowered in mercury trough, the vertical height of mercury level in tube is always found to be constant.

The space above mercury in the tube contains mercury vapour and its pressure can be neglected.

Let us consider points *B* and *A* as shown in the figure. Then, $p_A = p_B$ = atmospheric pressure, p_a.

Let h is the height of mercury column and ρ is the density of mercury,

So, $$p_A = p_B = p_a = h\rho g$$

By putting values atmospheric pressure,

$$h = 0.76 \, \text{m}$$
$$\rho = 13.6 \times 10^3 \, \text{kg}/\text{m}^3$$
$$g = 9.8 \, \text{m}/\text{s}^2$$
$$p_a = 0.76 \times 13.6 \times 10^3 \times 9.8$$
$$= 1.013 \times 10^5 \, \text{N}/\text{m}^2$$
$$= 1.013 \times 10^5 \, \text{Pa}$$

(This is the atmospheric pressure at the sea level).

The pressure can also be stated in terms of cm or mm of mercury (Hg). A pressure equivalent of 1 mm is called a **torr** named after Torricelli.

Open Tube Manometer

Open tube manometer is used to measure pressure difference. It consists of a U-shape tube containing a liquid having low density such as oil to measure the small pressure difference and mercury as the high density liquid to measure the large pressure differences. One end of the tube is open to the atmosphere and the other end is joined with a flask, whose pressure we want to know.

The arrangement is shown in figure.

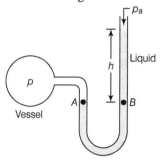

Open tube manometer

The pressure p at point *A* is equal to pressure at point *B*.

$\therefore$ $p_A = p_B$ (Pascal's law)

As $p_A = p_a + h\rho g$

So, $p_B = p_a + \rho g h$

Absolute Pressure and Gauge Pressure

The total or actual pressure p at a point is called absolute pressure. Gauge pressure is the difference between the actual pressure (or absolute pressure) at a point and the atmospheric pressure, i.e. $p_g = p - p_a = h\rho g$

The gauge pressure is proportional to h. Many pressure measuring devices directly measure the gauge pressure. These include the tyre pressure gauge and the blood pressure gauge (sphygmomanometer).

EXAMPLE |5| Absolute and Gauge Pressure in a Tank
What is the absolute and gauge pressure of the gas above the liquid surface in the tank shown in figure? Density of oil = 820 kg-m^{-3}, density of mercury = 13.6×10^3 kgm^{-3}. Given, 1 atm pressure = 1.01×10^5 Pa.   [NCERT]

Sol. As the points A and B are at the same level in the mercury column, so $p_A = p_B$

Now, $p_A = p + (1.50 + 1.00) \times 820 \times 9.8$

where, p is the pressure of the gas in the tank.

And $p_B = p' + (1.50 + 0.75) \times 13.6 \times 10^3 \times 9.8$

where, p' is the atmospheric pressure.

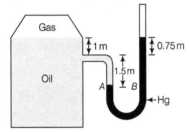

As, $p_A = p_B$

$p - p' = 2.25 \times 13.6 \times 10^3 \times 9.8 - 2.50 \times 820 \times 9.8$

$= 3 \times 10^5 - 0.2 \times 10^5 = 2.8 \times 10^5$ Pa

∴ Gauge pressure

= absolute pressure – atmospheric pressure.

$p_g = p - p' = 2.8 \times 10^5$ Pa $[\because p' = p_a]$

Absolute pressure

= gauge pressure + atmospheric pressure

$p = 2.8 \times 10^5 + 1.01 \times 10^5 = 3.81 \times 10^5$ Pa

Height of Atmosphere

The standard atmospheric pressure is 1.013×10^5 Pa. If the atmosphere of the earth has uniform density $\rho = 1.29$ kg/m^3, then the height h of the air column which exerts the standard atmospheric pressure is given by $h\rho g = 1.013 \times 10^5$

$$h = \frac{1.013 \times 10^5}{\rho g} = \frac{1.013 \times 10^5}{1.29 \times 9.8} \text{ m}$$

$$h = 7.95 \times 10^3 \text{ m} \approx 8 \text{ km}$$

In fact, both the density of air and the value of g decrease with height and the earth's atmosphere extends up to 100 km.

Different Units of Pressure

(i) **Atmosphere** (atm) It is the pressure exerted by 76 cm of Hg column (at 0°C, 95° latitude and mean sea level).

(ii) In meteorology, the atmospheric pressure is measured in bar and millibar. 1 bar

$$= 10^5 \text{ Pa} = 10^6 \text{ dyne/cm}^2$$

$$1 \text{ millibar} = 10^{-3} \text{ bar} = 100 \text{ Pa}$$

(iii) Atmospheric pressure is also measured in torr a unit named after Torricelli.

$$1 \text{ torr} = 1 \text{ mm of Hg} = 133 \text{ Pa}$$

$$1 \text{ atm} = 1.013 \text{ bar} = 760 \text{ torr}$$

Note
• A drop in the atmospheric pressure by 10 mm of Hg or more is a sign of an approaching storm.
• The gauge pressure may be positive or negative depending on $p > p_a$ or $p < p_a$. In inflated tyres or the human circulatory system, the absolute pressure is greater than atmospheric pressure, so gauge pressure is positive, called the **over pressure**.
• However, when we suck a fluid through a straw, the absolute pressure in our lungs is less than atmospheric pressure and so, the gauge pressure is negative.

Pascal's Law for Transmission of Fluid Pressure

Pascal's law states that, **whenever external pressure is applied on any part of a fluid contained in a vessel at rest, it is transmitted undiminished and equally in all directions.**

This is the Pascal's law for transmission of fluid pressure and has many applications in daily life.

Applications of Pascal's Law

(i) Hydraulic Lift

Hydraulic lift is an application of Pascal's law. It is used to lift heavy loads. It is a force multiplier.

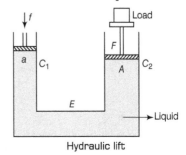

Hydraulic lift

It consists of two cylinders C_1 and C_2 connected to each other by a pipe E. These cylinders are fitted with water-tight frictionless pistons of different cross-sectional areas. These cylinders and the pipe contain a liquid.

Suppose, a downward force f is applied on the smaller piston of cross-sectional area a. Then, pressure exerted on the liquid,

$$p = \frac{f}{a}$$

According to Pascal's law, this pressure p is transmitted to the larger piston of cross-sectional area A, then upward force on larger piston C_2 is

$$F = p \times A = \frac{f}{a} \times A = \frac{A}{a} \times f$$

$$\boxed{\text{Upward force on a larger piston, } F = \frac{A}{a} f}$$

As, $A > a$, therefore, $F > f$.

This shows that the small forces applied on the smaller piston (acting downward) will be appearing as a very large force (acting upward) on the larger piston. As a result of it, a heavy load placed on the larger piston is easily lifted upwards.

EXAMPLE |6| Force Exerted by Larger Piston

Two syringes of different cross-sections (without needles) filled with water are connected with a tightly fitted rubber tube. Diameters of the smaller and larger piston are 1.0 cm and 3.0 cm, respectively.

(i) Find the force exerted on the larger piston when a force of 10 N is applied to the smaller piston.

(ii) If the smaller piston is pushed in through 6.0 cm, how much does the larger piston move out? **[NCERT]**

Sol. (i) Here, $A_1 = \pi \left(\frac{D_1}{2}\right)^2$, $A_2 = \pi \left(\frac{D_2}{2}\right)^2$

$$A_1 = \pi \left(\frac{3}{2} \times 10^{-2}\right)^2 \text{ m}^2,$$

$$A_2 = \pi \left(\frac{1}{2} \times 10^{-2}\right)^2 \text{ m}^2$$

∵ Pressure is transmitted undiminished through water, so,

$$\therefore \quad F_2 = \frac{A_2}{A_1} F_1 = \frac{\pi \left(\frac{3}{2} \times 10^{-2}\right)^2}{\pi \left(\frac{1}{2} \times 10^{-2}\right)^2} \times 10$$

$$\Rightarrow \quad F_2 = 90 \text{ N}$$

(ii) Volume covered by the movement of smaller piston inwards is equal to volume moved outwards due to

the larger piston.

∵ Water is incompressible

∴
$$L_1 A_1 = L_2 A_2$$

$$L_2 = \frac{A_1}{A_2} L_1 = \frac{\pi \left(\frac{1}{2} \times 10^{-2}\right)^2}{\pi \left(\frac{3}{2} \times 10^{-2}\right)^2} \times 6 \times 10^{-2}$$

$$L_2 = 0.67 \times 10^{-2} \text{ m} = 0.67 \text{ cm}$$

Atmospheric pressure is common to both pistons and has been ignored.

EXAMPLE |7| Pressure needed to lift a car

In a car lift compressed air exerts a force F_1 on a small piston having a radius of 5.0 cm. This pressure is transmitted to a second piston of radius 15 cm. If the mass of the car to be lifted to 1350 kg, calculate F_1. What is the pressure necessary to accomplish this task? $(g = 9.8 \text{ ms}^{-2})$. **[NCERT]**

Sol. Since, the pressure is transmitted undiminished through the fluid, calculate the force F_2 exerting by the car.

Given, $r_1 = 5 \text{ cm} = 0.05 \text{ m}$, $r_2 = 15 \text{cm} = 0.15 \text{ m}$, $m = 1350 \text{ kg}$

$$F_2 = mg = 1350 \times 9.81 \text{ N}$$

As the pressure through air is transmitted equally in all directions, so that the pressure p_1 and p_2 will be same.

$$p_1 = p_2$$

$$\Rightarrow \quad \frac{F_1}{A_1} = \frac{F_2}{A_2}$$

$$\Rightarrow \quad \frac{F_1}{\pi r_1^2} = \frac{F_2}{\pi r_2^2}$$

$$\therefore \quad F_1 = F_2 \times \left(\frac{r_1}{r_2}\right)^2$$

$$= 1350 \times 9.81 \times \left(\frac{5}{15}\right)^2$$

$$\approx 1.5 \times 10^3 \text{ N}$$

Now, the required air pressure necessary to lift the car can be calculated.

The air pressure p which will produce the force of

$$1.5 \times 10^3 \text{ N is } p = \frac{F_1}{A_1} = \frac{1.5 \times 10^3}{\pi (0.05)^2} \Rightarrow p = 1.9 \times 10^5 \text{ Pa}$$

EXAMPLE |8| Work Done by Hydraulic Lift

Consider the hydraulic lift having small cylindrical piston and larger piston with radii 4.0 cm and 16 cm, respectively. If a truck of mass 3000 kg is placed on the larger piston, then find out the force must be applied to the small piston to lift the truck. Also find how far must the small piston move down to lift the truck through a height of 0.20 m. Assume initially these two pistons are at the same height. (Take $g = 10 \text{ m/s}^2$)

A downward force F_1 is applied to a piston with a small area or smaller piston and a downward force with magnitude F_2 equal to the weight of the truck is applied on the larger piston.

Sol. Given, $r_1 = 4.0$ cm $= 0.04$ m,
$$r_2 = 16.0 \text{ cm} = 0.16 \text{ m},$$
$$m = 3000 \text{ kg}, d_2 = 0.20 \text{ m}$$
Force $F_2 =$ weight of the truck $= mg = 3000 \times 10$
$$F_2 = 30000 \text{ N}$$

From Pascal's law, the pressure at given level is the same throughout the hydraulic fluid. Since, the piston are at the same level. Therefore, the downward force on the smaller piston can be determined as

$$F_1 = \frac{A_1}{A_2} \times F_2$$

where, $A_1 = \pi r_1^2 = \pi (0.04)^2 = 0.005024$
$$A_2 = \pi r_2^2 = \pi (0.16)^2 = 0.080384 \text{ m}^2$$
$$F_1 = \frac{0.005024}{0.080384} \times 30000 = 1875 \text{ N}$$

Hence, a force of 1875 N on small piston can lift a truck weighing 30000 N.

Now, apply the conservation of energy as if we neglect friction, then the amount of work done by the applied force must equal to the work done to lift the truck. Thus,

$$W_1 = W_2$$
$$\Rightarrow \qquad F_1 d_1 = F_2 d_2 \qquad [\because \text{ given, } d_2 = 0.20 \text{ m}]$$
$$1875 \times d_1 = 30000 \times 0.20$$
$$d_1 = \frac{30000 \times 0.20}{1875} = 3.2 \text{ m}$$

(ii) Hydraulic Brakes

The working of the hydraulic brakes is also based on the Pascal's law.

It consists of a tube T containing brake oil. One end of the tube is connected to the wheel cylinder having two pistons P_1 and P_2. The pistons P_1 and P_2 are connected to the brake shoes S_1 and S_2, respectively and the other end of tube is connected to master cylinder fitted with the piston P.

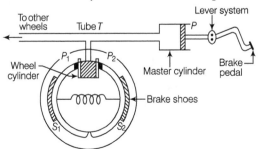

Constructional details of hydraulic brakes

The piston P is connected to the brake pedal through the lever system. The area of cross-section of the wheel cylinder is greater than that of master cylinder. The arrangement is shown in above figure.

Working of Hydraulic Brakes

(i) When the brake pedal is pressed, the lever system operates. The piston P is pushed.

The pressure is transmitted to pistons P_1 and P_2 in accordance with Pascal's law.

(ii) The pistons (P_1 and P_2) push the brake shoes away from each other. The brake shoes press against the inner rim of the wheel and retard the motion of the wheel.

(iii) Since, the area of the pistons of the wheel cylinder is greater than the area of piston P, therefore, a small force applied to the brake pedal produces a large thrust on the wheels and hence, the brake becomes operative.

(iv) When the pressure on the brake pedal is released, the brake shoes return to their normal pistons by the action of spring (i.e., it pulls the brake shoes away from the rim) which in turn force back the oil from wheel cylinder into the master cylinder.

(v) In order to apply equal pressure to all the wheels, the master cylinder is connected to all the wheels of the vehicle through tubes.

(vi) Hence, small force applied to the pedal exerts a much larger force on the wheel drums, which enables the driver to keep the vehicle under control.

BUOYANCY

When a body is partially or wholly immersed in a fluid at rest, it displaces the fluid. The displaced fluid exerts a thrust or an upward force on the body.

The upward force acting on the body immersed in a fluid is called **upward thrust** or **buoyant force** and the phenomenon is called **buoyancy**.

We know the weight of the body acts at its centre of gravity. But the buoyant force acts at the **centre of buoyancy** which is the centre of gravity of the liquid displaced by the body, when immersed in the liquid.

ARCHIMEDES' PRINCIPLE

The Archimedes' principle gives the magnitude of buoyant force on a body. It states that

when a body is immersed wholly or partially in a liquid at rest, it experiences an upthrust. The upthrust is equal to the weight of the liquid displaced by the immersed part of the body and its upthrust acts through the centre of gravity of the displaced fluid.

Explanation of Archimedes' Principle

Consider a cylindrical body of height h immersed in a fluid. The upward force (F_2) on the bottom of the body is more than the downward force (F_1) on its top. If p_1 and p_2 are the pressures at upper face and lower face of the body, respectively.

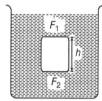

The resultant upward force on the body exerted by the fluid is equal to $(p_2 - p_1)A$.

As we know, $p_2 - p_1 = \rho g h$

So, $(p_2 - p_1)A = h\rho g A = mg$ $[\because m = Ah\rho]$

where, ρ = density of fluid and

A = cross-sectional area of the body

Thus, the upward force exerted by the fluid on the body is equal to the weight of the displaced fluid.

The following three cases are possible when the body is immersed in the fluid.

(i) If the weight of the body is greater than the upward force or upthrust by the fluid acting upwards, then the body sinks.

(ii) If the weight of the body is equal to the upthrust or the weight of the body is just balanced by upthrust, then the body floats fully immersed.

(iii) If the weight of the body is less than the upward force, then the body floats partly immersed.

If the total volume of the body is V_S and a part V_P of it is submerged in the fluid, then at equilibrium,

Weight of the body = Weight of fluid displaced

$$V_S \rho_S g = V_P \rho_l g$$

where, ρ_S and ρ_l are the densities of the body and fluid, respectively.

$$\boxed{\frac{\rho_S}{\rho_l} = \frac{V_P}{V_S}}$$

EXAMPLE |9| A Cube Placed in Water and Mercury

A tank contains water and mercury as shown in figure. An iron cube of edge 6 cm is in equilibrium as shown in figure. What is the fraction of cube inside the mercury? Given, density of iron = 7.7×10^3 kgm^{-3} and density of mercury = 13.6×10^3 kgm^{-3}.

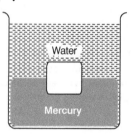

Sol. Let y be the depth of cube in mercury. The depth of cube in water will be $(0.06 - y)$ m. The buoyant force on cube due to mercury can be find out by using Archimedes' principle.

$$B_1 = (0.06)^2 \times y \times (13.6 \times 10^3) \times 9.8 \text{ N}$$

Similarly, due to water the buoyant force on cube is

$$B_2 = (0.06)^2 \times (0.06 - y) \times 10^3 \times 9.8 \text{ N}$$

When cube is in equilibrium, the sum of both the buoyant forces will be equal to the total weight of iron cube. $B_1 + B_2$ = weight of iron cube

or $(0.06)^2 \times 10^3 \times 9.8 [13.6 y + (0.06 - y)]$

$$= (0.06)^3 \times 7.7 \times 10^3 \times 9.8$$

$$\Rightarrow \quad y = \frac{0.396}{12.6} = 0.032 \text{ m}$$

Fraction of cube inside mercury = $\frac{0.032}{0.06}$

$$= 0.533 = 53\%$$

EXAMPLE |10| Up and Down Motion of a Fish

What is the principle behind the up and down motion of a fish in water?

Sol. An object can float on water if its density is less than water. A fish can adjust its density by expanding or contracting itself. The fish can move upward by decreasing its density and downward by increasing its density.

Note

When ice floats in a liquid and completely melts, then there could be following cases

(i) If $\rho_l > \rho_w$, the level of liquid will rise.

(ii) If $\rho_l < \rho_w$, the level of liquid decreases.

(iii) If $\rho_l = \rho_w$, the level of liquid will remain the same.

TOPIC PRACTICE 1

OBJECTIVE Type Questions

1. Average pressure p_{av} is defined as

   (a) $p_{av} = \dfrac{F}{A}$ (b) $p_{av} = \dfrac{V}{F}$

   (c) $p_{av} = \dfrac{A}{F}$ (d) $p_{av} = \dfrac{F}{V}$

Sol. (a) If F is the magnitude of the normal force acting over an area A, then the average pressure p is defined as the normal force acting per unit area.

$$p_{av} = \frac{F}{A}$$

2. The density of water at 4°C is

   (a) 1.0×10^3 kgm^{-3} (b) 4×10^2 kgm^{-3}

   (c) 6×10^3 kgm^{-3} (d) 3.2×10^3 kgm^{-3}

Sol. (a) The density of water at 4°C (277 K) is 1.0×10^3 kgm^{-3}.

3. Pressure at a point inside a liquid does not depend on
   (a) the depth of the point below the surface of the liquid.
   (b) the nature of the liquid.
   (c) the acceleration due to gravity at that point.
   (d) total weight of fluid in the beaker.

Sol. (d) $p = \dfrac{F}{A} = \rho g h$

∴ It does not depend on the weight of fluid.

4. Three liquids of densities d, $2d$ and $3d$ are mixed in equal proportion of weights. If density of water is d, then the specific gravity of the mixture is

   (a) $\dfrac{11}{7}$ (b) $\dfrac{18}{11}$ (c) $\dfrac{13}{9}$ (d) $\dfrac{23}{18}$

Sol. (b)

$$w_1 = w_2 = w_3$$
$$\Rightarrow \quad m_1 = m_2 = m_3 = m \text{ (say)}$$

Then, $V_1 = \dfrac{m}{d}, V_2 = \dfrac{m}{2d}, V_3 = \dfrac{m}{3d}$

∴ $d_{mix} = \dfrac{\text{Mass}}{\text{Volume}} = \dfrac{3m}{V_1 + V_2 + V_3} = \dfrac{18}{11}d$

So, specific gravity of mixture $= \dfrac{d_{mix}}{d_{water}} = \dfrac{18}{11}$

5. A hydraulic lift has 2 limbs of areas A and $2A$. Force F is applied over limb of area A to lift a heavy car. If distance moved by piston P_1 is x, then distance moved by piston P_2 is

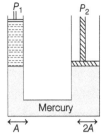

Mercury

     A $2A$

   (a) x (b) $2x$ (c) $\dfrac{x}{2}$ (d) $4x$

Sol. (c) As, $V_1 = V_2 \Rightarrow A_1 x_1 = A_2 x_2$

$$\Rightarrow \quad x_2 = \frac{A_1}{A_2} x_1 = \frac{Ax}{2A} = \frac{x}{2}$$

VERY SHORT ANSWER Type Questions

6. Three vessels have same base area and different neck area. Equal volume of liquid is poured into them, which will possess more pressure at the base?

Sol. If the volumes are same, then height of the liquid will be highest in which the cross-sectional area is least at the top. So, the vessel having least cross-sectional area at the top possess more pressure at the base (∵ $p = \rho g h$).

7. What is the use of open tube manometer?

Sol. Open tube manometer is used for measuring pressure difference.

8. A mercury barometer is placed in the mercury trough in a way that the angle made with the vertical is 60°. Find the height of mercury column.

Sol. The height of mercury in the inclined case will be 76 cm.

9. What is gauge pressure?

Sol. The difference between absolute pressure and atmospheric pressure is known as gauge pressure.

As, $p_{absolute} = p_a + \rho g h$

So, $p_{absolute} - p_a = \rho g h$ i.e. $p_{gauge} = \rho g h$

Here, ρ is the density of a fluid of depth h.

10. A vessel filled with water is kept on a weighing pan and the scale adjusted to zero. A block of mass M and density ρ is suspended by a massless spring of spring constant k.

This block is submerged inside into the water in the vessel. What is the reading of the scale? **[NCERT]**

Sol. The scale is adjusted to zero, therefore, when block suspended to a spring is immersed in water, then the reading of the scale will be equal to the thrust on the block due to water.

$$\text{Thrust} = V \rho_w g = \frac{m}{\rho} \rho_w g \qquad \left[\because V = \frac{m}{\rho} \right]$$

11. How will a mercury barometer's height change, if we introduce some water vapour into it.

Sol. Because water vapour exerts pressure. Thus, the barometric height decreases.

SHORT ANSWER Type Questions

12. A container of area $0.02 \, \text{m}^2$ is filled with water. Find the pressure at the bottom of the container if a weight is placed on the piston. (as shown in the figure).

Sol. The net force acting on the base

$$= (\rho g h) A + mg$$
$$F = 1000 \times 9.8 \times 1 \times 0.02 + 10 \times 9.8$$
$$= 294 \, \text{N}$$
$$\therefore \quad \text{Pressure} = \frac{\text{Thrust}}{\text{Area}} = \frac{294 \, \text{N}}{0.02} = 14700 \text{N}$$

13. A 50 kg girl wearing high heels shoes balances on a single heel. The heel is circular with a diameter 1.0 cm. What is the pressure exerted on the horizontal floor? **[NCERT]**

Sol. Given, mass of girl $(m) = 50 \, \text{kg}$

Diameter of circular heel $(2r) = 1.0 \, \text{cm}$

$\therefore$ Radius $(r) = 0.5 \, \text{cm} = 5 \times 10^{-3} \, \text{m}$

Area of circular heel $(A) = \pi r^2 = 3.14 \times (5 \times 10^{-3})^2 \, \text{m}^2$
$$= 78.50 \times 10^{-6} \, \text{m}^2$$

$\therefore$ Pressure exerted on the horizontal floor

$$p = \frac{F}{A} = \frac{mg}{A} = \frac{50 \times 9.8}{78.50 \times 10^{-6}} = 6.24 \times 10^6 \, \text{Pa}$$

14. If the required pressure in the tyre of a car is 199 kPa, then
   (i) what is the gauge pressure?
   (ii) what is the absolute pressure?

Sol. (i) Gauge pressure
$$\therefore \quad\quad\quad p_g = 199 \, \text{kPa}$$
(ii) Absolute pressure
$$p = p_a + p_g \quad\quad [\because \text{from Eq. (i)}]$$
$$= 101 \, \text{kPa} + 199 \, \text{kPa} = 300 \, \text{kPa}$$

15. A hydraulic automobile lift is designed to lift cars with a maximum mass of 3000 kg. The area of cross-section of the piston carrying the load is 425 cm². What maximum pressure would the smaller piston have to bear? **[NCERT]**

Sol. Given, maximum mass that can be lifted $(m) = 3000 \, \text{kg}$

Area of cross-section $(A) = 425 \, \text{cm}^2 = 4.25 \times 10^{-2} \, \text{m}^2$

$\therefore$ Maximum pressure on the bigger piston

$$p = \frac{F}{A} = \frac{mg}{A} = \frac{3000 \times 9.8}{4.25 \times 10^{-2}} = 6.92 \times 10^5 \, \text{Pa}$$

According to Pascal's law, the pressure applied on an enclosed liquid is transmitted equally in all directions.

$\therefore$ Maximum pressure on smaller piston

= maximum pressure on bigger piston

$$p' = p = 6.92 \times 10^5 \, \text{Pa}$$

16. Two vessels have the same base area but different shapes. The first vessel takes twice the volume of water than the second vessel required to fill upto a particular common height. Is the force exerted by the water on the base of the vessel the same in the two cases? If so, why do the vessels filled with water to that same height give different readings on a weighing scale? **[NCERT]**

Sol. The pressure exerted by a liquid column depends upon its height. The height of water in both vessels are same, therefore, the pressure on the base of each vessel will be same.

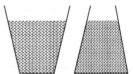

The area of the base of each vessel is also same and hence, force exerted by the water on the base of the vessels is same. Liquid also applies force on the walls of the vessel. As walls of the vessels are not perpendicular to the base, therefore, force exerted on the walls by the liquid has a non-zero vertical component, which is more in first vessel. Therefore, the two vessels filled with water to the same height give different readings on a weighing scale.

17. Torricelli's barometer used mercury. Pascal duplicated it using French wine of density 948 kg/m³. Determine the height of the wine column for normal atmospheric pressure. **[NCERT]**

The pressure exerted by a liquid column

where, $p = h\rho g$, h = height of liquid column
   ρ = density of liquid
   g = acceleration due to gravity.

Sol. Atmospheric pressure $(p) = 1.013 \times 10^5 \, \text{Pa}$

Density of French wine $(\rho) = 984 \, \text{kg/m}^3$

Let h be the height of wine column,

$$p = h\rho g, \quad h = \frac{p}{\rho g} = \frac{1.013 \times 10^5}{984 \times 9.8} = 10.5 \, \text{m}$$

18. A vertical off-shore structure is built to withstand a maximum stress of 10^9 Pa. Is the structure suitable for putting up on top of an oil well in the ocean? Take the depth of the ocean to be roughly 3 km and ignore ocean currents. **[NCERT]**

Sol. Given, depth of ocean $(h) = 3\,\text{km} = 3000\,\text{m}$

Density of water $(\rho) = 10^3\,\text{kg/m}^3$

Pressure exerted by water column

$$p = h\rho g = 3000 \times 10^3 \times 9.8$$

$$= 29.4 \times 10^6 = 2.94 \times 10^7\,\text{Pa}$$

Maximum stress which can be withstand by the vertical off-shore structure $= 10^9\,\text{Pa}$

As, $10^9\,\text{Pa} > 2.9 \times 10^7\,\text{Pa}$

Therefore, the vertical structure is suitable for putting up on top of an oil well in the ocean.

19. A balloon with hydrogen in it rises up but a balloon with air comes down, Why?

Sol. The density of hydrogen is less than air. So, the buoyant force on the balloon will be more than its weight in case of the hydrogen. So, in this case the balloon rises up. In case of air, the weight of balloon is more than the buoyant force acting on it, so balloon will come down. **[2]**

20. A body of mass 6 kg is floating in a liquid with 2/3 of its volume inside the liquid. Find ratio between the density of the body and density of liquid. Take $g = 10\,\text{m/s}^2$.

Sol. As we know that, for a floating body

Buoyant force = Weight of liquid displaced

Let V be the volume of the body $\dfrac{2}{3} V \rho_l g = V \rho_l g$

where, ρ_b = density of floating body

and ρ_l = density of liquid

∴ $\dfrac{\rho_b}{\rho_l} = \dfrac{2}{3}$

LONG ANSWER Type I Questions

21. Explain why?

(i) The blood pressure in humans is greater at the feet than the brain.

(ii) Atmospheric pressure at a height of about 6 km decreases to nearly half its value at the sea level though the height of the atmosphere is more than 100 km.

(iii) Hydrostatic pressure is a scalar quantity even though pressure is force divided by area.

[NCERT]

Sol. (i) The pressure of liquid column is given by $p = h\rho g$, where h is depth, ρ is density and g is acceleration due to gravity.

Therefore, pressure of liquid column increases with depth. The height of blood column in human body is more at feet than at the brain. Therefore, the blood pressure in humans is greater at the feet than the brain.

(ii) The density of air is maximum near the surface of the earth and decreases rapidly with height. At a height of 6 km, the density of air decreases to nearly half of its value at the sea level. Beyond 6 km height, the density of air decreases very slowly with height. Hence, the atmospheric pressure at a height of about 6 km decreases to nearly half of its value at the sea level.

(iii) When force is applied on a liquid, the pressure is transmitted equally in all directions inside the liquid. Therefore, hydrostatic pressure has no fixed direction and hence, it is a scalar quantity.

22. A U-tube contains water and methylated spirit separated by mercury. The mercury columns in the two arms are in level with 10.0 cm of water in one arm and 12.5 cm of spirit in the other. What is the specific gravity of spirit?   **[NCERT]**

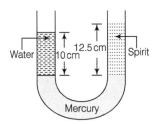

Sol. Height of water column, $h_1 = 10.0\,\text{cm}$

Density of water, $\rho_1 = 1\,\text{g/cm}^3$

Height of spirit column, $h_2 = 12.5\,\text{cm}$

Density of spirit, $\rho_2 = ?$

The mercury column in both arms of the U-tube are at same level, therefore, pressure in both arms will be same.

∴ Pressure exerted by water column = pressure exerted by spirit column

∴ $p_1 = p_2$

$$h_1 \rho_1 g = h_2 \rho_2 g$$

or $\rho_2 = \dfrac{h_1 \rho_1}{h_2} = \dfrac{10 \times 1}{12.5} = 0.80\,\text{g/cm}^3$

Specific gravity of spirit $= \dfrac{\text{Density of spirit}}{\text{Density of water}}$

$$= \dfrac{0.80}{1} = 0.80$$

23. In the previous question, if 15.0 cm of water and spirit each are further poured into the respective arms of the tube, what is the difference in the levels of mercury in the two arms? (specific gravity of mercury = 13.6) **[NCERT]**

Sol. When 15.0 cm of water is poured in each arm, then

Height of water column $(h_1) = 10 + 15 = 25\,\text{cm}$

Height of spirit column $(h_2) = 12.5 + 15 = 27.5$ cm

Density of water $(\rho_w) = 1$ g/cm^3

Density of spirit $(\rho_s) = 0.80$ g/cm^3

Density of mercury $(\rho_m) = 13.6$ g/cm^3

Let in equilibrium, the difference in the level of mercury in both arms be h cm.

$$\therefore \quad h\rho_m g = h_1\rho_w g - h_2\rho_s g$$

or
$$h = \frac{h_1\rho_w - h_2\rho_s}{\rho_m} = \frac{25 \times 1 - 27.5 \times 0.80}{13.6}$$

$$= 0.221 \text{ cm}$$

Therefore, mercury will rise in the arm containing spirit by 0.221 cm.

24. During blood transfusion, the needle is inserted in a vein where the gauge pressure is 2000 Pa. At what height must the blood container be placed so that blood may just enter the vein? (Use the density of whole blood from table). **[NCERT]**

Densities of Some Common Fluids at STP

Fluid	Density $\rho(\text{gm}^{-3})$
Water	1.00×10^3
Sea water	1.03×10^3
Mercury	13.6×10^3
Ethyl alcohol	0.806×10^3
Whole blood	1.06×10^3
Air	1.29
Oxygen	1.43
Hydrogen	9.0×10^{-2}
Interstellar space	$\approx 10^{-22}$

Sol. Given, gauge pressure $(p) = 2000$ Pa

Density of whole blood $(\rho) = 1.06 \times 10^3$ kg/m^3

$$g = 9.8 \text{ m/s}^2$$

Let the container be placed at height h metre.

Pressure exerted by the blood $(p) = h\rho g$

or
$$h = \frac{p}{\rho g} = \frac{2000}{1.06 \times 10^3 \times 9.8}$$

$$= 0.193 \text{ m} \approx 0.20 \text{ m}$$

25. A tank with a square base of area 1.0 m^2 is divided by a vertical partition in the middle. The bottom of the partition has a small hinged door of area 20 cm^2. The tank is filled with water in one compartment and an acid (of relative density 1.7) in the other, both to a height of 4.0. Compute the force necessary to keep the door close. **[NCERT]**

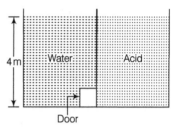

Sol. Given, height of water and acid $(h) = 4.0$ m

Density of water $(\rho_w) = 1 \times 10^3$ kg/m^3

Density of acid $(\rho_a) = 1.7 \times 10^3$ kg/m^3

Pressure exerted by water at the door

$$p_1 = h\rho_w g = 4 \times 1 \times 10^3 \times 9.8$$

$$= 39.2 \times 10^3 \text{ Pa}$$

Pressure exerted by acid at the door

$$p_2 = h\rho_a g = 4 \times 1.7 \times 10^3 \times 9.8$$

$$= 66.64 \times 10^3 \text{ Pa}$$

$\therefore$ Difference in pressure $(\Delta p) = p_2 - p_1$

$$= 66.64 \times 10^3 - 39.2 \times 10^3$$

$$= 27.44 \times 10^3 \text{ Pa}$$

Area of the door $(A) = 20$ cm^2

$$= 20 \times 10^{-4} \text{ m}^2$$

Force acting on the door $= \Delta p \times A \quad \left[\because \text{Pressure} = \frac{\text{force}}{\text{area}} \right]$

$$= 27.44 \times 10^3 \times 20 \times 10^{-4}$$

$$= 54.88 \text{ N} \approx 55 \text{ N}$$

Therefore, 55 N force is necessary to keep the door close.

ASSESS YOUR TOPICAL UNDERSTANDING

OBJECTIVE Type Questions

1. The key property of fluids is that
   (a) they offer very little resistance to shear stress
   (b) their shape changes
   (c) they offer very large resistance to shear stress
   (d) Both (a) and (b)

2. The two thin bones (femurs), each of cross-sectional area 10 cm^2 support the upper part of human body of mass 40 kg. Estimate the average pressure sustained by the femurs.
   (a) 2×10^5 Nm^{-2} (b) 3×10^4 Nm^{-2}
   (c) 2.5×10^3 Nm^{-2} (d) 6×10^4 Nm^{-2}

3. If two liquids of same volume but different densities ρ_1 and ρ_2 are mixed, then density of mixture is given by
   (a) $\rho = \dfrac{\rho_1 + \rho_2}{2}$ (b) $\rho = \dfrac{\rho_1 + \rho_2}{2\rho_1\rho_2}$
   (c) $\rho = \dfrac{2\rho_1\rho_2}{\rho_1 + \rho_2}$ (d) $\rho = \dfrac{\rho_1\rho_2}{\rho_1 + \rho_2}$

4. Pressure is applied to an enclosed fluid. It is
   (a) increased and applied to every part of the fluid
   (b) diminished and transmitted to the walls of the container
   (c) increased in proportion to the mass of the fluid and then transmitted
   (d) transmitted unchanged to every portion of the fluid and the walls of container

5. A uniformly tapering vessel is filled with a liquid of density 900 kgm^{-3}. The force that acts on the base of the vessel due to the liquid is (Take, $g = 10$ ms^{-2})

Area $=10^{-3}$ m2

0.4 m

Area $=2 \times 10^{-3}$ m2

   (a) 3.6 N   (b) 7.2 N   (c) 9.0 N   (d) 14.4 N

Answers

1. (d) | 2. (a) | 3. (a) | 4. (d) | 5. (b)

VERY SHORT ANSWER Type Questions

6. The blood pressure in humans is greater at the feet than at the brain, why?

7. What will be the following changes in the height of mercury in a barometer indicates?
   (i) Increase   (ii) Decrease

8. The thrust due to atmospheric pressure on us is around 15 tonne. How we withstand such a thrust?

SHORT ANSWER Type Questions

9. An ice cube floats in water. What will happen to the water level if the complete ice melts?

10. A block floats in water and this system is placed in an elevator. If the elevator starts accelerating downwards, will the block float with higher or lower immersed part in the water?

11. A dimension of base of vessel is 20 cm $\times$ 10 cm. Water is poured upto a height 5 cm. What is the pressure at the bottom of the vessel? Take $g = 10$ ms^{-2}.

12. Explain, why atmospheric pressure at a height about 6 km decreases to nearly half of its value at the sea level, though the height of the atmosphere is more than 100 km.

LONG ANSWER Type I Questions

13. A vertical off-shore structure is built to withstand a maximum stress of 10^{10} Pa. Is the structure suitable for putting up on top of an oil well in the ocean? Take the depth of the ocean to be roughly 31 km and ignore ocean currents.

14. A body floats in water with one-third of its volume outside water. While floating in another liquid its $\dfrac{3}{4}$th volume outside. Find out the density of other liquid. (given density of water = 1 g/cc)

15. If a column of 60 cm height of water supports a 45 cm column of an unknown liquid. Calculate the density of the liquid.
   (given density of water = 10^3 kg/m^3)

|TOPIC 2|
Surface Tension and Surface Energy

SURFACE TENSION

Surface tension arises due to the fact that the free surface of a liquid at rest has some additional potential energy. Due to it, a liquid surface tends to occupy a minimum surface area and behaves like stretched membrane.

e.g. A steel needle may be made to float on water, though the steel is more dense than water. This is because the water surface acts as a stretched elastic membrane and supports the needle. This property of a liquid is called **surface tension.**

Consider a line *AB* on the free surface of a liquid. The small elements of the surface on this line are in equilibrium because they are acted upon by equal and opposite forces, acting perpendicular to the line from either side as shown in figure.

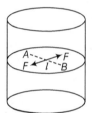

Definition of surface tension

The force acting on this line is proportional to the length of this line. If *l* is the length of imaginary line and *F* the total force on either side of the line, then

$$F \propto l \quad \Rightarrow \quad F = Sl$$

$$S = \frac{F}{l}$$

or $\boxed{\text{Surface tension, } S = \dfrac{\text{Force}}{\text{Length}}}$

From this expression, **surface tension can be defined as the force acting per unit length of an imaginary line drawn on the liquid surface, the direction of force being perpendicular to this line and tangential to the liquid surface.** It is denoted by *S* and it is a **scalar quantity.**

Units and Dimension of Surface Tension

SI units of surface tension = N/m

CGS unit of surface tension = dyne/cm

$$\text{Dimension of surface tension} = \frac{\text{Force}}{\text{Length}} = \frac{[MLT^{-2}]}{[L]}$$

$$= [ML^0 T^{-2}]$$

Factors Affecting Surface Tension

1. **Temperature** The surface tension of liquid decreases with rise in temperature and *vice-versa*.

   The surface tension of a liquid becomes zero at a particular temperature, called 'Critical temperature' of that liquid. For small temperature differences, surface tension decreases almost linearly as

   $$S_t = S_0(1 - \alpha t)$$

   where, S_t : Surface tension at $t°C$,

   S_0 : Surface tension at $0°C$ and

   (α : the temperature sufficient of surface tension)

   Due to this,
   (i) Hot soup taste better than cold soup as hot soup spread over a large area of tongue.
   (ii) Machinery parts get jammed in winter as surface tension of lubricating oil increases with decrease in temperature.

2. **Addition of Impurities** The surface tension of liquids changes appreciably with addition of impurities.(a) A highly soluble substance like sodium chloride increases the surface tension of water. (b)A sparingly soluble substance like phenol or soap reduces the surface tension of water.

Detergent and Surface Tension

Surface tension has a wide use in daily life. The detergents, used for cleaning the dirty clothes in our home is a very good example of surface tension.

Actually, water cannot wet oil stain on your clothes, that is why water alone cannot remove dirt from your clothes.

The molecule of detergent can get attached with water and dirt molecules and they take away the dirt with them when we wash the clothes with detergent.

Applications of Surface Tension

(i) Rain drops and drops of mercury placed on glass plate are spherical.

(ii) Hair of shaving brush/painting brush, when dipped in water spread out, but as soon as, it is taken out, its hair stick together.

(iii) A greased needle placed gently on the free surface of water in a beaker does not sink.

(iv) Oil drop spreads on cold water but does not change shape on hot water.

Measuring the Surface Tension of a Liquid

The surface tension of liquid can be measured experimentally as shown in figure. A flat vertical glass plate, below which a vessel filled with some liquid is kept. The plate is balanced by weights on the other side. The vessel is raised slightly until the liquid touches the glass plate and pulls it down because of the force of surface tension. Weights are added till the plate just detaches from water.

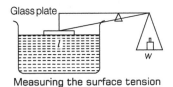

Measuring the surface tension

Suppose the additional weight required is mg.

$$S = (mg/2l)$$

where, m is the extra mass and l is the length of the plate edge.

SURFACE ENERGY

The free surface of a liquid always has a tendency to contract and possess minimum surface area. If it is required to increase the surface area of the liquid at a constant temperature, work has to be done. This **work done** is stored in the surface film of the liquid as its **potential energy**.

This potential energy per unit area of the surface film is called the **surface energy**.

Hence, the surface energy may be defined as the amount of work done in increasing the area of the liquid surface by unity. Thus,

$$\text{Surface energy} = \frac{\text{Work done in increasing the surface area}}{\text{Increase in surface area}}$$

The SI unit of surface energy is J/m^2.

Relation between Surface Energy and Surface Tension

Consider a rectangular frame $PQRS$. Here, wire QR is movable. A soap film is formed on the frame. The film pulls the movable wire QR inward due to surface tension.

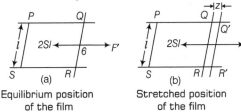

Equilibrium position   Stretched position
of the film   of the film

As, $\text{Surface tension} = \dfrac{\text{force}}{\text{length}} = \dfrac{F'}{2l}$

$$F' = S \times 2l$$

If QR is moved through a distance z by an external force F very slowly, then some work has to be done against this force.

∴   External work done = Force × distance
$$= S \times 2l \times z \quad [\because F' = F]$$

Increase in surface area of film $= 2l \times z$

[As soap film has two sides]

$$\text{Surface energy} = \frac{\text{Work done}}{\text{Surface area}} = \frac{S2lz}{2lz} = S$$

So, **value of surface energy of liquid is numerically equal to the value of surface tension.**

ANGLE OF CONTACT

The surface of liquid near the plane of contact with another medium is in curved shape.

The angle between tangent to the liquid surface at the point of contact and the solid surface inside the liquid is called as angle of contact. It is denoted by θ.

The value of angle of contact depends on the following factors

  (i) Nature of the solid and liquid in contact.

 (ii) Cleanliness of the surface in contact.

(iii) Medium above the free surface of the liquid.

(iv) Temperature of the liquid

e.g. Water forms droplets on lotus leaf shown in Fig. (a) while spreads over a clean plastic plate in Fig. (b).

Consider the three interfacial tensions at all the three interfaces such as

S_{sa} = surface tension between solid and air

S_{la} = surface tension between liquid and air

S_{sl} = surface tension between solid and liquid

At the line of contact, the surface forces between the three media must be in equilibrium. Resolving S_{la} into two rectangular components, we have $S_{la} \cos \theta$ acts along the solid surface and $S_{la} \sin \theta$ acts along the perpendicular to the solid surface.

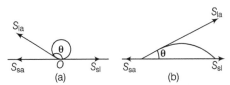

Different shapes of water drops with interfacial tensions

As the liquid on the surface of soild is at rest, so the molecules of these interfaces are in equilibrium. Thus, the net force on them is zero.

For the molecule O to be in equilibrium.

$$S_{sl} + S_{la} \cos\theta = S_{sa}$$

$$\boxed{\cos\theta = \frac{S_{sa} - S_{sl}}{S_{la}}}$$

The following cases arise

(i) If the surface tension at the solid-liquid S_{sl}, interface is greater than the surface tension at the liquid-air S_{la} interface, i.e. $S_{sl} > S_{la}$, then $\cos\theta$ is negative and $\theta > 90°$ (the angle of contact is **obtuse angle**). The molecules of a liquid are attracted strongly to themselves and weakly to those of solid. It costs a lot of energy to create a liquid-solid surface. The liquid then does not wet the solid.

   e.g. Water-leaf or glass-mercury interface.

(ii) If the surface tension at the solid-liquid S_{sl} interface is less than the surface tension at the liquid-air S_{la} interface, i.e. $S_{sl} < S_{la}$, then $\cos\theta$ is positive and $\theta < 90°$ (the angle of contact is **acute angle**). The molecules of the liquid are strongly attracted to those of solid and weakly attracted to themselves. It costless energy to create a liquid-solid surface and liquid wets the solid.

   e.g. When soap or detergent is added to water, the angle of contact becomes small.

Excess Pressure Inside a Liquid Drop

Suppose a spherical liquid drop of radius R and S be the surface tension of liquid. Due to its spherical shape, there is an excess pressure p inside the drop over that on outside. This excess pressure acts normally outwards. Due to this pressure, radius increases from R to $R + dR$, then extra surface energy can be determined.

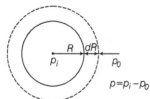

Excess pressure inside a liquid drop

Excess pressure inside the drop, $p = p_i - p_0$

where, p_i = total pressure inside the liquid drop

p_0 = atmospheric pressure

Initial surface area of the liquid = $4\pi R^2$

Final surface area of the liquid drop

$$= 4\pi(R + dR)^2$$
$$= 4\pi(R^2 + 2R\,dR + dR^2)$$
$$= 4\pi R^2 + 8\pi R\,dR$$

$$[dR^2 \text{ is very small and hence neglected}]$$

Increase in the surface area of liquid drop

$$= 4\pi R^2 + 8\pi R\,dR - 4\pi R^2$$
$$= 8\pi R\,dR$$

External work done in increasing the surface area of the drop

= Increase in surface energy

= Increase in surface area × Surface tension

$$= (8\pi R\,dR) \times S \qquad \ldots(i)$$

But work done

= Excess pressure × Area × Change in radius

$$= p \times 4\pi R^2 \times dR \qquad \ldots(ii)$$

From Eqs. (i) and (ii), we get

So, $$p \times 4\pi R^2 \times dR = 8\pi R\,dRS$$

$$\boxed{\text{Excess pressure, } p = \frac{2S}{R}}$$

So, **Pressure difference in a drop bubble,**

$$p_i - p_0 = \frac{2S}{R}$$

Excess Pressure Inside a Soap Bubble

From the above case, Increase in surface area = $8\pi R\,dR$

But a soap bubble has two free surfaces.

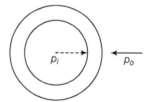

Excess pressure inside a soap bubble

So, effective increase in surface area of the soap bubble

$$= 2 \times 8\pi R\,dR = 16\pi R\,dR \qquad \ldots(i)$$

External work done in increasing the surface area of the soap bubble = Increase in surface energy

= Increase in surface area × surface tension

$$= 16\pi R\,dRS$$

But, work done = Force × change in radius

where, Force = Excess pressure × area = $(p \times 4\pi r^2)$

So, work done = $p \times 4\pi R^2 \times dR$ ...(ii)

From Eqs. (i) and (ii), we get

$$p \times 4\pi R^2 \times dR = 16\pi R dRS$$

$$\boxed{p = \frac{4S}{R}}$$

Pressure difference inside a soap bubble,

$$p_i - p_0 = \frac{4S}{R}$$

Excess pressure inside an air bubble in a liquid is similar to a liquid drop in air, it has only one free spherical surface. Hence, excess pressure is given by

$$p = \frac{2S}{R}$$

Note

• When an air bubble of radius R lies at a depth h below the free surface of a liquid of density ρ and surface tension S, the excess pressure inside the bubble will be

$$p = \frac{2S}{R} + h\rho g$$

• When an ice-skater slides over the surface of smooth ice, some ice melts due to the pressure exerted by the sharp metal edges of the skates. The tiny water droplets act as rigid ball bearings and help the skaters to run along smoothly.

EXAMPLE |1| Excess Pressure in Hemispherical Dubble
The lower end of a capillary tube of diameter 2 mm is dipped 8 cm below the surface of water in a beaker. What is the pressure required in the tube in order to blow a hemispherical bubble at its end in water? The surface tension of water at temperature of the experiments is 7.30×10^{-2} Nm^{-1}, 1 atm = 1.01×10^5 Pa, density of water = 1000 kg/m^3, $g = 9.80$ ms^{-2}. Also, calculate the excess pressure. **[NCERT]**

Sol. Given, $h = 0.08$ m, $d = 1000$ kg/m^3, $g = 9.80$ m/s^2 and we know that $p_0 = p_a + hdg$

p_0 is outside pressure

$$p_0 = 1.01 \times 10^5 \text{ Pa} + 0.08 \text{ m} \times 1000 \text{ kg/m}^3 \times 9.80 \text{ m/s}^2$$

$$p_0 = 1.01784 \times 10^5 \text{ Pa}$$

Calculate inside pressure required in tube in order to blow a hemispherical bubble

$$p_i = p_0 + \frac{2S}{r}$$

where $S = 7.30 \times 10^{-2}$ Pa-m

$$p_i = 1.01784 \times 10^5 + \frac{2 \times 7.3 \times 10^{-2}}{10^{-3}}$$

$$= (1.01784 + 0.00146) \times 10^5 \text{ Pa}$$

$$\Rightarrow \quad p_i = 1.02 \times 10^5 \text{ Pa}$$

where, the radius of the bubble is taken to be equal to the radius of capillary tube. Since, the bubble is hemispherical. The excess pressure in the bubble is 146 Pa.

CAPILLARITY

The term capilla means hair which is Latin word. A tube of very fine (hair-like) bore is called a **capillary tube**.

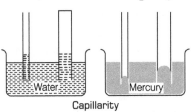

Capillarity

If a capillary tube of glass is dipped in liquid like water, the liquid rises in the tube, but when the capillary tube is dipped in a liquid like mercury, the level of liquid falls in the tube. This phenomenon of rise or fall of a liquid in the capillary is called **capillarity**.

Some examples are

1. We use towels for drying our skin.
2. In trees sap rises due to vessels. It is similar to capillary action.

Capillary Rise

One application of the pressure difference across a curved surface is the water rises up in a narrow tube (capillary) in spite of gravity. Consider a capillary of radius R is inserted into a vessel containing water.

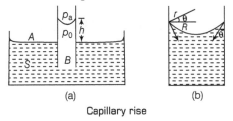

Capillary rise

The surface of water in the capillary becomes concave. It means that there must be a pressure difference between the two sides of the meniscus.

So, $\quad (p_a - p_0) = (2S/r) = 2S/(R \sec \theta)$

$$= (2S/R) \cos \theta \quad ...(i)$$

where, r = radius of curvature of the concave meniscus.

Now, consider two points A and B. According to Pascal's law, they must be at the same pressure,

$$p_0 + h\rho g = p_A = p_B = p_a$$

So, $\quad p_a = p_0 + h\rho g$

$$p_a - p_0 = \rho g h \quad ...(ii)$$

$$(p_a = \text{atmospheric pressure})$$

From Eqs. (i) and (ii), we get

$$\rho g h = \frac{2S}{R} \cos\theta$$

Height of rise of liquid in capillary, $h = \dfrac{2S \cos\theta}{\rho R g}$

This is the formula for the rise of liquid in a capillary. The liquids which met the glass surfaces, e.g. water, rises in the capillary and the liquids which do not wet the glass surface falls in the capillary.

Some common examples of capillarity are
 (i) Blotting paper absorbs ink due to capillarity.
 (ii) A towel soaks water on account of capillarity motion.
 (iii) Oil rises through the wicks due to capillarity.

EXAMPLE |2| Water Rise in Capillary
A capillary of radius 0.05 cm is immersed in water. Find the value of rise of water in capillary if value for the surface tension is 0.073 N/m and angle of contact is 0°.

Sol. Given, $S = 0.073$ N/m,

$$R = 0.05\,\text{cm} = 5 \times 10^{-4}\,\text{m}$$

$$\theta = 0°, h = ?$$

From the formula, $h = \dfrac{2S\cos\theta}{\rho g R}$

$$= \frac{2 \times 0.073 \times \cos 0°}{10^3 \times 9.8 \times 5 \times 10^{-4}} = 0.02979\,\text{m}$$

EXAMPLE |3| Different Liquid in Capillary Tube
In a glass capillary tube, water rises upto a height of 10.0 cm while mercury fall down by 5.0 cm in the same capillary. If the angles of contact for mercury glass is 60° and water glass is 0°, then find the ratio of surface tension of mercury and water.

Sol. For water, $h_1 = 10.0\,\text{cm} = 0.1$ m

$$\rho_1 = 10^3\,\text{kg/m}^3, \theta = 0°$$

For mercury, $h_2 = 5.0\,\text{cm} = 0.05$ m

$$\rho_2 = 13.6 \times 10^3\,\text{kg/m}^3, \theta = 60°$$

Suppose S_1 and S_2 are the surface tensions for water and mercury, respectively, then

$$S_1 = \frac{h_1 R \rho_1 g}{2\cos\theta_1} \quad \text{and} \quad S_2 = \frac{h_2 R \rho_2 g}{2\cos\theta_2}$$

The ratio of surface tension of mercury and water,

$$\frac{S_2}{S_1} = \frac{h_2 R \rho_2 g}{2\cos\theta_2} \times \frac{2\cos\theta_1}{h_1 R \rho_1 g}$$

$$\frac{S_2}{S_1} = \frac{h_2 \rho_2 \cos\theta_1}{h_1 \rho_1 \cos\theta_2}$$

$$= \frac{0.05 \times 13.6 \times 10^3 \times \cos 0°}{0.1 \times 1000 \times \cos 60°} = 13.6 : 1$$

| TOPIC PRACTICE 2 |

OBJECTIVE Type Questions

1. Surface tension is due to
   (a) frictional forces between molecules
   (b) cohesive forces between molecules
   (c) adhesive forces between molecules
   (d) Both (b) and (c)

   Sol. (d) Both cohesive and adhesive forces result in surface tension.

2. The value of surface tension of water is minimum at
   (a) 4° C   (b) 25° C
   (c) 50° C   (d) 75° C

   Sol. (d) Value of surface tension decreases with increase in temperature. So, it is minimum at 75°C.

3. In figure, pressure inside a spherical drop is more than pressure outside. (S = surface tension and r = radius of bubble)

   The extra surface energy if radius of bubble is increased by Δr is
   (a) $4\pi r\, \Delta r\, S$ (b) $8\pi r\, \Delta r\, S$
   (c) $2\pi r\, \Delta r\, S$ (d) $10\pi r\, \Delta r\, S$

   Sol. (b) Suppose a spherical drop of radius r is in equilibrium. If its radius increases by Δr. The extra surface energy is
   $$|4\pi(r + \Delta r)^2 - 4\pi r^2|S = 8\pi r\, \Delta r\, S$$

4. Radius of a soap bubble is increased from R to $2R$. Work done in this process in terms of surface tension is
   (a) $24\,\pi R^2 S$ (b) $48\,\pi R^2 S$
   (c) $12\pi R^2 S$ (d) $36\pi R^2 S$

   Sol. (a) $W = 8\pi T(R_2^2 - R_1^2) = 8\pi S[(2R)^2 - (R^2)] = 24\,\pi R^2 S$

5. The angle of contact at the interface of water-glass is 0°, ethyl alcohol-glass is 0°, mercury-glass is 140° and methyliodide-glass is 30°. A glass capillary is put in a trough containing one of these four liquids. It is observed that the meniscus is convex. The liquid in the trough is   **[NCERT Exemplar]**
   (a) water   (b) ethylalcohol
   (c) mercury   (d) methyliodide

Sol. (c) According to the question, the observed meniscus is of convex figure shape. Which is only possible when angle of contact is obtuse. Hence, the combination will be of mercury-glass (140°)

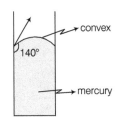

VERY SHORT ANSWER Type Questions

6. If a wet piece of wood burns, then water droplets appear on the other end, why?

Sol. When a piece of the wood burns, then steam formed and water appear in the form of drops due to surface tension on the other end.

7. Why, surface tension of all lubricating oils and paint is kept low?

Sol. So, they can spread over large area easily.

8. It becomes easier to spray the water in which some soap is dissolved, explain it.

Sol. When some soap is dissolved in water, the surface tension of water decreases. Thus, the less energy required to spray water.

9. Find the work done in increasing the radius of a soap bubble from 4 cm to 6 cm. The value of surface tension for the soap solution is 30 dyne cm^{-1}.

Sol. Given, $r_1 = 4$ cm, $r_2 = 6$ cm, $S = 30$ dyne cm^{-1}

So, change in surface area $= 2 \times 4\pi \, (6^2 - 4^2)$

[Soap solution has two surfaces]

$= 8\pi \, 20 = 160 \, \pi \, cm^2$

Work done $= S \times$ change in surface area

$= 30 \times 160 \times 3.142$

$= 15081.6$ erg

10. Find the work done required to make a soap bubble of radius 0.02 m. Given surface tension of soap 0.03 N/m.

Sol. Given, $S = 0.03$ N/m

Work done $=$ surface area $\times$ surface tension

$= 2 \times 4\pi r^2 \times S$

$= 2 \times 4 \times 3.14 \times (0.02)^2 \times 0.03$

$= 3 \times 10^{-4}$ J

11. Why soap bubble bursts after some time?

Sol. Soap bubble bursts after some time because the pressure inside it become more than the outside pressure.

12. How a raincoat become waterproof?

Sol. If the angle of contact between water and the material of the raincoat is obtuse, then rainy water does not wet the raincoat. Thus, the raincoat becomes waterproof.

SHORT ANSWER Type Questions

13. Fig.(a) shows a thin liquid film supporting a small weight $= 4.5 \times 10^{-2}$N. What is the weight supported by a film of the same liquid at the same temperature in Figs. (b) and (c)? Explain your answer physically. **[NCERT]**

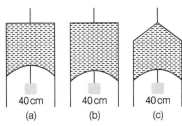

40 cm   40 cm   40 cm

(a)   (b)   (c)

Sol. As liquid is same, temperature is same and the length of the film supporting the weight is also same, therefore, in Figs. (b) and (c), the film will support same weight, i.e. 4.5×10^{-2}N.

14. The surface tension and vapour pressure of water at 20°C is 7.28×10^{-2}N/m and 2.33×10^3Pa, respectively. What is the radius of the smallest spherical water droplet which can form without evaporating at 20°C? **[NCERT]**

Sol. Given, surface tension of water, $S = 7.28 \times 10^{-2}$ N/m

Vapour pressure, $p = 2.33 \times 10^3$ Pa

The drop will evaporate, if the water pressure is greater than the vapour pressure.

Let a water droplet of radius R can be formed without evaporating.

∴ Vapour pressure $=$ Excess pressure in drop

∴ $\qquad p = \dfrac{2S}{R}$

or $\qquad R = \dfrac{2S}{p} = \dfrac{2 \times 7.28 \times 10^{-2}}{2.33 \times 10^3} \approx 6.25 \times 10^{-5}$ m

15. A liquid drop breaks into 27 small drops. If surface tension of the liquid is S, then find the energy released.

Sol. Let the radius of larger drop $= R$

and radius of each small drop $= r$

Volume of 27 small drops = Volume of the large drop

$$= 27 \times \frac{4}{3} \times \pi r^3 = \frac{4}{3} \pi R^3$$

So, $\qquad r = R/3$

Surface area of large drop $= 4\pi R^2$

Surface area of 27 small drops $= 27 \times 4\pi r^2$

$$= 27 \times 4\pi \left(\frac{R}{3}\right)^2 = 12\pi R^2$$

$\therefore$ Increase in surface area $= 12\pi R^2 - 4\pi R^2 = 8\pi R^2$

Increase in energy = Increase in surface area

$$\times \text{Surface tension}$$

$$= 8\pi R^2 \times S$$

16. Two soap bubbles of radii 6 cm and 8 cm coalesce to form a single bubble. Find the radius of the new bubble.

Sol. Surface energy of first soap bubble

$$= \text{Surface tension} \times \text{surface area}$$

$$= 2 \times 4\pi R_1^2 S = 8\pi R_1^2 S$$

Surface energy of second soap bubble $= 8\pi R_2^2 S$

Let the radius of the new soap bubble is R. So, the surface energy of new bubble $= 8\pi R^2 S$

By the law of conservation of energy,

$$8\pi R^2 S = 8\pi R_1^2 S + 8\pi R_2^2 S$$

$$R^2 = R_1^2 + R_2^2 = 36 + 64$$

$\therefore \qquad R^2 = 100 \text{ cm}^2 \Rightarrow R = 10 \text{ cm}$

17. A liquid drop of radius 4 mm breaks into 1000 identical drops. Find the change in surface energy. $S = 0.07 \text{ Nm}^{-1}$.

Sol. Volume of 1000 small drops = Volume of a large drop

$$1000 \times \frac{4}{3} \pi r^3 = \frac{4}{3} \pi R^3$$

$$r = \frac{R}{10}$$

Surface area of large drop $= 4\pi R^2$

Surface area of 1000 drop $= 4\pi \times 1000 \, r^2 = 40\pi R^2$

$\therefore$ Increase in surface area $= (40 - 4)\pi R^2 = 36 \pi R^2$

The increase in surface energy

$$= \text{Surface tension} \times \text{increase in surface area}$$

$$= 36\pi R^2 \times 0.07 = 36 \times 3.14 \times (4 \times 10^{-3})^2 \times 0.07$$

$$= 1.26 \times 10^{-4} \text{ J}$$

18. The sap in trees, which consists mainly of water in summer, rises in a system of capillaries of radius $r = 2.5 \times 10^{-5}$ m. The surface tension of sap is $S = 7.28 \times 10^{-2}$ N/m and angle of contact is $0°$. Does surface tension alone account for the supply of water to the top of all trees? **[NCERT]**

Sol. Given, radius $(r) = 2.5 \times 10^{-5}$ m

Surface tension $(S) = 7.28 \times 10^{-2}$ N/m

Angle of contact $(\theta) = 0°$,
density of water $(\rho) = 10^3$ kg/m^3

The maximum height which sap can rise in trees through capillarity action is given by

$$h = \frac{2S \cos \theta}{r\rho g}$$

$$h = \frac{2 \times 7.28 \times 10^{-2} \times \cos 0°}{2.5 \times 10^{-5} \times 1 \times 10^3 \times 9.8} = 0.59 \text{ m}$$

But, the height of many trees are more than 0.59 m, therefore, the rise of sap in all trees is not possible through capillarity action alone.

LONG ANSWER Type I Questions

19. A U-shaped wire is dipped in a soap solution and removed. The thin soap film formed between the wire and a light slider supports a weight of 1.5×10^{-2} N (which includes the small weight of the slider). The length of the slider is 30 cm. What is the surface tension of the film? **[NCERT]**

Sol. Length of the slider $(l) = 30$ cm

As a soap film has two free surfaces, therefore, total length of the film to be supported

$$l' = 2l = 2 \times 30 = 60 \text{ cm} = 0.60 \text{ m}$$

Let S be the surface tension of the soap solution.

Total force on the slider due to surface tension,

$$F = S \times 2l$$

$$F = S \times 0.60 \text{ N} \qquad \qquad ...(i)$$

Weight (w) supported by the slider $= 1.5 \times 10^{-2}$ N

In equilibrium,

Force on the slider due to surface tension = weight supported by the slider

$\therefore \qquad \qquad F = w$

$$S \times 0.60 = 1.5 \times 10^{-2}$$

or $\qquad S = \dfrac{1.5 \times 10^{-2}}{0.60} = 2.5 \times 10^{-2}$ N/m

20. What is the pressure inside the drop of mercury of radius 3.00 mm at room temperature? Surface tension of mercury at that temperature $(20°C)$ is 4.65×10^{-1} N/m. The atmospheric pressure is 1.01×10^5 Pa. Also, give the excess pressure inside the drop.

Excess pressure inside a liquid drop is given by

$\Delta p = \dfrac{2S}{R}$, where S = surface tension of the liquid,

R = radius of the drop. **[NCERT]**

Sol. Given, radius of drop $(R) = 3.00$ mm $= 3 \times 10^{-3}$ m

Surface tension of mercury $(S) = 4.65 \times 10^{-1}$ N/m

Atmospheric pressure $(p_0) = 1.01 \times 10^5$ Pa

Pressure inside the drop = Atmospheric pressure

+ Excess pressure inside the liquid drop $= p_0 + \dfrac{2S}{R}$

$$= 1.01 \times 10^5 + \dfrac{2 \times 4.65 \times 10^{-1}}{3 \times 10^{-3}}$$

$$= 1.01 \times 10^5 + 3.10 \times 10^2$$

$$= 1.01 \times 10^5 + 0.00310 \times 10^5$$

$$= 1.01310 \times 10^5 \text{ Pa}$$

Excess pressure inside the drop

$$(\Delta p) = \dfrac{2S}{R} = \dfrac{2 \times 4.65 \times 10^{-1}}{3 \times 10^{-3}}$$

$$= 3.10 \times 10^2 = 310 \text{ Pa}$$

21. Two mercury droplets of radii 0.1 cm and 0.2 cm collapse into one single drop. What amount of energy is released? The surface tension of mercury $S = 435.5 \times 10^{-3}$ N/m.

When two or more droplets collapse to form a bigger drop, then its surface area decreases and energy is released equal to $S \Delta A$. **[NCERT]**

Sol. Radii of mercury droplets, $r_1 = 0.1$ cm $= 1 \times 10^{-3}$ m

$$r_2 = 0.2 \text{ cm} = 2 \times 10^{-3} \text{ m}$$

Surface tension $(S) = 435.5 \times 10^{-3}$ N/m

Let the radius of the big drop formed by collapsing be R.

∴ Volume of big drop = Volume of small droplets

$$\dfrac{4}{3}\pi R^3 = \dfrac{4}{3}\pi r_1^3 + \dfrac{4}{3}\pi r_2^3$$

or $\qquad R^3 = r_1^3 + r_2^3$

$$= (0.1)^3 + (0.2)^3$$

$$= 0.001 + 0.008 = 0.009$$

or $\qquad R = 0.21$ cm $= 2.1 \times 10^{-3}$ m

∴ Change in surface area

$$\Delta A = 4\pi R^2 - (4\pi r_1^2 + 4\pi r_2^2)$$

$$= 4\pi \left[R^2 - (r_1^2 + r_2^2)\right]$$

∴ Energy released $= S \cdot \Delta A$

$$= S \times 4\pi \left[R^2 - (r_1^2 + r_2^2)\right]$$

$$= 435.5 \times 10^{-3} \times 4 \times 3.14 \left[(2.1 \times 10^{-3})^2 - (1 \times 10^{-6}\right.$$

$$\left. + 4 \times 10^{-6})\right]$$

$$= 435.5 \times 4 \times 3.14 \left[4.41 - 5\right] \times 10^{-6} \times 10^{-3}$$

$$= -32.27 \times 10^{-7} = -3.22 \times 10^{-6} \text{ J}$$

(Negative sign shows absorption)

Therefore, 3.22×10^{-6} J energy will be absorbed.

22. If a drop of liquid breaks into smaller droplets, it results in lowering of temperature of the droplets. Let a drop of radius R, break into N small droplets each of radius r. Estimate the lowering in temperature. **[NCERT]**

Sol. When a big drop of radius R, break into N droplets each of radius r, the volume remains constant.

∴ Volume of big drop $= N \times$ Volume of small drop

$$\dfrac{4}{3}\pi R^3 = N \times \dfrac{4}{3}\pi r^3$$

or $\qquad R^3 = Nr^3$ or $N = \dfrac{R^3}{r^3}$

Now, change in surface area $= 4\pi R^2 - N4\pi r^2$

$$= 4\pi (R^2 - Nr^2)$$

Energy released $= S \times \Delta A = S \times 4\pi (R^2 - Nr^2)$

Due to releasing of this energy, the temperature is lowered.

If ρ is the density and s is specific heat of liquid and its temperature is lowered by $\Delta\theta$, then

Energy released $= ms\Delta\theta$

$$S \times 4\pi (R^2 - Nr^2) = \left(\dfrac{4}{3}\pi \times R^3 \times \rho\right) s\Delta\theta$$

$$\Delta\theta = \dfrac{S \times 4\pi (R^2 - Nr^2)}{\dfrac{4}{3}\pi R^3 \rho \times s} = \dfrac{3S}{\rho s}\left[\dfrac{R^2}{R^3} - \dfrac{Nr^2}{R^3}\right]$$

$$= \dfrac{3S}{\rho s}\left[\dfrac{1}{R} - \dfrac{(R^3/r^3) \times r^2}{R^3}\right] \qquad \left[\because N = \dfrac{R^3}{r^3}\right]$$

$$\Delta\theta = \dfrac{3S}{\rho s}\left[\dfrac{1}{R} - \dfrac{1}{r}\right]$$

LONG ANSWER Type II Questions

23. If a number of little droplets of water, each of radius r, coalesce to form a single drop of radius R, and the energy released is converted into kinetic energy then find out the velocity acquired by the bigger drop.

Sol. Let n be the number of little droplets which coalesce to form single drop. Then,

Volume of n little droplets = Volume of single drop

or $\qquad n \times \dfrac{4}{3}\pi r^3 = \dfrac{4}{3}\pi R^3$ or $nr^3 = R^3$

Decrease in surface area

$$= n \times 4\pi r^2 - 4\pi R^2$$

$$= 4\pi \left[nr^2 - R^2\right] = 4\pi \left[\dfrac{nr^3}{r} - R^2\right]$$

$$= 4\pi \left[\dfrac{R^3}{r} - R^2\right] = 4\pi R^3 \left[\dfrac{1}{r} - \dfrac{1}{R}\right]$$

The energy released, $\qquad$ $[\because nr^3 = R^3]$

E = Surface tension × decrease in surface area

$$= 4\pi S R^3 \left[\frac{1}{r} - \frac{1}{R}\right]$$

The mass of bigger drop,

$$M = \frac{4}{3}\pi R^3 \times 1 = \frac{4}{3}\pi R^3$$

$\therefore \qquad E = \frac{4}{3}\pi S R^3 . 3\left[\frac{1}{r} - \frac{1}{R}\right]$

$$= 3SM\left[\frac{1}{r} - \frac{1}{R}\right] \qquad \left[\because M = \frac{4}{3}\pi R^3\right]$$

$\because$ KE of bigger drop = Energy released

$$\frac{1}{2}MV^2 = 3SM\left[\frac{1}{r} - \frac{1}{R}\right]$$

$\therefore \qquad V = \sqrt{6S\left(\frac{R-r}{Rr}\right)}$

24. What is the excess pressure inside a bubble of soap solution of radius 5.00 mm, given that the surface tension of soap solution at the temperature (20°C) is 2.50×10^{-2} N/m? If an air bubble of the same dimension were formed at a depth of 40.0 cm inside a container containing the soap solution (of relative density 1.20), what would be the pressure inside the bubble? (1 atm pressure is 1.01×10^5 Pa.)

💡 The excess pressure inside a soap bubble is given by $\Delta p = \frac{4S}{R}$. where S = surface tension of the soap solution, R = radius of the bubble.

[NCERT]

Sol. Given, surface tension of soap solution (S)

$$= 2.5 \times 10^{-2}\,\text{N/m}$$

Density of soap solution $(\rho) = 1.2 \times 10^3\,\text{kg/m}^3$

Radius of soap bubble $(r) = 5.00\,\text{mm} = 5.0 \times 10^{-3}\,\text{m}$

Radius of air bubble $(R) = 5 \times 10^{-3}\,\text{m}$

Atmospheric pressure $(p_0) = 1.01 \times 10^5\,\text{Pa}$

Excess pressure inside the soap bubble

$$= \frac{4S}{r} = \frac{4 \times 2.5 \times 10^{-2}}{5.0 \times 10^{-3}}$$

$$= 20\,\text{Pa}$$

Excess pressure inside the air bubble

$$= \frac{2S}{R} = \frac{2 \times 2.5 \times 10^{-2}}{5.0 \times 10^{-3}} = 10\,\text{Pa}$$

$\therefore$ Pressure inside the air bubble = Atmospheric pressure + Pressure due to 40 cm of soap solution column + Excess pressure inside the bubble

$= (1.01 \times 10^5) + (0.40 \times 1.2 \times 10^3 \times 9.8) + 10$

$= (1.01 \times 10^5) + 4.704 \times 10^3 + 10$

$= 1.01 \times 10^5 + 0.04704 \times 10^5 + 0.00010 \times 10^5$

$= 1.05714 \times 10^5\,\text{Pa} = 1.06 \times 10^5\,\text{Pa}$

25. Explain why?

(i) The angle of contact of mercury with glass is obtuse, while that of water with glass is acute.

(ii) Water on a clean glass surface tends to spread out while mercury on the same surface tends to form drops. (Put differently, water wets the glass while mercury does not.)

(iii) Surface tension of a liquid is independent of the area of the surface.

(iv) Water with detergents dissolved in it should have small angles of contact.

(v) A drop of liquid under no external forces is always spherical in shape. **[NCERT]**

Sol. (i) When a small quantity of a liquid is poured on a solid, three types of interfaces namely liquid-air, solid-air and solid-liquid are occured. The surface tension corresponding to these three interfaces are S_{LA}, S_{SA} and S_{SL}, respectively. If θ is the angle of contact between solid and liquid then,

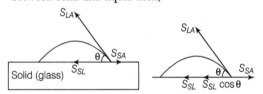

$$S_{SL} + S_{LA}\cos\theta = S_{SA}$$
$\Rightarrow \qquad S_{LA}\cos\theta = S_{SA} - S_{SL}$
$$\cos\theta = \frac{S_{SA} - S_{SL}}{S_{LA}} \qquad \ldots(i)$$

For mercury and glass $S_{SA} < S_{SL}$, therefore, from Eq. (i) $\cos\theta$ is negative and therefore, $\theta > 90°$, i.e. obtuse.

For water and glass $S_{SA} > S_{SL}$, therefore, from Eq. (i) $\cos\theta$ is positive and therefore, $\theta < 90°$, i.e. acute.

(ii) For equilibrium of a liquid drop on a solid surface

$$S_{SL} + S_{LA}\cos\theta = S_{SA}$$

In case of mercury and glass, $S_{SL} > S_{SA}$, therefore, for equilibrium $\cos\theta$ should be negative, i.e. θ should be obtuse. In order to achieve this obtuse value of angle of contact, the mercury tends to form a drop. In case of water and glass, $S_{SA} > S_{SL}$, therefore, for equilibrium $\cos\theta$ should be positive, i.e. θ should be acute.

In order to achieve this value of angle of contact, the water tends to spread.

(iii) Surface tension of a liquid is defined as the force acting per unit length on an imaginary line drawn tangentially to the liquid surface at rest. Therefore, surface tension is independent of the area of the liquid surface.

(iv) The rise of liquid in a capillary tube is given by

$$h = \frac{2S \cos \theta}{r \rho g},$$

i.e. $h \propto \cos \theta$

The cloth has narrow spaces in the form of fine capillaries. If angle of contact θ is small, then the value of $\cos \theta$ will be large and hence, detergent will rise more in fine capillaries in the cloth. Now, the detergent solution will penetrate more in cloth and remove stains and dust from the cloth.

(v) In the absence of external forces, the size of a liquid drop is decided only by the force due to surface tension. Due to surface tension, a liquid drop tends to acquire minimum surface area. As surface area is minimum for a sphere for a given volume of liquid. Therefore, under no external force a liquid is always spherical in shape.

26. Mercury has an angle of contact equal to $140°$ with sodalime glass. A narrow tube of radius 1.00 mm made of this glass is dipped in a trough containing mercury. By what amount does the mercury dip down in the tube relative to the liquid surface outside? Surface tension of mercury at the temperature of the experiment is 0.465 N/m. Density of mercury $= 13.6 \times 10^3 \text{kg/m}^3$.   **[NCERT]**

Sol. Given, angle of contact $(\theta) = 140°$

Radius of tube $(r) = 1$ mm $= 10^{-3}$ m

Surface tension $(S) = 0.465$ N/m

Density of mercury $(\rho) = 13.6 \times 10^3 \text{kg/m}^3$

Height of liquid rise or fall due to surface tension (h)

$$= \frac{2S \cos \theta}{r \rho g}$$

$$= \frac{2 \times 0.465 \times \cos 140°}{1 \times 10^{-3} \times 13.6 \times 10^3 \times 9.8}$$

$$= \frac{2 \times 0.465 \times (-0.7660)}{10^{-3} \times 13.6 \times 10^3 \times 9.8}$$

$$= -5.34 \times 10^{-3} \text{m}$$

$$= -5.34 \text{ mm}$$

Hence, the mercury level will depressed by 5.34 mm.

27. Two narrow bores of diameter 3.0 mm and 6.0 mm are joined together to form a U-tube open at both ends. If the U-tube contains water, what is the difference in its levels in the two limbs of the tube? Surface tension of water at the temperature of the experiment is $7.3 \times 10^{-2} \text{N/m}$. Take the angle of contact to be zero and density of water to be $1.0 \times 10^3 \text{kg/m}^3$.

$(g = 9.8 \text{ m/s}^2)$ **[NCERT]**

Sol. Given, surface tension of water $(S) = 7.3 \times 10^{-2} \text{N/m}$

Density of water $(\rho) = 1.0 \times 10^3 \text{kg/m}^3$

Acceleration due to gravity $(g) = 9.8 \text{ m/s}^2$

Angle of contact $(\theta) = 0°$

Diameter of one side, $2r_1 = 3.0$ mm

$\therefore$ $r_1 = 1.5$ mm $= 1.5 \times 10^{-3}$ m

Diameter of other side, $2r_2 = 6.0$ mm

$r_2 = 3.0$ mm $= 3.0 \times 10^{-3}$ m

Height of water column rises in first and second tubes

$$h_1 = \frac{2S \cos \theta}{r_1 \rho g} \Rightarrow h_2 = \frac{2S \cos \theta}{r_2 \rho g}$$

$\therefore$ Difference in levels of water rises in both tubes

$$\Delta h = h_1 - h_2 = \frac{2S \cos \theta}{\rho g}\left(\frac{1}{r_1} - \frac{1}{r_2}\right)$$

$$= \frac{2 \times 7.3 \times 10^{-2} \times \cos 0°}{1.0 \times 10^3 \times 9.8}\left[\frac{1}{1.5 \times 10^{-3}} - \frac{1}{3.0 \times 10^{-3}}\right]$$

$$= \frac{14.6}{9.8} \times 10^{-2}\left[\frac{2-1}{3}\right]$$

$$= \frac{14.6}{9.8 \times 3} \times 10^{-2}$$

$$= 0.497 \times 10^{-2} \text{m}$$

$$= 4.97 \times 10^{-3} \text{m}$$

$$= 4.9 \text{ mm}$$

ASSESS YOUR TOPICAL UNDERSTANDING

OBJECTIVE Type Questions

1. The surface tension of a liquid at its boiling point
   (a) becomes zero
   (b) becomes infinity
   (c) is equal to the value at room temperature
   (d) is half to the value at the room temperature

2. A liquid film is formed over a frame *ABCD* as shown in figure. Wire *CD* can slide without friction. Maximum value of mass that can be hanged from *CD* without breaking the liquid film is

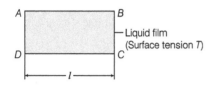

   (a) $\dfrac{Tl}{g}$
   (b) $\dfrac{2Tl}{g}$
   (c) $\dfrac{g}{2Tl}$
   (d) $T \times l$

3. The force required to separate two glass plates of $10^{-2}\,\text{m}^2$ with a film of water 0.05 mm thick between them, is (surface tension of water is $70 \times 10^{-3}\,\text{Nm}^{-1}$)
   (a) 28 N
   (b) 14 N
   (c) 50 N
   (d) 38 N

4. Why are drops and bubbles spherical?
   (a) Surface with minimum energy
   (b) Surface with maximum energy
   (c) High pressure
   (d) Low pressure

5. A capillary tube *A* is dipped in water. Another identical tube *B* is dipped in soap-water solution. Which of the following shows the relative nature of the liquid columns in the two tubes?

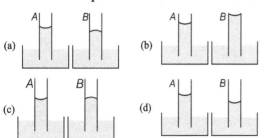

Answer

VERY SHORT ANSWER Type Questions

6. Find the pressure inside an air bubble of radius 5 cm which is 5 cm below the surface of water. Surface tension of water is $7 \times 10^{-2}\,\text{Nm}^{-1}$.

7. Find force to pull a circular disc of radius 2 cm from surface of water. Surface tension of water = 0.07 N/m.

8. Why two boats which are moving close to each other, pushed towards each other?

SHORT ANSWER Type Questions

9. The excess pressure inside a soap bubble of radius 4 cm is balanced by the weight of 20 mg, then find the value of surface tension.

10. Water rises upto height *h* in a capillary tube of certain diameter. This capillary tube is replaced by similar tube of half the diameter. Find out the height of water in that capillary.

LONG ANSWER Type I Questions

11. A frame made of metallic wire enclosing a surface area *A* is covered with a soap film. If the area of the frame of metallic wire is reduced by 50%, then what will be the change in energy of the soap.

12. A liquid rises in a capillary such that the surface tension balances its weight of 5×10^{-3} N of liquid, surface tension of liquid is $5 \times 10^{-2}\,\text{Nm}^{-1}$. Find the radius of the capillary.

LONG ANSWER Type II Questions

13. Two capillary tubes of same diameter are put vertically one each in two liquids whose relative densities are 0.8 and 0.6 and surface tensions are 60 and 50 dyne/cm, respectively. What is the ratio of heights of liquids in the two tubes?

14. The limbs of a manometer consist of uniform capillary tubes of radii 1.44×10^{-3} m and 7.2×10^{-4} m. Find out the correct pressure difference if the level of the liquid (density $10^3\,\text{kgm}^{-3}$ surface tension $72 \times 10^{-3}\,\text{Nm}^{-1}$) in the narrower tube stands 0.2 m above that in the broader tube.

|TOPIC 3|
Hydrodynamics

We have studied the fluids at rest or hydrostatics. Now, we will learn the branch of Physics which deals with the study of fluids in motion called **fluid dynamics** or **hydrodynamics**.

STREAMLINE, LAMINAR AND TURBULENT FLOW

Streamline Flow

Streamline flow of a liquid is that flow in which each particle of the liquid passing through a point travels along the same path and with the same velocity as the preceding particle passing through the same point. It is also defined as a curve whose tangent at any point is in the direction of the fluid velocity at that point.

Trajectory of a fluid particle

Properties of Streamline

(i) In streamline flow, no two streamlines can cross each other. If they do so, the particles of the liquid at the point of intersection will have two different directions for their flow, which will destroy the steady nature of the liquid flow.

(ii) The greater is the crowding of streamline at a place greater is the velocity of the liquid particles at that place and *vice-versa*.

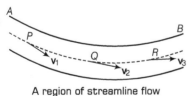
A region of streamline flow

Equation of Continuity

It states that, **during the streamline flow of the non-viscous and incompressible fluid through a pipe of varying cross-section, the product of area of cross-section and the normal fluid velocity (av) remains constant throughout the flow.**

Consider a non-viscous and incompressible liquid flowing through a tube AB of varying cross-section.

Let a_1 be the area of cross-section, v_1 at section A and the values of corresponding quantities at section B be a_2 and v_2, respectively. The density of flowing fluid is ρ.

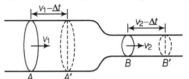
Fluid flow through pipe AB

As the fluid is incompressible, is constant

As, mass = volume × density

= Area of cross-section × length × density

∴ Mass of fluid that entering through section A in time Δt,

$$m_1 = a_1 v_1 \Delta t \rho_1$$

Mass of fluid that leaving through section B in time Δt,

$$m_2 = a_2 v_2 \Delta t \rho_2$$

According to conservation of mass, we get

$$m_1 = m_2$$

or $$a_1 v_1 \Delta t \rho = a_2 v_2 \Delta t \rho$$

ρ, is constant

Hence, $$a_1 v_1 = a_2 v_2$$

or $$\boxed{av = \text{constant}}$$

This is known as **equation of continuity**.

Laminar Flow

If the liquid flows over a horizontal surface in the form of layers of different velocities, then the flow of liquid is called **laminar flow**.

In laminar flow, the particle of one layer do not enter into another layer. In general, laminar flow is a streamline flow as shown in figure.

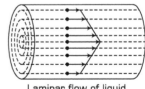
Laminar flow of liquid

Turbulent Flow

In rivers and canals, where speed of water is quite high or the boundary surfaces cause abrupt changes in velocity of the flow, then the flow becomes irregular.

Such flow of liquid is known as **turbulent flow**.

Thus, the flow of fluid in which velocity of all particles crossing a given point is not same and the motion of the fluid becomes irregular or disordered is called **turbulent flow** as shown in figure.

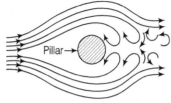

Turbulent flow of liquid

 Ideal Fluid

The motion of real fluids is very complicated. To understand fluid dynamics in a simpler manner, we assume that the fluid is ideal. An ideal fluid is one which is non-viscous, incompressible, and its flow is steady and irrotational.

BERNOULLI'S THEOREM

Bernoulli's principle is based on the law of conservation of energy and applied to ideal fluids. It states that **the sum of pressure energy per unit volume, kinetic energy per unit volume and potential energy per unit volume of an incompressible, non-viscous fluid in a streamlined irrotational flow remains constant at every cross-section throughout the liquid flow.**

Mathematically, it can be expressed as

$$p + \frac{1}{2}\rho v^2 + \rho g h = \text{constant}$$

where, p represents for pressure energy per unit volume $\frac{1}{2}\rho v^2$ for kinetic energy per unit volume and $\rho g h$ for potential energy per unit volume and ρ is density of flowing fluid (ideal).

The Swiss physicist **Daniel Bernoulli** developed this relationship in 1738.

Proof Consider an ideal fluid having streamline flow through a pipe of varying area of cross-section as shown in figure.

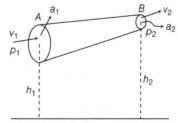

The flow of an ideal fluid in a pipe varying cross-section

Let p_1, a_1, h_1, v_1 and p_2, a_2, h_2, v_2 be the pressure, area of cross-section, height and velocity of flow at points A and B, respectively. Force acting on fluid at point $A = p_1 a_1$

Distance travelled by fluid in one second at point A
$$= v_1 \times 1 = v_1$$
Work done per second on the fluid at point A
= Force × distance travelled by fluid in one second.
$$W_1 = p_1 a_1 \times v_1$$
Similarly, work done per second by the fluid at point B,
$$W_2 = p_2 a_2 v_2$$
∴ Net work done on the fluid by pressure energy,
$$W = p_1 a_1 v_1 - p_2 a_2 v_2$$

But, $a_1 v_1 = a_2 v_2 = \dfrac{m}{\rho}$ (i.e. equation of continuity)

∴ Net work done on the fluid by the pressure energy,
$$W = \left(\frac{p_1 m}{\rho} - \frac{p_2 m}{\rho}\right)$$

Total work done by the pressure energy on the fluid increases the kinetic energy and potential energy of the fluid, when it flows from A to B.

∴ Increase in potential energy of fluid
$$= \text{KE at } B - \text{KE at } A$$
$$= \frac{1}{2}mv_2^2 - \frac{1}{2}mv_1^2 \quad [\because a_1 > a_2 \therefore v_2 > v_1]$$

Similarly, total increase in potential energy $= mgh_2 - mgh_1$

According to work energy theorem, work done on the fluid is equal to change in the energy of fluid.

i.e. work done by the pressure energy = total increase in energy

∴ $$\frac{p_1 m}{\rho} - \frac{p_2 m}{\rho} = (mgh_2 - mgh_1) + \left(\frac{1}{2}mv_2^2 - \frac{1}{2}mv_1^2\right)$$

$$\left(\frac{p_1 - p_2}{\rho}\right) = (gh_2 - gh_1) + \frac{1}{2}v_2^2 - \frac{1}{2}v_1^2$$

or $$\frac{p_1}{\rho} + \frac{1}{2}v_1^2 + gh_1 = \frac{p_2}{\rho} + \frac{1}{2}v_2^2 + gh_2$$

Hence, $$\frac{p}{\rho} + gh + \frac{1}{2}v^2 = \text{constant}$$

$$p + \frac{1}{2}\rho v^2 + \rho g h = \text{constant} \qquad \ldots(i)$$

Dividing both sides of Eq. (i) by ρg, we get
$$\frac{p}{\rho g} + h + \frac{v^2}{2g} = \frac{\text{constant}}{\rho g} = \text{new constant} \qquad \ldots(ii)$$

Here, $\dfrac{p}{\rho g}$ is called pressure head, h is called gravitational head and $\dfrac{v^2}{2g}$ is called velocity head.

Equation (ii) enable us to state Bernoulli's theorem in the streamline flow of an ideal liquid as the sum of pressure head, gravitational head and velocity head is always constant. If the fluid is flowing through a horizontal tube, two ends of the tube are at the same level. Therefore, there is no gravitational head (level difference), i.e. $h = 0$.

$$\frac{p}{\rho} + \frac{1}{2}v^2 = p + \frac{1}{2}\rho v^2 = \text{constant}$$

This shows, if p increases, v decreases and *vice-versa*. Thus, Bernoulli's theorem also states that in the streamline flow of an ideal liquid through a horizontal tube, the velocity increases where pressure decreases and *vice-versa*. This is also called **Bernoulli's principle**.

Bernoulli's Equation for the Fluid at Rest

When a fluid at rest, i.e. the velocity is zero everywhere, then the Bernoulli's equation becomes

$$p_1 + \rho g h_1 = p_2 + \rho g h_2$$

$$\boxed{p_1 - p_2 = \rho g (h_2 - h_1)}$$

Note
It must be noted that while applying the conservation of energy principle, then we assumed that there is no loss in energy due to friction. But in fact, when the fluid flow, some of the energy is lost due to friction. Generally, when the fluid flows in the different layers with different velocities. These layers exert frictional forces. This property of fluid is called **viscosity**.

Limitations of Bernoulli's Theorem

(i) Bernoulli's equation ideally applies to fluids with zero viscosity or non-viscous fluids.

(ii) The fluids must be incompressible, as the elastic energy of the fluid is also not taken into consideration.

(iii) Bernoulli's equation is applicable only to streamline flow of a fluid. It is not valid for non-steady or turbulent flow.

EXAMPLE |1| Water Flowing Through Two Pipes
Consider the two horizontal pipes of different diameters which are connected together and the water is flowing through these two pipes. In the first pipe, the pressure is $3.0 \times 10^4\,\text{N/m}^2$ and the speed of the water flowing is 5 m/s. If the diameters of the pipes are 4 cm and 6 cm, respectively, then what will be the speed and the pressure of the water in the second pipe? Density of the water is $10^3\,\text{kg/m}^3$.

Sol. According to the equation of continuity, we get

$$a_1 v_1 = a_2 v_2$$

$$\Rightarrow \qquad \pi r_1^2 v_1 = \pi r_2^2 v_2$$

$$\therefore \qquad v_2 = \left(\frac{r_1}{r_2}\right)^2 v_1$$

Given, $\quad r_1 = \dfrac{4}{2} = 2\,\text{cm} = 2 \times 10^{-2}\,\text{m}$

$$r_2 = \frac{6}{2} = 3\,\text{cm} = 3 \times 10^{-2}\,\text{m}$$

$$v_1 = 5\,\text{m/s}$$

$$v_2 = \left(\frac{2}{3}\right)^2 \times 5 = 2.22\,\text{m/s}$$

Now, applying the Bernoulli's theorem

$$p_1 + \frac{1}{2}\rho v_1^2 = p_2 + \frac{1}{2}\rho v_2^2$$

$$p_2 = p_1 + \frac{1}{2}\rho (v_1^2 - v_2^2)$$

$$= 3.0 \times 10^4 + \frac{1}{2} \times 10^3 (5^2 - 2.22^2)$$

$$= 3 \times 10^4 + 500 \times 20.08$$

$$p_2 \approx 4 \times 10^4\,\text{N/m}^2$$

Applications of Bernoulli's Theorem

(i) Speed of Efflux (Torricelli's Law)

According to Torricelli's, velocity of efflux i.e. the velocity with which the liquid flows out of an orifice (i.e. a narrow hole) is equal to that which a freely falling body would acquire in falling through a vertical distance equal to the depth of orifice below the free surface of liquid.

Speed of efflux The word efflux means the outflow of a fluid as shown in figure. Consider a tank containing a liquid of density ρ with a small hole on its side at height y_1 from the bottom and y_2 be the height of the liquid surface from the bottom and p be the air pressure above the liquid surface.

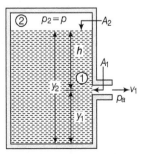

Fluid flow from an orifice

If A_1, A_2 are the cross-sectional areas and v_1, v_2 are the velocities of liquid at point 1 and 2, respectively, then from the equation of continuity, we get

$$A_1 v_1 = A_2 v_2 \quad \text{or} \quad v_2 = \frac{A_1}{A_2} v_1$$

If $A_2 \gg A_1$ so the liquid may be taken at rest at the top, i.e. $v_2 \approx 0$.

Applying the Bernoulli's theorem at points 1 and 2. The pressure $p_1 = p_a$ (the atmospheric pressure)

We get, $p_a + \frac{1}{2}\rho v_1^2 + \rho g\, y_1 = p + \rho g\, y_2 \qquad [\because\ v_2 \approx 0]$

or

$$\frac{1}{2}\rho v_1^2 = \rho g\,(y_2 - y_1) + (p - p_a)$$

$$y_2 - y_1 = h$$

Hence,

$$\frac{1}{2}\rho v_1^2 = \rho g h + (p - p_a)$$

Velocity of the liquid falls from orifice,

$$v_1 = \sqrt{2gh + \frac{2\,(p - p_a)}{\rho}}$$

(i) When the tank is open to the atmosphere,

$$p = p_a$$

and

$$v_1 = \sqrt{2gh}$$

Thus, the **velocity of efflux** of a liquid is equal to the velocity which a body acquires in falling freely from the free liquid surface to the orifice. This result is called **Torricelli's law.**

Distance at which the stream strikes the floor

$$x = 2\sqrt{h y_1}$$

EXAMPLE |2| Water is Emerging Out from an Orifice

If the water emerges from an orifice in a tank in which the gauge pressure is 4×10^5 N/m^2 before the flow starts then, what will be the velocity of the water emerging out? Take density of water is 1000 kgm^{-3}.

Sol. Here, $p = 4 \times 10^5$ N/m^2 and $\rho = 1000$ kgm^{-3}, $g = 10$m/s^2

Apply $p = h\rho g$,

$$\Rightarrow \quad h = \frac{p}{\rho g} = \frac{4 \times 10^5}{1000 \times 10}$$

Velocity of efflux,

$$v = \sqrt{2gh} = \sqrt{\frac{2 \times 10 \times 4 \times 10^5}{1000 \times 10}}$$

$$= \sqrt{800} = 28.28 \text{ m/s}$$

(ii) Venturimeter

It is a device used to measure the flow speed of incompressible fluid through a pipe. It is also called **flow meter** or **venturi tube**.

Construction It consists of a horizontal tube having wider opening of cross-section a_1 and a narrow neck of cross-section a_2. These two regions of the horizontal tube are connected to a manometer, containing a liquid of density p_m.

Working Let the liquid velocities be v_1 and v_2 at the wider and narrow region of the tube, respectively. Let p_1 and p_2 are liquid pressures at region A and B then,

According to the equation of continuity,

$$a_1 v_1 = a_2 v_2$$

or

$$\frac{a_1}{a_2} = \frac{v_2}{v_1}$$

Venturimeter

Using Bernoulli's equation for horizontal flow of liquid with density ρ.

$$p_1 + \frac{1}{2}\rho v_1^2 = p_2 + \frac{1}{2}\rho v_2^2$$

or

$$p_1 - p_2 = \frac{1}{2}\rho\,(v_2^2 - v_1^2)$$

$$p_1 - p_2 = \frac{1}{2}\rho v_1^2 \left(\frac{v_2^2}{v_1^2} - 1\right)$$

$$p_1 - p_2 = \frac{1}{2}\rho v_1^2 \left(\frac{a_1^2}{a_2^2} - 1\right)$$

...(i)

This pressure difference cause the liquid in the arm 2 of U tube connected at the narrow tube B to rise in comparison to other arm 1. The difference in height h of two arms of U tube measures the pressure difference.

$$p_1 - p_2 = h\rho_m g$$

$$h\rho_m g = \frac{1}{2}\rho v_1^2 \left(\frac{a_1^2}{a_2^2} - 1\right) \qquad \text{[using Eq. (i)]}$$

From above equation

$$\boxed{\text{Velocity of flow, } v_1 = \sqrt{\frac{2h\rho_m g}{\rho}\left(\frac{a_1^2}{a_2^2}-1\right)^{-1/2}}}$$

It is speed of liquid in the wider tube.

The volume of the liquid flowing per second through the wider tube is

$$V = a_1 v_1 = a_1 \sqrt{\frac{2h\rho_m g}{\rho}\left(\frac{a_1^2}{a_2^2}-1\right)^{-1/2}}$$

$$= a_1 a_2 \sqrt{\frac{2h\rho_m g}{\rho(a_1^2 - a_2^2)}} = a_1 a_2 \sqrt{\frac{2(p_1 - p_2)}{\rho(a_1^2 - a_2^2)}}$$

So, $$\boxed{\text{Volume of the liquid, } V = a_1 a_2 \sqrt{\frac{2(p_1 - p_2)}{\rho(a_1^2 - a_2^2)}}}$$

EXAMPLE |3| Blood Velocity

The flow of blood in a large artery of an anesthetised dog is diverted through a venturimeter. The wider part of the meter has a cross-sectional area equal to that of the artery, $a_1 = 8\,mm^2$. The narrower part has an area $a_2 = 4\,mm^2$. The pressure drop in the artery is 24 Pa. What is the speed of the blood in the artery? **[NCERT]**

Sol. The Bernoulli's equation for the horizontal flow is

$$p_1 + \frac{1}{2}\rho v_1^2 = p_2 + \frac{1}{2}\rho v_2^2$$

By equation of continuity,

$$a_1 v_1 = a_2 v_2 \text{ or } v_2 = \frac{a_1 v_1}{a_2}$$

$$\therefore \quad p_1 - p_2 = \frac{1}{2}\frac{\rho a_1^2 v_1^2}{a_2^2} - \frac{1}{2}\rho v_1^2 = \frac{1}{2}\rho v_1^2\left[\left(\frac{a_1^2}{a_2^2}\right)-1\right]$$

Here, $p_1 - p_2 = 24\,Pa$

$$\rho(\text{blood}) = 1.06 \times 10^3 \text{ kgm}^{-3}, a_1/a_2 = 8/4 = 2$$

$$\therefore \quad v_1 = \sqrt{\frac{2(p_1 - p_2)}{\rho\left(\frac{a_1^2}{a_2^2}-1\right)}}$$

$$= \sqrt{\frac{2 \times 24}{1.06 \times 10^3 \times (2^2 - 1)}} = 0.1228 \text{ m/s}$$

(iii) Atomizer or Sprayer

It is based on the Bernoulli's principle. The essential parts of an atomizer are shown in figure. The forward stroke of the piston produces a stream of air past the end of the tube. The air flowing past the open end of the tube reduces the pressure on the liquid. So, the atmospheric pressure acting on the surface of liquid forces, the liquid into the tube D. As a result the liquid rises up in the vertical tube A. When it collides with the high speed air in tube B, it breaks up into fine spray.

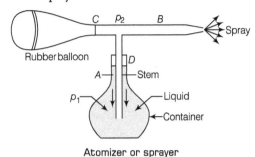

Atomizer or sprayer

(iv) Blood Flow and Heart Attack

Consider a case, where a person suffering from heart attack problem, whose artery gets constricted due to the accumulation of plaque on its inner walls.

According to Bernoulli's principle, the pressure inside artery becomes low and the artery may collapse due to external pressure. The activity of heart is further increased in order to force the blood through that artery. As the blood rushes through that artery, the internal pressure once again drops due to same reason. This will be leading to a repeat collapse. This phenomenon is called **vascular flutter** which can be heard on a stethoscope. This may result in a heart attack.

(v) Dynamic Lift

Dynamic lift is the force that acts on a body by virtue of its motion through a fluid. It is responsible for the curved path of a spinning ball and the lift of an aircraft wing.

(a) Ball Moving without Spin

When the velocity of the air above the ball is same as below the ball at the corresponding points resulting in zero pressure difference.

The air therefore, exerts no upward or downward force on the ball as shown in Fig. (a)

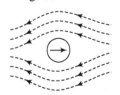

(a) Ball moving without spin

(b) Ball Moving with Spin

As the ball moves to the right, air rushes to the left with respect to the ball. Since the ball is spinning, it drags some air with it because of the roughness of its surface. The speed of air above the ball with respect to it is greater than below the ball. Hence, the pressure below the ball is greater than that above the ball. The force acts on the ball which makes it follow a curved path, as shown in Fig. (b).

The difference in lateral pressure, which causes a spinning ball to take a curved path which is curved towards the greater pressure side, is called **magnus effect**.

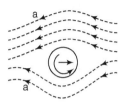

(b) Ball moving with spin

(c) Aerofoil, Lift of an Aircraft Wing

Aerofoil is a solid object shaped to provide an **upward dynamic lift** as it moves horizontally through air. This upward force makes aeroplane fly. The cross-section of the wing of an aeroplane looks like an aerofoil.

When the aeroplane moves through air, the air in the region above the wing moves faster than the air below as seen from the streamlines above the wing.

The difference in speed in the two regions makes the pressure in the region above lower than the pressure below the wing producing thereby a dynamic lift.

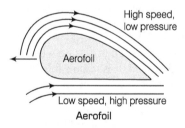

High speed, low pressure

Aerofoil

Low speed, high pressure
Aerofoil

EXAMPLE |4| A Boeing Aircraft

A fully loaded Boeing aircraft has a mass of 3.3×10^5 kg. Its total wing area is 500 m². It is in level flight with a speed of 960 km/h. (i) Estimate the pressure difference between the lower and upper surfaces of the wings (ii) Estimate the fractional increase in the speed of the air on the upper surface of the wing relative to the lower surface. [The density of air is $\rho = 1.2$ kgm^{-3}]   [NCERT]

Sol. (i) The weight of the boeing aircraft is balanced by the upward force due to the pressure difference

$$\Delta p \times A = mg = 3.3 \times 10^5 \times 9.8$$

So, $\Delta p = \dfrac{mg}{A}, \Delta p = \dfrac{3.3 \times 10^5 \times 9.8}{500}$

$$= 6.46 \times 10^3 \text{ N/m}^2$$

$$\therefore \qquad \Delta p \approx 6.5 \times 10^3 \text{ N/m}^2$$

(ii) Consider v_1 and v_2 are the speeds of air on lower and upper surfaces of the wings and p_1 and p_2 are the corresponding pressures.

From Bernoulli's principle

$$p_1 + \frac{1}{2}\rho v_1^2 = p_2 + \frac{1}{2}\rho v_2^2$$

$$\therefore \qquad p_1 - p_2 = \Delta p = \frac{\rho}{2}(v_2^2 - v_1^2)$$

$$(v_2 - v_1) = \frac{2\Delta p}{\rho(v_2 + v_1)}$$

Average speed, $v_{av} = \dfrac{v_2 + v_1}{2} = 960$ km/h $= 267$ m/s

So, $\dfrac{v_2 - v_1}{v_{av}} = \dfrac{\Delta p}{\rho v_{av}^2} = \dfrac{6.5 \times 10^3}{1.2 \times (267)^2} \approx 0.08 = 8\%$

Then, the speed above the wing needs to be only 8% higher than that below.

Roof can Blown off Without Damaging the House

During wind storm, the roofs of some huts are blown off without damaging the other parts of the house. The high wind blowing over the roof creates a low pressure p_2 in accordance with Bernoulli's principle.

The pressure p_1 below the roof is equal to the atmospheric pressure which is larger than p_2. This difference of pressure provides a vertical lift to the roof of hut. When lift is sufficient to overcome the gravity pull on the roof, the roof of the hut is blown off without causing any damage to the walls of hut.

VISCOSITY

When a solid body slides over another solid body, the force of friction opposes the relative motion of the solid bodies. In the same way, when a layer of fluid slides over another layer of the same fluid, a force of friction comes into play which is called **viscous force**. This force opposes the relative motion of the different layers of a fluid.

So, the tendency of fluids to oppose the relative motion of its layers is called **viscosity of fluid**. The backward dragging force called **viscous drag** or **viscous force**.

Cause of Viscosity

The velocities of the layers of the liquid increases uniformly from bottom to the top layer. For any layer of liquid, its lower layer pulls it backward while its upper layer pulls it forward direction. This type of flow is known as **laminar flow**.

Similar cases arise when the liquid, flowing in a pipe or a tube, then the velocity of the liquid is maximum along the axis of the tube and decreases gradually, as it moves towards the walls where it becomes zero.

Coefficient of Viscosity

Consider the flow of liquid as shown in figure. A portion of liquid which at some instant having the shape *MNOP* after the short interval of time (say Δt) the fluid is deformed and take the shape as *MQRP* since, the fluid has undergone the shear strain, stress in the solid is the force per unit area but in case of fluid, it depends on the rate of change of strain or strain rate.

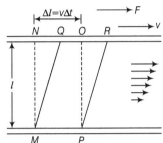

The layer of fluid is deformed under some stress

Strain $\dfrac{\Delta l}{l}$ and the rate of change of strain is $\dfrac{\Delta l}{l \Delta t} = \dfrac{v}{l}$.

Hence, the coefficient of viscosity is defined as the ratio of shearing stress to the strain rate

$$\eta = \frac{F/A}{v/l} = \frac{Fl}{vA}$$

$$\boxed{\text{Coefficient of viscosity, } \eta = \frac{Fl}{vA}}$$

or it can be written as, $\quad \eta = \dfrac{F/A}{\dfrac{dv}{dx}}$

Dimension of η

As, we know $\quad \eta = \dfrac{F}{A} \cdot \dfrac{l}{v}$

$\therefore \qquad \eta = \dfrac{[MLT^{-2}]}{[L^2 LT^{-1}]}[L] = [ML^{-1}T^{-1}]$

Units of η

(i) In CGS system, the unit of η is **dyne-s/cm^2** and it is called **poise**.

$$1 \text{ poise} = \frac{1 \text{ dyne}}{1 \text{ cm}^2} \times \frac{1 \text{ cm}}{1 \text{ cm/s}}$$

1 poise = 1 dyne-s / cm^2

The coefficient of viscosity of a liquid is said to be 1 poise, if a tangential force of 1 dyne cm^{-2} of the surface is required to maintain a relative velocity of 1 cm s^{-1} between two layers of the liquid 1 cm apart.

(ii) The SI unit of η is **Ns/m^2** or **kg/ms** and it is called **decapoise** or **poiseuille**.

$$1 \text{ poiseuille} = \frac{1 N}{1 \text{ m}^2} \cdot \frac{1 \text{ m}}{1 \text{ m/s}} = 1 \text{ Ns/m}^2$$

The coefficient of viscosity of a liquid is said to be 1 poiseuille or decapoise if a tangential force of $1 Nm^{-2}$ of the surface is required to maintain a relative velocity of $1 ms^{-1}$ between two layers of the liquid 1 m apart.

(iii) Relation between poiseuille and poise

1 poiseuille or 1 decapoise = 10 poise

The coefficient of viscosity is a scalar quantity.

Relative Viscosity

Relative viscosity of liquid $= \dfrac{\eta_{\text{liquid}}}{\eta_{\text{water}}}$

Relative viscosity of bloods remains constant between 0° C and 37°C.

Note

- Viscosity is just like friction force which converts kinetic energy into heat energy.
- No fluid has zero viscosity.
- Thin liquids like water, alcohol etc. are less viscous than thick liquids coal tar, blood, honey, glycerine etc.

Fluid friction force or force of viscosity

$$F = \eta A \frac{dv}{dz}$$

where, A = Area of layers

$\dfrac{dv}{dz}$ = Velocity gradient between two layers

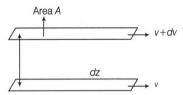

EXAMPLE |5| Shearing Stress at a River Bed
Near the surface of the river, the velocity of water is 160 kmh^{-1}. Find the shearing stress between horizontal layers of water, if the river is 6 m deep and the coefficient of viscosity of water is 10^{-2} poise.

Sol. Given, $v = 160 \text{ km/h} = 160 \times \dfrac{5}{18} \text{ m/s} = 44.44 \text{ m/s}$

$$l = 6 \text{ m and } \eta = 10^{-2} \text{ poise} = 10^{-3} \text{ Pa-s}$$

$$\text{Shearing stress} = \frac{F}{A} = \eta \frac{v}{l} = 10^{-3} \times \frac{44.44}{6}$$

$$\text{Shearing stress} = 7.407 \times 10^{-3} \text{ Nm}^{-2}$$

EXAMPLE |6| **Effect of Viscous Force**
A metal block of area 0.10 m² is connected to a 0.01 kg mass via a string that passes over an ideal pulley (considered massless and frictionless), as in figure. A liquid with a film thickness of 0.30 mm is placed between the block and the table. When released the block moves to the right with a constant speed of 0.085 ms⁻¹. Find the coefficient of viscosity of the liquid.

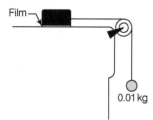

[NCERT]

Sol. Given, $m = 0.010$ kg, $g = 9.8$ m/s², $A = 0.10$ m²

$$F = T = mg = 0.010 \times 9.8 = 9.8 \times 10^{-2} \text{ N}$$

Shear stress on the fluid $= \dfrac{F}{A} = \dfrac{9.8 \times 10^{-2}}{0.10} = 0.98 \text{ N/m}^2$

The strain rate, $\quad \eta = \dfrac{\text{Stress}}{\text{Strain rate}}$

Strain rate $= \dfrac{v}{l} = \dfrac{0.085}{0.30 \times 10^{-3}}$

Now, the coefficient of viscosity of the liquid.

$$\eta = \dfrac{F\, l}{A v} = \dfrac{9.8 \times 10^{-2} \times 0.30 \times 10^{-3}}{0.10 \times 0.085}$$

$$\eta = 3.45 \times 10^{-3} \text{ Pa-s}$$

Difference between Viscous Force and Solid Friction

Viscous Force	Solid Friction
Viscous force is directly proportional to the area of layers in contact.	Solid friction is independent of the area of the surfaces in contact.
It is directly proportional to the relative velocity between the two liquid layers.	It is independent of the relative velocity between two solid surfaces.
It is independent of the normal reaction between the two liquid layers.	It is directly proportional to the normal reaction between the surfaces in contact.

Effect of Temperature on the Viscosity

The viscosity of liquids decreases with increase in temperature and increases with decrease in temperature.

i.e. $$\eta \propto \dfrac{1}{\sqrt{T}}$$

On the other hand, the viscosity of gases increases with the increase in temperature and *vice-versa*.

i.e. $$\eta \propto \sqrt{T}$$

CRITICAL VELOCITY

The critical velocity of a liquid is that limiting value of its velocity of flow upto which the flow is streamlined and above which the flow becomes turbulent.

The critical velocity v_c of a liquid flowing through a tube depends on

   (i) coefficient of viscosity of the liquid (η)

   (ii) density of the liquid (ρ)

   (iii) radius of the tube (r)

Consider, $\quad v_c = k \eta^a \rho^b r^c$

where, k is a dimensionless constant. Writing the above equation in dimensional form, we get

$$[M^0 L T^{-1}] = [ML^{-1}T^{-1}]^a [ML^{-3}]^b [L]^c$$

$$[M^0 L T^{-1}] = [M^{a+b} L^{-a-3b+c} T^{-a}]$$

Compare the powers of M, L and T on both sides, we get

$$a + b = 0$$
$$-a - 3b + c = 1$$
$$-a = -1$$

On solving, we get,

$$a = 1, b = -1, c = -1$$

$\therefore \qquad v_c = k \eta \rho^{-1} r^{-1} = \dfrac{k\eta}{\rho r}$

We get,

$$\boxed{\text{Critical velocity, } v_c = \dfrac{k\eta}{\rho r}}$$

For the flow to the streamline, value of v_c should be as large as possible. For this, η should be large, ρ and r should be small. So, we conclude that

   (i) The flow of liquids of higher viscosity and lower density through narrow pipes tends to be **streamlined**.

   (ii) The flow of liquids of lower viscosity and higher density through broad pipes tends to become **turbulent** because in that case the critical velocity will be very small.

STOKE'S LAW

When a small spherical body falls through a viscous fluid at rest, the layers of fluid in contact with the body are dragged alongwith it. But the layers of the fluid away from the body are at rest. This produces a relative motion between different layers of the fluid.

As a result, a **backward dragging** force (i.e. viscous force) comes into play, which opposes the motion of the body.

This backward dragging force increases with the increase in velocity of the moving body. Falling of a raindrop, swinging of a pendulum bob are the examples of such type of motion.

Sir George G Stokes (1819–1903), an English scientist found that the backward dragging force F acting on a small spherical body of radius r, moving through a fluid of coefficient of viscosity η, with velocity v is given by

$$\boxed{\text{Dragging force, } F = 6\pi\eta rv}$$

This is called **Stoke's law** of viscosity.

He observed that viscous drag (F) depends upon

(i) coefficient of viscosity (η) of the fluid.

(ii) velocity (v) of the body.

(iii) radius (r) of the spherical body.

Let $\qquad F = k\,\eta^a v^b r^c$

...(i)

As $\qquad [F] = [MLT^{-2}], [\eta] = [ML^{-1}T^{-1}]$

$$[v] = [LT^{-1}], [r] = [L]$$

So, $\quad [MLT^{-2}] = [ML^{-1}T^{-1}]^a[LT^{-1}]^b[L]^c$

$$[MLT^{-2}] = [M^a L^{-a+b+c} T^{-a-b}]$$

Compare powers both sides of M, L, T, we get

$$a = 1 \qquad\qquad\text{...(ii)}$$
$$-a+b+c = 1 \qquad\text{...(iii)}$$
$$-a-b = -2 \qquad\text{...(iv)}$$
or $\qquad a+b = 2 \qquad\qquad\text{...(v)}$

From Eqs. (iii) and (v), we get

$$c = 1, \quad b = 1$$

Substituting these values in Eq. (i), we get

$$F = 6\pi\eta rv$$

where, the value of k was found to be 6π experimentally.

Note

- This law is used in the determination of electronic charge with the help of Millikan's experiment.
- This law accounts the formation of clouds.
- This law accounts, why the speed of rain drops is less than that of a body falling freely with a constant velocity from the height of clouds.
- This law helps a man coming down with the help of a parachute.

EXAMPLE |7| **Dragging Force on Rain Droplets**

Consider a drop of rain having radius 0.4 mm and terminal velocity 2 m/s. Find the viscous force on the rain drops, if viscosity of air is 18×10^{-5} dyne cm^{-2}s.

The Stoke's law is an interesting example of retarding force which is proportional to velocity.

Sol. Given, radius, $r = 0.4$ mm $= 0.4 \times 10^{-3}$ m

Terminal velocity, $v = 2$ ms^{-1}

and viscosity of air, $\eta = 18 \times 10^{-5}$ dyne cm^{-2}s

$$= 18 \times 10^{-6}\text{Pa-s}$$

According to Stoke's law, the viscous force $F = 6\pi\eta rv$

$$= 6 \times 3.142 \times 18 \times 10^{-6} \times 0.4 \times 10^{-3} \times 2$$

$$F = 2.71 \times 10^{-7}\text{N}$$

TERMINAL VELOCITY

The maximum constant velocity acquired by a body while falling through a viscous fluid is called its **terminal velocity**.

Consider an example of raindrop in air. It accelerates initially due to gravity. The force of viscosity increases as the velocity of the body increases. A stage is reached, when the true weight of the body becomes just equal to the sum of the upthrust and the viscous force. Then, the body begins to fall with a constant velocity called **terminal velocity**.

Suppose a sphere of density ρ falls through a liquid of density σ. When the body attains terminal velocity v, upward thrust + force of viscosity = weight of the spherical body

Upward thrust = The weight of the fluid displaced

$$= \frac{4}{3}\pi r^3 \sigma g$$

Force of viscosity $= 6\pi\eta rv$, and weight of the spherical body

$$= \frac{4}{3}\pi r^3 \rho g \qquad\qquad [\because mV\rho]$$

Thus, $\quad \dfrac{4}{3}\pi r^3 \sigma g + 6\pi\eta rv = \dfrac{4}{3}\pi r^3 \rho g$

or $\qquad\qquad 6\pi\eta rv = \dfrac{4}{3}\pi r^3 (\rho - \sigma)\, g$

or $\boxed{\text{Terminal velocity, } v = \dfrac{2}{9}\cdot\dfrac{r^2(\rho-\sigma)\, g}{\eta}}$

where, $\quad r =$ radius of the spherical body,

$\qquad\qquad v =$ terminal velocity

and $\qquad \eta =$ coefficient of viscosity of fluid

EXAMPLE |8| **Velocity of a Spherical Droplet**

If 27 drops of rain were to be combine to form one new large spherical drop, then what should be the velocity of this large spherical drop? Consider the terminal velocity of 27 drops of equal size falling through the air is 0.20 ms^{-1}.

Sol. Let, the radius of the small drop is r and that of big drop is R. The volume of the big drop $= 27 \times$ volume of each small drop

$$\frac{4}{3}\pi R^3 = 27 \times \frac{4}{3}\pi r^3 \Rightarrow R = 3r$$

Let, the terminal velocities of small and big drop are v_1 and v_2, respectively. Then,

$$v = \frac{2r^2(\rho - \sigma)g}{9\eta} \Rightarrow v \propto r^2$$

Hence, $\frac{v_2}{v_1} = \frac{R^2}{r^2} \Rightarrow v_2 = v_1 \times \frac{R^2}{r^2} = 0.2\left(\frac{3r}{r}\right)^2 = 0.2 \times 9$

$$v_2 = 1.8 \text{ m/s}$$

REYNOLD'S NUMBER

Osborne Reynolds (1842-1912) observed that turbulent flow is less likely for viscous fluid flowing at low rates. He defined a dimensionless parameter whose value decides the nature of flow of a liquid through a pipe, i.e. whether a flow will be steady or turbulent, it is given by

$$\boxed{\text{Reynold's number, } R_e = \frac{\rho v D}{\eta}}$$

where, ρ = density of the liquid,

v = velocity of the liquid,

η = coefficient of viscosity of the liquid

and D = diameter of the pipe

(i) If R_e lies between 0 and 2000, then liquid flow is streamline or laminar.

(ii) If $R_e > 3000$, then liquid flow is turbulent.

(iii) If R_e lies between 2000 and 3000, then flow of liquid is unstable, it may change from laminar to turbulent and *vice-versa*.

The exact value at which turbulent sets in a fluid is called **critical Reynold's number**.

In another form, R_e can also be written as

$$R_e = \frac{\rho v D}{\eta} = \frac{\rho v^2}{\left(\eta \frac{v}{D}\right)} = \frac{\rho A v^2}{\eta \frac{Av}{D}} = \frac{\text{Inertial force}}{\text{Force of viscosity}}$$

Hence, Reynold's number represents the ratio of the inertial force per unit area to the viscous force per unit area.

EXAMPLE |9| **Finding the Nature of the Flow**
The flow rate of water is 0.58 L/mm from a tap of diameter of 1.30 cm. After some time, the flow rate is increased to 4 L/min. Determine the nature of the flow for both the flow rates. The coefficient of viscosity of water is 10^{-3}Pa - s and the density of water is 10^3 kg/m^3.

Sol. Given, diameter, $D = 1.30$ cm $= 1.3 \times 10^{-2}$m

Coefficient of viscosity of water, $\eta = 10^{-3}$Pa-s

Density of water, $\rho = 10^3$ kg/m^3

The volume of the water flowing out per second is

$$V = vA = v \times \pi r^2 = v\pi \frac{D^2}{4}$$

$\therefore$ Speed of flow, $v = \frac{4v}{\pi D^2}$

Reynold's number, $R_e = \frac{\rho v D}{\eta} = \frac{4\rho v}{\eta \pi D}$

Case I When $V = 0.58$ L / min

$$= \frac{0.58 \times 10^{-3} \text{m}^3}{1 \times 60 \text{ s}}$$

$$= 9.67 \times 10^{-6} \text{m}^3\text{s}^{-1}$$

$$R_e = \frac{4 \times 10^3 \times 9.67 \times 10^{-6}}{10^{-3} \times 3.14 \times 1.3 \times 10^{-2}} = 948$$

$\because R_e < 1000$, so the flow is steady or streamline

Case II When $V = 4$ L/min

$$= \frac{4 \times 10^{-3}}{60} \text{ m}^3\text{s}^{-1} = 6.67 \times 10^{-5} \text{m}^3\text{s}^{-1}$$

$$R_e = \frac{4 \times 10^3 \times 6.67 \times 10^{-5}}{10^{-3} \times 3.14 \times 1.3 \times 10^{-2}} = 6536$$

$\because R_e > 3000$, so the flow will be turbulent.

Poiseuille's Formula

The volume of a liquid flowing out per second through a horizontal capillary tube of length l, radius r, under a pressure difference p applied across its ends is given by

$$V = \frac{Q}{t} = \frac{\pi p r^4}{8\eta l}$$

This formula is called **Poiseuille's** formula.

| TOPIC PRACTICE 3 |

OBJECTIVE Type Questions

1. In a streamline flow,
   (a) the speed of a particle always remains same
   (b) the velocity of a particle always remains same
   (c) the kinetic energies of all the particles arriving at a given point are the same
   (d) the potential energies of all the particles arriving at a given point are the same

Sol. (b) Both velocity and direction of flow remain same.

2. Two water pipes of diameters 2 cm and 4 cm are connected with the main supply line. The velocity of flow of water in the pipe of 2 cm diameter is
   (a) 4 times that in the other pipe
   (b) $\frac{1}{4}$ times that in the other pipe
   (c) 2 times that in the other pipe
   (d) $\frac{1}{2}$ times that in the other pipe

Sol. (a) From equation of continuity, $av =$ constant

$$d_A = 2\,\text{cm} \quad \text{and} \quad d_B = 4\,\text{cm}$$

$$\therefore \quad r_A = 1\,\text{cm} \quad \text{and} \quad r_B = 2\,\text{cm}$$

$$\therefore \quad \frac{v_A}{v_B} = \frac{a_B}{a_A} = \frac{\pi(r_B)^2}{\pi(r_A)^2} = \left(\frac{2}{1}\right)^2 \Rightarrow v_A = 4v_B$$

3. A ball is moving without spinning in a straight line through a fluid (as shown)

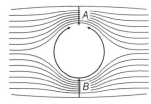

If p_A and p_B are pressure values at A and B, then

(a) $p_A < p_B$ (b) $p_B < p_A$

(c) $p_A \times p_B = 1$ (d) $p_A / p_B = 1$

Sol. (d) As the ball is not spinning, By Bernoulli's theorem,

$$p_A = p_B \Rightarrow \frac{p_A}{p_B} = 1$$

4. A tall cylinder is filled with viscous oil. A round pebble is dropped from the top with zero initial velocity. From the plot shown in figure, indicate the one that represents the velocity (v) of the pebble as a function of time (t). **[NCERT Exemplar]**

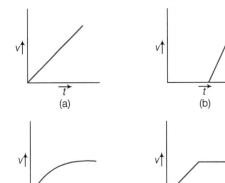

Sol. (c) When the pebble is falling through the viscous oil the viscous force is

$$F = 6\pi\eta r v$$

As the force is variable, hence acceleration is also variable so v-t graph will not be straight line. First velocity increases and then becomes constant known as terminal velocity.

5. The coefficient of viscosity for hot air is

(a) greater than the coefficient of viscosity for cold air

(b) smaller than the coefficient of viscosity for cold air

(c) same as the coefficient of viscosity for cold air

(d) increases or decreases depending on the external pressure

Sol. (a) For gases, viscosity increases with temperature.

VERY SHORT ANSWER Type Questions

6. Can two streamlines cross each other, why?

Sol. Two streamlines can never cross each other because if they cross them at the point of intersection, there will be two possible direction of flow of fluid which is impossible for streamlines.

7. Why does the velocity increase when liquid flowing in a wider tube enters a narrow tube? **[NCERT]**

Sol. This is due to equation of continuity, $a_1 v_1 = a_2 v_2$

$$\because \qquad a_1 > a_2$$

$$\therefore \qquad v_2 > v_1$$

8. Can Bernoulli's equation be used to describe the flow of water through a rapid in a river? Explain.

Sol. No, Bernoulli's equation cannot be used to describe the flow of water through a rapid in a river because Bernoulli's equation can be utilised only for streamline flow.

9. Does it matter if one uses gauge instead of absolute pressures in applying Bernoulli's equation? Explain.

Sol. No, it does not matter if one uses gauge instead of absolute pressures in applying Bernoulli's equation unless the atmospheric pressure at the two points where, Bernoulli's equation is applied are significantly different.

10. The height of water level in a tank is $H = 96\,\text{cm}$. Find the range of water stream coming out of a hole at depth $H/4$ from upper surface of water.

Sol. The depth of hole below the upper surface of water is

$$h = \frac{H}{4} = \frac{96}{4} = 24\,\text{cm}$$

The height of hole from ground is,

$$h' = 96 - 24 = 72\,\text{cm}$$

Horizontal range $= 2\sqrt{hh'}$

$$= 2\sqrt{24 \times 72}$$

$$= 48\sqrt{3}\,\text{cm}$$

11. A hot liquid moves faster than a cold liquid. Why?

Sol. The viscosity of liquid decreases with the increase in temperature. Therefore, viscosity of hot liquid is less than that of cold liquid. Due to this, hot liquid moves faster than the cold liquid.

12. On what factors does the critical speed of fluid flow depend?

Sol. The critical speed of a fluid depends on (a) diameter of tube, (b) density of fluid, (c) coefficient of viscosity of the fluid.

SHORT ANSWER Type Questions

13. Fill in the blanks using the word(s) from the list appended with each statement.

    (i) Surface tension of liquids generally......with temperature. (increases/decreases)

    (ii) Viscosity of gases......with temperature, whereas, viscosity of liquids......with temperature. (increases/decreases)

    (iii) For solids with elastic modulus of rigidity, the shearing force is proportional to......while for fluids, it is proportional to......(shear strain/rate of shear strain)

    (iv) For a fluid in a steady flow, the increase in flow speed at a constriction follows from......while the decrease of pressure there follows from......(conservation of mass/Bernoulli's principle).

    (v) For the model of a plane in a wind tunnel, turbulence occurs at a......speed that the critical speed for turbulence for an actual plane (greater/smaller) **[NCERT]**

Sol. (i) decreases

    (ii) increases, decreases

    (iii) shear strain, rate of shear strain

    (iv) conservation of mass, Bernoulli's principle

    (v) greater

14. In deriving Bernoulli's equation, we equated the work done on the fluid in the tube to its change in the potential and kinetic energy.

    (i) How does the pressure change as the fluid moves along the tube, if dissipative forces are present?

    (ii) Do the dissipative forces become more important as the fluid velocity increases? Discuss qualitatively. **[NCERT]**

Sol. (i) If dissipative forces are present, then a part of pressure energy is utilised in overcoming these forces. Due to which, the pressure decreases as the fluid moves along the tube.

    (ii) Yes, the dissipative forces become more important as the fluid velocity increases.

    The viscous drag is given by

$$F = -\eta A \frac{dv}{dx}$$

    As the velocity of fluid increases, the velocity gradient increases and hence, viscous drag increases i.e. dissipative force also increases.

15. Figs. (a) and (b) refer to the steady flow of a non-viscous liquid. Which of two figures is incorrect Why? **[NCERT]**

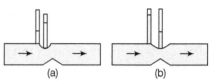

(a)   (b)

Sol. Fig. (a) is incorrect. According to equation of continuity, the speed of liquid is larger at smaller area.

From Bernoulli's theorem due to larger speed, the pressure will be lower at smaller area and therefore, height of liquid column will also be at lesser height, while in Fig. (a) height of liquid column at narrow area is higher.

16. At what speed will the velocity head of stream of water be 40 cm?

Sol. Given, $h = 40$ cm,

$$g = 980 \text{ cm/s}^2$$

We know that velocity head, $h = \dfrac{v^2}{2g}$

$$\therefore \qquad v = \sqrt{2gh} = \sqrt{2 \times 980 \times 40}$$

$$= 280 \text{ cms}^{-1}$$

17. In Millikan's oil drop experiment, what is the terminal speed of an uncharged drop of radius 2.0×10^{-5} m and density 1.2×10^3 kg/m³? Take the viscosity of air at the temperature of the experiment to be 1.8×10^{-5} Pa-s. How much is the viscous force on the drop at that speed? Neglect buoyancy of the drop due to air. **[NCERT]**

Sol. Given, radius of drop $(r) = 2.0 \times 10^{-5}$ m

Density of oil $(\rho) = 1.2 \times 10^3$ kg/m³

Viscosity of air $(\eta) = 1.8 \times 10^{-5}$ Pa-s

Terminal velocity, $v = \dfrac{2}{9} \dfrac{r^2 (\rho - \rho_0) g}{\eta}$

$$= \frac{2}{9} \times \frac{(2 \times 10^{-5})^2 \times (1.2 \times 10^3 - 0) \times 9.8}{1.8 \times 10^{-5}}$$

$$= 5.8 \times 10^{-2} \text{ m/s}$$

$\therefore$ Viscous force on the drop, (According to Stoke's law)

$$F = 6\pi \eta r v = 6 \times 3.14 \times 1.8 \times 10^{-5} \times 2 \times 10^{-5} \times 5.8 \times 10^{-2}$$

$$= 3.93 \times 10^{-10} \text{ N}$$

18. The terminal velocity of a copper ball of radius 2.0 mm falling through a tank of oil at 20°C is 6.5 cms⁻¹. Compute the viscosity of the oil at 20°C. Density of oil is 1.5×10^3 kg m⁻³, density of copper is 8.9×10^3 kg m⁻³. **[NCERT]**

Sol. Given, $v_t = 6.5 \times 10^{-2}$ m/s

$$r = 2 \times 10^{-3} \text{ m}, g = 9.8 \text{ m/s}^2$$

$$\rho = 8.9 \times 10^3 \text{ kg/m}^3, \sigma = 1.5 \times 10^3$$

$$\rho - \sigma = 8.9 \times 10^3 - 1.5 \times 10^3$$

$$= 7.4 \times 10^3 \text{ kg/m}^3$$

As, we know terminal velocity

i.e. $\quad v_t = \dfrac{2}{9} \dfrac{r^2(\rho - \sigma)}{\eta} g$

$$\eta = \dfrac{2}{9} \times \dfrac{(2 \times 10^{-3})^2 \times 9.8}{(6.5 \times 10^{-2})} \times 7.4 \times 10^3$$

$$\eta = 9.9 \times 10^{-1} \text{ kg/ms}$$

19. The velocity of water in a river is 18 kmh^{-1} near the surface. If the river is 5 m deep, find the shearing stress between horizontal layers of water. The coefficient of viscosity of water 10^{-2} poise.

Sol. As the velocity of water at the bottom of the river is zero,

$$dv = 18 \text{ kmh}^{-1} = 18 \times \dfrac{5}{18} = 5 \text{ ms}^{-1}$$

Also, $dx = 5$ m, $\eta = 10^{-2}$ poise $= 10^{-3}$ Pa-s

Force of viscosity, $F = \eta A \dfrac{dv}{dx}$

We know that, shearing stress $= \dfrac{F}{A}$

$\Rightarrow \qquad \dfrac{F}{A} = \eta \dfrac{dv}{dx} = \dfrac{10^{-3} \times 5}{5} = 10^{-3} \text{ Nm}^{-2}$

20. What should be the average velocity of water in a tube of radius 0.005 m so that the flow is just turbulent? The viscosity of water is 0.001 Pa-s.

Sol. Here, $r = 0.005$ m, diameter $D = 2r = 0.010$ m

$$\eta = 0.001 \text{ Pa-s}, \rho = 1000 \text{ kgm}^{-3}$$

For flow to be just turbulent, $R_e = 3000$

$\therefore \quad v = \dfrac{R_e \eta}{\rho D} = \dfrac{3000 \times 0.001}{1000 \times 0.010} = 0.3 \text{ ms}^{-1}$

LONG ANSWER Type I Questions

21. In a test experiment on a model aeroplane in a wind tunnel, the flow of speeds on the upper and lower surfaces of the wings are 70 m/s and 63 m/s respectively. What is the lift on the wings, if its area is 2.5 m^2? Take the density of air to be 1.3 kg / m^3. **[NCERT]**

Sol. Let the lower and upper surface of the wings of the aeroplane be at the same height h and speeds of air on the upper and lower surfaces of the wings be v_1 and v_2. Speed of air on the upper surface of the wings

$$v_1 = 70 \text{ m/s}$$

Speed of air on the lower surface of the wings

$$v_2 = 63 \text{ m/s}$$

Density of the air, $\rho = 1.3 \text{ kg/m}^3$

Area, $A = 2.5 \text{ m}^2$

According to Bernoulli's theorem,

$$p_1 + \dfrac{1}{2}\rho v_1^2 + \rho gh = p_2 + \dfrac{1}{2}\rho v_2^2 + \rho gh$$

or $\qquad p_2 - p_1 = \dfrac{1}{2}\rho(v_1^2 - v_2^2)$

$\therefore$ Lifting force acting on the wings,

$$F = (p_2 - p_1) \times A$$

$$= \dfrac{1}{2}\rho(v_1^2 - v_2^2) \times A \qquad [\because \text{ force } = \text{pressure} \times \text{area}]$$

$$= \dfrac{1}{2} \times 1.3 \times [(70)^2 - (63)^2] \times 2.5$$

$$= \dfrac{1}{2} \times 1.3 [4900 - 3969] \times 2.5$$

$$= \dfrac{1}{2} \times 1.3 \times 931 \times 2.5 = 1.51 \times 10^3 \text{ N}$$

22. Air is streaming past a horizontal air plane wing such that its speed is 120 ms^{-1} over the upper surface and 90 ms^{-1} at the lower surface. If the density of air is 1.3 kgm^{-3}, find the difference in pressure between the top and bottom of the wing. If wing is 10 m long and has an average width of 2 m, calculate the gross lift of the wing.

Sol. Given, $v_2 = 120$ m/s, $v_1 = 90$ m/s, $\rho_a = 1.3 \text{ kg/m}^3$,

$$h_1 = 10 \text{ m}, a_1 = 10 \times 2 = 20 \text{ m}^2$$

According to Bernoulli's theorem,

$$\dfrac{p_1}{\rho} + gh_1 + \dfrac{1}{2}v_1^2 = \dfrac{p_2}{\rho} + gh_2 + \dfrac{1}{2}v_2^2$$

For the horizontal flow, $h_1 = h_2$

$\therefore \qquad \dfrac{p_1}{\rho} + \dfrac{1}{2}v_1^2 = \dfrac{p_2}{\rho} + \dfrac{1}{2}v_2^2$

Given, $v_1 = 90$ m/s, $v_2 = 120$ m/s, $\rho = 1.3 \text{ kg/m}^3$

$\therefore \qquad \dfrac{p_1 - p_2}{\rho} = \dfrac{1}{2}(v_2^2 - v_1^2)$

$$(p_1 - p_2) = \dfrac{\rho(v_2^2 - v_1^2)}{2}$$

$$= 1.3 \times \dfrac{(14400 - 8100)}{2} = \dfrac{1.3 \times 6300}{2}$$

$$p_1 - p_2 = 4.095 \times 10^3 \text{ N/m}^2$$

It is the pressure difference between the top and the bottom of the wing.

Gross lift of wing $= (p_1 - p_2) \times$ Area of the wing

$$= 4.095 \times 10^3 \times 10 \times 2$$

$$= 8.190 \times 10^4 \text{ N}$$

23. A venturimeter is connected to two points in the mains where its radii are 20cm and 10cm, respectively, and the levels of water column in the tubes differ by 10 cm. How much water flows through the pipe per minute?

Sol. As we know that,

The volume of water flowing per second

$$V = a_1 a_2 \sqrt{\frac{2h\rho_m g}{\rho(a_1^2 - a_2^2)}}$$

$\because$
$$V = a_1 a_2 \sqrt{\frac{2hg}{a_1^2 - a_2^2}}$$

$\because$ $r_1 = 20$ cm, $a_1 = \pi r_1^2 = \pi(20)^2 \text{cm}^2$

$r_2 = 10$ cm, $a_2 = \pi r_2^2 = \pi(10)^2 \text{cm}^2$

$r_1 = 10$ cm, $g = 980 \text{cm/s}^2$

$\therefore$
$$V = \pi^2 (20)^2 \cdot (10)^2 \sqrt{\frac{2 \times 10 \times 980}{\pi^2((20)^4 - (10)^4)}} \text{ c.c/sec}$$

$$= \frac{175.93 \times 10^3}{\sqrt{15}} \text{ c.c/sec}$$

$$= \frac{175.93 \times 10^3}{\sqrt{15}} \times 60 \text{ c.c/min}$$

$$= 2728.7 \text{ litres/min}$$

24. (i) What is the largest average velocity of blood flow in an artery of radius 2×10^{-3}m, if the flow must remain laminar?

(ii) What is the corresponding flow rate? (Take, viscosity of blood to be 2.084×10^{-3}Pa-s) **[NCERT]**

Sol. Given, radius of artery $(r) = 2 \times 10^{-3}$ m

$\therefore$ Diameter of artery $D = 2r = 4 \times 10^{-3}$ m

Density of whole blood $(\rho) = 1.06 \times 10^3 \text{kg/m}^3$

Coefficient of viscosity of blood $(\eta) = 2.084 \times 10^3$ Pa-s

For laminar flow, maximum value of Reynold's number

$$R_e = 2000$$

(i) Critical velocity $(v_c) = \dfrac{R_e \eta}{\rho D}$

$$= \frac{2000 \times 2.084 \times 10^3}{1.06 \times 10^3 \times 4 \times 10^{-3}}$$

$$= 9.83 \times 10^5 \text{ m/s}$$

(ii) Flow rate of blood = Volume of blood flowing per second

$$= A v_c$$

$$= \pi r^2 \times v_c$$

$$= 3.14 \times (2 \times 10^{-3})^2 \times 9.83 \times 10^5$$

$$= 12.35 \text{ m}^3/\text{s}$$

25. Show that if n equal rain droplets falling through air with equal steady velocity of 10 cms^{-1} coalesce, the resultant drop attains a new terminal velocity of $10 n^{2/3} \text{cms}^{-1}$.

Sol. Volume of a bigger drop

$$= n \times \text{Volume of a smaller droplet}$$

or $\dfrac{4}{3} \pi R^3 = n \times \dfrac{4}{3} \pi r^3$ or $R^3 = nr^3$ or $R = n^{1/3} r$

Terminal velocity of a small droplet is given by

$$v_s = \frac{2}{9} \frac{r^2}{\eta} (\rho - \rho') g \qquad \dots(i)$$

Terminal velocity of a bigger drop is given by

$$v_b = \frac{2}{9} \frac{R^2}{\eta} (\rho - \rho') g \qquad \dots(ii)$$

Dividing Eq. (ii) by Eq. (i), we get $\dfrac{v_b}{v_s} = \dfrac{R^2}{r^2}$

But $R = n^{1/3} r$ and $v_s = 10$ cm/s

$$v_b = v_s \times \left(\frac{R^2}{r^2}\right) = 10 \times \frac{n^{2/3} r^2}{r^2}$$

$$v_b = 10 \, n^{2/3} \text{cm/s}$$

26. The flow rate of water from a tap of diameter 1.25 cm is 0.48 L/min. The coefficient of viscosity of water is 10^{-3}Pa-s. After some time the flow rate is increased to 3 L/min. Characterise the flow for both the flow rates. **[NCERT]**

Sol. Let the speed of the flow be v.

Given, diameter of tap = $d = 1.25$ cm

Volume of water flowing out per second.

$$Q = v \times \frac{\pi d^2}{4}$$

$\Rightarrow$
$$v = \frac{4Q}{d^2 \pi}$$

Estimate Reynold's number,

$$R_e = \frac{4\rho Q}{\pi d \eta}$$

$Q = 0.48 \text{ L/min} = 8 \times 10^{-3} \text{ L/s} = 8 \times 10^{-6} \text{ m}^3/\text{s}$

$$R_e = \frac{4 \times 10^3 \times 8 \times 10^{-6}}{3.14 \times 1.25 \times 10^{-2} \times 10^{-3}}$$

$R_e = 815$ [i.e. below 1000, the flow is steady]

After some time, when

$$Q = 3 \text{ L/min} = 5 \times 10^{-5} \text{ m}^3/\text{s},$$

$$R_e = \frac{4 \times 10^3 \times 5 \times 10^{-5}}{3.14 \times 1.25 \times 10^{-2} \times 10^{-3}} = 5095$$

$\therefore$ The flow will be turbulent.

27. The cylindrical tube of a spray pump has a cross-section of 8.0 cm^2 one end of which has 40 fine holes each of diameter 1.00 mm. If the liquid flow inside the tube is 1.5 m/min, what is the speed of ejection of the liquid through the holes? **[NCERT]**

Sol. Area of cross-section of tube $(A) = 8 \, cm^2 = 8 \times 10^{-4} m^2$

Number of holes, $N = 40$

Diameter of each hole, $2r = 1.0$ mm

$\therefore$ Radius of each hole, $r = 0.5 \, mm = 5 \times 10^{-4} m$

Velocity of liquid flow in tube $= 1.5 \, m/min = \dfrac{1.5}{60} \, m/s$

$\qquad\qquad = 2.5 \times 10^{-2} m/s$

Total area of holes $= N \times \pi r^2 = 40 \times 3.14 \times (5 \times 10^{-4})^2$

$\qquad\qquad = 3.14 \times 10^{-5} m^2$

From equation of continuity,

$$A_1 v_1 = A_2 v_2$$

or $\quad v_2 = \dfrac{A_1 v_1}{A_2} = \dfrac{8 \times 10^{-4} \times 2.5 \times 10^{-2}}{3.14 \times 10^{-5}}$

$\qquad\quad = \dfrac{20}{3.14} \times 10^{-1} = 0.64 \, m/s$

28. A cylindrical vessel filled with water upto a height of 2 m stands on a horizontal plane. The side wall of the vessel has a plugged circular hole touching the bottom. Find the minimum diameter of the hole so that the vessel begin to move on the floor, if the plug is removed. The coefficient of friction between the bottom of the vessel and the plane is 0.4 and total mass of water plus vessel is 100 kg.

Sol. Velocity of efflux through the hole, $v = \sqrt{2gh}$

$\because$ Distance moved by water in one second $v = \sqrt{2gh}$

$\therefore$ Rate of the momentum $= (\rho A \sqrt{2gh})(\sqrt{2gh}) = 2 \, ghA\rho$

According to Newton's second law of motion,

Force due to the velocity of efflux $= 2 \, gh \, A\rho$.

Now, according to Newton's third law of motion,

Force on the vessel = Rate of the momentum

Force on the vessel $= 2 \, gh \, A\rho$

The vessel will move, if force on the vessel = force of friction

or $\qquad 2gh \, A\rho = \mu Mg$

or $\qquad A = \dfrac{\mu M}{2h\rho} = \dfrac{0.4 \times 100}{2 \times 2 \times 1000} = \dfrac{1}{100}$

Since, the hole is circular.

$$A = \pi r^2 = \dfrac{\pi D^2}{4}$$

$\therefore \qquad D = \sqrt{\dfrac{4A}{\pi}} = \sqrt{\dfrac{4 \times 1}{100 \times 3.14}} = 0.113 \, m$

So, diameter of a hole $D = 0.113$ m

LONG ANSWER Type II Questions

29. Explain why?
   (i) To keep a piece of paper horizontal, you should blow over, not under it.
   (ii) When we try to close a water tap with our fingers, fast jets of water gush through the opening between our fingers.
   (iii) The size of the needle of a syringe controls flow rate better than the thumb pressure exerted by a doctor while administering an injection.
   (iv) A fluid flowing out of a small hole in a vessel results in a backward thrust on the vessel.
   (v) A spinning cricket ball in air does not follow a parabolic trajectory. **[NCERT]**

Note

According to Bernoulli's theorem, for horizontal flow of fluids,

$$p + \dfrac{1}{2}\rho v^2 = \text{constant}$$

Therefore, when velocity of a fluid increases, its pressure decreases and vice-versa.

Sol. (i) When we blow over a piece of paper, the velocity of air above the paper increases. So, in accordance with Bernoulli's theorem $\left(p + \dfrac{1}{2}\rho v^2 = \text{constant} \right)$, the pressure of air decreases above the paper. Due to the pressure difference of air between below and above the paper a lifting force acts on paper and hence, it remain horizontal.

(ii) According to equation of continuity, for steady flow of liquid the product of area of cross-section of the tube and velocity of liquid remains constant at each point, i.e. $A_1 v_1 = A_2 v_2$

When we try to close a water tap with our fingers, the area of cross-section of the outlet of water jet is reduced due to the restriction provided by the fingers and therefore, the velocity of water increases and fast jets of water gush through the openings between our fingers.

(iii) According to Bernoulli's theorem,

$$p + \dfrac{1}{2}\rho v^2 = \text{constant}$$

In this relation, pressure (p) occurs with one power while velocity (v) occurs with two powers. Therefore, the influence of velocity is higher than pressure. The size of the needle controls the velocity of flow and the thumb pressure controls pressure.

Therefore, size of the needle of a syringe controls flow rate better than thumb pressure.

(iv) A fluid flowing out of a small hole in a vessel have a large velocity and therefore, a large momentum. As no external force is acting, therefore, according to law of conservation of momentum equal momentum in opposite direction and hence, a backward velocity is attained by the vessel. Therefore, a backward thrust $\left(F = \dfrac{dp}{dt} \right)$ acts on the vessel.

(v) A spinning cricket ball in air does not follow a parabolic trajectory due to Magnus effect.

Let a spinning cricket ball is moving forward with a velocity v and spinning clockwise with velocity u. As ball moves forward, it leaves, a lower pressure region behind it.

To fill this region, air moves backward with velocity v. The layers of air in contact with the ball spin with ball with velocity u. Therefore, the resultant velocity of air above the ball is $(v - u)$ and below the ball is $(v + u)$. According to Bernoulli's theorem,

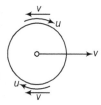

$$p + \frac{1}{2}\rho v^2 = \text{constant}$$

Therefore, pressure below the ball becomes lower than above the ball. Due to this pressure difference, a force acts on ball in downward direction. Therefore, the ball follows a curved path in spite of a parabolic trajectory.

30. A non-viscous liquid of constant density $1000\ \text{kgm}^{-3}$ flows in a streamline motion along a tube of variable cross-section. The tube is a kept inclined in the vertical plane as shown in figure. The area of cross-section of the tube at two points P and Q at heights of 2 m and 5 m are respectively, $4 \times 10^{-3}\ \text{m}^2$ and $8 \times 10^{-3}\ \text{m}^2$. The velocity of the liquid at point P is $1\ \text{ms}^{-1}$. Find the work done per unit volume by the pressure and the gravity forces as the fluid flows from point P to Q.

Sol. Given, $\rho = 1000\ \text{kg/m}^3$, $v_1 = 1\ \text{m/s}$, $a_1 = 4 \times 10^{-3}\ \text{m}^2$,

$$a_2 = 8 \times 10^{-3}\ \text{m}^2, h_1 = 2\ \text{m}, h_2 = 5\ \text{m}$$

Apply Bernoulli's theorem,

$$p_1 + \frac{1}{2}\rho v_1^2 + g\rho h_1 = p_2 + \frac{1}{2}\rho v_2^2 + g\rho h_2$$

$$(p_1 - p_2) = \frac{1}{2}\rho(v_2^2 - v_1^2) + \rho g(h_2 - h_1)$$

where,

$(p_1 - p_2) =$ Work done by pressure per unit volume

i.e. $\left(\dfrac{W}{\text{Volume}}\right)_p = \frac{1}{2}\rho(v_2^2 - v_1^2) + \rho g(h_2 - h_1)$ ...(i)

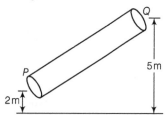

From equation of continuity,

$$a_1 v_1 = a_2 v_2$$

$$v_2 = \frac{a_1 v_1}{a_2} = \frac{4 \times 10^{-3} \times 1}{8 \times 10^{-3}} = 0.5\ \text{m/s}$$

$$\left(\frac{W}{\text{Volume}}\right)_p = \frac{1}{2} \times 1000\,[0.25 - 1] + 1000 \times 10\,(5 - 2)$$

$$= -375 + 30{,}000 = 29625\ \text{J/m}^3$$

Work done per unit volume by the gravitational force

$$= \rho g(h_1 - h_2)$$
$$= 1000 \times 10\,(2 - 5) = -3 \times 10^4\ \text{J/m}^3$$

31. If a sphere of radius r falls under gravity through a liquid of viscosity η, its average acceleration is half that of in starting of the motion. Then, show that the time taken by it to attain the terminal velocity is independent of the liquid density.

Sol. Let the density of sphere's material is ρ and that of liquid is σ. When the sphere just enters in the liquid. Downward force on the sphere, $F =$ weight of the sphere – weight of the fluid displaced by it.

$$F = \frac{4}{3}\pi r^3 \cdot \rho g - \frac{4}{3}\pi r^3 \cdot \sigma g$$

$\because$ Mass $=$ Volume $\times$ Density $= \frac{4}{3}\pi r^3 (\rho - \sigma)g$

$\therefore$ Acceleration of the sphere at this instant,

$$a = \frac{F}{m}$$

$$a = \frac{\frac{4}{3}\pi r^3 (\rho - \sigma)g}{\frac{4}{3}\pi r^3 \rho} = \left(1 - \frac{\sigma}{\rho}\right)g$$

When the sphere approches to terminal velocity, its acceleration becomes zero.

$\therefore$ Average acceleration of the sphere $= \dfrac{a + 0}{2}$

$$= \frac{\left(1 - \dfrac{\sigma}{\rho}\right)g}{2} = \left(1 - \frac{\sigma}{\rho}\right)\frac{g}{2}$$

If time t taken by the sphere to attain the terminal velocity As we know that,

Terminal velocity, $v = \dfrac{2}{9}\dfrac{r^2}{\eta}(\rho - \sigma)g$

$\because$ The sphere falls from rest,

$\therefore$ $\qquad u = 0$

Using $\qquad v = u + at$

Putting values $\dfrac{2}{9}\dfrac{r^2}{\eta}(\rho - \sigma)g = 0 + \left(1 - \dfrac{\sigma}{\rho}\right)\dfrac{g}{2} \cdot t$

$\therefore$ $\qquad t = \dfrac{4}{9}\dfrac{r^2 \rho}{\eta}$

Thus, t is independent of the liquid density.

32. If a liquid is flowing through a horizontal tube, write down the formula for the volume of the liquid flowing per second through it. Water is flowing through a horizontal tube of radius $2r$ and length l m at a rate of 60L/s, when connected to a pressure difference of h cm of water. Another tube of same length but radius r is connected in series with this tube and the combination is connected to the same pressure head. Find out the pressure difference across each tube and the rate of flow of water through the combination.

Sol. The volume of the liquid flowing per second through a horizontal tube, $V = \dfrac{\pi}{8} \cdot \dfrac{pr^4}{\eta l}$

where,
r = radius of the tube,
l = length of the tube,
P = pressure difference across the two ends of the tube
and η = coefficient of viscosity of the liquid

$\because$ $\qquad\qquad V = \dfrac{\pi}{8} \cdot \dfrac{pr^4}{\eta l}$

In first case,

$$= \dfrac{\pi}{8} \cdot \dfrac{h\rho g (2r)^4}{\eta l} \qquad [\because \ p = h\rho g]$$

$$\dfrac{\pi}{8} \cdot \dfrac{h\rho g (2r)^4}{\eta l} = 60 \qquad\qquad …(i)$$

In IInd case, the volume of liquid flowing per second V_1, through each tube is equal

$$V_1 = \dfrac{\pi}{8} \dfrac{\rho_1 (2r)^4}{\eta l} = \dfrac{\pi \rho_2 (r)^4}{8\eta l} \qquad …(ii)$$

$\because$ $\qquad \rho_1 + \rho_2 = h\rho g \qquad\qquad …(iii)$ [given]
From Eq. (ii),

$$\rho_1 = \dfrac{\rho_2}{16}$$

Putting this value into Eq. (iii), we get

$$\rho_2 = \dfrac{16h\rho g}{17}$$

Putting this value of ρ_2 into Eq. (ii)

$$V_1 = \dfrac{\pi}{8} \cdot \dfrac{16h\rho g}{17} \cdot \dfrac{r^4}{\eta l}$$

$$= \dfrac{1}{17} \cdot \dfrac{\pi}{8} \cdot \dfrac{h\rho g}{\eta l} (2r)^4$$

$$= \dfrac{1}{17} \times 60 \qquad\qquad \text{[using Eq. (i)]}$$

$$= 3.53 \text{L/s}$$

33. Glycerine flows steadily through a horizontal tube of length 1.5 m and radius 1.0 cm. If the amount of glycerine flowing per second at one end is 4.0×10^{-3}kg/s. What is the pressure difference between the two ends of the tube? (Density of glycerine = 1.3×10^3kg/m^3 and viscosity of glycerine = 0.83 Pa-s). (You may also like to check, if the assumption of laminar flow in the tube is correct). **[NCERT]**

Sol. Given, length of the tube $(l) = 1.5$ m
Radius of the tube $(r) = 1.0$ cm = 1×10^{-2} cm
Mass of glycerine flowing per second = 4×10^{-3} kg/s
Density of glycerine, $\rho = 1.3 \times 10^3$ kg/m^3
Viscosity of glycerine, $\eta = 0.83$ Pa-s
Volume of glycerine flowing per second, $V = \dfrac{m}{\rho}$

$$\left[\because \text{density} = \dfrac{\text{Mass}}{\text{Volume}} \right]$$

$$= \dfrac{4 \times 10^{-3}}{1.3 \times 10^3} \text{m}^3/\text{s} = \dfrac{4}{1.3} \times 10^{-6} \text{m}^3/\text{s}$$

According to Poiseuille's formula, the rate of flow of liquid through a tube

$$V = \dfrac{\pi}{8} \dfrac{pr^4}{\eta l}$$

where, p is the pressure difference between the two ends of the tube.

or $\qquad p = \dfrac{8\eta lV}{\pi r^4} = \dfrac{8 \times 0.83 \times 1.5 \times 4 \times 10^{-6}}{3.14 \times (1 \times 10^{-2})^4 \times 1.3}$

$$= 976 \text{ Pa}$$

To check the laminar flow in the tube, the value of Reynold's number should be less than 2000.

Reynold's number, $R_e = \dfrac{\rho D v_c}{\eta}$

where, v_c is the critical velocity and D is the diameter of the tube.

Critical velocity, $v_c = \dfrac{\text{Volume flowing out per second}}{\text{Area of cross-section}}$

$$= \dfrac{m/\rho}{A} = \dfrac{m}{\rho \pi r^2} \qquad [\because A = \pi r^2]$$

$\therefore$ Reynold's number, $R_e = \dfrac{\rho D}{\eta} \times \dfrac{m}{\rho \pi r^2}$

$$= \dfrac{2r \times m}{\eta \pi r^2} \qquad\qquad [\because D = 2r]$$

$$= \dfrac{2m}{\pi r \eta} = \dfrac{2 \times 4 \times 10^{-3}}{3.14 \times 10^{-2} \times 0.83} = 0.31$$

As $R_e < 2000$, therefore, flow of glycerine is laminar.

ASSESS YOUR TOPICAL UNDERSTANDING

OBJECTIVE Type Questions

1. Which of the following diagrams does not represent a streamline flow? **[NCERT Exemplar]**

(a)

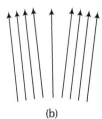

(b)

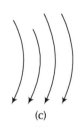

(c)

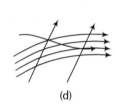

(d)

2. In a turbulent flow, the velocity of the liquid molecules in contact with the walls of the tube is
(a) zero
(b) maximum
(c) equal to critical velocity
(d) may have any value

3. According to Bernoulli's equation,

$$\frac{p}{\rho g} + h + \frac{1}{2}\frac{v^2}{g} = \text{constant}$$

The terms, $\frac{p}{\rho g}$, h and $\frac{1}{2}\frac{v^2}{g}$ are generally called respectively :
(a) Gravitational head, pressure head and velocity head
(b) Gravity, gravitational head and velocity head
(c) Pressure head, gravitational head and velocity head
(d) Gravity, pressure and velocity head

4. A cylinder of height 20 m is completely filled with water. The velocity of efflux of water (in ms^{-1}) through a small hole on the side wall of the cylinder near its bottom is
(a) 10
(b) 20
(c) 25.5
(d) 5

5. We have three beakers A, B and C containing three different liquids. They are stirred vigorously and placed on a table. Then, liquid which is
(a) most viscous comes to rest at the earliest
(b) most viscous comes to rest at the last
(c) most viscous slows down earliest but comes to rest at the last
(d) All of them come to rest at the same time

Very Short Answer Type Questions

6. What is the effect of temperature on viscosity of a liquid?

7. What is the net weight of a body when it falls with terminal velocity through a viscous fluid?

8. When water flows through a pipe, which layer moves faster?

9. Why the gas bubbles rise up through soda water bottle? Give one reason only.

10. Why the viscosity of the liquid decreases with increase in temperature?

11. Which fundamental law forms the basis of equation of continuity?

SHORT ANSWER Type Questions

12. When does the streamline become turbulent. How?

13. Why does the speed of a whirlwind in a tornado alarmingly high?

14. What do you mean by the term 'terminal velocity' for motion through a viscous medium?

LONG ANSWER Type I Questions

15. The relative velocity between two parallel layers of water is 8 cms^{-1} and the perpendicular distance between them is 0.1 cm. Calculate the velocity gradient. **[Ans. 80 cms^{-1}/cm]**

16. Water flows at a speed of 6 cms^{-1} through a pipe of tube of radius 1 cm. The coefficient of viscosity of water at room temperature is 0.01 poise. What is the nature of flow?
[Ans. R_e = 1200 < 2000 so, flow is laminar]

17. Find the critical velocity for air flowing through a tube of 2 cm diameter. For air, $\rho = 1.3 \times 10^{-3}$ g cm^{-3} and $\eta = 181 \times 10^{-6}$ poise. **[Ans. 140 cms^{-1}]**

LONG ANSWER Type II Questions

18. The reading of pressure meter attached with a closed pipe is 3.5×10^{5} Nm^{-2}. On opening the valve of the pipe, the reading of the pressure meter is reduced to 3.0×10^{5} Nm^{-2}. Calculate the speed of the water flowing in pipe. **[Ans. 10 m/s]**

19. A capillary tube 1 mm in diameter and 20 cm in length is fitted horizontally to a vessel kept full of alcohol. The depth of the centre of capillary tube below the surface of alcohol is 20 cm. If the viscosity and density of alcohol are 0.012 UGS unit and 0.8 gcm^{-3}, respectively, find the amount of the alcohol that will flow out in 5 min. Given that $g = 980 \text{ cms}^{-2}$

   [**Ans.** 38.4 g]

20. A liquid is kept in cylindrical vessel which is rotated along its axis. The liquid rises at the sides. If the radius of vessel is 0.05 m and the speed of rotation is 2 rev/s, find the difference in height of the liquid at the centre of the vessel and its sides.

   [**Ans.** 0.02 m]

21. Water flows through a horizontal pipe whose internal diameter is 2.0 cm, at a speed of 1.0 ms^{-1}. What should be the diameter of the nozzle, if the water is to emerge at a speed of 4.0 ms^{-1}?

   [**Ans.** 1.0 cm]

22. Check the dimensional consistancy of the Poiseuille's formula for the laminar flow in a tube
$$Q = \frac{\pi R^4 (p_1 - p_2)}{8 \eta l}$$

SUMMARY

- **Thrust** The total force exerted by the liquid at rest, on any surface in contact with it is called the thrust of the liquid on that surface.

- **Pressure**, $p = \dfrac{\text{Thrust}}{\text{Area}} = \dfrac{F}{A}$. Its SI unit is N/m^2 or Pascal (Pa).
  Pressure exerted by a liquid column
$$p = \rho g h$$
  where, $h =$ height of liquid column, $g =$ acceleration due to gravity, $\rho =$ density of liquid.

- **Pascal's law** It states that if an external pressure is applied to an enclosed liquid, it is transmitted undiminished equally to all other points of the liquid and to the walls of container.

- **Atmospheric pressure** The pressure exerted by the atmosphere is called atmospheric pressure.
  At sea-level, we have atmospheric pressure $= 1.013 \times 10^5 \text{ Nm}^{-2}$

- **Absolute Pressure and gauge pressure** The total or actual pressure p at a point is called absolute pressure. Gauge pressure is the difference between the actual pressure (absolute pressure) at a point and the atmospheric pressure. Thus,
$$p_g = p - p_a \text{ or } p = p_a + p_g$$
  Absolute pressure = Atmospheric pressure + Gauge pressure.

- **Buoyancy** It states that when a body is partially or fully dipped into a fluid, the fluid exerts an upward force on the body called as buoyant force and this phenomenon is called buoyancy.

- **Archimedes' principle** It states that when a body is partially or fully dipped in a fluid at rest, the fluid exerts an upward force of buoyancy equal to the weight of the displaced fluid.
  Weight of the body = Weight of fluid displaced
$$V_b \rho_b g = V_f \rho_f g$$
  $\therefore$ Denisity of body to fluid, $\dfrac{\rho_b}{\rho_f} = \dfrac{V_f}{V_b}$

- **Surface tension** (S) Surface tension is the property of a liquid due to which its free surface behaves like a stretched elastic membrane and tends to have least possible surface area.
  SI unit of surface tension is Nm^{-1} or Jm^{-2}.

- **Capillarity** The phenomenon of rise or fall of a liquid in the capillary tube is called capillarity.
  Height of rise of liquid in capillary is given by $h = \dfrac{2S \cos \theta}{\rho R g}$ where, $R =$ radius of capillary base.

- **Streamline and Turbulent Flow** Flow of a fluid is said to be streamlined if each element of the fluid passing through a particular point travels along the same path, with exactly the same velocity as that of the preceding element.

A special case of streamline flow is laminar flow, in which a fluid has a steady flow in the form of parallel layer and these do not mix with one another.

- **A turbulent flow** is the one in which the motion of the fluid particles is disordered or irregular. In such a flow, most of the energy used up in maintaining the flow, is spent in causing eddies in the fluid and only a small part of the energy is used for the actual forward flow.

- **Equation of continuity** It states that when an incompressible and non-viscous fluid flows steadily through a tube of non-uniform cross-section, then the product of area of cross-section and the velocity of flow is same at every point in the tube. $Av = $ constant

- **Bernoulli's theorem** It states that the sum of pressure energy, kinetic energy and potential energy per unit volume of an incompressible and non-viscous fluid in a streamlined irrotational flow remains constant at every cross-sectional throughout the liquid flow.

$$p + \frac{1}{2}\rho v^2 + \rho gh = \text{constant}$$

where, $p = $ pressure, $\frac{1}{2}\rho v^2 = $ kinetic energy per unit volume, $\rho gh = $ potential energy per unit volume.

- **Velocity of efflux** (Torricelli's theorem) The speed of liquid coming out through a hole at a depth (h) below the free surface is called velocity of efflux, $v = \sqrt{2hg}$

- **Viscosity** It is the property of a fluid due to which an opposing force comes into play whenever there is relative motion between its different layers.

- **Newton's formula for viscous force** The viscous drag between two parallel layers each of area A and having velocity gradient $\frac{dv}{dx}$ is given by $F = -\eta A \frac{dv}{dx}$

where, η is the coefficient of viscosity of the liquid.

- **Stoke's law** It states that the backward dragging force of viscosity acting on a spherical body of radius r moving with velocity v through a fluid of viscosity η is $F = 6\pi\eta rv$

- **Terminal velocity** It is the maximum constant velocity attained by a spherical body while falling through a viscous medium. The terminal velocity of a spherical body of density ρ and radius r moving through a fluid of density ρ' and viscosity η is given by $v = \frac{2}{9}\frac{r^2}{\eta}(\rho - \rho')g$

- **Reynold's number** It is a dimensionless number which determines the nature of the flow of the liquid. For a liquid of viscosity η, density ρ and flowing through a pipe of diameter D, Reynold's number is given by

$$R_e = \frac{\rho vD}{\eta}$$

If $R_e < 2000$, the flow is streamline or laminar.
If $R_e > 3000$, the flow is turbulent.
If $2000 < R_e < 3000$, the flow is unstable. It may change from laminar to turbulent and *vice-versa*.

- **Poiseuille's formula** The volume of a liquid flowing per second through a horizontal capillary tube of length l, radius r under a pressure difference p across its two ends is given by $V = \frac{\pi}{8} \cdot \frac{pr^4}{\eta l}$, where, η is coefficient of viscosity of the liquid.

CHAPTER PRACTICE

OBJECTIVE Type Questions

1. Pascal's law states that pressure in a fluid at rest is the same at all points, if
   (a) they are at the same height
   (b) they are along same plane
   (c) they are along same line
   (d) Both (a) and (b)

2. If two liquids of same masses but densities ρ_1 and ρ_2 respectively are mixed, then density of mixture is given by
   (a) $\rho = \dfrac{\rho_1 + \rho_2}{2}$
   (b) $\rho = \dfrac{\rho_1 + \rho_2}{2\,\rho_1\,\rho_2}$
   (c) $\rho = \dfrac{2\,\rho_1\rho_2}{\rho_1 + \rho_2}$
   (d) $\rho = \dfrac{\rho_1\rho_2}{\rho_1 + \rho_2}$

3. The excess pressure inside an air bubble of radius r just below the surface of water is p_1. The excess pressure inside a drop of the same radius just outside the surface is p_2. If T is surface tension, then
   (a) $p_1 = 2p_2$
   (b) $p_1 = p_2$
   (c) $p_2 = 2p_1$
   (d) $p_2 = 0,\ p_1 \neq 0$

4. In a soap bubble, pressure difference is
   (a) $\dfrac{2S_{la}}{r}$
   (b) $\dfrac{4S_{la}}{r}$
   (c) $\dfrac{S_{la}}{r}$
   (d) $\dfrac{8S_{la}}{r}$

5. Along a streamline,   [NCERT Exemplar]
   (a) the velocity of a fluid particle remains constant
   (b) the velocity of all fluid particles crossing a given position is constant
   (c) the velocity of all fluid particles at a given instant is constant
   (d) the speed of a fluid particle remains constant

6. An ideal fluid flows through a pipe of circular cross-section made of two sections with diameters 2.5 cm and 3.75 cm. The ratio of the velocities in the two pipes is   [NCERT Exemplar]
   (a) $9 : 4$
   (b) $3 : 2$
   (c) $\sqrt{3} : \sqrt{2}$
   (d) $\sqrt{2} : \sqrt{3}$

7. As the temperature of water increases, its viscosity
   (a) remains unchanged
   (b) decreases
   (c) increases
   (d) increases or decreases depending on the external pressure

8. Reynold's number (R_e) can be defined as
   (a) $\dfrac{\rho\eta}{vd}$
   (b) vd/ρ
   (c) $\dfrac{\rho vd}{\eta d}$
   (d) $d\rho v/\eta$

ASSERTION AND REASON

Direction (Q.Nos. 9-18) *In the following questions, two statements are given- one labelled Assertion (A) and the other labelled Reason (R). Select the correct answer to these questions from the codes (a), (b), (c) and (d) as given below*
   (a) Both Assertion and Reason are true and Reason is the correct explanation of Assertion.
   (b) Both Assertion and Reason are true but Reason is not the correct explanation of Assertion.
   (c) Assertion is true but Reason is false.
   (d) Assertion is false but Reason is true.

9. **Assertion** In steady flow, the velocity of each passing fluid particle remains constant in time.

   Reason Each particle follows a smooth path and the paths of the particle do not cross each other.

10. **Assertion** In streamline flow, $A \times v$ is constant.

    Reason For incompressive flow, mass in = mass out.

11. **Assertion** The stream of water flowing at high speed from a garden horse pipe tend to spread like a fountain when held vertically up, but tends to narrow down when held vertically down.

    Reason In any steady flow of an incompressible fluid, the volume flow rate of the fluid remains constant.

12. Assertion The shape of an automobile is so designed that its front resembles the streamline pattern of the fluid through which it moves.

Reason The resistance offered by the fluid is proportional to area.

13. Assertion The machine parts are jammed in winter.

Reason The viscosity of the lubricants used in the machine increases at low temperature.

14. Assertion For Reynold's number $R_e > 2000$, the flow of fluid is turbulent.

Reason Inertial forces are dominant as compared to the viscous forces.

15. Assertion A fluid will stick to a solid surface.

Reason Surface energy between fluid and solid is smaller than the sum of surface energies.

16. Assertion Smaller drop of liquid resists deforming forces better than the larger drops.

Reason Excess pressure inside a drop is directly proportional to its surface area.

17. Assertion The surface of water in the capillary tube is concave.

Reason The pressure difference between two sides of the tube is $\dfrac{2S}{a} \cos\theta$.

18. Assertion Ploughing a field reduces evaporation of water from the ground beneath.

Reason Results in lowering of surface area open to sunlight.

CASE BASED QUESTIONS

Direction (Q. Nos. 19-20) *These questions are case study based questions. Attempt any 4 sub-parts from each question.*

19. Fluid Dynamics

Consider the flow at two regions 1 (i.e. *BC*) and 2 (i.e. *DE*). Consider the fluid initially lying between *B* and *D*. In an infinitesimally time interval Δt, this fluid would have moved. Suppose v_1 is the speed at *B* and v_2 at *D*, then fluid initially at *B* has moved a distance $v_1 \Delta t$ to *C* ($v_1 \Delta t$ is small enough to assume constant cross-section along *BC*).

In the same interval Δt, the fluid initially at *D* moves to *E*, a distance equal to $v_2 \Delta t$. Pressures p_1 and p_2 act as shown on the plane faces of areas A_1

A_1 and A_2 binding the two regions as shown in figure

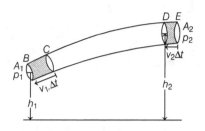

(i) The work done on the fluid at *BC* is
 (a) $p_1 A_1 \Delta t$ 	(b) $p_1 v_1 \Delta t$
 (c) $p_1 \Delta V$ 	(d) $A_1 \Delta V$

(ii) The work done on the fluid of *DE* is
 (a) $p_2 \Delta V$ 	(b) $-p_2 \Delta V$
 (c) $p_1 A_2 \Delta t$ 	(d) $p_2 v_2 \Delta t$

(iii) Total work done on the fluid is
 (a) $\dfrac{p_1 - p_2}{2} \Delta V$ 	(b) $p_2 \Delta V$
 (c) $p_1 \Delta V$ 	(d) $(p_1 - p_2) \Delta V$

(iv) The change in its kinetic energy is
 (a) $\dfrac{1}{2} \Delta V (v_2^2 - v_1^2)$

 (b) $\dfrac{1}{2} \rho \Delta V (v_2^2 - v_1^2)$

 (c) $\rho \Delta V (v_2^2 - v_1^2)$

 (d) $\dfrac{1}{2} \rho \Delta V (v_2^2 + v_1^2)$

(v) Expression of Bernoulli's equation is
 (a) $p + \dfrac{1}{2} \rho v^2 = \text{constant}$

 (b) $p + \dfrac{1}{2} \rho v^2 + \rho gh = \text{constant}$

 (c) $p + \rho v^2 + \dfrac{1}{2} \rho gh = \text{constant}$

 (d) $\dfrac{1}{2} \rho v^2 + \rho gh = \text{constant}$

20. Hydraulic Lift

Hydraulic lift is an application of Pascal's law. It is used to lift heavy loads. It is a force multiplier.

So, when small forces applied on the smaller piston (acting downward) will be appearing as a very large force (acting upward) on the larger piston. As a result of it, a heavy load placed on the larger piston is easily lifted upwards.

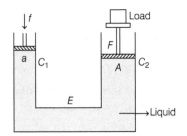

(i) Pascal's law states that pressure in a fluid at rest is the same at all points, if
(a) they are at the same height
(b) they are along same plane
(c) they are along same line
(d) Both (a) and (b)

(ii) Pressure is applied to an enclosed fluid as shown in the above figure. It is
(a) increased and applied to every part of the fluid
(b) diminished and transmitted to the walls of the container
(c) increased in proportion to the mass of the fluid and then transmitted
(d) transmitted unchanged to every portion of the fluid and the walls of container

(iii) Pressure at a point inside a liquid does not depend on
(a) the depth of the point below the surface of the liquid
(b) the nature of the liquid
(c) the acceleration due to gravity at that point
(d) total weight of fluid in the beaker

(iv) A hydraulic lift has 2 limbs of areas A and $2A$.

Force F is applied over limb of area A to lift a heavy car.

If distance moved by piston P_1 is x, then distance moved by piston P_2 is

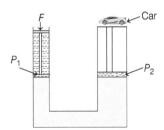

(a) x (b) $2x$ (c) $\dfrac{x}{2}$ (d) $4x$

(v) If work done by piston in the given figure on fluid is W_1, then work done by fluid in limbs on piston P_2 is
(a) $\dfrac{W_1}{4}$ (b) $4W_1$ (c) $\dfrac{W_1}{2}$ (d) W_1

VERY SHORT ANSWER Type Questions

21. How is the surface tension of a liquid explained on the basis of intermolecular forces?

22. From where the energy comes when a liquid rises against gravity in a capillary tube?

SHORT ANSWER Type Questions

23. A thin wire is bent in the form of a ring of diameter 3.0 cm. The ring is placed horizontally on the surface of soap solution and then raised up slowly. How much upward force is necessary to break the vertical film formed between the ring and the solution? $T = 3.0 \times 10^{-2}\,\text{Nm}^{-1}$
[Ans. $5.66 \times 10^{-3}\,\text{N}$ **]**

24. Prove that there is always excess of pressure on the concave side of the meniscus of a liquid. Obtain expression for the excess of pressure inside a liquid drop.

LONG ANSWER Type I Questions

25. Two cylindrical vessels placed on a horizontal table contain water and mercury, respectively up to the same heights. There is a small hole in the walls of each of the vessels at half the height of liquids in the vessels. Find out the ratio of the velocities of efflux of water and mercury from the holes. Which of the two jets of liquid will fall at a greater distance on the table from the vessel? Relative density of mercury with respect to water = 13.6

26. Water enters a horizontal pipe of non-uniform cross-section with a velocity or $0.6\,\text{ms}^{-1}$ and leaves the other end with a velocity of $0.4\,\text{ms}^{-1}$. At the first end, pressure of water is $1200\,\text{Nm}^{-2}$. Calculate the pressure of water at the other end. Density or water is $1000\,\text{kgm}^{-3}$. **[Ans.** $1300\,\text{N/m}^2$**]**

27. 27 identical drops of water are falling down vertically in air each with a terminal velocity $0.15\,\text{ms}^{-1}$. If they combine to form a single bigger drop, what will be its terminal velocity?
[Ans. 1.35 m/s**]**

28. Two soap bubbles have radii in the ratio 2 : 3. Compare the excess of pressure inside these bubbles. [**Ans.** 4/9]

29. If the sap in tree behaves like water in glass capillaries, what must be the diameter of the pores in the trunk of a teak tree 30 m high for the sap to reach the tap. Surface tension of sap $= 72 \times 10^{-3}$ N/m and angle.

LONG ANSWER Type II Questions

30. If a number of little droplets of water, all of the same radius r, coalesce to form a single drop of radius R, show that the rise in temperature will be given by $\dfrac{3T}{\rho J}\left(\dfrac{1}{r} - \dfrac{1}{R}\right)$, where T is the surface tension of water and J is the mechanical equivalent of heat.

31. If the terminal speed of a sphere of gold (density $= 19.5$ kg/m^3) is 0.2 m/s in viscous liquid (density $= 19.5$ kg/m^3) is 0.2 m/s in viscous liquid (density $= 1.5$ kg/m^3).

    Find out the terminal speed of a sphere of silver (density $= 10.5$ kg/m^3) of the same size in the same liquid.

    [**Ans.** 1.76×10^{-2} N/m]

32. During blood transfusion of a patient, the bottle of the blood is adjusted on a stand in such a way that blood is 1.3 m above the needle which has a radius of 0.18 mm and length of 3 cm. Calculate the viscosity of the blood if 4.5 cc of blood passes through needle in 60 s. Given density of blood is 1.02 g cm^{-3}. [**Ans.** 0.0238 Poise]

10

We are known to common sense notions of heat and temperature.

When heat is supplied to a body, the physical state of the body may be changed. These changes may follow certain laws. Thus, we can say that all the changes in characteristics (properties) of matter that appear due to heat are known as its thermal properties. Hence, in this chapter, we will deal with heat and its measurement and the process of heat transfer.

THERMAL PROPERTIES OF MATTER

|TOPIC 1|
Temperature and its Measurement

TEMPERATURE AND HEAT

Temperature

Temperature is the measure of degree of hotness or coldness of a body. The measurement of temperature of a body is a relative measure.

Consider, there are two bodies with temperatures T_1 and T_2 where $T_1 > T_2$, then the body with T_1 is called **hotter one** with respect to another one which is known as **colder body**.

Note

When a body is heated, the changes can take place in the body such as it may expand or its physical state may be changed.

Heat

Heat is the form of energy which flows from hotter body to colder body by virtue of temperature difference. The process of transfer of heat is a non-mechanical process i.e. there is no mechanical work involved in the process of heat transfer. The amount of heat is measured in Joule (SI unit). Another widely used unit for the heat is calorie (in CGS) where 1 joule equals 4.2 calorie (cal).

One calorie is equal to the amount of heat energy required to raise the temperature of one gram of water through 1°C (from 14.5°C to 15.5°C)

Caloric Theory of Heat

According to this theory, heat is an invisible, weightless and odourless fluid called **caloric**. When some calorie is added to a body, its temperature rises and when some calorie is removed, its temperature falls.

Dynamic Theory of Heat

According to this theory, all substances (solids, liquids and gases) are made of molecules. These molecules are in a state of continuous random motion.

Depending on the nature and temperature of the substance, the molecules may possess three types of motion

(i) **Translatory motion** This is the motion in a straight line which is common in gases.

Translatory motion

(ii) **Vibrational motion** This is the to and fro motion of the molecules about their mean positions. This is common in liquid and gases.

Vibrational motion

(iii) **Rotational motion** This is the motion of molecules about their axis. This type of motion occurs usually at high temperature.

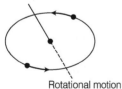

Rotational motion

Note
Every type of motion provides some kinetic energy to the molecules of the body. In fact, heat possessed by the body is the total thermal energy of the body which is the sum of kinetic energies of all individual molecules of the body due to translational, vibrational and rotational motion of the molecules.

Measurement of Temperature

As temperature is a fundamental physical quantity and it need measurement. The measurement of temperature is done by some specified scales.

These scales are commonly called **thermometers**. The thermometers are calibrated so that a numerical value may be assigned to a given temperature.

It measures the temperature of the body in the unit as **kelvin** (K), **degree centigrade** (°C), **degree fahrenheit** (°F), etc., among which kelvin (K) is taken as the SI unit of temperature. Many physical properties of materials change sufficiently with temperature to be used as the basis for constructing thermometers.

The commonly used properties are variation of the volume of a liquid with temperature, variation of pressure or volume of gas with temperature, the variation of resistance of metal with temperature, the variation of thermoemf with temperature of a junction in a thermocouple, etc.

As we know two reference points are needed to define any standard scale. In case of water, these points are ice point and steam point at which the pure water freezes and boils respectively under standard pressure.

The ice and steam point of water are 32°F and 212°F on the fahrenheit scale and 0°C and 100°C on celsius scale. On the celsius scale, there are 100 equal intervals between two reference points (i.e. ice and steam point) while on the fahrenheit scale, they are 180.

The graph of fahrenheit temperature (T_F) *versus* celsius or centigrade temperature (°C) is found to be

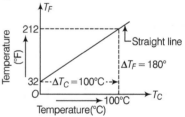

Celsius *versus* Fahrenheit graph

The equation of this straight line is given as

$$T_F = \frac{9}{5}T_C + 32$$

The size of the unit for kelvin temperature is the same celsius degree, so temperatures on these scales are related by

$$T_K = T_C + 273.15$$

Different Scales to Measure the Temperature

S. No.	Scale	Unit	Freezing or ice point (Lower fixed point)	Boiling or steam point (Upper fixed point)
1.	Celsius scale	Degree centigrade (°C)	0°C	100°C
2.	Fahrenheit scale	Degree Fahrenheit (°F)	32°F	212°F
3.	Reaumur scale	Degree Reaumur (°R)	0° R	80°R
4.	Kelvin scale	Kelvin (K)	273.15 K	373.15 K

Relation among the Temperatures Measured by Different Scales

The temperature measured by different scales is given as

$$\frac{C-0}{100} = \frac{F-32}{180} = \frac{R-0}{80} = \frac{K-273.15}{100}$$

Here, C, F, R and K are the readings of different scales.

Constant-Volume Gas Thermometer

If p_0, p_{100}, p_{tr} and p_r are the pressures of gas at temperatures $0°C$, $100°C$, triple point of water and unknown temperature ($t°C$) respectively, keeping the volume constant, then

$$t = \left(\frac{p - p_0}{p_{100} - p_0} \times 100 \right)°C$$

or

$$T = \left(273.16 \frac{p}{p_{tr}} \right)K$$

Platinum Resistance Thermometer

If R_0, R_{100}, R_{tr} and R_r are the resistances of a platinum wire at temperatures $0°C$, $100°C$, triple point of water and unknown temperature ($t°C$) respectively, then

$$t = \left(\frac{R - R_0}{R_{100} - R_0} \times 100 \right)°C \text{ or } T = \left(\frac{R_t}{R_{tr}} T_{tr} \right)K$$

$$= \left(\frac{R}{R_{tr}} \times 273.16 \right)K$$

IDEAL GAS EQUATION AND ABSOLUTE TEMPERATURE

A special type of thermometer named **liquid-in-glass thermometer** shows the various readings for the temperature other than the fixed points because of different expansion properties of liquids. But a thermometer that uses a gas gives the unique reading regardless of which gas is used.

At low densities, the gases exhibit same behaviour of expansion. There are three characteristics of a gas which describe its behaviour, these are pressure (p), volume (V) and temperature (T).

The relation among the characteristics of a gas is given by

(i) **Boyle's Law** It is given by English chemist Robert Boyle (1627–1691). According to this law,

$$p \propto \frac{1}{V} \qquad \text{(at constant temperature)}$$

i.e. $pV = \textbf{constant}$

(ii) **Charles' Law** It is given by French scientist Jacques Charles (1747–1823). According to this law,

$$V \propto T \qquad \text{(at constant pressure)}$$

i.e. $\dfrac{V}{T} = \textbf{constant}$

Ideal Gas Equation

On combining these two laws (above mentioned), we get

$$\frac{pV}{T} = \textbf{constant} \text{ (for a given quantity of gas)}$$

This relation is known as **ideal gas law.** It can be written in more general forms for a given amount of gas as

$$\boxed{pV = \mu RT}$$

where, μ is **number of moles** of a gas and R is known as **universal gas constant** valued $8.31\,\text{J mol}^{-1}\,\text{K}^{-1}$. This equation is known as **ideal gas equation.**

From the ideal gas equation, $pV \propto T$

This is the cause for a gas to be used to measure temperature by a volume gas thermometer (for which $p \propto T$ as volume of the gas is constant).

Absolute Zero Temperature

Theoretically, there is no limit for maximum temperature but there is a sharp point for minimum temperature that no body can have the temperature lower than this minimum value of temperature which is known as **absolute zero temperature.**

Absolute Zero Temperature from p-T Graph

The variation of pressure (p) with temperature $T(°C)$ is shown in figure.

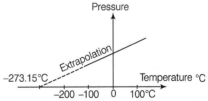

Graph of pressure *versus* temperature of a low density gas kept at constant volume

The graph is extrapolated, it meets the temperature axis at $-273.15°C$, Kelvin (after British Scientist Lord Kelvin) called this value of temperature as **absolute zero** (0 A) or (0 K). This is because at this temperature, pressure and volume of the gas become zero.

Hence, the lowest temperature of $-273.15°C$ at which gas is supposed to have zero volume (or zero pressure) and at which entire molecular motion stops, is called **absolute zero** of temperature. If we were imagine to going below this temperature, volume of gas would be negative, which is impossible. This suggests that the **lowest attainable temperature is absolute zero.**

The plot for pressure *versus* temperature and extrapolation of lines for low density gases (A, B and C) indicates the same absolute zero temperature is given below.

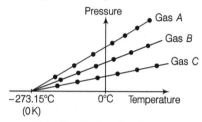

p-T diagram for low density gases

The absolute zero temperature is regarded as 0 K or $-273.15°C$. This implies 273.15 K $= 0°C$.

The temperature measured in Kelvin scale is known as absolute temperature and the scale itself is known as absolute scale.

THERMAL EXPANSION

It is generally observed that sealed bottles with metallic lids are so tightly screwed that it has to put the lid in hot water to open the lid. It would allow the metallic cover to expand and thereby loosening it to unscrew easily.

So, when heat is supplied to material, its dimensions (length, area and volume) can be changed due to change in its temperature.

The phenomenon of change in dimensions of an object due to heat supplied is known as **thermal expansion.**

Types of Thermal Expansion

There are three types of thermal expansion
  (i) Linear expansion
  (ii) Area (or superficial) expansion and
  (iii) Volume (or cubical) expansion

Linear Expansion

The expansion in length of a body due to increase in its temperature is called the **linear expansion.**

If a rod having initial length l_1 at temperature T_1 and final increased length l_2 at increased temperature T_2, then fractional change in its length is given by

$$\frac{\Delta l}{l_1} = \frac{(l_2 - l_1)}{l_1} = \alpha_l (T_2 - T_1) = \alpha_l \Delta T$$

Linear expansion

Here, $\Delta l \propto l_1$ and $\Delta l \propto \Delta T$ $\therefore$ $\Delta l \propto l_1 \Delta T$

$\Rightarrow$ $\boxed{\text{Expansion in length, } \Delta l = \alpha_l\, l_1\, \Delta T}$

The quantity, α_l is known as **coefficient of linear expansion.** It is a characteristic of the material of the rod. Normally, metals expand more and hence relatively high values of α_l.

$$\alpha_l = \frac{\Delta l}{l\Delta T}$$

$$= \frac{\text{Increase in length}}{\text{Original length} \times \text{Rise in temperature}}$$

Hence, the coefficient of linear expansion of a material of a solid rod is defined as increase in length per unit original length per degree rise in temperature. Its unit is $°C^{-1}$ or K^{-1}.

EXAMPLE |1| A Hardworking Blacksmith

A blacksmith fixes iron ring on the rim of the wooden wheel of a bullock cart. The diameter of the rim and the iron ring are 5.243 m and 5.231 m, respectively at 27°C. To what temperature should the ring be heated so as to fit the rim of the wheel?   ($\alpha = 1.20 \times 10^{-5} K^{-1}$)   [NCERT]

Sol. Given, initial temperature $T_1 = 27°C$
  Initial length, $l_1 = 5.231$ m
  Final length, $l_2 = 5.243$ m
  Now, $\alpha_l = \dfrac{\Delta l}{l_1 \Delta T} = \dfrac{l_2 - l_1}{l_1 \Delta T}$
  $\Rightarrow$ $l_2 = l_1 [1 + \alpha_l (T_2 - T_1)]$
  i.e. 5.243 m $= 5.231$m $[1 + 1.20 \times 10^{-5}$ K$^{-1} (T_2 - 27°C)]$
  This gives $T_2 = 218°C$

EXAMPLE |2| Shrinkage in the Shaft

A large steel wheel is to be fitted on to a shaft of the same material. At 27°C, the outer diameter of the shaft is 8.70 cm and the diameter of the central hole in the wheel is 8.69 cm. The shaft is cooled using 'dry ice' (solid carbon dioxide). At what temperature of the shaft does the wheel slip on the shaft? Assume coefficient of linear expansion of the steel to be constant over the required temperature range. $\alpha_{\text{steel}} = 1.20 \times 10^{-5}$ K^{-1}.   [NCERT]

  Sol. Given, $l_1 = 8.70$ cm, $l_2 = 8.69$ cm,
    $T_1 = 27 + 273 = 300$ K, $T_2 = ?$

As, $l_2 - l_1 = \alpha l_1 (T_2 - T_1)$

$\therefore$ $T_2 - T_1 = \dfrac{l_2 - l_1}{\alpha l_1}$

or $T_2 - 300 = \dfrac{8.69 - 8.70}{1.20 \times 10^{-5} \times 8.70} = -95.8$

or $T_2 = 300 - 95.8$

          $= 204.2\, \text{K} = -68.95°\, \text{C}$

Area Expansion

The expansion in the area of a surface due to increase in its temperature is called **area expansion**.

Area expansion

If a plate having initial area A_1 at temperature T_1 and final area A_2 at temperature T_2 then fractional change in its area is given by

$$\frac{\Delta A}{A_1} = \frac{(A_2 - A_1)}{A_1} = \alpha_A (T_2 - T_1) = \alpha_A \Delta T$$

Here, $\Delta A \propto A_1$ and $\Delta A \propto \Delta T$

$\therefore$ $\Delta A \propto A_1 \Delta T$

$\Rightarrow$ $\boxed{\text{Expansion in area, } \Delta A = \alpha_A A_1 \Delta T}$

where, α_A is known as **coefficient of area expansion**. It depends on nature of the material of the plate.

$$\alpha_A = \frac{\Delta A}{A_1 \Delta T}$$

$$\alpha_A = \frac{\text{Increase in surface area}}{\text{Original surface area} \times \text{Rise in temperature}}$$

Hence, coefficient of area expansion of metal sheet is defined as the increase in its surface area per unit original surface area per degree rise in its temperature. Its unit is $°\text{C}^{-1}$ or K^{-1}.

EXAMPLE |3| Expansion in Metal Ball

A metal ball having a diameter of 0.4 m is heated from 273 to 360 K. If the coefficient of area expansion of the material of the ball is 0.000034 K^{-1}, then determine the increase in surface area of the ball.

Sol. Given, Diameter = 0.4 m

Radius, $r = \dfrac{0.4}{2} = 0.2\, \text{m}$

          $\Delta T = T_2 - T_1 = 360\, \text{K} - 273\, \text{K} = 87\, \text{K}$

          $\alpha_A = 0.000034\, \text{K}^{-1}$

          $\Delta A = ?$

Apply, $\Delta A = \alpha_A A_1 \Delta T$

where, $A_1 = 4 \pi r^2 = 4 \times \pi \times (0.2)^2$

          $= 0.5024\, \text{m}^2$

          $\Delta A = 0.000034 \times 0.5024 \times 87$

          $\Delta A = 0.001486$

          $= 1.486 \times 10^{-3}\, \text{m}^2$

Volume Expansion

The expansion in the volume of an object due to increase in its temperature is known as **volume expansion**.

Volume expansion

The fractional change in volume of an object is given by

$$\frac{\Delta V}{V_1} = \frac{(V_2 - V_1)}{V_1} = \alpha_V (T_2 - T_1) = \alpha_V \Delta T$$

Here, $\Delta V \propto V_1$ and $\Delta V \propto \Delta T$

$\therefore$ $\Delta V \propto V_1 \Delta T$

$\Rightarrow$ $\boxed{\text{Expansion in volume, } \Delta V = \alpha_V V_1 \Delta T}$

where, α_V is known as coefficient of volume expansion.

$$\alpha_V = \frac{\Delta V}{V_1 \Delta T}$$

Hence, the coefficient of volume (cubical) expansion of a substance is defined as the increase in volume per unit original volume per degree rise in its temperature. Its unit is $°\text{C}^{-1}$ or K^{-1}.

It is also a characteristic of material of the object but not strictly a constant. The coefficient of volume expansion α_V depends generally on temperature, its value first increases with temperature and then becomes constant at a high temperature (above 500K). The dependency is shown alongside.

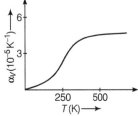

Coefficient of volume expansion of with temperature

The values of volume expansion for some substances are given in the table.

Note

The dimensions of all types of coefficients of expansion is $[\text{K}^{-1}]$ and SI unit is per Kelvin i.e. K^{-1}.

Relation among the Coefficients of Expansion

The coefficients of expansion can be given as

$$\alpha_l = \frac{\Delta l}{l_1 \Delta T} = \frac{\Delta l}{l \Delta T} \qquad \text{(When } l_1 = l)$$

$$\alpha_A = \frac{\Delta A}{A_1 \Delta T} = \frac{\Delta A}{A \Delta T} \qquad \text{(When } A_1 = A)$$

and $\quad \alpha_V = \frac{\Delta V}{V_1 \Delta T} = \frac{\Delta V}{V \Delta T} \qquad \text{(When } V_1 = V)$

Its ratio is given by

$$\alpha_l : \alpha_A : \alpha_V = 1 : 2 : 3$$

i.e. $\qquad \alpha_A = 2\alpha_l$

and $\qquad \alpha_V = 3\alpha_l$

Coefficient of Thermal Expansion at High Temperature

The coefficients α_l, α_A and α_V for a given solid are constants only at a given temperature. The value of these coefficients, however changes with change in the temperature range and become constant only at a high temperature.

EXAMPLE |4| Expansion of Solid Sheet

Show that the coefficient of area expansions (α_A) for rectangular solid sheet is twice of its linear expansion (α_l). **[NCERT]**

Sol. Consider a rectangular solid sheet having length a and breadth b as shown in figure.

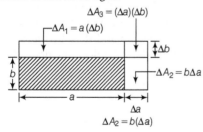

$$\Delta A_3 = (\Delta a)(\Delta b)$$
$$\Delta A_1 = a(\Delta b)$$
$$\Delta A_2 = b\Delta a$$
$$\Delta A_2 = b(\Delta a)$$

When temperature of sheet is increased by ΔT, its length a is increased by Δa and breadth is increased by Δb. Then,

$$\Delta a = \alpha_l a \Delta T$$

and $\qquad \Delta b = \alpha_l b \Delta T$

Increase in area of sheet is

$$\Delta A = \Delta A_1 + \Delta A_2 + \Delta A_3$$
$$\Delta A = a \Delta b + b \Delta a + (\Delta a)(\Delta b)$$
$$= a \alpha_l b \Delta T + b \alpha_l a \Delta T + (\alpha_l)^2 ab(\Delta T)^2$$
$$= \alpha_l ab \Delta T (2 + \alpha_l \Delta T)$$
$$= \alpha_l A \Delta T (2 + \alpha_l \Delta T)$$

For small values of α_l and ΔT, the value of $\alpha_l \Delta T$ would be much smaller so, it can be neglected then

$$\Delta A = 2\alpha_l ab \Delta T = 2\alpha_l A \Delta T \qquad ...(i)$$

As we know, $\Delta A = \alpha_A A \Delta T \qquad ...(ii)$

From Eqs. (i) and (ii), we get $\alpha_A = 2\alpha_l$

EXAMPLE |5| Expansion in a Glass Block

The volume of a glass block initially was 15000 cm^3 but when the temperature of that glass block increases from 20°C to 45°C, then its volume increases by 5cm^3. Determine the coefficient of linear expansion.

Sol. Given, $V_1 = 15000$ cm^3,

$$\Delta T = T_2 - T_1 = 45°C - 20°C = 25°C$$

Change in volume, $\Delta V = 5$ cm^3

Coefficient of volume expansion,

$$\alpha_V = \frac{\Delta V}{V_1 \Delta T} = \frac{5}{15000 \times 25}$$

$$\alpha_V = 0.0133 \times 10^{-3} \,°C^{-1}$$

Coefficient of linear expansion

$$\alpha_l = \frac{\alpha_V}{3} = \frac{0.0133 \times 10^{-3}}{3}$$

$$\alpha_l = 4.4 \times 10^{-6} \,°C^{-1}$$

Anomalous Expansion of Water

Water shows an anomalous behaviour, it contracts on heating between the temperature 0°C to 4°C. When water is cooled below the room temperature (i.e. normal temperature) the volume of given amount of water decreases.

Until its temperature reaches to 4°C and below 4°C, the volume increases (and hence density decreases). So, it is clear that water has maximum density (and hence minimum volume) at 4°C.

The figure shows the variation of volume of 1 kg of water with temperature (°C).

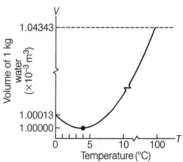

Abnormal behaviour of water

The lake cools towards 4°C water near the surface loses energy to the atmosphere becomes denser and sinks, the warmer, less dense water near the bottom rises.

However, once colder water on top reaches temperature below 4°C, it becomes less dense and remains at the surface, where it freezes. This phenomenon allows the marine animals to remain alive and move freely near the bottom.

Comparison of Expansions in Solids, Liquids and Gases

The expansion in solids and liquids is rather small as compared to the gases at ordinary temperature. The coefficient of volume expansion for the liquids is relatively independent of the temperature.

For an ideal gas, the volume expansion at constant pressure can be obtained from the equation,

$$pV = \mu RT \quad \Rightarrow \quad p\Delta V = \mu R\Delta T$$

$$\Rightarrow \quad \frac{\Delta V}{V} = \frac{\Delta T}{T} \quad \text{i.e. } \alpha_V = \frac{1}{T} \text{ for an ideal gas.}$$

At 0°C, $\alpha_V = 3.7 \times 10^{-3}$ K^{-1} which is much larger than the solids and liquids. For a gas, room temperature and constant pressure α_V is about 3300×10^{-6} K^{-1}.

The curve shows the variation of density of water with respect to temperature from 0°C to 10°C as shown in figure.

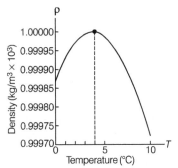

Variation of density of water w.r.t. temperature

THERMAL STRAIN AND THERMAL STRESS

When a metal rod whose ends are rigidly fixed so as to prevent the rod from expansion or contraction, undergoes a change in temperature, thermal strains and thermal stresses are developed in the rod. This is because if the temperature is increased, the rod has a tendency to expand. However, as it is fixed at two ends, the rod exerts a force on supports.

If a rod of length l is heated by a temperature ΔT, then increase in length of rod should have been $\Delta l = l\alpha\Delta T$.

But due to being fixed at ends rod does not expand and a compressive thermal strain is developed in it whose value is

$$\boxed{\text{Thermal (compressive) strain} = \frac{\Delta l}{l} = \alpha\,\Delta T}$$

Here, α = linear expansion coefficient of the material of rod. Due to this strain, a thermal stress is developed in the rod having a value.

Thermal stress = $Y \times$ thermal strain = $Y\alpha\,\Delta T$

$$\boxed{\text{Thermal stress} = Y\alpha\Delta T}$$

Here, Y = Young's modulus of the material of given rod. If A be the cross-section area of the rod, then force exerted by the rod on the supports will be $F = Y\alpha\,\Delta T\,A$.

EXAMPLE |6| Cool the Brass Wire

A brass wire 1.8 m long at 27°C is held taut with little tension between two rigid supports. If the wire is cooled to a temperature of −39°C, what is the tension developed in the wire, if its diameter is 2.0 mm? Coefficient of linear expansion of brass = 2.0×10^{-5}°C^{-1}, Young's modulus of brass = 0.91×10^{11} Pa. **[NCERT]**

Sol. Here, $l = 1.8$ m, $T_1 = 27°$C, $T_2 = -39°$C

$$r = \frac{2.0}{2} = 1.0 \text{ mm} = 1.0 \times 10^{-3} \text{ m}$$

$$\alpha = 2.0 \times 10^{-5}\,°\text{C}^{-1}, Y = 0.91 \times 10^{11} \text{ Pa}$$

As, $\Delta l = l\alpha(T_2 - T_1)$

$\therefore$ Strain, $\dfrac{\Delta l}{l} = \alpha(T_2 - T_1) = \alpha\Delta T$

Stress = Strain × Young's modulus

$$= \alpha(T_2 - T_1) \times Y = 2.0 \times 10^{-5} \times (-39 - 27) \times 0.91 \times 10^{11}$$

$$= -1.2 \times 10^8 \text{ Nm}^{-2}$$

$\therefore$ Tension developed in the wire

$$= \text{Stress} \times \text{Area of cross-section} = \text{Stress} \times \pi r^2$$

$$= -1.2 \times 10^8 \times 3.14 \times (1.0 \times 10^{-3})^2 = -3.77 \times 10^2 \text{ N}$$

EXAMPLE |7| Cool the Steel Wire

Consider the steel wire having diameter 3 mm is stretched between two clamps, calculate the tension in the wire when its temperature falls from 50°C to 40°C. Given α_l for steel is 1.1×10^{-6}°C^{-1} and Young's modulus 21×10^{11} dyne cm^{-2}.

Sol. Given, Diameter = 3 mm = 0.3 cm, $r = \dfrac{0.3}{2} = 0.15$ cm

Change in temperature, $\Delta T = 50°$C − 40°C = 10°C

Coefficient of linear expansion, $\alpha_l = 1.1 \times 10^{-6}\,°\text{C}^{-1}$

Young's modulus, $Y = 21 \times 10^{11}$ dyne cm^{-2}

Apply the formula for linear expansion.

$$\Delta l_1 = l_1 \alpha_l \Delta T = l_1 \times 1.1 \times 10^{-6} \times 10°C$$

$$\Rightarrow \qquad \Delta l = 11 \times 10^{-6}\, l_1$$

Young's modulus $(Y) = \dfrac{F \times l}{A \times \Delta l} = \dfrac{F \times l}{\pi r^2 \times \Delta l}$

$$F = \dfrac{Y \times \pi r^2 \times \Delta l}{l_1}$$

$$= \dfrac{21 \times 10^{11} \times \pi \times (0.15)^2 \times 11 \times 10^{-6}\, l_1}{l_1}$$

$$F = 16.32 \times 10^5 \text{ dyne}$$

TOPIC PRACTICE 1

OBJECTIVE Type Questions

1. Heat is associated with   **[NCERT Exemplar]**
   (a) kinetic energy of random motion of molecules
   (b) kinetic energy of orderly motion of molecules
   (c) total kinetic energy of random and orderly motion of molecules
   (d) kinetic energy of random motion in some cases and kinetic energy of orderly motion in other

Sol. (a) We know that as temperature increases vibration of molecules about their mean position increases hence, kinetic energy associated with random motion of these molecules increases. Thereby leading to production of heat.

2. The common physical property which is to be used as the basis for constructing thermometer is
   (a) the variation of the volume of a liquid with temperature
   (b) the variation of the pressure of a gas with temperature
   (c) the variation of the resistance of a wire with temperature
   (d) All of the above

Sol. (d) Any physical property which varies linearly with temperature can be used in constructing thermometers.

3. As the temperature is increased, the period of a pendulum
   (a) increases as its effective length increases even though its centre of mass still remains at the centre of the bob
   (b) decreases as its effective length increases even though its centre of mass still remains at the centre of the bob
   (c) increases as its effective length increases due to shifting to centre of mass below the centre of the bob

   (d) decreases as its effective length remains same but the centre of mass shifts above the centre of the bob

Sol. (a) As the temperature is increased length of the pendulum increases.

We know that, time period of pendulum $T = 2\pi\sqrt{\dfrac{L}{g}}$

$$\Rightarrow \qquad T \propto \sqrt{L}$$

As L, increases so, time period (T) also increases.

4. A bar of iron is 10 cm at 20°C. At 19°C, it will be (α of iron $= 11 \times 10^{-6}\,°C^{-1}$)
   (a) 11×10^{-6} cm longer   (b) 11×10^{-5} cm shorter
   (c) 11×10^{-6} cm shorter   (d) 11×10^{-5} cm longer

Sol. (b) According to linear expansion, we get

$$L = L_0\,(1 + \alpha\Delta\theta)$$

$$\dfrac{L_1}{L_2} = \dfrac{1 + \alpha\,(\Delta\theta_1)}{1 + \alpha\,(\Delta\theta_2)}$$

$$\Rightarrow \qquad \dfrac{10}{L_2} = \dfrac{1 + 11 \times 10^{-6} \times 20}{1 + 11 \times 10^{-6} \times 19}$$

$$\Rightarrow \qquad L_2 = 9.99989$$

Length is shorter by $= 10 - 9.99989 = 0.00011$
$$= 11 \times 10^{-5} \text{ cm}$$

5. An aluminium sphere is dipped into water. Which of the following is true? **[NCERT Exemplar]**
   (a) Buoyancy will be less in water at 0°C than that in water at 4°C
   (b) Buoyancy will be more in water at 0°C than that in water at 4°C
   (c) Buoyancy in water at 0°C will be same as that in water at 4°C
   (d) Buoyancy may be more or less in water at 4°C depending on the radius of the sphere

Sol. (a) Let volume of the sphere is V and ρ is the density of water, then we can write buoyant force

$$F = V\rho g \quad (g = \text{acceleration due to gravity})$$

$$\Rightarrow \qquad F \propto \rho \qquad (\because V \text{ and } g \text{ are almost constant})$$

$$\Rightarrow \qquad \dfrac{F_{4°C}}{F_{0°C}} = \dfrac{\rho_{4°C}}{\rho_{0°C}} > 1 \qquad (\because \rho_{4°C} > \rho_{0°C})$$

$$\Rightarrow \qquad F_{4°C} > F_{0°C}$$

Hence, buoyancy will be less in water at 0°C than that in water at 4°C.

VERY SHORT ANSWER Type Questions

6. Is it correct to call heat as the energy in transit?

Sol. Yes, it is perfect correct to call heat as the energy in transit because it is continuously flowing on account of temperature difference between bodies or parts of a system.

7. Give the relation between celsius, fahrenheit and reaumur scale temperature.

Sol. $\dfrac{C-0}{100-0} = \dfrac{F-32}{212-32} = \dfrac{R-0}{80-0}$

8. Can temperature on celsius scale and kelvin scale related?

Sol. $\qquad t(^\circ C) = T(k) - 273.15$

or $\qquad T(K) = t(^\circ C) + 273.15$

9. Two absolute scales A and B have triple points of water defined to be $200\,A$ and $350\,B$. What is relation between T_A and T_B? **[NCERT]**

Sol. $\dfrac{T_A}{T_B} = \dfrac{200}{350} = \dfrac{4}{7}$ or $T_A = \dfrac{4}{7}T_B$

10. Why should a thermometer bulb have a small heat capacity?

Sol. The thermometer bulb having small heat capacity will absorb less heat from the body whose temperature is to be measured. Hence, the temperature of that body will practically remain unchanged.

11. Why the temperature above 1200°C cannot be measured accurately by a platinum resistance thermometer?

Sol. This is because platinum begins to evaporate above 1200°C.

12. Each side of a cube increases by 0.01% on heating. How much is the area of its faces and volume increased?

Sol. The area of the faces will increased by 0.02% and the volume by 0.03%.

13. Why is a gap left between the ends of two railway lines in a railway track?

Sol. It is done to accommodate the linear expansion of railway line during summer. If the gap is not left in summer, the lines will bend causing a threat of derailment.

SHORT ANSWER Type Questions

14. Find out the temperature which has same numerical value on celsius and fahrenheit scale.

Sol. Let θ be the same numerical value of temperature on the both scales.

$\therefore \qquad \dfrac{T_C}{5} = \dfrac{T_F - 32}{9}$

$\Rightarrow \qquad \dfrac{\theta}{5} = \dfrac{\theta - 32}{9}$ $\qquad [\because \theta^\circ C = \theta^\circ F = \theta,\ \text{given}]$

$\Rightarrow \qquad 9\theta = 5\theta - 160$

$\qquad\qquad -4\theta = 160$

$\therefore \qquad\qquad \theta = -40^\circ$

$\qquad\qquad \theta = -40^\circ C$

$\qquad\qquad\quad = -40^\circ F$

15. In what ways are the gas thermometers superior to mercury thermometers?

Sol. A gas thermometer is more superior to a mercury thermometer, as its working is independent of the nature of gas (working substance) used. As the variation of pressure (or volume) with temperature is uniform, the range, in which temperature can be measured with a gas thermometer is quite large. Further, a gas thermometer is more sensitive than mercury thermometer.

16. Gas thermometers are more sensitive than mercury thermometers. Why?

Sol. The coefficient of increase of pressure (or volume) of a gas is $\dfrac{1}{273.15}\,^\circ C^{-1}$. It is very large as compared to coefficient of expansion of mercury. Therefore, for a certain increase in temperature, increase in volume of the gas will be large compared to that of mercury and hence a gas thermometer is more sensitive.

17. There is a slight temperature difference between the water fall at the top and the bottom. Why?

Sol. The potential energy of water at the top of the fall gets converted into heat kinetic energy at the bottom of the fall. When water hits the ground, a part of its kinetic energy gets converted into heat which increases its temperature slightly.

18. A steel tape 1 m long is correctly calibrated for a temperature of 27.0°C. The length of a steel rod measured by this tape is found to be 63.0 cm on a hot day when the temperature is 45.0°C.

What is the actual length of the steel rod on that day? What is the length of the same steel rod on a day when the temperature is 27.0°C? Coefficient of linear expansion of steel $= 1.20 \times 10^{-5}\,^\circ C^{-1}$? **[NCERT]**

Sol. Here, $t_1 = 27^\circ C$, $l_1 = 63$ cm,

$\qquad t_2 = 45^\circ C$, $\alpha = 1.20 \times 10^{-5}\,^\circ C^{-1}$

Length of the rod on the hot day is

$\qquad l_2 = l_1[1 + \alpha(t_2 - t_1)]$

$\qquad\quad = 63[1 + 1.20 \times 10^{-5}\,(45 - 27)]$

$\qquad\quad = 63.0136$ cm

As the steel tape has been calibrated for a temperature of 27°C, so length of the steel rod at 27°C = 63 cm.

19. The difference between length of a certain brass rod and that of a steel rod is claimed to be constant at all temperatures. Is this possible?

Sol. Yes, it is possible to describe the difference of length to remain constant. So, the change in length of each rod must be equal at all temperature. Let L_b and L_s be the length of the brass and the steel rod and α_b and α_s be the coefficients of linear expansion of the two metals. Let there is change in temperature be ΔT.

Then, $\qquad \alpha_b L_b \Delta T = \alpha_s L_s \Delta T$

or $\qquad \alpha_b L_b = \alpha_s L_s$

$\Rightarrow \qquad L_b / L_s = \alpha_s / \alpha_b$

Hence, the lengths of the rods must be in the inverse ratio of the coefficient of linear expansion of their materials.

20. There are two spheres of same radius and material at same temperature but one being solid while the other hollow. Which sphere will expand more if (i) they are heated to the same temperature (ii) same amount of heat is given to each of them?

Sol. (i) As thermal expansion of isotropic solids is similar to true photographic enlargement, the expansion of a cavity is same as if it were a solid body of the same material i.e. $\Delta V = \gamma V \Delta T$. As here V, γ and ΔT are same for both solid and hollow spheres, so the expansions of both will be equal.

(ii) If same amount of heat is given to the two spheres, then due to lesser mass, rise in temperature of hollow sphere will be more (as $\Delta T = Q/Mc$) and hence the expansion will be more as $\Delta V = \gamma V \Delta T$.

21. The coefficient of volume expansion of glycerine is $49 \times 10^{-5} \,°C^{-1}$. What is the fractional change in its density for a 30°C rise in temperature? **[NCERT]**

Sol. Let M be the mass of glycerine, ρ_0 its density at 0°C, ρ_t its density at t°C.

Then, $\qquad \gamma = \dfrac{V_t - V_0}{V_0 \Delta T} = \dfrac{\dfrac{M}{\rho_t} - \dfrac{M}{\rho_0}}{(M/\rho_0)\Delta T}$

$\qquad \gamma = \dfrac{\dfrac{1}{\rho_t} - \dfrac{1}{\rho_0}}{(1/\rho_0)\Delta T} = \dfrac{\rho_0 - \rho_t}{\rho_0 \Delta T}$

$\therefore$ Fractional change in density,

$\dfrac{\rho_0 - \rho_t}{\rho_0} = \gamma \Delta T$

$\qquad = 49 \times 10^{-5} \times 30 = 0.0147$

22. Two identical rectangular strips-one of copper and the other of steel are riveted to form a bimetallic strip. What will happen on heating?

Sol. The coefficient of linear expansion of copper is more than steel. On heating, the expansion in copper strip is more than the steel strip. The bimetallic strip will bend with steel strip on inner (concave) side.

LONG ANSWER Type I Questions

23. A celsius and fahrenheit thermometer are put in an hot bath. The reading of fahrenheit thermometer is 3/2 times the reading of celsius thermometer. What is the temperature of bath on celsius, fahrenheit and kelvin's scales.

Sol. Let if reading on celsius scale is θ.

Reading on $\qquad T_F = \dfrac{3}{2}\theta$

As $\qquad \dfrac{\theta}{100} = \dfrac{T_F - 32}{180}$

$\qquad \dfrac{\theta}{5} = \dfrac{\dfrac{3}{2}\theta - 32}{9}$

On solving, we get

$\qquad \theta = -106.67\,°C$

Temperature on kelvin's scale

$\qquad T_K = -106.67 + 273.15$

$\qquad = 166.48\,K$

24. The triple points of neon and carbon dioxide are 24.57 K and 216.55 K, respectively. Express these temperatures on the celsius and fahrenheit scales. **[NCERT]**

Sol. For neon Triple point $T = 24.57\,K$

$\therefore \quad T_C = T(K) - 273.15$

$\qquad = 24.57 - 273.15 = -248.58\,°C$

$\quad T_F = \dfrac{9}{5}T_C + 32 = \dfrac{9}{5} \times (-248.58) + 32 = -415.44\,°F$

For carbon dioxide Triple point, $T = 216.55\,K$

$\therefore \quad T_C = T(K) - 273.15$

$\qquad = 216.55 - 273.15 = -56.6\,°C$

$\quad T_F = \dfrac{9}{5}T_C + 32 = \dfrac{9}{5} \times (-56.6) + 32$

$\qquad = -69.88\,°C$

25. Two ideal gas thermometers A and B use oxygen and hydrogen, respectively. The following observations are made **[NCERT]**

Temperature	Pressure thermometer A	Pressure thermometer B
Triple point of water	1.250×10^5 Pa	0.200×10^5 Pa
Normal melting point of sulphur	1.797×10^5 Pa	0.287×10^5 Pa

(i) What is the absolute temperature of normal melting point of sulphur as read by thermometers A and B?

(ii) What do you think is the reason for slightly different answers from A and B? **[NCERT]**

Sol. (i) (a) For pressure thermometer A,

$$T_{tr} = 273 \text{ K}, \, p_{tr} = 1.250 \times 10^5 \text{ Pa},$$

$$p = 1.797 \times 10^5 \text{ Pa}$$

Normal freezing point of sulphur,

$$T = \frac{p}{p_{tr}} \times T_{tr}$$

$$= \frac{1.795 \times 10^5 \times 273}{1.250 \times 10^5} = 392.028 \text{ K}$$

(b) For pressure thermometer B,

$$T_{tr} = 273 \text{ K}, \, p_{tr} = 0.200 \times 10^5 \text{ Pa},$$

$$p = 0.287 \times 10^5 \text{ Pa}$$

$$\therefore \quad T = \frac{0.287 \times 10^5 \times 273}{0.200 \times 10^5} = 391.75 \text{ K}$$

(ii) The slight difference is due to the fact that oxygen and hydrogen do not behave strictly as ideal gases.

26. A metallic ball has a radius of 9.0 cm at 0°C. Calculate the change in its volume when it is heated to 90°C. Given that coefficient of linear expansion of metal of ball is 1.2×10^{-5} K^{-1}.

Sol. As radius of ball, $r_0 = 9.0$ cm $= 0.090$ m at 0°C, hence its

volume, $\quad V_0 = \frac{4}{3} \pi r_0^3 = \frac{4}{3} \times 3.14 \times (0.090)^3$

$$= 3.05 \times 10^{-3} \text{ m}^3$$

Again as, $\alpha = 1.2 \times 10^{-5}$ K^{-1},

$$\therefore \quad \gamma = 3\alpha = 3 \times 1.2 \times 10^{-5} = 3.6 \times 10^{-5} \text{ K}^{-1}$$

Moreover rise in temperature

$$\Delta T = 90°\text{C} - 0°\text{C} = 90°\text{C} = 90 \text{ K}$$

$\therefore$ Increase in volume, $\Delta V = V \gamma \Delta T$

$$= 3.05 \times 10^{-3} \times 3.6 \times 10^{-5} \times 90$$

$$= 9.88 \times 10^{-6} \text{ m}^3 = 9.88 \text{ cm}^3$$

27. A steel wire of 2.0 mm^2 cross-section is held straight (but under no tension) by attaching it firmly to two points a distance 1.50 m apart at 30°C. If the temperature now decreases to 5°C and if the two points remain fixed, what will be the tension in the wire?

Given that Young's modulus of steel $= 2 \times 10^{11}$ Nm^{-2} and coefficient of thermal expansion of steel $\alpha = 1.1 \times 10^{-5}$/ °C.

Sol. Given, cross-section area, $A = 2.0$ mm$^2 = 2 \times 10^{-6}$ m^2,

change in temperature, $\Delta T = 30 - 5 = 25°$ C,

Young's modulus of steel wire, $Y = 2 \times 10^{11}$ Nm^{-2} and coefficient of linear expansion of steel,

$$\alpha = 1.1 \times 10^{-5} / °\text{C}.$$

$\therefore$ Tension developed in the rod,

$$F = YA\alpha\Delta T$$

$$= 2 \times 10^{11} \times 2 \times 10^{-6} \times 1.1 \times 10^{-5} \times 25$$

$$F = 110 \text{ N}$$

28. The brass scale of a barometer gives correct reading at 0°C. Coefficient of linear expansion of brass is 2.0×10^{-5}/°C. The barometer reads 75.00 cm at 27°C. What is the true atmospheric pressure at 27°C?

Sol. As the brass scale of a barometer gives correct reading at $T_1 = 0°$ C, hence at temperature $T_2 = 27°$ C, the scale will expand and will not give correct reading.

In such a case, true value

$$= \text{observed scale reading} \times (1 + \alpha\Delta T)$$

$\therefore$ True pressure $= 75.00$ cm $\times [1 + 2.0 \times 10^{-5} \times (27 - 0)]$

$$= 75 \times (1 + 2.0 \times 10^{-5} \times 27)$$

$$= 75.00 (1 + 54 \times 10^{-5}) \text{ cm}$$

$$= 75.04 \text{ cm}$$

LONG ANSWER Type II Questions

29. The electrical resistance in Ohms of a certain thermometer varies with temperature according to the approximate law

$$R = R_0[1 + 5 \times 10^{-3}(T - T_0)]$$

The resistance is 101.6 Ω at the triple point of water and 165.5 Ω at the normal melting point of lead (600.5 K). What is the temperature when the resistance is 123.4 Ω? **[NCERT]**

Sol. When $T = 273$ K, $R = 101.6$ Ω

$$\therefore \quad 101.6 = R_0[1 + 5 \times 10^{-3}(273 - T_0)] \quad \text{...(i)}$$

Given, $\quad T = 600.5$ K, $R = 165.5$ Ω

$$\therefore \quad 165.5 = R_0[1 + 5 \times 10^{-3}(600.5 - T_0)] \quad \text{...(ii)}$$

Dividing Eq. (ii) by Eq. (i), we get

$$\frac{165.5}{101.0} = \frac{1 + 5 \times 10^{-3}(600.5 - T_0)}{1 + 5 \times 10^{-5}(273 - T_0)}$$

On solving, $\quad T_0 = -49.3$ K

Substituting in Eq. (i), we get

$$101.6 = R_0[1 + 5 \times 10^{-3}(273 + 49.3)]$$

or $\quad R_0 = \frac{101.6}{1 + 5 \times 10^{-3} \times 322.3} = 38.9$ Ω

For $R = 123.4$ Ω, we have

$$123.4 = 38.9[1 + 5 \times 10^{-3}(T + 49.3)]$$

On solving, we get $T = 384.8$ K

30. A brass rod of length 50 cm and diameter 3.0 mm is joined to a steel rod of the same length and diameter. What is the change in length of the combined rod at 250°C, if the original length are at 40.0°C? Is there a 'thermal stress' developed at the junction? The ends of the rod are free to expand. Coefficient of linear expansion of brass = $2.0 \times 10^{-5} °C^{-1}$ and that of steel = $1.2 \times 10^{-5} °C^{-1}$. **[NCERT]**

Sol. For brass rod,

$l = 50$ cm, $t_1 = 40° C$, $t_2 = 250° C$

$\alpha = 2.0 \times 10^{-5} °C^{-1}$

Change in length of brass rod is

$\Delta l = \alpha l(t_2 - t_1)$

$= 2.0 \times 10^{-5} \times 50 \times (250 - 40) = 0.21$ cm

For steel rod, $l = 50$ cm, $t_1 = 40° C$, $t_2 = 250° C$,

$\alpha = 1.2 \times 10^{-5} °C^{-1}$

Change in length of steel rod is

$\Delta l' = \alpha l(t_2 - t_1)$

$= 1.2 \times 10^{-5} \times 50 \times (250 - 40) = 0.13$ cm

Change in length of the combined rod at 250°C

$= \Delta l + \Delta l' = 0.21 + 0.13 = 0.34$ cm

As the rods expand freely, so no thermal stress is developed at the junction.

31. A hole is drilled in a copper sheet. The diameter of the hole is 4.24 cm at 27°C. What is the change in the diameter of the hole when the sheet is heated to 227°C? Coefficient of linear expansion of copper is 1.70×10^{-5}/°C. **[NCERT]**

Sol. Given, diameter of the hole $(d_1) = 4.24$ cm

Initial temperature $T_1 = 27 + 273 = 300$ K

Final temperature $T_2 = 227 + 273 = 500$ K

Coefficient of linear expansion $(\alpha) = 1.70 \times 10^{-5}$/°C

Coefficient of superficial expansion

$(\beta) = 2\alpha = 3.40 \times 10^{-5}$/°C

Initial area of hole at 27°C $(A_1) = \pi r^2 = \dfrac{\pi d_1^2}{4}$

$= \dfrac{\pi}{4}(4.24)^2 = 4.494\pi$ cm^2

Area of hole at 227°C $(A_2) = A_1(1 + \beta \Delta t)$

$= 4.494\pi[1 + 3.40 \times 10^{-5} \times (227 - 27)]$

$= 4.494\pi(1 + 3.40 \times 10^{-5} \times 200)$

$= 4.495\pi \times 1.0068 = 4.525\pi$ cm^2

If diameter of hole becomes d_2 at 227°C then $A_2 = \dfrac{\pi d_2^2}{4}$

or $\quad 4.525\pi = \dfrac{\pi d_2^2}{4} \Rightarrow d_2^2 = 4.525 \times 4$

$\Rightarrow \qquad d_2 = 4.2544$ cm

∴ Change in diameter $(\Delta d) = d_2 - d_1 = 4.2544 - 4.24$

$= 0.0144$ cm

$= 1.44 \times 10^{-2}$ cm

32. Show that the coefficient of volume expansion for a solid substance is three times its coefficient of linear expansion.

Sol. Consider a solid in the form of a rectangular parallelopiped of sides a, b and c respectively so that its volume $V = abc$.

If the solid is heated so that its temperature rises by ΔT, then increase in its sides will be

$\Delta a = a \cdot \alpha \cdot \Delta T$, $\Delta b = b \cdot \alpha \cdot \Delta T$ and $\Delta c = c \cdot \alpha \cdot \Delta T$

or $\quad a' = a + \Delta a = a(1 + \alpha \cdot \Delta T)$

$\quad b' = b + \Delta b = b(1 + \alpha \cdot \Delta T)$

and $\quad c' = c + \Delta c = c(1 + a \cdot \Delta T)$

∵ New volume, $V' = V + \Delta V = a'b'c'$

$= abc(1 + \alpha \cdot \Delta T)^3$

∴ Increase in volume,

$\Delta V = V' - V = [abc(1 + \alpha \cdot \Delta T)^3 - abc]$

∴ Coefficient of volume expansion,

$\gamma = \dfrac{\Delta V}{V \cdot \Delta T} = \dfrac{abc(1 + \alpha \cdot \Delta T)^3 - abc}{abc \cdot \Delta T}$

∴ $\quad \gamma = \dfrac{(1 + \alpha \cdot \Delta T)^3 - 1}{\Delta T}$

$= \dfrac{(1 + 3\alpha \cdot \Delta T + 3\alpha^2 \cdot \Delta T^2 + \alpha^3 \cdot \Delta T^3) - 1}{\Delta T}$

$= 3\alpha + 3\alpha^2 \Delta T + \alpha^3 \cdot \Delta T^2.$

However, as α has an extremely small value for solids, hence terms containing higher powers of α may be neglected. Therefore, we obtain the relation $\gamma = 3\alpha$

i.e. coefficient of volume expansion of a solid is three times of its coefficient of linear expansion.

ASSESS YOUR TOPICAL UNDERSTANDING

OBJECTIVE Type Questions

1. A glass of ice-cold water left on a table on a hot summer day eventually warms up whereas a cup of hot tea on the same table cools down because
   (a) its surrounding media are different
   (b) the direction of heat flow depends on the surrounding temperature with respect to the object
   (c) heating or cooling does not depend on surrounding temperature
   (d) Both (a) and (b)

2. On a hilly region, water boils at 95°C. The temperature expressed in fahrenheit is
   (a) 100°F   (b) 20.3°F
   (c) 150°F   (d) 203°F

3. A uniform metallic rod rotates about its perpendicular bisector with constant angular speed. If it is heated uniformly to raise its temperature slightly   **[NCERT Exemplar]**
   (a) its speed of rotation increases
   (b) its speed of rotation decreases
   (c) its speed of rotation remains same
   (d) its speed increases because its moment of inertia increases

4. Coefficient of volumetric expansion α_V is not a constant. It depends on temperature. Variation of α_V with temperature for metals is

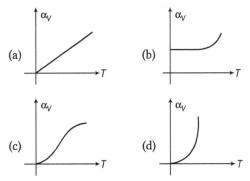

5. Variation of the density of water with respect to temperature from 0°C to 10°C is correctly represented by

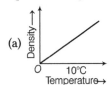

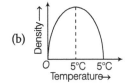

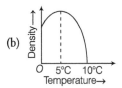

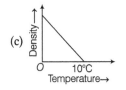

Answer

  1. (b) | 2. (d) | 3. (b) | 4. (c) | 5. (d)

VERY SHORT ANSWER Type Questions

6. Which physical quantity governs the direction of flow of heat?

7. A body at higher temperature contains more heat. Comment.

8. Why does a solid expand on heating?

9. A tightened glass stopper can be taken out easily by pouring hot water around the neck of the bottle. Why?

10. Why are gas thermometers are more sensitive than mercury thermometers?

SHORT ANSWER Type Questions

11. By how much the temperature of a copper rod to be raised so as to increase its length by 1%? Given that coefficient of linear expansion of copper $= 1.7 \times 10^{-5}$ K^{-1}.   **[Ans. 588.2°C]**

12. The length of a steel pan of a river bridge is 50 m and the bridge has to withstand temperature ranging from 4°C to 52°C.
    What allowance should be kept for its change in length with temperature? Given that for a steel, $\alpha = 1.1 \times 10^{-5}$ C.   **[Ans. 2.6 cm]**

13. The difference between the length of a certain brass rod and that of a steel rod is claimed to be constant at all temperature. Is this possible?

14. What is mean of metals and alloys, which have a greater value of temperatures coefficient of expansion and why?

15. At what temperature, if any, do the following pair of scales gives the same reading?
    Fahrenheit and Kelvin.   **[Ans. 574.6°]**

LONG ANSWER Type I Questions

16. Cooking is easier in pressure cooker but difficult on hills, why?

17. A clock with an iron pendulum keeps correct time at 20°C. How much will it lose or gain per day, if temperature changes to 40°C? Coefficient of cubical expansion of iron is $36 \times 10^{-6} \, °C^{-1}$.

[**Ans.** 10.368 s]

18. What are coefficients of linear, superficial and cubical expansions? What is the relation amongst them?

19. How does thermal expansion of liquids differ from that of solid? Is real expansion always greater than the apparent expansion?

LONG ANSWER Type II Questions

20. A resistance thermometer reads the resistance $R = 20.0 \, \Omega, 27.5 \, \Omega$ and $50.0 \, \Omega$ at the ice point (0°C), the steam point (100°C), the zinc point (420°C),

respectively. Assuming that the resistance varies with temperature as $R_t = R_0 (1 + \alpha t + \beta t^2)$, where t is temperature in Celsius scale. Determine the value R_0, α and β.

[**Ans.** 20 Ω, $3.8 \times 10^{-3} \, °C^{-1}$, $-5.6 \times 10^{-7} \, °C^{-2}$]

21. A circular disc made by iron is rotating about its axis of rotation with a uniform angular speed ω.

Determine the change in the linear speed of particle at the rim in percentage. The disc of rim is slowly heated from 20°C to 50°C keeping the angular speed uniform. Given that coefficient of linear expansion for the material of iron is $1.2 \times 10^{-5} \, °C^{-1}$.

[**Ans.** 3.6×10^{-2}]

22. What do you mean by thermal expansion, describe its types with units. Also, give the relation among the expansion coefficient?

23. A hole is drilled in a copper sheet. The diameter of the hole is 4.24 cm at temperature 27°C. What is the change in the diameter of the hole when the sheet is heated upto temperature 227°C. Given that coefficient of linear expansion for the copper is $1.7 \times 10^{-5} \, °C^{-1}$.

[**Ans.** 0.0144 cm]

|TOPIC 2|
Calorimetry and Heat Transfer

HEAT CAPACITY

The quantity of heat is given to any substance depends on its mass m, the change in temperature ΔT and the nature of substance which is being warmed. To change the temperature of substance, a given quantity of heat is absorbed or rejected by it, which is characterised by a quantity is known as **heat capacity**. The heat capacity is defined as amount of heat needed to change the temperature by unity i.e. 1°C, it is denoted by S and having SI unit JK^{-1}.

$$\text{Heat capacity}, S = \frac{\Delta Q}{\Delta T}$$

where, ΔQ = heat absorbed or rejected by body and

ΔT = change in temperature.

Dimensional formula of heat capacity = $[ML^2T^{-2}K^{-1}]$

Note

Mass of water having the same heat capacity as a given body is called **water equivalent** of the body. The unit of water equivalent is gram.

Specific Heat Capacity

The amount of heat needed to raise the temperature of unit mass of a substance by unity is known as the **specific heat capacity** or **specific heat**. It is denoted by s and its SI unit is $Jkg^{-1}K^{-1}$.

$$s = \frac{S}{m} = \frac{\Delta Q}{m\Delta T}$$

$\Rightarrow$ $$\boxed{\text{Specific heat capacity}, s = \frac{1}{m}\frac{\Delta Q}{\Delta T}}$$

where, m = mass of given substance.

The SI unit of specific heat capacity is $Jkg^{-1}K^{-1}$.

Note

Water has the highest specific heat capacity $(4.18 \times 10^3 \, Jkg^{-1}°C^{-1})$ compared to other substances. For this reason water is used as a coolant in automobile radiators as well as a heater in hot water bags.

Molar Specific Heat Capacity

The amount of heat needed to raise the temperature of one mole of a substance (gas) by unity is known as the **molar heat capacity** of that substance. It is denoted by C. Its SI unit is $Jmol^{-1}K^{-1}$.

$$C = \frac{S}{\mu} = \frac{\Delta Q}{\mu \Delta T}$$

where μ = number of moles of substance (gas).

$$\boxed{\text{Molar specific heat capacity, } C = \frac{\Delta Q}{\mu \Delta T}}$$

Relation between Specific Heat and Molar Specific Heat Capacity

As, number of moles, $\mu = \dfrac{m}{M}$

where, m = mass of the substance
and M = molecular mass

$$m = \mu M$$

$$C = \frac{1}{\mu}\left[\frac{\Delta Q}{\Delta T}\right] = M\left[\frac{\Delta Q}{m\Delta T}\right]$$

But, $\dfrac{\Delta Q}{m\Delta T} = s$

$$\boxed{C = Ms}$$

where, s = specific heat capacity,
M = molecular mass of the substance
and C = molar specific heat capacity.

Hence, molar specific heat capacity

= molecular mass × specific heat capacity.

Types of Molar Specific Heat Capacity

There are two types of molar specific heat capacity

(i) **Molar specific heat capacity at constant pressure** It is molar heat capacity of a gas at constant pressure i.e. the amount of heat required to raise the temperature of 1 mole of a gas by unity at constant pressure and is denoted by C_p.

(ii) **Molar specific heat capacity at constant volume** It is molar heat capacity of a gas at constant volume i.e. the amount of heat required to raise the temperature of 1 mole of gas through 1°C at constant volume and denoted by C_V.

The molar specific heat capacity and specific heat capacity play an important role in calorimetry.

EXAMPLE |1| A Drilling Machine

A 10 kW drilling machine is used to drill a bore in a small aluminium block of mass 8.0 kg. How much is the rise in temperature of the block in 2.5 min, assuming 50% of power is used up in heating the machine itself or lost to the surroundings. Specific heat of aluminium $= 0.91 \, Jg^{-1}{}^{\circ}C^{-1}$. **[NCERT]**

Sol. Given, power, $P = 10$ kW $= 10 \times 10^3$ W

Time, $t = 2.5$ min $= 2.5 \times 60$ s

Total energy used

$$= Pt = 10 \times 10^3 \times 2.5 \times 60$$

$$= 1.5 \times 10^6 \, J$$

Energy absorbed by aluminium block,

$$Q = 50\% \text{ of the total energy} = \frac{1.5 \times 10^6}{2}$$

$$= 0.75 \times 10^6 \, J$$

Also, $m = 8.0$ kg $= 8.0 \times 10^3$ g, $s = 0.91 \, Jg^{-1}{}^{\circ}C^{-1}$

As, $Q = ms \, \Delta T$

$\therefore \quad \Delta T = \dfrac{Q}{ms} = \dfrac{0.75 \times 10^6}{8.0 \times 10^3 \times 0.91}$

$$= 103.02°C$$

CALORIMETRY

It is the branch of science that deals with the measurement of heat. When a body at higher temperature is brought in contact with another body at lower temperature, then the heat flows from the body kept at higher temperature to the body kept at lower temperature till the both bodies acquire the same temperature.

Thus, the principle of calorimetry states that total heat given by a hotter body equals to the total heat received by colder body.

i.e. **Heat lost by hotter body = Heat gained by colder body**

If there are two bodies of masses m_1 and m_2 and having values of specific heats s_1 and s_2 respectively, then for temperature difference ΔT.

$$\Rightarrow \quad \boxed{m_1 s_1 \, \Delta T = m_2 s_2 \, \Delta T}$$

Note

A system is said to isolated one if no exchange of heat takes place between the system and surrounding. During calorimetry, it is assumed that no heat is allowed to escape to the surrounding.

Calorimeter

It is a device used for measuring the quantities of heat. It consists of a cylindrical vessel of copper provided with a stirrer. The vessel is kept inside a wooden jacket. The space between the calorimeter and the jacket is packed with a heat insulating material like glass wool, etc.

Thus, the calorimeter gets thermally isolated from the surroundings. The loss of heat due to radiation is further reduced by polishing the outer surface of the calorimeter and the inner surface of the jacket.

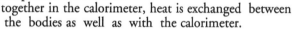

The lid is provided with holes for inserting a thermometer and a stirrer into the calorimeter.

When bodies at different temperatures are mixed together in the calorimeter, heat is exchanged between the bodies as well as with the calorimeter.

If there is no loss of heat to the surroundings, then according to the principle of calorimetry,

Heat gained by cold bodies = Heat lost by hot bodies

EXAMPLE |2| Experiment for Specific Heat

In an experiment on the specific heat of a metal, a 0.20 kg block of the metal at 150°C is dropped in a copper calorimeter (of water equivalent 0.025 kg) containing 150 cm^3 of water at 27°C. The final temperature is 40°C. Compute the specific heat of the metal.

Sol. Given, mass of metal block, $m = 0.20$ kg $= 200$ g

Fall in temperature of metal block,
$$\Delta T = 150° - 40° = 110°C$$

Let specific heat of metal block $= 5$ cal g^{-1} °C^{-1}

∴ Heat lost by metal block $= mc\ \Delta T = 200 \times 5 \times 110$ cal

Volume of water in calorimeter $= 150$ cm^3

Mass of water, $m' = 150$ g

Water equivalent of calorimeter, $w = 0.025$ kg $= 25$ g

Specific heat of water, $s' = 1$ cal g^{-1} °C^{-1}

∴ Heat gained by water and calorimeter
$$= (m' + w)\, s'\, \Delta T' = (150 + 25) \times 1 \times (40 - 27)\text{ cal}$$
$$= 175 \times 13\text{ cal}$$

According to principle of calorimetry, we get

Heat lost = Heat gained

∴ $$200 \times s \times 110 = 175 \times 13$$

or $$s = \frac{175 \times 13}{200 \times 110} = 0.1 \text{ cal g}^{-1}\text{°C}^{-1}$$

EXAMPLE |3| Energy Transfer through a Concrete Wall

A sphere made of aluminium of 0.047 kg placed for sufficient time in a vessel containing boiling water, so that the sphere is at 100° C.

After that it is allowed to transform to 0.14 kg copper calorimeter containing 0.25 kg of water kept at the temperature 20° C. The temperature of water rises and attains a steady state at 23° C. Calculate the specific heat capacity of aluminium. **[NCERT]**

Sol. Given, mass of aluminium, $m_1 = 0.047$ kg

Initial temperature of sphere $= 100°C$

Final temperature $= 23°C$

Change in temperature $(\Delta T) = (100°C - 23°C) = 77°C$

We have to find, $s_{Al} =$ specific heat of aluminium

The amount of heat lost by aluminium sphere
$$= m_1 s_{Al} \Delta T_1 = \Delta Q_1$$
$$= 0.047 \text{ kg} \times s_{Al} \times 77°C$$

Mass of water, $m_2 = 0.25$ kg

Mass of calorimeter, $m_3 = 0.14$ kg

Initial temperature calorimeter with water $= 20°C$

Final temperature (mixture) $= 23°C$

Change in temperature $(\Delta T_2) = 23°C - 20°C = 3°C$

Specific heat capacity of water $= s_w = 4.18 \times 10^3$ Jkg^{-1}K^{-1}

Specific heat capacity of copper
$$= s_{Cu} = 0.386 \times 10^3 \text{ Jkg}^{-1}\text{K}^{-1}$$

Thus, heat gained by water and calorimeter
$$\Delta Q_2 = m_2 s_w \Delta T_2 + m_3 s_{Cu} \Delta T_2$$
$$= (m_2 s_w + m_3 s_{Cu})\, \Delta T_2$$
$$\Rightarrow \Delta Q_2 = 0.25 \text{ kg} \times 4.18 \times 10^3 \text{ Jkg}^{-1}\text{K}^{-1} + 0.14 \text{ kg}$$
$$\times 0.386 \times 10^3 \text{ Jkg}^{-1}\text{K}^{-1}\, (23°C - 20°C)$$

According to the principle of calorimetry, we get

Heat lost by aluminium sphere = Heat gained by water and calorimeter
$$\Rightarrow 0.047 \text{ kg} \times s_{Al} \times 77°C$$
$$= (0.25 \text{ kg} \times 4.18 \times 10^3 \text{ Jkg}^{-1}\text{K}^{-1}$$
$$+ 0.14 \text{ kg} \times 0.386 \times 10^3 \text{ Jkg}^{-1}\text{K}^{-1})(3°C)$$
$$\Rightarrow s_{Al} = 0.911 \text{ kJ kg}^{-1}\text{K}^{-1}$$

CHANGE OF STATE

The process of converting one state of a substance into another state is known as **change of state** of a substance or matter. Matter generally exists in three states

(i) Solid   (ii) Liquid

(iii) Gas

These states can be changed into one another by absorbing heat or rejecting heat. The process is so called the **change of state**.

The common changes of states are
  (i) Solid to liquid (and *vice-versa*)
  (ii) Liquid to gas (and *vice-versa*)

The changes can be occur when the exchange of heat takes place between substance and its surroundings.

Note
- Besides these three states i.e. solid, liquid and gas, the fourth state of matter also exist which is known as **plasma.**
- When a substance is heated to a very high temperature, many electrons around the nucleus of the atom of the substance are free. The collection of these free electrons and the positive ions forms a plasma.

Effect of Heat on Ice

Take some cubes of ice in a beaker at 0°C. Start heating it slowly on a constant heat supplying source.

Note, the temperature after every minute and stir the mixture of water and ice continuously.

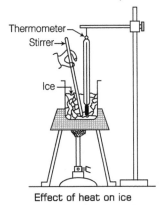

Effect of heat on ice

We will find a graph between temperature and time as shown in figure. It is also observed that there is no change in temperature for so long as there is ice in the beaker even heat being continuously supplied to the system.

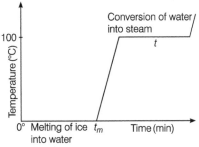

Plot of change of state of ice on heating

It is seen that the temperature remains constant until the entire amount of the solid substance (i.e. ice) melts. Thus, both the solid and liquid states of the substance co-exist in

thermal equilibrium during the change of state from solid to liquid. After the whole of ice gets melted into water and as we continue heating the beaker, we note that the temperature begins to increase till it reaches nearly 100°C when it again becomes steady. This point is t in the graph.

The heat supplied is now being used to change the state of water from liquid to vapour. It is noted that temperature remains constant until the entire amount of liquid is converted into vapour.

Note
For a constant heat supply, the change of state takes place with no variation in temperature of the system.

Terms Related to Change of State

There are some important terms related to change of state as given below

Melting and Melting Point

The process of change of state from solid to liquid is called **melting**. The temperature at which solid starts to liquify is known as the **melting point** of that solid.

Note
The melting point of a substance at standard atmospheric pressure is called **normal melting point.**

Fusion and Freezing Point

The process of change of state from liquid to solid is called **fusion**. The temperature at which liquid starts to freeze is known as the **freezing point** of the liquid.

Vaporisation and Boiling Point

The process of change of state from liquid to vapour (or gas) is called **vaporisation**. During the change of state (completely), the temperature remains constant which implies both liquid and vapour states of the substance co-exist in thermal equilibrium. The temperature at which the liquid and the vapour states of the substance co-exist is called the **boiling point** of the liquid.

Sublimation

The process of change of state directly from solid to vapour (or gas) is known as **sublimation**. There is no matter of liquid state of substance. The reverse process of sublimation is not possible e.g. camphor, nepthalene balls, etc.

Effect of Pressure on the Boiling Point of a Liquid

The boiling point of a liquid increases with the increase in pressure. The boiling point of water is 100°C at 1 atm pressure and it is 128°C at 2 atm pressure.

TRIPLE POINT

The temperature of a substance remains constant during its phase change (or change of state).

The graph between temperature and pressure of substance can be plotted which is called **phase diagram** or p-T diagram.

The diagram (phase diagram of water and CO_2) shows p-T plane divided into three regions i.e. solid region, liquid region and vapour region which are separated by **sublimation curve**, **fusion curve** and **vaporisation curve**.

These three curves represent the states in which solid and vapour phases, solid and liquid phases and liquid and vapour phases co-exist.

The temperature and pressure at which all three phases of a substance co-exist simultaneously is known as the **triple point** of the substance, e.g. The triple point for water is represented by temperature 273.16 K and pressure 6.11×10^{-3} Pa.

Two figures below show the phase diagram with triple point for (a) water (b) CO_2.

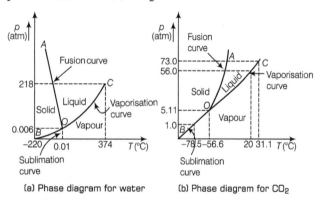

(a) Phase diagram for water   (b) Phase diagram for CO_2

The point on sublimation curve BO represents states in which the solid and vapour phases co-exist. The point on vaporisation curve co-represent the states in which the liquid and vapour phases co-exist.

The point on the fusion curve AO represents the states in which solid and vapour phases co-exist

LATENT HEAT

The amount of heat transferred per unit mass during the change of phase of a substance without any change in its temperature is called latent heat of the substance for particular change.

Latent heat is denoted by L and having SI unit J kg^{-1}. The value of latent heat is usually quoted at standard atmospheric pressure because it also depends upon the pressure.

Thus, if a mass m of a substance undergoes a change from one state to the other, then the quantity of heat required is given by

$$\boxed{Q = mL}$$

i.e.
$$\boxed{\text{Latent heat, } L = Q/m}$$

Hence, during the phase change, the heat required by the substance depends on the mass m of the substance and heat of transformation Q.

Types of Latent Heat

There are two types of latent heat of materials

(i) **Latent Heat of Fusion or Melting**

It is latent heat for solid-liquid state change. It is denoted by L_f and is given by

$$\boxed{\text{Latent heat of fusion, } L_f = \frac{Q}{m}}$$

Its SI unit is Jkg^{-1}.

(ii) **Latent Heat of Vaporisation**

It is in latent heat for liquid-gas state change. It is denoted by L_V and often referred to as heat of fusion and heat of vaporisation. It is given by

$$\boxed{\text{Latent heat of vaporisation, } L_V = \frac{Q}{m}}$$

and its SI unit is Jkg^{-1}. The latent heats of state change of some substances are given below in the table.

Variation of Temperature During Change of State

It is observed from the above graph as heat is added or removed during a change of state, the temperature remains constant, hence the slopes of the phase lines are not all the same, which indicates the specific heats of the various states are not equal.

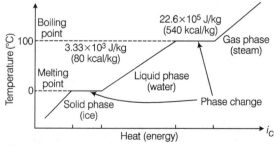

Temperature *versus* heat for water at 1 atm pressure

e.g. Water having $L_f = 3.33 \times 10^5$ Jkg^{-1} and $L_V = 22.6 \times 10^5$ Jkg^{-1}, it means 3.33×10^5 J of heat is needed to melt 1 kg of ice at $0°C$ and 22.6×10^5 J of heat is needed to convert 1 kg of water to steam at $100°C$.

EXAMPLE |4| Partial Melting

The ice of 0.15 kg mass at $0°C$ is mixed with 0.30 kg of water at $50°C$ in a container. The resulting temperature of the container (after mixing) is $6.7°C$. Determine the heat of fusion of ice if specific heat (s_w) for the water is 4186 Jkg^{-1}K^{-1}. **[NCERT]**

Sol. According to the calorimetry principle, we get

Heat lost by water $= ms_w (\theta_f - \theta_i)_w$
$$= (0.30 \text{ kg}) (4186 \text{ Jkg}^{-1}\text{K}^{-1}) (50.0 - 6.7)°C$$
$$= 54376.14 \text{ J}$$

Heat required to melt ice $=$ mass of ice $\times L_f$
$$= m_I L_f = (0.15 \text{ kg}) L_f$$

Heat required to raise temperature of ice water to final temperature (from the calorimetry)
$$= m_I s_w (\theta_f - \theta_i)_I$$
$$= (0.15 \text{ kg}) (4186 \text{ Jkg}^{-1}\text{K}^{-1}) (6.7°C - 0°C)$$
$$= 4206.93 \text{ J}$$

Principle of calorimetry i.e. heat lost = heat gained
$$\Rightarrow \quad 54376.14 \text{ J} = (0.15 \text{ kg}) L_f + 4206.93 \text{ J}$$
$$\Rightarrow \quad L_f = 3.34 \times 10^5 \text{ Jkg}^{-1}$$

This is required value of heat of fusion of ice.

EXAMPLE |5| Velocity of Bullet

A lead bullet penetrates into a solid object and melts. If half of its kinetic energy was used to heat it, calculate the initial velocity of the bullet. The initial temperature of the bullet is $27°C$ and the melting point of the material of bullet is $327°C$. Given that latent heat of fusion of lead is 2.5×10^4 J kg^{-1} and specific heat capacity of lead is 125 J kg^{-1}K^{-1}.

Sol. From the calorimetry, heat required $\Delta Q_1 = ms\Delta\theta_1$.

Let mass of bullet is m and given
$$s = 125 \text{ Jkg}^{-1}\text{ K}^{-1}$$
$$\Delta\theta = 327° - 27° = 300°C$$
$$\Rightarrow \quad \Delta Q_1 = m \times 125 \times 300 = m \times 3.75 \times 10^4 \text{ Jkg}^{-1}$$

Heat required to melt the bullet $\Delta Q_2 = mL_b$.
Latent heat of bullet, $L_b = 2.5 \times 10^4$ J kg^{-1}
$$\Rightarrow \quad \Delta Q_2 = m \times 2.5 \times 10^4 \text{ J kg}^{-1}$$

The kinetic energy of bullet $= \dfrac{1}{2} mv^2$, where v is velocity.

Half of kinetic energy $= \dfrac{1}{2}\left(\dfrac{1}{2}mv^2\right) = \dfrac{1}{4}mv^2$

From principle of calorimetry,
Loss in kinetic energy $= \Delta Q_1 + \Delta Q_2$
$$\therefore \quad 1/4\, mv^2 = m (3.75 + 2.5) \times 10^4 \text{ Jkg}^{-1}$$
$$\Rightarrow \quad v = 500 \text{ ms}^{-1}$$

EXAMPLE |6| Change of State of Ice

Calculate the heat required to convert 3 kg of ice at $-12°C$ kept in a calorimeter to steam at $100°C$ at atmospheric pressure.

Given, specific heat capacity of ice is 2100 Jkg^{-1}K^{-1}, specific heat capacity of water is 4186 Jkg^{-1}K^{-1}, latent heat of fusion of ice is 3.35×10^5 Jkg^{-1} and latent heat of steam is 2.256×10^6 Jkg^{-1}. **[NCERT]**

Sol. Heat required to convert ice at $-12°C$ to ice at $0°C$
$$Q_1 = ms_{ice} \Delta T_1.$$
Mass of ice, $m = 3$ kg; specific heat of ice,
$$s_{ice} = 2100 \text{ Jkg}^{-1}\text{ K}^{-1}$$
Change in temperatures $= [0 - (-12)]$
$$\Rightarrow \quad \Delta T_1 = 12°C$$
$$\therefore \quad Q_1 = 3 \text{ kg} \times 2100 \text{ J kg}^{-1}\text{ K}^{-1} \times 12°C$$
$$= 75600 \text{ J}$$
Heat required to melt ice at $0°C$ to water at $0°C$.
$$Q_2 = mL_{ice}$$
Latent heat of ice, $L_{ice} = 3.35 \times 10^5$ Jkg^{-1}
$$\therefore \quad Q_2 = 3 \text{ kg} \times 3.35 \times 10^5 \text{ Jkg}^{-1} = 1005000 \text{ J}$$
Heat required to convert water at $0°C$ to water at $100°C$,
$$Q_3 = ms_w\Delta T_2.$$
Specific heat of water, $s_w = 4186$ JKg^{-1} K^{-1}
Change in temperatures $= (100 - 0)°C$
$$\Rightarrow \quad \Delta T_2 = 100°C$$
$$\therefore \quad Q_3 = 3 \text{ kg} \times 4186 \text{ J kg}^{-1}\text{ K}^{-1} \times 100°C$$
$$= 1255800 \text{ J}$$
Heat required to convert water at $100°C$ to steam at $100°C$, $Q_4 = mL_{steam}$.
Latent heat of steam,
$$L_{steam} = 2.256 \times 10^6 \text{ J kg}^{-1}$$
$$\therefore \quad Q_4 = 3 \text{ kg} \times 2.256 \times 10^6 \text{ J kg}^{-1}$$
$$= 6768000 \text{ J}$$
Total heat is equal to sum of heat of individual thermodynamic process.
$$\Rightarrow \quad Q = Q_1 + Q_2 + Q_3 + Q_4$$
$$\Rightarrow \quad Q = 75600 \text{ J} + 1005000 \text{ J} + 1255800 \text{ J} + 6768000 \text{ J}$$
$$= 9.1 \times 10^6 \text{ J}$$

Mechanical Equivalent of Heat

The temperature of a body may also be increased by doing mechanical work on the system. The mechanical equivalent of heat gives how many joules of mechanical work is needed to raise the temperature of 1 g of water by 1°C.

It is denoted by J expressed in J/cal and can have only numerical values.

Thus, W is work done in Joule (SI unit) = JH heat given or taken out in calories (CGS unit).

HEAT TRANSFER

Heat is the form of energy which can flow from one body to another due to their temperature difference in the form of radiations, molecular vibrations, molecular displacement, etc. These processes of heat flow are collectively known as **heat transfer**. The processes of heat transfer are shown in figure.

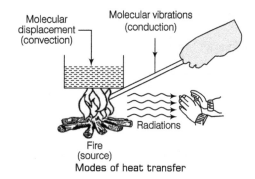

Modes of heat transfer

There are three modes of heat transfer namely
(i) Conduction (ii) Convection (iii) Radiation

Conduction

The transfer of heat taking place due to molecular vibrations (i.e. molecular collisions) is known as **heat conduction**. In this process, there is no change in average position of the molecule and hence there is no mass movement of matter generally in solids, heat is transferred by the process of conduction.

Thermal Conductivity

The ability of material to conduct the heat through it is known as **thermal conductivity**. Thus, heat conduction is defined as the time rate of heat flow in a material for a given temperature difference.

Consider a metal rod of length l and area of cross-section A. Let the ends of the rod are at the temperatures T_1 and T_2. Then, the rate of flow of heat (H) conducted through any section (in steady state) of the rod is directly proportional to the temperature difference ΔT, time t for which the heat

flows and the area of cross-section A and is inversely proportional to the length L of the rod.

Thus, the rate of heat transfer is given by

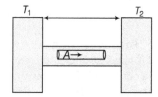

Calculation of thermal conductivity of a metal rod

$$\text{Rate of heat transfer} = \frac{\Delta Q}{\Delta t} = \frac{KA\,(T_1 - T_2)}{L}$$

$$H = KA\frac{\Delta T}{L}$$

$\because \qquad H = \dfrac{Q}{t}$

$\therefore \qquad \boxed{\text{Heat transfer, } Q = KA\frac{\Delta T}{L}\cdot t}$

Here, K is known as **coefficient of thermal conductivity** of material of rod. The greater value of K implies that material will conduct the heat more rapidly. The SI unit of K is $\text{Js}^{-1}\text{m}^{-1}\text{K}^{-1}$ or $\text{Wm}^{-1}\text{K}^{-1}$ and dimensions of K is $[\text{MLT}^{-3}\text{K}^{-1}]$. The value of thermal conductivity vary slightly with temperature, but it can be considered to be constant over normal temperature range. The term $\dfrac{\Delta T}{L}$ is known as **temperature gradient**.

If $A = 1, T_1 - T_2 = \Delta T = 1, L = 1$ and $t = 1$, then $Q = K$

Hence, the **coefficient of thermal conductivity of a material may be defined as the quantity of heat that flows per unit time through a unit cube of the material when its opposite faces are kept at a temperature difference of one degree.**

Note Steady state means that the temperature of each part of the body remains constant during the conduction of heat through it.

Also, the metals are much better conductors than the non-metals. This is because the metals have large number of free electrons which can carry heat from hotter part to colder part.

Thermal Current and Thermal Resistance

The rate of flow of heat is known as **heat current**. It is denoted by H.

SI unit of thermal current is J/s or Watt (W) and its dimensions $[\text{ML}^2\text{T}^{-3}]$

Thus, $$H = \frac{\Delta Q}{\Delta t} = KA \frac{(T_1 - T_2)}{L} = \frac{T_1 - T_2}{\left(\dfrac{L}{KA}\right)}$$

Thermal resistance, $R = \dfrac{\Delta T}{H} = \dfrac{T_1 - T_2}{H} = \dfrac{L}{KA}$

$\therefore$ Thermal resistance, $R = \dfrac{L}{KA}$

It is just resemble to current, $i = \dfrac{V_1 - V_2}{R}$
where, $V_1 - V_2 =$ voltage difference and $R =$ resistance.

So, the terms $\dfrac{T_1 - T_2}{(L/KA)}$ and $\dfrac{L}{KA}$ can be treated as thermal current (heat flow) and thermal resistance, respectively.
SI unit of thermal resistance (R) is K-s/J or K/W and its dimension is $[M^{-1}L^{-2}T^3K]$.

EXAMPLE |7| Heat Flow through a Glass

Calculate the rate of loss of heat through a glass window of area 1000 cm^2 and thickness 0.4 cm. When temperature inside is $37°C$ and outside is $-5°C$. Coefficient of thermal conductivity of glass is 2.2×10^{-3} cal s^{-1} cm^{-1} K^{-1}.

Sol. Given, $A = 1000 \text{ cm}^2$, $L = 0.4$ cm

$$\Delta T = T_1 - T_2 = 37 - (-5) = 42°C$$
$$K = 2.2 \times 10^{-3} \text{ cal s}^{-1} \text{cm}^{-1} \text{K}^{-1}$$

Rate of loss of heat,

$$H = \frac{Q}{T} = \frac{KA(T_1 - T_2)}{L} = \frac{2.2 \times 10^{-3} \times 1000 \times 42}{0.4}$$

$$H = 231 \text{ cal s}^{-1}$$

EXAMPLE |8| Heat Flow through Two Rods

Two rods A and B are of equal length. Each rod has its ends at temperatures T_1 and T_2. What are the conditions that will ensure equal rates of flow of heat through the rods A and B?

Sol. Heat transferred rate by rod A is $\dfrac{\Delta Q_1}{\Delta t}$.

Length of rod A is L and temperature difference,
$$\Delta T = T_1 - T_2$$
Area of cross-section of rod, $A = A_1$,
thermal conductivity $= K_1 \Rightarrow \dfrac{\Delta Q_1}{\Delta t} = K_1 A_1 \dfrac{\Delta T}{L}$

Heat transferred rate by rod B is $\dfrac{\Delta Q_2}{\Delta t}$.

Length of rod B is L, temperature difference $= T_1 - T_2$, area of cross-section of rod $B = A_2$,
Thermal conductivity $= K_2$

$$\Rightarrow \quad \frac{\Delta Q_2}{\Delta t} = K_2 A_2 \frac{\Delta T}{L}$$

For equal rate of heat transfer,
$$\frac{\Delta Q_1}{\Delta t} = \frac{\Delta Q_2}{\Delta t} \Rightarrow \frac{K_1 A_1 \Delta T}{L} = \frac{K_2 A_2 \Delta T}{L}$$

$$\Rightarrow \quad K_1 A_1 = K_2 A_2 \Rightarrow \frac{K_2}{K_1} = \frac{A_1}{A_2}$$

This is the required condition for equal **rate of heat transferred** from both the rods.

Connection of Rods with Different Thermal Conductivities

If two or more rods or conductors are connected with one another, the equivalent thermal conductivity as a whole may be altered.

(a) **Series combination of two thermal conductors**
We know that the series combination of resistances gives the equivalent resistance as $R_{eq} = R_1 + R_2$

This gives $\dfrac{L_1 + L_2}{K_{eq} A} = \dfrac{L_1}{K_1 A} + \dfrac{L_2}{K_2 A}$ $\left[\because R = \dfrac{L}{KA}\right]$

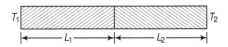

If $L_1 = L_2 = L$, then $\dfrac{2L}{K_{eq} A} = \dfrac{L}{K_1 A} + \dfrac{L}{K_2 A}$

$\Rightarrow$ Equivalent thermal conductivity, $K_{eq} = \dfrac{2K_1 K_2}{K_1 + K_2}$

Here, K_{eq} is the equivalent thermal conductivity of series connection of rods (as thermal conductor).

(b) **Parallel combination of two thermal conductors**
We know that the parallel combination of resistances gives the equivalent resistances as $\dfrac{1}{R_{eq}} = \dfrac{1}{R_1} + \dfrac{1}{R_2}$

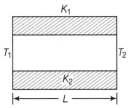

This gives, $\dfrac{1}{\dfrac{L}{K_{eq} 2A}} = \dfrac{1}{\left(\dfrac{L}{K_1 A}\right)} + \dfrac{1}{\left(\dfrac{L}{K_2 A}\right)}$

(For equal area of cross-sections and length)

$$\Rightarrow \qquad \frac{2A\,K_{eq}}{L} = \frac{K_1 A}{L} + \frac{K_2 A}{L}$$

$$\Rightarrow \qquad \boxed{\text{Equivalent thermal conductivity, } K_{eq} = \frac{K_1 + K_2}{2}}$$

EXAMPLE |9| Thermal Equivalence of Composite Bar

An iron bar having length $L_1 = 0.1$ m, area of cross-section $0.02\,m^2$ thermal conductivity $K_i = 79$ $Wm^{-1}K^{-1}$ and brass bar having length $L_2 = 0.1$ m area of cross-section, $A_2 = 0.02$ m^2 and thermal conductivity $K_2 = 109 Wm^{-1}K^{-1}$ are soldered end to end as shown in figure.

The terminal ends of two rods are maintained at 373 K and 273 K, respectively. Find the expression and compute

(i) the temperature of the junction of two bars.

(ii) equivalent thermal conductivity of composite bar and

(iii) the heat current through the composite bar [NCERT]

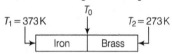

Sol. Given, $L_1 = L_2 = L = 0.1$ m

$$A_1 = A_2 = A = 0.02\,m^2$$

$$K_1 = 79\ Wm^{-1}K^{-1},\ K_2 = 109\ Wm^{-1}K^{-1}$$

$$T_1 = 373\ K \text{ and } T_2 = 273\ K$$

At steady state, heat transferred from each section of thermal conductor is same

i.e. $$H_1 = H_2 = H$$

$$\Rightarrow \qquad \frac{K_1 A_1 (T_1 - T_0)}{L_1} = \frac{K_2 A_2 (T_0 - T_2)}{L_2} \qquad ...(i)$$

For $A_1 = A_2 = A$ and $L_1 = L_2 = L$, Eq. (i) becomes

$$K_1 (T_1 - T_0) = K_2 (T_0 - T_2)$$

$$\Rightarrow \qquad T_0 = \frac{K_1 T_1 + K_2 T_2}{K_1 + K_2}$$

Therefore, heat current through each bar

$$H = \frac{K_1 A (T_1 - T_0)}{L} = \frac{K_2 A (T_0 - T_2)}{L}$$

$$= \frac{A(T_1 - T_2)}{L \left(\frac{1}{K_1} + \frac{1}{K_2} \right)}$$

$$= \frac{K_1 K_2 A (T_1 - T_2)}{L(K_1 + K_2)} \qquad ...(ii)$$

Now, heat current through composite bar of length $L_1 + L_2 = 2L$ and equivalent thermal conductivity K', can be given by

$$H' = \frac{K' A (T_1 - T_2)}{2L} = H \qquad ...(iii)$$

From Eqs. (ii) and (iii), we get

$$\Rightarrow \qquad K' = \frac{2K_1 K_2}{K_1 + K_2}$$

(i) So, the temperature of the junction of two bars is

$$T_0 = \frac{K_1 T_1 + K_2 T_2}{K_1 + K_2}$$

$$= \frac{79\,Wm^{-1}K^{-1} \times 373 K + 109 Wm^{-1}K^{-1} \times 273 K}{79\,Wm^{-1}K^{-1} + 109 Wm^{-1}K^{-1}}$$

$$= 315\ K$$

(ii) Equivalent thermal conductivity

$$K' = \frac{2K_1 K_2}{K_1 + K_2}$$

$$= \frac{2 \times 79\ Wm^{-1}K^{-1} \times 109\ Wm^{-1}K^{-1}}{79\ Wm^{-1}K^{-1} + 109\ Wm^{-1}K^{-1}}$$

$$= 91.6\ Wm^{-1}K^{-1}$$

(iii) Heat current through the composite bar

$$H' = H = \frac{K' A (T_1 - T_2)}{2L}$$

$$= \frac{91.6\ Wm^{-1}K^{-1} \times 0.02\ m^2 \times (373 - 273)\ K}{2 \times 0.1\ m}$$

$$= 916.1\ W$$

Convection

Convection is the process in which heat is transferred from one point to another by the actual motion of matter from a region of high temperature to a region of lower temperature. This process of heat transfer takes place only in liquids.

There are two types of convections

(i) **Forced Convection** This convection is the process in which heat is transferred from one place to other by actual transfer of heated material (or molecules). If heated material is forced to move say by a blower or a pump, the process of heat transfer is called **forced convection**. The heat transfer in human body is an example of forced convection.

(ii) **Natural or Free Convection** In the process of convection, if the heated material moves due to difference in density. This process of heat transfer is **called natural** or **free convection** such as heat transfer in water.

Land and Sea Breezes

During the day, the **land heats up faster than the sea**. This occurs because the water has greater specific heat and because mixing currents disperse the absorbed heat throughout the great volume of water.

The hot air above the land expands and becoming less dense and hence the warmer air rises and colder air from the sea takes it place. The warmer air from the land moves towards the sea to complete the cycle. This create a breeze from the sea to the land which is called a **sea breeze**.

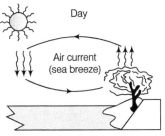

Land warmer than water

During the night, the opposite happens. The **land cools faster than sea**. The warm air above the sea rises. This warm air is replaced by colder air from the land creating a **land breeze**.

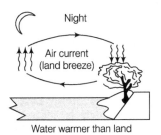

Water warmer than land

Formation of Trade Winds

As equatorial and polar regions of the earth receive unequal solar heat. At the equator, air near the earth's surface is hot while the air in upper atmosphere of the poles is cool.

So, there is a convection current in between two positions, air at the equatorial surface rising and moving out towards the poles, descending and streaming in towards the equator. The rotation of the earth, however, modifies this convection current because of this air has the Eastward speed of 1600 km/h.

While the speed of air closer to the poles is zero. So, air descends not at the poles but at 30° North latitude and returns to the equator. This is called **trade wind**. Hence, the steady wind blowing from North-East to equator, near the surface of Earth is called **trade wind**. It is an example of natural convection.

Radiation

It is a mode of heat transfer from one place to another without heating the intervening medium. The heat is transferred by the mean of thermal radiations, radiant energy or simply radiation. Here, the term radiation is used in two meanings. The first is the process by which the energy is emitted by a body, is transmitted in space and falls on another body. The second one is the energy itself is being transmitted in space.

The heat from the sun reaches to the earth by radiation. These are travelling millions of kilometers of empty space (i.e. without any material medium).

Thermal Radiation

The electromagnetic radiation emitted by a body, by virtue of its temperature like the radiation by a red hot iron or light form filament lamp is called **thermal radiation**.

Colour of a Body

When thermal radiation falls on some other body, it may partly reflected and partly absorbed. The amount of heat that a body absorbed by radiation depends on the colour of the body. The colour of object shows that radiation of that particular wavelength is reflected back by the body.

Black Body Radiation

A body that absorbs all the radiations falling on it is known as a **black body**. It emits the radiations at the fastest rate. The radiations emitted by a black body is known as **black body radiation**. The black body is also called the **ideal radiator**. A perfect body absorbs 100% of radiations falling on it, is only an ideal concept because within the universe there is no existence of black body. However, lamp black is close to a black body because, it reflects only 1% of radiation falling on it.

Absorptive and Emissive Powers and Emissivity

The ratio of the amount of thermal radiation absorbed by a body in a given time to the total amount of thermal radiations incident on the body in the same time is known as **absorptance** (a) or **absorptive power** of the body.

$$\Rightarrow \qquad \frac{\text{Energy absorbed}}{\text{Energy incident}}$$

The **emissive power** of a body at a given temperature and for a given wavelength λ is defined as the amount of radiant energy per unit time per unit surface area of the body within a unit wavelength range around the wavelength λ.

The ratio of emissive power (e) of a body to the emissive power (E) of a perfect black body at the same temperature is called **emissivity**. It is denoted by ε.

Thus, $$\boxed{\text{Emissivity}, \varepsilon = \frac{e}{E}}$$

Stefan-Boltzmann Law

Stefan-Boltzmann law states that the total energy emitted per second by a unit area of a perfect black body is proportional to the fourth power of its absolute temperature.

i.e. $$E \propto T^4$$

i.e. $$\boxed{\text{Total energy, } E = \sigma T^4}$$

where σ is a universal constant called Stefan-Boltzmann constant. $\sigma = 5.67 \times 10^{-8}$ Wm^{-2} K^{-4}

If the body is not a perfect black body and has emissivity ε, then above relations get modified as

$$E = \varepsilon \sigma T^4$$

where, $\quad \varepsilon$ = emissivity of that body

EXAMPLE |10| Perfect Black Body

Calculate the temperature (in K) at which a perfect black body radiates energy at the rate of 5.67 W/cm^2.
Given, $\sigma = 5.67 \times 10^{-8}$ Wm^{-2} K^{-4}

Sol. Given, $E = 5.67$ W / cm$^2 = 5.67 \times 10^4$ W / m^2

$$\sigma = 5.67 \times 10^{-8} \text{ Wm}^{-2} \text{ K}^{-4}$$

Apply Stefan's law, $E = \sigma T^4$

$$T^4 = \frac{E}{\sigma} \Rightarrow T = \left(\frac{E}{\sigma}\right)^{1/4} = \left(\frac{5.67 \times 10^4}{5.67 \times 10^{-8}}\right)^{1/4}$$

$$T = (10^{12})^{1/4} = 10^3$$

$$T = 1000 \text{ K}$$

EXAMPLE |11| Heat Lost by the Sheet

A thin brass rectangular sheet of sides 15.0 cm and 12.0 cm is heated in a furnace to 600°C, and taken out. How much electric power is needed to maintain the sheet at this temperature, given that its emissivity is 0.0250? Neglect heat loss due to convection.
(Stefan-Boltzmann constant, $\sigma = 5.67 \times 10^{-8}$ Wm^{-2}K^{-4}).

[NCERT]

Sol. As the energy is radiated from both surfaces of the sheet, so

$$A = 2 \times 15.0 \times 12.0 \times 10^{-4} \text{ m}^2$$

$$= 3.60 \times 10^{-2} \text{ m}^2$$

$$T = 600 + 273 = 873 \text{ K}$$

$$\varepsilon = 0.250,$$

$$\sigma = 5.67 \times 10^{-8} \text{ Wm}^{-2} \text{ K}^{-4}.$$

The rate of heat loss by the sheet,

$$H = \frac{Q}{t} = \varepsilon \sigma A T^4$$

$$= 0.250 \times 5.67 \times 10^{-8} \times 3.60 \times 10^{-2} \times (873)^4$$

$$= 296 \text{ Js}^{-1} = 296 \text{ W}.$$

Wien's Displacement Law

Wien's displacement law states that the wavelength (λ_m) corresponding to which the energy emitted by a black body is maximum and is inversely proportional to its absolute temperature (T).

Thus, $\quad \lambda_m \propto \dfrac{1}{T} \quad$ or $\quad \boxed{\lambda_m T = b}$

where, b = Wien's constant $= 2.9 \times 10^{-3}$ m K

EXAMPLE |12| A Hot Body Radiating Energy

A hot body having the surface temperature 1327°C. Determine the wavelength at which it radiates maximum energy. Given Wien's constant $= 2.9 \times 10^{-3}$ mK.

Sol. Given, $T = 1327 + 273 = 1600$ K

Wien's constant, $b = 2.9 \times 10^{-3}$ m K

$$\lambda_m = \frac{b}{T} = \frac{2.9 \times 10^{-3}}{1600} = 1.81 \times 10^{-6} \text{ m}$$

EXAMPLE |13| Rate of Energy Lost

Consider a filament which is indirectly heated. The radiating maximum energy having wavelength 3.4×10^{-5} cm. Determine the amount of heat energy lost per second per unit area if the temperature of surrounding air is 17°C.
Given, $\sigma = 5.67 \times 10^{-8}$ Wm^{-2} K^{-4}, $b = 2.9 \times 10^{-3}$ mK

Sol. Given, wavelength, $\lambda_m = 3.4 \times 10^{-5}$ cm $= 3.4 \times 10^{-7}$ m

Temperature surrounding,

$$T_0 = 17°C + 273 = 290 \text{ K}$$

$$\sigma = 5.67 \times 10^{-8} \text{ Wm}^{-2} \text{ K}^{-4}$$

$$b = 2.9 \times 10^{-3} \text{ mK}$$

According to Wien's law

$$T = \frac{b}{\lambda_m} = \frac{2.9 \times 10^{-3} \text{ mK}}{3.4 \times 10^{-7}} = 8529.4 \text{ K}$$

According to Stefan-Boltzmann law,

$$E = \sigma(T^4 - T_0^4) = 5.67 \times 10^{-8} [(8529.4)^4 - (290)^4]$$

$$E = 30016.98 \times 10^4 \text{ W / m}^2$$

NEWTON'S LAW OF COOLING

Newton's law of cooling states that the rate of cooling of a body is directly proportional to the temperature difference between the body and its surroundings, provided the temperature difference is small

i.e. Rate of loss of heat $\propto$ Temperature difference between the body and its surroundings.

$$-\frac{dQ}{dt} \propto (T - T_0)$$

$$\boxed{\text{Rate of loss of heat, } -\frac{dQ}{dt} = k(T - T_0)}$$

EXAMPLE |14| Temperature of Cool Body

A body cools in 7 min from 60°C to 40°C. What will be its temperature after the next 7 min? The temperature of the surroundings is 10°C.

Sol. According to the Newton's law of cooling, we have

$$\frac{dQ}{dt} = k\left(\frac{T_1 + T_2}{2} - T_0\right)$$

$$\frac{ms(T_1 - T_2)}{t} = k\left(\frac{T_1 + T_2}{2} - T_0\right)$$

$$\frac{ms(60 - 40)}{7 \times 60} = k\left(\frac{60 + 40}{2} - 10\right)$$

$$\frac{m \times 20}{420} = k \times 40$$

Suppose, after the next 7 min = 420 seconds, the temperature is T. Then,

$$\frac{ms(40 - T)}{420} = k\left(\frac{40 + T}{2} - 10\right) \qquad \ldots\text{(ii)}$$

On dividing Eq. (i) by Eq. (ii), we get

$$\frac{20}{40 - T} = \frac{40}{\left(\frac{40 + T}{2} - 10\right)}$$

On solving, we get $T = 28°\text{C}$

TOPIC PRACTICE 2

OBJECTIVE Type Questions

1. A normal diet furnishes 2000 kcal to a 60 kg person in a day. If this energy was used to heat the person with no losses to the surroundings, how much would the person's temperature increases? The specific heat of the human body is 0.83 $\text{calg}^{-1}\,^\circ\text{C}^{-1}$.

   (a) 8.2°C
   (b) 4.01°C
   (c) 6.0°C
   (d) 5.03°C

Sol. (b) Here, $m = 60$ kg $= 60 \times 10^3$ g, $c = 0.83$ cal $\text{g}^{-1}\,^\circ\text{C}^{-1}$

$$Q = 200 \text{ kcal} = 2 \times 10^5 \text{ cal}$$

Amount of heat required for a person,

$$\because \qquad Q = mc\Delta T$$

$$\Rightarrow \qquad \Delta T = \frac{Q}{mc} = \frac{2 \times 10^5}{60 \times 10^3 \times 0.83} = 4.016°\text{C}$$

2. When water boils or freezes, during these processes its temperature
   (a) increases
   (b) decreases
   (c) does not change
   (d) sometimes increase and sometimes deceases

Sol. (c) When water boils or freezes, its temperature does not change during these processes. Heat here is absorbed or liberated as latent heat.

3. At atmospheric pressure, water boils at 100°C. If pressure is reduced, then
   (a) it still boils at same temperature
   (b) it now boils at a lower temperature
   (c) it now boils at a higher temperature
   (d) it does not boil at all

Sol. (b) When pressure is increased, boiling point is elevated. *i.e.,* at higher pressure, water boils at temperature greater than 100°C. Similarly, at reduced pressure, water boils at a lower temperature.

4. A liquid boils when its vapour pressure is equal to
   (a) 6.0 cm of Hg column
   (b) atmospheric pressure
   (c) double of atmospheric pressure
   (d) 1000 Pa or more

Sol. (b) When vapour pressure is equal to atmospheric pressure, then boiling occurs.

5. The amount of heat that a body can absorb by radiation
   (a) depends on colour and temperature both of body
   (b) depends on colour of body only
   (c) depends on temperature of body only
   (d) depend on density of body

Sol. (a) The thermal radiation that falls on a body partly reflected and partly absorbed. The amount of heat that a body can absorb, by radiation depends on the colour of the body and temperature of body.

6. Due to the change in main voltage, the temperature of an electric bulb rises from 3000K to 4000K. What is the percentage rise in electric power consumed?
   (a) 216
   (b) 100
   (c) 150
   (d) 178

Sol. (a) Electric power consumed in first case,

$$P_1 = \sigma T_1^4 = \sigma(3000)^4 \qquad \ldots\text{(i)}$$

Electric power consumed in second case,

$$P_2 = \sigma T_2^4 = \sigma(4000)^4 \qquad \ldots\text{(ii)}$$

On dividing Eq. (ii) by Eq. (i), we get

$$\frac{P_2}{P_1} = \frac{(4000)^4}{(3000)^4} = \frac{256}{81}$$

As we know percentage rise in power

$$= \frac{P_2 - P_1}{P_1} \times 100 = \frac{256 - 81}{81} \times 100$$

$$= \frac{175}{81} \times 100 = 216\%$$

VERY SHORT ANSWER Type Questions

7. Why water is used as an coolant in the radiator of cars?

Sol. Because, specific heat of water is very high due to this it absorbs a large amount of heat. This helps in maintaining the temperature of the engine low.

8. Black body radiation is white. Comment.

Sol. The statement is true. A black body absorbs radiations of all wavelengths. When heated to a suitable temperature, it emits radiations of all wavelengths. Hence, a black body radiation is white.

9. Does the boiling point of water change with pressure?

Sol. The boiling point of water increases with the increase in pressure (and *vice-versa*).

10. If all the objects radiate electromagnetic energy, why do not the objects around us in everyday life become colder and colder?

Sol. According to the Principal of heat exchange, all the objects (above 0 K) not only radiate electromagnetic energy but also absorb at the same rate from their surroundings. Thus, they do not become colder.

11. White clothes are more comfortable in summer while colourful clothes are more comfortable in winter. Why?

Sol. White clothes absorb very little heat radiation and hence they are comfortable in summer. Coloured clothes absorb almost whole of the incident radiation and keep the body warm in winter.

12. Can we boil water inside in the earth satellite?

Sol. No, the process of transfer of heat by convection is based on the fact that a liquid becomes lighter on becoming hot and rise up. In condition of weightlessness, this is not possible. So, transfer of heat by convection is not possible in the earth satellite.

13. Stainless steel cooking pans are preferred with extra copper bottom. Why?

Sol. The thermal conductivity of copper is much larger than that of steel. The copper bottom allows more heat to flow into the pan and hence helps in cooking the food faster.

14. Why an ice box is constructed with a double wall?

Sol. An ice box is made of double wall and the space in between the walls is filled with some non-conducting material to provide heat insulation, so that the loss of heat can be minimised.

15. Why birds are often seen to swell their feathers in winter?

Sol. When the birds swell their feathers, they are able to enclose air in the feathers. Air, being a poor conductor of heat, so it prevents the loss of heat from the bodies of the birds to the surroundings and as such they do not feel cold in winter.

16. Two bodies at different temperatures T_1 and T_2, if brought in thermal contact do not necessarily settle at the mean temperature $\frac{(T_1 + T_2)}{2}$. Why?

Sol. The two bodies may have different masses and different materials i.e. they may have different thermal capacities.
In case the two bodies have equal thermal capacities, they would settle at the mean temperature $\frac{T_1 + T_2}{2}$.

17. Usually a good conductor of heat is a good conductor of electricity also. Give reason.

Sol. Electrons contribute largely both towards the flow of electricity and the flow of heat. A good conductor contains a large number of free electrons. So, it is both a good conductor of heat and electricity.

18. Place a safety pin on a sheet of paper. Hold the sheet over a burning candle, until the paper becomes yellow and charr. On removing the pin, its white trace is observed on the paper. Why?

Sol. The safety pin is made of steel which is good conductor of heat. So, the safety pin takes heat from the paper under it and transfer it away to the surroundings. The portion of the paper under the safety pin remains comparatively colder than the remaining part.

19. When we step barefoot into an office with a marble floor, we feel cold. Why?

Sol. This is because marble is a better conductor of heat than concrete. When we walk barefooted on a marble floor, heat flows our body through the feet and we feel cold.

20. Is it possible to convert water into vapour form without increasing its temperature, if temperature and pressure of water are 30°C and 1 atm respectively?

Sol. Yes, water at 30°C can be converted into vapour by reducing its pressure until it equals to the vapour pressure of water at 30°C.

21. Calorimeters are made of metals not glass. Why?

Sol. This is because metals are good conductors of heat and have low specific heat capacity.

22. Which object will cool faster when kept in open air, the one at $300°C$ or the one of $100°C$? Why?

Sol. The object at $300°C$ will cool faster than the object at $100°C$. This is in accordance with Newton's law of cooling.

As we know, rate cooling of an object $\propto$ temperature between the object and its surroundings.

SHORT ANSWER Type Questions

23. What kind of thermal conductivity and specific heat requirements would you specify for cooking utensils?

Sol. A cooking utensil should have (i) high conductivity, so that it can conduct heat through itself and transfer it to the contents quickly. (ii) low specific heat, so that it immediately attains the temperature of the source.

24. Two thermos flasks are of the same height and same capacity. One has a circular cross-section while the other has a square cross-section. Which of the two is better?

Sol. As both flasks have same height and capacity, the area of the cylindrical wall will be less than that of the square wall. Hence, the thermos flask of circular cross-section will transmit less heat as compared to the thermos flask of square cross-section and it will be better.

25. The coolant used in a nuclear reactor should have high specific heat. Why?

Sol. The purpose of a coolant is to absorb maximum heat with least rise in its own temperature. This is possible only if specific heat is high because $Q = mc\,\Delta T$. For a given value of m and Q, the rise in temperature ΔT will be small if c is large. This will prevent different parts of the nuclear reactor from getting too hot.

26. Given below are observations on molar specific heats at room temperature of some common gases. **[NCERT]**

Gas	Molar specific heat (C_V) (cal mol^{-1} K^{-1})
Hydrogen	4.87
Nitrogen	4.97
Oxygen	5.02
Nitric oxide	4.99
Carbon monoxide	5.01
Chlorine	6.17

The measured molar specific heats of these gases are markedly different from those for monoatomic gases. (Typically, molar specific heat of a monoatomic gas is 2.92 cal/mol K). Explain this difference. What can you infer from the somewhat larger (than the rest) value for chlorine?

Sol. A monoatomic gas has three degrees of freedom, while a diatomic gas possesses five degrees of freedom. Therefore, molar specific heat of a diatomic gas (at constant volume).

$$C_V = \frac{f}{2}R = \frac{5}{2}R = \frac{5}{2}\times\frac{8.31}{4.2}$$
$$= 5 \text{ cal mol}^{-1}\text{K}^{-1}$$

In the given table, all the gases are diatomic gases and for all of them (except chlorine), the value of C_V is about 5 cal mol^{-1}K^{-1}.

The slightly higher value of C_V for chlorine is due to the fact that even at room temperature, a chlorine gas molecule possesses the vibrational mode of motion also.

27. On a hot day, a car is left in sunlight with all the windows closed. After some time, it is found that the inside of the car is considerably warmer than the air outside. Explain, why?

Sol. Glass transmits about 50% of heat radiation coming from a hot source like the sun but does not allow the radiation from moderately hot bodies to pass through it. Due to this, when a car is left in the sun, heat radiation from the sun gets into the car but as the temperature inside the car is moderate, they do not pass back through its windows. Hence, inside of the car becomes considerably warmer.

28. Two vessels of different materials are identical in size and wall thickness. They are filled with equal quantities of ice at $0°C$.

If the ice melts completely in 10 and 25 min respectively, compare the coefficients of thermal conductivity of the materials of the vessels.

Sol. Let K_1 and K_2 be the coefficients of thermal conductivity of the materials and t_1 and t_2 be the times in which ice melts in the two vessels.

As the same quantity of ice melts in the two vessels, the quantity of heat flowed into the vessels must be same.

$$\because \quad Q = \frac{K_1 A\,(T_1 - T_2)\,t_1}{x} = \frac{K_2 A\,(T_1 - T_2)\,t_2}{x}$$
$$\Rightarrow \quad K_1 t_1 = K_2 t_2$$
$$\therefore \quad \frac{K_1}{K_2} = \frac{t_2}{t_1} = \frac{25 \text{ min}}{10 \text{ min}} = 5:2$$

29. A piece of paper wrapped tightly on a wooden rod is observed to get charred quickly when held over a flame as compared to a similar piece of paper when wrapped on a brass rod. Explain why?

Sol. Brass is a good conductor of heat. It quickly conducts away the heat. So, the paper does not alter its ignition point easily. On the other hand, wood is a bad conductor of heat and is unable to conduct away the heat. So, the paper quickly reaches its ignition point and is charred.

30. In a coal fire, the pockets formed by coals appear brighter than the coals themselves. Is the temperature of such a pocket higher than the surface temperature of a glowing coal?

Sol. The temperature of pockets formed by coals are not appreciably different from the surface temperature of glowing coals.

However, the pockets formed by coals act as cavities. The radiations from these cavities are black body radiations and so have maximum intensity. Hence, the pockets appear brighter than the glowing coals.

31. Woollen clothes are warm in winter. Why?

Sol. Woollen fibres enclose a large amount of air in them. Both wool and air are bad conductors of heat. The small coefficient of thermal conductivity prevents the loss of heat from our body due to conduction. So, we feel warm in woollen clothes.

32. Why rooms are provided with the ventilators near the roof?

Sol. It is done so to remove the harmful impure air and to replace it by the cool fresh air. The air we breath out is warm and so it is lighter. It rises upwards and can go out through the ventilator provided near the roof.

The cold fresh air from outside enters the room through the doors and windows. Thus, the convection current is set up in the air.

33. The earth constantly receives heat radiation from the sun and gets warmed up. Why does the earth not get as hot as the sun?

Sol. Because the earth is located at a very large distance from the sun, hence it receives only a small fraction of the heat radiation emitted by the sun. Further, due to loss of heat from the surface of the earth due to convection and radiation also, the earth does not become as hot as the sun.

34. If a drop of water falls on a very hot iron, it does not evaporate for a long time. Give reason.

Sol. When a drop of water falls on a very hot iron, it gets insulated from the iron by a layer of poor conducting water vapour. As the heat is conducted very slowly through this layer, it takes quite long for the drop to evaporate.

But if the drop of water falls on iron which is not very hot, then it comes in direct contact with iron and evaporates immediately.

35. Why it is much hotter above a fire than by its side?

Sol. Heat carried away from a fire sideways mainly by radiation. Above the fire, heat is carried by both radiation and convection of air but convection carries much more heat than radiation. So, it is much hotter above a fire than by its sides.

36. How does tea in a thermo flask remain hot for a long time?

Sol. The air between the two walls of the thermo flask is evacuated. This prevents heat loss due to conduction and convection.

The loss of heat due to radiation is minimised by silvering the inside surface of the double wall. As the loss of heat due to the three processes is minimised and the tea remains hot for a long time.

37. Two bodies of specific heats C_1 and C_2 having same heat capacities are combined to form a single composite body. What is the specific heat of the composite body?

Sol. As the heat capacities are equal, so $m_1 C_1 = m_2 C_2$.

Let C be the specific heat of the composite body. Then,
$$(m_1 + m_2) C = m_1 C_1 + m_2 C_2$$
$$= m_1 C_1 + m_1 C_1 = 2 m_1 C_1$$
or
$$C = \frac{2 m_1 C_1}{m_1 + m_2} = \frac{2 m_1 C_1}{m_1 + m_1 \frac{C_1}{C_2}} = \frac{2 C_1 C_2}{C_1 + C_2}$$

LONG ANSWER Type I Questions

38. Two vessels A and B of different materials but having identical shape, size and wall thickness are filled with ice and kept at the same place. Ice melts at the rate of $100\ g\ min^{-1}$ and $150 g\ min^{-1}$ in A and B, respectively. Assuming that heat enters the vessels through the walls only, calculate the ratio of thermal conductivities of their materials.

Sol. Let m_1 and m_2 be the masses of ice melted in same time ($t = 1$ min) in vessels A and B, respectively.

Then, the amounts of heat flowed into the two vessels will be
$$Q_1 = \frac{K_1 A (T_1 - T_2) t}{x} = m_1 L \qquad ...(i)$$
$$Q_2 = \frac{K_2 A (T_1 - T_2) t}{x} = m_2 L \qquad ...(ii)$$

where, L is latent heat of ice.

Dividing Eq. (i) by Eq. (ii), we get,

$$\frac{K_1}{K_2} = \frac{m_1}{m_2} = \frac{100\text{ g}}{150\text{ g}} = \frac{2}{3} = 2:3$$

39. A brass boiler has a base area of 0.15 m^2 and thickness 1.0 cm. It boils water at the rate of 6.0 kg min^{-1}, when placed on a gas stove. Estimate the temperature of the part of the flame in contact with the boiler. Thermal conductivity of brass $= 109\text{ Js}^{-1}\text{m}^{-1}{}^{\circ}\text{C}^{-1}$ and heat of vaporisation of water $= 2256\text{ Jg}^{-1}$. **[NCERT]**

Sol. Here, $A = 0.15\text{ m}^2$, $x = 1.0\text{ cm} = 0.01\text{ m}$,

$$K = 109\text{ Js}^{-1}\text{m}^{-1}{}^{\circ}\text{C}^{-1},\ L = 2256\text{ Jg}^{-1}$$
$$T_2 = 100{}^{\circ}\text{C},\ t = 1\text{ min} = 60\text{ s}$$

Let T_1 be the temperature of the part of the flame in contact with boiler. Then, amount of heat that flows into water in 1 min.

$$Q = \frac{KA(T_1 - T_2)t}{x}$$
$$= \frac{109 \times 0.15 \times (T_1 - 100) \times 60}{0.01}\text{ J}$$

Mass of water boiled per min $= 6\text{ kg} = 6000\text{ g}$
Heat used to boil water,

$$Q = mL = 6000\text{ g} \times 2256\text{ Jg}^{-1} = 6000 \times 2256\text{ J}$$

$\therefore \quad \dfrac{109 \times 0.15 \times (T_1 - 100) \times 60}{0.01} = 6000 \times 2256$

or $\quad T_1 - 100 = \dfrac{6000 \times 2256 \times 0.01}{109 \times 0.15 \times 60} = 138{}^{\circ}\text{C}$

or $\quad T_1 = 138 + 100 = 238{}^{\circ}\text{C}$

40. Explain the following
   (i) Hot tea cools rapidly when poured into the saucer from the cup.
   (ii) Temperature of a hot liquid falls rapidly in the beginning but slowly afterwards.
   (iii) A hot liquid cools faster if outer surface of the container is blackened.

Sol. (i) As surface area increases on pouring hot tea in saucer from the cup and the rate of loss of heat is directly proportional to surface area of the radiating surface, so the tea will cool faster in the saucer.
   (ii) Temperature of a hot liquid falls exponentially in accordance with Newton's law of cooling. In other words, rate of cooling is directly proportional to the temperature difference between hot liquid and the surroundings. It is due to this reason that a hot liquid cools rapidly in the beginning but slowly afterwards.
   (iii) When outer surface of container is blackened, the surface becomes good emitter of heat and so the hot liquid in it cools faster.

41. A thermocol cubical ice box of side 30 cm has a thickness of 5.0 cm. If 4.0 kg of ice are put in the box, estimate the amount of ice remaining after 6 h. The outside temperature is $45{}^{\circ}\text{C}$ and coefficient of thermal conductivity of thermocol $= 0.01\text{ Js}^{-1}\text{m}^{-1}{}^{\circ}\text{C}^{-1}$. Given, heat of fusion of water $= 335 \times 10^3\text{ J kg}^{-1}$ **[NCERT]**

Sol. Here, $A = 6 \times \text{side}^2 = 6 \times 30 \times 30$
$$= 5400\text{ cm}^2 = 0.54\text{ m}^2$$
$$x = 5\text{ cm} = 0.05\text{ m},\ t = 6\text{ h} = 6 \times 3600\text{ s}$$
$$T_1 - T_2 = 45 - 0 = 45{}^{\circ}\text{C},$$
$$K = 0.01\text{ Js}^{-1}\text{m}^{-1}{}^{\circ}\text{C}^{-1}$$
$$L = 335 \times 10^3\text{ J kg}^{-1}$$

Total heat entering the box through all the six faces,

$$Q = \frac{KA(T_1 - T_2)t}{x}$$
$$= \frac{0.01 \times 0.54 \times 45 \times 6 \times 3600}{0.05} = 104976\text{ J}$$

Let m kg of ice melt due to this heat. Then,

$$Q = mL$$

or $\quad m = \dfrac{Q}{L} = \dfrac{104976\text{ J}}{336 \times 10^3\text{ J kg}^{-1}} = 0.313\text{ kg}$

Mass of ice left after six hours $= 4 - 0.313 = 3.687\text{ kg}$

42. A copper block of mass 2.5 kg is heated in a furnace to a temperature of $500{}^{\circ}\text{C}$ and then placed on a large ice block. What is the maximum amount of ice that can melt? (specific heat of copper $= 0.39\text{ Jg}^{-1}{}^{\circ}\text{C}^{-1}$, and heat of fusion of water $= 335\text{ Jg}^{-1}$). **[NCERT]**

Sol. Mass of copper block, $M = 2.5\text{ kg} = 2.5 \times 10^3\text{ g}$
Specific heat of copper, $c = 0.39\text{ J g}^{-1}{}^{\circ}\text{C}^{-1}$

Fall in temperature, $\Delta T = 500 - 0 = 500{}^{\circ}\text{C}$
Heat lost by copper block $= mc\Delta T$
$$= 2.5 \times 10^3 \times 0.39 \times 500\text{ J}$$

Let mass of ice melted $= M$ gram
Heat of fusion of ice, $L = 335\text{ Jg}^{-1}$

Heat gained by ice $= ML = M \times 335\text{ J}$
$\because \quad$ Heat gained $=$ Heat lost
$\therefore \quad M \times 335 = 2.5 \times 10^3 \times 0.39 \times 500$

or $\quad M = \dfrac{2.5 \times 10^3 \times 0.39 \times 500}{335}$
$$= 1455.2\text{ g} = 1.455\text{ kg}$$

43. A fat man is used to consuming about 3000 kcal worth of food everyday. His food contains 50 g of butter plus a plate of sweets everyday, besides items which provide him with other nutrients (proteins, vitamins, minerals, etc.) in addition to fats and carbohydrates. The calorific value of 10 g of butter is 60 kcal and that of a plate of sweets is of average 700 kcal. What dietary strategy should he adopt to cut down his calories to about 2100 kcal per day? Assume the man cannot resist eating the full plate of sweets once it is offered to him.

Sol. The man intends to cut down =3000−2100=900kcal.

But avoiding sweets completely, he will cut down 700 kcal. To cut down another 200 kcal, he should cut down butter by $\dfrac{10}{60} \times 200 \simeq 33\,\text{g}$ per day.

He should not cut down consumption of food, that provides him with vitamins and other vital nutrients.

44. Two rods of the same area of cross-section, but of lengths l_1 and l_2 and conductivities K_1 and K_2 are joined in series. Show that the combination is equivalent of a material of conductivity

$$K = \dfrac{l_1 + l_2}{\left(\dfrac{l_1}{K_1}\right) + \left(\dfrac{l_2}{K_2}\right)}$$

Sol. It is given that conductivities K_1 and K_2 are in series, so rate of flow of heat energy is same. But the sum of the difference in temperature is the difference across their free ends.

$\therefore \quad (\theta_1 - \theta) + (\theta - \theta_2) = (\theta_1 - \theta_2)$

i.e. $\dfrac{\theta}{t} \cdot \dfrac{l_1}{K_1 A} + \dfrac{\theta}{t} \cdot \dfrac{l_2}{K_2 A} = \dfrac{\theta}{t} \cdot \dfrac{(l_1 + l_2)}{K_{eq} A}$

$\Rightarrow \quad \dfrac{l_1}{K_1} + \dfrac{l_2}{K_2} = \dfrac{l_1 + l_2}{K_{eq}}$

$\therefore \quad K_{eq} = \dfrac{l_1 + l_2}{\left(\dfrac{l_1}{K_1} + \dfrac{l_2}{K_2}\right)}$

LONG ANSWER Type II Questions

45. Answer the following.

(i) The triple point of water is a standard fixed point in modern thermometry. Why? What is wrong in taking the melting point of ice and the boiling point of water as standard fixed points (as was originally done in the celsius scale)?

(ii) There were two fixed points in the original celsius scale as mentioned above which were assigned the number 0°C and 100°C,

respectively. On the absolute scale, one of the fixed points is the triple point of water, which on the kelvin absolute scale is assigned the number 273.16 K. What is the other fixed point on this (kelvin) scale?

(iii) The absolute temperature (kelvin scale) T is related to the temperature t_c on the celsius scale by $t_c = T - 273.15$. Why do we have 273.15 in this relation and not 273.16?

(iv) What is the temperature of the triple point of water on an absolute scale whose unit interval size is equal to that of the fahrenheit scale?

[NCERT]

Sol. (i) The melting point of ice as well as the boiling point of water change with change in pressure. The presence of impurities also changes the melting and boiling points. However, the triple point of water has a unique temperature and is independent of external factors.

(ii) The other fixed point on Kelvin scale is absolute zero, which is the temperature at which the volume and pressure of any gas become zero.

(iii) As the triple point of water on celsius is 0.01°C (and not 0°C) and on kelvin scale 273.16 and the size of degree on the two scales is same, so

$$t_c - 0.01 = T - 273.16$$

$\therefore \qquad t_c = T - 273.15$

(iv) One degree on fahrenheit scale

$$= \dfrac{180}{100} = \dfrac{9}{5} \text{ divisions on celsius scale.}$$

But one celsius scale division is equal to one division on kelvin scale.

∴ Triple point on kelvin scale (whose size of a degree is equal to that of the fahrenheit scale)

$$= 273.16 \times 9 / 5 = 491.69$$

46. A child running a temperature of 101°F is given an antipyretic (i.e. a medicine that lowers fever) which causes an increase in the rate of evaporation of sweat from his body. If the fever is brought down to 98°F in 20 min. What is the average rate of extra evaporation caused by the drug? Assume the evaporation mechanism to be the only way by which heat is lost. The mass of the child is 30 kg. The specific heat of human body is approximately the same as that of water and latent heat of evaporation of water at that temperature is about 580 cal g^{-1}. **[NCERT]**

Sol. Mass of child, $M = 30\,\text{kg} = 30 \times 10^3\text{g}$

Fall in temperature, $\Delta T = 101 - 98 = 3°\text{F} = 3 \times \dfrac{5}{9} = \dfrac{5}{3}°\text{C}$

Specific heat of human body,

c = specific heat of water $= 1\,\text{cal g}^{-1}{}°\text{C}^{-1}$

Heat lost by child in the form of evaporation of sweat,
$$Q = Mc\,\Delta T = 30 \times 10^3 \times 1 \times \frac{5}{3}$$
$$= 50000 \text{ cal}$$

If M' gram of sweat evaporates from the body of the child, then heat gained by sweat
$$Q = M'L = M' \times 580 \text{ cal} \qquad [\because L = 580 \text{ calg}^{-1}]$$

$\because$ Heat gained = Heat lost
$$M' \times 580 = 50000$$
$$\Rightarrow \quad M' = \frac{50000}{580} = 86.2 \text{ g}$$

Time taken by sweat to evaporate = 20 min

$\therefore$ Rate of evaporation of sweat $= \dfrac{86.2}{20} = 4.31 \text{ g min}^{-1}$

47. Answer the following questions based on the p-T phase diagram of CO_2.

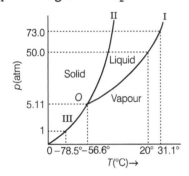

(i) CO_2 at 1 atm pressure and temperature $-60°C$ is compressed isothermally. Does it go through the liquid phase?

(ii) What happens when CO_2 at 4 atm pressure is cooled from room temperature at constant pressure?

(iii) Describe qualitatively the changes in a given mass of solid CO_2 at 10 atm pressure and temperature $-65°C$ as it heated upto room temperature at constant pressure.

(iv) CO_2 is heated to a temperature 70°C and compressed isothermally. What changes in its properties, do you expect to observe? **[NCERT]**

Sol. (i) No, when CO_2 at 1 atm pressure and at $-60°C$ is compressed isothermally, it changes directly from vapour phase to solid phase without going through the liquid phase.

This can be checked by drawing a vertical line at $-60°C$ which intersects the sublimation curve III.

(ii) CO_2 at 4 atm pressure and at temperature (say 25°C) is vapour. If it is cooled at constant temperature, it condenses directly into solid without going through liquid phase.

This can be checked by drawing a horizontal line at $p=4$ atm which intersects the sublimation curve III.

(iii) CO_2 at 10 atm pressure and at $-65°C$ is solid. As CO_2 is heated at constant pressure, it will go to liquid phase and then to the vapour phase. It is because, the horizontal line through the initial point intersects both the fusion and the vaporisation curves. The fusion and boiling points can be known from the points, where the horizontal line at 10 atm (initial point) intersects the respective curves.

(iv) When the carbon dioxide is heated to 70°C (which is greater than its critical temperature), it will not exhibit any clear phase transition to the liquid phase. At this state, it will deviate more and more from ideal gas behaviour, as its pressure increases.

48. Explain why

(i) a body with large reflectivity is a poor emitter.

(ii) a brass tumbler feels much colder than a wooden tray on a chilly day.

(iii) an optical pyrometer (for measuring high temperature) calibrated for an ideal black body radiation gives too low a value for the temperature of a red hot iron piece in the open, but gives a correct value for the temperature when the same piece is in the furnace.

(iv) the earth without its atmosphere would be inhospitably cold.

(v) heating systems based on circulation of steam are more efficient in warming a building than those based on circulation of hot water. **[NCERT]**

Sol. (i) A body with large reflectivity is a poor absorber of heat. According to Kirchhoff's law, a poor absorber of heat is a poor emitter. Hence, a body with large reflectivity is a poor emitter.

(ii) Brass is a good conductor of heat. When a brass tumbler is touched, heat quickly flows from human body to tumbler. Consequently, the tumbler appears colder. Wood is a bad conductor. So, heat does not flow from the human body to the tray in this case. Thus, it appears comparatively hotter.

(iii) Let T be the temperature of the hot iron in the furnace. Heat radiated per second per unit area, $E = \sigma T^4$

When the body is placed in the open at temperature T_0, the heat radiated/second/unit area, $E' = \sigma\,(T_4 - T_0^4)$.

Clearly, $E' < E$. So, the optical pyrometer gives too low a value for the temperature in the open.

(iv) Heat radiated out by the earth is reflected back by the atmosphere. In the absence of atmosphere, at night all heat would escape from the earth's surface and thereby the earth's surface would be inhospitably cold. Also, atmosphere helps in maintaining the temperature through convection current.

(v) Though steam and boiling water are at the same temperature but each unit mass of steam contains a larger amount of additional heat called the latent heat. e.g. each gram of steam has 540 cal of more heat than each gram of boiling water. Hence, steam loses more heat than boiling water.

49. Answer the following questions based on the *p-T* phase diagram of carbon dioxide as shown in the figure.

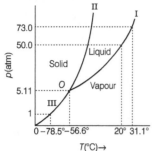

$T(°C) \rightarrow$

(i) At what temperature and pressure can the solid, liquid and vapour phases of CO_2 co-exist in equilibrium?

(ii) What is the effect of decrease of pressure on the fusion and boiling point of CO_2?

(iii) What are the critical temperature and pressure for CO_2? What is their significance?

(iv) Is CO_2 solid, liquid or gas at (a) – 70°C under 1 atm (b) – 60°C under 10 atm (c) 15°C under 56 atm? **[NCERT]**

Sol. (i) The solid, liquid and vapour phases of CO_2 co-exist in equilibrium at its triple point *O* for which

$$p_{tr} = 5.11 \text{ atm and } T_{tr} = -56.6°C$$

(ii) The vaporisation curve I and fusion curve II show that both the boiling point and fusion point of CO_2 decrease with decrease of pressure.

(iii) For CO_2, $p_c = 73.0$ atm and $T_c = 31.1°C$.
Above its critical temperature, CO_2 gas cannot be liquefied, however large pressure may be applied.

(iv) (a) – 70°C under 1 atm. This point lies in **vapour** region.
Therefore, at –70°C under 1 atm, CO_2 is vapour.
(b) – 60°C under 10 atm. This point lies in **solid** region. Therefore, CO_2 is **solid** at – 60°C under 10 atm.
(c) 15°C under 56 atm. This point lies in **liquid** region. Therefore, CO_2 is **liquid** at 15°C under 56 atm.

50. Distinguish between conduction, convection and radiation.
Sol.

	Conduction	Convection	Radiation
1.	It is the transfer of heat by direct physical contact.	It is the transfer of heat by the motion of a fluid.	It is the transfer of heat by electromagnetic waves.
2.	It is due to temperature difference. Heat flows from high temperature region to low temperature region.	It is due to difference in density. Heat flows from low density region to high density region.	It occurs from all bodies at temperatures above 0 K.
3.	It occurs in solids through molecular collisions, without actual flow of matter.	It occurs in fluids by actual flow of matter.	It can take place at large distances and does not heat the intervening medium.
4.	It is a slow process.	It is also a slow process.	It propagates at the speed of light.
5.	It does not obey the laws of reflection and refraction.	It does not obey the laws of reflection and refraction.	It obeys the laws of reflection and refraction.

51. A body cools from 80°C to 50°C in 5 min. Calculate the time it takes to cool from 60°C to 30°C, the temperature of the surrounding is 20°C. **[NCERT]**

Sol. According to Newton's law of cooling, when the temperature difference is not large, rate of loss of heat is proportional to the temperature difference between the body and the surroundings.

$$mc \frac{T_1 - T_2}{t} = K(T - T_0)$$

where, $T = \frac{T_1 + T_2}{2}$ = average of the initial and final

temperatures of the body and T_0 is the temperature of the surroundings.

Here, $T_1 = 80°C$, $T_2 = 50°$, $T_0 = 20°C$,
$t = 5$ min $= 300$ s

$$T = \frac{T_1 + T_2}{2} = \frac{80 + 50}{2} = 65°C$$

$$\therefore \quad mc \frac{80 - 50}{300} = K(65 - 20) \qquad \text{...(i)}$$

If the liquid takes *t* seconds to cool from 60°C to 30°C, then

$$T = \frac{60 + 30}{2} = 45°C$$

$$\therefore \quad mc \frac{60 - 30}{t} = K(45 - 20) \qquad \text{...(ii)}$$

Dividing Eq. (i) by Eq. (ii), we get

$$\frac{30}{300} \times \frac{t}{30} = \frac{45}{25}$$

or $$t = \frac{45}{25} \times 300 = 540s = 9 \text{ min}$$

ASSESS YOUR TOPICAL UNDERSTANDING

OBJECTIVE Type Questions

1. Time taken to heat water upto a temperature of $40°C$ (from room temperature) is t_1 and time taken to heat mustard oil (of same mass and at room temperature) upto a temperature of $40°C$ is t_2, then (given mustard oil has smaller heat capacity)
   (a) $t_1 = t_2$
   (b) $t_1 > t_2$
   (c) $t_2 > t_1$
   (d) t_1 and t_2 both are less than 10 min

2. Cooking is difficult on hills becuase
   (a) atmospheric pressure is higher
   (b) atmospheric pressure is lower
   (c) boiling point of water is reduced
   (d) Both (b) and (c)

3. Change of state from solid to vapour state without passing through the liquid state is called
   (a) regelation   (b) sublimation
   (c) condensation   (d) sedimentation

4. The bottoms of utensils for cooking food are blackened to
   (a) absorb minimum heat from fire
   (b) absorb maximum heat from fire
   (c) emit radiations
   (d) reflect heat to surroundings

5. The rate of loss of heat depends on
   (a) the sum of temperature of the body and its surroundings
   (b) the difference in temperature of the body and its surroundings
   (c) the product of temperature of the body and its surroundings
   (d) the ratio of temperature of the body and its surroundings

6. A spherical body with radius 12 cm radiates 450 W power at 500 K. If the radius were halved and the temperature doubled, what would be the power radiated?
   (a) 2000 W   (b) 1500 W
   (c) 1800 W   (d) 2500 W

VERY SHORT ANSWER Type Questions

7. In which unit the water equivalent of unit is measured?

8. What is the heat capacity of boiling water?

9. Heat and work are equivalent to each other. What does it mean?

10. What will be ratio of specific heat capacity and molar heat capacity of a material?

11. When hot liquid is mixed with a cold liquid, what will be effect on final temperature?

12. Out of three modes of transmission of heat, which one is fastest?

SHORT ANSWER Type I Questions

13. Why snow is a better heat insulator than ice?

14. Why do we use copper gauze in Davy's safety lamp?

15. Is it necessary that all black coloured objects should be considered black bodies?

16. Why felt rather than air is employed for thermal insulation?

LONG ANSWER Type I Questions

17. State and explain three different modes of transference of heat. Explain how the loss of heat due to these three modes are minimised in a thermo flask.

18. What is calorimetry? Briefly explain its principle.

19. Can a gas be liquified at any temperature by increase of pressure alone?

20. A cup of tea cools from $81°C$ to $79°C$ in 1 min. The ambient temperature is $30°C$. What time is needed for cooling of same cup of tea in same ambience from $61°C$ to $59°C$?

LONG ANSWER Type II Questions

21. Three rods of identical cross-sectional area and made from the same metal from the sides of an isosceles triangle ABC (shown in figure), right-angled at B. The points A and B are maintained at temperatures T and $\sqrt{2}T$, respectively. In the steady state, the temperature of the point C is T_C. Assuming that only heat conduction takes place. Then, determine the value of $\dfrac{T_C}{T}$.

Answers

1. (b)	**2.** (d)	**3.** (b)	**4.** (b)	**5.** (b)
6. (c)				

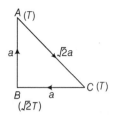

Hence, a, a and $\sqrt{2}a$ are the respective side lengths.

$$\left[\text{Ans. } \frac{3}{\sqrt{2}+1}\right]$$

22. Three rods of equal lengths of thermal conductivities $K, 2K$ and $3K$ are symmetrically joined to a point. If temperatures of ends are 0°C, 50°C and 100°C, respectively. Determine the temperature of junction point.

$$\left[\text{Ans. } \frac{200}{3}°\text{C}\right]$$

23. A copper cube of mass 200 g slides down on a rough inclined plane having inclination 37° at a constant speed. If any loss in mechanical energy goes into the copper block as thermal energy. Find the increase in the temperature of the block as it slides down through 60 cm. Given, specific heat of copper is 420 J kg^{-1} K^{-1}. [**Ans.** 8.6×10^{-3} °C]

24. On a winter day the temperature of the tap water is 20°C whereas the atmospheric temperature is 5°C. Water is stored in a tank of capacity 0.5 m^3 for household use. If it were possible to use the heat liberated by the water to left a 10 kg mass vertically. How high can it be lifted as the water comes to the room temperature. Take $g = 10$ ms^{-2}? [**Ans.** 315 km]

25. Explain what is meant by specific heat of a substance what are its units. Define two types of specific heat of gases and which one is greater?

SUMMARY

- **Temperature** is the property of a state of matter by virtue of which we predict its hotness or coldness, relative to some body.
- **Heat** is form of energy which determines the change in thermal state of a body. It flows from the body which is at a high temperature to the other at low temperature.
- The devices which are used to measure the temperature are termed as **thermometers**.
- **Relation between C, F and K Scales**
$$\frac{C}{5} = \frac{F-32}{9} = \frac{K-273.15}{5}$$
- **Boyle's Law** $p \propto \dfrac{1}{V}$ (at constant temperature)

  ∴ $pV = $ constant
- **Charles' Law** $V \propto T$ (at constant pressure)
$$\frac{V}{T} = \text{constant}$$
- **Ideal Gas Equation**
$$pV = \mu RT$$
where, p = pressure of gas, V = volume of gas, T = temperature of gas
μ = number of moles, R = universal gas constant $= 8.31$ Jmol^{-1}K^{-1}
- If a rod is having length l_0 at temperature T, then expansion in length of rod due to rise in temperature by ΔT, is given by
$$\Delta l = l_0 \Delta \alpha T$$
where, α is the coefficient of linear expansion, whose value depends on the nature of the material.
Final length, $l_f = l_0 + l_0 \alpha \Delta T = l_0 (1 + \alpha \Delta T)$
- Area expansion is valid only for solids. This is given by $A_f = A_0 (1 + \beta \times \Delta T)$
where, A_f is the area of body when temperature has been changed by ΔT, A_0 is the area of body at temperature T and β is the coefficient of superficial expansion.

- Volume after expansion, $V = V_0(1 + \gamma \Delta T)$, where, γ is the coefficient of cubical expansion.

- **Heat Capacity** The heat capacity of a body is the quantity of heat required by the body to raise its temperature by 1°C. It is also known as thermal capacity.
$$\text{Heat capacity} = ms \text{ (mass} \times \text{specific heat)}$$

- **Water Equivalent** It is the quantity of water whose thermal capacity is same as the heat capacity of the body. It is denoted by W.
$$W = ms = \text{Heat capacity of the body}$$

- **Specific Heat** The specific heat (s) of a substance is the quantity of heat in calorie required to raise the temperature of 1g of that substance by 1°C. Its unit is $\text{cal g}^{-1}\text{C}^{-1}$.

- **Molar Heat Capacity** The amount of heat required to change the temperature of unit mole of substance by 1°C is termed as its molar heat capacity.
$$C = \frac{Q}{\mu \Delta T} \text{ where, } \mu = \text{number of moles} = \frac{m}{M}$$

- **Calorimetry** Heat lost by hotter body = Heat gained by colder body $m_1 s_1 \Delta T = m_2 s_2 \Delta T$

- **Latent Heat** The heat required to change the state of a system is proportional to mass of the system, i.e.
$$Q \propto m \Rightarrow Q = mL$$
where, $L = $ **latent heat** of the material.

- **Transmission of Heat** There are three different ways in which heat can be transferred-conduction, convection and radiation.

- **Conduction** It is a process by which the heat is transferred in solid. In conduction, molecules vibrate about a fixed location and transfer the heat by collision.

- **Convection** It is a process by which heat is transferred in fluids (liquids and gases). In convection, transfer of heat takes place by transport of matter (in form of motion of particles).

- **Radiation** This mode of heat transfer doesn't require any medium, and it is the fastest mode of heat transfer. Instance of this mode of heat transfer is the radiation received by earth coming from sun.

- The amount of heat transmitted through a conductor is given by $Q = \dfrac{KA\Delta T t}{l}$

  Thermal resistance of heat is given by $|H| = \left|\dfrac{\Delta Q}{\Delta t}\right| = \dfrac{KA}{l}\Delta T = \dfrac{\Delta T}{l/KA}$

  The term $\dfrac{l}{KA}$ is generally called the **thermal resistance.**

- **Stefan's Law** The energy emitted per second per unit area of a black body (emissive power = 1) is proportional to the fourth power of the absolute temperature.
  i.e. $$E = \sigma T^4$$
  Here, $\sigma = $ Stefan's constant $= 5.67 \times 10^{-8} \text{Jm}^{-2}\text{s}^{-1}\text{K}^{-4}$
  For any other body $\quad e = \varepsilon \sigma T^{-4}$
  Here, $\varepsilon = $ emissivity of body ($\varepsilon = 1$ for a black body)
  If Q is the total energy radiated by the ordinary body, then $e = \dfrac{Q}{A \times t} = \varepsilon \sigma T^{-4} \Rightarrow Q = A\varepsilon \sigma T^{-4} t$

- **Wien's displacement law** It states that, "as temperature of black body T increases, the wavelength λ_m corresponding to maximum emission decreases' such that $\lambda_m \propto \dfrac{1}{T}$ or $\lambda_m T = b$

  where, b is known as Wien's constant and its value is $2.89 \times 10^{-3}\text{mK}$

- According to **Newton's law of cooling,** 'rate of cooling of a body is directly proportional to the temperature difference between the body and the surroundings provided that the temperature difference is small.'
  Mathematically, $-\dfrac{dT}{dt} \alpha (T - T_0), \quad -\dfrac{dT}{dt} = k(T - T_0)$
  where, k is a universal constant.

CHAPTER PRACTICE

OBJECTIVE Type Questions

1. Temperature of atmosphere in Kashmir falls below $-10°C$ in winter. Due to this water animal and plant life of Dal-lake
   (a) is destroyed in winters
   (b) frozen in winter and regenerated in summers
   (c) survives as only top layer of lake in frozen
   (d) None of the above

2. When temperature of water is raised from 0°C to 4°C, it
   (a) expands
   (b) contracts
   (c) expands upto 2°C and then contracts upto 4°C
   (d) contracts upto 2°C and then expands upto 4°C

3. A bimetallic strip is made of aluminium and steel $(\alpha_{Al} > \alpha_{steel})$. On heating, the strip will
   [NCERT Exemplar]
   (a) remain straight
   (b) get twisted
   (c) will bend with aluminium on concave side
   (d) will bend with steel on concave side

4. The radius of a metal sphere at room temperature T is R and the coefficient of linear expansion of the metal is α. The sphere heated a little by a temperature ΔT so that its new temperature is $T + \Delta T$. The increase in the volume of the sphere is approximately.
   [NCERT Exemplar]
   (a) $2\pi R\alpha \Delta T$ (b) $\pi R^2 \alpha \Delta T$
   (c) $4\pi R^3 \alpha \Delta T / 3$ (d) $4\pi R^3 \alpha \Delta T$

5. The latent heat of vaporisation of a substance is always
   (a) greater than its latent heat of fusion
   (b) greater than its latent heat of sublimation
   (c) equals to its latent heat of sublimation
   (d) less than its latent heat of fusion

6. If m mass of a substance undergoes a phase change, then amount of heat required will be
   (a) $\Delta Q = mL$ (b) $\Delta Q = mC_p \Delta T$
   (c) $\Delta = ms\Delta T$ (d) $\Delta Q = mC_V \Delta T$

7. Two rods of same length and material transfer a given amount of heat in 12 s, when they are joined end to end (i.e., in series). But when they are joined in parallel, they will transfer same heat under same temperature difference across thier ends in
   (a) 24 s   (b) 3 s
   (c) 38 s   (d) 1.5 s

8. The temperature of two bodies A and B are respectively, 727°C and 327°C. The ratio $H_A : H_B$ of the rates of heat radiated by them is
   (a) 727 : 327   (b) 5 : 3
   (c) 25 : 9   (d) 625 : 81

9. The rate of cooling due to conduction, convection, and radiation combined, is proportional to the difference in temperature, for
   (a) large temperature differences
   (b) small temperature differences
   (c) any temperature difference
   (d) None of the above

ASSERTION AND REASON

Direction (Q. Nos. 10-18) *In the following questions, two statements are given- one labelled Assertion (A) and the other labelled Reason (R). Select the correct answer to these questions from the codes (a), (b), (c) and (d) as given below*
   (a) Both Assertion and Reason are true and Reason is the correct explanation of Assertion.
   (b) Both Assertion and Reason are true but Reason is not the correct explanation of Assertion.
   (c) Assertion is true but Reason is false.
   (d) Assertion is false but Reason is true.

10. **Assertion** A hotter body has more heat content than a colder body.

    Reason Temperature is the measure of degree of 'hotness' of a body.

11. **Assertion** When heat transfer takes place between a system and surroundings, the total heat content of system or surroundings separately remains same.

    Reason Heat is a form of energy which follows the principle of conservation of energy.

12. **Assertion** The triple point of water is a standard fixed point in modern thermometry.

    Reason Melting point of ice and the boiling point of water change due to change in atmospheric pressure but triple-point of water does not change.

13. **Assertion** Water kept in an open vessel will quickly evaporate on the surface of the Moon.

    Reason The temperature at the surface of the Moon is much higher than boiling point of water.

14. **Assertion** Houses made of concrete roofs get very hot during summer days.

    Reason Thermal conductivity of concrete is much smaller than metal.

15. **Assertion** When temperature difference across the two sides of a wall is increased, its thermal conductivity increases.

    Reason Thermal conductivity depends on the nature of material of the wall.

16. **Assertion** A black body at higher temperature T radiates energy U. When temperature falls to one third, the radiated energy will be $U/81$.

    Reason $U^2 \propto T^4$

17. **Assertion** The SI unit of Stefan's constant is $Wm^{-2} K^{-4}$.

    Reason This follows from Stefan's law $E = \sigma T^4$

    $$\therefore \sigma = \frac{E}{T^4} = \frac{Wm^{-2}}{K^4}$$

18. **Assertion** The radiation from the sun's surface varies as the fourth power of its absolute temperature.

    Reason Sun is not a black body.

CASE BASED QUESTIONS

Direction (Q. Nos. 19-20) *These questions are case study based questions. Attempt any 4 sub-parts from each question.*

19. **Temperature of Junction**

    An iron bar ($L_1 = 0.1$ m, $A_1 = 0.02$ m^2, $K_1 = 79$ Wm^{-1}K^{-1}) and a brass bar ($L_2 = 0.1$ m, $A_2 = 0.02$ m^2, $K_2 = 109$ Wm^{-1}K^{-1}) are soldered end to end as shown in figure. The free ends of the iron bar and brass bar are maintained at 373 K and 273K, respectively.

$T_1 = 373$ K $\longrightarrow$ | Iron | Brass | $\longleftarrow T_2 = 273$ K

T_0

(i) What is the temperature of the junction of two bars in steady state?
  (a) 315 K (b) 420 K
  (c) 520 K (d) 600 K

(ii) Compute the equivalent thermal conductivity of the compound bar.
  (a) 100 Wm^{-1} K^{-1}
  (b) 91.6 Wm^{-1} K^{-1}
  (c) 110 Wm^{-1} K^{-1}
  (d) 120 Wm^{-1} K^{-1}

(iii) How much heat current flows through the compound bar?
  (a) 920 W (b) 916.1 W
  (c) 102.5 W (d) 112.5 W

(iv) Two rods of same length and material transfer a given amount of heat in 12 s, when they are joined end to end (*i.e.,* in series). But when they are joined in parallel, they will transfer same heat under same temperature difference across thier ends in
  (a) 24 s (b) 3 s
  (c) 38 s (d) 1.5 s

(v) The two ends of a metal rod are maintained at temperatures 100°C and 110°C. The rate of heat flow in the rod is found to be 4.0 J/s. If the ends are maintained at temperatures 200°C and 210°C, the rate of heat flow will be
  (a) 44.0 Js^{-1} (b) 16.8 Js^{-1}
  (c) 8.0 Js^{-1} (d) 4.0 Js^{-1}

20. **Heat Exchange**

    Consider a metallic bar of length L and uniform cross-section A with its two ends maintained at different temperatures. This can be done, *e.g.,* By putting the ends in thermal contact with large reservoirs at temperatures, say, T_C and T_D, respectively shown in figure. Let us assume the ideal condition that the sides of the bar are fully insulated so that no heat is exchanged between the sides and the surroundings.

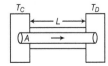

After sometime, steady state is reached; the temperature of the bar decreases uniformly with distance from T_C to T_D; $(T_C > T_D)$. The reservoir at C supplies heat at a constant rate, which transfers through the bar and is given out at the same rate to the reservoir at D.

It is found experimentally that in this steady state heat flow by conduction in a bar with its two ends maintained at temperatures T_C and T_D; $(T_C > T_D)$.

(i) The rate of flow of heat (H) is proportional to
  (a) $(T_D + T_C)$ (b) $(T_C - T_D)$
  (c) T_C (d) T_D

(ii) In $H = \dfrac{\Delta Q}{\Delta t} = \dfrac{KA}{L}(T_C - T_D)$, the proportionality constant K is called the
  (a) thermal conductivity
  (b) specific heat
  (c) latent heat
  (d) coefficient of linear expansion

(iii) The SI unit of K is
  I. $Js^{-1}m^{-1}K^{-1}$ II. WmK^{-1}
  III. $Wm^{-1}K^{-1}$ IV. $Js\,m^{-1}K$
  (a) Only III
  (b) Both I and III
  (c) Only IV
  (d) Only II

(iv) Heat is flowing steadily from A to B temperature T at P, at distance x from A is such that

  (a) T decreases linearly with x
  (b) T increases linearly with x
  (c) T decreases exponentially with x
  (d) T increases with x as $T \propto x^2$

(v) Calculate the rate of loss of heat through a glass window of area $1000\,\text{cm}^2$ and thickness $0.4\,\text{cm}$ when temperature inside is 37°C and outside is −5°C. Coefficient of thermal conductivity of glass is $2.2 \times 10^{-3}\ \text{cal s}^{-1}\text{cm}^{-1}\text{K}^{-1}$.
  (a) $450\ \text{cal s}^{-1}$ (b) $231\ \text{cal s}^{-1}$
  (c) $439\ \text{cal s}^{-1}$ (d) $650\ \text{cal s}^{-1}$

Answers

1. (c)	**2.** (b)	**3.** (d)	**4.** (d)	**5.** (a)
6. (a)	**7.** (b)	**8.** (d)	**9.** (b)	**10.** (d)
11. (d)	**12.** (a)	**13.** (c)	**14.** (b)	**15.** (d)
16. (c)	**17.** (c)	**18.** (c)		

19.	**(i)** (a)	**(ii)** (b)	**(iii)** (b)	**(iv)** (b)	**(v)** (d)
20.	**(i)** (b)	**(ii)** (a)	**(iii)** (b)	**(iv)** (a)	**(v)** (b)

VERY SHORT ANSWER Type Questions

21. A body at high temperature contains more heat. Comment.

22. Two copper balls having masses 5 g and 10 g collide with a target with the same velocity. If the total energy is used in heating the balls, which ball will attain higher temperature? Justify?

23. What should be the absorbing power and reflecting power of a perfectly black body?

SHORT ANSWER Type Questions

24. The density of mercury is $13.6 \times 10^3 \text{kg m}^{-3}$ at 0°C and its coefficient of volume expansion is $1.82 \times 10^{-4}\text{K}^{-1}$. Find the density at 50°C.
[**Ans.** $13.47 \times 10^3 \text{kg m}^{-3}$]

25. Figure shows two bars of iron and brass having same length and same area of cross-section in steady state. Determine temperature at common junction. Given that
$K_{\text{iron}} = 79\ \text{W m}^{-1}\text{K}^{-1}$
and $K_{\text{brass}} = 109\ \text{W m}^{-1}\ \text{K}^{-1}$.

[**Ans.** 315 K]

26. What should be the length of steel and copper rods at 0°C so that the length of the steel rod is 5 cm longer than the copper rod at any temperature? Given that linear expansion coefficient of steel $= 12 \times 10^{-5}/°\text{C}$ and for copper $= 1.6 \times 10^{-5}/°\text{C}$

27. An aluminium cube 10 cm on a side at 0°C is heated to 30°C. Find the change in its density. Given that coefficient of volume expansion of aluminium $= 7.2 \times 10^{-5}/°\text{C}$ and density of aluminium at 0°C $= 2700\ \text{kg}/\text{m}^3$.
[**Ans.** $-5.8\ \text{kg}/\text{m}^3$]

28. Determine the temperature at which a wooden block and a metallic block are equally cold or equally hot when touched.

29. Air is a bad conductor of heat why is it so that we do not feel warm without cloth?

30. Animal curl into a ball when they feel very cold. Why?

LONG ANSWER Type I Questions

31. A box having total surface area 0.05 m^2 and of 6 mm thick side walls is filled with melting ice and kept in a room. Calculate the thermal conductivity of the box material if 0.5 kg of ice melts in 1 h. The room temperature is 40°C and latent heat of fusion of ice = 3.33×10^5 J kg^{-1}.

[**Ans.** 0.42 W m^{-1}K^{-1}]

32. A copper block of mass 2.5 kg is heated in a furnace to a temperature of 500°C and then placed on a large ice block. What is maximum amount of ice that can melt? Given that specific heat of water = 390 J kg^{-1}K^{-1} and latent heat of fusion of water = 3.35×10^5 J kg^{-1}

33. A steel girder is 50 m long and has a cross-sectional area 250 cm^2. What is the force exerted by the girder when heated from 5°C to 25°C?

Given that $\alpha_s = 11 \times 10^{-6}/°C$ and $Y_s (\text{or } \alpha_V) = 2 \times 10^{11}/°C$

[**Ans.** 11×10^5 N]

34. The window panes of a room have an area of 4.8 m^2 and of 4 mm thickness. At what rate does the heat energy flow through the window if the temperature inside the room is 25°C and that outside is 10°C. Given that the thermal conductivity of glass is 0.75 W m^{-1}K^{-1}.

[**Ans.** 1.35×10^4 W]

35. A pan filled by hot food cools from 94°C to 86°C in 120 s when the room temperature is 293 K. How long will it take to cool from 71°C to 69°C?

[**Ans.** 42 s]

LONG ANSWER Type II Questions

36. Establish the relationship among thermal expansions α_l, α_A and α_V.

37. A specific book describes a new temperature scale called Z, in which boiling and freezing points of water are referred as 65°Z and $-15°$ Z, respectively.

(a) To what temperature on Fahrenheit scale would a temperature $-95°$Z correspond?

(b) What temperature change on the Z scale would correspond to a change of 40° on Celsius scale?

[**Ans.** (a) $-148°$ F (b) $32°Z$]

11

Thermodynamics is the field of Physics relating heat and work tansfer and the associated changes in the properties (such as pressure, volume, temperature, etc) of a working substance. Thermodynamics is a macroscopic science. It involves few macroscopic variables of the system. Thermodynamics avoids the molecular description all together. The state of a gas in thermodynamics is specified by macroscopic variables such as pressure, volume, temperature, mass and composition of gas.

THERMODYNAMICS

|TOPIC 1|
Heat and First Law of Thermodynamics

THERMODYNAMIC SYSTEM, SURROUNDINGS AND BOUNDARY

Thermodynamic system is an assembly of an extremely large number of particles (atoms or molecules) so that the assembly has a certain value of pressure, volume and temperature. The thermodynamic system may exist in the form of a solid, liquid or gas or a combination of two or more of these states.

Everything outside the system which has a direct effect on the system is called its **surroundings**. All space in universe outside the system is surroundings. e.g. Environment.

A system is separated from its surroundings by a **boundary**.

A system boundary is a real or imaginary two-dimensional closed surface that encloses the volume or region that a thermodynamic system occupies, through which energy exchange can or cannot be possible and work could be done on the system and by the system.

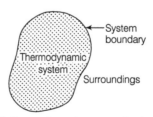

A thermodynamic system having boundary and surroundings

CLASSIFICATION OF THERMODYNAMIC SYSTEM

A thermodynamic system can be classified by the nature of the transfer of heat that are allowed to occur across its boundary.

A thermodynamic system may be open, closed and isolated.

(i) **Open System** It exchanges both energy and matter with the surroundings.

(ii) **Closed System** It exchanges only energy (not matter) with its surroundings.

(iii) **Isolated System** It exchanges neither energy nor matter with its surroundings.

THERMODYNAMIC EQUILIBRIUM

A thermodynamic system is said to be in thermodynamic equilibrium when macroscopic variables (like pressure, volume, temperature, mass, composition etc.) that characterise the system do not change with time.

e.g. Consider a gas inside a closed rigid container, completely insulated from its surroundings. Since, the pressure, volume, temperature, mass and composition of the gas do not change with time, therefore the gas is said to be in a state of thermodynamic equilibrium.

Whether or not a system is in a state of thermodynamic equilibrium, depends on the surroundings and the nature of the wall that separates the system from the surroundings. Consider two gases A and B occupying two different containers. Let the pressure and volume of the gases be (p_A, V_A) and (p_B, V_B), respectively.

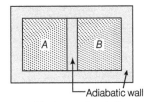

Systems A and B
separated by adiabatic wall

Suppose first that the two systems are put in proximity but are separated by an **adiabatic wall** (i.e. an insulating wall that does not allow flow of energy or heat from one to another). The system are insulated from the rest of the surroundings also by similar adiabatic walls.

The situation is shown schematically in figure. In **this case**, it is observed that any possible pair of values (p_A, V_A) will be in equilibrium with any possible pair of values (p_B, V_B).

THERMAL EQUILIBRIUM

Two systems are said to be in thermal equilibrium with each other if they are at the same temperature.

Again, consider the adiabatic wall separating the two gases A and B is replaced by **diathermic wall** (i.e. a wall that allows energy flow or heat from one to another). On account of flow of heat energy, the macroscopic variables of the two gases change spontaneously, either pressure or volume or both the pressure and volume of two gases may change.

Let the pressure and volume of two gases after change are (p'_A, V'_A) and (p'_B, V'_B) such that the new states of A and B are in equilibrium with each other. There is no more energy flow from one to another.

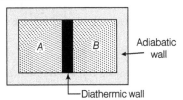

Two systems A and B in thermal equilibrium

Hence, the temperature of two gases become equal and the gases are said to be in thermal equilibrium with each other. This condition is shown in figure below.

Thus, two systems are said to be in thermal equilibrium with each other if they are at the same temperature.

- If there is no unbalanced force and torque is acting on the system, then the system is said to be in mechanical equilibrium.

- If the system does not undergo any spontaneous change in its internal structure due to chemical reaction, diffusion etc., then the system is said to be in chemical equilibrium.

- Two systems are said to be in thermal equilibrium, if there is no net flow of heat between them when they are brought into thermal contact.

ZEROTH LAW OF THERMODYNAMICS

This law was formulated by **RH Fowler** in 1931. The zeroth law of thermodynamics states that

If two systems A and B are separately in thermal equilibrium with a third system C, then A and B are in thermal equilibrium with each other.

Let us consider two systems A and B separated by a fixed adiabatic wall. The two systems A and B are in contact with a third system C through diathermic wall. The macroscopic variables of A and B will vary until both A and B come in thermal equilibrium with the third system C.

This shows that two systems A and B are separately in thermal equilibrium with a third system C. This condition is shown in Fig. (a)

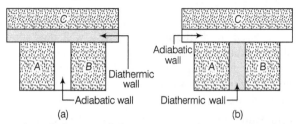

(a)   (b)

Let the adiabatic wall between A and B is replaced by a diathermic wall and an adiabatic wall insulates C from A and B. A and B are found in thermal equilibrium with each other. This condition is shown in Fig. (b), **both the experiments prove the zeroth law of thermodynamics.**

Concept of Temperature

Zeroth law of thermodynamics implies that temperature is a physical quantity which has the same value for all systems which are in thermal equilibrium with each other.

Hence, zeroth law says that if systems A and B are separately in thermal equilibrium with C, then

$$T_A = T_C \quad \text{and} \quad T_B = T_C \quad \Rightarrow \quad T_A = T_B$$

So, systems A and B will also be in thermal equilibrium with each other.

Some Definitions of Temperature

- Temperature is that thermodynamic variable which determines whether the two systems in contact will be in thermal equilibrium or not.
- Temperature of a body is that parameter which determine the degree of hotness or coldness of a body.
- Temperature of a body is that parameter which determine the direction of flow of heat when the body is brought in contact with another body.

HEAT, INTERNAL ENERGY AND WORK

Internal energy of a system is defined as the total energy possessed by the system due to molecular motion and molecular configuration. It is represented by U. The energy due to molecular motion is called **internal kinetic energy** U_K. The motion includes translational, rotational and vibrational motion of the molecules. The energy due to molecular configuration is called **internal potential energy** U_P. Then,

$$\boxed{\text{Internal energy}, U = U_K + U_P}$$

Thus, the internal energy of a system is the sum of molecular kinetic and potential energies in the frame of reference relative to which the centre of mass of the system is at rest.

Internal Energy of an Ideal Gas

In an ideal gas, there are no molecular forces of attraction so that the intermolecular forces are zero and the gas does not possess intermolecular potential energy, thus $U_P = 0$.

Hence, internal energy of an ideal gas is just the sum of kinetic energies associated with various random motions (i.e. translational, rotational and vibrational) of its molecules. Thus, the internal energy of an ideal gas depends on its temperature.

Internal Energy of a Real Gas

In a real gas, the intermolecular forces are not negligible. The molecules of a real gas exert mutual force of attraction on one another. Therefore, a definite amount of work has to be done in changing the distance between molecules.

Thus, internal energy of a real gas is the sum of internal kinetic energy and internal potential energy of the molecules of the gas. It would obviously depend on both the temperature and volume of the gas.

(i) The internal energy is a macroscopic state variable. The internal energy depends on the state of the system that depends on the values of pressure, volume, temperature, mass, composition etc., when the container is at rest as shown in Fig. (a)

(a) Container is at rest

(ii) The internal energy depends on the state of the system, but not on the path taken to achieve that state.

(iii) The internal energy of a gas can vary the macroscopic state variables of the gas, varies.

(iv) In thermodynamics, the KE of the system as a whole is not relevant. It means if the container of the gas is moving as a whole with some velocity as shown in Fig. (b), the KE of the container is not to be included in internal energy.

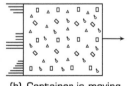

(b) Container is moving

Heat

It is the energy that exchanged between a system and its environment because of the temperature difference between them. SI unit of heat is joule. The amount of heat Q given to a body to raise its temperature from T_i to T_f depends on mass, nature of substance and change in its temperature.

i.e. $\Delta Q \propto m\Delta T$ or $\Delta Q \propto m(T_f - T_i)$

or   Change in heat, $\Delta Q = ms(T_f - T_i)$

where, m = mass of body, T_i = initial temperature
T_f = final temperature, s = specific heat of material

Work

By work, we mean work done by the system or on the system. Suppose, a gas is confined in a cylinder with a movable piston, if p is pressure on the piston and A is area of piston, then force exerted by the gas on the piston of cylinder, $F = pA$

When the piston is pushed outward an infinitesimal distance dx, then the work done by the gas

$$dW = Fdx = pA\, dx = p\, dV \qquad [\because Adx = dV]$$

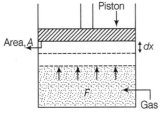

and for a finite volume change from V_i to V_f,

Work done, $W = \int_{V_i}^{V_f} dW$

$$\boxed{\text{Work done, } W = \int_{V_i}^{V_f} p\, dV}$$

Here, p could be variable or constant.

There are many ways to change the state of a gas. One way is represented by a plot between pressure of the gas and its volume and it is called an **indicator diagram**. The indicator diagram represents the variation of pressure (p) of the gas with the volume (V).

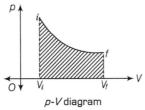

p-V diagram

On indicator diagram, the area bounded by p-V graph represents the work done

$$\text{Work} = \int_{V_i}^{V_f} p\, dV = \text{area under } p\text{-}V \text{ graph}$$

$$\text{From, } \Delta W = \int_{V_i}^{V_f} p\, dV$$

If system expands, $V_f > V_i$ i.e. W = positive

If system contracts, $V_f < V_i$ i.e. W = negative

Like heat, work done is also path dependent and so it is not a state function. In case of a cyclic process, work done is equal to the area enclosed under p-V diagram and it is positive, if cycle is clockwise and negative, if the cycle is anti-clockwise.

Ways to Change Internal Energy of a System

There are four ways to change the internal energy of a system.

(i) By doing work on the system ($\Delta W = -$ve).
(ii) If system is doing some work ($\Delta W = +$ve).
(iii) If some heat energy is given to the system ($\Delta Q = +$ve).
(iv) If some heat energy is taken out from the system. ($\Delta Q = -$ve).

We will use these sign conventions for ΔQ and ΔW in the topics coming ahead.

HEAT AND WORK–TWO DIFFERENT MODES OF ENERGY TRANSFER

To understand the concept, let us perform the following experiment

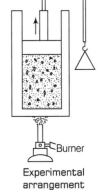

(i) Place a cylinder having some gas over a burner. Heat energy will flow from the burner to the gas. This will increase the internal energy of the gas.

(ii) To push the piston of the cylinder containing gas in the upward direction, some work is done by the gas, due to which the internal energy of the gas decreases.

Note that both these things could happen in the reverse directions too.

Experimental arrangement

If the gas, is in contact with a colder body then heat will flow from gas to the colder body and temperature of the gas will fall. Hence, internal energy of the gas will decrease. If the gas pushed the piston downwards, the work will be done on the gas. Therefore, the internal energy of the gas will increase.

Heat and work are two different modes to change the state of the system and to change the internal energy of the system.

Heat is the energy in transit. Heat is not a state variable of the system is described by internal energy of the system.

Hence, we can say that heat and work are not state variables. They are two modes of energy transfer that could change the internal energy of the system.

FIRST LAW OF THERMODYNAMICS AS ENERGY BALANCE

First law of thermodynamics is a statement of conservation of energy applied to any system in which energy transfer from or to the surroundings is taken into account.

It states that heat given to a system is either used in doing external work or it increases the internal energy of the system or both.

i.e. $\boxed{\text{Heat supplied, } \Delta Q = \Delta U + \Delta W}$

where,

ΔQ = Heat supplied to the system by the surroundings.

ΔW = Work done by the system on the surroundings

ΔU = Change in internal energy of the system.

ΔU depends only on the initial and final states.

Consider a gas in a cylinder with a massless and frictionless piston. Let the gas expands by a very small volume dV.

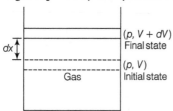

Experimental arrangement to prove
first law of thermodynamics

Let p is pressure and V is volume of the gas. A is area of cross-section of the piston, dx is the distance moved by the piston. Let the volume expansion is dV.

So, the work done by the gas

$$dW = \text{force} \times dx$$
or $\quad dW = pA \times dx = p(A\,dx) = pdV \quad [\because A dx = dV]$
$\therefore \qquad dW = pdV$

[For small displacement dx, the pressure is assumed to be constant.]

Thus, from first law $\Delta Q = \Delta U + pdV$

where,

ΔQ = heat transition between system and surroundings

ΔU = change in internal energy of the system.

EXAMPLE |1| Conversion of Water into Steam

1 g of water at 100°C is converted into steam of the same temperature. If the volume of steam is 1551 cm³, find out the change in internal energy of the water. Latent heat of steam = 2256×10^3 J/kg. Consider atm pressure.

Sol. Given, Mass of water, $m = 1\,g = 1 \times 10^{-3}\,kg$

Hence, pressure is $p = 1.013 \times 10^5\,N/m^2$

Volume of steam, $V_s = 1551\,cm^3 = 1551 \times 10^{-6}\,m^3$

Volume of water, $V_w = \dfrac{mass}{density} = \dfrac{1 \times 10^{-3}}{10^3} = 2 \times 10^{-6}\,m^3$

First law of thermodynamics gives

$$\Delta Q = \Delta U + p\Delta V$$
$$\Rightarrow \qquad mL = \Delta U + p(V_s - V_w)$$
$\therefore$ Change in internal energy is

$$\Delta U = mL - p(V_s - V_w)$$
$$= 1 \times 10^{-3} \times 2256 \times 10^3 - 1.013 \times 10^5$$
$$\times (1551 \times 10^{-6} - 10^{-6})$$
$$= 2256 - 0.1013 \times 1550 \cong 2099\,J$$

EXAMPLE |2| Different Types of Phases

The quantities in the following table represent four different paths for same initial and final states. Find the values of a, b, c, d, e, f and g.

S. No.	Q (J)	W (J)	ΔU (J)
Path I	− 80	−120	d
Path II	90	c	e
Path III	a	40	f
Path IV	b	− 40	g

Sol. For path I, $\Delta Q = \Delta W + \Delta U \Rightarrow \Delta U = \Delta Q - \Delta W$

$$= -80 - (-120) = 40\,J$$

As, ΔU = a state function, so $d = e = f = g = 40\,J$

Now for path II, $\Delta Q = \Delta W + \Delta U$

$$90 = c + 40 \Rightarrow c = 50\,J$$

Similarly, $\qquad a = 80\,J, b = 0$

EXAMPLE |3| Different Paths of System

Arrange four paths shown in ascending order on the basis of (i) change in internal energy (ii) work done by the gas (iii) magnitude of energy transferred or heat.

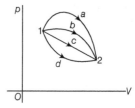

Sol. (i) As, ΔU depends on initial and final states but not on path, so for all a, b, c and d paths, ΔU is same.

(ii) Work done is given by area under curve and above volume axis so in ascending order, work done is d, c, b, a.

(iii) By first law, $\Delta Q = \Delta U + \Delta W$

and ΔU is same for all so, ΔQ is greatest for which ΔW is greatest. So, ascending order for ΔQ is d, c, b, a.

HEAT CAPACITY

If an amount of heat ΔQ is needed to change its temperature by ΔT, then **heat capacity** can be defined as

$$\boxed{\text{Heat capacity, } S = \frac{\Delta Q}{\Delta T}}$$

Heat capacity is numerically equal to the heat energy required to change the temperature of a body by unity. Its unit is J/K. Different amounts of heat may be needed for a unit rise in temperature at different temperatures.

Specific Heat Capacity

The amount of heat required to change the temperature of unit mass of a substance by unity is known as **specific heat capacity** of heat substance.

$$s = \frac{S}{m} = \frac{1}{m}\frac{\Delta Q}{\Delta T}$$

$$\boxed{\text{Specific heat capacity, } s = \frac{1}{m}\frac{\Delta Q}{\Delta T}}$$

where, s = specific heat capacity of the substance.

It depends on the nature of substance and its temperature. Its unit J/kg-K. Heat capacity per kg is known as **specific heat capacity**.

Molar Specific Heat Capacity

Heat capacity per mole is known as **molar specific heat capacity.**

$$C = \frac{S}{\mu} = \frac{1}{\mu}\left(\frac{\Delta Q}{\Delta T}\right)$$

$$\boxed{\text{Molar specific heat capacity, } C = \frac{1}{\mu}\frac{\Delta Q}{\Delta T}}$$

where, μ = number of moles.

The amount of heat required to raise the temperature of one gram mole of a substance through a unit is called **molar specific heat** capacity of the substance.

C depends on the nature of the substance, its temperature and the conditions under which heat is supplied. Its unit is J/mol-K.

Using the law of equipartition of energy, we can predict molar specific heat capacities of solids. In a solid consisting of N-atoms, the energy corresponding to vibration in each dimension about the mean position is given by

$$2 \times \frac{1}{2}K_B T = K_B T \qquad \dots(i)$$

Then, the average energy in three dimensions is $3K_B T$. For one mole of a solid, the total energy is

$$U = 3K_B T \times N_A = 3RT \qquad [\because K_B N_A = R] \dots(ii)$$

Now, at constant pressure

$$\Delta Q = \Delta U_{int} + p\,\Delta V \simeq \Delta U_{int}$$

Since, for a solid, ΔV is negligible.

Therefore, by using Eq. (ii)

$$C = \frac{\Delta Q}{\Delta T} = \frac{\Delta U_{int}}{\Delta T} = 3R$$

Specific and molar heat capacities of some solids at room temperature and atmospheric pressure

Substance	Specific heat $(J kg^{-1} K^{-1})$	Molar specific heat $(J\,mol^{-1} K^{-1})$
Aluminium	900.0	24.4
Carbon	506.5	6.1
Copper	386.4	24.5
Lead	127.7	26.5
Silver	236.1	25.5
Tungsten	134.4	24.9

SPECIFIC HEAT CAPACITY OF WATER

In old time, **calorie** is used as a unit of heat. Earlier it was defined as the amount of heat required to raise the temperature of 1 g of water by 1°C.

But later it was observed that specific heat of water varies slightly with temperature as shown in the figure below.

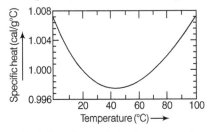

Variation of specific heat capacity of water with temperature

Specifically, one calorie is defined to be the amount of heat required to raise the temperature of 1 g of water from 14.5°C to 15.5°C.

As heat is a form of energy, hence joule, J is preferred to use the unit of heat, in SI unit, the specific heat capacity of water is 4186 J/kg-K or 4.186 J/g-K.

Mechanical Equivalent of Heat

Mechanical equivalent of heat is defined as the amount of work needed to produce 1 calorie of heat.
It is just a conversion factor.

1 calorie (heat energy) = 4.186 J $\simeq$ 4.2 J

Specific heat capacities of gases

For gases, their specific heat capacities depends on the process or under which condition heat exchange between the gases and the sourrounding is taking place.

There are two main specific heat capacities for a gas and defined as,

(i) **Molar heat capacity at constant volume, (C_V)** –

The amount of heat required to increase the temperature of one mole of the gas by 1°C (or 1K) at constant volume is known as molar heat capacity at constant volume. It is denoted by C_V.

(ii) **Molar heat capacity at constant pressure, (C_p)** –

The amount of heat required to increase the temperature of one mole of the gas by 1°C (or 1 K) at constant volume is known as molar heat capacity at constant pressure. It is denoted by C_p.

Note

For a gas, $C_p > C_V$ always, because at constant pressure, more heat is required to increase the temperature of one mole of the gas by 1°C (or 1K) as compare to that of at constant volume.

Relation between C_p and C_V (Mayer's Formula)

We can establish the relation between specific heat capacity at constant volume (C_V) and specific heat capacity at constant pressure (C_p) of a gas.

For an ideal gas, the relation between C_p and C_V is
$$C_p - C_V = R \qquad \text{...(i)}$$
This relation is known as **Mayer's Formula**.

To establish the relation, we begin with first law of thermodynamics for 1 mole of the gas
$$\Delta Q = \Delta U + p\Delta V$$

If heat ΔQ is absorbed at constant volume,

$\therefore$ $p\Delta V = 0$ and $\Delta Q = C_V \Delta T$ for one mole of a gas
$$\Delta V = 0$$

Then, $$C_V = \left(\frac{\Delta Q}{\Delta T}\right)_V = \left(\frac{\Delta U}{\Delta T}\right)_V = \left(\frac{\Delta U}{\Delta T}\right) \qquad \text{...(ii)}$$

where the subscript V is dropped in the last step, since U of an ideal gas depends only on temperature, not on volume.

Now, heat ΔQ is absorbed at constant pressure, then
$$\Delta Q = C_p \Delta T$$
$$C_p = \left(\frac{\Delta Q}{\Delta T}\right)_p = \left(\frac{\Delta U}{\Delta T}\right)_p + p\left(\frac{\Delta V}{\Delta T}\right)_p$$

The subscript p can be dropped from the first term since U of an ideal gas depends only on T, not on pressure.

Now, by using Eq. (ii), we have

or $$C_p = C_V + p\left(\frac{\Delta V}{\Delta p}\right)_p \qquad \text{...(iii)}$$

For one mole of an ideal gas, we can write $pV = RT$
If the pressure is kept constant
$$p\left(\frac{\Delta V}{\Delta T}\right)_p = R \qquad \text{...(iv)}$$

From Eqs. (iii) and (iv), we get
$$\boxed{C_p - C_V = R}$$

Here, C_p and C_V are molar specific heat capacities of an ideal gas at constant pressure and volume, respectively and R is the universal gas constant.

The ratio of C_p and C_V is notified by γ.
$$\gamma = C_p / C_V$$
It is also known as heat capacity ratio, then
$$C_V = \frac{R}{r-1} \text{ and } C_p = \gamma \frac{R}{r-1}$$

EXAMPLE |4| Mixture of Two Gases

A gaseous mixture enclosed in a vessel consists of 1g mole of a gas $A\left(\gamma = \frac{5}{3}\right)$ and some amount of gas $B\left(\gamma = \frac{7}{5}\right)$ at a temperature T. The gases A and B do not react with each other and are assumed to be ideal.

Find number of gram moles of the gas B, if γ for the gaseous mixture is $\left(\frac{19}{13}\right)$.

Sol. For an ideal gas,
$$\frac{C_p}{C_V} = \gamma \text{ and } C_p - C_V = R$$

So, combining above equations, we get
$$C_V = \frac{R}{\gamma - 1}$$
$$(C_V)_A = \frac{R}{\frac{5}{2} - 1} = \frac{3}{2}R$$

and $$(C_V)_B = \frac{5}{2}R$$

and $$(C_V)_{\text{mix}} = \frac{R}{\frac{19}{13} - 1} = \frac{13}{6}R$$

Now, from conservation of energy
$$U_{\text{mix}} = U_A + U_B$$
or $$\Delta U_{\text{mix}} = \Delta U_A + \Delta U_B$$
$$\Rightarrow (\mu_A + \mu_B)(C_V)_{\text{mix}} \Delta T = \mu_A (C_V)_A \Delta T + \mu_B (C_V)_B \Delta T$$

$$\Rightarrow \qquad (C_V)_{\text{mix}} = \frac{\mu_A (C_V)_A + \mu_B (C_V)_B}{\mu_A + \mu_B}$$

$$\Rightarrow \qquad \frac{13}{6} R = \frac{1 \times \frac{3}{2} R + \mu_B \times \frac{5}{2} R}{1 + \mu_B}$$

$$\Rightarrow \qquad 13 + 13\mu_B = 9 + 15\mu_B$$

$$\Rightarrow \qquad \mu_B = 2 \, \text{g-mol}$$

EXAMPLE |5| Monoatomic Gas

Find molar specific heat for the process $p = \dfrac{a}{T}$ for a monoatomic gas. $\left(a = \text{constant}, C_V = \dfrac{3}{2} R \right)$

Sol. From first law of thermodynamics,

$$\Delta Q = \Delta W + \Delta U$$

$$\Rightarrow \qquad C = \frac{\Delta Q}{\Delta T} = \frac{\Delta W}{\Delta T} + \frac{\Delta U}{\Delta T}$$

or $\qquad C = \dfrac{\Delta W}{\Delta T} + C_V \qquad [\because \Delta U = C_V \Delta T]$

$$C = \frac{p \Delta V}{\Delta T} + C_V \qquad [\because \Delta W = p \Delta V] \,\,...(\text{i})$$

For the process,

$$pV = RT \qquad [\because \text{ for monoatomic gas}, \mu = 1]$$

$$\Rightarrow \qquad V = \frac{RT}{p} = \frac{RT^2}{a}$$

$$\Rightarrow \qquad \frac{\Delta V}{\Delta T} = \frac{dV}{dT} = \frac{2RT}{a} \qquad\qquad ...(\text{ii})$$

Substituting value of Eq. (ii) in Eq. (i), we get

$$= p \left(\frac{2RT}{a} \right) + C_V = \frac{a}{T} \left(\frac{2RT}{a} \right) + C_V \qquad \left[\because p = \frac{a}{T} \right]$$

$$\Rightarrow \quad C = 2R + C_V = 2R + \frac{3}{2} R = \frac{7}{2} R$$

THERMODYNAMIC STATE VARIABLES AND EQUATION OF STATE

Every **equilibrium state** of a thermodynamic system is completely described by specific values of some macroscopic variables and these are called **state variables**. e.g. Pressure, volume, temperature and mass.

Equilibrium State

A system is not always in a equilibrium state but with time, it comes in mechanical and thermal equilibrium state.

e.g. A mixture of gases undergoing an explosive chemical reaction (e.g. a mixture of petrol vapour and air when ignited by a spark) is not an equilibrium state but with time the gas attains a uniform temperature and pressure and comes to thermal and mechanical equilibrium with its surroundings.

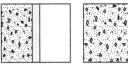

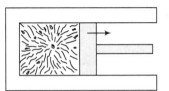

(a) Partition in the box is suddenly removed leading to free expansion of the gas

(b) A mixture of gases undergoing an explosive chemical reaction

Equation of State

The various state variables are not necessarily independent. The equation which represents the relationship between the state variables of a system is called its **equation of state**.

e.g. For an ideal gas, the equation of state is the ideal gas equation $\qquad pV = \mu RT$

For a fixed amount of gas given, there are thus only two independent variables, say p and V or T and V. The pressure-volume curve for a fixed temperature is called an **isotherm**.

EXTENSIVE AND INTENSIVE STATE VARIABLES

The state variables are of two types such as extensive and intensive

Extensive State Variables

Extensive state variables indicate the **size** of the system.

Let us consider that a system in equilibrium is divided into two equal parts. The variable whose values get halved in each part are **extensive**. e.g. Internal energy (U), volume (V), total mass (M) are extensive variables.

Intensive State Variables

These are state variables that do not depend on the size of the system. Again consider a system in equilibrium divided into two equal parts. The variables that remain unchanged for each part are **intensive**.

e.g. Pressure (p), temperature (T) and density (ρ) are intensive variables.

Note

The extensive variables change with the size of the system, but the intensive variables do not change with size.

THERMODYNAMIC PROCESSES

When state of a system changes or the state variables changes with time, then this process is known as **thermodynamic process.**

Quasi-Static Process

Quasi-static process is a hypothetical concept. Practically, processes that are sufficiently slow are considered as quasi-static.

The system changes its variables (p, T, V) so slowly that it remains in thermal and mechanical equilibrium with its surroundings throughout. In a quasi-static process, at every stage, the difference in the pressure of the system and the external pressure is infinitesimally small. The same is true for the temperature difference between the system and its surroundings.

To take a gas from the state (p, T) to another state (p', T') *via* a quasi-static process, we change the external pressure by a very small amount, allow the system to equalise its pressure with that of the surroundings and continue the process infinitely slowly until the system achieves the pressure p'.

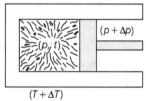

(T + ΔT)

Changes in temperature and
pressure in quasi-static process

Similarly, to change the temperature, we introduce an infinitesimal temperature difference between the system and the surrounding reservoirs and by choosing reservoirs of progressively different temperatures T to T'. The system achieves the temperature T'.

Note

The processes that do not involve accelerated motion of piston-large temperature gradient and pressure gradient are quasi-static.

Some Important Processes

(i) An **isothermal process** occurs at constant temperature.

e.g. Freezing of water at 0°C to form ice at 0°C.

(ii) An **isobaric process** occurs at constant pressure.

e.g. Boiling of water in a open container.

(iii) An **isochoric process** is one in which volume is kept constant, meaning that the work done by the system will be zero.

e.g. Heat given to a system with fixed walls.

(iv) An **adiabatic process** does not allow transfer of heat by or to the system.

e.g. Rapid compression, like filling of a cycle tube by a hand pump.

(v) **Cyclic and non-cyclic process** In cyclic process, initial and final states are same while in non-cyclic processes, they are different.

EXAMPLE |6| **Examples of Various Processes**

Give an example of each of given below

(i) Isobaric process   (ii) Isochoric process

(iii) Isothermal process   (iv) Adiabatic process

Sol. (i) **Isobaric process** Cooking in an open lid container.

(ii) **Isochoric process** Cooking in a pressure cooker.

(iii) **Isothermal process** Boiling of water at atmospheric pressure.

(iv) **Adiabatic process** Expulsion of air from a bursted tyre (tube).

EXAMPLE |7| **Condition of Adiabatic Process**

How an adiabatic can be carried practically?

Sol. For an adiabatic process, $\Delta Q = 0$. So, if a process is carried very fast so that heat cannot transferred from system to surroundings and *vice-versa*, it is an adiabatic process.

Work Done in an Isothermal Process

For an isothermal process, temperature remains constant.

For an ideal gas, the equation of state is given by

$$pV = \text{constant}$$

So, gas follows Boyle's law

$$p_i V_i = p_f V_f, \text{ for isothermal process}$$

p-V Diagram

On a p-V diagram, an isotherm is a curve that connects points of same temperature.

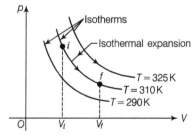

An isothermal expansion process

Work Done

Work done in an isothermal process = area under p-V graph

$$= \int_{V_i}^{V_f} p \, dV = \mu RT \int_{V_i}^{V_f} \frac{dV}{V} \left[\because PV = \mu RT \therefore P = \frac{\mu RT}{V} \right]$$

$$= \mu RT \ln(V)_{V_i}^{V_f} = \mu RT \ln(V_f - V_i)$$

$$W_{\text{iso}} = \mu RT \ln \left(\frac{V_f}{V_i} \right)$$

Work done, $\boxed{W_{\text{iso}} = 2.303 \, \mu RT \log \left(\frac{V_f}{V_i} \right)}$

As temperature of ideal gas remains constant.

$\therefore \qquad\qquad \Delta U = 0$

So, by first law of thermodynamics

$$\Delta Q = \Delta W + \Delta U$$

$$\Rightarrow \qquad \Delta Q = \Delta W = \mu RT \ln \left(\frac{V_f}{V_i} \right)$$

where, μ = number of moles, R = gas constant and T = temperature

V_f and V_i are the final and initial volumes of the gas, respectively.

i.e. Heat supplied in an isothermal change is used to do work against surroundings or if the work is done on the system, then the equal amount of heat energy will be liberate by the system.

Let us consider two cases for finding the nature of the work done.

Case I If $V_f > V_i$, then $W > 0$

Thus, it is an **isothermal expansion** which means the gas absorbs heat.

Case II If $V_f < V_i$, then $W < 0$

Thus, it is an **isothermal compression**, work is done on the gas by the environment and heat is released.

EXAMPLE |8| **Work Done in Isothermal Process**
Three moles of an ideal gas kept at constant temperature of 300 K are compressed from a volume of 4 L to 1 L. Calculate the work done in the process. Take R as 8.31 J/mol-K.

Sol. Given, $\mu = 3$, $T = 300$ K, $V_i = 4$ L, $V_f = 1$ L,

$$R = 8.31 \, \text{J/mol-K}, W = ?$$

Work done in isothermal process is given by

$$W = 2.303 \, \mu RT \log \frac{V_f}{V_i}$$

$$= 2.303 \times 3 \times 8.31 \times 300 \log \frac{1}{4} = -1.037 \times 10^4 \, \text{J}$$

WORK DONE IN AN ADIABATIC PROCESS

In an adiabatic process, there is no exchange of heat between system and the surroundings.

By first law, $\qquad \Delta Q = \Delta U + \Delta W$ ...(i)

For adiabatic process, $\quad \Delta Q = 0$

$\therefore \qquad\qquad \Delta U = -\Delta W$

For adiabatic process,

$$\boxed{pV^\gamma = \text{constant}}$$

where, $\qquad\qquad \gamma = \dfrac{C_p}{C_V}$

Thus, if we consider an ideal gas with the adiabatic range from (p_i, V_i) to (p_f, V_f), then

$$p_i V_i^\gamma = p_f V_f^\gamma = \text{constant}$$

In the propagation of sound in air, the compression and rare fraction of air molecules comes under adiabatic process. The air molecules oscillates, so fast that neither the heat comes in nor comes out from the oscillating particles region. That is why oscillation of particles during sound wave propagation comes under adiabatic process.

Note

Relation between p and T; V and T in an adiabatic process
$$p^{1-\gamma} \cdot T^\gamma = \text{Constant and } V^{\gamma-1} \cdot T = \text{Constant}$$

p-V Diagram

On a p-V diagram, the process is represented by an adiabatic curve as shown.

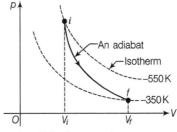

An adiabatic expansion process

A curve representing an adiabatic process is called an **adiabat**. If we differentiate pV^γ = constant, we get

$$dp \, V^\gamma + p\gamma V^{\gamma-1} \, dV = 0$$

$$\Rightarrow \qquad \frac{dp}{dV} = -\gamma \left(\frac{p}{V} \right)$$

So, slope of adiabatic curve $= -\gamma \left(\dfrac{p}{V} \right)$, which is γ times more than slope of an isotherm.

By definition of specific heat,

$$C = \frac{\Delta Q}{m \Delta T} = \frac{Q}{m \Delta T}, \Delta Q = 0 \text{ in adiabatic process.}$$

So, $C = 0$ (adiabatic process)

So, specific heat of a gas in adiabatic compression or expansion is zero.

Work Done

Also, work done in an adiabatic process

$$W = \int_{V_i}^{V_f} p \, dV = \int_{V_i}^{V_f} \frac{K}{V^\gamma} \, dV$$

$$\because \quad pV^\gamma = K \qquad\qquad\qquad [\text{constant}]$$

$$\therefore \quad p_i V_i^\gamma = p_f V_f^\gamma = K \qquad [\text{constant}]$$

where, $pV^\gamma = \text{constant} = K$

$$= K \left| \frac{V^{-\gamma+1}}{-\gamma+1} \right|_{V_i}^{V_f} = \frac{K}{1-\gamma} \left[\frac{1}{V_f^{\gamma-1}} - \frac{1}{V_i^{\gamma-1}} \right]$$

Thus, $W = \dfrac{1}{1-\gamma} \left[\dfrac{p_f V_f^\gamma}{V_f^{\gamma-1}} - \dfrac{p_i V_i^\gamma}{V_i^{\gamma-1}} \right] = \dfrac{p_i V_i - p_f V_f}{\gamma-1}$

$pV = \mu RT$, $p_i V_i = \mu RT_i$ and $p_f V_f = \mu RT_f$

$$\boxed{\text{Work done, } W = \frac{\mu R (T_i - T_f)}{\gamma-1}}$$

Now, by first law of thermodynamics

$$\Delta Q = \Delta U + \Delta W$$

As, $\Delta Q = 0 \Rightarrow \Delta U = -\Delta W$

So, if work is done by the system, the internal energy and so the temperature of system falls i.e. $W > 0$, $T_f < T_i$. Conversely, if work is done on the system, the internal energy and so the temperature of system increases.

i.e. $W < 0, T_f > T_i$

All nearly practical adiabatic processes occur so rapidly that no transfer of energy as heat occurs between the system and surroundings. e.g. Sudden bursting of bicycle tube and propagation of sound waves in air.

The p-V curves of an ideal gas for two adiabatic processes connecting two isotherms is shown in the figure

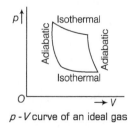

p-V curve of an ideal gas

EXAMPLE |9| **Compressing the Cylinder**
A cylinder containing one gram molecule of the gas was compressed adiabatically until its temperature lose from 27°C to 97°C. Calculate the work done and heat produced in the gas. Take γ as 1.5

Sol. Given, $T_i = 27°C = 27 + 273 = 300 \text{ K}$

$$T_f = 97°C = 97 + 273 = 370 \text{ K}, \gamma = 1.5$$

Work done in adiabatic compression is given by

$$W = \frac{R}{1-\gamma}(T_i - T_f) = \frac{8.31}{1-1.5}(300-370) = 1163.4 \text{ J}$$

Heat produced, $H = \dfrac{W}{J} = \dfrac{1163.4}{4.2} = 277 \text{ cal}$

Work Done in an Isochoric Process

In case of an isochoric process, volume of the system remains constant. So, if heat is added to system, its pressure increases and if heat is extracted from the system, pressure will be reduced.

Equation of State

In this process, p and T changes but $V = \text{constant}$. Gay-Lussac's law is obeyed.

$$\Rightarrow \quad p \propto T \Rightarrow \frac{p_1}{T_1} = \frac{p_2}{T_2}$$

where, $V = \text{constant}$

So, $\boxed{\text{Work done, } \Delta W = 0}$

$$\Rightarrow \quad \Delta W = p \, \Delta V = 0 \qquad [\because \Delta V = 0]$$

From first law of thermodynamics, $\Delta Q = \Delta U$

Hence, in an isochoric process, the entire heat given to or taken from the system goes to change its internal energy and temperature of the system.

The change in temperature can be determined by the equation.

$$\boxed{\Delta U = \mu C_V \, \Delta T}$$

WORK DONE IN AN ISOBARIC PROCESS

When a thermodynamic system undergoes a physical change at constant pressure, then this thermodynamic process is known as **isobaric process**.

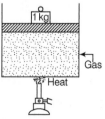

A simple arrangement to show isobaric process

e.g. A gas is heated in a piston cylinder arrangement with constant weight over the cylinder.

Suppose the pressure p of a gas remains constant and its volume changes from V_i to V_f, then the work done by the gas is

$$W = \int_{V_i}^{V_f} p \, dV = p \int_{V_i}^{V_f} dV = p(V_f - V_i)$$

$$\boxed{\text{Work done}, W = \mu R(T_f - T_i)} \qquad [\because pV = \mu RT]$$

As the temperature of the gas changes, so its internal energy also changes. Hence, in an isobaric process, the absorbed heat goes partly to increase internal energy and partly to do work.

EXAMPLE |10| Raising the Temperature of Ideal Gas

If 70 cal of heat is required to raise the temperature of 2 mol of an ideal gas at constant pressure from 30°C to 35°C, calculate

(i) work done by the gas

(ii) increase in internal energy of gas.
Take R = 2 cal/mol-K.

Sol. (i) In isobaric process, p = constant

and $\quad \Delta W$ = work done = $p\Delta V$

$\qquad = nR(\Delta T) = 2 \times 2 \times (35 - 30) = 20$ cal

(ii) $\Delta U = \Delta Q - \Delta W \qquad$ [from first law]

$\qquad = 70 - 20 = 50$ cal

EXAMPLE |11| Isobaric Process

Find the ratio of $\dfrac{\Delta Q}{\Delta U}$ and $\dfrac{\Delta Q}{\Delta W}$ in an isobaric process. The ratio of molar specific heats, $\dfrac{C_p}{C_V} = \gamma$.

Sol. In an isobaric process, p = constant

$\therefore \qquad C = C_p$

and $\qquad \dfrac{\Delta Q}{\Delta U} = \dfrac{nC_p \Delta T}{nC_V \Delta T} = \dfrac{C_p}{C_V} = \gamma$

also $\qquad \dfrac{\Delta Q}{\Delta W} = \dfrac{\Delta Q}{\Delta Q - \Delta U}$

$\qquad\qquad = \dfrac{nC_p \Delta T}{nC_p \Delta T - nC_V \Delta T} = \dfrac{C_p}{C_p - C_V} = \dfrac{\gamma}{\gamma - 1}$

EXAMPLE |12| Ratio of C_p and C_V

3 mol of an ideal gas at 300 K is isothermally expanded to five times its initial volume and heated at this constant volume so that the pressure is raised to its initial value before expansion.

In the whole process, heat supplied to the gas is 83.14 kJ. Calculate ratio C_p/C_V for the gas. [$\log_e 5 = 1.61$ and $R = 8.31$ J mol^{-1} K^{-1}]

Sol. Process is shown in the indicator diagram.

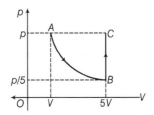

For isothermal process AB,

$$\Delta W = \mu RT \log_e (V_f/V_i)$$
$$= 3 \times 8.31 \times 300 \times \log_e 5$$
$$= 12.03 \text{ kJ}$$

As for isothermal process, $\Delta T = 0$

$\Rightarrow \qquad\qquad \Delta U = 0$

and by first law, $\Delta Q = \Delta W = 12.03$ kJ

For isochoric process BC,

$$V = \text{constant} \Rightarrow \Delta W = 0$$
$$\Delta U = \mu C_V \Delta T = 3C_V \Delta T$$

Now, for process BC, $\dfrac{p_B}{T_B} = \dfrac{p_C}{T_C}$

$\Rightarrow \qquad \dfrac{P/5}{300} = \dfrac{P}{T_C} \Rightarrow T_C = 1500$ K

$\Rightarrow \qquad \Delta T_{BC} = T_C - T_B = 1500 - 300 = 1200$ K

So, $\Delta U = \mu C_V \Delta T = 3 \times C_V \times 1200 = 3.6 \, C_V$ kJ

$\therefore \qquad (\Delta Q)_{\text{isochoric}} = 3.6 \, C_V$ kJ

Now, given that $\Delta Q_{\text{process } ABC} = 83.14$ kJ

$\Rightarrow \qquad \Delta Q_{ABC} = \Delta Q_{\text{isothermal}} + \Delta Q_{\text{isochoric}}$

$\Rightarrow \qquad 83.14 = 12.03 + 3.6 \, C_V \Rightarrow C_V = 19.75$ J/mol-K

and $\qquad C_p = C_V + R = 19.75 + 8.31$

$\qquad\qquad = 28.05$ J/mol -K

$\therefore \qquad \gamma = \dfrac{C_p}{C_V} = \dfrac{28.05}{19.75} = 1.42$

WORK DONE IN A CYCLIC PROCESS

A single process or a series of processes in which, after certain interchanges of heat and work, the system is restored to its initial state known as a **cyclic process**. As both initial and final states are same in a cyclic process, $\Delta U = U_f - U_i = 0$.

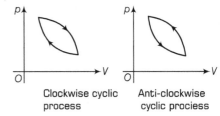

Clockwise cyclic process   Anti-clockwise cyclic process

For a cyclic process, p-V graph is a closed curve and area enclosed by the curve is equal to the work done.

From first law of thermodynamics,
$$\Delta Q = \Delta U + \Delta W$$
For cyclic process, $\Delta U = 0$ or $\Delta Q = \Delta W$

So, heat supplied to the system is converted into work done and *vice-versa*.

Let (V_1, p_1) shows the initial state of a gas and (V_2, p_2) shows the final state. The gas reached between A and B by both paths AB and BA.

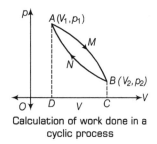

Calculation of work done in a cyclic process

So, work done by the gas for expansion from A to B, is
$$W_1 = \text{area } AMBCDA$$

Let the system return back to the initial state $A(V_1, p_1)$ by the path BA. The complete process is cyclic.

Work done on the gas for compression from B to A is
$$W = -\text{area } BNADCB$$

Net work done by the gas in the cyclic process
$$W_{A \to B \to A} = W_1 + W_2$$
$$= \text{area } AMBCDA - \text{area } BNADCB$$
$$= \text{area } AMBNA$$

Hence, the work done in a cyclic process is equal to the area enclosed by the loop.

- If the cycle is clockwise, work done is positive and if the cycle is anti-clockwise, the work done is negative.
- Cyclic processes are of great importance or mechanical machines like engines and refrigerators operates in cycles; in which the system do work by using influx of heat and is restored to its initial state.
- A process in which the system do not return to its initial state after undergoing a series of change is known as non-cyclic process.

Summary of thermodynamic processes

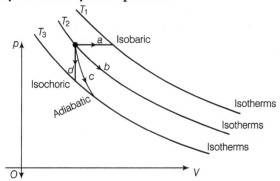

p-V diagram to represent various thermodynamic processes

Thermodynamic Processes

Process	Constant Quantity	Path	Heat/Work/Internal energy
Isobaric	p	a	$\Delta Q = nC_p \Delta T$, $\Delta W = p\Delta V$ $\Delta U = nC_V \Delta T$
Isochoric	V	d	$\Delta Q = \Delta U = nC_V \Delta T$ $\Delta W = 0$
Isothermal	T	b	$\Delta Q = \Delta W = nRT\ln V_f / V_i$ $\Delta U = 0$
Adiabatic	pV^γ	c	$\Delta Q = 0$; $\Delta W = -\Delta U$

EXAMPLE |13| Change of State

When a system goes from state A to state B, it is supplied with 400 J of heat and it does 100 J of work.

(i) For process $A \to B$, what is the change in internal energy?

(ii) If the system moves from B to A, what will be change in system, internal energy?

(iii) If in moving from A to B along a different path where, work done on the system is 400 J, how much heat does it absorb for this path?

Sol. (i) From first law of thermodynamics,
$$\Delta U_{AB} = \Delta Q_{AB} - \Delta W_{AB} = (400 - 100)\,\text{J} = 300\,\text{J}$$

(ii) As ΔU for a closed path is zero,
$$\Delta U_{AB} + \Delta U_{BA} = 0$$
$$\Delta U_{BA} = -\Delta U_{AB} = -300\,\text{J}$$

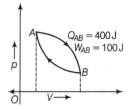

(iii) As ΔU_{AB} is same for any other path, so
$$\Delta U_{AB} = \Delta Q - \Delta W$$
$$300\,\text{J} = \Delta Q - (-400\,\text{J}) \Rightarrow \Delta Q = -100\,\text{J}$$

TOPIC PRACTICE 1

OBJECTIVE Type Questions

1. If two systems are in thermal equilibrium with each other, it means their
   (a) masses are equal, temperatures may be unequal
   (b) temperatures are equal
   (c) masses and temperatures are equal
   (d) None of the above

   Sol. (b) If two systems are in thermal equilibrium with each other, it means their temperatures must be same. Masses may be equal or unequal.

2. Choose the correct option.
   (a) Zeroth law gives the concept of temperature
   (b) Temperature measures the 'hotness' of the body
   (c) Heat flows from higher temperature to lower temperature until thermal equilibrium is attained
   (d) All of the above

   Sol. (d)

   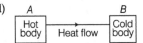

   Heat flows from body A to body B because temperature of body A is higher. At thermal equilibrium, $T_A{}' = T_B{}'$

   $\left.\begin{array}{l} A \text{ in equilibrium with } C \\ B \text{ in equilibrium with } C \end{array}\right\} \Rightarrow A$ in equilibrium with B

   zeroth law.

3. For isothermal expansion of an ideal gas,
   (a) $\Delta U = +$ ve   (b) $\Delta Q = +$ ve
   (c) $\Delta W = +$ ve   (d) Both (b) and (c)

   Sol. (d) For isothermal expansion,
   $$\Delta U = 0 \Rightarrow \Delta Q = \Delta W$$
   Here, $\Delta W \rightarrow +$ ve $\Rightarrow \Delta Q \rightarrow +$ ve

4. Heat capacity of a substance depends on
   (a) the mass of the substance
   (b) the temperature of the substance
   (c) Both (a) and (b)
   (d) Neither (a) nor (b)

   Sol. (c) S depends on the mass of the substance and its temperature.

   Heat capacity, $S = \dfrac{\text{Heat consumed by given mass}}{\text{Temperature raised}}$

   If given mass is increased, then S increases.

5. A system is provided with 200 cal of heat and the work done by the system on the surroundings is 40 J. Then, its internal energy
   (a) increases by 600 J   (b) decreases by 800 J
   (c) increases by 800 J   (d) decreases by 50 J

   Sol. (c) Given, $dQ = +200$ cal $= 200 \times 4.2 = 840$ J, $dW = +40$ J
   From first law of thermodynamics,
   $$dQ = dU + dW$$
   $$dU = dQ - dW = 840 - 40 = 800\,\text{J}$$
   So, the internal energy of the system increases by 800 J.

6. An ideal gas undergoes cyclic process $ABCDA$ as shown in given p-V diagram. The amount of work done by the gas is   **[NCERT Exemplar]**

   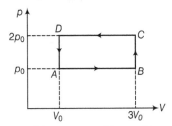

   (a) $6p_0 V_0$ (b) $-2p_0 V_0$ (c) $+2p_0 V_0$ (d) $+4p_0 V_0$

   Sol. (b) Consider the p-V diagram given in the question.
   Work done in the process $ABCD$
   $$= \text{area of rectangle } ABCDA$$
   $$= (AB) \times BC = (3V_0 - V_0) \times (2p_0 - p_0)$$
   $$= 2V_0 \times p_0 = 2\,p_0\,V_0$$
   As the process is going anti-clockwise, hence there is a net compression in the gas. So, work done by the gas $= -2\,p_0\,V_0$.

VERY SHORT ANSWER Type Questions

7. Can a system be heated and its temperature remain constant?   **[NCERT Exemplar]**

   Sol. If the system does work against the surroundings so that it compensates for the heat supplied, the temperature can remains constant.

8. Air pressure in a car tyre increases during driving. Explain.   **[NCERT Exemplar]**

   Sol. During driving, temperature of the gas increases while its volume remains constant. So, according to Charles' law, at constant V, $p \propto T$. Therefore, pressure of gas increases.

9. An electric heater supplies heat to a system at a rate of 100 W. If the system performs work at a rate of 75 J/s. At what rate, is the internal energy increasing?   **[NCERT]**

   Sol. Heat energy supplied per second by the heater
   $$\Delta Q = 100\,\text{W} = 100\,\text{J/s}$$
   Work done by the system $(\Delta W) = + 75$ J/s
   Rate of change in internal energy $(\Delta U) = ?$
   According to first law of thermodynamics,
   $$\Delta U = \Delta Q - \Delta W$$
   $$= 100 - 75 = 25\,\text{J/s}$$
   $$= 25\,\text{W}$$

10. If a gas is suddenly compressed, its temperature increases, why?

Sol. Because sudden compression of a gas is an adiabatic process. According to the first law of thermodynamics,

$$\Delta Q = \Delta U + \Delta W$$
$$\because \qquad \Delta Q = 0$$
$$\therefore \qquad \Delta U = -\Delta W$$

$\because \Delta W$ = negative because work done on the gas

Thus, ΔU increases and gas temperature rises.

11. Find the values of two molar specific heats of nitrogen. Given, $\gamma = 1.41$ and $R = 8.31 \, \text{J mol}^{-1}\text{K}^{-1}$.

Sol. Given, $R = 8.31 \, \text{J mol}^{-1}\text{K}^{-1}$ and $\gamma = 1.41$

We know, $C_V = \dfrac{R}{(\gamma - 1)} = \dfrac{8.31}{(1.41 - 1)} = 20.3 \, \text{Jmol}^{-1}\text{K}^{-1}$

$\because \qquad \dfrac{C_p}{C_V} = \gamma \Rightarrow C_p = C_V \cdot \gamma$

$\qquad\qquad = 20.3 \times 1.41 = 28.623 \, \text{J/mol-K}$

12. Write conditions for an isothermal process.

Sol. The conditions for an isothermal process are
   (i) The walls should be diathermic.
   (ii) The process should be quasi-static.

13. Why a gas is cooled when it expand?

Sol. When a gas expands, it does work on the surroundings. This work is done on the expense of internal energy and that is why its internal energy and so its temperature decreases.

14. Apply first law of thermodynamics for isothermal expansion of an ideal gas.

Sol. First law of thermodynamics gives, $\Delta Q = \Delta U + \Delta W$

For an isothermal expansion, $\Delta U = 0$.
So, $\qquad\qquad \Delta Q = \Delta W$

For an isothermal expansion of the ideal gas work done by the gas is equal to the heat given to the ideal gas.

15. Two isothermal curves do not intersect each other, why?

Sol. If two isothermal curves intersect, this implies that the pressure and volume of a gas are the same at two different temperatures, that's impossible.

16. When a bottle of cold carbonated drink is opened, a slight fog is formed around the opening, why?

Sol. In opening of bottle, adiabatic expansion of gas causes lowering of temperature.

17. Why air quickly leaking out of a balloon becomes cooler?

Sol. Leaking of air is adiabatic expansion and adiabatic expansion produces cooling.

SHORT ANSWER Type Questions

18. A person of mass 60 kg wants to lose 5 kg by going up and down a 10 m high stairs. Assume he burns twice as much fat while going up than coming down. If 1 kg of fat is burnt on expending 7000 kcal calories, how many times must he go up and down to reduce his weight by 5 kg?

[NCERT Exemplar]

Sol. Here, $m = 60 \, \text{kg}$, $g = 10 \, \text{m/s}^2$, $h = 10 \, \text{m}$

In going up and down once, number of kilocalories burnt

$$= (mgh + mgh/2) = \frac{3}{2} mgh$$

$$= \frac{3}{2} \times \frac{60 \times 10 \times 10}{4.2 \times 1000} = \frac{15}{7} \, \text{kcal}$$

Total number of kilocalories to be burnt for losing 5 kg of weight $= 5 \times 7000 = 35000 \, \text{kcal}$

$\therefore$ Number of times of the person has to go up and down

the stairs $= \dfrac{35000}{15/7} = \dfrac{35 \times 7}{15} \times 10^3 = 16.3 \times 10^3$ times

19. A system goes from P to Q by two different paths in the p-V diagram as shown in figure. Heat given to the system in path 1 is 1000 J. The work done by the system along path 1 is more than path 2 by 100 J. What is the heat exchanged by the system in path 2? [NCERT Exemplar]

Sol. For path 1, Heat given $\quad Q_1 = +1000 \, \text{J}$

Work done $\qquad\qquad\qquad = W_1$ [Let]

For path 2, Work done $W_2 = (W_1 - 100) \, \text{J}$

Heat given $\qquad\qquad Q_2 = ?$

As change in internal energy between two states for different path is same.

$$\Delta U = Q_1 - W_1 = Q_2 - W_2$$
$$1000 - W_1 = Q_2 - (W_1 - 100)$$
$$Q_2 = 1000 - 100 = 900 \, \text{J}$$

20. What amount of heat must be supplied to 2.0×10^{-2} kg of nitrogen (at room temperature) to raise its temperature by 45°C at constant pressure? (Molecular mass of $N_2 = 28$, $R = 8.3 \, \text{J mol}^{-1}\text{K}^{-1}$) [NCERT]

Sol. Here, mass of gas, $m = 2 \times 10^{-2} \, \text{kg} = 20 \, \text{g}$

Rise in temperature, $\Delta T = 45°C$

Heat required, $\Delta Q = ?$

Molecular mass, $M = 28$

Number of moles, $n = \dfrac{m}{M} = \dfrac{20}{28} = 0.714$

As nitrogen is a diatomic gas, molar specific heat at constant pressure is

$$C_p = \dfrac{7}{2}R = \dfrac{7}{2} \times 8.3 \, \text{J mol}^{-1}\text{K}^{-1}$$

As $\Delta Q = nC_p \Delta T$

$\therefore \quad \Delta Q = 0.714 \times \dfrac{7}{2} \times 8.3 \times 45 \, \text{J} = 933.4 \, \text{J}$

21. A geyser heats water flowing at the rate of 3.0 L/min from 27°C to 77°C. If the geyser operates on a gas burner, what is the rate of consumption of the fuel if its heat of combustion is 4.0×10^4 J/g?.   **[NCERT]**

Sol. Here, volume of water heated = 3.0 L/min

Mass of water heated, $m = 3000$ g/min

Rise in temperature, $\Delta T = 77 - 27 = 50°$ C

Specific heat of water, $C = 4.2 \, \text{J g}^{-1} \, °\text{C}^{-1}$

Amount of heat used, $\Delta Q = mC\Delta T = 3000 \times 4.2 \times 50$

$= 63 \times 10^4 \, \text{J/min}$

Heat of combustion $= 4 \times 10^4$ J/g

Rate of combustion of fuel $= \dfrac{63 \times 10^4}{4 \times 10^4}$

$= 15.75 \, \text{g / min}$

22. Two bodies at different temperatures T_1 and T_2 are brought in contact. Under what condition, they settle to mean temperature? (after they attain equilibrium)   **[NCERT Exemplar]**

Sol. Let m_1 and m_2 are masses of bodies with specific heats s_1 and s_2, then if their temperature after they are in thermal equilibrium is T.

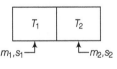

Then, if $T_1 > T > T_2$ and assuming no heat loss.

Heat lost by hot body = heat gained by cold body

$$m_1 s_1 (T_1 - T) = m_2 s_2 (T - T_2)$$

$\Rightarrow \quad \dfrac{m_1 s_1 T_1 + m_2 s_2 T_2}{m_1 s_1 + m_2 s_2} = T$ [equilibrium temperature]

So for, bodies to settle down to mean temperature,

$$m_1 = m_2 \quad \text{and} \quad s_1 = s_2$$

means bodies have same specific heat and have equal masses.

Then, $T = \dfrac{T_1 + T_2}{2}$ [mean temperature]

23. A cylinder with a movable piston contains 3 moles of hydrogen at standard temperature and pressure. The walls of the cylinder are made of a heat insulator and the piston is insulated by having a pile of sand on it. By what factor, does the pressure of the gas increase if the gas is compressed to half its original volume? **[NCERT]**

Sol. As no heat is allowed to be exchanged, the process is adiabatic.

$\therefore \quad p_2 V_2^{\gamma} = p_1 V_1^{\gamma}$ or $\dfrac{p_2}{p_1} = \left(\dfrac{V_1}{V_2}\right)^{\gamma}$

As $V_2 = \dfrac{1}{2}V_1$ or $\dfrac{p_2}{p_1} = \left(\dfrac{V_1}{1/2 V_1}\right)^{1.4} = 2^{1.4} = 2.64$

24. The initial state of a certain gas is (p_i, V_i, T_i). It undergoes expansion till its volume becomes V_f. Consider the following two cases

(i) The expansion takes place at constant temperature.

(ii) The expansion takes place at constant pressure.

Plot the p-V diagram for each case. In which of the two cases, is the work done by the gas more?   **[NCERT Exemplar]**

Sol.

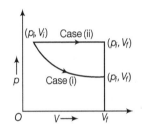

The p-V diagram for each case is shown in the figure.

In case (i) $p_i V_i = p_f V_f$, therefore process is isothermal.

In case (ii), pressure is constant, work done = area under the p-V curve, so work done is more when the gas expands at constant pressure.

25. When ice melts, then change in internal energy is greater than the heat supplied, why?

Sol. When ice melts, volume of water formed is less than that of ice. So, surroundings (environment) does work on the system (ice). And by first law,

$$\Delta Q = \Delta W + \Delta U$$

$\Rightarrow \quad \Delta U = \Delta Q - \Delta W$

(ΔW = negative as work is done on the system)

$\Rightarrow \quad \Delta U > \Delta Q$

LONG ANSWER Type I Questions

26. Explain, why?

(i) 500 J of work is done on a gas to reduce its volume by compression adiabatically. What is the change in internal energy of the gas?

(ii) The coolant in a chemical or a nuclear plant , i.e. the liquid used to prevent the different parts of a plant from getting too hot should have high specific heat.

(iii) The climate of a harbour town is more temperate than that of a town in a desert at the same latitude [NCERT]

Sol. (i) ∵ process is adiabatic

∴ $\Delta Q = 0$

Work done on the gas, $\Delta W = -500\text{J}$

According to the first law of thermodynamics.

$\Delta Q = \Delta U + \Delta W \Rightarrow \Delta U = -\Delta W = 500\text{J}$

(ii) This is because heat absorbed by a substance (coolant) is directly proportional to the specific heat of the substance.

(iii) This is because in a harbour town, the relative humidity is more than in a desert town. Hence, the climate of a harbour town is without extremes of hot and cold.

27. A thermodynamic system is taken from an original state D to an intermediate state E by the linear process shown in figure.

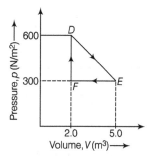

Its volume is then reduced to the original value from E to F by an isobaric process. Calculate the total work done by the gas from D to E to F. [NCERT]

Sol. From figure, change in pressure,
$$dp = DF = 600 - 300 = 300 \text{ Nm}^{-2}$$

Change in volume, $dV = EF = 5 - 2 = 3 \text{ m}^3$

Work done by the gas from D to E to F = area of ΔDEF

$$W = \frac{1}{2} \times EF \times DF = \frac{1}{2} \times 300 \times 3 = 450\text{J}$$

28. In changing the state of a gas adiabatically from an equilibrium state A to another equilibrium state B, an amount of work equal to 22.3 J is done on the system. If the gas is taken from state A to B via a process in which the net heat absorbed by the system is 9.35 cal, how much is the net work done by the system in the latter case? (Take, 1 cal = 4.19 J). [NCERT]

💡 According to first law of thermodynamics, if ΔQ heat energy is given (or taken) to a thermodynamic system which is partially utilised in doing work (ΔW) and remaining part increases (or decreases) the internal energy of the system.

Sol. Given, work done $(W) = -22.3$ J

Work done is taken negative as work is done on the system.

In an adiabatic change, $\Delta Q = 0$

Using first law of thermodynamics,
$$\Delta U = \Delta Q - W = 0 - (-22.3) = 22.3 \text{ J}$$

For another process between states A and B,

Heat absorbed $(\Delta Q) = + 9.35$ cal
$$= + (9.35 \times 4.19) \text{ J} = + 39.18 \text{ J}$$

Change in internal energy between two states via different paths are equal.

∴ $\Delta U = 22.3$ J

∴ From first law of thermodynamics,
$$\Delta U = \Delta Q - W$$
or $\qquad W = \Delta Q - \Delta U$
$$= 39.18 - 22.3 = 16.88 \text{ J} \approx 16.9 \text{ J}$$

29. A cycle followed by an engine (made of one mole of an ideal gas in a cylinder with a piston) is shown in figure. Find heat exchanged by the engine with the surroundings for each section of the cycle. $[C_V = (3/2)R]$

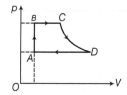

(i) AB : constant volume
(ii) BC : constant pressure
(iii) CD : adiabatic
(iv) DA : constant pressure [NCERT Exemplar]

Sol. (i) In figure, portion AB of the cycle involved increases in pressure/temperature of gas at constant volume. Therefore, the system gains heat from the surroundings.

$$Q_{AB} = U_{AB} \qquad\qquad [\because W = 0]$$
$$= \frac{3}{2}R(T_B - T_A) = \frac{3}{2}(p_B V_B - p_A V_A) \quad [\because \Delta U = nC_V \Delta T]$$
$$= \frac{3}{2}(p_B - p_A) V_A \qquad\qquad [\because V_B = V_A]$$

(ii) In the portion BC, the gas increases in volume at constant pressure. Heat required for this is gained from surroundings.

$$Q_{BC} = U_{BC} + W_{BC} = \frac{3}{2}(p_C V_C - p_B V_B) + p_B(V_C - V_B)$$
$$= \frac{5}{2}p_B(V_C - V_B) \qquad\qquad [\because p_C = p_B]$$
$$Q_{BC} = \frac{5}{2}p_B(V_C - V_A)$$

(iii) As CD represents an adiabatic change, therefore,
$$Q_{CD} = 0.$$

(iv) DA involves compression of gas from V_D to V_A at constant pressure p_A. Work is done on the gas (negative).

$$\Delta Q_{DA} = \Delta U_{DA} + \Delta W_{DA}$$
$$= \frac{3}{2}R(T_A - T_D) + p_A(V_A - V_D)$$
$$= \frac{3}{2}p_A(V_A - V_D) + p_A(p_A - V_D)$$
$$= \frac{5}{2}p_A(V_A - V_D)$$

30. Calculate the work done for adiabatic expansion of a gas.

Sol. Consider (say μ mole) an ideal gas, which is undergoing an adiabatic expansion. Let the gas expands by an infinitesimally small volume dV, at pressure p, then the infinitesimally small work done given by $dW = pdV$

The net work done from an initial volume V_1 to final volume V_2 is given by

$$W = \int_{V_1}^{V_2} pdV$$

For an adiabatic process, $pV^\gamma = $ constant $= K$

$$p = \frac{K}{V^\gamma} = KV^{-\gamma}$$

$$\therefore \quad W = \int_{V_1}^{V_2}(KV^{-\gamma})dV = K\left[\frac{V^{-\gamma+1}}{-\gamma+1}\right]_{V_1}^{V_2}$$

$$= \frac{KV_2^{-\gamma+1} - KV_1^{-\gamma+1}}{(1-\gamma)}$$

For an adiabatic process,

$$K = p_1 V_1^\gamma = p_2 V_2^\gamma$$

$$\Rightarrow \quad W = \frac{p_2 V_2^\gamma \cdot V_2^{-\gamma+1} - p_1 V_1^\gamma \cdot V_2^{-\gamma+1}}{(1-\gamma)}$$

$$= \frac{1}{(1-\gamma)}(p_2 V_2 - p_1 V_1)$$

For an ideal gas, $p_1 V_1 = \mu R T_1$ and $p_2 V_2 = \mu R T_2$. So, we have

$$W = \frac{1}{(1-\gamma)}[\mu R T_2 - \mu R T_1] = \frac{\mu R}{(\gamma-1)}[T_1 - T_2]$$

31. Consider one mole of perfect gas in a cylinder of unit cross-section with a piston attached (figure). A spring (spring constant k) is attached (unstretched length L) to the piston and to the bottom of the cylinder. Initially, the spring is unstretched and the gas is in equilibrium.

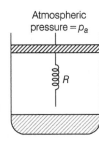

Atmospheric pressure $= p_a$

R

A certain amount of heat Q is supplied to the gas causing an increase of volume from V_0 to V_1.

(i) What is the initial pressure of the system?

(ii) What is the final pressure of the system?

(iii) Using the first law of thermodynamics, write down a relation between Q, p_a, V, V_0 and k.

Sol. (i) $p_i = p_a$

(ii) $p_f = p_a + \frac{k}{A}(V - V_0)$

(iii) According to first law of thermodynamics,

$$\Delta Q = \Delta U + \Delta W \text{ where,}$$

$$\Delta U = C_V(T - T_0), \Delta W = p_a(V - V_0) + \frac{1}{2}k(V - V_0)^2$$

$$\Delta Q = p_a(V - V_0) + \frac{1}{2}k(V - V_0)^2 + C_V(T - T_0)$$

where, $T_0 = p_a V_0/R$,

$$\Rightarrow \quad T = [p_a + (K/A) \times (V - V_0)]\, V/R$$

32. Consider a p-V diagram in which the path followed by one mole of perfect gas in a cylindrical container is shown.

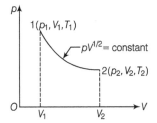

(i) Find the work done when the gas is taken from state 1 to state 2.

(ii) What is the ratio of temperatures T_1/T_2, if $V_2 = 2V_1$?

(iii) Given the internal energy for one mole of gas at temperature T is $(3/2)\,RT$, find the heat supplied to the gas when it is taken from states 1 to 2, with $V_2 = 2V_1$.   **[NCERT Exemplar]**

Sol. (i) Work done by the gas (let $pV^{1/2} = A$),

$$\Delta W = \int_{V_1}^{V_2} pdV = A\int_{V_1}^{V_2}\frac{dV}{\sqrt{V}} = A\left[\frac{\sqrt{V}}{1/2}\right]_{V_1}^{V_2}$$

$$= 2A(\sqrt{V_2} - \sqrt{V_1})$$

$$= 2p_1 V_1^{1/2}[V_2^{1/2} - V_1^{1/2}]$$

(ii) Since, $T = pV/nR = \frac{A}{nR}\cdot\sqrt{V}$

Thus, $\frac{T_2}{T_1} = \sqrt{\frac{V_2}{V_1}} = \sqrt{2}$

(iii) Then, the change in internal energy,

$$\Delta U = U_2 - U_1 = \frac{3}{2}R(T_2 - T_1) = \frac{3}{2}RT_1(\sqrt{2} - 1)$$

$$\Delta W = 2A\sqrt{V_1}(\sqrt{2} - 1) = 2RT_1(\sqrt{2} - 1)$$

According to first law of thermodynamics,

$$\Delta Q = \Delta U + \Delta W \Rightarrow \Delta Q = (7/2)RT_1(\sqrt{2} - 1)$$

LONG ANSWER Type II Questions

33. In the given p-V diagrams,   [NCERT Exemplar]
Find which curve
represents

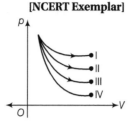

(i) isothermal process,

(ii) adiabatic process for
(a) monoatomic
(b) diatomic
(c) triatomic gas.

Sol. For isothermal process, $pV =$ constant

For adiabatic process, $pV^\gamma =$ constant

$$\gamma = \frac{5}{3} \text{ for monoatomic gas} = 1.66$$

$$\gamma = \frac{7}{5} = 1.4 \text{ for diatomic gas}$$

$$\gamma = \frac{8}{6} = 1.33 \text{ for triatomic gas}$$

and slope increases with γ so,
For Ist, $\gamma = 1$, an isotherm
For IInd, $\gamma = 1.33$
For IIIrd, $\gamma = 1.4$
For IVth, $\gamma = 1.66$
So, graph I is isothermal,
Graph II is triatomic adiabatic,
Graph III is diatomic adiabatic,
Graph IV is monoatomic adiabatic.

34. Consider that an ideal gas (n moles) is expanding in a process given by $p = f(V)$, which passes through a point (V_0, p_0). Show that the gas is absorbing heat at (p_0, V_0), if the slope of the curve $p = f(V)$ is larger than the slope of the adiabat passing through (p_0, V_0).

Sol. Slope of $p = f(V)$, curve at $(V_0, p_0) = f(V_0)$

Slope of adiabat at (V_0, p_0)
$$= K(-\gamma) V_0^{-1-\gamma} = -\gamma p_0/V_0$$

Now, heat absorbed in the process $p = f(V)$
$$dQ = dU + dW = nC_V dT + p dV$$
Since, $T = (1/nR) pV = (1/nR) V f(V)$
$$\therefore \quad dT = (1/nR)[f(V) + V f'(V)] dV$$

Thus, $\left. \dfrac{dQ}{dV} \right|_{V = V_0} = \dfrac{C_V}{R}[f(V_0) + V_0 f'(V_0)] + f(V_0)$

$$= \left[\frac{1}{\gamma - 1} + 1\right] f(V_0) + \frac{V_0 f'(V_0)}{\gamma - 1}$$

$$= \frac{\gamma}{\gamma - 1} p_0 + \frac{V_0}{\gamma - 1} f'(V_0)$$

Heat is absorbed when $dQ/dV > 0$ when gas expands, that is when $\gamma p_0 + V_0 f'(V_0) > 0$
$$f'(V_0) > -\gamma p_0/V_0$$

35. A cycle followed by a machine (made of one mole of perfect gas in a cylinder with a piston) is shown in figure

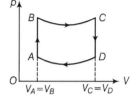

A to B : volume constant

B to C : adiabatic

C to D : volume constant

D to A : adiabatic

$$V_C = V_D = 2V_A = 2V_B$$

(i) In which part of the cycle, heat is supplied to the machine from outside?

(ii) In which part of the cycle, heat is being given to the surrounding by the machine?

(iii) What is the work done by the machine in one cycle? Write your answer in term of p_A, p_B, V_A.

(iv) What is the efficiency of the machine?

Take, $\gamma = \dfrac{5}{3}$ for the gas and

$$C_V = \frac{3}{2} R \text{ for one mole}$$
    [NCERT Exemplar]

Sol. (i) A to B because $T_B > T_A$, as $p \propto T$ [$\because V$ constant]

(ii) C to D because $T_C > T_D$, as $p \propto T$ [$\because V$ constant]

(iii) $W_{AB} = \int_A^B p dV = 0$ and $W_{CD} = 0$ [$\because V$ constant]

Similarly, $W_{BC} = \int_B^C p dV = K\int_B^C \dfrac{dV}{V^\gamma} = K\left[\dfrac{V^{-\gamma+1}}{-\gamma+1}\right]_{V_B}^{V_C}$

    [$\because pV^r = K$]

$$= \frac{1}{1-\gamma}(p_C V_C - p_B V_B)$$

Similarly, $W_{DA} = \dfrac{1}{1-\gamma}(p_A V_A - p_D V_D)$

Now, $p_C = p_B\left(\dfrac{V_B}{V_C}\right)^\gamma = 2^{-\gamma} p_B$ [$\because V_C = 2V_B$]

Similarly, $p_D = p_A 2^{-\gamma}$

Total work done $= W_{BC} + W_{DA}$

$$= \frac{1}{1-\gamma}[p_B V_B(2^{-\gamma+1} - 1) - p_A V_A(2^{-\gamma+1} - 1)]$$

$$= \frac{1}{1-\gamma}(2^{1-\gamma} - 1)(p_B - p_A) V_A \quad [\because V_A = V_B]$$

$$= \frac{3}{2}\left[1 - \left(\frac{1}{2}\right)^{2/3}\right](p_B - p_A) V_A$$

(iv) Heat supplied during process A to B

$dQ_{AB} = dU_{AB}$

$Q_{AB} = \dfrac{3}{2}nR(T_B - T_A) = \dfrac{3}{2}(p_B - p_A)V_A$

Efficiency $= \dfrac{\text{Net work done}}{\text{Heat supplied}} = \left[1 - \left(\dfrac{1}{2}\right)^{2/3}\right]$

36. What is a cyclic process? What is change in internal energy of the system in a cyclic process? In changing the state of a gas adiabatically from an equilibrium states A to B, an amount of 40.5 J of work is done on the system. If the gas is taken from states A to B *via* a process in which net heat absorbed by the system is 12.6 cal. How much is the net work done by the system in the later case?
(1 cal = 4.19 J) **[NCERT]**

Sol. A cyclic process restores the system back to its initial state after completion of the cycle.

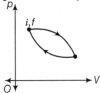

As internal energy is a state function, so its value at initial point is same as that at final point (initial state is same as that of final state).

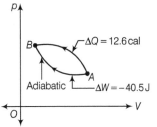

For adiabatic process $A \to B$,

$\Delta Q = 0$, so by first law of thermodynamics,

$$\Delta Q = \Delta W + \Delta U$$

or $\Delta U = -\Delta W = -(-40.5) = 40.5$ J

For another process, $A \to B$,

$\Delta Q = +12.6$ cal

$= 12.6 \times 4.19$ J $= 52.8$ J

and by first law of thermodynamics,

$$\Delta Q = \Delta W + \Delta U$$

$\Rightarrow \qquad \Delta W = \Delta Q - \Delta U$

$\Rightarrow \qquad \Delta W = 52.8 - 40.5 = 12.3$ J

[as ΔU is a state function, ΔU_{AB} is same for this process also]

ASSESS YOUR TOPICAL UNDERSTANDING

OBJECTIVE Type Questions

1. If a system is in thermodynamic equilibrium with its surroundings, it means
   (a) temperature of system and surroundings must be same
   (b) pressure, volume and temperature of system and surroundings must be same
   (c) pressure, volume and temperature of system and surroundings may be different
   (d) None of the above

2. According to Zeroth law, which physical quantity must have same value for the two systems to be in thermal equilibrium?
   (a) Pressure
   (b) Temperature
   (c) Volume
   (d) Composition

3. Specific heat capacity depends on
   (a) nature of the substance
   (b) on its mass
   (c) on its temperature
   (d) Both (a) and (c)

4. An ideal gas having molar specific heat capacity at constant volume is $\dfrac{3}{2}R$, the molar specific heat capacities at constant pressure is
   (a) $\dfrac{1}{2}R$ (b) $\dfrac{5}{2}R$
   (c) $\dfrac{7}{2}R$ (d) $\dfrac{9}{2}R$

5. If 150 J of heat is added to a system and the work done by the system is 110 J, then change in internal energy will be
   (a) 40 J   (b) 110 J   (c) 150 J   (d) 260 J

6. An ideal gas undergoes four different processes from the same initial state (figure). Four processes are adiabatic, isothermal, isobaric and isochoric. Out of 1, 2, 3 and 4 which one is adiabatic?

[NCERT Exemplar]

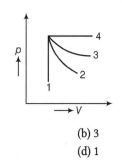

(a) 4   (b) 3
(c) 2   (d) 1

Answers

1. (a)	2. (b)	3. (d)	4. (b)	5. (a)
6. (c)				

VERY SHORT ANSWER Type Questions

7. What is meant by free expansion?

8. State why a gas can only expand at constant temperature, if a certain quantity of heat is supplied to it.

9. Is it possible to convert internal energy into work?

SHORT ANSWER Type Questions

10. Generally, a gas has two specific heat capacities, why? and which one is greater, explain it?

11. State the process in which air pressure in a car tyre increases during driving. Explain why?

12. Two samples of a gas initially at the same temperature and pressure are compressed from a volume V to a volume $V/2$. One sample is compressed isothermally and the other adiabatically. In which sample is the pressure greater? Justify.

LONG ANSWER Type I Questions

13. Explain the limitations of the first law of thermodynamics.

14. (i) Why does a gas have two molar specific heats?
(ii) Which one is greater and why?
(iii) What is the difference between the two molar specific heats and what is their ratio?

15. A monoatomic ideal gas $\left(\gamma = \dfrac{5}{3}\right)$ initially at 17°C is suddenly compressed to one-eight of its original volume.
Find the final temperature after compression.   **[Ans.** 887°C]

LONG ANSWER Type II Questions

16. Two containers P and Q of equal volume are connected to each other with a stopcock. The temperature and pressure in P is standard and in evacuated with no gas in it. Both the containers are thermally insulated. The stopcock is suddenly opened. Answer the following questions.
(i) What are the final pressures of the gases P and Q?
(ii) What is the change in internal energy of the gas in P?

17. A gas is expanded twice in a way so that the volume becomes twice the initial value. In first case, gas is expanded isothermally while in second case gas is expanded adiabatically.
(i) In which case, is the pressure is greater and why?
(ii) Which work done is more and why?

18. Figure shows a process PQR performed on an ideal gas. Find the net heat given to the system during the process.

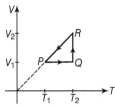

Ans. $nR\left[T_2 \ln \dfrac{V_2}{V_1} - (T_2 - T_1)\right]$

|TOPIC 2|
Second Law of Thermodynamics

SECOND LAW OF THERMODYNAMICS

There are many processes which are based on energy conservation but not possible in nature.

e.g. A ball lying on a floor could jump upto some height by itself gaining some heat energy from the ground. This process is possible according to first law (energy conservation) but not actually possible in nature.

It means that some additional basic principle of nature forbids the above process, even though it satisfy the energy conservation. The principle that put a restriction on the first law of thermodynamics is known as the **second law of thermodynamics.**

The second law of thermodynamics gives a fundamental limitation to the efficiency of a heat engine and the coefficient of performance of a refrigerator. Two statements of Kelvin-Planck and Clausius put restrictions on the possibility of perfect heat engine and perfect refrigerator, respectively.

KELVIN-PLANCK'S STATEMENT

No process is possible whose sole result is the absorption of heat from a reservoir and the complete conversion of the heat into work.

CLAUSIUS STATEMENT

No process is possible whose sole result is the transfer of heat from a colder object to a hotter object.

PMM1 AND PMM2

Any device that violates the first law of thermodynamics (by creating energy) is called a perpetual motion machine of the first kind (PMM1) and the device that violates the second law is called a perpetual motion machine of the second kind (PMM2).

EXAMPLE |1| **Conversion of Heat into Work**
Is it possible to convert all the heat extracted from a hot body into work?

Sol. No, heat cannot be converted into work completely because a part of heat is rejected and remaining part is converted into work.

REVERSIBLE AND IRREVERSIBLE PROCESS

Reversible Process

A process which could be reserved in such a way that the system and its surrounding returns exactly to their initial states with no other changes in the universe is known as **reversible process.**

e.g. If heat is absorbed in the direct process, then same amount of heat should be given out in the reverse process. If work is done on the working substance in the direct process, then the same amount of work should be done by the working substance in the reverse process.

The conditions for reversibility are

(i) There must be complete absence of dissipative forces such as friction, viscosity, electric resistance etc.

(ii) The direct and reverse processes must take place infinitely slowly.

(iii) The temperature of the system must not differ appreciably from its surroundings.

Some examples of reversible process are

(i) All isothermal and adiabatic changes are reversible if they are performed very slowly.

(ii) When a certain amount of heat is absorbed by ice, it melts. If the same amount of heat is removed from it, the water formed in the direct process will be converted into ice.

(iii) An extremely slow extension or contraction of a spring without setting up oscillations.

(iv) When a perfectly elastic ball falls from some height on a perfectly elastic horizontal plane, the ball rises to the initial height.

(v) Very slow evaporation or condensation.

It should be remembered that the conditions mentioned for a reversible process can never be realised in practice. Hence, a reversible process is only an ideal concept. In actual process, there is always loss of heat due to friction, conduction radiation, etc.

Ideal Engine is Practically not Possible

Reversibility is the rule of nature. It means that a change happened in the universe cannot be exactly reversed. That is why, any engine cannot have 100% efficiency. If we could eliminate all the resistive forces, the efficiency of an engine could be maximised.

For future, some trains are proposed that will move in a vacuum tunnel to eliminate the air friction and hence to increase the efficiency of the engine.

Irreversible Process

Any process which is not reversible exactly is an **irreversible process**. All natural processes such as conduction, radiation, radioactive decay etc., are irreversible processes. All practical processes such as free expansion, Joule-Thomson expansion, electrical heating of a wire are also irreversible.

Irreversibility arises mainly from two causes

(i) Many processes (like diffusion of gases, decay of organic matter) take the system to non-equilibrium states.

(ii) Many processes involve the dissipative forces like friction, viscosity, inelasticity, etc.

Some examples of irreversible processes are given below

(i) When a steel ball is allowed to fall on an inelastic lead sheet, its kinetic energy changes into heat energy by friction. The heat energy raises the temperature of lead sheet. No reverse transformation of heat energy occurs.

(ii) The sudden and fast stretching of a spring may produce vibrations in it. Now, a part of the energy is dissipated. This is the case of irreversible process.

(iii) Sudden expansion or contraction and rapid evaporation or condensation are examples of irreversible processes.

(iv) The passage of an electric current through a resistor is irreversible.

(v) Heat transfer between bodies at different temperatures is also irreversible.

(vi) Joule-Thomson effect is irreversible because on reversing the flow of gas, a similar cooling or heating effect is not observed.

CARNOT ENGINE

Carnot engine is an ideal heat engine proposed by **Sadi Carnot** in 1824. The reversible engine which operates between two temperatures of source (T_1) and sink (T_2) is known as **Carnot heat engine**.

The designed engine is a theoretical engine which is free from all the defects of a practical engine. This engine cannot be realised in actual practice, however, this can be taken as a standard against which the performance of an actual engine can be judged.

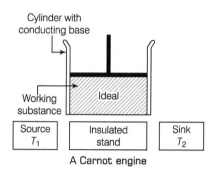

A Carnot engine

The main parts of Carnot engine are as follows

Cylinder

The cylinder has conducting base and insulating walls. It consists an ideal gas as a working substance insulating and frictionless piston is attached with it as shown in the figure.

Source

It is a hot reservoir at a temperature T_1 with conducting walls. It has infinite thermal capacity. Any amount of heat can be taken from it without changing the temperature.

Sink

It is a cold reservoir at temperature T_2. It has infinite thermal capacity so any amount of heat can be rejected to it without changing the temperature.

Working Substance

We use an ideal gas as a working substance in the cylinder.

Insulating Stand

The base of the cylinder could be placed on the insulating stand, to isolate it completely from the surroundings.

Carnot Cycle

As the engine works, the working substance of the engine undergoes a cycle known as **Carnot cycle**.

The Carnot cycle consists of the following four strokes

First Stroke (Isothermal Expansion)(Curve AB)

The cylinder containing one mole of an ideal gas as working substance allowed to expand slowly at the constant temperature T_1 by putting it on the source.

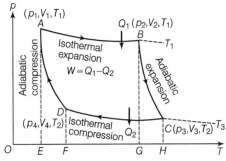

Various processes in Carnot cycle

Work done = heat absorbed by the system

$$W_1 = Q_1 = \int_{V_1}^{V_2} p\, dV$$

$$= RT_1 \log_e\left(\frac{V_2}{V_1}\right) = \text{area of } ABGEA$$

Second Stroke (Adiabatic Expansion) (Curve BC)

The cylinder is then placed on the non-conducting stand and the gas is allowed to expand adiabatically till the temperature falls from T_1 to T_2.

$$W_2 = \int_{V_2}^{V_3} p\, dV = \frac{R}{(\gamma - 1)}(T_1 - T_2) = \text{area } BCHGB$$

Third Stroke (Isothermal Compression) (Curve CD)

The cylinder is placed on the sink and the gas is compressed at constant temperature T_2.

Work done = heat released by the system

$$W_3 = Q_2 = -\int_{V_3}^{V_4} p\, dV = -RT_2 \log_e \frac{V_4}{V_3}$$

$$= RT_2 \log_e \frac{V_3}{V_4} = \text{area } CDFH$$

Fourth Stroke (Adiabatic Compression) (Curve DA)

Finally, the cylinder is again placed on non-conducting stand and the compression is continued so that gas returns to its initial stage.

$$W_4 = -\int_{V_4}^{V_1} p\, dV = -\frac{R}{\gamma - 1}(T_2 - T_1)$$

$$= \frac{R}{\gamma - 1}(T_1 - T_2) = \text{area of } ADFEA$$

Efficiency of Carnot Cycle (Engine)

The efficiency of engine is defined as the ratio of work done to the heat supplied, i.e.

$$\eta = \frac{\text{Work done}}{\text{Heat input}} = \frac{W_{\text{net}}}{Q_1}$$

Net work done during the complete cycle

$$W = W_1 + W_2 + (-W_3) + (-W_4)$$
$$= W_1 - W_3 = \text{area } ABCDA \quad [\text{as } W_2 = W_4]$$

$$\therefore \quad \eta = \frac{W}{Q_1} = \frac{W_1 - W_3}{W_1} = \frac{Q_1 - Q_2}{Q_1} = 1 - \frac{Q_2}{Q_1}$$

or

$$\eta = 1 - \frac{RT_2 \log_e(V_3/V_4)}{RT_1 \log_e(V_2/V_1)}$$

Since, points B and C lie on same adiabatic curve

$$\therefore \quad T_1 V_2^{\gamma-1} = T_2 V_3^{\gamma-1}$$

or

$$\frac{T_1}{T_2} = \left(\frac{V_3}{V_2}\right)^{\gamma-1} \qquad \ldots\text{(i)}$$

Also, points D and A lie on the same adiabatic curve

$$\therefore \quad T_1 V_1^{\gamma-1} = T_2 V_4^{\gamma-1}$$

or

$$\frac{T_1}{T_2} = \left(\frac{V_4}{V_1}\right)^{\gamma-1} \qquad \ldots\text{(ii)}$$

From Eqs. (i) and (ii), we get

$$\frac{V_3}{V_2} = \frac{V_4}{V_1}$$

or

$$\frac{V_3}{V_4} = \frac{V_2}{V_1}$$

$$\Rightarrow \quad \log_e\left(\frac{V_3}{V_4}\right) = \log_e\left(\frac{V_2}{V_1}\right)$$

So,

$$\boxed{\text{Efficiency of Carnot engine, } \eta = 1 - \frac{T_2}{T_1}}$$

- The efficiency of the Carnot engine depends only on the temperatures of source and sink.
- The efficiency of Carnot engine does not depend on the nature of the working substance.
- The efficiency of Carnot engine will be 100%, if the temperature of the sink is 0 K. As practically, we cannot attain a sink at 0 K, so it is not possible to have 100% efficiency.

Carnot Theorems

According to Carnot theorem,

(i) A heat engine working between the two given temperatures T_1 of hot reservoir i.e. source and T_2 of cold reservoir i.e. sink cannot have efficiency more than that of the Carnot engine.

(ii) The efficiency of the Carnot engine is independent of the nature of working susbtance.

We can prove the part (ii) of Carnot theorem as below.

Suppose a reversible Carnot engine R and an irreversible heat engine I, working between the same source T_1 and same sink T_2 as shown in figure.

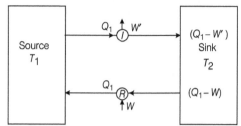

Reversible and irreversible heat engine act together

Suppose the two engines are coupled in such a way that irreversible engine I acts like a heat engine and reversible Carnot engine R acts like a refrigerator. In one complete cycle, the engine I absorbs heat Q_1 from the source, deliver work W' and release the balance $(Q_1 - W')$ to the sink. The engine R returns the same heat Q_1 to the source when work W is done on it in one full cycle. Therefore, it would take heat $(Q_1 - W)$ from the sink as shown in figure.

Let us assume that the efficiency of reversible engine R is less than that of I, i.e. $\eta_R < \eta_I$.

For Q_1, $W < W'$ and $(Q_1 - W) > (Q_1 - W')$

Thus, the coupled I-R system on whole extracts heat $(Q_1 - W) - (Q_1 - W') = (W' - W)$ from the sink and delivers the same amount of work $(W' - W)$ in one cycle without any change in the source. So, it is against the second law of thermodynamics.

Hence, the assertion $\eta_I > \eta_R$ is wrong. No engine can have efficiency greater than that of the Carnot engine. Thus, this proves the first part of Carnot theorem.

Coefficient of Performance of Carnot Engine

For Carnot refrigerator, $\dfrac{Q_1}{Q_2} = \dfrac{T_1}{T_2}$

$$\Rightarrow \quad \frac{Q_1 - Q_2}{Q_2} = \frac{T_1 - T_2}{T_2} \quad \text{or} \quad \frac{Q_2}{Q_1 - Q_2} = \frac{T_2}{T_1 - T_2}$$

So, $\boxed{\text{Coefficient of performance, } \beta = \dfrac{T_2}{T_1 - T_2}}$

where, T_1 = temperature of surrounding,
T_2 = temperature of cold body.
It is clear that $\beta = 0$ when $T_2 = 0$, i.e. the coefficient of performance will be zero, if the cold body is at the temperature equal to absolute zero.

EXAMPLE |2| **Carnot Cycle**

Consider a Carnot cycle operating between $T_1 = 500$ K and $T_2 = 300$ K producing 1 kJ of mechanical work per cycle. Find the heat transferred to/by the engine by/to the reservoir. **[NCERT Exemplar]**

Sol. Here, $T_1 = 500$ K, $T_2 = 300$ K, $W = 1$ kJ $= 1000$ J

As, efficiency, $\eta = \dfrac{W}{Q} = \dfrac{T_1 - T_2}{T_1}$

So, heat transferred to engine by the hot reservoir in cycle

$$Q_1 = \frac{W T_1}{T_1 - T_2} = \frac{1000 \times 500}{500 - 300} = 2500 \text{ J or 2.5 kJ}$$

and heat transferred by the engine to the cold reservoir in one cycle

$$Q_2 = Q_1 - W = 2.5 \text{ kJ} - 1 \text{ kJ} = 1.5 \text{ kJ}$$

EXAMPLE |3| **Power Consumed in Carnot Cycle**

A refrigerator has to transfer an average of 263 J of heat per second from temperature $-10°$ C to $25°$ C. Calculate the average power consumed, assuming no energy losses in the process.

Sol. Given, $Q_2 = 263$ J/s, $T_2 = -10°$ C $= -10 + 273 = 263$ K

and $T_1 = 25°$C $= 25 + 273 = 298$ K,

$$\beta = \frac{Q_2}{W} = \frac{T_2}{T_1 - T_2}$$

$\Rightarrow$ Average power, $W = \dfrac{Q_2(T_1 - T_2)}{T_2} = \dfrac{263\,(298 - 263)}{263}$

$$= 35 \text{ J/s} = 35 \text{ W}$$

EXAMPLE |4| **Coefficient of Performance of Carnot Engine**

A Carnot engine takes 10^6 cal of heat from a source at $827°$C and exhaust it to a sink $27°$C. How much work does it gives or output? What is engine efficiency? Also, find out the coefficient of performance of the engine, if it is used in reverse direction.

Sol. Given, $T_1 = 827 + 273 = 1100$ K

$$T_2 = 27 + 273 = 300 \text{ K}, Q_1 = 10^6 \text{ cal}$$

$$Q_2 = \frac{T_2}{T_1} \times Q_1 = \frac{300}{1100} \times 10^6 = 2.72 \times 10^5 \text{ cal}$$

Efficiency $(\eta) = \left(1 - \dfrac{T_2}{T_1}\right) \times 100\% = \left(1 - \dfrac{300}{1100}\right) \times 100$

$$= 72.72\%$$

As, $\beta = \dfrac{T_2}{T_1 - T_2}$ = coefficient of performance

$$= \frac{300}{1100 - 300} = \frac{300}{800} = 0.375$$

EXAMPLE |5| Freezing of Water

A Carnot engine with ideal gas is used for freezing water which is at 0°C. The engine is operated by a 600 W electric motor having an efficiency of 50%. Find time to freeze 25 kg of water. Take 25°C and 0°C as the source and sink. Latent heat of ice $= 333 \times 10^3 \, \text{Jkg}^{-1}$.

Sol. Given, $T_1 = 273 \, \text{K}$,

$$T_2 = 25 + 273 = 298 \, \text{K}$$
$$L = 333 \times 10^3 \, \text{J kg}^{-1}$$

Efficiency of electric motor = 50%

Find out the used power of the engine.

$$= 50\% \text{ of } 500 \, \text{W} = 250 \, \text{W}$$

Coefficient of performance, $\beta = \dfrac{Q_2}{W} = \dfrac{T_2}{T_1 - T_2}$

Heat extracted from water in unit time.

$$Q_2 = \frac{T_2}{T_1 - T_2} \times W = \frac{273}{298 - 273} \times 250 = 2730.0 \, \text{Js}^{-1}$$

Total heat extracted from 25 kg water to freeze it into ice,

$$Q = mL = 25 \times 333 \times 10^3 \, \text{J}$$

Total time taken in freezing water into ice

$$= \frac{Q}{Q_2} = \frac{25 \times 333 \times 10^3}{2730} = 3049.45 \, \text{s}$$

| TOPIC PRACTICE 2 |

1. Carnot engine is a
   (a) irreversible   (b) petrol engine
   (c) reversible   (d) diesel engine

Sol. (c) Process starts from p_1, V_1, T_1 and reverses back to p_1, V_1, T_1 after doing work (given by area enclosed). Here p, V, T reverse back, work done is not reversed back.

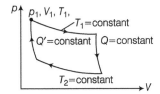

Carnot engine is a reversible engine working between two temperatures.

2. According to second law of thermodynamics,
   (a) a heat engine cannot have efficiency equal to 1
   (b) a refrigerator (or heat pump) could have infinite value of coefficient of performance
   (c) a heat engine can convert heat fully in to work
   (d) heat can flow from cold to hot body

Sol. (a) Second law puts limitation on the efficiency of a heat engine and on the coefficient of performance of a refrigerator. Heat engine cannot have efficiency equal to 1 and a refrigerator cannot have infinite value of coefficient of performance.

3. According to Carnot, which type of engine working between two temperatures T_1 and T_2 have maximum efficiency?
   (a) Reversible engine
   (b) Irreversible engine
   (c) External combustion engine
   (d) Diesel engine.

Sol. (a) For reversible engine, according to Carnot, efficiency is maximum.

4. The efficiency of a Carnot's engine working between steam point and ice point is
   (a) 26.81%   (b) 29%
   (c) 30%   (d) 10%

Sol. (a) $T_1 = (100 + 273) = 373 \, \text{K}$

$$T_2 = (0 + 273) = 273 \, \text{K}$$

Efficiency $(\eta) = 1 - \dfrac{T_2}{T_1} = 1 - \dfrac{273}{373} = \dfrac{100}{373}$

$$\% \eta = \frac{100}{373} \times 100 = 26.81 \, \%$$

VERY SHORT ANSWER Type Questions

5. Can a ship be moved with the energy of the sea water?

Sol. No, a ship cannot be moved in a sea by the use of the energy of sea water because refrigerator is against the second law of thermodynamics.

6. Is reversible process possible in nature?

Sol. A reversible process is never possible in nature because of dissipative forces and condition for a quasi-static process is not practically possible.

7. What are the forces which make any process irreversible?

Sol. All sorts of dissipative forces, e.g. force of friction, viscous drag, electrical resistance, non-elasticity, thermal radiation, convection etc., make a real process irreversible.

8. On what factors, the efficiency of a Carnot engine depends?

Sol. The efficiency of a carnot engine depends, on the temperature of source of heat and the sink.

9. If the temperature of the sink is increased, what will happen to the efficiency of Carnot engine?

Sol. Efficiency, $\eta = 1 - \dfrac{T_2}{T_1}$

By increasing T_2, the efficiency of the Carnot engine will decrease.

10. Find the efficiency of the Carnot engine working between boiling point and freezing point of water.

Sol. Efficiency of Carnot engine, $\eta = 1 - \dfrac{T_2}{T_1}$

$$= 1 - \dfrac{273\,\text{K}}{373\,\text{K}} = \dfrac{100}{373}$$

$$= 0.268 = 26.8\%$$

11. Can we design a reversible Carnot engine in practice?

Sol. No, we cannot design an ideal Carnot engine in practice.

12. Which thermodynamic law put restrictions on the complete conversion of heat into work?

Sol. According to second law of thermodynamics, heat energy cannot converted into work completely.

13. What type of process is a Carnot cycle?

Sol. Carnot cycle is a reversible cyclic process through which heat is converted into mechanical work.

SHORT ANSWER Type Questions

14. Consider a Carnot cycle operating between $T_1 = 500\,\text{K}$ and $T_2 = 300\,\text{K}$ producing 1 kJ of mechanical work per cycle. Find the heat transferred to the engine by the reservoirs.

[NCERT Exemplar]

Sol. As we know, $\quad \dfrac{Q_2}{Q_1} = \dfrac{T_2}{T_1} = \dfrac{3}{5}$

$$\because \qquad 1 - \dfrac{Q_2}{Q_1} = 1 - \dfrac{T_2}{T_1}$$

$$\Rightarrow \qquad \dfrac{Q_1 - Q_2}{Q_1} = \dfrac{500 - 300}{500} \quad [\because Q_1 - Q_2 = W]$$

$$\Rightarrow \qquad \dfrac{W}{Q_1} = \dfrac{2}{5}$$

$$\therefore \qquad Q_1 = 10^3 \times \dfrac{5}{2} = 2500\,\text{J}$$

15. A Carnot engine is operating between 600 K and 200 K. Consider that the actual energy produced is 2 kJ per kilocalorie of heat absorbed. Compare the real efficiency with the efficiency of Carnot engine.

Sol. Given, $T_1 = 600\,\text{K}$, $T_2 = 200\,\text{K}$

Efficiency of Carnot engine,

$$\eta = \dfrac{T_1 - T_2}{T_1} = \dfrac{600 - 200}{600}$$

$$= \dfrac{400}{600} = \dfrac{2}{3} = 66\%$$

Real efficiency $= \dfrac{\text{Energy output}}{\text{Energy input}} = \dfrac{2}{1 \times 4.2} = 0.47 = 47\%$

$$\therefore \quad \dfrac{\text{Real efficiency}}{\text{Carnot engine efficiency}} = \dfrac{47}{66} = 0.71$$

16. Draw p-V diagram of a Carnot cycle.

Sol. p-V diagram for Carnot cycle

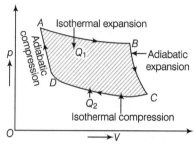

17. Under what condition, an ideal Carnot engine has 100% efficiency?

Sol. Efficiency of a Carnot engine is given by $\eta = \left(1 - \dfrac{T_2}{T_1}\right)$

where, T_2 = temperature of sink

and $\quad T_1$ = temperature of sink source.

So, for $\eta = 1$ or 100%, $T_2 = 0\,\text{K}$ or heat is rejected into a sink at 0 K temperature.

LONG ANSWER Type I Questions

18. Temperatures of the hot and cold reservoirs of a Carnot engine is raised by equal amounts. How the efficiency of the Carnot engine affected?

Sol. Let the initial temperatures of hot and cold reservoirs were T_1 and T_2. The efficiency of the Carnot engine is given by

So, initially $\qquad \eta = \dfrac{T_1 - T_2}{T_1}$ ...(i)

As given the temperature of both the reservoirs is raised by equal amount t, so $T_1' = T_1 + t$ and $T_2' = T_2 + t$. The final efficiency of the Carnot engine will be

$$\eta' = \dfrac{T_1' - T_2'}{T_1'} = \dfrac{(T_1 + t) - (T_2 + t)}{(T_1 + t)}$$

$$= \dfrac{T_1 - T_2}{(T_1 + t)}$$ ...(ii)

Dividing Eq. (ii) by Eq. (i), we have

$$\dfrac{\eta'}{\eta} = \dfrac{\left(\dfrac{T_1 - T_2}{T_1 + t}\right)}{\left(\dfrac{T_1 - T_2}{T_1}\right)} = \dfrac{T_1}{T_1 + t}$$ ...(iii)

As $\eta' < \eta$, i.e. the efficiency of Carnot engine decreases.

19. Two Carnot engines A and B are operated in series. The first one A receives heat at 900 K and rejects it to a reservoir at temperature T. The second engine B operates on this reservoir and rejects heat to a reservoir at 400 K. Calculate temperature T when

    (i) efficiencies of both A and B are equal.

    (ii) the work outputs of both A and B are equal.

Sol. **(i)** Efficiency of A = efficiency of B

$$\eta_A = \eta_B$$
$$\Rightarrow \quad 1 - \frac{T}{900} = 1 - \frac{400}{T}$$
$$\Rightarrow \quad T^2 = 900 \times 400$$
$$\Rightarrow \quad T = 600\,\text{K}$$

(ii) Let the first engine take Q_1 heat as input at temperature, $T_1 = 800$ K and gives out heat Q_2 at temperature T_0 The second engine receive Q_2 as input and give is out heat Q_3 at temperature $T_3 = 300$K to the sink.

Work done by first (A) engine = work done by second (B) engine.

Thus, $\quad Q_1 - Q_2 = Q_2 - Q_3$

Dividing both sides by Q_1

$$1 - \frac{Q_2}{Q_1} = \frac{Q_2}{Q_1} - \frac{Q_3}{Q_1}$$
$$\Rightarrow \quad 1 - T/T_1 = \frac{Q_2}{Q_1}\left(1 - \frac{Q_3}{Q_2}\right)$$
$$\Rightarrow \quad 1 - T/T_1 = \frac{T}{T_1}(1 - T_3/T)$$
$$\Rightarrow \quad T_1/T - 1 = 1 - \frac{T_3}{T} \Rightarrow \frac{T_1}{T} + \frac{T_3}{T} = 2$$
$$\Rightarrow \quad \frac{1}{T}(T_1 + T_3) = 2 \Rightarrow T = \frac{T_1 + T_3}{2}$$
$$\Rightarrow \quad T = \frac{900 + 400}{2} = 650\,\text{K}$$

20. Find out whether these phenomena are reversible or not.

    (i) Waterfall and   (ii) Rusting of iron.

Sol. **(i) Waterfall** The falling of water cannot be reversible process. During the water fall, its potential energy convert into kinetic energy of the water.

On striking the ground, some part of potential energy converts into heat and (sound not possible that heat and the sound). In nature, it automatically convert the kinetic energy and potential energy so that the water will rise back so waterfall is not a reversible process.

(ii) Rusting of iron In rusting of iron, the iron become oxidised with the oxygen of the air as it is a chemical reaction, it cannot be reversed.

LONG ANSWER Type II Questions

21. Two cylinders A and B of equal capacity are connected to each other *via* a stopcock. A contains a gas at standard temperature and pressure. B is completely evacuated. The entire system in thermally insulated. The stopcock is suddenly opened.

Answer the following

    (i) What is final pressure of the gas in A and B?

    (ii) What is the change in internal energy of the gas?

    (iii) What is the change in temperature of the gas?

    (iv) Do the intermediate states of the system (before settling to the final equilibrirum state) lie on its p-V-T surface?   **[NCERT]**

Sol. **(i)** Let capacity of each cylinder be V and atmospheric pressure be p.

$$p_1 = p$$

Initial volume of gas = Volume of the cylinder A

$$\therefore \quad V_1 = V$$

When stopcock is opened, then volume available for gas becomes $2V$

$$\therefore \quad V_2 = 2V$$

Final pressure $(p_2) = ?$

As system is thermally insulated, therefore there is no change in temperature during the process and hence it is an isothermal process.

For an isothermal process (according to Boyle's law),

$$p_1 V_1 = p_2 V_2$$
$$\text{or} \quad p_2 = p_1 \frac{V_1}{V_2} = p \times \frac{V}{2V}$$
$$= \frac{p}{2} = \frac{1}{2}\,\text{atm}$$
$$= 0.5\,\text{atm}$$

(ii) Change in internal energy, $\Delta U = 0$, as no work is done on or by the gas.

(iii) Change in temperature of the gas is zero as gas does no work in expansion.

(iv) No, because free expansion of gas is rapid and cannot be controlled. The intermediate states are non-equilibrium states and do not satisfy the gas equation. Therefore, the intermediate state of the gas does not be on the p-V-T surface.

22. Explain with the suitable example that a reversible process must be carried slowly and a fast process is necessarily irreversible.

Sol. A reversible process must pass through equilibrium states which are very close to each other so that when process is reversed, it passes back through these equilibrium states.

Then, it is again decompressed or it passes through same equilibrium states, system can be restored to its initial state without any change in surroundings.

e.g. If a gas is compressed as shown

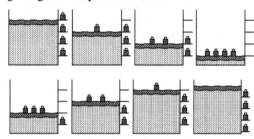

But a reversible process can proceeds without reaching equilibrium in intermediate states.

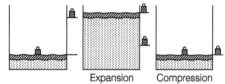

Expansion   Compression

23. The efficiency of a Carnot engine is 1/2. If the sink temperature is reduced by 100°C, then engine efficiency becomes 2/3. Find

(i) sink temperature

(ii) source temperature

(iii) Explain, why a Carnot engine cannot have 100% efficiency?

Sol. (i) Efficiency, $\eta = 1 - \dfrac{T_2}{T_1}$

where, T_2 = sink temperature

T_1 = source temperature.

$$1 - \frac{T_2}{T_1} = \frac{1}{2} \qquad \qquad ...(i)$$

$$1 - \left(\frac{T_2 - 100}{T_1} \right) = \frac{2}{3} \qquad \qquad ...(ii)$$

From Eq. (i), $\dfrac{T_2}{T_1} = \dfrac{1}{2}$ and Eq. (ii)

$$\frac{T_2 - 100}{T_1} = \frac{1}{3}$$

On dividing, we get

$$\frac{T_2}{T_2 - 100} = \frac{3}{2} \Rightarrow T_2 = 300\text{K}$$

(ii) Substituting in Eq. (i), $T_1 = 600\,\text{K}$

(iii) As efficiency, $\eta_2 \Rightarrow 1 - \dfrac{T_2}{T_1}$

$\therefore$ It equals to 1 only when $\dfrac{T_2}{T_1} = 0$ or $T_2 = 0\text{K}$

But absolute zero is not possible.

24. Two Carnot engines A and B are operated in series. The first one A receives heat at 800 K and rejects to a reservoir at temperature T K. The second engine B receives the heat rejected by the first engine and in turn rejects to a heat reservoir at 300 K. Calculate the temperature T K for the following cases.

(i) When the outputs of the two engines are equal.

(ii) When the efficiencies of the two engines are equal.

Sol. **For engine A,** $T_1 = 800\,\text{K}, T_2 = T\,\text{K}$

Efficiency, $\qquad \eta_A = 1 - \dfrac{T_2}{T_1} = 1 - \dfrac{T}{800}$

Also, $\qquad \dfrac{Q_2}{Q_1} = \dfrac{T_2}{T_1} = \dfrac{T}{800}$

Work output, $W_A = Q_1 - Q_2 = \eta_A \times Q_1$

$$\left[\because \eta_A = 1 - \frac{Q_2}{Q_1} \right]$$

or $\qquad W_A = \left(1 - \dfrac{T}{800} \right) Q_1$

For engine B, $T_1' = T\,\text{K}, T_2' = 300\,\text{K}$

Efficiency, $\qquad \eta_B = 1 - \dfrac{T_2'}{T_1'} = 1 - \dfrac{300}{T}$

Work output, $W_B = Q_1' - Q_2' = \eta_B \times Q_1' = \left(1 - \dfrac{300}{T} \right) Q_1'$

Since, the engine B absorbs the heat rejected by the engine A, so

$$Q_1' = Q_2 \quad \therefore \quad W_B = \left(1 - \frac{300}{T} \right) Q_2$$

(i) When outputs of the two engines are equal,

$W_A = W_B$

or $\qquad \left(1 - \dfrac{T}{800} \right) Q_1 = \left(1 - \dfrac{300}{T} \right) Q_2$

or $\qquad \left(1 - \dfrac{T}{800} \right) = \left(1 - \dfrac{300}{T} \right) \dfrac{Q_2}{Q_1} = \left(1 - \dfrac{300}{T} \right) \dfrac{T}{800}$

On solving, we get $T = 550\,\text{K}$

(ii) When the efficiencies are equal, $\eta_A = \eta_B$

or $\qquad 1 - \dfrac{T}{800} = 1 - \dfrac{300}{T}$

or $\qquad T^2 = 24 \times 10^4$

$\therefore \qquad T = 489.9\,\text{K}$

ASSESS YOUR TOPICAL UNDERSTANDING

OBJECTIVE Type Questions

1. Reversibility is not possible because of
   (a) resistive force present everywhere
   (b) every process around us is Quasi-static
   (c) gases are viscous.
   (d) gases have density

2. Which condition is true for an ideal Carnot engine which have 100% efficiency?
   (a) Temperature of sink source $T_1 = 0$K
   (b) Temperature of sink $T_2 = 0$K
   (c) Temperature of sink source $T_1 = 1.0$ K
   (d) None of the above

Answers
   1. (a) | 2. (b)

VERY SHORT ANSWER Type Questions

3. What is the significance of second law of thermodynamics ?

4. How is the efficiency of a Carnot engine affected by the nature of the working substance?

SHORT ANSWER Type Question

5. A Carnot engine takes in a thousand kilocalories of heat from a reservoir at 827°C and exhausts it to a sink at 27°C.

   (i) How much work does it perform?
   (ii) What is the efficiency of the engine?
   [**Ans.** (i) 2.720×10^5 cal (ii) 72.72 %]

LONG ANSWER Type I Questions

6. An ideal Carnot engine takes heat from a source at 317°C, does some external work and delivers the remaining energy to a heat sink at 117°C. If 500 kcal of heat is taken from the source.
   (i) How much work is done?
   (ii) How much heat is delivered to the sink?
   [**Ans.** (i) 710 kg (ii) 331 kcal]

7. A Carnot engine absorbs 6×10^5 cal at 227°C. Calculate work done per cycle by the engine if its sink is maintained at 127°C.   [**Ans.** 5.04×10^5 J]

LONG ANSWER Type II Questions

8. Heat cannot flow itself from a body at lower temperature to a body at higher temperature, is a consequence of which law of thermodynamics?

9. (i) Explain second law of thermodynamics.
   (ii) Write a paragraph explaining Carnot engine efficiency (η) and its relation with temperature.

SUMMARY

- **Thermodynamics** It is the branch of physics which deals with the study of transformation of heat energy into other forms of energy.

- **System** Thermodynamic system is an assembly of an extremely large number of particles so that the assembly has a certain value of pressure, volume and temperature.

- **Surroundings** Everything outside the system which has a direct effect on the system.

- **Boundary** A system is separated from its surroundings.

- **A thermodynamic** system is said to be in thermodynamical equilibrium when macroscopic variables that characterise the system do not change with time.

- Two systems are said to be in thermal equilibrium with each other if they are at the same temperature.

- **Zeroth law of thermodynamics** If two systems A and B are separately in thermal equilibrium with a third system C, then A and B are in thermal equilibrium with each other.

- **Heat** It is the energy that is transferred between a system and its environment.
$$\Delta Q = ms \, (T_f - T_i)$$

- **Internal energy** The total energy possessed by the system due to molecular motion and molecular configuration, i.e.
$$U = U_k + U_p$$

- Work done by or on the system is given by $W = \int_{V_i}^{V_f} p\,dV$

  where, V_i = initial volume of gas, V_f = final volume of gas, p = pressure

- **Heat capacity** An amount of heat ΔQ is needed to change its temperature ΔT. Its unit is J/K.
$$S = \frac{\Delta Q}{\Delta T}$$

- **Specific heat capacity** The amount of heat required to change the temperature of unit mass of a substance by unity. Its unit is J/kg-K.
$$S = \frac{1}{m}\frac{\Delta Q}{\Delta T}$$

- **Molar specific heat capacity** The amount of heat required to raise the temperature of one gram mole of a substance through a unit degree.
$$C = \frac{1}{\mu}\frac{\Delta Q}{\Delta T}$$

  Its unit is J/mol-K

- The relation between C_p and C_V is given by, $C_p - C_V = R$

- **First law of thermodynamics** The heat given to system is either used in doing work (ΔW) or it increases the internal energy (ΔU) the system, i.e. $\Delta Q = \Delta U + \Delta W$

- When state of a system changes or the state variables changes with time, then this process is known as thermodynamic system.

- The processes that do not involve accelerated motion of piston-large temperature gradient and pressure gradient are quasi-static.

- An **isothermal process** occurs at constant temperature and work done in an isothermal process is given by the following equation.
$$W = 2.303\,\mu RT \log\left(\frac{V_f}{V_i}\right)$$

- An isobaric process occurs at constant pressure and work done is an isobaric process is given by the following equation.
$$W = \mu R\,(T_f - T_i)$$

- An **isochoric process** is one in which volume is kept constant, meaning that the work done by the system will be zero.

- An adiabatic process does not allow transfer of heat by or to the system and work done in this process is given by the following equation
$$W = \frac{\mu R\,(T_i - T_f)}{\gamma - 1}$$

- In cyclic process, initial and final states are same while in non-cyclic processes, they are different.

- **Kelvin-Planck statement** No process is possible whose sole result in the absorption of heat from a reservoir and the complete conversion of heat into work.

- **Clausius statement** No process is possible whose sole result is the transfer of heat from a colder object to hotter object.

- **Carnot engine** The reversible engine which operates between two temperatures of source and sink.

- Carnot cycle consists four strokes and each stroke having own work which is given by the following equations.
$$W_1 = RT_1 \log_e \frac{V_2}{V_1}, \qquad W_2 = (T_1 - T_2)\frac{R}{\gamma - 1}(T_1 - T_2)$$
$$W_3 = RT_2 \log_e \frac{V_3}{V_4}, \qquad W_4 = \frac{R}{\gamma - 1}(T_1 - T_2)$$

- **Carnot's theorem**
  (i) A heat engine working between the two given temperature T_1 of hot reservoir, i.e. source and T_2 of cold reservoir, i.e. sink cannot have efficiency of more than that of Carnot engine.
  (ii) The efficiency of the Carnot engine is independent of the nature of working substance.

- Coefficient of performance of Carnot engine is given by the following equation.
$$\beta = \frac{T_2}{T_1 - T_2}$$

- where, T_1 = temperature of surroundings and T_2 = temperature of cold body

CHAPTER PRACTICE

OBJECTIVE Type Questions

1. According to first law of thermodynamics
   (a) any process that involves energy conservation is possible in nature
   (b) $\Delta Q = \Delta U + \Delta W$
   (c) Both (a) and (b)
   (d) Neither (a) nor (b)

2. $(\Delta Q - \Delta W)$ is
   (a) path dependent
   (b) path independent
   (c) equal to ΔU
   (d) Both (b) and (c)

3. Mechanical equivalent of heat is equal to the amount of
   (a) work done to produce 1 cal heat
   (b) a conversion factor between calorie and joule
   (c) Both (a) and (b)
   (d) Neither (a) nor (b)

4. Choose the state variable from the given options.
   (a) Heat
   (b) Work
   (c) Internal energy
   (d) All of these

5. A mixture of gases undergoing explosive chemical reaction
   (a) is not in equilibrium state during explosion
   (b) may have variable temperature and pressure values during explosion
   (c) finally the gas will attained equilibrium state with its surroundings
   (d) All of the above

6. A gas is expanded isothermally from volume V_1 to V_2 at a constant temperature T, the work done by the gas in this expansion is
   (a) $\mu RT \log \dfrac{V_1}{V_2}$
   (b) $\mu RT \times \dfrac{V_1}{V_2}$
   (c) $\mu RT \log \dfrac{V_2}{V_1}$
   (d) $\mu RT \times \dfrac{V_2}{V_1}$

7. For Carnot engine, which process should be chosen to take the working substance from T_1 to T_2 or *vice-versa* ?
   (a) Isochoric
   (b) Isothermal
   (c) Adiabatic
   (d) Isobaric

ASSERTION AND REASON

Direction (Q. Nos. 8-15)   *In the following questions, two statements are given- one labelled Assertion (A) and the other labelled Reason (R). Select the correct answer to these questions from the codes (a), (b), (c) and (d) as given below*
   (a) Both Assertion and Reason are true and Reason is the correct explanation of Assertion.
   (b) Both Assertion and Reason are true but Reason is not the correct explanation of Assertion.
   (c) Assertion is true but Reason is false.
   (d) Assertion is false but Reason is true.

8. **Assertion** Thermodynamics deals with the concepts of heat and temperature.
   Reason The temperature of an ideal gas depends on its molecular kinetic energy.

9. **Assertion** If the temperature of two systems is not same it means that they must not be in thermodynamic equilibrium.
   Reason If the temperature of two systems is same, it means that they must be in thermal equilibrium.

10. **Assertion** By doing some work on the system, we can change the internal energy of a system.
    Reason If work is done by the system, its internal energy may decrease.

11. **Assertion** Specific heat capacity and molar specific heat capacity both have same units.
    Reason Specific heat capacity and molar specific heat capacity both do not depend on mass.

12. **Assertion** State variables are required to specify the equilibrium state of the system.
    Reason Pressure is an intensive state variable.

13. **Assertion** In isothermal process for ideal gas, change in internal energy is zero.
    Reason No heat is supplied to system or rejected by system, in an isothermal process.

14. **Assertion** First law of thermodynamics is based on energy conservation.
    Reason Second law of thermodynamics put limitations on first law.

15. Assertion Reversible Carnot engine with one particular substance can not be more efficient than the one using another substance.

Reason Efficiency of Carnot engine = T_2/T_1.

CASE BASED QUESTIONS

Direction (Q. Nos. 16-17) *These questions are case study based questions. Attempt any 4 sub-parts from each question.*

16. Equilibrium State

An equilibrium state of a gas is completely specified by the values of pressure, volume, temperature and mass (and composition, if there is a mixture of gases). A gas allowed to expand freely against vacuum is not an equilibrium state. During the rapid expansion, pressure of the gas may not be uniform throughout. Similarly, a mixture of gases undergoing an explosive chemical reaction is not an equilibrium state, again its temperature and pressure are not uniform. Now consider following system.

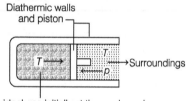

Diathermic walls and piston

T →

T

→Surroundings

p

An ideal gas initially at thermodynamic and mechanical equilibrium

(i) If the external pressure is reduced suddenly, then
  (a) the gas will expand suddenly which has non-equilibrium intermediate stages
  (b) the piston will accelerate outwards
  (c) Both (a) and (b)
  (d) Neither (a) nor (b)

(ii) If a finite temperature difference exists between system and surroundings.
  (a) there will be a rapid exchange of heat between system and surroundings with non-equilibrium intermediate stages
  (b) after sometime the temperature and pressure of surroundings and system will become same
  (c) Both (a) and (b)
  (d) Neither (a) nor (b)

(iii) Choose the correct option.
  (a) Thermodynamics is a microscopic science
  (b) Thermodynamics results based on molecular description of the molecules of the gas
  (c) p, V and T are state variables
  (d) Q is a state variable

(iv) The internal energy of the given system could be changed
  (a) by extracting heat from the system
  (b) by doing work done on the system
  (c) if system do some work on the surroundings
  (d) All of the above

(v) A mixture of gases undergoing explosive chemical reaction
  (a) is in equilibrium state during explosion
  (b) have constant temperature and pressure values during explosion
  (c) finally the gas will attained equilibrium state with its surroundings
  (d) Both (b) and (c)

17. First Law of Thermodynamics

First law of thermodynamics is a statement of conservation of energy applied to any system in which energy transfer from or to the surroundings is taken into account.

It states that heat given to a system is either used in doing external work or it increases the internal energy of the system or both.

i.e.   Heat supplied, $\Delta Q = \Delta U + \Delta W$

where, ΔQ = heat supplied to the system by the surroundings,

    ΔW = work done by the system on the surroundings

and ΔU = change in internal energy of the system.

(i) For an ideal gas, internal energy depends on
  (a) only molecular kinetic energy
  (b) only potential energy of the molecules
  (c) Both kinetic and potential energies of the molecules
  (d) None of the above

(ii) The internal energy of a system could be changed
  (a) by extracting heat from the system
  (b) by doing work done on the system
  (c) if system do some work on the surroundings
  (d) All of the above

(iii) $(\Delta Q - \Delta W)$ is
  (a) path dependent
  (b) path independent
  (c) equal to ΔU
  (d) Both (b) and (c)

(iv) Using first law of thermodynamics, which is true for isothermal expansion of an ideal gas,
  (a) $\Delta U = +$ ve   (b) $\Delta Q = +$ ve
  (c) $\Delta W = +$ ve   (d) Both (b) and (c)

(v) A system is provided with 200 cal of heat and the work done by the system on the surroundings is 40J, then its internal energy
  (a) increases by 600 J
  (b) decreases by 800 J
  (c) increases by 800 J
  (d) decreases by 50 J

Answers

1. (c)	2. (d)	3. (c)	4. (c)	5. (d)
6. (c)	7. (c)	8. (b)	9. (d)	10. (a)
11. (d)	12. (b)	13. (c)	14. (b)	15. (c)
16. (i) (c)	(ii) (c)	(iii) (c)	(iv) (d)	(v) (c)
17. (i) (a)	(ii) (d)	(iii) (d)	(iv) (d)	(v) (c)

VERY SHORT ANSWER Type Questions

18. When work done is positive?

19. Is it possible to increase the temperature of a gas without heating it?

20. What is a thermodynamic system?

21. What do you mean by an adiabatic wall and a diathermic wall?

22. Can a system be heated and its temperature remains constant?

23. Find value of specific heat of a gas in isothermal process.

SHORT ANSWER Type Questions

24. Which one a solid, a liquid or a gas of same mass and at the same temperature has greatest internal energy? Give reason.

25. Why water at the base of a waterfall is slightly warmer than the top?

26. Two blocks of same metal having masses 5 g and 10 g collide against a target with same velocity. If total energy is used in heating the balls, which will attain higher temperature?

27. Why is conversion of heat into work not possible without a sink at lower temperature?

28. Explain coolant fluid used in a chemical plant or in a car radiator should have high specific heat. Is water a suitable coolant?

LONG ANSWER Type I Questions

29. Find work done during the cyclic process shown in indicator diagram.

$$\left[\textbf{Ans. } \pi\left(\frac{V_2 - V_1}{2}\right)\left(\frac{p_2 - p_1}{2}\right)\right]$$

30. Draw indicator diagram for an adiabatic process. Find the slope of an adiabatic at any point.

31. Two identical samples of a gas are at a pressure p_1 and volume V_1. The two samples are allowed to expand so as to acquire a volume V_2. But one sample expands isothermally while the other expands adiabatically. In which case, more work is done and why ?

32. State second law of thermodynamics. Write a difference between heat engine and refrigerator.

33. Milk is poured into a cup of tea and is mixed with a spoon. Is this an example of a reversible process? Give reason.

34. Define reversible process. Write two characteristics of reversible process.

LONG ANSWER Type II Questions

35. What is Carnot engine? On what factors does it depend? Define also the efficiency of a Carnot engine.

36. A Carnot cycle is performed by 1 mole of air ($r = 1.4$) initially at 327° C. Each stage represents a compression or expansion in the ratio 1: 6. Calculate
  (i) the lowest temperature
  (ii) network done during each side
  (iii) efficiency of the engine
  Take, $R = 8.31$ J/mol-K

  [**Ans.** (i) 20° C (ii) 457232 J (iii) 51.2%]

37. Explain the construction and various operations for Carnot heat engine working between two temperatures. Hence, derive the relation coefficient of performance and efficiency of refrigerator.

38. What do you understand by reversible and irreversible processes? Give example what are the necessary conditions for a process to be reversible.

39. Find the V-T and T-p diagrams for cyclic process on p-V diagram.

12

Kinetic theory of gas explains the behaviour of gases based on the idea that the gas consists of rapidly moving atoms or molecules. Interatomic forces which are short range forces can be neglected in gases, this explains the rapid movement of gases.

KINETIC THEORY

|TOPIC 1|
Behaviour and Kinetic Interpretation of Gases

MOLECULAR NATURE OF MATTER

In 20th century, **Richard Feynman**, one of the great physicists discovered that matter is made up of atoms.

The scientific atomic theory is usually credited to **John Dalton** (1766-1844), an English chemist. He proposed the atomic theory to explain the laws of definite and multiple proportions obeyed by elements when they combine into compounds.

(i) **Law of definite proportion** states that any given compound has a fixed proportion by mass of its constituents.

(ii) **Law of multiple proportion** states that when two elements combined to form more than one compound, for a fixed mass of one element, the masses of other elements are in ratio of small integers.

About 200 years ago, John Dalton suggested that 'the smallest constituents of an element are atoms. Atoms of one element are identical but differ from those of other elements. A small number of atoms of each element combine to form a molecule of the compound.'

As number of atoms combine to form a molecule so Dalton's atomic theory is also referred as molecular theory of matter.

In 19th century, Gay Lussac stated that

'when gases combine chemically to yield another gas, their volumes are in the ratio of small integers.'

Amedeo Avogadro (1776-1856) helped to understand the combination of different gases in a simple manner. Avogadro's law says that,

equal volumes of all gases at the same temperature and pressure have equal number of molecules when Avaggadro's law combined with Daltons' theory to explain Gay Lussac's law.

Atomic Hypothesis

All things are made of atoms. The atoms are little particles that move around in perpetual motion, attracting each other when they are a little distance apart, but repelling upon being squeezed into one another. Advancement in science and technology enable us to see the molecules with the help of electron microscope and scanning tunneling microscope.

So, the size of atom is of the order 10^{-10} m

i.e. one angstrom (1 Å) $= 10^{-10}$ m.

States of Matter

Solids are the substances which have definite shape, size and volume. In solid, the interatomic spacing is least (about 2 Å) and interatomic force of attraction is maximum.

Liquids are the substances which have definite volume but no definite shape and size. In liquid, the interatomic spacing is greater in comparison to solid but less in comparison to gas and interatomic force of attraction is relatively weaker in comparison to solid. This enables liquid to flow.

Gases are the substances which do not have fixed shape, size and volume. In gases, the interatomic spacing is maximum (about 10 Å). Interatomic force of attraction is least in comparison to solids and liquids.

Motion of Molecules in a Gas

The average distance, a molecule can travel without colliding is called the **mean free path** (discussed later in detail). The mean free path in gases is of the order of thousands of Angstrom, due to this reason, atoms of gases are much free to move and can travel long distances without colliding. Due to this property of gases, they get dispersed away if they are not enclosed.

Modern theories had proved that atoms are no longer indivisible or elementary. Every atom consists of nucleus and electrons, the nucleus itself is made up of protons and neutrons, protons and neutrons are again made up of quarks. It may be possible in future that quarks may be further subdivided into some sort of elementary particles.

BEHAVIOUR OF GASES

Nature of gases are easier to understand as the molecules are far from each other and their mutual interactions are negligible except when two molecules collide.

So, gases at low pressure and high temperature much above that at which they liquify (or solidify) follow a relation.

$$pV = KT \qquad \qquad \ldots(i)$$

where, p = pressure and V = volume.

T is absolute temperature (i.e. in Kelvin scale)

K is a constant that varies with volume or with number of atoms or molecules (N) of gas in the given sample.

K can also be written as $K = Nk$ $\qquad \ldots(ii)$

The observation tells that k is same for all gases and is denoted by k_B.

So, Eq. (ii) becomes $K = Nk_B$ $\qquad \ldots(iii)$

where, k_B = Boltzmann constant and its value in SI unit is 1.38×10^{-23} J/K

From Eqs. (i) and (iii), we have

$$pV = Nk_B T$$

or $\qquad \dfrac{pV}{NT} = k_B = \text{constant}$

So, for different gases, we may write

$$\frac{p_1 V_1}{N_1 T_1} = \frac{p_2 V_2}{N_2 T_2} = \frac{p_3 V_3}{N_3 T_3} \cdots = k_B = \text{constant}$$

If p, V and T are same, then N will be same for all gases and this is **Avogadro's hypothesis.**

In other word, according to Avogadro's hypothesis, equal volumes of all gases under identical conditions of pressure and temperature will contain equal number of molecules.

It is established that 22.4 L of any gas at STP (Standard Temperature 273 K and Pressure 1 atm) contain same number of molecules and is represented by N_A.

Avogadro's number $(N_A) = 6.023 \times 10^{23}$.

The perfect gas equation can be written as,

$$pV = \mu RT$$

where, μ is number of moles and $R = N_A k_B$ is universal constant and T is absolute temperature in kelvin.

$$\mu = \frac{M}{M_0} = \frac{N}{N_A}$$

where, M = mass of the gases

In terms of density, perfect gas equation is

$$p = \frac{\rho RT}{M_0}$$

where, ρ = mass density of the gas,

M_0 = molar mass of the gas,
(mass of one mole of the gas)

$R = 8.314$ J mol^{-1}K^{-1}

and k_B = Boltzmann's constant = 1.38×10^{-23} J/K.

Note
- The mass of 22.4 L of any gas at STP is equal to its molecular weight in grams. This amount is called **one mole**.
- 1 mole of a substance contains 6.023×10^{23} atoms or molecules.
- 22.4 L of any gas at STP contains 1 mole of atoms or molecules.

EXAMPLE |1| Applying the Perfect Gas Equation

A vessel contains two non-reacting gases, i.e. neon (monoatomic) and oxygen (diatomic). The ratio of their partial pressures is 3 : 2. Estimate the ratio of (i) number of molecules and (ii) mass density of neon and oxygen in the vessel. Atomic number of Ne = 20.2, molecular mass of $O_2 = 32.0$. **[NCERT]**

Sol. (i) As V and T are same for the two gases, we can write

$$p_{Ne}V = \mu_{Ne}RT$$

and $$p_{O_2}V = \mu_{O_2}RT$$

or $$\frac{p_{Ne}}{p_{O_2}} = \frac{\mu_{Ne}}{\mu_{O_2}}$$

$\therefore$ $$\frac{p_{Ne}}{p_{O_2}} = \frac{3}{2} \Rightarrow \frac{\mu_{Ne}}{\mu_{O_2}} = \frac{3}{2}$$

If N_{Ne} and N_{O_2} are the number of molecules of the two gases and N_A is Avogadro's number, then

$$\frac{\mu_{Ne}}{\mu_{O_2}} = \frac{N_{Ne}/N_A}{N_{O_2}/N_A} = \frac{3}{2}$$

$\Rightarrow$ $$\frac{N_{Ne}}{N_{O_2}} = 1.5$$

(ii) Now, $$\mu_{O_2} = \frac{m_{O_2}}{M_{O_2}} \text{ and } \mu_{Ne} = \frac{m_{Ne}}{M_{Ne}}$$

$\therefore$ $$\frac{\rho_{Ne}}{\rho_{O_2}} = \frac{m_{Ne}/V}{m_{O_2}/V} = \frac{m_{Ne}}{m_{O_2}} = \frac{\mu_{Ne}M_{Ne}}{\mu_{O_2}M_{O_2}}$$

$$= \frac{3}{2} \times \frac{20.2}{32} = 0.947$$

EXAMPLE |2| Fractional Change in Volume of Water Vapour

The density of water is 1000 kgm^{-3}. The density of water vapour at 100°C and 1 atm pressure is 0.6 kg m^{-3}. The volume of a molecule multiplied by the total number gives, which is called, molecular volume. Estimate the ratio of the molecular volume to the total volume occupied by the water vapour under the above conditions of temperature and pressure. **[NCERT]**

Sol. For a given mass of water molecule i.e.

$$\text{Volume} \propto \frac{1}{\text{Density}}$$

$\therefore$ Ratio of the molecular volume to the total volume of water vapour

$$= \frac{\text{Density of water vapour}}{\text{Density of water}}$$

$$= \frac{0.6 \text{ kgm}^{-3}}{1000 \text{ kgm}^{-3}} = 6 \times 10^{-4}$$

EXAMPLE |3| Molecular Volume of a Water

Estimate the volume of a water molecule using the data in example 2. **[NCERT]**

Sol. Molecular mass of water = 18

$\therefore$ Number of molecules in 18 g or 0.018 kg of water
$$= 6 \times 10^{23}$$

Mass of 1 molecule of water $= \dfrac{0.018}{6 \times 10^{23}}$

$$= 3 \times 10^{-26} \text{kg}$$

In the liquid phase, the molecules of water are closely packed, so density of water molecules may be taken equal to the density of bulk water = 1000 kgm^{-3}

$\therefore$ Volume of a water molecule $= \dfrac{\text{Mass}}{\text{Density}}$

$$= \frac{3 \times 10^{-26}}{1000}$$

$$= 3 \times 10^{-29} \text{ m}^3$$

EXAMPLE |4| Interatomic Distance in Water Molecule

What is the average distance between atoms in water? Use the data given in examples 2 and 3. **[NCERT]**

Sol. Volume of water in vapour state

$$= \frac{1}{6 \times 10^{-4}} \times \text{(volume of water in liquid state)}$$

$$= 1.67 \times 10^3 \times \text{volume of water in liquid state}$$

This is also the increase in amount of volume available for each molecule of water.

When volume V increases by 10^3 times, then radius increases by $V^{1/3}$ or 10 times.

But volume of a water molecule

$$\frac{4}{3}\pi r^3 = 3 \times 10^{-29} \text{ m}^3$$

$\therefore$ $$r = \left(\frac{9}{4\pi} \times 10^{-29}\right)^{1/3}$$

$$\approx 2 \times 10^{-10} \text{ m} = 2 \text{ Å}$$

Increased radius $= 10 \times 2 = 20$ Å

Average distance $= 2 \times$ Increased radius $= 40$ Å

EXAMPLE |5| Ratio of Number of Molecules

Two non-reactive gases are kept in a container. The ratio of their partial pressures is given 5 : 3. Find the ratio of number of molecules.

Sol. As two non-reactive gases are mixed in a container, so the value of V and T will be same for both with partial pressures, p_1 and p_2.

For gas I $p_1 V = \mu_1 RT$ ...(i)

For gas II $p_2 V = \mu_2 RT$ ...(ii)

Dividing Eq. (i) by Eq. (ii), we get

$$\frac{p_1}{p_2} = \frac{\mu_1}{\mu_2} \qquad \text{...(iii)}$$

$$\mu_1 = N_1/N_A \qquad \text{...(iv)}$$

$$\mu_2 = N_2/N_A \qquad \text{...(v)}$$

Dividing Eq. (iv) by Eq. (v)

$$\frac{\mu_1}{\mu_2} = \frac{N_1}{N_2} \qquad \text{...(vi)}$$

From Eqs. (iii) and (vi), we get

$$\frac{N_1}{N_2} = \frac{\mu_1}{\mu_2} = \frac{p_1}{p_2} \implies \frac{N_1}{N_2} = \frac{p_1}{p_2} \text{ or } \frac{N_1}{N_2} = \frac{5}{3}.$$

Behaviour of Real Gas and Ideal Gas

An ideal gas is a theoretical model of a gas and no real gas is truly ideal. However, a real gas behaves as an ideal gas most closely at low pressure and high temperature. This is because at low pressure and high temperature, the molecules of gas are far apart due to which molecular force of attraction is negligible.

As $pV = \mu RT$ (ideal gas equation)

where, μ is the number of moles of the gas and $R = N_A k_B$ = universal constant, called gas constant for one gram mole of the gas.

$\therefore$ $\dfrac{pV}{\mu T} = R = \text{constant}$

There is a graph drawn between $\dfrac{pV}{\mu T}$ and p as shown in the figure below.

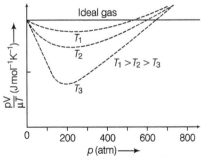

Behaviour of real gases approach ideal gas at low pressure and high temperature

If we plot same graph for real gases at three different temperatures T_1, T_2, T_3 $(T_1 > T_2 > T_3)$, then we find the curve as shown in figure by dotted lines.

Solid line showing ideal gas approach and dotted line showing real gas approach. From the observation of this graph, we will find that all curves for real gas approach ideal gas behaviour at low pressure and high temperature.

LAWS FOR AN IDEAL GAS

Boyle's Law

It states that for a given mass of a gas at constant temperature, the volume of that mass of gas is inversely proportional to its pressure, i.e. $V \propto \dfrac{1}{p}$

According to ideal gas equation, we get $pV = \mu RT$

At constant temperature, $pV = \text{constant}$

$\Rightarrow$ Boyle's law, $p_1 V_1 = p_2 V_2 = p_3 V_3 \cdots = \text{constant}$

The figure below shows the comparison between experimental p-V curves and the theoretical curves predicted by Boyle's law.

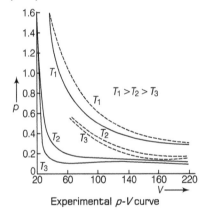

Experimental p-V curve

EXAMPLE |6| Change in Volume

A gas at 27°C in a cylinder has a volume of 4 L and pressure 100 N/m². If the gas is first compressed at constant temperature so that the pressure is 150 N/m². Estimate the change in volume.

Sol. Given, $V_1 = 4$ L, $V_2 = ?$, $p_1 = 100$ N/m²

$$p_2 = 150 \text{ N/m}^2, \Delta V = ?$$

Using Boyle's law for constant temperature, we have

$$p_1 V_1 = p_2 V_2$$

$$\Rightarrow \quad V_2 = \frac{p_1 V_1}{p_2} = \frac{100 \times 4}{150} = 2.667 \text{ L}$$

$\therefore$ Change in volume, $\Delta V = V_1 - V_2 = 4 - 2.667 = 1.33$ L

Charles' Law

It states that for a given mass of an ideal gas at constant pressure, volume (V) of a gas is directly proportional to its absolute temperature T. i.e.

$$V \propto T$$

From ideal gas equation, $\dfrac{V}{T} = \dfrac{\mu R}{p}$

At constant pressure, $\dfrac{V}{T}$ = **constant**

$\Rightarrow$ Charles' law, $\dfrac{V_1}{T_1} = \dfrac{V_2}{T_2} = \dfrac{V_3}{T_3} = \cdots$ = constant

The figure below shows the comparison between experimental T-V curves and the theoretical curves predicted by Charles' law.

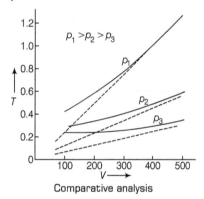

Comparative analysis

EXAMPLE |7| Change in Temperature
A gas is filled in a cylinder at 300K. Calculate the temperature upto which it should be heated so that its volume becomes $\dfrac{4}{3}$ of its initial volume.

Sol.   Given, $T_1 = 300$ K, $T_2 = ?$

$$V_1 = V, \quad V_2 = \dfrac{4}{3} V$$

According to Charles' law, we get

$$\dfrac{V_2}{V_1} = \dfrac{T_2}{T_1}$$

$\Rightarrow$ $T_2 = T_1 \dfrac{V_2}{V_1} = 300 \times \dfrac{4}{3} = 400$ K

Dalton's Law of Partial Pressure

It states that the total pressure of a mixture of non-interacting ideal gases is equal to the sum of partial pressures exerted by individual gases in the mixture.

i.e. $$p = p_1 + p_2 + p_3 + \cdots$$

Consider a mixture of non-interacting ideal gases. Let gas 1 has μ_1 moles, gas 2 has μ_2 moles and so on.

Suppose the net volume of the mixture is V, temperature of mixture is T and pressure of mixture is p.

Equation of state for the mixture

$$pV = (\mu_1 + \mu_2 + \cdots) RT$$
$$p = \dfrac{\mu_1 RT}{V} + \dfrac{\mu_2 RT}{V} + \cdots$$

Dalton's law, $p = p_1 + p_2 + p_3 + \cdots$

Here, $p_1 = \dfrac{\mu_1 RT}{V}$ is the pressure of gas 1 would exert at the same condition of volume and temperature if no other gases are present.

Graham's Law of Diffusion

It states that the rate of diffusion of a gas is inversely proportional to the square root of its density.

$$r \propto \dfrac{1}{\sqrt{\rho}} \qquad \ldots(i)$$

where, r = rate of diffusion and ρ = density of the gas.

From the ideal gas equation, $pV = \mu RT$

$$= \dfrac{M}{M_0} RT$$

$\Rightarrow$ $$\dfrac{M}{V} = \dfrac{p M_0}{RT} \qquad \ldots(ii)$$

where, M = mass of gas

and M_0 = molecular mass of gas

Density of gas, $\rho = \dfrac{M}{V}$

From Eq. (ii), we get

$$\rho = \dfrac{p M_0}{RT} \qquad \ldots(iii)$$

From Eqs. (i) and (iii), we get

$$r \propto \dfrac{1}{\sqrt{M_0}}$$

Let r_1 and r_2 be the rates of diffusion of gases 1 and 2 respectively, then

$$\dfrac{r_1}{r_2} = \sqrt{\dfrac{\rho_2}{\rho_1}} = \sqrt{\dfrac{M_{02}}{M_{01}}}$$

where, ρ_1 is density of gas 1 and ρ_2 is density of gas 2.

EXAMPLE |8| Identifying the Gas

From a certain apparatus, the diffusion rate of hydrogen has an average value of $28.7 \text{ cm}^3 \text{s}^{-1}$. The diffusion of another gas under the same conditions is measured to have an average rate of $7.2 \text{ cm}^3 \text{s}^{-1}$. Identify the gas.   **[NCERT]**

Sol. According to Graham's law of diffusion, we get

$$\frac{r_1}{r_2} = \sqrt{\frac{M_2}{M_1}}$$

where, r_1 = rate of diffusion of hydrogen = $28.7 \text{ cm}^3 \text{s}^{-1}$

r_2 = rate of diffusion of unknown gas = $7.2 \text{ cm}^3 \text{s}^{-1}$

M_1 = molecular mass of hydrogen = 2 unit

M_2 = molecular mass of unknown gas = ?

$$\therefore \quad \frac{28.7}{7.2} = \sqrt{\frac{M_2}{2}} \Rightarrow M_2 = \left(\frac{28.7}{7.2}\right)^2 \times 2 = 31.78 \approx 32$$

which is molecular mass of oxygen. So, unknown gas is oxygen.

EXAMPLE |9| Pressure Exerted on an Air Bubble

An air bubble of volume 1.0 cm^3 rises from the bottom of a lake 40 m deep at a temperature of 12°C. To what volume does it grow when it reaches the surface, which is at a temperature of 35°C ?

Given, 1 atm = 1.01×10^5 Pa.   **[NCERT]**

Sol. Initially, when air bubble is at 40 m deep. Then,

$V_1 = 1 \text{ cm}^3 = 1 \times 10^{-6} \text{ m}^3$,

$T_1 = 12° = 273 + 12 = 285$ K

$p_1 = 1 \text{ atm} + h_1 \rho g$

$= 1.01 \times 10^5 + 40 \times 10^3 \times 9.8 = 493000$ Pa

Firstly, when air bubble reaches at the surface, then

$T_2 = 35° \text{C} = 273 + 35 = 308$ K

$p_2 = 1 \text{ atm} = 1.01 \times 10^5 \text{ Pa}, V_2 = ?$

As we know, $\dfrac{p_1 V_1}{T_1} = \dfrac{p_2 V_2}{T_2} \Rightarrow V_2 = \dfrac{p_1 V_1 T_2}{T_1 p_2}$

Final volume i.e.

$$V_2 = \frac{(493000) \times (1 \times 10^{-6}) \times 308}{285 \times 1.01 \times 10^5}$$

$$= 5.275 \times 10^{-6} \text{ m}^2$$

Work Done on Compressing a Gas

The expansion and compression of ideal gases follow the expression.

$$pV^n = \text{constant} \qquad \qquad \text{...(i)}$$

where n is number of moles of the gas. Ideal gases also follow the combined gas law

$$\frac{pV}{T} = \text{constant} \qquad \qquad \text{...(ii)}$$

Dividing Eq. (i) by $\dfrac{pV}{T}$, we get

$$pV^n \div \frac{pV}{T} = \text{constant} \qquad \text{...(iii)}$$

$$\Rightarrow \qquad pV^n \cdot \frac{T}{pV} = \text{constant} \qquad \text{...(iv)}$$

$$\Rightarrow \qquad TV^{n-1} = \text{constant} \qquad \text{...(v)}$$

Eq. (ii) can now be rewritten as

$$V = \text{constant} \cdot \frac{T}{p} \qquad \text{...(vi)}$$

Putting this value is Eq. (i), we get

$$\frac{pT^n}{p^n} = \text{constant} \qquad \text{...(vii)}$$

$$\Rightarrow \qquad \frac{T}{p^{\frac{n-1}{n}}} = \text{constant} \qquad \text{...(viii)}$$

Work done by a gas which is compressing from state 1 to state 2 is given by

$$W = -\int_1^2 p \, dV \qquad \text{...(ix)}$$

From Eq. (i), we have

$$p = \frac{C}{V^n} \qquad \text{...(x)}$$

Putting this value in equation (ix), we get

$$W = -\int_1^2 V^{-n} \, dV \qquad \text{...(xi)}$$

On integration it leads to

$$W = C \left(\frac{V^{-n+1}}{-n+1}\right)\Bigg|_1^2 \qquad \text{...(xii)}$$

Using equation $pV^n = C$, we have

$$W = -\left(pV^n \frac{V^{1-n}}{1-n}\right)\Bigg|_1^2 \qquad \text{...(xiii)}$$

$$W = -\left(\frac{pV}{1-n}\right)\Bigg|_1^n \qquad \text{...(xiv)}$$

$$\Rightarrow \qquad \boxed{W = -\frac{(p_2 V_2 - p_1 V_1)}{1-n}} \qquad \text{...(xv)}$$

Ideal gas law also follows the equation

$$p_1 V_1 = mRT_1 \qquad \text{...(xvi)}$$

$$p_2 V_2 = mRT_2 \qquad \text{...(xvii)}$$

Work done now becomes

$$W = -\frac{mR(T_2 - T_1)}{1-n} \qquad \text{...(xviii)}$$

Note Similar expressions are obtained by similar methods for work done during expansion of gas but starting from

$$W = \int_1^2 p\,dV$$

We obtain,

$$W = \frac{p_2 V_2 - p_1 V_1}{n-1}$$

$$W = \frac{mR(T_2 - T_1)}{n-1}$$

KINETIC THEORY OF IDEAL GAS

The main founders of kinetic theory of gases are

(i) James Clerk Maxwell (1831-1879), a Scottish physicist

(ii) Ludwig Boltzmann (1844-1906) from Austria.

Kinetic theory of gases is based on the molecular picture of matter. It correlates the macroscopic properties (e.g. pressure and temperature) of gases to microscopic properties (e.g. speed and kinetic energy) of gas molecules.

Assumptions of Kinetic Theory of Gases

(i) A given amount of gas consists of a very large number of molecules (of the order of Avogadro's number 10^{23}) and all molecules are identical in all respect.

(ii) The molecules of a gas are in a state of incessant random motion in all directions with different speeds, move freely in straight lines following Newton's first law.

(iii) The size of a molecule is much smaller than the average separation between the molecules. At ordinary pressure and temperature, the average distance between molecules is about 20 Å, whereas size of a molecule is 2 Å.

(iv) There is no intermolecular forces between molecules of gas except during collision.

(v) The collision between molecules among themselves or between molecules and walls are perfectly elastic (i.e. total momentum and total kinetic energy of molecules are conserved, however only their velocities will change).

(vi) The duration of collision between two molecules is negligible as compared to time interval of two successive collisions, i.e. collisions are instantaneous.

(vii) The density and the distribution of molecules is uniform throughout the gas.

Pressure of an Ideal Gas

Consider an ideal gas consisting of N molecules in a container of volume V. The container is a cube with edges of length l. Consider a molecule of mass m moving with velocity (v_x, v_y, v_z).

As molecule collides with the wall parallel to yz-plane elastically, its x-component of velocity is reversed, while its y and z-components of velocity remain unaltered i.e. velocity after collision is $(-v_x, v_y, v_z)$.

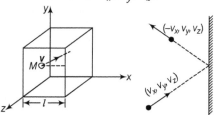

Elastic collision of a gas molecule along
x-component of velocity

So, the change in momentum of the molecule is

$$\Delta p_x = (p_x)_{\text{final}} - (p_x)_{\text{initial}}$$
$$\Delta p_x = -mv_x - (mv_x)$$
$$\Delta p_x = -2mv_x$$

$\because$ Impulse = Change in momentum of molecule

$$\Rightarrow \qquad F\,\Delta t = \Delta p_x = -2mv_x \qquad \text{...(i)}$$

where, F is the average force on the molecule by the wall.

For molecule to collide with same wall, twice it must travel a distance $2l$ in x-direction (as the molecule has to travel from $+x$ to $-x$-directions between two walls).

So, time interval between two collisions with same wall is

$$\Delta t = \frac{2l}{v_x}$$

The average force exerted on a molecule by the wall for each collision is

$$F = \frac{-2mv_x}{\Delta t} = \frac{(-2mv_x)}{(2l/v_x)} = \frac{-mv_x^2}{l}$$

By Newton's Third Law,

The average force exerted by a molecule on the wall is $\frac{mv_x^2}{l}$. If there are N molecules, so total force on the wall will be

$$F_{\text{wall}} = \frac{m}{l}(v_{x_1}^2 + v_{x_2}^2 + \cdots + v_{x_N}^2)$$

It can be rewritten as

$$F_{\text{wall}} = \frac{Nm}{l}\bar{v}_x^2 \qquad \text{...(ii)}$$

where, $$\bar{v}_x^2 = \frac{v_{x_1}^2 + v_{x_2}^2 + \cdots + v_{x_N}^2}{N}$$

Now, $$\bar{v}^2 = \bar{v}_x^2 + \bar{v}_y^2 + \bar{v}_z^2$$

[as velocity has 3 components v_x, v_y, v_z]

Since, motion is completely random, so average values $\bar{v}_x^2, \bar{v}_y^2$ and $\bar{v}_z^2$ are equal to each other [i.e. $\bar{v}_x^2 = \bar{v}_y^2 = \bar{v}_z^2$]

$\therefore \qquad \bar{v}^2 = 3\bar{v}_x^2$ or $\bar{v}_x^2 = \frac{1}{3}\bar{v}^2$ ...(iii)

From Eqs. (ii) and (iii), we get, $F_{\text{wall}} = \frac{N}{3}\left(\frac{m}{l}\bar{v}^2\right)$ ...(iv)

Here, F_{wall} is normal force on the wall.

Pressure on the wall, $p = \dfrac{F_{\text{wall}}}{\text{Area}} = \dfrac{F_{\text{wall}}}{l^2}$

$\Rightarrow \qquad p = \frac{1}{l^2}\left(\frac{N}{3}\frac{m\bar{v}^2}{l}\right)$ or $p = \frac{1}{l^3}\left(\frac{Nm\bar{v}^2}{3}\right)$

or, $$p = \frac{1}{V}\left(\frac{Nm\bar{v}^2}{3}\right) \qquad [\because \text{volume } V = l^3]$$

or, $$\boxed{p = \frac{1}{3}\left(\frac{N}{V}\right)m\bar{v}^2}$$

$\Rightarrow$ Pressure exerted by an ideal gas, $p = \frac{1}{3}nm\bar{v}^2$ ...(v)

where, p = pressure exerted on wall,
n = number density (i.e. number of molecules per unit volume) of gas,
m = mass of one molecule,
$\bar{v}^2$ = mean square speed

and $p = \frac{1}{3}nm\bar{v}^2$ is known as expression for pressure exerted by an ideal gas and also called **kinetic gas equation**.

From the above derivations, we conclude

(i) The shape of vessel is immaterial because area A and time interval Δt do not appear in the final result. For a vessel of arbitrary shape, we can always choose a small infinitesimal planar area and carry through all the steps.

(ii) As per Pascal's law, pressure in one portion of the container as the gas in equilibrium is the same as anywhere else.

(iii) In this derivation, we have ignored any collisions amongst molecules. It can be shown that if these collisions are not too frequent and the time spent in such collision is negligible compared to time between collisions, then mutual molecular collisions do not affect the final result.

Relation between Pressure exerted by an Ideal Gas and its Density

Let M be the mass of all molecules of a given ideal gas enclosed in a vessel of volume V having density ρ, then

$n \times m$ = Number of molecules per unit volume
$\qquad \times$ mass of one molecule
$\qquad$ = Total mass of all molecules per unit volume
$\qquad = \dfrac{M}{V}$

$\Rightarrow \qquad n \times m = \rho \qquad \left[\because \text{Density } [\rho] = \dfrac{\text{Mass}}{\text{Volume}}\right]$ ...(vi)

From Eqs. (v) and (vi), we get

$$p = \frac{1}{3}\rho\bar{v}^2$$

EXAMPLE |10| Behaviour of an Ideal Gas

A container is filled with a gas at a pressure of 76 cm of mercury at a certain temperature. The mass of a gas is increased by 50% by introducing more gas in the container at same temperature. Calculate the final pressure of the gas.

Sol. According to kinetic theory of gases,

$$pV = \frac{1}{3}Mv_{\text{rms}}^2$$

At constant temperature, v_{rms}^2 is constant. As V is also constant.

$\therefore \qquad\qquad p \propto M$

When the mass of the gas is increased by 50%, pressure also increased by 50%.

$\therefore$ Resultant pressure $= 76 + \dfrac{50}{100} \times 76 = 114$ cm of Hg

Kinetic Interpretation of Temperature

The average KE of a molecule depends on the absolute temperature of the gas. It is the kinetic interpretation of temperature. Let us consider a sample of an ideal gas having N number of molecules. Let the volume of the gas is V, pressure is p and temperature is T.

From the pressure expression of an ideal gas

$$p = \frac{1}{3}nm\bar{v}^2 \qquad\qquad \text{...(i)}$$

Multiplying both sides with V, we get

$\Rightarrow \qquad pV = \frac{1}{3}(nV)m\bar{v}^2$

or, $\qquad pV = \frac{2}{3}(nV)\frac{1}{2}m\bar{v}^2$

$\Rightarrow \qquad pV = \frac{2}{3}N\left(\frac{1}{2}m\bar{v}^2\right) \qquad \text{...(ii)}$

Here, number of molecules in the sample, $N = nV$

Here, $\dfrac{1}{2}m\bar{v}^2$ is the average kinetic energy of the molecules of the gas.

So, total internal energy of the gas

$$E = N\left(\dfrac{1}{2}m\bar{v}^2\right) \qquad \ldots\text{(iii)}$$

From Eqs. (ii) and (iii), we get

$$pV = \dfrac{2}{3}E \qquad \ldots\text{(iv)}$$

For ideal gas, we can write

$$pV = \mu RT$$

or, $$pV = \mu k_B N_A T = k_B(\mu N_A)T$$

or, $$pV = k_B NT \qquad \ldots\text{(v)}$$

$$[N = \mu N_A = \text{total number of molecules}]$$

Combining Eqs. (iv) and (v), we get

$$\dfrac{2}{3}E = k_B NT \quad \Rightarrow \quad \dfrac{E}{N} = \dfrac{3}{2}k_B T \qquad \ldots\text{(vi)}$$

or $$\dfrac{1}{2}mv^2 = \dfrac{3}{2}k_B T \qquad \ldots\text{(vii)}$$

$\Rightarrow \qquad$ Average kinetic energy, $\dfrac{1}{2}mv^2 \propto T$

It is clear that **average kinetic energy of a molecule is directly proportional to the absolute temperature of the gas.** It is independent of pressure, volume and the nature of the ideal gas. This is a fundamental result that relates temperature of the gas to average kinetic energy of a molecule.

If $T = 0$, then $\dfrac{1}{2}m\bar{v}^2 = 0$ but $m \neq 0$ so $\bar{v}^2 = 0$

Thus, **absolute zero of temperature may be defined as that temperature at which the mean square speed of the gas molecules reduces to zero.**

Root Mean Square Speed

The square root of the mean square speed $\bar{v}^2$ is known as **root mean square speed.**

From kinetic interpretation,

$$\dfrac{1}{2}m\bar{v}^2 = \dfrac{3}{2}k_B T$$

So, $$\bar{v}^2 = \dfrac{3k_B T}{m}$$

Taking square root of both the sides

$$\sqrt{\bar{v}^2} = \sqrt{\dfrac{3k_B T}{m}}$$

Root mean square speed, $v_{rms} = \sqrt{\dfrac{3k_B T}{m}}$

where, m = mass of one molecule,

k_B = Boltzmann constant

and T = absolute temperature.

EXAMPLE |11| Energy Stored in a Balloon

A balloon has 5.0 g mole of helium at 7°C. Calculate
(i) the number of atoms of helium in the balloon.
(ii) the total internal energy of the system.

[NCERT Exemplar]

Sol. (i) Here, $\mu = 5.0$, $T = 7°\text{C} = 273 + 7 = 280$ K

Number of atoms $= \mu N_A = 5.0 \times 6.02 \times 10^{23}$

$\approx 30 \times 10^{23}$

(ii) Average kinetic energy per molecule $= \dfrac{3}{2}k_B T$

$\therefore$ Total internal energy $= \dfrac{3}{2}k_B T \times N$

$= \dfrac{3}{2} \times 30 \times 10^{23} \times 1.38 \times 10^{-23} \times 280 = 1.74 \times 10^4$ J

EXAMPLE |12| Root Mean Square Speed

In a container, two gases neon and argon are filled. Find the ratio of the root mean square speed of the molecules of the two gases. $M_{Ne} = 20.2$ and $M_{Ar} = 39.9$. The temperature of the system is 30°C.

Sol. Given, $M_{Ne} = 20.2$, $M_{Ar} = 39.9$

Temperature $(T) = 30°$ C

We know that, $\dfrac{1}{2}mv_{rms}^2 = \dfrac{3}{2}k_B T$

Temperature is same for both the gases. Now, we can find the ratio of v_{rms} for the two gases.

$$\dfrac{(v_{rms}^2)_{Ne}}{(v_{rms}^2)_{Ar}} = \dfrac{(M)_{Ar}}{(M)_{Ne}}$$

Now, we can easily find the numerical value of ratio of two v_{rms}.

$$\dfrac{(v_{rms})_{Ne}}{(v_{rms})_{Ar}} = \sqrt{\dfrac{39.9}{20.2}} \approx 1.40$$

Maxwell's Speed Distribution

In a given sample of gas, all molecules don't move with same speed. They move randomly in different directions, but the distribution of velocities among the molecules remain fixed. Maxwell first studied molecular speed distribution and derived an equation giving distribution of molecules as follows.

If dN represents the number of molecules having speed between v and $v + dv$ then,

$$dN = 4\pi N \left(\frac{m}{2\pi k_B T}\right)^{3/2} v^2 e^{-\frac{mv^2}{2k_B T}} \, dv$$

where, v = molecular speed of the gas,

m = the molecular mass of the gas,

T = temperature of the gas in kelvin,

N = total number of molecules of the gas

and k_B = Boltzmann constant.

The fraction of molecules with speed v and dv is equal to area of strip shown in figure,

i.e. $\dfrac{dN}{N} = f(v)\, dv$ = area of the strip

Total area of the curve will be unity, as it represents all molecules. Above figure shows the Maxwell's distribution function $f(v)$ of a gas at three different temperatures. Each

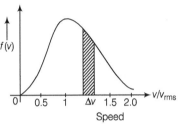

graph has a peak which represents the maximum fraction of total molecules having maximum speed (v_{max}) due to this reason v_{max} is also called most probable speed. As the temperature increases, the curve become flatter and its maximum points (peak points) shifts towards higher speed.

Note

- **Most probable speed** The speed possessed by the maximum number of molecules in a gas at a given temperature.

$$V_{mp} = \sqrt{\frac{2k_B T}{m}}$$

- **Mean or Average speed** The arithmetic mean of the speed of the molecules of a gas at a given temperature.

$$V_{av} = \sqrt{\frac{8k_B T}{\pi m}}$$

EXAMPLE |13| RMS Speed of a Gas Molecule

The molecules of a given mass of a gas have root mean square speeds of 100 ms^{-1} at 27°C and 1.00 atm pressure. What will be the root mean square speeds of the molecules of the gas at 127°C and 2.0 atm pressure? [NCERT Exemplar]

Sol. According to ideal gas equation, we get

$$\frac{p_1 V_1}{T_1} = \frac{p_2 V_2}{T_2}$$

or $\quad \dfrac{V_1}{V_2} = \dfrac{p_2 T_1}{p_1 T_2} = \dfrac{2 \times 300}{1 \times 400} = \dfrac{3}{2}$

$$p_1 = \frac{1}{3}\frac{M}{V_1}(v_{rms})_1^2, \quad p_2 = \frac{1}{3}\frac{M}{V_2}(v_{rms})_2^2$$

$\therefore \quad (v_{rms})_2^2 = (v_{rms})_1^2 \times \dfrac{V_2}{V_1} \times \dfrac{p_2}{p_1} = (100)^2 \times \dfrac{2}{3} \times 2$

or $\quad (v_{rms})_2 = \dfrac{200}{\sqrt{3}}$ m s^{-1}

EXAMPLE |14| A Nuclear Fission

Uranium has two isotopes of masses 235 and 238 units. If both are present in uranium hexafluoride gas, which would have the larger average speed? If atomic mass of fluorine is 19 units, estimate the percentage difference in speeds at any temperature. How is the above concept of difference in speeds utilised in the enrichment of uranium needed for nuclear fission? [NCERT]

At a fixed temperature, the average energy = $\frac{1}{2}mv_{rms}^2$ is constant. So, smaller the mass of a molecule, faster will be its speed. Clearly,

Speed of molecule $\propto \dfrac{1}{\sqrt{\text{molecular mass}}}$

Sol. Molecular mass of ^{235}U hexafluoride

$$= 235 + 6 \times 19 = 349$$

Molecular mass of ^{238}U hexafluoride

$$= 238 + 6 \times 19 = 352$$

$\therefore \quad \dfrac{v_{349}}{v_{352}} = \left(\dfrac{352}{349}\right)^{1/2} = 1.0044$

Percentage difference in speeds,

$$\frac{\Delta v}{v} \times 100 = 0.0044 \times 100 = 0.44\%$$

^{235}U is the isotope needed for nuclear fission. To separate it from the more abundant isotope ^{238}U, the mixture is surrounded by a porous cylinder. The porous cylinder must be thick and narrow, so that the molecule wanders through individually, colliding with the walls of the long porous, as shown in figure.

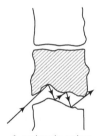

A molecule going through a porous wall

The faster molecule will leak out more than the slower one and so there is more of the lighter molecule (enrichment) outside the porous cylinder. The method is not very efficient and has to be repeated several times for sufficient enrichment.

| TOPIC PRACTICE 1 |

OBJECTIVE Type Questions

1. Interatomic forces are

   (a) attractive in long range

   (b) repulsive in short range

   (c) negligible in gases

   (d) All (a), (b) and (c)

Sol. (d) Interatomic forces are attractive in long range and repulsive in short range and negligible in gases.

2. According to atomic hypothesis
   (a) atoms attract each other when they are little distance apart
   (b) atoms repel if they being squeezed into one another
   (c) Both (a) and (b)
   (d) Neither (a) nor (b)

Sol. (c) Atoms attract when they are little distance apart and repel, if they being squeezed into one another.

3. Boyle's law is applicable for an [NCERT Exemplar]
   (a) adiabatic process   (b) isothermal process
   (c) isobaric process   (d) isochoric process

Sol. (b) Boyle's law is applicable when temperature is constant

   i.e., $pV = nRT = $ constant
   $\Rightarrow$ $pV = $ constant (at constant temperature)
   i.e., $p \propto \dfrac{1}{V}$ [where , p=pressure, V= volume]

   So, this process can be called as isothermal process.

4. The collisions of the molecules of an ideal gas are
   (a) elastic
   (b) inelastic
   (c) completely inelastic
   (d) partially elastic

Sol. (a) According to kinetic theory of gases the collision among molecules and the collision of molecule with the walls of container are elastic.

5. The root mean square speed of a nitrogen molecule at 300K is
   (a) $\sqrt{534}$ ms^{-1} (b) 534 ms^{-1}
   (c) 267 ms^{-1} (d) $\sqrt{216}$ ms^{-1}

Sol. (c) $v_{rms} = \sqrt{\dfrac{3RT}{M}} = \sqrt{\dfrac{3 \times 8.314 \times 300}{28}}$

   $= 267.2 \, \text{ms}^{-1}$

VERY SHORT ANSWER Type Questions

6. Under what conditions, real gases behave as an ideal gas?

Sol. At low pressure and high temperature, real gases behave as an ideal gas.

7. Calculate the number of atoms in 39.4 g gold. Molar mass of gold is 197g mol^{-1}. [NCERT Exemplar]

Sol. Molar mass of gold is 197g mol^{-1}, the number of atoms
   $= 6.0 \times 10^{23}$
   $\therefore$ Number of atoms in 39.4 g
   $= \dfrac{6.0 \times 10^{23} \times 39.4}{197} = 1.2 \times 10^{23}$

8. The given graph shows the variation of p-V versus p graph for different gases at constant temperature. Which of the following gas is ideal and why?

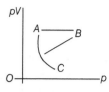

Sol. Gas A is ideal because pV is constant for gas A so, gas A obeys Boyle's law for all values of pressure.

9. When air is pumped into a cycle tyre, the volume and pressure of the air in the tyre, both are increased. What about Boyle's law in this case? [NCERT Exemplar]

Sol. When air is pumped, more molecules are pumped in Boyle's law, is stated for situation where number of molecules remain constant.

10. The volume of a given mass of a gas at 27°C, 1 atm is 100 cc. What will be its volume at 327°C? [NCERT Exemplar]

Sol. Keeping p constant, we have
   $$V_2 = \dfrac{V_1 T_2}{T_1} = \dfrac{100 \times 600}{300} = 200 \, \text{cc}$$

11. What is the minimum possible temperature on the basis of Charles' law?

Sol. The minimum possible temperature on the basis of Charles' law is $-273.15°$C.

12. If a vehicle runs on the road for a long time, then the air pressure in the tyres increases. Explain.

Sol. Due to the presence of friction between the road and tyres, the tyres get heated as a result of which temperature of air inside the tyre increases and hence pressure in tyre also increases.

13. According to kinetic theory of gases, explain absolute zero.

Sol. Absolute zero is the temperature at which the molecules of a gas becomes motionless. i.e. $\bar{v}_{rms} = 0$

14. Two molecules of a gas have speeds of 9×10^6 ms^{-1} and 1×10^6 ms^{-1}, respectively. What is the root mean square speed of these molecules? [NCERT Exemplar]

Sol. $v_{rms} = \sqrt{\dfrac{v_1^2 + v_2^2}{2}} = \sqrt{\dfrac{(9 \times 10^6)^2 + (1 \times 10^6)^2}{2}}$

   $= \sqrt{\dfrac{(81 + 1) \times 10^{12}}{2}} = \sqrt{41} \times 10^6 \, \text{ms}^{-1}$

15. What would be the effect on rms velocity of gas molecules, if the temperature of the gas is increased by a factor 4?

Sol. As, $v_{rms} \propto \sqrt{T}$

   If temperature of the gas is increased 4 times, then v_{rms} will be doubled.

16. If a gas is heated, its temperature increases. On the basis of kinetic theory of gases, explain.

Sol. If a gas is heated, then the root mean square velocity of its molecules is increased.

$\because \quad v_{rms} \propto \sqrt{T}$

$\therefore$ The temperature of the gas increases.

SHORT ANSWER Type Questions

17. Molar volume is the volume occupied by 1 mol of any (ideal) gas at standard temperature and pressure (STP : 1 atm pressure, 0°C). Show that, it is 22.4 L. **[NCERT]**

Sol. As, for one mole of ideal gas, $pV = \mu RT$ $[\mu = 1]$

$$pV = RT$$

$$\Rightarrow \quad V = \frac{RT}{p}$$

Putting, $R = 8.31 \text{ J mol}^{-1} \text{ K}^{-1}$, $T = 273\text{K}$

$$p = 1 \text{ atm} = 1.013 \times 10^5 \text{ N-m}^{-2}$$

$$V = \frac{8.31 \times 273}{1.013 \times 10^5} = 0.0224 \text{ m}^3$$

$$= 22.4 \text{ L} \qquad [\because 1\text{m}^3 = 10^3\text{L}]$$

18. Estimate the total number of air molecules (inclusive of oxygen, nitrogen, water vapour and other constituents) in a room of capacity 25.0 m³ at a temperature of 27°C and 1 atm pressure. ($k_B = 1.38 \times 10^{-23} \text{ JK}^{-1}$) **[NCERT]**

Sol. Given, $V = 25.0 \text{ m}^3$, $T = 273 + 27 = 300$ K

$$k_B = 1.38 \times 10^{-23} \text{ JK}^{-1}$$

Now, $pV = \mu RT$

$\Rightarrow \quad pV = \mu(N_A k_B)T$

$\Rightarrow \quad pV = N' k_B T$

[N' is total number of molecules]

$$\therefore \quad N' = \frac{pV}{k_B T} = \frac{(1.01 \times 10^5) \times 25}{(1.38 \times 10^{-23}) \times 300}$$

$$= 6.10 \times 10^{26}$$

19. Estimate the fraction of molecular volume to the actual volume occupied by oxygen gas at STP. Take the diameter of an oxygen molecule to be 3 Å. **[NCERT]**

Sol. Given, $d = 3$ Å

$$r = \frac{d}{2} = 1.5 \times 10^{-10} \text{ m} = 1.5 \times 10^{-8} \text{ cm}$$

Molecular volume, $V = \frac{4}{3}\pi r^3 N$

$$= \frac{4}{3} \times 3.14 \times (1.5 \times 10^{-8})^3 \times 6.023 \times 10^{23} = 8.52 \text{ cc}$$

Actual volume occupied by 1 mole of oxygen at STP,

$$V' = 22400 \text{ cc}$$

$$\therefore \quad \frac{V}{V'} = \frac{8.52}{22400} = 3.8 \times 10^{-4}$$

20. A flask contains argon and chlorine in the ratio of 2 : 1 by mass. The temperature of the mixture is 27°C. Obtain the ratio of

(i) average kinetic energy per molecule and

(ii) root mean square speed (v_{rms}) of the molecules of the two gases. Atomic mass of argon = 39.9 u; Molecular mass of chlorine = 70.9 u. **[NCERT]**

Sol. (i) The average kinetic energy per molecule of any gas is $\frac{3}{2}k_B T$. It depends only on temperature and not on the nature of the gas. As both argon and chlorine have the same temperature in the flask, the ratio of average KE per molecule of the two gases is 1 : 1.

(ii) If m is mass of single molecule and M is the molecular mass, then

$$\frac{1}{2}mv_{rms}^2 = \frac{3}{2}k_B T$$

= constant at a given temperature

$$\therefore \quad \frac{(v_{rms}^2)_{Ar}}{(v_{rms}^2)_{Cl_2}} = \frac{(m)_{Cl_2}}{(m)_{Ar}} = \frac{M_{Cl_2}}{M_{Ar}} = \frac{70.9}{39.9} = 1.777$$

or $\quad \frac{(v_{rms})_{Ar}}{(v_{rms})_{Cl_2}} = \sqrt{1.777} = 1.333$

21. We have 0.5 g of hydrogen gas in a cubic chamber of size 3 cm kept at NTP. The gas in the chamber is compressed keeping the temperature constant till a final pressure of 100 atm. Is one justified in assuming the ideal gas law, in the final state? (Hydrogen molecules can be considered as spheres of radius 1 Å). **[NCERT Exemplar]**

Sol. We have, $0.25 \times 6 \times 10^{23}$ molecules, each of volume 10^{-30}m^3.

Molecular volume = $2.5 \times 10^{-7} \text{ m}^3$

Supposing, ideal gas law is valid.

Final volume = $\frac{V_{in}}{100} = \frac{(3)^3 \times 10^{-6}}{100} \approx 2.7 \times 10^{-7} \text{ m}^3$

Which is about the molecular volume. Hence, intermolecular forces cannot be neglected. Therefore, the ideal gas situation does not hold.

22. Three vessels of equal capacity have gases at the same temperature and pressure. The first vessel contains neon (monoatomic), the second contains chlorine (diatomic) and the third contains uranium hexafluoride (polyatomic). Do the vessels contain equal number of respective molecules?

Is the root mean square speed of molecules, the same in the three cases? If not, in which case is v_{rms}, the largest? **[NCERT]**

Sol. As three vessels are identical i.e. they have same volume. Now at constant pressure, temperature and volume, the three vessels will contain equal number of molecules (by Avogadro's law) and is equal to Avogadro's number, $N_A = 6.023 \times 10^{23}$.

$$\because \quad v_{rms} = \sqrt{\frac{3k_B T}{m}} \Rightarrow v_{rms} \propto \frac{1}{\sqrt{m}}$$

where, m is mass of single gas molecule as neon has the smallest mass, so rms speed will be greatest in case of neon.

23. A tank used for filling helium balloons has a volume of 0.6 m³ and contains 2.0 mol of helium gas at 20.0°C. Assuming that the helium behaves like an ideal gas.

    (i) What is the total translational kinetic energy of the molecules of the gas?

    (ii) What is the average kinetic energy per molecule?

Sol. (i) We know that $(KE)_{trans} = \frac{3}{2}nRT$

    Given, $\quad n = 2$ mol, $T = 273 + 20 = 293$ K

$$\Rightarrow (KE)_{trans} = \frac{3}{2}(2)(8.31)(293) = 7.3 \times 10^3 \text{ J}$$

    (ii) Average KE per molecule

$$= \frac{1}{2}m\bar{v}^2_{rms} = \frac{3}{2}kT = \frac{3}{2}(1.38 \times 10^{-23})(293)$$
$$= 6.07 \times 10^{-21} \text{ J}$$

24. At what temperature, is the root mean square speed of an atom in an argon gas cylinder equal to the rms speed of a helium gas atom at −20°C? (Atomic mass of Ar = 39.9 u, He = 4.0 u). **[NCERT]**

Sol. Let C and C' be the rms velocity of argon and a helium gas atoms at temperatures TK and T'K, respectively.

Here, $\quad M = 39.9, M' = 4.0, T = ?,$
$$T' = -20 + 273 = 253 \text{ K}$$

Now, $\quad v = \sqrt{\frac{3RT}{M}} = \sqrt{\frac{3RT}{39.9}}$

and $\quad v' = \sqrt{\frac{3RT'}{M'}} = \sqrt{\frac{3R \times 253}{4}}$

Since, $v = v'$, therefore $\sqrt{\frac{3RT}{39.9}} = \sqrt{\frac{3R \times 253}{4}}$

or $\quad T = \frac{39.9 \times 253}{4} = 2523.7\text{K}$

25. A gas mixture consists of molecules of types A, B and C with masses, $m_A > m_B > m_C$. Rank the three types of molecules in decreasing order of (i) average KE (ii) rms speed. **[NCERT Exemplar]**

Sol. The average KE will be same as conditions of temperature and pressure are same.

$$v_{rms} \propto \frac{1}{\sqrt{m}}$$

$\because \quad\quad\quad m_A > m_B > m_C$

$\Rightarrow \quad\quad\quad v_C > v_B > v_A$

26. A gas is contained in a closed vessel. How pressure due to the gas will be affected if force of attraction between the molecules disappear suddenly?

Sol. As force of attraction between molecules disappears, then molecules will hit the wall with more speeds, hence, rate of change of momentum will increase.

As we know $F = \frac{\Delta p}{\Delta t}$,

where F is average force on the wall due to molecules. Δp is change in momentum and Δt is the time duration. Due to increase in Δp, force F will also increase, hence pressure, $p = \frac{F}{A}$ will increase. Here, A is area of one wall.

LONG ANSWER Type I Questions

27. Write the difference between ideal gas and real gas.

Sol.

	Ideal Gas	Real Gas
(i)	It obeys ideal gas equation, $pV = \mu RT$ at all temperatures and pressures.	It does not obey, $pV = \mu RT$ at all values of temperature and pressure.
(ii)	The volume of the molecules of an ideal gas is zero.	The volume of the molecules of a real gas is non-zero.
(iii)	There is no intermolecular force between the molecules.	There is intermolecular force of attraction or repulsion depending on whether intermolecular separation is larger or small.
(iv)	There is no intermolecular potential energy (U) because intermolecular force (F) is zero.	Potential energy (U) does not equal to zero as intermolecular force (F) is not zero.
(v)	It has only kinetic energy.	It has both kinetic and potential energy.
(vi)	At absolute zero, the volume, pressure and internal energy become zero.	All real gases get liquified before reaching absolute zero. The internal energy of the liquified gas is not zero.

28. Estimate the average thermal energy of a helium atom at (i) room temperature (27°C) (ii) the temperature on the surface of the sun (6000 K), (iii) the temperature of 10 million kelvin (the typical core temperature in the case of a star). **[NCERT]**

💡 Thermal energy represents that part of internal energy which is translational kinetic in nature. This is equal to $\frac{3}{2}k_BT$; which only depends on absolute temperature of the gas.

Sol. (i) Given, $T = 27°C = (273.15 + 27) = 300.15$ K

Average thermal energy, $E = \frac{3}{2}k_BT$

(where, k_B = Boltzmann constant

$$= 1.38 \times 10^{-23} \text{ J K}^{-1})$$

$$E = \frac{3}{2} \times 1.38 \times 10^{-23} \times 300.15 = 6.21 \times 10^{-21} \text{ J}$$

(ii) At the temperature, $T = 6000$ K (surface of the sun)

Average thermal energy, $E = \frac{3}{2}k_BT$

$$= \frac{3}{2} \times 1.38 \times 10^{-23} \times 6000 = 1.241 \times 10^{-19} \text{ J}$$

(iii) At temperature, $T = 10^7$ K

Average thermal energy,

$$E = \frac{3}{2}k_BT = \frac{3}{2} \times 1.38 \times 10^{-23} \times 10^7$$

$$= 2.07 \times 10^{-16} \text{ J}$$

29. (i) Write ideal gas equation in terms of density.

(ii) If molar volume is the volume occupied by 1 mole of any (ideal) gas at STP, show that it is 22.4 L (take $R = 8.313 \text{ mol}^{-1}\text{K}^{-1}$).

Sol. (i) Refer to text on page no. 511.

(ii) $p = 1$ atm $= 0.76$ m of Hg

$$= 0.76 \times (13.6 \times 10^3) \times 9.8 \text{ Pa}$$

$\Rightarrow \quad T = 273$ K, $R = 8.31 \text{ J mol}^{-1}\text{K}^{-1}$, $\mu = 1$ mole

As $pV = \mu RT$

or, $V = \dfrac{\mu RT}{p} = \dfrac{1 \times 8.31 \times 273}{0.76 \times (13.6 \times 10^3) \times 9.8}$

$$= 22.4 \times 10^{-3} \text{ m}^3 = 22.4 \text{ L}$$

30. Explain, why

(i) there is no atmosphere on moon.

(ii) there is fall in temperature with altitude.

[NCERT Exemplar]

Sol. (i) The moon has small gravitational force and hence the escape velocity is small. As the moon is in the proximity of the earth as seen from the sun, the moon has the same amount of heat per unit area as that of the earth. The air molecules have large range of speeds.

Even though the rms speed of the air molecules is smaller than escape velocity on the moon, a significant number of molecules have speed greater than escape velocity and they escape.

Now, rest of the molecules arrange the speed distribution for the equilibrium temperature. Again, a significant number of molecules escape as their speeds exceed escape speed. Hence, over a long time the moon has lost most of its atmosphere.

(ii) As the molecules move higher, their potential energy increases and hence kinetic energy decreases and hence temperature reduces.

At greater height, more volume is available and gas expands and hence some cooling takes place.

31. A meter long narrow bore held horizontally (and closed at one end) contains a 76 cm long mercury thread which traps a 15 cm column of air. What happens, if the tube is held vertically with the open end at the bottom? **[NCERT]**

Sol. If the tube is held horizontally, the mercury thread of length 76 cm traps a length of air = 15 cm. A length of 9 cm of the tube will be at the open end, Fig. (a). The pressure of air enclosed in tube will be atmospheric pressure. Let area of cross-section of the tube be 1 sq. cm.

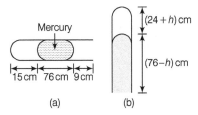

(a) (b)

$\therefore \qquad p_1 = 76$ cm and $V_1 = 15$ cm^3

If the tube is held vertically, 15 cm air gets another 9 cm of air (filled in the right handside in the horizontal position) and let h cm of mercury flow out to balance the atmospheric pressure, Fig. (b). Then, the heights of air column and mercury column are $(24 + h)$ cm and $(76 - h)$ cm, respectively.

The pressure of air $= 76 - (76 - h) = h$ cm of mercury

$\therefore \qquad V_2 = (24 + h)$ cm^3

and $\qquad p_2 = h$ cm

If we assume that temperature remains constant, then

$$p_1V_1 = p_2V_2 \text{ or } 76 \times 15 = h \times (24 + h)$$

or $\qquad h^2 + 24h - 1140 = 0$

or $\qquad h = \dfrac{-24 \pm \sqrt{(24)^2 + 4 \times 1140}}{2}$

$$= 23.8 \text{ cm or } -47.8 \text{ cm}$$

Since, h cannot be negative (because more mercury cannot flow into the tube), therefore $h = 23.8$ cm. Thus, in the vertical position of the tube, 23.8 cm of mercury flows out.

32. The container shown in figure has two chambers, separated by a partition of volumes $V_1 = 2.0$ L and $V_2 = 3.0$ L. The chambers contain $\mu_1 = 4.0$ and $\mu_2 = 5.0$ moles of a gas at pressures $p_1 = 1.00$ atm and $p_2 = 2.00$ atm. Calculate the pressure after the partition is removed and the mixture attains equilibrium.   **[NCERT Exemplar]**

V_1	V_2
μ_1	μ_2
p_1	p_2

Sol. Given, $V_1 = 2.0$ L, $V_2 = 3.0$ L, $\mu_1 = 4.0$ moles, $\mu_2 = 5.0$ moles

$$p_1 = 1.00 \text{ atm}, \ p_2 = 2.00 \text{ atm}$$
$$p_1 V_1 = \mu_1 R T_1, \ p_2 V_2 = \mu_2 R T_2$$
$$\mu = \mu_1 + \mu_2, \ V = V_1 + V_2$$

For 1 mole, $pV = \dfrac{2}{3}E$

For μ_1 mole, $p_1 V_1 = \dfrac{2}{3}\mu_1 E_1$

For μ_2 mole, $p_2 V_2 = \dfrac{2}{3}\mu_2 E_2$

Total energy is $(\mu_1 E_1 + \mu_2 E_2) = \dfrac{3}{2}(p_1 V_1 + p_2 V_2)$

$$pV = \dfrac{2}{3}E_{\text{total}} = \dfrac{2}{3}\mu E_{\text{per mole}}$$

$$p(V_1 + V_2) = \dfrac{2}{3} \times \dfrac{3}{2}(p_1 V_1 + p_2 V_2)$$

$$p = \dfrac{p_1 V_1 + p_2 V_2}{V_1 + V_2} \qquad \ldots(i)$$

$$= \left(\dfrac{1.00 \times 2.0 + 2.00 \times 3.0}{2.0 + 3.0}\right) = \dfrac{8.0}{5.0} = 1.60 \text{ atm}$$

33. An oxygen cylinder of volume 30 L, has an initial gauge pressure of 15 atm and a temperature of 27 °C. After some oxygen is withdrawn from the cylinder, the gauge pressure drops to 11 atm and its temperature drops to 17 °C. Estimate the mass of oxygen taken out of the cylinder ($R = 8.31 \text{ mol}^{-1}\text{K}^{-1}$, molecular mass of $O_2 = 32$ u).   **[NCERT]**

☼ Whenever masses are taken out of the closed system, no more it is a closed system, hence ideal gas equation should be applied to calculate the change in mass. First, number of moles removed should be calculated and then by multiplying with molecular mass of the gas, the same can be converted into mass of the gas removed.

Sol. Given, absolute pressure, $p_1 = (15 + 1)$ atm
[∵ absolute pressure = gauge pressure + 1 atm]
$$= 16 \times 1.013 \times 10^5 \text{ Pa}$$
$$V_1 = 30 \text{ L} = 30 \times 10^{-3}\text{ m}^3$$

$$T_1 = 273.15 + 27 = 300.15 \text{ K}$$

Using ideal gas equation, $pV = nRT$

or $n = \dfrac{pV}{RT} = \dfrac{p_1 V_1}{RT_1} = \dfrac{16 \times 1.013 \times 10^5 \times 30 \times 10^{-3}}{8.314 \times 300.15}$

$$= 19.48$$

Final $p_2 = (11 + 1) = 12 \text{ atm} = 12 \times 1.013 \times 10^5 \text{ Pa}$

$$V_2 = 30 \text{ L} = 30 \times 10^{-3}\text{ m}^3$$

$$T_2 = 273.15 + 17 = 290.15 \text{ K}$$

Number of moles
$$= \dfrac{p_2 V_2}{RT_2} = \dfrac{12 \times 1.013 \times 10^5 \times 30 \times 10^{-3}}{8.314 \times 290.15} = 15.12$$

Hence, moles removed $= 19.48 - 15.12 = 4.36$
Mass removed $= 4.36 \times 32$ g
$$= 139.52 \text{g} = 0.1395 \text{ kg}$$

LONG ANSWER Type II Questions

34. A gas in equilibrium has uniform density and pressure throughout its volume. This is strictly true only if there are no external influences. A gas column under gravity, e.g. does not have uniform density (and pressure). As you might expect, its density decreases with height. The precise dependence is given by the so called law of atmosphere.

$$n_2 = n_1 \exp[-mg(h_2 - h_1)/k_B T]$$

where, n_2 and n_1 refer to number density at heights h_2 and h_1, respectively. Use this relation to derive the equation for sedimentation equilibrium of a suspension in a liquid column.

$$n_2 = n_1 \exp[-mg N_A(\rho - \rho')(h_2 - h_1)/(\rho RT)]$$

where, ρ is the density of the suspended particle and ρ', that of surrounding medium.

[∵ N_A is Avogadro's number and R is the universal gas constant.]   **[NCERT]**

Sol. According to the law of atmospheres,
$$n_2 = n_1 \exp\left[-\dfrac{mg}{k_B T}(h_2 - h_1)\right] \qquad \ldots(i)$$

where, n_2 and n_1 refer to number density of particles at heights h_2 and h_1, respectively.

If we consider the sedimentation equilibrium of suspended particles in a liquid, then in place of mg, we will have to take effective weight of the suspended particles.

Let, V = average volume of a suspended particle, ρ = density of suspended particle, ρ' = density of liquid, m = mass of one suspended particle, m' = mass of equal volume of liquid displaced.

According to Archimedes' principle, effective weight of one suspended particle
= Actual weight − weight of liquid displaced = $mg - m'g$

$$= mg - V \rho' g = mg - \left(\frac{m}{\rho}\right)\rho' g = mg\left(1 - \frac{\rho'}{\rho}\right)$$

Also, Boltzmann constant, $k_B = \dfrac{R}{N_A}$

where, R is gas constant and N_A is Avogadro's number.

Putting, $mg\left(1 - \dfrac{\rho'}{\rho}\right)$ in place of mg and value of k_B in

Eq. (i), we get

$n_2 = n_1 \exp\left[-\dfrac{mg N_A}{RT}\left(1 - \dfrac{\rho'}{\rho}\right)(h_2 - h_1)\right]$, which is

required relation.

35. Given below are densities of some solids and liquids. Give rough estimate of the size of their atoms. **[NCERT]**

Substance	Atomic Mass (u)	Density $(10^{-3}\,kg\,m^{-3})$
(i) Carbon (diamond)	12.01	2.22
(ii) Gold	197.00	19.32
(iii) Nitrogen (liquid)	14.01	1.00
(iv) Lithium	6.94	0.53
(v) Fluorine (liquid)	19.00	1.14

Sol. We know, that, density of an element

$$\rho = \frac{\text{Mass}}{\text{Volume}} = \frac{\text{Mass of 1 mole}}{\substack{\text{Total volume of molecules in}\\ \text{1 mole when closely packed}}}$$

$$\rho = \frac{M(\text{in grams})}{\left(\frac{4}{3}\pi r^3\right)N_A} = \frac{3\,M \times 10^{-3}\,\text{kg}}{4\pi r^3 \cdot N_A}$$

$$\Rightarrow \quad r = \left[\frac{3\,M \times 10^{-3}}{4\pi N_A \cdot \rho}\right]^{1/3},$$

where, N_A = Avogadro's number $\simeq 6 \times 10^{23}$

(i) For carbon (diamond),

$M = 12.01$, $\rho = 2.22 \times 10^3$ kg /m^3

$\therefore$ Radius of carbon atom

$$r = \left[\frac{3 \times 12.01 \times 10^{-3}}{4 \times 3.14 \times 6 \times 10^{23} \times 2.22 \times 10^3}\right]^{1/3}$$

$= 1.29 \times 10^{-10}$ m

$= 1.29$ Å

(ii) For gold, $M = 197.00, \rho = 19.32 \times 10^3$ kg/m^3

$\therefore$ Radius of gold atom

$$r = \left[\frac{3 \times 197 \times 10^{-3}}{4 \times 3.14 \times 6 \times 10^{23} \times 19.32 \times 10^3}\right]^{\frac{1}{3}}$$

$= 1.59 \times 10^{-10}$ m $= 1.59$ Å

(iii) For nitrogen (liquid),

$M = 14.01$, $\rho = 1.00 \times 10^3$ kg / m^3

$\therefore$ Radius of nitrogen atom

$$r = \left[\frac{3 \times 14.01 \times 10^{-3}}{4 \times 3.14 \times 6 \times 10^{23} \times 1.0 \times 10^3}\right]^{\frac{1}{3}}$$

$= 1.77 \times 10^{-7}$ m $= 1.77$ Å

(iv) For lithium, $M = 6.94$, $\rho = 0.53 \times 10^3$ kg/m^3

$\therefore$ Radius of lithium atom

$$r = \left[\frac{3 \times 6.94 \times 10^{-3}}{4 \times 3.14 \times 6 \times 10^{23} \times 0.53 \times 10^3}\right]^{\frac{1}{3}}$$

$= 1.73 \times 10^{-10}$ m $= 1.73$ Å

(v) For flourine (liquid),

$M = 19.00$ and $\rho = 1.14 \times 10^3$ kg /m^3

$\therefore$ Radius of fluorine atom

$$r = \left[\frac{3 \times 19.0 \times 10^{-3}}{4 \times 3.14 \times 6 \times 10^{23} \times 1.14 \times 10^3}\right]^{\frac{1}{3}}$$

$= 1.88 \times 10^{-10}$ m $= 1.88$ Å

36. You are given, the following data about a group of particles, where n_i represents the number of molecules with speed v_i

n_i	2	4	8	6	3
$v_i\,(ms^{-1})$	1.0	2.0	3.0	4.0	5.0

Calculate   (i) average speed

(ii) rms speed

(iii) most probable speed.

Sol.   (i) Average speed

$$= \frac{n_1 v_1 + n_2 v_2 + n_3 v_3 + n_4 v_4 + n_5 v_5}{n_1 + n_2 + n_3 + n_4 + n_5}$$

$$= \frac{2 \times 1 + 4 \times 2 + 8 \times 3 + 6 \times 4 + 3 \times 5}{2 + 4 + 8 + 6 + 3} = 3.17 \text{ m / s}$$

(ii) Root mean square speed

$$= \sqrt{\frac{n_1 v_1^2 + n_2 v_2^2 + n_3 v_3^2 + n_4 v_4^2 + n_5 v_5^2}{n_1 + n_2 + n_3 + n_4 + n_5}}$$

$$= \sqrt{\frac{2 \times 1^2 + 4 \times 2^2 + 8 \times 3^2 + 6 \times 4^2 + 3 \times 5^2}{2 + 4 + 8 + 6 + 3}}$$

$= 3.36$ m / s

(iii) The most probable speed is that speed which is possessed by maximum number of molecules.

Most probable speed $(v_{mp}) = \sqrt{\dfrac{2 k_B T}{m}} = \sqrt{\dfrac{3 k_B T}{m}} \times 2/3$

$$v_{mp} = \sqrt{\frac{2}{3}} \times \sqrt{\frac{3 k_B T}{m}} = \sqrt{\frac{2}{3}} v_{rms} = \sqrt{\frac{2}{3}} \times 3.36 \text{ m/s}$$

$= 0.816 \times 3.36$ m/s $= 2.74$ m/s

37. Figure shows plot of pV/T *versus* p for 1.00×10^{-3} kg of oxygen gas at two different temperatures.

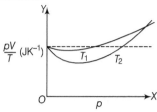

(i) What does the dotted plot signify?

(ii) Which is true, $T_1 > T_2$ or $T_1 < T_2$?

(iii) What is the value of pV/T, where the curves meet on the Y-axis?

(iv) If we obtain similar plots for 1.00×10^{-3} kg of hydrogen, would we get the same value of pV/T at the point where the curves meet on the Y-axis? If not, what mass of hydrogen yields the same value of pV/T (for low pressure, high temperature region of the plot)? (Molecular mass of H_2 = 2.02 u, O_2 = 32.0 u, R = 8.31 Jmol^{-1}K^{-1}). [NCERT]

Sol. (i) Dotted plot shows that $\dfrac{pV}{T}$ is a constant quantity $\left(\dfrac{pV}{T} = mR \right)$ which is independent of pressure. It signifies the ideal gas behaviour.

(ii) As curve at temperature T_1 is closer to the dotted plot than the curve at temperature T_2. Since, the behaviour of a real gas approaches the behaviour of perfect gas when temperature is increased, so $T_1 > T_2$.

(iii) The value of $\dfrac{pV}{T}$, where the curves meet on Y-axis is equal to μR.

Now, given mass of oxygen gas = 1.00×10^{-3} kg = 1 g

$\therefore \qquad \dfrac{pV}{T} = \mu R = \left(\dfrac{1}{32} \right) \times 8.31 \text{ JK}^{-1}$

$\qquad\qquad = 0.26 \text{ JK}^{-1}$

(iv) If we use 1.00×10^{-3} kg of hydrogen, then we will not get same value of $\dfrac{pV}{T}$ at the point where the curves meet on Y-axis because molecular mass of hydrogen is different from oxygen.

Now, to get same value of $\dfrac{pV}{T}$, mass of hydrogen required is obtained from

$\dfrac{pV}{T} = \mu R = \dfrac{m}{2.02} \times 8.31 = 0.26$

$\Rightarrow \qquad m = \dfrac{2.02 \times 0.26}{8.31} = 6.32 \times 10^{-2}$ g

38. Consider an ideal gas with following distribution of speeds. [NCERT Exemplar]

Speed (m/s)	% of molecules
200	10
400	20
600	40
800	20
1000	10

(i) Calculate v_{rms} and hence $T (m = 3.0 \times 10^{-26}$ kg)

(ii) If all the molecules with speed 1000 m/s escape from the system, calculate new v_{rms} and hence T.

Sol. This problem is designed to give an idea about cooling by evaporation

(i) $v^2_{rms} = \dfrac{\sum\limits_i n_i v_i^2}{\sum n_i}$

$= \dfrac{\left[\begin{array}{l} 10 \times (200)^2 + 20 \times (400)^2 \\ + 40 \times (600)^2 + 20 \times (800)^2 + 10 \times (1000)^2 \end{array} \right]}{100}$

$= \dfrac{10 \times 100^2 \times (1 \times 4 + 2 \times 16 + 4 \times 36 + 2 \times 64 + 1 \times 100)}{100}$

$= 1000 \times (4 + 32 + 144 + 128 + 100)$

$= 408 \times 1000 \text{ m}^2/\text{s}^2$

$\therefore \quad v_{rms} = 639 \text{ m/s}$,

$\dfrac{1}{2} m v^2_{rms} = \dfrac{3}{2} kT$

$\therefore \quad T = \dfrac{1}{3} \dfrac{m v^2_{rms}}{k}$

$= \dfrac{1}{3} \times \dfrac{3.0 \times 10^{-26} \times 4.08 \times 10^5}{1.38 \times 10^{-23}}$

$= 2.96 \times 10^2 = 296 \text{ K}$

(ii) $v^2_{rms} = \dfrac{\left[\begin{array}{l} 10 \times (200)^2 + 20 \\ \times (400)^2 + 40 \times (600)^2 + 20 \times (800)^2 \end{array} \right]}{90}$

$= \dfrac{10 \times 100^2 \times (1 \times 4 + 2 \times 16 + 4 \times 36 + 2 \times 64)}{90}$

$v^2_{rms} = 10000 \times \dfrac{308}{9}$

$v^2_{rms} = 342 \times 1000 \text{ m}^2/\text{s}^2$

$v_{rms} = 584 \text{ m/s}$

$T = \dfrac{1}{3} \dfrac{m v^2_{rms}}{k} = 248 \text{ K}$

ASSESS YOUR TOPICAL UNDERSTANDING

OBJECTIVE Type Questions

1. Which of the following options is correct about the flow of a liquid?
   (a) In liquids the atoms are not as rigidly fixed as in solid
   (b) In liquids the atoms are more rigidly fixed as in gas
   (c) In liquid the separation between atoms are spaced about 1 Å
   (d) All of the above

2. The mass of 22.4 L of any gas is equal to its molecular weight in grams at
   (a) 270 K and 1 atm
   (b) 273 K and 1 atm
   (c) 273 K and 10 atm
   (d) 270 K and 10 atm

3. Which one of the following graphs represents the behaviour of an ideal gas?

   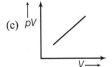
   (a)

   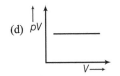
   (b)

   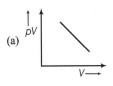
   (c)

   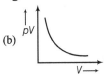
   (d)

4. A cylinder containing an ideal gas is in vertical position and has a piston of mass M that is able to move up or down without friction (figure). If the temperature is increased **[NCERT Exemplar]**

   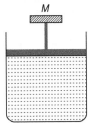

   (a) both p and V of the gas will change
   (b) only p will increase according to Charles' law
   (c) V will change but not p
   (d) p will change but not V

5. Oxygen and hydrogen are at the same temperature T. The ratio of the mean kinetic energy of oxygen molecules to that of the hydrogen molecules will be
   (a) 16 : 1   (b) 1 : 1   (c) 4 : 1   (d) 1 : 4

Answers

1. (a) | **2.** (b) | **3.** (d) | **4.** (c) | **5.** (b)

VERY SHORT ANSWER Type Questions

6. We have two different gases at the same temperature, then what will be the ratio of their average kinetic energies?

7. If 4 : 9 is ratio of densities of two gases at the given temperature. Find out the ratio of their rms speeds?
   [Ans. 3:2]

8. Draw temperature-volume graph of an ideal gas at constant pressure.

9. What are the characteristics of gas molecules?

10. State Boyle's law in terms of pressure and density.

SHORT ANSWER Type Questions

11. Is it possible to increase the temperature of a gas while keeping its pressure and volume constant. Explain it?

12. Draw p-V graph that shows the comparison of experimental and theoretical variations of p with V at constant temperature.

13. The value of root mean square speed for O_2 is 400 m/s. Find the temperature of the O_2.
    [Ans. $\approx$ 200 K]

14. If value of most probable speed for an ideal gas is 500 m/s. Find the value of root mean square speed for this gas. **[Ans. 390 m/s]**

15. Find the temperature at which rms speed of a gas is half of its value of 0°C, pressure remaining constant. **[Ans. 68.25 K]**

LONG ANSWER Type I Questions

16. Write the assumptions of kinetic theory of gases.

17. Find the expression for the average kinetic energy of a molecule of an ideal gas.

18. At what temperature, will the molecules in a sample of helium gas have an rms speed of 1.0 km/s?
    [Ans. 160K]

19. If the pressure of a gas filled in closed container is increased by 0.2%. When temperature is increased by 1 K, calculate the initial temperature of the gas.
    [Ans. 500 K]

20. If the ratio of molecular weights of two gases is 4. What will be ratio of the v_{rms} values for the molecules of those two gases? [**Ans.** 0.5]

LONG ANSWER Type II Questions

21. A box of $1.00 \, m^3$ is filled with nitrogen at 1.5 atm at 300 K. The box has a hole of an area $0.010 \, mm^2$. How much time is required for the pressure to reduce by 0.10 atm, if the pressure outside is 1 atm. [**Ans.** $1.38 \times 10^5 \, s$]

22. An oxygen cylinder of volume 30 L has an initial gauge pressure of 15 atm and a temperature of 27°C.

After some oxygen is withdrawn from the cylinder, the gauge pressure drop to 11 atm and its temperature drops to 17°C. Estimate mass of oxygen taken out of the cylinder ($R = 8.3 \, J \, mol^{-1} \, K^{-1}$, molecular mass of $O_2 = 32$) [**Ans.** 141 g]

23. An electric bulb of volume $250 \, cm^3$ was sealed off during manufacture at a pressure of 10^{-3} mm of mercury at 27°C.

Compute the number of air molecules contained in the bulb.

Given that, $R = 8.31 \, J/mol/K$
and $N_A = 6.02 \times 10^{23} \, mol^{-1}$. [**Ans.** 8×10^{15}]

|TOPIC 2|
Motion of Gas Molecules

DEGREE OF FREEDOM

The total number of coordinates or independent quantities required to describe completely the position and configuration of a dynamical system is known as number of **degrees of freedom** of the system. It is represented by f and expressed as

Degree of freedom, $f = 3N - K$

where, N is the number of particles in a system and K is number of independent relations between the particles.

(i) In case of monoatomic gas, such as helium, neon argon, have translational degree of freedom.

If $N = 1$ and $K = 0$, then $f = 3 \times 1 - 0 = 3$

(ii) In case of diatomic gas, such as oxygen, hydrogen, nitrogen etc., each molecule has two rotational degrees of freedom in addition to three translational degrees of freedom.

∴ $f = 5$

(iii) The gas like SO_2, H_2S etc., has three molecules, i.e. they are triatomic gases. In case of triatomic gases,

$f = 7$ for linear molecules

and $f = 6$ for non-linear molecules

LAW OF EQUIPARTITION OF ENERGY

It states that

'For a dynamic system in thermal equilibrium, the total energy is distributed equally amongst all the degree of freedom and the energy associated with each molecule per degree of freedom is $\frac{1}{2} k_B T$.'

Where, $k_B = 1.38 \times 10^{-23} \, JK^{-1}$ is Boltzmann constant and T is absolute temperature of system on the kelvin scale. For a monoatomic gas in thermal equilibrium at temperature T, the average value of translational energy of the molecule is

$$\langle E_t \rangle = \left\langle \frac{1}{2} mv_x^2 \right\rangle + \left\langle \frac{1}{2} mv_y^2 \right\rangle + \left\langle \frac{1}{2} mv_z^2 \right\rangle$$

Translational energy of the molecules, $\langle E_t \rangle = \frac{3}{2} k_B T$

Since, there is no preferred direction, then the above equation can be written as

$$\left\langle \frac{1}{2} mv_x^2 \right\rangle = \frac{1}{2} k_B T, \left\langle \frac{1}{2} mv_y^2 \right\rangle = \frac{1}{2} k_B T, \left\langle \frac{1}{2} mv_z^2 \right\rangle = \frac{1}{2} k_B T$$

Thus, energy associated with each molecule per degree of freedom is $\frac{1}{2}k_B T$, which is law of equilibrium of energy.

Therefore, total energy of a diatomic gas molecule is the sum of translational energy E_t and rotational energy E_r

$$E_t + E_r = \left(\frac{1}{2}mv_x^2 + \frac{1}{2}mv_y^2 + \frac{1}{2}mv_z^2\right) + \left(\frac{1}{2}I_1\omega_1^2 + \frac{1}{2}I_2\omega_2^2\right)$$

where, ω_1 and ω_2 are angular speeds about the axes 1 and 2 and I_1 and I_2 are moment of inertia.

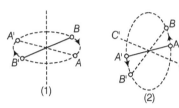

(1)   (2)

Rotation of a diatomic molecule

In case of diatomic/polyatomic gas, molecules may not be a **rigid rotator** having no vibration. Molecules like CO at moderate temperatures have a mode of vibration and contributes a vibrational energy E_v to total energy

$$E_v = \frac{1}{2}m\left(\frac{dy}{dt}\right)^2 + \frac{1}{2}ky^2$$

where, k = force constant of the oscillator
and y = vibrational coordinate
$\therefore$ Total energy, $E = E_t + E_v + E_r$

SPECIFIC HEAT CAPACITY (C)

In this topic, we will deal with the specific heat capacity of gases having different degree of freedom. It can be calculated by applying the law of equipartition of energy of gases.

Monoatomic Gases

In monoatomic gases, a molecule has three translational degrees of freedom. By law of equipartition of energy, average energy per molecule per degree of freedom $=\frac{1}{2}k_B T$.

So, average energy per molecule with three degrees of freedom $= 3 \times \frac{1}{2}k_B T = \frac{3}{2}k_B T$

Now, total internal energy of one mole of monoatomic gas

$$U = \frac{3}{2}k_B T \times N_A = \frac{3}{2}RT \quad (\text{as } R = N_A k_B)$$

$\therefore$ $U = \frac{3}{2}RT$ ...(i) [for monoatomic gas]

If dU is a small amount of heat energy required to raise the temperature of 1g mole of the gas at constant volume through at temperature dT. Then,

$$C_V = \frac{dU}{dT} \qquad [\because \mu = 1]...(ii)$$

where, C_V = specific heat of gas at constant volume.
Putting, $U = \frac{3}{2}RT$ in Eq. (ii), we have

$$C_V = \frac{d}{dT}\left(\frac{3}{2}RT\right) = \frac{3}{2}R$$

$\therefore$ $C_V = \frac{3}{2}R$

If C_p is molar specific heat at constant pressure, then
$$C_p - C_V = R$$
$\Rightarrow$ $C_p - \frac{3}{2}R = R$

$\therefore$ $C_p = \frac{5}{2}R$

Now, ratio of specific heat, $\gamma = \dfrac{C_p}{C_V} = \dfrac{\left(\frac{5}{2}\right)R}{\left(\frac{3}{2}\right)R} = \dfrac{5}{3} = 1.67$

Ratio of specific heat capacities for monoatomic gases
$$\gamma = 1.67$$

EXAMPLE |1| Kinetic Energy in Helium Atom
Calculate the molecular kinetic energy of 1 g of helium (molecular weight 4) at 127°C. (Given, $R = 8.31\ \text{Jmol}^{-1}\text{K}^{-1}$)

Sol. Given, $T = 273 + 127 = 400\,\text{K}$

Helium is monoatomic gas.

$\therefore$ Average kinetic energy per mole of helium $= \frac{3}{2}RT$

Average kinetic energy of 1 g of helium

$$= \frac{3}{2}\frac{RT}{M} = \frac{3 \times 8.31 \times 400}{2 \times 4} = 1246.5\,\text{J}$$

Diatomic Gases

In case of diatomic gases, if the vibrational mode is not considered, then it has five degrees of freedom (three translational and two rotational) at room temperature.

According to law of equipartition of energy, total internal energy of one mole of such type of gas is

$$U = 5 \times \left(\frac{1}{2}k_B T\right) \times N_A$$

Thus, $U = \frac{5}{2}RT$ $[\because R = k_B N_A]$

The molar specific heat C_V is given by,

So, $$C_V = \frac{dU}{dT} = \frac{d}{dT}\left(\frac{5}{2}RT\right)$$

∴ $$C_V = \frac{5}{2}R$$

Now, $$C_p = C_V + R \implies C_p = \frac{5}{2}R + R = \frac{7}{2}R$$

So, $$C_p = \frac{7}{2}R$$

So, $$\gamma = \frac{C_p}{C_V} = \frac{\left(\frac{7}{2}\right)R}{\left(\frac{5}{2}\right)R} \implies \gamma = \frac{7}{5} = 1.40$$

Ratio of specific heat capacities for diatomic gases
$$\gamma = 1.40$$

EXAMPLE |2| Diatomic Gas Molecule

Calculate the total number of degrees of freedom possessed by the molecules in $1\,cm^3$ of H_2 gas at temperature 273 K and 1 atm pressure? **[NCERT Exemplar]**

Sol. At 273 K temperature and 1 atm pressure mean STP condition.

∴ Number of H_2 molecules on $22400\,cm^3$ at STP
$$= 6.02 \times 10^{23}$$

∴ Number of H_2 molecules in $1\,cm^3$ at STP
$$= \frac{6.02 \times 10^{23}}{22400} = 2.6875 \times 10^{19}$$

Number of degrees of freedom associated with each H_2 (diatomic) molecule = 5

∴ Total number of degrees of freedom associated with $1\,cm^3$ of gas $= 2.6875 \times 10^{19} \times 5 = 1.34375 \times 10^{20}$

EXAMPLE |3| Specific Heat at Constant Volume

Find the value of internal energy of one mole of a diatomic gas, which do not show vibrational mode. Also, find the value of C_V for the sample of above gas.

Sol. Molecule of diatomic gas will have three translational and two rotational degrees of freedom. So,

Degrees of freedom $(f) = 3 + 2 = 5$

Total energy $$(E) = 5\left(\frac{1}{2}k_B T\right) = \frac{5}{2}k_B T$$

As the gas is one mole, so the total number of molecules is N_A. So, total energy of one mole of gas could be found.
$$U = \frac{5}{2}k_B T \times N_A = \frac{5}{2}k_B N_A T = \frac{5}{2}RT$$

We can find the value of C_V by applying, $C_V = \frac{dU}{dT}$

$$C_V = \frac{d}{dT}\left(\frac{5}{2}RT\right) \implies C_V = \frac{5}{2}R$$

Triatomic Gas

In case of such kind of gases (linear triatomic gas), there are seven degrees of freedom. Using law of equipartition of energy, total internal energy of one mole of such gases is

$$U = 7 \times \left(\frac{1}{2}k_B T\right) \times N_A = \frac{7}{2}RT \; [\because k = k_A N_B]$$

Now, $$C_V = \frac{dU}{dT} = \frac{d}{dT}\left(\frac{7}{2}RT\right) = \frac{7}{2}R$$

$$\implies C_V = \frac{7}{2}R$$

Now, $$C_p = C_V + R = \frac{7}{2}R + R \implies C_p = \frac{9}{2}R$$

∴ $$\gamma = \frac{C_p}{C_V} = \frac{\left(\frac{9}{2}\right)R}{\left(\frac{7}{2}\right)R} = \frac{9}{7}$$

$$\implies \gamma = \frac{9}{7} = 1.28$$

Ratio of specific heat capacities for triatomic gases,
$$\gamma = 1.28$$

Polyatomic Gas

A polyatomic gas molecule in general has three translational, three rotational degrees of freedom and with certain number (let f) of vibrational modes.

Using law of equipartition of energy, total internal energy of one mole of such gases is

$$U = \left[\frac{3}{2}k_B T + \frac{3}{2}k_B T + f k_B T\right] \times N_A$$

$$\implies U = (3 + f)RT$$

Now, $$C_V = \frac{dU}{dT}$$

$$= \frac{d(3+f)RT}{dT} = (3+f)R$$

$$\implies C_V = (3 + f)R$$

∴ $$C_p = C_V + R = (3 + f)R + R$$

$$\implies C_p = (4 + f)R$$

So, $$\boxed{\gamma = \frac{C_p}{C_V} = \frac{(4+f)}{(3+f)}}$$

Taking $$f = 6$$

Ratio of specific heat capacities for polyatomic gas, $\gamma = 1.11$

Determination of γ from the Degrees of Freedom

If a polyatomic gas molecule has f degrees of freedom, then internal energy of one mole of the gas is

$$U = f \times \left(\frac{1}{2} k_B T\right) \times N_A = \frac{f}{2} RT$$

Now,

$$C_V = \frac{dU}{dT} = \frac{d}{dT}\left(\frac{f}{2} RT\right) = \frac{f}{2} R$$

$$C_V = \frac{f}{2} R$$

$\therefore$

$$C_p = C_V + R = \frac{f}{2} R + R = \left(\frac{f}{2} + 1\right)R$$

$$C_p = \left(\frac{f}{2} + 1\right)R$$

So, specific heat ratio is

$$\gamma = \frac{C_p}{C_V} = \frac{\left(\frac{f}{2} + 1\right)R}{\frac{f}{2} R}$$

$\Rightarrow$

$$r = \left(1 + \frac{2}{f}\right)$$

which is required relation between γ and f.

EXAMPLE |4| An Isolated Container

An isolated container containing monoatomic gas of molar mass m is moving with a velocity v_0. If the container is suddenly stopped, find the change in temperature.

[NCERT Exemplar]

Sol. Loss in kinetic energy of gas $= \Delta E = \frac{1}{2}(mn) v_0^2$

where, n is number of moles and m is molar mass.

If its temperature changes by ΔT, then

$$n\frac{3}{2} R\Delta T = \frac{1}{2} mn\, v_0^2$$

$\therefore$ Change in temperature, $\Delta T = \dfrac{mv_0^2}{3R}$

Specific Heat Capacity of Solids

In solids, each atom vibrates about its mean position, let us consider one mole of solid containing N_A atoms. By law of equipartition of energy, average energy associated with an atom due to its oscillation in one dimension is

$$= 2 \times \left(\frac{1}{2} k_B T\right) = k_B T$$

$\therefore$ In three dimension (3D) average energy per atom $= 3 k_B T$.

$\therefore$ Total energy of one mole of solid is

$$U = (3 k_B T) \times N_A = 3\, RT \quad [\because k_B N_A = R]$$

According to first law of thermodynamics

$$\Delta Q = \Delta U + \Delta W \quad \text{or} \quad \Delta Q = \Delta U + p\Delta V$$

In case of solid, ΔV is negligible

$\therefore$ $\quad \Delta Q \approx \Delta U$

Molar specific heat of solid, $C = \dfrac{\Delta Q}{\Delta T} = \dfrac{\Delta U}{\Delta T}$

Specific heat capacity of solids, $C = 3R$

$\Rightarrow \quad C = 24.93 \text{ Jmol}^{-1}\text{K}^{-1} \ [\because R = 8.31 \text{ Jmol}^{-1}\text{K}^{-1}]$

Specific Heat Capacities of Some Solids at Room Temperature and Atmospheric Pressure

Substance	Specific Heat $(\text{Jkg}^{-1}\text{K}^{-1})$	Molar Specific Heat $(\text{Jmol}^{-1}\text{K}^{-1})$
Aluminium	900.0	24.4
Carbon	506.5	6.1
Copper	386.4	24.5
Lead	127.7	26.5
Silver	236.1	25.5
Tungsten	134.4	24.9

From this table, it is clear that the prediction generally agrees with experimental values at ordinary temperature except i.e. carbon.

Note

The temperature at which all metals have constant C_V is called **Debye temperature**.

Specific Heat Capacity of Water

If we consider water molecule as a solid made up of 3 atoms (2 hydrogen and 1 oxygen) and each atom is free to vibrate in three dimensions about its mean position.

By using law of equipartition of energy, average energy associated with one atom of water molecule

$$= 2 \times \left(\frac{1}{2} k_B T\right) = k_B T$$

In three dimension, the average energy per atom of water molecule $= 3k_B T$

$\therefore$ Total energy of one molecule of water is

$$= 3 \times (3k_B T) = 9k_B T$$

Now, total energy of 1 mole of water is

$$U = 3 \times 3k_B T \times N_A = 9RT$$

$\therefore$ Molar specific heat of water,

$$C = \frac{\Delta Q}{\Delta T} = \frac{\Delta U}{\Delta T} = 9R$$

Specific heat capacity of water, $C = 9R$

$\Rightarrow \qquad C = 74.79 \text{ J mol}^{-1}\text{K}^{-1}$

$$[\because R = 8.31 \text{ J mol}^{-1} \text{ K}^{-1}]$$

EXAMPLE |5| A Mixture of Gases

A gas mixture consists of 2.0 moles of oxygen and 4.0 moles of neon at temperature T. Neglecting all vibrational modes, calculate the total internal energy of the system. (oxygen has two rotational modes) **[NCERT Exemplar]**

Sol. O_2 has five degrees of freedom.

Therefore, energy per mole $= \dfrac{5}{2}RT$

$\therefore$ For 2 moles of O_2, energy $= 5RT$

Neon has three degrees of freedom

$\therefore \qquad$ Energy per mole $= \dfrac{3}{2}RT$

$\therefore$ For 4 moles of neon, energy

$$= 4 \times \dfrac{3}{2}RT = 6RT$$

$\therefore \qquad$ Total energy $= 5RT + 6RT = 11RT$.

MEAN FREE PATH (λ)

Every gas consists of a large number of molecules undergoing frequent collision, therefore they cannot move straight or unhindered, these molecules are in a state of continuous and random motion. Also, they undergo perfectly elastic collision against each other. The average distance travelled by a molecule between two successive collisions is known as **the mean free path of the molecule.**

Expression for Mean Free Path

Let d be the diameter of each molecule of the gas, then a particular molecule will suffer collision with any molecule that comes within a distance d between centres of two molecules.

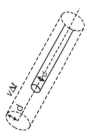

Volume swept by a molecule in time Δ

If $\bar{v}$ is average speed of molecule, then from figure, the volume swept by the molecule in small time Δt in which any molecule will collide with it

$$= \pi d^2 \langle v \rangle \Delta t$$

If n is number of molecules per unit volume of the gas, then number of collision suffered by the molecule in time Δt

$$= \pi d^2 \langle v \rangle \Delta t \times n.$$

So, number of collisions per second

$$= \dfrac{\pi d^2 \langle v \rangle \Delta t \times n}{\Delta t} = n\, \pi d^2 \langle v \rangle$$

$\therefore$ Average time between two successive collisions

i.e. $\qquad \tau = \dfrac{1}{n\, \pi d^2 \langle v \rangle}$

$\therefore$ Mean free path = average distance between two

successive collision

$\Rightarrow \quad \lambda = \tau \times \text{mean velocity} = \dfrac{1}{n\, \pi d^2 \langle v \rangle} \times \bar{v} = \dfrac{1}{n\, \pi d^2}$

$$\boxed{\text{Mean free path, } \lambda = \dfrac{1}{n\, \pi d^2}}$$

where, d = diameter of each molecule

and $\quad n$ = number of molecules per unit volume.

Basic Assumptions on Mean Free Path

(i) The molecules of gas are considered as hard spheres, each of diameter d.

(ii) The collision between gas molecules are perfectly elastic.

(iii) All molecules of a gas except the molecule under consideration are at rest.

(iv) A molecule of the gas under consideration collides with all those molecules whose centre are at distance d from centre of molecule under consideration.

In the above derivation of λ, we imagined the other molecules to be at rest. But actually all molecules are moving, which will result into the following more accurate value.

$$\lambda = \dfrac{1}{\sqrt{2}n\, \pi d^2} \qquad \qquad \ldots(i)$$

where, $\quad T$ = temperature of gas (in kelvin),

d = molecules diameter

and $\quad \lambda$ = mean free path.

Note

Mean free path, $\lambda = \dfrac{K_B T}{\sqrt{2}\pi d^2 P}$ (in terms of temperature and pressure)

- The mean free path of a given gas is (i) directly proportional to its absolute temperature, and (ii) inversely proportional to its pressure.

- Using kinetic theory of gases, the Bulk measurable properties like viscosity, heat conductivity and rate of diffusion are easily related to the microscopic parameters like molecular size.

EXAMPLE |6| Flying with Planes

Ten small planes are flying at a speed of 150 km/h in total darkness in an air space that is $20 \times 20 \times 1.5$ km^3 in volume. You are in one of the planes, flying at random within this space with no way of knowing where the other planes are. On the average about how long a time will elapse between near collision with your plane. Assume for this rough computation that a safety region around the plane can be approximated by a sphere of radius 10 m. [NCERT Exemplar]

Sol. Given, $v = 150$ km/h, $V = 20 \times 20 \times 1.5$,

$$N = 10, \ d = 2 \times 10 = 20 \text{ m}$$

Time taken by plane, $t = \lambda/v$ and mean free path

i.e. $\lambda = \dfrac{1}{\sqrt{2}\pi d^2 n}$

where, d = diameter and n = number of density

So, $n = \dfrac{N}{V} = \dfrac{10}{20 \times 20 \times 1.5} = 0.0167 \text{ km}^{-3}$

and time elapse between collision,

$$t = \dfrac{1}{\sqrt{2}\pi d^2 (N/V) \times v}$$

$$= \dfrac{1}{1.414 \times 3.14 \times (20)^2 \times 0.0167 \times 10^{-3} \times 150} = 0.225 \text{ h}$$

EXAMPLE |7| Mean Free Path

The average speed of air molecules is 485 m/s. At STP the number density is 2.7×10^{25} /m^3 and diameter of the air molecule is 2×10^{-10} m. Find the value of mean free path (λ) for the air molecule and average time (τ) between successive collisions.

Sol. To find the mean free path, we need the values of d and n. Just put these values in the formula of mean free path.

$$\lambda = \dfrac{1}{\sqrt{2}n\,\pi d^2} = \dfrac{1}{\sqrt{2}\,\pi \times 2.7 \times 10^{25}(2 \times 10^{-10})^2}$$

$$= 2.9 \times 10^{-7} \text{ m}$$

The value of $\tau = \dfrac{l}{v}$

Now, put the values and get the value of τ .

$$\tau = \dfrac{2.9 \times 10^{-7}}{485} = 5.9 \times 10^{-10} \text{ s}$$

BROWNIAN MOTION

In 1827, a Scottish Botanist, Robert Brown saw the pollen grains moving continuously in *zig-zag* random motion while observing the pollen grains of a flower under a microscope. Brownian motion is the *zig-zag* motion of the particles of microscope of size suspended in water, air or some other fluid. This motion can be explained on the basis of kinetic theory.

A very small particle (of the order of 10^{-5} m) suspended in a fluid is continuously bombarded from all sides by the molecules of the fluid. The impulses and the torque acting on the suspended particle due to continuous bombardment do not sum to zero exactly, therefore, a net torque or impulse in one or the other direction exists. It is due to the net torque that the suspended particle moves continuously in a random motion.

The Brownian motion depends upon the following factors as

   (i) Size of the suspended particle
  (ii) Density of the fluid
 (iii) Temperature of the medium
  (iv) Viscosity of the medium

In 1987, Ahmed Zewall, an Egyptian scientist observed the detailed interactions by illuminating them with flashes of laser light for very short duration of order 10 femto seconds (1 femto-seconds = 10^{-15} s).

| TOPIC PRACTICE 2 |

OBJECTIVE Type Questions

1. The average energy associated with each translational degree of freedom is

   (a) $\dfrac{3}{2} k_B T$ (b) $k_B T$

   (c) $\dfrac{1}{2} k_B T$ (d) $2 k_B T$

   Sol. (c) Average energy associated with each translational degree of freedom is $\dfrac{1}{2} k_B T$.

2. Diatomic molecule (rigid rotator) has
   (a) 3 translational degrees of freedom
   (b) 2 rotational degrees of freedom
   (c) Both (a) and (b)
   (d) All of the above

   Sol. (c) The diatomic molecules (without vibrational mode) like O_2 and N_2 has three translational degrees of freedom and two rotational degrees of freedom.

3. Law of equipartition of energy is used to
   (a) predict the specific heats of gases
   (b) predict the specific heats of solids
   (c) Both (a) and (b)
   (d) Neither (a) nor (b)

   Sol. (c) Law of equipartition of energy is used to predict the specific heat of gases and solids.

4. The internal energy of 2 moles of a monoatomic gas is

(a) $\frac{3}{2}RT$ (b) $3RT$ (c) $2RT$ (d) $5RT$

Sol. (b) Internal energy, $U = \left(\frac{3}{2}k_BT\right)2N_A$

$$= 3(k_B \times N_A)T = 3RT.$$

5. The mean free path for air molecule with average speed 18.5 ms^{-1} at STP is

(Take, $d = 2 \times 10^{-10}$ m and $n = 2.7 \times 10^{25} \text{ m}^{-3}$)

(a) 3.5×10^{-7} m   (b) 4×10^{-7} m

(c) 2.9×10^{-7} m   (d) 5×10^{-7} m

Sol. (c) For air at STP, $n = 2.7 \times 10^{25} \text{ m}^{-3}$

$$d = 2 \times 10^{-10} \text{ m}$$

$$\Rightarrow \qquad l = \frac{1}{\sqrt{2}n\pi d^2}$$

On putting values, $l = 2.9 \times 10^{-7}$ m

VERY SHORT ANSWER Type Questions

6. What is the number of degree of freedom of a bee flying in a room?

Sol. Three, because bee is free to move along x-direction or y-direction or z-direction.

7. How degree of freedom of a gas molecule is related with the temperature?

Sol. Degree of freedom will increase when temperature is very high because at high temperature, vibrational motion of the gas will contribute to the kinetic energy. Hence, there is an additional kinetic energy associated with the gas, as a result of increased degree of freedom.

8. Is molar specific heat of a solid, a constant quantity?

Sol. Yes, the molar specific heat of a solid is a constant quantity as its value is $3R \text{ J/mol}^{-K}$.

9. The specific heat of argon at constant volume is $0.075 \text{ kcal kg}^{-1}\text{K}^{-1}$, then what will be its atomic weight? [Given, $R = 2 \text{ cal mol}^{-1}\text{K}^{-1}$]

Sol. Argon is a monoatomic gas, so

$$C_V = \frac{3}{2}R = \frac{3}{2} \times 2 = 3 \text{ cal mol}^{-1}\text{K}^{-1}$$

$$C_V = Mc_V$$

$$\Rightarrow \qquad M = \frac{C_V}{c_V} = \frac{3}{0.075} = 40$$

10. Name an experimental evidence in support of random motion of gas molecules.

Sol. Brownian motion and diffusion of gases provide experimental evidence in support of random motion of gas molecules.

11. What is mean free path of a gas?

Sol. The average distance travelled by a molecule between two successive collisions is known as mean free path of the molecule.

12. How is mean free path depends on number density of the gas?

Sol. The mean free path is inversely proportional to the number density of the gas.

13. Calculate the ratio of the mean free paths of the molecules of two gases having molecular diameters 1 Å and 2 Å. The gases may be considered under identical conditions of temperature, pressure and volume.

[NCERT Exemplar]

Sol. As, we know, mean free path, $\lambda \propto \frac{1}{d^2}$

Given, $d_1 = 1$Å and $d_2 = 2$Å

$\Rightarrow \quad \lambda_1 : \lambda_2 = 4 : 1$

14. If a molecule having N atoms has k number of constraints, how many degrees of freedom does the gas possess?

Sol. Degree of freedom, $f = 3N - K$.

15. If there are f degrees of freedom with n moles of a gas, then find the internal energy possessed at a temperature T.

Sol. For 1 mole with f degrees of freedom,

Internal energy, $U = 1 \times C_V \times T = \frac{f}{2}RT$

For n moles, $\quad U = nC_V\,T = \frac{nf}{2}RT$

SHORT ANSWER Type Questions

16. Equal masses of monoatomic and diatomic gases are supplied heat at the same temperature, pressure and volume.
If same amount of heat is supplied to both the gases, which of them will undergo greater temperature rise?

Sol. For monoatomic gas, temperature rise will be greater because monoatomic gas possesses only translational degree of freedom whereas diatomic gas translation, rotation and vibrational (at higher temperature), so temperature rise for diatomic gases is lower.

17. At room temperature, diatomic gas molecule has five degrees of freedom, at high temperature. It has seven degrees of freedom, explain?

Sol. At low temperature, diatomic gas has three translational and two rotational degrees of freedom, so total number of degrees of freedom is 5.

But at high temperature, gas molecule starts to vibrate which give two additional degrees of freedom i.e. 7.

18. Calculate the number of degrees of freedom in 15 cm^3 of nitrogen at NTP.

Sol. Number of nitrogen molecules in 22400 cm^3 of gas at NTP $= 6.023 \times 10^{23}$

∴ Number of nitrogen molecules in 15 cm^3 of gas at NTP

$$= \frac{6.023 \times 10^{23} \times 15}{22400} = 4.03 \times 10^{20}$$

Number of degrees of freedom of nitrogen (diatomic) molecule at 273 K = 5

∴ Total degrees of freedom of 15 cm^3 of gas

$$= 4.03 \times 10^{20} \times 5$$
$$= 2.015 \times 10^{21}$$

19. A diatomic gas is heated in a vessel to a temperature of 10000 K. If each molecule possess an average energy E_1. After sometime, a few molecule escape into the atmosphere at 300 K. Due to which, their energy changes to E_2. Calculate the ratio of $\frac{E_1}{E_2}$.

Sol. Number of degrees of freedom of diatomic gas at 10000 K = 7.

Number of degrees of freedom of diatomic gas at 300 K = 5

$$\therefore \quad \frac{E_1}{E_2} = \frac{\left(\frac{7}{2}\right) k_B T_1}{\left(\frac{5}{2}\right) k_B T_2} = \frac{7}{5} \times \frac{T_1}{T_2} = \frac{7}{5} \times \frac{10000}{300} = \frac{140}{3}$$

20. What will be the internal energy of 8 g of oxygen at STP?

Sol. Oxygen is a diatomic gas.

Number of moles of O_2 gas

$$= \frac{\text{Atomic wt.}}{\text{Molecular wt.}} = \frac{8}{32}$$
$$= \frac{1}{4} = 0.25$$

∴ Energy associated with 1 mole of oxygen

$$U = \frac{5}{2} RT$$

∴ Internal energy of 8 g of oxygen

$$= 0.25 \times \frac{5}{2} RT$$
$$= 0.25 \times \frac{5}{2} \times 8.31 \times 273 = 1417.9 \text{ J}$$

21. Give a formula for mean free path of the molecules of a gas. Briefly explain, how its value is affected by (i) change in temperature and (ii) change in pressure.

Sol. As, we know that the value of mean free path of the molecules of a given gas is given by

Mean free path, $\quad \lambda = \frac{1}{\sqrt{2}\pi n d^2}$

Here, n = number of gas molecules present in unit volume of given gas and d = molecular diameter.

(i) **Effect of temperature** As temperature of a gas is increased at constant pressure, volume of gas increases and hence n, the number of molecules per unit volume decrease. In fact

$$n \propto \frac{1}{V} \text{ and } V \propto T,$$

Thus, $\quad n \propto \frac{1}{T}$

Due to decrease in molecular number density, the value of mean free path of the gas increase i.e. $\lambda \propto \frac{1}{n} \propto T$. Thus, pressure remaining constant, the mean free path of a gas is directly proportional to its absolute temperature.

(ii) **Effect of pressure** At constant temperature, on increasing pressure, the volume V decrease, the molecular number density n increases and consequently, the mean free path decreases

i.e. $\qquad p \propto \frac{1}{V} \propto n$

∴ $\qquad \lambda \propto \frac{1}{n}$

or $\qquad \lambda \propto \frac{1}{p}$

Thus, at a constant temperature, the mean free path of a gas is inversely proportional to its pressure.

22. What is basic law followed by equipartition of energy?

Sol. The law of equipartition of energy for any dynamical system in thermal equilibrium, the total energy is distributed equally amongst all the degrees of freedom.

The energy associated with each molecule per degree of freedom is $\frac{1}{2} k_B T$, where k_B is Boltzmann's constant and T is temperature of the system.

23. Explain qualitatively, how the extent of Brownian motion is affected by the
   (a) size of the Brownian particle,
   (b) density of the medium,
   (c) temperature of the medium,
   (d) viscosity of the medium?   [NCERT]

Sol. The effect of the various factors on the Brownian motion is as follows

	Factors	Effects
(a)	Decrease in the size of the Brownian particle.	Increase of Brownian motion.
(b)	Decrease in the density of the medium.	Increase of Brownian motion.
(c)	Increase in temperature of the medium.	Increase of Brownian motion.
(d)	Increase in viscosity of the medium.	Decrease of Brownian motion.

24. Calculate the mean free path of a molecule of a gas at a room temperature and one atmospheric pressure. The radius of the gas molecules (avg) is 2×10^{-10} m?

Sol. Given, $T = 27°C = 273 + 27 = 300$ K,

$$P = 1\,\text{atm} = 1.01 \times 10^5\,\text{N/m}^2$$

$$d = 2 \times 2 \times 10^{-10}\,\text{m} = 4 \times 10^{-10}\,\text{m}$$

$\because$ Mean free path, $\lambda = K_B T / \sqrt{2}\pi d^2 p$

$$= \frac{1.38 \times 10^{-23} \times 300}{1.414 \times 3.14 (4 \times 10^{-10})^2 1.013 \times 10^5}$$

$$= 5.75 \times 10^{-8}\,\text{m}$$

25. Although velocity of air molecules is very fast but fragnance of a perfume spreads at a much slower rate, explain?

Sol. This is because scent vapour molecules do not travel uninterrupted, they undergo a number of collisions and trace a *zig-zag* path, due to which their effective displacement per unit time is small, so spreading is at a much slower rate.

LONG ANSWER Type I Questions

26. Calculate the temperature atoms at which rms speed of Argon gas is equal to the rms speed of Helium gas atoms at $-10°C$? (Atomic mass of Ar = 39.9 u, that of He = 4u)

Sol. As we know that, $V_{\text{rms}} = \sqrt{\dfrac{3RT}{M}}$

Thus, $\qquad V_{\text{rms}} / Ar = V_{\text{rms}} / \text{He}$

$$\Rightarrow \qquad \sqrt{\frac{T_{\text{Ar}}}{M_{\text{Ar}}}} = \sqrt{\frac{T_{\text{He}}}{M_{\text{He}}}}$$

$$T_{\text{Ar}} = ? \quad T_{\text{He}} = 273 - 10 = 263\,\text{K}$$

$$M_{\text{Ar}} = 39.9\text{u}, \ M_{\text{He}} = 4\text{u}$$

Thus, $\qquad \dfrac{T_{\text{Ar}}}{39.9} = \dfrac{263}{4}$

$$T_{\text{Ar}} = \frac{263 \times 39.9}{4} = 2623.43\,\text{K}$$

27. If one mole of a monoatomic gas is mixed with three moles of a diatomic gas. What is the molar specific heat of mixture at constant value? [Take, $R = 8.31$ J mol^{-1}K^{-1}]

Sol. Given, for monoatomic gas, $\mu_1 = 1, C_{V_1} = \dfrac{3}{2} R$ and for a diatomic gas, $\mu_2 = 3$ and $C_{V_2} = \dfrac{5}{2} R$

$\therefore$ Total heat energy required to raise the temperature of mixture by ΔT.

$$\Delta U = \mu_1 C_{V_1} \Delta T + \mu_2 C_{V_2} \Delta T$$

$$\Delta U = 1 \times \frac{3}{2} R\Delta T + 3 \times \frac{5}{2} R\Delta T = 9R\Delta T \quad ...(\text{i})$$

Let C_{V_m} be the molar specific heat of the mixture at constant volume and as total number of moles of mixture.

$$\mu_m = 1 + 3 = 4$$

$\therefore$ Heat energy required

$$\Delta U = \mu_m C_{V_m} \Delta T$$

$$\Rightarrow \qquad \Delta U = 4 C_{V_m} \Delta T \qquad ...(\text{ii})$$

From Eqs. (i) and (ii), we have

$$9R\Delta T = 4 C_{V_m} \Delta T$$

$$\Rightarrow \qquad \Delta C_{V_m} = \frac{9}{4} R = 2.25 R$$

28. A cylinder of fixed capacity contains 44.8 L of helium gas at STP. Calculate the amount of heat required to raise the temperature of container by 15°C?
[given $R = 8.31$ J mol^{-1}K^{-1}]

Sol. At STP, 1 mole of gas occupy 22.4 L of volume.

$\therefore$ Moles of helium in container, $\mu = \dfrac{44.8}{22.4} = 2$ moles

Now, helium is monoatomic, so, $C_V = \dfrac{3}{2} R$

Change in temperature,

$$\Delta T = T_2 - T_1 = 15°C = 15\,\text{K}$$

$\therefore$ Volume of gas remain constant

$\therefore \qquad \Delta W = p\Delta V = 0 \Rightarrow \Delta Q = \Delta U + \Delta W$

Amount of heat required, $\Delta Q = \Delta U = \mu C_V \Delta T$

$$= 2 \times \frac{3}{2} R \times 15 = 45\,R$$

$$= 45 \times 8.31 = 374\,\text{J}$$

29. A gaseous mixture contain 16 g of helium and 16 g of oxygen, then calculate the ratio of C_p / C_V of the mixture.

Sol. Moles of helium $(\mu_{\text{He}}) = \dfrac{16}{4} = 4$

Moles of oxygen $(\mu_{O_2}) = \dfrac{16}{32} = \dfrac{1}{2}$

As helium is monoatomic, so degrees of freedom of helium, $f = 3$, so $C_{V_{He}} = \dfrac{f}{2}R = \dfrac{3}{2}R$

As oxygen is diatomic, so degrees of freedom of oxygen, $f = 5$, so

$$C_{V_{O_2}} = \dfrac{f}{2}R = \dfrac{5}{2}R$$

$$\therefore \quad C_{V\,\text{mixture}} = \dfrac{\mu_{He}C_{V_{He}} + \mu_{O_2}C_{V_{O_2}}}{\mu_{He} + \mu_{O_2}}$$

$$= \dfrac{4 \times \dfrac{3}{2}R + \dfrac{1}{2} \times \dfrac{5}{2}R}{4 + \dfrac{1}{2}} = \dfrac{29}{18}R$$

$$\gamma = \dfrac{C_p}{C_V} \qquad \text{[of mixture]}$$

$$\gamma_{\text{mixture}} = 1 + \dfrac{R}{C_{V\,\text{mixture}}} = 1 + \dfrac{R}{\dfrac{29}{18}R} = 1.62$$

$$[\text{as } C_p - C_V = R]$$

30. Three moles of a diatomic gas is mixed with two moles of monoatomic gas. What will be the molecular specific heat of the mixture at constant volume? [given, $R = 8.31\,\text{J mol}^{-1}\text{K}^{-1}$]

Sol. For a monoatomic gas, i.e. $\gamma = \dfrac{5}{3}$

$$C_{V_\gamma} = \dfrac{R}{\gamma - 1} = \dfrac{R}{\dfrac{5}{3} - 1} = \dfrac{3}{2}R$$

For a diatomic gas, i.e. $\gamma = \dfrac{7}{5}$

$$C_V = \dfrac{R}{\dfrac{7}{5} - 1} = \dfrac{5}{2}R$$

By conservation of energy,

$$C_{V_{\text{mixture}}} = \dfrac{\mu_1 C_{V_1} + \mu_2 C_{V_2}}{\mu_1 + \mu_2}$$

$$= \dfrac{2 \times \dfrac{3}{2}R + 3 \times \dfrac{5}{2}R}{2 + 3} = \dfrac{3R + 7.5\,R}{5} = 2.1\,R$$

31. What will be the mean free path of nitrogen gas at STP of given diameter of nitrogen molecule $= 2\,\mathring{A}$?

Sol. Given, diameter of nitrogen molecule, $d = 2\,\mathring{A}$

$$= 2 \times 10^{-10}\,\text{m}$$

At STP, one mole of gas (or 22.4 L) of gas have

$$N_A = 6.023 \times 10^{23}\ \text{molecules}$$

$\therefore$ Number density of nitrogen molecules

$$n = \dfrac{N_A}{22.4\,\text{L}} = \dfrac{6.023 \times 10^{23}}{22.4 \times 10^{-3}\,\text{m}^3} = 2.69 \times 10^{25}\,\text{m}^{-3}$$

$\therefore$ Mean free path of nitrogen at STP condition,

$$\lambda = \dfrac{1}{\sqrt{2}\,\pi n d^2}$$

$$\lambda = \dfrac{1}{1.414 \times 3.142 \times (2.69 \times 10^{25}) \times (2 \times 10^{-10})^2}$$

$$= 2.1 \times 10^{-7}\,\text{m}$$

LONG ANSWER Type II Questions

32. A box of $1.00\,\text{m}^3$ is filled with nitrogen at 1.50 atm at 300 K. The box has a hole of an area is $0.010\,\text{mm}^2$. How much time is required for the pressure to reduce by 0.10 atm, if the pressure outside is 1 atm. **[NCERT Exemplar]**

Sol. Given, volume of the box, $V = 1.00\,\text{m}^3$

Area, $a = 0.010\,\text{mm}^2 = 10^{-8}\,\text{m}^2$

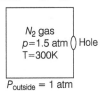

Temperature outside = Temperature inside

Initial pressure inside the box = 1.50 atm.

Final pressure inside the box = 0.10 atm.

Assuming,

v_{ix} = Speed of nitrogen molecule inside the box along x-direction.

n_1 = Number of molecules per unit volume in a time interval of Δt, all the particles at a distance $(v_{ix}\Delta t)$ will collide the hole and the wall, the particle colliding along the hole will escape out reducing the pressure in the box.

Let area of the wall is A, number of particles colliding in time, Δt

$$= \dfrac{1}{2}n_1(v_{ix}\Delta t)A$$

$\dfrac{1}{2}$ is the factor because all the particles along x- direction are behaving randomly. Hence, half of these are colliding against the walls on either side.

Inside the box, $v_{ix}^2 + v_{iy}^2 + v_{iz}^2 = v_{\text{rms}}^2$

$$\Rightarrow \qquad v_{ix}^2 = \dfrac{v_{\text{rms}}^2}{3} \qquad [\because v_{ix} = v_{iy} = v_{iz}]$$

If particles collide along hole, they move out. Similarly, outer particles colliding along hole will move in.

If a = area of hole

Then, net particle flow in time,

$$\Delta t = \frac{1}{2}(n_1 - n_2)\frac{k_B T}{m}\Delta ta \qquad \left[\because v_{rms} = \sqrt{\frac{3k_B T}{m}}\right]$$

[Temperature inside and outside the box are equal]

Let n = number of density of nitrogen

$$n = \frac{\mu N_A}{V} = \frac{pN_A}{RT} \qquad \left[\because \frac{\mu}{V} = \frac{p}{RT}\right]$$

Where, N_A = Avogadro's number

If after time Δt, pressure inside changes from p to p_1'

$$\therefore \qquad n_1' = \frac{p_1' N_A}{RT}$$

Now, number of molecules gone out = $n_1 V - n_1' V$

$$= \frac{1}{2}(n_1 - n_2)\sqrt{\frac{k_B T}{m}}\Delta ta$$

$$\therefore \quad \frac{p_1 N_A}{RT}V - \frac{p_1' N_A}{RT}V = \frac{1}{2}(p_1 - p_2)\frac{N_A}{RT}\sqrt{\frac{k_B T}{m}}\Delta ta$$

$$\Rightarrow \qquad \Delta t = 2\left(\frac{p_1 - p_1'}{p_1 - p_2}\right)\frac{V}{a}\sqrt{\frac{m}{k_B T}}$$

Putting the values from the data given,

$$\Delta t = 2\left(\frac{1.5 - 1.4}{1.5 - 1.0}\right)\frac{1 \times 1.00}{0.01 \times 10^{-6}}\sqrt{\frac{46.7 \times 10^{-27}}{1.38 \times 10^{-23} \times 300}}$$

$$= \frac{2}{5} \times 3.358 \times 10^5 = \frac{6.717}{5} \times 10^5 = 1.343 \times 10^5 \, s$$

33. (i) Define mean free path.

(ii) Derive an expression for mean free path of a gas molecule.

Sol. (i) The mean free path of a gas molecule is defined as the average distance travelled by a molecule between two successive collisions.

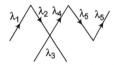

According to figure, if a molecule covers free path $\lambda_1, \lambda_2, \lambda_3 \cdots$ after successive collisions, then its mean free path is given by

$$\lambda = \frac{\lambda_1 + \lambda_2 + \lambda_3 \cdots}{\text{(total number of collisions)}}$$

(ii) Refer to text on page 476.

34. (i) What do you understand by specific heat capacity of water?

(ii) If one mole of ideal monoatomic gas ($\gamma = 5/3$) is mixed with one mole of diatomic gas ($\gamma = 7/5$). What is the value of γ for the mixtures?

(here, γ represents the ratio of specific heat at constant pressure to that at constant volume)

Sol. (i) Refer to text on pages 475 and 476.

(ii) For monoatomic gas, $C_V = \frac{3}{2}R$

For diatomic gas, $C_V' = \frac{5}{2}R$

Let, μ and μ' be moles of mono and diatomic gases then, C_V (mixture) $= \frac{\mu C_V + \mu' C_V'}{\mu + \mu'}$

$$C_V = \frac{1 \times \frac{3}{2}R + 1 \times \frac{5}{2}R}{1 + 1} = 2R$$

$$\gamma \text{ (mixture)} = 1 + \frac{R}{C_{V\text{(mixture)}}} = 1 + \frac{R}{2R} = 1.5$$

35. Estimate the mean free path and collision frequency of a nitrogen molecule in a cylinder containing nitrogen at 2.0 atm and temperature 17°C. Take the radius of a nitrogen molecule to be roughly 1.0 Å. Compare the collision time with the time, the molecule moves freely between two successive collisions

(molecular mass of $N_2 = 28.0$ u). **[NCERT]**

Sol. Let n be the number of molecules per unit volume of the gas. Now, $pV = NkT$, where N = number of molecules in volume V of the gas

$$\therefore \qquad n = \frac{N}{V} = \frac{p}{kT}$$

Here, $p = 2 \times 1.01 \times 10^5 \, N/m^2, k = 1.38 \times 10^{-23} \, J/K$

$T = 273 + 17 = 290$ K

$$\therefore \qquad n = \frac{2 \times 1.01 \times 10^5}{(1.38 \times 10^{-23}) \times (290)}$$

$$= 5.05 \times 10^{25} \text{ molecules/m}^3$$

Mean free path,

$$\lambda = \frac{1}{4\pi\sqrt{2}\,r^2 n}$$

Here, $r = 1.0$ Å $= 1.0 \times 10^{-10}$ m,

$n = 5.05 \times 10^{25}$ molecules/m^3

$$\therefore \qquad \lambda = \frac{1}{4\pi\sqrt{2} \times (1.0 \times 10^{-10})^2 \times 5.05 \times 10^{25}}$$

$$\lambda = 1.11 \times 10^{-7} \, m$$

Now, $v_{rms} = \sqrt{\frac{3RT}{M}} = \sqrt{\frac{3 \times 8.31 \times 290}{28 \times 10^{-3}}} = 508.14$ m/s

$\therefore$ Collision frequency,

$$f = \frac{v_{rms}}{\lambda} = \frac{508.14}{1.11 \times 10^{-7}}$$

$$= 4.58 \times 10^9 \text{ collisions/s}$$

ASSESS YOUR TOPICAL UNDERSTANDING

OBJECTIVE Type Questions

1. A molecule moving along a straight line possess .... degree of freedom.
   (a) one   (b) two   (c) three   (d) four

2. The value of γ for a diatomic molecule (vibrational mode) is
   (a) $\dfrac{9}{7}$ (b) $\dfrac{7}{9}$ (c) $\dfrac{7}{5}$ (d) $\dfrac{5}{7}$

3. During an adiabatic process, the pressure of a gas is found to be proportional to the cube of its temperature. The ratio of $\dfrac{C_p}{C_V}$ for the gas is
   (a) $\dfrac{4}{3}$ (b) 2   (c) $\dfrac{5}{3}$ (d) $\dfrac{3}{2}$

4. The value of C_V for solids is
   (a) $3R$ (b) $2R$
   (c) $4R$ (d) $3/2 R$

5. As temperature tends to zero i.e., $T \rightarrow 0$
   (a) specific heat of all substances approaches zero
   (b) specific heat of all substances approaches infinity
   (c) specific heat of all substances may be zero or infinity
   (d) None of the above

6. We took two separate gases with the same number densities for both. If the ratio of the diameters of their molecules is 4 : 1, then ratio of their mean free paths is
   (a) 1 : 4   (b) 4 : 1   (c) 2 : 1   (d) 1 : 16

Answer

1. (a)	2. (a)	3. (d)	4. (a)	5. (a)
6. (d)				

VERY SHORT ANSWER Type Questions

7. What is the value of degree of freedom for a diatomic rigid rotator (which do not show vibrational mode)?

8. The speed of gas molecule is around the speed of sound, so why gas takes considerable time to diffuse?

9. If the formula of mean free path is considered to be as $\bar{l} = \dfrac{1}{n\pi d^2}$, then find the condition for this particular formula.

10. Which type of gas when the value of γ for a gas is $\dfrac{9}{7}$?

11. Why diatomic molecule contributes only two rotational degrees of freedom?

SHORT ANSWER Type Questions

12. What is the value of degree of freedom for a rotating fan?

13. Find the value of degree of freedom for a cricket ball in projectile motion.

14. Find the value of specific heat capacity for solids.

15. Calculate the value of specific heat capacity for one mole of water in J/kg.
    [**Ans.** 75 J/kg , for 1 mole]

16. Does, $C_p - C_V = R$, is applicable for any type of gas whether it is mono, di and polyatomic? Discuss it in brief.

LONG ANSWER Type I Questions

17. Describe law of equipartition of energy with the help of two examples.

18. Estimate the value of γ for (i) monoatomic,
    (ii) diatomic and (iii) polyatomic gases.

19. Calculate the mean free path and collision frequency of a nitrogen molecule in a cylinder containing nitrogen at 2 atm and temperature 17°C. Take the radius of a nitrogen molecule to be roughly 1.0 Å. Compare the collision time with the time, the molecule moves freely between two successive collisions. Molecular mass of N_2 = 28.0 u.
    [**Ans.** 500 times]

20. Explain the concept of absolute zero temperature on the basis of kinetic theory of gases.

21. Three vessels of equal capacity have gases at the same temperature and pressure. The first vessel contains neon (monoatomic), the second contains chlorine (diatomic) and the third contains uranium hexafluoride (polyatomic). Do the vessels contain equal number of respective molecules same in three cases ? If not, in which case, v_{rms} is largest?

LONG ANSWER Type II Questions

22. Estimate the average thermal energy of a helium atom at
    (i) room temperature 27°C,
    (ii) at 10^5 K and
    (iii) at 5000 K

    [**Ans.** (i) $[6.2 \times 10^{-21}$ J] (ii) $[2.1 \times 10^{-18}$ J]
    (iii) $[10.5 \times 10^{-20}$ J]

23. Four moles of an ideal gas having $\gamma = 1.67$ are mixed with 2 moles of another ideal gas having $\gamma = 1.4$. Find the value of γ for resulting mixture of gases.

    [**Ans.** 1.54]

24. Calculate the change in internal energy of 3 mole of neon gas when its temperature is raised by 20°C.
    (Take, $R = 8.31$ J mol^{-1}K^{-1})

    [**Ans.** 7.48 J]

SUMMARY

- **Behaviour of gases** Gases at low pressure and high temperature much above that at which they liquify (or solidify), follow a relation.

$$pV = Nk_B T \text{ or } \frac{pV}{NT} = k_B = \text{constant}$$

For different gases, $\frac{p_1 V_1}{N_1 T_1} = \frac{p_2 V_2}{N_2 T_2} = \frac{p_3 V_3}{N_3 T_3} \ldots = k_B = \text{constant}$ where, k_B = Boltzmann's constant and its value in SI unit is 1.38×10^{-23} J/K.

- **Boyle's law** It states that for a given mass of a gas at constant temperature, the volume of that mass of gas is inversely proportional to its pressure.

    i.e. $V \propto \dfrac{1}{p}$

    $\Rightarrow$ $p_1 V_1 = p_2 V_2 = p_3 V_3 \ldots = \text{constant}$

- **Charles' law** It states that for a given mass of an ideal gas at constant pressure, volume (V) of a gas is directly proportional to its absolute temperature T

    i.e. $V \propto T$

    $\Rightarrow$ $\dfrac{V_1}{T_1} = \dfrac{V_2}{T_2} = \dfrac{V_3}{T_3} \ldots = \text{constant}$

- **Dalton's law of partial pressure** It states that the total pressure 'of a mixture of non-interacting ideal gases is the sum of partial pressures exerted by individual gases in the mixture.

    i.e. $p = p_1 + p_2 + p_3 + \ldots$
    Dalton's law, $p = p_1 + p_2 + p_3 + \ldots$

- **Graham's law of diffusion** It state that the rate of diffusion of a gas is inversely proportional to the square root of its density. $r \propto \dfrac{1}{\sqrt{\rho}}$

    where, r = rate of diffusion and ρ = density of the gas.

- **Kinetic theory of ideal gas** Kinetic theory of gases is based on the molecular theory of matter. It correlates the macroscopic properties like pressure and temperature of gases to microscopic properties like speed and kinetic energy of gas molecules.

- **Root mean square speed** The square root of average of square velocities of gas molecules is known as root mean square speed. It is abbreviated as v_{rms}.

    Root mean square speed, $v_{\text{rms}} = \sqrt{\dfrac{3k_B T}{m}}$

    where, m = mass of one molecule
    k_B = Boltzmann's constant and T = absolute temperature of the gas.

- **Mean square velocity** The average of square velocity of the gas is known as mean square velocity. It is abbreviated as
$$\overline{v}^2 = (v_{rms})^2$$

- **Most probable speed** The approximate speed with which maximum number of gas molecules move is known as most probable speed. The most probable speed is abbreviated as v_{rms} and given by
$$v_{mp} = \sqrt{\frac{2kT}{m}}$$

- **Average speed** The average speed of ideal gas molecules is given by
$$v_{av} = \frac{v_1 + v_2 + v_3 + \dots v_n}{2} = \sqrt{\frac{8RT}{\pi m}}$$

- **Degree of freedom** The total number of coordinates axes of independent quantities required to describe completely the position and configuration of dynamical system (gaseous) is known as number of degrees of freedom of the system. It is represented by f and expressed as
$$f = 3N - K$$
where, N is the number of particles and K is number of coordinates of the particles.

- **Law of equipartition of energy** For a dynamic system in thermal equilibrium, the total energy is distributed equally amongst all the degree of freedom and the energy associated with each molecule per degree of freedom is
$$\frac{1}{2} k_B T.$$

- where, f = degree of freedom, N = number of particles and K = number of coordinates of the particles

- **Molar specific heat of gases** The molar specific heat of gases is the heat given per mole of the gas per unit rise in the temperature. Molar specific heat has two kind

  (i) Molar specific heat constant volume
  $$C_V = \left(\frac{\Delta Q}{\Delta T}\right)_V \text{ or } C_V = \frac{f}{2}R$$

  (ii) Molar specific heat at constant pressure
  Relation between C_p and C_V is given by
  $$C_p = C_V + R \text{ or } C_p = \left(\frac{f}{2} + 1\right)R = \frac{1}{n}\left(\frac{\Delta A}{\Delta T}\right)_P$$

- **Mean free path** It is the average distance between two successive collisions of a gas molecules and is given by
$$\lambda = \frac{1}{\sqrt{2}\pi d^2 n}$$
where, d = diameter of a molecule and n = number of molecules per unit volume.
It is also called the **number density** of the molecules.

CHAPTER PRACTICE

OBJECTIVE Type Questions

1. Temperature remaining constant, the pressure of gas is decreased by 20%. The percentage change in volume
   (a) increases by 20%   (b) decreases by 20%
   (c) increases by 25%   (d) decreases by 25%

2. The internal energy of an ideal gas is in the form of
   (a) kinetic energy of molecules
   (b) potential energy of molecules
   (c) Both kinetic and potential energy of molecules
   (d) gravitational potential energy of molecules

3. According to the kinetic theory of gases, the temperature of a gas is a measure of average
   (a) velocities of its molecules
   (b) linear momenta of its molecules
   (c) kinetic energies of its molecules
   (d) angular momenta of its molecules

4. An inflated rubber balloon contains one mole of an ideal gas, has a pressure p, volume V and temperature T. If the temperature rises to 1.1 T, and the volume is increased to 1.05 V, the final pressure will be   **[NCERT Exemplar]**
   (a) 1.1 p (b) p
   (c) less than p (d) between p and 1.1

5. At what temperature the kinetic energy of gas molecule is half of the value at 27°C?
   (a) 13.5°C   (b) 150°C   (c) 75 K   (d) $-123°$ C

6. The two gases with the ratio 3 : 2 of their masses in a container are at a temperature T. The ratio of the kinetic energies of the molecule of two gases is
   (a) 3 : 2   (b) 9 : 4   (c) 1 : 1   (d) 4 : 9

7. The ratio of the molar heat capacities of a diatomic gas at constant pressure to that at constant volume is
   (a) $\dfrac{7}{2}$ (b) $\dfrac{3}{2}$
   (c) $\dfrac{3}{5}$ (d) $\dfrac{7}{5}$

8. The gases carbon monoxide (CO) and nitrogen (N_2) at the same temperature have kinetic energies E_1 and E_2, respectively. Then,
   (a) $E_1 = E_2$
   (b) $E_1 > E_2$
   (c) $E_1 < E_2$
   (d) E_1 and E_2 cannot be compared

9. The total energy for one mole of solid is
   (a) $2\,RT$ (b) $3\,RT$ (c) $4\,RT$ (d) $3/2\,RT$

ASSERTION AND REASON

Direction (Q.Nos. 10-14) *In the following questions, two statements are given- one labelled Assertion (A) and the other labelled Reason (R). Select the correct answer to these questions from the codes (a), (b), (c) and (d) as given below*
   (a) Both Assertion and Reason are true and Reason is the correct explanation of Assertion.
   (b) Both Assertion and Reason are true but Reason is not the correct explanation of Assertion.
   (c) Assertion is true but Reason is false.
   (d) Assertion is false but Reason is true.

10. **Assertion** Molecules attract when they are little distance apart and repels when they come very close to each other.
    Reason $F = -\dfrac{dU}{dr}$

11. **Assertion** In gases, the molecules move faster and move long distances without colliding.
    Reason In gases, the interatomic forces are negligible.

12. **Assertion** The total translational kinetic energy of all the molecules of a given mass of an ideal gas is 1.5 times the product of its pressure and its volume.
    Reason The molecules of a gas collide with each other and the velocities of the molecules change due to the collision.

13. **Assertion** A gas can be liquified at any temperature by increase of pressure alone.
    Reason On increasing pressure, the temperature of gas increases.

14. **Assertion** Internal energy of an ideal gas does not depend upon volume of the gas.

    Reason Internal energy of ideal gas depends on temperature of gas.

CASE BASED QUESTIONS

Direction (Q. Nos. 15-16) *These questions are case study based questions. Attempt any 4 sub-parts from each question. Each question carries 1 mark.*

15. **Law of Equipartition of Energy**

    For a dynamic system in thermal equilibrium, the total energy is distributed equally amongst all the degree of freedom and the energy associated with each molecule per degree of freedom is $\frac{1}{2}k_B T$

    where, $k_B = 1.38 \times 10^{-23} \text{JK}^{-1}$ is Boltzmann constant and T is absolute temperature of system on the kelvin scale. For a monoatomic gas in thermal equilibrium at temperature T, the average value of translational energy of the molecule is

    $$\langle E_t \rangle = \left\langle \frac{1}{2}mv_x^2 \right\rangle + \left\langle \frac{1}{2}mv_y^2 \right\rangle + \left\langle \frac{1}{2}mv_z^2 \right\rangle$$

    Translational energy of the molecules,

    $$\langle E_t \rangle = \frac{3}{2}k_B T$$

    (i) Law of equipartition of energy is used to
    (a) predict the specific heats of gases
    (b) predict the specific heats of solids
    (c) Both (a) and (b)
    (d) Neither (a) nor (b)

    (ii) Diatomic molecule (rigid rotator) has
    (a) 3 translational degrees of freedom
    (b) 2 rotational degrees of freedom
    (c) Both (a) and (b)
    (d) All of the above

    (iii) Choose the correct option.
    (a) Each translational mode contributes $\frac{1}{2}k_B T$ average energy.
    (b) Each rotational mode contributes $\frac{1}{2}k_B T$ average energy.
    (c) Vibrational mode contributes $k_B T$ average energy.
    (d) All of the above

    (iv) Molecules of CO at moderate temperature have energy
    (a) $\frac{7}{2}k_B T$ (b) $\frac{5}{2}k_B T$
    (c) $\frac{3}{2}k_B T$ (d) $\frac{1}{2}k_B T$

    (v) The mean kinetic energy of one mole of gas per degree of freedom (on the basis of kinetic theory of gases) is
    (a) $\frac{1}{2}k\,T$ (b) $\frac{3}{2}k\,T$
    (c) $\frac{3}{2}R\,T$ (d) $\frac{1}{2}R\,T$

16. **Collision**

    A molecule of gas collides with the wall of a container elastically.

    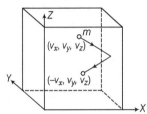

    As collision is elastic only the x-component of the velocity changes after collision. It become reversed y and z-components of velocity do not change.

    (i) Momentum imparted to the wall due to collision of the molecule is
    (a) $2mv_y$ (b) $2mv_x$ (c) $2mv_z$ (d) mv_x

    (ii) The total momentum imparted to the wall in time Δt on the area A of the wall due to molecules of velocity v_x is
    (a) $nmv_x^2 A\Delta t$ (b) $nmv_x A\,\Delta t$
    (c) $\frac{1}{2}nmv_x^2 A\,\Delta t$ (d) $\frac{1}{2}nm\,v_x\,A\,\Delta t$

    (iii) The expression of pressure due to the collision of molecules of velocity v_x is
    (a) nmv^2 (b) nmv_x^2
    (c) nmv_x (d) $\frac{1}{2}nmv_x^2$

    (iv) The expression of total pressure to the group of molecules having velocities along the X-axis is
    (a) nmv_x^2 (b) $nm\bar{v}_x^2$
    (c) $nm\,v_x^2$ (d) None of these

(v) The general expression of pressure due to a gas is

(a) $\frac{1}{2} nm \bar{v}^2$

(b) $\frac{1}{3} nm \bar{v}^2$

(c) $nm \bar{v}$

(d) None of these

where, $\bar{v}^2$ is mean of the square speed of a molecule.

Answers

1. (c)	2. (a)	3. (c)	4. (d)	5. (d)
6. (c)	7. (d)	8. (a)	9. (b)	10. (a)
11. (a)	12. (b)	13. (d)	14. (b)	
15. (i) (c)	(ii) (c)	(iii) (d)	(iv) (a)	(v) (d)
16. (i) (b)	(ii) (a)	(iii) (b)	(iv) (b)	(v) (b)

VERY SHORT ANSWER Type Questions

17. Can an ideal gas be really obtained in practice?

18. Write the rms speed of molecules of a gas in terms of its pressure.

19. How rms speed of a gas vary with temperature?

20. Mention two conditions under which the real gases obey the ideal gas equation.

21. Smell of a scent spreads in whole room when few drops of it are poured on the table. Which phenomenon is responsible for it?

22. Name the factors on which degree of freedom of a gas depends.

23. What is the value of γ to monoatomic gas?

[**Ans.** 1.67]

SHORT ANSWER Type Questions

24. Draw p-V curves showing deviations from ideal behaviour for a given mass of a gas for two different temperatures.

25. What is Brownian motion?

26. Why does specific heat of gases increases with their atomicity?

27. For an ideal gas, show that, $C_p - C_V = \dfrac{R}{J}$.

28. What do you understand by degree of freedom?

29. What is the rms speed of hydrogen gas molecules at STP. Given, density is 0.09 kg m^{-3}.

[**Ans.** 1.8×10^3 ms^{-1}]

30. Why temperature less than 0 K is not possible?

LONG ANSWER Type I Questions

31. Calculate the temperature at which the rms speed of CO_2 gas molecule will be 1 kms^{-1}. Given that molecular mass of $CO_4 = 44$ u

[**Ans.** 1.8×10^3 K]

32. What is the kinetic energy of translation of one molecule of a gas at 300 K ? Gas is having three degree of freedom. $k_B = 1.38 \times 10^{-23}$ JK^{-1}.

[**Ans.** 6.21×10^{-21} J]

33. State Charles' law, obtain it from kinetic theory of gases.

34. Establish ideal gas equation.

35. From kinetic theory of gases, can we obtain ideal gas equation? If yes, how?

36. State Dalton's law of partial pressure. Obtain it from kinetic theory of gases.

37. One mole of a monoatomic gas is mixed with three moles of a diatomic gas. What is the molar specific heat of the mixture at constant volume. ($R = 8.31$ J mol^{-1} K^{-1})

[**Ans.** 2.25 R]

LONG ANSWER Type II Questions

38. Calculate the mean free path of nitrogen gas at STP. Given the diameter of nitrogen molecule is 4 Å. [**Ans.** 5×10^{-8} m]

39. What are the postulates of kinetic theory of gases? What will be expression for the pressure exerted by an ideal gas ?

40. Using the law of equipartition of energy, show that for an ideal gas having f degree of freedoms is given by $\gamma = 1 + 2/f$.

41. What is Maxwell Boltzmann law with regard to speed distribution amongst molecules, state and explain?

42. What is the difference between atomic mass and atomic weight? Also, state what is the difference between NTP and STP.

13

In previous chapters, we have studied that the motion is the change in position of an object with respect to time and its reference point. On the basis of path traced and various other properties, motion can be classified into several categories. These motions are given as below,

   (i) Non-repetitive motions like rectilinear motion and projectile motion, etc.
   (ii) Periodic motion like circular motion or orbital motion, motion of a bouncing ball, etc.
   (iii) Oscillatory motion, like the motion of a pendulum.

OSCILLATIONS

|TOPIC 1|
Introduction to Oscillation

We can notice a number of phenomena in our daily life, illustrating oscillatory motion, e.g. motion of vibrating strings of sitar or guitar, vibration of air molecules helping in propagation of sound, vibration of atoms about their equilibrium positions in a solid, oscillatory motion of AC voltage (going positive and negative about the mean value).

PERIODIC AND OSCILLATORY MOTION
Periodic Motion

A motion that repeats itself after regular intervals of time is called **periodic motion**. e.g. Revolution of planets around the sun, rotation of the earth about its polar axis, etc.

Oscillatory Motion

A motion in which a body moves to and fro or back and forth repeatedly about a fixed point in a regular interval of time is called **oscillatory motion**. This fixed point is known as mean/equilibrium position or centre of oscillation.

e.g. Motion of a simple pendulum as it moves to and fro about its mean position.

Periodic Motion *vs* Oscillatory Motion

Every oscillatory motion is periodic, but every periodic motion need not be oscillatory. e.g. Motion of the planet around the sun is periodic but not oscillatory, body undergoing periodic motion has an equilibrium position somewhere on its path. The body is at this position during its motion, no net force acts on it. So, if it is left there at rest, it remains there forever.

If the body is given a small displacement from its mean position, a force called restoring one comes into play which tries to bring the body back to the equilibrium point. This process repeats itself again and again causing oscillation.

e.g. A ball placed in a bowl will be in equilibrium at the bottom. If it is displaced a little from the mean position, it will start oscillatory in the bowl.

Period and Frequency

Period

The smallest interval of time after which a periodic motion is repeated, is called its **period**. Its SI unit is second and it is denoted by the symbol T.

Period of oscillation should have a very high range of accuracy. So, its unit varies with the necessity.

e.g.
- (i) Period of vibration of a quartz crystal is expressed in units of microsecond (10^{-6} s) i.e. μs.
- (ii) Period of revolution of the planet mercury is 88 earth days.
- (iii) Period of revolution of Halleys Comet is 76 years, so it appears after every 76 years.

Frequency

The number of oscillations/vibrations preformed by a oscillating body about its mean position in a unit time is known as its frequency. The SI unit of frequency of oscillation is hertz (Hz) on the name of Heinrich Rudolph Hertz (1857-1894) who discovered radio waves.

Frequency can also be defined as reciprocal of time period, it is denoted by ν.

Thus,
$$\boxed{\text{Frequency, } \nu = \frac{1}{T}}$$

and 1 hertz = 1 Hz = 1 oscillation per sec = $1 s^{-1}$

This will go down, after frequency. When frequency of an oscillatory motion is very high, then motion is called **vibrational motion**.

EXAMPLE |1| Human Heart

On an average, a human heart is found to beat 75 times in a minute. Calculate its beat frequency and period.

[NCERT]

Sol. The beat frequency of heart

$$= \frac{\text{Number of beats}}{\text{Time taken}} = \frac{75}{60} = 1.25\, s^{-1} = 1.25\, \text{Hz}$$

Beat period, $T = \dfrac{1}{\text{frequency}} = \dfrac{1}{1.25\, s^{-1}} = 0.8\, s$

Displacement

In general, the name displacement is given to a change in position of a particle with respect to origin. In oscillation, we use term displacement as the change in position with respect to mean position (or equilibrium position) or reference position.

Illustrations for Displacement of a Particle

(i) Consider a block is attached to a spring at one of its end, the other end of which is fixed to a rigid wall. Generally, it is convenient to measure the displacement variable (x) as the deviation of the block from the mean position of the oscillation with time, as given in the diagram below.

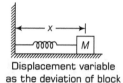

Displacement variable as the deviation of block

(ii) In a simple pendulum, the displacement variable is its angular deviation (θ) from the vertical during oscillations with time as given in the diagram below.

Displacement variable as the deviation of simple pendulum

Note
Displacement variable is measured as a function of time having both positive and negative values.

Periodic Function

The displacement can be represented by a mathematical function of time. The function which repeats its value in regular interval of time or period is called **periodic function**. One of the simplest periodic function is given by

$$f(t) = A \cos \omega t \qquad \text{...(i)}$$

The time period for this function will be, $T = 2\pi/\omega$ because when we add 2π with the argument ωt of the function, then its value remains same.

Thus, $f(t) = f(t + T)$

Similarly, if we consider a sine function then

$$f(t) = A \sin \omega t$$

Also, $f(t) = A \sin \omega t + B \cos \omega t \qquad \text{...(ii)}$

is a periodic function with time period T.

Now taking, $A = D \cos \phi$

and $B = D \sin \phi$

Thus, Eq. (ii) can be written as

$$f(t) = D \sin(\omega t + \phi)$$

where, $D = \sqrt{A^2 + B^2}$ and $\phi = \tan^{-1}\left(\dfrac{B}{A}\right)$

An important result given by the French mathematician, Jean Baptiste Joseph Fourier (1768-1830) is that **any periodic function can be expressed as a superposition of sine and cosine function of different time periods with suitable coefficients.**

EXAMPLE |2| Periodic and Non-periodic Motion

Which of the following functions of time represent (a) periodic and (b) non-periodic motion? Give the period for each case of periodic motion. [ω is any positive constant]. **[NCERT]**

(i) $\sin \omega t + \cos \omega t$

(ii) $\sin \omega t + \cos 2\omega t + \sin 4\omega t$

(iii) $e^{-\omega t}$

(iv) $\log(\omega t)$

Sol. (i) Given, $x(t) = \sin \omega t + \cos \omega t$

$$= \sqrt{2}\left[\sin \omega t \cos \frac{\pi}{4} + \cos \omega t \sin \frac{\pi}{4}\right]$$

$$x(t) = \sqrt{2}\sin\left(\omega t + \frac{\pi}{4}\right)$$

Moreover, $x\left(t + \dfrac{2\pi}{\omega}\right) = \sqrt{2}\sin\left[\omega\left(t + \dfrac{2\pi}{\omega}\right) + \dfrac{\pi}{4}\right]$

$$= \sqrt{2}\sin\left(\omega t + 2\pi + \frac{\pi}{4}\right)$$

$$= \sqrt{2}\sin\left(\omega t + \frac{\pi}{4}\right) = x(t)$$

$[\because \sin(2\pi + \theta) = \sin \theta]$

Hence, $\sin \omega t + \cos \omega t$ is a periodic function with time period equal to $\dfrac{2\pi}{\omega}$.

(ii) Given, $x(t) = \sin \omega t + \cos 2\omega t + \sin 4\omega t$

$\sin \omega t$ is a periodic function with period

$$= \frac{2\pi}{\omega} = T$$

$\cos 2\omega t$ is a periodic function with period

$$= \frac{2\pi}{2\omega} = \frac{\pi}{\omega} = \frac{T}{2}$$

$\sin 4\omega t$ is a periodic function with period

$$= \frac{2\pi}{4\omega} = \frac{\pi}{2\omega} = \frac{T}{4}$$

Clearly, the function $x(t)$ repeats after a minimum time, $T = \dfrac{2\pi}{\omega}$. Hence, the given function is periodic.

(iii) The function $e^{-\omega t}$ decreases monotonically to zero as $t \to \infty$. It is an exponential function with a negative exponent of e, where $e \approx 2.71828$. It never repeat its value. So, it is non-periodic.

(iv) The function $\log(\omega t)$ increases monotonically with time. As $t \to \infty$, $\log(\omega t) \to \infty$. It never repeat its value. So, it is non-periodic.

EXAMPLE |3| Standard Equation of Waves

The equation of a wave is given by $y = 6\sin 10\pi t + 8\cos 10\pi t$, where y is in centimetre and t in second. Determine the constants involved in the standard equation of the wave.

Sol. Given, $\quad\quad y = 6\sin 10\pi t + 8\cos 10\pi t \quad\quad$ ...(i)

The general equation of wave is

$$y = A\sin(\omega t + \phi)$$

$$= A\sin \omega t \cos \phi + A\cos \omega t \sin \phi$$

$$= (A\cos \phi)\sin \omega t + (A\sin \phi)\cos \omega t \quad\quad \text{...(ii)}$$

Comparing Eqs. (i) and (ii), we get

$$A\cos \phi = 6 \quad\quad\quad \text{...(iii)}$$

$$A\sin \phi = 8 \quad\quad\quad \text{...(iv)}$$

and $\quad\quad\quad \omega t = 10\pi t$ or $\omega = 10\pi$

$\therefore$ Time period, $T = \dfrac{2\pi}{\omega} = \dfrac{2\pi}{10\pi} = 0.2$s

Squaring and adding Eqs. (iii) and (iv), we get

$$A^2(\cos^2 \phi + \sin^2 \phi) = 6^2 + 8^2$$

$$= 36 + 64 = 100$$

or $\quad\quad\quad A^2 = 100$

$\therefore \quad\quad\quad A = 10$ cm

Dividing Eq. (iv) by Eq. (iii), we get

$$\tan \phi = \frac{8}{6} = 1.3333$$

$\therefore \quad\quad\quad \phi = \tan^{-1}(1.3333) = 53°8'$

SIMPLE HARMONIC MOTION

A special type of periodic motion in which a particle moves to and fro repeatedly about a mean position under the influence of a restoring force is known as **Simple Harmonic Motion (SHM)**.

Characteristic of Restoring Force in SHM

The restoring force is always directed towards the mean position and its magnitude at any instant is directly proportional to the displacement of the particle from its mean position at that instant.

As the restoring force is directed towards the mean position at any point in its oscillation, thus, displacement of a simple harmonic motion is always a sinusoidal function of time.

Equation of SHM

Consider a particle oscillating back and forth about the origin of an x-axis between the limits $+A$ and $-A$ as given in the figure below.

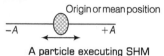

Origin or mean position

$-A$ $+A$

A particle executing SHM

This oscillatory motion of the particle is said to be SHM if the displacement x of the particle from the origin varies with time as

> Displacement, $x(t) = A \cos(\omega t + \phi)$

Where, A, ω and ϕ are constants.

Given, the time t is taken as zero when the particle is at position $+A$ and it returns to same point with position $+A$ at time $t = T$.

Let at an instant t, the particle be at P, if O is taken as mean position of the particle, then $OP = x$ (say), i.e. the displacement of the particle from the mean position.

$-A$ $O \xrightarrow{x} +A$

        P

The restoring force F acting on the particle at that instant is

$$F = -kx$$

where, k is a force constant having SI unit N/m. The negative sign shows that the restoring force F is always directed towards the mean position.

The relation $F = -kx$ is known as **force law** for SHM.

Location of the Particle Executing SHM at the Discrete Value of Time t

The figure below shows the positions of a particle executing SHM are at discrete values of time. It must be noted that each interval of time being $\dfrac{T}{4}$.

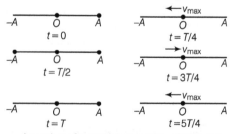

Location of a particle executing SHM with different time

Observations from the figures are

(i) The time after which motion repeats itself is T.

(ii) T will remain fixed, i.e. it doesn't vary with variation in initial location ($t = 0$).

(iii) The speed is maximum for zero displacement at $x = 0$ and zero at the extremes of motion.

EXAMPLE |4| Periodicity of an SHM

Which of the following functions of time represent (a) simple harmonic motion (b) periodic but not simple harmonic? Give the period for each function when functions are

   (i) $\sin \omega t - \cos \omega t$ (ii) $\sin^2 \omega t$ **[NCERT]**

Sol. (i) Given, function is

$$\sin \omega t - \cos \omega t = \sin \omega t - \sin\left(\frac{\pi}{2} - \omega t\right)$$

$$= 2\sin\left(\frac{\omega t + \dfrac{\pi}{2} - \omega t}{2}\right) \cdot \sin\left(\frac{\omega t - \dfrac{\pi}{2} + \omega t}{2}\right)$$

Given function $= 2\sin\left(\dfrac{\pi}{4}\right) \cdot \sin\left(\omega t - \dfrac{\pi}{4}\right)$

$$= \sqrt{2} \sin\left(\omega t - \frac{\pi}{4}\right)$$

This function represents a simple harmonic motion having a period of $T = \dfrac{2\pi}{\omega}$ and a phase angle $\left(-\dfrac{\pi}{4}\right)$ or $\left(-\dfrac{7\pi}{4}\right)$.

(ii) Also, $\sin^2 \omega t = \dfrac{1 - \cos 2\omega t}{2} = \dfrac{1}{2} - \dfrac{1}{2}\cos 2\omega t$

The function is periodic having a period of $T = \dfrac{\pi}{\omega}$. It also represents a harmonic motion with the point of equilibrium occurring at $\dfrac{1}{2}$ instead of zero.

EXAMPLE |5| SHM on a Straight Line

Two particles execute SHM of the same amplitude and frequency along close parallel lines. They pass each other moving in opposite directions, each time their displacement is half their amplitude. What is their phase difference?

Sol. In SHM, $x = A \sin(\omega t + \phi)$ ...(i)

Velocity, $v = \dfrac{dx}{dt} = A \omega \cos(\omega t + \phi)$ ...(ii)

At $t = 0$, $x = \dfrac{A}{2}$, then from Eq. (i), $\dfrac{A}{2} = A \sin \phi$

or $\sin \phi = \dfrac{1}{2} = \sin \dfrac{\pi}{6}$ or $\sin \dfrac{5\pi}{6}$

$\therefore$ $\phi = \dfrac{\pi}{6}$ or $\dfrac{5\pi}{6}$

$x = -A$ $x = 0$ $x = \dfrac{A}{2}$ $x = A$

If $\phi = \dfrac{\pi}{6}$, displacement and velocity both are positive.

When $\phi = \dfrac{5\pi}{6}$, displacement is positive and velocity is negative. Therefore, displacement-time equations of two particles will be

$$x_1 = A \sin\left(\omega t + \dfrac{\pi}{6}\right)$$

and $$x_2 = A \sin\left(\omega t + \dfrac{5\pi}{6}\right)$$

∴ Phase difference

$$\Delta\phi = \dfrac{5\pi}{6} - \dfrac{\pi}{6} = \dfrac{4\pi}{6} = \dfrac{2\pi}{3}\,\text{rad}$$

SIMPLE HARMONIC MOTION AND UNIFORM CIRCULAR MOTION
(GEOMETRICAL INTERPRETATION OF SHM)

Consider a particle P starting from X is moving with a uniform speed along the circumference of a circle of radius A, with centre at O. This circle is known as **circle of reference**, while the particle P is known as **reference particle**.

Let P' be the foot of perpendicular drawn from the point P to the diameter XOX'. P' is known as **projection** of the particle P at diameter XOX'.

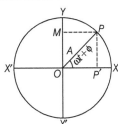

Circular representation of SHM

As P moves along the circle from X to Y, Y to X', X' to Y' and Y' to X, the projection of the particle P i.e. P' moves from X to O, O to X', X' to O and O to X, respectively.

Thus, P revolves along the circumference of the circle while its projection P' moves to and fro about the point O along the diameter XOX'. Hence, the motion of P' about point O is said to be **simple harmonic.**

Therefore, the projection of uniform circular motion upon a diameter of the circle executes simple harmonic motion.

The motion of projection of reference particle along any other diameter of the circle of reference will also be simple harmonic motion.

Hence, **SHM can be geometrically defined as the projection of a uniform circular motion on any diameter of the circle of reference.**

EXAMPLE |6| Circular Motion of a Particle Executing SHM

Figure below shows a circular motion of a particle. All the parameters are labelled in the figure. Obtain the corresponding equation for simple harmonic motion of the revolving particle P.

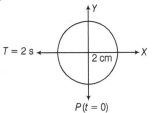

Sol. Suppose the particle moves from P to P' in time t.

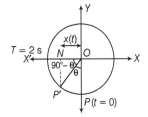

The angle swept by the radius vector

$$\theta = \omega t = \dfrac{2\pi}{T}t = \dfrac{2\pi}{2}\cdot t = \pi t\,\text{rad}$$

Displacement $ON = OP'\cos\left(\dfrac{\pi}{2} - \theta\right) = 2\cos\left(\dfrac{\pi}{2} - \theta\right)$

$$-x(t) = 2\sin\theta$$

[negative sign shows displacement being to left from O]

$$\Rightarrow \qquad x(t) = 2\sin\pi t$$

CHARACTERISTICS OF SIMPLE HARMONIC MOTION

Some of the important parameters which define the characteristics of a simple harmonic motion are given below.

(i) Displacement

The displacement of a particle executing SHM at an instant is given by the distance of the particle from the mean position at that instant.

The values of displacement as a continuous function of time can be represented as a graph given below.

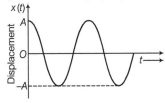

Displacement as a continuous function of time

Here, $\boxed{\text{Displacement, } x\,(t) = A\cos(\omega t + \phi)}$

The function containing sine or cosine term is known as sinusoidal function.

(ii) Amplitude

The magnitude of maximum displacement of a particle executing SHM is called **amplitude** of the oscillation of that particle. Amplitude is measured on either side of mean position.

The displacement varies between the extremes $+A$ and $-A$ because the sinusoidal function of time varies from $+1$ to -1.

Two SHM may have same ω (angular frequency) and ϕ (phase constant) but different amplitudes A and B.

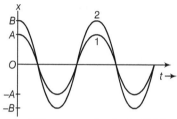

Different amplitudes in SHM

(iii) Phase

If amplitude A is fixed for a given SHM, then the state of motion i.e. position and velocity of the particle at any time t is determined by the argument $(\omega t + \phi_0)$ in the sinusoidal function. This quantity $(\omega t + \phi_0)$ is called phase of the motion.

For $t = 0$, phase $\omega t + \phi_0 = \phi_0$. Thus, ϕ_0 is called **phase constant** or **phase angle**. Two SHM may have the same A (amplitude) and ω (angular frequency) but different phase angle ϕ.

This can be shown in the graph below

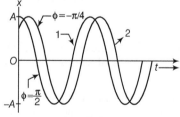

Phase determination

As in above graph, the curve 1 has phase constant of $\pi/2$ (i.e. $\phi = \pi/2$) and amplitude of A, the curve 2 has phase constant of $\dfrac{\pi}{4}$ $\left(\text{i.e. } \phi = +\dfrac{\pi}{4}\right)$ and amplitude of A.

(iv) Angular Frequency

Angular frequency of a body executing periodic motion is equal to the product of frequency of the particle with factor 2π.

It is denoted by ω and its SI unit is radian per second.

We know that, $T = \dfrac{2\pi}{\omega} \Rightarrow \omega = \dfrac{2\pi}{T} = 2\pi\nu$

where, ν = frequency of the particle.

Since, the motion is periodic with a period T, the displacement $x\,(t)$ must return to its initial value after one period of the motion i.e. $x\,(t)$ must be equal to $x\,(t+T)$ for all t.

Consider the equation, $x\,(t) = A\cos\omega t$

$$A\cos\omega t = A\cos\omega\,(t+T)$$

Now, the cosine function is periodic with period 2π i.e. it first repeats itself when the argument changes by 2π. Therefore,

$\Rightarrow \qquad \omega\,(t+T) = \omega t + 2\pi$

$\Rightarrow \qquad \boxed{\text{Angular frequency, } \omega = \dfrac{2\pi}{T}}$

Thus, angular frequency ω is 2π times the frequency of oscillation $\dfrac{1}{T}$.

Two SHM may have the same amplitude (A) and phase angle (ϕ) but different angular frequency ω.

This can be represented on the graph as below

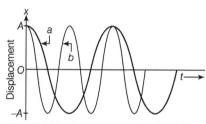

Two SHM having same amplitude and phase

In above wave diagram, curve (b) has half the period and twice the frequency of the curve (a).

(v) Velocity

The velocity of a particle executing SHM at any instant, is defined as the time rate of change of its displacement at that instant.

$$\boxed{\text{Velocity, } v = \omega\sqrt{A^2 - x^2}}$$

At mean position, $x = 0$

$\therefore \qquad\qquad v = \omega A \qquad\qquad$ [maximum velocity]

At extreme position $\qquad x = A$

$\therefore \qquad\qquad v = 0 \qquad\qquad$ [minimum velocity]

The velocity can also be calculated as

$$v(t) = \frac{d}{dt}[x(t)] = \frac{d}{dt}[A\cos(\omega t + \phi)]$$

$$\boxed{\text{Velocity, } v(t) = -\omega A \sin(\omega t + \phi)}$$

(vi) Acceleration

The acceleration of the particle executing SHM at any instant is defined as the time rate of change of its velocity at that instant.

$$\boxed{\text{Acceleration, } a = -\omega^2 x}$$

At mean position, $x = 0$

$\therefore \qquad\qquad a = 0 \qquad\qquad$ [minimum acceleration]

At extreme position $x = A$,

$\therefore \qquad\qquad a = -\omega^2 A \quad$ [maximum acceleration]

The acceleration can also be calculated as

i.e. $\qquad\qquad a(t) = \frac{d}{dt}[v(t)]$

$$= \frac{d}{dt}[-\omega A \sin(\omega t + \phi)]$$

$$\boxed{\text{Acceleration, } a(t) = -\omega^2 A \cos(\omega t + \phi)}$$

EXAMPLE |7| Period and Velocity

Consider an SHM as $x(t) = 2\cos(4\pi t + \pi/6)$ where x is in metres and t in seconds. Determine the time period and initial velocity of the oscillating body.

Sol. Given equation of SHM

$$x(t) = 2\cos(4\pi t + \pi/6) \qquad \text{...(i)}$$

We know that, $x(t) = A\cos(\omega t + \phi) \qquad \text{...(ii)}$

Comparing Eq. (i) with Eq. (ii), we get

$\therefore$ Amplitude, $A = 2$

$$\omega = 4\pi \quad \text{or} \quad \frac{2\pi}{T} = 4\pi$$

$$\Rightarrow \qquad T = \frac{1}{2} = 0.5\,\text{s}$$

The velocity of the particle can be found by differentiating displacement w.r.t time

$\therefore$ Velocity, $v = \dfrac{dx}{dt} = \dfrac{d}{dt}[2\cos(4\pi t + \pi/6)]$

$$= -2\sin\left(4\pi t + \frac{\pi}{6}\right) \times 4\pi$$

or velocity, $v = -8\pi\sin\left(4\pi t + \dfrac{\pi}{6}\right)$

The initial velocity is the velocity of the oscillating body at time $t = 0$

$\therefore$ Initial velocity $= \dfrac{dx}{dt}\bigg|_{t=0} = -8\pi\sin\left(4\pi \times 0 + \dfrac{\pi}{6}\right)$

$$= -8\pi\sin\left(\dfrac{\pi}{6}\right)$$

Initial velocity $= -4\pi$ m/s $\qquad \left[\because \sin\dfrac{\pi}{6} = \dfrac{1}{2}\right]$

EXAMPLE |8| Finding the Characteristics of SHM

A simple harmonic motion is represented by

$$x = 12\sin(10t + 0.6)$$

Find out the amplitude, angular frequency, frequency, time period and initial phase if displacement is measured in metre and time in seconds.

Sol. Given equation, $x = 12\sin(10t + 0.6)$

On comparing with $x(t) = A\sin(\omega t + \phi)$

We have,

(i) Amplitude, $A = 12$ m

(ii) Angular frequency, $\omega = 10$ rad/s

(iii) Frequency, $\nu = \dfrac{\omega}{2\pi} = \dfrac{10}{2\pi} = 1.59$ Hz

(iv) Time period, $T = \dfrac{2\pi}{\omega} = \dfrac{1}{1.59} = 0.628$ s

(v) Initial phase, $\omega t + \phi|_{t=0} = 10t + 0.6|_{t=0}$

$$= 0.6 \text{ rad}$$

EXAMPLE |9| A Periodic Motion

A particle executes SHM with a time period of 2 s and amplitude 5 cm. Find

(i) displacement   (ii) velocity and

(iii) acceleration after 1/3 s starting from the mean position.

Sol. Here, $T = 2$ s, $A = 5$ cm, $t = \dfrac{1}{3}$ s

(i) For the particle starting from mean position, (i.e. $\phi = 0$) displacement,

$$x = A\sin\omega t = A\sin\frac{2\pi}{T}t$$

$$= 5\sin\frac{2\pi}{2} \times \frac{1}{3} = 5\sin\frac{\pi}{3}$$

$$= 5 \times \frac{\sqrt{3}}{2} = 4.33\,\text{cm}$$

(ii) Velocity, $v = \dfrac{dx}{dt} = \dfrac{d(A\sin\omega t)}{dt} = A\omega\cos\omega t$

$$= \frac{2\pi A}{T}\cos\frac{2\pi}{T}t = \frac{2\pi \times 5}{2}\cos\frac{\pi}{3}$$

$$= 5 \times 3.14 \times 0.5 \qquad \left[\because \cos\frac{\pi}{3} = 0.5\right]$$

$$= 7.85 \text{ cm s}^{-1}$$

(iii) Acceleration, $a = \dfrac{dv}{dt} = \dfrac{d(A\omega \cos \omega t)}{dt} = -A\omega^2 \sin \omega t$

$$= -\frac{4\pi^2 A}{T^2}\sin\frac{2\pi}{T}t$$

$$= -\frac{4 \times 9.87 \times 5}{4}\sin\frac{\pi}{3}$$

$$= -9.87 \times 5 \times \frac{\sqrt{3}}{2}$$

$$= -42.73 \text{ cm s}^{-2}$$

$$\therefore \qquad |a| = 42.73 \text{ cm s}^{-2}$$

EXAMPLE |10| Displacement, Speed and Acceleration

A body oscillates with SHM according to the equation,

$$x = (5.0 \text{ m}) \cos [(2\pi \text{ rad s}^{-1})\, t + \pi/4].$$

At $t = 1.5$ s, calculate displacement, speed and acceleration of the body. **[NCERT]**

Sol. Equation of SHM,

$$x(t) = (5.0 \text{ m}) \cos[(2\pi \text{ rad s}^{-1})\, t + \pi/4]$$

time, $t = 1.5$ s

$$x(t) = 5.0 \times \cos[2\pi \times 1.5 + \pi/4]$$

$$= 5.0 \times \cos\left(3\pi + \frac{\pi}{4}\right)$$

$$= -5.0 \cos\frac{\pi}{4}$$

$$= -5.0 \times 0.707$$

$$x(t) = -3.535 \text{ m}$$

$$v = \frac{dx}{dt} = \frac{d}{dt}\left[5.0 \cos\left(2\pi t + \frac{\pi}{4}\right)\right]$$

$$= -5.0 \times \sin\left(2\pi t + \frac{\pi}{4}\right) \times 2\pi$$

$$= -10\pi \sin\left(2\pi t + \frac{\pi}{4}\right)$$

$$\therefore \quad \left.\frac{dx}{dt}\right|_{t=1.5} = -10\pi\sin\left(3\pi + \frac{\pi}{4}\right) = 10\pi \times 0.707$$

$$= 22.22 \text{ m/s} \qquad [\because \sin(3\pi + \theta) = -\sin\theta]$$

$$a = \frac{dv}{dt} = \frac{d}{dt}\left[-10\pi \sin\left[2\pi t + \frac{\pi}{4}\right]\right]$$

$$= -10\pi \times 2\pi \cos\left(2\pi t + \frac{\pi}{4}\right)$$

$$\left.\frac{dv}{dt}\right|_{t=1.5} = -20\pi^2 \cos\left(3\pi + \frac{\pi}{4}\right) = 139.56 \text{ m/s}^2$$

Displacement, Velocity and Acceleration of a Body Executing SHM

Displacement $x(t) = A\cos\omega t$	Velocity $v(t) = -\omega A\sin\omega t$	Acceleration $a(t) = -\omega^2 A\cos\omega t$
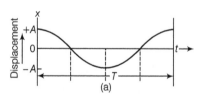	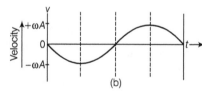	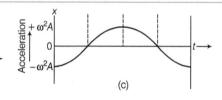
(a)	(b)	(c)
Sinusoidal in nature, x varies from $-A$ to A. It has zero phase difference.	Sinusoidal in nature. $v(t)$ varies from $-\omega A$ to ωA. It has a phase difference of $\dfrac{\pi}{2}$ w.r.t. $x(t)$	Sinusoidal in nature. $a(t)$ varies from $-\omega^2 A$ to $\omega^2 A$. It has a phase difference of π w.r.t. $x(t)$.

TOPIC PRACTICE 1

OBJECTIVE Type Questions

1. The motion of satellites and planets is
   (a) periodic   (b) oscillatory
   (c) simple harmonic   (d) non-periodic

   Sol. (a) The motion of planets and satellites are repetitive and repeats itself after a fixed interval of time. These type of motions are known as periodic motion.

2. The periodic function $f(t) = A\sin(\omega t)$ repeats itself with periodic function of
   (a) 2π (b) 3π
   (c) π (d) $\pi/2$

   Sol. (a) A periodic function repeats itself after a time period T.
   and $f(t) = f(t + T)$
   As, $\sin(\omega t) = \sin(\omega t + 2\pi)$
   $\therefore$ Period of function is 2π.

3. SHM could be related to
   (a) non-uniform circular motion
   (b) uniform circular motion
   (c) straight line motion
   (d) projectile motion

   Sol. (b) SHM could be related to uniform circular motion. The projection of uniform circular motion on a diameter of the circle follows simple harmonic motion.

4. The displacement of a particle in SHM varies according to the relation $x = 4 (\cos \pi t + \sin \pi t)$. The amplitude of the particle is
   (a) -4 (b) 4 (c) $4\sqrt{2}$ (d) 8

   Sol. (c) Given, equation $x(t) = 4 (\cos \pi t + \sin \pi t)$
   Now, comparing above equation with general form
   $$x(t) = A \cos \omega t + B \sin \omega t$$
   We get, $A = 4$ and $B = 4$
   As, the resultant amplitude for such a equation is
   $$= \sqrt{A^2 + B^2}$$
   $\therefore$ Amplitude $= \sqrt{4^2 + 4^2} = 4\sqrt{2}$

5. At extreme position, velocity of the particle executing SHM that has amplitude A is
   (a) $\omega^2 A$ (b) 0
   (c) ωA (d) $\dfrac{\omega A}{2}$

   Sol. (b) Velocity of the particle executing SHM is given as
   $$v = \omega \sqrt{A^2 - x^2}$$
   At extreme position, $x = A$
   $\Rightarrow$ $v = 0$

VERY SHORT ANSWER Type Questions

6. What are the basic properties required by a system to oscillate?

   Sol. Inertia and elasticity are the properties which are required by a system to oscillate.

7. All oscillatory motions are periodic and *vice-versa*. Is it true?

   Sol. No, there are other types of periodic motions also. Circular motion and rotatory motion are periodic but non-oscillatory.

8. State the conditions when motion of a particle can be an SHM.

   Sol. For SHM, the restoring force on the particle must be proportional to its displacement and directed towards mean position.

9. Give the name of three important characteristics of a SHM.

   Sol. Three important characteristics of an SHM are amplitude, time period (or frequency) and phase.

10. If the body is given a small displacement from the mean position, a force comes in to play which tends to bring the body back to the mean point, this give rise to vibrations. Define phase of a vibrating particle.

    Sol. The phase of a vibrating particle at any instant of time is the state of particle as regards to its position and state of motion.

11. The piston in the cylinder head of a locomotive has a stroke (twice the amplitude) of 1.0 m. If the piston executes simple harmonic motion with an angular frequency of 200 rad/min, then what is its maximum speed?   **[NCERT]**

    Sol. Given, angular frequency of the piston, $\omega = 200$ rad/min
    Stroke length $= 1$ m
    $\therefore$ Amplitude of SHM,
    $$A = \frac{\text{Stroke length}}{2} = \frac{1}{2} = 0.5 \text{ m}$$
    Now, $v_{\max} = \omega A = 200 \times 0.5 = 100$ m/min

SHORT ANSWER Type Questions

12. Which of the following examples represent periodic motion?
    (i) A swimmer completing one (return) trip from one bank of a river to the other and back.
    (ii) A freely suspended bar magnet displaced from its *N-S* direction and released.
    (iii) A hydrogen molecule rotating about its centre of mass.

(iv) An arrow released from a bow.   [NCERT]

💡 If the motion is repeated after certain interval of time, then, it is periodic. Circular motion is periodic.

Sol. (i) There is no repetition of the motion as the swimmer just completes one trip, hence not periodic.
(ii) The motion is repeated after a certain interval of time, hence periodic. In fact, the bar magnet oscillates about its mean position with a definite period of time.
(iii) Rotatory motion is periodic as repeating after fixed time-interval.
(iv) There is no repetition, hence not periodic.

13. Figures depict four x-t plots for linear motion of a particle. Which of the plots represent periodic motion? What is the period of motion (in case of periodic motion)?   [NCERT]

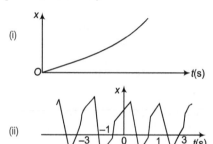

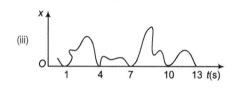

💡 As the graphs are plot between displacements *versus* time, we shall check for repetition to ascertain, whether periodic or not. Also, the minimum time span after which the plot repeats itself will be time period of the motion.

Sol. (i) No repetition of motion. Its a unidirectional, linear but non-uniform motion of the particle.
(ii) Motion repeats after every 2 s. Hence, periodic with time period 2 s.
(iii) Repetition of one position or a few positions (but not all) is not enough for motion to be periodic, the entire motion during one period must be repeated successively. Hence, the given x-t plot is not periodic, though there is repetition of a single position ($x = 0$ at every 3 s) but other positions are not repeated.
(iv) Clearly, the motion repeats itself after every 2 s. Hence, periodic motion having a time-period of 2s.

14. Which of the following examples represent (nearly) simple harmonic motion and which represent periodic but not simple harmonic motion?
(i) The rotation of earth about its axis.
(ii) Motion of an oscillating mercury column in a U-tube.
(iii) Motion of a ball bearing inside a smooth curved bowl, when released from a point slightly above the lower most point.
(iv) General vibrations of a polyatomic molecule about its equilibrium position.   [NCERT]

💡 Every SHM is periodic but every periodic motion is not SHM. Only that periodic motion which are governed by the force law i.e. $F = -kx$, is simple harmonic.

Sol. (i) There is no to and fro motion which is a must for a periodic motion to be SHM. Hence, rotation of earth about its axis is not SHM.
(ii) This is a periodic motion and as it follows $F = -kx$ (about mean position, to and fro motion) hence SHM.
(iii) A periodic motion, oscillatory in nature about lower most point as mean position following SHM force law, hence, it is SHM.
(iv) A polyatomic molecule has a number of natural frequencies. So, in general, its vibration is a superposition of SHMs of a number of different frequencies. Thus, superposition is periodic but not necessarily SHM.

15. Every SHM is periodic motion, but every periodic motion need not to be a simple harmonic motion. Do you agree? Give an example to justify your statement.

Sol. Yes, every periodic motion need not to be SHM. e.g. the motion of the earth round the sun is a periodic motion, but not simple harmonic motion as the back and forth motion is not taking place.

16. Which of the following relationships between the acceleration a and the displacement x of a particle involve simple harmonic motion?   [NCERT]

(i) $a = 0.7x$ (ii) $a = -200x^2$
(iii) $a = -10x$ (iv) $a = 100x^3$

💡 All SHM follows the condition acceleration $\propto$ –displacement or acceleration = – constant × displacement.

Sol. (i) No negative sign on RHS, hence, not SHM.
(ii) Displacement on RHS is squared, hence not SHM.
(iii) $a = -10x$ follows the condition of SHM, acceleration $\propto$ – displacement hence, SHM.
(iv) No negative sign on RHS and displacement appears as cubed, hence, not SHM.

17. The maximum acceleration of a simple harmonic oscillator is a_0 and the maximum velocity is v_0. What is the displacement amplitude?

Sol. Let A be the displacement amplitude and ω be the angular frequency of the simple harmonic oscillator.

Then, $a_0 = \omega^2 A$ and $v_0 = \omega A$

On dividing, $\dfrac{v_0^2}{a_0} = \dfrac{\omega^2 A^2}{\omega^2 A} = A$

or $A = \dfrac{v_0^2}{a_0}$

LONG ANSWER Type I Questions

18. A particle is in linear simple harmonic motion between two points A and B, 10 cm apart. Take the direction from A to B as the positive direction and give the signs of velocity, acceleration and force on the particle when it is

(i) at the end A.
(ii) at the end B.
(iii) at the mid-point of AB going towards A.
(iv) at 2 cm away from B going towards A.
(v) at 3 cm away from A going towards B.
(vi) at 4 cm away from B going towards A. [NCERT]

💡 At either extreme positions in SHM, the velocity is 0 but not the acceleration and force. Acceleration is always direct towards the mean position (point about which SHM is taking place). Further, acceleration decides the direction of force.

Sol. Visualise the situation using the diagram below

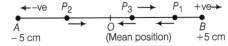

Now,

		Velocity	Acceleration	Force
(i)	A	0	+	+
(ii)	B	0	−	−
(iii)	O	−	0	0
(iv)	P_1	−	−	−
(v)	P_2	+	+	+
(vi)	P_3	−	−	−

19. A body describes simple harmonic motion with an amplitude of 5 cm and a period of 0.2 s. Find the acceleration and velocity of the body when the displacement is (i) 5 cm, (ii) 3 cm and (iii) 0 cm. [NCERT]

Sol. Given, amplitude, $A = 5$ cm $= 0.05$ m,

Time period, $T = 0.2$ s

(i) When displacement is $x = 5$ cm $= 0.05$ m

Acceleration, $a = -\omega^2(x) = -\left(\dfrac{2\pi}{T}\right)^2(x)$

$= -\left(\dfrac{2\pi}{0.2}\right)^2(0.05) = -5\pi^2 \text{ m/s}^2$

Velocity, $v = \omega\sqrt{A^2 - x^2}$

$= \left(\dfrac{2\pi}{T}\right)\sqrt{(0.05)^2 - (0.05)^2}$

$= \left(\dfrac{2\pi}{T}\right) \times 0 = 0$

(ii) When displacement is $x = 3$ cm $= 0.03$ m

Acceleration, $a = -\left(\dfrac{2\pi}{0.2}\right)^2(0.03) = -3\pi^2 \text{ m/s}^2$

and velocity, $v = \omega\sqrt{A^2 - x^2}$

$= \left(\dfrac{2\pi}{0.2}\right)\sqrt{(0.05)^2 - (0.03)^2} = 0.4\pi \text{ m/s}$

(iii) When displacement is $x = 0$

Acceleration, $a = -\omega^2 x = 0$

Velocity, $v = \omega\sqrt{A^2 - x^2}$

$= \left(\dfrac{2\pi}{0.2}\right)\sqrt{(0.05)^2 - (0)^2}$

$= 0.5\pi \text{ m/s}$

20. A particle performs SHM on a rectilinear path. Starting from rest, it travels x_1 distance in first second and in the next second, it travels x_2 distance. Find out the amplitude of this SHM.

Sol. Because the particle starts from rest, so its starting point will be extreme position.

Thus, the displacement of the particle from the mean position after one second

$A - x_1 = A\cos\omega t = A\cos\omega$ ...(i) [putting $t = 1$ s]

where, A is amplitude of the SHM and for next second

$A - (x_1 + x_2) = A\cos\omega t$

$= A\cos 2\omega$ [putting $t = 2$ s]

$= A[2\cos^2\omega - 1]$ ...(ii)

$[\because \cos 2\omega = 2\cos^2\omega - 1]$

From Eq. (i) and Eq. (ii), we have

$A - (x_1 + x_2) = A\left[2\cdot\left(\dfrac{A - x_1}{A}\right)^2 - 1\right]$

$= \dfrac{1}{A}[2A^2 + 2x_1^2 - 4Ax_1 - A^2]$

$\Rightarrow A^2 - A(x_1 + x_2) = A^2 + 2x_1^2 - 4Ax_1$

$\Rightarrow A[3x_1 - x_2] = 2x_1^2$

$\therefore A = \dfrac{2x_1^2}{3x_1 - x_2}$

21. Figures correspond to two circular motions. The radius of the circle, the period of revolution, the initial position and the sense of revolution (i.e. clockwise or anti-clockwise) are indicated on each figure.

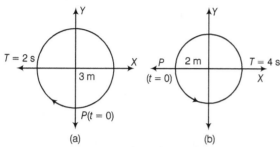

(a)　　　　　　(b)

Obtain the corresponding simple harmonic motions of the X-projection of the radius vector of the revolving particle P, in each case. **[NCERT]**

💡 The projection on the required axis gives the displacement. Initial phase is found from the position of the particle at $t = 0$.
The displacement is considered as a function of time and equated to the graphical displacement to get the required equation.

Sol. If the particle moves from P to P' in time-interval t, then angle moved by position vector (or radius vector)

$$\theta = \omega t = \frac{2\pi}{T} t = \frac{2\pi}{2} t = \pi t \text{ rad}$$

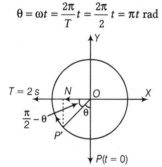

Displacement suffered by the particle

$$ON = OP' \cos\left(\frac{\pi}{2} - \theta\right) = OP' \sin\theta$$

But　$ON = -x(t)$
As it is left to mean position O, hence, negative sign.

$\Rightarrow$　$-x(t) = 3\sin\theta$　　$[\because OP = 3 \text{ cm}]$
or　$x(t) = -3\sin\theta$
or　$x(t) = -3\sin\pi t$ as $\theta = \pi t$

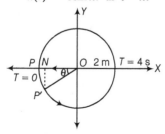

If the particle moves from P to P' in the time-interval t. Angle swept by radius vector

$$\theta = \omega t = \frac{2\pi}{T} t = \frac{2\pi}{4} t = \frac{\pi t}{2} \text{ rad}$$

Displacement,　$ON = OP' \cos\theta$

or　$-x(t) = 2\cos\frac{\pi t}{2}$　　$[\because OP = 1 \text{cm}]$

Negative sign to indicate left to mean position.

$\Rightarrow$　$x(t) = -2\cos\left(\frac{\pi t}{2}\right)$

22. The following figures depict two circular motions. The radius of the circle, the period of revolution, the initial position and the sense of revolution are indicated on the figures.

Obtain the simple harmonic motion of the x-projection of the radius vector of the rotating particle P in each case.　　**[NCERT]**

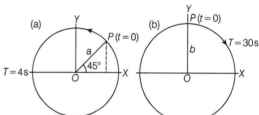

Sol.

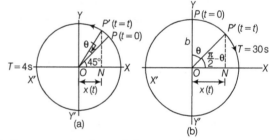

(a)　　　　　　(b)

In figure, suppose the particle moves in the anti-clockwise sense from P to P' in time t as shown in Fig.(a). Angle swept by the radius vector,

$$\theta = \omega t = \frac{2\pi}{T} t = \frac{2\pi}{4} t \qquad [\because T = 4 \text{ s}]$$

N is the foot of perpendicular drawn from P' on the XOX'-axis.

Displacement,　$ON = OP' \cos(\theta + \pi/4)$

or　$x(t) = a \cos\left(\frac{2\pi}{4} t + \frac{\pi}{4}\right)$

This equation represents SHM of amplitude a, period 4 s and an initial phase of $\frac{\pi}{4}$ rad.

Now, in Fig. (b), suppose the particle moves in the clockwise sense from P to P' in time t.
Angle swept by the radius vector,

$$\theta = \omega t = \frac{2\pi}{T} t = \frac{2\pi}{30} t \qquad [\because T = 30 \text{ s}]$$

Displacement,

$$ON = OP' \cos\left(\frac{\pi}{2} - \theta\right)$$

or

$$x(t) = b \cos\left(\frac{\pi}{2} - \frac{2\pi}{30}t\right)$$

or

$$x(t) = b \cos\left(\frac{2\pi}{30}t - \frac{\pi}{2}\right) [\because \cos(-\theta) = \cos\theta]$$

This equation represents SHM of amplitude b period 30 s and an initial phase of $-\frac{\pi}{2}$ rad.

23. A man stands on a weighing machine placed on a horizontal platform. The machine reads 50 kg. By means of a suitable mechanism, the platform is made to execute harmonic vibrations up and down with a frequency of two vibrations per second. What will be the effect on the reading of the weighing machine? The amplitude of vibrations of platform is 5 cm. Take, $g = 10 \text{ ms}^{-2}$.

Sol. Here, $m = 50 \text{ kg}, \nu = 2 \text{ s}^{-1}, A = 5 \text{ cm} = 0.05 \text{ m}$

Maximum acceleration

$$a_{max} = \omega^2 A = (2\pi\nu)^2 A = 4\pi^2\nu^2 A$$

$$= 4 \times \left(\frac{22}{7}\right)^2 \times (2)^2 \times 0.05 = 7.9 \text{ ms}^{-2}$$

∴ Maximum force felt by the man

$$m(g + a_{max}) = 50(10 + 7.9) = 895.0 \text{ N} = 89.5 \text{ kgf}$$

Minimum force felt by the man

$$= m(g - a_{max}) = 50(10 - 7.9)$$
$$= 105.0 \text{ N} = 10.5 \text{ kgf}$$

Hence, the reading of the weighing machine varies between 10.5 kgf and 89.5 kgf.

24. A particle is executing SHM. If v_1 and v_2 are the speeds of the particle at distance x_1 and x_2 from the equilibrium position, show that the frequency of oscillations is

$$f = \frac{1}{2\pi}\left(\frac{v_1^2 - v_2^2}{x_2^2 - x_1^2}\right)^{1/2}$$

Sol. The displacement of a particle executing SHM is given by

$$x = A\cos\omega t$$
$$\frac{dx}{dt} = -\omega A \sin\omega t$$

∴ Velocity, $v = \frac{dx}{dt}$

or
$$v^2 = A^2\omega^2 \sin^2\omega t$$
$$= A^2\omega^2(1 - \cos^2\omega t)$$
$$= \omega^2(A^2 - x^2)$$

Hence, $\quad v_1^2 = \omega^2(A^2 - x_1^2)$ ...(i)

and $\quad v_2^2 = \omega^2(A^2 - x_2^2)$ ...(ii)

Subtracting the above equations,

$$v_1^2 - v_2^2 = \omega^2(x_2^2 - x_1^2)$$

$$\omega^2 = \frac{v_1^2 - v_2^2}{x_2^2 - x_1^2}$$

$$\Rightarrow \quad \omega = \left(\frac{v_1^2 - v_2^2}{x_2^2 - x_1^2}\right)^{1/2}$$

But $\quad \omega = 2\pi f$

$$f = \frac{1}{2\pi}\left(\frac{v_1^2 - v_2^2}{x_2^2 - x_1^2}\right)^{1/2}$$

LONG ANSWER Type II Questions

25. Which of the following functions of time represent (i) simple harmonic (ii) periodic but not simple harmonic and (iii) non-periodic motion? Give period for each case of periodic motion (ω is any positive constant). [NCERT]

(a) $\sin\omega t - \cos\omega t$ (b) $\sin^3\omega t$

(c) $3\cos\left(\frac{\pi}{4} - 2\omega t\right)$ (d) $\cos\omega t + \cos 3\omega t + \cos 5\omega t$

(e) $\exp(-\omega^2 t^2)$ (f) $1 + \omega t + \omega^2 t^2$

Any periodic function can be expressed as a superposition of sine and cosine functions of different time periods with suitable coefficients.

Sol. (a) Assuming $x(t) = \sin\omega t - \cos\omega t$

$$= \sqrt{2}\left[\frac{1}{\sqrt{2}}\sin\omega t - \frac{1}{\sqrt{2}}\cos\omega t\right]$$

$$= \sqrt{2}\left[\cos\frac{\pi}{4}\sin\omega t - \sin\frac{\pi}{4}\cos\omega t\right]$$

$$= \sqrt{2}\sin\left(\omega t - \frac{\pi}{4}\right)$$

Clearly, the above equation is of the form

$$x = A\sin(\omega t \pm \phi)$$

represents SHM.

Again, if $t = \frac{2\pi}{\omega}$ is the period of SHM, then

$$x\left(t + \frac{2\pi}{\omega}\right) = \sqrt{2}\sin\left[\omega\left(t + \frac{2\pi}{\omega}\right) - \frac{\pi}{4}\right]$$

$$= \sqrt{2}\sin\left(\omega t + 2\pi - \frac{\pi}{4}\right)$$

$$= \sqrt{2}\sin\left(\omega t - \frac{\pi}{4}\right) = x(t)$$

Hence, the period $T = \frac{2\pi}{\omega}$

and phase angle $= -\frac{\pi}{4}$ or $\left(2\pi - \frac{\pi}{4}\right)$

(b) Let $x(t) = \sin^3 t \Rightarrow x(t) = \frac{1}{4}(3\sin\omega t - \sin 3\omega t)$

Using, $\sin 3\theta = 3\sin\theta - 4\sin^3\theta$

The above equations represent two SHMs in combination. The combination is periodic but not SHM.

Period of $\frac{3}{4}\sin\omega t = \frac{2\pi}{\omega} = T$

Period of $\frac{1}{4}\sin 3\omega t = \frac{2\pi}{3\omega} = T' = \frac{T}{3}$

Thus, period of the combination = Minimum time after which the combined function repeats

$$= \text{LCM of } T \text{ and } \frac{T}{3} = T$$

(c) $x(t) = 3\cos\left(\frac{\pi}{4} - 2\omega t\right) = 3\cos\left(2\omega t - \frac{\pi}{4}\right)$

As $\cos(-\theta) = \cos\theta$

The above equation is of the form
$$x(t) = A\cos(\omega t \pm \phi)$$

Hence, SHM with period $T = \frac{2\pi}{2\omega} = \frac{\pi}{\omega}$

(d) $x(t) = \cos\omega t + \cos 3\omega t + \cos 5\omega t$

$\cos\omega t$ represents SHM with period $= \frac{2\pi}{\omega} = T$ (say)

$\cos 3\omega t$ represents SHM with period $= \frac{2\pi}{3\omega} = \frac{T}{3}$

$\cos 5\omega t$ represents SHM with period $= \frac{2\pi}{5\omega} = \frac{T}{5}$

The minimum time after which the combined function repeats its value is T. Hence, the given function represents periodic function but not SHM, with period T.

(e) $x(t) = \exp(-\omega^2 t^2)$

The given function is an exponential function. It decreases monotonically $x(t) \to 0$ as $t \to \infty$

There is no repetition of the values. Hence, it represents a non-periodic function.

(f) $x(t) = 1 + \omega t + \omega^2 t^2$

Here, as $t \to \infty$, $x(t) \to \infty$

No repetition of values. Hence, it represents non-periodic function.

26. The motion of a particle executing simple harmonic motion is described by the displacement function, $x(t) = A\cos(\omega t + \phi)$

If the initial ($t = 0$) position of the particle is 1 cm and its initial velocity is ω cm/s, then what are its amplitude and initial phase angle? The angular frequency of the particle is $\pi\,\text{s}^{-1}$. If instead of the cosine function, we choose the sine function to describe the SHM, $x = B\sin(\omega t + \alpha)$, then what are the amplitude and initial phase of the particle with the above initial conditions? **[NCERT]**

Sol. Given, $x(t) = A\cos(\omega t + \phi)$ ...(i)

At $t = 0$; $x(0) = 1$ cm, velocity $v = \omega$ cm/s

Angular frequency $\omega = \pi s^{-1} \Rightarrow 1 = A\cos(\omega t + \phi)$

For $t = 0$, $1 = A\cos\phi$ ...(i)

Now, $v(t) = \frac{dx(t)}{dt} = \frac{d}{dt}A\cos(\omega t + \phi)$

$$= -A\omega\sin(\omega t + \phi)$$

Again at $t = 0$, $v = \omega$ cm/s

$\Rightarrow \quad \omega = -A\omega\sin\phi \Rightarrow -1 = A\sin\phi$ ...(ii)

Squaring and adding Eqs. (i) and (ii),

$$A^2\cos^2\phi + A^2\sin^2\phi = (1)^2 + (-1)^2$$
$$A^2 = 2 \Rightarrow A = \pm\sqrt{2}\text{ cm}$$

Hence, the amplitude $= \sqrt{2}$ cm

Dividing Eq. (ii) by Eq. (i), we have

$$\frac{A\sin\phi}{A\cos\phi} = \frac{-1}{1} \text{ or } \tan\phi = -1$$

$\Rightarrow \qquad \phi = -\frac{\pi}{4} \text{ or } \frac{7\pi}{4}$

Now, if instead of cosine, we choose the sine function, then $x(t) = B\sin(\omega t + \alpha)$

At $t = 0$, $x = 1$ cm $\Rightarrow 1 = B\sin(0 + \alpha)$

or $B\sin\alpha = 1$ ...(iii)

Velocity $v(t) = \frac{dx(t)}{dt} = \frac{d}{dt}[B\sin(\omega t + \alpha)]$

$$= +B\omega\cos(\omega t + \alpha)$$

Again at $t = 0$, $v(t) = \omega$ cm/s

$$\omega = +B\omega\cos(0 + \alpha)$$
$$B\cos\alpha = +1$$ ...(iv)

Squaring and adding Eqs. (iii) and (iv),

$$B^2\sin^2\alpha + B^2\cos^2\alpha = (1)^2 + (+1)^2$$
$\Rightarrow \qquad B^2\sin^2\alpha + B^2\cos^2\alpha = 2$
$$B^2(\sin^2\alpha + \cos^2\alpha) = 2$$
$$B^2 1 = 2 \Rightarrow B = \pm\sqrt{2}\text{ cm}$$

Hence, amplitude of motion $= \sqrt{2}$ cm

Dividing Eq. (iii) by Eq. (iv), we get

$$\frac{B\sin\alpha}{B\cos\alpha} = \frac{1}{1} \text{ or } \tan\alpha = 1$$

$\therefore \qquad \alpha = \frac{\pi}{4}$

27. Plot the corresponding reference circle for each of the following simple harmonic motions. Indicate the initial ($t = 0$) position of the particle, the radius of the circle and the angular speed of the rotating particle. For simplicity, the sense of rotation may be fixed to be anti-clockwise in every case (x is in cm and t is in second).

(a) $x = -2\sin\left(3t + \dfrac{\pi}{3}\right)$

(b) $x = \cos\left(\dfrac{\pi}{6} - t\right)$

(c) $x = 3\sin\left(2\pi t + \dfrac{\pi}{4}\right)$

(d) $x = 2\cos\pi t$ **[NCERT]**

💡 The given functions are first converted into cosine functions through manipulation and then compared with standard SHM equation to get the parameter values. The same is depicted graphically.

Sol. (a) Given, $x = -2\sin\left(3t + \dfrac{\pi}{3}\right)$

$$= 2\cos\left(3t + \dfrac{\pi}{3} + \dfrac{\pi}{2}\right) = 2\cos\left(3t + \dfrac{5\pi}{6}\right)$$

On comparing with standard equation for SHM,

$x = A\cos\left[\dfrac{2\pi}{T}t + \phi\right]$, we get amplitude $A = 2$ cm

Phase angle, $\phi = \dfrac{5\pi}{6} = 150°$

Angular velocity, $\omega = \dfrac{2\pi}{T} = 3$ rad/s

This corresponding reference circle is plotted as below

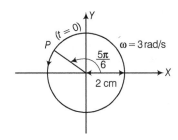

(b) $x = A\cos\left(\dfrac{2\pi}{T}t + \phi\right)$ is the standard SHM equation.

The given equation, $x = \cos\left(\dfrac{\pi}{6} - t\right)$

$$= \cos\left(t - \dfrac{\pi}{6}\right) \quad [\text{as } \cos(-\theta) = \cos\theta]$$

On comparison, amplitude $A = 1$ cm

Phase angle, $\phi = -\dfrac{\pi}{6} = -30°$

Angular velocity, $\omega = \dfrac{2\pi}{T} = 1$ rad/s

The reference circle is plotted below.

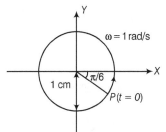

(c) Given equation, $x = 3\sin\left(2\pi t + \dfrac{\pi}{4}\right)$

$$= -3\cos\left[\left(2\pi t + \dfrac{\pi}{4}\right) + \dfrac{\pi}{2}\right]$$

$$\left[\because \cos\left(\dfrac{\pi}{2} + \theta\right) = -\sin\theta\right]$$

or $x = 3\cos\left(2\pi t + \dfrac{3\pi}{4}\right)$

On comparing with standard SHM equation

$$x = A\cos\left(\dfrac{2\pi}{T}t + \phi\right)$$

We get, $A = 3$ cm

Phase angle, $\phi = \dfrac{3\pi}{4} = 135°$ and $\omega = \dfrac{2\pi}{T} = 2\pi$ rad/s

The reference circle of the motion of the particle is plotted below.

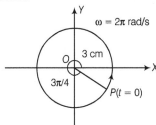

(d) Given, $x = 2\cos\pi t$

Standard SHM equation, $x = A\cos\left(\dfrac{2\pi}{T}t + \phi\right)$

Then, we get amplitude, $A = 2$ cm

Phase angle, $\phi = 0$

Angular velocity, $\omega = \pi$ rad/s

The reference circle of the motion is plotted below.

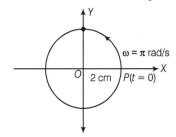

ASSESS YOUR TOPICAL UNDERSTANDING

OBJECTIVE Type Questions

1. The motion of a swing is
   (a) periodic but not oscillatory
   (b) oscillatory
   (c) linear simple harmonic
   (d) circular motion.

2. When frequency of oscillations is high then motion is called
   (a) periodic   (b) non-periodic
   (c) vibratory   (d) rotatory

3. A particle executing a simple harmonic motion has a period of 6 s. The time taken by the particle to move from the mean position to half the amplitude, starting from the mean position is
   (a) $\frac{1}{4}$ s   (b) $\frac{3}{4}$ s
   (c) $\frac{1}{2}$ s   (d) $\frac{3}{2}$ s

4. A particle executing SHM has a maximum speed of 30 cm/s angular frequency 10 rad/s. The amplitude of oscillation is
   (a) 3 cm   (b) 6 cm
   (c) 1 cm   (d) 60 cm

5. The relation between acceleration and displacement of four particles are given below   [NCERT Exemplar]
   (a) $a_x = +2x$ (b) $a_x = +2x^2$
   (c) $a_x = -2x^2$ (d) $a_x = -2x$
   Which, one of the particle is suggesting simple harmonic motion?

Answers

| 1. (b) | 2. (c) | 3. (c) | 4. (a) | 5. (d) |

VERY SHORT ANSWER Type Questions

6. What is the phase difference between particle velocity and particle displacement in SHM?   [**Ans.** $-\pi/2$]

7. When are two SHMs said to be in anti-phase ?

SHORT ANSWER Type Questions

8. Show that in a simple harmonic motion, particle velocity is ahead in phase by $\frac{\pi}{2}$ rad as compared to its displacement and acceleration is further ahead in phase by $\frac{\pi}{2}$ as compared to velocity.

9. A simple harmonic motion is given by
   $x = 6.0 \cos\left(100\, t + \frac{\pi}{4}\right)$, where x is in cm and t in second. What is the (i) displacement amplitude, (ii) frequency?   [**Ans.** (i) – 6.0 cm, (ii) 16 Hz]

10. The maximum acceleration in a simple harmonic motion is a_m and the maximum velocity is v_0. What is the displacement amplitude of simple harmonic motion? $\left[\textbf{Ans. } \dfrac{v_0^2}{a_0}\right]$

LONG ANSWER Type I Questions

11. A body oscillates with SHM according to the equation $x(t) = 5 \cos\left(2\,\pi t + \frac{\pi}{4}\right)$, where x is in metres and t is in seconds.
    Calculate the following
    (a) displacement at time $t = 0$,
    (b) angular frequency
    (c) magnitude of maximum velocity
    [**Ans.** (a) 3.54 m, (b) 6.28 s^{-1}, (c) 31.4 m/s]

12. A body oscillates with SHM according to the equation (in SI units)
    $x = 5 \cos [2\,\pi\,\text{rad s}^{-1} \cdot t + \pi/4]$
    At $t = 1.5$ s, calculate the (a) displacement, (b) speed and (c) acceleration of the body.

LONG ANSWER Type II Questions

13. A particle is subjected to two simple harmonic motions in the same direction having equal magnitude and equal frequency.
    If the resultant amplitude is equal to the amplitude of the individual motion. Find the phase difference between two individual motions.   [**Ans.** $2\pi/3$]

14. A particle moving with SHM in a straight line has a speed of 6 m/s when 4 m from the centre of oscillation and a speed of 8 m/s when 3 m from the centre of oscillation. Find the amplitude of oscillation and the shortest time taken by the particle in moving from the extreme position to a point mid way between the extreme position and the centre.   [**Ans.** ± 5 m and $\pi/6$ s]

15. Derive an expression for the acceleration in the simple harmonic motion and also distinguish the displacement, velocity and acceleration of SHM in a uniform circular motion.

|TOPIC 2|
Force and Energy in SHM and Systems Executing SHM

FORCE LAW FOR SIMPLE HARMONIC MOTION

Whenever a body is displaced a little from its equilibrium position (i.e. mean position), a **restoring force** acts on the body in a direction opposite to its displacement in order to bring the body back to its equilibrium position.

This restoring force is proportional to the displacement, provided the displacement is small. If the body is left there, it returns back to its mean position, under the restoring force.

Then, the body gains some kinetic energy which helps to overshoot its mean position and body goes to other side. Again, a restoring force is set up which slows it down and brings the body back to the mean position and so on.

In this way, the restoring force helps in oscillating the body back and forth about the mean position with a definite period.

Now, from Newton's second law of motion

We know that, $\qquad F = ma$

For a body executing SHM, we have studied earlier that $a(t) = -\omega^2 x(t)$

Thus, $\qquad F(t) = -m\omega^2 x(t)$

$\Rightarrow \qquad \boxed{\text{Restoring force, } F(t) = -kx(t)} \qquad \ldots(i)$

where, $\qquad k = m\omega^2 \quad$ or $\quad \omega = \sqrt{\dfrac{k}{m}}$

The force law is expressed by Eq. (i) and can be taken as an alternative definition of simple harmonic motion. It states that **simple harmonic motion is the motion executed by a particle subjected to a force, which is proportional to the displacement of the particle and is always directed towards the mean position.**

EXAMPLE |1| Block Fastened With Two Springs
Two identical springs of spring constant k are attached to a block of mass m and to fixed supports as shown in figure. Show that when the mass is displaced from its equilibrium position on either side, it executes a simple harmonic motion. Find the period of oscillations. **[NCERT]**

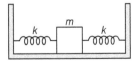

Let the mass m is displaced by the small length x to the right side of the mean position. Then, the left spring gets elongated by distance x and right spring gets compressed by distance x.

Sol. Force exerted by left spring, trying to pull the mass towards the mean position.

$$F_1 = -kx$$

Similarly, force exerted by the right spring, trying to push the mass towards the mean position,

$$F_2 = -kx$$

The net force acting on the mass due to both the springs is

$$F = F_1 + F_2 = -2kx$$

Thus, the force acting on the mass is proportional to its displacement x and is directed towards its mean position. Hence, the motion of the mass m is simple harmonic.

Comparing the equation,

$$F = -2kx \text{ with } F = -k'x.$$

We have, force constant $k' = 2k$.

∴ The time period of oscillation is

$$T = 2\pi\sqrt{\dfrac{m}{k'}} = 2\pi\sqrt{\dfrac{m}{2k}}$$

EXAMPLE |2| A Huge Piston
The vertical motion of a huge piston in a machine is simple harmonic with a frequency of $0.50\,\text{s}^{-1}$. A block of 10 kg is placed on the piston. What is the maximum amplitude of the piston's SHM for the block and the piston to remain together?

Sol. As, $\quad v = \dfrac{1}{2\pi}\sqrt{\dfrac{k}{m}}$

∴ $\qquad k = 4\pi^2 mv^2$

For maximum displacement $y_{max} = A$
Maximum restoring force,

$$F = -kA = -mg$$

or $\qquad A = \dfrac{mg}{k} = \dfrac{mg}{4\pi^2 mv^2} = \dfrac{g}{4\pi^2 v^2}$

$$= \dfrac{9.8}{4 \times (3.14)^2 \times (0.50)^2}$$

$$= 0.99 \text{ m}$$

EXAMPLE |3| A Block Attached to a Spring

Consider a block of mass 700 g is fastened to a spring having spring constant of 70 N/m. Find out the following parameters if block is pulled a distance of 14 cm from its mean position on a frictionless surface and released from rest at $t = 0$.

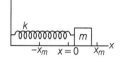

(i) The angular frequency, the frequency and the period of the resulting motion.

(ii) The amplitude of the oscillation.

(iii) The maximum speed of the oscillating block.

(iv) The maximum acceleration of the block.

(v) The phase constant and hence the displacement function $x(t)$.

💡 The spring block system forms a linear simple harmonic oscillation with block undergoing SHM. Linear means the restoring force $(F = -kx)$ is proportional to x rather than power of x. For a spring, the spring constant being, $k = m\omega^2$.

Sol. (i) The angular frequency is given by

$$\omega = \sqrt{\frac{k}{m}} = \sqrt{\frac{70\,\text{N/m}}{0.700\,\text{kg}}} = 10\,\text{rad/s}$$

Frequency, $f = \dfrac{\omega}{2\pi} = \dfrac{10}{2\pi} \approx 1.59\,\text{Hz}$

The period, $T = \dfrac{1}{f} = \dfrac{1}{1.59} = 0.63 = 630\,\text{ms}$

Since, there is no friction involved, the mechanical energy of the spring block system is conserved. The block is released from rest 14 cm from its equilibrium or mean position. The block will have zero kinetic energy whenever it is again 14 cm from its equilibrium position, which means it will never farther than 14 cm.

(ii) The maximum amplitude of the oscillation

= maximum displacement

$\therefore \qquad x_m = 14\,\text{cm} = 0.14\,\text{m}$

(iii) The maximum speed v_m is given by

$$v_m = \omega\, x_m = 10 \times 0.14 = 1.4\,\text{m/s}$$

(iv) The maximum acceleration of the block is given by

$$a_m = \omega^2 x_m = 100 \times 0.14 = 14\,\text{m/s}^2$$

At time $t = 0$, the block is located at position, $x = x_m$

(v) Then, from $x(t) = x_m \cos(\omega t + \phi)$

$$x_m = x_m \cos(0 \times \omega + \phi)$$

$$\cos\phi = 1 \implies \phi = 0$$

The displacement

$$x(t) = x_m \cos(\omega t + \phi) = 0.14 \times \cos(10t + 0)$$

$$x(t) = 0.14 \cos 10t$$

ENERGY IN SIMPLE HARMONIC MOTION

A particle executing SHM posseses both kinetic energy and potential energy. When a body is displaced from its equilibrium position by doing work upon it, it acquires potential energy. When the body is released, it begins to move back with a velocity, thus acquiring kinetic energy.

Both kinetic and potential energies of a particle in SHM vary between zero and their maximum values.

Kinetic Energy

At any instant, the displacement of a particle executing SHM is given by

$$x = A \cos(\omega t + \phi)$$

$\therefore$ Velocity, $\qquad v = \dfrac{dx}{dt} = -\omega A \sin(\omega t + \phi)$

Hence, kinetic energy of the particle at any displacement x is given by

$$K = \frac{1}{2}mv^2 = \frac{1}{2}m\omega^2 A^2 \sin^2(\omega t + \phi)$$

But, $A^2 \sin^2(\omega t + \phi) = A^2[1 - \cos^2(\omega t + \phi)]$

$$= A^2 - A^2 \cos^2(\omega t + \phi) = A^2 - x^2$$

Thus, $\qquad K = \dfrac{1}{2}kA^2 \sin^2(\omega t + \phi) \quad [\because k = m\omega^2]$

$$= \frac{1}{2}m\omega^2(A^2 - x^2) = \frac{1}{2}k(A^2 - x^2)$$

$$\boxed{\text{Kinetic energy, KE} = \frac{1}{2}k(A^2 - x^2)}$$

Hence, kinetic energy is also a periodic function of time, being **zero when the displacement is maximum**.

Kinetic energy is **maximum when the particle is at the mean position**.

Period of kinetic energy is $T/2$.

Potential Energy

When the displacement of a particle from its equilibrium position is x, then restoring force acting on it given as

$$F = -kx$$

If we displace the particle further through a small distance dx, then work done against the restoring force is given by

$$dW = -Fdx = -kx\,dx$$

The total work done in moving the particle from mean position $(x = 0)$ to displacement x is given by

$$W = \int dW = -\int_0^x kx\,dx = -k\left[\frac{x^2}{2}\right]_0^x = -\frac{1}{2}kx^2$$

This work done against the restoring force is stored as the potential energy of the particle. Hence, potential energy of a particle at displacement x is given by

$$U = -W = \frac{1}{2}kx^2 = \frac{1}{2}m\omega^2 x^2$$

$$\boxed{\text{Potential energy, } U = \frac{1}{2}kx^2}$$

$$= \frac{1}{2}m\omega^2 A^2 \cos^2(\omega t + \phi)$$

$$U = \frac{1}{2}kA^2 \cos^2(\omega t + \phi)$$

Thus, potential energy of a particle executing simple harmonic motion is also periodic with period $T/2$.

Potential energy is **zero at the mean position and maximum at the extreme position.**

Total Energy

At any displacement x, the total energy of a harmonic oscillation is given by

$$E = K + U = \frac{1}{2}k(A^2 - x^2) + \frac{1}{2}kx^2$$

$$\boxed{\text{Total energy, } E = \frac{1}{2}kA^2}$$

$$E = \frac{1}{2}m\omega^2 A^2 = 2\pi^2 m\nu^2 A^2 \quad [\because \omega = 2\pi\nu]$$

Thus, **the total mechanical energy of a harmonic oscillation is independent of time or displacement, while it depends on the maximum displacement i.e. amplitude.**

Hence, in the absence of any frictional force, the total energy of a harmonic oscillation is **conserved.**

Hence, the total energy of particle in SHM is directly proportional to the mass m of the particle, the square of its frequency ν, and the square of its vibrational amplitude A.

Graphical Representation of Energy in SHM

At mean position, $x = 0$

(i) Kinetic energy, $K = \frac{1}{2}k(A^2 - 0^2) = \frac{1}{2}kA^2$

(ii) Potential energy, $U = \frac{1}{2}k(0^2) = 0$

Hence, at **mean position, the entire mechanical energy is in the form of kinetic energy.**

At extreme positions, $x = \pm A$

(i) Kinetic energy, $K = \frac{1}{2}k(A^2 - A^2) = 0$

(ii) Potential energy, $U = \frac{1}{2}kA^2$

Hence, at **the two extreme positions, the energy is totally potential i.e. kinetic energy is zero.**

From above results, the graph for kinetic energy K, potential energy U and total energy E with displacement x is given below.

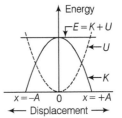

K, U and E as functions of displacement x for a harmonic oscillation

Plot for variation of energies K, U and E of a harmonic oscillator with time t is given below.

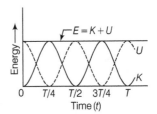

K, U and E as functions of time t for a harmonic oscillation

From the graph, we note that PE or KE completes two vibrations in a time during which SHM completes one vibration, (i.e. PE and KE both repeat after a period $T/2$) **Thus, the frequency of PE or KE is double than that of SHM. But, the total energy remains constant at all t or x.**

EXAMPLE |4| **Energy in an SHM**
A particle is executing SHM of amplitude A. At what displacement from the mean position is the energy half kinetic and half potential?

Sol. As, $\qquad E_k = E_p$

$$\therefore \qquad \frac{1}{2}m\omega^2(A^2 - x^2) = \frac{1}{2}m\omega^2 x^2$$

$$\Rightarrow \qquad A^2 - x^2 = x^2 \text{ or } 2x^2 = A^2$$

$$\Rightarrow \qquad x^2 = \frac{A^2}{2} \text{ or } x = \pm\frac{A}{\sqrt{2}}$$

Thus, the energy will be half kinetic and half potential at displacement $\dfrac{A}{\sqrt{2}}$ on either side of the mean position.

EXAMPLE |5| Energy of a Body Executing SHM

A body of mass 0.2 kg and velocity with 1s after it passes through it, mean position be 6 m/s executes SHM. Find out the total energy and potential energy of the body if time period of the body is 8s during the SHM?

Sol. Given, $m = 0.2\,\text{kg}$, $T = 8\,\text{s}$, $\omega = \dfrac{2\pi}{T} = \dfrac{2\pi}{8} = \dfrac{\pi}{4}\,\text{rad/s}$

When $t = 1\,\text{s}$, $v = 6\,\text{m/s}$

$$v(t) = \omega A \cos \omega t$$

$$6 = \frac{\pi}{4} \times A \cos\left(\frac{\pi}{4} \times 1\right) \Rightarrow 6 = \frac{\pi}{4} \times A \times \frac{1}{\sqrt{2}}$$

$$A = \frac{4\sqrt{2} \times 6}{\pi} = \frac{24\sqrt{2}}{\pi}\,\text{m}$$

The total energy of the body

$$E = \frac{1}{2} m \omega^2 A^2 = \frac{1}{2} \times 0.2 \times \left(\frac{\pi}{4}\right)^2 \times \left(\frac{24\sqrt{2}}{\pi}\right)^2$$

$$= \frac{230.4}{32} = 7.2\,\text{J}$$

Potential energy, $PE = E - KE = 7.2 - \dfrac{1}{2} m v^2$

$$= 7.2 - \frac{1}{2} \times 0.2 \times (6)^2 = 7.2 - 3.6$$

Potential energy $= 3.6\,\text{J}$

EXAMPLE |6| Energy of body attached with spring

A block whose mass is 1 kg is fastened to a spring. The spring has a spring constant of 50 Nm^{-1}. The block is pulled to a distance $x = 10$ cm from its equilibrium position at $x = 0$ on a frictionless surface from rest at $t = 0$. Calculate the kinetic, potential and total energies of the block when it is 5 cm away from the mean position. **[NCERT]**

Sol. Given, $m = 1\,\text{kg}$, $k = 50\,\text{Nm}^{-1}$, $A = 10\,\text{cm} = 0.1\,\text{m}$, $x = 5\,\text{cm} = 0.05\,\text{m}$

Kinetic energy, $K = \dfrac{1}{2} k (A^2 - x^2)$

$$K = \frac{1}{2} \times 50 \times [(0.1)^2 - (0.05)^2] = 0.1875\,\text{J}$$

Potential energy of a block,

$$U = \frac{1}{2} k x^2 = \frac{1}{2} \times 50 \times (0.05)^2 = 0.0625\,\text{J}$$

Total energy, $E = K + U = 0.1875 + 0.0625$

$$E = 0.25\,\text{J}$$

We also know that at maximum displacement, KE is zero and hence the total energy of the system is equal to PE. Therefore, the total energy of the system

$$= \frac{1}{2} (k \times A^2) = \frac{1}{2} \times 50\,\text{Nm}^{-1} \times 0.1 \times 0.1$$

$$= 0.25\,\text{J} \qquad [\because \text{here}, x = A = 0.1\,\text{m}]$$

Which is same as the sum of two energies at a displacement of 5 cm. This is in confirmity with the principle of conservation of energy.

SOME SYSTEMS EXECUTING SIMPLE HARMONIC MOTION

A pure simple harmonic motion is not possible unless some conditions are not applied on it. Let us consider some of the examples of pure simple harmonic motion under certain conditions.

1. OSCILLATION DUE TO A SPRING

To study oscillation due to a spring, let us consider a massless spring lying on a frictionless horizontal table. Its one end is attached to a rigid support and the other end to a block of mass m.

If the block is pulled towards right through a small distance x and released, it starts oscillating back and forth about its equilibrium position under the action of the restoring force.

$$F = -kx$$

where, k is the force constant (restoring force per unit deformation of the spring). The negative sign indicates that the force is directed oppositely to x.

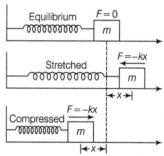

Three different positions of the oscillation due to a spring

If $\dfrac{d^2 x}{dt^2}$ is the acceleration of the body, then

$$m \frac{d^2 x}{dt^2} = -kx \qquad \left[\because F = ma = m \frac{d^2 x}{dt^2}\right]$$

or

$$\frac{d^2 x}{dt^2} = \frac{-k}{m} x = -\omega^2 x$$

Thus, **acceleration is proportional to displacement x and acts opposite to it.**

Hence, the block executes simple harmonic motion. Its time period is given by

$$T = \frac{2\pi}{\omega} = \frac{2\pi}{\sqrt{k/m}} \quad \text{or} \quad \boxed{\text{Time period}, T = 2\pi\sqrt{\frac{m}{k}}}$$

Frequency of oscillation can also be calculated as

$$\text{Frequency, } \nu = \frac{1}{T} = \frac{1}{2\pi}\sqrt{\frac{k}{m}}$$

Clearly, the time period T will be small or frequency ν large if the spring is highly stiff (high k) and attached body is light (small m)

EXAMPLE |7| SHM of Body Attach with Spring

A 5 kg collar is attached to a spring of spring constant $500\,\mathrm{Nm}^{-1}$. It slides without friction over a horizontal rod. The collar is displaced from its equilibrium position by 10.0 cm and released. Calculate

  (i) the period of oscillation,

  (ii) the maximum speed and

  (iii) maximum acceleration of the collar.   **[NCERT]**

Sol. Draw the figure containing collar of 5 kg attached to a spring of spring constant 500 N /m.

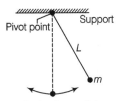

  (i) Given, $m = 5\,\mathrm{kg}$, $k = 500\,\mathrm{N/m}$, $A = 10\,\mathrm{cm} = 0.1\,\mathrm{m}$

The period of oscillation is given by

$$T = 2\pi\sqrt{\frac{m}{k}} = 2\pi \times \sqrt{\frac{5}{500}} = 0.628\,\mathrm{s}$$

  (ii) Maximum speed of the collar, $v_{\max} = \omega A$

$$v_{\max} = \sqrt{\frac{k}{m}} \cdot A = \sqrt{\frac{500}{5}} \times 0.1 = 1\,\mathrm{m/s}$$

  (iii) Maximum acceleration of the collar,

$$a_{\max} = \omega^2 A = \frac{k}{m} \cdot A = \frac{500}{5} \times 0.1 = 10\,\mathrm{m/s}^2$$

2. SIMPLE PENDULUM

An ideal simple pendulum consists of a point mass suspended by an inextensible and weightless string which is fixed at the other end as shown in figure. But this type of pendulum is not possible to make practically.

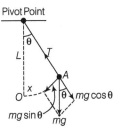

A simple pendulum

So, practically, a simple pendulum is obtained by suspending a small metal bob by a long and fine cotton thread from a support as given in the figure along side.

Expression for Time Period of a Simple Pendulum

Consider a simple pendulum, a small bob of mass m tied to an inextensible massless string of length L.

In the equilibrium position, the bob of a simple pendulum lies vertically below the point of suspension. If the bob is slightly displaced on either side and then released, it begins oscillation about the mean position.

An oscillating pendulum

Let us consider that at any instant during oscillation, the bob lies at position A when its displacement is $OA = X$ and the thread makes an angle θ with the vertical.

The forces acting on the bob are

  (i) Weight mg of the bob acting vertically downwards.

  (ii) Tension T along the string.

The force mg has two rectangular components

  (i) The component $mg\cos\theta$ acting along the thread is balanced by the tension T in the thread and

  (ii) The tangential force $mg\sin\theta$ will provide the restoring torque, which tends to bring the bob back to its mean position. Thus, the restoring torque of the force $mg\sin\theta$ about the pivot point is given by

$$\tau = -(mg\sin\theta)L = -mgL\sin\theta \qquad \text{...(i)}$$

where, the negative sign shows that the torque acts to reduce θ. L is the length of the simple pendulum. For rotation, the torque can be given as

$$\tau = I\alpha \qquad \text{...(ii)}$$

where, I = pendulum's moment of inertia about the pivot point.

    α = angular acceleration about the pivot point.

From Eqs. (i) and (ii), we get

$$-mgL\sin\theta = I\alpha$$

$$\Rightarrow \qquad\qquad \alpha = \frac{-mgL\sin\theta}{I}$$

If θ is in radian, $\sin\theta$ can be expressed as

$$\sin\theta = \theta - \frac{\theta^3}{3!} + \frac{\theta^5}{5!} - \ldots$$

Now, if θ is small, $\sin\theta$ can be approximated by θ

$$\therefore \qquad\qquad \alpha \approx \frac{-mgL\theta}{I}$$

Therefore, the acceleration of the pendulum is proportional to the angular displacement θ but in opposite sign. Thus, as the pendulum moves to the right, it's pull to the left increases until it stops and begins to return to the left.

Similarly, when it moves towards left, its acceleration to the right tends to return it to the right and so on as it swings to and fro as SHM. Hence, the motion of a simple pendulum swinging through small angles is approximately SHM.

Equation $\alpha = \dfrac{-mgL}{I}\theta$ is the angular analogue of equation $a = -\omega^2 x$.

On comparing these equations, we have

$$\omega = \sqrt{\frac{mgL}{I}}$$

$$\Rightarrow \qquad \frac{2\pi}{T} = \sqrt{\frac{mgL}{I}} \Rightarrow T = 2\pi\sqrt{\frac{I}{mgL}} \qquad \text{...(iii)}$$

where, T = time period of pendulum.

All the masses of a simple pendulum is centered in the mass m of the bob (taken as a point) which is at a distance of L from the pivot point. Therefore, $I = mL^2$. On putting this value in Eq. (iii)

$$T = \frac{1}{2\pi}\sqrt{\frac{mL^2}{mgL}} = \frac{1}{2\pi}\sqrt{\frac{L}{g}}$$

$$\Rightarrow \qquad \boxed{\text{Time period of pendulum, } T = 2\pi\sqrt{\frac{L}{g}}}$$

Obviously, the time period of a simple pendulum depends on its length L and acceleration due to gravity g and is independent of the mass m of the bob.

$T = 2\pi\sqrt{\dfrac{L}{g}}$ is valid only for small length.

If length is large, then $T = 2\pi\sqrt{\dfrac{R}{\left(1+\dfrac{R}{L}\right)g}}$

as $L \to \infty$, $T = 2\pi\sqrt{\dfrac{R}{g}}$

as $L = R$, $T = 2\pi\sqrt{\dfrac{R}{2g}}$

where, R = distance between the pivot point and the centre of mass of the pendulum.

EXAMPLE |8| Second Pendulum
What is the length of a simple pendulum, which ticks seconds?

The time period of simple pendulum which ticks seconds is 2s and called as **second pendulum**.

Sol. Given, $T = 2$s and $g = 9.8$ m/s^2

$$T = 2\pi\sqrt{\frac{L}{g}} = 2\pi\sqrt{\frac{L}{9.8}}$$

$$2^2 = 4\pi^2 \times \frac{L}{9.8} \Rightarrow L = \frac{9.8}{\pi^2} = 0.992\,\text{m} \approx 1.0\,\text{m}$$

TOPIC PRACTICE 2

OBJECTIVE Type Questions

1. In simple harmonic motion, the force
   (a) is constant in magnitude only.
   (b) is constant in direction only.
   (c) varies in magnitude as well as in direction
   (d) is constant in both magnitude and direction.

   Sol. (c) In SHM, force varies in magnitude as well as in direction. As, for the particle executing SHM, the force subjected to it is always proportional to the displacement of the particle and is directed towards the mean position.

2. In SHM,
   (a) PE is stored due to elasticity of system
   (b) KE is stored due to inertia of system
   (c) Both KE and PE are stored by virtue of elasticity of system.
   (d) Both (a) and (b)

   Sol. (d) In SHM, potential energy depends on its elastic behaviour and kinetic energy on its inertial behaviour. In case of mass m oscillating on spring. KE is due to motion of m and PE is due to stretching of spring.

3. Natural length of the spring is 40 cm and its spring constant is 4000 Nm^{-1}. A mass of 20 kg is hung from it. The extension produced in the spring is ($g = 9.8$ ms^{-2})
   (a) 4.9 cm   (b) 0.49 cm
   (c) 9.4 cm   (d) 0.94 cm

   Sol. (a) In equilibrium, $kx = mg$

   $\therefore$ Extension, $x = \dfrac{mg}{k}$

   $$x = \frac{20 \times 9.8}{4000}$$

   $$x = 0.049\,\text{m}$$

   $$x = 4.9\,\text{cm}$$

4. A body of mass 400g connected to a spring with spring constant 10 Nm^{-1}, executes simple harmonic motion, time period of oscillation is

(a) $4\pi \times 10^{-1}$ s   (b) 0.3 π s

(c) 2 s   (d) 5×10^{-1} s

Sol. (a) Here, $m = 400g = 400 \times 10^{-3}$ kg

As, $R = 10$ Nm^{-1}

$$T = 2\pi\sqrt{\frac{m}{R}}$$

$$= 2\pi\sqrt{\frac{400 \times 10^{-3}}{10}} = 4\pi \times 10^{-1}\text{s}$$

5. Two spring of force constants k_1 and k_2 are connected to a mass m as shown in figure. The frequency of oscillation of the mass is f. If both k_1 and k_2 are made four times their original values, the frequency of oscillation becomes

(a) $f/2$ (b) $f/4$

(c) $4f$ (d) $2f$

Sol. (d) Frequency of oscillation,

$$f = \frac{1}{2\pi}\sqrt{\frac{k_1 + k_2}{m}}$$

and $$f' = \frac{1}{2\pi} \cdot 2\sqrt{\frac{k_1 + k_2}{m}} = 2f$$

VERY SHORT ANSWER Type Questions

6. What is the force equation of a SHM?

Sol. According to force equation of SHM, $F = -kx$,

where, k is a constant known as force constant.

7. Under what condition is the motion of a simple pendulum be simple harmonic? [NCERT Exemplar]

Sol. When the displacement amplitude of the pendulum is extremely small as compared to its length.

8. What is the ratio between the distance travelled by the oscillator in one time period and amplitude?   [NCERT Exemplar]

Sol. Total distance travelled by an oscillator in one time period, from its mean position to one extreme position, then to other extreme position and finally back to mean position is 4 A, where A is the amplitude of oscillation.

Hence, the ratio $= \dfrac{4A}{A} = 4$

9. A simple pendulum is transferred from earth to the surface of moon. How will its time period be affected?

Sol. As value of g on moon is less than that on earth, in accordance with the relation $T = 2\pi\sqrt{l/g}$, the time period of oscillations of a simple pendulum on moon will be greater.

10. If the length of a simple pendulum is increased by 25%, then what is the change in its time period?

Sol. $\because$ Time period, $T = 2\pi\sqrt{\dfrac{l}{g}}$

or $T \propto \sqrt{l}$

$\therefore$ % increase in time period

$$\frac{\Delta T}{T} \times 100 = \frac{1}{2} \cdot \frac{\Delta l}{l} \times 100$$

$$= \frac{1}{2} \times 25 = 12.5\%$$

11. How much is KE for displacement equal to half the amplitude?

Sol. $\because$ $x = A/2$, So

$$KE = \frac{1}{2} m\omega^2 (A^2 - x^2)$$

$$= \frac{1}{2} m\omega^2 [A^2 - (A/2)^2]$$

$$= \frac{1}{2} \times \frac{3}{4}[m\omega^2 A^2] = \frac{3}{4}(KE)_{max}$$

It is 3/4 th of maximum KE.

SHORT ANSWER Type Questions

12. In case of an oscillating simple pendulum what will be the direction of acceleration of the bob at (a) the mean position, (b) the end points?

Sol. The direction of acceleration of the bob at its mean position is radial i.e. towards the point of suspension.

At extreme points, however, the acceleration is tangential towards the mean position.

13. Justify the following statements

(i) The motion of an artificial satellite around the earth cannot be taken as SHM.

(ii) The time period of a simple pendulum will get doubled if its length is increased four times.

Sol. (i) The motion of an artificial satellite around the earth is periodic as it repeats after a regular interval of time. But it cannot be taken as SHM because it is not a to and fro motion about any fixed point that is, mean position.

(ii) Time period of simple pendulum,

$$T = 2\pi\sqrt{\frac{l}{g}},$$

i.e. $T \propto \sqrt{l}$

Clearly, if the length is increased four times, the time period gets doubles.

14. A body of mass 12 kg is suspended by coil spring of natural length 50 cm and force constant 2.0×10^3 Nm^{-1}. What is the stretched length of the spring? If the body is pulled down further stretching the spring to a length of 5.9 cm and then released, then what is the frequency of oscillation of the suspended mass? (Neglect the mass of the spring)

Sol. Given, $m = 12$ kg, original length $l = 50$ cm,
$$k = 2.0 \times 10^3 \text{ Nm}^{-1}$$
As, $F = ky$
$$\therefore \quad y = \frac{F}{k} = \frac{mg}{k} = \frac{12 \times 9.8}{2 \times 10^3} = 5.9 \times 10^{-2} \text{ m} = 5.9 \text{ cm}$$
$\therefore$ Stretched length of the spring $= l + y = 50 + 55.9$ cm
$$= 105.9 \text{cm}$$
Frequency of oscillations, $\nu = \dfrac{1}{T} = \dfrac{1}{2\pi}\sqrt{\dfrac{k}{m}}$
$$= \frac{1}{2 \times 3.14}\sqrt{\frac{2 \times 10^3}{12}} = 2.06 \text{ s}^{-1}$$

15. A spring compressed by 0.1 m develops a restoring force 10 N. A body of mass 4 kg placed on it. Deduce
    (i) the force constant of the spring.
    (ii) the depression of the spring under the weight of the body (take $g = 10$ N/kg)
    (iii) the period of oscillation, the body is distributed and
    (iv) frequency of oscillation

Sol. Here, $F = 10$ N, $\Delta l = 0.1$ m, $m = 4$ kg

(i) $k = \dfrac{F}{\Delta l} = \dfrac{10}{0.1} = 100 \text{ Nm}^{-1}$

(ii) $y = \dfrac{mg}{k} = \dfrac{4 \times 10}{100} = 0.4$ m

(iii) $T = 2\pi\sqrt{\dfrac{m}{k}} = 2 \times \dfrac{22}{7}\sqrt{\dfrac{4}{100}} = 1.26$ s

(iv) Frequency, $\nu = \dfrac{1}{T} = \dfrac{1}{1.26} = 0.8$Hz

16. A circular disc of mass 10 kg is suspended by a wire attached to its centre. The wire is twisted by rotating the disc and released. The period of torsional oscillations is found to be 1.5 s. The radius of the disc is 15 cm. Determine the torsional spring constant of the wire. (Torsional spring constant α is defined by the relation, $J = -\alpha\theta$, where J is the restoring couple and θ the angle of twist.) **[NCERT]**

This is a question based on torsion pendulum for which $\quad T = 2\pi\sqrt{\dfrac{I}{\alpha}}$

where, I = moment of inertia of the disc about axis of rotation, α = torsion constant which is restoring couple per unit twist.

Sol. Given, Mass of the disc, $m = 10$ kg
Radius of the disc, $r = 15$ cm $= 0.15$ m
$$T = 1.5 \text{ s}$$
I is the moment of inertia of the disc about the axis of rotation which is perpendicular to the plane of the disc and passing through its centre.
$$\therefore \quad I = \frac{1}{2}mr^2 = \frac{1}{2} \times (10) \times (0.15)^2$$
$$= 0.1125 \text{ kg-m}^2$$
Time period, $T = 2\pi\sqrt{\dfrac{I}{\alpha}}$
$$\alpha = \frac{4\pi^2 I}{T^2} = \frac{4 \times (3.14)^2 \times 0.1125}{(1.5)^2}$$
$$= 1.972 \text{ N-m/rad}$$

17. Define the restoring force and it characterstic in case of an oscillating body.

Sol. A force which takes the body back towards the mean position in oscillation is called restoring force.
Characteristic of Restoring force
The restoring force is always directed towards the mean position and its magnitude of any instant is directly proportional to the displacement of the particle from its mean position of that instance.

18. A particle executes SHM of period 8 s. After what time of its passing through the mean position, will be energy be half kinetic and half potential?

Sol. Given,   PE $=$ KE
i.e. $\dfrac{1}{2}m\omega^2 x^2 = \dfrac{1}{2}m\omega^2(A^2 - x^2)$
$$x^2 = A^2 - x^2 \Rightarrow x = \frac{A}{\sqrt{2}}$$
Now, $\quad x = A\sin\omega t = A\sin\left(\dfrac{2\pi}{T}\right)t$
So, $\quad \dfrac{A}{\sqrt{2}} = A\sin 2\pi\dfrac{t}{8}$
or $\quad \sin\dfrac{\pi t}{4} = \dfrac{1}{\sqrt{2}} = \sin\dfrac{\pi}{4}$
or $\quad \dfrac{\pi t}{4} = \dfrac{\pi}{4}$ or $t = 1$ s

LONG ANSWER Type I Questions

19. A spring balance has a scale that reads from 0 to 50 kg. The length of the scale is 20 cm. A body suspended from this spring, when displaced and released, oscillates with a period of 0.60 s. What is the weight of the body? **[NCERT]**

Sol. The length of the scale 20 cm reads upto 50 kg.

So, $F = mg = 50 \times 9.8$ N and $y = 20$ cm $= 0.20$ m

Now, force constant, $k = \dfrac{F}{y} = \dfrac{50 \times 9.8}{0.20} = 2450 \text{Nm}^{-1}$

Suppose the spring oscillates with time period of 0.60 s when loaded with a mass of M kg. Then,

$$T = 2\pi \sqrt{\dfrac{M}{k}} \quad \text{or} \quad T^2 = 4\pi^2 \dfrac{M}{k}$$

$$M = \dfrac{T^2 k}{4\pi^2} = \dfrac{(0.60)^2 \times 2450}{4 \times (3.14)^2} = 22.36 \text{ kg}$$

$\therefore$ Weight $= Mg = 22.36 \times 9.8 = 219.13$ N

20. A spring of force constant 1200 Nm^{-1} is mounted on a horizontal table. A mass of 3.0 kg is attached to the free end of the spring, pulled sideways to a distance of 2.0 cm and then released.

  (i) What is the frequency of oscillation of the mass?

  (ii) What is the maximum acceleration of the mass?

  (iii) What is the maximum speed of the mass?

[NCERT]

Sol. Here, $k = 1200 \text{Nm}^{-1}$, $m = 3.0$ kg

and $A = 2.0$ cm $= 2.0 \times 10^{-2}$ m

(i) Frequency of oscillation of the mass,

$$\nu = \dfrac{1}{2\pi} \sqrt{\dfrac{k}{m}} = \dfrac{1}{2 \times 3.14} \sqrt{\dfrac{1200}{3.0}} = \dfrac{1}{2 \times 3.14} \times 20$$

$$= 3.18 \text{s}^{-1} \approx 3.2 \text{s}^{-1}$$

(ii) Angular frequency,

$$\omega = \sqrt{\dfrac{k}{m}} = \sqrt{\dfrac{1200}{3.0}} = 20 \text{s}^{-1}.$$

$\therefore$ Maximum acceleration of the mass

$$= \omega^2 A = (20)^2 \times 2.0 \times 10^{-2} = 8.0 \text{ ms}^{-2}.$$

(iii) Maximum speed of the mass

$$= \omega \cdot A = 20 \times 2.0 \times 10^{-2} = 0.40 \text{ ms}^{-1}.$$

21. The acceleration due to gravity on the surface of moon is 1.7 m/s^2. What is the time period of a simple pendulum on the surface of moon, if its time period on the surface of earth is 3.5 s? (g on the surface of earth is 9.8 m/s^2.) **[NCERT]**

💡 Consider the two time periods separately. Then, get the ratio and put the given values to get the result.

Sol. Given, acceleration due to gravity on the moon $(g_m) = 1.7 \text{ m/s}^2$

Acceleration due to gravity on the earth, $(g_e) = 9.8 \text{ m/s}^2$

Time period on the earth, $T_e = 3.5$ s

Time period on the moon, $T_m = ?$

On the surface of the earth, time period $= T_e$

$\therefore$ $\qquad T_e = 2\pi \sqrt{\dfrac{l}{g_e}} \qquad$ ...(i)

On the surface of the moon, time period $= T_m$

$\therefore$ $\qquad T_m = 2\pi \sqrt{\dfrac{l}{g_m}} \qquad$ ...(ii)

Suppose g_e, g_m are accelerations due to gravity on the earth and the moon surface, respectively.

On dividing Eq. (i) by Eq. (ii), we get

$$\dfrac{T_e}{T_m} = \dfrac{2\pi}{2\pi} \sqrt{\dfrac{l}{l} \times \dfrac{g_m}{g_e}}$$

$\Rightarrow \qquad \dfrac{T_e}{T_m} = \sqrt{\dfrac{g_m}{g_e}}$

$\Rightarrow \qquad T_m = \left(\sqrt{\dfrac{g_e}{g_m}} \right) T_e$

Putting the values, we get

$$T_m = \sqrt{\dfrac{9.8}{1.7}} \times 3.5 = 8.4 \text{ s}$$

22. A mass attached to a spring is free to oscillate, with angular velocity ω in a horizontal plane without friction or damping. It is pulled to a distance x_0 and pushed towards the centre with a velocity v_0 at time $t = 0$. Determine the amplitude of the resulting oscillations in terms of the parameters ω, x_0 and v_0. **[Hint** Start with the equation $x = a\cos(\omega t + \theta)$ and note that the initial velocity is negative.**]** **[NCERT]**

💡 If in a spring mass system, the mass is displaced and given a velocity, also, it will perform SHM but with an amplitude more than the amount of extension.

Sol. We have for SHM

$x = A \cos(\omega t + \theta) \qquad$ ...(i)

where, $x = $ displacement, $A = $ amplitude

$\theta = $ phase constant, we get

On differentiating with respect to t,

$$\dfrac{dx}{dt} = -A\omega \sin(\omega t + \theta)$$

$\Rightarrow \qquad v = -A\omega \sin(\omega t + \theta) \qquad$ ...(ii)

where, $v = $ instantaneous velocity of the particle at t.

Now, at $t = 0$, $x = x_0$

From Eq. (i),

$\Rightarrow \qquad x_0 = A \cos \theta \qquad \qquad ...(iii)$

Again at $t = 0$, $v = -v_0$

From Eq. (ii),

$$-v_0 = -A\omega \sin\theta$$

or $\qquad \dfrac{v_0}{\omega} = A \sin\theta \qquad \qquad ...(iv)$

On squaring and adding Eqs. (iii) and (iv), we get

$$A^2(\cos^2\theta + \sin^2\theta) = x_0^2 + \left(\dfrac{v_0}{\omega}\right)^2$$

$\Rightarrow \qquad A^2 = x_0^2 + \left(\dfrac{v_0}{\omega}\right)^2$

or $\qquad A = \sqrt{x_0^2 + \left(\dfrac{v_0}{\omega}\right)^2}$

23. The length of a second pendulum on the surface of earth is 1 m. What will be the length of a second pendulum on the moon?

[NCERT Exemplar]

Sol. A second pendulum means a simple pendulum having time period, $T = 2$ s

For a simple pendulum, $T = 2\pi\sqrt{\dfrac{l}{g}}$

where, l = length of the pendulum and g = acceleration due to gravity on surface of the earth.

$$T_s = 2\pi\sqrt{\dfrac{l_e}{g_e}} \qquad \qquad ...(i)$$

On the surface of the moon,

$$T_m = 2\pi\sqrt{\dfrac{l_m}{g_m}} \qquad \qquad ...(ii)$$

Dividing Eq. (i) by Eq. (ii), we get

$\therefore \qquad \dfrac{T_s}{T_m} = \dfrac{2\pi}{2\pi}\sqrt{\dfrac{l_e}{g_e}} \times \sqrt{\dfrac{g_m}{l_m}}$

$T_s = T_m$ to maintain the second pendulum time period.

$\therefore \qquad 1 = \sqrt{\dfrac{l_e}{l_m} \times \dfrac{g_m}{g_e}} \qquad \qquad ...(iii)$

But the acceleration due to gravity at moon is 1/6 of the acceleration due to gravity at earth, i.e. $g_m = \dfrac{g_e}{6}$

Squaring Eq. (iii) and putting this value,

$$1 = \dfrac{l_e}{l_m} \times \dfrac{g_e/6}{g_e} = \dfrac{l_e}{l_m} \times \dfrac{1}{6}$$

$\Rightarrow \qquad \dfrac{l_e}{6l_m} = 1$

or $\qquad l_m = \dfrac{1}{6}l_e = \dfrac{1}{6} \times 1 = \dfrac{1}{6}$ m

24. Answer the following questions.

(i) Time period of a particle in SHM depends on the force constant k and mass m of the particle $T = 2\pi\sqrt{\dfrac{m}{k}}$. A simple pendulum executes SHM approximately. Then, why is the time period of a pendulum independent of the mass of the pendulum?

(ii) The motion of a simple pendulum is approximately simple harmonic for small angle oscillations. For larger angles of oscillation, a more involved analysis shows that T is greater than $2\pi\sqrt{\dfrac{l}{g}}$. Think of a qualitative argument to appreciate this result.

(iii) A man with a wristwatch on his hand falls from the top of a tower. Does the watch give correct time during the free fall?

(iv) What is the frequency of oscillation of a simple pendulum mounted in a cabin that is freely falling under gravity? [NCERT]

Sol. (i) For a simple pendulum, k is proportional to m the mass of the particle, hence $\dfrac{m}{k}$ becomes constant and does not affect the time period.

(ii) If we replace $\sin\theta \approx \theta$ for large angles, then actually $\sin\theta < \theta$. Now, since this factor is multiplied to the restoring force $mg\sin\theta$ is replaced by $mg\theta$ which means an effective reduction in g for large angles. Hence, there is an increase in time period T over that given by the formula

$$T = 2\pi\sqrt{\dfrac{l}{g}}$$

as compared to the case which it is assumed $\sin\theta \approx \theta$.

(iii) Yes, since the motion of hands of a wristwatch to indicate time depends on action of the spring and has nothing to do with acceleration due to gravity.

(iv) In a free fall the effective $g = 0$, i.e. gravity disappears (also called **weightlessness**)

$\therefore$ Time period $T = 2\pi\sqrt{\dfrac{l}{g}} = 2\pi\sqrt{\dfrac{l}{0}} = \infty$

Frequency, $v = \dfrac{1}{T} = 0$

i.e. frequency of oscillation is zero.

25. A simple pendulum of length l and having a bob of mass M is suspended in a car. The car is moving on a circular track of radius R with a uniform speed v. If the pendulum makes small oscillations in a radial direction about its equilibrium position, then what will be its time period?

[NCERT]

For a simple pendulum $T = 2\pi\sqrt{\dfrac{l}{g_{\text{eff}}}}$; so you should always find the g_{eff} in the situation; the pendulum is oscillating and then calculate the time period.

Sol. The bob is subjected to two simultaneous, accelerations perpendicular to each other *viz*, acceleration due to gravity g and radial acceleration, $a_R = \dfrac{v^2}{R}$ towards the centre of the circular path.

∴ Effective acceleration, $g_{\text{eff}} = \sqrt{g^2 + \left(\dfrac{v^2}{R}\right)^2}$

∴ Time period of the simple pendulum

$$T = 2\pi\sqrt{\frac{l}{g_{\text{eff}}}} = 2\pi\sqrt{\frac{l}{\left(g^2 + \left(\dfrac{v^2}{R}\right)^2\right)^{1/2}}}$$

$$= 2\pi\sqrt{\frac{l}{\left(g^2 + \dfrac{v^4}{R^2}\right)^{1/2}}}$$

26. An air chamber of volume V has a neck area of cross-section a into which a ball of mass m just fits and can move up and down without any friction (see figure). Show that when the ball is pressed down a little and released, it executes SHM. Obtain an expression for the time period of oscillations assuming pressure-volume variations of air to be isothermal.   **[NCERT]**

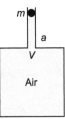

 This is a system executing SHM. So, proceed in the order finding restoring force, proving SHM and find force constant to determine time period.

Sol. Before pressing the ball, the pressure inside the chamber = pressure outside the chamber = atmospheric pressure.

Let now the ball is depressed by x units. As a result, the volume will decrease and this would increase the pressure inside.

Decrease in the volume of air, $\Delta V = ax$

where, a = cross-sectional area of the neck

Volume strain = $\dfrac{\text{Change in volume}}{\text{Original volume}} = \dfrac{\Delta V}{V} = \dfrac{ax}{V}$

Volume stress = Bulk stress = p

As, $B = \dfrac{-p}{\left(\dfrac{ax}{V}\right)}$ where, negative sign shows the decrease in volume.

∴ Increases in the pressure, $p = -\dfrac{Bax}{V}$

The restoring force on the ball

$$F = pa = -\frac{Bax}{V}\cdot a = \frac{-Ba^2 x}{V} \qquad \left[\because \frac{Ba^2}{V} = \text{constant}\right]$$

$$F \propto -\text{ displacement }(x)$$

Hence, motion is SHM.

∴ $T = 2\pi\sqrt{\dfrac{m}{k}} = 2\pi\sqrt{\dfrac{mV}{Ba^2}}$

27. One end of a U-tube containing mercury is connected to a suction pump and the other end to atmosphere. A small pressure difference is maintained between the two columns.

Show that when the suction pump is removed, the column of mercury in the U-tube executes simple harmonic motion.   **[NCERT]**

 Start from the beginning, find the restoration force and then apply the rule to determine time period in typical SHM.

Sol. Let area of cross-section of each arm of the U-tube be A. When a small pressure difference be maintained between two columns then liquid column falls through height h in one arm.

Now, difference in liquid column in two arms = $2h$

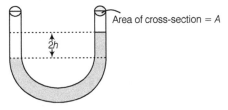

Density of mercury column = ρ
Acceleration due to gravity = g
Restoring force

$\quad F = -$ Weight of mercury column in excess of one arm
$\quad\quad = -$ (Volume × Density × g)
$\quad\quad = -(A \times 2h \times \rho \times g)$
$\quad\quad = -2A\rho gh = -k \times \text{Displacement in one arm }(h)$

Clearly, $2A\rho g = \text{constant} = k$ (say)   [as $F = -kx$]
$$F \propto -h$$

Hence, motion is SHM, $k = 2A\rho g$

∴ Time period, $T = 2\pi\sqrt{\dfrac{m}{k}} = 2\pi\sqrt{\dfrac{m}{2A\rho g}}$

where, m = mass of the mercury column of length l

If ρ_{Hg} is density of mercury,

Then, $\qquad m = Al\rho$

$\Rightarrow \qquad T = 2\pi \sqrt{\dfrac{Al\rho}{2A\rho g}} = 2\pi \sqrt{\dfrac{l}{2g}}$

28. In the previous question, let us take the position of mass when the spring is unstreched as $x = 0$ and the direction from left to right as the positive direction of x-axis. Given x as a function of time t for the oscillating mass, if at the moment we start the stopwatch ($t = 0$), the mass is

(i) at the mean position,

(ii) at the maximum stretched position and

(iii) at the maximum compressed position.

In what way do these functions for SHM differ from each other, in frequency, in amplitude or the initial phase? **[NCERT]**

💡 Standard equation for SHM should be used with different initial phases.

Sol. Assuming the standard equation

$x(t) = A \sin(\omega t + \phi)$

(i) When $t = 0$, $x = 0$ [mean position]

$\Rightarrow \qquad 0 = A \sin(\omega \times 0 + \phi)$

$A \sin \phi = 0$ [as $A \neq 0$]

or $\qquad \sin \phi = 0 \quad \therefore \quad \phi = 0$

∴ Required function is

$x(t) = A \sin(\omega t + 0)$ or $x(t) = A \sin \omega t$

where, $\quad \omega = \sqrt{\dfrac{k}{m}} = \sqrt{\dfrac{1200}{3.0}} = 20$ rad/s

$\therefore \qquad x(t) = A \sin 20t$ or $x(t) = 2 \sin 20t$

(ii) When $t = 0$, $x = +A$ (maximum stretched position)

$x(t) = A \sin(\omega t + \phi)$ at $t = 0$ and $x = +A$

$+A = A \sin(\omega \times 0 + \phi)$ or $1 = \sin \phi \Rightarrow \phi = \dfrac{\pi}{2}$

$\therefore \qquad x(t) = A \sin\left(\omega t + \dfrac{\pi}{2}\right)$

$= A \cos \omega t = A \cos 20t = 2 \cos 20t$

(iii) When the spring is at maximum compressed position.

At $t = 0$, $x(t) = -A$

$\Rightarrow \quad -A = A \sin(\omega \times 0 + \phi)$ or $-1 = \sin \phi$ or $\phi = \dfrac{3\pi}{2}$

$\therefore \quad x(t) = A \sin\left(\omega t + \dfrac{3\pi}{2}\right) = -A \cos \omega t = -2 \cos 20t$

So, the equations only differ in initial phase and in no other factors.

29. A body weighing 10 g has a velocity of 6 cm s^{-1} after one second of its starting from mean position. If the time period is 6 s, then find the kinetic energy, potential energy and the total energy.

Sol. Here, $m = 10$ g, $T = 6$ s

$$\omega = \dfrac{2\pi}{T} = \dfrac{2\pi}{6} = \dfrac{\pi}{3} \text{ rad s}^{-1}$$

When $t = 1$ s, $v = 6$ cm s^{-1}

As $\qquad v = A\omega \cos \omega t$

$6 = A \times \dfrac{\pi}{3} \cos \dfrac{\pi}{3} \times 1 = A \times \dfrac{\pi}{3} \cos 60°$

$= A \times \dfrac{\pi}{3} \times \dfrac{1}{2} = \dfrac{\pi A}{6}$ or $A = \dfrac{36}{\pi}$ cm

Total energy, $E = \dfrac{1}{2} mA^2 \omega^2$

$$= \dfrac{1}{2} \times 10 \times \left(\dfrac{36}{\pi}\right)^2 \times \left(\dfrac{\pi}{3}\right)^2 = 720 \text{ erg}$$

Kinetic energy $= \dfrac{1}{2} mv^2 = \dfrac{1}{2} \times 10 \times 6^2 = 180$ erg

∴ Potential energy = Total energy − Kinetic energy

$= 720 - 180 = 540$ erg

30. Show that for a particle in linear SHM, the average kinetic energy over a period of oscillation equals the average potential energy over the same period. **[NCERT]**

Sol. Suppose a particle of mass m executes SHM of period T. The displacement of the particle at any instant t is given by

$$y = A \sin \omega t$$

∴ Velocity, $v = \dfrac{dy}{dt} = \omega A \cos \omega t$

Kinetic energy, $E_k = \dfrac{1}{2} mv^2 = \dfrac{1}{2} m\omega^2 A^2 \cos^2 \omega t$

Potential energy, $E_p = \dfrac{1}{2} m\omega^2 y^2 = \dfrac{1}{2} m\omega^2 A^2 \sin^2 \omega t$

∴ Average KE over a period of oscillation,

$$E_{k_{av}} = \dfrac{1}{T} \int_0^T E_k \, dt = \dfrac{1}{T} \int_0^T \dfrac{1}{2} m\omega^2 A^2 \cos^2 \omega t \, dt$$

$$= \dfrac{1}{2T} m\omega^2 A^2 \int_0^T \dfrac{(1 + \cos 2\omega t)}{2} \, dt$$

$$= \dfrac{1}{4T} m\omega^2 A^2 \left[t + \dfrac{\sin 2\omega t}{2\omega}\right]_0^T$$

$$= \dfrac{1}{4T} m\omega^2 A^2 (T) = \dfrac{1}{4} m\omega^2 A^2 \; [\because \sin 2\omega T = 0] \;...(i)$$

Average PE over a period of oscillation,

$$E_{p_{av}} = \dfrac{1}{T} \int_0^T E_p \, dt = \dfrac{1}{T} \int_0^T \dfrac{1}{2} m\omega^2 A^2 \sin^2 \omega t \, dt$$

$$= \dfrac{1}{2T} m\omega^2 A^2 \int_0^T \dfrac{(1 - \cos 2\omega t)}{2} dt$$

$$= \dfrac{1}{4T} m\omega^2 A^2 \left[t - \dfrac{\sin 2\omega t}{2\omega}\right]_0^T$$

$$= \frac{1}{4T} m\omega^2 A^2 (T) = \frac{1}{4} m\omega^2 A^2 \qquad ...(ii)$$

Clearly, from Eqs. (i) and (ii),

$$E_{k_{av}} = E_{p_{av}}$$

LONG ANSWER Type II Questions

31. A cylindrical piece of cork of base area A, density ρ and height L floats in a liquid of density ρ_L. The cork is depressed slightly and then released. Show that the cork oscillates up and down simple harmonically and find its time period of oscillations.   **[NCERT]**

Sol. Consider a cylinder of mass m, length L, density of material ρ and uniform area of cross-section A. Therefore,

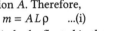

$$m = AL\rho \qquad ...(i)$$

Let the cylinder be floated in the liquid of density ρ_L.

In equilibrium, let l be the length of cylinder dipping in liquid.

In equilibrium, weight of cylinder = Weight of liquid displaced

$$mg = Al\,\rho_L\, g$$
$$m = Al\,\rho_L \qquad ...(ii)$$

Let the cylinder be pushed down by y, then

Total upward thrust, $F_2 = A(l + y)\rho_L\, g$

Restoring force, $F = -(F_2 - mg)$

$$F = -[A(l + y)\rho_L\, g - Al\,\rho_L\, g] = -A\rho_L\, gy \qquad ...(iii)$$

In SHM, $F \propto -y$

$$F = -ky \qquad ...(iv)$$

From Eq. (iii) and Eq. (iv),

Spring factor, $k = A\rho_L g$

Inertia factor, $m = AL\rho$

Time period, $T = 2\pi \sqrt{\dfrac{\text{Inertia factor}}{\text{Spring factor}}}$

$$T = 2\pi \sqrt{\frac{AL\rho}{A\rho_L g}} = 2\pi \sqrt{\frac{L\rho}{\rho_L g}} \qquad ...(v)$$

Using, $m = Al\rho_L = AL\rho$

So, $l\rho_L = L\rho$

So, another form of time period

$$T = 2\pi \sqrt{\frac{l\,\rho_L}{g\,\rho_L}} = 2\pi \sqrt{\frac{l}{g}}$$

32. A person normally weighing 50 kg stands on a massless platform which oscillates up and down harmonically at a frequency of $2.0\ s^{-1}$ and an amplitude 5.0 cm. A weighing machine on the platform gives the persons weight against time.

(a) Will there be any change in weight of the body, during the oscillation?

(b) If answer to part (a) is yes, then what will be the maximum and minimum reading in the machine and at which position?

[NCERT Exemplar]

Sol. (a) This is a case of variable acceleration. In accelerated motion, weight of body depends on the magnitude and direction of acceleration for upward or downward motion.

Hence, the weight of body changes.

(b) Considering the situation in two extreme positions, as their acceleration is maximum in magnitude.

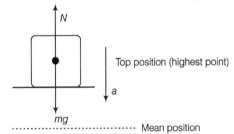

We have, $mg - N = ma$

Note, at the highest point, the platform is accelerating downward.

$$\Rightarrow \qquad\qquad N = mg - ma$$

But $a = \omega^2 A \qquad$ (in magnitude)

$$\therefore \qquad\qquad N = mg - m\omega^2 A$$

where, A = amplitude of motion.

Given, $m = 50$ kg, frequency $\nu = 2\ s^{-1}$

$$\therefore \qquad \omega = 2\pi\nu = 4\pi\ \text{rad/s}$$
$$A = 5\ \text{cm} = 5 \times 10^{-2}\ \text{m}$$

$$\therefore \qquad N = 50 \times 9.8 - 50 \times (4\pi)^2 \times 5 \times 10^{-2}$$
$$= 50[9.8 - 16\pi^2 \times 5 \times 10^{-2}]$$
$$= 50[9.8 - 7.89] = 50 \times 1.91 = 95.5\ \text{N}$$

When the platform is at the lowest position of its oscillation,

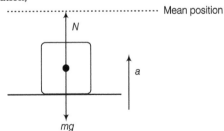

It is accelerating towards mean position that is vertically upwards.

Writing equation of motion

$$N - mg = ma = m\omega^2 A$$

or $N = mg + m\omega^2 A$
$$= m[g + \omega^2 A]$$

Putting the data, $N = 50[9.8 + (4\pi)^2 \times 5 \times 10^{-2}]$
$$= 50[9.8 + (12.56)^2 \times 5 \times 10^{-2}]$$
$$= 50[9.8 + 7.88] = 50 \times 17.68$$
$$= 884.4 \text{ N}$$

Now, the machine reads the normal reaction. It is clear that
maximum weight = 884.4 N (at lowest point)
minimum weight = 95.5 N (at top point)

33. Fig. (a) shows a spring of force constant k clamped rigidly at one end and a mass m attached to its free end. A force F applied at the free end stretches the spring. Fig. (b) shows the same spring with both ends free and attached to a mass m at either end. Each end of the spring in Fig. (b) is stretched by the same force F.

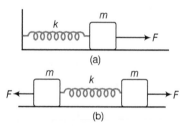

(a)

(b)

(i) What is the maximum extension of the spring in both the cases?

(ii) If the mass in Fig. (a) and the two masses in Fig. (b) are released, then what is the period of oscillation in each case? **[NCERT]**

Draw the free body diagram to find the extension in the spring in two cases.
In both cases, the system would perform SHM. In the first, the mean position will be the position of mass for unstretched case of the spring whereas in second case it will be centre of mass of the spring block system which will be the mean position for oscillation.

Sol. (i) For **Case** (a), as we know that, $F = -kx \Rightarrow |F| = kx$

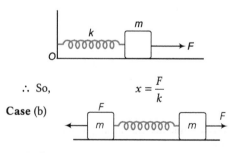

∴ So, $x = \dfrac{F}{k}$

Case (b)

If x' is the extension in the spring, then drawing free body diagram of either mass (as the system under applied force is under equilibrium).

$kx' \cdots$ ~~~~~ ▭ → F

$$kx' = F$$
∴ $$x' = \dfrac{F}{k}$$

In both the cases, extension is the same $\left(\dfrac{F}{k}\right)$.

(ii) The period of oscillation in case (a),
As, $$F = -kx$$
where, x = given extension
But $$F = ma$$
∴ $$ma = -kx$$
⇒ $$a = -\left(\dfrac{k}{m}\right)x \qquad \ldots(i)$$
$$a \propto -x \qquad [\text{as}, \dfrac{k}{m} \text{ is a constant}]$$

On comparing Eq. (i) with $a = -\omega^2 x$, we get
∴ $$\omega = \sqrt{\dfrac{k}{m}}$$

Period of oscillation, $T = \dfrac{2\pi}{\omega} = 2\pi\sqrt{\dfrac{m}{k}}$

Case (b)

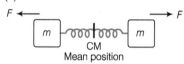

CM
Mean position

The system is divided into two similar systems with spring divided in two equal halves. $k' = 2k$
Hence, $$F = -k'x$$
$k' = 2k$ (on cutting a spring in two halves, its k doubles)
⇒ $$F = -2kx$$
But $$F = ma$$
∴ $$ma = -2kx$$
⇒ $$a = -\left(\dfrac{2k}{m}\right)x \qquad \ldots(ii)$$
⇒ $$a \propto -\text{displacement} \qquad [\text{as} \dfrac{2k}{m} \text{ is a constant}]$$

On comparing Eq. (ii) with $a = -\omega^2 x$, we get
$$\omega = \sqrt{\dfrac{2k}{m}}$$

Period of oscillation,
$$T = \dfrac{2\pi}{\omega} = 2\pi\sqrt{\dfrac{m}{2k}}$$

ASSESS YOUR TOPICAL UNDERSTANDING

OBJECTIVE Type Questions

1. For simple harmonic motion of an object of mass m,
   (a) $\mathbf{F} = -m\omega^2 x$
   (b) $\mathbf{F} = -m\omega x$
   (c) Force always acts in the opposite direction of displacement
   (d) Both (a) and (c)

2. The expression for displacement of an object in SHM is $x = A\cos(\omega t)$. The potential energy at $t = T/4$ is
   (a) $\frac{1}{2}kA^2$ (b) $\frac{1}{8}kA^2$ (c) $\frac{1}{4}kA^2$ (d) zero

3. A simple pendulum suspended from the roof of a lift oscillates with frequency ν when the lift is at rest. If the lift falls freely under gravity, its frequency of oscillations becomes
   (a) zero   (b) ν (c) 2ν (d) infinite

4. If we do an experiment by swinging a small ball by a thread of length 100 cm, what will be the approximate time for complete to and fro periodic motion?
   (a) 4 s   (b) 2 s   (c) 6 s   (d) 1 s

5. A block is left in the equilibrium position as shown in the figure. If now it is stretched by $\frac{mg}{k}$, the net stretch of the spring is
   (a) $\frac{mg}{k}$ (b) $\frac{mg}{2k}$ (c) $\frac{2mg}{k}$ (d) $\frac{mg}{4k}$

Answers

1. (d) | 2. (d) | 3. (a) | 4. (b) | 5. (c)

VERY SHORT ANSWER Type Questions

|1 Mark|

6. Two simple pendulums of equal length cross each other at mean position. What is their phase difference? **[Ans. π rad, i.e. 180°]**

7. A body executes SHM with a period of $11/7$ s and an amplitude of 0.025 m. What is the maximum value of acceleration? **[Ans. -0.4 m/s^2]**

SHORT ANSWER Type Questions

8. When a particle oscillates simple harmonically, its potential energy varies periodically. If ν is the frequency of oscillation of the particle, then what is the frequency of variation of potential energy? **[Ans. 2ν]**

LONG ANSWER Type I Questions

9. Derive the expression for total energy in oscillations.

10. When the mass is displaced a little to one side, one spring gets compressed and another is elongated. Due to which the combination of spring works as parallel combination of springs. Here, effective spring factor k will be given by
    $k = k_1 + k_2 = 600 + 600 = 1200$ Nm^{-1}
    [Ans. $T = 0.314$ s, $v_{\max} = 1$ ms^{-1}, $E = 1.5$ J]

LONG ANSWER Type II Questions

11. A point particle of mass 0.1 kg is executing SHM with amplitude of 0.1 m. When the particle passes through the mean position, its kinetic energy is 8×10^{-3} joule. Obtain the equation of motion of this particle, if the initial phase of oscillation is 45°.

12. A mass of 1 kg is executing SHM which is given by $x = 6.0\cos\left(100t + \dfrac{\pi}{4}\right)$ cm. What is the maximum kinetic energy? **[Ans. -18 J]**

13. In the figure shown below, two identical springs of spring constant 7580 N/m are attached to a block of mass 0.245 kg. What is the frequency of oscillation on the frictionless floor? **[Ans. 39.6 Hz]**

14. A spring of force constant 1200 Nm^{-1} is mounted on a horizontal table as shown in figure. A mass of 3 kg is attached to the free end of the spring, pulled sideways to a distance of 2.0 cm and released. What is
    (i) the speed of the mass, if the spring is compressed?
    (ii) the potential energy of the mass, when the mass comes to rest?
    (iii) total energy of the mass during oscillation? **[Ans. 0.35 ms^{-1}, 0.24 J, 0.24 J]**

SUMMARY

- **Periodic motion** A motion which repeats itself after a regular interval of time is called a **periodic motion**.

- **Oscillatory motion** A motion in which a body moves to and fro or back and forth repeatedly about a fixed point (called mean position) is called **oscillatory** or **vibratory motion**.

- **Simple harmonic motion** It is a special type of periodic motion in which the body moves to and fro repeatedly about a mean position under the influence of a restoring force is known as simple harmonic motion (SHM). The restoring force is directly proportional to its displacement from the mean position.

$$F \propto x \text{ or } F = -kx$$

  where, k is the force constant or spring constant.

- **Displacement in SHM** The displacement of a particle executing SHM is expressed as, $y = A\sin(\omega t + \phi)$

  where, A is amplitude of SHM, ω is the angular frequency $\left(\text{where}, \omega = \dfrac{2\pi}{T} = 2\pi\nu\right)$ and ϕ is the initial phase of SHM.

- **Time period** It is the time taken by a particle to complete one oscillation about its mean position. It is denoted by T.

- **Frequency** It is the number of oscillations completed per second by a particle about its mean position. It is denoted by ν and is equal to the reciprocal of time period. Thus, $\nu = \dfrac{1}{T}$. Frequency is measured in hertz.

$$1 \text{ hertz} = 1\,\text{Hz} = 1\,\text{oscillation per second} = 1\text{s}^{-1}.$$

- **Angular frequency** It is the quantity obtained by multiplying frequency ν by a factor of 2π. It is denoted by ω. Thus, $\omega = 2\pi\nu = \dfrac{2\pi}{T}$. SI unit of $\omega = \text{rad s}^{-1}$.

- **Phase** The phase of vibrating particle at any instant gives the state of the particle as regards its position and the direction of motion at that instant. It is denoted by ϕ.

- **Velocity in SHM** The velocity of particle executing SHM is defined as the time rate of change of its displacement at particular instant. Velocity, $v = \omega\sqrt{A^2 - y^2}$

  At mean position $(y = 0)$ during its motion, $v = A\omega = v_{\max}$ and at extreme positions $(y = \pm A), v = 0$.
  where, $v_{\max}$ velocity amplitude $= A\omega$ or Velocity, $v(t) = -\omega A\sin(\omega t + \phi)$

- **Acceleration in SHM** The acceleration of a SHM at an instant is defined as the time rate of change of velocity at that instant. Acceleration, $a = -\omega^2 y$

- The acceleration is also variable. At mean position $(y = 0)$, acceleration, $a = 0$ and at extreme position $(y = \pm A)$, acceleration is $a_{\max} = \mp A\omega^2$.

  where, $a_{\max}$, Acceleration amplitude $= A\omega^2$ or Acceleration, $a(t) = \omega^2 A\cos(\omega t + \phi)$

  Time Period in SHM Time period of SHM, $T = \dfrac{2\pi}{\omega} = 2\pi\sqrt{\dfrac{|y|}{|a|}} = 2\pi\sqrt{\dfrac{\text{Displacement}}{\text{Acceleration}}}$

- **Energy in SHM** If a particle of mass m executes SHM, then at a displacement x from mean position, the particle possesses potential and kinetic energy.
  At any displacement x,

  (i) Potential energy, $U = \dfrac{1}{2}m\omega^2 x^2 = \dfrac{1}{2}kx^2$ (iii) Total energy, $E = U + K = \dfrac{1}{2}m\omega^2 A^2 = 2\pi^2 m\nu^2 A^2$

  (ii) Kinetic energy, $K = \dfrac{1}{2}m\omega^2(A^2 - x^2) = \dfrac{1}{2}k(A^2 - x^2)$

- **Simple pendulum** A simple pendulum, in practice, consist of a heavy but small sized metallic bob suspended by a light, inextensible and flexible string. The motion of a simple pendulum is simple harmonic whose time period and frequency are given by

$$T = 2\pi\sqrt{\dfrac{l}{g}} \text{ and } \nu = \dfrac{1}{2\pi}\sqrt{\dfrac{g}{l}}$$

CHAPTER PRACTICE

OBJECTIVE Type Questions

1. Choose the correct option.
   (a) Every periodic motion is oscillatory
   (b) Every oscillatory motion is periodic
   (c) Both (a) and (b)
   (d) Neither (a) nor (b)

2. The function $\log_a(\omega t)$
   (a) is a periodic function
   (b) is a non-periodic function
   (c) could represents oscillatory motion
   (d) can represent circular motion.

3. Which of the following expression does not represent simple harmonic motion?
   (a) $x = A\cos\omega t + B\cos\omega t$
   (b) $x = A\cos(\omega t + \alpha)$
   (c) $x = B\sin(\omega t + \beta)$
   (d) $x = A\sin\omega t\cos^2\omega t$

4. A body performing simple harmonic motion is expressed by the displacement equation $y = 4\sin 2t$. The magnitude of maximum acceleration of the body is
   (a) 12   (b) 8
   (c) 16   (d) 20

5. Two simple harmonic motions of angular frequency 100 rads^{-1} and 1000 rads^{-1} have the same displacement amplitude. The ratio of their maximum acceleration is
   (a) $1:10$ (b) $1:10^2$
   (c) $1:10^3$ (d) $1:10^4$

6. A particle executing simple harmonic motion with an amplitude A and angular frequency ω. The ratio of maximum acceleration to the maximum velocity of the particle is
   (a) ωA (b) $\omega^2 A$
   (c) ω (d) $\dfrac{\omega^2}{A}$

7. For a SHM, if the maximum potential energy become double, choose the correct option.
   (a) Maximum kinetic energy will become double

   (b) The total mechanical energy will become double
   (c) Both (a) and (b)
   (d) Neither (a) nor (b)

8. The ratio of frequencies of two pendulums oscillating are $2:3$, then their lengths are in ratio
   (a) $\sqrt{2/3}$ (b) $\sqrt{3/2}$
   (c) 4/9   (d) 9/4

9. The acceleration due to gravity on the surface of the moon is 1.7ms^{-2}. The time period of a simple pendulum on the moon, if its time period on the earth is 3.5 s is
   (a) 2.2 s   (b) 4.4 s
   (c) 8.4 s   (d) 16.8 s

10. A simple pendulum is mounted in a satellite revolving around the earth. Then, choose the correct one.
    (a) Frequency of oscillation is zero.
    (b) Gravitational acceleration is absent inside the satellite.
    (c) Both (a) and (b)
    (d) Neither (a) nor (b)

ASSERTION AND REASON

Directions (Q.Nos. 11-15) *In the following questions, two statements are given- one labelled Assertion (A) and the other labelled Reason (R). Select the correct answer to these questions from the codes (a), (b), (c) and (d) as given below*
    (a) Both Assertion and Reason are true and Reason is the correct explanation of Assertion.
    (b) Both Assertion and Reason are true but Reason is not the correct explanation of Assertion.
    (c) Assertion is true but Reason is false.
    (d) Assertion is false but Reason is true.

11. **Assertion** Vibrations and oscillations are two different types of motion.

    Reason For vibration frequency is more and for oscillation the frequency is less.

12. **Assertion** $x(t) = A\sin(\omega t)$ is periodic but cannot represent an oscillatory motion.

    Reason $\sin\theta$ is a sinusoidal periodic function.

13. **Assertion** $x = A\cos(\omega t)$ and $x = A\sin(\omega t)$ can represent same motion depending on initial position of particle.

   Reason Phase constant depends on position of particle at $t = 0$.

14. **Assertion** In $X = A\cos(\omega t)$, ω represents the angular velocity of a particle moving on a circular path.

   Reason The uniform circular motion and simple harmonic motion can be correlated.

15. **Assertion** For force ($\mathbf{F}$) that represents spring force, $\mathbf{F} = -m\omega^2\mathbf{x}$.

   Reason Magnitude of spring force is directly proportional to net stretch in the spring.

CASE BASED QUESTIONS

Directions (Q. Nos. 16-17) *These questions are case study based questions. Attempt any 4 sub-parts from each question. Each question carries 1 mark.*

16. **Energy in SHM**

   A particle executing SHM posseses both kinetic energy and potential energy. When a body is displaced from its equilibrium position by doing work upon it, it acquires potential energy. When the body is released, it begins to move back with a velocity, thus acquiring kinetic energy.

   Both kinetic and potential energies of a particle in SHM vary between zero and their maximum values

   (i) In SHM,
      (a) PE is stored due to elasticity of system
      (b) KE is stored due to inertia of system
      (c) Both KE and PE are stored by virtue of elasticity of system.
      (d) Both (a) and (b)

   (ii) The expression for displacement of an object in SHM is $x = A\cos(\omega t)$. The potential energy at $t = T/4$ is
      (a) $\dfrac{1}{2}kA^2$ (b) $\dfrac{1}{8}kA^2$
      (c) $\dfrac{1}{4}kA^2$ (d) zero

   (iii) For a SHM, if the maximum potential energy become double, choose the correct option.
      (a) Maximum kinetic energy will become double
      (b) The total mechanical energy will become double
      (c) Both (a) and (b)
      (d) Neither (a) nor (b)

(iv) A block is in simple harmonic motion as shown in the figure on a frictionless surface. i.e. $\mu = 0$.
   Choose the correct option.

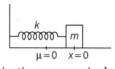

   (a) The kinetic energy varies between a maximum value and zero.
   (b) The potential energy varies between a maximum value and zero.
   (c) Total energy remains constant.
   (d) All of the above

(v) In simple harmonic motion, let the time period of variation of potential energy is T_1 and time period of variation of position is T_2, then relation between T_1 and T_2 is
   (a) $T_1 = T_2$ (b) $T_1 = 2T_2$
   (c) $2T_1 = T_2$ (d) None of these

17. **Spring-Mass System**

   A system of two blocks is attached with a spring and stretched by two equal and opposite forces as shown in the figure. Let the maximum stretch of spring towards each block is $\dfrac{X}{2}$.

   (i) The magnitude of spring force on block B is
      (a) kx (b) $\dfrac{kx}{2}$
      (c) $2kx$ (d) None of these

   (ii) The equation of SHM for block B when F from both blocks is removed, is
      (a) $F_{SHM} = -m\omega^2 x$ (b) $F_{SHM} = -\dfrac{m\omega^2 x}{2}$
      (c) $F_{SHM} = -kx$ (d) None of these

   (iii) The time period of the two blocks system is
      (a) $2\pi\sqrt{\dfrac{m}{k}}$ (b) $2\pi\sqrt{\dfrac{2m}{k}}$
      (c) $2\pi\sqrt{\dfrac{m}{2k}}$ (d) $2\pi\sqrt{\dfrac{m}{4k}}$

   (iv) In SHM,
      (a) PE is stored due to elasticity of system
      (b) KE is stored due to inertia of system
      (c) Both KE and PE are stored by virtue of elasticity of system.
      (d) Both (a) and (b)

(v) I. Time period of a spring-mass system depends on its amplitude.

II. Time period of a spring-mass system depends on its mass.

III. Time period of a spring-mass system depends on spring constant.

Choose the correct option regarding the above statements.

(a) I and II
(b) I and III
(c) II and III
(d) All of these

Answers

1.	(b)	2.	(b)	3.	(d)	4.	(c)	5.	(b)
6.	(c)	7.	(c)	8.	(d)	9.	(c)	10.	(c)
11.	(d)	12.	(d)	13.	(a)	14.	(a)	15.	(b)

16.	(i)	(d)	(ii)	(d)	(iii)	(c)	(iv)	(d)	(v)	(c)
17.	(i)	(a)	(ii)	(b)	(iii)	(c)	(iv)	(d)	(v)	(c)

VERY SHORT ANSWER Type Questions

18. What is the period of each of the function, $\sec \omega t$ and $\csc \omega t$?

19. Name the quantity which is conserved during the collision.

20. Two identical springs of force constant k each are connected in parallel. What will be the equivalent spring constant?

21. A pendulum clock is thrown out of an aeroplane. What will be its time period and how it will be effected in free fall?

22. How will a simple pendulum behave if it is taken to the moon?

23. What would be the effect on the time period if the amplitude of a simple pendulum increases?

24. A simple pendulum moves from one end to the other in $\frac{1}{4}$ second. What is its frequency?

25. Write the relation between time period T, displacement x and acceleration a of a particle in SHM.

26. Write the relation between acceleration, displacement and frequency of a particle executing SHM.

SHORT ANSWER Type Questions

27. What is meant by phase of an oscillating particle?

28. On what factors does the energy of a harmonic oscillator depend?

29. What would be the time period of a simple pendulum at the centre of the earth?

30. A simple harmonic motion of acceleration a and displacement x is represented by $a + 4\pi^2 x = 0$.

What is the time period of SHM?

LONG ANSWER Type I Questions

31. Write down the differential equation for SHM. Give its solution. Hence, obtain expression for the time period of SHM.

32. Obtain an expression for the velocity of a particle executing SHM, when is this velocity (i) maximum and (ii) minimum.

33. The relation between the acceleration a and displacement x of a particle executing SHM is

$a = -\left(\dfrac{p}{q}\right) y$, where p and q are constants.

LONG ANSWER Type II Questions

34. Draw the graphical representation of simple harmonic motion showing the
 (i) displacement-time curve
 (ii) velocity-time curve and
 (iii) acceleration-time curve

35. Explain the relation in phase between displacement, velocity and acceleration in SHM, graphically as well as theoretically.

36. Define the terms harmonic oscillator, displacement, amplitude, cycle, time period, frequency, angular frequency and phase with reference to an oscillatory system.

37. Show that simple harmonic motion may be regarded as the projection of uniform circular motion along a diameter of the circle. Hence, derive an expression for the displacement of a particle in SHM.

14

A wave is a periodic disturbance that travels through a medium (or vacuum). In general, a wave transports energy and momentum from one part of the medium (or vacuum) to the other part of it, without any bulk motion of the material of medium. All our communications essentially depend on transmission of signals through waves.

WAVES

|TOPIC 1|
Waves and Their Superposition

Waves occur when a system is disturbed from its equilibrium position and this disturbance travels or propagates from one region of the system to other. In a wave, both information and energy propagate (in the form of signals) from one point to another but there is no motion of matter as a whole through a medium.

Types of Waves

We usually deal with three types of waves as given below

Mechanical Wave

The waves requiring a material medium for their propagation are called mechanical waves. These waves are also called **elastic waves** because their propagation depend on the material media which possess elasticity and inertia. e.g. Water waves, sound waves and seismic waves, energy waves that travel through the earth's layers. These waves are governed by Newton's laws of motion and can exist only in a material medium such as water, air and rock, strings, etc.

Electromagnetic Wave

These types of waves travel in the form of oscillating electric and magnetic fields are called electromagnetic waves.

Electromagnetic waves do not require any material medium for their propagation and are also called **non-mechanical waves**.

CHAPTER CHECKLIST
- Waves and Their Superposition
- Types of Waves
- Characteristics of Wave Motion
- Transverse & Longitudinal Wave
- Displacement Relation in a Progressive Wave
- Speed of a Travelling Wave
- Principle of Superposition of Waves
- Reflection of Waves
- Standing Waves and Normal Modes
- Vibrations of Air Columns
- Beats

e.g. Visible and ultraviolet light, X-rays, radio and television waves, microwaves etc. All the electromagnetic waves travel through the vacuum at the same speed c given as

$$c = 29,97,92,458 \text{ m/s} \qquad [\text{speed of light}]$$

$$\simeq 3 \times 10^8 \text{ m/s}$$

Matter Wave

These types of waves are associated with microscopic particles i.e. electrons, protons and other fundamental particles and even atoms and molecules when they are in motion are called matter waves or de-Broglie waves.

e.g. electron microscope is associated with electrons present in matter wave.

> ### Dual Nature of Light
> - Light wave is an electromagnetic wave. Every radiation that we get from the sun comes under electromagnetic waves. Actually, light shows dual nature. Light behaves as wave, as well as particle.
> - In the same way, a moving particle could behave as wave. Matter wave is the wave associated with a moving particle.

Characteristics of Wave Motion

  (i) In a wave motion, the disturbance travels through the medium due to repeated periodic oscillations of the particles of the medium about their mean positions.

  (ii) The energy is transferred from one place to another without any actual transfer of the particles of the medium.

  (iii) There is a continuous phase difference between two successive particles because each particle receives disturbance a little later than its preceding particle.

  (iv) The velocity with which a wave travels is different from the velocity of the particles with which they vibrate simple harmonically about their mean positions.

  (v) In a given medium, the wave velocity remains constant, while the particle velocity changes continuously during its vibration about the mean position.

     The particle's velocity is maximum at the mean position and zero at the extreme position.

  (vi) For the propagation of a mechanical wave, the medium must possess the properties of inertia, elasticity as well as friction.

Spring Model for the Propagation of a Wave

Consider a collection of springs connected to one another and one end is fixed to a rigid support. If the spring at one end is pulled suddenly and released, the disturbance travels to the other end.

A collection of springs connected to each other

The reason behind this is when the first spring is pulled, it gets stretched. Due to elasticity, a restoring force is developed in the first spring.

This restoring force brings the first spring back to its mean position and stretches the second spring and so on. Thus, the disturbance moves from one end to the other, but each spring oscillating about its equilibrium.

Propagation of Sound Wave through Air

Consider the small region of air as a spring. It is connected to the neighbouring regions or springs. As sound waves pass through air, it compresses and expands a small region of air. This causes a change in density and pressure of that region.

According to Boyle's law,

$$\text{Change in pressure } (\Delta p) \propto \frac{1}{\text{Change in volume } (\Delta V)}$$

$$\Rightarrow \qquad (\Delta p) \propto (\Delta \rho)$$

As the pressure is force per unit area, so a restoring force is proportional to the disturbance or change in density is developed just like in an extended or compressed spring.

If a region is compressed, its molecules tend to move out to the adjacent region, thereby, increasing the density or creating compression in that region. The air in the first region undergoes rarefaction due to decrease in its density in the first region.

But, if a region is comparatively rarefied, the surrounding air will rush in making the rarefaction move to the adjoining region. Thus, the compression or rarefaction moves from one region to another, making the propagation of a disturbance possible in air.

Propagation of Sound Wave in a Solid

In a crystalline solid, various atoms can be considered as end points, with springs connected between pairs of them. In this, each atom or group of atoms is in equilibrium due to forces from the surrounding atoms because the forces exerted by the other atoms are cancelled out.

When the sound wave propagates, the atom is displaced from its equilibrium position and a restoring force is developed. This disturbance produced by the force travels to the next atom and so on. Thus, the wave propagates through the solid.

TRANSVERSE WAVE

Transverse wave motion is that wave motion in which the individual particles of the medium execute simple harmonic motion about their mean positions in a direction perpendicular to the direction of propagation of the wave. The wave itself is known as **transverse wave**.

e.g. Waves in string, ripples on the surface of water. Movement of string of stringed musical instruments like sitar, guitar.

Illustration for Transverse Wave

Consider a horizontal spring with its one end held in the hand and other end fixed to a rigid support as shown in figure.

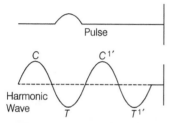

Transverse wave along the stretched string

If we give its free end a smart upward jerk, an upward kink or pulse is created there, which travels along the string towards the fixed end. Hence, if we continuously give up and down jerks to the free end of the string, the string successively undergoes a disturbance about its mean position and a number of sinusoidal waves begin to travel along the string. So that, the waves in the string are transverse in nature.

The points $(C, C', \ldots)$ called **crest** show the position of maximum displacement in the positive direction i.e. upward direction.

The points $(T, T', \ldots)$ called **trough** show the position of maximum displacement in the negative direction i.e. downward direction.

Media for Transverse Waves

In transverse waves, the particle's motion is perpendicular to the direction of propagation of the wave. As the wave propagates, each element of the medium undergoes a **shearing strain**.

Transverse waves can, therefore, be propagated only in those media which can sustain **shearing stress**, such as solids and springs but not in fluids.

LONGITUDINAL WAVE

The waves in which the individual particles of the medium execute simple harmonic motion about their mean positions along the direction of propagation of the wave are called **longitudinal waves**.

e.g. Waves in spring, sound waves, vibration of air column in organ pipes, etc.

Illustration for Longitudinal Wave

Consider the production of waves in a long pipe filled with air has a piston at one end.

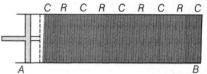

Production of Longitudinal waves in a cylinder by moving a piston back and forth.

If we push the piston suddenly towards right, a small layer of air just near the piston head is compressed and after being compressed, this layer moves towards right and compresses the next layer and so on, the compression reaches the other end. Thus, the motion of air and the changes in air pressure (due to the change in density of the medium in compression) travel towards the right as a pulse.

Now, if the piston is pulled towards left, there is rarefied in the layer adjacent to the piston occured resulting in the fall of pressure. The air from the next layer moves to restore pressure. Consequently, the next layer is rarefied. In this way, a pulse of rarefaction moves towards right.

Due to continuous pushing and pulling of the piston in a simple harmonic manner, a sinusoidal wave travels in the cylinder in the form of **compressions** and **rarefactions**, (marked C, R, C, R, etc.) resulting a temporary reduction in volume and consequent increase in density.

As the motion of the oscillation of the elements of air is parallel to the direction of propagation of wave along the pipe, the sound waves produced in air are **longitudinal** waves.

A compression is a region of the medium in which the distance between any two consecutive particles of the medium is less than the normal distance. Hence, temporarily there will be decrease in volume, increase in density.

A rarefaction is a region of the medium in which the distance between any two consecutive particles of the medium is more than the normal distance. Consequently, there will be increase in volume and decrease in density of the medium temporarily.

Media for Longitudinal Waves

Fluids as well as solids can sustain compressive strain, therefore, longitudinal waves can propagate in all elastic media.

Few characteristics of a media for propagation of wave

(i) A medium like a steel bar, both transverse and longitudinal waves can propagate while air can sustain only longitudinal waves.

(ii) Transverse and longitudinal waves travel with different speeds, when they propagate through the same medium.

(iii) In a wave motion, only the disturbance travels through a medium. The medium does not travel with the disturbance.

(iv) Waves may be one-dimensional, two-dimensional or three-dimensional. Mode of dimension will be according to the propagation of energy in one, two or three dimension.

(v) Transverse waves along a string are one-dimensional, ripples on water surface are two-dimensional and sound waves produced from a point source are three-dimensional.

EXAMPLE |1| Identifying the Waves

Given below are some examples of wave motion. State in each case if the wave motion is transverse, longitudinal or a combination of both.

(i) Motion of a kink in a longitudinal spring produced by displacing one end of the spring side ways.

(ii) Waves produced in a cylinder containing a liquid by moving its piston back and forth.

(iii) Waves produced by a motorboat sailing in water.

(iv) Ultrasonic waves in air produced by a vibrating quartz crystal. **[NCERT]**

Sol. (i) Transverse and longitudinal
(ii) Longitudinal
(iii) Transverse and longitudinal
(iv) Longitudinal

Displacement Relation in a Progressive Wave

To describe travelling wave mathematically, we need position x and time t. Consider the wave travelling in positive x-direction. The displacement $y(x, t)$ denotes the transverse displacement of the element at position x at time t and is given by

$$\boxed{\text{Displacement, } y(x, t) = a \sin (kx - \omega t + \phi)} \quad \dots \text{(i)}$$

The above equation can also be represented by using linear combination of sine and cosine functions such as

$$y(x, t) = A \sin (kx - \omega t) + B \cos (kx - \omega t)$$

where, $\quad a = \sqrt{A^2 + B^2}$ and $\phi = \tan^{-1} \left(\dfrac{B}{A} \right) \quad \dots \text{(ii)}$

Clearly from above equation, we can say that the constituents of the medium at different positions execute SHM.

As the above equation is written in terms of position x, it can be used to find the displacements of all the elements of the string as a function of time.

Thus, it can tell us the shape of the wave at any given time and how that shape changes as the wave moves along the string and hence, how the wave progress.

The wave travelling in the negative direction of X-axis can be, represented by

$$y(x, t) = a \sin (kx + \omega t + \phi) \quad \dots \text{(iii)}$$

where,

$y(x, t)$ = displacement of vibrating element or particle as a function of position x and time t.

$\quad a$ = amplitude of the vibrating element or particle

$\quad \omega$ = angular frequency of the wave

$\quad x$ = position of vibrating element

$\quad k$ = angular wave number.

$(kx - \omega t + \phi)$ = phase of a vibrating element at time t and position x. ϕ is phase constant at $x = 0$, $t = 0$.

The figure below shows the plots of Eq. (i) for different values of time and position. In the plot, crest is the point of maximum positive displacement and trough is the point of maximum negative displacement.

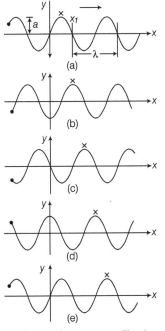

Plots for a harmonic wave travelling in positive
-direction at different time

To analyse the motion, we have represented dot (•) and cross (×) in the figure.

Amplitude and Phase

The magnitude of the maximum displacement of the particles from their equilibrium position, as a wave passes through them is known as **amplitude** of the particle.

In Eq. (i), the displacement $y(x, t)$ varies between a and $-a$. Here, a represents the maximum displacement of the constituents of the medium from their mean position.

The displacement y may be positive or negative but a is positive. It is called the **amplitude** of the particle. The quantity $(kx - \omega t + \phi)$ is called the **phase** of the wave which appears as the argument of the sine or cosine function.

Wavelength and Angular Wave Number

The minimum distance between two particles having the same phase is called the **wavelength** of the wave, usually denoted by λ.

Or

The distance travelled by a wave during the time in which any particle of the medium completes one vibration about its mean position is known as **wavelength** of the wave.

As, $y(x, t) = a \sin(kx - \omega t + \phi)$

Taking $\phi = 0$ in the displacement at $t = 0$, $y(x, 0) = a \sin kx$

Because, the sine function is having period 2π.

$$\therefore \quad \sin kx = \sin(kx + 2n\pi) = \sin k\left(x + \frac{2n\pi}{k}\right)$$

The displacement will be same at points x and $x + \dfrac{2n\pi}{k}$ with $n = 1, 2, 3, \ldots$. The least distance between two points with same phase will be

$$\lambda = \frac{2\pi}{k} + x - x \text{ (for } n = 1)$$

$$\boxed{\text{Wavelength, } \lambda = \frac{2\pi}{k}}$$

$$\Rightarrow \quad \text{Angular wave number, } k = \frac{2\pi}{\lambda} \text{ rad m}^{-1}.$$

where, k is called **angular wave number**. Hence, the angular wave number also known as **propagation constant** is 2π times the number of waves that can be accommodated per unit length.

Period, Angular Frequency and Frequency

Figure below shows a sinusoidal plot. It describes the shape as well as displacement. We are monitoring the motion of the element by putting $\phi = 0$ and $x = 0$ in equation given as

$$y(x, t) = a \sin(kx - \omega t + \phi)$$

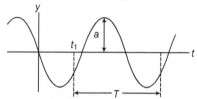

Graph for displacement time period, amplitude and frequency

We will get $y(0, t) = a \sin(-\omega t) = -a \sin \omega t$

Time period

The time taken by a wave to travel a distance equal to one wavelength is known as the **time period** of wave.

If period of sine function is T measured from an arbitrary time t_1, then

$$\Rightarrow \quad -a \sin \omega t_1 = -a \sin \omega (t_1 + T)$$
$$= -a \sin (\omega t_1 + \omega T)$$

Because, sine function repeats after every 2π.

$$\therefore \quad \omega T = 2\pi$$

$$\Rightarrow \quad \boxed{\text{Angular frequency, } \omega = \frac{2\pi}{T}}$$

where, ω is called the **angular frequency**, SI unit is rad s^{-1}. The number of complete vibrations or oscillations produced by a wave in one second is known as the **frequency** of the wave. The frequency ν of a wave is defined as $\dfrac{1}{T}$ and is related to the angular frequency ω by

$$\boxed{\text{Frequency, } \nu = \frac{1}{T} = \frac{\omega}{2\pi}}$$

where, $\nu =$ frequency of the wave
ν is usually measured in hertz (Hz).

The relation between the wavelength λ and velocity v of the wave is given as $\quad \lambda = \dfrac{v}{n}$

Note

The frequency of a wave will remain unchanged during any type of interaction that the wave suffers because it depends only on the frequency of the source.

EXAMPLE |2| Formation of the Progressive Wave

If a progressive wave travelling in positive x-direction having the amplitude of 6 cm, frequency 200 Hz and velocity is 400 m/s, then write the equation of that progressive wave.

Sol. Given, $A = 6\,cm = 0.06\,m$

$$v = 200\,Hz$$

$$k = \frac{2\pi}{\lambda} = \frac{2\pi}{v/\nu} \qquad \left[\because \lambda = \frac{v}{\nu}\right]$$

$$k = \frac{2\pi\nu}{v} = \frac{2\pi \times 200}{400} = \pi\,m^{-1}$$

$$\omega = 2\pi\nu = 2\pi \times 200 = 400\pi\,rad/s$$

The standard equation of the progressive wave is

$$y(x, t) = A\sin(kx - \omega t)$$

put the values to get the equation

$$y(x, t) = 0.06\sin(\pi x - 400\pi t)\,m$$

EXAMPLE |3| Wave in a String

A wave travelling along a string is described by $y(x,t) = 0.005\sin(80.0x - 3.0t)$ in which the numerical constants are in SI units (0.005 m, 80.0 rad m^{-1} and 3.0 rad s^{-1}). Calculate

(i) the amplitude of particle,

(ii) the wavelength and

(iii) the period and frequency of the wave. Also, calculate displacement y of the particle at a distance $x = 30.0$ cm and time $t = 20$ s ? **[NCERT]**

Sol. Given, $y(x, t) = 0.005\,\sin(80.0x - 3.0t)$

Then, $y(x, t) = a\sin(kx - \omega t)$

Now, compare the given equation with standard equation to find out all the physical quantities.

$$a = 0.005\,m$$

$$k = 80.0\,rad/m$$

$$\omega = 3.0\,rad/s$$

The physical quantities by using the given fundamental physical quantities.

(i) Amplitude, $a = 0.005\,m = 5\,mm$

(ii) Wavelength, $\lambda = \dfrac{2\pi}{k} = \dfrac{2\pi}{80} = 7.85\,cm$

(iii) Time period, $T = 2\pi/\omega = \dfrac{2\pi}{3} = 2.09\,s$

and frequency, $v = \dfrac{1}{T} = \dfrac{1}{2.09}$

$$= 0.478 \simeq 0.48\,Hz$$

Now, the displacement y of the particle at a distance.

$$x = 30.0\,cm = 0.3\,m \text{ and time } t = 20\,s$$

$$y(0.3, 20) = 0.005\,\sin(80 \times 0.3 - 3.0 \times 20)$$

$$y(0.3, 20) = 0.005\,\sin(24 - 60)$$

$$= 0.00495\,m \simeq 5\,mm$$

Speed of a Travelling Wave

We can fix our attention on any particular point on the wave to determine the speed of propagation. It is convenient to look at the motion of the crest. In the figure shown below, we have shown the shape of the wave at two instants of time t and $t + \Delta t$ and the wave pattern shifted by distance Δx.

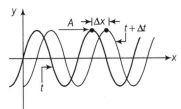

Wave moves to right with velocity v

As shown in above waveform, each point of the moving waveform, such as point A marked on a peak, retain its displacement y.

Here, it must be noted that the points on the string do not retain this displacement but points on the waveform do. As point A retains its displacement as it moves, the phase in the equation of the displacement $y(x,t)$ is constant. Thus,

$\Rightarrow \qquad kx - \omega t = $ constant

$\Rightarrow$ If x changed to $x + \Delta x$ and t to $t + \Delta t$

$\Rightarrow \qquad kx - \omega t = k(x + \Delta x) - \omega(t + \Delta t)$

or $\qquad k\Delta x = \omega \Delta t \Rightarrow \dfrac{\Delta x}{\Delta t} = \dfrac{\omega}{k} = v$

$\Rightarrow \qquad v = \dfrac{2\pi\nu}{k} = \nu \times \left(\dfrac{2\pi}{k}\right) = \nu\lambda$

$\therefore \qquad \boxed{\text{Speed of travelling wave, } v = \nu\lambda = \dfrac{\lambda}{T}}$

The above equation is general relation for all progressive waves, shows that the wave pattern travels a distance equal to the wavelength of the wave.

Speed of a Transverse Wave on Stretched String

The speed of a mechanical wave is related with the restoring force set up in the medium due to the disturbance produced. For wave on a string, it will be provided by the tension (T).

We will use dimensional method to get the equation for speed.

Combining dimensions of mass per unit length (or linear mass density) μ of the string as $[\text{ML}^{-1}]$ and tension T of the string as $[\text{MLT}^{-2}]$, we get

$$\frac{[\text{MLT}^{-2}]}{[\text{ML}^{-1}]} = [\text{L}^2\text{T}^{-2}]$$

As dimension for v is $[LT^{-1}]$

$$\boxed{\text{Speed of a transverse wave, } v = c\sqrt{\frac{T}{\mu}}}$$

where, c is a dimensionless constant, c is turned out to be 1.

$$\Rightarrow \qquad v = \sqrt{\frac{T}{\mu}}$$

The speed of the wave along a stretched ideal string depends only on the tension and the linear mass density of the string and does not depend on the frequency of the wave.

The frequency of the wave is determined by the source that generates the wave. The wavelength is then given in the form

$$\lambda = \frac{v}{\nu}$$

EXAMPLE |4| Stretched Wire

A wave moves with speed 300 m/s on a wire which is under tension of 400 N. Find how much tension must be changed to increase the speed to 315 m/s?

Sol. We know speed, $v = \sqrt{\frac{T}{\mu}}$

$$\Rightarrow \qquad \frac{dv}{dT} = \frac{1}{2\sqrt{\mu T}}$$

$$\Rightarrow \qquad \frac{dv}{v} = \frac{1}{2}\frac{dT}{T} \qquad \left[\text{putting }\sqrt{\mu} = \frac{\sqrt{T}}{V}\right]$$

$$\Rightarrow \qquad dT = (2T)\frac{dv}{v}$$

$$= 2 \times 400 \times \left(\frac{315-300}{300}\right)$$

$$= \frac{2 \times 4}{3} \times 15 = 2 \times 4 \times 5 = 40\text{ N}$$

Hence, tension should be increased by 40 N.

or

Alternate Method

As speed $v = \sqrt{\frac{T}{\mu}}$

$$\Rightarrow \qquad \frac{v_2}{v_1} = \sqrt{\frac{T_2}{T_1}} \qquad [\mu \text{ is same}]$$

$$\frac{T_2}{T_1} = \left(\frac{v_2}{v_1}\right)^2 = \left(\frac{315}{300}\right)^2 = \left(\frac{300+15}{300}\right)^2$$

$$\frac{T_2}{T_1} = \left(1+\frac{15}{300}\right)^2 = \left(1+\frac{1}{20}\right)^2$$

$$\frac{T_2}{T_1} = 1 + 2 \times \frac{1}{20} \qquad [\text{use Binomial theorem}]$$

$$\frac{T_2}{T_1} = 1 + \frac{1}{10}$$

$$\frac{T_2}{T_1} - 1 = \frac{1}{10} \quad \Rightarrow \quad \frac{T_2 - T_1}{T_1} = \frac{1}{10}$$

$$\Delta T = \frac{1}{10} \times T_1 = \frac{1}{10} \times 400 = 40\text{ N}$$

Hence, tension should be increased by 40 N.

(Previous method is not familiar for the student, so, the given solution gives more comfort to the student).

EXAMPLE |5| Tension in a Cord

A uniform cord have a mass 0.2 kg and length 6 m. If tension is maintained in the cord by suspending a mass of 3 kg from one end, then find out the speed of a pulse on this cord. Also find the time, it takes the pulse to travel from the wall to the pulley.

Sol. Given, Mass of a suspended block, $m = 3$ kg

Mass of the cord = 0.2 kg

Length of the cord = 6 m

Speed of the cord = ?

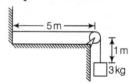

Tension, T = weight of mass of 3 kg = $m \times g$

$$= 3 \times 9.8 = 29.4\text{ N}$$

$$\mu = \frac{m}{l} = \frac{0.2}{6}$$

$$= 0.033\text{ kg/m}$$

As we know the wave speed or speed of a pulse on the cord is given by

$$v = \sqrt{\frac{T}{\mu}}$$

Put the values to get the speed of the pulse.

$$v = \sqrt{\frac{T}{\mu}} = \sqrt{\frac{29.4}{0.033}} \simeq 29.85\text{ m/s}$$

Thus, the time for this speed to travel from the wall to pulley i.e. a distance of 5 m.

$$\text{Time} = \frac{5}{29.85} = 0.168\text{ s}$$

Speed of a Longitudinal Wave
(Speed of Sound)

In a longitudinal wave, the constituents of the medium oscillate forward and backward in the direction of wave propagation. In case of sound wave, it will be compression and rarefactions formed in air.

The Bulk modulus of the medium,

$$B = -\frac{\Delta p}{\Delta V / V}.$$

Where, Δp = change in pressure,

ΔV = change in volume

V = initial volume

B has a SI unit Pa.

Combining dimensions of $B[ML^{-1}T^{-2}]$ and density $\rho[ML^{-3}]$, we will get

$$\frac{[ML^{-1}T^{-2}]}{[ML^{-3}]} = [L^2T^{-2}]$$

$$\Rightarrow \qquad v = c\sqrt{\frac{B}{\rho}}$$

By experiment, $c = 1 \Rightarrow v = \sqrt{\frac{B}{\rho}}$

For a linear medium like a solid bar, the modulus of elasticity will be Young's modulus (Y). By analysing the dimensional analysis as previous the speed of longitudinal waves in a solid bar is given by

$$v = \sqrt{\frac{Y}{\rho}}$$

where, Y is the Young's modulus of the material of the bar and ρ is density. Table below gives the speed of sound in some media.

Speed of Sound in Different Media

Medium	Speed ($m\ s^{-1}$)
Gases	
Air (0°C)	331
Air (20°C)	343
Helium	965
Hydrogen	1284
Liquids	
Water (0°C)	1402
Water (20°C)	1482
Seawater	1522
Solids	
Aluminium	6420
Copper	3560
Steel	5941
Granite	6000
Vulcanised rubber	54

Speed of Mechanical Waves

The speed of a mechanical wave, in a medium, depends upon the properties of the medium. For given type of waves (in a given medium), this speed, however does not change with a change in the characteristics (amplitude, wavelength or frequency) of the wave. e.g. the speeds of different types of sound waves, infrasonic, audible or ultrasonic, in a given medium, are all given by

$$\boxed{\text{Speed of mechanical waves, } v = \sqrt{\frac{E}{\rho}}}$$

where, E is the (appropriate) elastic constant and ρ is the density of the medium. The speed is thus, dependent only on the properties of the medium.

Speed of Electromagnetic Waves

The speed of propagation of electromagnetic waves is also determined by the characteristics of the medium through which they are propagating. Electromagnetic waves, as we know, are a combination of the oscillations of electric and magnetic fields in mutually perpendicular directions. The relevant properties of the medium, determining their speed of propagation, are the permittivity and the permeability of the medium.

In vacuum, the speed of propagation (c) of all types of electromagnetic waves, is given by $c = \dfrac{1}{\sqrt{\mu_0 \varepsilon_0}}$

Here, μ_0 = permeability of vacuum and ε_0 = permittivity of vacuum.

In any other material medium, the speed of propagation (v) of electromagnetic waves, is given by

$$\boxed{\text{Speed of electromagnetic waves, } v = \frac{1}{\sqrt{\mu \varepsilon}}}$$

where, μ = permeability of the medium and ε = permittivity of the medium. It however, turns out that the values of μ and ε, of a material medium, are not quite the same for electromagnetic waves of different frequencies.

EXAMPLE |6| Speed of Sound in Aluminium
An aluminium rod of length 90 cm and of mass is clamped at its mid-point and is set into longitudinal vibrations by stroking it with resined cloth. Assume that the rod vibrates in its fundamental mode of vibration. The density of aluminium is 2.6 g/cm³ and its Young's modulus is 7.80×10^{10} N/m². Find the speed of the sound in aluminium. If the wavelength is 180 m then, find frequency of vibration.

Sol. Given, Young's modulus, $Y = 7.80 \times 10^{10}$ N/m^2

Density of aluminium, $\rho = 2.6$ g/cm$^3 = \dfrac{2.6 \times (100)^3}{1000}$ kg/m^3

$$\rho = 2600 \text{ kg/m}^3$$

Wavelength, $\lambda = 180$ m

Speed of the sound in aluminium,

$$v = \sqrt{\frac{Y}{\rho}} = \sqrt{\frac{7.80 \times 10^{10} \text{ N}/\text{m}^2}{2600 \text{ kg}/\text{m}^3}}$$

$$v = 5477 \text{ m/s}$$

As, $\lambda = \dfrac{v}{\nu} \Rightarrow \nu = \dfrac{v}{\lambda} = \dfrac{5477 \text{ m/s}}{180 \text{ m}} = 30.42$ Hz

Liquids and solids generally have higher speeds of sound than in gases.

Speed of the Longitudinal Wave in an Ideal Gas

For an ideal gas, we know that $pV = Nk_B T$

where, p is pressure, V is volume, N is molecular density, k_B is Boltzmann constant and T is the temperature on absolute scale (Kelvin).

For isothermal change, $\Delta T = 0$

$\Rightarrow \quad V\Delta p + p\Delta V = 0 \Rightarrow -\dfrac{\Delta p}{\Delta V/V} = p$

As, $\quad B = -\dfrac{\Delta p}{\Delta V/V}$

$\therefore \quad B = p$

Hence, $\quad v = \sqrt{\dfrac{B}{\rho}}$

or Speed of longitudinal waves in an ideal gas, $v = \sqrt{\dfrac{p}{\rho}}$

This is known as **Newton's formula.**

EXAMPLE |7| Moving with the Speed of Sound

Estimate the speed of sound in air at STP. The mass of 1 mole of air is 29.0×10^{-3} kg. **[NCERT]**

Sol. We know that volume of any gas at STP is 22.4 litre.

Density of air at STP is

$$\rho_0 = \left(\frac{\text{mass}}{\text{volume at STP}}\right)_{\text{for one mole of air}}$$

$$= \frac{29.0 \times 10^{-3} \text{ kg}}{22.4 \times 10^{-3}} = 1.29 \text{ kgm}^{-3}$$

According to Newton's formula,

Speed of sound, $v = \left[\dfrac{1.01 \times 10^5 \text{ Nm}^{-2}}{1.29 \text{ kgm}^{-3}}\right]^{1/2} = 280$ ms^{-1}

Laplace Correction

The result obtained as the speed of sound in air at STP is 280 ms^{-1} which is about 15% smaller as compared to the experimental value of 331 ms^{-1}. The mistake in the formula was pointed out by Laplace and he told that the changes in pressure and volume of a gas, when sound waves are propagated through it, are not isothermal, but adiabatic.

Hence, we will apply

$$pV^\gamma = \text{constant}$$

$$\Rightarrow \quad p\gamma V^{\gamma-1}\Delta V + V^\gamma \Delta p = 0$$

The adiabatic bulk modulus,

$$B_{ad} = -\frac{\Delta p}{\Delta V/V} = \gamma p$$

where, γ is the ratio of two specific heats C_p/C_V. The speed of sound is therefore, given by,

Speed of sound, $v = \sqrt{\dfrac{\gamma p}{\rho}}$

This modification of Newton's formula is referred to as the **Laplace correction.** For air, $\gamma = 7/5$.

By this formula, we will get a value of 331.3 ms^{-1}, which agree with the practical value.

Note
- Speed of longitudinal wave in term of temperature of the gas

$$V = \sqrt{\frac{rRT}{M}}$$

where, T is temperature of the gas
M is molar mass of the gas
- According to the standard gas equation

$$pV = RT$$

$$\Rightarrow \quad p = \frac{RT}{V} \quad ...(i)$$

$\therefore$ Speed of sound $v = \sqrt{\dfrac{rp}{\rho}} = \sqrt{\dfrac{\gamma RT}{\rho \times V}} = \sqrt{\dfrac{\gamma RT}{M}}$

Substituting value of ρ, where $\rho \times v = M$

PRINCIPLE OF SUPERPOSITION OF WAVES

This principle states that when two or more pulses overlap, the resultant displacement is the algebraic sum of the displacements due to each pulse.

Consider the two waves travelling together along the same stretched string in opposite directions.

They meet and pass through each other, and move on independently as shown in figure.

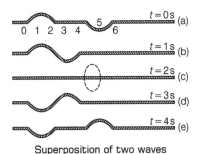

Superposition of two waves

In the graph (c), the displacement due to the two pulses have exactly cancelled each other and there is zero displacement throughout.

Three important applications of superposition principle are:

1. Stationary waves
2. Beats
3. Interference of waves

Interference of Wave

Wave interference is the phenomenon that occurs when the two or more waves pass through the same medium. The interference of waves causes the medium to take on a shape that results from the net effect of the two individual waves upon the particles of the medium.

Let the two waves disturbances in the medium having displacements $y_1(x, t)$ and $y_2(x, t)$.

Then, the net displacement $y(x, t)$ is

$$y(x, t) = y_1(x, t) + y_2(x, t)$$

For n waves superimposing with each other

$$y = f_1(x - vt) + f_2(x - vt) + \ldots + f_n(x - vt)$$
$$= \sum_{i=1}^{n} f_i(x - vt)$$

Here, function is represented for the moving waves. This principle of superposition is basic to the phenomenon of interference.

To illustrate the principle, we will consider two harmonic travelling waves having the same angular frequency ω and wave number $k = 2\pi/\lambda$. Let us assume that their amplitudes are identical.

If the two waves are out of phase by a phase constant ϕ, then the two waves are represented as

$$y_1(x, t) = a \sin(kx - \omega t)$$
and
$$y_2(x, t) = a \sin(kx - \omega t + \phi)$$

By the principle of superposition, the net displacement of the resultant wave

$$y(x, t) = y_1(x, t) + y_2(x, t)$$
$$= a \sin(kx - \omega t) + a \sin(kx - \omega t + \phi)$$
$$= a \left[2 \sin \left\{ \frac{(kx - \omega t) + (kx - \omega t + \phi)}{2} \right\} \frac{\cos \phi}{2} \right]$$

(by using the trigonometrical relation)

$$y(x, t) = 2 a \cos \frac{\phi}{2} \sin \left(kx - \omega t + \frac{\phi}{2} \right)$$

Clearly, it shows that the resultant wave is a harmonic travelling wave in positive direction of X-axis with same frequency and wavelength. The phase angle of resultant wave is $\frac{\phi}{2}$.

And the amplitude is $A(\phi) = 2 a \cos \frac{\phi}{2}$

Case I For $\phi = 0$ i.e. the two waves are in phase.

$$y(x, t) = 2 a \sin(kx - \omega t)$$

i.e. the resultant wave will has amplitude $2a$ (amplitude will be maximum).

Case II For $\phi = \pi$ i.e. the two waves are out of phase by 180°.

$$y(x, t) = 0$$

(i.e. zero displacement everywhere at all times)

Constructive and Destructive Interference

When waves interfere in phase, it is called **constructive interference** and when they interfere in phase opposition, that is called **destructive interference**.

Note
In generalised form For constructive interference.
- Phase difference, $\phi = 2n\pi$
- Path difference = $\Delta x = n\lambda$

For destructive interference
- Phase difference, $\phi = (2n + 1)\pi$
- Path difference, $\Delta x = (2n + 1)\lambda/2$
  where, $n = 0, 1, 2, \ldots$
  λ is the wavelength.

The phenomenon of constructive and destructive interference are shown in the figures (a) and (b), respectively.

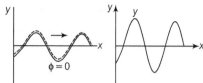

(a) Constructive interference

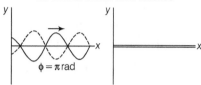

(b) Destructive interference

(i) In constructive interference, if a wave meets a crest of another wave of same frequency at the same point, then the magnitude of the displacement is the sum of the individual magnitudes as shown in Fig. (a).

(ii) In destructive interference, if a crest of one wave meets a trough of another wave, then the magnitude of the displacements is equal to the difference in the individual magnitudes as shown in Fig. (b).

(iii) If two sinusoidal waves of the same amplitude and wavelength travel in the same direction along a stretched string, they interfere to produce a resultant sinusoidal wave travelling in that direction.

(iv) For interference between sources of amplitudes A_1, A_2 and associated intensities I_1, I_2 as $I \propto A^2$.

$$\frac{I_{max}}{I_{min}} = \left(\frac{\sqrt{I_1} + \sqrt{I_2}}{\sqrt{I_1} - \sqrt{I_2}}\right)^2$$

When $I_1 = I_2 = I_0$, then $I_{resultant} = 4I_0 \cos^2 (\phi/2)$ where, ϕ is the phase difference.

(v) These principles are valid for sound and light waves as well provided sources must be coherent i.e. these phase differences must not change with passage of time.

EXAMPLE |8| **Let us Mix with Each Other**
Two waves of equal frequencies have their amplitudes in the ratio of 3 : 5. They are superimposed on each other. Calculate the ratio of I_{max}/I_{min}.

Sol. $\dfrac{A_1}{A_2} = \dfrac{3}{5} \Rightarrow \sqrt{\dfrac{I_1}{I_2}} = \dfrac{3}{5}$

Now, $\dfrac{I_{max}}{I_{min}} = \left(\dfrac{\sqrt{I_1} + \sqrt{I_2}}{\sqrt{I_1} - \sqrt{I_2}}\right)^2 = \left(\dfrac{\sqrt{I_1/I_2} + 1}{\sqrt{I_1/I_2} - 1}\right)^2$

$= \left(\dfrac{3/5 + 1}{3/5 - 1}\right)^2 = \dfrac{64}{4} = \dfrac{16}{1}$

| TOPIC PRACTICE 1 |

OBJECTIVE Type Questions

1. Water waves produced by a motorboat sailing in water are   [NCERT Exemplar]
   (a) neither longitudinal nor transverse
   (b) Both longitudinal and transverse
   (c) only longitudinal
   (d) only transverse

Sol. (b) Water waves produced by a motorboat sailing in water are both longitudinal and transverse, because the waves produced are due to the transverse as well as lateral vibrations in the particles of the medium.

2. The frequency of a sound wave is n and its velocity is v. If the frequency is increased to $4n$, the velocity of the wave will be
   (a) v (b) $2v$
   (c) $4v$ (d) $v/4$

Sol. (a) Velocity of sound is independent of frequency. Therefore, it is same (v) for frequency n and $4n$.

3. A steel wire has linear mass density 6.9×10^{-3} kg m^{-1}. If the wire is under a tension of 60 N, then the speed of the transverse waves on the wire is
   (a) 63 ms^{-1} (b) 75 ms^{-1}
   (c) 73 ms^{-1} (d) 93 ms^{-1}

Sol. (d) Linear mass density = 6.9×10^{-3} kg m^{-1}

Tension, $T = 60$ N

Thus, speed of wave on the wire is given by

$$v = \sqrt{\frac{T}{\mu}} = \sqrt{\frac{60 \text{ N}}{6.9 \times 10^{-3} \text{ kg m}^{-1}}} = 93 \text{ ms}^{-1}$$

4. The displacement of the wave given by equation $y(x, t) = a \sin (kx - \omega t + \phi)$, where $\phi = 0$ at point x and $t = 0$ is same as that at point
   (a) $x + 2n\pi$ (b) $x + \dfrac{2n\pi}{k}$
   (c) $kx + 2n\pi$ (d) Both (a) and (b)

Sol. (b) $y(x, 0) = a \sin kx = a \sin (kx + 2n\pi)$

$= a \sin k \left(x + \dfrac{2n\pi}{k}\right)$

$\Rightarrow$ The displacement at points x and $\left(x + \dfrac{2n\pi}{k}\right)$

are the same where, $n = 1, 2, 3, \ldots$

5. Two pulses having equal and opposite displacements moving in opposite directions overlap at $t = t_1$s. The resultant displacement of the wave at $t = t_1$s is
   (a) twice the displacement of each pulse
   (b) half the displacement of each pulse
   (c) zero
   (d) Either (a) or (c)

Sol. (c) The displacement due to two pulses will exactly cancel out each other. Thus, there will be no displacement throughout.

VERY SHORT ANSWER Type Questions

6. What is the quantity transmitted with propagation of longitudinal waves through a medium? [NCERT Exemplar]

Sol. Propagation of longitudinal waves through a medium leads to transmission of energy through the medium.

7. Is Newton's law of motion applicable for material waves? Is this applicable for electromagnetic waves?

Sol. Newton's laws of motion are applicable for material waves but not applicable for electromagnetic waves.

8. Does a vibrating source always produce sound?

Sol. A vibrating source produces sound when it vibrates in a medium and frequency of vibration lies within the audible range (20 Hz to 20 kHz).

9. How speed of sound waves in air varies with humidity? [NCERT Exemplar]

Sol. Speed of sound waves in air increases with increase in humidity. This is because, presence of moisture decreases the density of air.

10. The displacement of an elastic wave is given by the function $y = 3\sin\omega t + 4\cos\omega t$
    where, y is in cm and t is in second. Calculate the resultant amplitude. [NCERT Exemplar]

Sol. The resultant amplitude will be
$$y = \sqrt{y_1^2 + y_2^2} = \sqrt{9 + 16} = \sqrt{25} = 5\,\text{cm}$$

11. Sound waves of wavelength λ travelling in a medium with a speed of v m/s enter into another medium where, its speed is $2v$ m/s. Wavelength of sound waves in the second medium is [NCERT Exemplar]

Sol. Frequency in the first medium, $\nu = \dfrac{v}{\lambda}$

Frequency will remain same in the second medium, as the source.
$$\Rightarrow \quad v' = v \Rightarrow \frac{2v}{\lambda'} = \frac{v}{\lambda} \Rightarrow \lambda' = 2\lambda$$

SHORT ANSWER Type Questions

12. A steel wire has a length of 12 m and a mass of 2.10 kg. What will be the speed of a transverse wave on this wire when a tension of 2.06×10^4N is applied? [NCERT Exemplar]

Sol. $l = 12$ m, $M = 2.10$ kg, $T = 2.06 \times 10^4$N, $v = ?$
$$\mu = \frac{M}{l} = \frac{2.10}{12}\,\text{kg/m}$$
$$v = \sqrt{\frac{T}{\mu}} = \sqrt{\frac{2.06 \times 10^4}{2.10/12}}$$
$$= 3.43 \times 10^2\,\text{m/s}$$

13. A steel wire has a length of 12.0 m and a mass of 2.10 kg. What should be the tension in the wire so that speed of a transverse wave on the wire equals the speed of sound in dry air at $20°C = 343\,\text{ms}^{-1}$? [NCERT]

Sol. Given, $l = 12.0$ m, $M = 2.10$ kg, $T = ?$, $v = 343$ m/s
$$\mu = \text{mass per unit length}$$
$$= \frac{M}{l} = \frac{2.10}{12} = 0.175\,\text{kgm}^{-1}$$
As we know that, $v = \sqrt{\dfrac{T}{\mu}}$
$$\Rightarrow \qquad T = v^2\mu = (343)^2 \times (0.175)$$
$$\Rightarrow \qquad T = 2.06 \times 10^4\,\text{N}$$

14. A string of mass 2.5 kg is under a tension of 200 N. The length of the stretched string is 20.0 m. If the transverse jerk is struck at one end of the string, the disturbance will reach the other end in [NCERT Exemplar]

Sol. Here, $\mu = \dfrac{2.5}{20}\,\text{kg/m}$, $T = 200$ N
$$v = \sqrt{\frac{T}{\mu}} = \sqrt{\frac{200}{2.5/20}} = \sqrt{\frac{200 \times 20}{2.5}}$$
$$= \sqrt{\frac{4 \times 10^4}{25}} = \frac{2 \times 10^2}{5}$$
$$= \frac{20 \times 10}{5} = 40\,\text{m/s}$$
So, $\quad t = \dfrac{l}{v} = \dfrac{20}{40} = 0.50$ s

15. Equation of a plane progressive wave is given by $y = 0.6\sin 2\pi\left(t - \dfrac{x}{2}\right)$. On reflection from a denser medium, its amplitude becomes 2/3 of the amplitude of incident wave. What will be equation of reflected wave? [NCERT Exemplar]

Sol. On reflection from the denser medium, there will be a phase change of 180°.

Net amplitude $= \dfrac{2}{3} \times 0.6 = 0.4$

Hence, equation of reflected wave will be

$$y = 0.4 \sin 2\pi \left[t + \dfrac{x}{2} + \pi \right]$$

$$= -0.4 \sin 2\pi (t + x/2)$$

16. At what temperature (in °C) will the speed of sound in air be 3 times its value at 0°C?

[NCERT Exemplar]

Sol. We know that, speed, $v \propto \sqrt{T}$

By formula $v = \dfrac{\chi RT}{\rho}$

where, T is in kelvin.

$$\dfrac{v_t}{v_0} = \sqrt{\dfrac{273 + t}{273 + 0}} = 3$$

$$\Rightarrow \qquad \dfrac{273 + t}{273} = 9$$

$$\Rightarrow \qquad t = 9 \times 273 - 273$$

$$= 2184 °C$$

17. You have learnt that a travelling wave in one dimension is represented by a function $y = f(x,t)$ where, x and t must appear in the combination $x - vt$ or $x + vt$, i.e. $y = f(x \pm vt)$. Is the converse true? Examine if the following functions for y can possibly represent a travelling wave

(i) $(x - vt)^2$

(ii) $\log[(x + vt)/x_0]$

(iii) $1/(x + vt)$ **[NCERT Exemplar]**

Sol. Conceptual question based on fundamentals of characteristics of a travelling wave.

The converse is not true means if the function can be represented in the form $y = f(x \pm vt)$, it does not necessarily express a travelling wave. As the essential condition for a travelling wave is that the vibrating particle must have finite displacement value for all x and t.

(i) For $x = 0$,

If $t \to 0$, then $(x - vt)^2 \to 0$ which is finite, hence, it is a wave as it passes the two tests.

(ii) $\log\left(\dfrac{x + vt}{x_0} \right)$

At $x = 0$ and $t = 0$,

$$f(x,t) = \log\left(\dfrac{0 + 0}{x_0} \right)$$

$$= \log 0 \to \text{ not defined}$$

Hence, it is not a wave.

(iii) $\dfrac{1}{x + vt}$

For $x = 0, t = 0$, $f(x) \to \infty$

Though the function is of $(x \pm vt)$ type still at $x = 0$, it is infinite, hence, it is not a wave.

LONG ANSWER Type I Questions

18. Earthquakes generate sound waves inside the earth. Unlike a gas, the earth can experience both transverse (S) and longitudinal (P) sound waves. Typically the speed of S wave is about 4.0 kms^{-1} and that of P wave is 8.0 kms^{-1}. A seismograph records P and S waves from an earthquake. The first P wave arrives 4 min before the first S wave. Assuming the waves travel in straight line, at what distance does the earthquake occur? **[NCERT]**

Sol. Let v_1, v_2 be the velocities of S wave and P wave and t_1, t_2 be the time taken by these waves to reach the seismograph.

l = distance of occurrence of earthquake from the seismograph

$$v_1 t_1 = v_2 t_2$$

$$\Rightarrow \qquad v_1 = 4 \text{ km s}^{-1}, v_2 = 8 \text{ km s}^{-1}$$

$$\Rightarrow \qquad 4t_1 = 8t_2 \Rightarrow t_1 = 2t_2 \qquad \text{...(i)}$$

$$t_1 - t_2 = 4 \text{ min} = 240 \text{s} \qquad \text{...(ii)}$$

On solving Eqs. (i) and (ii), $t_2 = 240$s

$$\Rightarrow \qquad t_1 = 2t_2 = 2 \times 240 = 480 \text{s}$$

$$\Rightarrow \qquad l = v_1 t_1 = 4 \times 480 = 1920 \text{km}$$

19. A stone dropped from the top of a tower of height 300 m in high splashes into the water of a pond near the base of the tower. When is the splash heard at the top, given that the speed of sound in air is 340 ms^{-1}? (Take, $g = 9.8$ ms^{-2})

[NCERT]

Sol. Given, $h = 300$ m, $g = 9.8$ m/s^2, $v = 340$ ms^{-1}

t_1 = time taken by stone to strike the water surface

$$t_1 = \sqrt{\dfrac{2h}{g}} = \sqrt{\dfrac{300}{4.9}} = 7.82 \text{ s} \quad \left(\text{As } h = 0 + \dfrac{1}{2} g t_1^2 \right)$$

t_2 = time taken by the splash's sound to reach top of the tower

$$t_2 = \dfrac{h}{v} = \dfrac{300}{340} = 0.882 \qquad \left[\because v = \dfrac{h}{t_2} \right]$$

Total time, t = time to hear splash of sound

$$= t_1 + t_2 = 7.82 + 0.882 = 8.702$$

20. If c is rms speed of molecules in a gas and v is the speed of sound waves in the gas, show that c/v is constant and independent of temperature for all diatomic gases. **[NCERT Exemplar]**

Sol. From kinetic theory of gases,

$$p = \frac{1}{3}\rho c^2, \text{ where } c \text{ is rms speed of molecules of gas.}$$

$$\Rightarrow \qquad c = \sqrt{\frac{3p}{\rho}} \qquad \qquad ...(i)$$

$$v = \text{speed of sound in the gas} = \sqrt{\frac{\gamma p}{\rho}} \qquad ...(ii)$$

$\Rightarrow$ from Eqs. (i) and (ii),

$$\frac{c}{v} = \sqrt{\frac{3p}{\rho} \times \frac{\rho}{\gamma p}} = \sqrt{\frac{3}{\gamma}}$$

For diatomic gases, $\gamma = 1.4 = $ constant

$$\Rightarrow \qquad \frac{c}{v} = \sqrt{\frac{3}{1.4}} = 1.46 = \text{constant}]$$

21. One end of a long string of linear mass density $8.0 \times 10^{-3} \text{kg m}^{-1}$ is connected to an electrically driven tuning fork of frequency 256 Hz. The other end passes over a pulley and is tied to a pan containing a mass of 90 kg. The pulley end absorbs all the incoming energy so that reflected waves at the end have negligible amplitude. At $t = 0$, the left and (fork end) of the string $x = 0$ has zero transverse displacement ($y = 0$) and is moving along positive y-direction. The amplitude of the wave is 5.0 cm. Write down the transverse displacement y as function of x and t that describes the wave on the string.
[NCERT]

Sol. $v = 256 \text{ Hz}, T = m \times g, T = 90 \times 9.8 = 882 \text{ N}$

$$\mu = \frac{m}{L} = 8.0 \times 10^{-3} \text{ kgm}^{-1}$$

Amplitude, $a = 5 \text{ cm} = 0.05 \text{ m}$
Velocity of the transverse wave

$$\Rightarrow \qquad v = \sqrt{\frac{T}{\mu}} = \sqrt{\frac{882}{8 \times 10^{-3}}} = 3.32 \times 10^2 \text{ m/s}$$

$$\omega = 2\pi v = 2 \times 3.14 \times 256$$
$$= 1.61 \times 10^3 \text{ rad/s}$$

$$\lambda = \frac{v}{v} = \frac{3.32 \times 10^2}{256}$$

$$k = \frac{2\pi}{\lambda} = \frac{2 \times 3.14 \times 256}{3.32 \times 10^2} = 4.84 \text{ m}^{-1}$$

As wave propagating along positive X-axis
$$Y = a \sin(\omega t - kx)$$
$$= 0.05 \sin(1.61 \times 10^3 t - 4.84 x)$$

Here x, y are in metre and t is in second.

22. For the wave $y(x, t) = 3.0 \sin(36t + 0.018x + \pi/4)$, plot the displacement (y) versus (t) graph for $x = 0, 2$ and 4 cm. What are the shapes of these graphs? In which aspects does the oscillatory motion in travelling wave differ from one point to another amplitude, frequency or phase?
[NCERT]

Sol. The transverse harmonic wave is

$$y(x, t) = 3.0 \sin\left[36t + 0.018x + \frac{\pi}{4}\right]$$

It is the equation of travelling wave along negative direction of x.
For $\qquad x = 0, \qquad \qquad ...(i)$
$$y(x, t) = 3.0 \sin[36t + \pi/4]$$
Here, $\qquad \omega = \frac{2\pi}{T} = 36, \quad T = \frac{2\pi}{36} = \frac{\pi}{18} \text{ s}$

For different values of t, we calculate y using Eq. (i). These values are tabulated below

t	0	T/8	2T/8	3T/8	4T/8	5T/8	6T/8	7 T/8	T
y	$3/\sqrt{2}$	3	$3/\sqrt{2}$	0	$-3/\sqrt{2}$	-3	$-3/\sqrt{2}$	0	$3/\sqrt{2}$

On plotting y versus t graph, we obtain a sinusoidal curve as shown in figure below.

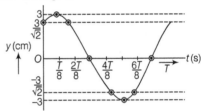

Similar graphs are obtained for $x = 2$ cm and $x = 4$ cm.
The oscillatory motion in travelling wave differs from one point to another only in terms of phase. Amplitude and frequency of oscillatory motion remain the same in all the three cases.

23. A transverse harmonic wave on a string is described by $y(x, t) = 3.0 \sin(36t + 0.018x + \pi/4)$ Where, x and y are in cm and t in seconds. The positive direction of x is from left to right.

  (i) Is this a travelling wave or a stationary wave? If it is travelling, what are the speed and direction of its propagation?
  (ii) What are its amplitude and frequency?
  (iii) What is the initial phase at the origin?
  (iv) What is the least distance between two successive crests in the wave? **[NCERT]**

Sol. Given equation is $y(x, t) = 3.0 \sin(36t + 0.018x + \pi/4)$
Comparing with standard equation
$$y(x, t) = a \sin(\omega t + kx + \phi)$$

(i) The given equation represents a transverse harmonic wave travelling from right to left (i.e. along negative x-axis). It is not a stationary wave.

By comparing, we get $\omega = 36$ rad/s, $k = 0.018$/cm

$\therefore$ Speed of wave, $v = \dfrac{\omega}{k} = \dfrac{36}{0.018} = 2000$ cm/s

(ii) By comparing amplitude, $a = 3$ cm

$\Rightarrow$ $\qquad 2\pi v = 36$

$\Rightarrow$ $\qquad v = \dfrac{36}{2\pi} = 5.73$ Hz

(iii) Initial phase, $\phi = \dfrac{\pi}{4}$

(iv) $\omega = 36$, $k = \dfrac{2\pi}{\lambda} = 0.018$

$\Rightarrow$ $\lambda =$ least distance $= \dfrac{2\pi}{k} = \dfrac{2\pi}{0.018}$ cm

$\qquad\qquad\qquad = 349.1$ cm

24. A source of frequency 250Hz produces sound waves of wavelength 1.32 m in a gas at STP. Calculate the change in the wavelength, when temperature of the gas is 40°C

Sol. We have, $v_0 = 250$ Hz, $T_0 = 273$ K

$\qquad T_1 = 273 + 40 = 313$ K; $\lambda_0 = 1.32$ m

$\therefore$ Speed of sound, $v_0 = v_0 \cdot \lambda_0 = 250 \times 1.32 = 330$ m/s

As we know that,

Speed of sound, $v \propto \sqrt{T}$

Thus, $\qquad \dfrac{v_1}{v_0} = \sqrt{\dfrac{T_1}{T_0}}$

$\qquad v_1 = v_0 \sqrt{\dfrac{T_1}{T_0}} = 330 \sqrt{\dfrac{313}{273}} = 353.34$ m/s

$\because \qquad v_1 = v_0 \lambda_1$

$\qquad \lambda_1 = \dfrac{353.34}{250} = 1.41$ m

$\therefore$ Change in the wavelength,

$\qquad \Delta\lambda = \lambda_1 - \lambda_0 = 1.41 - 1.32 = 0.09$ m

LONG ANSWER Type II Questions

25. The earth has a radius of 6400 km. The inner core of 1000 km radius is solid. Outside it, there is a region from 1000 km to a radius of 3500 km which is in molten state. Then, again from 3500 km to 6400 km the earth is solid. Only longitudinal (P) waves can travel inside a liquid. Assume that the P wave has a speed of 8 kms^{-1} in solid parts and of 5 kms^{-1} in liquid parts of the earth. An earthquake occurs at some place close to the surface of the earth. Calculate the time after

which it will be recorded in a seismometer at a diametrically opposite point on the earth if wave travels along diameter? **[NCERT Exemplar]**

Sol. Consider the diagram shown below

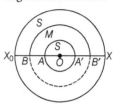

The wave is travelling along the diameter $X_0 X$.

(i) $x_1 =$ distance through solid portion

$\qquad = X_0 B + AA' + B'X$

$\qquad = (2900 + 2 \times 1000 + 2900)$ km $= 7800$ km

(ii) $x_2 =$ distance through molten portion

$\qquad = BA + A'B' = (2500 + 2500)$ km $= 5000$ km

Now, $v_1 = 8$ km/s, $v_2 = 5$ km/s, $t =$ total time

$$\left[\text{Time} = \dfrac{\text{Distance}}{\text{Speed}}, t = \dfrac{x}{v} \right]$$

$= t_1 + t_2 = \dfrac{x_1}{v_1} + \dfrac{x_2}{v_2} = \dfrac{7800}{8} + \dfrac{5000}{5}$

$t = 975 + 1000 = 1975$ s $= 32$ minutes 55 seconds

26. In the given progressive wave,

$$y = 5 \sin(100\pi t - 0.4\pi x)$$

where, y and x are in m, t is in seconds. What is the

(i) amplitude, (ii) wavelength,

(iii) frequency, (iv) wave velocity,

(v) particle velocity amplitude? **[NCERT Exemplar]**

Sol. Comparing with the standard form of equation

$\qquad y = a \sin[\omega t - kx]$

(i) Amplitude, $a = 5$ m

(ii) $\omega = \dfrac{2\pi}{T} = 100\pi$

$\qquad k = \dfrac{2\pi}{\lambda} = 0.4\pi \Rightarrow \lambda = \dfrac{2}{0.4} = \dfrac{20}{4} = 5$ m

(iii) $\omega = 2\pi v = 100\pi \Rightarrow v = 50$ Hz

(iv) Wave velocity, $v = v\lambda = 50 \times 5 = 250$ m/s

(v) Particle velocity $= \dfrac{dy}{dt} = a\omega \cos(\omega t - kx)$

$\qquad \left(\dfrac{dy}{dt}\right)_{max} = a\omega = 5 \times 100\pi = 500\pi$ m/s

27. Use the formula, $v = \sqrt{\dfrac{\gamma p}{\rho}}$ to explain, why the speed of sound in air

(i) is independent on pressure,

(ii) increases with temperature,

(iii) increases with humidity. **[NCERT]**

Sol. (i) Effect of pressure

v = speed of sound in a gas = $\sqrt{\dfrac{\gamma p}{\rho}}$

p = pressure, ρ = density, $\dfrac{M}{V}$ $\Rightarrow$ $v = \sqrt{\dfrac{\gamma pV}{M}}$

When T is constant, pV = constant $\Rightarrow$ v = constant

Hence, velocity of sound is independent of the change in pressure of the gas provided temperature remains constant.

(ii) Formula for velocity, $v = \sqrt{\dfrac{\gamma p}{\rho}}$

According to standard gas equation,

$$pV = RT$$

$$\Rightarrow \qquad p = \frac{RT}{V}$$

$$\Rightarrow \qquad v = \sqrt{\frac{\gamma \times RT}{pV}} = \sqrt{\frac{\gamma RT}{M}}$$

Where, $M = pV$ = molecular weight of the gas

$$\Rightarrow \qquad v \propto \sqrt{T}$$

Hence, v increases with temperature.

(iii) Due to presence of water vapours in air density changes. Hence, velocity of sound changes with humidity.

Let ρ_m = density of moist, ρ_d = density of dry air

v_m = velocity of sound in moist air

v_d = velocity of sound in dry air

$$v_m = \sqrt{\frac{\gamma p}{\rho_m}}, v_d = \sqrt{\frac{\gamma p}{\rho_d}}$$

$$\frac{v_m}{v_d} = \sqrt{\frac{\rho_d}{\rho_m}} \text{ as } \rho_d > \rho_m \Rightarrow v_m > v_d$$

28. For the harmonic travelling wave
$y = 2\cos 2\pi(10t - 0.0080x + 3.5)$
where, x and y are in cm and t is in second.
What is the phase difference between the oscillatory motion at two points separated by a distance of

(i) 4 m (ii) 0.5 m (iii) $\dfrac{\lambda}{2}$

(iv) $\dfrac{3\lambda}{4}$ (at a given instant in time)?

(v) What is the phase difference between the oscillation of a particle located at $x = 100$ cm, at $t = T$ s and $t = 5$ s? **[NCERT Exemplar]**

Sol. Given equation is $y = 2\cos 2\pi(10t - 0.008x + 3.5)$

Comparing with standard equation,

$$y = a\cos(\omega t - kx + \phi)$$

$$a = 2 \text{ cm}, \omega = \frac{2\pi}{T} = 20\pi, \ T = 0.1 \text{ s}$$

$$k = \frac{2\pi}{\lambda} = 0.008 \times 2\pi$$

$$\Rightarrow \qquad \lambda = \frac{2\pi}{2\pi \times 0.008} = 1.25 \text{ m}$$

$$\phi = 2\pi \times 3.5 = 7\pi \text{ rad}$$

(i) $\phi_1 = \dfrac{2\pi}{\lambda} \times 4 = \dfrac{2\pi}{1.25} \times 4 = 6.4\pi$ rad

(ii) $\phi_2 = \dfrac{2\pi}{\lambda} \times x = \dfrac{2\pi}{1.25} \times 0.5 = 0.8\pi$ rad

(iii) When $x = \lambda/2$

$$\phi_3 = \frac{2\pi}{\lambda} \times \lambda/2 = \pi \text{ rad}$$

(iv) When $x = \dfrac{3\lambda}{4}$; $\phi_4 = \dfrac{2\pi}{\lambda} \times \dfrac{3\lambda}{4} = \dfrac{3\pi}{2}$ rad

(v) At $t = T$; $\phi = \dfrac{2\pi}{T} = \dfrac{2\pi}{0.1} = 20\pi$ rad

and at $t = 5$s; $\phi' = \dfrac{2\pi}{0.1} \times 5.100\pi$ rad

$\therefore$ Phase difference $\phi' - \phi = 100\pi - 20\pi = 80\pi$ rad

29. A travelling harmonic wave on a string is described by $y(x,t) = 7.5\sin(0.0050x + 12t + \pi/4)$.

(i) What are the displacement and velocity of oscillation of a point at $x = 1$ cm, and $t = 1$ s? Is this velocity equal to the velocity of wave propagation?

(ii) Locate the points of the string which have the same transverse displacements and velocity as the $x = 1$ cm point at $t = 2$ s, 5 s and 11 s. **[NCERT]**

Sol. The travelling harmonic wave is

$$y(x, t) = 7.5\sin(0.0050x + 12t + \pi/4)$$

At $x = 1$ cm and $t = 1$ s

$$y(1, 1) = 7.5\sin(0.005 \times 1 + 12 \times 1 + \pi/4)$$
$$= 7.5\sin(12.005 + \pi/4) \qquad \text{...(i)}$$

Now, $\theta = (12.005 + \pi/4)$ rad

$$= \frac{180}{\pi}(12.005 + \pi/4) \text{ degree}$$

$$= \frac{12.79 \times 180}{22/7} = 732.55°$$

$\therefore$ From Eq. (i), $y(1, 1) = 7.5\sin(732.55°)$

$$= 7.5\sin(720 + 12.55°)$$
$$= 7.5\sin 12.55° \text{ cm}$$
$$= 7.5 \times 0.2173 = 1.63 \text{ cm}$$

Velocity of oscillation,

$$v = \frac{d}{dt}\{y(1, 1)\}$$

$$= \frac{d}{dt}\left[7.5\sin\left(0.005x + 12t + \frac{\pi}{4}\right)\right]$$

$$= 7.5 \times 12\cos\left[0.005x + 12t + \frac{\pi}{4}\right]$$

(i) At, $x = 1$ cm, $t = 1$ s

$v = 7.5 \times 12 \cos(0.005 + 12 + \pi/4)$

$= 90 \cos(732.55°) = 90 \cos(720 + 12.55)$

$v = 90 \cos(12.55°) = 90 \times 0.9765 = 87.89$ cm/s

Comparing the given equations with the standard form

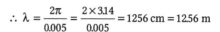

$\Rightarrow y(x, t) = a \sin(kx + \omega t + \phi)$

We get, $a = 7.5$ cm, $\omega = 12$, $2\pi v = 12$ or

$v = \dfrac{6}{\pi}$

$\dfrac{2\pi}{\lambda} = 0.005$

$\therefore \lambda = \dfrac{2\pi}{0.005} = \dfrac{2 \times 3.14}{0.005} = 1256$ cm $= 12.56$ m

Velocity of wave propagation,

$v = v\lambda = \dfrac{6}{\pi} \times 12.56$ m/s $= 24$ m/s

We find that velocity at $x = 1$ cm, $t = 1$ s is **not equal to velocity of wave propagation**.

(ii) Now, all points which are at a distance of $\pm\lambda, \pm 2\lambda, \pm 3\lambda$ from $x = 1$ cm will have same transverse displacement and velocity. As $\lambda = 12.56$ m, therefore, all points at distances ± 12.6 m, ± 25.2 m, ± 37.8 m from $x = 1$ cm will have same displacement and velocity, as $x = 1$ cm point at $t = 2$ s, 5 s and 11 s.

ASSESS YOUR TOPICAL UNDERSTANDING

OBJECTIVE Type Questions

1. The wave generated from up and down jerk given to the string or by up and down motion of the piston at end of the pipe is
   - (a) transverse
   - (b) longitudinal
   - (c) Both (a) and (b)
   - (d) electromagnetic wave

2. With propagation of longitudinal waves through a medium, the quantity transmitted is [NCERT Exemplar]
   - (a) matter
   - (b) energy
   - (c) energy and matter
   - (d) energy, matter and momentum

3. Speed of sound wave in air [NCERT Exemplar]
   - (a) is undependent of temperature
   - (b) increases with pressure
   - (c) increases with increase in humidity
   - (d) decreases with increase in humidity

4. Equation of progressive wave is

   $y = a \sin\left(10\pi x + 11\pi t + \dfrac{\pi}{3}\right)$

   The wavelength of the wave is
   - (a) 0.2 unit
   - (b) 0.1 unit
   - (c) 0.5 unit
   - (d) 1 unit

5. Two sine waves travel in the same direction in a medium. The amplitude of each wave is A and the phase difference between the two waves is $120°$. The resultant amplitude will be
   - (a) A
   - (b) $2A$
   - (c) $4A$
   - (d) $\sqrt{2}A$

Answer

1. (c) | 2. (b) | 3. (c) | 4. (a) | 5. (a)

VERY SHORT ANSWER Type Questions

6. A wave pulse is described by $y(x,t) = ae^{-(bx-at)^2}$ where a, b and c are positive constants. What is the speed of this wave? [Ans. c/b]

7. The density of oxygen is 16 times the density of hydrogen. What is the relation between the speed of sound in two gases? [Ans. $V_{H_2} = 4 V_{O_2}$]

8. The velocity of sound in a tube containing air at $27°C$ and a pressure of 76 cm of mercury is 330 m/s. What will it be when pressure is increased to 100 cm of mercury and the temperature is kept constant? [Ans. will remain same]

9. The ratio of the amplitudes of two waves are $3 : 4$. What is the ratio of the intensities of two waves? [Ans. $9 : 16$]

SHORT ANSWER Type Questions
|2 Marks|

10. Write expression for the intensity related with a string through which a wave is passing.

11. If the speed of a transverse wave on a stretched string of length 1 m is 60 m/s. What is the fundamental frequency of vibration? [Ans. 30 Hz]

12. The equation of a wave travelling on a string stretched along the x-axis is given by

    $$Y = ke^{-\left(\frac{x}{b} + \frac{t}{T}\right)^2}$$

    where, is the maximum of the pulse located at $t = T$? At $t = 2T$? [Ans. $x = -b$ and $x = -2b$]

LONG ANSWER Type I Questions

13. Two identical sinusoidal waves travel along a stretched string in the positive direction of x-axis. Show graphically resultant wave formed due to their superposition when phase difference between them is (i) 0   (ii) π.

14. Write condition for constructive and destructive interferences.

15. A certain 120 Hz wave on a string has an amplitude of 0.160 mm. How much energy exists in an 80 g length of the string?   [**Ans.** 0.58 mJ]

16. A travelling wave pulse is given by $y = \dfrac{10}{5 + (x + 2t)^2}$

    Here, x and y are in metre and t in second. In which direction and with what velocity is the pulse propagating? What is the amplitude of pulse?

    [**Ans.** velocity = 2 m/s; amplitude = 2 m; along negative X-axis]

LONG ANSWER Type II Questions

17. A transverse wave of amplitude 0.5 mm and frequency 100 Hz is produced on a wire stretched to a tension of 100 N. If the wave speed is 100 m/s. What average power is the source transmitting to the wire?   [**Ans.** 49 mm]

18. Discuss Newton's formula for the velocity of longitudinal waves in air. What correction was applied by Laplace and why?

19. Find condition for constructive interference of sound wave in terms of phase difference.

20. A wire of variable mass per unit length $\mu = \mu_0 \, y$ is hanging from the ceiling as shown in figure. The length of wire is l_0. A small transverse disturbance is produced at its lower end. Find the time after which the disturbance will reach to the other end.

    $$\left[\textbf{Ans. } \sqrt{\dfrac{8l_0}{g}}\right]$$

21. The figure shows a snap photograph of a vibrating string at $t = 0$. The particle P is observed moving up with velocity $20\sqrt{3}$ cm/s. The tangent at P makes an angle 60° with x-axis

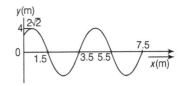

(i) Find the direction in which the wave is moving.

(ii) Write the equation of the wave.

(iii) The total energy carried by the wave per cycle of the string. Assuming that the mass per unit length = 50 g/m of the string.

[**Ans.** (i) Negative x. (ii) $Y = (0.4 \text{ cm})$

$$\sin\left(10\pi t + \frac{\pi}{2}x + \frac{\pi}{4}\right), \text{(iii)} 1.6 \times 10^{-5} \text{ J}]$$

|TOPIC 2|
Stationary Waves and Doppler's Effect

REFLECTION OF WAVES

If a pulse or wave meets a rigid boundary, they get reflected e.g. echo. If the boundary is not completely rigid, a part of the incident wave is reflected and a part is transmitted into the second medium.

If a wave is incident obliquely on the boundary between two different media, the transmitted wave is called the **refracted wave**. The incident and refracted waves obey Snell's law of refraction and incident and reflected waves obey usual laws of reflection.

Reflection of a pulse meeting a rigid boundary is shown in the figure below

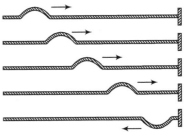

Reflection of pulse meeting a rigid boundary

In the above diagram, the travelling pulse is moving towards the non-absorptive wall (i.e. there is no absorption of energy at the boundary). As the displacement of connecting point at the boundary must be zero, hence by the principle of superposition, the reflected wave must have equal amplitude as well as phase difference of π.

If boundary point is completely free to move, the reflected pulse has the same phase and amplitude as the incident pulse. The net maximum displacement at the boundary will be twice of amplitude of each pulse.

Let the incident travelling wave is

$$y(x, t) = a \sin (kx - \omega t)$$

At the rigid boundary, the reflected wave is given by

$$y_r (x, t) = a \sin (kx - \omega t + \pi)$$
$$= - a \sin (kx - \omega t)$$

At an open boundary, the reflected wave is given by

$$y_r (x, t) = a \sin (kx - \omega t + 0)$$
$$= a \sin (kx - \omega t)$$

At the rigid boundary, $y' = y + y_r = 0$ at all times.

STANDING WAVES AND NORMAL MODES

Standing Waves

A new set of waves formed when two sets of progressive wave trains of the same type, i.e. both transverse or both longitudinal having the same amplitude and same time period/frequency/wavelength and travelling with same speed along the same straight line in opposite directions superimpose are called **standing waves** or **stationary waves**.

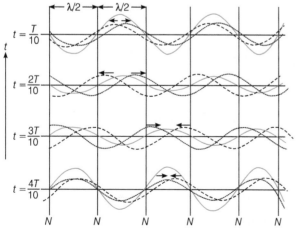

Stationary waves arising from superposition of two harmonic waves travelling in opposite directions

The resultant waves do not propagate in any direction, there is no transfer of energy in the medium.

When we are considering reflections at two or more boundaries (a string fixed at both ends or an air column in a pipe with both ends closed) here due to interference between incident and reflected wave, a steady wave pattern will set up on the string. Such wave patterns are called **standing waves** or **stationary waves**.

Now, consider wave equations

$y_1 (x, t) = a \sin (kx - \omega t)$ (for wave along +ve X-axis)

$y_2 (x, t) = a \sin (kx + \omega t)$ (for wave along −ve X-axis)

Resultant wave, $y(x, t) = y_1 (x, t) + y_2 (x, t)$
$$= a [\sin (kx - \omega t) + \sin (kx + \omega t)]$$

$$\boxed{\text{Net resultant wave, } y(t) = 2a \sin kx \cos \omega t}$$

Here, the amplitude of the standing/stationary wave is $2a \sin kx$.

Thus, in this wave pattern, the amplitude varies from point to point, but each element of the string oscillates with the same angular frequency ω or time period and there is no phase difference.

As the wave pattern remains stationary, the amplitude is fixed at a given location but different at different locations.

Normal Modes

Points having zero amplitude (i.e. where, there is no motion are called **Nodes** and the points having largest amplitude are known as **Antinodes**.

The significant feature of stationary waves is that the system cannot oscillate with any arbitrary frequency, but is characterised by a set of natural frequencies or **normal modes** of oscillation.

Now, let us determine these normal modes for a stretched string fixed at both ends.

From above equation for **nodes,** the amplitude is zero for values of kx that give $\sin kx = 0$

$\sin kx = 0 \Rightarrow kx = n\pi; n = 0, 1, 2, 3, 4, \ldots$

$$\Rightarrow \boxed{\text{For nodes, } x = \frac{n\pi}{k}}$$

$$x = \frac{n\pi}{2\pi / \lambda} = \frac{n\lambda}{2}; n = 0, 1, 2, 3 \ldots$$

So, the first node is formed at $x = 0$. The second node is formed at $x = \frac{\lambda}{2}$ and so on.

Hence, distance between two successive nodes is $\frac{\lambda}{2}$.

For **antinodes**, the maximum value of amplitude is $2a$ which occurs for values of kx that give $|\sin kx| = 1$

$\Rightarrow \qquad kx = \left(n + \dfrac{1}{2}\right)\pi \; ; n = 0, 1, 2, 3\ldots$

$\Rightarrow \qquad \boxed{\text{For antinodes, } x = (2n + 1)\dfrac{\lambda}{4}}$

$\qquad n = 0, 1, 2, \ldots \left(\because k = \dfrac{2\pi}{\lambda}\right) \qquad \ldots(i)$

Thus, the amplitude of wave will be maximum at the position of string given by above equation. The first maximum amplitude will be at $x = \dfrac{\lambda}{4}$. The second maximum amplitude will be at $x = \dfrac{3\lambda}{4}$ and so on.

Hence, distance between two consecutive antinodes is $\dfrac{\lambda}{2}$.

EXAMPLE |1| Wave function

The two individual wave functions are
$y_1 = (5 \text{ cm}) \sin (4x - t)$ and $y_2 = (5 \text{ cm}) \sin (4x + t)$
where, x and y are in centimeters. Find out the maximum displacement of the motion at $x = 2.0$ cm. Also, find the positions of nodes and anti-nodes.

 As from the given equations, it is clear that these two waves are travelling in opposite direction, i.e. one is moving in $+x$-direction and other in $-x$-direction. If these two waves are summed, the resulting wave will be a stationary wave.

Sol. Given, $\qquad y_1 = (5 \text{ cm}) \sin (4x - t)$
$\qquad\qquad y_2 = (5 \text{ cm}) \sin (4x + t)$
The resulting wave
$\qquad y = (2A \sin kx) \cos \omega t$
Now, compare the given equation.
$\qquad y_1 = (5 \text{ cm}) \sin (4x - t)$ with $y_1 = A \sin (kx - \omega t)$.
$\qquad A = 5$ cm, $k = 4$ and $\omega = 1$ rad/s
$\qquad y = (2A \sin kx) \cos \omega t$
$\qquad y = (10 \sin 4x) \cos t$
The maximum displacement of the motion at position
$\qquad x = 2 \cdot 0$ cm
$\qquad y_{\max} = 10 \sin 4x \big|_{x = 2.0}$
$\qquad\qquad = 10 \sin (4 \times 2) = 10 \sin (8 \text{ rad})$
$\qquad y_{\max} = 9.89$ cm
The wavelength by using the relation between wavelength and wave number.
$\qquad k = \dfrac{2\pi}{\lambda} = 4$
$\Rightarrow \qquad \lambda = \dfrac{2\pi}{4} = \dfrac{\pi}{2}$ cm

The nodes and anti-nodes can be given as
$\qquad$ Nodes at $x = \dfrac{n\lambda}{2} = n \times \left(\dfrac{\pi}{4}\right)$ cm,
$\qquad$ where $n = 0, 1, 2, \ldots$
$\qquad$ Antinodes at $x = (2n+1)\dfrac{\lambda}{4} = (2n+1) \times \left(\dfrac{\pi}{8}\right)$ cm,
$\qquad$ where $n = 0, 1, 2, \ldots$

Vibration of String Fixed at Both Ends

Consider a stretched string having length L fixed at both ends. The one end be at $x = 0$ fixed while the other one at $x = L$. These are the boundary conditions.

As, $\qquad L = \dfrac{n\lambda}{2} ; n = 1, 2, 3\ldots$

$\Rightarrow$ Possible wavelengths of stationary waves are
$\qquad \lambda = \dfrac{2L}{n} ; n = 1, 2, 3\ldots$

and corresponding frequencies are

Frequency of the vibration, $\nu = \dfrac{nv}{2L}$ for $n = 1, 2, 3\ldots$

Here, v is the speed of the wave.

Modes of Vibration

The manner in which the string vibrates and give rise to a standing wave is known as **mode of vibration** of the string.

First Mode of Vibration

The mode of vibration in which string will vibrate in one segment or the lowest possible natural frequency (as shown in figure) is called **fundamental mode** or **first harmonic**.

As, $L = \dfrac{n\lambda}{2}$ for first harmonic, put $n = 1$ then,

$$L = \dfrac{\lambda_1}{2} \quad \text{and} \quad \nu = \dfrac{v}{2L}$$

Second Mode of Vibration

The mode of vibration in which string will vibrate in two segments (as shown in figure) is called **second harmonic** or **first overtone**. For the second harmonic, put $n = 2$ in

$L = \dfrac{n\lambda}{2}$

For this, $L = \lambda_2$ and $\nu_2 = \dfrac{2v}{2L}$ or $2\nu_1$

As, $\qquad\qquad \nu = \dfrac{nv}{2L}$

Third Mode of Vibration

If $n = 3$, the frequency , $\nu = \dfrac{3v}{2L}$ or $\nu = 3\nu_1$ is called **third harmonic** and so on.

Figure below shows the first four harmonics of a stretched string fixed at both ends.

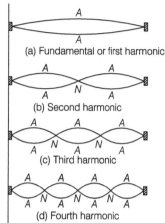

(a) Fundamental or first harmonic

(b) Second harmonic

(c) Third harmonic

(d) Fourth harmonic

The vibration of a string will be a superposition of different modes. Some modes may be strongly excited and some less.

Note Musical instruments like sitar or violin are based on this principle. Where the string is plucked or bowed, determines which modes are more prominent than others.

EXAMPLE |2| **Let's Play the Guitar**

A guitar string is 100 cm long and has a fundamental frequency of 125 Hz. Where should it be pressed to produce a fundamental frequency of 200 Hz ?

Sol. Fundamental frequency of a string fixed at both end is

$$\nu = \frac{v}{2L}$$

$$\nu = \frac{1}{2L}\sqrt{\frac{T}{\mu}} \qquad \left[\because v = \sqrt{\frac{T}{\mu}}\right]$$

As T and μ are fixed

$$\frac{\nu_1}{\nu_2} = \frac{L_2}{L_1} \Rightarrow L_2 = \frac{\nu_1}{\nu_2}L_1$$

$$\Rightarrow \qquad L_2 = \frac{125\,\text{Hz}}{200\,\text{Hz}} \times 100 = \frac{125}{2} = 62.5\,\text{cm}$$

Vibration of a String Fixed at one End

Standing waves can also be produced on a string which is fixed at one end and whose other end is free to move in a transverse direction. Here, in this case, we will have antinode at the free end and node at the fixed end.

Now, consider the equation of standing wave

$$y\,(x,t) = 2a\sin kx\cos\omega t$$

As we are having antinode at the end, $x = L$

$$\Rightarrow \qquad \sin kL = \pm 1$$

$$kL = (2n+1)\frac{\pi}{2}, \quad \text{where } n = 0, 1, 2, \ldots$$

$$\Rightarrow \quad \frac{2\pi}{\lambda} \times L = (2n+1)\frac{\pi}{2} \Rightarrow \frac{2L}{\lambda} = (2n+1)\times\frac{1}{2}$$

$$\Rightarrow \qquad \frac{2L\nu}{v} = (2n+1)\frac{1}{2}$$

$$\boxed{\text{Frequency of the vibration, } \nu = \frac{(2n+1)}{4L}v}$$

where, $n = 0, 1, 2$

where, ν is frequency and v is the speed of the wave.

The above frequencies are the normal frequencies of vibration. The fundamental frequency is obtained when $n = 0$.

$$\nu_0 = \frac{v}{4L} \qquad\qquad \text{[first harmonic]}$$

The overtone frequencies are

$$\nu_1 = \frac{3v}{4L} = 3\nu_0 \qquad\qquad \text{[third harmonic]}$$

$$\nu_2 = \frac{5v}{4L} = 5\nu_0 \qquad\qquad \text{[fifth harmonic]}$$

$$\nu_3 = \frac{7v}{4L} = 7\nu_0 \qquad\qquad \text{[seventh harmonic]}$$

$$\nu_0 : \nu_1 : \nu_2 : \nu_3 \ldots = 1 : 3 : 5 : 7 : \ldots$$

Here, we see that only odd harmonics are present. (i.e. contains odd multiples of the fundamental frequency)

The figure below shows shapes of the string.

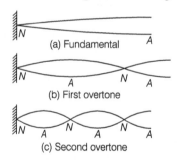

(a) Fundamental

(b) First overtone

(c) Second overtone

Laws of Transverse Vibration of String

- For a given string under a tension (T), the frequency of the vibrating string is inversely proportional to the vibrating length (L) of the string.
  i.e. $\nu \propto \dfrac{1}{L}$

- The frequency of the uniform string of given length is proportional to square root of tension (T) in the string
  i.e. $\nu \propto \sqrt{T}$

- For a given vibrating length and tension of the string, the frequency of the vibrating string is inversely proportional to the square root of the mass per unit length of the string.
  i.e. $\nu \propto \dfrac{1}{\sqrt{\mu}}$

- The fundamental frequency of a vibrating string is determined by a device known as sonometer.

- The laws of vibration of a string are also verified by using sonometer.

EXAMPLE |3| Fundamental Frequency

A 50 cm long wire of mass 20 g supports a mass of 1.6 kg as shown in figure. Find the fundamental frequency of the portion of the string between the wall and the pulley. Take, $g = 10 \text{ m/s}^2$.

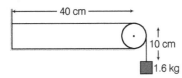

Sol. Here, mass/length; $m = \dfrac{20 \times 10^{-3}}{50/100} = 0.04 \text{ kg/m}$

$$T = 1.6 \text{ kg} = 1.6 \times 10 \text{ N} = 16 \text{ N}$$

Length that vibrates, $L = 50 - 10 = 40 \text{ cm} = 0.4 \text{ m}$

$$\therefore \ v = \frac{1}{2L}\sqrt{\frac{T}{m}} = \frac{1}{2 \times 0.04}\sqrt{\frac{16}{0.04}} = \frac{20}{0.8} = 25 \text{ Hz}$$

EXAMPLE |4| Identical Wires

Two identical wires of length L and $2L$ vibrate with fundamental frequencies 100 Hz and 150 Hz, respectively. What is the ratio of their tensions?

Sol. Let, $\mu_1 = \mu_2 = \mu$

$$v_1 = 100 = \frac{1}{2L}\sqrt{\frac{T_1}{\mu}}$$

$$v_2 = 150 = \frac{1}{2(2L)}\sqrt{\frac{T_2}{\mu}}$$

$$\frac{v_1}{v_2} = \frac{100}{150} = 2\sqrt{\frac{T_1}{T_2}}$$

$$\frac{T_1}{T_2} = \left(\frac{1}{3}\right)^2 = \frac{1}{9}$$

$$T_2 = 9\, T_1$$

VIBRATIONS OF AIR COLUMN

The vibrating air column in organ pipes is a common example of stationary waves. An organ pipe is a cylindrical tube which may be closed at one end (closed organ pipe) or open at both ends (open organ pipe).

If the air in pipe at its open end is made to vibrate, longitudinal wave is produced. This wave travels along the pipe towards its far end and is reflected back. Thus, due to superposition of **incident** and **reflected waves**, stationary waves are formed in pipe.

Closed Organ Pipe

Now, consider normal modes of oscillation of an air column with one end closed and the other open (i.e. closed organ pipe). A glass tube partially filled with water illustrates this system. The end in contact with water is a node having maximum pressure change, while the open end is an antinode having least pressure change.

If we are taking the end in contact with water to be $x = 0$, the other end, $x = L$ is an antinode.

In this case, we will have

$$|\sin kx| = 1 \ \Rightarrow \ |\sin kL| = 1$$

$$\Rightarrow \qquad kL = \left(n + \frac{1}{2}\right)\pi$$

$$\Rightarrow \qquad L = (2n+1)\frac{\lambda}{4}; \ n = 0, 1, 2, 3, \dots \left[\because k = \frac{2\pi}{\lambda}\right]$$

$$\Rightarrow \qquad \boxed{\text{Frequency, } v = (2n+1)\frac{v}{4L};} \ n = 0, 1, 2, 3, \dots$$

For fundamental frequency, $n = 0$ and $v = \dfrac{v}{4L}$

The higher frequencies are odd harmonics i.e. $\dfrac{3v}{4L}, \dfrac{5v}{4L}$, etc.

Thus, in a closed end pipe, only odd harmonics are present.

Figure below shows odd harmonics of air column with one end closed and the other is open.

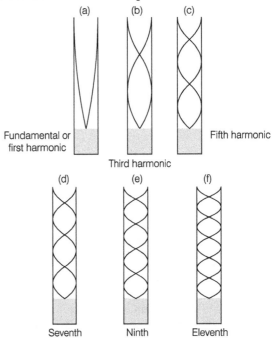

Note

- If the external frequency is close to one of the natural frequencies, the system is said to be in **resonance**.
- Normal modes of a circular membrane rigidly clamped to the circumference are determined by boundary condition that no point on the circumference of the membrane vibrates.
- The standing waves in closed organ pipe is similar to the standing wave on a string fixed at one end.

Open Organ Pipe

For a pipe opened at both ends, each (i.e. an open organ pipe) end is an antinode. It is then easily seen that an open air column at both ends generates all harmonics. The equation for the frequency will be same as that of string fixed at both ends.

$$\boxed{\text{Frequency, } v = \frac{nv}{2L}} \text{ for } n = 1, 2, 3, \dots$$

At both ends, antinodes will present and nodes will be alternate to antinodes.

The diagram is shown below

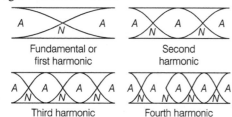

Fundamental or | Second
first harmonic | harmonic

Third harmonic | Fourth harmonic

For $n = 1$, $\quad v_1 = \dfrac{v}{2L}$

[fundamental frequency or first harmonic]

For $n = 2$, $\quad v_2 = \dfrac{v}{L} = 2v_1$

[second harmonic, first overtone]

For $n = 3$, $\quad v_3 = \dfrac{3v}{2L} = 3v_1$

[third harmonic, second overtone]

For $n = 4$, $\quad v_4 = \dfrac{4v}{2L} = 4v_0$

[fourth harmonic, third overtone]

$$v_1 : v_2 : v_3 : \dots = 1 : 2 : 3 : \dots$$

Note

- The sound produced by open organ pipe is more shriller than that produced by closed organ pipe.
- The quality of sound produced by an open organ pipe is better than produced by the closed organ pipe.
- The standing waves formed in open organ pipe is similar to standing waves formed on a string fixed at both ends.

EXAMPLE |5| Open and Closed Flute

A pipe 30.0 cm long is opened at both ends. Which harmonic mode of the pipe resonates with a 1.1 kHz source? Will resonance with the same source be observed, if one end of the pipe is closed? Take the speed of sound in air as 330 ms^{-1}. **[NCERT]**

Sol. Here, $L = 30.0$ cm $= 0.3$ m

Let nth harmonic of open pipe resonate with 1.1 kHz source,

i.e. $\qquad v_n = 1.1 \text{ kHz} = 1100 \text{ Hz}$

As, $\qquad v_n = \dfrac{nv}{2L}$

$\therefore \qquad n = \dfrac{2L v_n}{v} = \dfrac{2 \times 0.30 \times 1100}{330} = 2$

i.e. **2nd harmonic** resonates with open pipe.

If one end of pipe is closed, its fundamental frequency put $n = 0$ in $v = (2n + 1)\dfrac{v}{4L}$

$$v_1 = \frac{v}{4L} = \frac{330}{4 \times 0.3} = 275 \text{ Hz}$$

As odd harmonics alone are produced in a closed organ pipe, therefore, possible frequencies are $3 v_1 = 3 \times 275 = 825$ Hz, $5 v_1 = 5 \times 275 = 1375$ Hz and so on. As the source frequency is 1100 Hz, therefore, **no resonance** can occur when the pipe is closed at one end.

BEATS

This phenomenon arises from interference of waves having nearly same frequencies. The periodic variation in the intensity of sound wave caused by the superposition of two sound waves of nearly same frequencies and amplitude travelling in the same direction are called **beats**.

One rise and one fall in the intensity of sound constitutes **one beat** and the number of beats per second is called **beat frequency**.

The frequency of two sources or two waves should not differ by more than 10 Hz because, if it is more than 10 Hz, then it becomes difficult to distinguish between rise and fall in intensity of sound due to persistence of hearing.

Tuning the Instruments

Artists use the phenomenon of beat while tuning their instruments with each other. They go on tuning until their sensitive ears do not detect any beats. In this way, they match the frequencies of different instruments of the band.

Analytical Method of Beats

Let us consider two harmonic sound waves of nearly equal angular frequency ω_1 and ω_2 and suppose we are concerned with $y = 0$ only. Then, we can write the equations of waves as

$$y_1 = a \cos \omega_1 t \text{ and } y_2 = a \cos \omega_2 t$$

Here, we are considering sound wave hence, waves are represented by y_1, y_2 to show longitudinal displacement.

Now, by principle of superposition, the resultant displacement (y) is

$$y = y_1 + y_2 = a [\cos \omega_1 t + \cos \omega_2 t]$$
$$= 2a \cos \frac{(\omega_1 - \omega_2) t}{2} \cos \frac{(\omega_1 + \omega_2) t}{2}$$

$$= 2a \cos \omega_b t \cos \omega_a t$$

where, $\omega_b = \dfrac{\omega_1 - \omega_2}{2}$ and $\omega_a = \dfrac{\omega_1 + \omega_2}{2}$

Now, if we assume $|\omega_1 - \omega_2| < < \omega_1, \omega_2$ which means $\omega_a >> \omega_b$. This can be interpreted as the resultant wave is oscillating with the average angular frequency ω_a. The amplitude will be maximum when $|\cos \omega_b t|$ is 1.

Hence, the resultant wave, waxes and wanes with a frequency which is $2\omega_b = \omega_1 - \omega_2$.

Hence, beat frequency,

$$\boxed{\text{Beat frequency, } v_{\text{beat}} = v_1 - v_2.}$$

The figures below illustrate the phenomenon of beats for two harmonic waves of frequencies 11 Hz and 9 Hz. The amplitude of the resultant wave shows beats at a frequency of 2 Hz.

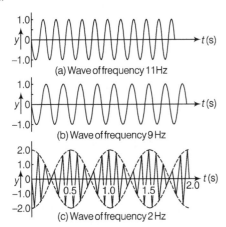

(a) Wave of frequency 11 Hz

(b) Wave of frequency 9 Hz

(c) Wave of frequency 2 Hz

Musical Pillars

Temples often have some pillars. The rock used produces basic notes.

Musical pillars are categorised into three types.

Shruti pillar It can produce the basic note 'swaras'.

Ganga Thoongal It produces the basic tunes which make up the 'ragas'.

Laya Thoongal It produces 'taal' (beats) when tapped.

EXAMPLE |6| An Amazing Sitar

Two sitar strings A and B playing the note 'Dha' are slightly out of tune and produce beats of frequency 5 Hz. The tension of string B is slightly increased and the beat frequency is found to decrease to 3 Hz. What is the original frequency of B, if the frequency of A is 427 Hz? [NCERT]

Sol. Here, frequency of $A = 427$ Hz

As number of beats/sec $(m) = 5$ Hz

$\therefore$ Possible frequencies of B are (427 ± 5) Hz = 432 Hz or 422 Hz.

When tension of B is increased, its frequency increases. Number of beats/s decreases to 3.

Therefore, m is negative.

Hence, original frequency of $B = 427 - 5 = 422$ Hz.

EXAMPLE |7| Identical Piano Strings

Consider the two identical piano strings, each tuned exactly to the 420 Hz. The tension in any one of the strings is increased by 2.0%. If they are now struck, what is the beat frequency between the fundamentals of the two strings? Take, length of the strings = 65 cm.

As the tension in one of the strings is changed, its fundamental frequency changes. Therefore, when both strings are played, they will have different frequencies and beats will be heard.

Sol. If v_1, v_1, T_1 and v_2, v_2, T_2 are the frequencies, velocity and tension in the first and second strings, respectively, then

$$\dfrac{v_2}{v_1} = \dfrac{v_2/2L}{v_1/2L} = \dfrac{v_2}{v_1} \quad \Rightarrow \quad \dfrac{v_2}{v_1} = \dfrac{\sqrt{T_2/\mu}}{\sqrt{T_1/\mu}} = \sqrt{\dfrac{T_2}{T_1}}$$

Given that the tension in one string is 2.0% larger than the other

i.e. $T_2 = T_1 + \dfrac{2}{100} T_1 = 1.02\, T_1$

The ratio of frequencies $\dfrac{v_2}{v_1} = \sqrt{\dfrac{1.02\, T_1}{T_1}} = 1.01$ Hz

Now, solve for the frequency of the tightened string.

$$v_2 = 1.01\, v_1 = 1.01 \times 420 = 424.2 \text{ Hz}$$
$$[\text{given, } v_1 = 420 \text{ Hz}]$$

Thus, the beat frequency,

$$v_{\text{beat}} = v_2 - v_1 = 424.2 - 420 = 4.2 \text{ Hz}$$

| TOPIC PRACTICE 2 |

OBJECTIVE Type Questions

1. A standing wave is generated on a string. Which of the following statement(s) is/are correct for the standing waves?
   (a) The amplitude of standing wave varies from point to point but each element of the string oscillates with the same angular frequency 'ω' or time period
   (b) The string as a whole vibrates in phase with differing amplitudes at different points
   (c) The wave pattern in neither moving to the right nor to the left
   (d) All of the above

Sol. (d) There is no phase difference between oscillations of different elements of the wave. However, the string as a whole vibrates in phase with different amplitudes at different points. Also, there is zero movement of the wave pattern. Hence, they are called standing or stationary waves.

2. Let a wave $y(x,t) = a \sin(kx - \omega t)$ is reflected from an open boundary and then the incident and reflected waves overlaps. Then the amplitude of resultant wave

(a) $2a \cos(kx)$ (b) $2a \sin(kx)$

(c) $2a \sin\left(\dfrac{kx}{2}\right)$ (d) $a \sin(kx)$

Sol. (b) We have incident wave $y_1 = a \sin(kx - \omega t)$

So the reflected wave is $y_2 = a \sin(kx + \omega t)$

From principle of superposition, the standing wave equation obtained after superimposing y_1 and y_2, we get

$$y(x, t) = 2a \sin kx \, \cos \omega t$$

Thus, the resultant amplitude is

$$A(x) = 2a \sin kx$$

3. At nodes in stationary waves

(a) change in pressure and density are maximum

(b) change in pressure and density are minimum

(c) strain is zero

(d) energy is maximum

Sol. (b) In stationary waves, all particles except nodes oscillate with same frequency but amplitude is zero at nodes and maximum at anti-nodes. Thus, change in pressure and density is minimum at nodes.

4. Following two wave trains are approaching each other.

$$y_1 = a \sin 2000 \, \pi t$$
$$y_2 = a \sin 2008 \, \pi t$$

The number of beats heard per second is

(a) 8   (b) 4

(c) 1   (d) zero

Sol. (b) Beat frequency $= f_2 - f_1 = \dfrac{\omega_2 - \omega_1}{2\pi}$

$$= \dfrac{2008\pi - 2000\pi}{2\pi} = 4 \text{ Hz}$$

VERY SHORT ANSWER Type Questions

5. Why should the difference between the frequencies be less than 10 to produce beats?

Sol. Human ear cannot identify any change in intensity is less than $\left(\dfrac{1}{10}\right)$th of a second. So, difference should be less than 10.

6. In a hot summer day, pitch of an organ pipe will be higher or lower?

Sol. The speed of sound in air is more at higher temperature, as $v \propto \sqrt{T}$. As we know, frequency $v = \dfrac{v}{\lambda}$ as v is more, hence, v will be more and accordingly pitch will be more.

7. Show that when a string fixed at its two ends vibrates in 1 loop, 2 loops, 3 loops and 4 loops, the frequencies are in the ratio $1:2:3:4$.

[NCERT Exemplar]

Sol. In case of a string fixed at two ends, when the string vibrates in n loops

$$v_n = \dfrac{n}{2l}\sqrt{\dfrac{T}{\mu}} \implies v_n \propto n$$

Hence, when the string vibrates in 1 loop, 2 loops, 3 loops, 4 loops, the frequencies are in the ratio $1:2:3:4$.

8 A hospital uses an ultrasonic scanner to locate tumours in a tissue. What is the wavelength of sound in the tissue in which the speed of sound is 1.7 kms^{-1}? The operating frequency of the scanner is 4.2 MHz. **[NCERT]**

Sol. $v = 1.7 \text{ km/s} = 1700 \text{ m/s}, v = 4.2 \text{ MHz} = 4.2 \times 10^6 \text{ Hz}$

$$\lambda = \dfrac{v}{v} = \dfrac{1700}{4.2 \times 10^6}$$

$$= 0.405 \times 10^{-3} \text{ m} = 0.405 \text{ mm}$$

$$\approx 4.1 \times 10^{-4} \text{ m}$$

9. When two waves of almost equal frequencies n_1 and n_2 reach at a point, simultaneously. What is the time interval between successive maxima?

[NCERT Exemplar]

Sol. Number of beats/s $= (n_1 - n_2)$

Hence, time interval between two successive beats = time interval between two successive maxima $= \dfrac{1}{n_1 - n_2}$

10. A sonometer wire is vibrating in resonance with a tuning fork. Keeping the tension applied same, the length of the wire is doubled. Under what conditions would the tuning fork still be in resonance with the wire? **[NCERT Exemplar]**

Sol. The sonometer frequency is given by

$$v = \dfrac{n}{2L}\sqrt{\dfrac{T}{\mu}}$$

Now, as it vibrates with length L, we assume $v = v_1$

$$n = n_1$$

$$\therefore \qquad v_1 = \dfrac{n_1}{2L}\sqrt{\dfrac{T}{\mu}} \qquad \qquad ...(i)$$

When length is doubled, then $v_2 = \dfrac{n_2}{2 \times 2L}\sqrt{\dfrac{T}{\mu}}$ ...(ii)

Dividing Eq. (i) by Eq. (ii), we get

$$\dfrac{v_1}{v_2} = \dfrac{n_1}{n_2} \times 2$$

To keep the resonance, $\dfrac{v_1}{v_2} = 1 = \dfrac{n_1}{n_2} \times 2$

$\Rightarrow \qquad n_2 = 2n_1$

Hence, when the wire is doubled, the number of loops also get doubled to produce the resonance. That is, it resonates in second harmonic.

SHORT ANSWER Type Questions

11. A metre-long tube open at one end, with a movable piston at the other end, shows resonance with a fixed frequency source (a tuning fork of frequency 340 Hz) when the tube length is 25.5 cm or 79.3 cm. Estimate the speed of sound in air at the temperature of the experiment. The edge effects may be neglected. **[NCERT]**

Sol. As, there is piston at one end, it behaves as a closed organ pipe. Hence, it will produce odd harmonics only. Hence, resonant frequencies will be first and third harmonic.

In the fundamental mode, $\dfrac{\lambda}{4} = 25.5$ cm

$\Rightarrow \qquad \lambda = 4 \times 25.5 = 102$ cm $= 1.02$ m

Speed of sound in air

$v = v\lambda = 340 \times (1.02) = 346.8$ m/s

12. A tuning fork A, marked 512 Hz, produces 5 beats per sec, where sounded with another unmarked tuning fork B. If B is loaded with wax, the number of beats is again 5 per sec. What is the frequency of the tuning fork B when not loaded? **[NCERT Exemplar]**

Sol. Frequency of A, $v_0 = 512$ Hz

Number of beats/s $= 5$

Frequency of $B = 512 \pm 5 = 517$ or 517 Hz

On loading its frequency decreases from 517 to 507, so that number of beats/s remain 5.

Hence, frequency of B when not loaded $= 517$ Hz.

13. A steel rod 100 cm long is clamped at its middle. The fundamental frequency of longitudinal vibrations of the rod are given to be 2.53 kHz. What is the speed of sound in steel? **[NCERT]**

Sol. Given, $L = 100$ cm $= 1$ m,

$v = 2.53$ kHz $= 2.53 \times 10^3$ Hz

As the given rod is clamped at middle, hence, there will be a node at the middle..

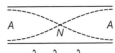

Hence, length, $L = \dfrac{\lambda}{4} + \dfrac{\lambda}{4} = \dfrac{\lambda}{2}$

$\Rightarrow \qquad \lambda = 2L = 2$ m

Speed, $v = v\lambda = 2.53 \times 10^3 \times 2$

$\qquad\qquad = 5.06 \times 10^3$ ms^{-1}

14. A pipe 20 cm long is closed at one end. Which harmonic mode of the pipe is resonantly excited by a source of 1237.5 Hz? (sound velocity in air $= 330$ ms^{-1}) **[NCERT Exemplar]**

Sol. Length of pipe $(l) = 20$ cm $= 20 \times 10^{-2}$ m

$$v_{funda} = \dfrac{v}{4L} = \dfrac{330}{4 \times 20 \times 10^{-2}}$$

$$v_{funda} = \dfrac{330 \times 100}{80} = 412.5 \text{ Hz}$$

$$\dfrac{v_{given}}{v_{funda}} = \dfrac{1237.5}{412.5} = 3$$

Hence, 3rd harmonic mode of the pipe is resonantly excited by the source of given frequency.

15. (i) For the wave on a string described by $Y = 0.06 \sin 2\pi/3x \cos(120\pi t)$, do all the points on the string oscillate with the same (a) frequency, (b) phase, (c) amplitude? Explain your answers.

(ii) What is the amplitude of a point 0.375 m away from one end? **[NCERT]**

Sol. (i) All the points except the nodes on the string have the same frequency and phase but not the same amplitude.

(ii) Given, $Y = 0.06 \sin \dfrac{2\pi}{3}x \cos(120\pi t)$

Putting $x = 0.375$ m

Amplitude, $Y = 0.06 \sin \dfrac{2\pi}{3} \times (0.375)$

$$= 0.06 \sin \dfrac{\pi}{4} = \dfrac{0.06}{\sqrt{2}} = 0.042 \text{ m}$$

16. A narrow sound pulse (e.g. a short pip by a whistle) is sent across a medium.

(i) Does the pulse have a definite (a) frequency, (b) wavelength, (c) speed of propagation?

(ii) If the pulse rate is 1 after every 20 s, (that is the whistle is blown for a split of second after every 20 s), is the frequency of the note produced by the whistle equal to 1/20 or 0.05 Hz? **[NCERT]**

Sol. (i) A short pip by a whistle
  (a) will not have a fixed frequency.
  (b) will not have fixed wavelength.
  (c) will have definite speed that will be equal to speed of sound in air.
  (ii) 0.05 Hz will be the frequency of repetition of the short pip.

17. A sitar wire is replaced by another wire of same length and material but of three times the earlier radius. If the tension in the wire remains the same, then by what factor will the frequency change? **[NCERT Exemplar]**

Sol. $v_1 = \dfrac{1}{l_1 D_1} \sqrt{\dfrac{T_1}{\pi \rho_1}}$

where, D = diameter of wire

$$v_2 = \frac{1}{l_2 D_2} \sqrt{\frac{T_2}{\pi \rho_2}}$$

$l_1 = l_2, \rho_2 = \rho_1$
$T_2 = T_1, D_2 = 3D_1$

$\Rightarrow \qquad v_2 = \dfrac{v_1}{3}$

New frequency is $\dfrac{1}{3}$rd of the original frequency.

18. Two sitar strings A and B playing the note 'Ga' are slightly out of tune and produce beats of frequency 6 Hz. The tension in the string A is slightly reduced and the beat frequency is found to reduce to 3 Hz. If the original frequency of A is 324 Hz, then what is the frequency of B? **[NCERT]**

💡 The difference in frequencies is the number of beats. If tension in the wire is increased, then the frequency is also increased and *vice-versa*.

Sol. Given, frequency of A, $f_A = 324$ Hz

Now, frequency of B, $f_B = f_A \pm$ beat frequency

$\qquad\qquad = 324 \pm 6$

or $\qquad\qquad f_B = 330$ or 318 Hz

Now, if tension in the string is slightly reduced, its frequency will also reduce from 324 Hz.

Now, if $f_B = 330$ and f_A reduces, then beat frequency should increase which is not the case but if $f_B = 318$ Hz and f_A decreases, the beat frequency should decrease, which is the case and hence, $f_B = 318$ Hz.

19. A wire stretched between two rigid supports vibrates in its fundamental mode with a frequency of 45 Hz. The mass of the wire is 3.5×10^{-2} kg and its linear mass density is 4.0×10^{-2} kgm^{-1}. What is (i) the speed of a transverse wave on the string and (ii) the tension in the string? **[NCERT]**

Sol. Here, given $v = 45$ Hz, $M = 3.5 \times 10^{-2}$ kg

$$\mu = \frac{\text{Mass}}{\text{Length}} = 4.0 \times 10^{-2} \text{ kgm}^{-1}$$

$$l = \frac{M}{\mu} = \frac{3.5 \times 10^{-2}}{4 \times 10^{-2}} = \frac{7}{8} \text{ m}$$

$$l = \frac{\lambda}{2} = \frac{7}{8} \Rightarrow \lambda = \frac{7}{4} \text{ m} = 1.75 \text{ m}$$

(i) Speed, $v = v \times \lambda = 45 \times 1.75 = 78.75$ m/s

(ii) As $v = \sqrt{\dfrac{T}{\mu}} \Rightarrow T = v^2 \times \mu$

$\Rightarrow T = (78.75)^2 \times 4 \times 10^{-2}$

$\Rightarrow T = 248.06$ N

20. A bat emits ultrasonic sound of frequency 1000 kHz in air. If the sound meets a water surface, then what is the wavelength of (i) the reflected sound, (ii) the transmitted sound? Speed of sound in air is 340 ms^{-1} and in water 1486 ms^{-1}. **[NCERT]**

Sol. Given, $v = 1000$ kHz $= 10^6$ Hz

$v_a = 340$ m/s, $v_w = 1486$ m/s

Wavelength of reflected sound,

$$\lambda_a = \frac{v_a}{v} = \frac{340}{10^6} = 3.4 \times 10^{-4} \text{ m}$$

Wavelength of transmitted sound,

$$\lambda_w = \frac{v_s}{v} = \frac{1486}{10^6} = 1486 \times 10^{-6}$$

$$\lambda_w = 1.486 \times 10^{-3} \text{ m}$$

LONG ANSWER Type I Questions

21. The pattern of standing waves formed on a stretched string at two instants of time are shown in figure. The velocity of two waves superimposing to form stationary waves is 360 m/s and their frequencies are 256 Hz.

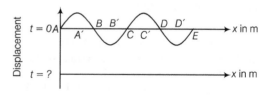

(i) Calculate the time at which the second curve is plotted.
(ii) Mark nodes and antinodes on the curve.
(iii) Calculate the distance between A' and C'.
[NCERT Exemplar]

Sol. Here, $v = 360$ m/s, $v = 256$ Hz

(i) In the figure, second curve represents all the particles passing simultaneously through mean position. This happens at $t = \dfrac{T}{4}\left(T = \dfrac{1}{256}\text{s}\right)$.

$$= \dfrac{1}{4 \times 256}\,\text{s} = 9.8 \times 10^{-4}\,\text{s}$$

(ii) Nodes are at points A, B, C, D, E and antinodes are at A', B', C', D'

(iii) Distance between A' and C'

$$= \dfrac{2\lambda}{2} = \lambda = \dfrac{v}{v} = \dfrac{360}{256} = 1.41\,\text{m}$$

22. The wave pattern on a stretched string is shown in figure. Interpret what kind of wave this is and find its wavelength?

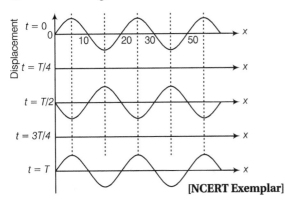

[NCERT Exemplar]

Sol. The wave pattern shown represent stationary wave.

t	x (cm)
0	0
$\dfrac{T}{2}$	10
T	20

At the above time and position and similarly for next interval and position. These points are at rest and called nodes.

Distance between successive nodes $= \dfrac{\lambda}{2} = 10$ cm

$\Rightarrow \qquad\qquad\qquad \lambda = 20$ cm

23. A tuning fork vibrating with a frequency of 512 Hz is kept close to the open end of a tube filled with water shown in figure. The water level in the tube is gradually lowered. When the water level is 17 cm below the open end, maximum intensity of sound is heard.

If the room temperature is 20°C, then calculate

(i) speed of sound in air at room temperature.

(ii) speed of sound in air at 0°C.

(iii) if the water in the tube is replaced with mercury, will there be any difference in your observations? **[NCERT Exemplar]**

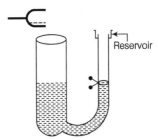

Reservoir

Sol. (i) $v = \dfrac{v}{4l}$

$\Rightarrow v = (v)(4l) = (512)\left(\dfrac{4 \times 17}{100}\right)$ m/s $= 348.16$ m/s

(ii) $v_0 = v_t \sqrt{\dfrac{T_0}{T}} = 348.16 \sqrt{\dfrac{273}{273 + 20}} = 336.1$ m/s

(iii) There will not be any change in resonance length, as frequency will remain same. As mercury acts as reflector intensity may change to some extent.

24. A pipe 20 cm long is closed at one end. Which harmonic mode of the pipe is resonantly excited by a 430 Hz source? Will the same source be in resonance with the pipe if both ends are open? (speed of sound in air is 340 ms⁻¹) **[NCERT]**

Sol. Given, $L = 20$ cm $= 0.2$ m, $v_n = 430$ Hz, $v = 340$ m/s

It will behave as closed organ pipe

$$v_n = (2n-1)\dfrac{v}{4L}, \text{ where } n = 1, 2, 3, \ldots$$

$\Rightarrow \qquad 430 = (2n-1)\dfrac{v}{4L} = (2n-1) \times \dfrac{340}{4 \times 0.2}$

$\Rightarrow (2n-1) = \dfrac{430 \times (0.8)}{340} \Rightarrow 2n = \dfrac{(430)(0.8)}{340} + 1$

$\Rightarrow \qquad n = \dfrac{43 \times 4}{340} + \dfrac{1}{2} = \dfrac{2 \times 172 + 340}{340 \times 2} = \dfrac{684}{680} = 1.006$

Hence, it will be the 1st normal mode or harmonic mode of vibration.

In a pipe open at both ends, $v_n = n \times \dfrac{v}{2l} = \dfrac{n \times 340}{2 \times 0.2} = 430$

$\Rightarrow \qquad n = \dfrac{430 \times 2 \times 0.2}{340} = \dfrac{43 \times 2 \times 2}{340} = 0.5$

As n is not integer, hence, open organ pipe cannot be in resonance with the source.

LONG ANSWER Type II Questions

25. Explain why (or how)

(i) in a sound wave, a displacement node is a pressure antinode and *vice-versa*?

(ii) bats can ascertain distances, directions, nature and sizes of the obstacles without any eyes?

(iii) a violin note and sitar note may have the same frequency, yet we can distinguish between the two notes?

(iv) solids can support both longitudinal and transverse waves but only longitudinal waves can propagate in gases, and

(v) the shape of a pulse gets distorted during propagation in a dispersive medium? **[NCERT]**

Sol. (i) **Node** It is a point where the amplitude of oscillation is zero, i.e. displacement is minimum. As pressure is inversely related with displacement, i.e. when displacement will be minimum, pressure will be maximum.

Antinode At this point displacement is maximum, i.e. amplitude of oscillation will be maximum and hence, pressure will be minimum as it is inversely related.

(ii) Bats emit ultrasonic waves of large frequencies. These waves will be reflected by the obstacles in their path. The reflected rays received by the bat will give idea about the obstacle, i.e. distance, direction, size and nature.

(iii) As overtones produced and relative strengths of notes are different in two notes of violin and sitar.

Although frequencies are same, we will distinguish by their strengths.

(iv) The reason behind is that solids have both the elasticity of volume as well as shape, whereas gases have only the volume elasticity.

(v) As in the dispersive medium wavelengths are different, hence the velocities, therefore, the shape of the pulse gets distorted.

ASSESS YOUR TOPICAL UNDERSTANDING

OBJECTIVE Type Questions

1. To increase the frequency from 100 Hz to 400 Hz the tension in the string has to be changed by
   (a) 4 times
   (b) 16 times
   (c) 2 times
   (d) None of these

2. A resonating column has resonant frequencies as 100 Hz, 300 Hz, 500 Hz. Then it may
   (a) an open pipe
   (b) a pipe closed at both ends
   (c) pipe closed at one end
   (d) Data insufficient

3. When two harmonic sound waves of close (but not equal) frequencies are heard at the same time, we hear
   (a) a sound of similar frequency
   (b) a sound of frequency which is the average of two close   frequencies
   (c) audibly distinct waxing and waning of the intensity of the sound with a frequency equal to the difference in the two close frequencies
   (d) All of the above

4. A person blows into an open end of a long pipe. As a result, a high pressure pulse of air travels down the pipe. When this pulse reaches the other end of the pipe,
   (a) a high pressure pulse starts travelling up the pipe, if the other end f the pipe is open
   (b) a low pressure pulse starts travelling up the pipe, if the other end of the pipe is open
   (c) a low pressue pulse starts travelling down the pipe, if the other end of the pipe is closed
   (d) None of the above

Answer

| 1. (b) | 2. (c) | 3. (d) | 4. (b) |

VERY SHORT ANSWER Type Questions

5. When are standing waves formed? Of the closed and open organ pipes, which one will produce better musical sound and why?

6. What are echo and acoustics?

7. In case of a stationary wave, where will a man hear maximum sound, at the node or at the antinode?

8. A string vibrates according to the equation
   $y = 5\sin\dfrac{\pi x}{3} \cos 40\pi t$, where x and y are in centimetres and t is in second. What is the speed of the component wave? **[Ans.** 120 cm/s**]**

9. Two tuning forks of frequencies 250 Hz and 252 Hz are being vibrated simultaneously. If a loud sound is produced just now, after what time would the sound be again equally loud?

SHORT ANSWER Type Questions

10. Third overtone of a closed organ pipe is in unison (resonance) with fourth harmonic of an open organ pipe. Find the ratio of lengths of the pipes. **[Ans.** 7 : 8**]**

11. What are beats? When are beats formed? What is their frequency?

12. By drawing figures, show the formation of first four harmonic setup in a vibrating string or wire fixed at its two ends. Mark nodes and antinodes.

LONG ANSWER Type I Questions

13. What do you mean by the terms, overtones and harmonics? Briefly explain. Find frequency of first harmonics for a string fixed at one end.

14. A guitar string is 90 cm long and has a fundamental frequency of 124 Hz. Where should it be pressed to produce a fundamental frequency of 180 Hz?
    [**Ans.** 60 cm]

15. A standing wave is formed by two harmonic waves, $Y_1 = A \sin(kx - \omega t)$ and $Y_2 = A \sin(kx + \omega t)$ travelling on a string in opposite directions. Mass density of the string is ρ and area of cross-section is s. Find the total mechanical energy between two adjacent nodes on the string.
    [**Ans.** $\dfrac{\rho A^2 \omega^2 \pi s}{k}$]

LONG ANSWER Type II Questions

16. Discuss formation of different modes of vibration in (i) an open end, (ii) a closed end air column. Draw neat diagram also.

17. A wire of length 40 cm which has a mass of 4 g oscillates in its second harmonic and sets the air column in the tube to vibration in its fundamental mode as shown in figure. $v = 340$ m/s for sound. Find the tension in the wire. [**Ans.** 11.57 N]

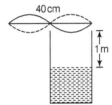

SUMMARY

- **Wave motion** It is a kind of disturbance which travels through a medium due to the repeated vibrations of the particles of the medium about their mean positions, the disturbance being handed over from one particle to the next.

- Three basic types of waves

  (i) Mechanical waves   (ii) Electromagnetic waves   (iii) Matter waves

- **Transverse waves** These are the waves in which particles of the medium vibrate about their mean positions in a direction perpendicular to the direction of propagation of the disturbance. These waves can propagate in those media which have a shear modulus of elasticity. e.g. Solids.

- **Longitudinal waves** These are the waves in which particles of the medium vibrate about their mean positions along the direction of propagation of the disturbance. These waves can propagate in those media having a bulk modulus of elasticity and are therefore, possible in all media: solids, liquids and gases.

- **Progressive wave** A wave that moves from one point of medium to another is called a progressive wave.

- **Displacement relation in a progressive wave** $y(x, t) = a \sin(kx - \omega t + f)$ for +ve x-direction.
  $y(x, t) = a \sin(kx - \omega t + f)$ for −ve x-direction.

- **Amplitude (A)** It is the maximum displacement suffered by the particles of the medium from the mean position during the ropagation of a wave.

- **Time period (T)** It is the time in which a particle of the medium completes one vibration about its mean position.

- **Frequency (v)** It is the number of waves produced per second in a given medium.

- **Wavelength (λ)** It is the distance covered by a wave during the time a particle of the medium completes one vibration about its mean position. It is the distance between two nearest particles of the medium which are vibrating in the same phase.

- **Characteristics of waves** Wavelength and angular wave number $\lambda = \dfrac{2\pi}{k}$

- Period, angular frequency and frequency $\omega = \dfrac{2\pi}{T}, v = \dfrac{1}{T}$

- Speed of a travelling wave $v = \nu\lambda = \dfrac{\lambda}{T}$

- Transverse wave on stretched spring $v = \sqrt{T/\mu}$

- **Principle of superposition of waves** When two or more pulses overlap, the resultant displacement is the algebraic sum of the displacements due to each pulse $y'(x, t) = y_1(x, t) + y_2(x, t)$

- **Interference of waves** The phenomenon that occurs when the two waves meet while travelling along the same medium.

$$y(x, t) = 2a\cos\frac{\phi}{2}\sin\left(kx - \omega t + \frac{\phi}{2}\right)$$

- If $f = 0$, two waves are in phase $y(x, t) = 2a\sin(kx - \omega t)$

- If $\phi = \pi$, two waves are out of phase by 180°,

$$y(x, t) = 0$$

- **Constructive interference** When waves interfere in phase $\phi = 2n\pi$, $\Delta x = n\lambda$

- **Destructive interference** When waves interfere in phase opposition $\phi = (2n + 1)\pi$, $\Delta x = \dfrac{(2n+1)\lambda}{2}$

- **Vibrations of air column** Closed organ pipe, $v = (2n + 1)\dfrac{v}{4L}$

  Open organ pipe, $v = \dfrac{nv}{2L}$

- **Relation between phase difference, path difference and time difference** Relation between phase difference, path difference and time difference is given by

  Phase difference $(\phi) = \dfrac{2\pi}{\lambda} \times$ Path difference (x)

  $\Rightarrow \phi = \dfrac{2\pi x}{\lambda} \Rightarrow x = \dfrac{\phi\lambda}{2\pi}$

  Speed of mechanical wave, $v = \sqrt{\dfrac{E}{\rho}}$

  Where E = The modulus of elasticity of the
  and ρ = The density of the medium

- **Speed of a transverse wave on stretched string**

$$v = \sqrt{\dfrac{T}{\mu}}$$

  Where, T = Tension in the string and μ = Linear mass density

- **Velocity of longitudinal waves in elastic medium** Solid medium $v = \sqrt{\dfrac{Y}{\rho}}$

  Where, Y is the Young's modulus of elasticity and ρ is its density.

- **Liquid medium** $v = \sqrt{\dfrac{B}{\rho}}$

  Where, B is the Bulk modulus of liquid and ρ is its density.

- **Gas medium** $v = \sqrt{\dfrac{p}{\rho}}$ where, p is the pressure of gas and ρ is its density.

$$v_{\text{Solid}} > v_{\text{Liquid}} > v_{\text{Gaseous}}$$

- **Laplace's correction** He pointed out that the propagation of sound in gaseous medium is not an isothermal process but an adiabatic process. Thus, $v = \sqrt{\dfrac{\gamma p}{\rho}}$

  where, γ is the ratio of specific heat of the gas at constant pressure p to that at constant volume.

- **Beats** It is the difference of nearly same frequencies and amplitudes.
  Beat frequency, $v_{\text{beat}} = v_1 - v_2$

CHAPTER PRACTICE

OBJECTIVE Type Questions

1. The picture of a progressive transverse wave at a particular instant of time gives
   (a) shape of the wave
   (b) motion of the particle of the medium
   (c) velocity of the wave
   (d) None of the above

2. In a longitudinal wave, the elastic property of the constituents of the medium that determines the stress under compressional strain is
   (a) Young's modulus (Y) (b) bulk modulus (B)
   (c) shear modulus (S) (d) Either (b) or (c)

3. A student plotted the following four graphs representing the variation of velocity of sound in a gas with the pressure p at constant temperature. Which one is correct?

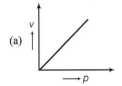
(a)
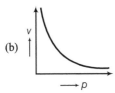
(b)

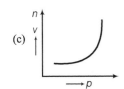
(c)
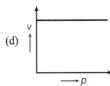
(d)

4. A wave equation is given by
$$y = 4 \sin\left[\pi\left(\frac{t}{5} - \frac{x}{9} + \frac{1}{6}\right)\right]$$
where, x is in cm and t is in second. The wavelength of the wave is
   (a) 18 cm   (b) 9 cm
   (c) 36 cm   (d) 6 cm

5. The equation of a progressive wave can be given by $y = 15 \sin(660\pi t - 0.02\pi x)$ cm. The frequency of the wave is
   (a) 330 Hz   (b) 342 Hz
   (c) 365 Hz   (d) 660 Hz

6. Two waves of equal amplitude A and equal frequency travel in the same direction in a medium. The amplitude of the resultant wave is
   (a) 0   (b) A
   (c) $2A$ (d) between 0 to $2A$

7. If a propagating wave meets a boundary which is not completely rigid or is an interface between two different elastic media, then which of the statements is/are correct?
   (a) A part of the incident wave is reflected and a part is transmitted into the second medium
   (b) The incident wave is completely reflected from the boundary
   (c) Only part of the wave is reflected and the remaining part disappears
   (d) None of the above

8. The air column in a pipe open at both ends is oscillating with certain frequency. Which of the given statement (s) is/are correct for the open air column at both ends?
   (a) Each end of the pipe acts as an antinode
   (b) An open air column at both ends generates all harmonics
   (c) Each end of the pipe is a node
   (d) Both (a) and (b)

ASSERTION AND REASON

Directions (Q.Nos. 9-14) *In the following questions, two statements are given- one labelled Assertion (A) and the other labelled Reason (R). Select the correct answer to these questions from the codes (a), (b), (c) and (d) as given below*
   (a) Both Assertion and Reason are true and Reason is the correct explanation of Assertion.
   (b) Both Assertion and Reason are true but Reason is not the correct explanation of Assertion.
   (c) Assertion is true but Reason is false.
   (d) Assertion is false but Reason is true.

9. **Assertion** The light emitted by stars, which are hundreds of light years away, reaches us through inter-stellar spaces even though the inter-stellar spaces are practically vacuum.
   Reason Light is an electromagnetic wave and do not necessarily require a medium for propagation, they can even travel in vacuum.

10. **Assertion** The amplitude $A(\phi)$ of the resultant of the two right travelling waves given by equations
    $$y_1(x, t) = A \sin (kx - \omega t)$$
    and $y_2(x, t) = A \sin (kx - \omega t + \phi)$
    is decreasing as ϕ increases from 0 to π.

    Reason The amplitude of the resultant of the two waves is given by $A(\phi) = 2A \cos \phi/2$ which is decreasing for $0 \le \phi \le \pi$.

11. **Assertion** Transverse waves are possible in solids and strings (under tension) but not in fluids.

    Reason Solids and strings have no zero shear modulus that is they can sustain shearing stress but fluids yield to shearing stress and hence they do not have shape of their own.

12. **Assertion** Longitudinal waves can be propagated through solids and fluids both.

    Reason Solids as well as fluids have non zero bulk modulus, that is they can sustain compressive stress and longitudinal waves involve compressive stress (pressure).

13. **Assertion** Speed of sound is more in liquids and solids than gases.

    Reason Liquids and solids have higher densities than gases.

14. **Assertion** Superposition of two harmonic waves, one of frequency 11 Hz and the other of frequency 9 Hz gives rise to beats of frequency 2 Hz.

    Reason Harmonic waves of nearly equal frequencies interfere to give rise to beat having beat frequency, $\nu_{beat} = |\nu_1 - \nu_2|$.

CASE BASED QUESTIONS

Directions (Q.Nos. 15-16) *These questions are case study based questions. Attempt any 4 sub-parts from each question. Each question carries 1 mark.*

15. **Displacement of Wave**

    A stone is dropped in a liquid at rest in a tank. The Fig. (a) below shows circular wave fronts. The waves produced at the centre of a circular ripple tank. Two corks A and B, floats on the water and moves up & down on the surface as the wave passes. The wavelength of the wave is 8.0 cm.

    The Fig. (b) shows how the displacement of A varies with time.

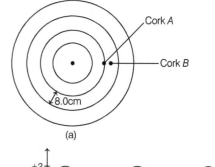

(a)

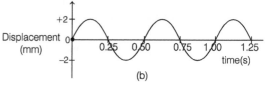

(b)

(i) Name the type of waves produced on water surface.
   (a) Longitudinal wave   (b) Transverse wave
   (c) Sound wave   (d) EM wave

(ii) What is the amplitude of the vibrations of A as wave passes?
   (a) 2 mm   (b) 0.25 mm
   (c) 0.50 mm   (d) 8 mm

(iii) The horizontal distance between A and B is half the wavelength of the wave, then the displacement of B with time is
   (a) same as that of A with equal magnitude
   (b) opposite to that of A with equal magnitude
   (c) double in magnitude as that of A
   (d) half in magnitude as that of A

(iv) What is the frequency of the wave?
   (a) 4 Hz   (b) 0.4 Hz
   (c) 2 Hz   (d) 0.2 Hz

(v) If the distance between the centre of the ripple tank and its edge is 40 cm, then the time taken by the wave to travel from the centre of the tank to the edge is
   (a) 5 s   (b) 2.5 s
   (c) 3 s   (d) 4.5 s

16. **Ultrasound**

    Ultrasound is an example of longitudinal wave having high frequency. These types of waves are the one in which the individual particles of the medium execute simple harmonic motion about their mean positions along the direction of propagation of the wave.

    Ultrasound is used to investigate the internal organs of a human body as it can penetrate into matter.

Figure below shows how ultrasound is used to produce an image of the heart.

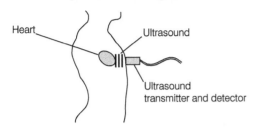

(i) What is the frequency range of ultrasound?
  (a) 20 Hz   (b) 20 kHz
  (c) Less than 20 Hz   (d) More than 20 kHz

(ii) Which of these can produce ultrasound?
  (a) Bats   (b) Dolphins
  (c) Porpoises   (d) All of these

(iii) When ultrasound wave passes through a body, then the particles in the body have motion in
  (a) forward and backward direction
  (b) parallel to direction of motion
  (c) perpendicular to direction of motion
  (d) Both (a) and (b)

(iv) There are small bubbles of gas in a body. When the body is kept in the path of ultrasound, then
  (a) bubbles gets expanded
  (b) bubbles gets contracted
  (c) Both (a) and (b)
  (d) No change occur

(v) The ultrasound of wavelength 1.2×10^{-3} m has a speed of 1500 m/s in a human body. The frequency is
  (a) 1.25×10^{-6} Hz   (b) 1.25×10^{6} Hz
  (c) 1.2×10^{-4} Hz   (d) 2×10^{6} Hz

Answer

1.	(a)	2.	(b)	3.	(d)	4.	(a)	5.	(a)
6.	(d)	7.	(a)	8.	(d)	9.	(a)	10.	(a)
11.	(a)	12.	(a)	13.	(b)	14.	(a)		

15.	(i) (b)	(ii) (a)	(iii) (b)	(iv) (c)	(v) (b)
16.	(i) (d)	(ii) (d)	(iii) (d)	(iv) (c)	(v) (b)

VERY SHORT ANSWER Type Questions

17. Is an oscillation, a wave, why?

18. Give two examples of each of longitudinal and transverse waves.

19. What is the audible range of sound frequencies? **[Ans.** 20 Hz to 20 kHz]

20. Two sound waves produce 12 beats in 4 s. By how much do their frequencies differ? **[Ans.** 3 beats/s]

SHORT ANSWER Type Questions

21. In a resonance tube, the second resonance does not occur exactly at three times the length of first resonance, why?

22. Establish the relation, $v = \nu\lambda$ for a wave motion.

23. What is the direction of oscillations of the particles of a medium through which (i) transverse, (ii) longitudinal wave is propagating?

24. A progressive wave of frequency 500 Hz is travelling with a velocity of 360 m/s. How far particles are two points 60° out of phase? **[Ans.** 0.12 m]

25. State few important use of phenomenon of beats.

LONG ANSWER Type I Questions

26. A tuning fork of frequency 200 Hz is in resonance with a sonometer wire. How many beats will be heard if tension in the wire is increased by 2%? **[Ans.** 2 beats]

27. What are stationary waves? Explain their formation analytically in case of a string fixed at both of its ends.

LONG ANSWER Type II Questions

28. State Newton's formula for velocity of sound in air. Point out the error and hence, discuss Laplace's correction and calculate the temperature at which the speed of sound will be two times of its value at 0°C. **[Ans.** 819°C]

29. Two tuning forks A and B give 5 beats/s.

A resounds with a closed column of air 15 cm long and B with an open column of air 30.5 cm long.

Calculate their frequencies. Neglect and correction. **[Ans.** 305 Hz, 300 Hz]

Hint Use $m = v_1 - v_2$

30. Stationary waves are set up by the superposition of two waves given by $y_1 = 0.05\sin(5\pi t - x)$ and $y_2 = 0.05\sin(5\pi t + x)$, where x and y are in metre and t in second. Calculate the amplitude of a particle at a distance of $x = 1$ m. **[Ans.** 0.054 m]

SAMPLE QUESTION PAPER 1

A HIGHLY SIMULATED SAMPLE QUESTION PAPER FOR CBSE CLASS XI EXAMINATIONS

PHYSICS (FULLY SOLVED)

GENERAL INSTRUCTIONS

1. All questions are compulsory. There are 33 questions in all.
2. This question paper has five sections: Section A, Section B, Section C, Section D and Section E.
3. **Section A** contains ten very short answer questions and four assertion reasoning MCQs of 1 mark each, **Section B** has two case based questions of 4 marks each, **Section C** contains nine short answer questions of 2 marks each, **Section D** contains five short answer questions of 3 marks each and **Section E** contains three long answer questions of 5 marks each.
4. There is no overall choice. However internal choice is provided. You have to attempt only one of the choices in such questions.

TIME : 3 HOURS   **MAX. MARKS : 70**

SECTION-A

All questions are compulsory. In case of internal choices, attempt anyone of them.

1. To break a wire, a force of 10^6 Nm^{-2} is required. If the density of the material is 3×10^3 kgm^{-3}, then calculate the length of the wire which will break by its own weight.

2. A body is rotating with angular velocity, $\omega = (3\hat{i} - 4\hat{j} - \hat{k})$. What is the linear velocity of a point having position vector $r = (5\hat{i} - 6\hat{j} + 6\hat{k})$?

3. What is the torque of a force $7\hat{i} + 3\hat{j} - 5\hat{k}$ about the origin whose position vector is $\hat{i} - \hat{j} + \hat{k}$?

4. Find the dimensions of a/b in the equation $F = a\sqrt{x} + bt^2$, where F is force, x is distance and t is time.

   Or

   5.74 g of a substance occupies 1.2 cm^3. Express its density by keeping the significant figures in view.

5. Temperature remaining constant, the pressure of a gas is decreased by 20%. What is the percentage change in volume?

   Or

   An ideal gas at 27°C is heated at constant pressure so as to triple its volume. What is the increase in temperature of the gas?

6. Can transverse waves be produced in air?

7. An ideal gas has molar specific heat capacity at constant volume equal to $\frac{3}{2}R$.

   Find the molar specific heat capacity at constant pressure.

8. What is the function of the wooden box in the sonometer?

   Or

   A truck is moving with a speed of 90 kmh^{-1} towards a hill. Truck blows horn at a distance of 1800 m from the hill and a echo is heard after 8 s. Calculate the speed of sound (in ms^{-1}).

9. If a wire is pressed over a slab of ice as shown in the figure, then what happens to the wire and the slab?

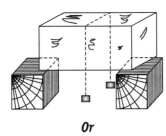

Or

The graph shows variation of temperature (T) of one kilogram of a material with the heat supplied (H) to it. At 0, the substance is in the solid state.

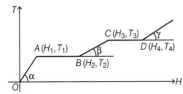

From the graph, what can we conclude?

10. A body covers a distance of 20 m in 7th second and 24 m in 9th second. If the motion is uniformly accelerated, then find the value of acceleration.

For question numbers 11, 12, 13 and 14, two statements are given-one labelled Assertion (A) and the other labelled **Reason** (R). Select the correct answer to these questions from the codes (a), (b), (c) and (d) as given below.

   (a) Both A and R are true and R is the correct explanation of A.
   (b) Both A and R are true but R is not the correct explanation of A.
   (c) A is true but R is false.
   (d) A is false and R is also false.

11. **Assertion** At highest point of a projectile, dot product of velocity and acceleration is zero.

   Reason At highest point, velocity and acceleration are mutually perpendicular.

12. **Assertion** When a body is dropped or thrown horizontally from the same height, it would reach the ground at the same time.

   Reason Horizontal velocity has no effect on the vertical direction.

13. **Assertion** In isothermal process, whole of the heat energy supplied to the body is converted into internal energy.

Reason According to the first law of thermodynamics, $\Delta Q = \Delta U + \Delta W$.

14. **Assertion** Longitudinal waves can be propagated through solids and fluids both.

   Reason Solids as well as fluids have non-zero bulk modulus, that is they can sustain compressive stress and longitudinal waves involve compressive stress (pressure).

SECTION-B

Questions 15 and 16 are case study based questions and are compulsory. Attempt any 4 sub parts from each question. Each question carries 1 mark.

15. **The Centre of Gravity**

The centre of gravity of a rigid body is a point through which the total weight of the body act. Centre of gravity can lie within the body or not. For small objects, centre of mass always coincides with centre of gravity. But in case of large bodies whose dimensions are comparable to the size of earth, centre of mass and centre of gravity will be at different locations.

In the given figure, balancing of a cardboard on the tip of a pencil is done. The point of support, G is the centre of gravity.

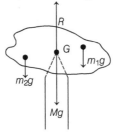

   (i) If the $\mathbf{F}_{net, ext}$ is zero on the cardboard, it means
      (a) $R = Mg$
      (b) $m_1 g = Mg$
      (c) $m_2 g = Mg$
      (d) $R = m_1 / g$

   (ii) Choose the correct option.
      (a) τ_{Mg} about CG $= 0$
      (b) τ_R about CG $= 0$
      (c) Net τ due to $m_1 g, m_2 g \cdots m_n g$ about CG $= 0$
      (d) All of the above

(iii) The centre of gravity and the centre of mass of a body coincide when
(a) g is negligible   (b) g is variable
(c) g is constant   (d) g is zero

(iv) If value of g varies, the centre of gravity and the centre of mass will
(a) coincide
(b) not coincide
(c) become same physical quantities
(d) None of the above

(v) Where will be the centre of gravity of the following rigid body?

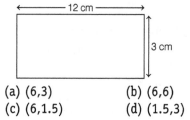

(a) (6,3)   (b) (6,6)
(c) (6,1.5)   (d) (1.5,3)

16. Hydraulic Lift

Hydraulic lift is an application of Pascal's law. It is used to lift heavy loads. It is a force multiplier.

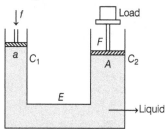

So, when small forces applied on the smaller piston (acting downward) will be appearing as a very large force (acting upward) on the larger piston. As a result of it, a heavy load placed on the larger piston is easily lifted upwards.

(i) Pascal's law states that pressure in a fluid at rest is the same at all points, if
(a) they are at the same height
(b) they are along same plane
(c) they are along same line
(d) Both (a) and (b)

(ii) Pressure is applied to an enclosed fluid as shown in the above figure. It is
(a) increased and applied to every part of the fluid
(b) diminished and transmitted to the walls of the container
(c) increased in proportion to the mass of the fluid and then transmitted
(d) transmitted unchanged to every portion of the fluid and the walls of container

(iii) Pressure at a point inside a liquid does not depend on
(a) the depth of the point below the surface of the liquid
(b) the nature of the liquid
(c) the acceleration due to gravity at that point
(d) total weight of fluid in the beaker

(iv) A hydraulic lift has 2 limbs of areas A and $2A$. Force F is applied over limb of area A to lift a heavy car. If distance moved by piston P_1 is x, then distance moved by piston P_2 is

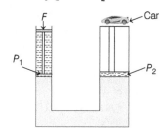

(a) x (b) $2x$
(c) $\dfrac{x}{2}$ (d) $4x$

(v) If work done by piston in the given figure on fluid is W_1, then work done by fluid in limbs on piston P_2 is
(a) $\dfrac{W_1}{4}$ (b) $4W_1$
(c) $\dfrac{W_1}{2}$ (d) W_1

SECTION-C

All questions are compulsory. In case of internal choices, attempt anyone.

17. Determine the tensions T_1 and T_2 in the strings shown in following figure:

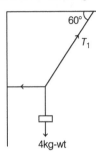

Or

A car of mass 1500 kg is moving with a speed of 12.5 ms^{-1} on a circular path of radius 20 m on a level road. What should be the frictional force between the car and the road, so that the car does not slip? What should be the value of the coefficient of friction to attain this force?

18. A bolt of mass 0.3 kg falls from the ceiling of an elevator moving down with an uniform speed of 7 ms^{-1}. It hits the floor of the elevator (length of the elevator = 3 m) and does not rebound. What is the heat produced by the impact? Would your answer be different if the elevator were stationary?

[NCERT]

Or

In a hydroelectric power station, the water is flowing at 2 ms^{-1} in the river which is 100m wide and 5m deep. Find the maximum power output from the river.

19. (i) Is rms speed same as the average speed? Write an expression of rms and average speed.

(ii) Why does molecular motion increase at 0 K?

20. Two particles are projected from the same point with same speed u at an angle of projection α and β from horizontal. If the maximum heights attained by them are h_1 and h_2 respectively for same range R, then find the relation between h_1, h_2 and R.

Or

A bullet fired at an angle of 30° with the horizontal hits the ground 3 km away. By adjusting its angle of projection, can one hope to hit a target 5 km away? Assume the muzzle speed to be fixed and neglect air resistance.

21. Two sound waves whose equations are

$$y_1 = 3\sin 200\pi \left(t - \frac{x}{300} \right) \text{ m and}$$

$$y_2 = 5\sin 208\pi \left(t - \frac{x}{300} \right) \text{ m}$$

are super-imposed.

(i) What is the name of the phenomenon that arises due to their superposition?

(ii) What is the frequency heard by a person?

22. A particle at the end of a spring executes simple harmonic motion with a period t_1, while the corresponding period for another spring is t_2. What is the period of oscillation when the two springs are connected in series?

23. (i) Using first law of thermodynamics, show why

(a) in an isothermal process, all heat energy given gets converted into work done?

(b) in an isochoric process, all heat energy given gets used up to increase the internal energy of the system?

(ii) First law of thermodynamics does not give any condition of flow of heat from lower temperature to high temperature. Comment.

24. 0.15 kg of ice at 0°C is mixed with 0.30 kg of water at 50°C in a container. The resulting temperature is at 6.7°C.
Find heat of fusion of ice.
(Given, specific heat of water is 4186 Jkg^{-1}K^{-1})

25. (i) Explain the need for banking of curved tracks.

(ii) State principle of conservation of angular momentum.

SECTION-D

All questions are compulsory. In case of internal choices, attempt anyone.

26. (i) The expression of a displacement function $x(t)$ varying with time t is given as

$$x(t) = -A\cos(\omega t)$$

Express this equation graphically and explain why it is a SHM.

(ii) Derive an expression for kinetic energy of a simple harmonic oscillator.

Or

(i) Why does a tuning fork have two prongs?

(ii) Explain the factors on which the pitch of a tuning fork depends.

27. Derive an expression for the moment of inertia of a thin uniform rod about an axis through its centre and perpendicular to its length. Also, determine the radius of gyration about the same axis.

Or

From a uniform disc of radius R, a circular section of radius $\dfrac{R}{2}$ is cut out. The centre of the hole is at $\dfrac{R}{2}$ from the centre of the original disc. Locate the centre of gravity of the resulting flat body.

28. (i) If C and R denote capacitance and resistance, then find the dimension of CR.

(ii) Check whether the following quantities are dimensionless or not.

(a) $\dfrac{\text{Work}}{\text{Energy}}$ (b) $\sin\theta$

(c) $\dfrac{\text{Momentum}}{\text{Time}}$

29. (i) A man standing on a hill top projects a stone horizontally with speed v_0 as shown in the given figure. Taking the coordinate system as given in the figure, find the coordinates of the point, where the stone will hit the hill surface.

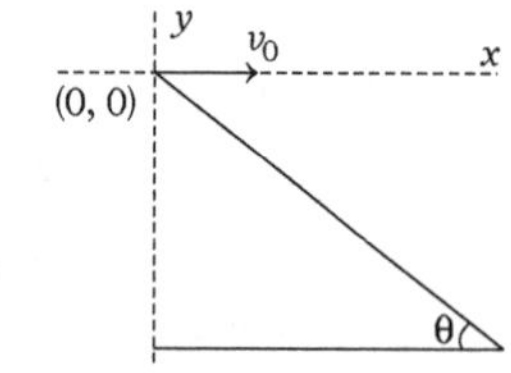

(ii) Two cars A and B move along concentric circular paths of radii r_A and r_B with velocities v_A and v_B respectively, maintaining a constant distance. Find $\dfrac{v_A}{v_B}$.

30. A trolley of mass 200 kg moves with a uniform speed of 36 km/h on a frictionless track. A child of mass 20 kg runs on the trolley from one end to the other (10 m away) with a speed of 4 ms^{-1} relative to the trolley in a direction opposite to its motion, and jumps out of the trolley. What is the final speed of the trolley? How much has the trolley moved from the time the child begins to run?   [NCERT]

SECTION-E

All questions are compulsory. In case of internal choices, attempt anyone.

31. (i) Mention any two conditions under which the weight of a person can become zero.

(ii) Calculate the period of revolution of the neptune around the sun, given that diameter of its orbit is 30 times the diameter of the earth's orbit around the sun. Assume both the orbits to be circular.

Or

(i) What do you mean by binding energy of a satellite? Write an expression for it.

(ii) Calculate the escape velocity for an atmospheric particle 1600 km above the earth's surface. (Given, radius of earth $= 6400$ km and $g = 9.8$ m/s^2)

32. (i) A spring balance is attached to the ceiling of a lift. A man hangs his bag on the spring and the spring reads 49 N, when the lift is stationary. What will be the reading of the spring balance, if the lift moves downward with an acceleration of 5 ms^{-2}?

(ii) A body tied to a string is made to revolve in a vertical circle. Derive an expression for the velocity and tension in an string at any point. Hence, find the tension at the bottom and the top of the circle.

Or

(i) Why is force of static friction called a self adjusting force?

(ii) Define angle of friction. Write its relation with coefficient of friction.

(iii) Define angle of repose. Deduce its relation with coefficient of static friction.

33. (i) Find the surface tension of soap solution, if the excess pressure inside a soap bubble of radius 6 mm is balanced by 2 mm column of oil of relative density 0.8.

(ii) Derive an expression for the excess pressure inside a soap bubble. Also, write the expression for excess pressure when an air bubble of radius R lies at a depth h below the free surface of liquid of density ρ.

Or

(i) When the load of a wire is increased from 3 kg-wt to 5 kg-wt, the length of that wire changes from 0.61 mm to 1.02 mm. Calculate the change in the elastic potential energy of the wire.

(ii) If the ratio of diameters, lengths and Young's moduli of steel and brass wires shown in the figure are p, q and r respectively, what will be the corresponding ratio of increase in their lengths?

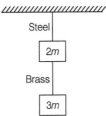

SOLUTIONS

1. Length of the wire which will break by its own weight,

$$L = \frac{F}{\rho g} = \frac{10^6}{3 \times 10^3 \times 10}$$

$$= \frac{100}{3} = 33.3\, \text{m} \approx 34\, \text{m}$$ [1]

2. Given, $\omega = 3\hat{i} - 4\hat{j} - \hat{k}$, $r = 5\hat{i} - 6\hat{j} + 6\hat{k}$

As, $\mathbf{v} = \omega \times \mathbf{r} = \begin{vmatrix} \hat{i} & \hat{j} & \hat{k} \\ 3 & -4 & -1 \\ 5 & -6 & 6 \end{vmatrix}$

$$= \hat{i}(-24 - 6) - \hat{j}(18 + 5) + \hat{k}(-18 + 20)$$

$$= -30\hat{i} - 23\hat{j} + 2\hat{k}$$ [1]

3. It is given that,

$$\mathbf{r} = \hat{i} - \hat{j} + \hat{k} \quad \text{and} \quad \mathbf{F} = 7\hat{i} + 3\hat{j} - 5\hat{k}$$

$\therefore$ Torque, $\tau = \mathbf{r} \times \mathbf{F} = \begin{vmatrix} \hat{i} & \hat{j} & \hat{k} \\ 1 & -1 & 1 \\ 7 & 3 & -5 \end{vmatrix}$

$$= (5 - 3)\hat{i} - (-5 - 7)\hat{j} + [3 - (-7)]\hat{k}$$

$$\Rightarrow \qquad \tau = 2\hat{i} + 12\hat{j} + 10\hat{k}$$ [1]

4. As, $F = a\sqrt{x} + bt^2$, $[a\sqrt{x}] = [F]$ and $[bt^2] = [F]$

$$\Rightarrow \qquad [a] = \frac{[F]}{[\sqrt{x}]} = \frac{[MLT^{-2}]}{[L^{1/2}]} = [ML^{1/2}T^{-2}]$$

$$[b] = \frac{[F]}{[t^2]} = \frac{[MLT^{-2}]}{[T^2]} = [MLT^{-4}]$$

$$\therefore \qquad [a/b] = \frac{[ML^{1/2}T^{-2}]}{[MLT^{-4}]} = [L^{-1/2}T^2]$$ [1]

Or

There are 3 significant figures in the measured mass, whereas there are only 2 significant figures in the measured volume. Hence, the density should be expressed only upto 2 significant figures.

$$\therefore \qquad \text{Density} = \frac{\text{Mass}}{\text{Volume}} = \frac{5.74}{1.2}$$

$$= 4.8\, \text{g cm}^{-3}$$ [1]

5. According to Boyle's law,

$$p_1V_1 = p_2V_2$$

As the pressure is decreased by 20%, so

$$p_2 = \frac{80}{100}p_1 \Rightarrow p_1V_1 = \frac{80}{100}p_1V_2 \Rightarrow V_1 = \frac{80}{100}V_2$$

Percentage increase in volume $= \frac{V_2 - V_1}{V_1} \times 100$

$$= \frac{100 - 80}{80} \times 100 = 25\%$$ [1]

Or

According to Charles' law, $\frac{V_1}{V_2} = \frac{T_1}{T_2}$

Given, $T_1 = 27°C = 27 + 273 = 300$ K

$\therefore \quad \dfrac{1}{3} = \dfrac{300 \text{ K}}{T_2}$

$\Rightarrow \quad T_2 = 900 \text{ K} = 900 - 273 = 627°C$

$\Rightarrow \quad \Delta T = 627 - 27 = 600°C$ [1]

6. No, transverse waves involve change in shape because they travel in the form of crests and troughs. It can be produced in a medium which has elasticity of shape. As air has no elasticity of shape, hence transverse waves cannot be produced in it. [1]

7. As, $C_V = \dfrac{3}{2}R$ ...(i)

Since, $C_p - C_V = R$ [1/2]

$\Rightarrow \quad C_p = R + C_V$

$= R + \dfrac{3}{2}R = \dfrac{5}{2}R$ [from Eq. (i)]

[1/2]

8. The function of the wooden box in a sonometer is to increase the sound intensity by its forced vibrations. It decreases the duration of emission of sound energy. [1]

Or

The speed of the truck is 90 kmh^{-1}

$= 90 \times \dfrac{5}{18} = 25 \text{ ms}^{-1}$

The distance travelled by truck in 8 s

$= 8 \times 25 = 200 \text{ m}$

Hence, the distance travelled by sound in reaching the hill and coming back to the moving driver

$= 1800 + (1800 - 200) = 3400 \text{ m}$

So, the speed of sound $= \dfrac{3400}{8} = 4.25 \text{ ms}^{-1}$ [1]

9. The wire passes through the ice slab. This happens due to the fact that just below the wire, ice melts at lower temperature due to increase in pressure. [1]

Or

From the graph, we see that temperature remains constant in the regions AB and CD even though heat H supplied increases. In these two parts, there is change of state. $H_2 - H_1$ represents latent heat of fusion, i.e. heat required to change solid to liquid state and $H_4 - H_3$ represents latent heat of vaporisation, i.e. heat required to change liquid to gaseous state. [1/2]

In the regions OA and BC as H increases, temperature T also increases linearly, i.e. rise in temperature is directly proportional to heat supplied. [1/2]

10. Given, $s_{7th} = u + \dfrac{a}{2}(2 \times 7 - 1) = 20$

$\Rightarrow \quad u + \dfrac{13}{2}a = 20$ ...(i)

and $s_{9th} = u + \dfrac{a}{2}(2 \times 9 - 1) = 24$

$\Rightarrow \quad u + \dfrac{17}{2}a = 24$ ...(ii)

[1/2]

Subtracting Eq. (i) from Eq. (ii), we get

$2a = 4 \Rightarrow a = 2 \text{ m/s}^2$ [1/2]

11. (a) Velocity is horizontal and acceleration is vertical, i.e. both are perpendicular to each other and hence their dot product is zero.

Therefore, both A and R are true and R is the correct explanation of A. [1]

12. (a) Both bodies will take same time to reach the earth because vertical downward component of velocity for both the bodies will be zero and time of descent $t = \sqrt{\dfrac{2h}{g}}$. And it is because horizontal velocity has no effect on the vertical direction.

Therefore, both A and R are true and R is the correct explanation of A. [1]

13. (d) As there is no change in internal energy of the system during an isothermal change. So, the energy taken by the gas is utilised by doing work against external pressure.

According to first law of thermodynamics,

$\Delta Q = \Delta U + \Delta W$

As, $\Delta U = 0 \Rightarrow \Delta Q = \Delta W$

Hence, whole heat energy supplied to the body in an isothermal process is converted into work done. Therefore, Assertion is incorrect but Reason is correct.

14. (a) Longitudinal wave involve compressive stress (pressure). Since, solids as well as fluids have Bulk modulus, i.e. they can sustain compressive stress, so longitudinal waves can be propagated through solids and fluids both.

Therefore, both A and R are true and R is the correct explanation of A. [1]

15. (i) (a) The tip of the pencil provides a vertically upward force due to which the cardboard is in equilibrium. As shown in figure the reaction of the tip is equal and opposite to Mg, the total weight of the cardboard, i.e. $R = Mg$. [1]

(ii) (d) Net τ due to all the forces of gravity $m_1g, m_2g, \cdots, m_ng$ about CG is zero.

τ of reaction **R** about CG is also zero as it is at CG.

Point G is the centre of gravity of the cardboard and it is so located that the total torque on it due to forces $m_1\mathbf{g}, m_2\mathbf{g} \cdots m_n\mathbf{g}$ is zero.

It means $\tau_g = \Sigma \, \tau_i = \Sigma \, \mathbf{r}_i \times m_i\mathbf{g} = 0$.

CG could be defined as the point where the total gravitational torque on the body is zero. **[1]**

(iii) (c) In $\tau_g = \Sigma\mathbf{r}_i \times m_i\mathbf{g} = 0$

$\qquad\qquad$ (τ_g = total gravitational torque)

$\qquad \Sigma \, \mathbf{r}_i \times m_i\mathbf{g} = 0$

If g is constant, $\quad (\Sigma m_i\mathbf{r}_i) \times \mathbf{g} = \mathbf{g}\Sigma m_i \mathbf{r}_i$

As $\mathbf{g} \neq 0$, so $\Sigma \, m_i \mathbf{r}_i = 0$

It is the condition, where the centre of mass (CM) of the body lies at origin. And here origin is considered at centre of gravity (CG). **[1]**

(iv) (b) If the value of g varies, then CM and CG will not coincide. Keep in mind that CG and CM both are two different concepts. CM has nothing to do with CG. **[1]**

(v) (c) In this CG will coincide with CM.

$\therefore$ The CG of this rigid body will be half of 3 cm from X-axis and half of 12 cm from Y-axis, due to symmetry. Thus, the CG will be at (6, 1.5). **[1]**

16. (i) (a) Pascal's law states that pressure in a fluid at rest is the same at all points, if they are at the same height. **[1]**

(ii) (d) Due to Pascal's law, when the pressure is applied, it will be transmitted unchanged to every portion of the fluid and the walls of containers. **[1]**

(iii) (d) $p = \dfrac{F}{A} = \rho gh$

$\therefore$ It does not depend on the weight of fluid. **[1]**

(iv) (c) $V_1 = V_2 \Rightarrow A_1 x_1 = A_2 x_2$

$\Rightarrow x_2 = \dfrac{A_1}{A_2} x_1 = \dfrac{Ax}{2A} = \dfrac{x}{2}$ **[1]**

(v) (d) Work done by both pistons is always same. **[1]**

17. Resolve the tension T_1 along horizontal and vertical directions as shown in the following figure

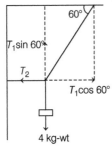

As the body is in equilibrium, so

$T_1 \sin 60° = 4\text{kg-wt} = 4 \times 9.8\,\text{N}$ $\qquad$ …(i)

and $T_1 \cos 60° = T_2$ $\qquad$ …(ii)

From Eq. (i), we get

$T_1 = \dfrac{4 \times 9.8}{\sin 60°} = \dfrac{4 \times 9.8 \times 2}{\sqrt{3}} = 45.26\,\text{N}$ **[1]**

From Eq. (ii), we get

$T_2 = T_1\cos 60° = 45.26 \times \dfrac{1}{2} = 22.63\,\text{N}$ **[1]**

Or

Given, $m = 1500\,\text{kg}, v = 12.5\,\text{ms}^{-1}, r = 20\,\text{m}$

As, frictional force = required centripetal force

$\therefore \qquad f = \dfrac{mv^2}{r} = \dfrac{1500 \times 12.5 \times 12.5}{20}$

$\qquad\qquad = 1.172 \times 10^4\,\text{N}$ **[1]**

Now, $\qquad f = \mu R = \mu mg \qquad [\because R = mg]$

$\therefore$ Coefficient of friction, $\mu = \dfrac{f}{mg} = \dfrac{1.172 \times 10^4}{1500 \times 9.8} = 0.8$ **[1]**

18. Given, mass of bolt, $m = 0.3\,\text{kg}$, height through which bolt falls $h = 3\,\text{m}$.

When the bolt falls on floor of elevator and does not rebound, it suffers a loss of potential energy

$\Delta U = mgh = 0.3 \times 9.8 \times 3 = 8.82\,\text{J}$ **[1]**

$\therefore$ Amount of heat produced = Loss of potential energy = 8.82 J, because there is no gain in KE at all.

The answer is true when either the elevator is at rest or in state of uniform motion because potential energy of bolt has no connection with velocity of elevator. **[1]**

Or

Mass of water flowing per unit time, $m = A\rho v$

$\qquad = 100 \times 5 \times 2 \times 10^3 = 10^6\,\text{kg}$

Kinetic energy of water, $K = \dfrac{1}{2}mv^2 = \dfrac{1}{2} \times 10^6 \times 2 \times 2$

$\qquad\qquad\qquad = 2 \times 10^6\,\text{J}$ **[1]**

Power output of the power station $= \dfrac{2 \times 10^6\,\text{J}}{1\text{s}}$

$\qquad\qquad = 2 \times 10^6\,\text{W}$

$\qquad\qquad = 2\,\text{MW}$ **[1]**

19. (i) The rms speed of molecules of a gas is the square root of the mean of the squared velocities of the molecules of a gas. rms speed is different from average speed

rms speed, $v_{\text{rms}} = \sqrt{\dfrac{v_1^2 + v_2^2 + v_3^3}{3}}$

and average speed, $\bar{v} = \dfrac{v_1 + v_2 + v_3}{3}$ **[1]**

(ii) According to kinetic theory of gases,

$$\bar{E} = \frac{3}{2} k_B T$$

or

$$T = \frac{2\bar{E}}{3k_B}$$

As, $T \propto \bar{E}$ (average kinetic energy of molecules)

∴ When temperature is 0K, average kinetic energy $= 0$

Hence, molecular motion increases at 0K. **[1]**

20. As range becomes equal for complementary angles, so

$$\alpha = 90° - \beta \text{ or } \beta = 90° - \alpha$$

The maximum heights attained by the projectiles are

$$h_1 = \frac{u^2 \sin^2 \alpha}{2g} \qquad \ldots(i)$$

and

$$h_2 = \frac{u^2 \sin^2 \beta}{2g} = \frac{u^2 \cos^2 \alpha}{2g} \qquad \ldots(ii)$$
[1]

$$[\because \beta = 90° - \alpha]$$

Multiplying Eq. (i) and Eq. (ii), we get

$$h_1 h_2 = \frac{u^4 \sin^2 \alpha \cos^2 \alpha}{4g^2}$$

$$\Rightarrow \quad \sqrt{4h_1 h_2} = \frac{u^2 \sin\alpha \cos\alpha}{g} = \frac{u^2 \sin 2\alpha}{2g}$$

$$[\because \sin 2\theta = 2\sin\theta \cos\theta]$$

$$\Rightarrow \quad 4\sqrt{h_1 h_2} = \frac{u^2 \sin 2\alpha}{g} = R \quad [\because R = \frac{u^2 \sin 2\theta}{g}]$$
[1]

Or

Angle of projection, $\theta = 30°$

Horizontal range, $R = 3$ km $= 3000$ m

Horizontal range, $R = \frac{u^2 \sin 2\theta}{g}$

or

$$\frac{u^2}{g} = \frac{R}{\sin 2\theta}$$

or

$$\frac{u^2}{g} = \frac{3000}{\sin 60°} = \frac{3000}{\sqrt{3}/2}$$

$$\frac{u^2}{g} = \frac{6000}{\sqrt{3}} \qquad \ldots(i)$$
[1]

When bullet is fired at an angle of projection 45°, then horizontal range is maximum.

$$\therefore \quad R_{max} = \frac{u^2 \sin(2 \times 45°)}{g} = \frac{u^2}{g}$$

$$= \frac{6000}{\sqrt{3}} = 2000\sqrt{3} = 3464 \text{ m}$$

Therefore, bullet cannot be fired up to 5000 m with the same muzzle speed. **[1]**

21. General equation of a progressive wave is

$$y = A\sin\omega\left(t - \frac{x}{v}\right)$$

Comparing the given two equations with above equation, we get

For first wave $\omega_1 = 200\pi$ rad s^{-1}

Frequency, $f_1 = \frac{\omega_1}{2\pi} = \frac{200\pi}{2\pi} = 100$ Hz

For second wave $\omega_2 = 208\pi$ rad s^{-1}

Frequency, $f_2 = \frac{\omega_2}{2\pi} = \frac{208\pi}{2\pi} = 104$ Hz **[1]**

(i) There is a slight difference between both frequencies, therefore the phenomenon arising due to the superposition of these waves is beats. **[1/2]**

(ii) Frequency of sound, i.e. heard by a person,

$$f = \frac{f_1 + f_2}{2} = \frac{100 + 104}{2} = 102 \text{ Hz}$$
[1/2]

22. A force F applied to the series combination produces displacements x_1 and x_2 in the two springs, then

$$F = -k_1 x_1 = -k_2 x_2$$

∴

$$x_1 = -\frac{F}{k_1} \text{ and } x_2 = -\frac{F}{k_2}$$

Total extension,

$$x = x_1 + x_2 = -F\left[\frac{1}{k_1} + \frac{1}{k_2}\right] = -F\left[\frac{k_1 + k_2}{k_1 k_2}\right]$$

or

$$F = -\frac{k_1 k_2}{k_1 + k_2} x$$
[1]

∴ Force constant of the series combination,

$$k_s = \frac{k_1 k_2}{k_1 + k_2}$$

Period of oscillation for the series combination,

$$T = 2\pi \sqrt{\frac{m}{k_s}} = 2\pi \sqrt{\frac{m(k_1 + k_2)}{k_1 k_2}} = 2\pi \sqrt{\frac{m}{k_1} + \frac{m}{k_2}}$$

or

$$T^2 = 4\pi^2 \left(\frac{m}{k_1} + \frac{m}{k_2}\right)$$

$$= \left(2\pi \sqrt{\frac{m}{k_1}}\right)^2 + \left(2\pi \sqrt{\frac{m}{k_2}}\right)^2$$

or

$$T^2 = t_1^2 + t_2^2$$
[1]

23. (i) According to first law of thermodynamics,

$$\Delta Q = \Delta U + \Delta W$$

or

$$\Delta Q = \Delta U + p\Delta V \quad [\because \Delta W = p\Delta V]$$

(a) In an isothermal process, the temperature of system remains constant. So, there is no change in internal energy (U) of the system, i.e.

$$\Delta U = 0$$
$$\Rightarrow \qquad \Delta Q = \Delta W$$

i.e. All heat energy given gets converted to work.

(b) In an isochoric process, the volume of the system remains constant, i.e.

$$\Delta V = 0$$
$$\Rightarrow \qquad \Delta W = p\Delta V = 0$$
$$\Rightarrow \qquad \Delta Q = \Delta U$$

i.e. All heat energy Q given goes to increase the internal energy U. [1]

(ii) First law of thermodynamics tells us about the conversion of mechanical work into heat energy and *vice-versa*. It does not put any condition as to why heat cannot flow from lower temperature to higher temperature. [1]

24. Heat lost by water $= m_f c_w (\theta_i - \theta_f)_w$

$$= (0.30 \text{ kg}) (4186 \text{ J kg}^{-1} \text{ K}^{-1}) (50.0°C - 6.7°C)$$

$$= 54376.14 \text{ J}$$

Heat required to melt ice $= m_i L_f = (0.15 \text{ kg}) L_f$ [1]

Heat required to raise temperature of ice water to final temperature $= m_i c_w (\theta_f - \theta_i)_f$

$$= (0.15 \text{ kg}) (4186 \text{ J kg}^{-1}\text{K}^{-1}) (6.7°C - 0°C)$$

$$= 4206.93 \text{ J}$$

Heat lost = Heat gained

$$54376.14 \text{ J} = (0.15 \text{ kg}) L_f + 4206.93 \text{ J}$$

$$L_f = 3.34 \times 10^5 \text{ Jkg}^{-1}$$ [1]

25. (i) When the circular track is banked, the wear and tear of the tyres are reduced. The horizontal component of the normal reaction of the road provides the necessary centripetal force for the vehicle to move along the curved path. [1]

(ii) **Law of conservation of angular momentum** The law of conservation of angular momentum states that if no external torque acts on a system, then its angular momentum remains constant, i.e. if $\Sigma \tau_{ext} = 0$, then $\mathbf{L}$ = constant. e.g. When a planet approaches the sun while revolving in its elliptical orbit, the moment of inertia of the planet about the sun decreases. To conserve the angular momentum, its angular speed increases. [1/2]

i.e. $\qquad f_k \propto R$ or $f_k = \mu_k R$
$$\Rightarrow \qquad \mu_k = \frac{f_k}{R}$$

The proportionality constant μ_k is called coefficient of kinetic friction. [1/2]

26. (i) From the equation,

$$x(t) = -A\cos(\omega t), \text{ we get} \qquad \ldots(i)$$

At $\qquad t = 0, x(0) = -A\cos 0° = -A$

At $\qquad t = \dfrac{T}{4}, x(T/4)$

$$= -A\cos\left(\frac{2\pi}{T} \times \frac{T}{4}\right) = 0$$

$$t = \frac{T}{2}, \quad x = +A$$ [1/2]

So, the expression can be represented by an x-t graph as shown below

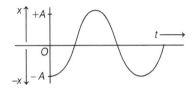

It is a SHM because the displacement varies periodically with time. [1]

(ii) At any instant, the displacement of a particle executing SHM is represented as

$$x = A\cos(\omega t + \phi_0) \qquad \ldots(i)$$

$\therefore$ Velocity, $u = \dfrac{dx}{dt} = -\omega A\sin(\omega t + \phi_0)$ [1/2]

Hence, kinetic energy $= \dfrac{1}{2}m\omega^2 A^2 \sin^2(\omega t + \phi_0)$

But, $A^2 \sin^2(\omega t + \phi_0) = A^2[1 - \cos^2(\omega t + \phi_0]$

$$= A^2 - A^2\cos^2(\omega t + \phi_0)$$

$$= A^2 - x^2 \qquad \text{[from Eq. (i)]}$$

$\therefore \qquad KE = \dfrac{1}{2}m\omega^2(A^2 - x^2)$

$$= \frac{1}{2}k(A^2 - x^2) \quad (\because k = m\omega^2)$$ [1]

Or

(i) The two prongs of a tuning fork set each other in resonance and help to maintain vibration for a longer time. [1]

(ii) The pitch of a tuning fork depends on

(a) **Length of the prongs** (*l*) It is inversely proportional to the square of length,

i.e. $\qquad$ Pitch $\propto \dfrac{1}{l^2}$

(b) **Thickness of prongs** (*b*) It is directly proportional to the thickness of prongs,

i.e. pitch $\propto b$

(c) **Elasticity of material** (*Y*) It is directly proportional to the square root of the Young's modulus of elasticity (*Y*),

i.e. $\qquad$ Pitch $\propto \sqrt{Y}$

(d) **Density of material** (ρ) It is inversely proportional to the square root of density of the material, i.e.

$$\text{Pitch} \propto \frac{1}{\sqrt{\rho}}$$

[2]

27. Consider a thin uniform rod AB of length L and mass M, free to rotate about an axis YY' through its centre O and perpendicular to its length.

$\therefore$ Mass per unit length $= \dfrac{M}{L}$

If we consider a small mass element of length dx at a distance x from O, mass of the element $= \dfrac{M}{L}dx$

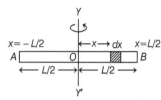

Moment of inertia of small element dx about YY',

$$dI = \frac{M}{L}dx \times x^2$$

Now, moment of inertia of the whole rod about YY' will be

$$I = \int dI = \int_{-L/2}^{L/2} \frac{M}{L}x^2 dx$$

$$I = \frac{ML^2}{12} \qquad \ldots(i)$$

[2]

As, $\qquad I = Mk^2$

$\Rightarrow \qquad Mk^2 = \dfrac{ML^2}{12}$

$\Rightarrow \qquad k^2 = \dfrac{L^2}{12}$

(where, k = radius of gyration of the rod about YY')

$\therefore$ Radius of gyration, $\quad k = \dfrac{L}{2\sqrt{3}}$

[1]

Or

Let mass per unit area of the disc be m.

$\therefore$ Mass of the disc (M) = Total area of disc $\times$ Mass per unit area = $\pi R^2 m$

Mass of the portion removed from the disc (M')

$$= \pi\left(\frac{R}{2}\right)^2 m = \frac{\pi R^2}{4}m = \frac{M}{4}$$

The centre of mass of the original disc is O and the centre of mass of the removed part is O_1 and let centre of mass of the remaining part be O_2.

According to the question, figure can be drawn as

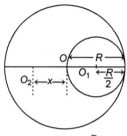

Here, $\qquad OO_1 = \dfrac{R}{2}$

The remaining portion of the disc can be considered as a system of two masses M at O and $-M' = -\dfrac{M}{4}$ at O_1.

If the distance of the centre of mass of the remaining part from the centre O is at a distance x, then

$$x = \frac{M \times 0 - M' \times \dfrac{R}{2}}{M - M'} = \frac{-\dfrac{M}{4} \times \dfrac{R}{2}}{M - \dfrac{M}{4}}$$

$$= -\frac{MR}{8} \times \frac{4}{3M} = -\frac{R}{6}$$

Therefore, centre of mass of the remaining part is at $\dfrac{R}{6}$ to the left of centre O.

[3]

28. (i) The capacitance of a conductor is defined as the ratio of the charge given to the rise in the potential of the conductor.

i.e. $\qquad C = \dfrac{q}{V} = \dfrac{q^2}{W} \qquad \left(\because V = \dfrac{W}{q}\right)$

$\Rightarrow \qquad C = \dfrac{\text{ampere}^2\text{-sec}^2}{\text{kg -metre}^2/\text{sec}^2}$

Hence, dimensions of C are $[M^{-1}L^{-2}T^4A^2]$.

From Ohm's law, $V = iR$

$\Rightarrow \qquad R = \dfrac{V}{i} = \dfrac{\text{Volt}}{\text{Ampere}} = \text{kg -metre}^2\text{sec}^{-3}\text{ampere}^{-2}$

$\therefore$ Dimensions of $R = [ML^2T^{-3}A^{-2}]$

$\therefore$ Dimensions of $CR = [M^{-1}L^{-2}T^4A^2][ML^2T^{-3}A^{-2}]$

$\qquad\qquad = [M^0L^0TA^0]$

[1½]

(ii) (a) Since, work and energy both have the same dimensions [ML^2T^{-2}], their ratio is a dimensionless quantity.

(b) In $\sin\theta$, θ represents an angle. An angle is the ratio of two lengths, i.e. arc length and radius. Therefore, θ is dimensionless and hence $\sin\theta$ is dimensionless.

(c) $\left[\dfrac{\text{Momentum}}{\text{Time}}\right] = \left[\dfrac{MLT^{-1}}{T}\right] = [MLT^{-2}]$

Hence, the given ratio is not dimensionless. **[1½]**

29. (i) Let C be the point, where the stone hits the hill surface, then from $\triangle ABC$,

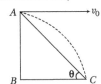

$$\frac{AB}{BC} = \frac{\frac{1}{2}gt^2}{v_0 t} = \tan\theta$$

$$\therefore \qquad t = \frac{2v_0 \tan\theta}{g}$$

Now, x-coordinate at $C = v_0 t = \frac{2v_0^2 \tan\theta}{g}$

and y-coordinate at $C = -\frac{1}{2}gt^2 = -\frac{2v_0^2 \tan^2\theta}{g}$ [2]

(ii) Angular velocity ω is constant.

$$\therefore \qquad v \propto r \text{ or } \frac{v_A}{v_B} = \frac{r_A}{r_B} \qquad (\because v = r\omega)$$ [1]

30. Let there be an observer travelling parallel to the trolley with the same speed. He will observe the initial momentum of the trolley of mass M and child of mass m as zero. When the child jumps in opposite direction, he will observe the increase in the velocity of the trolley by Δv. Let u be the velocity of the child. He will observe child landing at velocity $(u - \Delta v)$.

Therefore, final momentum $= M\Delta v - m(u - \Delta v)$

From the law of conservation of momentum, we have

$$M\Delta v - m(u - \Delta v) = 0 \implies \Delta v = \frac{mu}{M + m}$$ [1]

Putting various values, we have

$$\Delta v = \frac{4 \times 20}{20 + 220} = 0.33 \text{ ms}^{-1}$$ [1]

$\therefore$ Final speed of trolley is 10.36 ms^{-1}
The child takes 2.5 s to run on the trolley.
Therefore, the trolley moves a distance

$$= 2.5 \times 10.36 \text{ m} = 25.9 \text{ m}$$ [1]

31. (i) Weight of a person can become zero under the following conditions
   (a) When the person is at the centre of the earth (as $g = 0$ at the centre of the earth) because

$$g_d = g\left(1 - \frac{d}{R}\right), \text{ at centre } d = R,$$

   Hence $g_d = g\left(1 - \frac{R}{R}\right) = 0$

   (b) When the person is standing in a freely falling lift. [2]

(ii) According to Kepler's third law,

$$\frac{T_n^2}{T_e^2} = \frac{R_n^3}{R_e^3}$$ [1]

where subscripts n and e refer to the neptune and the earth, respectively.

$$\therefore \qquad T_n^2 = T_e^2 \times \left(\frac{R_n}{R_e}\right)^3$$

$$= 1 \times (30)^3$$ [1]

[$\because$ time period of the earth's revolution = 1 year and ratio of radii (hence, diameters) of the neptune and the earth is 30]

$$\therefore \qquad T_n = 1 \times \sqrt{(30)^3}$$
$$T_n = 30\sqrt{30} = 164.3 \text{ yr}$$ [1]

Or

(i) The energy needed by a satellite to leave its orbit around the earth and escape to infinity is called its binding energy.

The total energy of a satellite is $-\frac{GMm}{2r}$. To make total energy equal to zero, it has to supply an extra energy equal to $+\frac{GMm}{2r}$ in order to escape to infinity.

Hence, binding energy of a satellite $= \frac{GMm}{2r}$

Because $E = KE + PE = +\frac{1}{2}\frac{GMm}{r} - \frac{GMm}{r} = -\frac{GMm}{2r}$

$\left(\text{here, KE due to orbital motion of satellite} \right.$

$\left. \frac{1}{2}mv_0^2 = \frac{1}{2}m\left(\frac{GM}{r}\right) \text{ and PE} = -\frac{GMm}{r}\right)$ [2]

(ii) Escape velocity at a height h above the earth's surface, $v_e = \sqrt{2g_h(R + h)}$

$$\therefore \qquad g_h = \frac{gR^2}{(R + h)^2}$$

$$v_e = \sqrt{\frac{2 \times gR^2}{(R + h)^2} \times (R + h)} = \sqrt{\frac{2gR^2}{R + h}}$$

Given, $g = 9.8 \text{ ms}^{-2}$, $R = 6.4 \times 10^6 \text{ m}$,

$$h = 1600 \text{ km} = 1.6 \times 10^6 \text{ m}$$

$$\therefore \quad R + h = (6.4 + 1.6) \times 10^6 = 8 \times 10^6 \text{ m}$$

$$v_e = \sqrt{\frac{2 \times 9.8 \times (6.4 \times 10^6)^2}{8 \times 10^6}}$$

$$= 10.02 \times 10^3 \text{ ms}^{-1}$$

$$= 10.02 \text{ km s}^{-1}$$ [3]

32. (i) **When the lift is stationary** The reaction of the spring is equal to weight of the bag.

$$\therefore \qquad R = mg = 49\,\text{N}$$

$$\Rightarrow \qquad m = \frac{49}{g} = \frac{49}{9.8} = 5\,\text{kg}$$

When the lift moves downward

Reaction, $R' = m(g - a) = 5(9.8 - 5)$

$$= 24\,\text{N} \qquad \text{[1]}$$

(ii) Consider a body of mass m tied to one end of a string and rotated in a vertical circle of radius r.

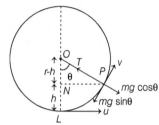

Velocity of body at any point

When the body passes through lowest point L with velocity u and through any point P with velocity v, it has moved up through a vertical height $LN = h$

According to law of conservation of energy,

$$(KE + PE) \text{ at } L = (KE + PE) \text{ at } P$$

$$\frac{1}{2}mu^2 + 0 = \frac{1}{2}mv^2 + mgh$$

$$v = \sqrt{u^2 - 2gh} \qquad \ldots(i) \quad \text{[2]}$$

Tension along the string at any point P

The various forces acting at any point P in the circle are :

(a) weight mg acting vertically downwards

(b) tension T along the string

Hence, $T - mg\cos\theta = \dfrac{mv^2}{r}$

$$\Rightarrow \qquad T = mg\cos\theta + \frac{mv^2}{r} \qquad \ldots(ii)$$

From $\triangle OPN, \quad \cos\theta = \dfrac{ON}{OP} = \dfrac{r - h}{r} \qquad \ldots(iii)$

Using Eqs. (i) and (iii), we get

$$T = mg\left(\frac{r - h}{r}\right) + \frac{m}{r}(u^2 - 2gh) \quad \text{[from Eq. (i)]}$$

$$= \frac{m}{r}(gr - gh + u^2 - 2gh)$$

$$T = \frac{m}{r}(u^2 + gr - 3gh)$$

As the bottom of circle,

$$h = 0$$

$$\Rightarrow \qquad T = \frac{m}{r}(u^2 + gr)$$

At the top of circle, $h = 2r$

$$\Rightarrow \qquad T = \frac{m}{r}(u^2 - 5gr) \qquad \text{[2]}$$

Or

(i) As the applied force increases, the force of static friction also increases and becomes equal to the applied force. Hence, it's a self adjusting force. **[1]**

(ii) **Angle of friction** The angle of friction may be defined as the angle which the resultant of the limiting friction and the normal reaction makes with the normal reaction. **[1/2]**

Relation between angle of friction and coefficient of friction

The coefficient of static friction is equal to the tangent of the angle of friction, i.e. $\tan\theta = \mu_s$ **[1/2]**

(iii) Angle of repose is defined as the minimum angle of inclination of a plane with the horizontal, such that a body placed on the plane just begins to slide down the line. It is represented by α and its value depends on material and nature of the surfaces in contact.

Consider a body of mass m placed on an inclined plane. The angle of inclination α of the inclined plane is so adjusted that a body placed on it just begins to slide down. Thus, α is the angle of repose. **[1]**

The various forces acting on the body are

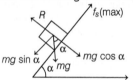

(a) The weight mg of the body acting vertically downwards.

(b) The limiting friction $f_{s(max)}$ acting along the inclined plane is in the upward direction. It balances the component $mg\sin\alpha$ of the weight mg.

Thus, $\qquad f_{s(max)} = mg\sin\alpha \qquad \ldots(i)$

(c) The normal reaction R acts at right angle to the inclined plane in the upward direction. It balances the component $mg\cos\alpha$ of the weight mg. Thus,

$$R = mg\cos\alpha \qquad \ldots(ii)$$

Dividing Eq. (i) by Eq. (ii), we get

$$\frac{f_{s(max)}}{R} = \frac{mg\sin\alpha}{mg\cos\alpha} \quad \text{or} \quad \mu_s = \tan\alpha$$

Thus, the coefficient of static friction is equal to the tangent of the angle of repose.

As, $\qquad \mu_s = \tan\theta = \tan\alpha$

$$\therefore \qquad \theta = \alpha$$

Thus, the angle of friction is equal to the angle of repose. **[2]**

33. (i) Given, $R = 6$ mm $= 6 \times 10^{-3}$ m,

$\qquad h = 2$ mm $= 2 \times 10^{-3}$ m,

$\qquad \rho = 0.8 \times 10^3$ kg/m^3

Excess pressure inside soap bubble = Pressure exerted by 2 mm oil column

or $\quad \dfrac{4\sigma}{R} = h\rho g$

$\Rightarrow \quad \sigma = \dfrac{1}{4} h R \rho g$

$\qquad = \dfrac{1}{4} \times 2 \times 10^{-3} \times 6 \times 10^{-3} \times 0.8 \times 10^3 \times 9.8$

$\qquad = 2.35 \times 10^{-2}$ Nm^{-1} $\qquad$ **[2]**

(ii) **Excess pressure inside a soap bubble** In case of a soap bubble, there are two surfaces which expand, so

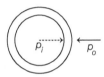

Increase in surface area of a soap bubble

$\qquad = 2 \times 8\pi R \, dR = 16\pi R \, dR$

External work done in increasing the surface area of the soap bubble = Increase in surface energy

= Increase in surface area × Surface tension

$= 16\pi \, R \, dRS$ $\qquad$ …(i)

But, work done = force × change in radius

where, force = excess pressure × area

$\qquad = (p \times 4\pi R^2)$

So, work done $= p \times 4\pi R^2 \times dR$ $\qquad$ …(ii)

From Eqs. (i) and (ii), we get

$\qquad p \times 4\pi R^2 \times dR = 16\pi \, RdRS$

$\Rightarrow \qquad\qquad p = \dfrac{4S}{R}$

Pressure difference inside a soap bubble,

$\qquad p_i - p_0 = \dfrac{4S}{R}$ $\qquad$ **[1½]**

Excess pressure inside an air bubble in a liquid is similar to a liquid drop in air, it has only one free spherical surface. Hence, excess pressure is given by

$\qquad p = \dfrac{2S}{R}$

When an air bubble of radius R lies at a depth h below the free surface of a liquid of density ρ and

surface tension S, the excess pressure inside the bubble will be

$\qquad p = \dfrac{2S}{R} + h\rho g$ $\qquad$ **[1½]**

Or

(i) Here, $F_1 = 3$ kg-f $= 3 \times 9.8$N $= 29.4$N

$\qquad \Delta l_1 = 0.61$ mm $= 6.1 \times 10^{-4}$m

$\qquad F_2 = 5$ kg-f $= 5 \times 9.8 = 49$N

$\qquad \Delta l_2 = 1.02$ mm $= 1.02 \times 10^{-3}$m

$\therefore \qquad U_1 = \dfrac{1}{2} F_1 \cdot \Delta l_1 = \dfrac{29.4 \times 6.1 \times 10^{-4}}{2}$

$\qquad\qquad = 8.96 \times 10^{-3}$ J

and $\quad U_2 = \dfrac{1}{2} F_2 \cdot \Delta l_2 = \dfrac{49 \times 1.02 \times 10^{-3}}{2}$

$\qquad\qquad = 24.99 \times 10^{-3}$ J

$\therefore$ Change in elastic potential energy of the wire,

$\qquad \Delta U = U_2 - U_1$

$\qquad\qquad = 24.99 \times 10^{-3} - 8.96 \times 10^{-3}$

$\qquad\qquad = 16.03 \times 10^{-3}$ J $\qquad$ **[2½]**

(ii)

$$\text{//////////////////////}$$

Steel

$\boxed{2m}$

Brass

$\boxed{3m}$

As Young's modulus, $Y = \dfrac{FL}{A\Delta L} = \dfrac{4FL}{\pi D^2 \Delta L}$

where, the symbols have their usual meanings.

$\therefore \qquad \Delta L = \dfrac{4FL}{\pi D^2 Y}$

$\therefore \qquad \dfrac{\Delta L_S}{\Delta L_B} = \dfrac{F_S}{F_B} \dfrac{L_S}{L_B} \dfrac{D_B^2}{D_S^2} \dfrac{Y_B}{Y_S}$

where, subscripts S and B refer to steel and brass, respectively.

Here, $\quad F_S = (2m + 3m) g = 5mg$

$\qquad F_B = 3mg$

$\qquad \dfrac{L_S}{L_B} = q,$

$\qquad \dfrac{D_S}{D_B} = p, \dfrac{Y_S}{Y_B} = r$

$\therefore \qquad \dfrac{\Delta L_S}{\Delta L_B} = \left(\dfrac{5mg}{3mg}\right)(q)\left(\dfrac{1}{p}\right)^2\left(\dfrac{1}{r}\right) = \dfrac{5q}{3p^2 r}$ $\qquad$ **[2½]**

SAMPLE QUESTION PAPER 2

A HIGHLY SIMULATED SAMPLE QUESTION PAPER FOR CBSE CLASS XI EXAMINATIONS

PHYSICS (UNSOLVED)

GENERAL INSTRUCTIONS

1. All questions are compulsory. There are 33 questions in all.
2. This question paper has five sections: Section A, Section B, Section C, Section D and Section E.
3. **Section A** contains ten very short answer questions and four assertion reasoning MCQs of 1 mark each, **Section B** has two case based questions of 4 marks each, **Section C** contains nine short answer questions of 2 marks each, **Section D** contains five short answer questions of 3 marks each and **Section E** contains three long answer questions of 5 marks each.
4. There is no overall choice. However internal choice is provided. You have to attempt only one of the choices in such questions.

TIME : 3 HOURS   **MAX. MARKS : 70**

SECTION-A

All questions are compulsory. In case of internal choices, attempt anyone of them.

1. The figure given below is the part of a horizontal stretched net. In this section, AB is stretched with a force of 10N, then find the force in the section BC.   [Ans. 10 N]

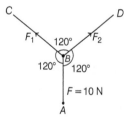

Or

A force of 98 N is required to just start moving a body of mass 100 kg over ice. What is the coefficient of static friction?   [Ans. 0.1]

2. There are two spheres of same radius and material at same temperature but one being solid while the other hollow. Which sphere will expand more, if they are heated to same temperature?

3. A liquid X of density 3.36 g/cm^3 is poured in a U-tube in right arm with height 10 cm, which contains Hg. Another liquid Y is poured in left arm with height 8 cm. Upper levels of X and Y are same. What is the density of Y? (Given, density of Hg = 13.6 g/cc)   [Ans. 0.8 g/cc]

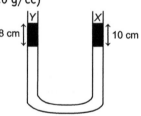

4. During an adiabatic process, the pressure of a gas is found to be proportional to the cube of its absolute temperature. What is the ratio $\dfrac{C_p}{C_V} = \gamma$ for the gas?   [Ans. 3/2]

Or

Find the value of C_V for solids m.

5. If the displacement of an object in simple harmonic motion is given by $x = A\cos(\omega t)$, then what will be its potential energy at $t = \dfrac{T}{4}$?   [Ans. zero]

Or

Find the force on an object of mass m executing SHM.

6. The phase difference between two points separated by 0.8 m in a wave of frequency 120 Hz is 0.5π. What will be the velocity of wave? **[Ans. 384 ms^{-1}]**

7. The speed of light is about 3×10^8 m/s. Express it in terms of astronomical unit per minute. **[Ans. 0.12 AU/m]**

Or

Justify the statement: 'Torque and energy have the same dimensions'.

8. A silver atom in a solid oscillates in SHM in a certain direction with a frequency of 10^{12} s^{-1}. What is the force constant of the bonds connecting one atom with the other? (Molecular weight of silver = 108) **[Ans. 7.1 Nm–1]**

9. A spherical body of volume V and density σ is suspended from a string, the other end of the string is connected to the roof of a sealed container filled with an ideal fluid of density ρ. If the container accelerates towards right with a constant acceleration a, then find the force exerted by the liquid on the body, when body is in equilibrium w.r.t. fluid.

10. When a body accelerates by βt, what is the velocity after time t, if it starts from rest?

For question numbers 11, 12, 13 and 14, two statements are given-one labelled Assertion (A) and the other labelled Reason (R). Select the correct answer to these questions from the codes (a), (b), (c) and (d) as given below.

(a) Both A and R are true and R is the correct explanation of A.

(b) Both A and R are true but R is not the correct explanation of A.

(c) A is true but R is false.

(d) A is false and R is also false.

11. **Assertion** Moon has no atmosphere.

Reason The escape speed for the moon is much smaller. Gas molecules, if formed on the surface of the moon having velocities larger than escape speed will escape the gravitational pull of the moon.

12. **Assertion** The dimensional method cannot be used to obtain the dependence of the work done by a force **F** on the angle θ between force **F** and displacement x.

Reason All trigonometric functions are dimensionless.

13. **Assertion** A body of mass 10 kg is placed on a rough inclined surface ($\mu = 0.7$). The surface is inclined to horizontal at angle 30°. Acceleration of the body down the plane will be zero.

Reason Work done by friction is always negative.

14. **Assertion** Smaller drop of liquid resists deforming forces better than the larger drops.

Reason Excess pressure inside a drop is directly proportional to its surface area.

Answers

11. (a)   12. (a)   13. (c)   14. (c)

SECTION-B

Questions 15 and 16 are case study based questions and are compulsory. Attempt any 4 sub parts from each question. Each question carries 1 mark.

15. **Racing on Bike**

Two bikers having same racing skills are competing against each other. Biker 1 has a bike of 1500 HP while Biker 2 has a bike of 1000 HP. Biker 1 defeated biker 2 in a race by 10 seconds.

Later biker 1 explained biker 2 that he can also win if he had 1500 HP bike. Moreover the weight also has a huge impact on the speed of the bike. More power and less weight makes a bike faster whereas less power and more weight makes a bike go slower.

(i) 1 Horse power (HP) .... watt
   (a) 446   (b) 746
   (c) 766   (d) 674

(ii) If the biker applied the brakes instantly, he goes from 10 ms^{-1} to 0 ms^{-1} in 7s. Assume that brakes apply 70 N, the work done on the road is equal to
   (a) 700 J   (b) 0.7 J
   (c) Zero   (d) None of these

(iii) Which of the following is largest unit of power?
   (a) Watt   (b) HP
   (c) Joule   (d) erg

(iv) The 1500 HP engine produce ...... joule per second energy.
   (a) 1.1×10^6
   (b) 3.8×10^6
   (c) 1.1×10^4
   (d) 3.8×10^4

(v) If the weight of 1500 HP bike is 100 kg, then find the maximum speed it can attain.
   (a) 380 km/h
   (b) 360 km/h
   (c) 340 km/h
   (d) 400 km/h

16. Moment of Inertia

A heavy wheel called flywheel is attached to the shaft of steam engine, automobile engine etc., because of its large moment of inertia, the flywheel opposes the sudden increase or decrease of the speed of the vehicle. It allows a gradual change in the speed and prevents jerky motion and hence ensure smooth ride of passengers.

(i) Analogue of mass in rotational motion is
   (a) moment of inertia
   (b) angular momentum
   (c) gyration
   (d) None of the above

(ii) Moment of inertia of a body depends upon
   (a) axis of rotation
   (b) torque
   (c) angular momentum
   (d) angular velocity

(iii) If a girl rotating on a chair bends her hand as shown in figure, the (neglecting frictional force)

   (a) I_{girl} will reduce   (b) I_{girl} will increase
   (c) ω_{girl} will reduce   (d) None of these

(iv) Two masses are joined with a light rod and the system is rotating about the fixed axis as shown in the figure. The MI of the system about the axis is

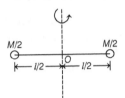

   (a) $Ml^2/2$ (b) $Ml^2/4$
   (c) Ml^2 (d) $Ml^2/6$

(v) One solid sphere A and another hollow sphere B are of same mass and same outer radius. Their moments of inertia about their diameters are respectively, I_A and I_B such that
   (a) $I_A = I_B$ (b) $I_A > I_B$
   (c) $I_A < I_B$ (d) None of these

Answers

15. (i) c   (ii) c   (iii) b   (iv) a   (v) b
16. (i) a   (ii) a   (iii) a   (iv) b   (v) c

SECTION-C

All questions are compulsory. In case of internal choices, attempt anyone.

17. Three sinusoidal waves of same frequency travel along a string in +ve x –direction. Their amplitudes are y, $\dfrac{y}{2}$, and $\dfrac{y}{3}$ and their phase constants are 0, $\dfrac{\pi}{2}$ and π respectively.

What are the
(a) amplitude
(b) phase constant of the resultant wave?

[**Ans.** (a) 0.83 y, (b) 37°]

18. (i) 10 mol of an ideal gas at constant temperature, 500 K is compressed from 50 L to 5L. Calculate the work done in this process.

(Given, $R = 8.31$ J mol^{-1}K^{-1})

[Ans. -9.6×10^4 J]

(ii) An electric heater supplies heat to a system at a rate of 50W. If the system performs work at a rate of 30 J/s. At what rate is the internal energy increased?   [Ans. 20 W]

19. (i) Two containers of equal volume contain the same gas at pressures p_1 and p_2 and absolute temperatures T_1 and T_2, respectively. When both the vessels are joined together, the gas reaches a common pressure p and common temperature T. Determine the ratio p/T.

(ii) At a given temperature, equal masses of monoatomic and diatomic gases are supplied equal quantities of heat. Which of the two gases will suffer larger temperature rise?

20. Define the term beats. How are they formed?

21. (i) Action and reaction are equal and opposite. Why cannot they cancel each other?

(ii) According to Newton's third law, every force is accompanied by an equal and opposite force. How can a movement ever take place?

Or

(i) Why do we consider gravitational force as a conservative force?

(ii) Potential energy depends on the reference point. Justify this statement.

22. Find the moment of inertia of a ring which is formed by bending a thin wire of mass M and length L about its axis.

Or

A hollow cylinder and solid sphere of mass m and radius r are rotating about an axis passing through its centre. If torques of equal magnitude are applied to them, then find the ratio of angular accelerations produced.

23. How can we locate the centre of mass of rigid bodies of regular geometrical shape and having uniform mass distribution? Give examples.

Or

When is a rigid body said to be in equilibrium? State the necessary conditions for a body to be in equilibrium.

24. What will be mass of air in a room that measures 5.0 m $\times 8.0$ m $\times 3.0$ m? (The density of air is $\dfrac{1}{800}$ times of that of water)

[Ans. 150 kg]

25. A balloon has 5.0 g mole of helium at 7°C. Calculate

(i) the number of atoms of helium in the balloon.   [Ans. 30×10^{23}]

(ii) the total internal energy of the system.

[Ans. 1.74×10^4 J]

SECTION-D

All questions are compulsory. In case of internal choices, attempt anyone.

26. A monkey of mass 40 kg climbs on a rope which can withstand a maximum tension of 600 N. Determine in the following cases whether the rope will break or not.

(i) The monkey climbs up with an acceleration of 6 ms^{-2}.

(ii) The monkey climbs down with an acceleration of 4 ms^{-2}.

(iii) The monkey climbs up with a uniform speed of 5 ms^{-1}. (Take, $g = 10$ ms^{-2}) Ignore the mass of the rope.

27. (i) A bowler throws a ball giving it a horizontal velocity and a small downward velocity. Determine the resultant speed of the ball at the bottom.

(ii) If the speed of a projectile at the maximum height is $\dfrac{1}{2}$ of its initial speed, then show that $\dfrac{4}{\sqrt{3}}$ is the ratio of range of projectile to the maximum height attained.   [Ans. $4/\sqrt{3}$]

Or

Show that vectors $\mathbf{A} = 2\hat{\mathbf{i}} - 3\hat{\mathbf{j}} - \hat{\mathbf{k}}$ and $\mathbf{B} = -6\hat{\mathbf{i}} + 9\hat{\mathbf{j}} + 3\hat{\mathbf{k}}$ are parallel.

UNSOLVED

28. (i) If frequency (F), velocity (v) and density (D) are considered as fundamental units. Then find the dimensional formula for momentum.

[Ans. Dv^4F^{-3}]

(ii) Which group of Physics has recently came into existence?

(iii) Quantitative measurement plays major role in Physics, why?

29. A transverse harmonic wave on a string is given by $y(x, t) = 3 \sin\left(36t + 0.2x + \dfrac{\pi}{4}\right)$ for $x = 0, 2$ cm, where y is in cm and t is in s. The displacements at different instants of time is shown below:

t	0	$\dfrac{T}{8}$	$\dfrac{2T}{8}$	$\dfrac{3T}{8}$	$\dfrac{4T}{8}$	$\dfrac{5T}{8}$	$\dfrac{6T}{8}$	$\dfrac{7T}{8}$	T
y	$\dfrac{3}{\sqrt{2}}$	3	$\dfrac{3}{\sqrt{2}}$	0	$-\dfrac{3}{\sqrt{2}}$	-3	$-\dfrac{3}{\sqrt{2}}$	0	$\dfrac{3}{\sqrt{2}}$

(i) Interpret the table with the help of a graph and write the nature of the graph.

(ii) How do amplitude, frequency or phase differ from one point to another in oscillatory motion of a travelling wave in the graph?

30. (i) If the breaking force for a wire is F, then determine the breaking force for
(a) two parallel wires of the same size
(b) for a single wire of double thickness?

(ii) The Young's modulus of a wire of length L and radius r is Y. If the length is reduced to $L/2$ and radius to $r/4$, what will be its Young's modulus? Explain.

Or

(i) Prove that the value of molar specific heat at constant volume for a monoatomic gas is $\dfrac{3}{2} R$.

(ii) Write the ratio of specific heats of a diatomic gas.

[Ans. 7/5]

(iii) Draw the volume- temperature graph at atmospheric pressure for a monoatomic gas (V in m^3, T in °C).

SECTION-E

All questions are compulsory. In case of internal choices, attempt anyone.

31. (i) A projectile is projected upward at an angle θ with the vertical with velocity u. Obtain the expression for
(a) time of flight,
(b) maximum height and
(c) horizontal range.

(ii) A projectile is fired from the surface of the earth with a velocity of 5 ms^{-1} at angle θ with the horizontal. Another projectile fired from another planet with a velocity of 3 ms^{-1} at the same angle follows a trajectory of the projectile fired from the earth. What is the value of the acceleration due to gravity on the planet (in ms^{-2})? (Given, $g = 9.8$ ms^{-2})

[Ans. 3.5 ms^{-2}]

Or

(i) Express the condition under which the three equations of motion can be used.

(ii) A girl is riding a bicycle with a speed of 5 ms^{-1} towards north direction on the road and raindrops start falling vertically downwards. On increasing the speed to 15 ms^{-1} rain appears to fall making an angle of 45° of the vertical. Find the magnitude of velocity of rain.

[Ans. $5\sqrt{5}$ ms^{-1}]

32. (i) Determine the ratio of the kinetic energy required to be given to the satellite to escape earth's gravitational field to the kinetic energy required to be given, so that the satellite moves in a circular orbit just above earth atmosphere.

[Ans. 2:1]

(ii) Two satellites A and B go round a planet P in circular orbits in circular orbits having radii $4R$ and R respectively. If the speed of the satellite A is $3v$, what will be the speed of the satellite B?

[Ans. 6 v]

(iii) For a satellite, escape velocity is 11 kms^{-1}. If the satellite is launched at an angle of 60° with the vertical, then what will be the escape velocity?

[Ans. 11 kms^{-1}]

(iv) Orbital velocity of earth's satellite near the surface is 7 kms^{-1}. When the radius of the orbit is 4 times than that of the earth's radius, what will be the orbital velocity in that orbit? [**Ans.** 3.5 kms^{-1}]

Or

(i) The masses and radii of the earth and moon are M_1, R_1 and M_2, R_2 respectively. Their centres are distance d apart. Determine the minimum velocity with which a particle of mass m should be projected from a point mid-way between their centres, so that it escapes to infinity.

(ii) If mass of earth is M, radius is R and gravitational constant is G, then what will be the work done to take 1 kg mass from earth surface to infinity?

(iii) Escape velocity of a body of 1 kg mass on a planet is 100 ms^{-1}. Calculate the gravitational potential energy of the planet. [**Ans.** − 5000 J]

33. (i) An ideal liquid of constant density ρ flows in a streamline motion along a tube of variable cross-section. The tube is kept inclined in the vertical plane as shown in figure. The area of cross-section of the tube at two points P and Q at heights of h_1 metre and h_2 metre are respectively, a_1 and a_2.

The velocity of the liquid at point P is 1 ms^{-1}. Find the expression for work done per unit volume by the pressure.

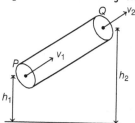

(ii) A venturimeter is connected to two points in the mains where its radii are 20cm and 10cm respectively and the levels of water column in the tubes differ by 10 cm. How much water flows through the pipe per minute? [**Ans.** 2728.7 litre/min]

Or

(i) A metallic ball has a radius of 9.0 cm at 0°C. Calculate the change in its volume when it is heated to 90°C. Given that coefficient of linear expansion of metal of ball is 1.2×10^{-5} K^{-1}. [**Ans.** 9.88 cm^3]

(ii) Two rods of the same area of cross-section, but of lengths l_1 & l_2 and conductivities K_1 & K_2 are joined in series. Find the equivalent conductivity of the given combination.

SAMPLE QUESTION PAPER 3

A HIGHLY SIMULATED SAMPLE QUESTION PAPER FOR CBSE CLASS XI EXAMINATIONS

PHYSICS (UNSOLVED)

GENERAL INSTRUCTIONS

1. All questions are compulsory. There are 33 questions in all.
2. This question paper has five sections: Section A, Section B, Section C, Section D and Section E.
3. **Section A** contains ten very short answer questions and four assertion reasoning MCQs of 1 mark each, **Section B** has two case based questions of 4 marks each, **Section C** contains nine short answer questions of 2 marks each, **Section D** contains five short answer questions of 3 marks each and **Section E** contains three long answer questions of 5 marks each.
4. There is no overall choice. However internal choice is provided. You have to attempt only one of the choices in such questions.

TIME : 3 HOURS

MAX. MARKS : 70

SECTION-A

All questions are compulsory. In case of internal choices, attempt any one of them.

1. If the speed of the wave shown in the figure is 330 ms^{-1} in the given medium, then find the equation of the wave propagating in the positive x-direction (all quantities are in MKS units).

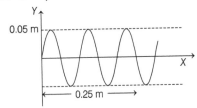

2. Force (F) and density (d) are related as $F = \dfrac{\alpha}{\beta + \sqrt{d}}$. What are the respective dimensions of α and β ?

3. A man of mass 50 g stands on a frame of mass 30 g. He pulls on a light rope which passes over a pulley. The other end of the rope is attached to the frame. For the system to be in equilibrium, what force man must exert on the rope? [**Ans.** 40 g]

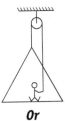

Or

A weight w is suspended from the mid-point of a rope, whose ends are at the same level. In order to make the rope perfectly horizontal, how much force much be applied to each of its ends? [**Ans.** Infinity]

4. When the temperature of a rod increases from t to $t + \Delta t$, its moment of inertia increases from I to $I + \Delta I$. If α be the coefficient of linear expansion of the rod, then what is the value of $\dfrac{\Delta I}{I}$?

5. A constant torque of 90 N-m rotates a body at its point of action by an angle of 60°. Find the work done by the torque. [**Ans.** 30 π J]

6. Write the expression for excess pressure inside a bubble of radius r in a liquid of surface tension T.

7. If the velocity of a particle is given by the expression $v(x) = 3x^2 - 4x$, where x is distance covered by the particle. Find the acceleration of the particle.

Or

Define frame of reference and its types.

8. Three forces $\mathbf{F}_1$, $\mathbf{F}_2$ and $\mathbf{F}_3$ are acting on a particle of mass m, such that $\mathbf{F}_2$ and $\mathbf{F}_3$ are mutually perpendicular and under their effect, the particle remains stationary. What will be the acceleration of the particle, if the force $\mathbf{F}_1$ is removed?

9. Two simple harmonic motions are represented by $y_1 = 5 (\sin 2\pi t + \sqrt{3} \cos 2\pi t)$ units

and $y_2 = 5 \sin \left(2\pi t + \dfrac{\pi}{4} \right)$ units, calculate the ratio of their amplitudes.   [Ans. 2 : 1]

Or

The equation of a sound wave is given as $y = 0.005 \sin(62.4x + 316t)$ units. Calculate the wavelength of this wave.   [Ans. 0.1 unit]

10. Write different systems of units.

Or

Calculate the value of total internal energy for one mole of diatomic molecule in its vibrational mode.

For question numbers 11, 12, 13 and 14, two statements are given-one labelled Assertion (A) and the other labelled **Reason** (R). Select the correct answer to these questions from the codes (a), (b), (c) and (d) as given below.

(a) Both A and R are true and R is the correct explanation of A.

(b) Both A and R are true but R is not the correct explanation of A.

(c) A is true but R is false.

(d) A is false and R is also false.

11. **Assertion** Pressure of a gas is $\dfrac{2}{3}$ times translational kinetic energy of gas molecules.

Reason Translational degree of freedom of any type of gas is three, whether the gas is monoatomic, diatomic or polyatomic.

12. **Assertion** The escape speed for the moon is 2.3 kms^{-1} which is five times smaller than that for the earth.

Reason The escape speed depends on acceleration due to gravity on the moon and radius of the moon and both of them are smaller than that of earth.

13. **Assertion** The unit based for measuring nuclear cross-section is 'barn'.

Reason 1 barn $= 10^{-14}$ m^2.

14. **Assertion** A string has a mass m. If it is accelerated, tension is non-uniform and if it is not accelerated, tension is uniform.

Reason Tension force is not an electromagnetic force.

Answers

11. (b) | 12. (a) | 13. (c) | 14. (d)

SECTION-B

Questions 15 and 16 are case study based questions and are compulsory. Attempt any 4 sub parts from each question. Each question carries 1 mark.

15. **First Law of Thermodynamics**

First law of thermodynamics is a statement of conservation of energy applied to any system in which energy transfer from or to the surroundings is taken into account. It states that heat given to a system is either used in doing external work or it increases the internal energy of the system or both.

i.e.   Heat supplied, $\Delta Q = \Delta U + \Delta W$

where, ΔQ = heat supplied to the system by the surroundings,

     ΔW = work done by the system on the surroundings

and ΔU = change in internal energy of the system.

(i) For an ideal gas, internal energy depends on

(a) only molecular kinetic energy

(b) only potential energy of the molecules

(c) Both kinetic and potential energies of the molecules

(d) None of the above

(ii) The internal energy of a system could be changed
- (a) by extracting heat from the system
- (b) by doing work done on the system
- (c) if system do some work on the surroundings
- (d) All of the above

(iii) $(\Delta Q - \Delta W)$ is
- (a) path dependent
- (b) path independent
- (c) equal to ΔU
- (d) Both (b) and (c)

(iv) Using first law of thermodynamics, which is true for isothermal expansion of an ideal gas,
- (a) $\Delta U = + ve$
- (b) $\Delta Q = + ve$
- (c) $\Delta W = + ve$
- (d) Both (b) and (c)

(v) A system is provided with 200 cal of heat and the work done by the system on the surroundings is 40 J. Then, its internal energy
- (a) increases by 600 J
- (b) decreases by 800 J
- (c) increases by 800 J
- (d) decreases by 50 J

16. Collision

A collision is an isolated event in which two or more colliding bodies exert strong forces on each other for a relatively short time. For a collision to take place, the actual physical contact is not necessary.

At the time of collision, the two colliding objects are deformed and may be momentarily at rest with respect to each other. If the initial velocities and final velocities of both the bodies are along the same straight line, then it is called a one-dimensional collision or head-on collision.

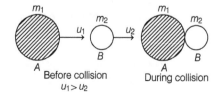

Before collision
$u_1 > u_2$

During collision

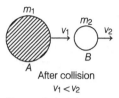

After collision
$v_1 < v_2$

(i) In elastic collision,
　I. initial kinetic energy is equal to the final kinetic energy.
　II. kinetic energy during the collision time Δt is constant.
Which of the following above option(s) is/are correct?
- (a) Only I
- (b) Only II
- (c) Both I and II
- (d) None of these

(ii) In an inelastic collision,
- (a) conservation of momentum is not followed
- (b) conservation of mechanical energy is not followed
- (c) conservation of mechanical energy is followed
- (d) None of the above

(iii) A particle of mass m_1 moves with velocity v_1 collides with another particle at rest of equal mass. The velocity of second particle after the elastic collision is
- (a) $2v_1$
- (b) v_1
- (c) $- v_1$
- (d) 0

(iv) A molecule in a gas container hits a horizontal wall with speed 200 ms^{-1} at an angle 30° with the normal and rebounds with the same speed. Which statement is true?
- (a) Momentum is conserved
- (b) Elastic collision
- (c) Inelastic collision
- (d) Both (a) and (b)

(v) A particle of mass 1g moving with a velocity $v_1 = 3\hat{i} - 2\hat{j}$ ms^{-1} experiences a perfectly elastic collision with another particle of mass 2 g and velocity $v_2 = 4\hat{j} - 6\hat{k}$ ms^{-1}. The velocity of the particle is
- (a) 2.3ms^{-1}
- (b) 4.6 ms^{-1}
- (c) 9.2 ms^{-1}
- (d) 6 ms^{-1}

Answers

15. (i) a　(ii) d　(iii) d　(iv) d　(v) c
16. (i) a　(ii) c　(iii) b　(iv) d　(v) b

SECTION-C

All questions are compulsory. In case of internal choices, attempt anyone.

17. Give the mean kinetic energy of one mole of gas per degree of freedom at 300 K.
[Ans. 1.24 kJ]

18. Two trains 120 m and 80 m in length are running in opposite directions with velocities 42 kmh^{-1} and 30 kmh^{-1}. In what time will they completely cross each other?
[Ans. 10 s]

19. A body covers 12 m in 2 s and 20 m in 4 s. How much distance will it cover in 4 s after the 5 s?
[Ans. 136 m]

20. Figure shows two bars of iron and brass having same length and same area of cross-section in steady state. Determine temperature at common junction. Given that

$$K_{\text{iron}} = 79 \text{ Wm}^{-1}\text{K}^{-1}$$
and $K_{\text{brass}} = 109 \text{ Wm}^{-1}\text{K}^{-1}$

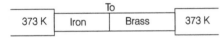

[Ans. 315 K]

21. (i) An object placed on a ground is in stable equilibrium. If object is slightly pushed, then what will be the effect on the position of centre of gravity?

(ii) Why is it easier to open a tap with two fingers than with one finger?

Or

On the application of a constant torque, a wheel is turned from rest through 800 rad in 20 s.

(i) Find angular acceleration. [Ans. 4 rads⁻²]

(ii) If same torque continues to act, what will be angular velocity of the wheel after 30 s from start? [Ans. 120 rads⁻¹]

22. The extension in a string obeying Hooke's law is η. The speed of sound in the stretched string is *v*. If the extension in the sting is increased to 1.5 η, then find the speed in newly stretched string. [Ans. 1.22 *v*]

Or

Define free oscillation with two examples.

23. State four important features of gravitational force.

24. The dot product of two vectors vanishes when vectors are orthogonal and has maximum value when vectors are parallel to each other. Explain.

Or

The angle between vectors **A** and **B** is 60°. What is the ratio of **A · B** and $|\mathbf{A} \times \mathbf{B}|$?
$\left[\text{Ans. } \dfrac{1}{\sqrt{3}}\right]$

25. (i) Write any two characteristics of elastic collision.

(ii) Write any one example of elastic and inelastic collision.

SECTION-D

All questions are compulsory. In case of internal choices attempt anyone.

26. (i) Define terminal velocity.

(ii) A capillary tube *A* is dipped in water and another identical tube *B* is dipped in soap solution. Draw the diagram showing the nature of liquid columns in both the tubes and explain.

(iii) What happens when a capillary tube of insufficient length is dipped in a liquid?

27. (i) On a certain day, rain was falling vertically with a speed of 9 m/s. A wind started blowing after sometime with a speed of 3 m/s in East to West direction. Find the resultant velocity and in which direction should the boy waiting at a bus stop hold his umbrella.
[Ans. 81.26°]

(ii) If $\mathbf{A} \times \mathbf{B} = \mathbf{C} \times \mathbf{B}$, show that **C** need not to be equal to **A**.

Or

(i) The position coordinate of a moving object given by $x = 10 + 16t + 8t^2$, where *x* is in meters and *t* in second. What is the velocity at $t = 3$ s? [Ans. 64 m/s]

(ii) What will be the effect on horizontal range of a projectile when its initial velocity is doubled keeping the angle of projection same?

(iii) Find the angle between $(\mathbf{A} + \mathbf{B})$ and $(\mathbf{A} \times \mathbf{B})$.

28. A particle is vibrating in SHM, when the displacements of the particle from its equilibrium positions are x_1 and x_2, it has velocities u_1 and u_2, respectively.

   (i) Show that its time period is given by $T = 2\pi \sqrt{x_1^2 - x_2^2 / v_2^2 - v_1^2}$.

   (ii) Find the ratio of velocities v_1 & v_2 in terms of x_1, x_2 and amplitude A.

Or

A particle performs SHM on a rectilinear path. Starting from rest, it travels x_1 distance in first second and in the next second, it travels x_2 distance. Find out the amplitude of this SHM.

29. **(i)** The frequency of vibration f of a mass m suspended from a spring of spring constant k is given by a relation of the type $f = Cm^x k^y$, where C is a dimensionless constant. Give the values of x and y.   **[Ans.** (i) $x = -1/2$, $y = 1/2$]

   (ii) Write the difference between Angstrom (Å) and astronomical unit (AU).

   (iii) Write the difference between nm, Nm and mN.

30. The equation of simple harmonic wave is given by the following equation

$$y = a \sin 2\pi \left(\frac{t}{T} - \frac{x}{\lambda} \right) \qquad \text{...(i)}$$

where, y is the displacement of particle, x is the position of particle and t is the time. The graph for Eq. (i) is drawn as

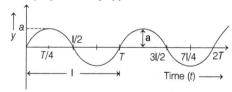

If the value of x for a particle is zero, then the equation of simple harmonic wave is given by

$$y = \sin 2\pi \frac{t}{T}$$

The above equation shows that the displacement y of the particle depends on t. The displacement y of a particle at different instants of time is given in the table as below:

t	0	$\frac{T}{4}$	$\frac{T}{2}$	$\frac{3T}{4}$	T	$\frac{5T}{4}$	$\frac{3T}{4}$	$\frac{7T}{4}$	$2T$
y	0	$+a$	0	$-a$	0	$+a$	0	$-a$	0

At $t = \frac{3T}{2}$ in Eq. (i), we get

$$y = a \sin 2\pi \left(\frac{3}{2} - \frac{x}{\lambda} \right)$$

In the different position x of the particles, the displacement are given in the table as below:

x	0	$\frac{\lambda}{4}$	$\frac{\lambda}{2}$	$\frac{3\lambda}{4}$	λ	$\frac{5\lambda}{4}$	$\frac{3\lambda}{2}$	$\frac{7\lambda}{4}$	2λ
y	0	$+a$	0	$-a$	0	$+a$	0	$-a$	0

Read the above paragraph carefully and give the graphical representation of (i) table-1 (graph y-t) and (ii) table-2 (graph y-x).

SECTION-E

All questions are compulsory. In case of internal choice attempt anyone.

31. **(i)** Prove that the mass of a planet m can be measured by equation $M = \dfrac{gR^2}{G}$

   where, $g =$ acceleration of gravity on planet, $R =$ radius of planet and $G =$ gravitational constant.

   (ii) The mean radius of the earth is R, its angular speed on its own axis is ω and the acceleration due to gravity at the earth's surface is g.

   Prove that the radius of the orbit of geo-stationary satellite is $\left[\dfrac{gR^2}{\omega^2} \right]^{1/3}$.

   (iii) If mass of satellite revolving around the earth is suddenly doubled, then what is the effect on its orbital speed?

Or

(i) Gravitational force between point masses m and M separated by a distance is F. Now if a point mass $5m$ is placed next to m, what will be the
(a) force on M due to m
(b) and total force on M? [Ans. 6 F]

(ii) The escape velocity from the surface of the earth is v_e. Give the escape velocity from the surface of a planet whose mass and radius are three times those of the earth.

(iii) Write the value of gravitational potential (a) for $r = $ infinity and (b) at the surface of earth.

32. (i) Define capillarity.

(ii) Find the height of liquid, if a capillary tube has a base radius of 0.05 cm and surface tension 0.073 Nm^{-1}.[Ans. 2.98 cm]

(iii) At what speed will the velocity of a stream of water be equal to 20 cm of mercury column? (Take, $g = 10$ ms^{-2})
[Ans. 7.37 ms^{-1}]

Or

(i) Identify the substances which can be stretched to cause large strains.

(ii) The diameter of a brass rod in 4 mm and Young's modulus of brass is $9 \times 10^{10} N/m^2$.
Calculate the force required to stretch by 0.1% of its length. [Ans. 360π N]

(iii) To what depth must a rubber ball be taken in deep sea, so that its volume is decreased by 0.1%?
(Take, density of sea water $= 10^3$ $kg m^{-3}$, bulk modulus of rubber $= 9 \times 10^8$ Nm^{-2} and $g = 10$ ms^{-2})
[Ans. 90 m]

(iv) The upper end of a wire of radius 4 mm and length 100 cm is clamped and its

other end is twisted through an angle of 30°. Then, find angle of shear.
[Ans. 0.12°]

33. (i) A body is sliding down a rough inclined plane. Derive an expression for the acceleration of the body.

(ii) An acrobat of mass 30 kg climbs on a rope which can stand a maximum tension of 400 N. In which of the following cases will the rope break?
The acrobat
(a) climbs up with an acceleration of 5 ms^{-2}.
(b) climbs down with an acceleration of 3 ms^{-2}.
(c) climbs up with a uniform speed of 4 ms^{-1}.

Or (i) State two advantages of friction in daily life.

(ii) A 100 kg gun fires a ball of 1 kg horizontally from a cliff of height 500 m.
It falls on the ground at a distance of 400m from the bottom of the cliff. What will be the recoil velocity of the gun? [Ans. − 0.4 m/s]

(iii) A block of wood of mass 5 kg is resting on the surface of a rough inclined plane making angle 60° as shown in figure. If the coefficient of static friction is 0.3, calculate the forces.

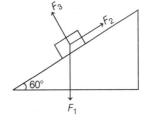

[Ans. 50.8 N]

SAMPLE QUESTION PAPER 4

A HIGHLY SIMULATED SAMPLE QUESTION PAPER FOR CBSE CLASS XI EXAMINATIONS

PHYSICS (UNSOLVED)

GENERAL INSTRUCTIONS

1. All questions are compulsory. There are 33 questions in all.
2. This question paper has five sections: Section A, Section B, Section C, Section D and Section E.
3. **Section A** contains ten very short answer questions and four assertion reasoning MCQs of 1 mark each, **Section B** has two case based questions of 4 marks each, **Section C** contains nine short answer questions of 2 marks each, **Section D** contains five short answer questions of 3 marks each and **Section E** contains three long answer questions of 5 marks each.
4. There is no overall choice. However internal choice is provided. You have to attempt only one of the choices in such questions.

TIME : 3 HOURS   **MAX. MARKS : 70**

SECTION-A

All questions are compulsory. In case of internal choices, attempt anyone of them.

1. What are the dimensions of a and b in the relation : $F = a + bx$, where F is force and x is distance ?

2. The displacement equation of a particle performing simple harmonic motion is given as $x = 4 \sin\left(10\pi t + \dfrac{\pi}{4}\right)$ cm. What is maximum velocity of the particle?
   [Ans. 40π cm/s]

3. A body is projected with a velocity of 30 ms^{-1} at an angle of $30°$ with the vertical. Find the horizontal range.   [Ans. 79.53 m]

   Or

   If the vectors $\mathbf{A} = 2\hat{\mathbf{i}} + \lambda\hat{\mathbf{j}} + \hat{\mathbf{k}}$ and $\mathbf{B} = 4\hat{\mathbf{i}} - 2\hat{\mathbf{j}} - 2\hat{\mathbf{k}}$ are perpendicular to each other, then find the value of λ.   [Ans. 3]

4. The displacement of a particle in a medium can be expressed as
   $$y = 10^{-6} \sin(100t + 20x + \frac{\pi}{4})\ \text{m}$$
   where, x is in metre and t is in second. What is the speed of the wave?   [Ans. 5 ms^{-1}]

5. An ideal gas is initially at temperature T and volume V. Its volume is increased by ΔV due to an increase in temperature ΔT, pressure remaining constant. Show how the physical quantity $\delta = \dfrac{\Delta T}{V\Delta T}$ varies with temperature.

   Or

   A gas at 27°C in a cylinder has a volume of 4L and pressure 100 N/m^2. If the gas is compressed at constant temperature, so that the pressure becomes 150 N/m^2, estimate the change in volume.   [Ans. 1.33 L]

6. A material is having Poisson's ratio 0.2. A load is applied on it, due to which it suffers the longitudinal strain 3.0×10^{-3}, then find out the percentage change radius.
   [Ans. 0.06%]

7. If $x = a + bt + ct^2$, where x is in metre and t in second, then what is the unit of c?

8. Obtain the dimensional formula for coefficient of viscosity.

9. Sound waves of wavelength λ travelling in a medium with a speed of v m/s enter into another medium, where its speed is $2v$ m/s.

Find the wavelength of sound waves in the second medium.

10. A mass M split into two parts m and $(M - m)$, which are then separated by a certain distance. Show that the gravitational force between the two parts becomes maximum, when the ratio of $\dfrac{m}{M} = \dfrac{1}{2}$. [Ans. 1/2]

Or

A satellite does not need any fuel to circle around the earth. Why?

For question numbers 11, 12, 13 and 14, two statements are given-one labelled Assertion (A) and the other labelled **Reason** (R). Select the correct answer to these questions from the codes (a), (b), (c) and (d) as given below.

(a) Both A and R are true and R is the correct explanation of A.

(b) Both A and R are true but R is not the correct explanation of A.

(c) A is true but R is false.

(d) A is false and R is also false.

11. **Assertion** If the surface between the blocks A and B is rough, then work done by friction on block B is always negative.

Reason Total work done by friction in both the blocks is always zero.

12. **Assertion** A force (**F**) that represents spring force is given as $\mathbf{F} = -m\omega^2\mathbf{x}$ is used for SHM.

Reason Magnitude of spring force is directly proportional to net stretch in the spring.

13. **Assertion** For motion along a straight line and in the same direction, the magnitude of average velocity is equal to the average speed.

Reason For motion along a straight line and in the same direction, the magnitude of displacement is equal to the path length.

14. **Assertion** Degree of freedom of a monoatomic gas is always three, whether we consider vibrational effects or not.

Reason At all temperatures (low or high), vibrational kinetic energy of an ideal gas is zero.

Answers

11. (c) | 12. (b) | 13. (a) | 14. (c) |

SECTION-B

Questions 15 and 16 are case study based questions and are compulsory. Attempt any 4 sub parts from each question. Each question carries 1 mark.

15. **Law of Equipartition of Energy**

For a dynamic system in thermal equilibrium, the total energy is distributed equally amongst all the degree of freedom and the energy associated with each molecule per degree of freedom is $\dfrac{1}{2} k_B T$

where, $k_B = 1.38 \times 10^{-23}\,\text{JK}^{-1}$ is Boltzmann constant and T is absolute temperature of system on the kelvin scale. For a monoatomic gas in thermal equilibrium at temperature T, the average value of translational energy of the molecule is

$$\langle E_t \rangle = \left\langle \frac{1}{2}mv_x^2 \right\rangle + \left\langle \frac{1}{2}mv_y^2 \right\rangle + \left\langle \frac{1}{2}mv_z^2 \right\rangle$$

Translational energy of the molecules,

$$\langle E_t \rangle = \frac{3}{2} k_B T$$

(i) Law of equipartition of energy is used to
   (a) predict the specific heats of gases
   (b) predict the specific heats of solids
   (c) Both (a) and (b)
   (d) Neither (a) nor (b)

(ii) Diatomic molecule (rigid rotator) has
   (a) 3 translational degrees of freedom
   (b) 2 rotational degrees of freedom
   (c) Both (a) and (b)
   (d) All of the above

(iii) Choose the correct option.
   (a) Each translational mode contributes $\dfrac{1}{2} k_B T$ average energy.
   (b) Each rotational mode contributes $\dfrac{1}{2} k_B T$ average energy.
   (c) Vibrational mode contributes $k_B T$ average energy.
   (d) All of the above

(iv) Molecules of CO at moderate temperature have energy

(a) $\frac{7}{2} k_B T$ (b) $\frac{5}{2} k_B T$

(c) $\frac{3}{2} k_B T$ (d) $\frac{1}{2} k_B T$

(v) The mean kinetic energy of one mole of gas per degree of freedom (on the basis of kinetic theory of gases) is

(a) $\frac{1}{2} kT$ (b) $\frac{3}{2} kT$

(c) $\frac{3}{2} RT$ (d) $\frac{1}{2} RT$

16. Vectors

Vectors are the physical quantities which have both magnitudes and directions and obey the triangle/parallelogram laws of addition and subtraction.

It is specified by giving its magnitude by a number and its direction. e.g. Displacement, acceleration, velocity, momentum, force, etc. A vector is represented by a bold face type and also by an arrow placed over a letter

i.e. $\mathbf{F}, \mathbf{a}, \mathbf{b}$ or $\vec{F}, \vec{a}, \vec{b}$

The length of the line gives the magnitude and the arrowhead gives the direction.

The point P is called head or terminal point and point O is called tail or initial point of the vector OP.

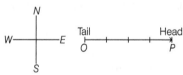

(i) Consider the quantities, pressure, power, energy, impulse, gravitational potential, electrical charge, temperature, area. Out of these, the only vector quantity/ies is/are
   (a) impulse, pressure and area
   (b) impulse
   (c) area and gravitational potential
   (d) impulse and pressure

(ii) The relation between the vectors $\mathbf{A}$ and $-2\mathbf{A}$ is that,
   (a) both have same magnitude
   (b) both have same direction
   (c) they have opposite directions
   (d) None of the above

(iii) If $\mathbf{A}$ is a vector with magnitude A, then the unit vector $\hat{a}$ in the direction of vector $\mathbf{A}$ is

   (a) AA (b) $\mathbf{A} \cdot \mathbf{A}$ (c) $\mathbf{A} \times \mathbf{A}$ (d) $\frac{\mathbf{A}}{|\mathbf{A}|}$

(iv) Find the correct option about vector subtraction.
   (a) $\mathbf{A} - \mathbf{B} = \mathbf{A} + \mathbf{B}$ (b) $|\mathbf{A} - \mathbf{B}| = |\mathbf{B} - \mathbf{A}|$
   (c) $\mathbf{A} - \mathbf{B} = \mathbf{A} + (-\mathbf{B})$
   (d) None of these

(v) $\mathbf{A}$ and $\mathbf{B}$ are two inclined vectors. R is their sum.

   Choose the correct figure for the given description.

(a) 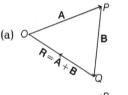   (b)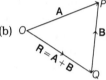

(c) 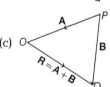   (d)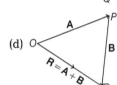

Answers

15. (i) c   (ii) c   (iii) d   (iv) a   (v) d
16. (i) b   (ii) c   (iii) d   (iv) c   (v) d

SECTION-C

All questions are compulsory. In case of internal choices, attempt anyone.

17. If the volume of a block of metal changes by 0.2% when it is heated through 40°C, what is the coefficient of linear expansion of metal?   [**Ans.** $1.67 \times 10^{-5}\,^{\circ}C^{-1}$]

18. At a metro station, a girl walks up a stationary escalator in time t_1. If she remains stationary on the escalator, then escalator takes her up in time t_2. Find the time taken by her to walk upon the moving escalator.

$$\left[\textbf{Ans. } \frac{t_1 t_2}{t_1 + t_2} \right]$$

Or

A balloon is ascending at the rate of 9.8 ms^{-1} at a height of 39.2 m above the ground when a food packet is dropped from the balloon. After how much time and with what velocity does it reach the ground? (Take, $g = 9.8$ ms^{-2})   [**Ans.** $- 29.4$ ms^{-1}]

19. Two billiard balls each of mass 0.5 kg moving in opposite directions with speed 6 m/s collide and rebound with the same speed. What is the impulse imparted to each ball due to the other?   [**Ans.** 3 kg-m/s]

20. At temperature T_0, a gas is compressed suddenly such that its pressure becomes $\dfrac{1}{q}$th of the original pressure. Show that the final temperature of gas becomes $T_0 q^{\frac{1-t}{t}}$, if $\gamma = t$.

21. 10 g of ice cubes at 0°C are released in a tumbler (water equivalent 55g) at 40°C. Assuming that negligible heat is taken from the surrounding, find the temperature of water in tumbler. [Given, $L = 80$ cal/g]   [**Ans.** 22°C]

Or

Define thermal capacity. Find the thermal capacity of 40 g of aluminium, if specific heat of aluminium. (Given, $s = 0.2$ cal/g-K)   [**Ans.** 33.6 J/°C]

22. Write the difference between elastic and inelastic collision.

23. What do you mean by rotational equilibrium and translational equilibrium?

24. A stone thrown upwards from the top of a tower 85 m high, reaches the ground in 5s. Find
(i) the greatest height above the ground   [**Ans.** 82.2 m]
(ii) and the velocity with which it reaches the ground. (Take, $g = 10$ms^{-2})   [**Ans.** 42 ms^{-1}]

25. A liquid drop of radius 4 mm breaks into 1000 identical drops. Find the change in surface energy. (Given, $S = 0.07$ Nm^{-1})   [**Ans.** 1.26×10^{-4} J]

Or

The volume of a glass block initially was 15000 cm^3 but when the temperature of that glass block increases from 20°C to 45°C, then its volume increases by 5cm^3. Determine the coefficient of linear expansion.   [**Ans.** 4.4×10^{-6} °C^{-1}]

SECTION-D

All questions are compulsory. In case of internal choices, attempt anyone.

26. Write the displacement equation of simple harmonic motion and define (i) displacement, (ii) amplitude and (iii) phase.

27. A solid cylinder of mass 10 kg rotates about its axis with angular speed of 100 rad/s. The radius of cylinder is 0.5 m. What is the kinetic energy associated with the rotation of the cylinder?
What is the magnitude of angular momentum of the cylinder about its axis?   [**Ans.** 125 kg-m^{2}s^{-1}]

Or

A solid cylinder rolls up an inclined plane of angle of inclination 30°. At the bottom of inclined plane, the centre of mass of cylinder has a speed of 5 ms^{-1}. How far will the cylinder go up the plane?   [**Ans.** 1.91 m]

28. A stone is tied to a string of length l and is whirled in a vertical circle with the other end of the string as the centre. At a certain instant of time, the stone is at its lowest position and has a speed u. Find the magnitude of the change in velocity as it reaches a position where the string is horizontal (g being acceleration due to gravity).

Or

A long spring of spring constant 500 N/m is attached to a wall horizontally and surface below the spring is rough with coefficient of friction 0.75. A 100 kg mass block moving with a speed $10\sqrt{2}$ ms^{-1} strikes the spring. Find the maximum compression of the spring. (Take, $g = 10$ ms^{-2})   [**Ans.** 5 m]

29. (i) Why are stationary waves called so?
(ii) The shape of a pulse gets distorted as it passes through a dispersive medium. Why?
(iii) Why do sound waves travel faster in warm air than cool air?

30. Two vectors **A** and **B** having equal magnitude of 8 units are inclined to each other by 60°. The magnitude of sum of these vectors is calculated as:

Sum of given vectors **A** and **B** is calculated by resolving them along two perpendicular directions X and Y, as shown in figure.

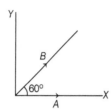

If F_X and F_Y are resolved parts of vectors **A** and **B** along X and Y directions, then

$$F_X = A\cos 0° + B\cos 60°$$
$$= 8 \times 1 + 8 \times \frac{1}{2} \quad [A = B = 8]$$
$$= 12$$

Similarly, $F_Y = A\sin 0° + B\sin 60°$
$$= 8\sin 0° + 8\sin 60°$$
$$= 0 + 8 \cdot \frac{\sqrt{3}}{2} = 4\sqrt{3}$$

∴ Sum of vectors

$$|\mathbf{A} + \mathbf{B}| = \sqrt{F_X^2 + F_Y^2} = \sqrt{12^2 + (4\sqrt{3})^2}$$
$$= \sqrt{192} = 8\sqrt{3} \text{ units}$$

Suggest an alternate method to find the
(i) magnitude of sum of these two vectors
[**Ans.** $8\sqrt{3}$ units]
(ii) angle that the resultant of these vectors makes with X-axis. [**Ans.** 30°]

SECTION-E

All questions are compulsory. In case of internal choices, attempt anyone.

31. (i) One end of a string 0.5 m long is fixed to a point A and the other end is fastened to a small object of weight 8 N. The object is pulled aside by a horizontal force F, until it is 0.3 m from the vertical through A. Find the magnitudes of the tension T in the string and the force F.

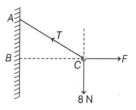

[**Ans.** 6 N]

(ii) A body of weight 200 N is suspended with the help of strings as shown in figure given below, find the tensions T_1 and T_2.

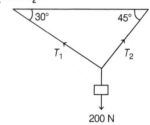

[**Ans.** $T_1 = 146.4$ N, $T_2 = 179.3$ N]

Or

Calculate the net acceleration produced in the arrangements shown below :
[Take, $g = 10 \text{ m/s}^2$]

(i)

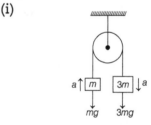

[**Ans.** 5 m/s²]

(ii)

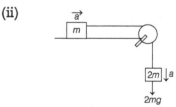

[**Ans.** 6.67 m/s²]

(iii)

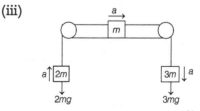

[**Ans.** 1.67 m/s²]

(iv)

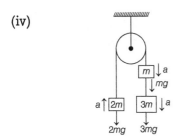

[**Ans.** 3.33 m/s^2]

(v)

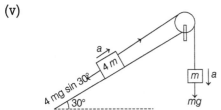

[**Ans.** 2 m/s^2]

32. (i) Give the relation between gravitational potential and gravitational field. Does any negative sign occur in the relation between them? What is the significance of the negative sign?

(ii) What are earth satellites? Derive an expression for period of revolution T of a satellite revolving in a circular orbit at a height h above the earth.

(iii) Show that a satellite revolving very close to the surface of the earth, i.e. $h \ll R_E$ (where R_E is the radius of the earth) has a time period of approximately 85 min. [Take, $g = 9.8$ ms^{-2}, $R_E = 6400$ km]

[**Ans.** 85 min]

Or

(i) A body of mass m is projected upward against gravity and reaches at a height h from the surface of earth. Derive an expression for work done with respect to earth whose mass and radius are M and R, respectively.

(ii) Two stationary particles of masses M_1 and M_2 are a distance d apart. A third particle lying on the line joining the particles, experiences no resultant gravitational force. What is the distance of this particle from M_1?

33. (i) Steam at 100°C is passed into 20 g of water at 10°C. If water acquires a temperature of 80°C, then find the mass of water present. [Take, specific heat of water $= 1$ cal g^{-1}°C^{-1} and latent heat of steam $= 540$ cal g^{-1}]

[**Ans.** 22.5 g]

(ii) Certain quantity of water cools from 70°C to 60°C in the first 5 min and to 54°C in the next 5 min. Find the temperature of the surroundings.

[**Ans.** 45°C]

Or

(i) Two spherical raindrops of equal size are falling vertically through air with a terminal velocity of 1 ms^{-1}. What would be the terminal speed, if these two drops were to coalesce to form a large spherical drop?

[**Ans.** 1.587 ms^{-1}]

(ii) Calculate the energy released when 1000 small water drops each of radius 10^{-7} m coalesce to form one large drop. The surface tension of water is 7.0×10^{-2} Nm^{-1}.

[**Ans.** 7.9 × 10^{-12} J]

SAMPLE QUESTION PAPER 5

A HIGHLY SIMULATED SAMPLE QUESTION PAPER FOR CBSE CLASS XI EXAMINATIONS

PHYSICS (UNSOLVED)

GENERAL INSTRUCTIONS

1. All questions are compulsory. There are 33 questions in all.
2. This question paper has five sections: Section A, Section B, Section C, Section D and Section E.
3. **Section A** contains ten very short answer questions and four assertion reasoning MCQs of 1 mark each, **Section B** has two case based questions of 4 marks each, **Section C** contains nine short answer questions of 2 marks each, **Section D** contains five short answer questions of 3 marks each and **Section E** contains three long answer questions of 5 marks each.
4. There is no overall choice. However internal choice is provided. You have to attempt only one of the choices in such questions.

TIME : 3 HOURS   **MAX. MARKS : 70**

SECTION-A

All questions are compulsory. In case of internal choices, attempt anyone of them.

1. A bullet travelling with a velocity of 16 ms^{-1} penetrates a tree trunk and comes to rest in 0.4 m. Find the time taken during the retardation.   **[Ans.** 0.05 s**]**

2. Two balls of same masses start moving towards each other due to gravitational attraction. If the initial distance between them is l, then at what distance they will meet?

$$\overset{m}{\underset{\longleftarrow l \longrightarrow}{\bigcirc\!\!\to F \qquad\qquad F\leftarrow\!\!\overset{m}{\bigcirc}}}$$

Or

A satellite is orbitting the earth with speed v_0. To make the satellite escape, what minimum percentage increase in its velocity is required?   **[Ans.** 41.4%**]**

3. A particle executing a simple harmonic motion has a period of 6 s. Find the time taken by the particle to move from the mean position to half the amplitude, starting from the mean position.   **[Ans.** (1/2) s**]**

4. A nucleus explodes into two lighter nuclei as shown in figure. Find the ratio of v_1 and v_2.

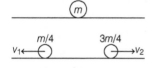

   [Ans. 3 : 1**]**

5. If velocity of light, acceleration due to gravity and atmospheric pressure are taken as the fundamental units. What will be the value of 9 m?   **[Ans.** 10^{-15} new unit**]**

6. A flywheel rotating at 420 rpm slows down to a constant rate of 2 rad s^{-2}. How much time it takes to stop the flywheel? **[Ans.** 22 s**]**

7. A 2 m by 3 m plate of aluminium has a mass of 324 kg. What is the thickness of plate?

   [$\rho = 2.70 \times 10^3$ kg/m^3]   **[Ans.** 2 cm**]**

Or

Planck's constant h, speed of light c and gravitational constant G are used to form a unit of mass M. How is mass related to c?   **[Ans.** $c^{1/2}$**]**

8. Even when rain is falling vertically downwards, the front screen of a moving car gets wet while the back screen remains dry. Why?

Or

When an observer is standing on earth, the trees and houses appear stationary to him. However, when he is sitting in a moving train, all these objects appear to move in backward direction. Why?

9. Write the expression of coefficient of performance for a refrigerator.

Or

Show that internal energy of an ideal gas is expressed as $U = \dfrac{pV}{(\gamma - 1)}$.

10. A block attached to a spring is executing simple harmonic motion with displacement, $x = A\cos(\omega t + \phi)$. What is the relation between T_1 and T_2, if the time period of variation of velocity is T_1 and time period of variation of KE is T_2. [Ans. $T_1 = 2T_2$]

For question numbers 11, 12, 13 and 14, two statements are given-one labelled Assertion (A) and the other labelled Reason (R). Select the correct answer to these questions from the codes (a), (b), (c) and (d) as given below.

(a) Both A and R are true and R is the correct explanation of A.

(b) Both A and R are true but R is not the correct explanation of A.

(c) A is true but R is false.

(d) A is false and R is also false.

11. **Assertion** In isothermal process for ideal gas change in internal energy is zero.

    Reason No heat is supplied to system or rejected by system, in an isothermal process.

12. **Assertion** Pressure has the dimensions of energy density.

    Reason Energy density $= \dfrac{\text{Energy}}{\text{Volume}}$

13. **Assertion** As we go up the surface of the earth, we feel light weighed than on the surface of the earth.

Reason The acceleration due to gravity decreases on going up above the surface of the earth.

14. **Assertion** The value of a_x depends on $\dfrac{dv}{dt}$.

    Reason Acceleration means rate of change of distance.

Answers

11. (c) | 12. (a) | 13. (a) | 14. (d) |

SECTION-B

Questions 15 and 16 are case study based questions and are compulsory. Attempt any 4 sub parts from each question. Each question carries 1 mark.

15. **Kinetic Energy**

The energy possessed by a body by virtue of its motion is called kinetic energy. In other words, the amount of work done, a moving object can do before coming to rest is equal to its kinetic energy.

∴ Kinetic energy, $KE = \dfrac{1}{2}mv^2$

where, m is a mass and v is the velocity of a body.

The units and dimensions of KE are Joule (in SI) and $[ML^2T^{-2}]$, respectively.

Kinetic energy of a body is always positive. It can never be negative.

(i) Which of the diagrams shown in figure most closely shows the variation in kinetic energy of the earth as it moves once around the sun in its elliptical orbit?

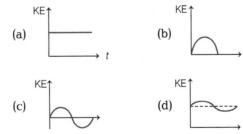

(ii) A force which is inversely proportional to the speed is acting on a body. The kinetic energy of the body starting from rest is

(a) a constant
(b) inversely proportional to time
(c) directly proportional to time
(d) directly proportional to square of time

(iii) The kinetic energy of an air molecule $(10^{-21}$ J) in eV is
(a) 6.2 meV   (b) 4.2 meV
(c) 10.4 meV   (d) 9.7 meV

(iv) Two masses of 1 g and 4 g are moving with equal kinetic energy. The ratio of the magnitudes of their momentum is
(a) 4 : 1   (b) $\sqrt{2}$: 1   (c) 1 : 2   (d) 1 : 16

(v) An object of mass 10 kg is moving with velocity of 10 ms^{-1}. Due to a force, its velocity become 20 ms^{-1}. Percentage increase in its KE is
(a) 25%   (b) 50%
(c) 75%   (d) 300%

16. Application of Pascal's Law

The transmission of fluid pressure in a closed system is based on Pascal's law and it has many applications in daily life.

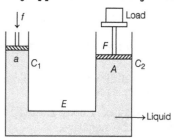

One such system (a hydraulic lift) is shown in figure, which consists of two cylinders C_1 and C_2 connected to each other by a pipe E. These cylinders are fitted with water-tight frictionless pistons of different cross-sectional areas. These cylinders and the pipe contain a liquid.

Suppose, a downward force f is applied on the smaller piston of cross-sectional area a. Then, pressure exerted on the liquid,

$$p = \frac{f}{a}$$

and upward force on a larger piston, $F = \dfrac{A}{a} f$

(i) Pressure is a scalar quantity, because
(a) it is the ratio of force to area and both force and area are vectors
(b) it is the product of the magnitude of the force to area

(c) it is the ratio of the component of the force normal to the area
(d) it does not depend on the size of the area chosen

(ii) Pressure at a point inside a liquid does not depend on
(a) the depth of the point below the surface of the liquid
(b) the nature of the liquid
(c) the acceleration due to gravity at that point
(d) total weight of fluid in the beaker

(iii) Pascal's law states that pressure in a fluid at rest is the same at all points, if
(a) they are at the same height
(b) they are along same plane
(c) they are along same line
(d) Both (a) and (b)

(iv) A hydraulic lift has 2 limbs of areas A and $2A$. Force F is applied over limb of area A to lift a heavy car. If distance moved by piston P_1 is x, then distance moved by piston P_2 is

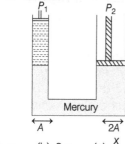

(a) x (b) $2x$ (c) $\dfrac{x}{2}$ (d) $4x$

(v) A uniformly tapering vessel is filled with a liquid of density 900 kgm^{-3}. The force that acts on the base of the vessel due to the liquid is (take, $g = 10$ ms^{-2})

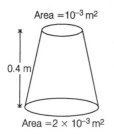

(a) 3.6 N   (b) 7.2 N
(c) 9.0 N   (d) 14.4 N

Answers

15. (i) d   (ii) c   (iii) a   (iv) c   (v) d
16. (i) c   (ii) d   (iii) a   (iv) c   (v) b

SECTION-C

ll questions are compulsory. In case of internal hoices, attempt anyone.

17. (i) A 3L glass flask contains some mercury. It is found that at all temperatures, the volume of the air inside the flask remains the same. What will be the volume of the mercury inside the flask? (Take, α for glass $= 9 \times 10^{-6}/°C$ and γ for mercury $= 1.8 \times 10^{-4}/°C$)

[Ans. 450 cc]

(ii) Two absolute scales have triple point 200 X and 300Y. Write the relation between the two temperatures on absolute scales. $\left[\text{Ans. } T_x = \frac{2}{3} T_y\right]$

18. The p-V diagram of an ideal gas two different masses m_1 and m_2 are drawn (as shown) at constant temperature T.

State whether $m_1 > m_2$ or $m_2 > m_1$?

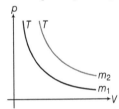

19. Explain inertial and gravitational masses of the ordinary objects. Do they differ in magnitude?

20. What is simple harmonic motion? Show that the acceleration of a particle in simple harmonic motion is proportional to its displacement.

Or

Prove that the displacement equation $x(t) = a \sin \omega t + b \cos \omega t$ represents a simple harmonic motion and find its amplitude and phase constant.

21. Write the name of frictional force which acts during rolling motion of a body. Discuss it with the help of a suitable diagram. What is the cause of this frictional force?

Or

Derive an expression for the angle, a cyclist will have to make with vertical while taking a circular turn.

22. Define surface tension. Give two examples which illustrate surface tension.

Or

If a capillary tube is immersed first in cold water and then in hot water, the height of capillary rise is smaller in the second case than the first one.

23. The potential energy of a 1 kg particle free to move along the X-axis is given by

$$U(x) = \left[\frac{x^4}{4} - \frac{x^2}{2}\right] J.$$ The total mechanical energy of the particle is 2 J. Find the maximum speed of the particle in ms^{-1}.

$\left[\text{Ans. } \frac{3}{\sqrt{2}} \text{ ms}^{-1}\right]$

24. Two forces whose magnitudes are in the ratio of 3 : 5, give a resultant of 35 N. If the angle of inclination be 60°, calculate the magnitude of each force. [Ans. 25 N]

25. A cyclist speeding at 18 km/h on a level road takes a sharp circular turn of radius 3m without reducing the speed. The coefficient of static friction between the tyres and the road is 0.1. Will the cyclist slip while taking the turn?

SECTION-D

All questions are compulsory. In case of internal choices, attempt anyone.

26. A smooth rod of length l rotates freely in a horizontal plane with angular velocity ω about a stationary vertical axis 0. The moment of inertia of the rod is equal to I relative the axis. A small ring of mass m is located on the rod close to the rotation axis and is tied to it by a thread. When the thread is burnt, the ring starts sliding radially outwards along the rod. Find the velocity of the ring relative to the rod as a function of its distance r from the rotation axis.

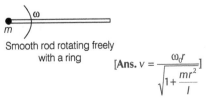

Smooth rod rotating freely with a ring

$\left[\text{Ans. } v = \dfrac{\omega_0 r}{\sqrt{1 + \dfrac{mr^2}{I}}}\right]$

Or

(i) A man standing near the top of an old wooden step ladder feels unstable. Why?

(ii) Why does a belly dancer fold her arms and bring the stretched leg close to the other leg?

(iii) What is instantaneous rotational power? Write its expression.

27. From a tower of height H, a particle is thrown vertically upwards with a speed u. The time taken by the particle to hit the ground is n times of that taken to reach the highest point of its path. What is the relation between H, u and n ?

28. (i) Two strings 1 and 2 are taut between two fixed supports (as shown in figure) such that the tension in both strings is same. Mass per unit length of 2 is more than that of 1. Explain which string is denser for a transverse travelling wave.

(ii) If a wave $y(x, t) = a \sin(kx - \omega t)$ is reflected from an open boundary and then the incident and reflected waves overlap. What will be the amplitude of the resultant wave?

Or

A uniform cord have a mass 0.2 kg and length 6 m. If tension is maintained in the cord by suspending a mass of 3 kg from one end, then find out the speed of a pulse on this cord. Also find the time, it takes the pulse to travel from the wall to the pulley.

[**Ans.** 0.168 s]

29. (i) A simple harmonic wave is expressed by equation

$$y = 7 \times 10^{-6} \sin\left(800\pi t - \frac{\pi}{42.5}x\right)$$

where, y and x are in cm and t is in second.

Calculate

(a) amplitude　　(b) frequency

(c) wavelength　　(d) and wave velocity.

[**Ans.** (a) $a = 7 \times 10^{-6}$ cm, $\nu = 400$ Hz,

(c) $\lambda = 85$ cm and $v = 340$ m/s]

(ii) In an experiment, it was found that a tuning fork and a sonometer wire gave

5 beats per second, both when the length of wire was 1 m and 1.05 m. Calculate the frequency of the fork.

[**Ans.** $\nu = 205$ Hz]

30. A vessel of volume $V = 5$ L contains 1.4 g of nitrogen at a temperature $T = 1800$ K. If 30% of nitrogen gas is dissociated into atoms at this temperature, then situation can be represented

$$\underset{\substack{1-x}}{N_2} \rightleftharpoons \underset{\substack{2x = (1+x)}}{2N = 1}$$

From an ideal gas equation

$$pV = nRT = (1+x)\frac{m}{M_0}RT$$

where, x = increase in the number of particles in the vessel

M_0 = Molecular mass of nitrogen

$$\Rightarrow \quad p = \frac{(1+0.3)mRT}{M_0 V}$$

Given, $V = 5\,l = 5 \times 10^{-3}$ cm^3,

$T = 1800$ K

$R = 8.3$ and $m = 1.4$ g

$$\therefore \quad p = \frac{1.3 \times 1.4 \times 8.3 \times 1800}{5 \times 10^{-3} \times 28 \times 10^{-3}}$$

$$= 1.94 \times 10^5 \text{ N/m}^2$$

Suggest an alternative method to calculate the pressure of gas in vessel.

[**Ans.** 1.94×10^5 N/m^2]

SECTION-E

All questions are compulsory. In case of internal choices, attempt anyone.

31. (i) A truck tows a trailer of mass 1200 kg at a speed of 10 ms^{-1} on a level road. The tension in

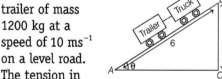

the coupling is 1000 N. What is the power extended on the trailer? Find the tension in the coupling when the truck ascends a road having an inclination of 1 in 6 as shown in given figure.

Assume that the frictional resistance on the inclined plane is same as that on the level road.

[**Ans.** 2960 N]

(ii) A block of weight 20 N is placed on a horizontal table and a tension T, which can be increased to 8 N before the block begins to slide, is applied at the block as shown in figure. A force of 4 N keeps the block moving at constant speed once it has been set in motion. Find the coefficient of static and kinetic friction.

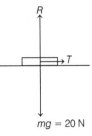

$mg = 20$ N

[Ans. 0.40, 0.20]

Or

(i) A railway car of mass 20 tonne moves with an initial speed of 54 kmh^{-1}. On applying brakes, a constant negative acceleration of 0.3 ms^{-2} is produced.
   (a) What is the braking force acting on the railway car? [Ans. -6000 N]
   (b) In what time it stops? [Ans. 50 s]

(ii) A trolley of mass 20 kg rests on a horizontal surface. A massless string tied to the trolley passes over a frictionless pulley and a load of 5 kg is suspended from the other end of string.
If coefficient of kinetic friction between trolley and surface is 0.1, find the acceleration of trolley and tension in the string. (Take, $g = 10$ ms^{-2}) [Ans. 44 N]

32. (i) State Stoke's law and derive its expression dimensionally.

(ii) The graph shows the behaviour of a length of wire in the region for which the substance obeys Hooke's law. What are P and Q representing in this graph?

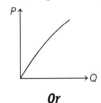

Or

(i) A stone of mass m is tied to one end of a wire of length L. The diameter of the wire is D and it is suspended vertically. The stone is now rotated in a horizontal plane and makes an angle θ with the vertical. If Young's modulus of the wire is

Y, then find the increase in the length of the wire in terms of Y.

(ii) If the diameter of a brass rod is 4 mm and Young's modulus of brass is 9×10^{10} Nm^{-2}. Then, how much force is required to stretch it by 0.1% of its original length? [Ans. $360\ \pi$N]

(iii) A uniform rod of length L and density ρ is being pulled along a smooth floor with a horizontal acceleration α as shown below. What is the magnitude of the stress at the transverse cross- section through the mid-point of the rod?

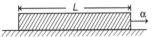

33. (i) Discuss the variation of g (acceleration due to gravity) with altitude.

(ii) The maximum and minimum velocities of a planet are 3×10^4 ms^{-1} and 1×10^3 ms^{-1}, respectively. What is the minimum distance of the planet from the sun, if maximum distance is 4×10^4 km? $\left[\text{Ans. } \dfrac{4}{3} \times 10^3 \text{km} \right]$

(iii) The radius of a planet is twice that of the earth but their average densities are same. If the escape velocities at the planet and at the earth are v_p and v_e respectively, then prove that $v_p = 2v_e$

Or

(i) State and explain the Kepler's laws of planetary motion.

(ii) A planet of radius $R = 1 / 10 \times$ (radius of earth) has the same mass density as earth. Scientists dig a well of depth $R/5$ on it and lower a wire of the same length and of linear mass density 10^{-3} kgm^{-1} into it. If the wire is not touching anywhere, then what amount of force is applied at the top of the wire by a person holding it in place? (Take, the radius of earth $= 6 \times 10^6$ m and the acceleration due to gravity of earth is 10 ms^{-2}) [Ans. 1080 N]

(iii) Three particles each of mass m are kept at vertices of an equilateral triangle of side L. What is the gravitational potential at the centre due to these particles?

Lightning Source UK Ltd.
Milton Keynes UK
UKHW051929131022
410412UK00003B/10

9 789326 196246